THE IMAGE OF THE BLACK IN LATIN AMERICAN AND CARIBBEAN ART

David Bindman, Alejandro de la Fuente, and Henry Louis Gates, Jr.
GENERAL EDITORS

Sheldon Cheek
ASSOCIATE EDITOR

David Bindman, Alejandro de la Fuente, and Henry Louis Gates, Jr.

GENERAL EDITORS

Sheldon Cheek

ASSOCIATE EDITOR

Hutchins Center for African & African American Research
Harvard University

Distributed by Harvard University Press
Cambridge, Massachusetts and London, England

The Image of the Black in Latin American and Caribbean Art

BOOK 2 The Modern World

Copyright © 2023 by the President and Fellows of Harvard College
All rights reserved
Printed in China

First printing

Library of Congress Cataloging-in-Publication Data

Names: Bindman, David, editor. | de la Fuente, Alejandro, editor. | Gates, Henry Louis, Jr., editor. | Cheek, Sheldon, editor. | Hutchins Center for African & African American Research.
    Title: The Image of the Black in Latin American and Caribbean Art. Book 2: The Modern World / David Bindman, Alejandro de la Fuente, Henry Louis Gates, Jr., general editors; Sheldon Cheek, associate editor | Hutchins Center for African & African American Research.
    Description: Cambridge, Massachusetts: Hutchins Center for African & African American Research, 2023. | Includes bibliographical references and index.
    Identifiers: Library of Congress Control Number: 2023942908 | ISBN 9780674248878. paper).
    Subjects: LCSH: Blacks in Art. | Art and race. | Art, Latin American. |
    Classification: LCC N8232 .I46 2023 | DDC 704.03/96-dc23 LC record available at https://lccn.loc.gov/2023942908.

CONTENTS

vii   **Preface** — DAVID BINDMAN, ALEJANDRO DE LA FUENTE, and HENRY LOUIS GATES, JR.

xi   Acknowledgments

15   Introduction — DAVID BINDMAN, ALEJANDRO DE LA FUENTE, and HENRY LOUIS GATES, JR.

PART III   Race and New Nations

27   1   The Configuration of the Afro-Brazilian Body, 1800–1900: Race, Slavery, Agency, and Celebration — MARCUS WOOD

42   2   Abolition and Post-Abolition in the Visual Culture of Latin America: Colombia, Brazil, Argentina, and Peru — MARÍA DE LOURDES GHIDOLI

68   3   The Image of the Black in the Formation of Latin American Nations — MARÍA DOLORES BALLESTEROS PÁEZ

85   4   *Costumbrismo*: Mapping Blackness in the New Nations of Mexico, Colombia, and Peru — HELEN MELLING

103   5   The War on Blackness ca. 1888: Religious Expression, Repression, and Resistance in Brazil — AMY BUONO

124   6   The Unrepresentable: Navigating Black Agency during Times of Transition — E. CARMEN RAMOS

148   7   Individual and Type: The Limits of Self-Representation in the Era of Portraiture, 1800–1880 — NATALIA MAJLUF

PART IV   New Nations Assert Themselves

169   8   Black Visualities in Puerto Rico and the Dominican Republic: 19th and 20th Centuries — EDWARD J. SULLIVAN

212   9   The Image of the Black in Select 20th-Century Works of Art in Haiti, Martinique, and Guadeloupe — JERRY PHILOGENE

247   10   Race and the Latin American Avant-Gardes, 1920s–1930s — ALEJANDRO DE LA FUENTE and RAFAEL CARDOSO

302   11   Image of the Black and More: Visual Thought and Creative Expression in the Caribbean and Brazil, 1939–1959 — YOLANDA WOOD

PART V   History and the Contemporary World

334   12   Sound, Fury, and Freedom: Monuments against Slavery — ROBERTO CONDURU

375   13   The Image of the Black in 20th-Century Anglo-Afro-Caribbean Art — PETRINE ARCHER

426   14   The Art of Black Mobilization, 1960s–2010s — ALEJANDRO DE LA FUENTE

458   15   Surface Viewing: On Blackness, Skin, and Photography in Contemporary Jamaican Art — KRISTA THOMPSON

479   16   Prismatic Blackness: Art, Being, and Aesthetics in the Global Caribbean — ERICA MOIAH JAMES

535   Notes

569   Illustrations

580   Index

PREFACE

DAVID BINDMAN, ALEJANDRO DE LA FUENTE, and HENRY LOUIS GATES, JR.

This is the second of two books that make up the second companion volume to the series *The Image of the Black in Western Art,* completed in five volumes (ten books) between 2010 and 2014. Three of the volumes (antiquity, the Middle Ages, and the nineteenth century) were reprints with new introductions of volumes that first appeared between 1976 and 1989, while the third volume (in three books), Renaissance to revolution, and the fifth volume, on the twentieth century (in two books) had not appeared before. They were followed by *The Image of the Black in African and Asian Art,* which appeared in 2017.

Why an extended study of *The Image of the Black in Latin American and Caribbean Art*? Essays on both Latin America and the Caribbean had appeared in previous volumes. Apart from images from the early years of the Spanish presence in Latin America, Dutch rule in Brazil in the seventeenth century is discussed in volume III, part 2, *casta* painting in Mexico in volume III, part 3, and Latin American and Caribbean art in volume V, part 1.[1] Though these essays were excellent accounts of their respective subjects, we felt that substantially more needed to be said about images of those of African descent (referred to in the present volume as Afrodescendants) than there had been space for in previous volumes. This feeling was heightened by the creation of the Afro-Latin American Research Institute at the Hutchins Center for African & African American Research at Harvard University and by the development of Afro-Latin American studies as a field more generally.

This ambition was entirely in line with the original intentions for *The Image of the Black in Western Art* series, which had been initiated in the 1960s by Dominique and Jean de Menil, who were then based in Houston, Texas, at the height of the struggle for civil rights for African Americans. Along with the de Menils' interventions in politics, the volumes were broadly intended to provide a positive alternative to the omnipresent demeaning visual stereotypes used to support and justify segregation. The objective of the series, as stated by Dominique de Menil in an introduction to the first volume, was to use European art of the past to demonstrate that relations between peoples of African and European descent had not always been governed by the enslavement of the former by the latter. The great art of the past, she argued—perhaps a bit naïvely—offered glimpses of the possibility of mutual respect and renewed understanding between different peoples, though she was well aware that European art was often used to reinforce and naturalize slavery.

In the preface to *The Image of the Black in Western Art,* David

Bindman and Henry Louis Gates, Jr., wrote at some length about the intellectual ancestry of the project and in particular about the influence of the great African American scholar Alain Locke (1886–1954) and the more immediate influence of the Polish-French author Jean Malaquais (1908–1998).[2] We also told the complex story of the genesis of the project, from its beginnings as a photographic archive (in two different locations, originally in Houston and Paris, and now at the Harvard University's Hutchins Center and the University of London's Warburg Institute), to the first publication of three volumes, consisting of five books, published in both French and English, between 1975 and 1989, under the editorship of Ladislas Bugner in Paris, then its revival in 2005–2006 under the aegis of the Du Bois Institute at Harvard (now the Hutchins Center), and the completion of the previously missing volume.

We also reflected on the problems of republishing and bringing up to date a project that had been initiated and carried out in a rather different political and intellectual climate. The concern of the de Menils to see the representation of those of African descent entirely through the lens of "Western art," though honorable, now looks a little dated, and we were able to contemporize the already published volumes by adding new introductions that specifically addressed recent political and art historical developments.

Many of these discussions have coalesced around the general title of the original series, *The Image of the Black in Western Art,* every word of which (including "the") is open to contention. First of all, what do we mean by "the Black" in the title? The short answer is persons of sub-Saharan African descent, in whatever proportion of ancestry, and not those who may also have dark skin but, as far as we know, originate from elsewhere. It goes without saying that one cannot always tell in a work of visual art (as one cannot always tell in person) just by looking whether a person is of African descent. In practice, however, the vast majority of Western representations are not of individuals but depend on stereotypes widely shared in European countries and those settled by Europeans. Additionally, there are several cases in commemorations of heroes of Latin American independence where those known to have been of at least partly African descent have undergone a process of "whitening."

Why then "The Image of the Black" and not "Images of Blacks or blacks"? This perhaps is more difficult to answer, but we would argue that the singular noun "the Black" gives a clearer sense of the ambition of the series—not always completely fulfilled—to give a comprehensive picture, covering all periods and most continents, of the representation of African peoples in all their variety and complexity.

Then there is the question of "Art." This presents an intriguing fault line between the first publication of *The Image of the Black in Western Art* in the 1970s and 1980s and the second series from 2010 to the present. Generally speaking, the de Menils and those who worked on the first series were committed to a view that anything worthy of the name of art rather than mere representation was inherently elevated and spiritual; it could reveal the humanity of those it might represent even against the ostensible beliefs of those who commissioned it. Artists, and especially the great artists—Rembrandt, Rubens, Velázquez, and the like—were believed to have had a special insight and feeling for the humanity of those they painted that transcended the master-slave relationship.

Whether this is so or not, from the nineteenth century onward, artists themselves have questioned the boundaries between art and non-art, especially between elite and popular imagery, while in recent years art historians have tended to argue not so much for a difference between the two but a continuum from one to the other. It is interesting that Hugh Honour in his superb 1989 volume on the nineteenth century in *The Image of the Black in Western Art* discusses only a small number of caricatures and wholly omits photography, while in volume III, part 2, published in 2011, Jean-Michel Massing takes an interest in the crude designs on tobacco wrappers. In volume III, part 3, English eighteenth-century caricatures are fully discussed in relation to the image of Africans, while nineteenth-century photography is brought fully into consideration in an essay in the twentieth-century volume by Deborah Willis, as is anthropological photography by Elizabeth Edwards.

The consideration of popular imagery inevitably raises the question of the deeply distasteful and offensive imagery associated with the rise of European imperialism and Jim Crow segregation in the United States, which was printed in overwhelming quantities with incalculable effects on people's perceptions of racial difference. Though it cannot and should not be ignored, to treat it comprehensively in the context of these volumes would swamp all other imagery. The solution we adopted in the twentieth-century volume was a single essay by Tanya Sheehan and Henry Louis Gates, Jr., entitled "Marketing Racism: Popular Imagery in the United States and Europe," illustrated by twelve plates, which show the most familiar tropes of such imagery, especially the most insidious. In the present volume we have given due attention to popular imagery such as cigar wrappers and newspaper illustrations without seeking to represent the subject in its entirety.

The previous volume, *The Image of the Black in African and Asian Art*, was the first to move beyond a European perspective on the imagery of Africans, and this volume might seem to be a reversion back to a "European" perspective. But that would greatly oversimplify the matter. One of the justifications for moving the series into the twentieth century (the original volumes had been intended to stop at around 1920) in the first place was that it enabled it to come to terms with the momentous change that occurred when Black people took charge of their own representation, something that happened mainly in the course of the twentieth century, though there were earlier precedents.

With the growing recognition and visibility of Black artists, particularly in the United States, the question becomes, as is noted in the preface to *The Image of the Black in African and Asian Art*, "Who are we?" rather than "Who are they?"[3] With the burgeoning presence of Black artists, the balance shifted almost totally, to the extent that the second book of the twentieth century volume of *The Image of the Black in Western Art* is called *The Rise of Black Artists*.

The visibility of Afrodescendants in general and of artists, intellectuals, professionals, and activists in particular has increased significantly in Latin America as well during that last few decades. The rise of social, cultural, and community organizations demanding recognition, rights, and inclusion for people of African descent across the region has forced many societies to grapple with the long-term effects of slavery, racism, and discrimination. These movements demand new histories, including new art histories, where the authorship and contributions of artists of African descent are acknowledged and studied properly. Our access to this production is still rather uneven, however. In some countries, like Brazil, there have been major attempts to retrieve and reevaluate the contributions of Afrodescendant artists since colonial times, but even there much work remains to be done. We have tried to mine wherever we could sources of information in each Latin American and Caribbean country, but we know that there must be many important paintings hanging in small museums and private collections that we did not discover in time to publish them. But it is our fervent hope that a number will turn up in the next few years, partly as a consequence of the publication of the present books.

Finally, a note on language. All words in our text denoting racial difference, even the phrase "racial difference" itself, are governed by historical usage, and therefore can sometimes appear outdated, anachronistic, jarring, or even offensive to readers. Genetic science long ago debunked the notion that the concept of "race" was a biological classification; rather, it is commonly understood that race is a social construct, though the former was taken for granted throughout the nineteenth century and most of the twentieth. But if one is writing about the past, it is virtually impossible to avoid using such terms in some form, and even more so with the very common use in the past of phrases like "mixed race" and variations that often connote demeaning associations, among them *mestizo, métis, mulatto, Mulâtresse*. We use the word "Black" to denote peoples of sub-Saharan African descent, replacing "colored," "Negro," or "negro," unless these words appear in a direct quote from an original source. We also use the term "Afrodescendants" for people of African descent throughout Latin America. Coined at the regional preparatory conference (Santiago de Chile, 2000) for the World Conference against Racism, Racial Discrimination, Xenophobia and Related Intolerance (Durban, 2001), this label was produced by race-justice activists from the region to constitute a group with legal, cultural, and ethical implications in the arenas of international justice and human rights.

ACKNOWLEDGMENTS

This is the second of two books that constitute the second companion volume to *The Image of the Black in Western Art,* following *The Image of the Black in African and Asian Art,* which appeared in 2017. Like the latter, it concentrates on a region rather than a time period, one that can broadly be described as "Western." The idea for the volume and its structure came out of discussions between the editors working at the Hutchins Center for African & African American Research at Harvard University and the contributors, who met together at a workshop at Harvard in December 2018.

The contributors were chosen after extensive consultation and discussion, and they range from the senior and very eminent to junior scholars, many from Latin America and the Caribbean, others from Britain, France, and the United States. It has been an enormous privilege and pleasure to work with such gifted people, as it has been with our colleagues and friends at the Hutchins Center, especially Amy Gosdanian, Bronia Greskovicova-Chang, Krishna Lewis, and Abby Wolf. The volumes owe a great deal to conversations with visiting fellows of the Hutchins Center, especially Petrina Dacres and Peter Hulme, and to Marial Iglesias Utset. Particular thanks go to Katherine Mills, a graduate student in the History of Art and Architecture Department at Harvard, for creating a website for this volume and to Jeffrey Blossom of Harvard's Center for Geographic Analysis for his composition of the maps used in the introduction.

As ever, we thank former Harvard President Derek Bok and Dean of the Faculty of Arts & Sciences Henry Rosovsky for establishing the conditions under which the Image Archive could be housed at what was then the Du Bois Institute at Harvard. President Neil L. Rudenstine oversaw with great dedication the relocation of the archive from the Menil Collection in Houston to Cambridge. In the 2000s, Presidents Lawrence H. Summers, Drew Gilpin Faust, and Lawrence S. Bacow also each contributed in myriad ways to the success and expansion of the Hutchins Center. This growth would not have been possible without the enthusiastic support of former Deans of the Faculty of Arts & Sciences Michael D. Smith and Claudine Gay (who is now the first Black president of Harvard) and Dean Lawrence D. Bobo.

Though she did not work on the present volume, it bears the indelible stamp of Karen Dalton, who was Dominique de Menil's assistant before she came to the Hutchins Center. Virtually from the beginning of the series, Karen's contribution to the project was tremendous, and we owe her an incalculable debt.

The editing of the text was carried out in exemplary fashion by Julie Wolf, and the books were designed with great care and sensitivity by Lorraine Ferguson Weinberg. We have once again enjoyed working with Richard Philpott of Zooid Pictures, Ltd., who had the daunting task of gathering the photographs and illustrations for the volumes and obtaining permissions, a monumental undertaking that he carried out with amazing efficiency and good humor.

DAVID BINDMAN
ALEJANDRO DE LA FUENTE
HENRY LOUIS GATES, JR.
SHELDON CHEEK

The Image of the Black
in Latin American and Caribbean Art

BOOK 2   The Modern World

INTRODUCTION

DAVID BINDMAN, ALEJANDRO DE LA FUENTE, and HENRY LOUIS GATES, JR.

"Without the black, Cuba would not be Cuba." This curious statement by the anthropologist and ethnographer Fernando Ortiz, which strikes us as obvious today, but which bore the tone of a profound revelation when he wrote it in 1943, applies equally to the whole of the Americas. (The same can be said about the presence of Europeans, of course, but that, apparently, didn't occur to Ortiz, which inadvertently tells us something important about the politics of race in Cuba at the time.) Without the eleven million Africans who survived the forced transport of the Middle Passage and arrived between the fifteenth and nineteenth centuries, and their legions of descendants, Latin America and the Caribbean as we know them today, simply put, would not be; in fact, the histories of colonialism, capitalism, modernity, culture, and nation-making in the Americas would have evolved profoundly and dramatically differently.[1]

It is impossible to determine precisely when the first sub-Saharan Africans arrived in the New World, but we know that it was very early. Africans and people of African descent are likely to have been part of the earliest European expeditions. By the time Christopher Columbus set sail in search of a faster route to the reaches of the Far East, Mediterranean Spain was home to a considerable African population. Many of them, enslaved and free, were North African Muslims, victims of the conflicts and displacements produced by the wars between Christendom and Islam since the Middle Ages. Many others, however, were enslaved sub-Saharan Africans, a group that was growing fast in southern Iberia by the late fifteenth century, since the trans-Saharan slave trade had been delivering enslaved Africans to the Mediterranean at least since the eleventh century.[2] ("Portuguese successes in this field," the historian John Thornton notes, "have been described as the victory of the 'caravel over the camel.'")[3] Columbus stopped for provisions in the Canary Islands, which were already undergoing colonization by Spain that would produce one of the earliest Atlantic slave societies. Slave raids to the continent's Barbary Coast had been common since the 1460s, and slave raiding on the West African coast started as soon as navigation there was possible, in the mid-fifteenth century.[4] More formalized trading started in the 1460s following Diogo Gomes's establishment of diplomatic relations with the coastal kingdoms like Great Jolof and the Mandinkas' on the Gambia River. Such expeditions were common in the 1470s. When the Europeans set foot on The Bahamas in October 1492, Africa and Africans were part of the social, cultural, and demographic fabric of Iberia. Lisbon, Seville, and Valencia were the slave capitals of Western Europe.[5]

It is not particularly surprising, then, that Africans and individuals of African descent appear in the earliest extant records among conquistadors and colonizers, so many that they have been described as "a ubiquitous and pivotal part of Spanish conquest campaigns in the Americas."[6] A singular early example is that of Juan Moreno, also referred to as "Juan Prieto," a servant of Christopher Columbus who apparently accompanied him on his first voyage in 1492. It is impossible to determine whether Moreno was enslaved or free. He was still living in Hispaniola in 1500 when he was called to testify about Columbus. Of African or Portuguese birth, he joined one of the expeditionary forces that reached Tierra Firme, or the Isthmus of Panama. By 1515 he was living in Santa María la Antigua del Darién, on the northern coast of today's Colombia.[7]

Perhaps the best-known Black conquistador is Juan Garrido (ca. 1480–ca. 1550), who in 1538 issued a "*probanza*," or declaration of merits, addressed to the king. As is typical of these documents, Garrido offered an autobiographical account in which he highlighted his service to the crown, which spanned several decades. Arriving in Hispaniola around 1503, probably as the personal servant of a Spaniard, Garrido participated in the forces under the command of Ponce de León that conquered Puerto Rico in 1508 and in the expeditionary forces that Diego Velázquez gathered to colonize Cuba in 1511. In 1515, Velázquez informed the king that "many black slaves" had participated in the conquest of Cuba and requested more to build fortifications. Several years later, when Hernán Cortés sailed from the southern coast of Cuba to Mexico, he also took a number of servants and enslaved Africans with him. Among those accompanying Cortés in his expedition to central Mexico was Juan Garrido, who settled in Mexico City and died there.[8]

Neither Garrido nor Moreno was exceptional. By the early decades of the sixteenth century, the number of Africans and people of sub-Saharan African descent in the initial Spanish settlements in the Caribbean was steadily and surely growing. As early as 1503 the governor of Hispaniola, Nicolás de Ovando, called to halt the importation of "*negros*" because those who had been arriving in the colony ran away with the native "Indians" and could not be forced to work on the extraction of gold. To stimulate permanent settlements in the colonies, the kings began to issue "*licencias*," or special permits, to some of their vassals to import enslaved sub-Saharan Africans in the colonies, tax-free. One such license, issued in 1502, specified that the beneficiary was allowed to transport to Hispaniola *cuantos negros quisieran* ("as many blacks as they wish").[9] Starting in 1518, usually in exchange for large payments, the kings of Spain began to issue monopolistic trade licenses that regulated the number of Africans to be imported in the American colonies. Thus began the infamous transatlantic slave trade, which would span almost four centuries and result in the forced migration of some 12.5 million Africans. Of the nearly 11 million who survived, almost all of them arrived in Latin America and the Caribbean; remarkably, only about 4 percent arrived in what is today the United States.[10]

Africans came from many different regions and linguistic families in the continent, from Senegambia bordering the Atlantic in the west, all the way south to the West Central African regions of Congo and Angola, and extending—to a dramatically lesser degree—as far east as Mozambique in southeast Africa, and even to the island of Madagascar in the Indian Ocean. The existence of multiple cultures among Africans was noticed by slaveholders and traders as early as the sixteenth century. The Europeans classified Africans according to a number of "nations" (*naciones*, in Spanish), a term that had ethnolinguistic and geographic connotations, even though they did not refer to geopolitical units in the African continent. As John Thornton has shown, however, the individuals designated under these naciones were frequently members of broadly similar linguistic communities. Thornton notes that the enslaved Africans from Upper Guinea (Senegambia and Rivers of Guinea) belonged to two linguistic families, West Atlantic and Mande, and that, despite significant differences, cultural distance among them was lessened by commerce and frequent communication. Some groups like the Mandinka, Jolofo (Wolof), and Fulo or Fula were Muslims and considered rebellious and problematic by Spanish enslavers. Those from Lower Guinea, from the Windward Coast to the Bight of Biafra (from today's Ivory Coast to eastern Nigeria and Cameroon), spoke a range of different languages. From the Kwa family, Akan was spoken among some peoples in what is today the country of Ghana. The Fon and Yoruba, around the Bight of Benin, in what is today western Nigeria, spoke related languages, but the languages did not allow them to understand each other. Igbo speakers, moreover, came from the Bight of Biafra in eastern Nigeria, and their language was unintelligible to Yoruba speakers. The Arara and Arda were Fon speakers, whereas the Lucumi were Yoruba speakers, and the Carabalí consisted of subgroups who spoke languages often indecipherable to each other, such as Efik and Igbo. The Spanish missionary Alonso de Sandoval, however, who catechized enslaved Africans in Cartagena in the early seventeenth century, asserted that Africans from this vast region understood each other, a preposterous claim considering all the above examples. More likely, he was describing a second language, a lingua franca that had been forged for purposes of trade and social interactions. The Congo-Angola from West Central Africa were more homogeneous, as all these people spoke languages of the Bantu group, especially Kikongo and Kimbundu, but these are analogous to the similarities between Spanish and French, rather than between Spanish and Portuguese.[11]

The areas of origin of enslaved Africans varied across time, depending on European access to provisions, a source of bitter imperial rivalries, on the expansion of European colonization in the Americas, and on the organization of the trade. Up to the mid-1590s, when the Spanish crown began to rent out the administration of the slave trade to private merchants in exclusivity, in what came to be known as the system of the *asientos*, most Africans came from Senegambia and the Rivers of Guinea region. The Portuguese were well positioned in this region thanks to their colonial settlement in the Cabo Verde islands, which became a major slave entrepôt in the sixteenth century. Traders of Portuguese descent also lived along the coast with the approval of African rulers, and the Portuguese established a few fortified trading factories in the region, such as one at Cacheu. But in the late sixteenth century, other European powers began to compete with the Portuguese for control of this region. The islands of Cabo Verde were attacked by the English and the Dutch in 1578, 1585, and 1596.[12]

With the establishment of the Portuguese colony of Angola in 1575, the character of the slave trade from Africa changed dramatically, as we might expect. The origins of what would come to be called the "Angolan Wave" had a lot to do with the wars in which Portugal became involved, following 1579. Accordingly, it is not surprising that with the first asiento with the Portuguese merchant Pedro Gomes Reinel in 1595, the supply of enslaved Africans to Spanish America moved south to Angola and Congo, as the volume of trade reported in the 1590s makes clear. The Portuguese merchants who benefited from this monopoly had a personal stake in the Angolan slave trade. The second *asientista*, João Rodrigues Coutinho, was the governor of the colony, and the contract was transferred to his brother Gonzalo Vaez Coutinho after his death in 1603. Eighty percent of the Africans arriving in the Spanish colonies by 1610 came from West Central Africa; 90 percent by 1620, most of them through the port city of Cartagena de Indias, which supplied the viceroyalty of Peru.[13] Mexico and Peru were the main destination of most enslaved Africans in the Spanish colonies between 1520 and 1650. By then, Africans and their descendants represented between 10 and 15 percent of the population of Peru.[14] This Angolan Wave is quite significant to subsequent culture formation of Africans in Latin America because of the creolized nature of this region (the kingdom of Kongo converted to Roman Catholicism in 1491 and soon developed its own form of the religion), and because of the relative homogeneity of the population culturally.

By the early seventeenth century, however, a new and insatiable market became the main enforced destination for most enslaved Africans: Brazil. Sugar production in the Brazilian Northeast depended initially on indigenous labor, but between the 1560s and the 1630s, a transition to African enslaved labor took place gradually.[15] The association between sugar production and African slavery intensified first in the Atlantic Islands (São Tomé, Madeira, Canary Islands) and then in Hispaniola, home to the first slave society in the Americas, during the sixteenth century.[16]

This association would reach new heights, however, during the seventeenth and eighteenth centuries when, in addition to Brazil, the English, the French, and the Dutch developed new slave-based sugar plantation economies in their Caribbean colonies.[17] The slave trade reached its peak during this period. Brazil, which would receive almost 5 million Africans over the course of the slave trade, became the destination of more than 2.7 million enslaved Africans between 1660 and 1808, but the "sugar islands" of the Caribbean followed closely, led by Jamaica (1 million), Haiti (0.8 million), and Barbados (0.5 million). Even the smaller islands in the Lesser Antilles, such as Grenada and St. Kitts, became home to hundreds of thousands of enslaved Africans. Spanish America declined in importance during this period, receiving only 7 percent of the enslaved Africans transported to the New World between 1701 and 1820. But this began to change in the early nineteenth century with the dramatic expansion of the sugar economy in Cuba after its collapse on Saint-Domingue, following the Haitian Revolution. The result of the migration of this industry was the importation to Cuba of the huge number of 720,000 enslaved Africans between 1804 and 1866. Furthermore, a significant number of Africans introduced by the English and the Dutch in their colonies found their way to other territories across the Caribbean via regional trade links. Although the slave trade was illegal for most of the nineteenth century, Brazil and Cuba received over 2 million enslaved Africans during these years, and it was not until the 1860s that the trade in enslaved Africans to Brazil and Cuba was brought to a halt.[18]

The exponential growth of the transatlantic slave trade after 1650 reached not only all of Atlantic Africa, from Upper Guinea to Bengela in West Central Africa, but also Mozambique and even Madagascar in the southeast. During the eighteenth century, a large number of Africans arrived in the Caribbean from the Gold Coast, the Bight of Benin, and the Bight of Biafra, areas where English and Dutch slave traders were firmly established. Large numbers of West Central Africans continued to be brought to the New World during the same period, mostly to Brazil. West Central Africans were also well represented among Brazilian and Cuban imports during the 1800s, followed by those from the Bights of Benin and Biafra, and even as far to the southeast as Mozambique.

In an act of unparalleled epistemic violence, the European enslavers collapsed all this cultural richness and diversity into a metonym derived from a single phenotypic characteristic, their supposed skin color, "Black," itself a metaphor for the wide range of skin colors among the peoples of sub-Saharan Africa. Across imperial boundaries, enslavers consolidated Africans of many different origins, languages, and ethnicities into *negros*, *Negroes*, *noirs*, legal and political categories of debasement that sought to erase lineages, memories, and personal and collective histories.[19] This process of erasure and reconstitution was neither smooth nor completely successful, however, as numerous "African" cultural, religious, and oral traditions were reproduced on New World soils. (It is important to recall that Wolof and Fulani, Yoruba and Igbo, only became "Africans" with the onset of the slave trade.) Indeed, in numerous areas of the Americas, and for extended periods of time, the numbers of Africans were so large that they may have been able to create parallel religious systems and "polycultural" communities, though this is highly speculative.[20]

In countries such as Cuba and Brazil, where large numbers of Africans continued to arrive into the nineteenth century, some groups were large enough to sustain their languages and other cultural practices under captivity for extended periods of time. The large concentration of Nagôs (Yoruba) in early-nineteenth-century Bahia, for instance, was behind the African-Muslim rebellion of 1835, the largest urban slave revolt known in the Americas. The enslaved Carabalí in the Guacamaro region in western Cuba relied on links of "solidarity and kinship" to plot a major slave revolt in 1825. Africans of similar origins also took advantage of existing institutional spaces to create their own *cabildos* and mutual aid societies, which functioned as spaces of cultural reproduction and community formation along various ethnic lines. Scholars acknowledge that various forms of cultural and social mixing, creolization and hybridity eventually took place, and Africans and their descendants were, of course, active and crucial participants in these processes, which were marked by both conflict and negotiation.[21]

The intensity and duration of the slave trade produced dramatically different demographic and cultural configurations in the New World over time. Brazil eventually became the second largest Black nation in the world, after Nigeria. Key expressions of its national culture, from *Candomblé* to *samba*, are clearly linked to African practices and influences. At the other end of the spectrum, countries such as Mexico, the recipient of large numbers of Africans during the early colonial period, up to 1650, directly from Africa and up to the early eighteenth century through the intra-American slave trade, experienced processes of intense creolization and intermarriage that rendered the majority of people of African descent officially demographically invisible, though distinct regions of Afro-Mexican culture still exist. The demographic recovery of the indigenous population during the

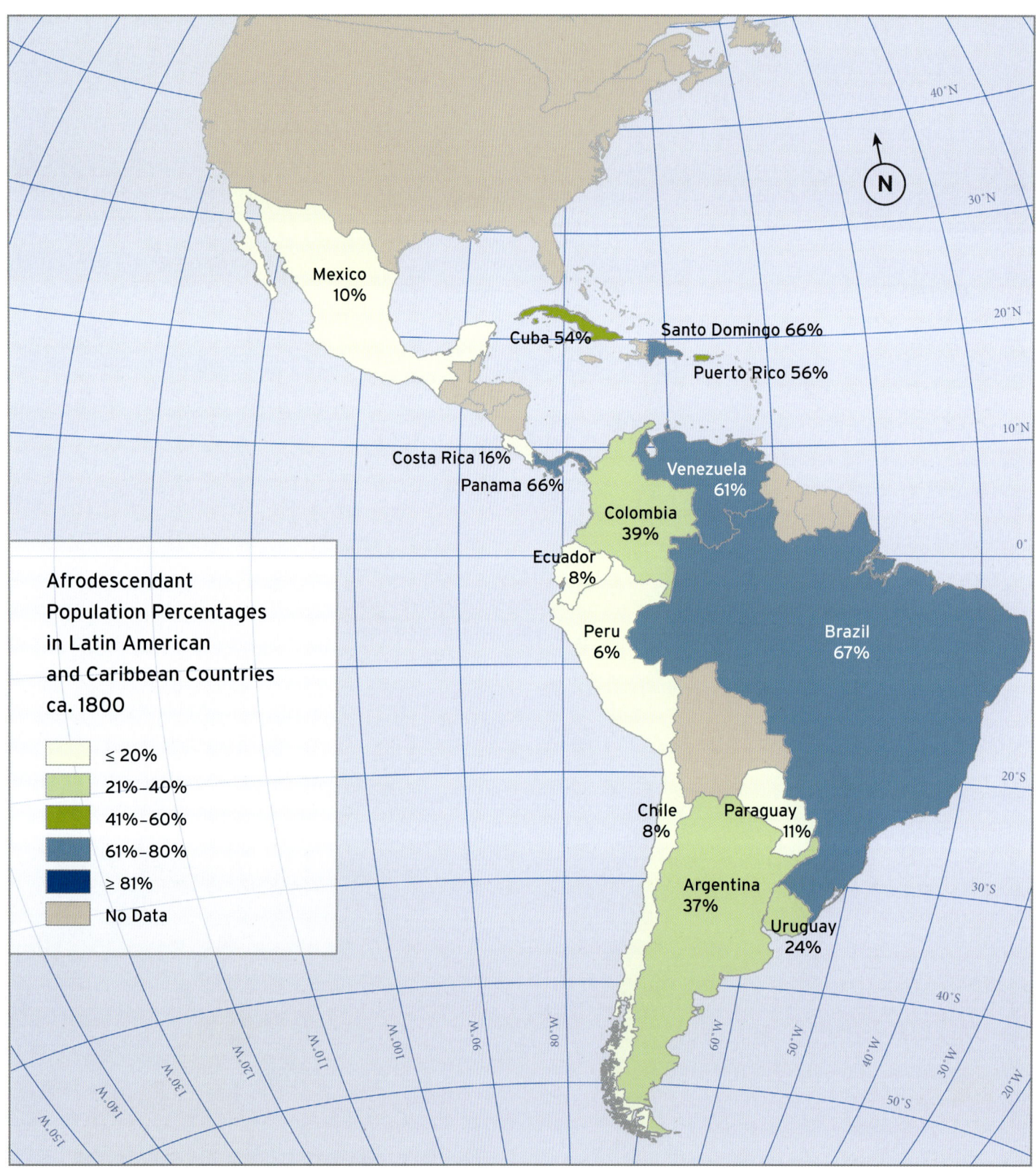

Map with population data ca. 1800. Geographical boundaries reflect the current distribution of states as depicted by Natural Earth Data. Population percentages are from George Reid Andrews's book *Afro-Latin America, 1800–2000*.

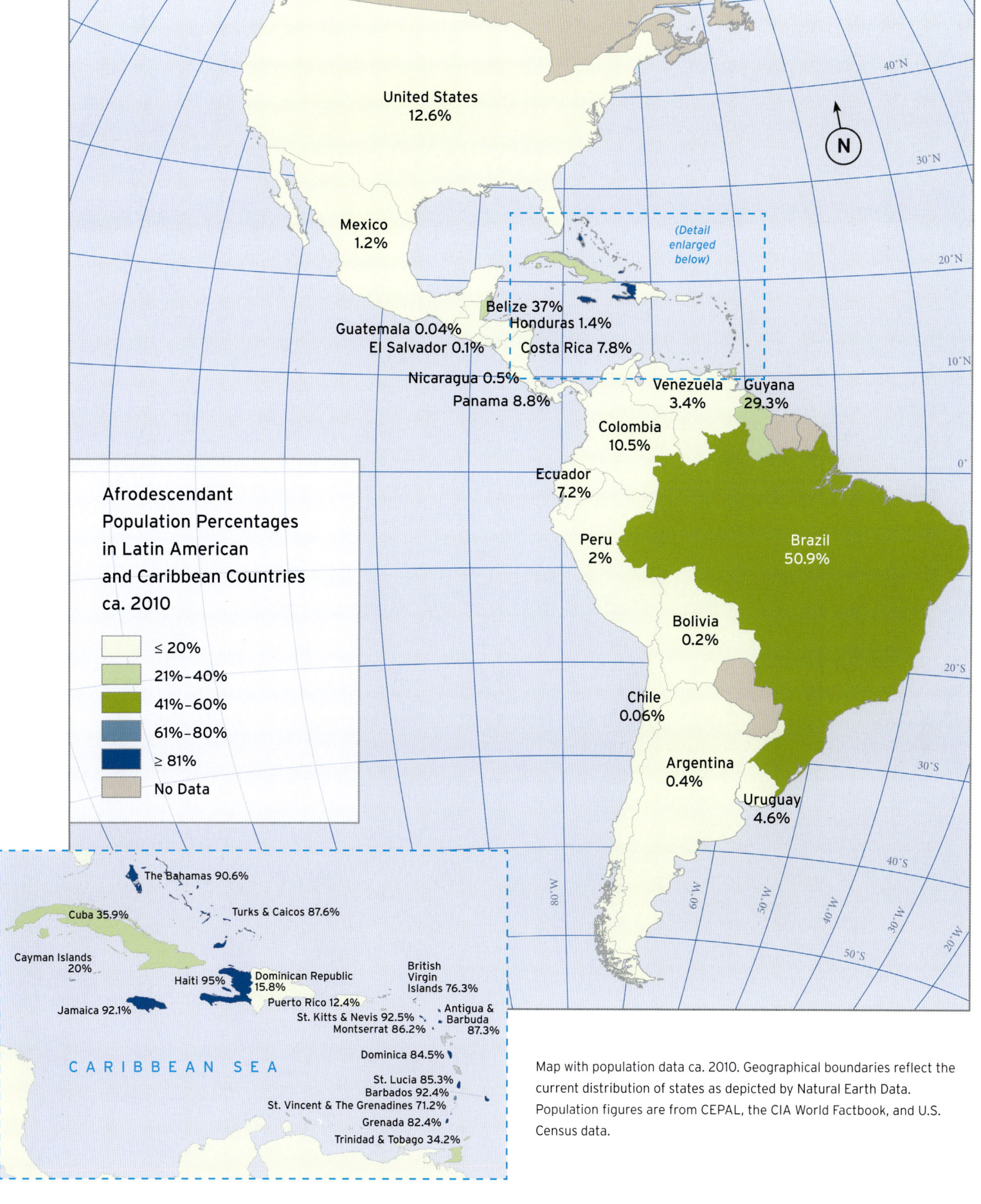

Map with population data ca. 2010. Geographical boundaries reflect the current distribution of states as depicted by Natural Earth Data. Population figures are from CEPAL, the CIA World Factbook, and U.S. Census data.

1700s facilitated this process. In Yucatan, for instance, a significant population of Africans and individuals of African descent in the early seventeenth century had officially disappeared by the early nineteenth century. Those previously identified as "negros" or "*mulatos*" were folded into an expanding category of "*mestizos*" that was later infused with nationalist meanings.[22] It is only recently, and under intense pressure from Afrodescendant social movements, that Mexican authorities have taken steps to acknowledge the importance of Africans and their descendants in the formation of Mexico as a nation and in contemporary society. And, of course, genetic traces of African origins are quite common among Mexicans living along the coasts, particularly those around Veracruz on the Gulf of Mexico and the Costa Chica region in the state of Oaxaca on the Pacific. The point we seek to emphasize in these volumes, however, is that even in areas that are not currently associated with the enslavement of Africans, their presence and contributions were significant at various points during the colonial period. Further migration movements during the twentieth century brought people of African descent into areas where their presence was previously limited, as in some countries in Central America.

How did visual representations intervene in these processes of cultural reproduction, conflict, creolization, and migration? How have individual Africans and, more generally, Black subjects—the negros, Negroes, and noirs of imperial Europe—been represented visually, from the colonial period to the present? How have those representations evolved over time?

Those are some of the questions that these volumes seek to answer. At the very least, we want to highlight the existence and importance of this visual corpus in order to facilitate access to these images and to promote their study by scholars interested in the five-hundred-year history of Africans and Afrodescendants in this hemisphere across different disciplines. We also seek to underline the urgent need for future research in this area, particularly with reference to representations produced by individuals of African descent. Painting and sculpting were understood as manual occupations in colonial Iberian societies, a mechanical trade undertaken by artisans of mostly African descent. Yet much of this production remains understudied and unidentified, not to mention the vast body of ritual art that Africans and their descendants produced in what the art historian Leslie King-Hammond has described as "safe and sacred 'spaces of blackness.'"[23] It will be difficult to recover this production, but we must at least try. By the late seventeenth century, we can identify a handful of artists of African descent. These include Juan Correa (1646–1716) in Mexico; Manuel da Cunha (1737–1809), Antônio Francisco Lisboa (Aleijadinho) (1738–1814), and Valentim da Fonseca e Silva (Mestre Valentim) (ca. 1745–1813) in Brazil; José Campeche (1751–1809) in Puerto Rico; Vicente Escobar (1762–1834) in Cuba; and José Gil de Castro (1785–1841) in Peru. The number of known artists of African descent increases significantly by the twentieth century. However, additional research is badly needed even for more recent historical periods and for artists who, although known to a small number of specialists, remain largely ignored by scholars of culture and the general public in the region. The traditional canon is hopelessly racialized and genderized.

We include essays and representations that encompass Latin America and the Caribbean, two regions that are frequently treated separately based on ethnolinguistic distinctions that owe much to French nineteenth-century imperial racial fantasies.

Too often, even in contemporary books and exhibitions, "Latin American" art is associated with European influences, which are racially coded as white.[24] Although there are themes for which it may make sense to distinguish between the Iberian colonial experience and that of other European powers, we did not think that dividing visual representations of Blacks and Blackness along European imperial lines made much sense. It is not only that most of the territories that we now associate with Latin America and the Caribbean share common histories of colonialism, imperial expansion, African slavery, the production of export commodities, and environmental degradation, but that ideas of race and Blackness were produced, codified, and represented across imperial and later national boundaries. The caste system, with all its racist phantasmagoric gradations of mixture, may have been a Castilian invention, grounded in notions of religious blood purity, but such notions found echo in other colonial societies, across linguistic barriers. As the racist defender of slavery Edward Long noted in his infamous *History of Jamaica* (1774), "the intermixture of Whites, Blacks, and Indians, has generated several different casts, which have all their proper denominations, invented by the Spaniards, who make this a kind of science among them."[25] North American constructions of race and Blackness often paled in size and absurdity compared to the many dubious homegrown Latin American and Caribbean "racial" classification schemes that emerged in places such as Haiti, the Dominican Republic, Cuba, and especially Brazil over the long, tortured history of "racial science" throughout Latin America and the Caribbean. These supposedly "scientific" schemes not only reflected and shaped imperial understandings and policies in the circum-Caribbean area, but had a concrete impact on local societies across the region, from Puerto Rico to Panama, from Nicaragua to Cuba, the Dominican Republic, and Haiti. Later in the century, different forms of anticolonialism and Black radicalism, as well as Pan-African ideologies of race and justice, again crossed national and linguistic barriers, with concrete (and frequently beautiful) reflections in the visual arts. Idioms of race and nation adopt locally specific forms, but the association between the two itself operates all over the region. Nationalist metaphors of racial inclusion can be found from Jamaica to Brazil, or Cuba.

Furthermore, Latin America spills into the Caribbean and vice versa. It was, after all, in the Caribbean that Spanish colonialism in the Americas lasted the longest, in Cuba and Puerto Rico. Some of the British West Indian islands, such as Jamaica, were first under Spanish control. The influence of the British West Indies also spills over to Central and South America, not to mention some of the Spanish-speaking islands of the Caribbean, many of which are home to Afro-Caribbean communities from the former British colonies as well as Haiti. In the early twentieth century, tens of thousands of Haitians and British West Indian workingmen and -women left their islands of origin to find employment across the circum-Caribbean, in Panama, Cuba, Costa Rica, Venezuela, Puerto Rico, and the Dominican Republic. That is why in the mid-1920s Cuba was home to the largest number of chapters of the Jamaican Marcus Garvey's Universal Negro Improvement Association outside the United States.[26] Many of these migrants eventually settled in the United States and Europe, recreating communities in numerous locations across the globe, from South Florida and New York City to London and Paris.

These Caribbean crossroads were also traversed by many of the artists included in our volumes. In these travels, they incorporated colors, images, traditions, and visions of race, culture, and nation that shaped their artistic work. The French impressionist master Camille Pissarro (1830–1903) was born in the Danish West Indies (since 1917 the U.S. Virgin Islands), but spent a formative period in Venezuela with the Danish painter Fritz Melbye (1826–1869) before settling in Paris. The Puerto Rican artist Juan Botello (1913–1986) was born in Spain but died in San Juan after living for long periods of time in Havana, Port-au-Prince, and Santo Domingo. It was precisely while living in Port-au-Prince, in 1945, that Botello met another traveling artist, the Afro-Cuban painter Wifredo Lam (1902–1982). Lam fled Paris during the Second World War and went to Havana after a stopover in Martinique, where he befriended the poet Aimé Césaire (1913–2008). André Breton (1896–1966) also traveled from New York City to Port-au-Prince in 1945 to offer lectures in support of Lam's exhibitions. Haiti had been a place of literal and fictive pilgrimage for many African American artists during the Harlem Renaissance. It continued to hold a special place in the artistic Black imaginary well into the 1940s.[27]

National boundaries do not define the work of these or many other of the artists represented in these pages. Were Pissarro's paintings of Caracas Danish, French, or Venezuelan? Is Botello's *Le forêt des pins* (*The Pinetree Forest*, 1945) a Haitian, Spanish, or Puerto Rican painting? Many masterpieces of the Latin American avant-garde of the 1920s and 1930s were produced in Paris. Others were produced in Mexico or New York. We follow this production, reconstructing routes, conversations, exchanges, and influences. Whenever possible, we also seek to bridge the divide that traditionally separates Brazil from Spanish-speaking countries. Several chapters in the book look at developments in Brazil side by side with other countries, something that art historians rarely do. These connections and exchanges have been central to the production of ideas and representations of Blackness since colonial times. At some points they may have served to consolidate race as a category of difference, as with the famous colonial *casta* paintings. In more recent times, however, the visual arts have been and remain at the forefront of antiracist struggles in the Americas.

III

Race and New Nations

1

THE CONFIGURATION OF THE AFRO-BRAZILIAN BODY, 1800–1900: RACE, SLAVERY, AGENCY, AND CELEBRATION

MARCUS WOOD

> Rigid behavioural alternatives have never existed in the history of slavery, and the stress on them stultifies any enquiry.
> —M. I. Finley, *Ancient Slavery and Modern Ideology*[1]

The antique and ancient Afro-Brazilian syncretic and folk art which is the focus of the following discussion is usually seen as the preserve of anthropology or cultural history: messy, ephemeral, and not part of the canonical materials of the Brazilian nineteenth-century art history archive proper. The official visual archive of slavery remains dominated by the superb productions of visiting European artists. Black bodies in Brazil proliferate from the seventeenth-century masterpieces of Albert Eckhout (ca. 1610–1665) to the genre works and illustrated travel books of Jean-Baptiste Debret (1768–1848) and Johann Moritz Rugendas (1802–1858), and the watercolor sketches of Thomas Ender (1793–1875), which hold center stage a century and a half after Eckhout. A magnificent photographic archive was generated in Brazil's big Northeast cities in the second half of the nineteenth century. A host of celebrated photographers, among them Marc Ferrez (1843–1923), Augusto Stahl (1828–1877), Alberto Henschel (1827–1882), and Luís Ferreira (fl. 1870–1900), emerged as some of the greatest early-stills photographers working anywhere in the world. This photographic archive has recently become internationally recognized, along with its unique representations of Black slave bodies. The thousands of images documenting the institution of slavery—primarily the individuals exploited by it—generated by the abolition debates in the illustrated journalism and lithographic print satire of Brazil have begun to be taken seriously, particularly in relation to the genius of Angelo Agostini (1843–1910), known as the "Brazilian Daumier."[2] I have devoted much of my life to writing monographs which open up this archive of paintings, prints, and photographs to a global readership.

And yet the archive of Afro-Brazilian syncretic religion, the artistic and sacred objects generated by the religions Candomblé, Umbanda, Macumba, and Xangô over four centuries, continue to be largely cordoned off by a sort of theoretical apartheid. These productions are positioned as historically, culturally, and semiotically the preserve of Brazilian Blacks, of enslaved men and women and their descendants. The ritual objects and costumes associated with these religions may be marginally studied by social anthropologists and granted a certain space within some Afro-Brazilian museums, or even be given a case or a room in museums displaying Brazilian "folklore" alongside "Indian" art.

Yet the objects discussed below are not just significant and aesthetically magnificent in their own right. Instead, they signify within a cultural space that should not be partitioned off solely as a Black aesthetic preserve or reservation. Let me explain by way of anecdote why I have written this piece. This narrative demonstrates that things in Brazil are not often what they seem at first sight, particularly when the subject in question is the reception by white elites—both European and Brazilian—of Afro-Brazilian cultural production.

The first time I went to Brazil from England, in 1985, I stayed in São Paulo with some Brazilian artist friends, a famous and influential couple. Both husband and wife worked full-time as artists, moving in the rarefied atmosphere of international biennales and group shows. Both had work in major international blue-chip collections, including the Museum of Modern Art in New York. After being in São Paulo for a couple of weeks, I started to spend time with a Portuguese-Brazilian artist friend who came from a different artistic and cultural milieu. He had a passionate interest in and knowledge of the Black urban religious cults that flourish in the suburbs of São Paulo as healthily as they do in Rio or Salvador, Bahia. Given my interest in slavery and its legacies, I told him I wanted to find out more about the syncretic cults and the ways they engaged with Brazil's slave histories, and I also hoped to buy some of the religious paraphernalia connected with them. He took me to a shabby old store, an enormous sort of shrine/warehouse in a slum area, its shelves filled with gods, metal ritual religious objects, herbs, spices, beads, and ceremonial clothing. I was about to buy a random selection of plaster gods and goddesses, some blood-red glass Umbanda drinking goblets in the form of human skulls, but the owner of the shop refused to sell me the stuff until he had divined which two *Orixás* (gods) guarded me. (Followers of Umbanda believe that each person has a number of gods, usually two primary ones, who watch over them.) He also insisted on making up a package, a *bolsa*, containing various herbs and powders, a fragment of a wolf's tooth, and a dried wolf's eye—or so he claimed.[3] Clearly this object was designed to put me in touch with my *axé*, the sacred life energy which is a fundamental concept shared by certain West African and Afro-Brazilian cultures.[4]

Upon my return, my upscale artist friends were curious about where I had been. As I sat in the well-appointed minimalist apartment, unpacking my purchases from their dirty newspaper wrappers, with piles of crumpled pages, smelly string, discarded Sellotape worms, and garish plaster and glass figures spreading out around me on their pristine hardwood floor, the mood changed. My hosts went quiet, eyeing me with pitying consternation, embarrassed for me and my naïve concern with this primitive trash. They professed to know nothing about nor to have any interest in this aspect of Brazilian culture and its flotsam and jetsam which now contaminated their home. I hid the stuff away, and the conversation turned to Hélio Oiticica's influence on modern installation art.

Two days later I found my friends in the midst of a heated argument. About a year earlier, the husband had been in a nasty car accident on his way to a meeting; his face had been cut, and he had nearly lost an eye, which was still badly damaged. When he left the room, his wife burst into tears. She had pleaded with her husband not to go out that evening, she wailed. Earlier, she had been talking to their house servant, a very Black, very old lady who had raised her husband since childhood. She had begged him to stay home, too. The Mãe de Santo (spiritual leader) at her local *terreiro* (temple) learned that the housekeeper had consulted Ifa through divination. A spell had been cast on him, she was told, and as punishment for being untrue in love, Xangô, the god of fire and lightning, was going to blind him. Prior to that, the servant told the wife, the husband had always heeded the advice of his old caretaker when she told him the gods had sent a message. Not that night, though. He had disobeyed her, taking a beautiful young woman to an exhibition instead of staying in. In a hissing whisper, his wife repeated over and over again, "Xangô punished him; Xangô punished him." In that moment I learned a vital lesson: as a white European visitor, when it comes to the white elite and Brazilian syncretism, what you see is most definitely not what you get.[5] I also realized that the early forms of representation in which enslaved people recorded their bodies, myths, and beliefs relate to the living memory of slavery for Brazilians in profound ways.

It has taken me three decades since that encounter to make at least some progress in my understanding of how, in so many ways, Brazil's inheritance from its history of slavery has an amplitude that a majority of European and North American academics ignore. This inheritance goes back a long way, to the arrival of the first Africans at Brazil's slave ports, and remains intact. My artist friends had inherited their proximity to these traditions through the Afro-Brazilians who brought them up and made their food and looked after them physically and emotionally when they were children. When it mattered, the white artists could be as intense, genuine, and beautifully atavistic about this belief system as the poorest Black fetishists you might meet in Bahia from the eighteenth century to the present day. Yet this astonishingly powerful, imaginative, and metaphorically diverse area of Brazil's art history remains cordoned off and hidden. Why else does the first great commentator and recorder of Afro-Brazilian art and cultural life, the Bahian Manuel Querino (1851–1923), remain virtually unknown even in Brazil and untranslated outside of the country? Why is his remarkable archive of photography, devoted to the recording of ancient syncretic Afro-Brazilian works of art, costumes, religious altars, and ceramics, not part of the cultural mainstream of slavery studies? Why is Querino essentially invisible when the elitist French interlopers Pierre Verger (1902–1996) and Roger Bastide (1898–1974), in quest of a purist African aesthetic to encrust upon Afro-Brazilian art, became and remained so celebrated, especially among Brazil's white cultural elite?

From 1800 to 1900, Brazil generated some of the most artistically powerful, imaginative embodiments of Black humans ever made. This century covers the heyday of the Brazilian slave trade and extends through the institution's demise, culminating in the official abolition of slavery with the passage of the so-called Golden Law in May 1888 and the founding of the republic shortly thereafter. In reality, of course, the inheritance of slavery did not just vanish as if by magic because of a piece of legislation. Exploring the representation of the Black body in Brazil up to the end of the nineteenth century, and including a variety of Afro-Brazilian sacred representations, allows for a perspective on how aspects of the semiotic inheritance of slavery lived in the Black imaginary through and after slavery, and how this inheritance was challenged. Representations of the Black body in Brazil occurred within the context of a variety of popular Afro-Brazilian cultures, and it is vital that this archive be represented.

The popular and sacred material discussed below is frequent-

1 Unidentified artist. *The Slave Anastácia*. Undated. Impromptu altar. Beads, quartz crystal. Rio de Janeiro, Museu do Negro.

ly hard to tie down within conventional rules of chronology or provenance, but it is no less valuable for that. This discussion insists that enslaved women and men themselves created extraordinary narratives and artistically powerful and politically empowered representations of Black bodies that exist outside the art history canon and that now need to be taken seriously, read deeply, and treasured aesthetically.

In the following analysis, I will pay special attention to the manner in which syncretic Afro-Brazilian religions imaginatively and creatively construct Black bodies. Key sites are isolated around the worship, narrativization, and fetishization of specific figures. Crucial test cases that follow are the Marian conflations of the Candomblé deity Iemanjá, who often appears as a Black female and is an all-powerful goddess; the *calunga* dolls, which embody the spirits of the enslaved ancestors; and the protean figure of Sacy-Pererê, who remains little known outside Brazil to this day but takes the form of a dark-skinned and mischievous one-legged Black youth.

How Black Bodies Register in 19th-Century Syncretic and Folkloric Art: Test Cases

Black bodies perform and proliferate within the emblematic, allegorical, and typological structures of visual representation generated by Afro-Brazilian forms of syncretism, from the costumes and accompanying symbolic attributes of the participants in Candomblé to the myriad mystical subdivisions of African- and slave-evolved religious communities. Black bodies also flood the iconography of Brazilian Catholic art under the magic touch of its Afro-Brazilian practitioners, whether in the form of miracle paintings, votive sculptures, or in the individual hybrid gods which mix and match Yoruban-evolved deities with the pantheon of Afro-Brazilian Catholic saints. Sometimes these are canonized Black saints, with Black skin but with non-African bodies and faces, and are recognized by Roman Catholicism, as in the case of St. Benedict or the Black Virgins, who proliferated for at least a millennium across the Old and New Worlds. At other times these Black statues become Africanized, as seen in a late-eighteenth-century sculpture of St. Benedict. Still other examples are peculiar to Afro-Brazilian thought and ritual, existing beyond the place of official canonization, as in the case of the twins Cosme and Damião, or of St. Expedite, or perhaps most spectacularly in the terrible forms of the tortured head of Escrava Anastácia.[6] The image of Anastácia, a beautiful Black woman locked into a ghastly dirt-eating metal mask, appeared in the late nineteenth century and was adapted from a lithograph depicting a young enslaved male in a European travel book. Her image still flourishes, and she is simultaneously perceived as a rape victim; the Yoruban deity of freshwaters, Iansã; a Catholic martyr; and a Black enslaved female.

Apart from these figures, hooked at various levels onto or encrusted upon Catholic martyrology and hagiography, there are many Black folkloric figures who may or may not have any relation to the narratives and symbols of Catholicism or Afro-Brazilian syncretism. The more I have studied specific figures within Candomblé and Umbanda and the manner in which Black bodies can morph into different narrative, religious, and racial configurations, the more I feel that it may be impossible to ascertain how these figures work according to the types of rigid symbolic and imagistic configurations with which Western art history feels methodologically secure. Figures move in and out; they are not

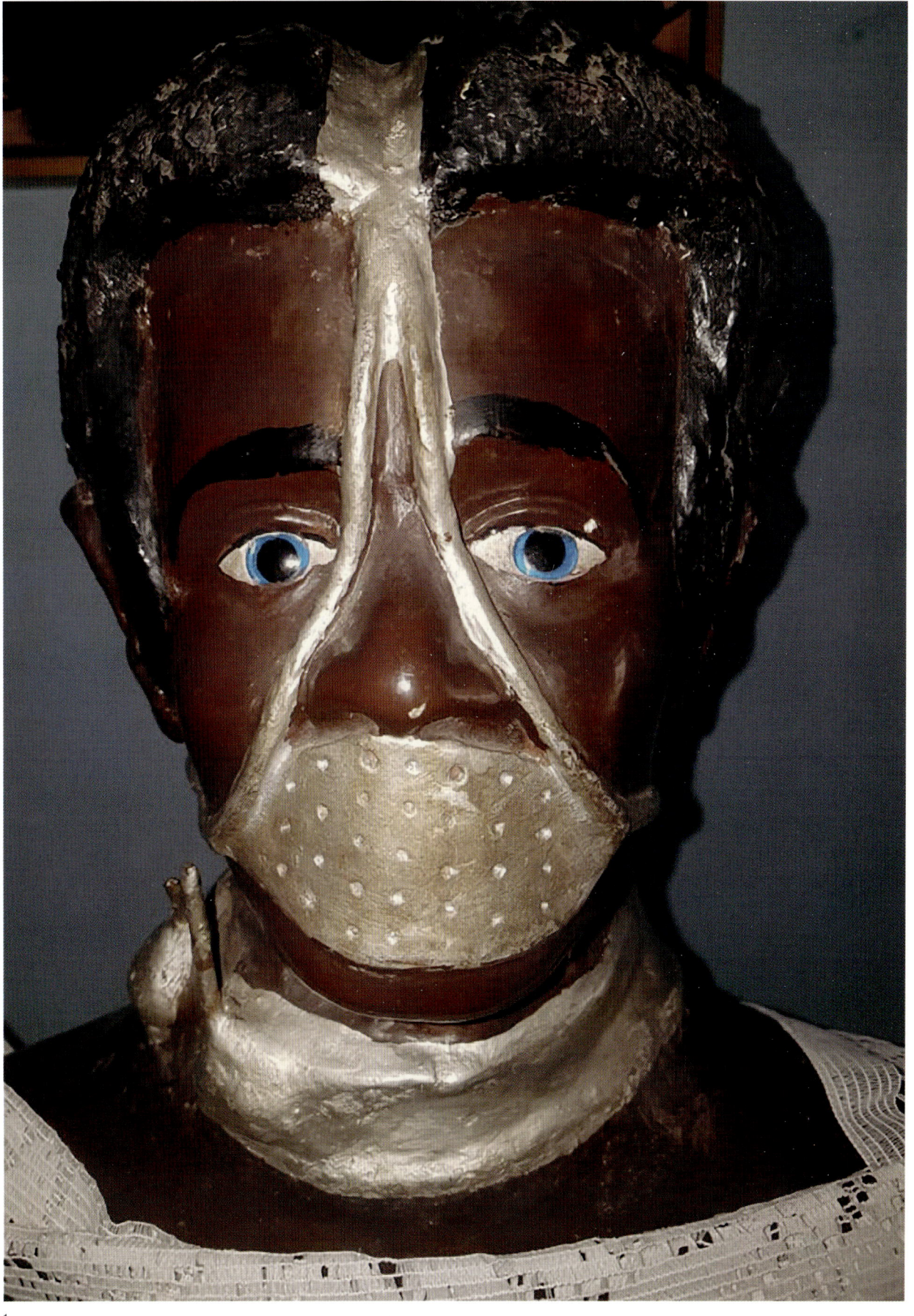

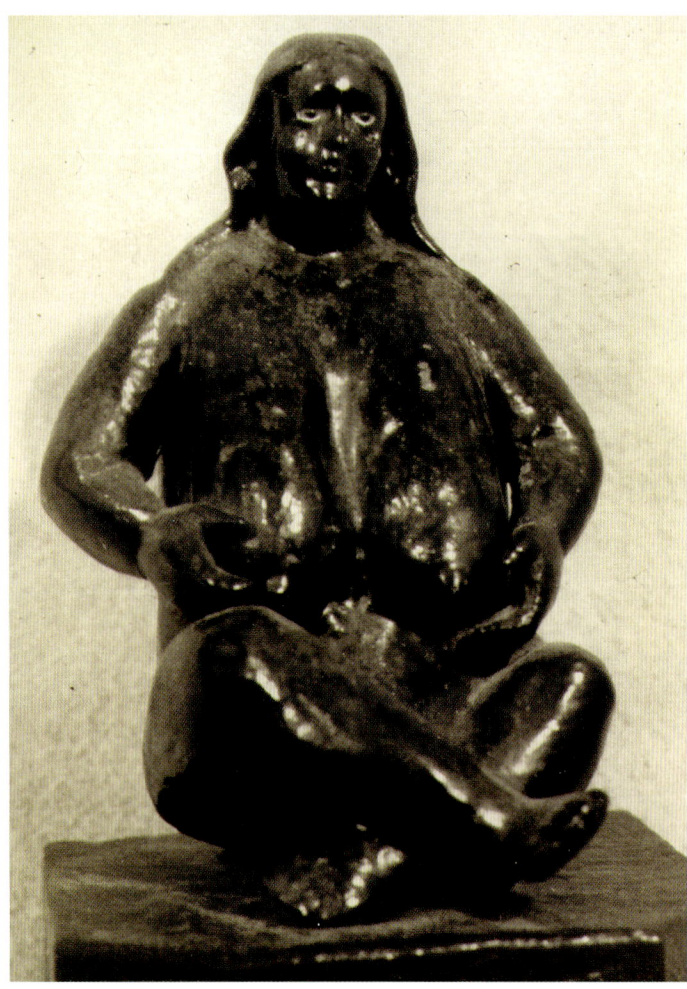

2 Unidentified artist. *Iemanjá Fertility Goddess*. Ca. 1850. Coal tar. Pernambuco, Brazil.

stable; often, the origins and precise racial significations of particular figures are indeterminate. There is a huge array of possible figures to draw upon in terms of Afro-Brazilian folklore and syncretism which has prioritized and transformed Black bodies—male and female, adult and child—or which has turned white progenitors Black, for any number of reasons. I want to take four examples that give some insight into the complexity, and perhaps finally the untranslatability, of these processes.

On the face of it, the figure of the Candomblé goddess Iemanjá is well known. It is difficult to date many of the older "folk art" representations of Iemanjá, so I will restrict myself to examples which are most probably from the late eighteenth century or early nineteenth century, and which certainly predate abolition. As a number of cultural anthropologists and art historians have proved, Iemanjá can be blond and blue-eyed; she can be completely Black and blue-eyed, or Black and black-eyed, or any shade in between. Iemanjá can easily manifest herself as a prim and proper all-white Virgin Mary. I have written elsewhere about the capacity of Candomblé to transform a Barbie doll into the goddess Iemanjá by the simple addition of a nylon fishtail pulled over her legs. She can be a replica of the famous Little Mermaid statue: cheap, plastic tourist fare imported from Copenhagen and sold in a fetish shrine outside the Church of the Bonfim in Salvador Bahia.[7] Then again, Iemanjá can take the form of a huge-breasted, pneumatic mother goddess carved from coal tar, looking like a Black version of the Venus of Willendorf.

This strong, Black, essentially female form of Iemanjá, carved somewhere in the middle to late nineteenth century, emerges as a primal maternal force. Plentiful body fat and pendulous breasts threaten to overwhelm the carving's small, fragile head with its fine-featured face, which may be Black, white, or somewhere in between. What is indisputable is that this figure is one of fertility, motherhood, and female abundance.

When looking at syncretic renditions of Iemanjá, maybe the crucial element is that she eludes binary categorizations around race or pigmentation. It is not a question of setting out provenance; neither is it a question of considering Black superior to white, nor of white being more aesthetically pleasing than Black.

In the liminal spaces of syncretism and the creolized imaginary, all comers are welcome. It is also crucial that they operate in semiotic terms outside any easy race dialectic.[8] Iemanjás both Black and white have leaped beyond Jean-Paul Sartre's antagonistic model of racial aesthetics. Famously in *Orpheo Negro*, Sartre could see the celebration of the Black body's beauty as imprisoned within racial antithesis. He could only see Black beauty in relation to, or defined by, the primary stage of his race dialectic, namely the thesis that white was beautiful. Frantz Fanon and Aimé Césaire were outraged by this position and drew their ideological swords against Sartre. They set out a model not of thesis, antithesis, and synthesis, but of synchronization, synchronicity, and syncretism. Their goddess is not lodged within an agonistic aesthetic dead end but has already sailed out beyond synthesis and into an endless space of female beauty, a space in which all colors and all forms of the essence of the female are beautiful. We like to hope that when the enslaved people placed their Black Iemanjás beneath the altar of a white Catholic Madonna, they were not usurping her but aesthetically conjoining with her. I now want to move into more contested aesthetic waters relating to the limits of syncretic signification, when the sexual exploitation of the woman's body within the power relations of slavery is considered.

Slave, *Calunga*, Madonna, Goddess, Whore:
How Should We Read the Syncretic Female Slave Body?
The analysis of a single remarkable work of art allows us to confront the terrible complicities of syncretistic association when the Black female form divine goes back on today's virtual auction block.

Syncretic Black artists and white artists working in eighteenth- and nineteenth-century Brazil apparently had no difficulty absorbing style and form. They took what they needed when they needed it to make a lovely mixed-race goddess of the sea and of childbirth. Iemanjá might exist in a votive shrine as a pair of Black breasts, but she might exist equally well as a baroque, polychrome sculpture, produced not in the shadow of a white Madonna but in her own light.

This ravishing work came up for sale recently and quietly disappeared into a private collection. In terms of the old rules of art historical connoisseurship, she had no provenance and still has none. She can only be approximately dated at some period between the last half of the eighteenth century and the first half of the nineteenth. It is intriguing that the upmarket website specializing in religious three-dimensional artworks on which she came up for sale was unsure about what to do with her, and as a result ended up treating her in a slightly obscene manner. The sellers introduced the lot as follows:

Provenance: Items quantity: 1
Material: Sculpture Wood
The black Madonna, Yemaja [sic], carved and polychromed
exotic wood processional statue, glass eyes and natural
hair for hairstyle. Slender body type, presented with
an elongated face with regular traits, almond-shaped eyes,
long straight nose and thin mouth; pierced ears with
pendant earrings; articulated arms. Included tunic and coat.
South America, Brazil, 18th Century.
Total height: 64.5 cm (25 ¼ in.)
Few accidents notably on right hand's fingers.

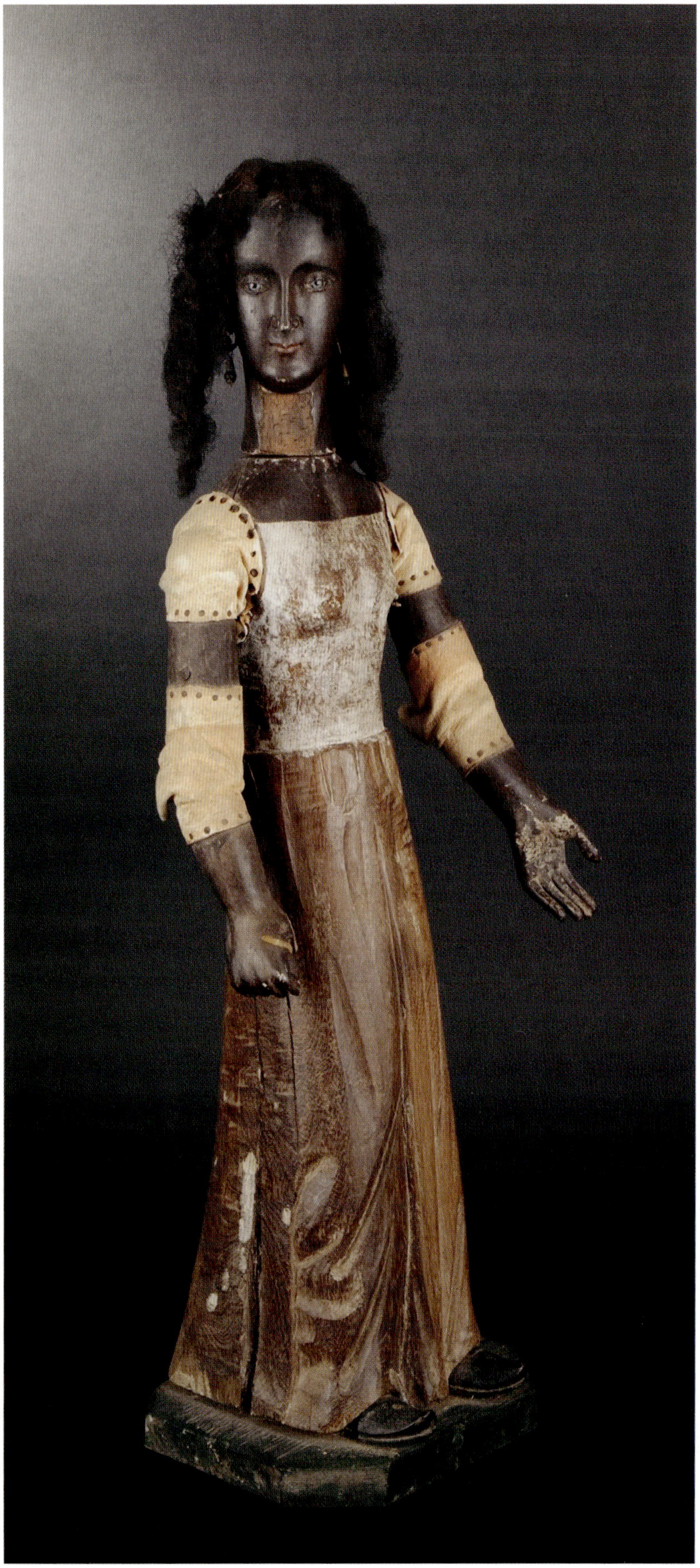

3a

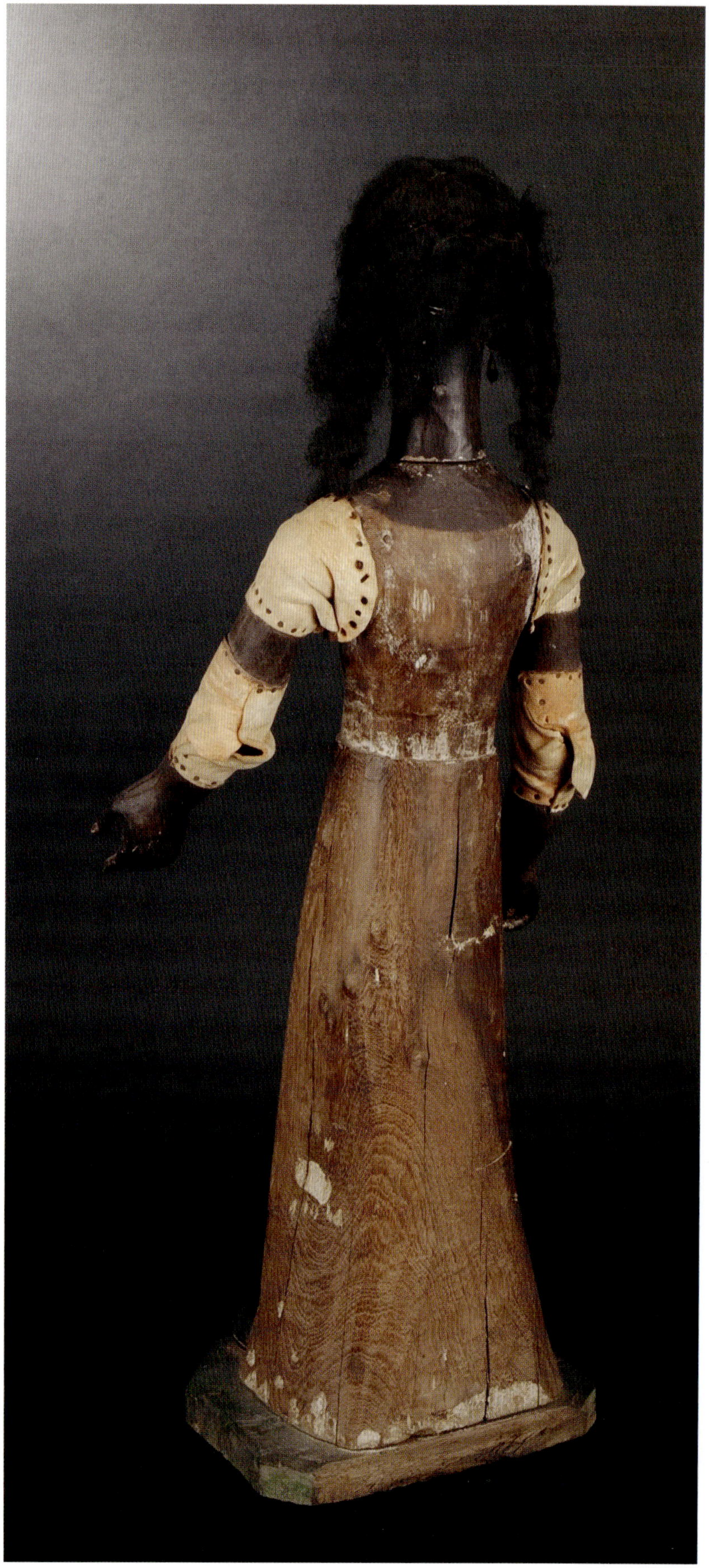

3b

3a, 3b Unidentified artist. *Iemanjá/Calunga*. Ca. 1820-1830. Two views. Wood, polychromed gesso, fiber. Private collection.

This precise description, so dry and forensic, is reminiscent of a runaway-slave advertisement. It is ironic that this Black female, on the auction block once again, is described factually, mythically, theologically, ambiguously. She seems to be any number of things except for the thing that cannot be explicitly spoken: namely, an enslaved young female. She is a "black Madonna," an epithet tying her to the vast global tradition of Black Virgins reaching back into early medieval Europe[9]—a tradition represented in Brazil by probably the most famous Black Virgin of them all, Nossa Senhora da Conceição Aparecida, the Virgin of the Apparition of the Immaculate Conception. Officially the patron saint of the people of Brazil, Nossa Senhora now has her own shrine, her own town, her own marketing industry, her own body of art history scholarship, and her own saint's day. Yet she is simultaneously described as "Yemaja," meaning "Iemanjá." Her glass eyes are noted, but not mentioned is the crucial fact that they are a piercing blue. This is of course not naturalistic. The deep azure eyes relate to her divine function as a water goddess and raise her above the corporeal and into the sphere of Afro-Brazilian divinity.

Yet the precise observation of body type and features appear intensely naturalistic, a fact which forces the prose to lean toward a character portrait of a certain kind of beautiful young woman. It is in the terrifying tension between her divine power and her beautiful, vulnerable physicality that the power of this work emerges. In the slender figure, carved with a sensuous, gentle "S" bend working through the entire body, William Hogarth's languorous rococo line of beauty is up and running. The curve of her back and bottom, the indentation of her waist, and the slight bust are all there in the living limewood, delicate, sensual, intensely feminine, and vulnerable. The hair, falling in ringlets—real human hair—is clearly not African. Combined with the attenuated face and carefully rouged thin lips, the loose-hanging locks create the effect of an indisputable female type. Neither white nor African, this is a *mulata*, and, significantly, a mulata on display. The sellers of this sacred Black female fetish try to square the circle of her syncretic essence, pushing forward with the sales pitch. Having given a rather flat opening attempt at forensic itemization, the sellers attempt prose that is slightly more ambitious:

> Imported to Brazil by black slaves, the African divinity Iemanjá or Yemaja, was adapted by the Church to be assimilated with the Virgin Mary figure. Strongly encouraged by Brazilian clergy, this syncretism facilitated dialogue between this population torn from their ancestral home. According to the Yoruba people from West African tradition, she was originally an aquatic divinity, protector of women particularly pregnant women.[10]

The prose is still invested in the same power dynamics that enabled the moral depravity of slavery before 1888. Note that the prose credits the state-backed Catholic Church with taking the lead on the syncretic fusion of Yoruba goddess and Catholic icon; the Catholic clergy become the master puppeteers behind inculcating the enslaved into the mysteries of Catholico-Yoruban nirvana.

It is not now possible to know precisely what the function of this figure would have been. Was it carried in a procession, and if so, what sort of procession was it? A Catholic procession, perhaps, or was it Candomblé or Umbanda? If the clothing is contemporary, then the sculpture did not function purely as a

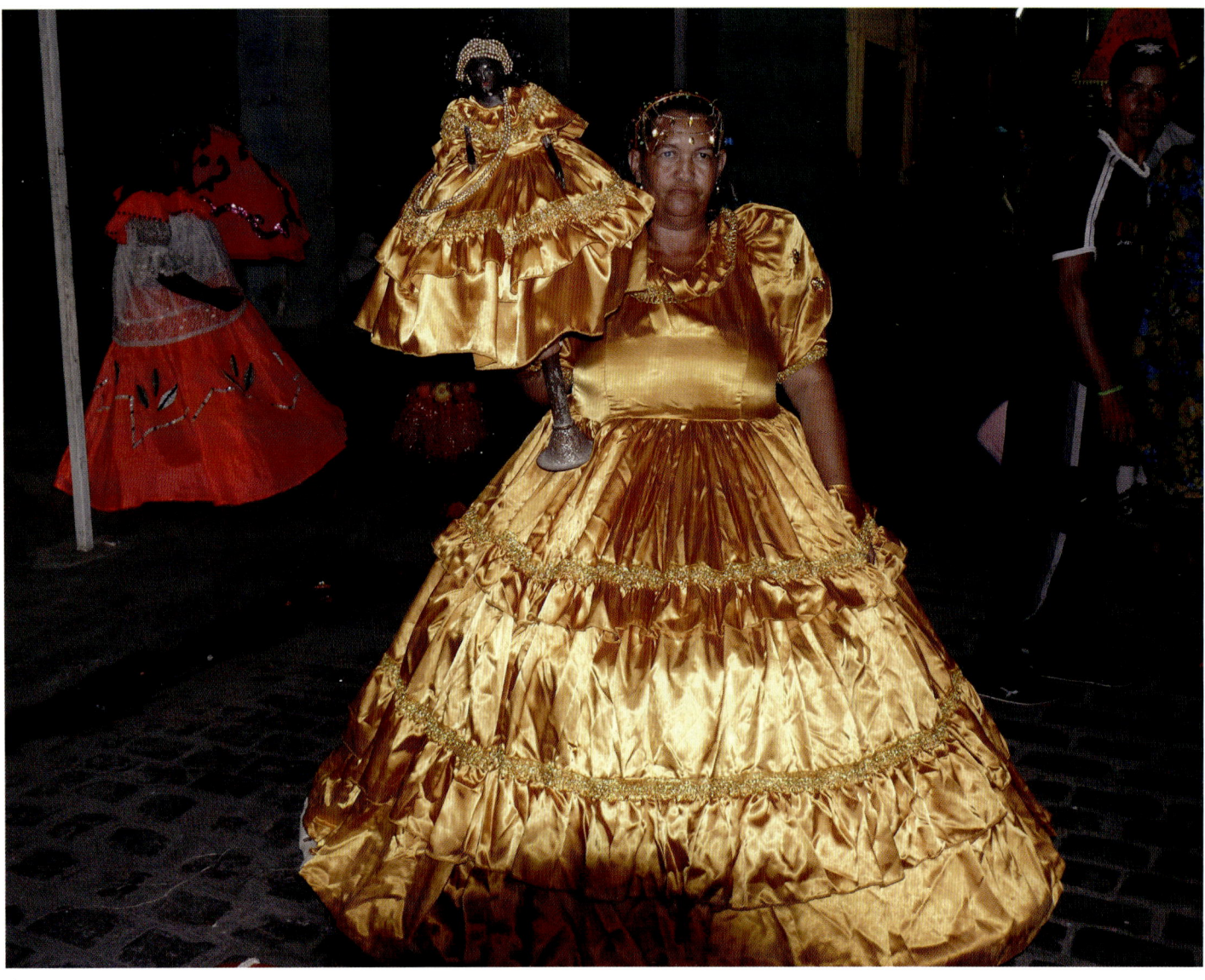

4

version or variant on Nossa Senhora da Conceição Aparecida. Given that this dark Virgin was found in a freshwater river area, her association with Iemanjá is not natural, for Iansa, not Iemanjá, is the goddess of streams and rivers. Nor apart from her blue eyes does she possess any attributes of Iemanjá. In fact, the fusion of the Virgin Mary with a water goddess who could incorporate freshwater, fountains, and the salt ocean had some theological basis in the symbolism of Catholic Marian litany. For example, the *Illustrated Litany of Loretto*, popular from its appearance in the mid-eighteenth century and into the nineteenth, promoted a fundamental association of Mary with the ocean. A fusion of freshwater and saltwater, of what would be Iansa and Iemanjá, is enacted in the engraving and text presenting Mary as "Mother of Divine Grace." She is both "represented as a fountain whose waters are gushing in every part" and as "Mary whose name *a Mari from the sea* abounds in Graces; and as all rivers flow into the sea, so all various graces which are found dispersed amongst the angels and saints, are all congregated in Mary." In the extraordinary rococo engraving that accompanies this insight, Mary appears as a fountain with jets streaming out of her breast and heart, the waters then descending upon a weird collection of mermaid-putti (cherubs), humanized dolphins, and other unstable marine fictions.[11]

There are, however, many other contexts in which this statue might have performed. Considering the look of the costume and of those almond eyes, was this figure related to indigenous Indian representation? Was she designed for a Maracatu procession? Given her size, there is also a strong possibility that she func-

4 Marcus Wood. *Calungas and Black Dancers*. 2007. Photograph. Recife, Brazil, Night of the Silent Drums.

tioned as a calunga—a Black female fetish sculpture central to the performance known as *Maracatu nação*, which has happened for two hundred years (and still does) during the Carnival in Recife in Brazil's Northeast region.

In the carnival groups of the Maracatu, one group of women, the Damas de Paço, dance to themselves and for themselves. As they move to the beat of the *caixa de guerra*, they exist in a space of their own and only secondarily for the human audience, who function as mere onlookers. Each woman, regardless of her age, holds a calunga doll out in her right hand and then dances to it and with it. The doll is neither an appendage nor an extension of the dancer's body, but a partner. In fact, it represents a threshold of communication with the spirit world of the ancestors, specifically those who were enslaved. The calunga figures are fetish dolls embodying their memory. The women who dance to and with their dolls on the Night of the Silent Drums are, in other words, communicating with the spirits of the enslaved ancestors. This single-sex dance, a self-portrait of sorts, performed with an effigy, enacted to communicate with the spirits of the dead, is typical of a number of West African communal dance forms.[12]

After the carnival, the calunga is taken back and kept as a sacred sculpture in the terreiro, or spiritual house of the *nação*, or group to which she belongs.

It is another element, terrifying and repressed, that really energizes this sculpture of a Black woman. Surely her primary signification as she stands there, on display, is as a young enslaved woman up for sale to the highest bidder, which ironically is precisely the position in which art marketplace economics have now placed her. Not only must she suffer the indignity of being sold and resold, but she is displayed uncovered to the buyers, her simple frock with its fringes at the collar and sleeve end, and her equally modest and unembellished shawl, stripped from her. We can inspect her as slave traders would examine their "goods," eyeing her for damage: looking at those broken fingers; at the chipped gesso which has fallen from the throat; at the stiff, articulated joints of the mannequin. We can look her over and then buy her or reject her. I find the whole process of looking at these sales photographs deeply disturbing, not to say pornographic.

This female sculpture is put up for the male scopophiliac, and even the female scopophiliac gaze, to gorge itself on. Does she function as a fetish object, a doll, a commodity fetish, a bondage fetish, or indeed as an African fetish doll? Perhaps that is the heart of her mystery: that she functions as an ur-fetish—transplanted, African, magical; a primitive African embodiment of Europe's most extreme sadomasochistic fantasies, ironically coined by Portuguese sailors when they first saw West African sculptural forms. It is as if the aesthetic marketplace now is still cutting up, stripping down, and laying out female flesh for our enjoyment, purchase, and investment. The sculpture has a precise market value now just as the enslaved mulata she represents historically had a value before 1888.

One way out of the semiotic bind posed by these photographs for sale lies in the insistence that syncretism celebrates Blackness by making it unexceptional. The relativity of Blackness and whiteness when faced with the transformative energies of the syncretic imagination melt away. Iemanjá's simultaneous manifestation as a Yoruban water goddess, a Black Virgin Mary, and a quintessentially beautiful young Black woman who may well have European, African, and indigenous Indian blood, can all coexist. Yes, we must take the suppressed and disguised aspects of this figure's

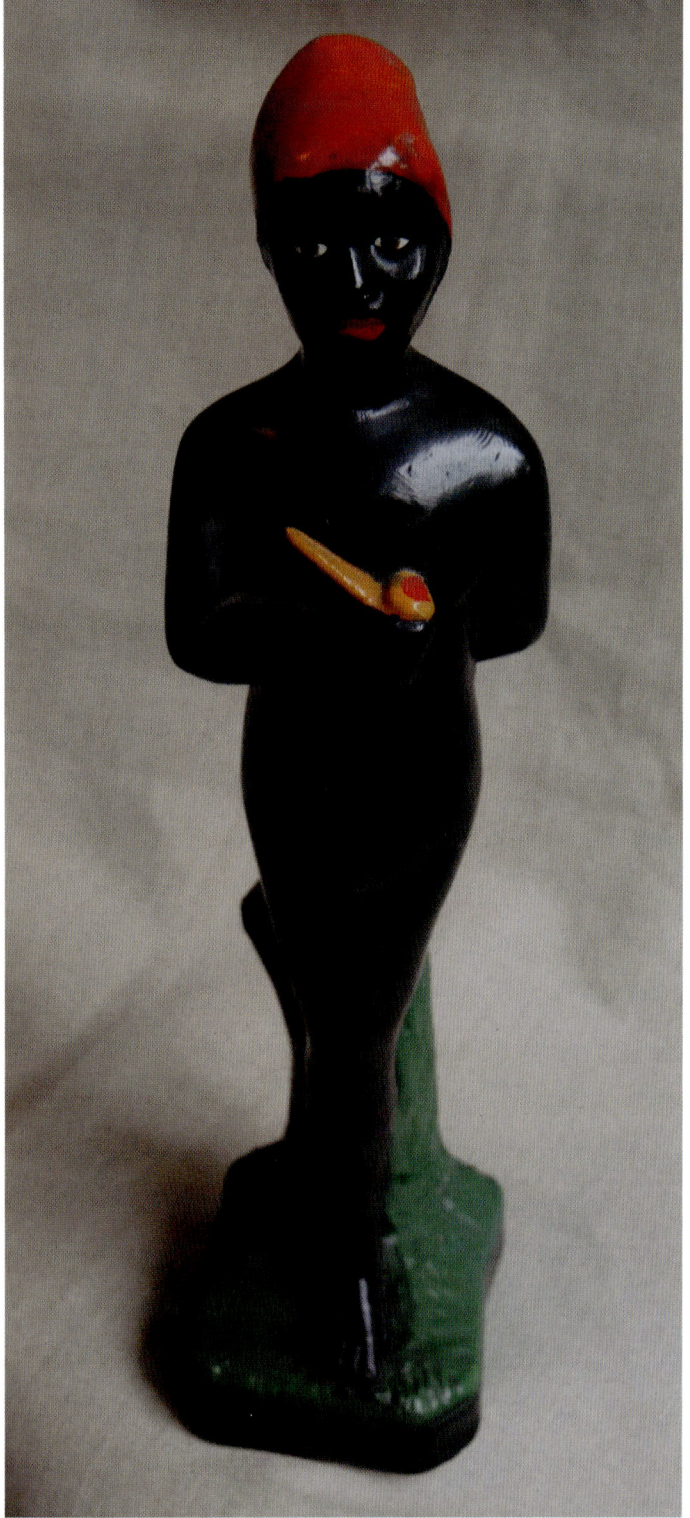

5

5 Unidentified artist. *Sacy-Pererê*. Ca. 1970. Molded and painted plaster.

divine significations seriously, yet the crucial fact to realize is that this depiction of a young female Black body remains contaminated by its relation to the memory of slavery and sexual depravity.

Saucy, Sassy Sacy-Pererê:
A Protean Man-Boy Existing on the Peripheries of Syncretism
The figure of Sacy-Pererê provides a fascinating example of the differences between Brazilian cultural constructions of the Black male body in slavery and afterward. Although little known outside Brazil, Sacy-Pererê means many different things to many different cultures within the country. He cannot in any direct way be connected to Catholic iconography or narratology, and his relation to Afro-Brazilian syncretic religions is debated, disputed, and certainly ambivalent and tangential. In some quarters he is absorbed into the Bahian Umbanda pantheon, but in an erratic manner; and he certainly does not share the clear symbolic and narrative functions of the major gods and goddesses of Candomblé. Almost all the information surrounding Sacy-Pererê has evolved out of oral storytelling and hearsay. He is genuinely folkloric, and although he evolved out of Brazilian cultures under slavery, he remains very much alive and kicking, ever morphing and with fluid meaning. He is a truly protean Black body in popular art. It is no exaggeration to say that all in all, Sacy-Pererê is one of the most semiotically unstable and symbolically rich configurations of Black corporeality in the whole of the Atlantic slave diaspora.

He is a striking figure. Brightly painted figurines of Sacy-Pererê's likeness are commonly available at shrine shops in Recife, Salvador Bahia, Rio, and São Paulo otherwise devoted to selling the more stable figures related to Bahian syncretic religions. He is also embedded within Brazilian children's literature, having become a hugely popular staple in nursery books and comic books in the 1960s. Illustrated journals and graphic novels often depicted him in the fashion of grotesque white-evolved racist stereotypes of Black people, along with his mother, who closely resembles the North American "mammy."[13]

As a Black figure within the popular imagination of Brazil, and as an ambiguous Black male figure in terms of age and gender, one who reaches back into the significations of Brazil's history of slavery, Sacy-Pererê is both fascinating and vibrant. He can be amusing, irritating, or terrifying. He can occupy a liminal space, his persona hovering somewhere between that of an annoying child or simply a mischievous one. He can be the formidable embodiment of revolutionary energy and ultimate slave resistance. Exactly how old his mythic base might be or what cultures it evolved out of cannot be forensically ascertained with any accuracy. It has been argued that he was a fusion of combined elements from African, Portuguese, and indigenous Brazilian folklore. In the interior it is said that he began as a Guarani deity, a brown monkey complete with tail or an exotic bird of the rainforest. He then became heavily saturated in African myth as he narratively migrated up to the slave coast of Brazil's Northeast region in the sixteenth century, picking up the African griot's pipe, only to be finally imbued with a series of European qualities typical of the imp.[14]

All Brazilians, from small children onward, know what Sacy-Pererê looks like, or they have their version of him and what he does. Yet his lineage, parenthood, and chronology are lost in a maze of crisscrossing oral narratives. He has also become a ghostly symbol of the damaged, wandering slave, the ultimate form of the displaced traveler who lacks any agency. Adopting his name as their own, the Brazilian migrant musical band Sacy-Pererê argues that he operates as a sort of mythic, Black, diminutive variant of the Ancient Mariner: "The name stems from a Brazilian legend: Along with other slaves, Sacy Pererê was carried off from Africa to Brazil. Due to a punishment imposed by his master, Sacy lost his leg. Since then Sacy, the one-legged boy with the red cap, has been the spirit which guides meandering travelers by whispering his story into their ears."[15] He is a common sight on household syncretic altars, and there are statues of Sacy-Pererê made of wood, coal tar, stone, and polychrome plaster that date back well into the nineteenth century, although his origins are undoubtedly much older than this.

Sacy-Pererê is ubiquitous, and his outward physical appearance tends to be relatively consistent. His Black skin is always very dark, and he is depicted as a naked male, a boy or youth with no visible genitalia. He wears a red bonnet, smokes a pipe, and stands on one leg. How is this strange figure to be symbolically and hermeneutically read? The absence of genitalia is significant because it indicates that Sacy is not to be aligned with the Yoruban-evolved trickster deities of Candomblé and Umbanda. His lack of endowment exists in stark contrast to the flamboyantly erect and ribaldly ithyphallic trickster god Exu, who in his male manifestation is very much a grown man, and not the least bit shy about openly displaying the fact.

There are several narratives explaining the single leg. Particularly prevalent is the explanation that he was not born a monopedic figure, but that he lost his other leg in a *capoeira* (dance/martial art) contest fighting another enslaved person. This suggests that Sacy existed at the heart of Black slave culture and that

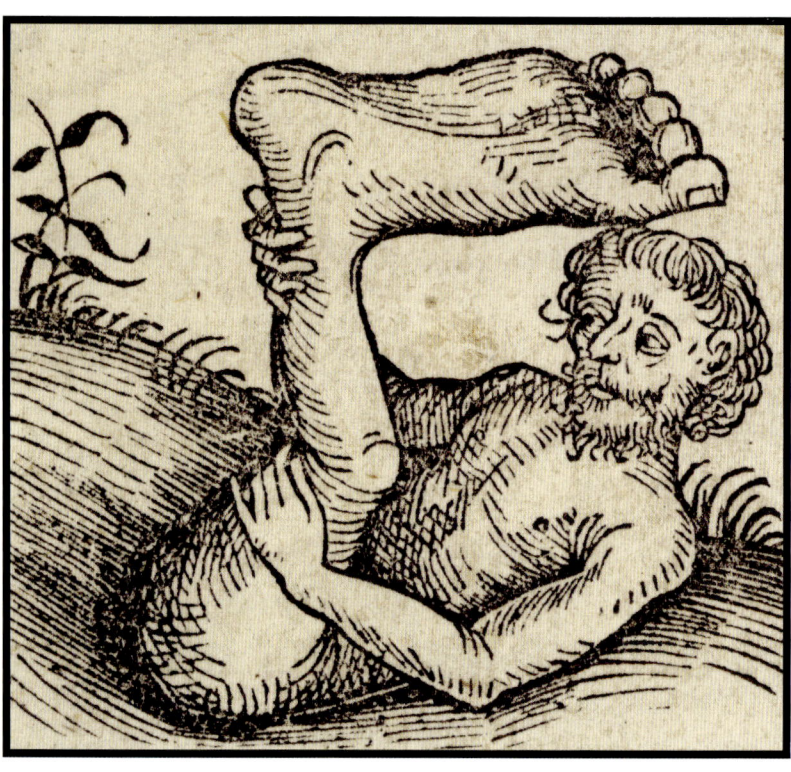

6

6 Michel Wolgemut, workshop. *A Sciopod*. Woodcut. Hartmann Schedel, *Nuremberg Chronicle*, 1493.

7 Unidentified artist. *Sacy Shoe Polish*. Ca. 1930. Advertisement. Lithograph.

he was a part of an active and potentially violent slave resistance. Then again, the amputation of a foot was an extreme form of punishment exacted on people held in slavery for multiple attempts at running away. Sacy's single leg might then allude to mutilation for attempted self-liberation.

In this context, it is relevant to note that Sacy always wears a red cap. This is undeniably reminiscent of the Liberty Cap or *bonnet rouge* of the French Jacobins, which had come via various cultural meanderings to represent Latin American revolutionary sympathies in nineteenth-century Brazil.[16] He smokes a pipe and often appears suddenly in a cloud of smoke. His association with smoke and burning sometimes leads to stories where he is related to the devil, or indeed is a small devil himself. In this sense he aligns with constructions of Satan as the first rebel. Yet he is also embedded in white myths connecting Black bodies with damnation and hellfire. Several popular tales specify that he shuns any image or ritual object related to the Catholic Church. In this sense he exists starkly outside the forms of typological fusion which typify other syncretic deities. For example, as noted, Iemanjá is fused with the Virgin Mary through the association of the Virgin's blue and white vestments with the ocean, while St. George, because of his armor, is fused with Ogun, god of war, iron, and weaponry. One story tells of how Sacy can be captured: the holy beads of a rosary cast into the smoke cloud in which he appears will lasso him. He is a form of trickster god, often presented as one who sets up benign practical jokes around the house, such as hiding and misplacing objects, but who is also capable of more extreme malevolence, such as spoiling or poisoning food. Here he might be acting spitefully much as a disaffected "house slave" would surreptitiously and secretly act against a slaveholder.

Sacy-Pererê's racial origins and parenthood draw on a number of narratives. By far the most common tale concerns his mother, who is presented as a large "house slave" or *mae praeta*, commonly at work in the kitchen making sweets and pastries. Little formal anthropological work has been done on the narratives of Sacy's parentage.[17] When it comes to the association of the one-legged man with the Black African, however, there are well-established literary analogs going back to Pliny and working their way through the earliest travel narratives produced in early modern Europe.

Probably the most notorious textual precursor of Sacy-Pererê in illustrated European literature is found in the remarkable account of Africans or Ethiopians in *The Voiage and Travayle of Sir John Maundeville, Knight*, which first appeared in the middle of the fourteenth century. In the fifty-first chapter, "Of the lande of Ethiope," Mandeville describes Africans with economy, conclud-

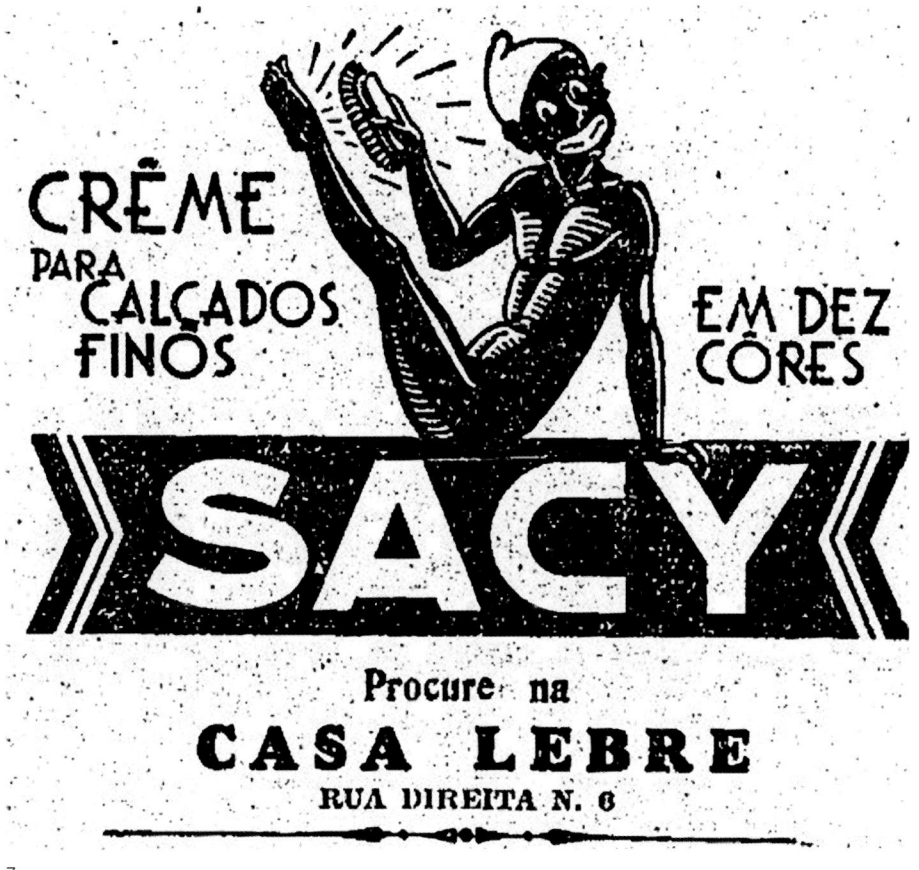

7

ing: "In Ethiope are such men as have but one foote, and they go so fast that it is a great marvaill, and that is a large foot that the shadow thereof covereth the body from son or rayne when they lye uppon their backs, and when their children are first borne they loke like russet, and when they waxe olde they be all blacke."[18] Yet as Mandeville's first great editor John Knight noted, these Ethiopians bear a strange similarity to an Asian Indian people described by Pliny: "… in India is another race of men, who have only one leg but are able to leap with a surprising agility."[19] Mandeville's text was a contemporary bestseller, translated into Latin and all the major European languages of the Middle Ages, so Sacy-Pererê's single Black leg might have come from Pliny's Indians via Africa and into Brazil. Mandeville gives no explanation as to why his Black Africans should have but one leg; they are, quite simply, marvelous in his eyes. Maybe this stark mark of difference is at a deep level a way of marking pigmental difference as an absolute divide between us and them, Black and white. It is also significant that early manuscript images and then woodcut illustrations proliferated, making this one-legged Ethiop a familiar figure to an educated European readership.

There is a fundamental similarity between the woodcuts of white European configurations of the one-legged African and the coarse woodcut imagery of late-nineteenth- and early-twentieth-century advertising showing Sacy. In the example above, Sacy bends to show off his capacity to polish his one Black foot until it shines, while the European image of the sciapodic Ethiop from nearly four hundred years earlier shows the Black man, who strangely is not Black, shielding his face from the sunshine with his one mighty foot. Sacy is ultimately a triumphant creation, a testimony to the protean capacities of Afro-Brazilian symbiology. He runs in and out of adult folklore and children's literature; he vacillates between supernatural being and enslaved victim, between an irritating impish spirit and an embodiment of slave resistance. Above all, he, in common with other Afro-Brazilian symbolic figures, has a capacity for cultural adaptation which the more stable icons and narratives of European-evolved thought and art do not.

7

2

ABOLITION AND POST-ABOLITION IN THE VISUAL CULTURE OF LATIN AMERICA: COLOMBIA, BRAZIL, ARGENTINA, AND PERU

MARÍA DE LOURDES GHIDOLI

The abolition of slavery is commemorated on specific dates, which vary in Latin America from country to country, but its achievement was the culmination of a slow process over the course of the nineteenth century. It is thus useful to understand the historical and political contexts of different regions and how abolition came about. In general, abolition was preceded by several judicial processes, including laws providing that children born of enslaved mothers would henceforth be free (often called Law of the Free Womb), prohibition of the further importation of enslaved Africans, gradual or immediate abolition, and compensation to former enslavers.[1] There were also several strategies for gaining freedom before the cumbersome political process came to fruition. For example, individual manumissions were possible, mainly through grants of freedom, usually through provisions of a will upon the death of an enslaver. Self-manumission took place when enslaved people bought freedom for themselves or family members. Other alternatives reflecting the agency of enslaved people included court cases challenging the slave system, flight and rebellion, and the creation of Maroon communities—isolated geographical enclaves where groups of runaway slaves lived (called *palenques* in Colombia, *quilombos* in Brazil).

How was the emancipation process represented in images? What images shaped the visual culture of abolition and the period following the end of slavery?

A widely disseminated iconography of emancipation emerged from British abolitionist propaganda and the abolition medallion. The image of the kneeling Black man became the icon of the British campaign begun by the Society for Effecting the Abolition of the Slave Trade, established in 1787. The society commissioned Josiah Wedgwood to design the medallion, which bore the caption "Am I not a Man and a Brother?" The subordinate posture of the figure, which suggests that freedom was a gift conceded by the enslaver, has been well circulated, a portrayal of the enslaved person as a passive subject eternally thanking a benefactor. That role was often played by such female allegories as Liberty and Justice or representations of the various nations involved. Marcus Wood has analyzed this motif in light of arguments Frantz Fanon developed, calling on the abstract analytical model of Hegel's master-slave, in the specific dynamic of the racialized power central to the African diaspora: "What Fanon demands that we see in the organization of this colossal fantasy, so consistent across the Black Atlantic, is nothing less than a brilliantly constructed aesthetic system for the control of white guilt and black suffering, and for the disguise of white culpability and black outrage."[2]

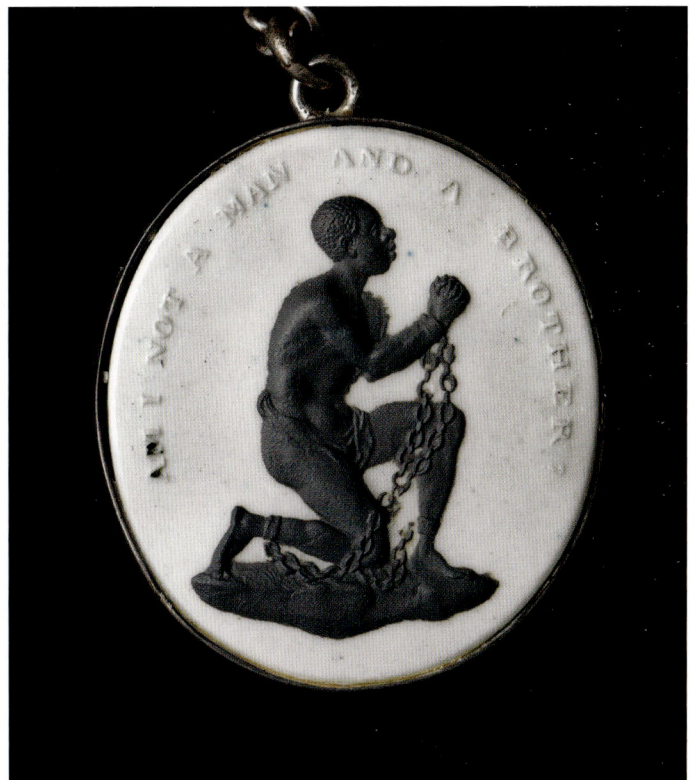

8 Josiah Wedgwood. *Am I not a Man and a Brother?* Ca. 1787. Antislavery medallion. Black jasperware. Washington, DC, Smithsonian National Museum of American History.

This visual trope, which spread profusely in all sorts of ways, also reached South America. And as we shall see, the givers of freedom were not allegorical figures, but real people.

Representing the Gradual Process of Abolition: Colombia

We will first deal with an image from Colombia, one of the allegorical bronze bas-reliefs on the pedestal of the first monument to Simón Bolívar, erected in Bogotá in 1846. The organizer of the project, José Ignacio Paris, who had been a friend of Bolívar, commissioned the monument from the Italian sculptor Pietro Tenerani and added to the homage with a commemorative medal and the publication of a book, *Intorno alla statua di Bolívar* (1845) by Filippo Gerardo, which included six steel engravings of the statue. The choice of Tenerani may have been a result of his familiarity with the iconography of Colombia's national hero; in 1831 and 1836 he had sculpted busts of Bolívar. Historically, the themes of the allegorical reliefs have been attributed to Tenerani's supposed knowledge of Bolívar's ideas and actions.[3] Vanegas Carrasco suggests that the monument should be interpreted as a political statement.[4] As context, between 1839 and 1841, just a few years before the statue was installed, the republic of Nueva Granada was immersed in a civil war, called the *Guerra de Los Supremos*, after the nickname given to regional *caudillos*, or supreme leaders. The war started as a dispute between the government and the Catholic Church and gave rise to other conflicts between supporters of the legacy of Bolívar and supporters of the legacy of Francisco de Paula Santander.[5] The four bas-relief plaques on the statue's pedestal recall several of Bolívar's major policy actions: the proclamation of independence; the oath to uphold the constitution; the granting of clemency to the vanquished enemy; and the abolition of slavery. The scenes were thus intended to extol the national hero's civic and moral virtues.

The plaque representing the emancipation of the enslaved Blacks includes a quotation from the speech with which Bolívar opened the Congress of Angostura on February 15, 1819: "I yield to your sovereign decision to change or reject any of my laws and decrees; but I beg you to confirm the absolute freedom of the slaves, as much as I would beg for my life, and the life of the republic."[6] The choice of this theme for the obverse of the commemorative medal shows how important it was to José Ignacio Paris. It should also be pointed out that as of 1846, the year of Paris's sculpture, slavery still existed in what is now Colombia. Only a free womb law, providing that children born of enslaved

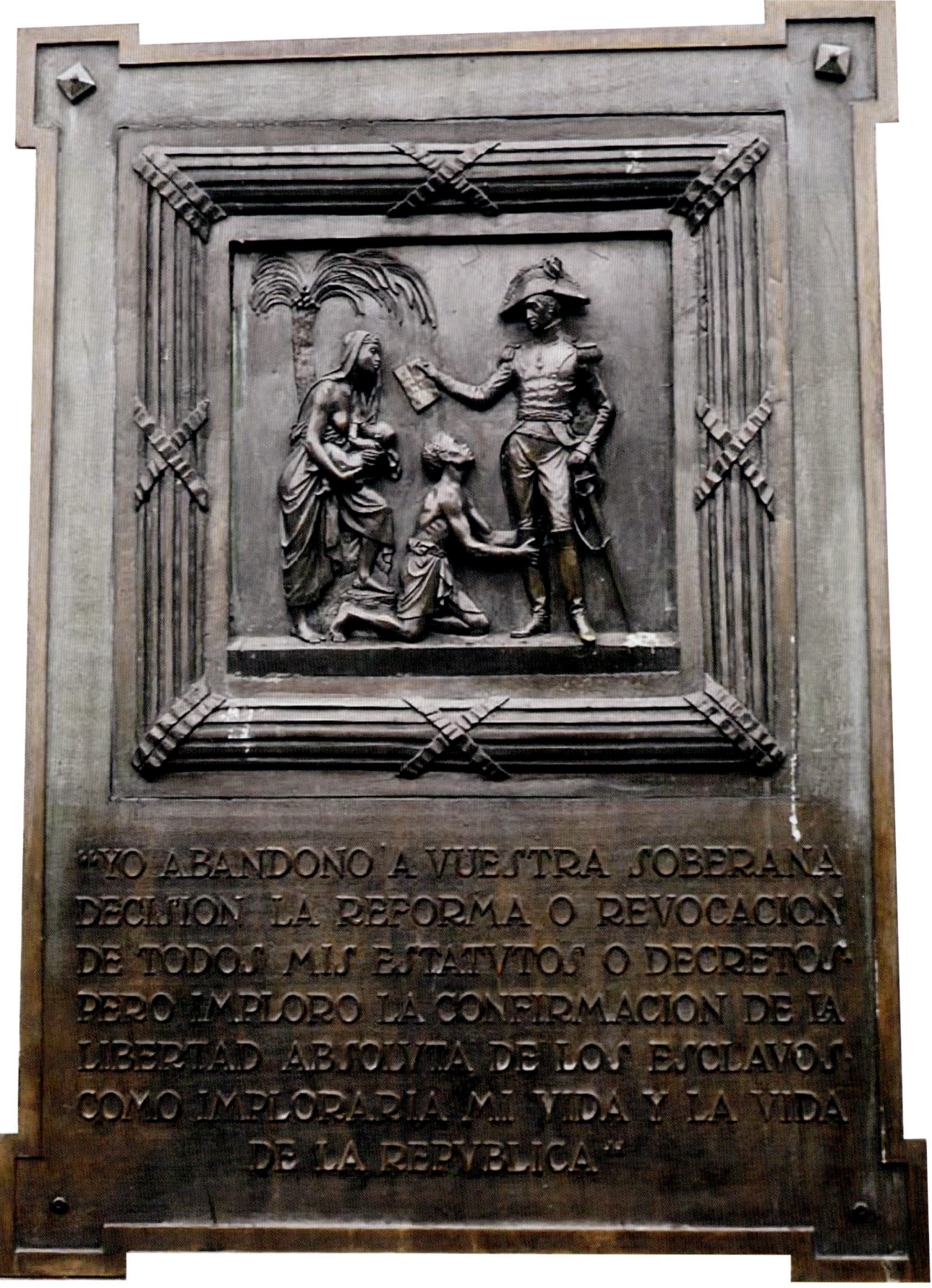

9 Pietro Tenerani. *The Abolition of Slavery*. 1846. Front relief, base of monument to Simón Bolívar. Bronze. Bogotá, Colombia, Plaza de Bolívar.

10 Pietro Tenerani, after. *The Abolition of Slavery*. Front relief, base of monument to Simón Bolívar. Steel engraving. Bogotá, Museo Nacional de Colombia.

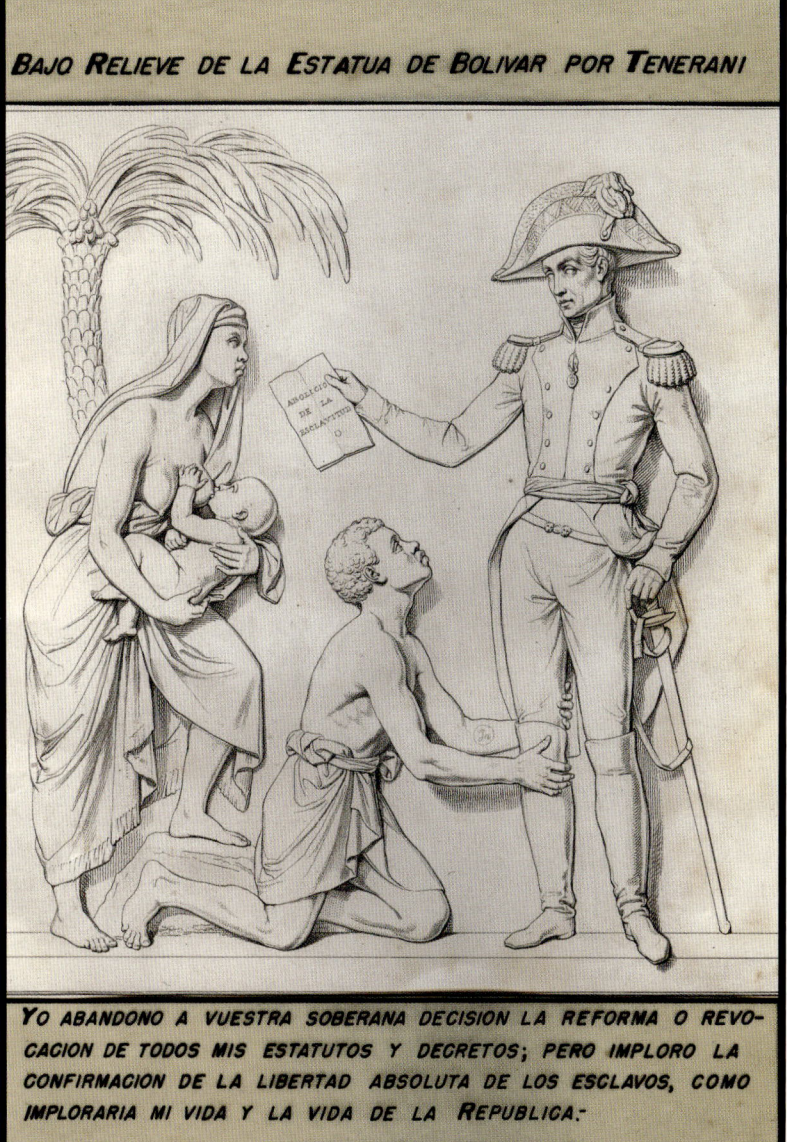

10

mothers would henceforth be free, had been included in the 1821 Constitution of Cúcuta and was applied to the territory of Gran Colombia (the present-day Colombia, Panama, Venezuela, and Ecuador).

The bas-relief plaque, the published engraving, and the medallion all show the same scene: an Afrodescendant woman and man next to Bolívar. The woman holds a nursing baby in her arms and is wearing a cloth wrap that goes from her head down to her ankles, open to leave her breasts exposed. The kneeling man, his upper body bare, grasps the right leg of the Liberator, who is dressed in a military uniform with sword and bicorn hat.

The man and woman are barefoot, a feature that symbolized, according to travel accounts[7] and many images in which it can be inferred, the enslaved condition of Afrodescendant people in the Americas. That is confirmed in the image in which Bolívar extends in his right hand a proclamation labeled "Abolition of Slavery" and again in the text below the bas-relief. The addition of a palm tree, hinting at a tropical landscape, completes the scene.

The contrasting ways the artist decided to display the faces of the figures should be noted. Bolívar's, in three-quarter view, is clearly a portrait.[8] The enslaved people, however, are in full profile. One might assume that the artist did this to emphasize facial

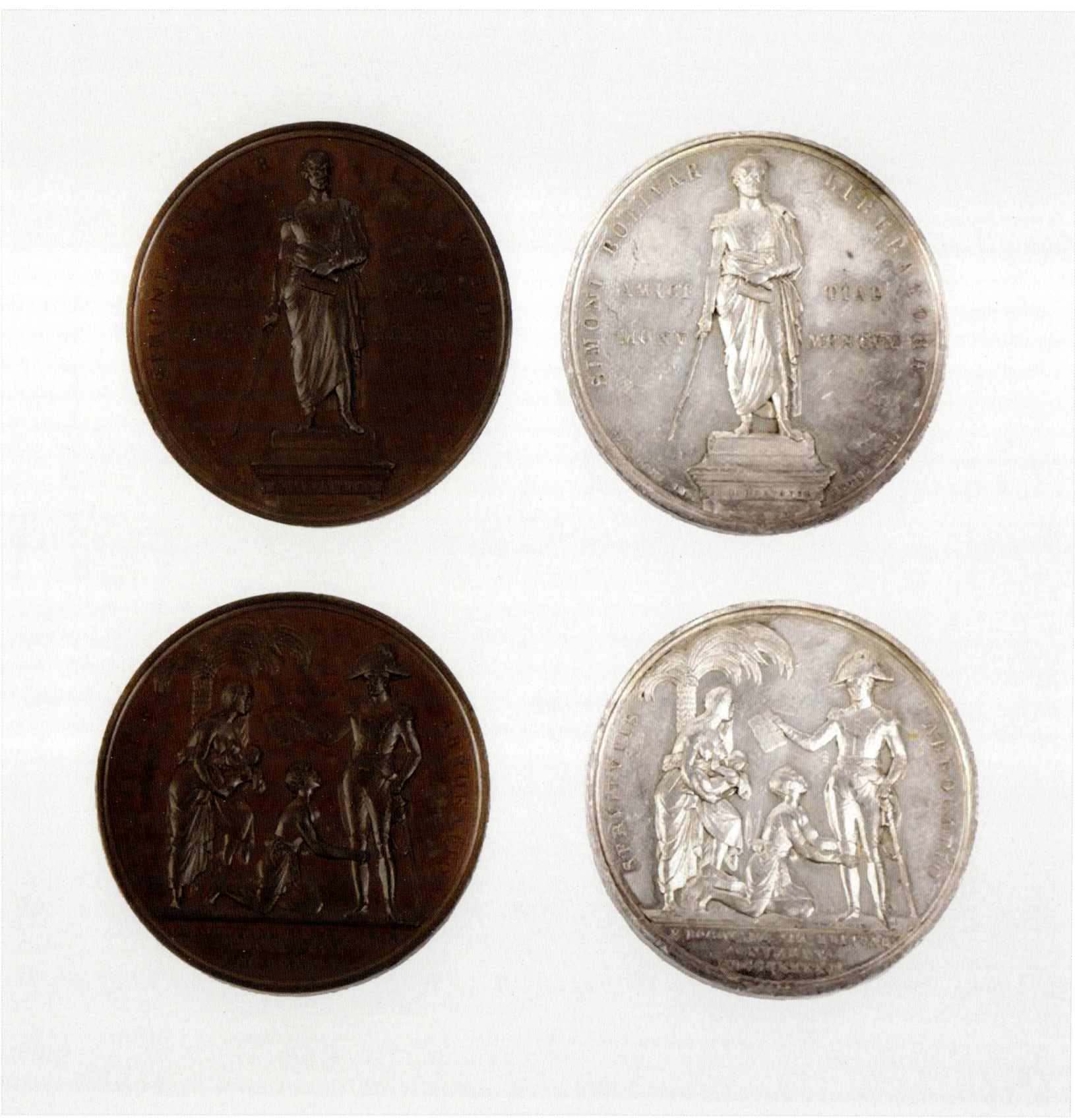

11 Karl Friedrich Voigt, Munich. *Simón Bolívar, Liberator of the Slaves.* Commemorative medal, bronze and silverplate versions. 1846. *Obverse:* Bolívar with thankful formerly enslaved family. Reverse: Statue of Bolívar from his monument, Bogatá, Colombia.

12 Angelo Agostini. *Back from Paraguay.* Illustration. Published in *A Vida Fluminense* (June 11, 1870).

13 A. D. Bressae. *Allegory on the Law of the Free Womb.* Ca. 1871. Polychromed plaster. Rio de Janeiro, Museu Histórico Nacional.

characteristics associated with people of African descent.⁹ But the image is derived mainly from the abolitionist propaganda discussed above.

In this example, the chains of the abolition medallion have been omitted, and a complete family is shown, with only the man kneeling. The woman leans toward the benefactor. The childlike representation of the Black man, facing a much larger Bolívar, is also reminiscent of the medallion. Recalling that Tenerani was trained in the neoclassical tradition,¹⁰ it is possible that the iconographic motif is not meant to represent Bolívar's concrete ideas and actions. Instead, the artist may have used a conventional representation that was common in Europe which, without Bolívar present, could be adapted to any other context. While the palm intrudes into the blank background typical of neoclassical bas-reliefs, palm trees were a common feature in Colombia's Cauca Valley, where slave labor was important.

Brazil
In imperial Brazil, we will deal with two milestones in the country's gradual abolition process that have been represented in images: the Rio Branco, or Law of the Free Womb of 1871, and the so-called Golden Law of 1888, which ended slavery. The Law of the Free Womb was approved at the end of the War of the Triple Alliance, which lasted from 1864 to 1870 and pitted Paraguay against the Triple Alliance of Argentina, Brazil, and Uruguay, and the return of victorious Black soldiers from the field of battle. That is the context for a cartoon by Angelo Agostini, an Italian artist living in Rio de Janeiro.¹¹

In the caption of the image, the artist draws an analogy between the enslavement of Africans and their descendants and a supposedly dictatorial government in an independent country, which had been the Triple Alliance's justification for that ignominious conflict.¹² The same analogy had been made earlier in the discourse surrounding the Latin American independence movements.¹³ The image itself denounces slavery in Brazil, as the decorated soldier returns and sees a person being whipped, then emphasizes the brutality of slavery by introducing an emotional element that hits the readers of the magazine even harder: the person being whipped is the soldier's own mother. The body language of the soldier is notable, starting with the look of horror and the hand raised to his forehead, indicating despair at not being able to stop the whipping. For someone who had just come from a struggle where he had put his life on the line, that would be contradictory. The left hand, clenched in a fist, indicates a sense of helplessness in the face of slavery's legality. In the composition of the work, the figures are in a realistic space divided into three planes: first the soldier, then the scene of the whipping, then the hills indicating the landscape. Considering Agostini's abolitionist sentiments, it might be suggested that with this formal composition he was trying to establish a timeline. The present would be the foreground with the figure of the soldier, a Black man who is free or about to be freed by his service in the war, and the past would be the plane in which the whipping takes place. The latter is almost directly taken from the images of the flagellation of enslaved Blacks in Latin America, and specifically in Brazil (by Jean-Baptiste Debret, Johann Moritz Rugendas, and others).

Two other works that are completely different from Agostini's cartoon but which represent the Law of the Free Womb are A. D. Bressae's polychromed plaster sculpture *Alegoría à lei do ventre livre* (*Allegory on the Law of the Free Womb*) and an oil painting

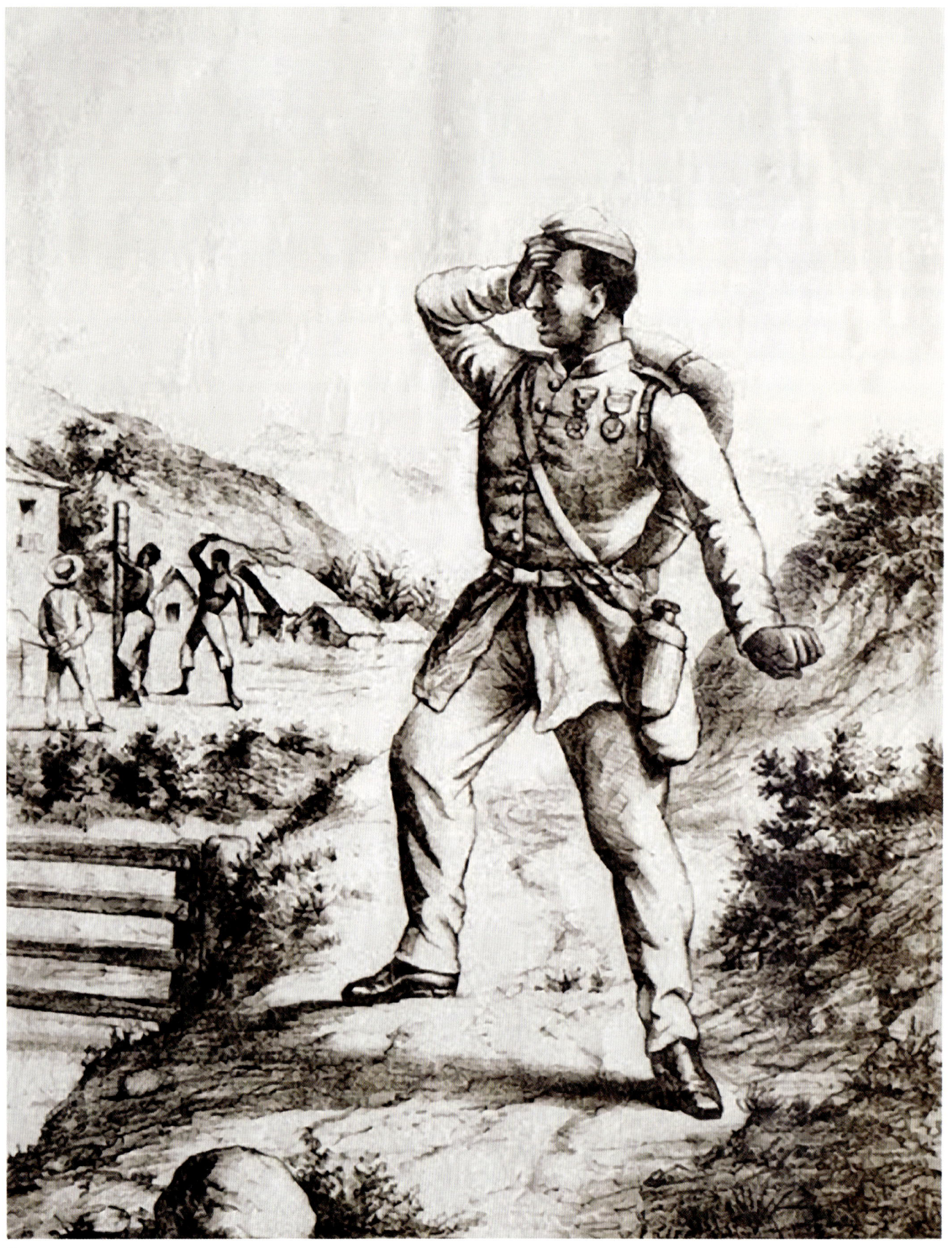
12

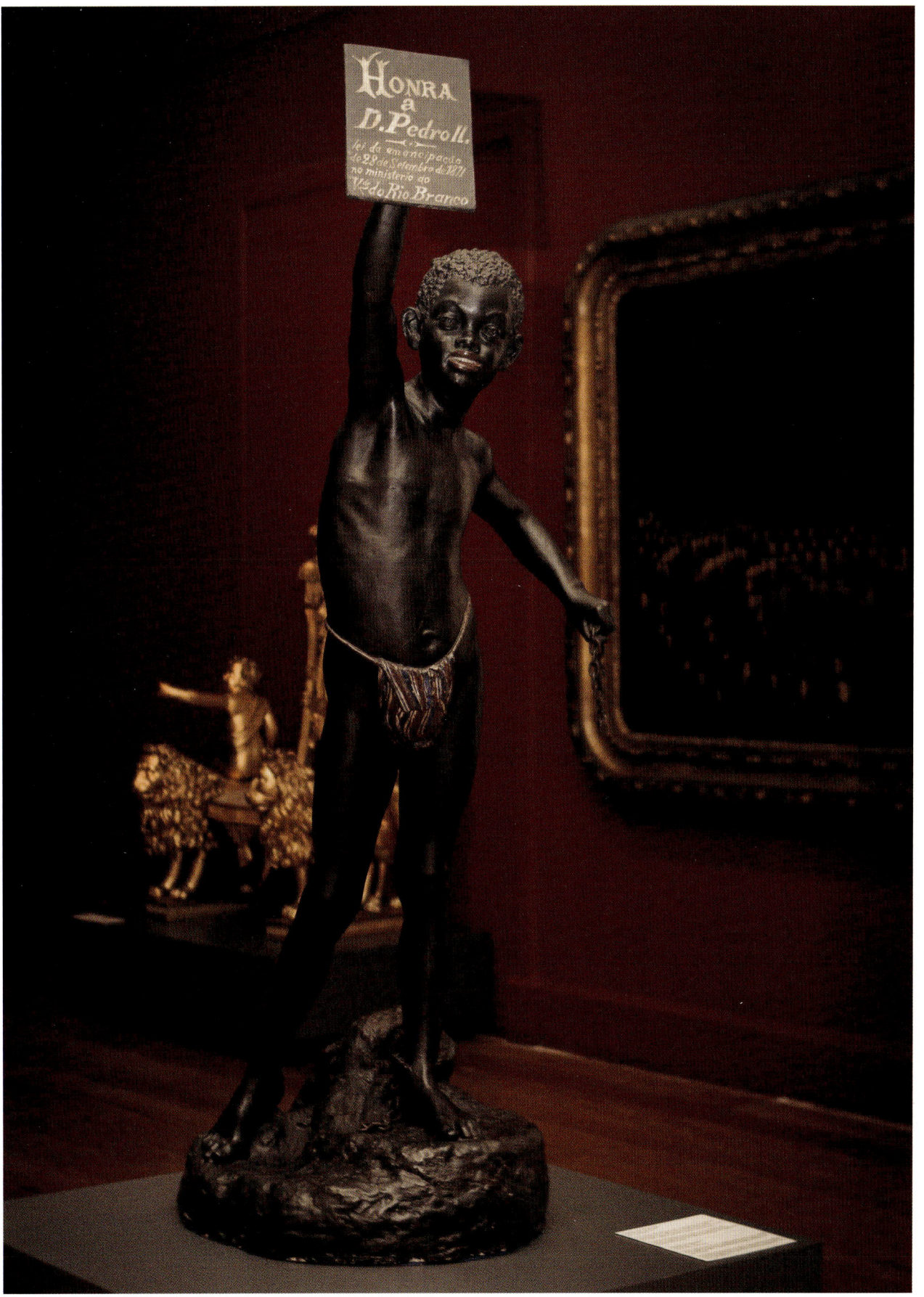

13

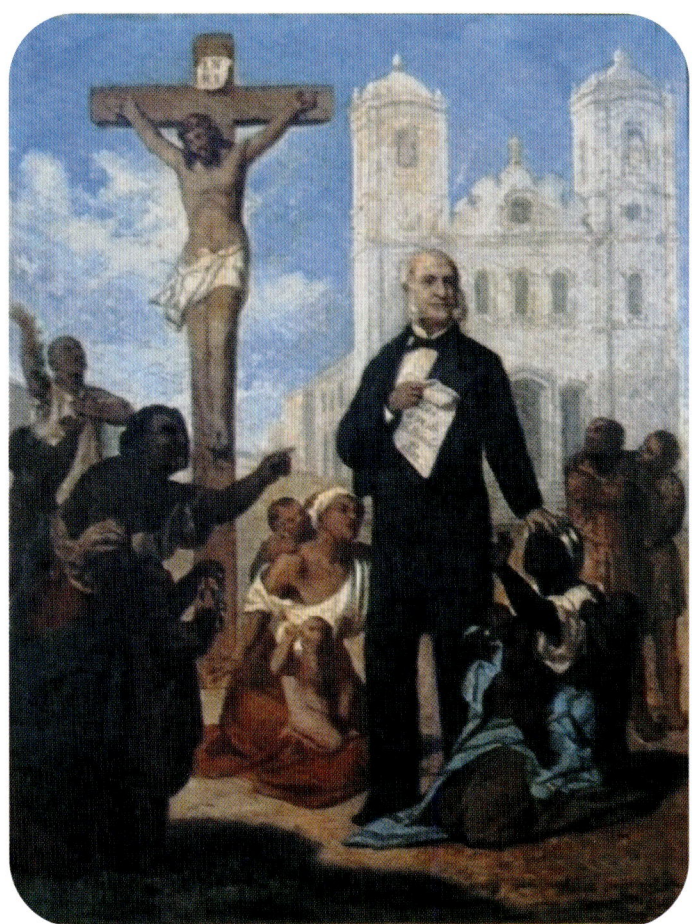

14 Miguel Navarro y Cañizares. *Allegory on the Law of the Free Womb*. Ca. 1871. Oil on canvas. Salvador, Bahia, Brazil, Basilica de Bonfim. Museu dos Ex-votos.

with the same title by Miguel Navarro y Cañizares. The first is one of the few works representing Black people in the collection of the National Historical Museum in Rio de Janeiro.[14] It is the statue of a boy—something uncommon in the sculpture of the era—who in one hand holds up a placard with the inscription "*Honra a D. Pedro II/lei de emancipação/28 de setembro de 1871/no ministerio do/V^{de} do Rio Branco*" ("Honor to Emperor Pedro II/law of emancipation/28 September 1871/in the Ministry of the Viscount of Rio Branco"). Here the benefactors do not appear as images, but only in the text (Pedro II, viscount of Rio Branco). In the boy's other hand is part of a broken chain, a common feature of images referring to the abolition of slavery. The rest of the chain lies at his feet. In contrast to the other images analyzed here, the boy is standing. His broad smile and posture show how happy he is to be proclaiming the good news that beginning in January 1872 the children born to enslaved mothers would be free. In reality, that long-sought freedom would not be immediate. The law provided that the children affected by the law, who would be called *ingênuos* (innocents), would be kept by their mothers' enslavers until they were eight years old, suggesting that under the law their lives would not be much different from if they had been enslaved from birth. At that point the mother's enslaver could free the child and collect an indemnity, or keep the ingênuo and make use of his or her labor until granting final freedom at age twenty-one.

Cañizares, a Spaniard who arrived in Brazil in 1876 and lived in Salvador, Bahia, until 1882, completed a painting with the same theme and title in about 1878. He was an expert portraitist as well as a painter of allegories and religious themes.[15] In this oil he brought all those skills to bear. The picture was commissioned as a votive offering and is now displayed in the museum of *ex-vo-*

tos (tokens left by seekers of healing) of Bonfim church with a silver medallion inscribed "*MILAGRE/O Senhor do Bonfim protege o Visconde do Rio Branco e este consegue a Lei de emancipacão do elemento servil/28 de 7ᵇʳᵒ de 1871*" ("MIRACLE/The Lord of Bonfim protects the Viscount of Rio Branco who achieves the Law of emancipation of the slaves/28 September 1871").[16] In this allegory, the viscount of Rio Branco appears in front of the church of Bonfim together with a large Christ on the cross, surrounded by people of African descent. The benefactor, in a condescending gesture, places his hand on the head of one of the women kneeling at his feet without looking at her. The women raise their gaze and their arms up to Rio Branco in gratitude. The ensemble includes a jumble of people in a space that is too narrow, in which the verticality of the crucified Christ and Rio Branco contrasts with the subordinate postures of the surrounding figures. Recognizing the racial mixture across the Brazilian population, the painter took care to display a gradation of skin colors, especially in the women. The number of children is also notable, consonant with the event the painting was intended to immortalize.

Allegory on the Law of the Free Womb is closely linked to another work by Cañizares, *Alegoria à lei áurea* (*Allegory on the Golden Law*), which commemorated the law abolishing slavery in Brazil on May 13, 1888. The religious reference, understandable in the votive offering, is again evident, but with no obvious explanation here. This painting is much larger, allowing many figures to be included, and divided into three vertical registers, suggesting an ascent from the earthly to the celestial. Two Afrodescendant women, one holding a baby, together with an apparently white woman, are kneeling on the lower level. Again the artist gives the women differing skin tones, this time reaching near whiteness in one. While the feet of the two Afrodescendant women are bare, the white woman's feet are covered, an indication that perhaps she is not enslaved, but her presence remains unexplained. One of the Black women and the child reach toward Princess Isabel, the woman offering her what appears to be a palm frond.[17] Only these lower figures show any sign of emotion. All the others seem to be indifferent to the event being commemorated,[18] and like Rio Branco in the other Cañizares work, they avoid looking at the kneeling women.

The middle register includes portrait images of men involved in the abolition campaign and the political process resulting in the law ending slavery, on the left side in civilian dress and on the right in the military-style uniforms of the Brazilian nobility.[19] Princess Isabel, who signed the law, together with one of her children, her husband, and busts of the emperor and empress, occupy a higher position, seeming to draw a connection to the celestial realm above. Isabel is dressed in white and surrounded by angels, immersed in an aura of glorification. She holds a large cross with "God, Charity" inscribed on the vertical post and "Redemption" on the cross bar.

While Bressae's allegorical sculpture was intended to honor Emperor Pedro II, Cañizares's painting goes further, to the quasi-religious glorification of the princess.[20] In both cases the participation of enslaved and free Blacks in the abolition process is erased,[21] taking away their capacity for agency.[22] These sorts of visual representations of emancipation thus become an extension of the power of the institution of slavery, confirmed by the reality that most of the Black population remained in the lower strata of society, occupied as they had been under slavery.

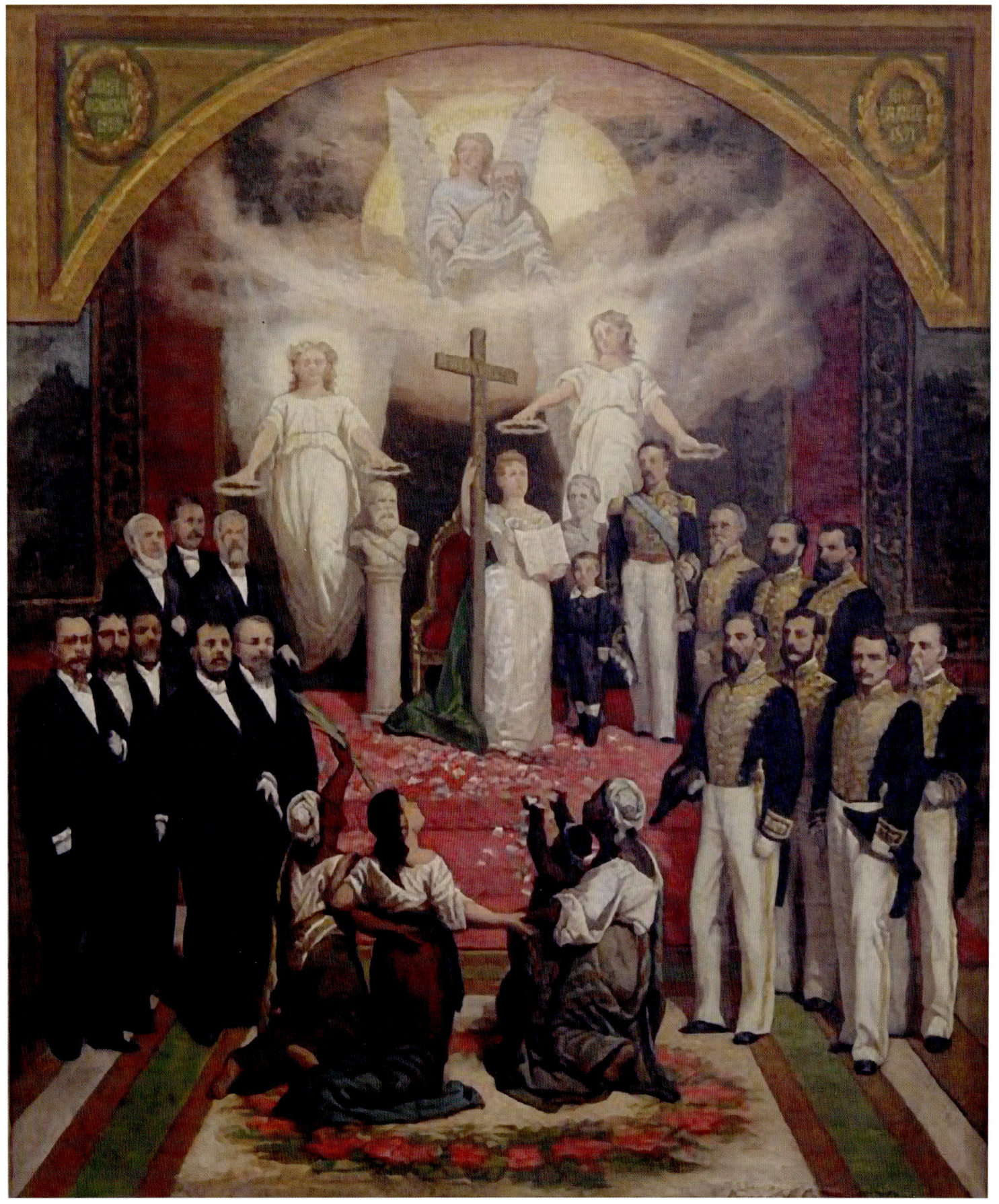

15 Miguel Navarro y Cañizares. *Allegory on the Golden Law*. 1888. Oil on canvas. Salvador, Bahia, Brazil, Escola de Belas Artes da Universidade Federal de Bahia.

16 D. Plot. *The Female Slaves of Buenos Aires Show That They Are Free and Grateful to Their Noble Liberator*. 1841. Oil on cloth. Buenos Aires, Argentina, Museo Histórico Nacional.

Argentina

For Argentina, I will focus on a specific iconographic example of enslaved people expressing gratitude to their benefactor: *Las esclavas de Buenos Aires demuestran ser libres y gratas a su noble libertador* (*The Female Slaves of Buenos Aires Show That They Are Free and Grateful to Their Noble Liberator*). Done in oil on unframed cloth, it is signed and dated at an angle in the lower right corner, "*San^s Lug^s de Rosas Mayo 1º de 1841 por D. de Plot*" (Holy Sites of Rosas, May 1, 1841, by D. Plot), an amateur artist about whom little is known.[23]

Juan Manuel de Rosas is an archetypical figure in Argentine history, not only because of his long periods in power (1829–1832 and 1835–1852), but also because, for the opponents who finally took him down, he became a defining reference point in subsequent political disputes. The frequent association of Rosas with Afrodescendant people allowed later discourse to connect both Rosas and Blacks with barbarism. Since the opponents of Rosas saw his fall from power as a return to civilized society, that connection facilitated the elimination of Afrodescendant people from the definition of what constituted the Argentine nation.

The painting shows a large group of Afrodescendant women, along with a few old men and children, approaching Rosas at the camp called Holy Sites of Rosas, the location of a large military unit and detention center. For his opponents, the prison held all the rabble or plebeian society that supported Rosas—indigenous people, Black women, common soldiers—whether as detainees or as free residents.[24] The women in the painting carry banners with the slogans of the Rosas regime: "*Viva el Restaurador de las Leyes*" ("Long Live the Restorer of the Laws") and "*Mueran los salbages* [*sic*] *unitarios*" ("Death to the Savage Unitarians"), adding a third one, "*Viva la libertad*" ("Long Live Freedom"). Rosas holds out a proclamation that promises "*Federación, Livertad* [*sic*], *no más Tiranos*" ("Federation, Freedom, No More Tyrants"). Above the scene flies an allegorical figure of Fame holding a banner labeled "Freedom" and trumpeting the news in verse: "Now in the Plata (i.e., Argentina), not one slave will moan in chains/ His bitter weeping ceased since humane Rosas/Proud, compassionate, and generous/Lavished the precious gift of freedom on the unfortunate African." The inclusion of a date and place, the impression that a procession is advancing toward Rosas, and the offerings of broken chains and shackles, another symbol of freedom, at the feet of the benefactor, all suggest that the image commemorates an event that occurred two years previously—the signing of a treaty with Great Britain on May 24, 1839, prohibiting the transatlantic slave traffic. That agreement did not change the legal status of enslaved people already in Argentina, though the Afrodescendant community might have seen it as a sign of progress toward abolition.

Though it is not known how this painting might have been circulated, it has been suggested that the image was to be used as propaganda for the regime.[25] But that puts the focus solely on the figure of Rosas. Such a perspective often leads to the conclusion that Afrodescendant people were manipulated by others and once again relegates them to a passive role. I prefer to focus on the group of Afrodescendant women who in the painting are put on a par with the ruler. Agreeing with Ricardo Salvatore,[26] I believe the leading role given to the women is witness to their capacity for agency. The image presents two political actors coming together in the struggle for the freedom of Africans and their descendants, but the two parties have different reasons for working toward that

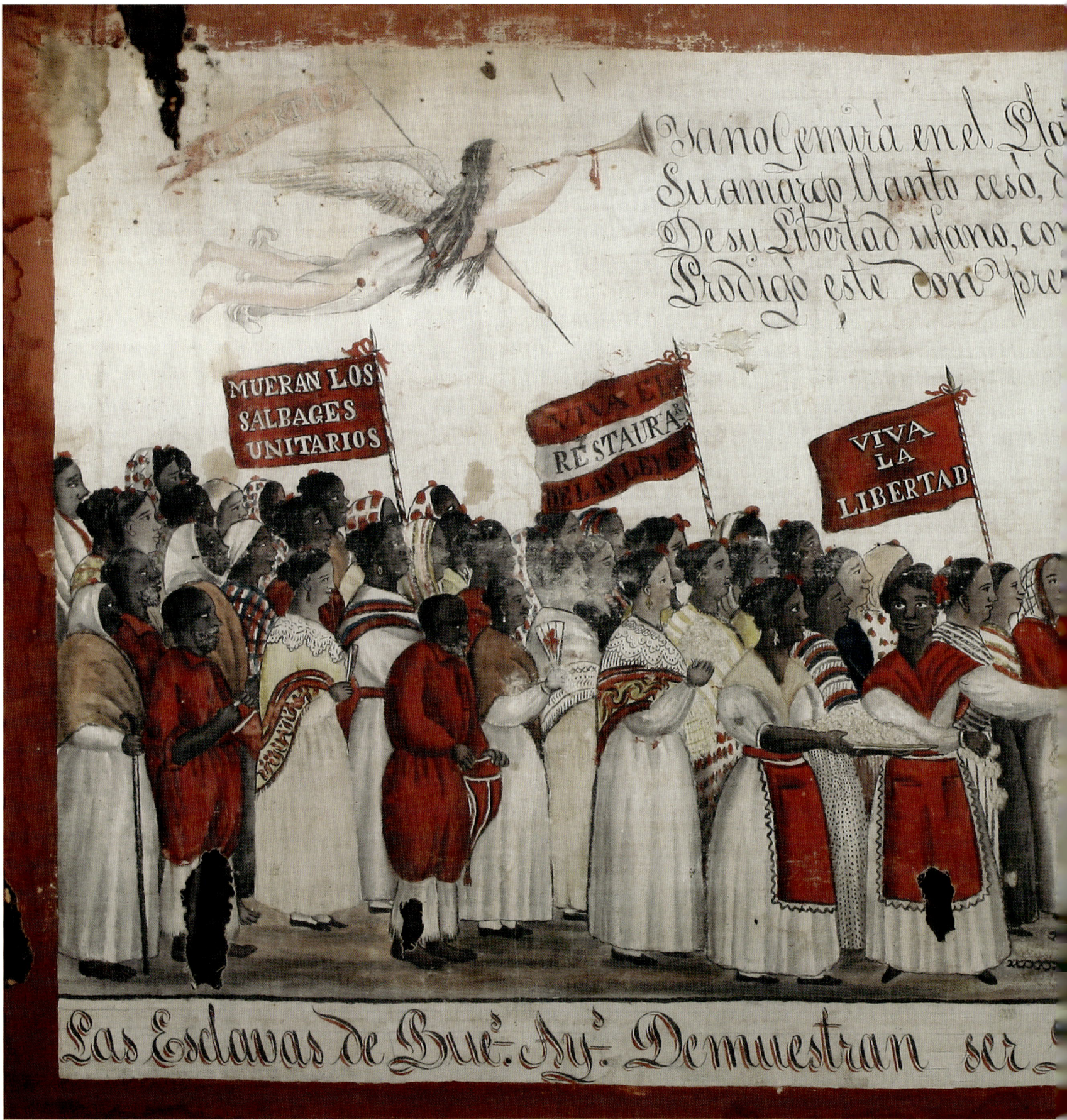

16

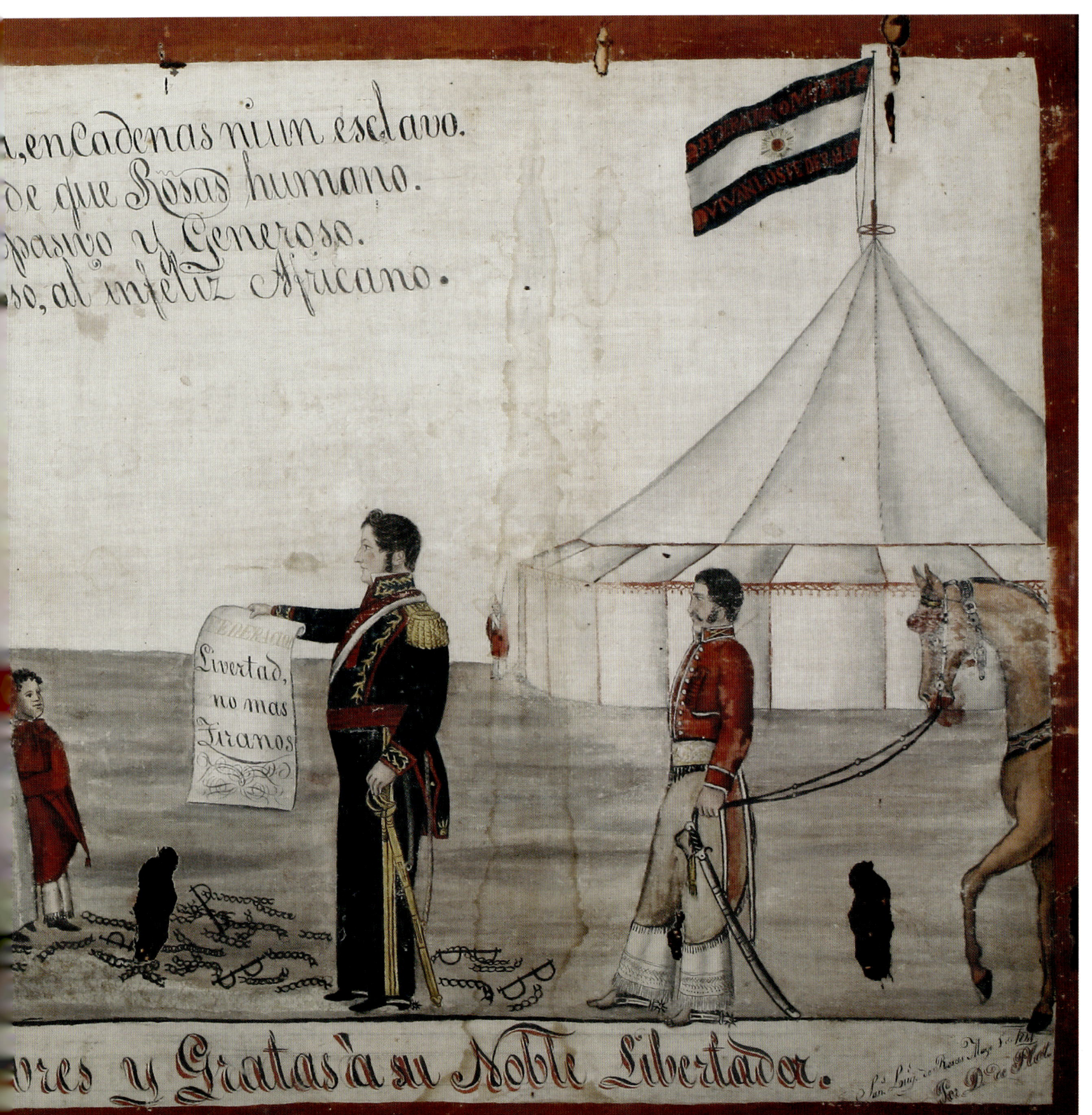

17 Prilidiano Pueyrredón. *Patio in Buenos Aires in 1850*. Ca. 1860. Oil on copper. Buenos Aires, Argentina, Museo Nacional de Bellas Artes.

common goal. Rosas wanted Afrodescendants as loyal followers, but he also hoped to gain a position in international affairs that European countries, especially Great Britain, respected, as well as to be recognized as a legitimate government. For Afro-Argentines, governmental decisions on their behalf meant the much sought-after possibility of achieving freedom, a promise that dated from the revolution for independence of May 1810[27] and the Free Womb Law of 1813.[28]

Afrodescendant People in the Post-Abolition Era: Argentina

In Argentina, after nearly a decade with the state (former province) of Buenos Aires coexisting as a nation separate from the Argentine Confederation, the 1860s saw the beginnings of a unified territory. Other important developments were the influx of a significant number of immigrants, the beginning of the transformation of the capital from a village to a city, and the abolition of slavery. Taken together, three paintings by Prilidiano Pueyrredón —*Patio porteño en 1850* (*Patio in Buenos Aires in 1850*), *Esquina porteña* (*Buenos Aires Street Corner*), and *El naranjero* (*The Orange Vendor*)—provide a glimpse into the conflicts that arose from a national project for a society that was not racially homogeneous. Pueyrredón is important not only as a portraitist but also as a painter of both rural and urban settings in the genre of *costumbrismo*. He is best known for bucolic scenes closely linked to this idealizing tradition that contributed to the construction of a national memory based on the idea of the rural society around Buenos Aires as the prototype of the nation's self-image, based on similarities of kinship and race (as a contemporary observer wrote).[29] But as Roberto Amigo has noted, the apparently conflict-free racial homogeneity of Pueyrredón's rural scenes does not extend to his depictions of urban society.[30] In the city, the inclusion of Afro-Argentines becomes relevant.

I have analyzed *Patio porteño en 1850* (ca. 1860) elsewhere,[31] so I will confine these comments to aspects of the image that are of present interest, beginning with the Afrodescendant servant who presents eggs to a woman we assume to be her employer. The latter, who is getting on in years, turns her head to the servant with a look of disdain, revealing a complex universe of tensions and racial hierarchies. Both women are protagonists in the narrative, despite being placed on the side of the image. To balance the composition, the painter included a young girl on the opposite side, who is apparently indifferent to the fraught situation across the patio. The figure on the right also lets the viewer imagine two perspectives that bring forth different visions of Buenos Aires society in the second half of the nineteenth century. One might think of the two people in dispute, an older woman and a Black servant who have lived together for a long time, as symbols of a world on the wane, while the young girl, outside the conflict, represents the future.

Esquina porteña and *El naranjero* were painted in 1865, just four years after the abolition of slavery in Buenos Aires.[32] After 1861, all descendants of Africans, whether from elsewhere or native-born, would have the same rights and duties as other citizens, at least in theory. *Esquina porteña* shows four people, two men and two women, in front of a food store on a Buenos Aires street corner. The center of the scene is filled by what a chronicler of the time described as a "a black woman in her Sunday best, who sweeps the street with silk."[33] She flaunts a showy red dress, with a green shawl over her shoulders and mantilla on her

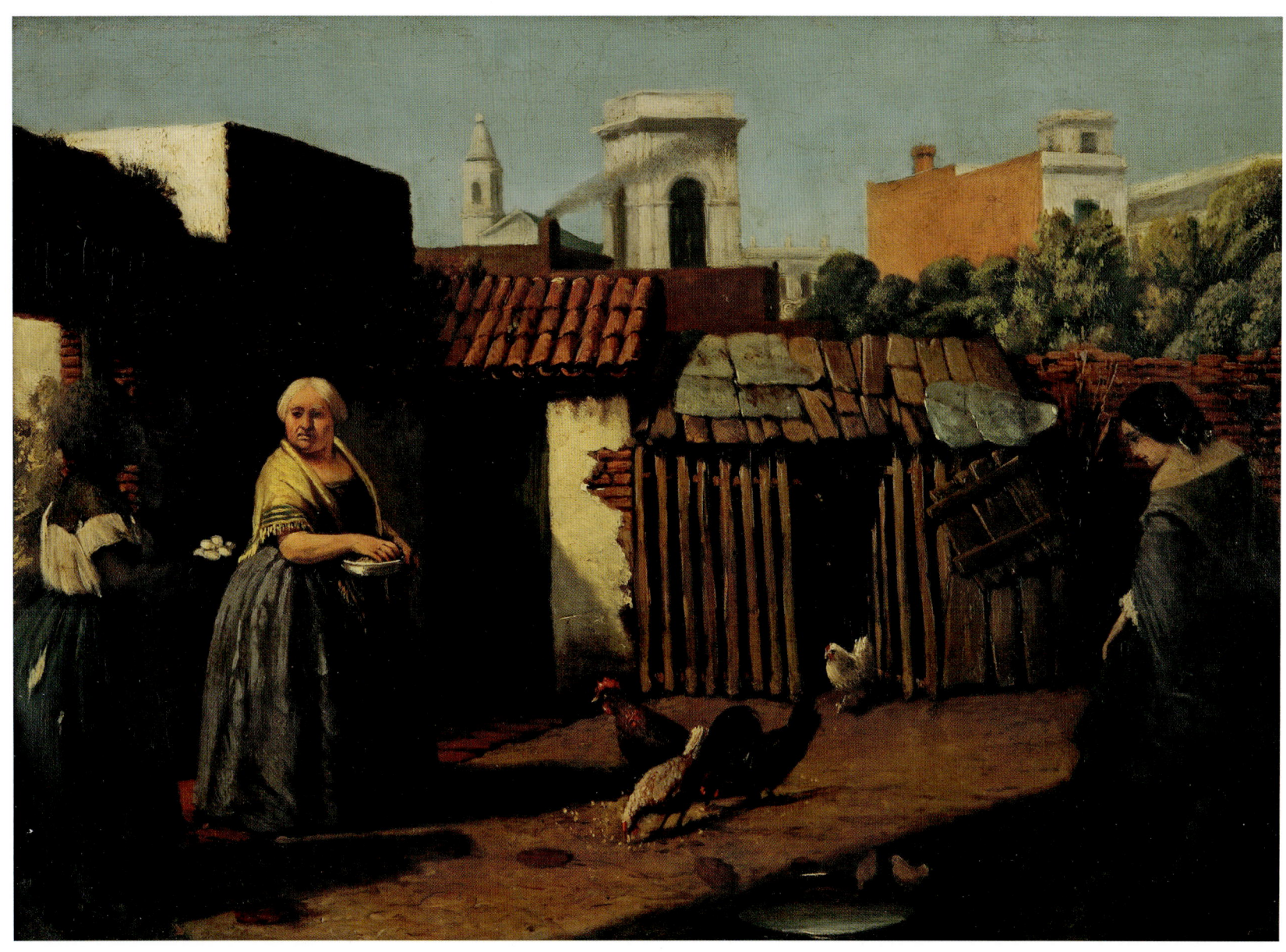

18 Prilidiano Pueyrredón. *Buenos Aires Street Corner*. 1865.
Oil on canvas. Private collection.

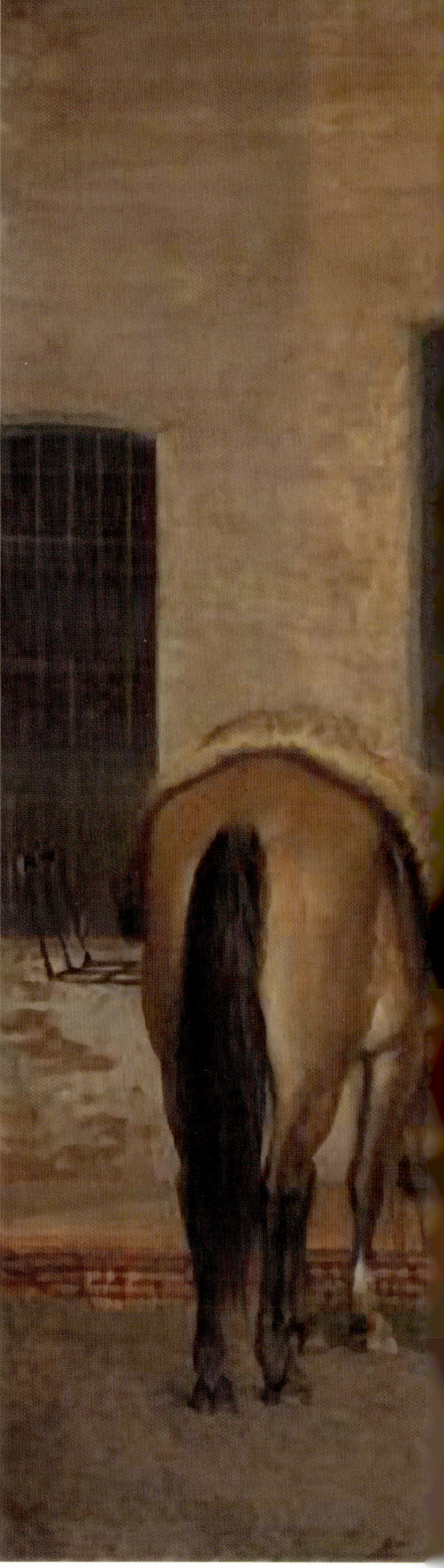

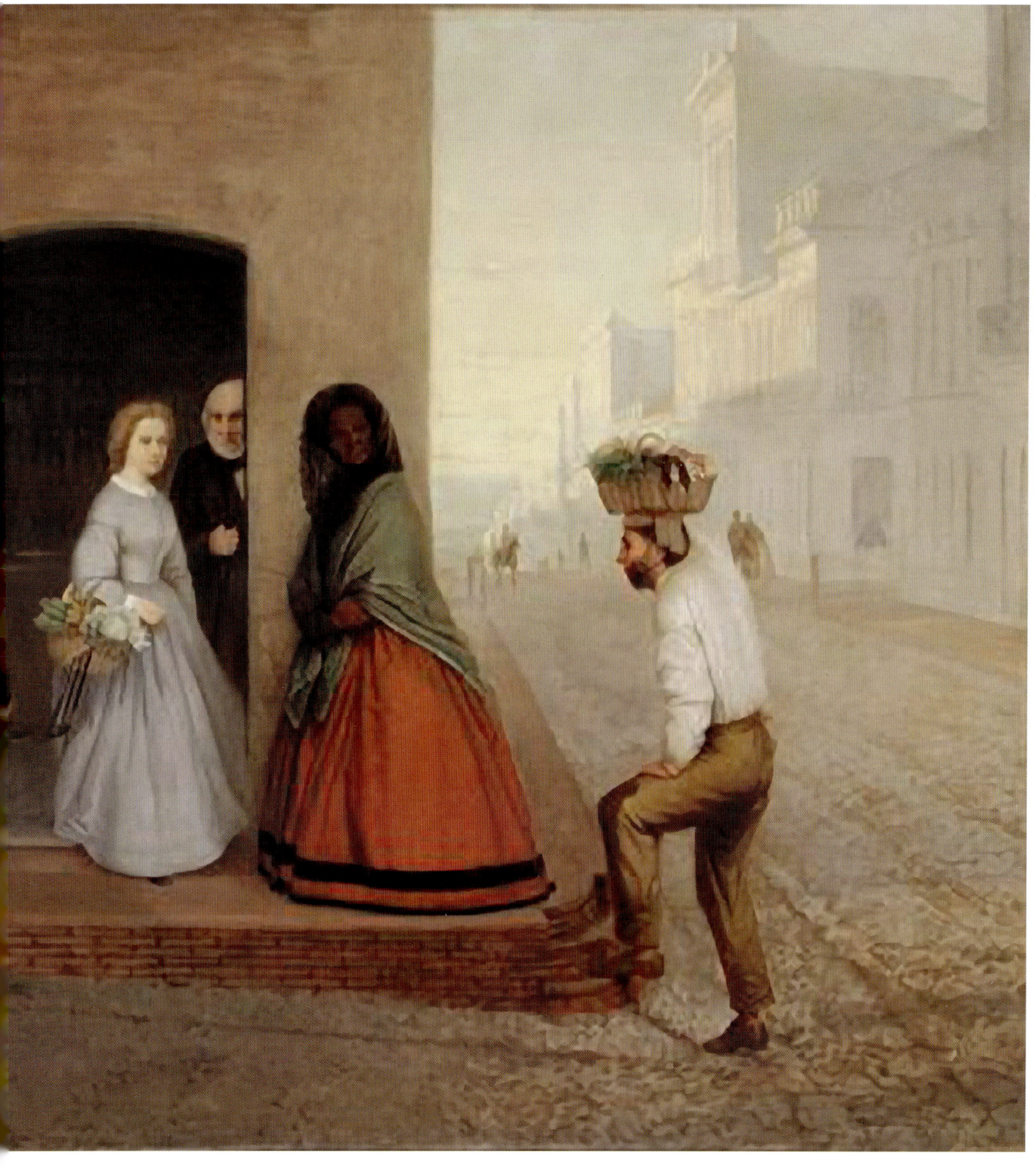

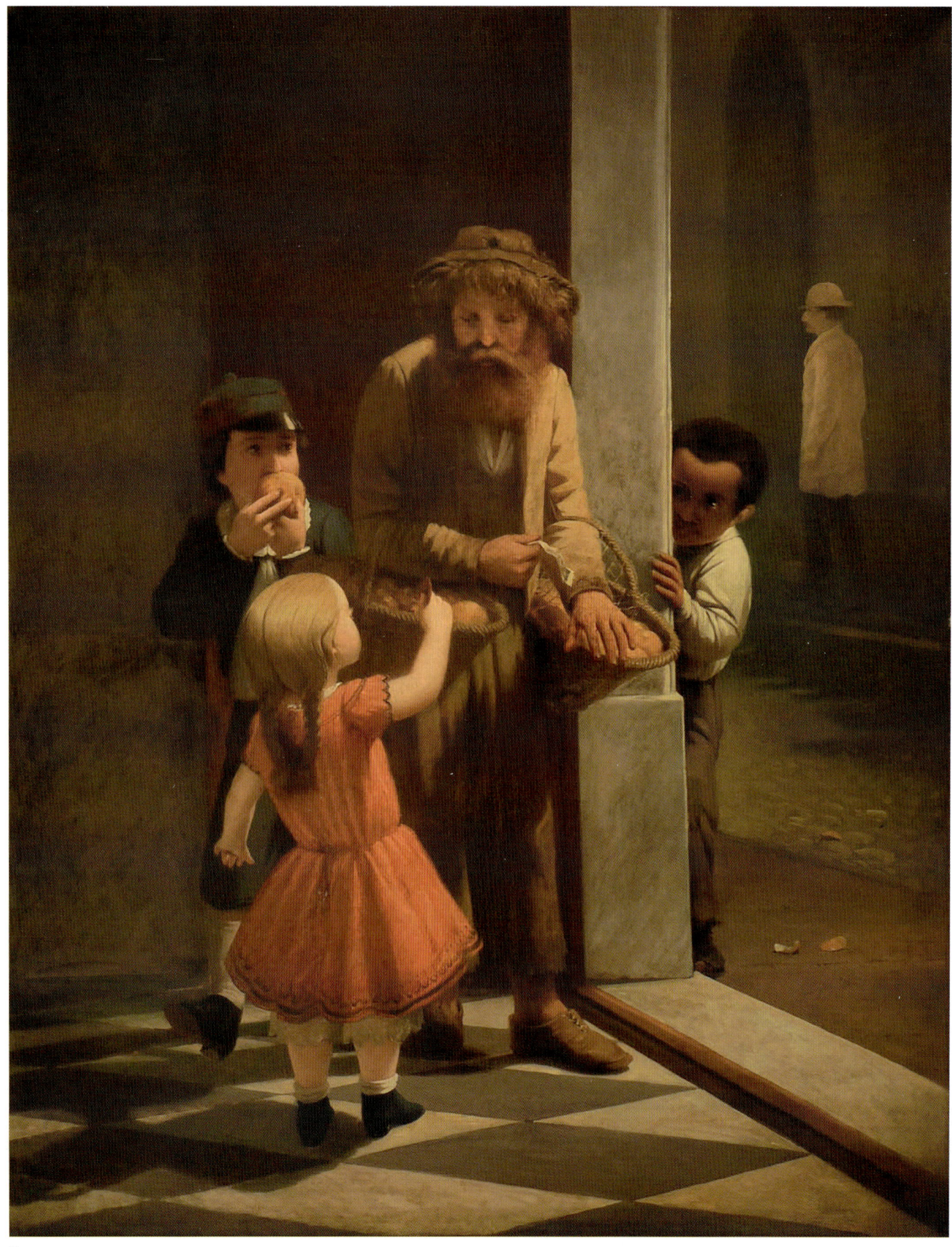

19 Prilidiano Pueyrredón. *The Orange Vendor*. 1865. Oil on canvas. Private collection.

head. As a counterpoint, the other woman, apparently younger, wears a simple light blue dress with white collar and cuffs, lacking decoration. The colors of the clothing recall the symbolism of the period dominated by Juan Manuel de Rosas, when light blue was the color of the Unitarian Party and red was associated with Rosas's Federation. It seems likely that Pueyrredón intended to suggest the common and stigmatizing association of Afro-Argentines with Rosas; contemporary viewers probably made that connection.

In *El naranjero,* Pueyrredón shows a typical character from the streets of Buenos Aires in the entryway of a house, as a boy and girl buy oranges from him. Another boy, this one Afrodescendant, lurks behind the wall and thus occupies a different space, the public space of the street. Both the vendor and the Black boy are poorly dressed, with worn-out footwear and threadbare pants, with the added detail that one of the boy's toes protrudes through a hole in his shoe. Since the Black boy is hiding, the writer of a contemporary newspaper article assumed that he is about to commit petty theft, "intent on swiping an orange from the vendor at the first careless moment."[34] At the Black boy's feet are orange peels, left unexplained. The writer did not consider that the peelings might have been tossed in the street by a previous customer, nor the possibility that the vendor (an Italian, according to the same writer, thus closer to social class of the supposed thief than to the small customers), might have given the boy an orange earlier. Eighty years later, José León Pagano, a pioneer of Argentine historiography, made the same suggestion regarding the Black boy's intentions: "With [the vendor], on his right, are *two children*, a boy and a girl. The latter, who has *blond hair* . . . holds out her right hand to give the vendor a coin. The boy, with *white complexion* . . . raises an orange to his mouth to suck it. A *negrito* [little Black boy] in white shirt and blue pants is next to the door frame, waiting for the moment when he can take a fruit from the baskets without being seen."[35] We don't know how contemporary viewers interpreted the painting, but they were probably not influenced by the opinions put forth by specialists in the field.

The titles of these works raise some questions. A neutral name like *El naranjero* suggests just another picturesque image of one of the street people of Buenos Aires. But the lurking Black boy intrudes on that expected neutrality. His presence suggests a possible action, presumably criminal. It raises a set of issues related to the poverty and marginality of Afrodescendant people, bordering on criminality.[36]

Esquina porteña, in contrast, is quite different from most depictions of Afrodescendants in Argentina. The prominence and centrality of the Black woman, her dress, the impossibility of thinking of her as subservient, her presence not justified by work of some kind (she is not shown as nearly all Blacks were: as a servant, accompanying an employer, or making or selling something)—all make this a provocative image, although we don't know precisely what the artist meant to convey.

With *Patio porteño* and *El naranjero,* along with the contemporary texts that describe them, a universe of hierarchies of race and class in Buenos Aires society is brought into relief. But *Esquina porteña* seems to subvert that situation. The two women are looking at the middle-aged white man on the right side (described by a contemporary writer as a native of Ferrol, in the Spanish region of Galicia),[37] who is carrying on his head a basket that belongs to the Black woman. The contemporary article

20 León Williez, editor. Manuel María del Mazo, illustrator. From the *Nonsense* series. 1855. Lithograph. Museo de Arte de Lima.

makes that assumption: "The contrast is odd—the black woman is the pot of the fable who is afraid of darkening by coming in contact with the pure flame of the fire, and *a real person* in our ultra-democratic customs, which have not only emancipated the slaves, but have provided them with servants of the Caucasian race, in fair and . . . provocative retaliation."[38]

These works recognize the racial diversity of Buenos Aires, despite the dominant elite narrative regarding the imminent disappearance of Blacks in Argentina.[39] It was probably an uncertain time for those who had abolished slavery as it was for those who had gained freedom. What did the future hold for this society? What part would Afrodescendant people play not only in the economy, but in education, politics, public opinion? Can we see this uncertainty in Pueyrredón's work? What was he suggesting in these images, particularly in *Esquina porteña*? Was his intention merely to show the city's racial diversity, or was he warning of the dangers of the abolition of slavery or what abolition might mean for the future?

Peru

In Peru, slavery was abolished by Ramón Castilla in a decree of December 3, 1854, as an opportunistic measure in the larger context of the so-called Liberal Revolution of that year.[40] The insurrection had begun in Arequipa, when President José Rufino Echenique was accused of rampant corruption in his administration. In April 1854 the Revolutionary Junta of Arequipa proclaimed Castilla, who had served as president prior to Echenique as well, provisional president. In an effort to build popular support, both leaders took measures to appeal to the lower classes. Five months before Castilla abolished slavery, he also ended indigenous tribute. An interesting image was created in Peru in this context, in the *Adefecios* (*Nonsense*) series of cartoons drawn by Manuel María del Mazo and published by León Williez in Lima in 1855. In a nearly symmetrical composition, the artist placed Marshal Castilla in the middle holding broken chains signifying Indian tribute and slavery, flanked by men in civilian dress. On the left side José Gálvez Egúsquiza, who contributed to ending tribute, faces a kneeling indigenous man. On the right side Manuel Toribio Ureta, who wrote the abolition decree, breaks the chains of an enslaved Black man who is kneeling. This print and the collection of which it is part belong to the genre of political satire directed at both Echenique and Castilla.[41]

Francisco Laso is considered to be the first painter of Peru's independent era and a pioneer in creating a national iconography. He was also a writer. In 1859, just a few years after abolition, Laso painted *Las tres razas, o la igualdad ante la ley* (*The Three Races, or Equality before the Law*), an oil depicting three young people playing cards in a domestic setting. Natalia Majluf notes that the image is heavily allegorical. It goes beyond the anecdotal quality of the genre of costumbrismo and "tries to resolve, on the surface of the canvas, the contradictions of the society in which [Laso] lived."[42] Gonzalo Portocarrero sees a utopian quality in this painting, not as something impossible but as something that could be achieved, as "equality and play replace the hierarchy and violence that were the prevalent features of interethnic relations in 19th-century Peru."[43] As he did in his writing, in this painting Laso sought to criticize the racial inequality that permeated Peruvian society.[44]

The card game takes place on some sort of bed or couch. This immediately suggests intimacy, the need for the play involving

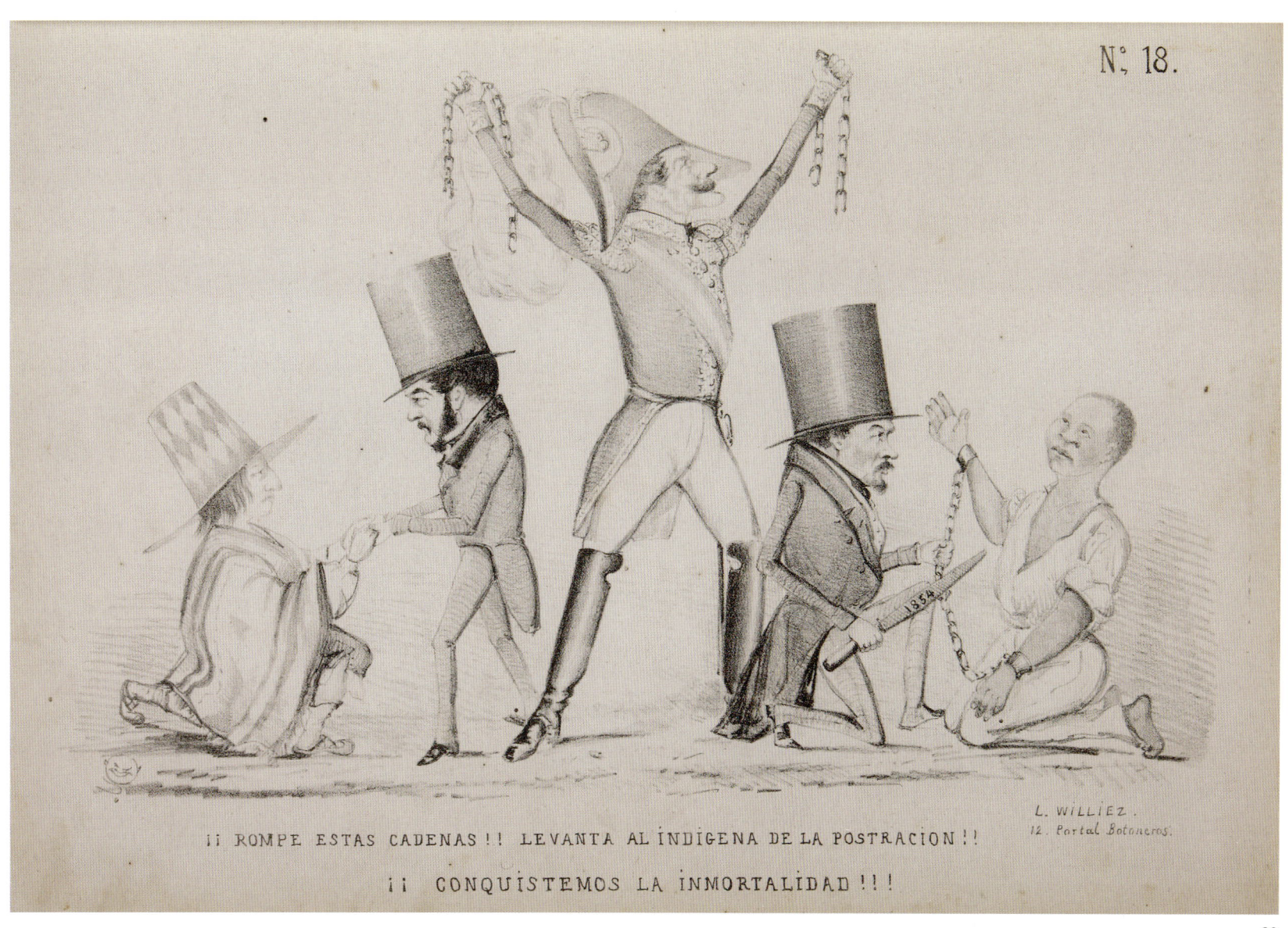

¡¡ROMPE ESTAS CADENAS!! LEVANTA AL INDÍGENA DE LA POSTRACION!!

¡¡CONQUISTEMOS LA INMORTALIDAD!!!

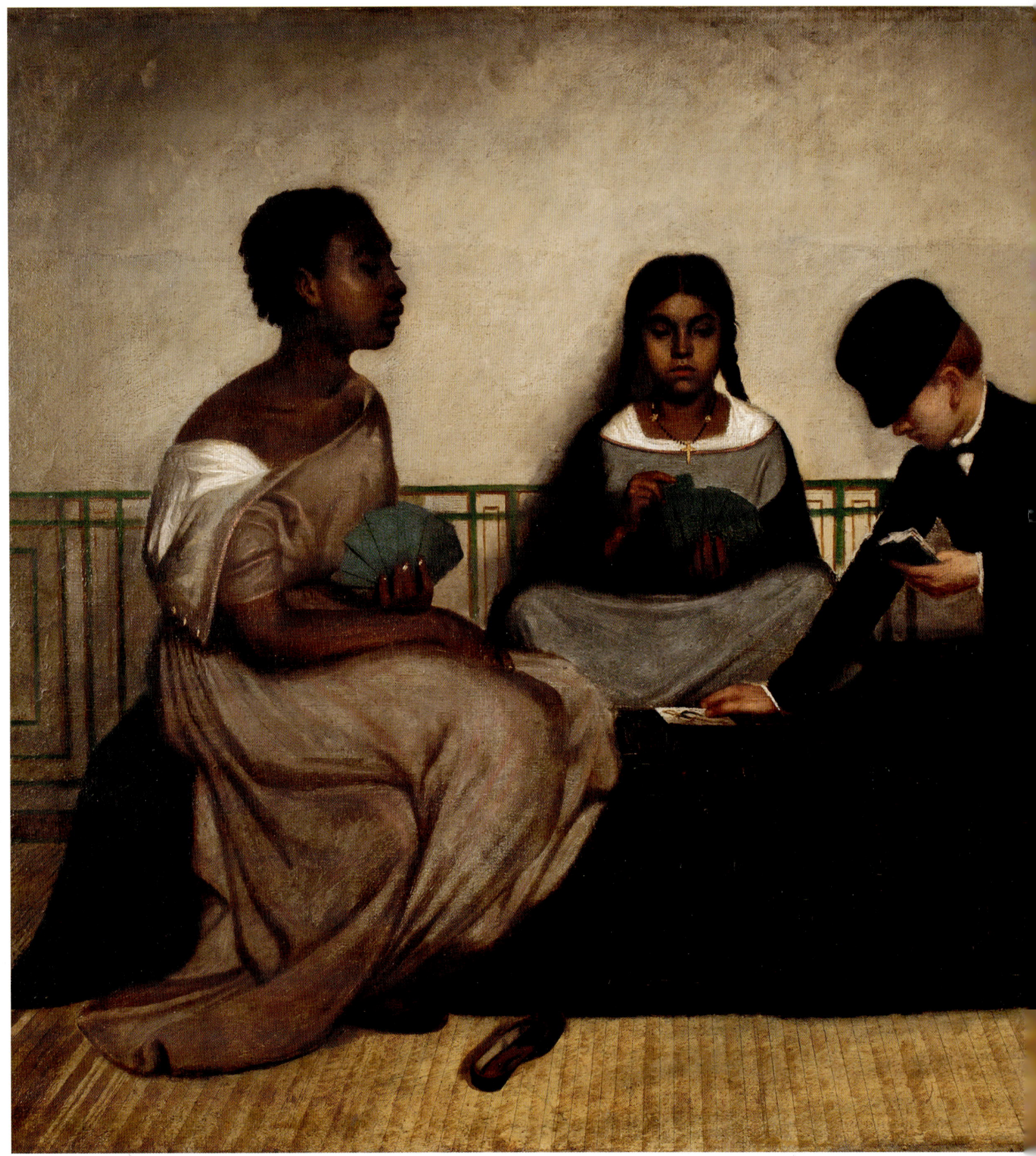

21

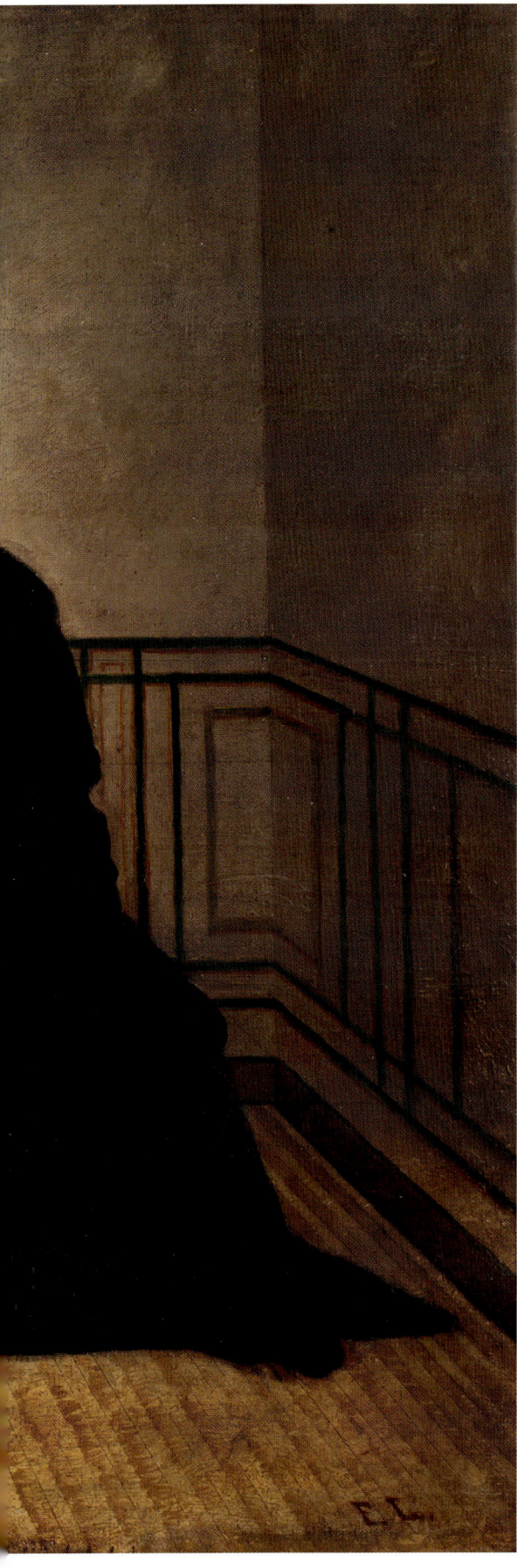

21 Francisco Laso. *The Three Races, or Equality before the Law*. Ca. 1859. Oil on canvas. Museo de Arte de Lima.

the child-employer, the indigenous child-servant, and the young Afrodescendant-servant (nanny?) to be located beyond the gaze of others in the household. In the apparent sequence of the play, the white boy has just put down a card, the Indian girl is about to play hers, and the young Black woman waits her turn. Might this be seen as a metaphor on racial and patriarchal ranks of Lima society? Laso's pyramidal composition places the indigenous girl in a privileged place, facing front and center. The Black girl, however, is a monumental presence, not only for being older, which makes for two main points of focus. Other elements direct our attention toward her—the light-colored clothing, her look at the boy's play, her pose, the dress that falls loose at the neck, the slipper that has fallen off. On the last two points, might the artist have intended to suggest a certain indolence on her part, and by extension on the part of Black people in general? Did he let us see the white blouse as a pictorial counterpoint to her dark skin? Was it the common visual trope, seen in both America and Europe, of showing Afrodescendant women with low-cut clothing? As for the fallen slipper, keeping in mind that being barefoot was associated with slavery, might that hint at an intermediate state between slavery and its recent abolition?

When this painting was exhibited for the first time, a commentator described it briefly as "depicting a boy accompanied by a *chola* [mixed-race indigenous/white girl] and a *zamba* [mixed-race indigenous/Black girl] playing cards; three entirely different types whom Laso has been able to differentiate skillfully."[45] Like the Argentine historian commenting on *El naranjero*, different types of terms are used for the different racial categories. The native-born white children are simply called boys or girls. Others get a diminutive term denoting skin color, such as *negrito* (little

ABOLITION AND POST-ABOLITION IN THE VISUAL CULTURE OF LATIN AMERICA   65

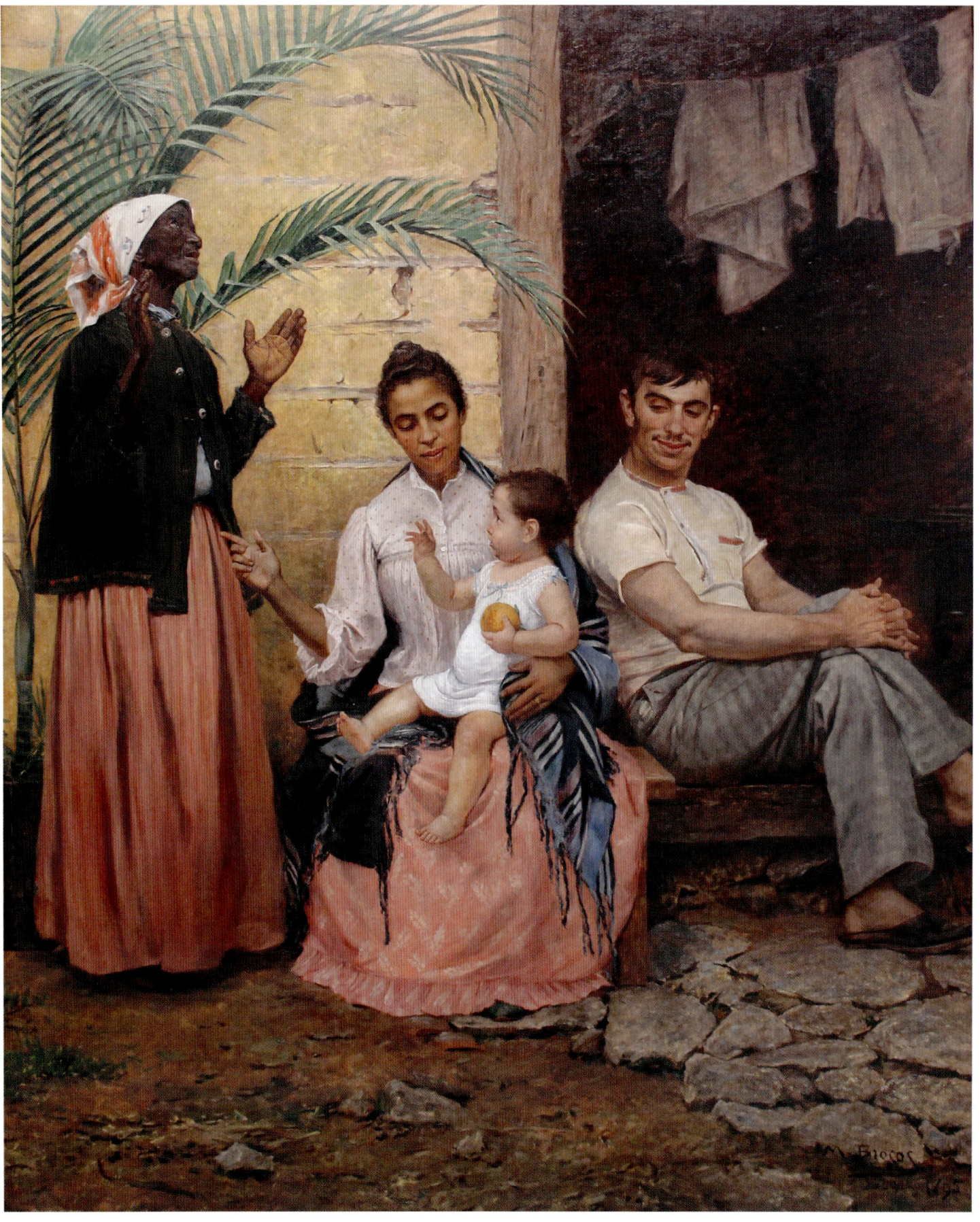
22

22 Modesto Brocos. *The Redemption of Ham*. 1895. Oil on canvas. Rio de Janeiro, Museu Nacional de Belas Artes.

Black boy), or racialized terms as *chola* or *zamba*, which originated in the colonial era and identify racial mixing.[46]

The white elite's expectation, or desire, that society would become whiter was widespread in the South American nations. That racial ideology, supported by contorted scientific theories, assumed that with race mixing, white people, being stronger and more adaptable, would win out over the indigenous and Afrodescendant groups. To this end, several governments in the region promoted European immigration. A paradigmatic image on this theme is *A redenção de Cam* (*The Redemption of Ham*), by Modesto Brocos, a Spanish painter living in Brazil. The title refers to an incident in the book of Genesis known as the "curse of Ham,"[47] which, as commerce in human beings progressed, was used to justify the enslavement of Africans. By portraying a Brazilian family made up of father, mother, baby, and grandmother, the artist shows the possibility of whitening through the range of skin colors. At the same time, as Tatiana Lotierzo suggests, gender issues are juxtaposed with those involving race.[48] The supposed superiority of the European is shown by the white male who has brought about the whitening of the male child. Other elements appear in the work, including references to Christian iconography—the Black grandmother in a pose of prayer; the mixed-race mother and child whose hand is raised in a gesture of blessing, suggesting the Virgin Mary and Jesus; and the father sitting somewhat to the side, who might be associated with Joseph.[49]

Rafael Cardoso notes that contemporary viewers would not have interpreted this image in a negative light, and that "such a reading . . . remained in place as late as 1911, when the director of Brazil's National Museum purportedly used the painting to illustrate a paper presented at the First Universal Races Congress in London, in which he predicted that black people and those of mixed race would become extinct in one hundred years' time through the 'influence of sexual selection.'"[50]

Although the result is not intentional, only two of the works selected for analysis in this chapter (*Patio porteño* and *Esquina porteña*) do not include children. In all the others, children appear either in a prominent position (as in Bressae's allegorical sculpture, *Las tres razas,* and *El naranjero*) or as secondary figures with their mothers—as if freedom, and especially social and racial equality, were a promise for the future.

3

THE IMAGE OF THE BLACK IN THE FORMATION OF LATIN AMERICAN NATIONS

MARÍA DOLORES BALLESTEROS PÁEZ

It was during the nineteenth century that Latin American countries constructed their nations, their history, and the image that they wanted to project to the rest of the world. Their methods had much in common from country to country; their national narratives emphasized differences from the former empire, their neighbors, and the pre-Iberian past. After the proclamation of independence came its celebration, commemorated by contemporary painters and the production of new imagery designed to symbolize the nation. Conflicts with neighbors followed, with new nations trying to establish borders and find scapegoats for their own troubles by depicting differences with surrounding nations. In the wake of this conflict-fueled instability, art academies under government patronage began to build narratives of the construction of each nation, its origin and its key moments, all of which were reenacted and reconstructed through painful memories shared mainly by light-skinned people. The Black population, with some exceptions, was usually excluded.

The new political leaders determined to develop a shared identity among the population, an identification with the new national state and their new role as citizens. Local and foreign artists contributed with *costumbrista* scenes and paintings of historical independence celebrations; national academies commissioned historical paintings to be displayed in newly established museums, which by the twentieth century would be reproduced on currency and in textbooks.[1] These images defined the idea of themselves and others that the political leaders wanted to promote.

Fireworks, Flags, and Freedom:
Celebrating Independence

After the heavy death toll of war and the years of suffering, the new Latin American countries were faced with the challenge of replacing the image and symbols of the Spanish king, with enacting "the visual transformation of the State from the Old Regime to political modernity."[2] The king's portrait, name, and coat of arms had circulated in the Spanish American lands in the form of paintings, coins, and stamped papers, but with independence, those likenesses had to be replaced, the coins redesigned, and sovereignty reconfigured.[3] To justify independence, to compensate for those who died to gain freedom from the imperial yoke, and to create nothing short of a new nation, the new countries needed to accentuate the differences from the empire.

Initially, the indigenous past was chosen as the main differentiating characteristic with which to fashion a new image of the nation. In countries such as Mexico and Peru, cities were given

23 Theubet de Beauchamp. 1827. *View of Mexico Square, September 16, 1827*. Watercolor. Madrid, Real Biblioteca.

old Aztec and Incan names, and ancient symbols, such as the Aztec prickly pear with an eagle and a snake, or the Incan sun, were incorporated in coins and national coats of arms.[4] The faces of the leaders of independence—the new nations' new heroes—replaced the king's image. Painted portraits, wax effigies, and sculptures were hung in city councils and shared among the people through cheap copies.[5] Depending on the political direction of the government, some heroes, such as Bolívar, San Martín, and Hidalgo were portrayed more frequently than others.[6] Several countries developed portrait galleries of military men and politicians, continuing the colonial tradition of the viceroys.[7] The representation of the leaders of independence began to decline by 1840 with the rise of academies: "the archaic rigidity" of the portraits yielded to a "neoclassical glow" and "romantic seductions."[8]

Another debate was how to celebrate the anniversary of the cornerstone moment of their nations, the civic festivals at which each state had to present an official view of itself.[9] Most countries referred back to religious celebrations and colonial festivals: fireworks, raffles, and liturgical services accompanied by patriotic speeches.[10] But the organizers had to replace Spain and the conquistadors with new heroes.[11] In Mexico, the celebrations included "*tableaux vivants* of indigenous figures armed with bows"; in Argentina, dancers dressed as Spaniards and Americans; and in Lima, Peru, there were reenactments of the Inca Empire, using "the Indigenous past as a justification for independence."[12]

Besides the references to freedom in poems and discourses, some independence celebrations were also accompanied by the manumission of people who were enslaved. During Colombia's national festivities, the birth of a new political order celebrated positive elements of the republican system, equating the liberation of the enslaved with political freedom.[13] On December 26, 1822, in Bogotá, thirteen enslaved people were freed,[14] and on September 16, 1825, in Mexico City, President Guadalupe Victoria issued an order to end slavery when government funds allowed, encouraging enslavers to free voluntarily those they held in bondage.[15] The patriotic fund to free slaves amounted to 2,000 pesos, allowing the manumission of twelve enslaved people.[16]

Two years later, in Mexico in 1827, eight enslaved individuals were liberated, among whom a woman attracted the attention of an important Mexican figure, the statesman and historian Carlos María de Bustamante. He wrote in his diary that when she heard "the nation retracting slavery according to the liberal principles that were adopted, etcetera, she fixed her eyes on Azcárate and her beautiful eyes were clouded with tears."[17] Although we do not have an image capturing the tears, the Swiss artist Theubet de Beauchamp did paint the ceremony.

Theubet de Beauchamp arrived in New Spain in 1816 and remained there until 1828.[18] Besides depicting costumbrista scenes and location views, he represented civic deeds of the independent government, such as the entrance and coronation of Iturbide and the celebrations of September 16, 1827. Theubet identifies important buildings in the main square and enslaved people being freed in the ceremony by President Guadalupe Victoria. The image, included in an album offered to King Ferdinand VII in 1830, follows in the tradition of *casta* paintings and drawings by Joaquín Antonio de Basarás of landscapes, costumes, and scenes to promote the new Mexican nation.[19]

Elsewhere in the region, local artists also represented costumbrista scenes and political celebrations.[20] In Peru, the watercolors of Francisco "Pancho" Fierro became the greatest manifestation

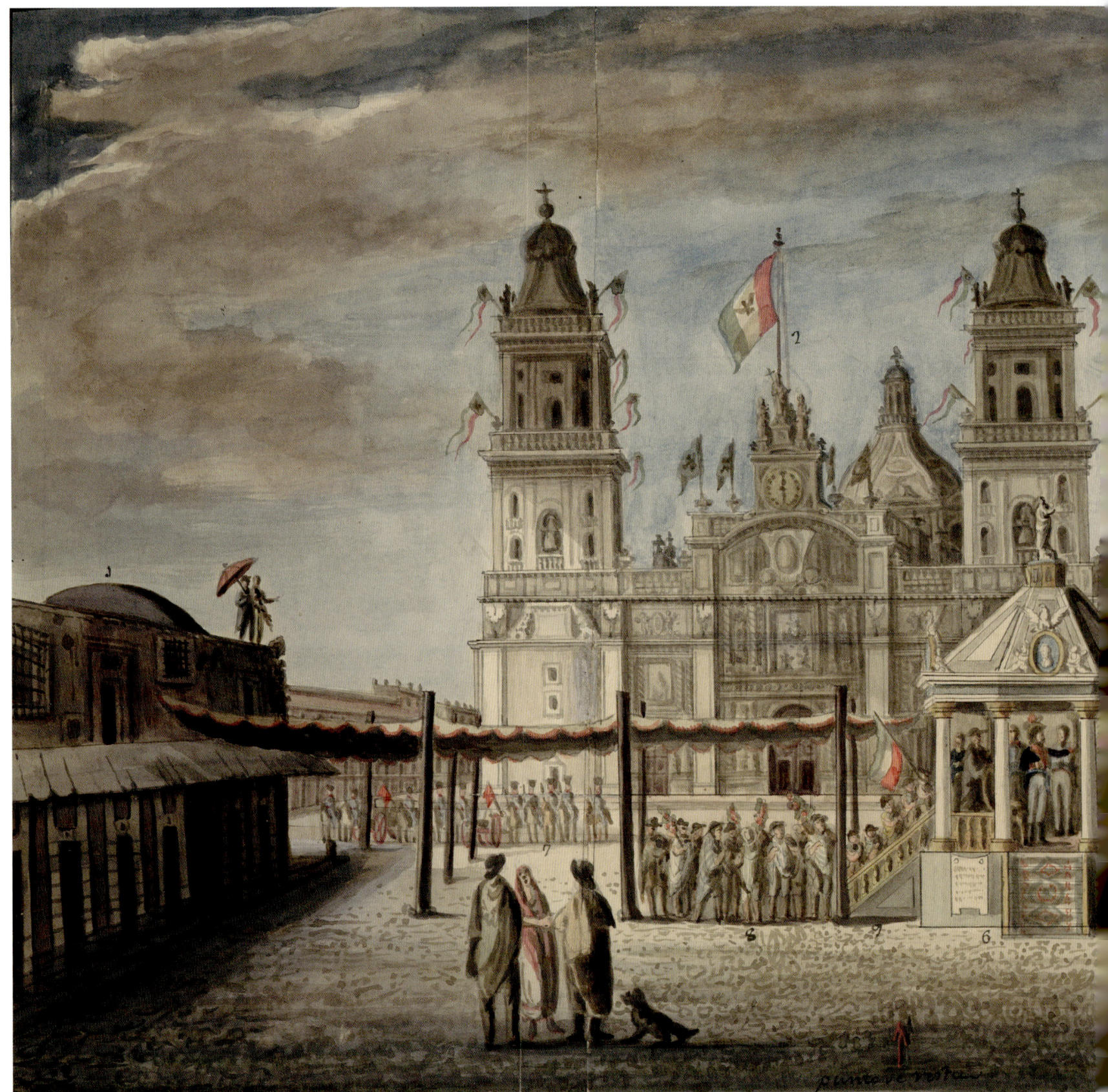

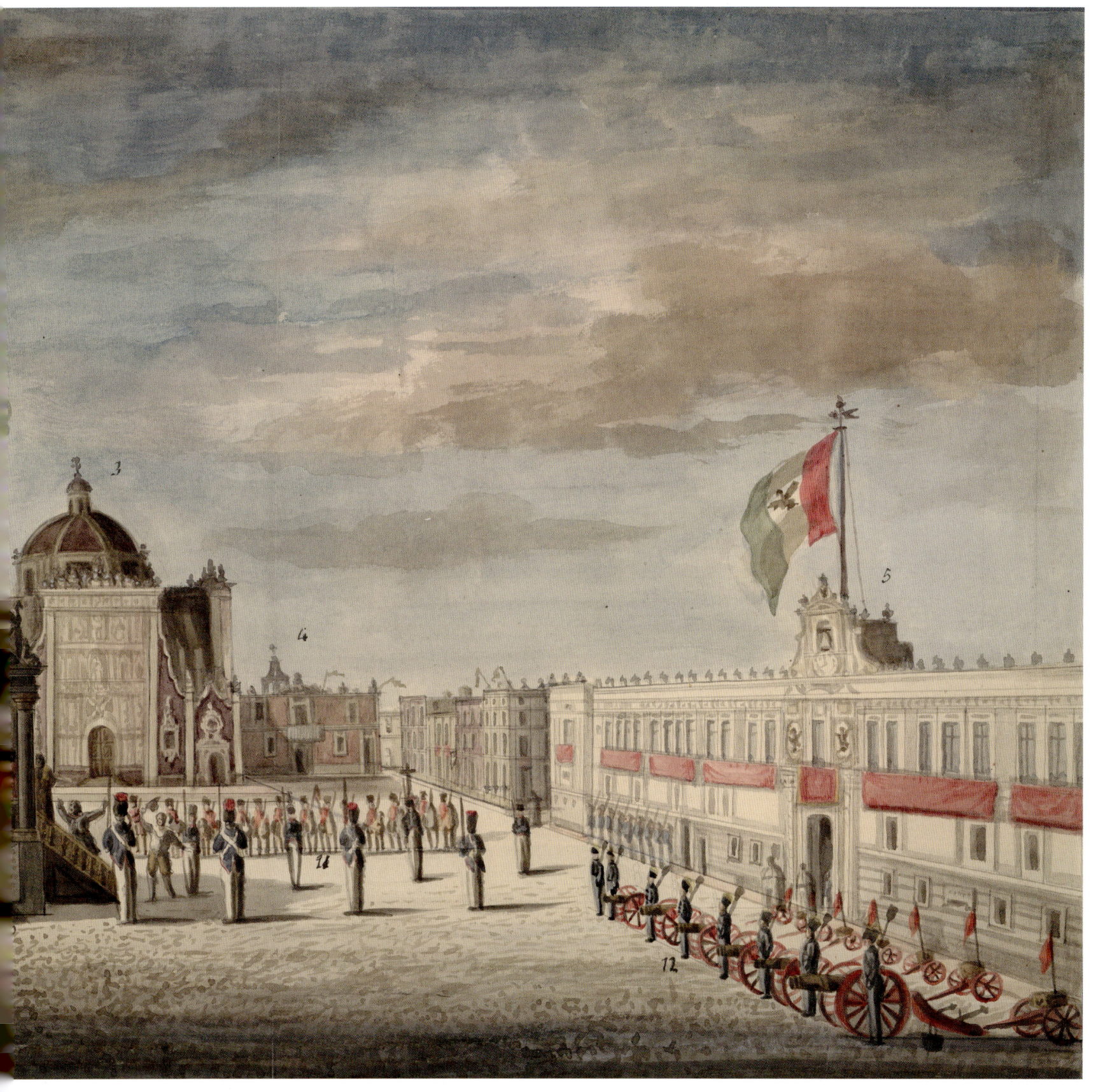

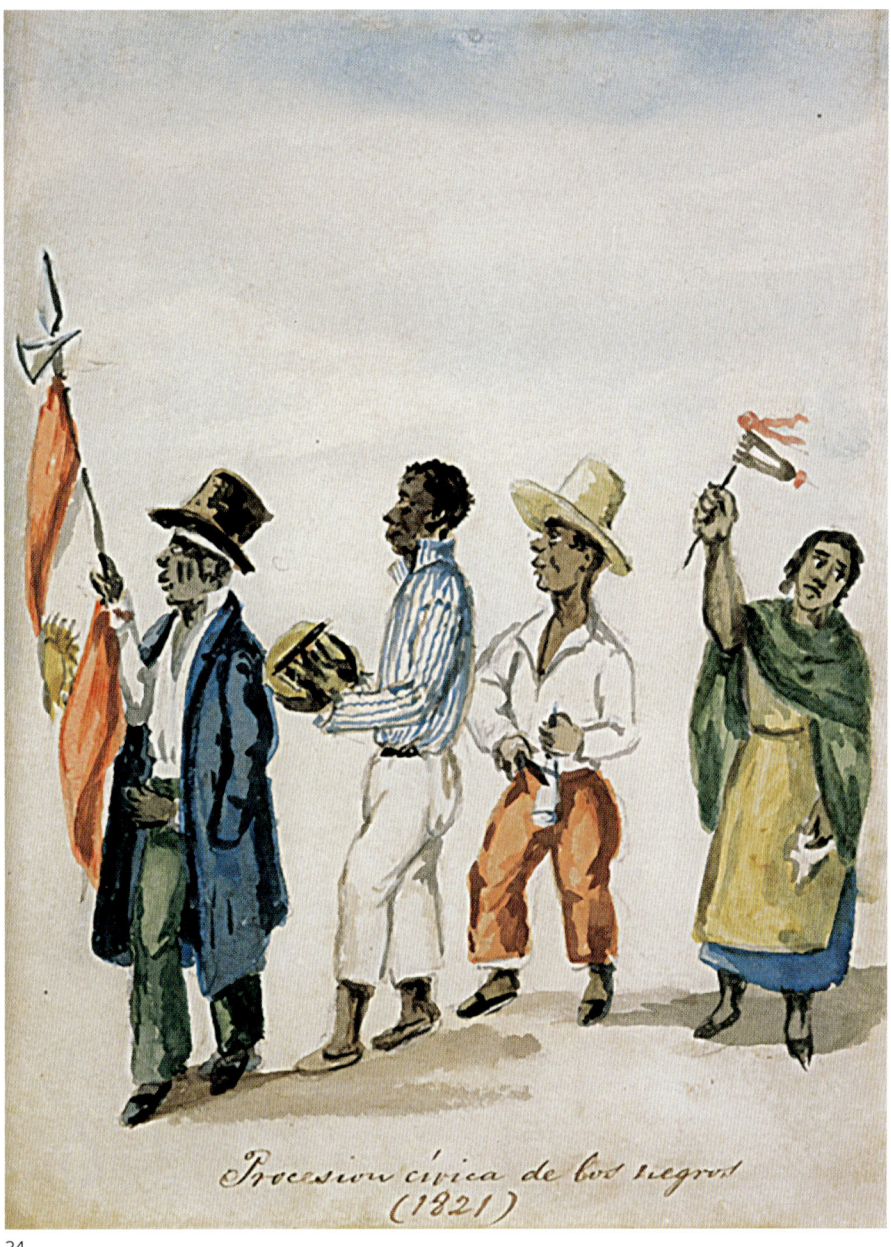

24

24 Francisco "Pancho" Fierro. *Civic Procession of the Blacks (1821)*. Undated. Watercolor on paper. Lima, Peru, Pinacoteca Municipal Ignacio Merino.

25 Unidentified artist. *Black over White*. 1867. Illustration. *Cabichui*. 1867.

of costumbrista, embodying the traditional memory of nineteenth-century Lima. He contributed to the construction of *criollismo* by rendering social diversity and the "harmony" of dances, street vendors, religious processions, and civic festivities.[21] The civic processions of the republic incorporated the hustle and bustle of the religious processions which marked colonial life. Music, dances, flowers, liquor, and fireworks[22] shared the public space with new flags and politic discourses, all of which contributed to a Creole identity.

In the year of Peru's declaration of independence, Francisco Fierro produced a trilogy depicting the Black community celebrating through musicians parading with flags and playing instruments. As Helen Melling noted, these groups include men, women, and children of different ages and socioeconomic status, according to their attire.[23] Fierro incorporated the representation of "black subjects within the body politic" and their participation in the "political sphere within the visual tradition."[24] He returns to a heterogeneous view of the Black population's presence in Peruvian society in his images of Black *cofradías* (confraternities, or Christian voluntary organizations) that was also emphasized by foreign artists.[25]

Taking the colonial framework as a reference, the new Latin

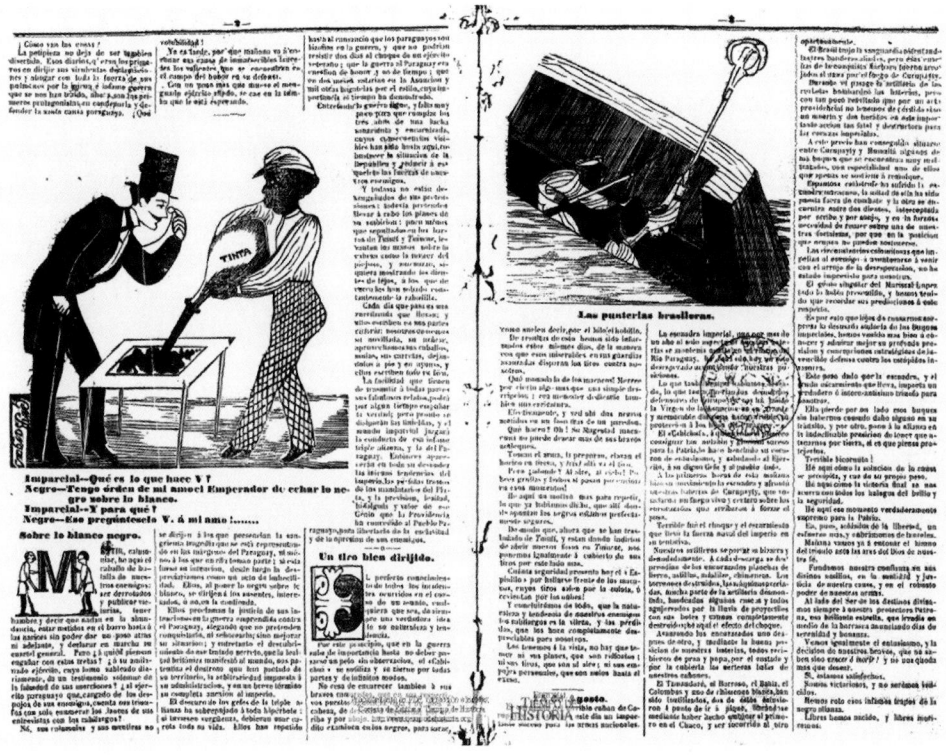

25

American countries started to construct an image of themselves that celebrated their freedom through civic ceremonies. Black people participated in and celebrated the battle for independence and participated in subsequent anniversaries either as symbols of the recently freed nation or by actively taking part in the celebration committee. Such postcolonial diversity was part of the exoticism of costumbrismo; Black people were exceptional figures who became part of the nation when they were freed, but then were generally written out of the national memory of independence.

One Nation, One Enemy?
The Construction of the Nation through War
One of the ways that Latin American countries defined themselves was through war against their neighbors, emphasizing their differences from them. Most countries suffered constant instability throughout the nineteenth century, with conflicts redrawing their borders, like the Mexican-U.S. War, the Triple Alliance, and the Pacific Wars. This necessitated the creation and reinforcement of distinctions from neighbors, who became "an object of difference, certainty, but one that can be fetishized and made familiar through the use of the stereotype."[26] Most nations identified themselves with universal values such as progress and order, valorizing the nation's European roots or occasionally its mixed biological and linguistic origins. In the meantime, colonial and racial stereotypes were assigned to the neighboring enemies in an effort to justify invasion and violence against people with whom they shared the continent.[27]

In 1865, a war pitting Paraguay against an alliance consisting of Argentina, Uruguay, and Brazil broke out and shook South America for five years. New technology transformed the information received at the fighting front in the form of the trench newspaper. The government of Paraguay produced four such newspapers to disseminate its views on the war to the public.[28] The government controlled the printing houses and the materials needed to produce newspapers, to teach the troops, and build their sense of identity.[29]

The *Cabichuí* claimed that Paraguay's position in relation to Brazil was a conflict of political systems: democracy against monarchy, freedom against slavery.[30] In print, enemy soldiers suffered racist comments and representations: dark figures with big lips and a title image of a monstrous dark figure being attacked by Paraguayan bees.[31] In the August 13, 1867, edition, *Cabichuí* published an engraving titled "Black over White." The article that accompanied the picture emphasizes the desire of the Paraguayan people to be free from slavery and oppression, justifying the war against Brazil.[32]

25

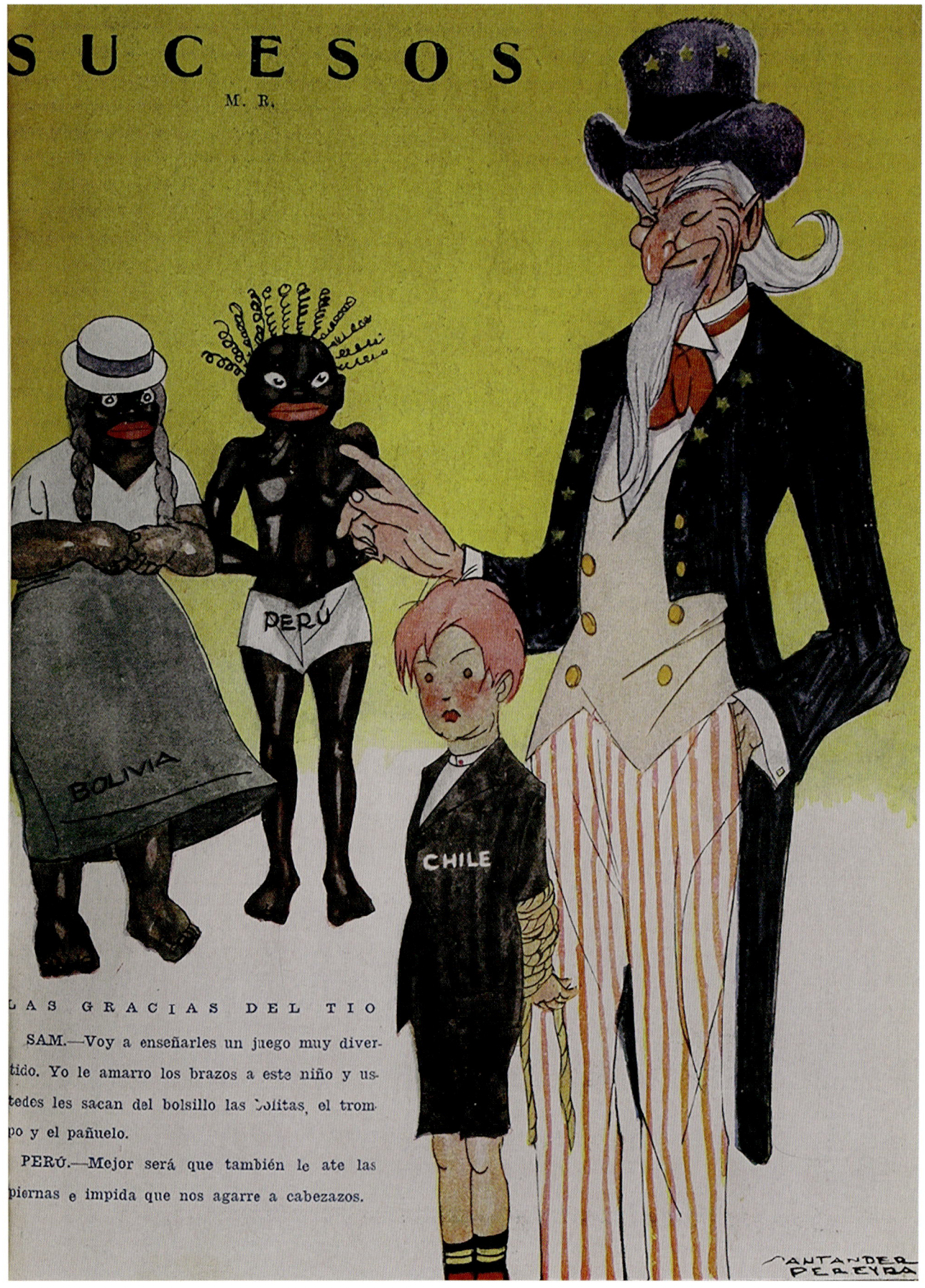

26 Santander Pereira. 1927. Illustration. *Revista Sucesos*.

27 Pedro Américo. *Battle of Avaí*. 1874-1877. Oil. Rio de Janeiro, Museo Nacional de Bellas Artes.

This dynamic of differentiation continued into the twentieth century in, for example, the racist discourse articulated by Chile in its conflict with Peru. The Chilean nationalist discourse was based on a dichotomy between civilization and barbarity, emphasizing racial and cultural attributes of Peruvians to justify the war. In the same period, scientific racism, embraced and endorsed by the European-descended elites, argued that there was a natural hierarchy of races.[33] Chile's racial exceptionalism in the Latin American context found expression through a white and uniform Chilean identity as opposed to the "exoticism" and "otherness" of Peru and Bolivia.[34] This discourse filled the pages of two of Chile's most important magazines, *Sucesos* (1902–1932) and *Corre-Vuela* (1908–1928). Both published images that ridiculed the Peruvian population as "black" people, assigning to them negative attributes like cowardice and foolishness.

In October 1927, Santander Pereira created a caricature representing the important role of the United States in the conflict. Chile is portrayed as a white boy, just like "Uncle Sam," while Peru is represented as a Black child, barefoot and seminaked, with extreme physical features "emphasizing its 'primitivism.'"[35] The text complementing the image asserts the superiority of the Chilean war capacity over those of Peru and Bolivia. Using a dark skin color, the cartoonists "ridiculed the 'other' through satirical paintings."[36] Caricatures by definition are not accurate portrayals of their subjects, and in their effort to denigrate Peru's multicultural population, these artists often relied on grotesquely exaggerated racist depictions of phenotypical and cultural elements that would be recognizable to their audience.

In the nineteenth century, as throughout the ages, art served not only an aesthetic function, but had a potential to teach and influence opinion. Historical paintings may appear to be representations of "an event which can be identified in time and space" and "a truthful reproduction of something that happened,"[37] but they were also "considered a noble artistic genre," representing moral precepts as well as historical facts.[38] In Brazil, the artistic production of the Imperial Academy of Fine Arts was dominated by allegories emphasizing the role of the emperor, accompanied by symbols of tropical exuberance. In 1872, the minister of empire commissioned the commemoration of key moments in Brazilian military history, including the Battle of Avaí, when Brazilian troops overcame Paraguayan resistance.[39] Pedro Americo painted a fifty-square-meter canvas between 1874 and 1877, which was well received by critics in Florence before traveling to Brazil. Black soldiers appear among the Brazilian troops, but their participation is minimized.

Yet the Black population had been an active part of armies since the colonial period.[40] They fought on both sides of the independence movement, and they were prominent in the ranks of the new independent nations.[41] Some Black fighters made the transition from fighters for independence to soldiers for their new nation. Claudio Linati in Mexico, Anton Goering in Venezuela, Francisco Fierro in Peru, Auguste Le Moyne in Colombia, and Juan Manuel Blanes in Uruguay all portrayed Black soldiers either as groups without resources, as in the work of the first two artists, or in immaculate uniforms, as in the last three.[42] Although Black soldiers participated in the construction of several new Latin American nations, in these images the artists who created them all but ignored their significant contributions.

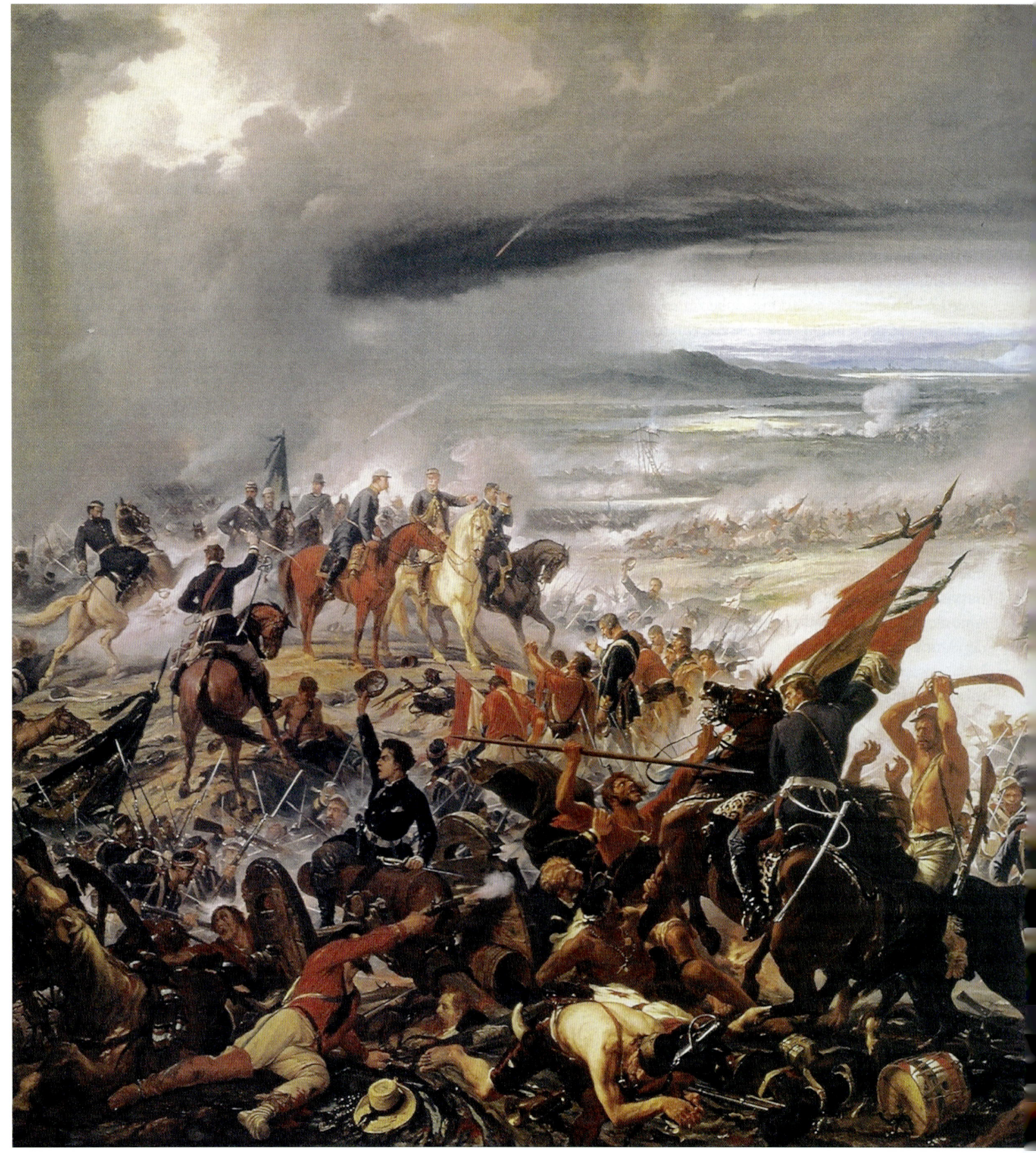

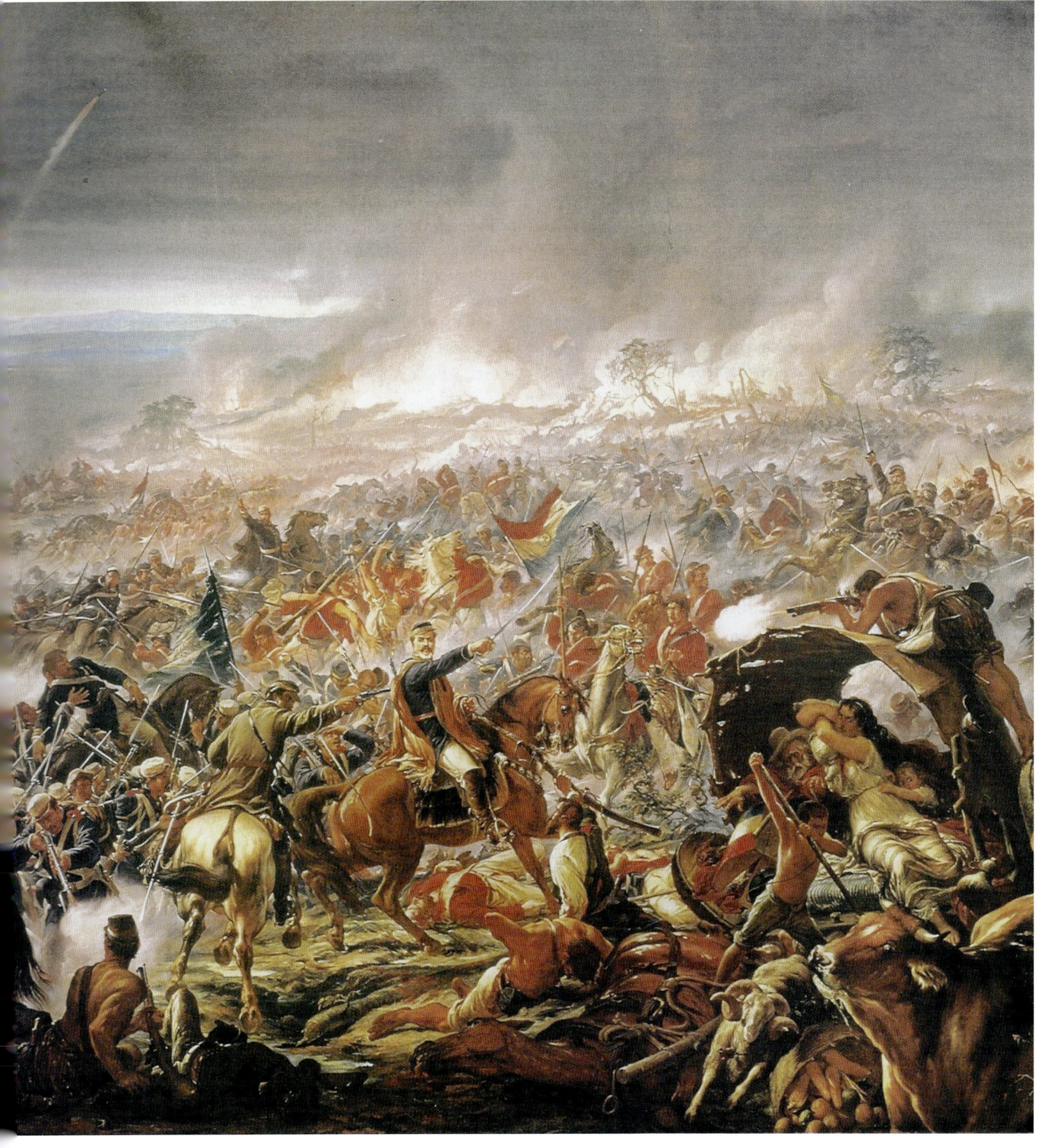

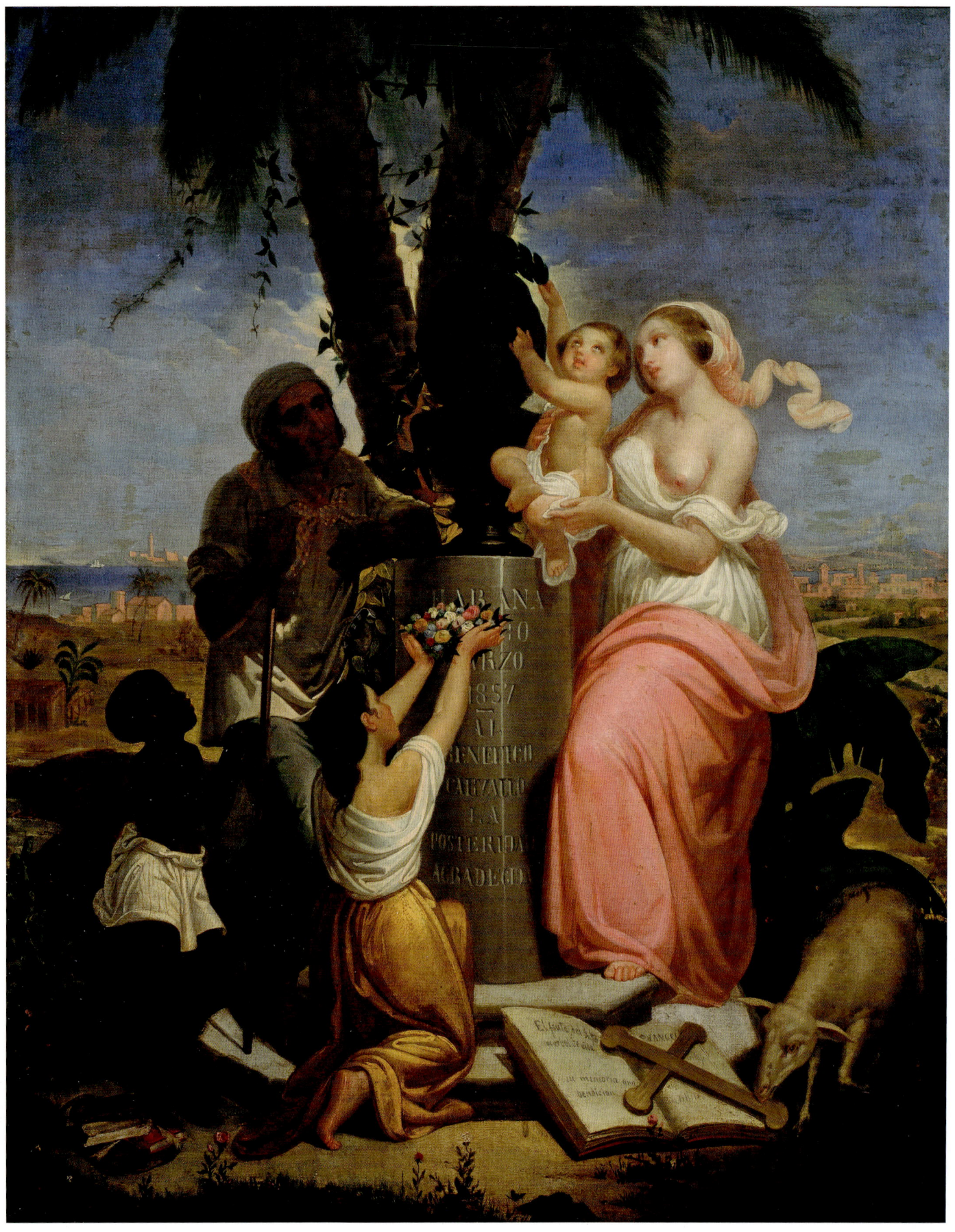

28 Hércules Morelli. *Christian Charity Crowning the Bust of Francisco Carvallo*. 1857. Oil on canvas. Havana, Museo Nacional de Bellas Artes de Cuba.

Nation Building: Remembering Independence

Academies took root in Ibero-America at the end of the eighteenth century and the beginning of the nineteenth, starting with the creation of the Royal Academy of San Carlos in Mexico City in New Spain in 1785 and followed by others in Peru, Guatemala, Chile, and Cuba, culminating in the creation of the latter's School of Painting and Sculpture of San Alejandro in Havana by 1818.[43] These academies struggled to stabilize and consolidate themselves because of the constant political instability and financial uncertainty of the new states.[44] Brazil, however, achieved a considerable quantity and quality of artistic production during the nineteenth century after the establishment of the Portuguese monarchy in Brazil in 1808.

After decades of conflict and instability, art academies across South America began to construct a narrative of the nation, its origin and key moments, through allegorical and historical paintings. They would hang on the walls of the academy and public buildings in Latin American countries, "liv[ing] outside of the historical time and the space of the citizen," while providing "an original narrative" located in an antiquity that anchors the national identity beyond the confines of history.[45]

From the outset, the academies focused on allegory. For example, the traditional *Alegoría de Carlos IV y el Imperio Español* (*Allegory of Charles IV and the Spanish Empire*) included symbolic representations of an "African force" building the empire. In Cuba, since the creation of the San Alejandro Academy in 1818, allegories attracted the most official commissions.[46] The Italian artist Hércules Morelli painted *La Caridad Cristiana coronando el busto de Francisco Carvallo, fundador de la Escuela y Hospital de Belén* (*Christian Charity Crowning the Bust of Francisco Carvallo*). The representation of the historical figure who founded the hospital and school of Belén in Cuba is accompanied by a white man who symbolizes the *guajiro* (agricultural worker), and also a Black child, an infantile representation of the Afro-Cuban population.

In the second half of the nineteenth century, historical paintings were a priority of these academies, exemplified by the Brazilian academy. The nation-state as a hegemonic political organization was in harmony with the hegemonic genre of historical painting in the same period.[47] Political power was represented in terms of "the representation of the community in the past," with artists having to satisfy the ideals and wishes of those in power.[48] These paintings could indicate the development of a national identity, as if the construction of a nation had its origin in the one that created these institutions and funded their paintings.[49]

In Colombia, in 1919, the Beautification Society of Bogotá and the Patriotic Festivities Committee of Colombia commissioned for 1,000 pesos from Francisco Antonio Cano a canvas based on a sketch made by the artist.[50] This painting represents the epic journey of troops, led by Francisco de Paula Santander, across the Andes, a trek which cost three hundred soldiers their lives.[51] Among the men at the forefront, a Black figure accompanies Santander, although he is far from the main focus of the painting. The decision of the painter to feature only one Black individual was a relatively common choice, as in Juan Lepiani's painting *Proclamación de la independencia del Perú* (*Proclamation of the Independence of Peru*). Devoting his career to historical and patriotic oil paintings,[52] Lepiani demonstrated elegance and rigid solemnity in this work.[53] Inspired by Antonio Ciseri's *Ecce Homo*, the composition is divided into two spaces: the balcony

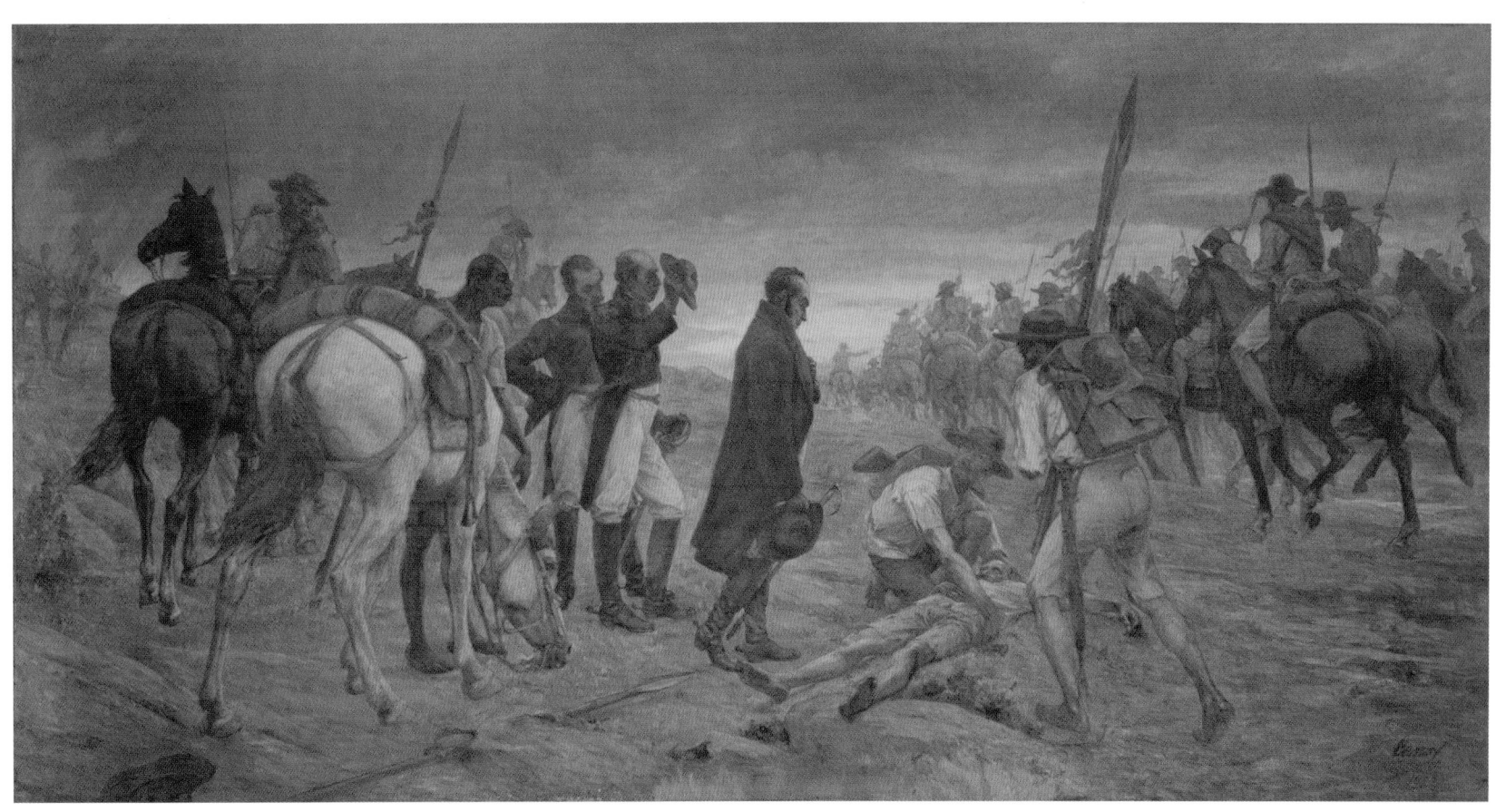

29 Francisco Antonio Cano. *Passage of the Liberating Army through the Páramo de Pisba*. 1922. Oil. Bogatá, Colombia, Colección Casa Museo Quinta de Bolívar. MinCultura.

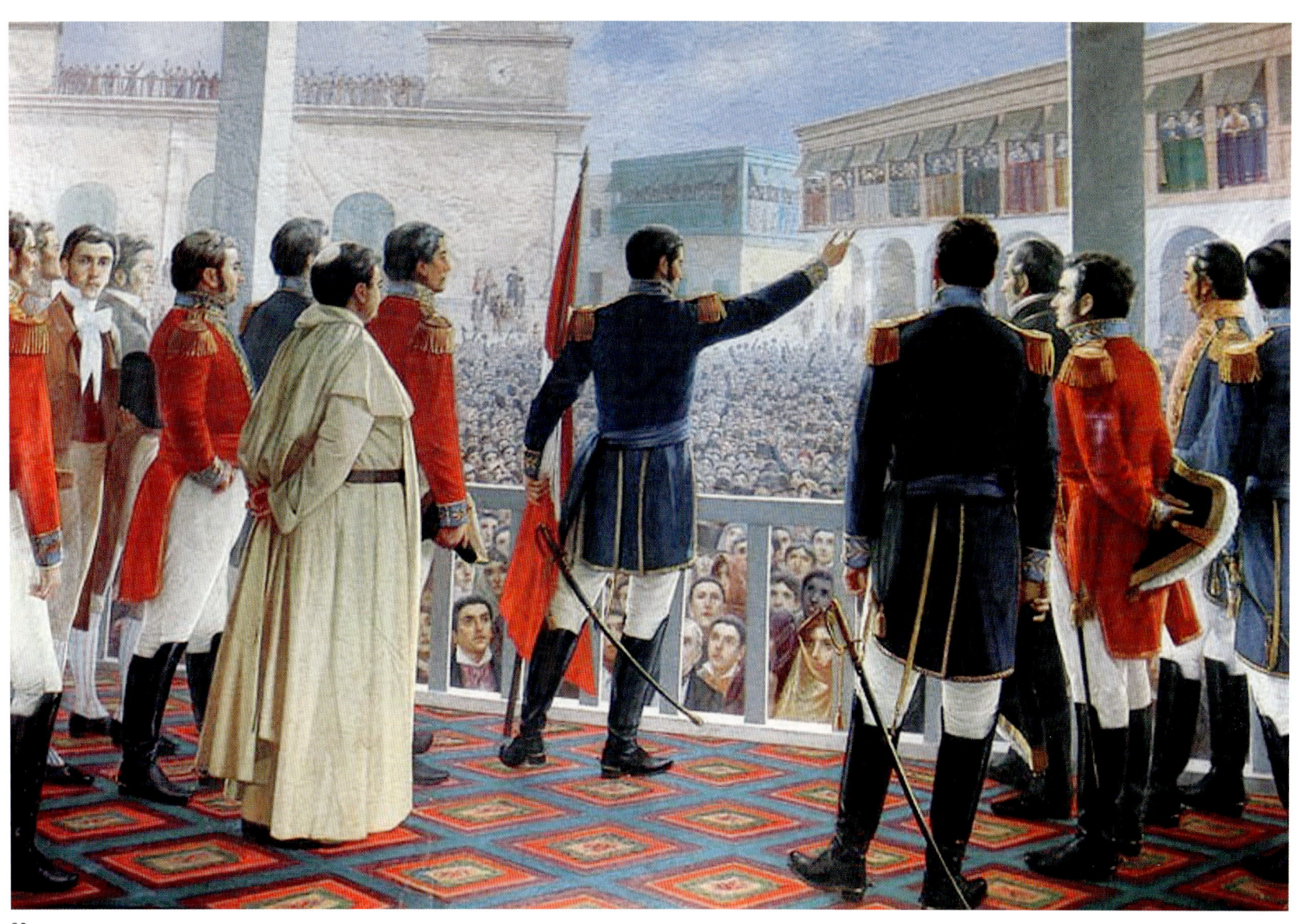

30 Juan Lepiani. *Proclamation of the Independence of Peru*. 1904. Oil. Lima, National Museum of Archaeology, Anthropology and History of Peru.

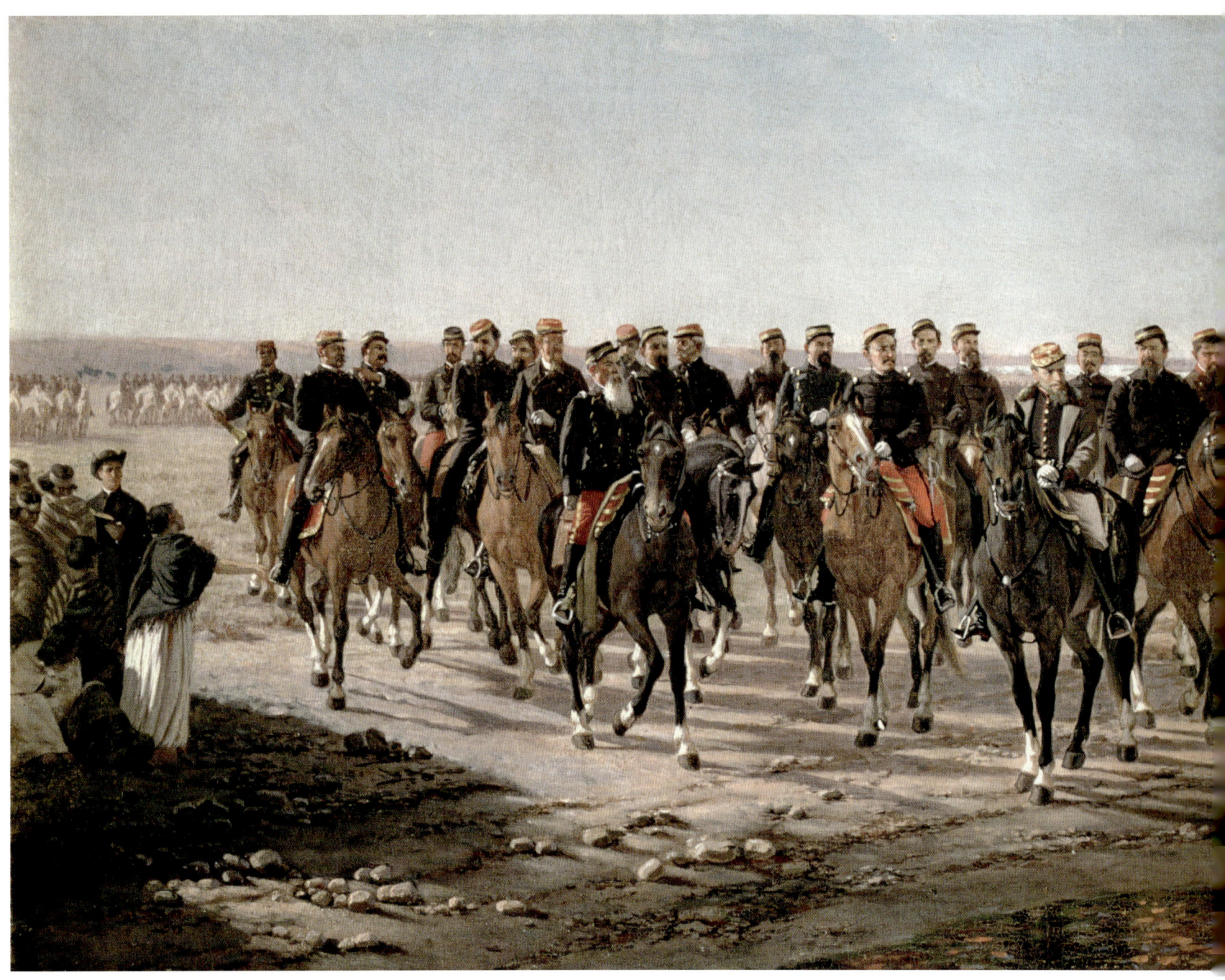

31

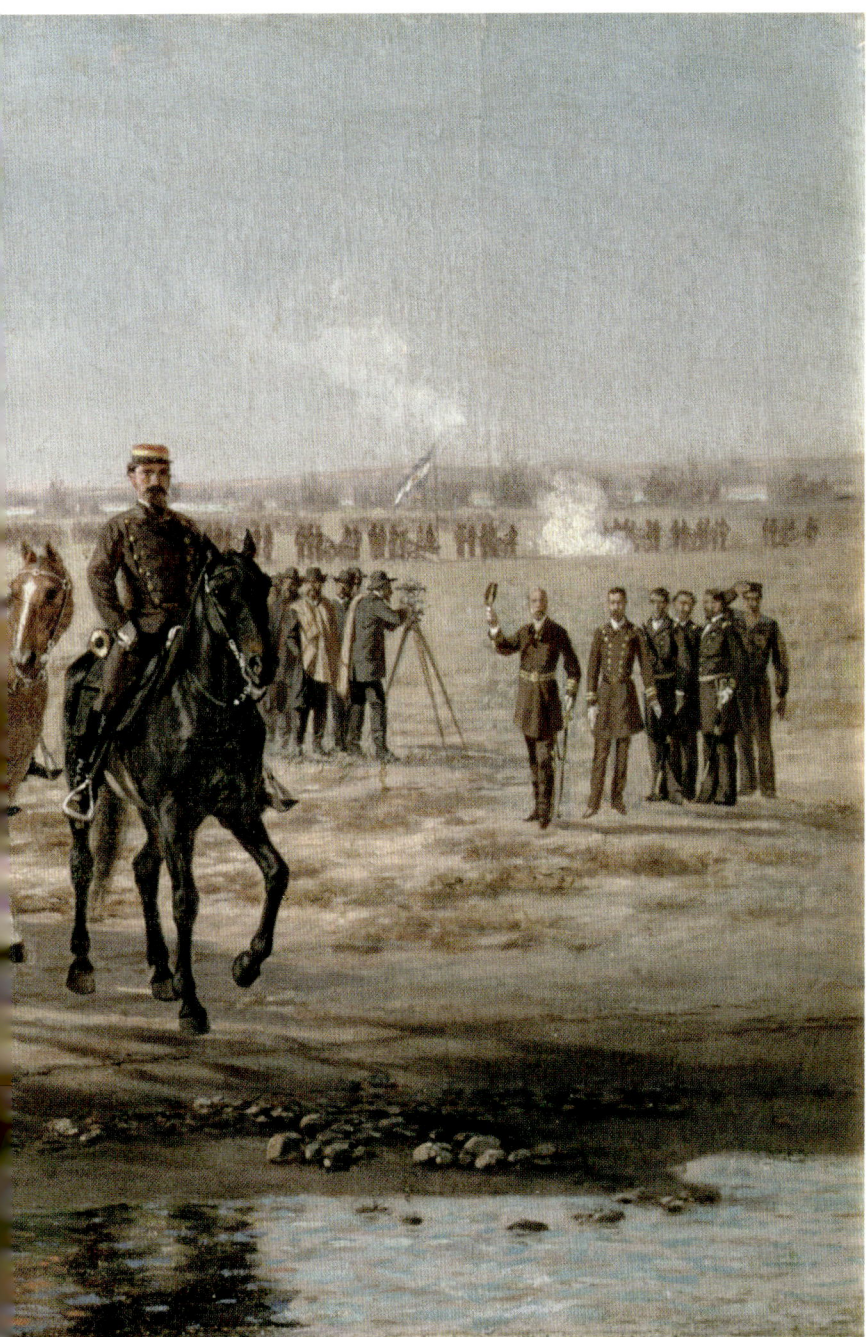

31 Juan Manuel Blanes. *The Conquest of the Desert*. 1896. Buenos Aires, Argentina, Museo Histórico Nacional.

with the independence leaders such as San Martín holding the Peruvian flag and the public square with Lima's people celebrating the historic event.⁵⁴ Among the overwhelmingly *criollo* crowd, a person of African descent is represented in one of the first rows.⁵⁵

As in the first representations of the conquest,⁵⁶ a Black person is included in each painting as an allegorical figure, as a part of the nation, but never as a main figure. Black people are rendered as infantilized symbols in the foundation paintings of their nations, essentially erased from the greater national narrative. As the construction of a collective memory of a civil war continued to the beginning of the twentieth century, academic paintings discounted or denied entirely the participation of Afrodescendant people in freeing their nations.

In Mexico, after the restoration of the republic in 1867, the academy chose to focus on pre-Hispanic themes, such as *El descubrimiento del pulque (The Discovery of Pulque)* (a fermented beverage) by José María Obregón in 1869, *El senado de Tlaxcala (The Senate of Tlaxcala)* by Rodrigo Gutiérrez in 1875, and *La tortura de Cuauhtémoc* (*The Torture of Cuauhtémoc*) by Leandro Izaguirre in 1893. In these paintings the narrative focuses on the indigenous past (represented by European figures) rather than on the diversity of Mexican social reality. Similarly, by the end of the nineteenth century, the governing class in Argentina, as in many other Latin American countries, was eager to achieve political and cultural homogeneity in the country. In 1896, two years before the opening of the National Historical Museum, Juan Manuel Blanes created a very large historical painting, measuring 11 × 4 meters, that became the official national expression of the "civilizing process," which justified the Argentinian government's relocation of indigenous groups to *estancias* (rural estates, usually cattle ranches) at the hands of the military.[57] The painting focuses on military figures as "heroes of civilization," whereas indigenous people are confined to a corner, and a captured woman appears before the group.[58] The landscape is a mythical desert, devoid of human presence. The ethnic diversity of the country is downplayed, despite the presence in the rear of a Black soldier, and there is no reference to the expulsion of indigenous groups to the estancias, where they were accompanied by Black workers.[59]

After the independence movements, Latin American elites worked to transform their nations into modern and progressive countries guided by liberalism in emulation of European and American nationalism. These European countries had either "no significant black or indigenous populations" or segregated them, as was done in the post–Civil War United States; Latin American nations, however, had "large numbers of *mestizos*, blacks and indigenous people."[60] By the beginning of the twentieth century, Latin American elites had absorbed the racial determinism of European theories of human development, but they governed nations with far less homogenous populations. Some chose to celebrate the *mestizo,* rejecting the idea that racial mixture was synonymous with degeneracy, yet still expressing "[bias] towards whiteness" and promoting immigration from European countries.[61] Although nations like Peru and Mexico elevated the figure of the Indian of ancient civilization by encouraging the idea of *indigenismo,* the Black population was rarely represented in the same way. Even in countries with very large Black populations, like Cuba and Brazil, their representation was rare, and they were looked on positively only insofar as they were on a path toward integration.[62]

The images we have seen in this essay were designed to create a shared memory, constructed around two circumstances: "the violent rupture of the Independence wars and the sociological basis created by multiple ethnicities."[63] Either as mestizos, criollos, or "Spanish Americans," the discourse was designed to differentiate the new nations from their original conquered inhabitants and their biological descendants, who were considered inferior and problematic, and from the descendants of enslaved Blacks brought over during the colonial period.[64] In defining a new national identity for the Latin American nations, the Black presence was diminished and/or deleted from the shared memory, represented by paintings and images, especially those displayed in museums. The virtual silence in such paintings about the past contribution of Black populations to the formation of Latin American nations speaks volumes about the construction of national memory by the elites.

4

COSTUMBRISMO:

MAPPING BLACKNESS IN THE NEW NATIONS OF MEXICO, COLOMBIA, AND PERU

HELEN MELLING

Most images of Black subjects in nineteenth-century Latin America were produced and circulated within the popular iconography forged by *costumbrismo*, as seen through the romantic and ethnographic gaze of both foreign and local artists. The depiction of local manners, types, and customs enshrined in this genre played a foundational role in the formation of social, racial, and national identities in the aftermath of the wars of independence throughout the region. This highly transitional period witnessed the emergence of recalibrated social hierarchies. The official rejection of colonial caste terminology and the frequently drawn-out process toward the abolition of slavery were fundamental both to this recalibration and to the shaping of cultural and national discourses surrounding the continent's Afrodescendant population. Costumbrismo contributed to new national imaginaries that sought to reconcile republican discourses of equality with socioracial distinctions and hierarchies that were predicated on notions of white racial superiority.[1] The genre produced paradigmatic visual representations of the region's Afrodescendant populations rooted in a typology of Black subjects as subservient, immoral, exotic, and picturesque, representations which would go on to have a lasting currency through their widespread repetition and circulation via popular media such as the watercolor and the lithograph.

While the greatest number and most familiar images of Black subjects during this period were produced in Cuba and Brazil, this essay considers the comparatively lesser-known examples of Mexico, Colombia, and Peru. In doing so, it traces parallels and contrasts in the depiction of Black subjects across these new nations, framed according to their distinct regional demographics, topographies, and histories. Although Mexico and Peru were important centers of slavery from the earliest moments of the colonial period, they have both been regarded in contemporary scholarship as part of "*mestizo*" America, countries of predominantly mixed-race and indigenous populations in which indigenous and mestizo-based narratives have been central in imaginings of the nation.[2] Colombia, meanwhile, owing to its larger Afrodescendant demographic and Black-white racial continuum, forms part of what has been broadly been considered as Afro-Latin America.[3] What links these three places in the nineteenth century is the way Blackness was mapped onto their national geographies via *costumbrista* iconography, which systematically locates Black types in specific localities and provinces, contributing to these regions becoming racialized and coded as "Black" in the national imagination. The place of these regions within the hierarchical racial order, vis-à-vis their perceived spatial and cultural proximity or distance from centers of political power and "whiteness,"

32 Claudio Linati, design. *Man from the Coast: Black Man from the Vicinity of Veracruz (Santa Fe) in His Sunday Clothes*. Hand-colored lithograph. *Costumes civils, militaires et réligieux du Mexique* (Brussels, Belgium, 1828).

in large measure determines both the nature and the extent of the representation of Black subjects in costumbrista art. Notwithstanding their demographic differences, in Colombia and Mexico we find that Black regions and Blackness were codified as coastal, tropical, and consequently marginal to national imaginaries. In Peru, meanwhile, the Afrodescendant population is primarily associated with Lima, resulting in a proliferation of images of Black subjects and their symbolic centrality in the emergence of a Creole-centered national identity.[4]

It is important to stress that in spite of its purported realism, costumbrisma art presents a deliberately constructed and frequently idealized world, described by Natalia Majluf in the case of Peru as the first important "invention of tradition" in Latin America.[5] Continuities can undoubtedly be traced back to Enlightenment visual culture, as secular movements that focused on typologies of peoples through the construction of social, racial, and gendered identities, shaped by the colonial gaze and representations of difference and otherness.[6] There is also a continued desire in the post-independence period to represent practices of *mestizaje* (racial mixing) and to acknowledge the resulting diversity of the new nations' populations, rooted in the visual language of "types," in which peoples are classified according to a variety of physical, phenotypical, and cultural attributes. The distinct criteria, function, and modes of production of costumbrismo, however, produce a fundamental rupture with classificatory projects of the Enlightenment,[7] disrupting the center-periphery dynamic of colonial imagery. The primacy of quotidian scenes and local subjects gives a marked focus to the clothing, occupations, and traditions of the lower and middle classes. Within this cast of types, Black subjects are largely associated with low-income occupations and tropical coastal climates, which contribute to their subordinated, peripheral place in the social hierarchy. This essay considers such transnational motifs of Blackness produced and circulated by costumbrista art, alongside a small number of works that also exceed aspects of this dominant paradigm. It also considers the role of Afrodescendants as authors of these representations in the case of the Afro-Peruvian artist Francisco "Pancho" Fierro.

A crucial consideration in examining this iconography is the impact of emancipation in shaping and reinforcing stereotypes of the Afrodescendant population and their exclusion from nation-building discourses of the late nineteenth century. In Mexico and Colombia, most costumbrista images of Black subjects were produced in the years that followed emancipation (1829 and 1851 respectively), whereas in Peru a significant number were produced prior to abolition in 1854. In spite of this, Peruvian costumbrista art is entirely devoid of images that portray the violence and abuse routinely inflicted on the enslaved population, in notable contrast to the scenes of torture that were produced by traveler-artists in Brazil. An overt social commentary or critique of slavery was clearly not part of the artistic agenda, which largely privileges harmonious, picturesque depictions and tends to gloss over sources of social conflict. The reality of Black freedom and agency was conceived as a threat both to economic prosperity and national homogeneity by the region's ruling elites, one that had to be discursively contained and "domesticated." The post-emancipation period also witnesses the concomitant rise of a disappearing narrative with regard to the Afrodescendant population across much of Latin America, in which abolition and mestizaje are invoked as the driving forces behind its inevitable

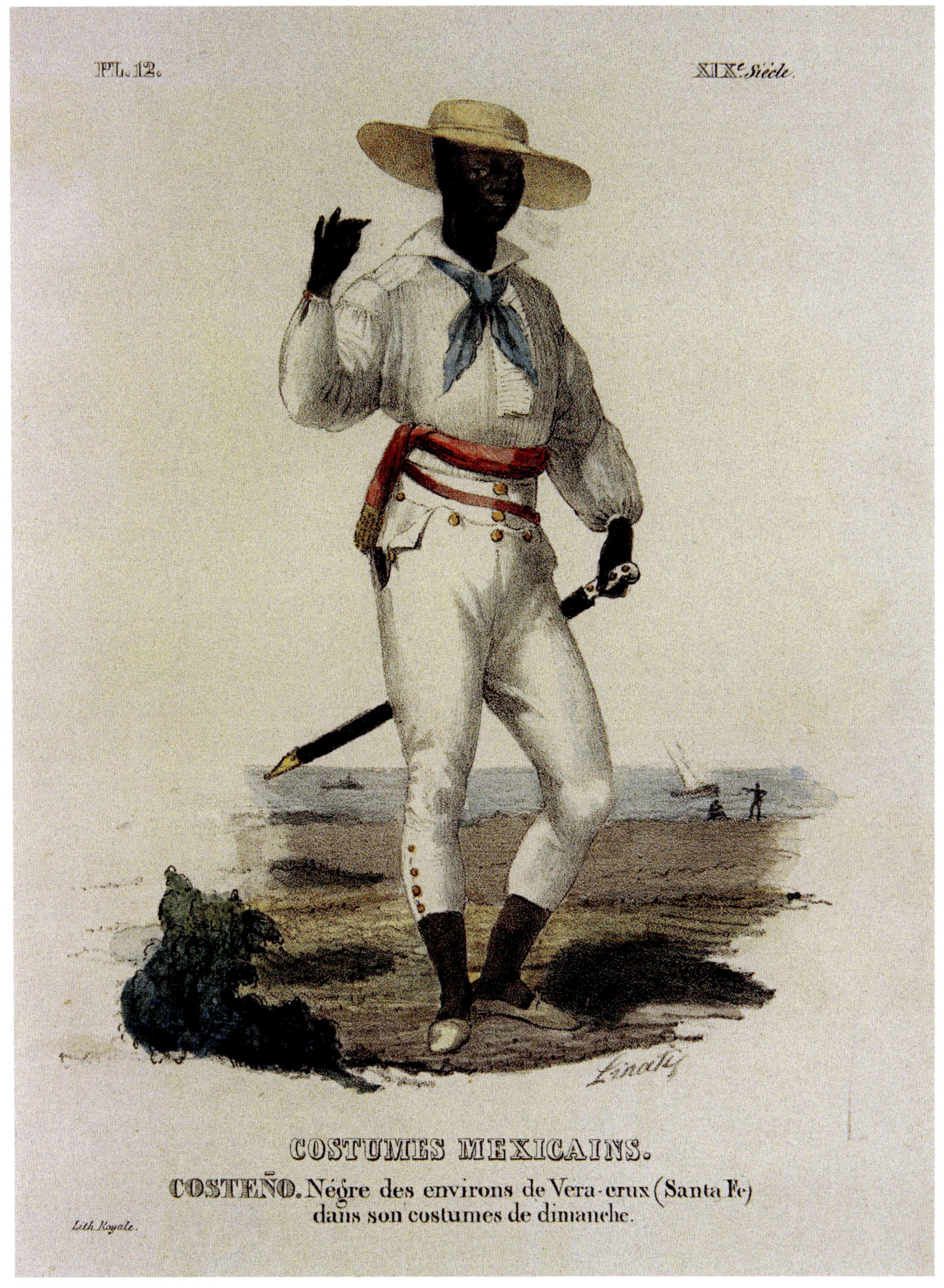

COSTUMES MEXICAINS.
COSTEÑO. Nègre des environs de Vera-crux (Santa Fe) dans son costumes de dimanche.

demise.⁸ This discourse was particularly accentuated in Peru and Mexico, alongside other countries with smaller Afrodescendant populations, and influenced the nature, circulation, and contextualization of costumbrista images of Black subjects in these new nations.

Mexico and Colombia:
"Tropical" Blackness on the Margins of the Nation
Although the presence of peoples of African descent is in evidence in the art of New Spain throughout the seventeenth and eighteenth centuries, this diminishes considerably following independence in 1821 and the abolition of slavery in 1829. It is particularly striking that the breadth of Black types that feature in eighteenth-century casta paintings⁹ does not translate into nineteenth-century republican iconography. In this respect, it is possible to speak of a relative "oblivion" of Blackness in Mexican costumbrismo.¹⁰ This is symptomatic of the broader marginalization of the Afrodescendant population from nation-building narratives that focused on a bipolar model of Indians and whites and hinged on the figure of the mestizo and the recuperation of Mexico's indigenous past.¹¹ The emphasis on the ideal of the mestizo is abundantly clear in *Los mexicanos pintados por si mismos* (1853–1855), described by Erica Segre as Mexico's seminal costumbrista compilation,¹² and which includes *criollos*, mestizos, and a lesser number of indigenous types, but a total absence of Afrodescendant types.

Free and enslaved Africans and their descendants were a vital rural and urban presence throughout New Spain. In the early republican period, however, in the national imagination, this population becomes limited to Mexico's coastal regions, in part owing to the historical arrival of enslaved Blacks through the ports of Veracruz and Acapulco. This regionalization of Blackness in Mexico is considerably bolstered by the emergence of the post-emancipation discourse of the Black population's "disappearance." As early as 1836, for example, the liberal politician and historian José María Luisa Mora alludes to their concentrated presence on the coast—implicitly invoked as the periphery of the nation—as evidence of their overall demographic decline: "*pues los cortos retos de ellos que han quedado en las costas del Pacifico y en las del atlantico son enteramente insignificantes….*"¹³

When they do appear, Afrodescendants are almost entirely linked with the Caribbean coast and Veracruz in particular, with its attendant tropical associations and stereotypes. These images, produced primarily by foreign traveler-artists and aimed at a predominantly European audience, fall within the context of exoticizing and frequently derogatory portrayals, as seen in the works of the Italian artist Claudio Linati (1790–1832). Linati introduced the technology of lithography to Mexico and worked within the tradition of costume books. Published in Brussels in 1828, Linati's *Trajes civiles, militares y religiosos de Mexico* features forty-eight lithographs of Mexican types. Each image is accompanied by a textual description that includes observations on Mexican costumes and traditions, rooted in a Eurocentric social and moral commentary of the subjects portrayed. As a whole, the album reinforces a sociracial hierarchy headed by the criollo elite and promotes negative stereotypes about Mexico's mixed-race, indigenous, and Afrodescendant populations. His racialized and pejorative representations of Black types appear in three images. In *Nègre des environs de Veracruz dans son costumes de Dimanche,* the emblematic figure of the *costeño* or *jarocho* (coastal dweller

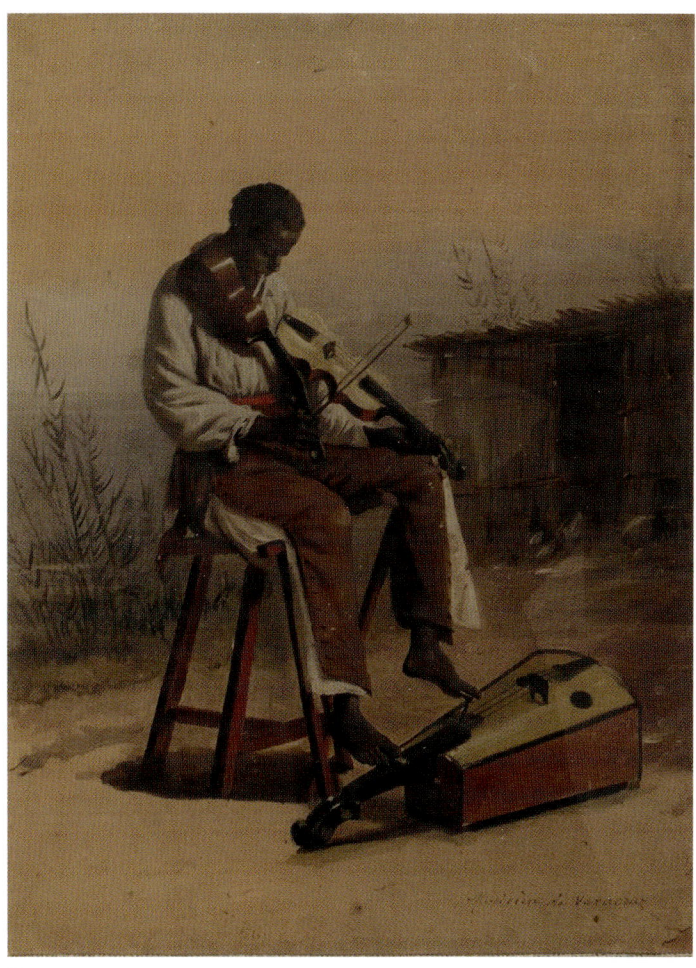

33 Édouard Pingret. *Musician from Veracruz*. Ca. 1850. Oil on cardboard. Colección Banco Nacional de México.

of Veracruz) is situated on the seafront in a leisurely scene; he is portrayed smoking, dressed in clothing typical of the region and identified as his "Sunday costume." In the textual accompaniment, Linati denigrates and ridicules the subject's appearance by likening it to that of a vaudeville harlequin. In a deeply pejorative second image, *Negre etendu dans son hamac*, Linati expresses his disdain for the leisurely lifestyle of the Black costeño, portraying him reclining in a hammock, holding a cigarette in his left hand and whipping his wife with his right. While Linati lauds the abolition of slavery in the passage that accompanies the lithograph, he portrays the Afro-Mexican population as inherently undeserving of their freedom owing to their indolence and degeneracy, corresponding with post-abolition fears prevalent in Latin America that peddled these stereotypes and prejudices regarding peoples of African descent.

In other cases, we encounter more romanticized depictions, as in *Músico de Veracruz* (ca. 1850) by the French artist Édouard Pingret (1788–1875).[14] The musician is shown intently engaged in tuning or fixing several string instruments. His bare feet and tattered clothing, coupled with the modest shack in the background, denote his rural location and working-class status, and the scene reinforces the association of Blackness both with the coast and music from the region. As Mey-Yen Moriuchi contends, although Pingret depicts popular types as dignified, hardworking, and poor, these images nevertheless perpetuated and fed attendant stereotypes regarding Mexico's mixed-race, indigenous, and Afrodescendant populations.[15] In this instance, although the subject's pose is attributable to his activity, the combination of his slumped back, downcast eyes, and humble clothing and surroundings lend a downtrodden, melancholic quality to the image.

While foreign artists produced the majority of costumbrista images of Afro-Mexicans, with this in itself comprising a reduced number of their output as a whole, the Mexican academy wholly ignored as a subject the Afrodescendant population.[16] This is partly attributable to the fact that the academy sidelined costumbrismo in favor of neoclassicism and historical or bibli-

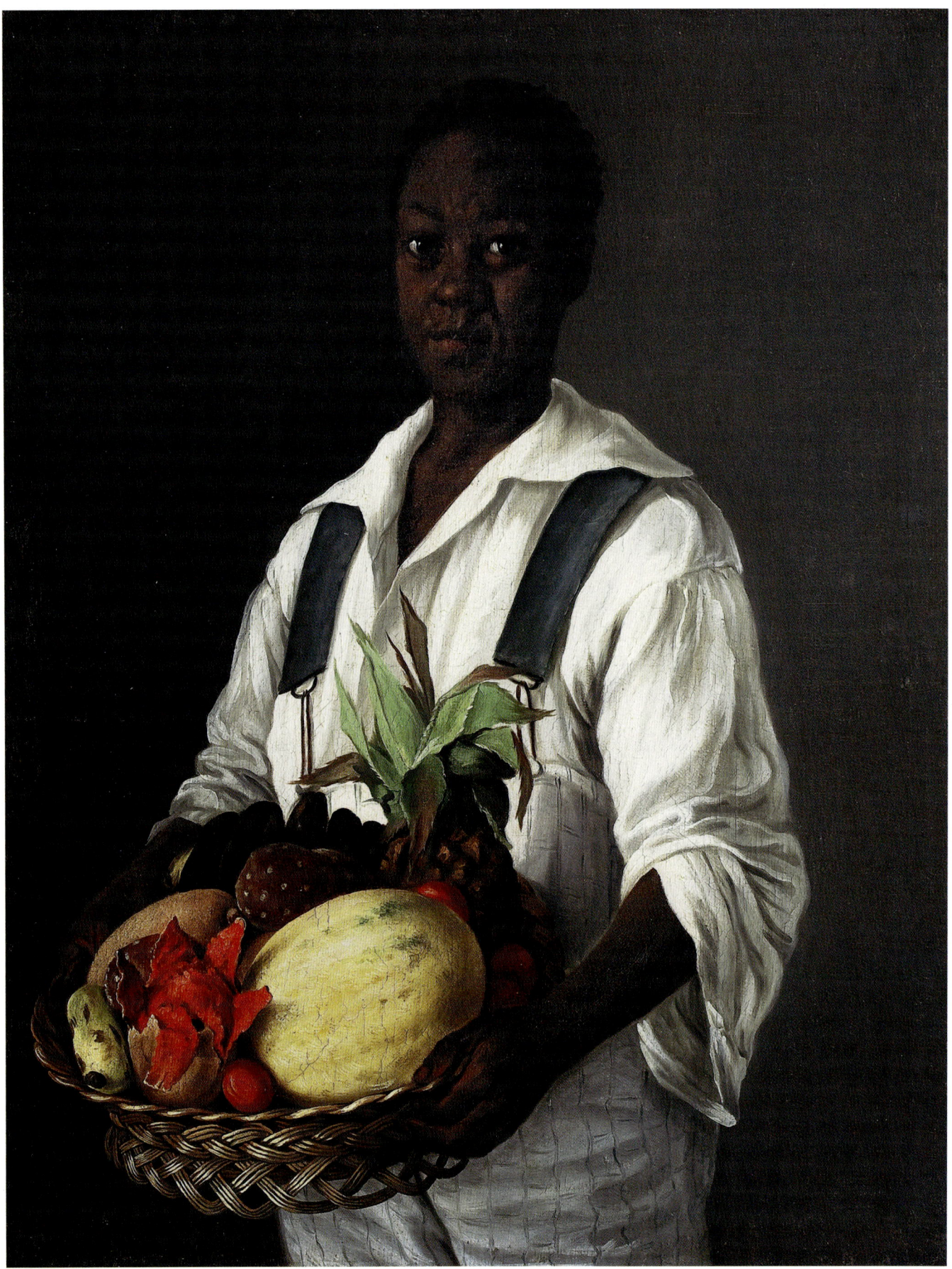

34

34 José Agustín Arrieta. *Young Man from the Coast*. After 1843. Oil on canvas. New York, Hispanic Society of America.

35 Felipe Santiago Gutiérrez. *Portrait of a Mulatto Woman*. 1875. Bogatá, Colombia, Proyecto Bachué.

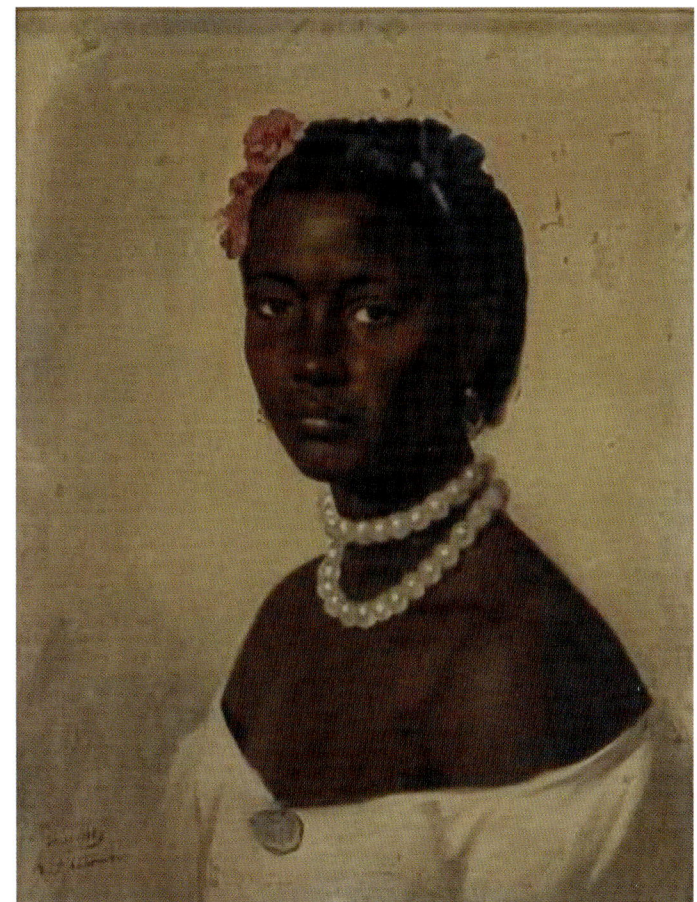

35

cal narratives.[17] Two artists removed from the capital, however, did incorporate figures of African descent into their academic paintings. We encounter a significant counterpoint to the traveler-artist's representations in Jose Agustín Arrieta's *El costeño* (1843), described by Edward Sullivan as among Arrieta's "most outstanding and singular achievements."[18] Arrieta (1803–1874) was Mexico's most renowned costumbrista artist, best known for his paintings of the peoples and customs of Puebla, where his career developed. In *El costeño*, the tropes of Black servitude and exoticism are clearly in evidence; the young man bears a basket of tropical fruits and vegetables, no doubt intended for the table of his superiors. This basket both denotes his serving occupation and reinforces the affiliation of the Afrodescendant population with the coast and its natural bounty. What is striking about the painting is that Arrieta breaks with the convention of confining servile figures to the periphery of the pictorial frame, instead relocating one such figure to the center as subject. As Sullivan observes, he also gives the young man lifesize, almost monumental proportions, "creating of him a noble protagonist."[19] The dignity inherent in this portrayal derives in no small measure from the subject's confident stance and steady gaze, neither of which betrays a hint of inferiority nor deference. The lesser-known Veracruzan painter José Justo Montiel (1824–1899) in *Negrito fumando* (1868) similarly portrays a young man of African descent in an oil painting, wrapped in a *rebozo* (shawl) and smoking a cigar.

Intriguingly, Felipe Santiago Gutiérrez (1824–1904), a Mexican artist and educator who resided in Colombia in the 1870s, presents a similar treatment of his Afro-Colombian subject in *Retrato de mulata* (1875).[20] As in Arrieta's painting, the identity of the sitter here remains subsumed beneath her role as representative of a socioracial type. In contrast, however, no occupational role is suggested here. She is elegantly attired and exquisitely rendered, and although the combination of attributes points to certain well-worn stereotypes of Black female sensuality (her exposed shoulders, hair adorned with flowers), this is a dignified depiction, one emphasized by her evident poise and confident

36 Carmelo Fernández. *White Women, Ocaña Province.* 1850. Watercolor. Bogotá, Biblioteca Nacional de Colombia. Colección de la Comisión Corográfica.

gaze. It is particularly rare to see an oil painting of a woman of African descent at this time executed with grace and respect.

More broadly, the majority of costumbrista images that depict Black subjects in Colombia are derived from the Chorographic Commission, founded in 1850 by the government of New Granada. One of the most ambitious cartographic expeditions of the period, the commission was led by a team of both foreign and national intellectuals who recorded the country's diverse topography, geography, and human population. A significant number of watercolors were produced as part of the project, and alongside paintings of landscapes and historic sites, these included human typologies situated in and particular to specific, differentiated localities and regions. These ideologically driven, racialized representations formed part of a broader objective of classifying and ordering the nation's territories and peoples, in order to better facilitate state-led governance and control.[21]

The commission has been identified as a foundational moment in establishing the primacy of region in the Colombian national imaginary.[22] It reified a geographical hierarchy predicated on oppositions between the "Black" coasts, the "white-mestizo" interior, and the "Indian" Amazon lowlands.[23] In contrast to Peru and Mexico, Colombian Indians comprised a small minority of the total population. In spite of the existence of a considerably larger Afrodescendant demographic, their visual representation is still subordinated and marginalized within the commission's illustrations, and within Colombian costumbrismo as a whole.[24] The Afrodescendant population is primarily associated with and located in the tropical, pacific coasts and lowlands of the country, although in reality there were also large numbers on the Caribbean coast, as well as a more dispersed demographic in Antioquia.[25]

In the broader context of Afro-Latin America, Blacks have been included in symbolic constructions of the nation to a much lesser extent in Colombia, and in more consistently disparaging ways.[26] Its Creole elite was the first of the Andean republics to entirely attribute the country's economic backwardness to racial inferiority.[27] As a result, the commissioners envisaged the nation's future economic prosperity and coherence as predicated on racial and cultural homogeneity, via mestizaje characterized as *blanqueamiento*, or whitening.[28]

The northeastern and northwestern Andean provinces and their inhabitants figure in these illustrations as national models of "progress." Despite their documentation of local heterogeneity, both the visual and textual descriptions aim to paint these populations as overwhelmingly white in appearance; Black types constitute a minor presence. In Carmelo Fernández's (1809–1887) *Mujeres blancas, provincia de Ocaña* (1850), the woman of apparent African descent goes unmentioned in the title. Dressed in a black cloak that covers most of her body, she stands behind the elegantly attired white women who appear oblivious to her presence. Her face and body are turned away from them and from the viewer, revealing only her profile. She carries a textile, likely a rug to be used in church by the white women, which further underlines her servile role. She is publicly displayed as a luxury attribute that confers wealth and status, one that frames and defines their "whiteness."[29] The type of the Afrodescendant public escort is a prominent motif in Latin American iconography of the period and is a notable component of Peruvian costumbrista renderings of Lima's *tapadas* in particular.[30]

While Fernández privileges light-skinned mestizo and white types, those of African descent feature more prominently in some

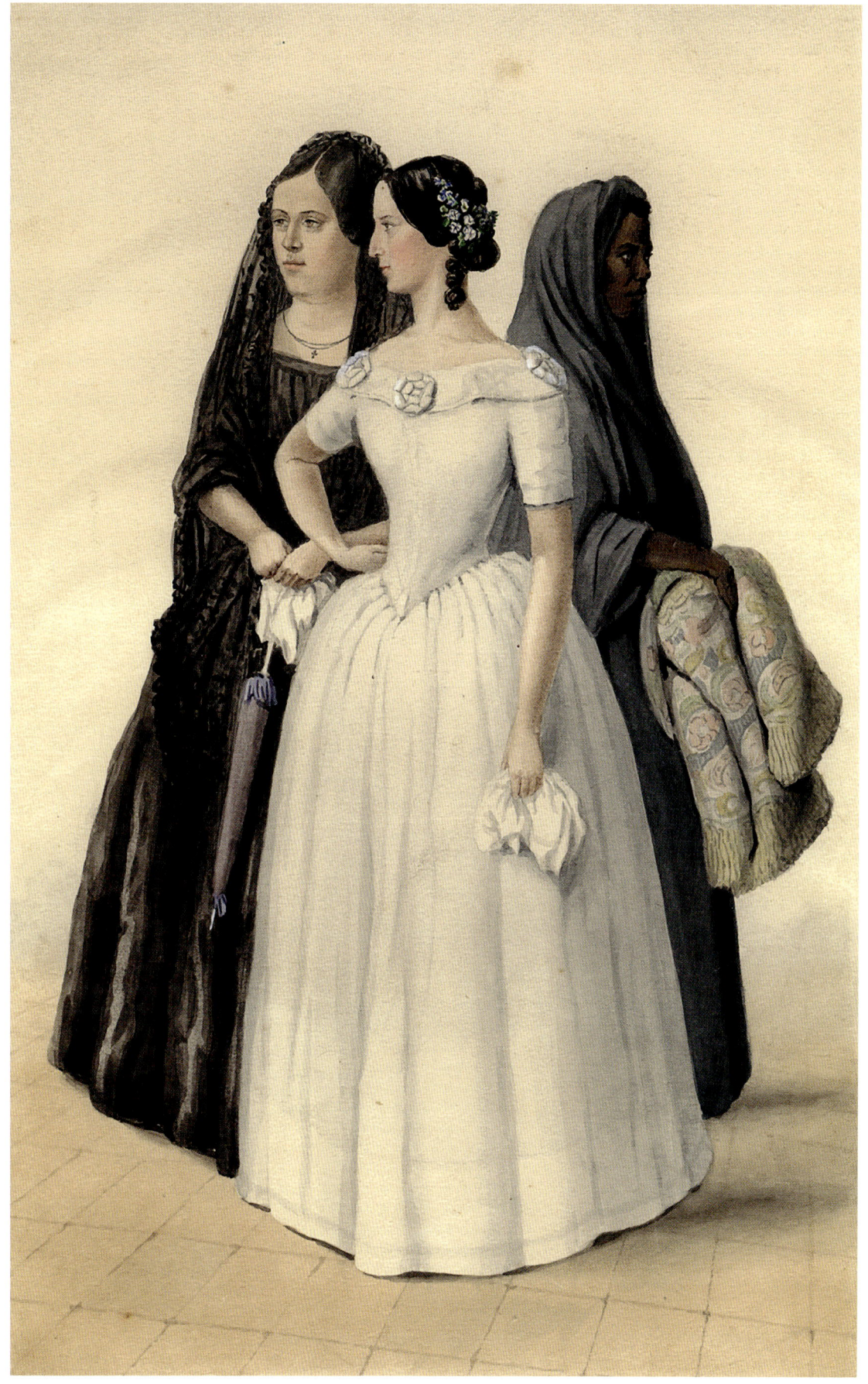
36

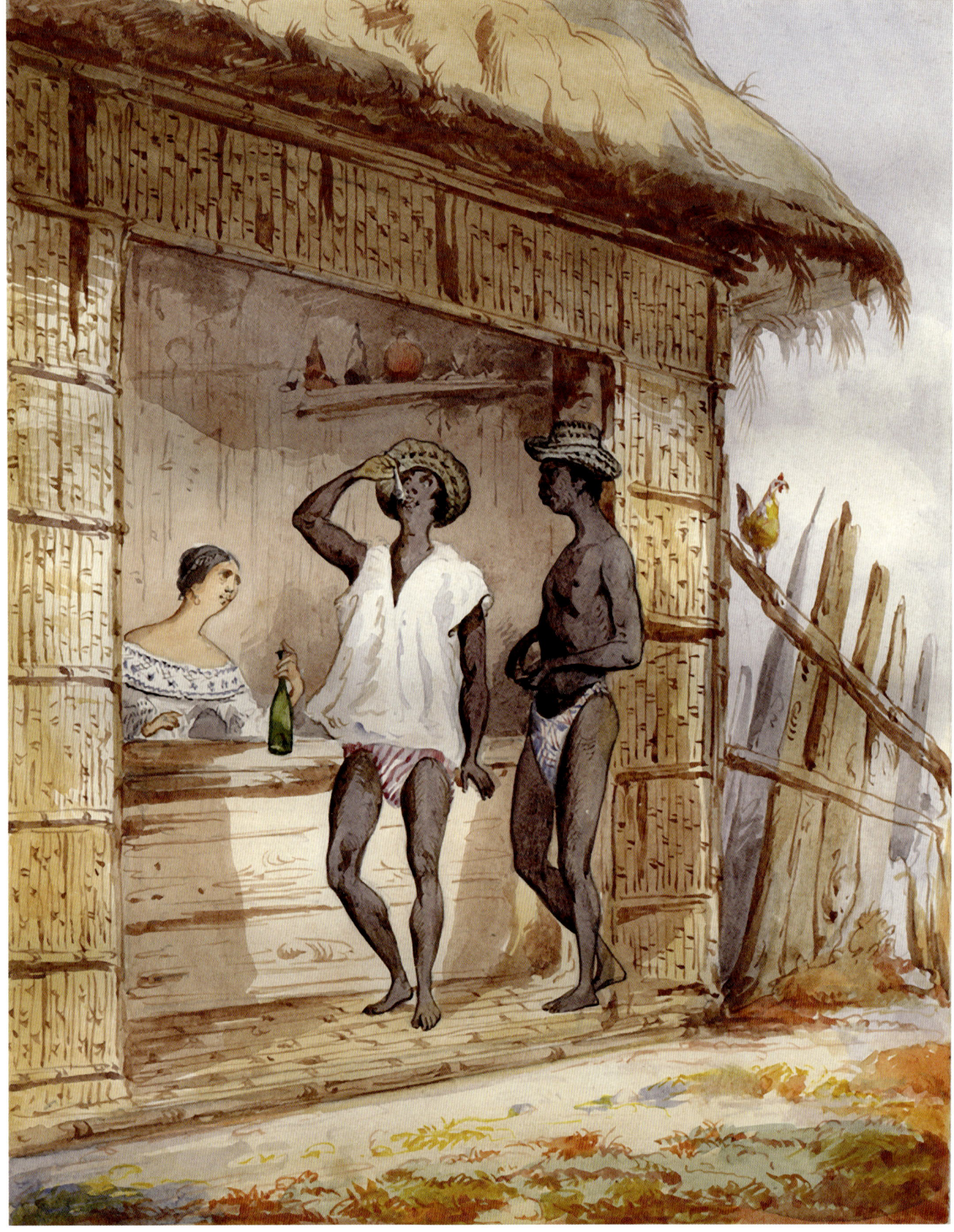
37

37 Manuel María Paz. *Sale of Liquor in the Village of Lloró, Province of Chocó*. 1853. Watercolor. Bogatá, Biblioteca Nacional de Colombia. Colección de la Comisión Corográfica.

of Henry Price's (1819–1863) best known watercolors. His exceptional portrait of an elegantly dressed Black woman in Medellín was not included in the commission's official collection for unknown reasons.[31] It is undoubtedly an incongruous representation in view of the derogatory tone of the commission's imagery of Black subjects as whole, particularly keeping in mind the fact that Medellín and the province of Antioquia had already gained a reputation as a largely white region by this time.[32]

With a small number of exceptions, this artwork anchors Afrodescendant types visually and discursively in the Pacific coastal region, which is described as "a grave for the white race" by the commission's leader, Agustín Codazzi.[33] Removed from the highland centers of progress, interracial mixing, and "whiteness," the inhabitants of Chocó and the neighboring provinces of Buenaventura and Barbacoas are portrayed as uncivilized, backward, and an obstacle to the nation's envisioned modernization and prosperity.[34] These illustrations articulate the fears and prejudices of the elite in the face of a recently emancipated population, alongside eighteenth- and nineteenth-century scientific and cultural conceptions about the unhealthy nature of tropical climates and their effects on human bodies.[35] The racialized nature of these illustrations is exemplified in *Venta de aguardiente en el pueblo de Lloró, provincia de Chocó*.[36] As analyzed by Beatriz Balanta Rodriguez, what may appear to some viewers as a picturesque, rustic scene in fact exerts considerable symbolic violence on the Black body; the figures are seminaked and appear to be figuratively distorted, in surroundings that convey a rural, isolated, and impoverished environment.[37] The activity itself also links the Black population to the consumption of alcohol and to attendant stereotypes of indolence, reluctance to work, and im-

morality. The distortion of Black faces and bodies is also identifiable in other images, such as *Aspecto esterior de las casas de Nóvita, provincia del Chocó*,[38] in which two semiclothed men or youths are juxtaposed with the elegantly clothed "white" couple lounging in the doorway. The bodies of the former appear to be almost atrophied in terms of their proportions, although the couple alongside them is diminutive in size as well. While this could be attributed to Paz's limitations as a figurative painter and with regard to perspective, other artists employ similar traits in scenes of the region that feature Black types, among them Léon Gauthier (1822–1901) in *Modo de lavar oro, provincia de Barbacoas*. The droopy, outsize bodies and blurred faces of these figures, coupled with their seminakedness and "closeness" to nature, makes these representations particularly dehumanizing.[39]

Notwithstanding the commission's deeply racist depictions of the Afrodescendant population, they clearly believed that the Pacific region and its inhabitants could be integrated into the nation's narrative of progress and modernization via imposed cultural change.[40] Afrodescendants are essentially identified as a demographic to be subjugated, controlled, and transformed through enforced labor and "white" settlement or colonization. *Plaza de Quibdó, provincia del Chocó* illustrates the potentially beneficial, domesticating influence of "white" settlers.[41] The clothing of the mother and child are highly reminiscent of the "white" woman portrayed alongside them, with the exception of their bare feet, a recognized symbol of servitude.[42]

Peru: Blackness as Part of a Lima-centric National Identity

The existence of an expansive visual archive of Black subjects originating in a country primarily identified with its indigenous

38 Léon Gauthier. *How Gold Is Washed, Province of Barbacoas*. 1853. Watercolor. Bogatá, Biblioteca Nacional de Colombia. Colección de la Comisión Corográfica.

population and pre-Columbian civilizations may come as something of a surprise to specialists and general readers alike. This visual corpus is rooted in representations of late-eighteenth- and nineteenth-century Lima and coastal Peru, the heart of which consists of costumbrista iconography. Peruvian slavery was a markedly urban phenomenon, with the largest demographic of enslaved and free Afrodescendants residing in Lima and on the coast, the primary sites settled and populated by Spanish colonialists. This enforced geographical and cultural proximity meant that Peru's Afrodescendant population played a crucial role in shaping coastal culture, which would later become the predominant model of integration and national identity after independence.

Peruvian costumbrismo developed primarily in Lima. The genre in turn was instrumental in the construction of *criollismo*, or a modern Creole identity. Within a dichotomous image of the nation, *criollo* became a synonym of Lima and the coast, in direct opposition to the indigenous and Andean.[43] Consequently, Peruvian costumbrismo makes Black subjects visible on an unprecedented scale. They take center stage in early republican iconography, in which the breadth of the Black presence in nineteenth-century Lima is articulated and acknowledged. From domestic and day-labor enslaved persons to market vendors and business owners, a wide range of Black subjects are integrated within a cross-section of Lima society that gives a marked focus to the representation of its multiethnic, popular classes, resulting in their symbolic centrality in costumbrista imaginings of the nation.[44]

The Peruvian archive presents a unique case in the figure of the *mulato* artist Francisco "Pancho" Fierro (ca. 1807–1879). A self-taught aquarellist, Fierro was nineteenth-century Lima's foremost illustrator and its greatest exponent of Peruvian costumbrismo. Although much of his output was aimed at a thriving tourist market of Europeans and North Americans, his imagery also circulated within Peru and was instrumental in the self-fashioning of a Creole identity. Crucially, his work presents images of Black subjects crafted at the hands of an artist of African descent, something exceptional at a time when artist-travelers and the white imagination dominated visual and indeed textual representations of Blackness. Key artist-travelers who produced images of Black subjects in Peru include the German artist Johann Moritz Rugendas (1802–1858) and the French vice-consul Léonce Angrand (1808–1886).

Iconic motifs of Blackness in the national imagination are derived from the extensive portrayal of Afro-Peruvians as the agents of Lima's popular processions, music, and dance practices. This is exemplified in Fierro's images of the carnival dance the "*son de los diablos*," believed to have originated in the participation of Afrodescendant religious confraternities in the Corpus Christi processions of colonial Lima. Although Fierro is the only artist to depict the dance, the leisure activities associated with the *fiesta de Amancaes*, a quintessential *limeño* tradition, are also a subject matter in the works of Angrand and Rugendas. Primarily associated with the city's Afrodescendant and mixed-race population, this event also attracted a cross-section of Lima society, all of whom converged in the pampas to have picnics, ride their horses, and dance. Festive, often elegantly dressed Afrodescendant women are especially prominent in scenes of Amancaes by Angrand (*La chichería*, 1837) and Rugendas (*San Juan en Amancaes*, 1843), in which they feature as revelers and dancers and on horseback. The *zamacueca*, a courtship dance that originated as

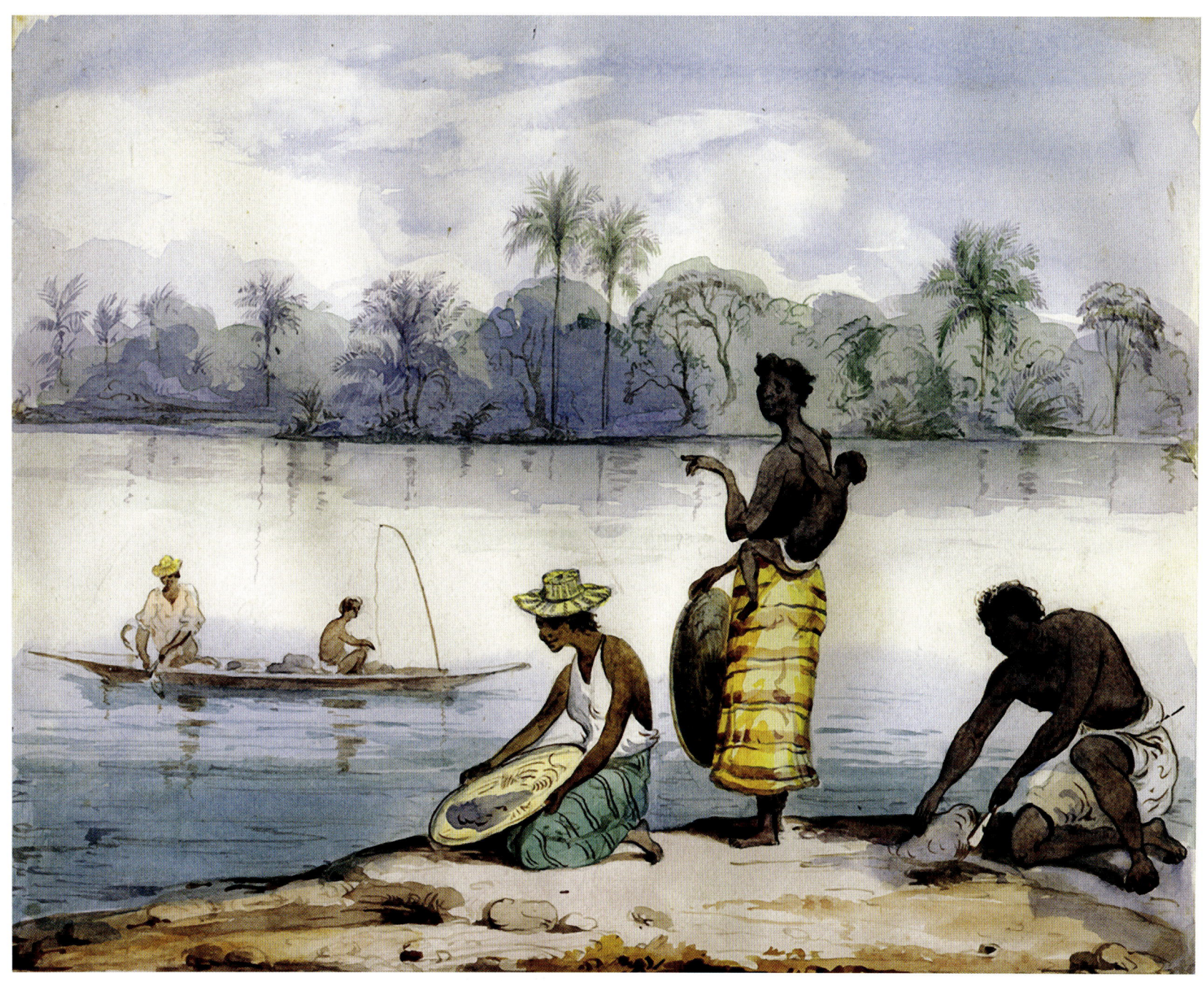

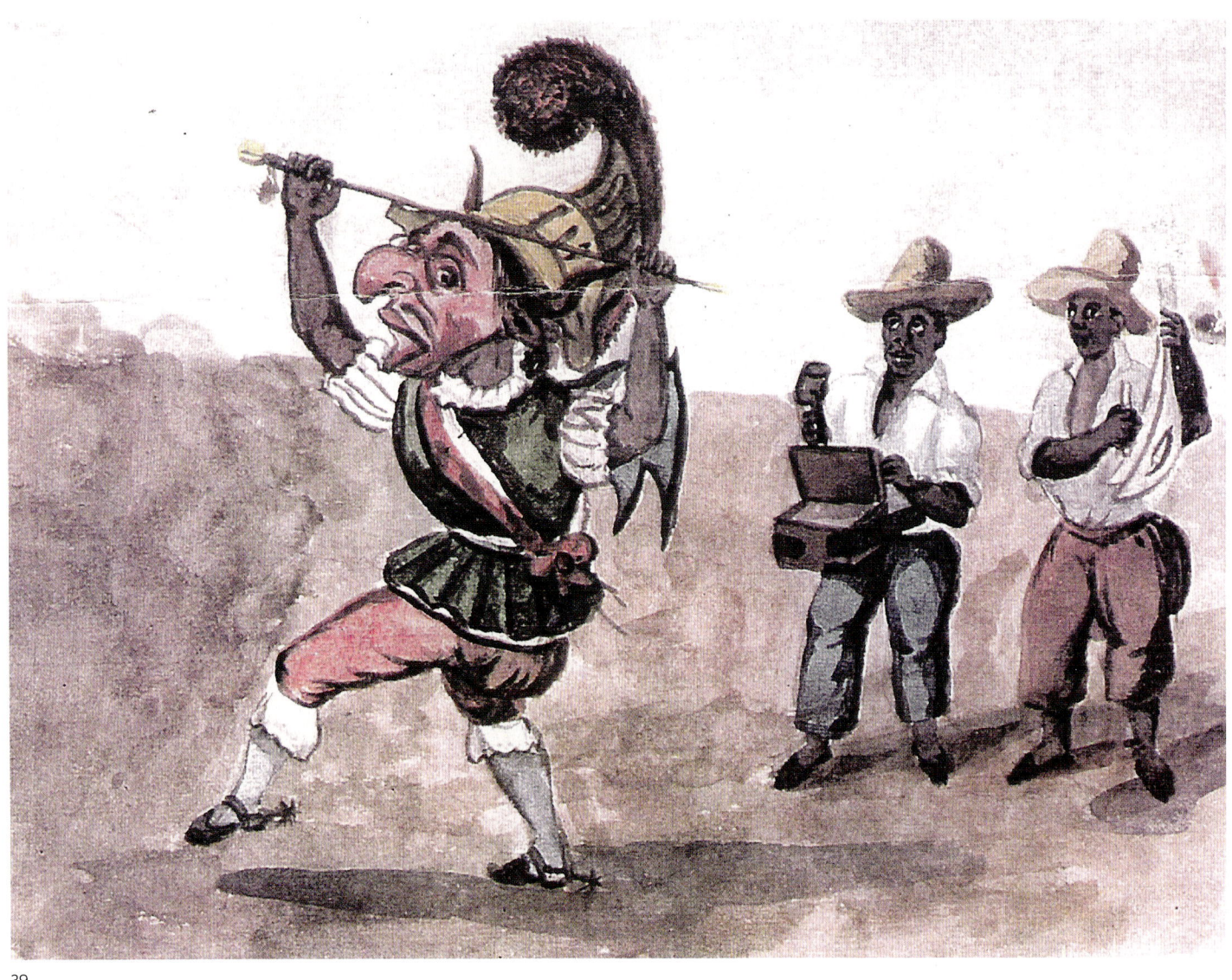

39

a Black social dance, was a central feature of Amancaes and is overwhelmingly associated with Lima's Black population in costumbrista iconography. Believed to be an early precursor of Peru's national dance from the coast, the *marinera*, the zamacueca is a recurring motif in Fierro's oeuvre.

Fierro was a foundational figure in nineteenth-century Peruvian art, elevated to the level of a cultural icon by elite advocates of limeño costumbrismo. His watercolors have long enjoyed a patrimonial status in Peru, and writers and artists such as José Antonio de Lavalle and Teófilo Castillo conceived of his body of work as a spontaneous and authentic expression of Creole culture.[45] As Majluf has argued, the fact that he is known primarily as "Pancho" Fierro is indicative of his renown as a popular painter and character within the criollo tradition, and his mystification within Peruvian historiography partly derives from his ethnic ancestry and stereotypical notions of Black subjectivity. This, coupled with his status as an untrained artist working in a "lesser" artistic genre, shapes a narrative that emphasizes the supposedly intuitive, spontaneous, and unrestrained approach to his art. Fierro is one of a number of Afrodescendant artists who were important contributors to colonial and republican art in Latin America, an area that merits further research and exploration

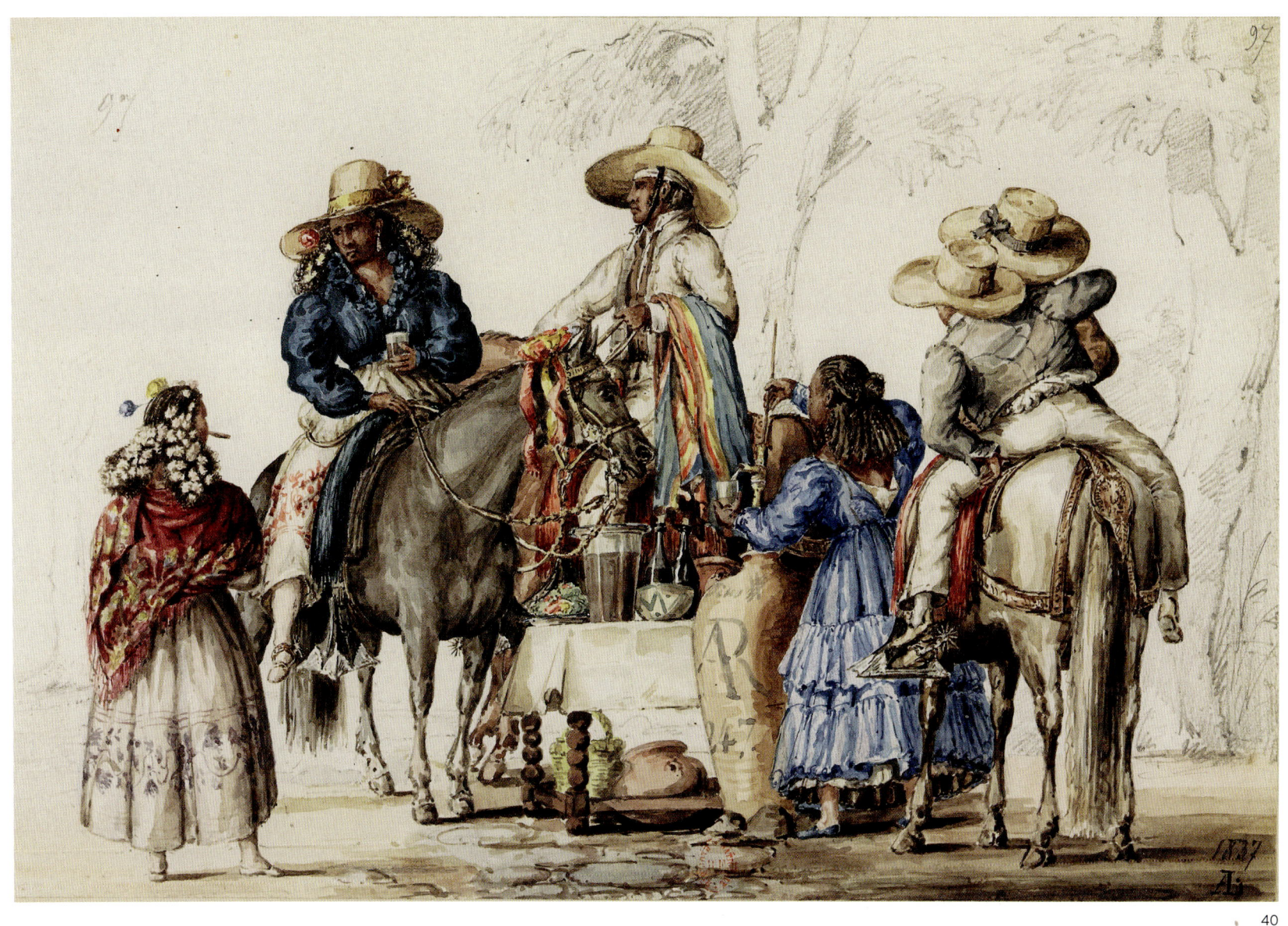

39 Francisco "Pancho" Fierro. *Dancing to the Sound of the Devils*. Undated. Watercolor on paper. Lima, Peru, Pinacoteca Municipal Ignacio Merino.

40 Léonce Angrand. *Woman Selling Chicha*. 1837. Watercolor. Paris, Bibliothèque nationale de France.

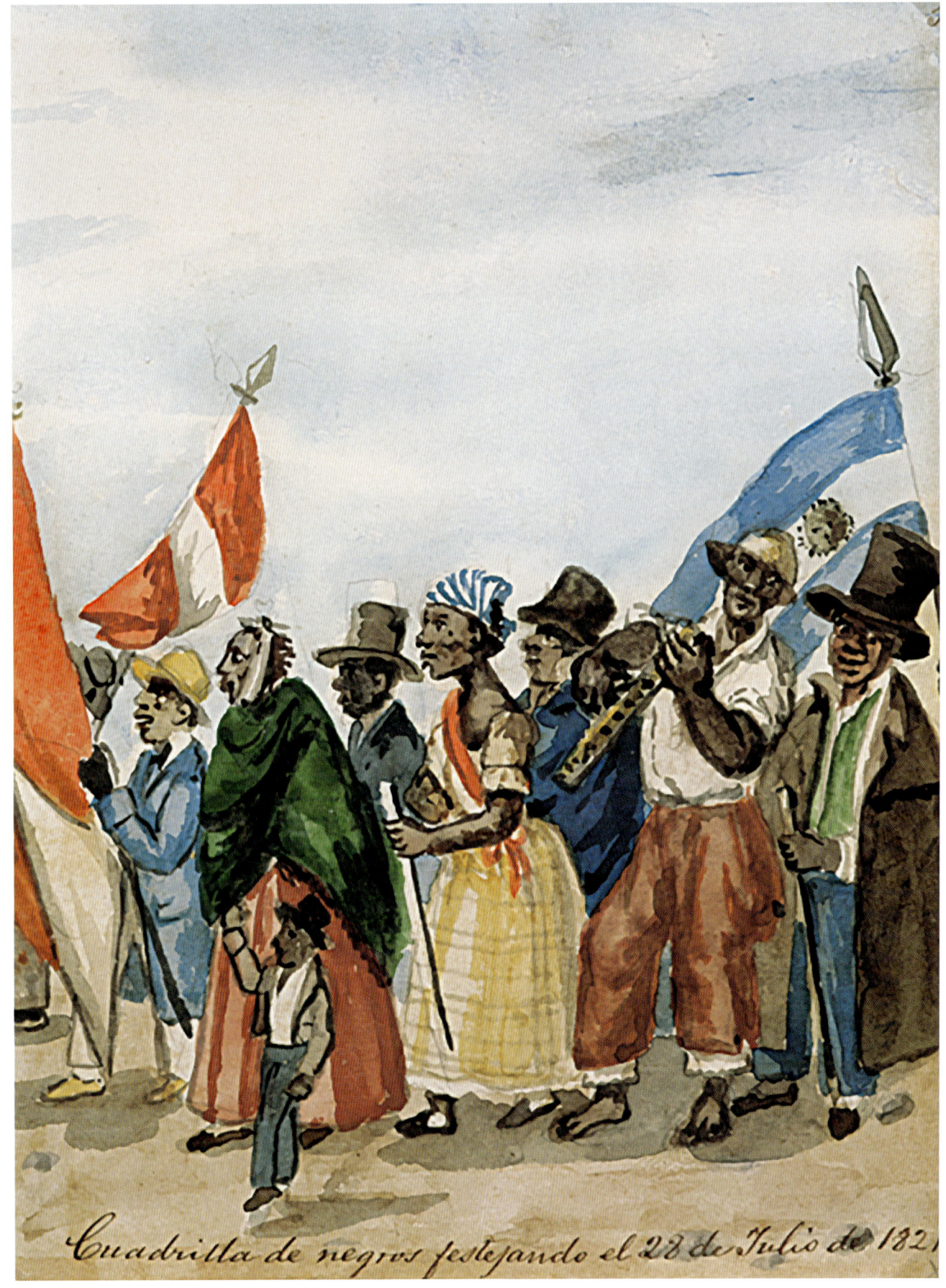

41 Francisco "Pancho" Fierro. *Group of Blacks Celebrating the 28th of July, 1821*. Undated. Watercolor on paper. Lima, Peru, Pinacoteca Municipal Ignacio Merino.

as pointed out by Alejandro de la Fuente.[46] As he makes clear, however, "their creative work cannot be placed outside broader processes of colonialism, slavery and imperial expansion." In this respect, it is undeniable that Fierro's art, alongside works by Angrand, Rugendas, and others, contributed to a broader image of Lima constructed by the Creole elite, which incorporated Afro-Peruvians and the multiethnic plebeian sector as marginal, picturesque counterparts to aristocratic society. This is most notably the case in Manuel Atanasio Fuentes's (1820–1889) *Lima; or Sketches of the Capital of Peru* (1866). In this lavishly illustrated study, the most iconic motifs of Blackness are distilled and reproduced via woodcuts and lithographs and inserted within a hierarchical framework of the capital that paradoxically conceives of the Black population in terms of its "disappearance" or "extinction" via mestizaje. Archetypal figures such as the Black water carrier and fruit vendor are an essential part of this urban landscape, as subsidiary figures to frame and underpin the image of a fundamentally "white" Creole Lima.[47]

A number of Fierro's works, however, can also be seen to exceed this paradigm and approximate a more complex image of their experience, subjectivity, and participation in Peruvian society.[48] The visible incorporation of Black subjects within the military and the body politic, for example, is unique to his oeuvre. His scenes of Black independence celebrations evoke the role of Afro-Peruvians as historical actors and political subjects in early republican Peru, themes that are largely marginalized or omitted altogether in both visual and textual discourses of the period. It is nonetheless important to acknowledge that there is undeniably a degree of stereotypical baggage that comes with the celebration of Black citizenship framed in the context of music practices, "as if no other form of black political demonstration was conceivable," de la Fuente remarks.[49] In a related vein, it could also be argued that this imagery contributes to a romantic, idealized, and reassuring vision of limeño society that is characteristic of much costumbrista art in general. Notwithstanding these important considerations, these images among others are significant in recognizing aspects of the wider visibility of the Black experience and its constituent role in the new Creole civic identity. This more diverse view of the Black population's presence is also reflected in visual representations of their activities within another pillar of the nation—the church—as seen through representations of their confraternities and their legacy in shaping a Creole religious and cultural identity.[50]

This partial overview reveals that in Colombia and Mexico, Black subjects were marginalized both geographically and discursively in nineteenth-century costumbrista art. This iconography contributed to wider discourses that limited peoples of African descent to the tropical lowlands and coastal regions in these national imaginaries. Although these areas were the sites of the historic arrival of the enslaved and/or those in which they and their descendants were concentrated in the greatest numbers, this regionalization of Blackness also partly stems from the colonial Spanish belief that peoples of African descent were "naturally" adapted to tropical weather. Contemporary scholarship shows that this coding of tropical areas as "Black" persists throughout much of Latin America and continues to obscure the contemporary presence and history of Afrodescendant peoples in other national regions.[51]

In Peru, however, owing to the affiliation of the Afrodescendant population with the traditional colonial center and capital of the republic, we encounter a proliferation of images of Black subjects in Peruvian costumbrismo. While this association is once again coastal and historically determined by slavery, the urban context of Lima means that Black types are necessarily portrayed in spatial and cultural proximity to modernity, progress, and Creole "whiteness." Blackness in costumbrista art therefore appears as a symbolically central, subordinated component of the syncretic ideology of criollismo or a Creole identity, which in official terms gives greater recognition to the European portion of its heritage and influences.

In spite of the fact that the Chorographic Commission's images were hidden from public view until the mid-twentieth century, they have since become ubiquitous in present-day Colombia.[52] In Peru this ubiquity finds parallels with the works of Fierro in particular, and those of nineteenth-century traveler-artists. Scholars have highlighted the continued uncritical use and reproduction of costumbrista imagery—and in particular those of Afrodescendant and indigenous types—frequently without key information necessary for contextualization and interpretation. By implicitly invoking the supposed verisimilitude of these images as "documentary" evidence of the past, such reproductions contribute to the reification and naturalization of socioracial difference enshrined in the genre, with a lasting impact in perpetuating stereotypes of Black inferiority and subordination in the popular imagination.[53]

5

THE WAR ON BLACKNESS CA. 1888:
RELIGIOUS EXPRESSION, REPRESSION, AND RESISTANCE IN BRAZIL

AMY BUONO

On the night of September 2, 2018, a fire broke out at the National Museum of Brazil. Inside the Rio de Janeiro institution was one of the most important collections of ethnographic and archaeological materials in the country. The fire destroyed the vast majority of the twenty million artifacts housed within its walls, among them the nation's oldest collections of indigenous, African, and Afro-Brazilian materials.[1] Though at the time of this writing a full account of the surviving two thousand artifacts remains unavailable, it is known that the fire ripped through the permanent exhibition spaces of the museum, including the rooms that held the *Kumbukumbu: Africa, Memory, and Heritage* exhibition. On display in *Kumbukumbu* were 185 objects produced by Africans and their descendants in Brazil, representing a small portion of the seven hundred artifacts of African cultural memory in the museum's larger repositories. Brazil's various colonial trajectories were illuminated by such items as those from the royal collections and libraries that had been brought to Rio from Lisbon when the Portuguese court fled in 1808, and were used to inaugurate the Royal Museum in 1821.

The collections of African and Afro-Brazilian objects, however, have their origins in more global histories of colonialism, slavery, and its aftermath. In these collections are diplomatic gifts given by King Adandozan of Dahomey to Prince Dom João in 1810, as well as objects that were acquired in museum expeditions across the African continent in the early to mid-twentieth century, were produced by Africans and their descendants in Brazil between 1880 and 1950, or were confiscated by the civil police during periods of repression of cultural and religious practices of Brazil's complex matrix of Afrodescendants. Poignantly, the name of the National Museum of Brazil's exhibit, *Kumbukumbu*—a Swahili word for objects and memory—recalls people and events from the past.[2] The ties between objects and cultural memory, between religious expression, repression, and resistance in the African diaspora, is precisely the topic of this essay.

This chapter examines the so-called war on Blackness in late-nineteenth- and early-twentieth-century Brazil, especially as it pertains to African and Afrodescendant religious expression and ceremonial. Using the year 1888 as a temporal pivot, when slavery was abolished in Brazil and when vast collections of African material culture were amassed across the Americas, this essay interrogates various forms of institutions in the Afro-Brazilian world in the context of slavery and its cultural, social, and political aftermath: legal and medical collections; art academies; spiritual temples; civic urbanization projects; and museums. Al-

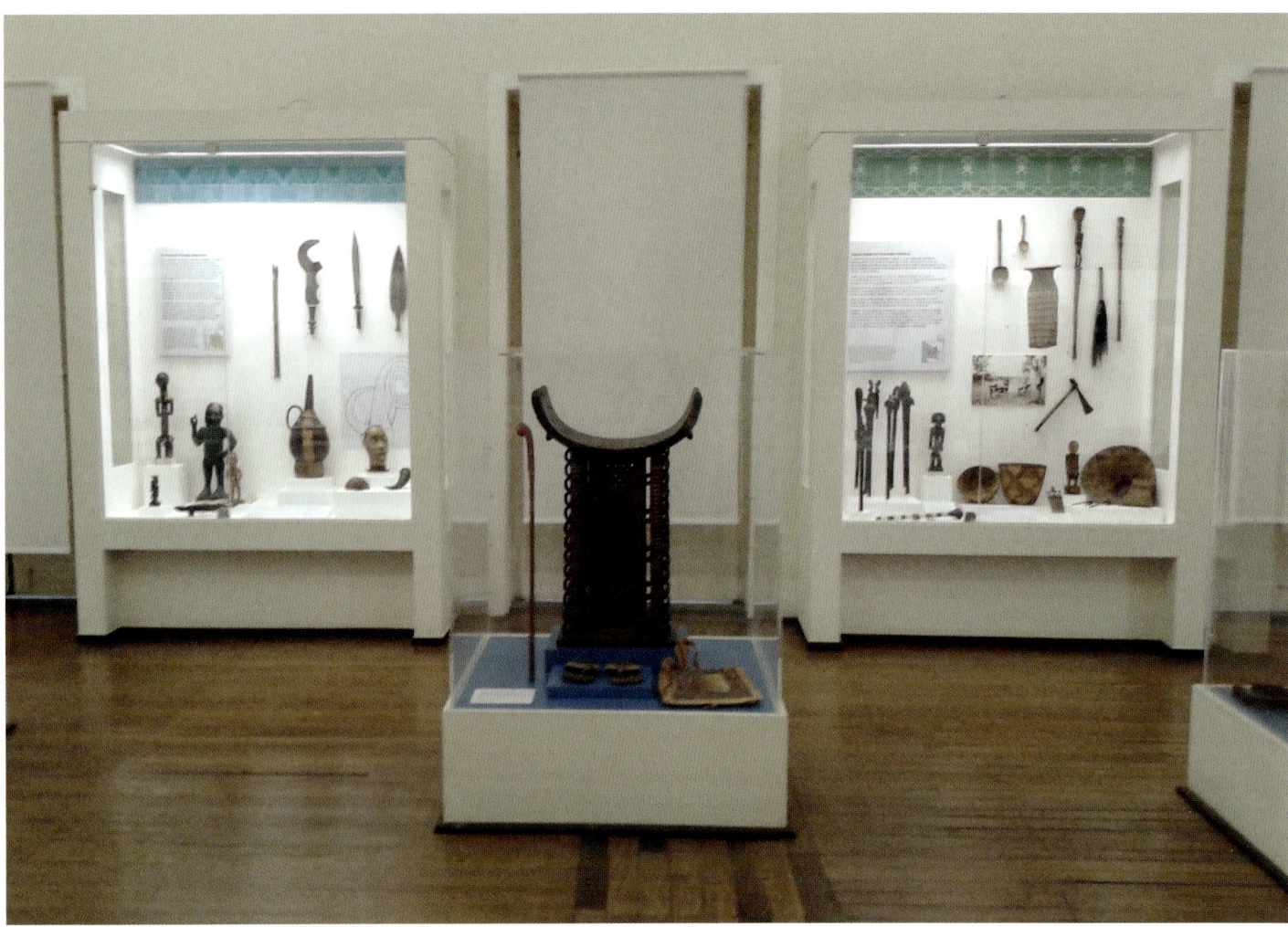

42

though several key locations in the Americas offer case studies of the diverse ways in which Afro-American religious and cultural expressions were articulated, repressive techniques of racial control were enacted, and cultural resistance was manifested, the focus in this essay is on the Brazilian cities of Rio de Janeiro and Salvador.

In particular, this essay examines the flourishing of Afro-Brazilian religious expression in the practices of Candomblé and Umbanda, across Brazil, as well as the intellectual circuits that made these spiritual and cultural practices visible to a broader viewing public. I explore the coding of Afro-Brazilian religious expressions with Blackness and the legacies of slavery, as well as the practice of governmental agencies in associating temples and other spiritual sites with political subversion.

The main visual and material culture discussed in this essay includes lithographs pertaining to the (il)legalities of *capoeira* as a "dance" and *lundu* as a musical form; artifacts from the legal and medical collections of seized Afro-Brazilian ritual objects (Rio, Salvador, Rio Grande do Sul); the principal temples of spiritual worship and photographs of their founders and advocates; and finally, the large-scale urbanization projects of the 1920s that reshaped cities like Rio, containing Blackness within designated spatial zones of the urban landscape: *favelas*. In the course of this essay, I will situate cultural institutions, from police museums as sites of repression to heritage museums as sites of preservation, within a larger historical and cultural frame. I will conclude with the contemporary *terreiro* (temple) museum Ilê Axé Opô Afonjá in Salvador, now a Brazilian heritage site of the Instituto do

42 *Kumbukumbu: Africa, Memory, and Heritage.* Installation at the National Museum of Brazil/UFRJ, Rio de Janeiro (pre-fire).

Patrimônio Histórico e Artístico Nacional (National Historic and Artistic Heritage Institute, or IPHAN), as an important example of temple sites within the context of current debates concerning intangible heritage preservation across the Americas.

Brazil legally abolished slavery on May 13, 1888, the last nation in the Western world to do so, ending a long and drawn-out process of abolition that extended back a half century. Weighing heavily upon Brazil's elite in the decision to take this action was evidence of successful slave revolts across the Americas, especially that of the French colony of Saint-Domingue, which began in 1791 and ended in 1804 with the Haitian Revolution.[3] With the official end of the institution of slavery in Brazil came new systems of social stratification, jurisprudence, and societal race relations.[4] By 1890, with Brazil's First Republic and the expansion of state authority, a new penal code was inaugurated, ushering in a modern state-sponsored apparatus of repression, one that had previously been controlled by Brazil's slaveholding class.[5] In the new urban fabric of Brazilian cities like Rio de Janeiro, the population of which expanded tremendously after the move there of the royal court in 1808, police repression had racial and spatial dimensions; now, with the elimination of slavery, Brazil's largest cities had a growing mixed-race urban underclass. The new penal code of 1890 sought to control and enforce public behavior through measures that addressed commonplace public-order issues, such as murder, theft, assault, drunkenness, begging, vagrancy, and violation of curfew, as well as addressing techniques by which police could identify purported magical practices.[6] Ordinances against "offenses to public order" primarily targeted cultural and racial differences, including practices associated with African heritage and religion. Examples of activities deemed illegal in this context were capoeira (a martial arts system of physical discipline and dancelike movement) and "sorcery" (witchcraft and magical practices).[7] State penal codes persecuted those engaged in "illegal practices of medicine, of magic, and of faith healing" as practitioners of witchcraft or magic, and established an office within the police force to deal with the identification and analysis of objects of "witchcraft" seized during police raids of homes and terreiros.[8] Civil criminal codes imposed substantial prison sentences and heavy fines for a variety of so-called magical practices, which covered an array of activities that included Spiritism, the casting of spells, the use of talismans and fortune-telling cards, the practice of medicine (including dentistry, pharmacy, homeopathy, hypnotism, and animal magnetism), and the use of psychotropic substances.[9] By 1890, the state had begun to intervene in practices that were taking place in temples.

The criminalization of capoeira, however, was directly tied to fears concerning the power of this cultural practice among those of African descent in Brazil. Long before the abolition of slavery, in the first decades of the nineteenth century, capoeira was described as a "violent, warlike dance"; as a case in point, lithographs by the German artist Johann Moritz Rugendas (1802–1858) depict early-nineteenth-century Brazil through the eyes of a foreigner. Period sources indicate that capoeira exasperated authorities, was thought to disturb the peace, and caused bloodshed and brawls.[10] Capoeira rituals took place in circles of three hundred or four hundred Africans, grouped by African nation, mainly from West Central Africa, thus indicating it was likely a form of communal and cultural memory.[11] During the time of slavery, capoeira was permissible on certain occasions, such as on Sundays and feast days. In its longer colonial history, howev-

43 Augustus Earle. *Capoeira*. 1824. Watercolor. Canberra, National Library of Australia.

er, it developed associations with slave revolts and runaway-slave communities called *quilombos,* and thus with fears concerning Black solidarity and rebellion. Moreover, as the historian Thomas Holloway notes, capoeira societies (called *maltas*), included free persons as well, and thus "connected those on the bottom of society, slave and free, in opposition to the order and state power."[12] The extensive network of surveillance directed against capoeira and Afro-Brazilian religions sought explicitly to control the city's Black population.

The English painter Augustus Earle (1793–1838) produced a striking watercolor of the capoeira in the early decades of the nineteenth century. The watercolor shows two men—African or Afrodescendant—engaged in the powerful, rhythmic dance. Muscular, intensely focused, and tensely poised, the men circle one another in a prelude to their battle, while one of the seated onlookers provides the drumbeat, the musical accompaniment for the event, which was also declared illegal in the period. A woman and child watch the pair, and an onlooker peers at the scene from an upper window of a colonial house. To the left of the combatants, a white police officer clambers over a fence, ready to capture the men in the act of a prohibited activity.

Like capoeira, the musical form and dance called lundu (alternately known as *landu, ondu,* and *landum*) was also charged with Africanness in the Luso-Brazilian world of the early to mid-nineteenth century, and, like capoeira, is thought to have roots in the Atlantic slave trade. During the seventeenth and eighteenth centuries, lundu was connected both to ideas of witchcraft by Europeans, likely stemming from earlier colonial histories, when the term "*lundus*" (a synonym for *calundús*) appeared in a Portuguese Inquisition testimonial of 1694 in reference to "demons or malignant spirits."[13] According to the historian James Sweet, the term became a generic reference to Central African religious traditions of ritual acts of possession and divination. By the seventeenth century in Brazil, it was used as a term for spirit possession within the enslaved and free-Black communities, and by the eighteenth century, white people in Brazil began to seek out the healing potential of calundús.[14]

In fact, lundu was also popularized in Portugal in the eighteenth century and early nineteenth centuries, where it was widely performed during theater intermissions in Lisbon, as well as in halls, circuses, and theaters across Brazil, Argentina, Uruguay, Chile, Peru, and Bolivia.[15] Dancers included those of both European and African descent, and as Martha Tupinambá de Ulhôa and Luiz Costa-Lima have argued, lundu must be considered a deeply transnational dance.[16] One of the most canonical images in the colonial record of lundu is Rugendas's *Danse landu (Lundu Dance)*. This image testifies to the oft-noted "lascivious" connotations of the dance, an issue commented upon throughout the colonial period by travelers to Brazil. A white couple face one another in the dance circle, not unlike the intense figuring of capoeira opponents, but in this instance, the dance signifies seduction rather than war. The man holds castanets, his arms elevated above his body, and the woman, with hands on her hips, swings to the rhythms of the guitar being played by the man seated in the right foreground.

In the colonial Brazilian context, understandings of Africanness in the public sphere were thus intertwined with dance and musical forms, such as in capoeira and lundu. Furthermore, expressions of religious and cultural identity through ritual acts of possession, divination, and healing were tightly linked with the

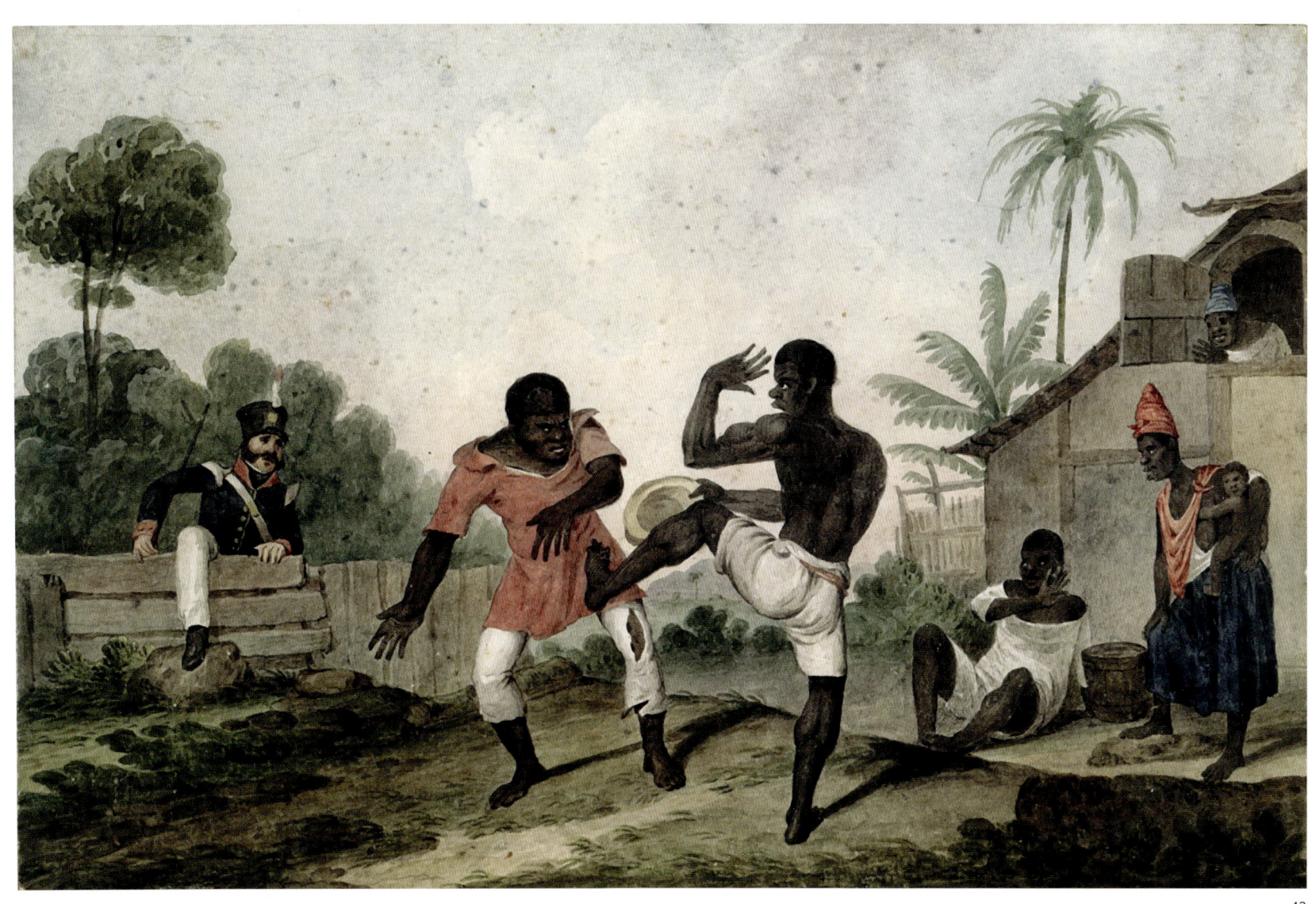

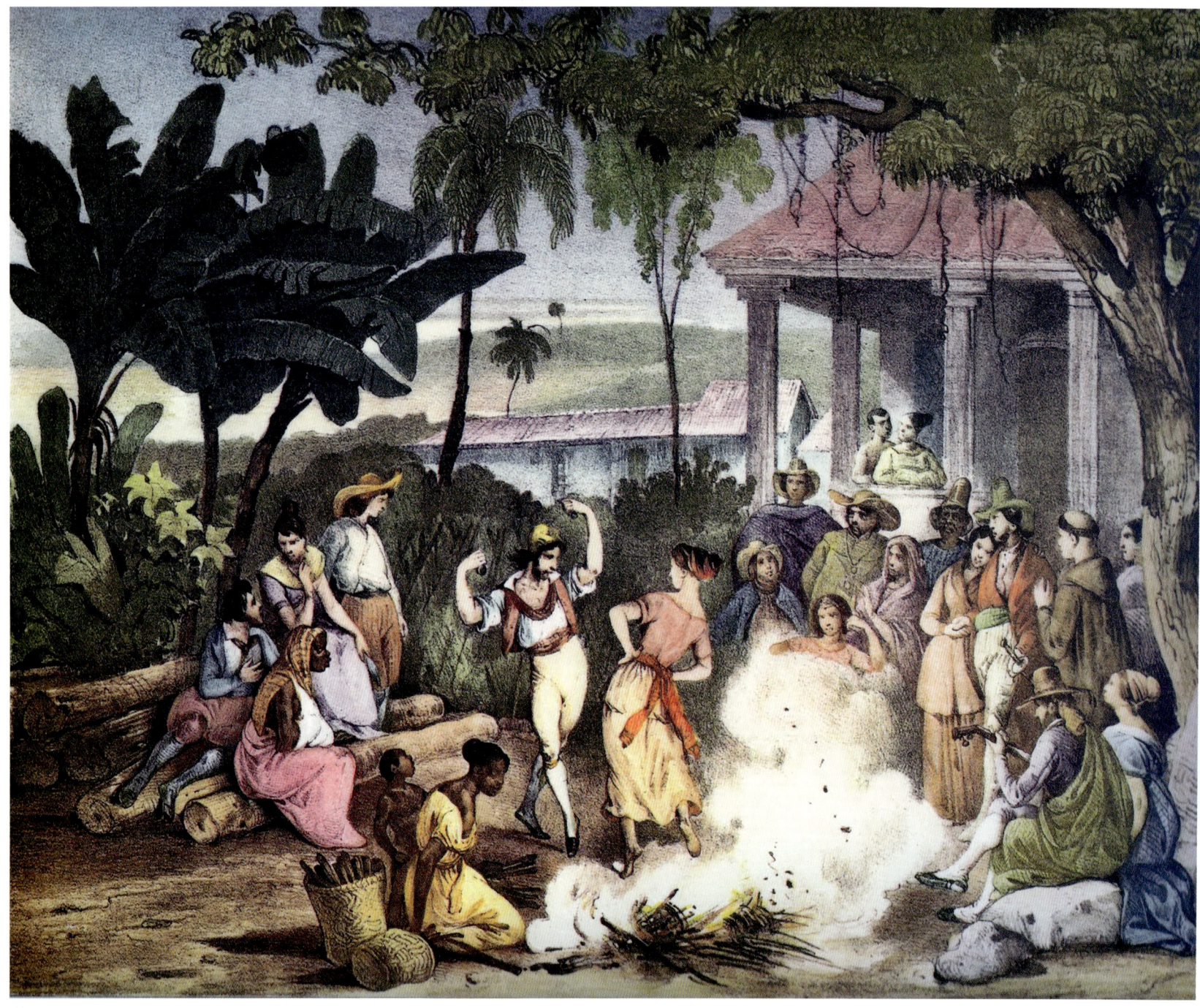
44

44 Johann Moritz Rugendas. *Lundu Dance*. 1835. Lithograph. In Rugendas, *Malerische Reise in Brasilien* (Paris, 1835).

legacies of the displacement and enslavement of Africans brought to Brazil from the sixteenth through nineteenth centuries and to the building and maintenance of physical and spiritual spaces of resistance. By the late nineteenth century, the major Brazilian cities of Salvador and Rio de Janeiro were crucial loci of culture and memory within the Black Atlantic, figuring as important sites for understanding both the development of Afro-Brazilian religious forms and the simultaneous preservation and suppression of their physical, spiritual, and material manifestations.

Salvador

An estimated 1.3 million Africans reached Bahia, in northeastern Brazil, from the Bight of Benin and West Central Africa, with the early capital city of Salvador becoming Brazil's "Black Rome," its center of African life and spirituality.[17] The Afro-Brazilian religion Candomblé was a product of the transatlantic slave trade and the creolization of various religious beliefs: Portuguese Catholicism, West Central African religions (Yoruba, Fon, and Bantu), and Amerindian sacred expressions.[18] Lacking a strict organizational structure, Candomblé has many variations and divisions roughly based on ethnic identities stemming from the port of embarkation in Africa. The core elements of the religion involve the worship of *Orixás* (deities), the veneration of ancestors, divination, and healing.[19] Centered in Salvador and its environs, Candomblé was an Afro-Brazilian religion practiced by both free and enslaved Blacks, with temples acting as the sacred precincts or anchors of religious practice. Candomblé temples also functioned as sites of community where the new disposable income of their practitioners could be invested in objects procured from various locales across Brazil and Africa; participating in the mobile networks through which these artifacts were acquired in turn bestowed social prestige within the local community. In post-slavery Bahia, with its population predominantly of African descent, authorities sought to suppress Afro-Brazilian religious assemblies for fear their religious leaders would revolt against the white, Christian ruling class. The possibility of an armed insurrection—especially considering the historical precedents of the successful Haitian Revolution of 1804 and, closer to home, Bahia's Muslim uprising of 1835—was always within sight.[20] Thus, for political and religious authorities, the suppression of Afro-Brazilian religious expression was invariably couched as a "public health" issue, entailing a refusal to recognize Candomblé and related spiritual practices as forms of religion at all, and instead categorizing them as sorcery or "fetishism," in a manner similar to the calundús, or demonic spirits, mentioned in seventeenth-century Portuguese Inquisition trials.

In many of these nineteenth-century accounts, spaces of Blackness in Brazil were associated with illness, racial degeneration, and political subterfuge. In addition, there were generalized fears that emancipation and insurgency would directly result from fraternization and communal gatherings of Africans and their descendants.[21] Perhaps the most poignant reminder of the deep legacies of slavery in Brazil is a recognition that this denigration of Afro-Brazilian religions as social, medical, and political threats persisted well into the twentieth century. It was only with the Penal Code Reform of 1940, under the national policies of the Getúlio Vargas regime's *Estado Novo*, that Afro-Brazilian religions (as well as capoeira) were decriminalized. The general trend toward suppression notwithstanding, the vigilance with which Afro-Brazilian religious spaces were surveilled was ambiv-

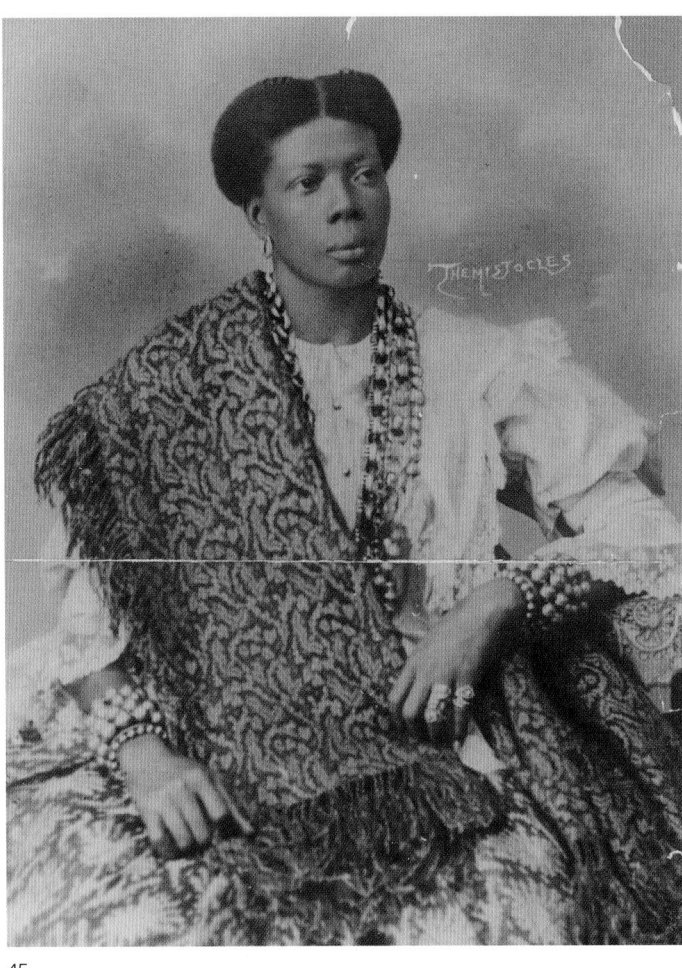

45

45 Unidentified photographer. *The Iyalorixá Eugênia Anna dos Santos (Mãe Aninha)*. Ca. 1890. Photograph. Washington, DC, National Anthropological Archives.

46 Unidentified artist. Amulets. 19th century. Gold and other materials. Vitória, Salvador, Brazil, Carlos Costa Pinto Museum.

alent at best; the governing white elites of Bahia intermittently accommodated Afro-Brazilian temples, allowing these sites in Salvador and elsewhere to become places of intellectual and cultural exchange and debate, where cultural identities and memories were constructed and performed, and out of which the initial large-scale ethnographies of Afro-Brazilian religions were first written.

Undoubtedly the most important Brazilian figure to write about Afro-Brazilian religious expression in the period was Raimundo Nina Rodrigues (1862–1906), a Bahia doctor recognized as the founder of "legal medicine," a predecessor to forensics that was infused with the antiblack racist views anchoring criminal anthropology and similar fields, and one of the first ethnographers of Afro-Brazilian religious practices such as Candomblé.[22] Along with many of his successors in the medical and legal realms, Nina Rodrigues occupied contradictory positions in the worlds they were studying, at once suppressing and preserving Afro-Brazilian cultural heritage. Many figures in the field of legal medicine in Brazil during this time considered Afro-Brazilian religious possession a form of mental illness, categorizing the objects associated with these rituals as instruments of disturbed and illegal practices. Working within an ambit of positivism and scientific racism, Nina Rodrigues and his colleagues studied Candomblé in the contexts of medicine, psychology, and criminology. Nonetheless, Nina Rodrigues, like so many Bahian elite of the period, was also a Candomblé initiate himself, actively participating in and advancing the culture of Candomblé temples. Additionally, Nina Rodrigues exhibited his own collection of Afro-Brazilian religious objects in the Faculty of Medicine in Salvador in the 1890s—the only institution of higher learning in Bahia and one directly linked to the elite governing body.[23] He and his contemporaries, among them politicians and foreign researchers,

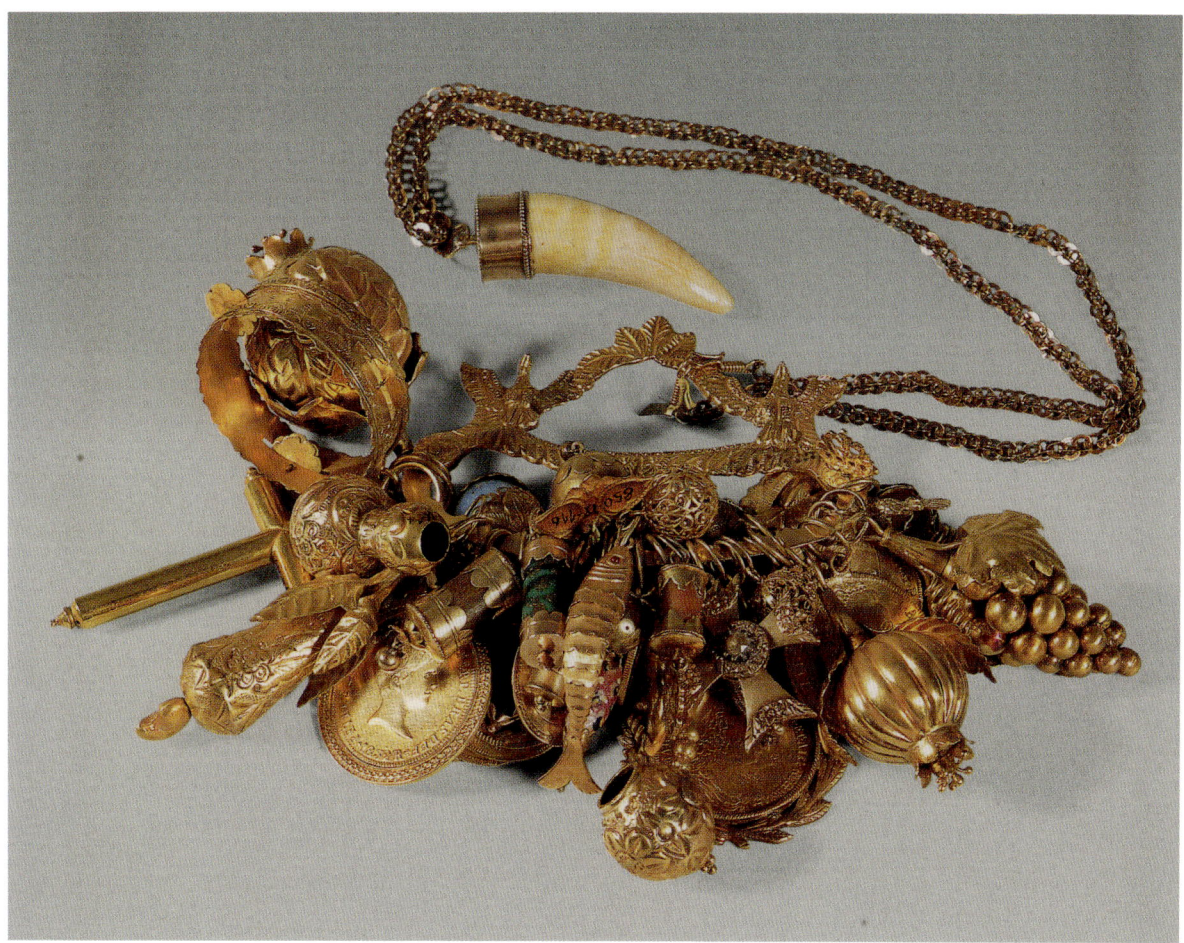

46

also frequented the Terreiro do Gantois in Salvador.[24] The temple, headed by a female priestess, was one of the key centers of Candomblé in late-nineteenth-century Salvador.

Studies of late-nineteenth-century Candomblé houses across Salvador, and in Bahia as a whole, provide fertile ground for understanding the powerful role that Afro-Brazilian women had in the formation and recognition of Candomblé culture writ large. Some of the earliest photographs associated with Candomblé temples depict female leaders. The rare photograph of a young Eugênia Anna dos Santos (1869–1938), or Mãe Aninha, from 1890 stands out as a case in point, revealing aspects of material culture of the period, important in understanding art making and Afro-Brazilian identity in late colonial Brazil. Dressed beautifully, she wears a pristine lace blouse; an ornate, likely handwoven shawl; and elaborate silverwork jewelry.[25] Such opulent silver-filigreed bracelets and necklaces were prevalent in formal portraits of Afro-Brazilian women during the period, revealing her elevated status and self-fashioning, as well as the metalworking traditions of the Fanti-Ashanti, Baule, and Yoruba groups that were brought to Brazil.[26] In the nineteenth century, both free and enslaved women would have worn such ornate jewelry, depending on their status and social position. Some of the more elaborate examples of jewelry from this period include what were known as *pencas de balangandãs*, beautifully wrought chains of amulets, usually worn around the waist of women of African descent in photographs from the late nineteenth century. Crafted in the same religious workshops that produced silver monstrances and reliquaries, these amulets took the shape of animals, fruits, Christian and African symbols, and tokens of everyday life.[27]

The sitter's strength is demonstrable in the image, conveying ideals of Black racial dignity that are at the heart of Candomblé. The photograph coincides with the arrival of the Lagosian Cul-

THE WAR ON BLACKNESS CA. 1888   111

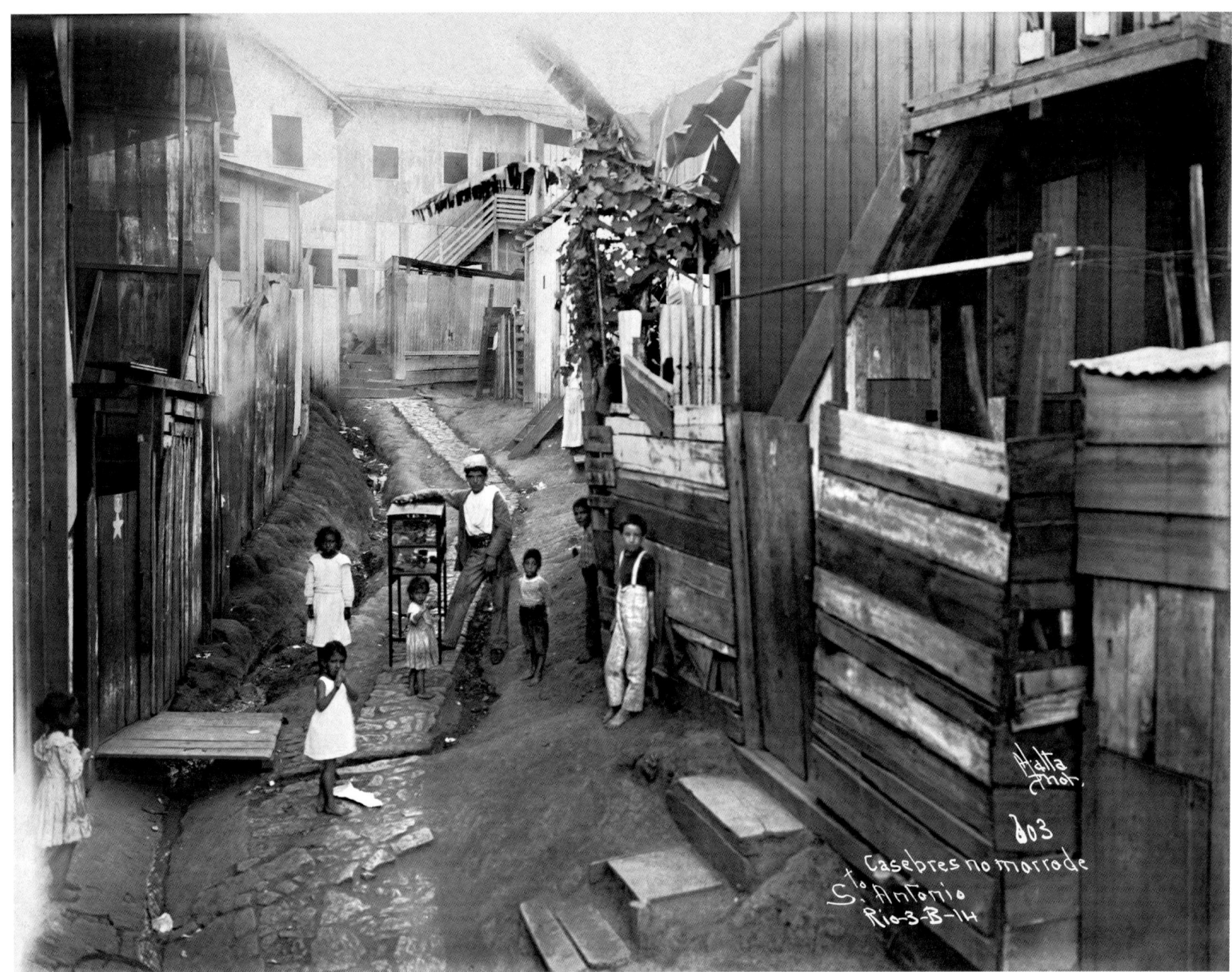

47 Augusto Malta. *Shanties in the Morro de Santo Antonio*. 1914. Photograph.

tural Renaissance, brought to Bahia by Afro-Brazilian travelers, which, combined with Black nationalism, informed Bahian Candomblé temples of this period, revealing their deeply cosmopolitan intellectual and spiritual frameworks.[28] Printed on cardstock, this photograph captures the power of the founder of the Salvador Candomblé house of Ilê Axé Opó Afonjá, of the Nagô "nation," those African descendants of Yoruba origin. The Ilê Axé Opó Afonjá temple, in fact, still stands as one of the most important historic heritage sites in Brazil, the second Afro-Brazilian site of worship to receive such status. As Kim Butler has shown, Mãe Aninha, who went on to found the Bahian temple in 1910, was a keen defender of Yoruba traditions in Bahia; she and her devotees adopted Yoruba customs and language in the house.[29] In this process, Aninha demarcated her ethnicity and lineage as part of the Nagô nation. Lineage determined succession within Candomblé, and as a result of a combination of her parentage and her training as a devotee, Aninha successfully assumed an African identity within the context of the religion, thus "becoming" African.[30] This shows the remarkable powers of Afro-Brazilian religion to redefine ethnicity and to create spaces of cultural resistance and female power in post-abolition Brazil.

Rio de Janeiro

By the late nineteenth century, in the wake of the abolition of slavery, Brazil's capital city grew exponentially, with freed people from across Brazil arriving in search of a better life, Europeans immigrating to (and through) Rio to find work in the city and on nearby plantations, and veterans from the War of the Triple Alliance seeking employment opportunities. Between 1872 and 1890, the population of Rio doubled; by 1890, with 522,651 inhabitants in the official census record, the city's population was three times that of Salvador.[31] This population influx had consequences on both the urban infrastructure of the city, with suburbs and shantytowns proliferating, and on the sociocultural dynamics of the local economy, where formerly enslaved men and women of African descent had difficulties securing official employment and thus were forced to continue to work at the margins of the official economy. Urban reform projects geared toward modernizing and "civilizing" the city, including the addition of streetlights, streetcars, water systems, public sanitation, gas, and telephone lines, led to the increased racialization of Rio's neighborhoods. A photograph taken by Augusto Malta (1864–1957) from the early twentieth century gives texture to these spatial dynamics of the city and to the demands of such projects in Rio. In 1903, Augusto Malta was invited by Francisco Pereira Passos, the politician and engineer who served as Rio's mayor from 1902 to 1906, to be the official photographer of the municipality, a position Malta maintained until 1934 and that he held when this particular photograph was taken.[32] Malta was given the task of documenting favelas, neighborhoods, and buildings across Rio, particularly the ruinous dilapidation of its tenements, as well as the consequent advances of the city administration in remedying these problems. Hygiene ranked high among the concerns of the municipality during this period, with epidemics of smallpox and yellow fever ravaging the city, disproportionately affecting the densely populated areas around the former slave port. In *Casebres no morro do Santo Antônio (Shanties in the Morro de Santo Antonio)*, a black and white photograph from 1914, Malta depicts the infamous neighborhood of Santo Antônio, an area of Old Rio de Janeiro, near the eighteenth-century Carioca Aqueduct, which connected Santa

Theresa to Santo Antônio Hill. Santo Antônio Hill had recently been made newsworthy among Rio's literary class by the writings of the journalist, short-story teller, and playwright João do Rio (1881–1921), who only six years earlier had published a chronicle in *Gazeta de Notícias* about his nocturnal visit to the hill.[33] Using spatialized language, Rio, himself a Carioca, or native of Rio de Janeiro, described Santo Antônio as a "non-city" within a city, employing analogies to remote geographies across Brazil—to the *roça* (countryside) and *sertão* (scrubland)—to describe a place where "poor workers *waited* for proper housing."[34] Malta's photograph shows the precarious incline of Santo Antônio, built on rock, with crude wooden shacks densely built to accommodate the residents on either side. An open drainage canal to the side of the narrow passageway between the houses must have carried off not only rainwater by also effluvia from the overcrowded neighborhoods. Featured in the photograph are seven barefoot children of various ages and an adult street vendor at the center, their darker skin a testament to the racial and social mapping of the neighborhood.

Civic reforms across Rio and the demands of imposing new public order left an impact not only on the streets and the lived urban fabric of the city as seen in Malta's photographs, but also on Rio's administrative institutions. Just as had been done in late-nineteenth-century Salvador, the police were trained to identify disturbances to the public order, including acts of so-called sorcery. Since the early colonial period, Brazil had judicial procedures to deal with accusations directed at witches and sorcerers, laws that originated in early-modern Iberia and traveled to colonial Brazil. A city increasingly notorious for the "con game," where notions of trickery in criminal behavior were widely discussed by criminologists, psychologists, and many novelists of the period, Rio was well known as a site of high crime.[35] In Rio, the institution of the police had its beginnings before Independence, in the early nineteenth century. Based on a French model introduced into Portugal in the mid-eighteenth century, the office of the General Intendent of Police of the Court, charged with the surveillance of the population at large, had both judicial and police functions.[36] Until the devastating fire of the National Museum of Rio de Janeiro in 2018, there had survived a small corpus of Afro-Brazilian religious objects from the late-nineteenth century, all associated with the office of Rio's General Intendent. Devoured by the blaze, these objects were the earliest known Afro-Brazilian ritual objects in Rio, bearing witness to the repression of Afro-Brazilian religious expression during the 1880s and techniques of police control in seizing such objects from Candomblé and Umbanda temples and homes, the Afro-Brazilian religious spaces of worship, such as the small statue of Xangô from the National Museum in Rio de Janeiro. Umbanda, a syncretic religion like Candomblé, blends aspects of Afro-Brazilian religious practices with Catholicism, Spiritism, and indigenous lore and was historically connected to suburban regions around the city, largely practiced by Rio's white middle class. The exquisitely crafted iron ceremonial objects once on display in the National Museum were associated with particular Orixás of Candomblé and Umbanda. Orixás, for example, were made manifest through miniature bows and arrows, staffs, spears, armlets, swords, and knives, all featured as part of the visual and material pantheon used in ceremonies; specifically, arrows were associated with the deity Oxóssi and fans associated with Oxum.[37] In Afro-Brazilian religions, deities are not represented in human form, as are the figurative saints of Ca-

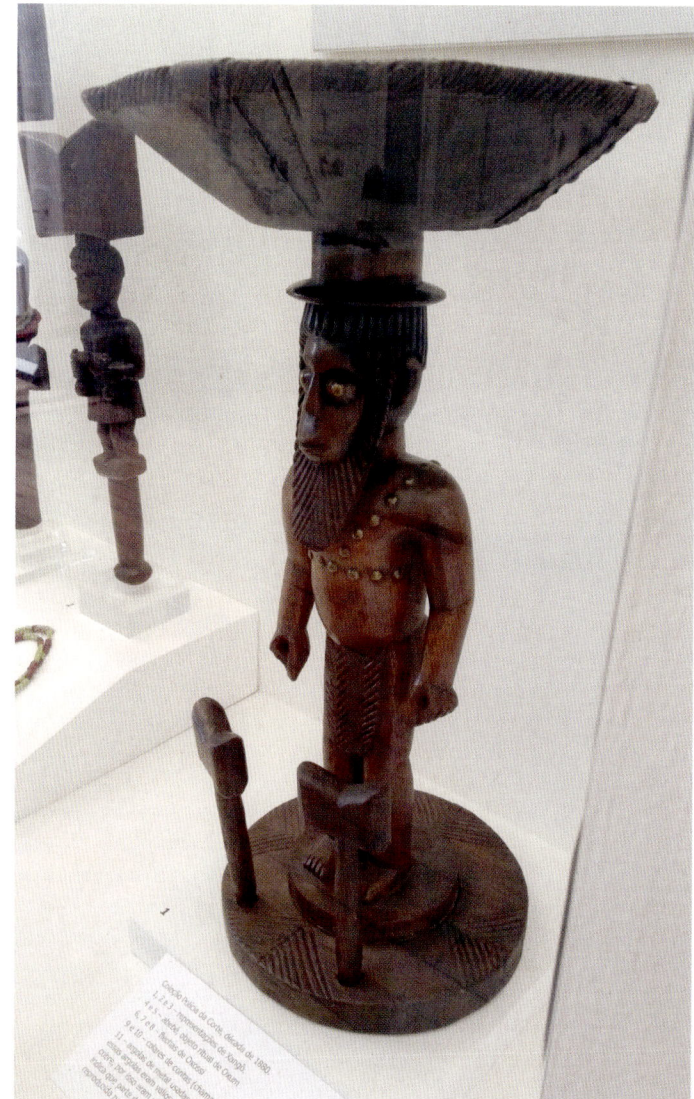

48 Afro-Brazilian objects. Rio de Janeiro, National Museum of Brazil / UFRJ (pre-fire). Xangô figure.

tholicism and other religions, but their presence is made manifest in acts of possession of the initiated. Therefore, the objects that adorn shrines and other Afro-Brazilian religious spaces are attributes and insignias, as initiates invoke and incorporate Orixás in acts of ritual transformation between bodies.[38]

Collections of the earliest Afro-Brazilian religious objects in Brazil are found outside Brazil, dispersed following the widespread practice of cracking down by authorities on Afro-Brazilian religious practices and the myriad seizures of religious objects. Most notable of these is the rare corpus of Afro-Brazilian objects that comprise the Wilhelm Pietzker collection, housed in the Ethnological Museum in Berlin. Pietzker, who claimed the sixty-seven Afro-Brazilian ritual objects were seized in police raids on the temples of Rio Grande do Sul in the 1870s, donated the cache to the German museum in 1880.[39] It is one of the largest collections of nineteenth-century Afro-Brazilian religious artifacts in existence. The objects range from insignia or tools of the Orixás, ornamentation of the initiates, to containers and figurative representations. The collection's geographic origin is most unusual, as Rio Grande do Sul is the southernmost province in Brazil and one not typically associated with Afro-Brazilian identity and religiosity. Rio Grande do Sul was, however, part of the internal slave trade in Brazil during the late eighteenth and early nineteenth century.[40] Objects such as these have in fact been seized objects all over Brazil, from Rio Grande do Sul in the south to Salvador in the northeast. And today, given the tragedy of the catastrophic fire in the National Museum, these remaining objects, part of their own diaspora, hold even greater importance.

THE WAR ON BLACKNESS CA. 1888   115

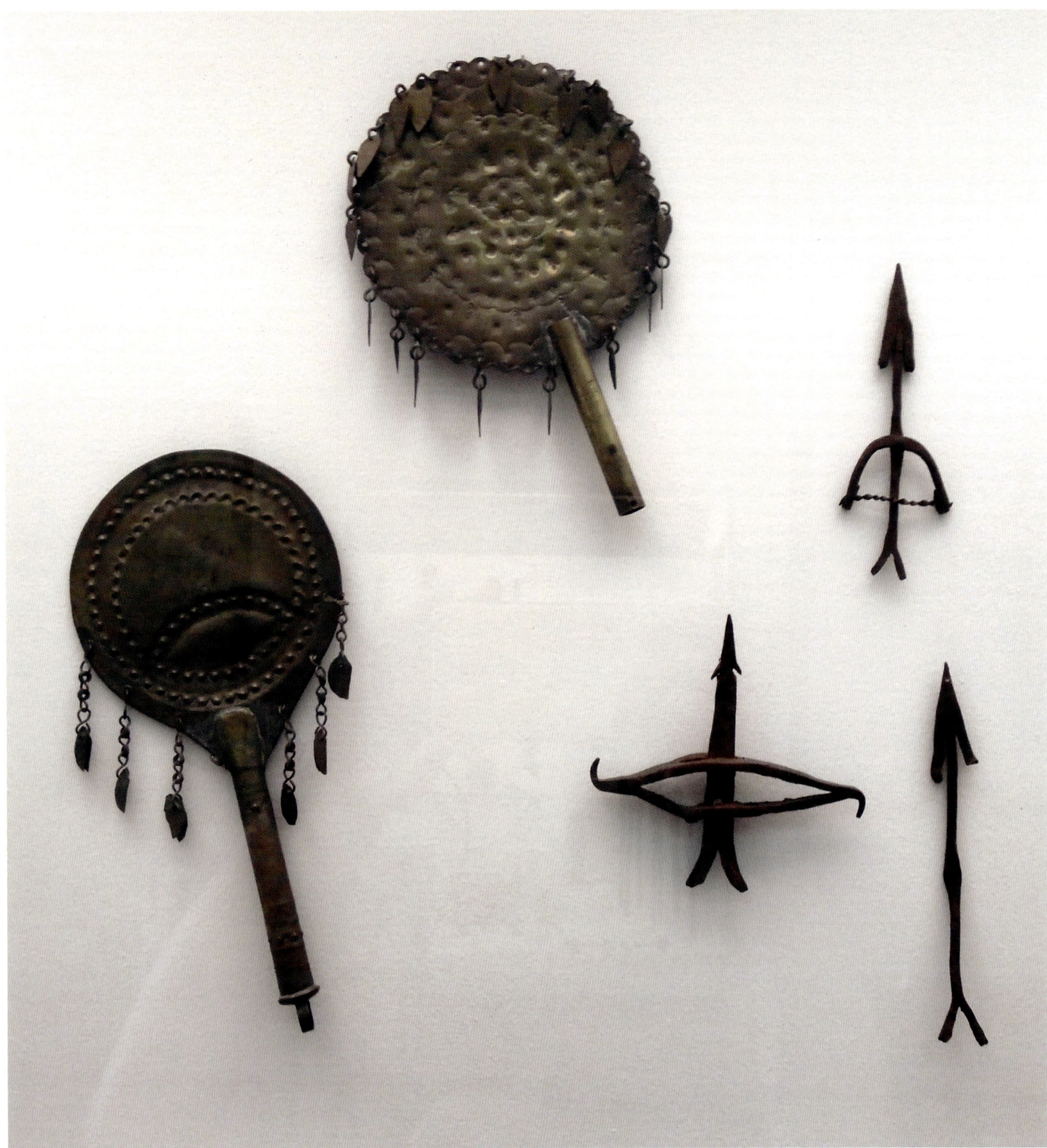

49

49 Afro-Brazilian objects. Ca. 1880. Berlin, Ethnological Museum. Wilhelm Pietzker Collection.

50 Afro-Brazilian object. Ca. 1880. Berlin, Ethnological Museum. Wilhelm Pietzker Collection.

51a Afro-Brazilian object. Ca. 1880. Berlin, Ethnological Museum. Wilhelm Pietzker Collection.

51b Afro-Brazilian object. Ca. 1880. Berlin, Ethnological Museum. Wilhelm Pietzker Collection.

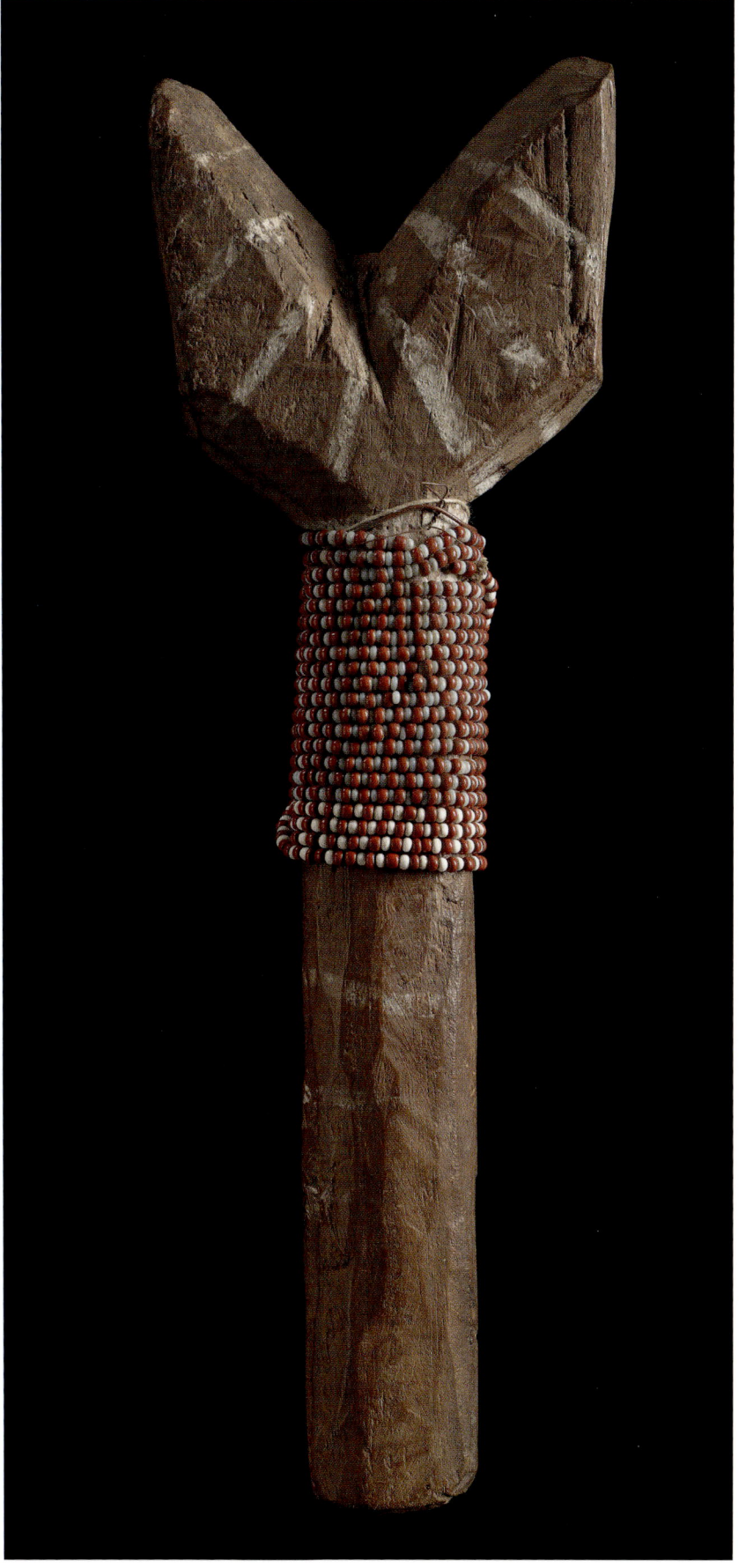

50

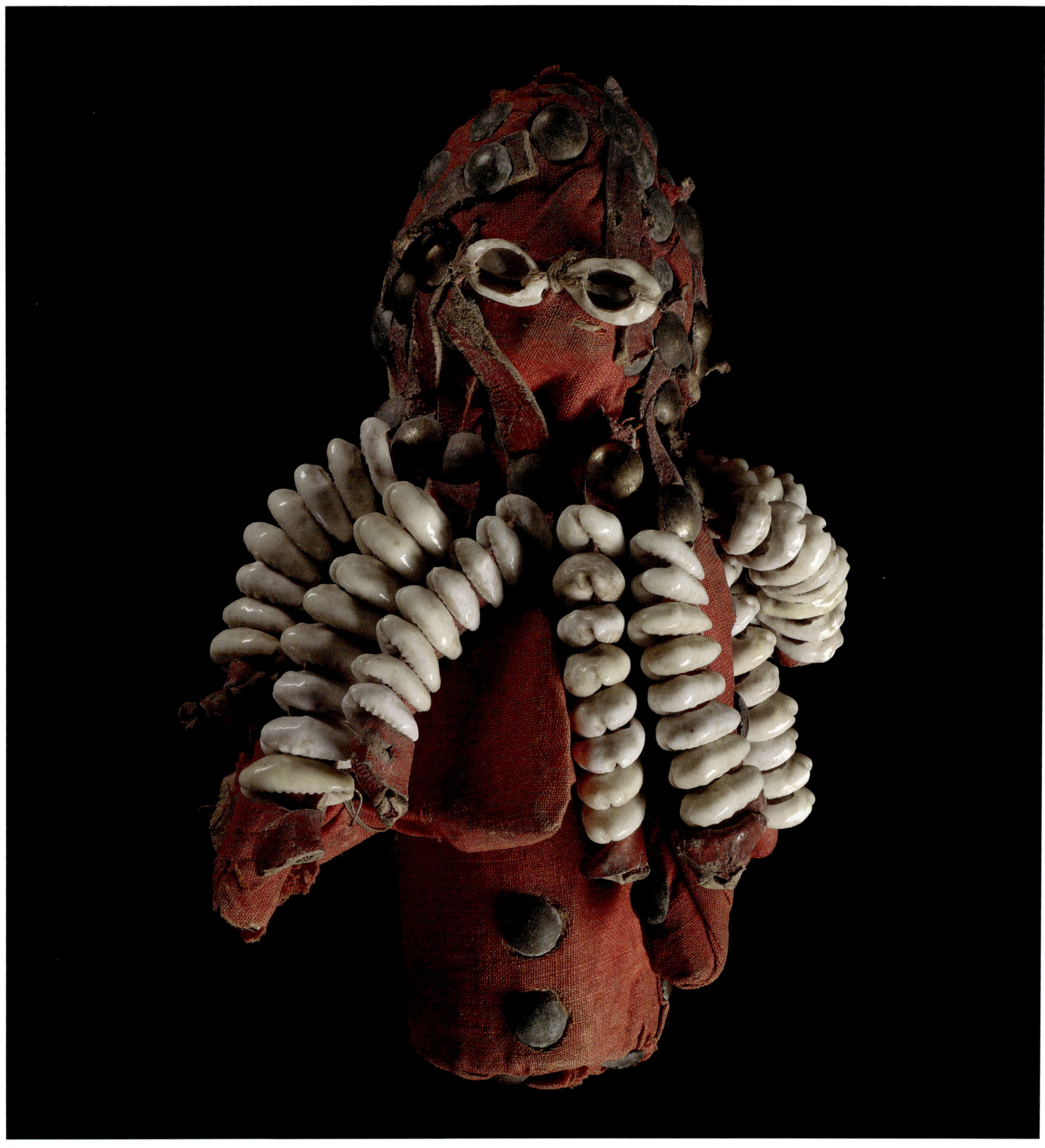
51a

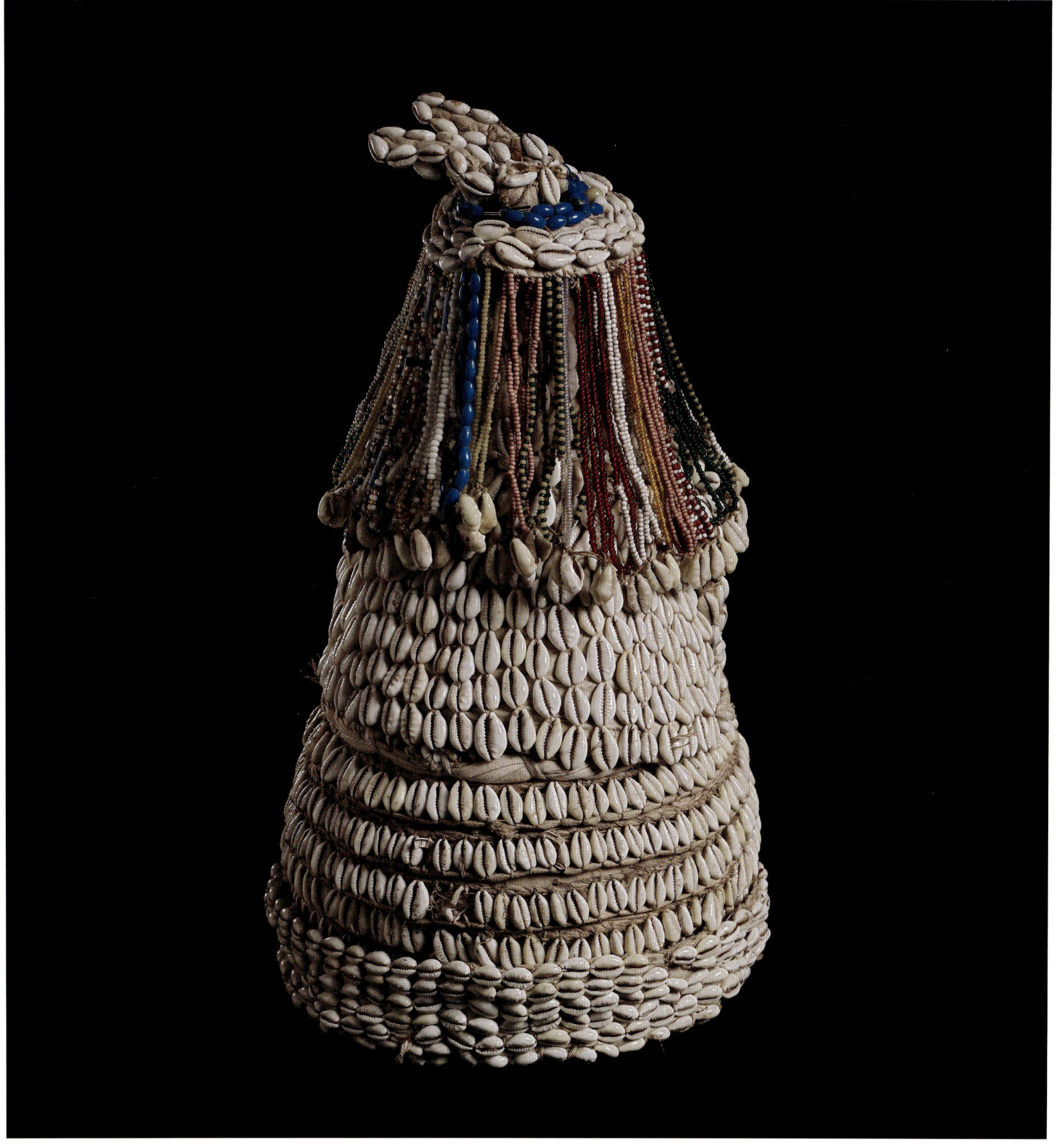

51b

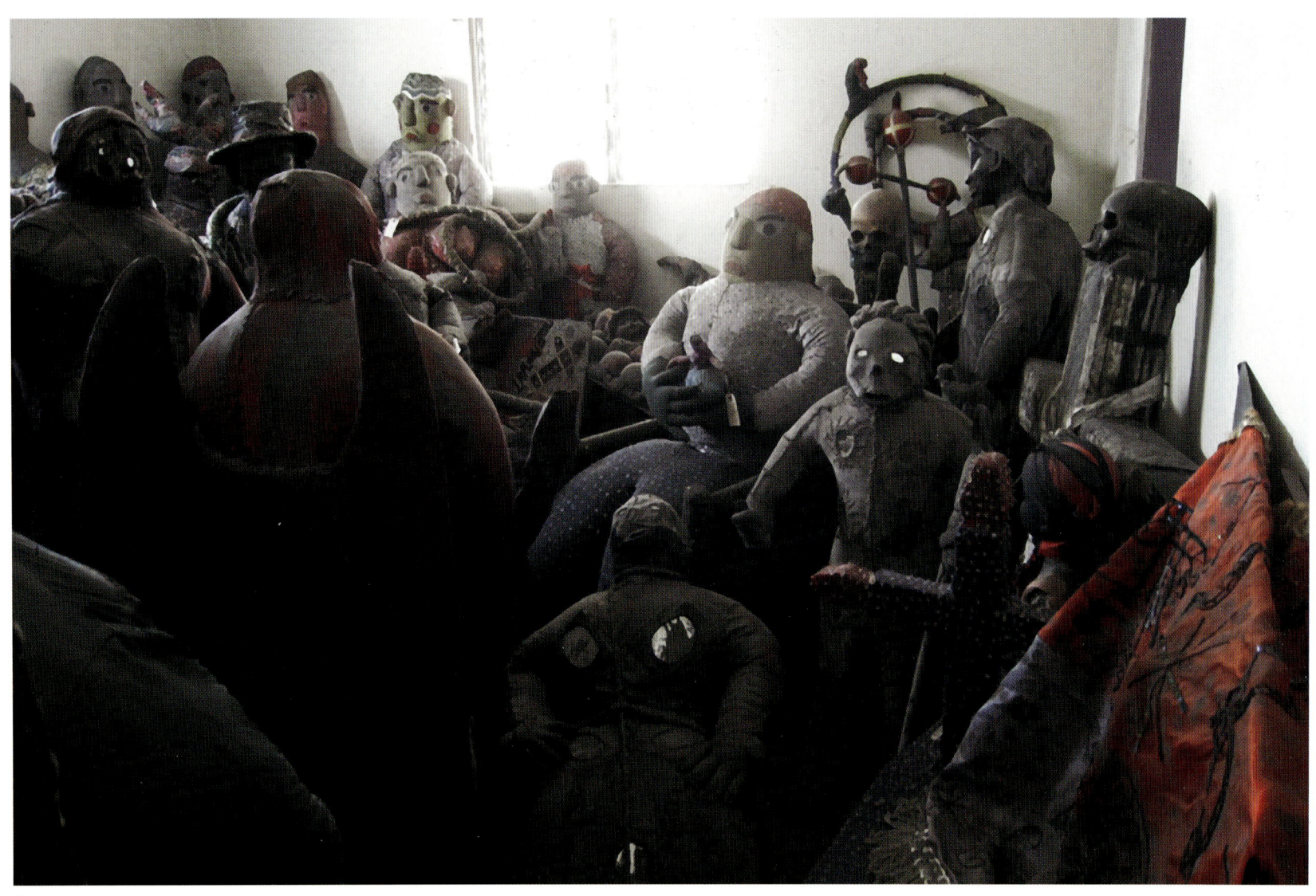

52

52 Haitian Vodou Bizango statues and other objects awaiting processing.

53 Haitian Vodou drum, confiscated in 1916. Philadelphia, Penn Museum, University of Pennsylvania.

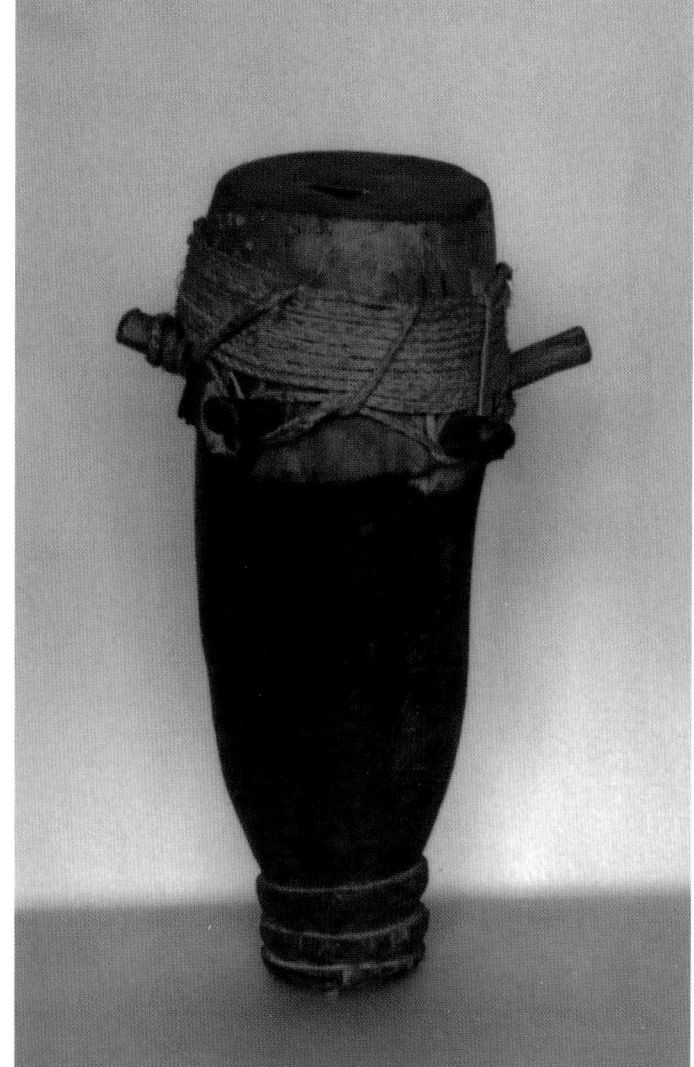
53

Thus, the issue of Afro-Brazilian religiosity and its relationship to the state was deeply connected to the intertwined histories of legal medicine and the civil police in Brazil. On February 2, 1912, the civil police of the state of Rio de Janeiro established their own museum collection, the Museum of Crime and the Museum of Methodology; today the collection is known as the Civil Police Museum of Rio de Janeiro.[41] As an administrative unit of the police academy, the museum was located in a lavish set of rooms in the upper stories of the central headquarters on the Rua de Relação in downtown Rio; it expanded into lateral spaces decades later. The primary function of the museum was to train police academy students. Only secondarily was it a museum open to Rio's general population, which was intermittently admitted to and barred from the museum over most of the twentieth century.

As an institution, the Civil Police Museum and its collections linked police training with collecting and visuality, resulting in an institution that uniquely shaped what today we would understand as an aspect of Brazil's Afro-Brazilian cultural heritage.

The concept of "deception" is critical for understanding the museum and its collection. The Museum of Black Magic within the larger museum exemplifies this. Starting in 1936, the museum served essentially as a jail for the potent, spiritually dynamic objects and images of Afro-Brazilian religions such as Candomblé and Umbanda. During the *Estado Novo* (1937–1945) under the dictatorship of Gétulio Vargas, Candomblé and Umbanda practitioners became the subjects of police surveillance throughout Brazil. Candomblé temples were suspected by the state of promoting communism and other potentially subversive practices

THE WAR ON BLACKNESS CA. 1888   121

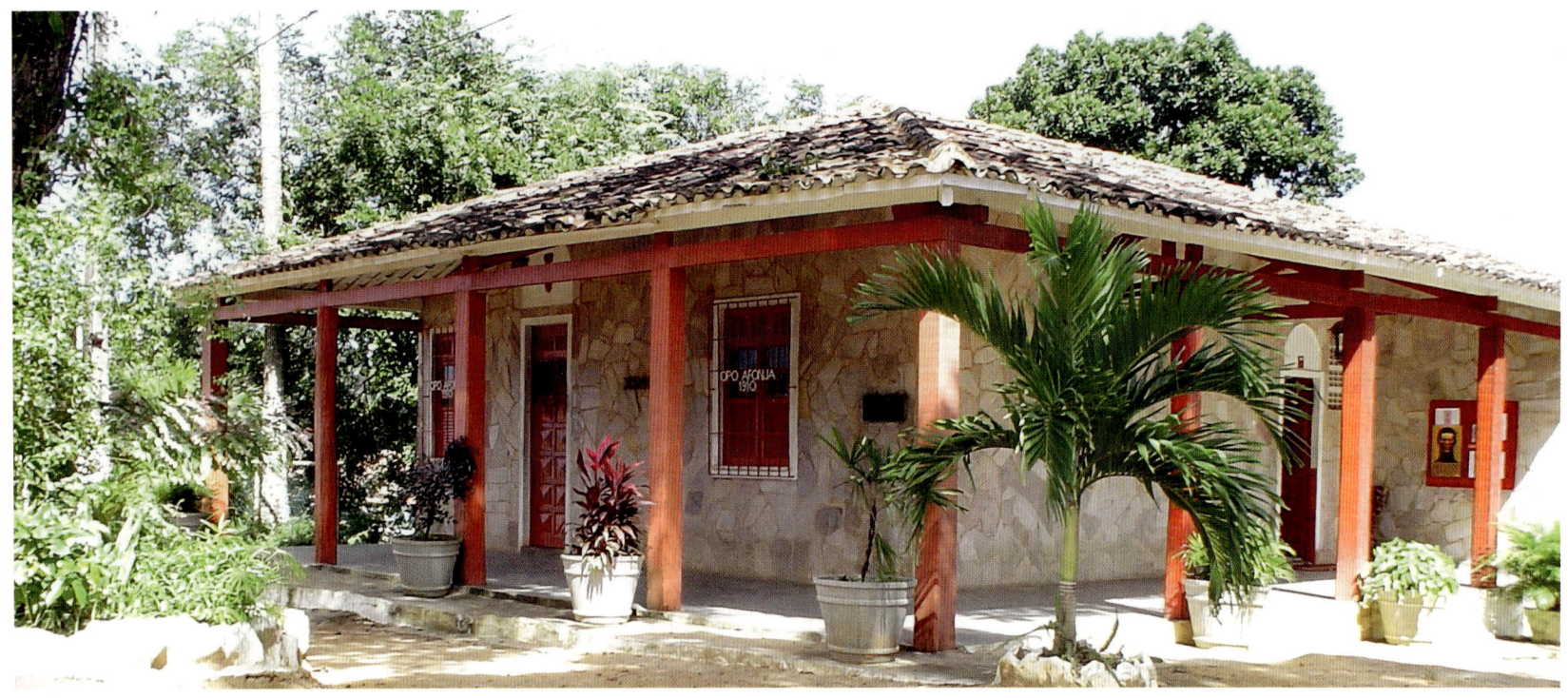

54

such as drug and alcohol abuse, gambling, and prostitution.⁴² Temple houses had to apply for special registration to function freely. This was characteristic of the Vargas regime, which either suppressed or promoted Afro-Brazilian religious practices, depending on the political pressures of the moment.

The civil police were under orders to confiscate objects associated with "fetishistic" or "animistic" religions, and, as the Brazilian sociologist Alexandre Fernandes Corrêa has discussed, to place anything "sinister," "strange," "primitive," or "grotesque," or with "immaterial and intangible ritual dimensions"—a list which conflates aesthetic criteria with legal and religious discrimination—into the Museum of Black Magic.⁴³ Paradoxically, though, the very act of incarcerating these objects had the effect of officially confirming and at some level perpetuating the real presence of their magical powers. The museum kept these objects isolated from public view and documented the histories of their usage and their seizure; thus they acquired a particular narrative and even spiritual powers within the academy. The objects within this collection play a crucial role in parsing out the complicated relationship between state institutions and the collection of religious objects, between state repression and religious practice, and between disciplines that segregate the study of material and visual culture from the politics of state. The seeming paradox of helping to preserve and even perpetuate Candomblé and Umbanda through police raids and seizures correlates to the moment in which the preservation of cultural heritage in Brazil received an institutional foundation.

Ostensibly, these police procedures were meant to suppress

54 Ilê Axé Opô Afonjá Museum, Salvador, Bahia, Brazil.

Afro-Brazilian religious practices, but intriguingly, once the ritual items were in police possession, they were arranged in the layout of a terreiro, or temple, within the museum space, thereby recreating the physical environment from which they had been seized. As the anthropologists Yvonne Maggie and Ulisse Rafael have noted, spirits of light were separated from those of darkness, and objects used to effect positive interventions were kept carefully segregated from those used to cause malevolent ones.[44] Here again, the suggestion is that the police understood in some detail the beliefs associated with these objects, and may have shared in them. In at least two very real senses, the purpose of the exercise was to *discipline* these artifacts. The museum attempted to contain and restrict the power of these objects—quite literally to incarcerate them—and it subjected them to a scholarly process of categorization and historicization. Because of the imperatives of rational police methods, as well as the pedagogical needs of the police academy, coupled with the registration practices of the museum, the police officers who seized these objects ended up acting as ethnographers, historians, and, by default, curators. Thus, these objects were politicized and, as a result of their removal from social uses inserted into a museum context, disciplined. In this instance, the Museum of Black Magic, as it was officially named in 1936, was created within an already established museum and contextualized with other objects and images of crime. How these objects were treated once they were in the museum demonstrates the contradictory ways in which the police officers initially repressed and yet ultimately sustained their spiritually efficacious nature. It should also be noted that, by the 1930s, the demographics of the civil police force had changed. Trainee officers were no longer upper-class law students, no longer Rio's elite, but increasingly drawn from populations with humbler origins, many coming from the same Rio communities they were tasked with suppressing, especially from the neighboring city of Niterói, one of the traditional centers of Umbanda practice in the region. Earlier in the century, Nina Rodrigues and his associates had frequented Candomblé temples in Salvador; now Rio's civil police officers were following suit, simultaneously enmeshed in the practices of suppression, beliefs in the efficacy of magic, and, through their detailed writings and collection of objects, inadvertently involved in the preservation of Afro-Brazilian religions.

In 1935, a year before the Museum of Black Magic was founded, the Brazilian poet, novelist, musicologist, art critic, and photographer Mário de Andrade (1893–1945), himself of Afro-Brazilian descent, co-founded and became the director of the Department of Culture in São Paulo (under the auspices of the National Artistic Patrimony Service). In this capacity, he issued a decree to preserve this very collection as Brazil's first corpus of cultural patrimony.[45] The National Congress approved de Andrade's proposal in 1938. The collections of the Civil Police Museum reveal the interlocking histories of state institutions with cultural memory and repression, and highlight the importance of understanding the *longue durée* of colonial institutions to understand how objects shift in meaning, and the contradictory ways by which cultural heritage is preserved.

6

THE UNREPRESENTABLE:
NAVIGATING BLACK AGENCY DURING TIMES OF TRANSITION

E. CARMEN RAMOS

The nineteenth century was a defining epoch in the construction and circulation of the Black image in Latin America, a time of rapid if halting racial and national emancipation. These projects were deeply interrelated, especially in the Spanish Caribbean, which lived with the threat or promise of the Haitian Revolution (1791–1804) and whose ties to Spanish colonialism largely endured until 1898. In Latin America, stories and images of the Haitian Revolution graphically laid out the stakes during these turbulent and transitional times. Works like Manuel Lopéz Lopéz's print *Desalines* [sic] (1806) not only depicted the unprecedented rise of Black leaders like this governor-general and later emperor of Haiti, but also advanced ideas of Black savagery.[1] Outfitted in a grand uniform and with eyes ablaze, Jean-Jacques Dessalines holds the decapitated head of a white woman. This print is a visceral reminder of the pervasive white fear of slave rebellions throughout the Americas. Latin American artists wrestled with representations of Black subjects as their respective regions sought to establish their rightful authority as nations—particularly as national autonomy was predicated on notions of white superiority. Black agency, the efforts of Afrodescendant populations to control their own destinies and not be passive subjects, had to be carefully orchestrated or avoided at all costs. Black representations did not exist in a vacuum but rather gave image to debates in the public sphere. Even as the bulk of images relegate African descendants to the lowest ranks of society, there were spaces of Black agency. Visual images created and controlled by Black people were few and far between, yet it is still productive to speak of the content and/or multivalence of racialized images during the colonial period.

The discussion that follows focuses on Cuba and to a lesser extent Puerto Rico, the two most artistically productive colonies in the Spanish Caribbean during the nineteenth century. While independence was earned in Mexico and across South America by 1825, Cuba and Puerto Rico remained Spanish colonies until the end of the Cuban Spanish American War of 1898. At this time Spain ceded Puerto Rico to the United States, and Cuba became a protectorate of the United States until 1902. Cuba had a thriving sugar economy that capitalized on Haiti's demise, which relied on thousands of enslaved Africans to work on plantations from the late eighteenth century until 1886, when slavery was officially abolished.[2] A strong independence movement did not develop in Puerto Rico following an unsuccessful revolt in 1868, yet Cuba witnessed several battles for independence in which the abolition of slavery and racial equality were central to the struggles.

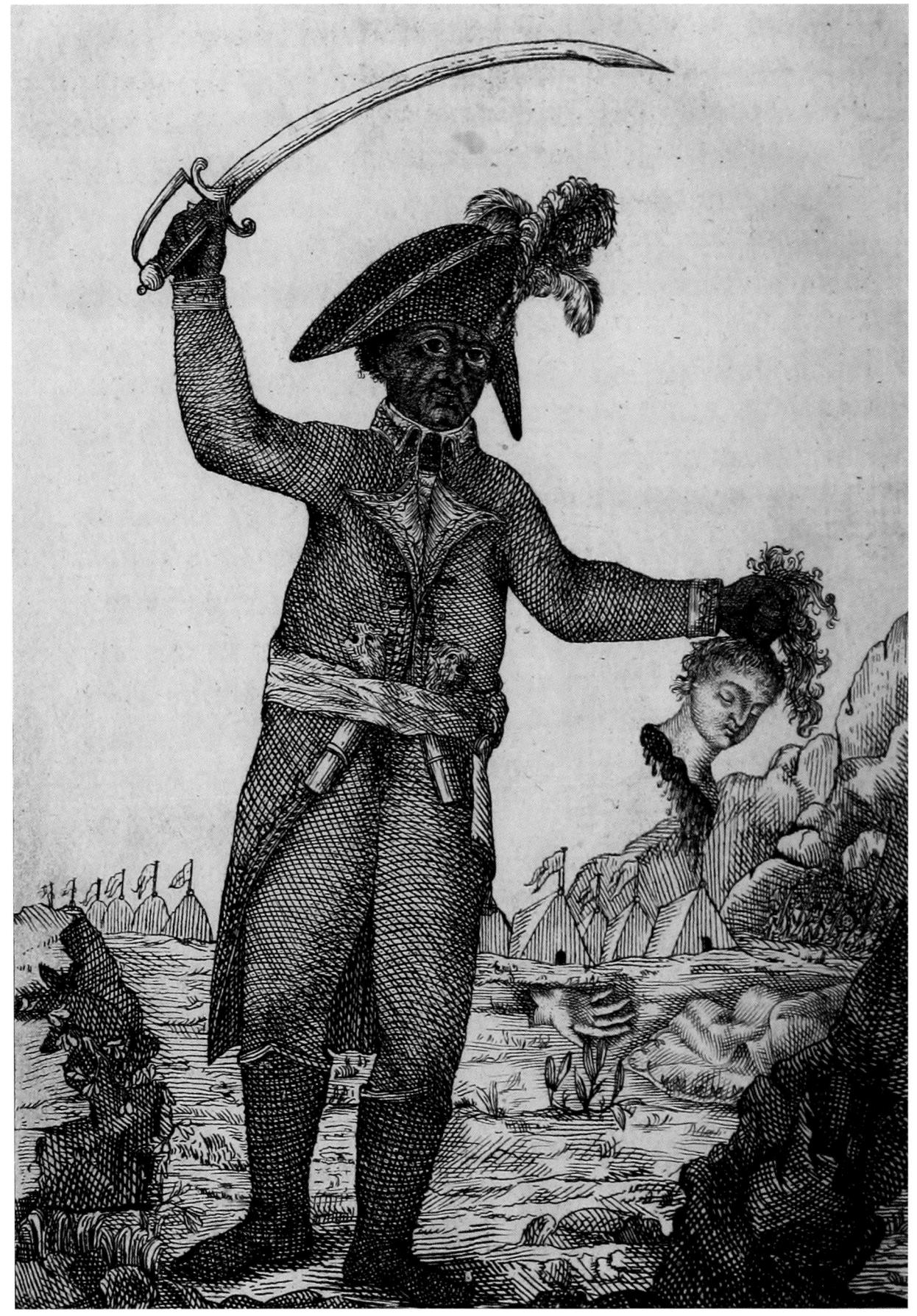
55

55 Manuel López López Iodibo. *Desalines* [*sic*]. Engraving. Louis Dubroca, *Life of J. J. Dessalines, Leader of the Negroes of Santo Domingo* (Mexico, 1806).

56 José Campeche. *Governor Miguel Antonio de Ustáriz*. Ca. 1789-1790. Oil on canvas. San Juan, Instituto de Cultura Puertorriqueña.

Starting with the Ten Years' War (1868–1878), Cuban insurrectionists fought against Spain with a multiracial rank and file and with prominent men of color leading Cuban forces. Cuba is also the site of one of the richest repositories of African diasporic culture in the Americas, which shaped the island's cultural and religious life. For these and other reasons, the images produced in the Spanish Caribbean are important case studies of the malleability of Black imagery within the context of anticolonial nationalist projects. How did artists and image makers come to terms with Black agency or its possibility when nationalist projects required a subdued Black body containable within the norms of Westernized nations? How was Blackness visually negotiated?

The majority of images of Black people during the nineteenth century circulated within popular genres like *costumbrismo* and political caricature. Costumbrismo was a literary and visual genre that catalogued the social types and customs of a given place. In the Caribbean and elsewhere, it trafficked in subservient, picturesque, and in some cases immoral Black subjects deemed representative of local traditions. These images were not usually produced by people of African descent themselves, but by the ruling Spanish and Creole classes who benefited from Black labor. Importantly, costumbrismo did not confine itself to paintings and prints only accessible to a few. Such representations, particularly imagery that dehumanized and trivialized Black people, appeared in objects of domestic and personal adornment like costumbrista anthologies, illustrated weeklies like *La Ilustración Española y Americana*, and cigarette packaging that was often collected and arranged in scrapbooks meant to edify and entertain. This distribution gave these images access to private spaces with the potential to affect socially colonial subjects and emergent citizens. The more uninhibited space of political caricature—which often drew on real historical figures and events—was more flexible in imagining the possibility of Black agency, if only to highlight the danger it posed, or its complete impossibility.

Black Artists and White Sympathizers

One must not discount the importance of artists of African descent who worked productively during the colonial period in Puerto Rico and Cuba. While the conventions of the day did not support or encourage them to focus on Black life, their active careers are a testament to their talent, industry, and determination during a time when slavery was still thriving. Artists of color, whether of indigenous or African ancestry, were common in many parts of Latin America because of the apparent lower status of art and artists within a guild and workshop system. Puerto Rico's José Campeche (1751–1809) was the most successful Caribbean artist working during the eighteenth and early nineteenth centuries.[3] He trained in his father's workshop and later studied with the Spanish rococo artist Luis Paret y Alcázar (1746–1799), who was temporarily in exile in San Juan, Puerto Rico. The son of a formerly enslaved father and a Canary Islander mother, Campeche became best known for his religious paintings and portraits of the most distinguished members of Puerto Rican society. Campeche used the conventions of the day to confer status on his sitters. His portrait of Governor Miguel Antonio de Ustáriz presents the governor in an elaborate rococo interior, where he points to a map of the city he had helped to modernize. The background features a view of San Juan with enslaved people paving the streets of the city, a project initiated by Ustáriz. Similar to early *casta* paintings in Mexico, Campeche's scene presents the

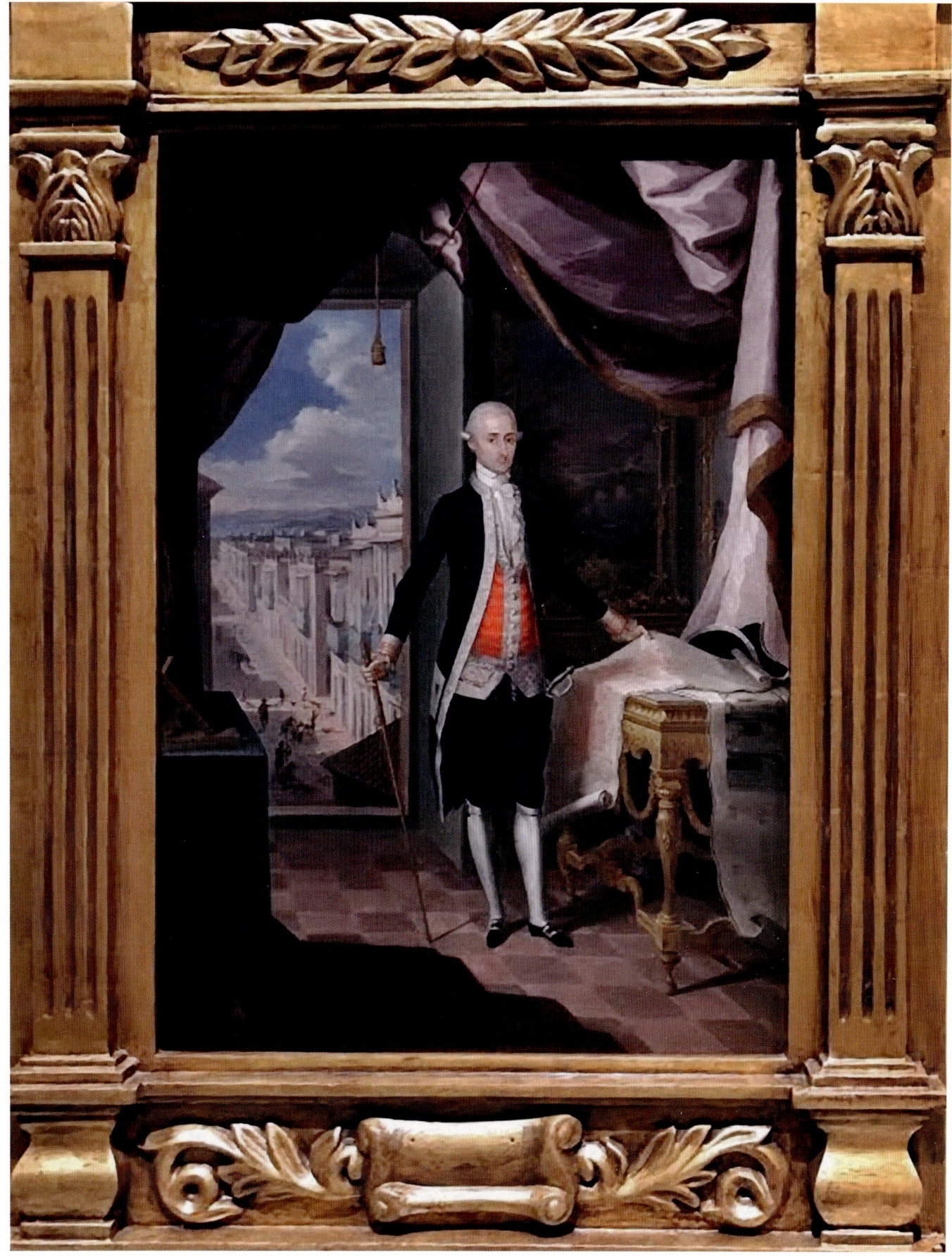

56

colony as an orderly place with a stable racial hierarchy. On the left side of the composition, the artist juxtaposes Ustáriz's hand grasping his cane with enslaved laborers, suggesting they have submitted to his authority. The street scene includes a commanding figure whose posture mimics that of Ustáriz and who directs the work of the enslaved Blacks.

Similarly, self-taught mixed-race artisans produced most Cuban painting during the early colonial period. The colonial government, churches, and private individuals commissioned artists like Vicente Escobar (1762–1834) to paint religious works and portraits of prominent people. The initiative to establish an art school in Cuba had much to do with the racial makeup of the colony's first artists. Outspoken Creoles, white settlers, like José Antonio Saco hoped that an art school would nurture white artisans in Cuba, thereby bringing the colony in line with other civilized nations.[4] The desire of Creoles to nurture the fine arts should be seen as part of an effort to raise the colony's cultural and racial status vis-á-vis a European standard. Episodes like this reveal the extent to which the initiative of Black people, even when not overtly rebellious, was monitored and debated within a racialized colonial context.

The Creole intelligentsia walked a fine line, arguing for the need to elevate the arts by wresting it from the hands of Black artists while at the same time urging artists to focus on Black life as evidence of Cuba's cultural uniqueness. The Cuban artist Juan Jorge Peoli (1825–1893) heeded this call when he illustrated Anselmo Suárez y Romero's 1843 costumbrista essay "*El guardiero*," or "The Caretaker."[5] An acknowledged masterpiece of literary costumbrismo, the essay itself is a poetic and nostalgic evocation of the Cuban countryside titled after an aging enslaved man who tends to animals on his enslaver's estate. The image shows a humbly clothed Black man standing in front of a hut-like dwelling or *bohío*, leaning against a makeshift cane, surrounded by a dog and hens. The figure's old age—conveyed through his graying hair, wrinkled forehead, and feeble posture—consolidates his unthreatening nature. Here, Peoli visually crystallizes and localizes a recurring representational trope in slave societies: the docile slave.[6]

The Puerto Rican artist Francisco Oller (1833–1917) painted ambitious works that prominently feature Afro-Puerto Rican subjects and demonstrate that it was possible to portray Black figures favorably within a colonial context. Oller was a highly accomplished international figure active in European academic, realist, and impressionist circles who devoted many of his later works to Puerto Rican subjects, notably in *The School of Master Rafael Cordero* (ca. 1890–1892). Cordero was a free person of color and tobacco worker who opened a school for poor young boys that eventually served elite children as well, a fact suggested by the broad range of skin tones among the students pictured around him. In his painting, Oller represents Cordero, wearing a turban on his head, as a bastion of humility, patience, kindness, and moral authority, conveyed by the religious paintings that surround him.[7]

Oller's acknowledged masterpiece, *The Wake*, is decidedly more ambivalent in its depiction of Black subjects. The monumental painting, which measures eight feet high by thirteen feet wide, at once relates to realist currents in Europe and costumbrista practices focused on eradicating supposedly immoral traditions from the lower classes. The painting presents a cacophonous view of a *baquiné*, the celebratory wake of an infant.[8] Within a crowded and humble rural dwelling of indigenous origin, mourners

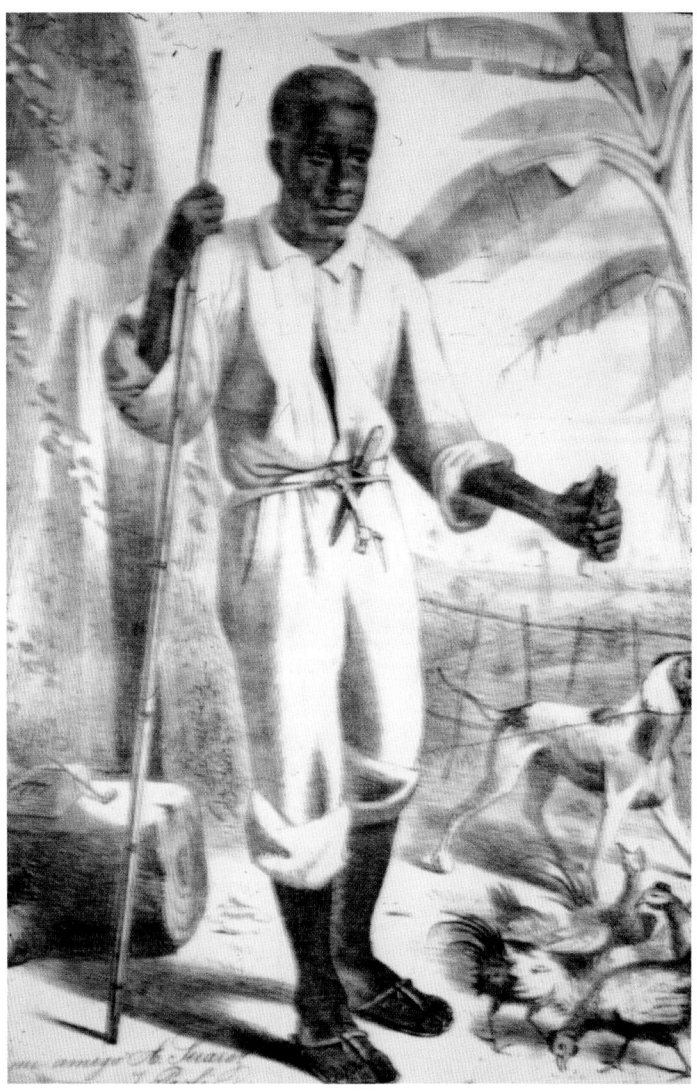

57 Juan Jorge Peoli. *The Caretaker*. 1853. Lithograph. *La Revista de La Habana*. Havana, Biblioteca José Martí.

appear more focused on the roasted pig hanging from the ceiling than on the solemn occasion that brought them together. The mother of the dead child, identifiable by the bandanna on her forehead, smiles at the viewer, inviting them into the celebration. The painting registers Oller's anti-clerical stance, as well as his own white elite class position, which led him to condemn rural customs as backward, including the baquiné that was informed by West African Kongo practices.[9] Some scholars situate Oller's subject within elite debates over the downward spiral of the colony due to racial mixing, while others view it as a compendium of Puerto Rican traditions or a statement on the tragic fate of people of color in the post-emancipation period.[10] Oller's own description of the painting, however, elevates the Black man and dead child seen in the center of the composition from the ruckus that surrounds them.[11] Only the elderly Black man, himself formerly enslaved, fully grasps the tragedy of the occasion.

Scenes of Subjugation

Oller's nuanced representations of Black subjects were the exception rather than the rule. Most nineteenth-century images in the Spanish Caribbean render Black life as subjugated to a colonial and white supremacist system or as an expression of moral and biological degeneracy (thereby justifying the colony's white supremacy). As in other slave societies, images of Black subjects appeared as unnamed props in portraits of the elite. In 1828, the French artist Jean-Baptiste Vermay, the first director of Cuba's art academy San Alejandro (fl. 1818), created one such painting to commemorate and record the opening festivities of El Templete, a new civic building constructed between 1827 and 1828 at the site of the founding of Havana.[12] The monumental painting was

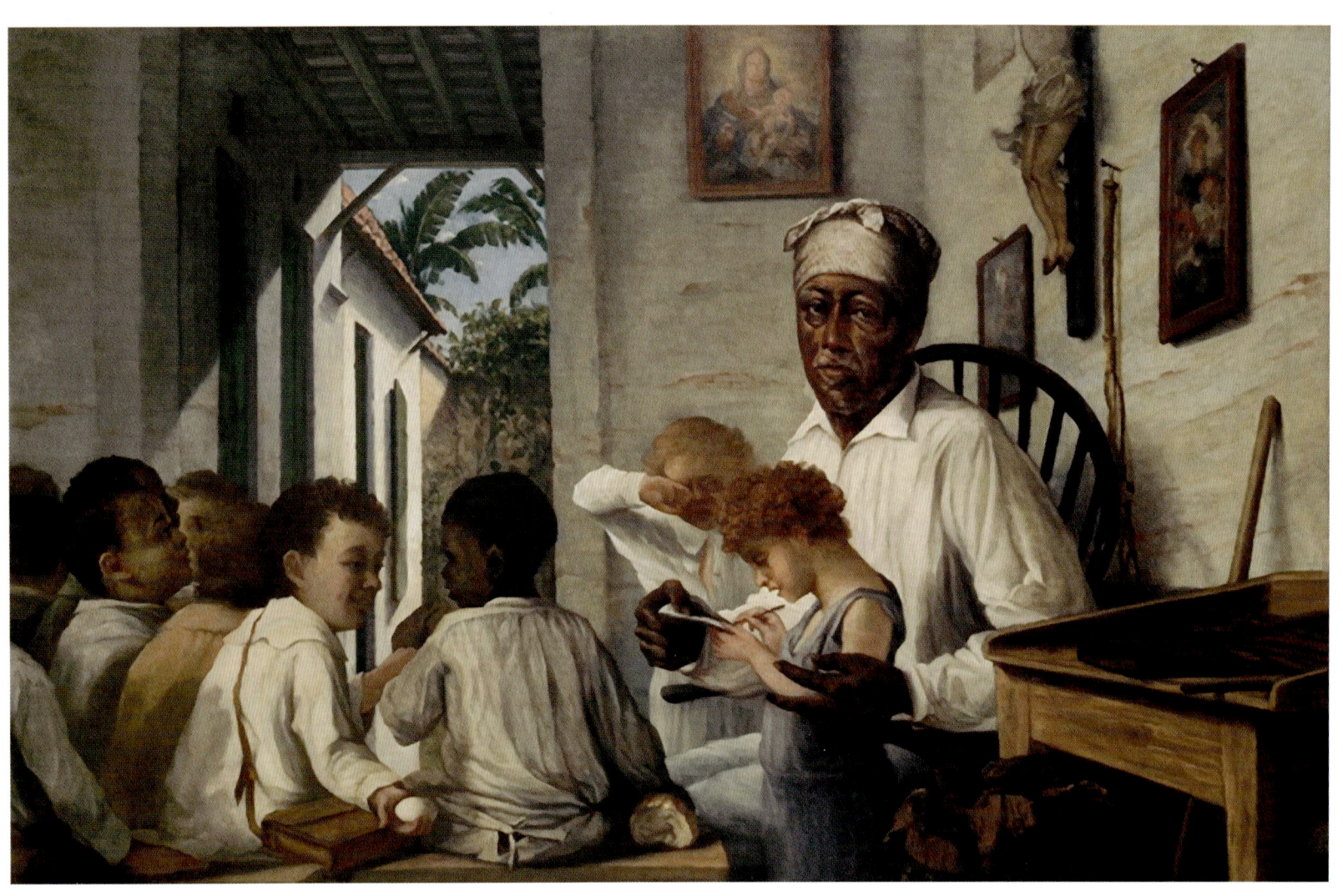

58

58 Francisco Oller. *The School of Master Rafael Cordero*. 1890-1892.
Oil on canvas. San Juan, Ateneo Puertorriqueño.

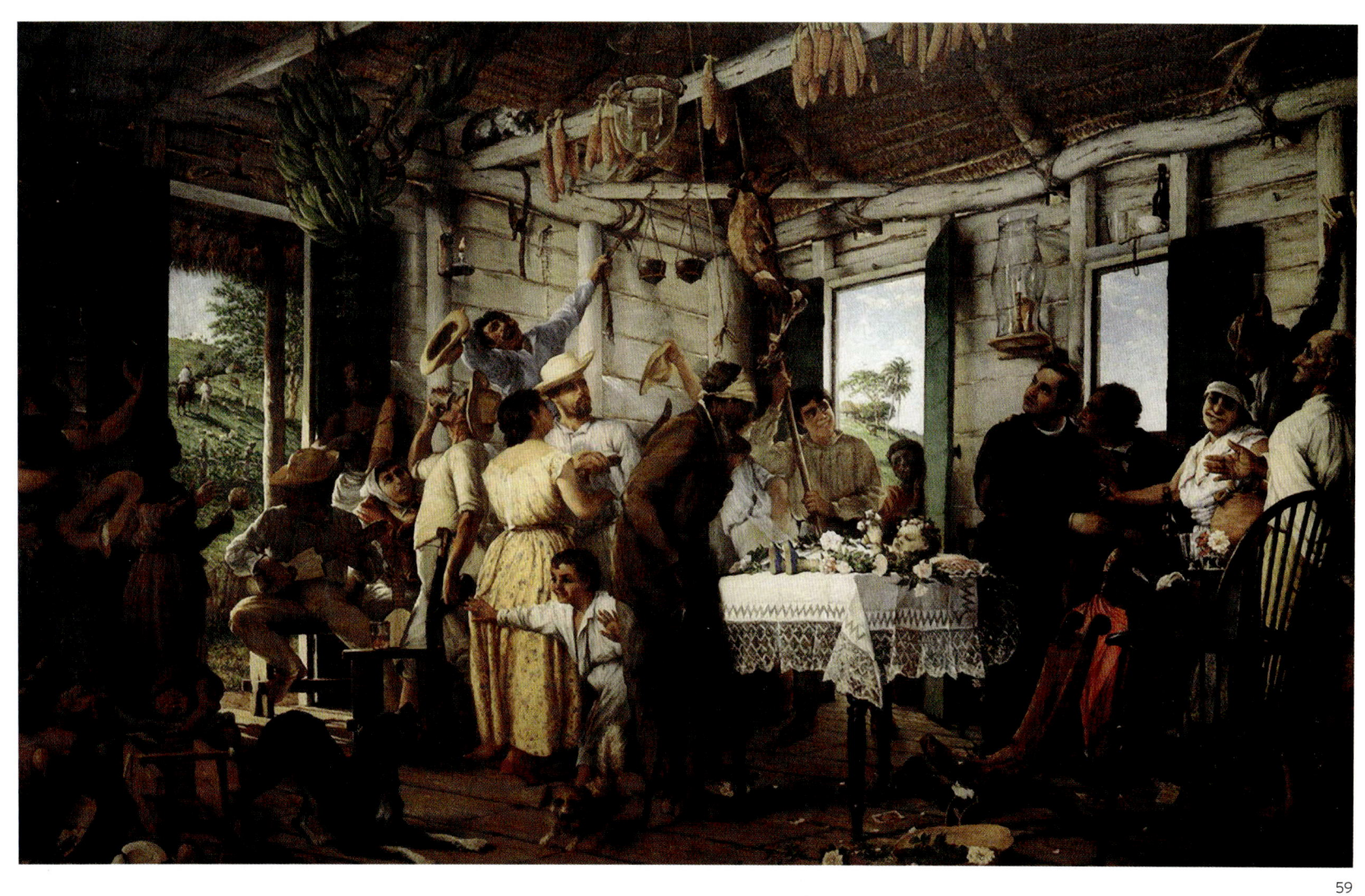

59 Francisco Oller. *The Wake*. Ca. 1893. Oil on canvas. San Juan, Museo de Historia, Antropología y Arte de la Universidad de Puerto Rico, Río Piedras.

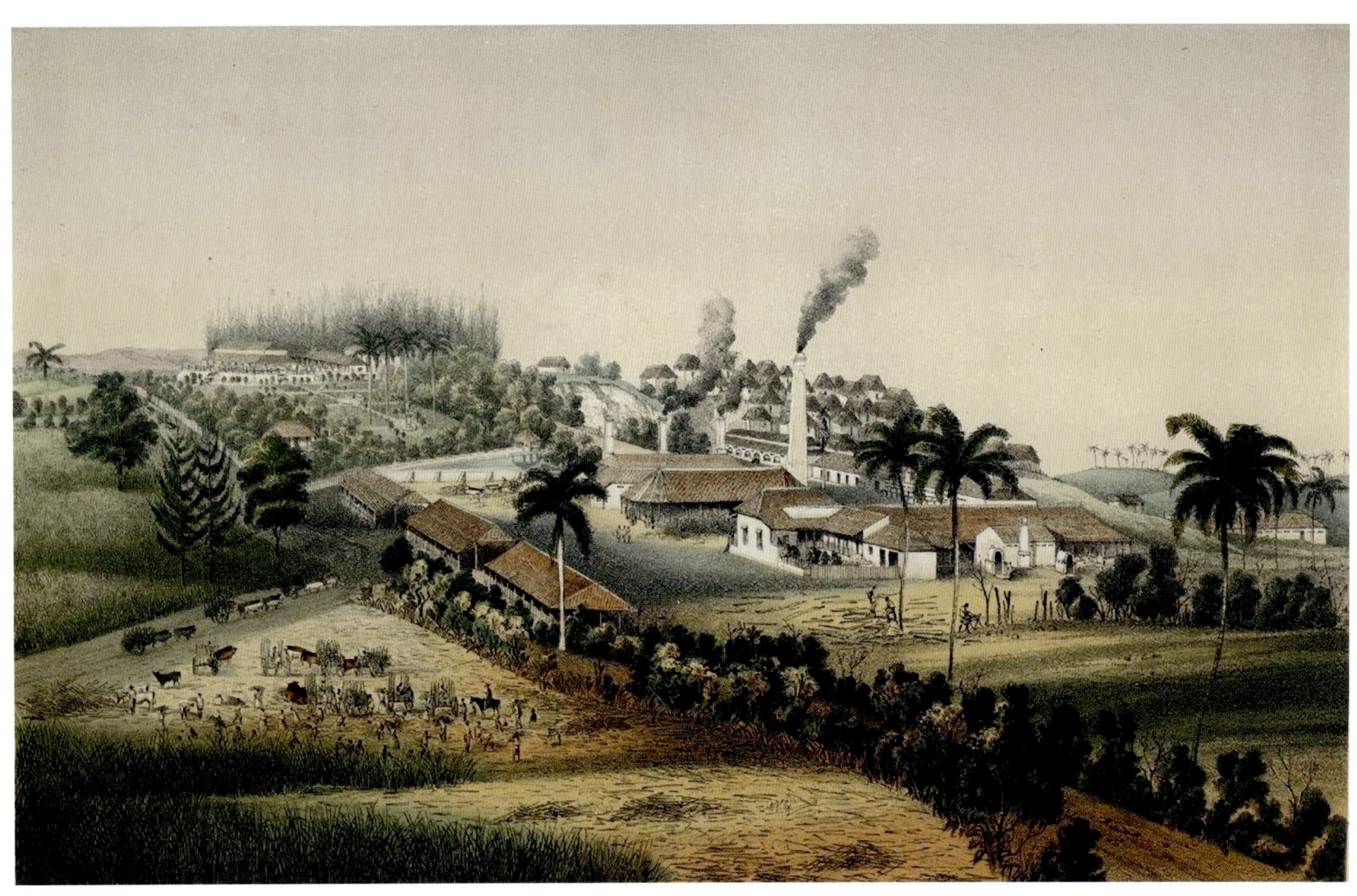

60

60 Eduardo Laplante. *Sugar Mill Owned by Conde de Fernandina in Cuba*. Lithograph. Justo G. Cantero, *Los ingenios: Colección de vistas de los principales ingenios de azúcar de la Isla de Cuba* (Havana, 1857).

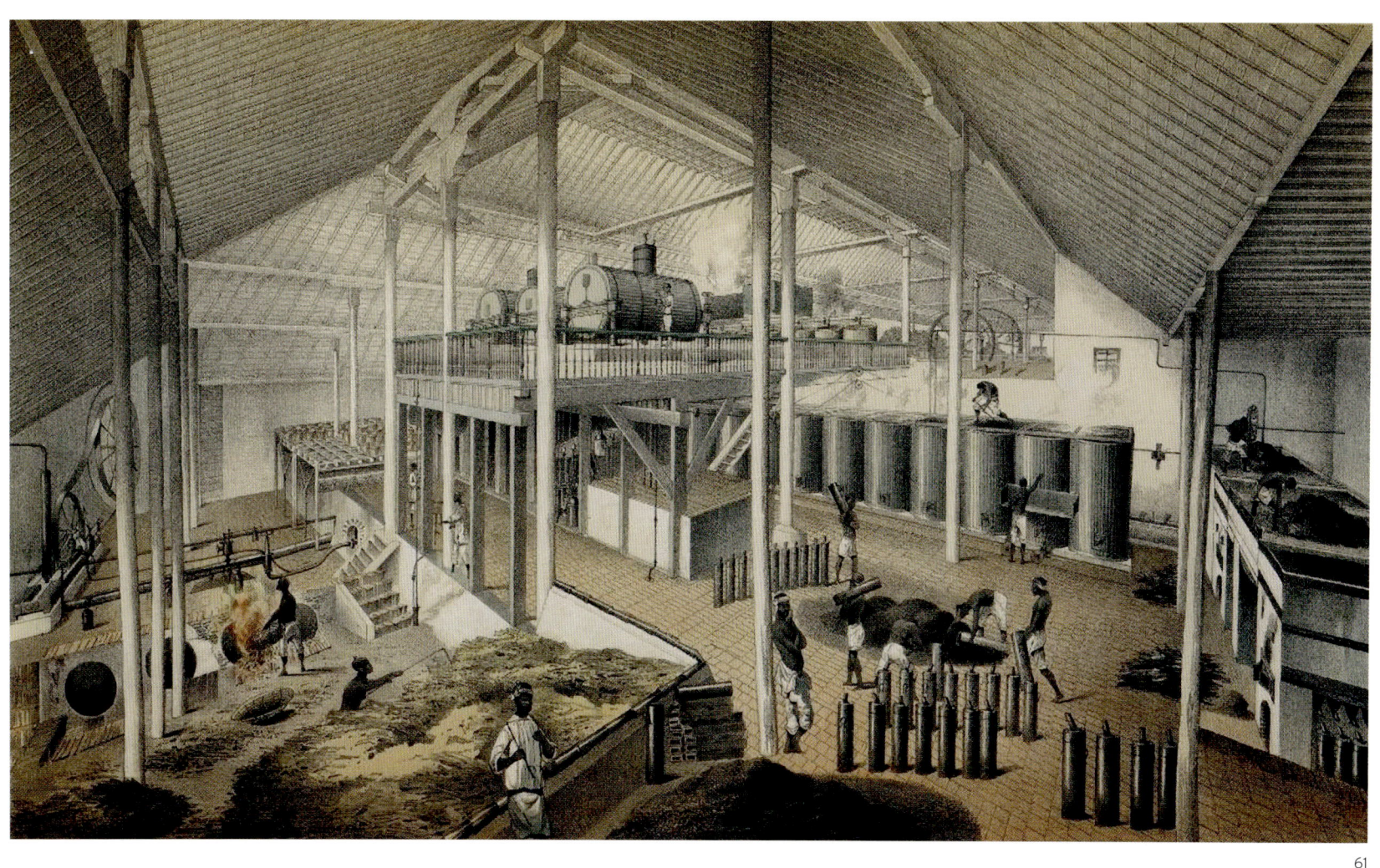

61 Eduardo Laplante. *Boiling House of Asunción Sugar Plantation.* Lithograph. Justo G. Cantero, *Los ingenios: Colección de vistas de los principales ingenios de azúcar de la Isla de Cuba* (Havana, 1857).

62 Víctor Patricio de Landaluze. *Judith Liberates Cuba from the Separatist Rebellion*. Published in *La Sombra* (March 29, 1874). Havana, Biblioteca Nacional José Martí.

modeled after Jacques-Louis David's work for Napoleon, *The Coronation of the Emperor and Empress (1805–1807)* and features portraits of Havana's most prominent residents and their Black domestic workers or enslaved laborers who accompanied them. Despite their anonymity, the Black female handmaiden on the left side of the painting, who gazes intently at the sky, and the finely dressed page or *calesero* (coach driver) near the center of the composition display provocative poses and prominent positions within the scene.[13]

Many images confine Black life to the context of labor, whether in the urban *casa grande* or on the plantation. Eduardo Laplante's lithographs, featured in the 1857 album *The Sugar Mills: Collection of Vistas of the Principal Sugar Mills of Cuba*, imagines slavery in idyllic terms. Laplante (1818–1860) was a French citizen commissioned by a Creole planter to depict the most prominent sugar plantations on the island. The book included descriptive text and statistical breakdowns detailing the modern machinery and productivity profile of each plantation.[14] Over a series of thirteen landscapes and "machinescapes" that shift between panoramic pastoral scenes of sugar estates and indoor views of sugar mill technology in use, Laplante constructs a sanitized image of Cuba's primary industry. Whether the anonymous enslaved people are working with hot, steam-powered machinery or toiling in the fields, slave life is rendered at an emotional and physical distance. The enslaved are either cogs in a mechanical system or thin Black bodies scattered in a natural landscape. It is important to realize that the viewer is not privy to life in the *barracon* (slave quarters), where enslaved Blacks lived under crowded and unhygienic conditions. In depicting prosperous plantations as efficient and orderly places of industry, the project by default claims slavery and sugar cultivation to be a civilizing and modernizing force.[15]

The most significant generator of images of Black people in Cuba was the Spanish artist and caricaturist Víctor Patricio de Landaluze (1828–1889), who moved to the island in 1850. The extensive nature of his production and its ubiquitous presence in books on Cuban history and culture to this day warrant a sustained discussion. Despite his expressed desire for Cuba to remain a Spanish colony—a conviction that led him to join the volunteer military force Los Voluntarios in defense of colonialism—Landaluze was responsible for costumbrista imagery that came to symbolize Cuban cultural sovereignty. He illustrated the first Latin American costumbrista anthology, *Los cubanos pintados por sí mismos* (1851) and later the more lavish *Tipos y costumbres de la isla de Cuba* (1881), which prominently featured Afro-Cuban types. His costumbrista practice occurred simultaneously with his political satire, much of it published in his own journals, that addressed both Creole politics and eventually the Cuban independence movement. His caricatures were especially virulent during the Ten Years' War, when he mocked Black insurgents as intellectually incapable of leadership. In an 1874 caricature, Landaluze retools Johannes Stradanus's 1638 image of Amerigo Vespucci discovering America to portray Spain awakening to a disheveled allegory of the Cuban insurrection, inadequately guarded by a slumming Black man.

To fully grasp the significance of Landaluze's costumbrismo, it is necessary to see it not so much as an inventory of Cuban types and scenes as a representation of the social and racial tensions of his day. While current scholarship has not sufficiently addressed Landaluze's market, it is likely that elite Cuban and Spanish residents purchased and/or commissioned his paintings. Cuban

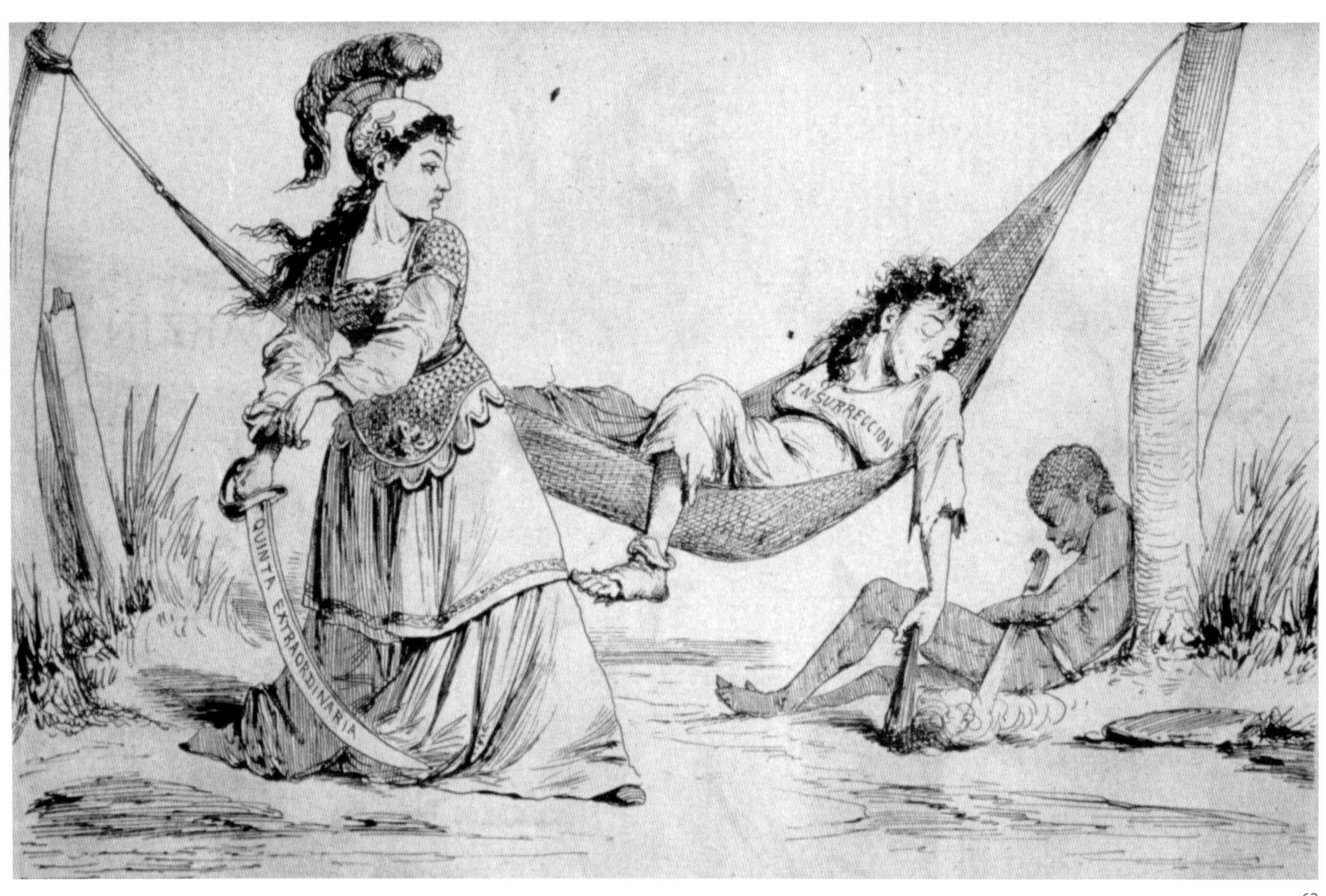

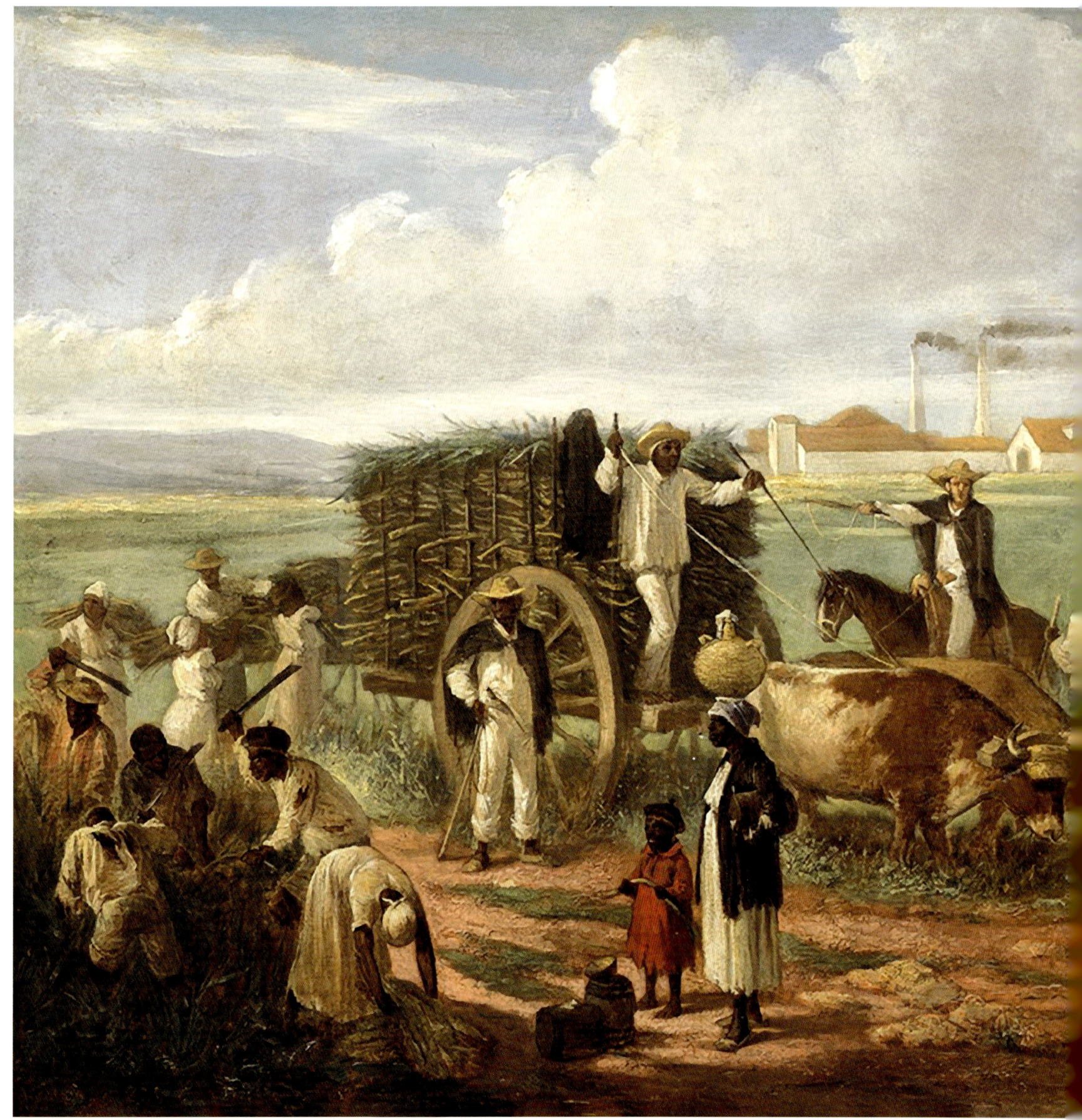

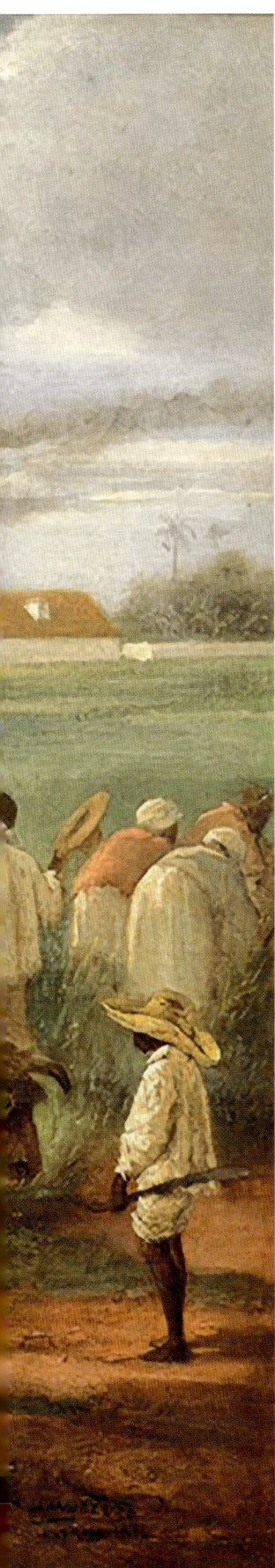

63 Victor Patricio de Landaluze. *Sugarcane Cutting*. 1874. Oil on canvas. Havana, Museo Nacional de Bellas Artes de Cuba.

photography and Landaluze's paintings themselves often depict elite, domestic spaces populated with paintings and prints.¹⁶ In these spaces, Landaluze's works served as emblems of racial power.¹⁷

Unlike much of his costumbrista illustrations that pictured single, isolated figures, Landaluze produced complex narrative paintings that foreground Black degeneracy and the need for continued Spanish colonialism. In fact, many of these paintings function as pairs that reinforce these interrelated ideas. Landaluze's *Corte de caña*, on the one hand, presents a verdant and productive plantation scene that paints a favorable view of the status quo. Here enslaved people of all ages labor peacefully and subordinately under the watchful eye and whip of an overseer, whose position astride a horse allows him to tower above his charges. Landaluze's Epiphany painting, *Día de Reyes en la Habana*, on the other hand, depicts the exact opposite, a world without white authority. It portrays a local variant of the annual Christian celebration held every January 6 in remembrance of the day when the three kings brought gifts to the infant Jesus. As the central scene of the painting readily conveys, in colonial Cuba Epiphany was commonly associated with enslaved and free people of color who came together for a day of carnival-like celebration that inverted the social order. On this occasion, Afro-Cubans would parade, often in ritual garb based on recreated African traditions, and perform in urban centers. Landaluze depicts one costumed reveler splayed on all fours like an animal on the streets of Havana. He also centers our view on an Afro-Cuban "Hottentot Venus" clad in a vivid green dress whose large buttocks indicate her physical depravity.¹⁸ Contemporaneous accounts conform to these interpretations. One nineteenth-century spectator described the scene: "Countless groups of *comparsas* of African negroes go through

THE UNREPRESENTABLE 137

64 Victor Patricio de Landaluze. *Epiphany in Havana*. Early to mid-1870s. Oil on canvas. Havana, Museo Nacional de Bellas Artes de Cuba.

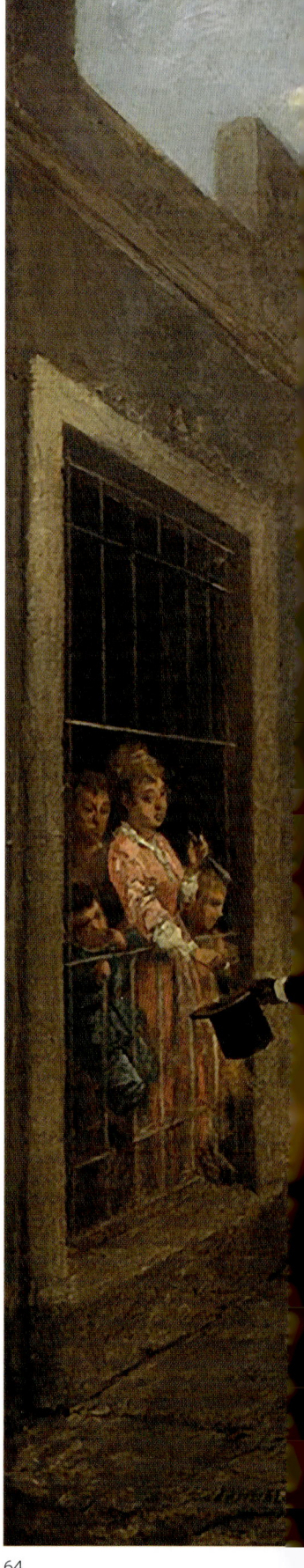

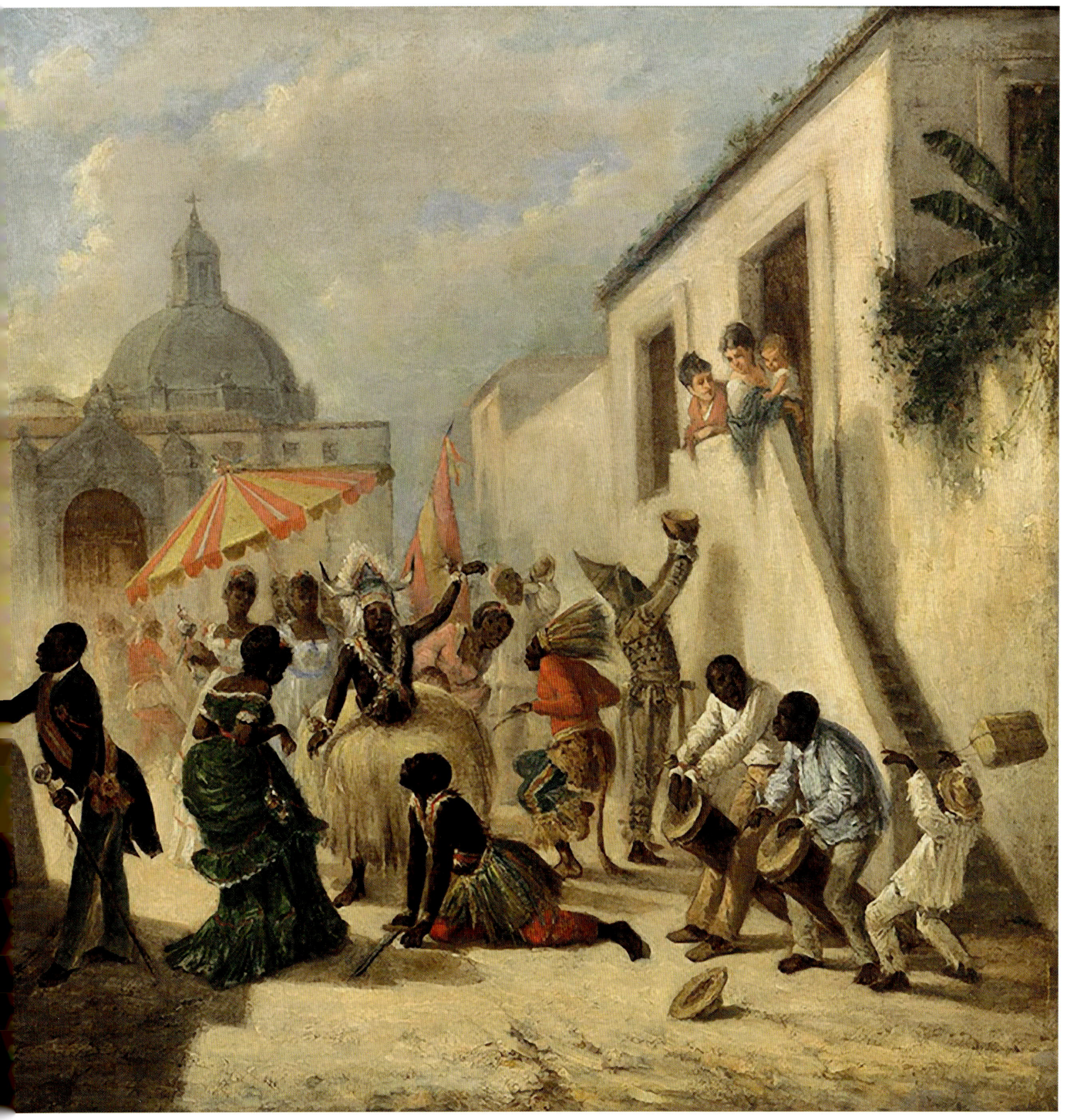

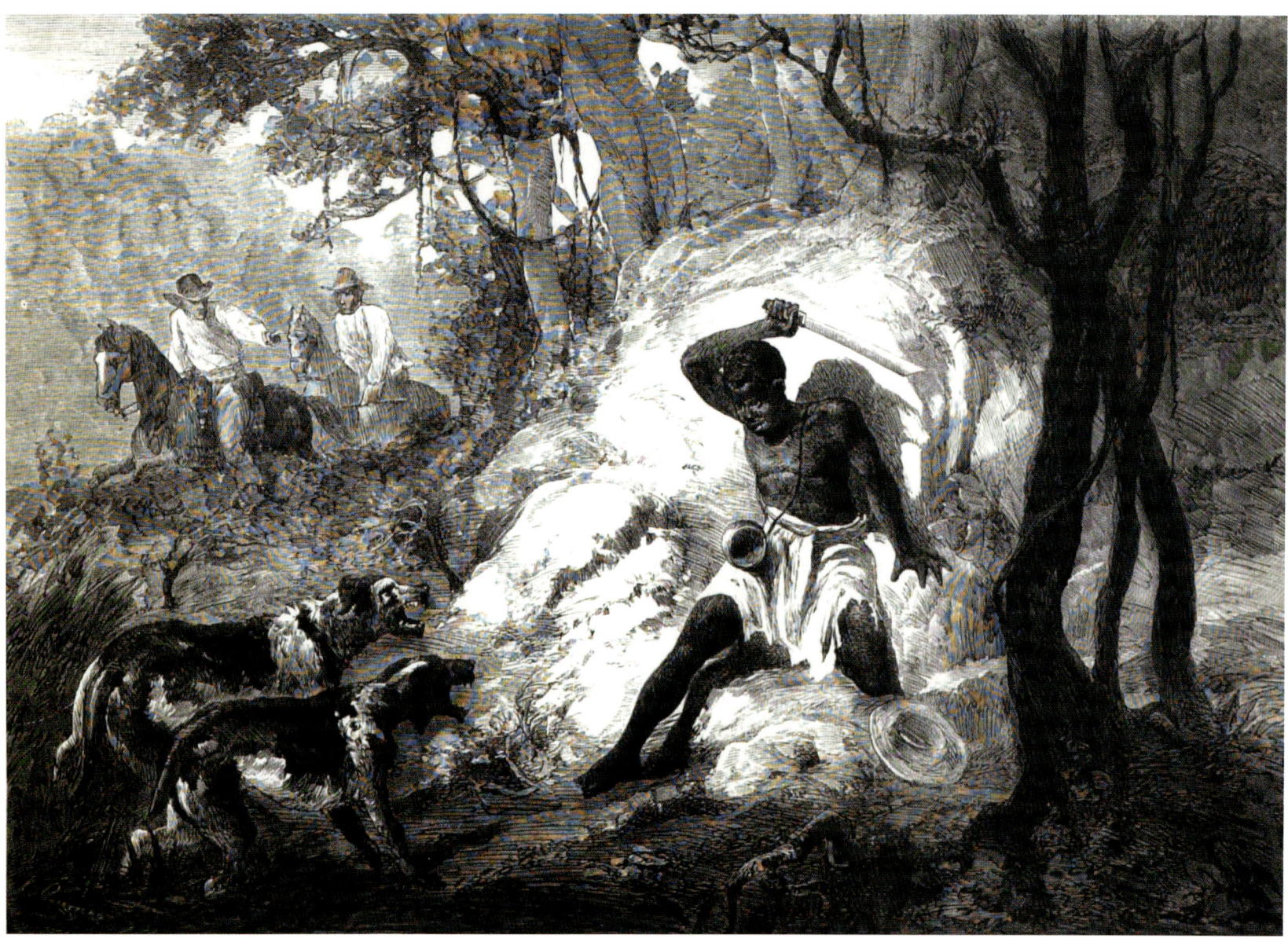
65

the streets of the capital; the crowd is huge, its aspect horrific. … The costumes of the negro kings [include] lambskin complete with tail. … All half-naked, kings and subjects, in their different groups, form the most repugnant sight possible to the eyes of civilized man."[19] Created during Cuba's first war of independence, Landaluze's works tap into the fear and idea that only a Spanish presence could forestall Cuba's racial demise into Blackness.

The messages encoded in Landaluze's paintings reached a wide audience because many were reproduced and discussed in popular illustrated weeklies like *La Ilustración Española y Americana*. The articles that accompany representations of freed and enslaved Afro-Cubans hail their good life on plantations and in wealthy homes, advocate continued Spanish colonialism, and generally express a disdain for Black life. One issue from 1875 presents an image of a runaway slave, which is based on a painting by Landaluze and the Cuban landscapist Esteban Chartrand (1840–1883).[20] In both the painting and reproduction, a runaway slave in tattered clothes wields his machete to protect himself

65 Victor Patricio de Landaluze and Esteban Chartand, after. *Runaway Slave*. 1875. Wood engraving. *La Ilustración Española y Americana* (September 22, 1875).

against two violent attack dogs ready to maul him. In the painting, an orangey-red stain on the ground suggests that the dogs have already successfully attacked. In the related article, the Spanish writer José Triay uses the occasion to debate whether poetry or painting is a more truthful art form. How is it possible to argue aesthetics over an image that pits vicious animals against a human being? To do so reveals a disturbing disregard for the value of Black life.

Landaluze's costumbrismo and caricature also focused intently on the figure of the *mulata* as a key type that captured Cuba's cultural uniqueness and represented the island's racial quagmire. Since the beginning of the conquest, the lack of female colonists meant that Spanish men sought sexual partners among native and African women on the island. The norm for these unions was concubinage, and the demographic result was a significant mixed-race population. Over time, this history coalesced into what can be called the lore of the mulata—a kind of informally inherited knowledge that legitimized racialized sexual exploitation by blaming the victim. By the first half of the nineteenth century, these stories found their way into scientific texts, theater productions, popular music, and early manifestations of costumbrista literature, cementing a picture of the mulata as a hypersexual, transgressive, and at times tragic female type, attracted to white and Black suitors alike. Themes of racial intermixture infiltrated political discourse as well, as some elite Creoles advocated for *blanqueamiento*, or whitening through a continual process of racial mixing, by welcoming white, working-class settlements.

The lore of the mulata found its most elaborate expression in small cigarette lithographs called *marquillas*, which were used to bundle and sell cigarettes.[21] Tobacco was a major industry in Cuba, second only to sugar, and by the 1850s cigarettes had become widely popular among all sectors of Cuban society. During the 1860s, cigarette manufacturers turned to chromolithography to create attractive and visually seductive packaging that often employed a full range of marketing gimmicks intended to encourage repeat customers.[22] Marquilla images that focused on aspects of Cuban life were a legacy of costumbrismo.

These tiny and attractive works of art (most were around four by five inches in size), recirculated other manifestations of Cuban visual culture, like Laplante's ascetic views of Cuban plantations, and regularly traded in racial caricatures that portrayed grotesque and animal-like Black bodies. Several brands manufactured serial productions devoted to the life and death of the mulata. The brand La Charanga de Villergas—titled after a satirical journal that collaborated with Landaluze into the late 1850s—produced the most extensive of all. Over a series of fifteen narrative scenes, consumers see and read about the birth and demise of the mulata. The first scene pictures her origin: she derives from the coupling of a Black woman and a humble white Spaniard. In the third part of the story, a very young mulata prematurely solicits a young white boy. Later scenes show the mulata in her prime, being courted by wealthy suitors donning top hats. By the end of the narrative, her moral downfall has begun, suggested by her disheveled state and renewed contact with other Afro-Cubans. *The Life and Death of the Mulata* is both moralistic and voyeuristic and recalls William Hogarth's *A Harlot's Progress*.[23] As in Hogarth's narrative, the mulata's moral corruption eventually leads to her death. This tragic culmination of the mulata's life reinforces ideas found in popular scientific studies of social degeneracy in Cuba. One of the most virulent treatises, *Prostitution*

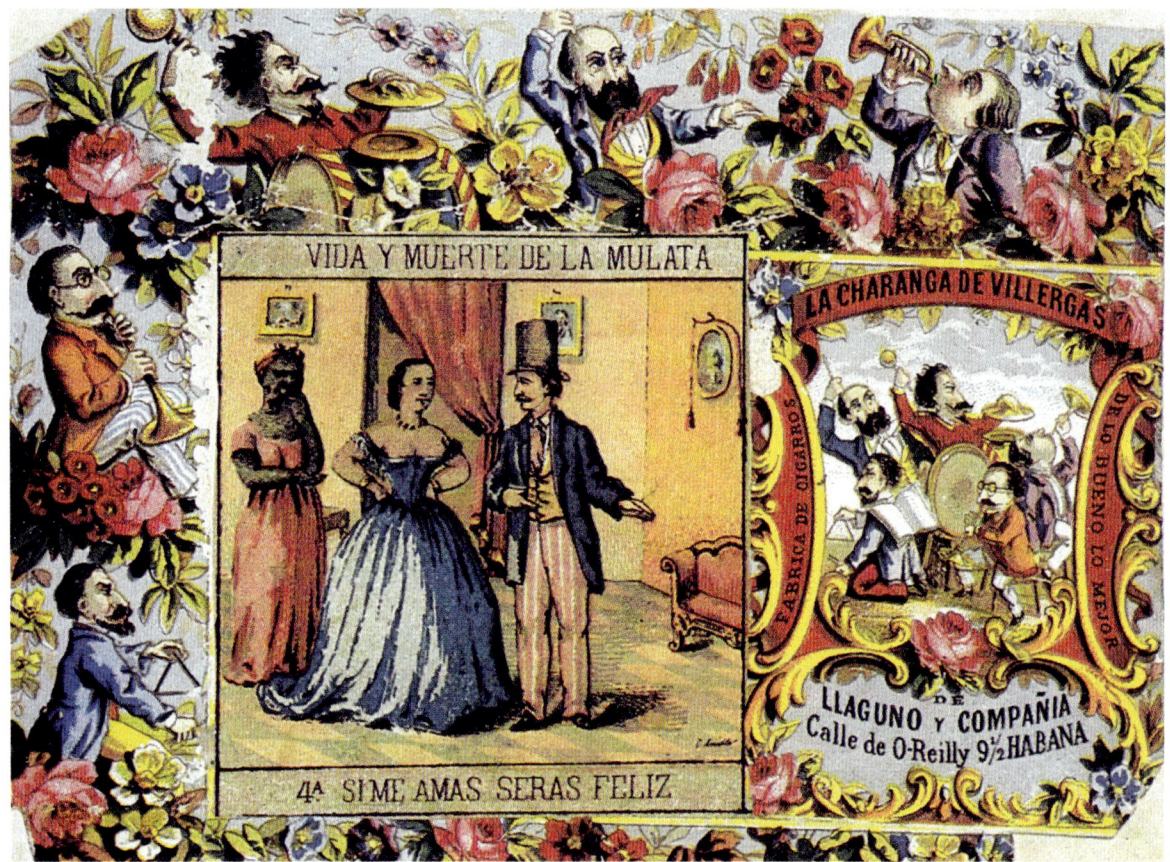

66

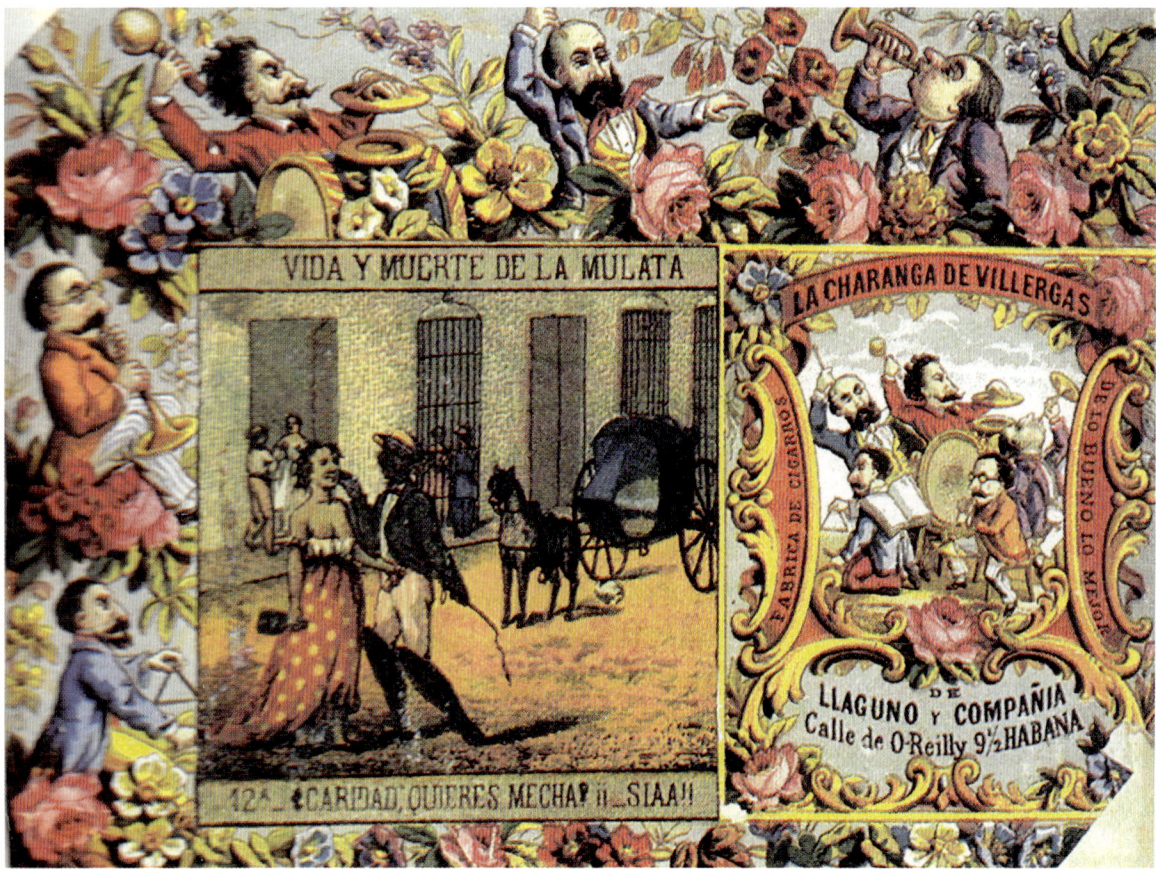

67

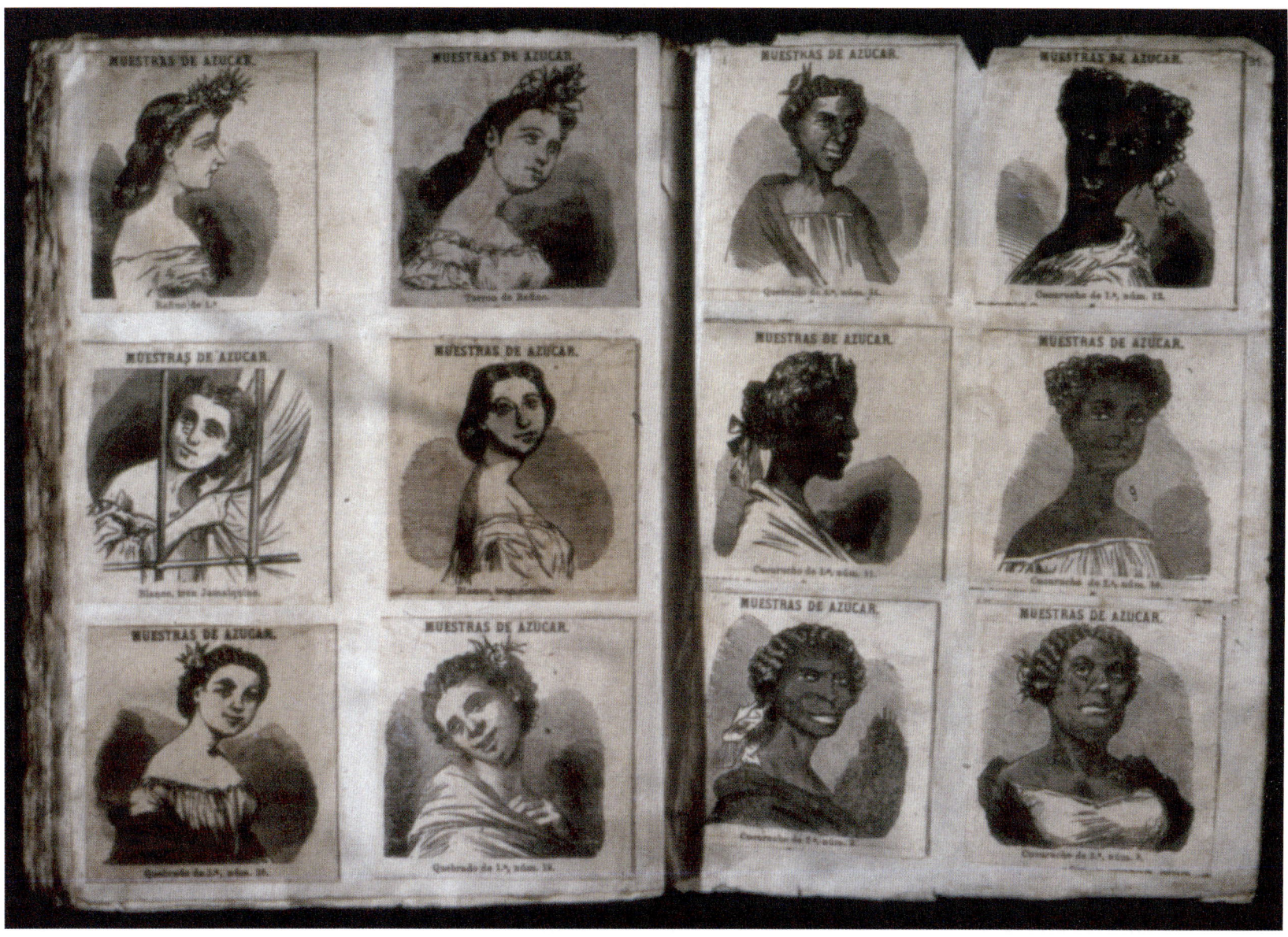

66 La Charanga de Villergas (cigarette factory). *"If You Love Me, You Will Be Happy."* 1860s. Color lithograph. From the series *Life and Death of the Mulata*, no. 4. Havana, Biblioteca Nacional José Martí.

67 La Charanga de Villergas (cigarette factory). *"Caridad, Want Me to Light You Up?"* 1860s. Color lithograph. From the series *Life and Death of the Mulata*, no. 12. Havana, Biblioteca Nacional José Martí.

68 Album of cigarette covers with different Havana brands. 1864. Seville, Spain, Archivo General de Indias.

69 Víctor Patricio de Landaluze. *Spirit Dancer*. 1881. Lithograph. New York Public Library.

in the City of Havana (1888), speaks to the discomfort many Creoles felt in accepting the new social order after emancipation. Written by the Creole social hygienist Benjamin de Céspedes, he presents the mulata as the paradigmatic prostitute. For Céspedes, "the black race is the origin of all or our misfortunes … and the vehicle of our misery."[24]

As the marquillas themselves reveal, costumbrismo insidiously penetrated daily life. Marquillas and journal illustrations were actively collected and arranged in scrapbooks meant to be studied and enjoyed in times of leisure. A scrapbook deposited in the Archive of the Indies in Seville features images from one of Landaluze's satirical journals that compared women of different racial hues to a hierarchy of grades of sugar. The maker of this album repeated (and internalized) Landaluze's hierarchy and placed white women at the apex of the group, mulatas near the middle, and the darkest-skinned (and most visually caricatured) women at the very bottom.

New Readings and Black Responses
Many costumbrista representations function like double-edged swords: they capture aspects of emergent diasporic culture, yet strip people of African descent of their intellectual and social worth. For example, we now recognize that Landaluze's detailed rendition of a ñáñigo, or a member of the all-male Abakuá secret society, evinces the strong links between Afro-Cuban and West African Ekpe/Ngbe ritual costuming practices.[25] Yet when this image was published in *Tipos y costumbres de la isla de Cuba* in 1881, Enrique Fernández Carrillo, the second chief of the Havana police, wrote the accompanying essay describing ñáñigos as atavistic and savage criminals.[26] In his early writings, the Cuban ethnologist and cultural critic Fernando Ortiz concurred. Ortiz treats many of Landaluze's preferred Afro-Cuban types in his first major book *The Afro-Cuban Underworld: The Black Witches* (1906). Written under the influence and guidance of the Italian criminologist and positivist Cesare Lombroso, Ortiz presented Afro-Cuban spirituality under the umbrella of criminality and notions of biologically determined social deviance.[27] The disdain that characterizes Ortiz's turn-of-the-century study is more resonant with how many nineteenth-century audiences viewed Afro-Cuban subjects rather than Ortiz's later, more reformed perspectives that hailed Afro-Cuban culture as a Cuban national treasure.

Even though Landaluze and others shrouded African diasporic practices in a veil of barbarism, they also inadvertently recorded the reinvention of tradition in a new context. An 1860s carte de visite of an Epiphany festival comparsa offers another view of Afro-Cuban types that figure prominently in Cuban costumbrismo. As Judith Bettelheim has noted, the staging of this ensemble conveys a knowledge of *cabildo* practices that suggests the participation of the sitters.[28] (Cabildos were mutual aid societies sanctioned by the Spanish government that allowed people of the same African cultural group to meet and gain emotional sustenance and financial support during times of need.) The centrality of the cabildo queen, the drummers' position astride their *yuka* drums, and their costuming which resurrects known African traditions, convey not only the resourcefulness of the diaspora, but its defiant response to oppression.

The Afro-Cuban press, especially in the decade following the Ten Years' War, defended Afrodescendant populations, and to a limited degree, employed images in their fight. In response to

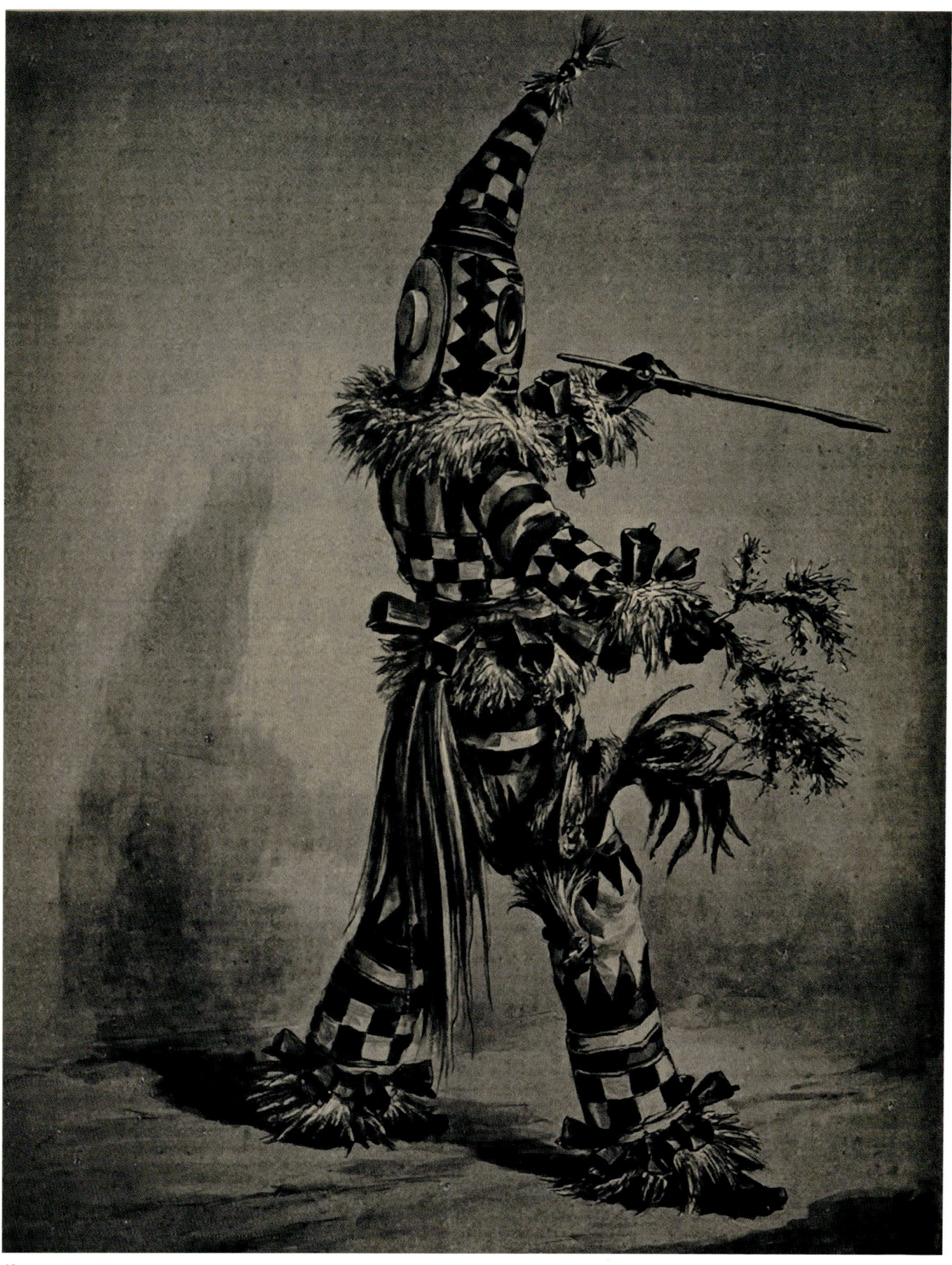
69

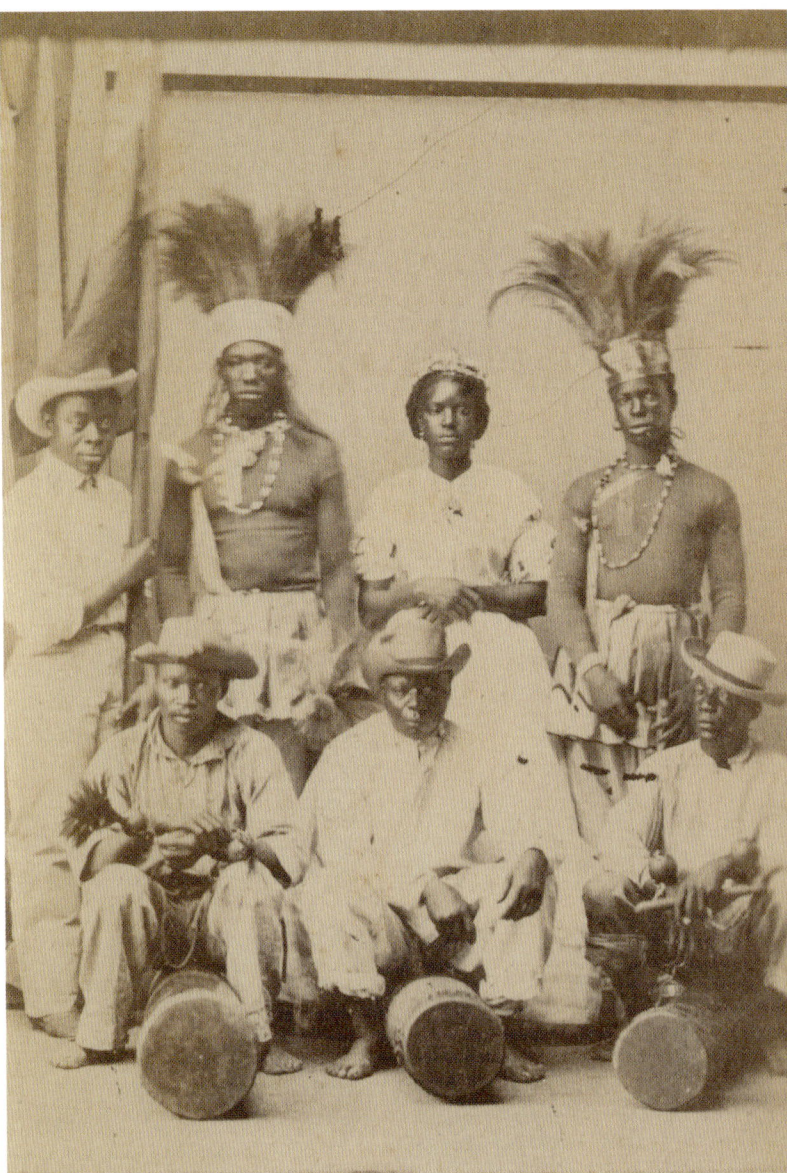

70

70 C. D. Fredricks. *Cabildo Group Carte de Visite*. Havana. 1860. New York, Schomburg Center for Research in Black Culture.

rampant public claims of Black female immorality, middle-class Afro-Cuban writers offered dramatically different narratives about Black and white sexual relations. Africa Céspedes explains that Afro-Cuban virgins, or *señoritas*, fell victim to the insatiable sexual desires of the white men who enslaved them. In doing so, she presents Afro-Cuban women as victims rather than as instigators of sexual immorality.[29] In 1888, the journal *Minerva* became the first publication catering to Afro-Cuban women. The modest journal published prose, poetry, and instructional articles meant to support and hail the domestic role of Black women as wives and mothers. In one instance, the journal presented a formal portrait of one of its contributors, Úrsula de Valverde, whose nickname was Cecilia, in a manner suggesting her individuality and married status were connoted by the "de" before her surname.[30] Demurely looking off to the side, dressed in a formal gown that covers her shoulders and arms, this portrait image shrouds Sra. Valverde in an aura of social respectability commonly conferred on white Creole women. This image adopts the conventions of European portraiture to contest the rampant image of Black female immorality that actively circulated in popular culture.

Black imagery produced and circulated during the pivotal years when Cuba and Puerto Rico struggled for independence

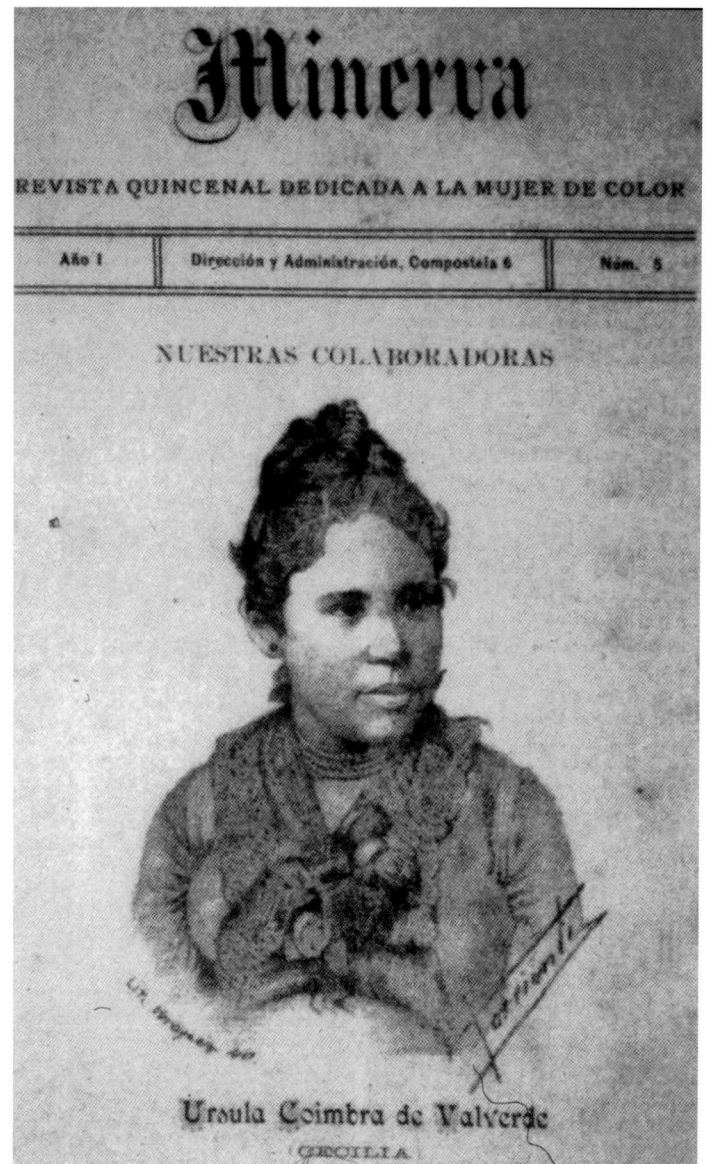

71

71 Torriente. *Úrsula de Valverde,* editor of the Cuban periodical *Minerva* in 1888–1889. Havana, Instituto de Literatura y Lingüísticas.

and emancipation both reinforced oppressive racial and colonial regimes and at times upheld the humanity of Black subjects, even if primarily in retrospect. Images of Black people appeared in civic spaces, churches, domestic homes, and journals and on consumer objects, where they stimulated public debates about who belongs, and in what way, to striving but not yet fully formed nations. The works discussed here had the power to shape the beliefs of emergent citizens, as well as to inform the foundational historical narratives of an important region within Latin America at the cusp of the twentieth century.

7

INDIVIDUAL AND TYPE:
THE LIMITS OF SELF-REPRESENTATION IN THE ERA OF PORTRAITURE, 1800-1880

NATALIA MAJLUF

José Gil de Castro (Lima, 1785–1837), the man who portrayed the most important Creole leaders of South American independence, did not paint his own portrait. No image of him has survived, and it is improbable that one would have existed. From a family who was formerly enslaved, he had trained in the painting workshops of colonial Lima before establishing himself as the most prestigious portraitist of Chile. Yet unlike Mexico, where painters emerged from the middle sectors of Spanish or Creole descent, in the Andean region, and especially in the viceroyalty of Peru, painting was a profession largely assumed by Indians, Afrodescendants, and people of mixed ethnicities. This could help explain that while a number of self-portraits of Mexican artists exist, no South American painter of this period is known to have painted a portrait of himself.[1] In a broader perspective, portraiture would come remarkably late to Afrodescendants in Spanish America, even in the course of the nineteenth century, the period that saw the greatest democratization of the genre.

In the case of Gil de Castro, it could be argued that this visual absence is somehow compensated for by his textual presence, through the more than one hundred narrative signatures painted on the front or back of his numerous portraits of the leaders of Independence. In 1821, for example, he signed the portrait of the Chilean head of government Bernardo O'Higgins with the inscription: "He was faithfully painted by army Captain José Gil, second cosmographer, member of the topographic table and Antigraphist (portraitist) of the Supreme Director: Year 1821." In other signatures he described himself as "citizen," "first portraitist," or "professor," among various designations. In the changing forms of writing his own name, one can read the aspirations of a man who was keenly aware of the revolutionary promises of an egalitarian society, formed by citizens equal before the law. Yet what may be deduced about his own life from fragmentary documentation allows us to imagine that these aspirations were not borne out in the early years of the republic. Independence, no more than freedom from slavery, did not end discrimination against Afrodescendants nor change their subaltern social status. In a society marked by racism, in which the gaze is deployed as an active instrument in the definition of ethnic categories, the self-portrait of an Afrodescendant would expose his skin color, the very element upon which society based its structures of discrimination. One could speculate that his extended signatures allowed Gil de Castro to assert his presence and achievements in the abstract terms of textual inscriptions, an option that avoided exposing himself to the racist gaze.[2]

72

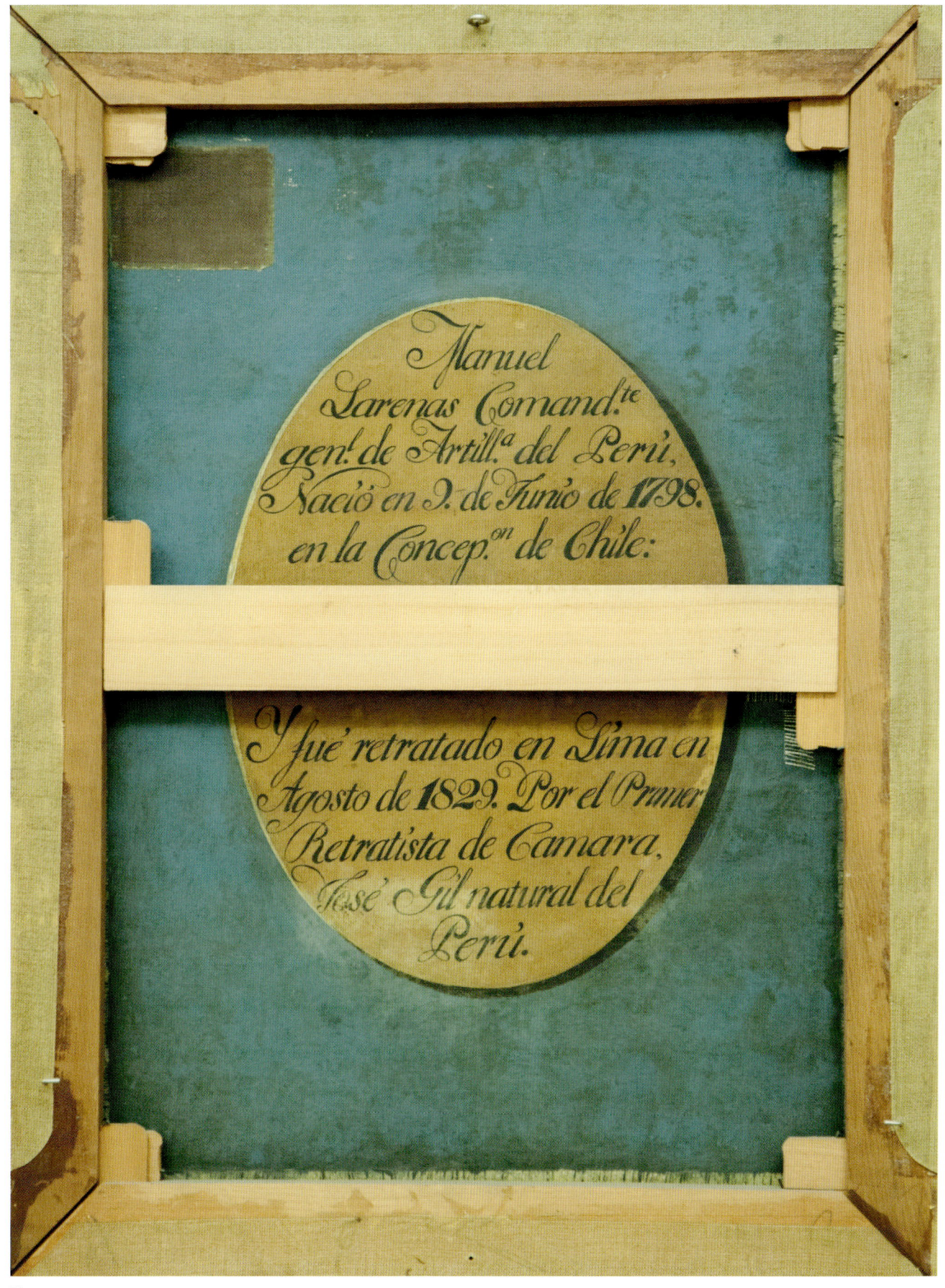

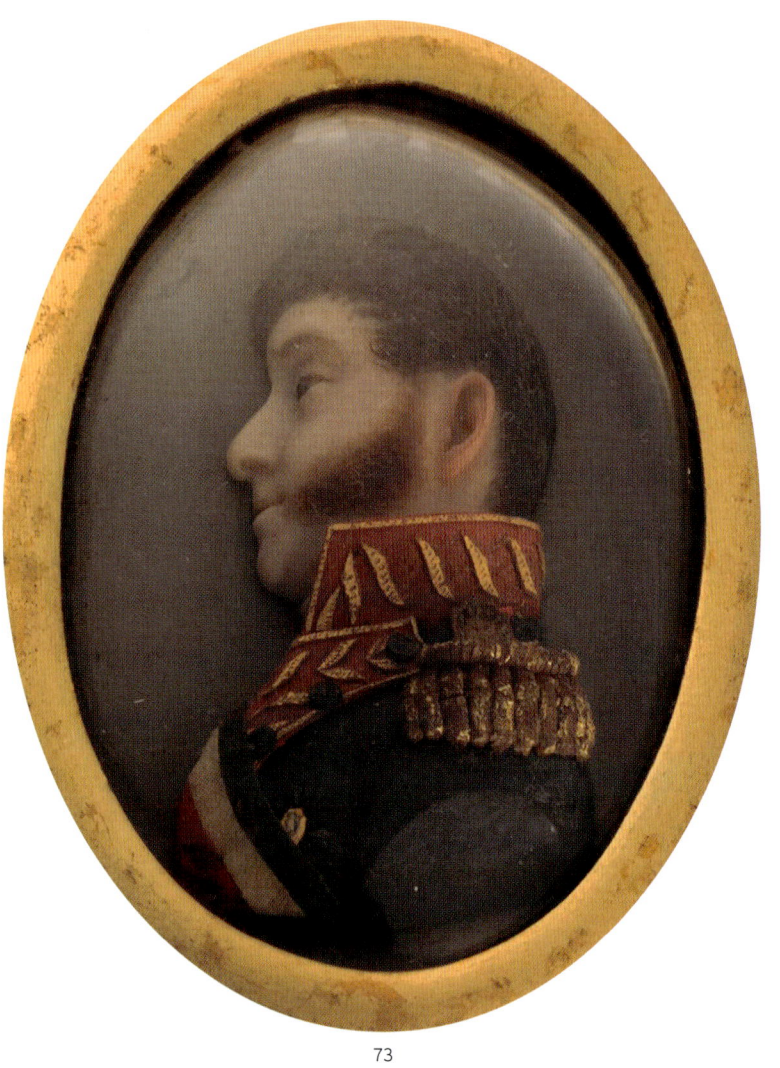

73

72 José Gil de Castro. Reverse of the *Portrait of Manuel Larenas y Álvarez Rubio*. 1829. Oil on canvas. Santiago, Chile, Museo Histórico Nacional.

73 José Francisco Rodríguez. *Vicente Guerrero*. Ca. 1828. Wax. Mexico City, Museo Nacional de Historia, INAH.

74 Carlos Guevara. *Juan Álvarez*. 1853. Oil on canvas. Mexico City, Museo Nacional de Historia, INAH.

Of the large number of portraits Gil de Castro painted over a period of more than two decades, most represent Europeans or Creoles of the highest social standing. The one exception is his posthumous full-length portrait of the indigenous hero José Olaya, commissioned by the Peruvian state (Museo Nacional de Arqueología, Antropología e Historia del Perú, Lima). One may imagine that Gil de Castro somehow identified with Olaya, whose skin he painted in a tone so dark that many have confused it with a portrait of an Afrodescendant.[3] One may also consider a similar degree of identification or at least an affinity with the figure of the liberator Simón Bolívar, broadly denounced by his detractors as leading an army of Blacks and of being himself of mixed origin.

In the early portraits, based on previous representations, Gil de Castro painted his skin color in darker tones, an element that, significantly, changed drastically in the official portraits Bolívar later commissioned directly from the painter in Lima.[4]

The wars of Spanish American independence had in fact been fought by armies composed largely of people of indigenous or African descent.[5] Yet very few such soldiers and officers emerged from anonymity in the foundational narratives and imagery produced in the years following the wars, an invisibility that is very literally borne out in the scarce number of known portraits, limited to figures who rose above the limitations of racial inequality to achieve prominent positions in postcolonial society.[6] Such is the

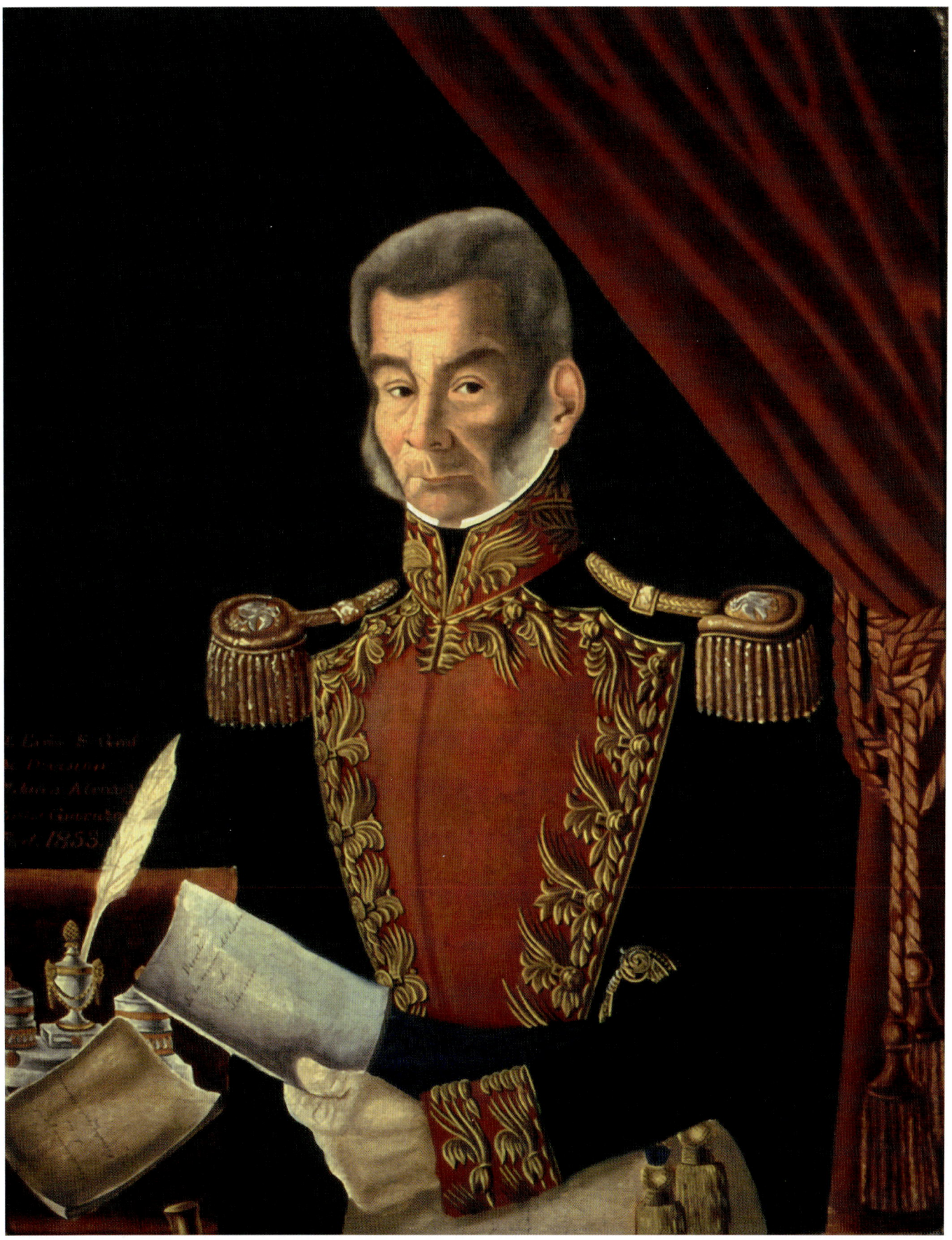
74

75 Unidentified artist. *José Romero*. Ca. 1850–1865. Oil on canvas. Santiago, Chile. Museo Histórico Nacional.

case of Vicente Guerrero (Tixtla, 1782–Cuilapan, Oaxaca, 1831), the military hero and politician who held the Mexican presidency in 1829. Guerrero was no doubt one of the most influential Afrodescendants in early republican Mexico, which probably explains the significant number of portraits of him that have come down to us. As María Dolores Ballesteros Páez has noted, his images are marked by stark contrasts, between those that portray him with light skin and straight hair to those that only slightly emphasize signs of a darker skin color and curled hair. The ambivalence is a sign of how contested his ethnic standing could be in contemporary political discussion, in which his enemies generally framed their attacks through offenses relating to his origins and ethnic status.[7] Among his earliest portraits, produced in his lifetime and probably from contemporary likenesses, are a group of wax miniatures, part of a popular typology produced for broad consumption.[8] And while there are few elements that would allow an evaluation of how faithful they were to the original, they were most likely not directly commissioned by Guerrero but instead created as part of a much broader commercial production of heroic imagery that circulated widely in early republican Mexico.

The distinction is crucial for portraiture and identity, as it brings into sight the complex issue of agency, the crucial matter of who assumes power over representation. So it is significant that the portrait of Guerrero's fellow insurgent and politician Juan Álvarez (Atoyac, 1790–La Providencia, 1867) was in all likelihood commissioned directly by the sitter. Painted during the period in which Álvarez served as governor of Guerrero, the state he had contributed to found in 1849, it was probably intended to be hung in the seat of regional government, much like the painting of his friend and partner in arms Vicente Guerrero he had previously commissioned for the regional congress at Chilpancingo.[9] He sits in full military dress next to a table that signals his office and clasps in his hand the founding decree of the state of Guerrero, which he holds out to the viewer. The painting was made in 1853, at a moment when his political ambitions were at their height, merely months before his participation in the Plan of Ayutla, which led to the overthrow of President Antonio López de Santa Anna and, subsequently, gained Álvarez the Mexican presidency in 1855.[10] Painted by Carlos Guevara, a forgotten regional artist, it stands as one of the few portraits of the period known to have been directly commissioned by an Afrodescendant. No doubt made from life, the artist sought to offer a true likeness of the aging politician, one that could stand as a memorial to this notable cacique, or local leader. It is significant that it was painted for a region in which he was a respected and powerful figure and not in the capital, where he is known to have been subjected to racist attacks and where Álvarez himself claimed not to feel at home.[11] Clearly, even those who rose to the highest political office could not overcome the social stigma associated with Afrodescendant status. The relative position of different groups in the social hierarchy had not changed substantially with independence.

As expected from societies where Afrodescendants rarely rose above the lesser ranks in politics and in the military, portraits of other Black protagonists of the wars of independence are extremely rare. Among the exceptions is that of the Chilean officer José Romero (Santiago, 1794–1858), made sometime in the 1850s, shortly before his death. Doubtless painted from life, he is shown seated and in uniform, bearing the silver medal of Maipú, awarded to those who bravely fought in one of the major battles of the South American wars. Significantly, though Gil de Castro

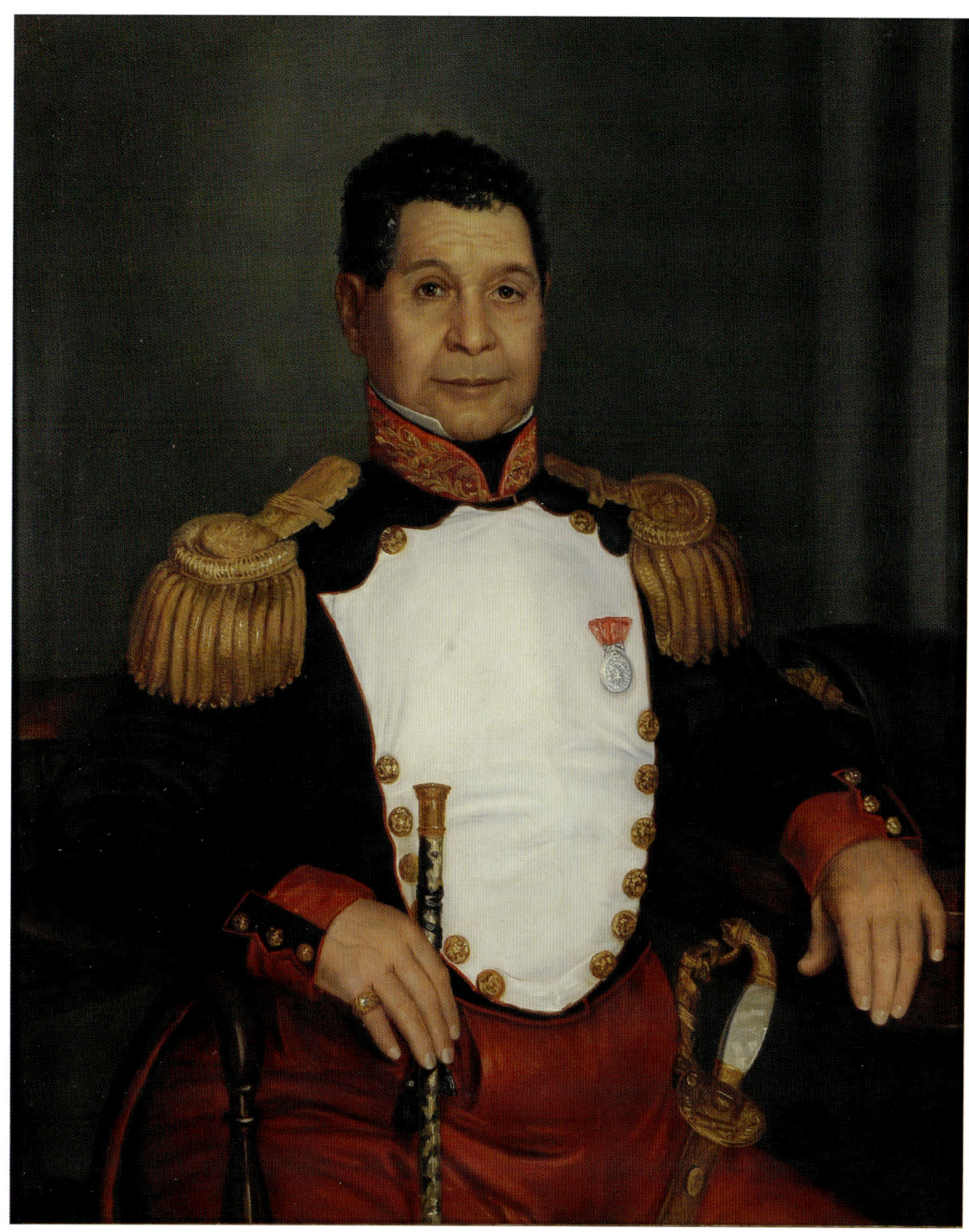
75

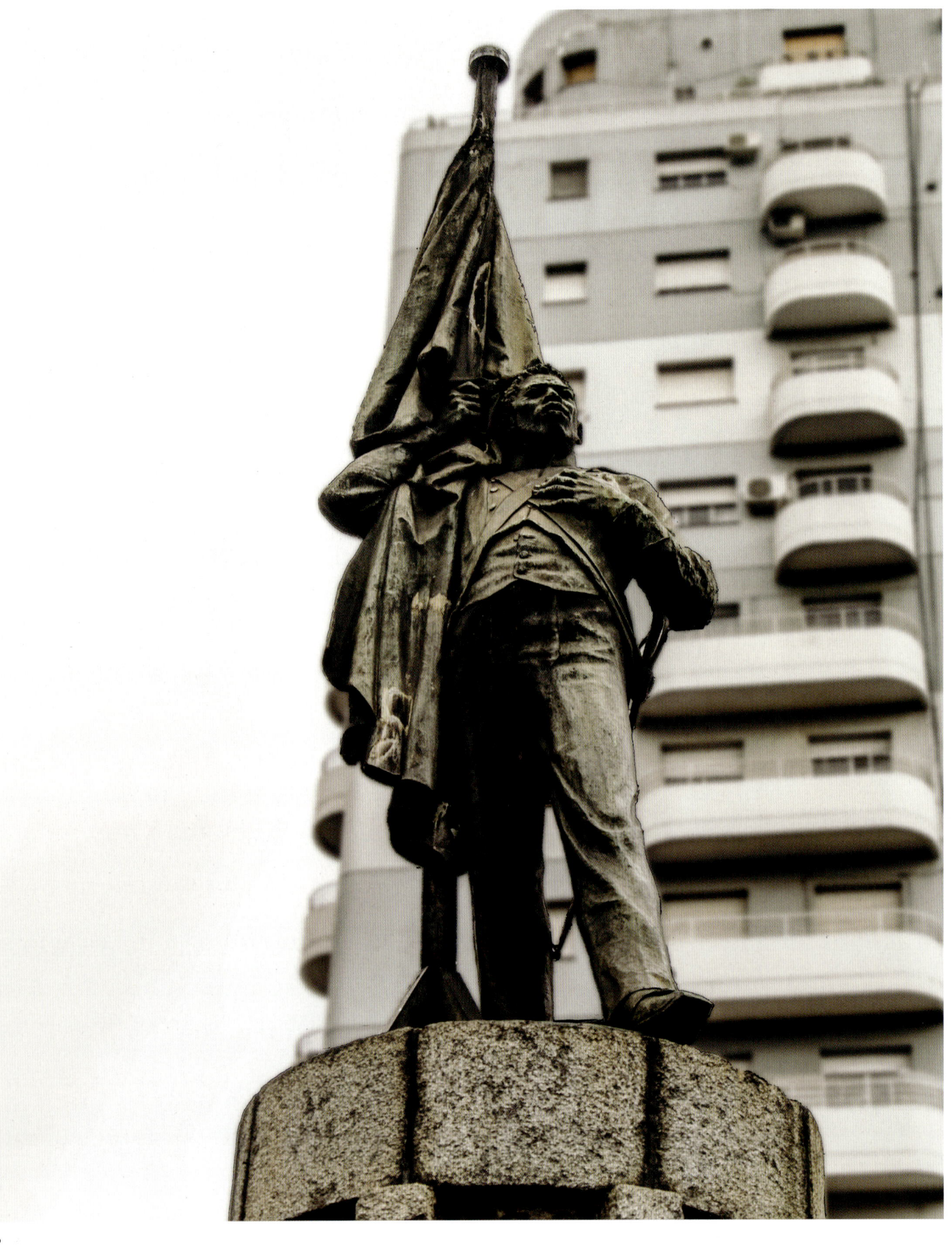

76

76 Lucio Correa Morales. *Public Monument to Antonio Ruiz ("Falucho").* 1897. Bronze. Buenos Aires, Argentina.

briefly coincided with him in the same battalion of Afrodescendants known as the Infantes de la Patria, he did not paint Romero's portrait, though he did portray most high-ranking foreign and Creole officers of the patriot armies in the years immediately following independence.[12] Nothing is known of the circumstances of the commission, though we may assume Romero had some degree of participation in the making of his own portrait. Though not a man of means, since the early 1830s he had served as officer and aide-de-camp of the Chamber of Deputies and had emerged as a sort of popular benefactor and philanthropist who attended petitions, visited prisons, and used his access to power to lobby for pardons. By the time of his death in 1858, he had achieved great popularity. His funeral, attended by prominent politicians and artisan guilds alike, became a public event of some importance in Santiago, to the point that the poet Mercedes Marín del Solar devoted a poem to his memory.[13] There is evidence that, over the following decades, his portrait would be broadly distributed through prints and photographs.[14] Romero had become the ideal citizen for Chilean elites, a token Afrodescendant who could be instrumental as a model figure in the construction of popular allegiances.

A similar role was given to the figure of Antonio Ruiz, whose heroic death was first narrated, and possibly invented, by the Argentine statesman Bartolomé Mitre. It is significant that although there is no evidence of the soldier's existence, his story, and not that of better-documented Afrodescendant heroes of independence, should have become the exemplary foundational narrative of Black Argentina. Popularly known as Falucho, a name that was commonly used to designate Afrodescendants in the revolutionary armies of the River Plate,[15] Ruiz's historical intangibility would in fact be one of the explicit reasons he came to be elevated above his peers by Argentinian elites.[16] "Let us honor in Falco," the congressman Francisco Quesada stated in 1894, "that race of valiant Blacks."[17] The public monument sculpted by Lucio Correa Morales that was erected in Buenos Aires in 1897 was thus actually the portrait of a race rather than of a historical figure, more a type than a portrait. The use of a nickname itself can be read as a sign of condescension, in many ways no different from the ubiquitous "*mulato*" preceding every mention of Gil de Castro's name, or from the derogatory "*Zambo-peluca*" commonly used for Sergeant Mayor José Romero, designations that wrest dignity and individuality from these historical figures while also demoting them to the status of social types. In more than one way, Falucho, too, came to be remembered as an anonymous soldier with a proper name.

In the arena of public representation, full formal names were largely the privilege of elites, as was the production of paintings.[18] During the colonial period Afrodescendants had barely even appeared as anonymous subsidiary figures in other people's portraits, whether as enslaved people or servants.[19] Individual portraits were altogether exceptional, and only a few religious paintings in which castes appear as proud donors or devoted Christians have been identified. One rare case is an Ecuadorian portrait of a musician kneeling next to his instrument in pious devotion before a court of saints and celestial figures engaged in music. He is depicted schematically, within an allegorical system of representation in which images had an essentially religious function and were not intended to provide a true likeness of the subject portrayed. Such devotional portraits in fact only surface in the very late eighteenth century, in the context of the rise of

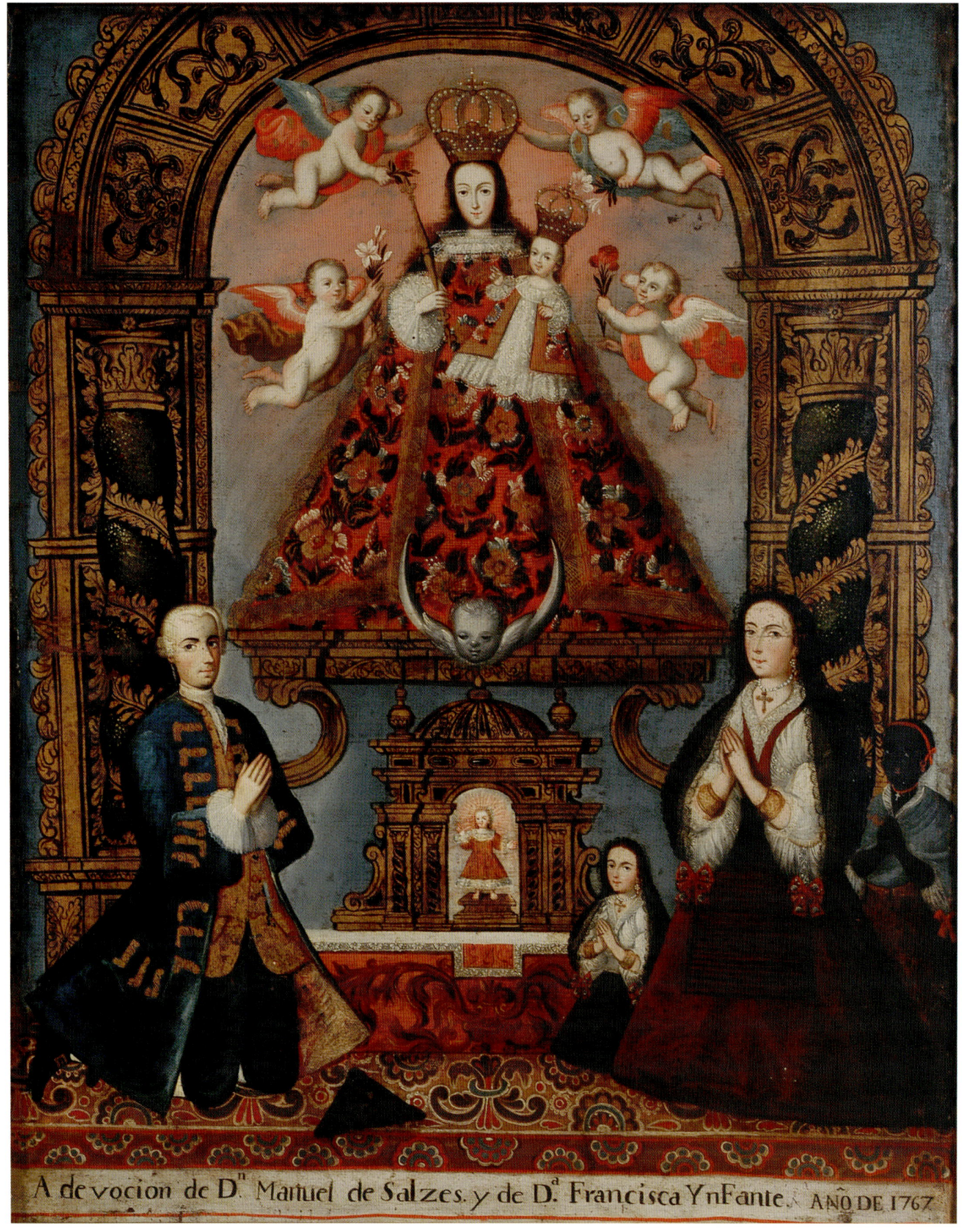

77

77 Unidentified artist. *Virgin with Donors Don Manuel de Salzes y de Doña Francisca Infante*. 1767. Oil on canvas with gold leaf. Santiago, Chile, Museo Nacional de Bellas Artes.

78 Juan Lovera. *Lino Gallardo*. 1830. Oil on canvas. Caracas, Venezuela, Galería de Arte Nacional.

79 Unidentified artist. *Eladia Gallardo*. Ca. 1822. Oil on canvas. Caracas, Venezuela, Galería de Arte Nacional.

portraiture and the greater opportunities for social mobility that were open to artisans and tradespeople in urban contexts.[20]

The rarity of such images responds not only to the high price of acquiring a portrait of oneself, especially an oil painting, but also to factors relating to specific cultural habits and the relative social rank of Afrodescendants in different cities across the Americas. In places like Caracas, where Afrodescendants comprised almost half of the total population, their social and political presence was also greater than in other Spanish American cities. Not all Afrodescendants shared the same status. The higher standing of lighter-skinned *pardos beneméritos* was gained through participation in militias, *gracias al sacar*,[21] and other means of social ascent, all of which usually involved separating themselves from less privileged Afrodescendants.[22]

The portrait of the *pardo* musician Lino Gallardo (Ocumare del Tuy, ca. 1773–Caracas, 1837), composer, violinist, and founder of a music academy and a philharmonic society in Caracas, asserts his high social standing. In this work by Juan Lovera (Caracas, 1776–1841), himself a distinguished Afrodescendant who taught painting in the same institution where Gallardo offered music lessons, he is shown proudly holding his instrument, a sign of his cultivated profession. In the lower corner, a sheet of music with a patriotic composition emphasizes his early adherence to the cause of independence.[23] Contrary to the schematic nature of late-eighteenth-century devotional images, the portrait clearly conveys the sitter's individuality. Yet, like the painting of his daughter Eladia, made around 1822 by an unidentified artist in Caracas, his ethnic status is not emphasized. Social standing was still largely predicated upon the possibility of assimilating into Creole society.

Portraits of this period thus rarely seek to affirm the subject's Afrodescendant traits. An exception is the painting of Micaela Vilela by Ildefonso Páez, the only identified painted portrait of an Afrodescendant in the Andean region in the nineteenth century. Vilela was as exceptional as her portrait. Her grandson, the writer Enrique López Albújar, would evoke her transition from "tenant to owner, from honest storekeeper to dame and mistress of a hotel and a factory, from poor *cuarterona*, buried away in a sad alley, to woman of respect and lady of a house full of movement and provincial luxury."[24] Painted in 1853 as pendant to Páez's portrait of her husband, Agustín López, both paintings hung together in the grand family living room in Piura, in northern Peru. Yet while the portrait of her Creole husband follows conventional pictorial formulas, her image stands out for the sense of presence it conveys, a reflection not only of the strength of her personality but also of the challenge that painting an Afrodescendant must have presented to the painter. From her grandson's recollections, it would seem as if Vilela stood above Piura society, bypassing and even challenging customs and uses of the city's established families. Her grandson recalled the flair with which she had outdone the provincial outlook of Piura elites by sending her children to Lima and Europe for an education. Her pride and self-assurance are evident in the portrait, which shows her sitting in a chair, looking out almost defiantly at the viewer. She is dressed elegantly in a black dress, with flowers in her hair, large pendant earrings, a gold necklace, and a ring on each finger of both her hands. In every way, Vilela's painting is a true modern portrait, a self-fashioned representation of character through which she asserts her social position as a status gained by force of personal merit. It is also a work that assertively and proudly foregrounds her ethnicity.

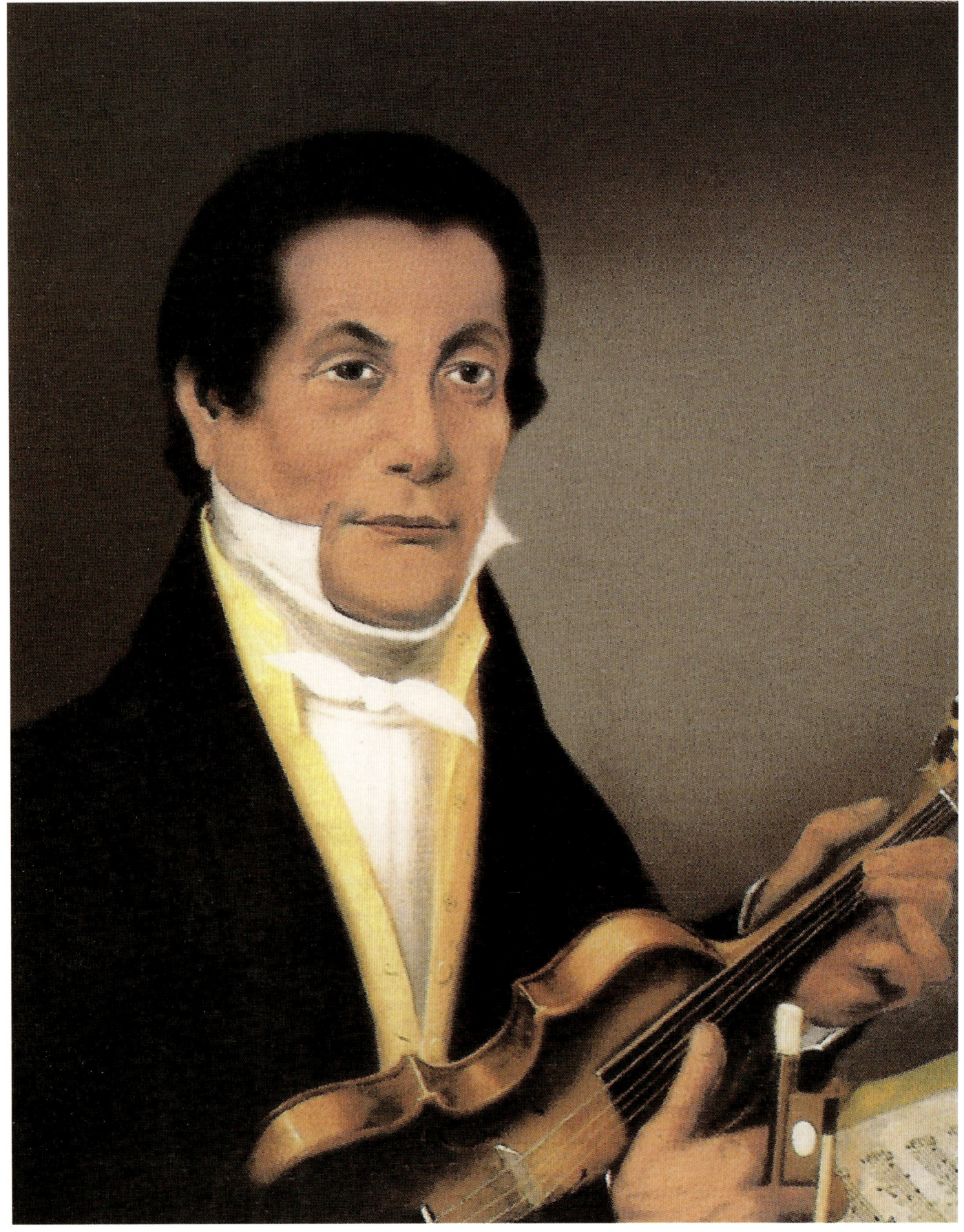

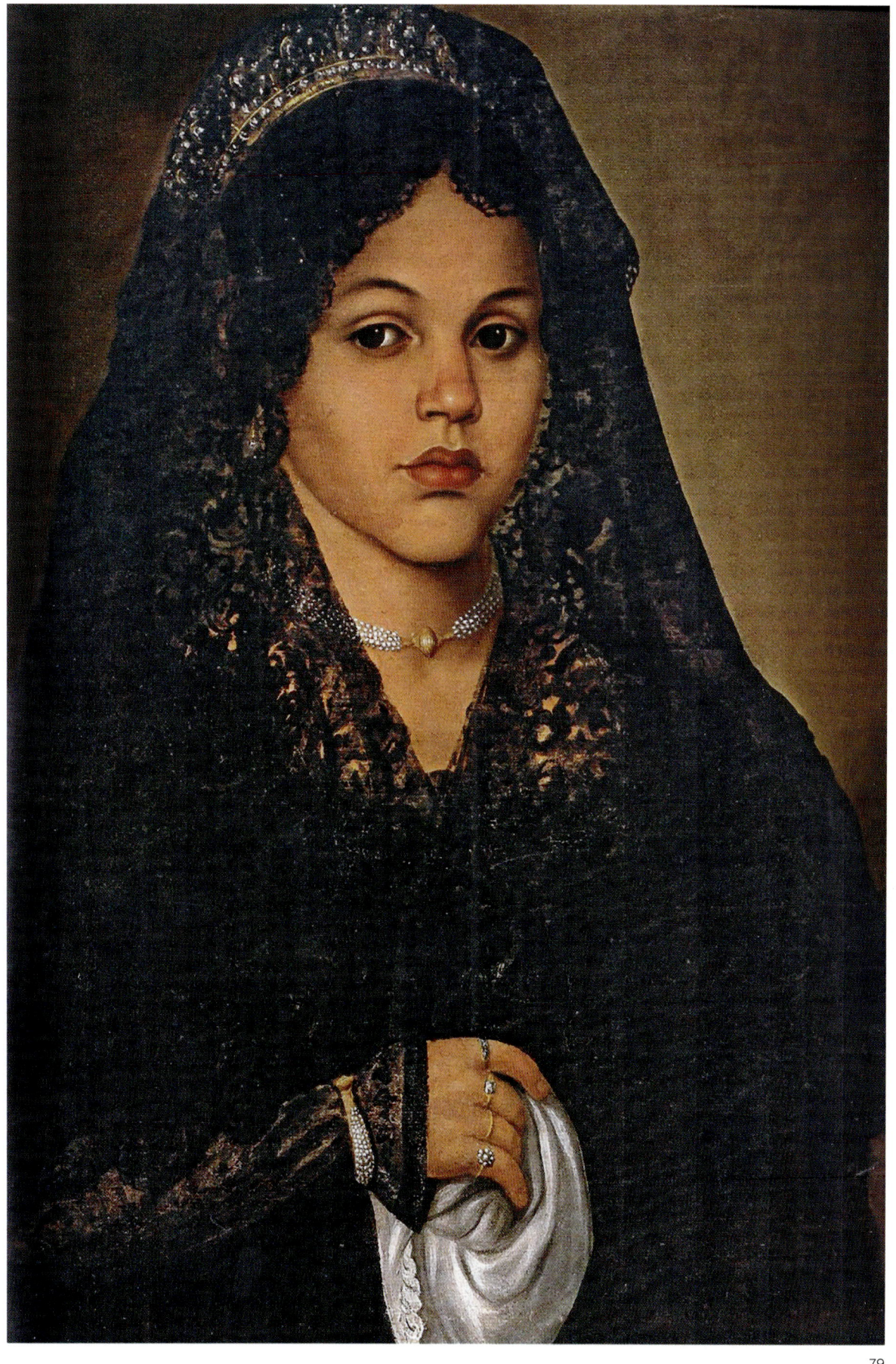

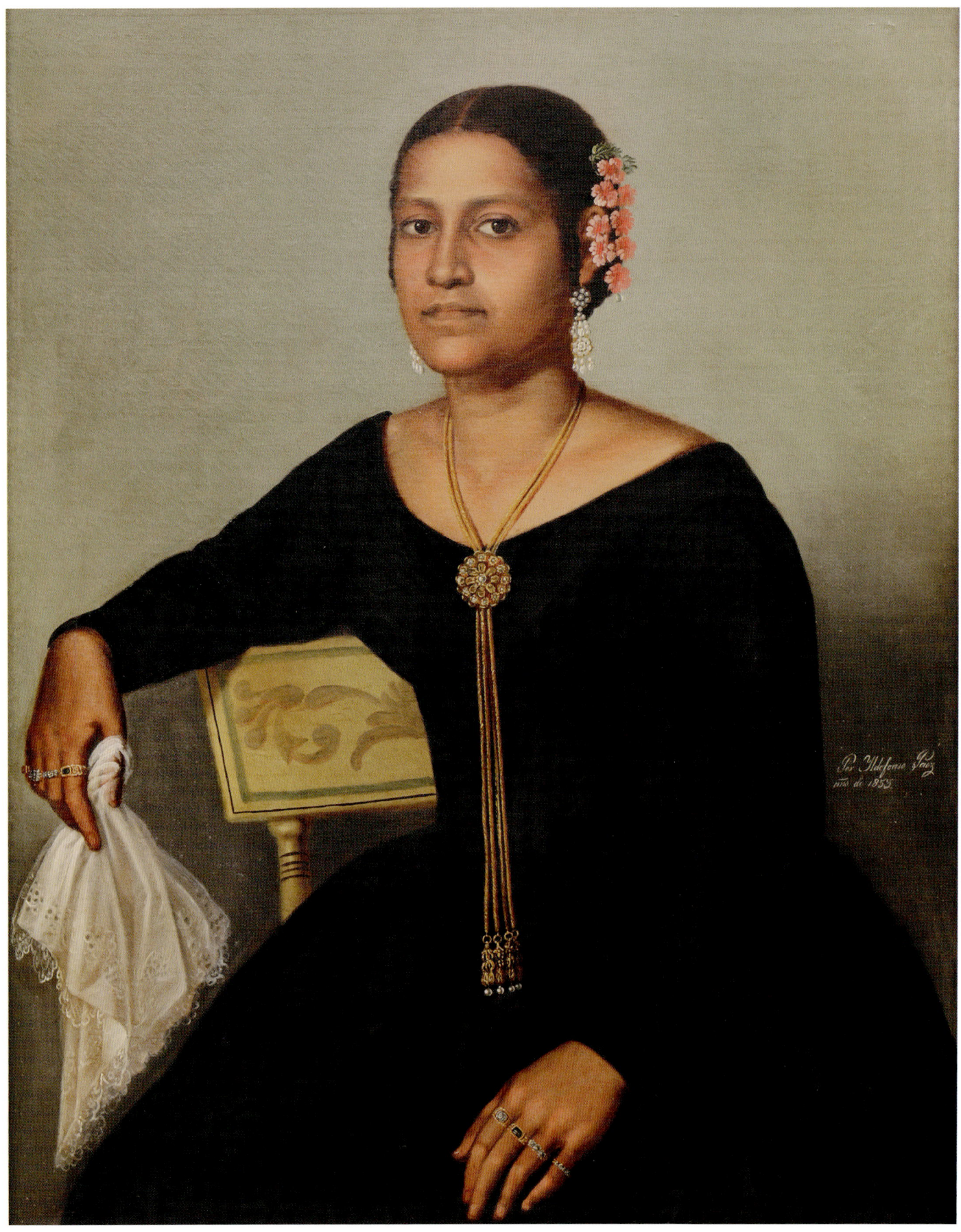

80 Ildefonso Páez. *Micaela Vilela de López, Piura*. 1853. Oil on canvas. Museo de Arte de Lima.

In this and other ways, Vilela's portrait stands out well above other images of identified Afrodescendants in nineteenth-century visual culture. Most drawings and paintings made from life after Afrodescendant sitters in this period were largely created in academic contexts and have remained anonymous, their names wholly forgottten. The rare named figures in the period's visual record are those that emerged from anonymity in the nostalgic narratives of *costumbrismo*, the tradition centered on the depiction of social types and customs. It is significant that they should appear in a genre framed by a nostalgic discourse, which sought to preserve in texts and images traditional ways of life that were thought to be vanishing in the face of modernization. The genre that gave them visibility paradoxically associated the passing of these traditions with the supposed disappearance of Afrodescendants from society, a generalized discourse common to many countries in the region.[25]

Among the innumerable images of generic figures from street sellers to upper-class women that costumbrismo produced, the genre exceptionally considered special figures identified by name who were, significantly, largely Afrodescendants. In Peru, caricatures of urban characters like the bullfighter Esteban Arredondo, the dancing master Maestro Hueso, or the bandit León Escobar appear among the subjects of Francisco "Pancho" Fierro's extensive repertoire of watercolors.[26] Whether real or imaginary, the fact that they purport to represent specific individuals allows us to consider them as portraits. In the context of Argentina, María de Lourdes Ghidoli has discussed the implications of characters like Don Eusebio de la Santa Federación, a delusional burlesque figure associated with Juan Manuel de Rosas, or "Tía Rosa" (Buenos Aires, n.d.–ca. 1902), a well-known sweet seller in Buenos Aires, as portrayals that in fact alternate between individualization and typology, an ambiguity that reveals the limitations of conceiving visual genres as fixed categories.[27]

In the case of such figures, popularized through literature, commercial imagery, and the press, individualization rarely translates into precise knowledge of full proper names or biographical and historical accuracy. The recurrent use of nicknames further evokes the paternalist condescension that framed these images. But even more significant is the fact that these portrayals were produced as part of *costumbrista* repertoires, a genre itself devoted to the representation of anonymous types. In such a context, names lose relevance, as they are framed through images that reveal a constant slippage between individual and group identities. Their function is not biographical but sociological.

The portrait of Juan José Cabezudo (Ica, ca. 1780–Lima, n.d.), a popular Lima cook who appears in numerous texts and images produced between the 1820s and 1870s, reveals the way in which such figurations subsume particularity in the discursive framework of costumbrismo. Like most caricatures of identifiable characters represented through the genre, Cabezudo is defined as a marginal figure with respect to established social norms. In some of the earliest known images, watercolors attributed to Francisco Javier Cortés, he is described as "Comesuelas," "*maricón principal de Lima*"—"main homosexual of Lima"—associating him with dissident forms of sexuality, a recurring strategy in representations of the Afrodescendant population.[28] In a photograph produced decades later by the Courret Studio, he is presented in a careful staging of the roles he had earlier played in images and texts. Cabezudo is here but part of a larger sequence of urban street sellers and tradespeople, which would have been acquired

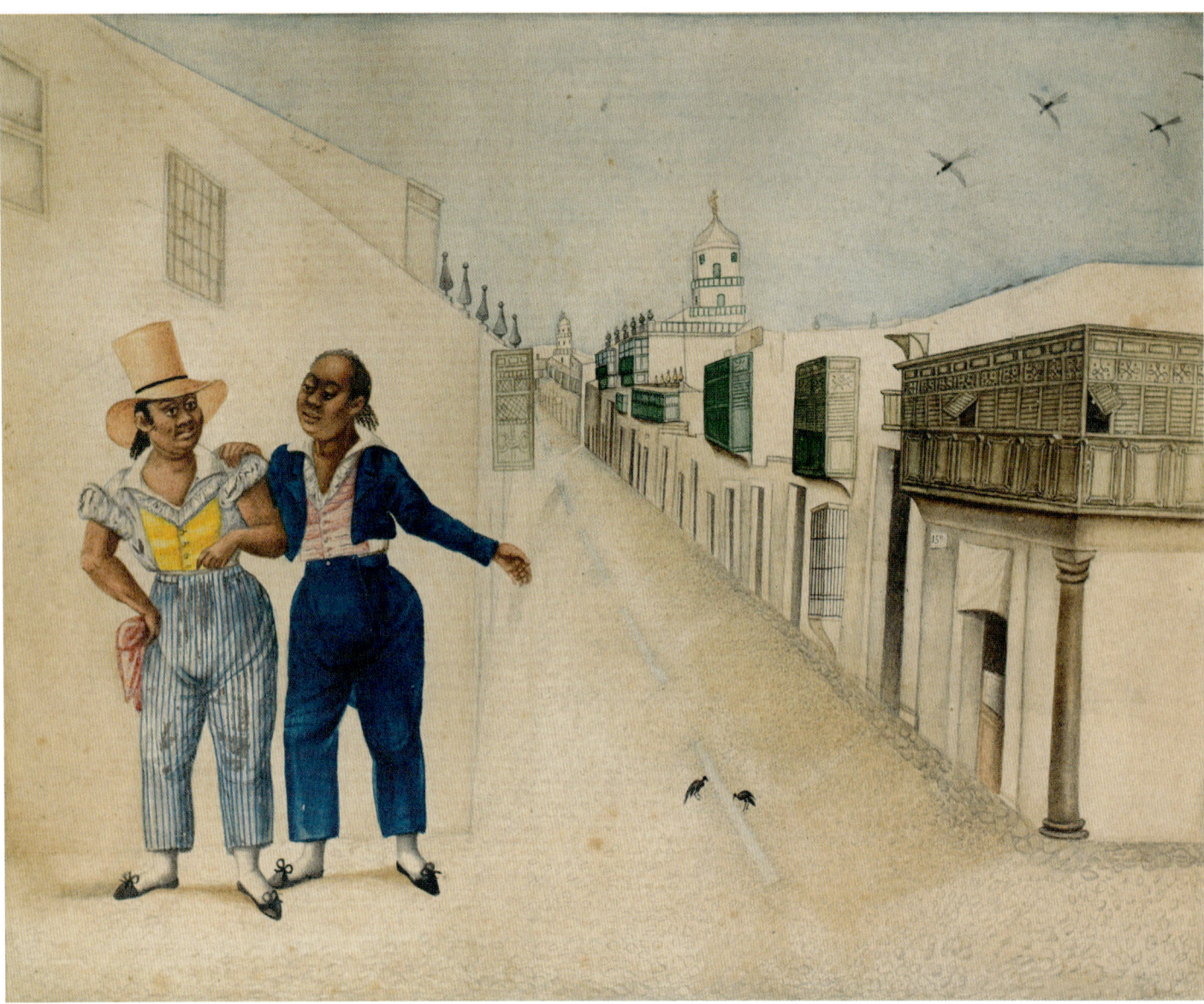

81

81 Francisco Javier Cortés, attributed. *Juan José Cabezudo ("Comesuelas") and His Friend*. Ca. 1827. Watercolor on paper. Museo de Arte de Lima.

82 Courret Studio (Lima). *The Cook Juan José Cabezudo ("Comesuelas")*. Ca. 1860. From a gelatin silver print. Lima, Biblioteca Nacional del Perú, Archivo Courret.

83 Courret Studio (Lima). *Francisco "Pancho" Fierro*. Ca. 1870-1879. Gelatin silver print. Lima, Biblioteca Nacional del Perú, Archivo Courret.

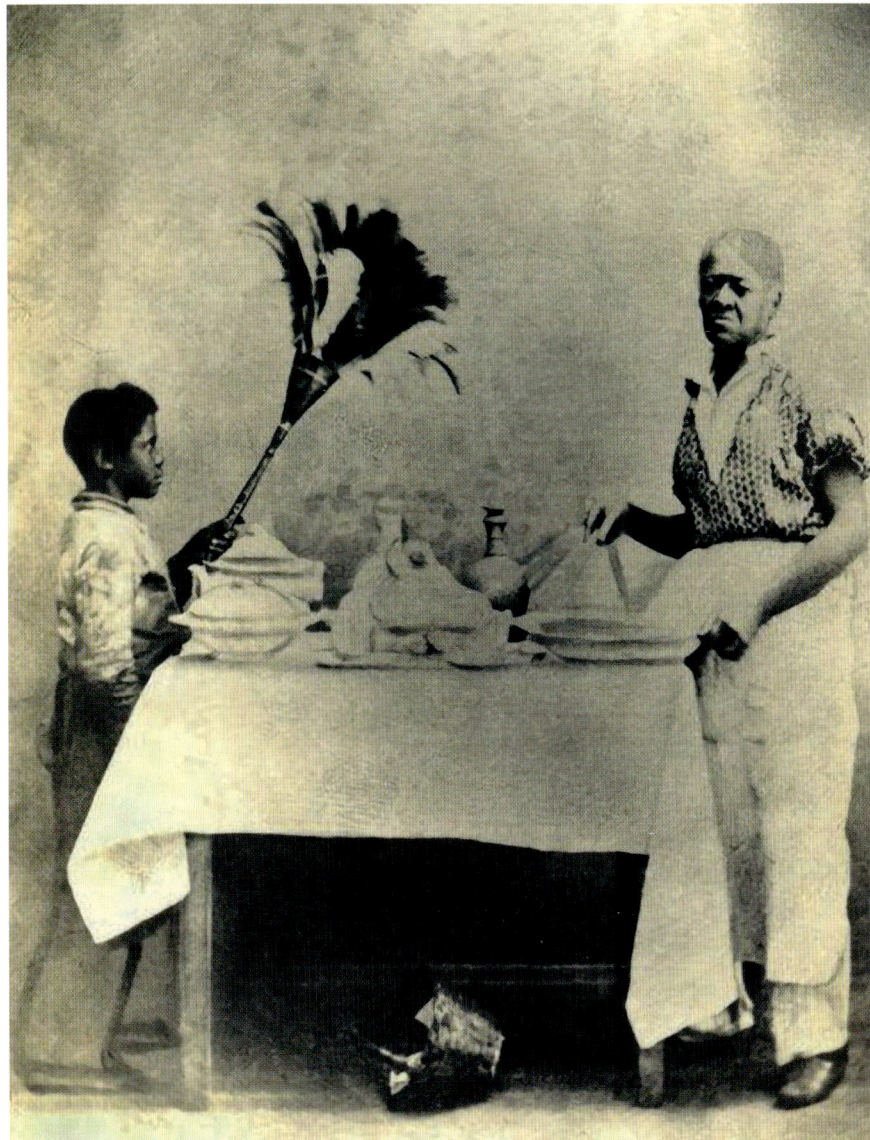
82

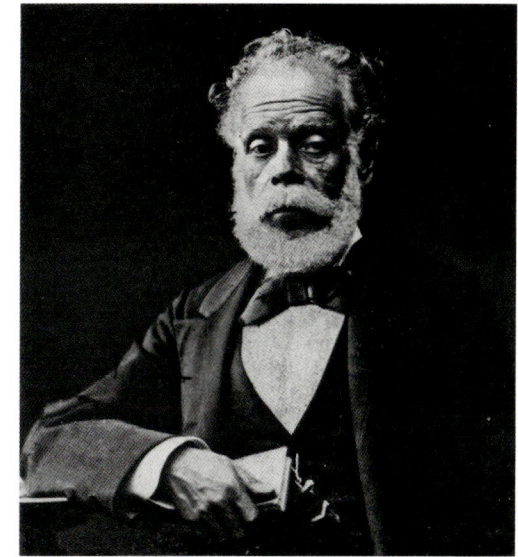
83

as collectible images in the carte de visite format, to be gathered in souvenir albums of Lima. The photograph can only be considered a portrait in that it stands as a trace of the man's actual presence before the camera. In every other regard it remains as an objectified figure, transformed into a token symbol of the capital's Afro-Creole culture.

It is revealing that the artist who was responsible for the greater part of Peruvian costumbrista visual production, the painter Francisco "Pancho" Fierro, himself of mixed ethnic origin and, significantly, generally known through a nickname, should have been portrayed in the literature as a "type" emerging from Lima's Afrodescendant culture.[29] Countering these representations is his photographic portrait, surviving as a glass plate in the Courret Archive in Lima, which shows him in old age, proudly posing in full suit and holding a book in his hand, an attribute of literacy that appears regularly in other portraits of this period. Fierro's image, probably taken during the 1870s, is one of the earliest known Peruvian photographic portraits of an identified Afrodescendant subject. Throughout the region, photography had emerged in the early 1860s as a critical element in the transformation of the genre from the privilege of elites to a vehicle of self-representation for broader sectors of the population. Yet portraiture only became widely used by Afrodescendants precisely as the genre lost its sumptuary character, when photography transformed the nature and uses of portraiture, broadening its range as a central element of personal ties and affections.

INDIVIDUAL AND TYPE   163

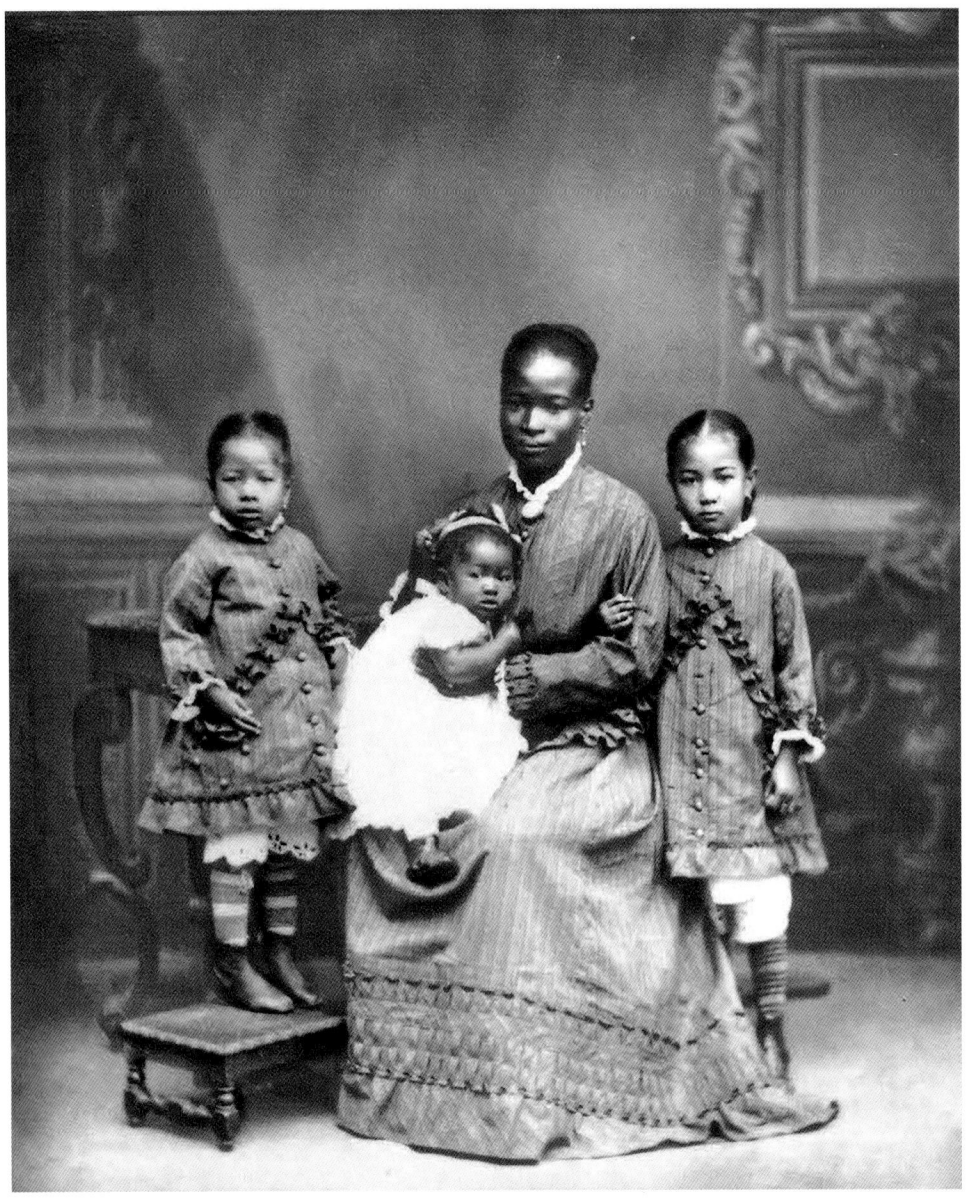

84

Numerous photographic images produced during the 1870s and 1880s reveal the visual contours of what could be defined as a new Afrodescendant bourgeoisie, everywhere appearing the same, as defined by the dress codes of the middle classes and the conventions fixed by commercial studio portraiture.³⁰ Such is the case of the Silva family in a photograph from the Courret Archive, showing an elegantly attired woman posing with her three children, surrounded by the props that served to construct the standardized regularity of the studio portrait in the last third of the nineteenth century.³¹ Images such as this have generated extended debate regarding the relative agency of the subjects portrayed in the fashioning of their own images.³² That they largely conformed to extended bourgeois norms does not deny the character of these photographs as images of personal identity and social affirmation. Like fashionable dress, photography, too, allowed the insertion of previously excluded groups into the modern spaces of consumption, visibility, and citizenship.³³ Specific research of individual biographies could doubtless lead to a more precise understanding of particular images, giving us more nuanced perspectives on the larger social processes that shaped new middle classes.³⁴

Some photographs contain enough information to allow us to speculate on their subject's history. One of the rare images of Afrodescendants in the Courret Archive identified by name is the portrait of a girl named Natalia Paz Soldán, doubtless in the service of the prominent family of the same name, taken in the

84 Courret Studio (Lima). *The Silva Family*. Ca. 1890. Gelatin silver print. Lima, Biblioteca Nacional del Perú, Archivo Courret.

85 Courret Studio (Lima). *Natalia Paz Soldán*. Ca. 1890. Gelatin silver print. Lima, Biblioteca Nacional del Perú, Archivo Courret.

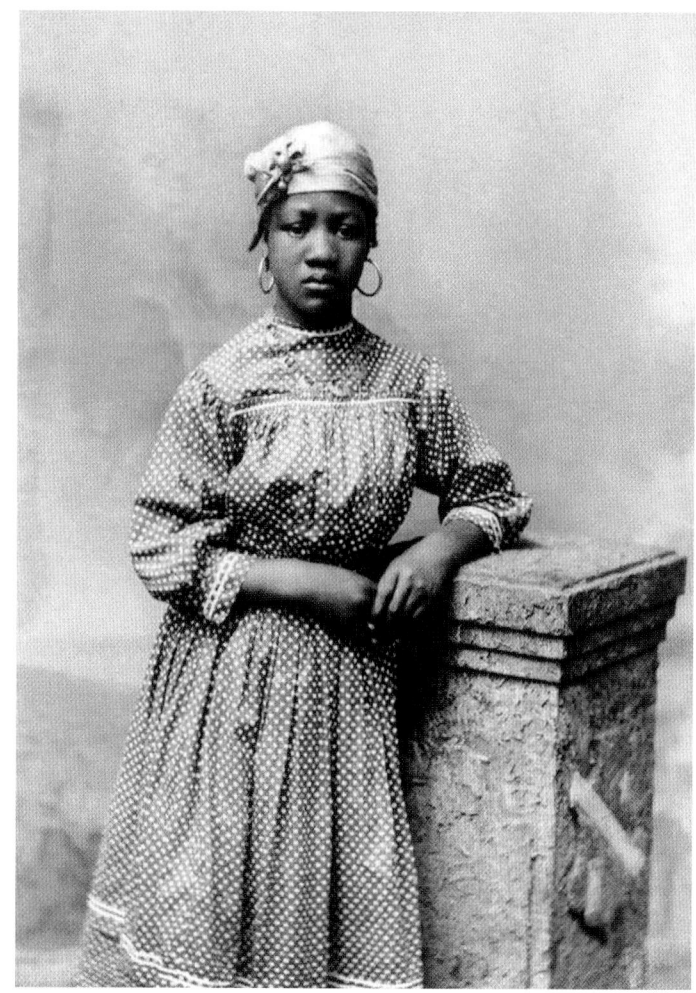

last years of the nineteenth century. Her status is made evident through her clothes, which are, however, not those that were typically used by household servants in Lima in those years. Rather, her crisp new polka-dotted dress, the headscarf, and the hoop earrings are evidently inspired by stereotypical images of North American Afrodescendant women, which had by then become widely popular through books, prints, and advertising. That we should know her name is merely circumstantial. The image in fact seems to deny the young girl all individuality and agency. Unlike colonial portraits, in which enslaved people and servants served merely as foils to establish the hierarchy and status of white sitters, here the photograph omits the person whom the girl serves. Yet the family she works for is subtly evoked through her dress, strangely a disguise of servitude, one most likely imposed rather than chosen. The image in fact recalls earlier forms of control of enslaved workers and servants, largely subjected to dress codes imposed by their owners or masters.[35] The individuality of the proper name is here obliterated by the dense layers of stereotype and imposed role playing.

This broad survey of nineteenth-century Afrodescendant portraiture in Spanish America reveals the tensions, difficulties, and daunting challenges of self-representation in societies marked by discrimination and racism. Generally associated with the emergence of modern ideas of subjectivity and individuality, portraiture of Afrodescendants would stand in permanent tension with stereotypes and expectations defining rigidly stratified societies. Even after portraiture became more widely accessible, images of Afrodescendants continued to conform to notions of social ascent invariably defined by normative bourgeois cultural forms. Larger social transformations and new notions of ethnicity and culture in the twentieth century would allow for the broader emergence of alternative forms of self-representation that boldly affirmed Afrodescendant identities through the assertion of difference.

IV

New Nations Assert Themselves

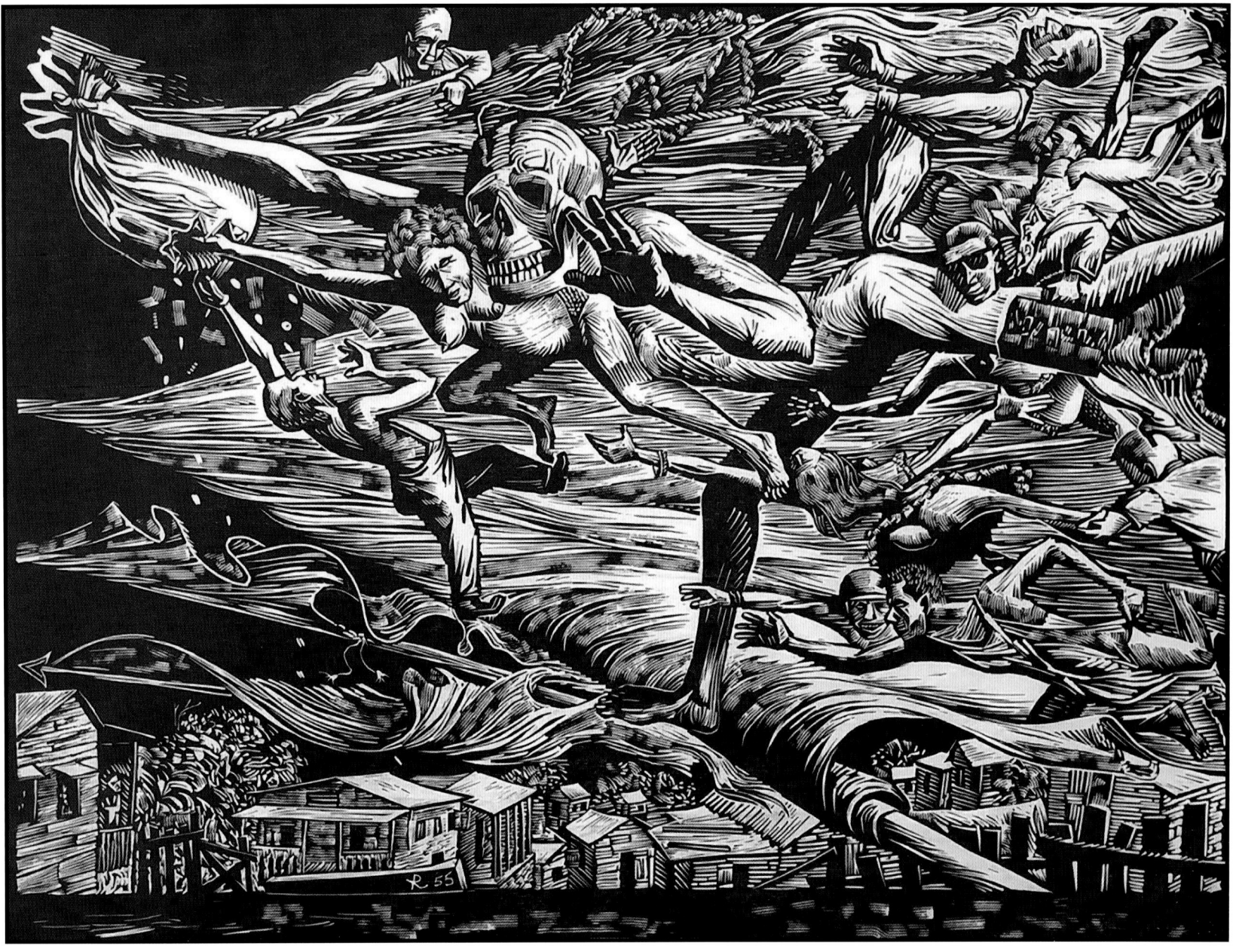

86 Carlos Raquel Rivera. *The Hurricane of the North*. 1955. Linocut on paper. Boston, Museum of Fine Arts.

8

BLACK VISUALITIES IN PUERTO RICO AND THE DOMINICAN REPUBLIC: 19TH AND 20TH CENTURIES

EDWARD J. SULLIVAN

Introduction: Engagements with the Colossus of the North
What follows is a partial, fragmentary recounting of Blackness in various forms of visuality in two Caribbean nations that form part of the Greater Antilles: Puerto Rico and the Dominican Republic (which shares the island of Hispaniola with Haiti). What links these two places is their geographic proximity as well as the same ties that bind virtually every other island or mainland country along the Caribbean Sea's basin or other political entity of the region. Both include a rich history of indigenous civilizations, among them the Taíno, Lucayans, Caribs, and Arawaks, and a long period of colonization principally by Spain beginning with the first of Christopher Columbus's voyages in 1492. The Caribbean places I discuss have also held the positions as loci of enslavement from Africa. Additionally, like many other Caribbean countries, Puerto Rico and the Dominican Republic have had a particularly fraught relationship, especially after the later nineteenth century, with the United States.

The tensions between these two places and what has been called the "Colossus of the North" have been a constant source of exacerbation of ongoing societal pressures and personal distress for their citizens. This trauma was eloquently illustrated by the Puerto Rican graphic artist Carlos Raquel Rivera (1923–1999) in his 1955 print *El huracán del norte* (*The Hurricane of the North*), in which a skeletal figure representing the United States sweeps over the urban landscape of La Perla, a socioeconomically underserved district in the historic center of Old San Juan, Puerto Rico, home to thousands of Afrodescendant people and people of mixed Taíno, African, and Spanish blood. This ghostly presence carries but does not distribute bags of money as he soars over the island accompanied by other specters representing the ravages of capitalism and U.S. influence in the island's cultural and political fate. The Afro-Puerto Rican artist Raquel Rivera, whose 1957 portrait by Rafael Tufiño is shown in this chapter, is one of the most distinguished members of the 1950s generation of Puerto Rican artists, a founding member of the Centro de Arte de Puerto Rico, and a major architect of modernizing the arts of the island in the mid-twentieth century.

The Spanish-American War of 1898 effectively displaced the last vestiges of Spanish colonialism in the Caribbean. The American victory and the effects of its considerable military prowess accounted for the loss of Spain's last two colonies in the region, Cuba and Puerto Rico (as well as the Philippines and Guam in the Pacific). Cuba became a de facto economic colony of the United States, remaining so virtually until the Cuban Revolution. Puerto

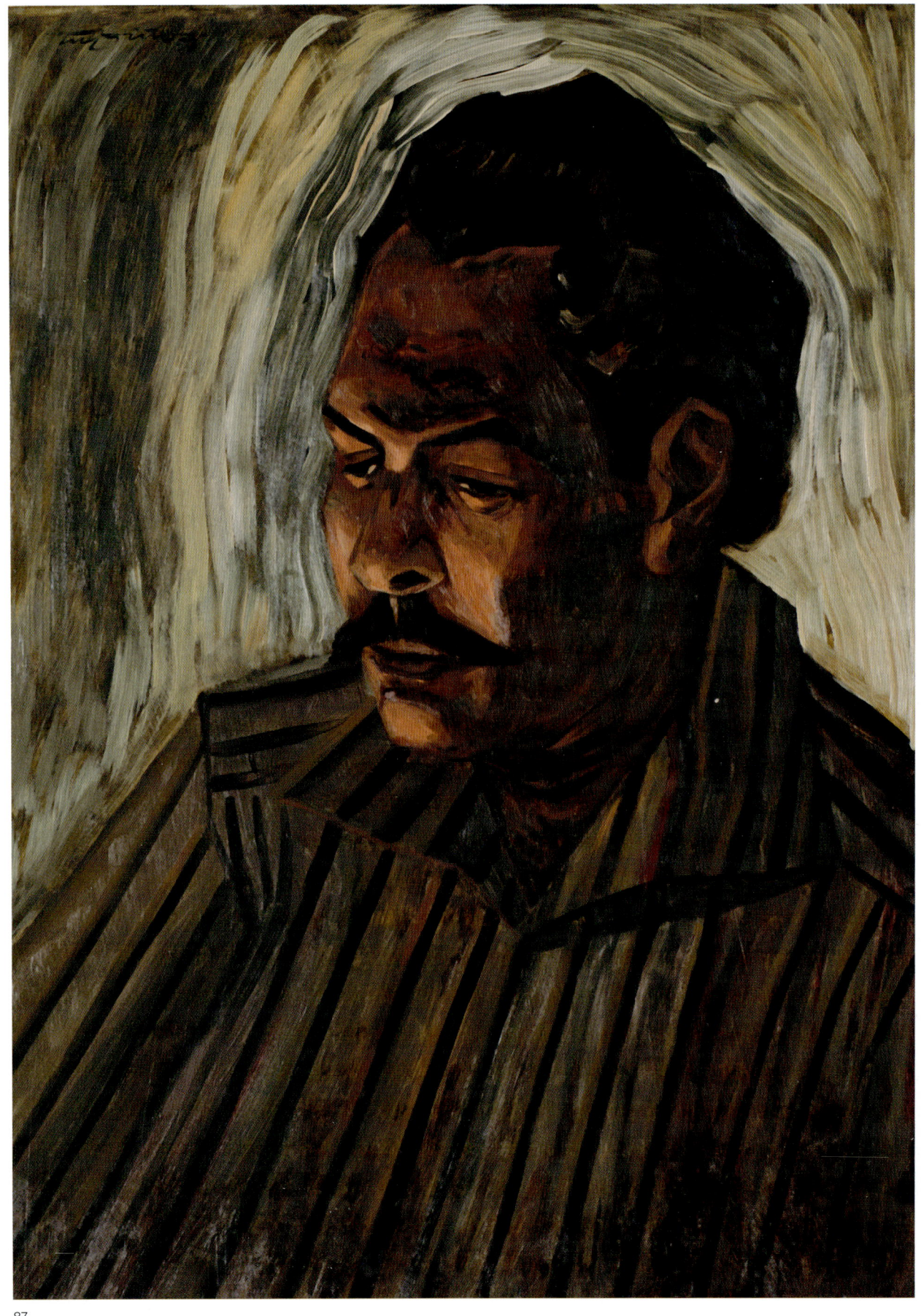
87

87 Rafael Tufiño. *Carlos Raquel Rivera*. 1957. Oil on wood. San Juan, Museo de Arte de Puerto Rico.

Rico was annexed as a territory and eventually proclaimed a "Free Associated State" or "Commonwealth." Its inhabitants became American citizens, but without the right to vote in federal elections, as of 1917 and the passage by the U.S. Congress of the Jones Act.[1] The euphemisms accorded to the political delineation of Puerto Rico mask the fact that it is indeed a colony of the United States, and one that is often a forgotten stepchild of Washington, D.C., as demonstrated so conspicuously in 2017–2018: when Hurricane María ravaged the island, the physical and psychological devastation inflicted by the storm was shockingly neglected by authorities in the North American capital.

The Dominican Republic was proclaimed an independent entity in 1844. Spain's oldest colony and its first colonial capital city, Santo Domingo, had been of great naval and economic importance in the early phases of Spanish imperial venture, but by the late eighteenth and early nineteenth centuries, it was dramatically neglected by Madrid. The eastern portion of the island of Hispaniola had been subsumed under Haitian control in 1801 during the heady days following the successful (but immensely costly in all ways) Haitian Revolution. The Dominican Republic has been the site of numerous incursions into its national territory on the part of U.S. naval and military forces in the nineteenth and twentieth centuries, and these events served to shape a contentious yet often dependent relationship with the North American superpower. The events are intricately intertwined with questions of race and the position of people of various gradations of color within the country throughout its modern history.

In 1869, shortly after the end of the Civil War in the United States, President Ulysses S. Grant sent Marines to occupy the Dominican Republic to protect U.S. commercial shipping interests in surrounding waters. This was followed in 1916 by an eight-year-long occupation of national territory by the U.S. Marines, seeking to "stabilize" the volatile political situation of the Dominican Republic which had witnessed a series of revolutions since the departure of the last contingent of U.S. troops more than forty years earlier. (U.S. Marines, in the meantime, had begun an occupation of Haiti that would last until 1934.) The direct intervention and control of political affairs led as well to an impact on daily life that would have far-reaching consequences for future generations. Dominicans ultimately formed the core of post-1960 Hispanic immigration to the United States. Since the 1960s, the boroughs of Manhattan and the Bronx in New York City became the principal venues for the fifth largest Hispanic diaspora in North America.

The U.S. invasion had other consequences for the future history of the Dominican Republic. After the occupying troops left the country in 1924, the rise of power of the national police force and, eventually, the Dominican Secret Police played ever greater roles in the political panorama of the country. The chief protagonist in the racially charged story of Dominican politics and foreign affairs was Rafael Leonidas Trujillo, the notorious head of the national police and after 1930 president and then iron-fisted dictator of the country until his assassination in 1961. The United States held a nominally "hands-off" position vis-à-vis Trujillo's most heinous activities. President Franklin D. Roosevelt condemned the infamous slaughter of upward of thirty-five thousand Haitians on the northwestern border in 1937's so-called Parsley Massacre instigated by Trujillo (himself of partial Haitian and African ancestry).[2] Nonetheless, the United States' Good Neighbor Policy of benign acceptance of many questionable policies of

88 Ramón Frade. *Our Daily Bread*. 1905. Oil on canvas. San Juan, Instituto de Cultura Puertorriqueña.

governments throughout Latin America and the Caribbean accounted for a de facto support of Trujillo, who would likely have been unable to withstand external pressures without the covert backing of the United States.

U.S. forces again landed on Dominican soil, ordered there in April 1965 by President Lyndon B. Johnson. Acting in the midst of the Cold War, Johnson was wary of the island nation succumbing to the same influences that had accounted for the rise of the Castro regime and revolution in Cuba. The Marines arrived after the overthrow of Juan Bosch, who had been elected president one year after Trujillo's death. Although they remained for only several weeks, the Marine presence was a clear sign of the prowess of American military might and an instantiation of the forced hegemony of American ideology in the region.

It is also important to point out that not only has the Caribbean been the theater of colonial conflict throughout the centuries, it has also been the proverbial crossroads of cultures, conflicted interests—both commercial and cultural—and a virtual laboratory of racial and ethnic blending and fusion. In the remarks that follow, it is particularly challenging to refer specifically to the image of "the Black." Blackness in the places that I have chosen to discuss (as well as throughout the region) is both a relative term and one that has many subtleties and points of contention. The African presence is, of course, pervasive throughout. Yet the comingling of persons of indigenous heritage, those of Asian background (especially in other island nations such as Cuba or Trinidad and Tobago), as well as those of European ethnic derivation provides a landscape of ethnicity, skin tone, and cultural identification that spans a wide spectrum and must be respected when attempting to assess the visualities of persons of color within our context. To take one example, we might examine the definition of the word *jíbaro*. In Puerto Rico, the jíbaro is a person of the central mountain ranges. The term is a slippery one, as it refers in common parlance to someone who is of the countryside, who lives in an economically precarious state, yet who has often served the function as the symbolic "heart and soul" of the country in literature and art. What is the ethnicity of this person? There are as many opinions and circumstances as there are authors who have written on this question. Whiteness is emphasized by some, but Blackness to one degree or another is a central factor in the ethnic identification of the jíbaro—yet Blackness is more often associated with inhabitants of the coast, such as those who were enslaved and their descendants who worked on sugar plantations. The Puerto Rican art historian Marimar Benítez has problematized this identification of the jíbaro with whiteness, stating that "the image of the white *jíbaro* crops up constantly in literature and conveys a distorted view of the island's population, which has in fact undergone considerable racial intermarriage."[3]

Thus, in one of the most iconic images of early-twentieth-century Puerto Rican art, *El pan nuestro* (*Our Daily Bread*) (1905) by Ramón Frade (1875–1954), we observe an older man in a mountainous setting holding a handful of plantains, proffering it to the viewer with the understanding that this staple of the Puerto Rican diet is one of the most essential qualities of existence on the island. The man himself is clearly an individual of mixed race. He is symbolic of the sacredness of peasant existence and the values most highly prized by a public who had so recently experienced the transition of colonial transfer—from the mandate of Spain to that of the United States—and who has come out the other side of this societal shock with a renewed reverence for autochthonous

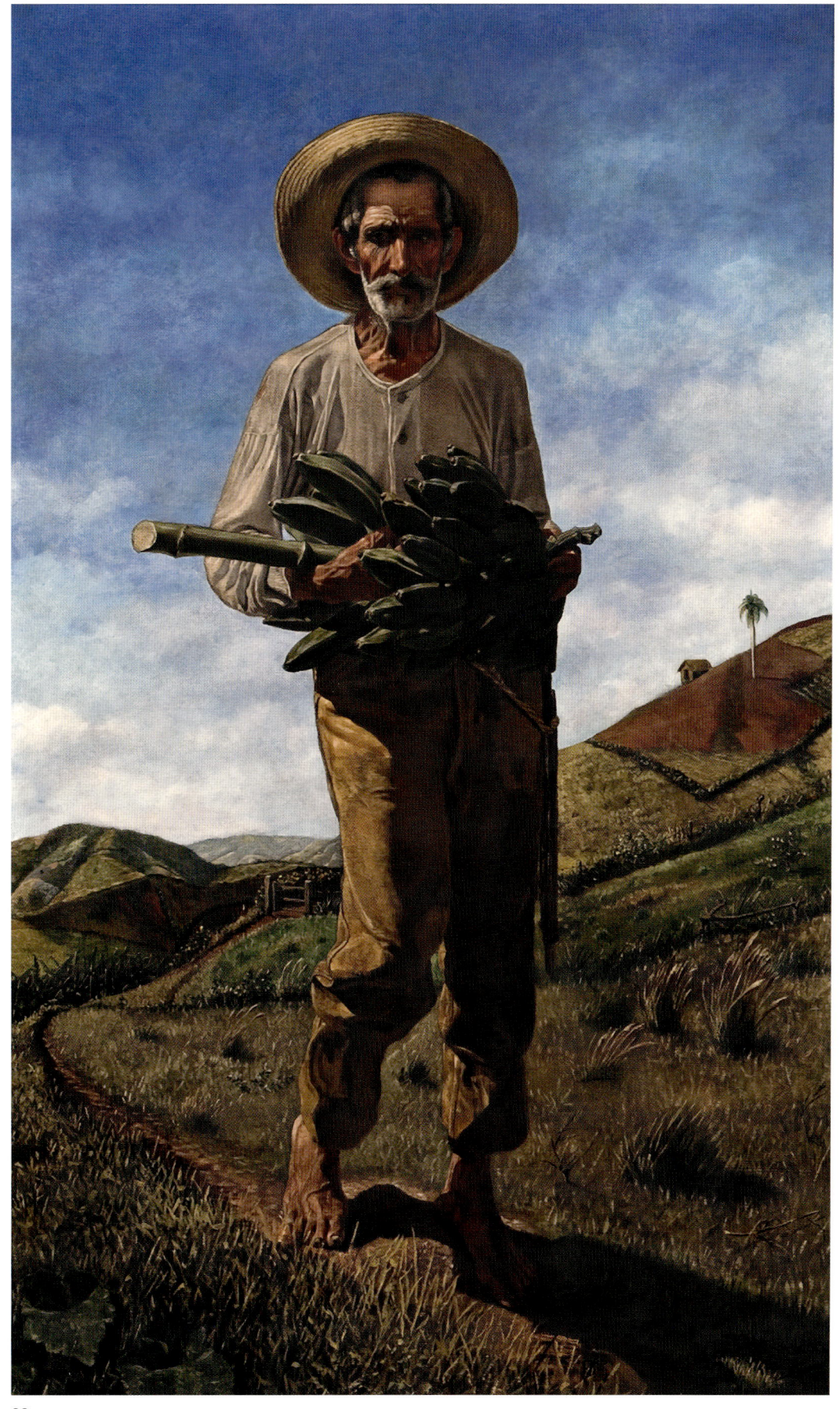
88

89 Unidentified artist. *The Three Kings*. Carved and polychromed wood. Washington, DC, Smithsonian American Art Museum.

values of the countryside, including the persona of the iconic Puerto Rican as a blend of Black, indigenous, and white. Such a scenario of racial mixing is repeated in the case of the Dominican Republic, where racial discourse is comprised of a quite different set of factors. I hope to be able to suggest some of the subtleties of these distinctions in the following series of remarks.

Borinquen

Borinquen is the indigenous name for the island of Puerto Rico. Derived from the Taíno word *Borikén*, it is often used in contemporary times in a way that defines a sense of pride and national self-identification with the island's heritage. This heritage is, of course, deeply imbricated with Blackness. First sighted by Christopher Columbus on his second journey of exploration and exploitation in 1493, Borikén was colonized shortly thereafter by Juan Ponce de León, who brought several several enslaved persons he owned to the island. In 1495 the Flemish entrepreneur known in Spanish as Gerónimo de Bruselas initiated the active slave trade, importing a small number of African-born enslaved individuals to work in his metal foundry. In the early 1500s the Hieronymite order of monks was given permission from the Spanish government to import Africans to Puerto Rico. By 1517 more than one thousand enslaved Africans were working for them. Thereafter, they worked in the gold mines and the sugar plantations that began operation in earnest after circa 1600. Relatively little remains of the material culture of Afro-Puerto Ricans from the initiation of slavery until the nineteenth century. Archaeological excavations undertaken in San Juan's Ballajá and Santo Domingo districts, areas of concentration of enslaved and free persons of color, have revealed pottery remains that may be linked to the everyday lives of slave populations.[4]

Tangible evidence of depictions of Blackness within the realm of the visual arts may be found in the tradition of *santos*, carved wood figures of saints, the Holy Family, and other sacred figures of Christianity. The colonial city of San Germán was the center of this industry, with groups of artisans such as the members of the Espada family creating works for private consumption to adorn home altars and small private chapels.[5] As in other countries, such as Brazil, where the large concentration of Afrodescendant people, especially in the northeast, explains the popularity of Black saints within the wood-carving traditions, this phenomenon is observed in Puerto Rico. The most famous of such Black saints is St. Balthazar, traditionally called the King of Arabia, one of the three magi who visited the infant Christ in the stable in Bethlehem shortly after his birth.

José Campeche y Jordán (1751–1809) is the first major figure within the Western-based traditions of painting to emerge from the island. Campeche's father, Tomás de Rivafrecha Campeche, a formerly enslaved Afrodescendant, was a painter of sacred images of both two and three dimensions. Campeche's mother was white, and her family came from the Canary Islands. Nothing of Tomás's work survives, and we therefore cannot know to what extent Campeche learned from him. Much better documented is the professional relationship between the young Campeche and the Spanish artist Luis Paret y Alcázar (1746–1799), who was in Puerto Rico from 1775 to 1778.

Paret y Alcázar was a painter in Madrid at the time of King Charles III, and the king's brother Don Luis was his principal patron. After a scandal involving illicit sexual relationships on the part of the prince, Paret, who was implicated in the affair, was

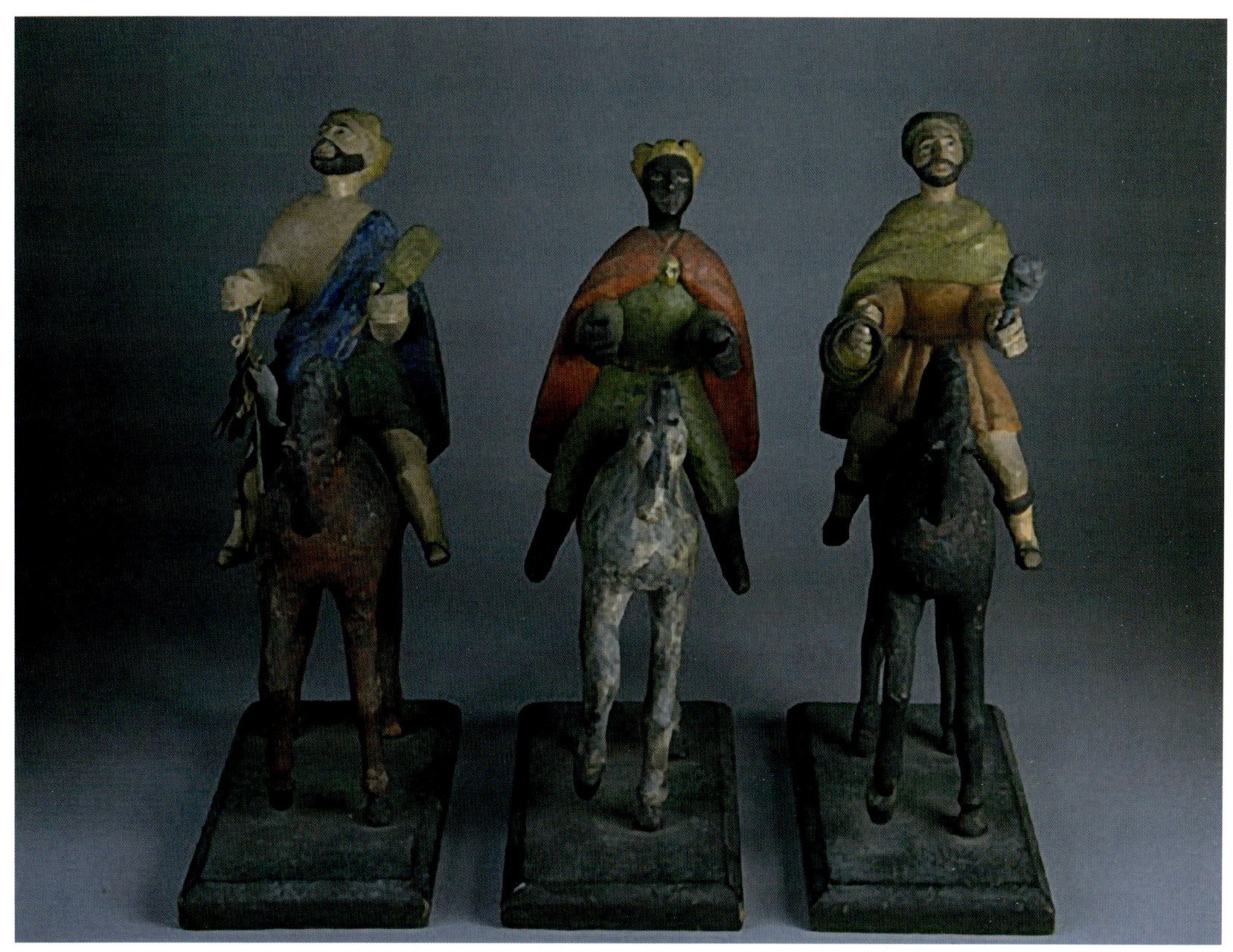

89

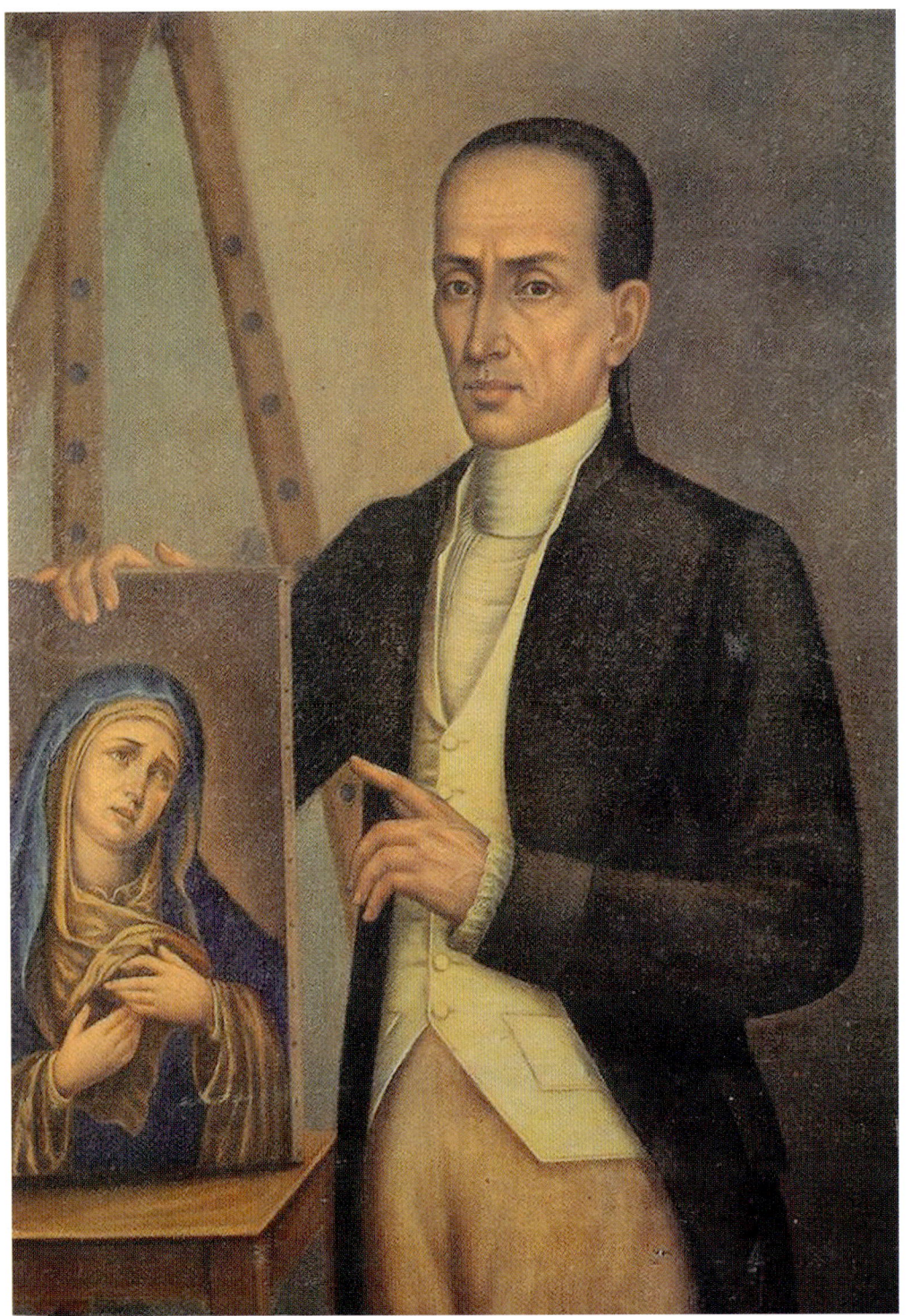

90

90 Ramón Atiles. *Portrait of José Campeche* (copy). Undated. Oil on canvas. Alpine, NJ, Collection of Mrs. Carmen Ana Unanue.

exiled to Puerto Rico for three years. Paret is one of a generation of artists in the 1770s and 1780s who brought a French-inspired rococo form of expression to Spanish painting and is credited with importing the rococo to the Caribbean. He imparted his teaching to his most accomplished student, Campeche. In Campeche's many portraits of military and political officials, depictions of women of high society in San Juan, and his numerous sacred scenes for churches and private collectors, he displays sensitivity to this new mode of brightly colored and airy compositions.

There are few images of people of color in his art. However, a copy of a lost self-portrait by his younger contemporary Ramón Atiles (1804–1875), who was also an artist of local elites, displays the dark-skinned Campeche standing before his easel, gesturing to a painting of the Virgin of Sorrows that he has just completed.

An exception to the scarcity of Black figures in the work of Campeche is found in an 1809 *Ex voto of the Holy Family*. A heavenly apparition of the Holy Family, the saints Anne and Joachim occupy the bulk of the space. The central figure is the Christ child who, together with the dove of the Holy Spirit and God the Father emerging from clouds above, constitutes a Holy Trinity. At lower left there is a nun, adoring the sacred vision. She is dressed in the habit of a Carmelite and may be, according to the art historian Arturo Dávila, Sister Margarita de la Concepción Calderón, who died in January 1803 at the Carmelite Convent in San Juan.[6]

For our purposes, the most significant images are the three Black individuals who accompany the nun. Two young women and a young man kneel behind her. They are all dressed in formal attire. The women wear veils, and all three participants in this scene hold bouquets of flowers. These people are almost certainly enslaved by the white nun. As was the case in many parts of the Spanish American world, members of the religious elite owned at least one enslaved person, but sometimes many more, attending to their needs in the convent. Perhaps the most famous example is that of Sor Juana Inés de la Cruz, the seventeenth-century Mexican nun and renowned poet and essayist who lived with numerous servants and enslaved people in the Convent of San Jerónimo in Mexico City. Campeche's painting is, according to Dávila, "the first representation of slaves in Puerto Rican art."[7]

José Campeche's art became a touchstone of inspiration in the visual arts of Puerto Rico. The Puerto Rican historian Cayetano Coll y Toste wrote a 1916 biography of the artist for the *Boletín Histórico de Puerto Rico*. He states that: "At the death of Campeche we were left with no representative within the pictorial arts until Maestro Oller."[8] Coll y Toste cites the artist Francisco Oller y Cestero (1833–1917) as the principal heir to the visual traditions established by Campeche. Oller was indeed a great admirer of Campeche, expressing his esteem for him in an 1891 speech given at the opening of the drawing academies he founded in San Juan: "Campeche! … Lost light of that dark time when art in Puerto Rico remained a secret.…"[9]

Francisco Oller became the most famous late-nineteenth- and early-twentieth-century painter not only in his own country but, arguably, within the Caribbean Basin during the second half of the 1800s.[10] He has been described as a "realist impressionist," a pioneer in the movements of impressionism, realism, and naturalism during his four extensive study trips to Europe, and the source of a renewed spirit of modernity in the Spanish-speaking Caribbean. His work was well known in his own country and exhibited in Cuba during his lifetime. Oller was also the first artist in Puerto Rico to dedicate a considerable portion of his visual

91 José Campeche y Jordán. *Ex voto of the Holy Family*. Ca. 1809. Oil on wood. San Juan, Instituto de Cultura Puertorriqueña.

output to depictions of Black persons in both urban and rural contexts.

Although Oller was tutored as a boy in San Juan by the less well-known painter Juan Cleto Noa, his more substantial formal training took place at the Academia de San Fernando in Madrid (1851–1853), where he studied with Federico de Madrazo (1815–1894), a pupil of the French neoclassicist Jean-Auguste-Dominique Ingres (1780–1867) and a renowned portraitist in his own right. Later, in Paris, where he spent considerable time, Oller became friendly with members of the impressionist circle, especially Camille Pissarro (1830–1903), a native of the island of St. Thomas in the Danish (later American) West Indies. Oller showed his work in at least four of the Paris Salon exhibitions.

Oller's career in San Juan and nearby towns developed at a time fraught with conflict. Movements to liberate the island had begun to emerge in the 1860s, concurrent with those organized in Cuba. The most significant of these was the *Grito de Lares* (*Cry of Lares*), named for the town where the unsuccessful rebellion began. Abolition of slavery did not come about until 1873, and throughout the century, landholders feared slave-led revolutions of the sort that had successfully turned Haiti into the first Black republic in the Caribbean, or slave rebellions, such as occurred in Martinique and Jamaica in 1831, as well as several unsuccessful revolts in Puerto Rico itself.

The sentiments of Francisco Oller, a white elite painter, a descendant of a well-known family of Catalan origin, were clearly pro-abolition. His friends and contemporaries included prominent politicians such as Ramón Baldorioty de Castro, a delegate to the Spanish Parliament in the 1860s where he formed part of the forefront of the antislavery movement, speaking forcefully against the practice in the *Cortes* in the mid-1860s. José Julián Acosta was likewise a staunch abolitionist and activist for the end of enslavement in Madrid. Like Baldorioty de Castro, he was a founding member of the Autonomist Party of Puerto Rico. Baldorioty and Acosta had met as children when they were both been pupils in the modest San Juan school of Maestro Rafael Cordero, an Afrodescendant teacher depicted in Francisco Oller's 1890–1892 portrait painted for the Gallery of Illustrious Puerto Ricans in the Ateneo Puertorriqueño, one of the island's main cultural institutions, founded in 1876 (see fig. 58). The painting remains there to this day.

In this work we see the subject of the portrait sitting in an interior space on a Windsor chair. To his left is a work table on which there are tobacco leaves and instruments for making cigars and cigarettes, a means of support we know that Cordero practiced. His principal occupation, however, was caring for and nurturing his students. Rafael Cordero opened the first school for male children of enslaved parents as well as free Black youths in 1810 on the Calle Luna in what is today called Old San Juan. (It is within the original walled precincts of the city established in colonial times.) Born free in 1790, Cordero inherited his freedom from his parents, who were born into bondage but who obtained their freedom prior to their children's birth. His parents encouraged his interest in literature and the arts. Cordero and his sisters, Gregoria and Celestina (who also opened a school for girls of color), had had no opportunity for formal study, as there were no schools on the island for Black children.[11]

We know a good deal about Cordero's biography from the account published in 1868 by Lorenzo Puente Acosta.[12] Cordero is revered as the founder of education for all, and there are many

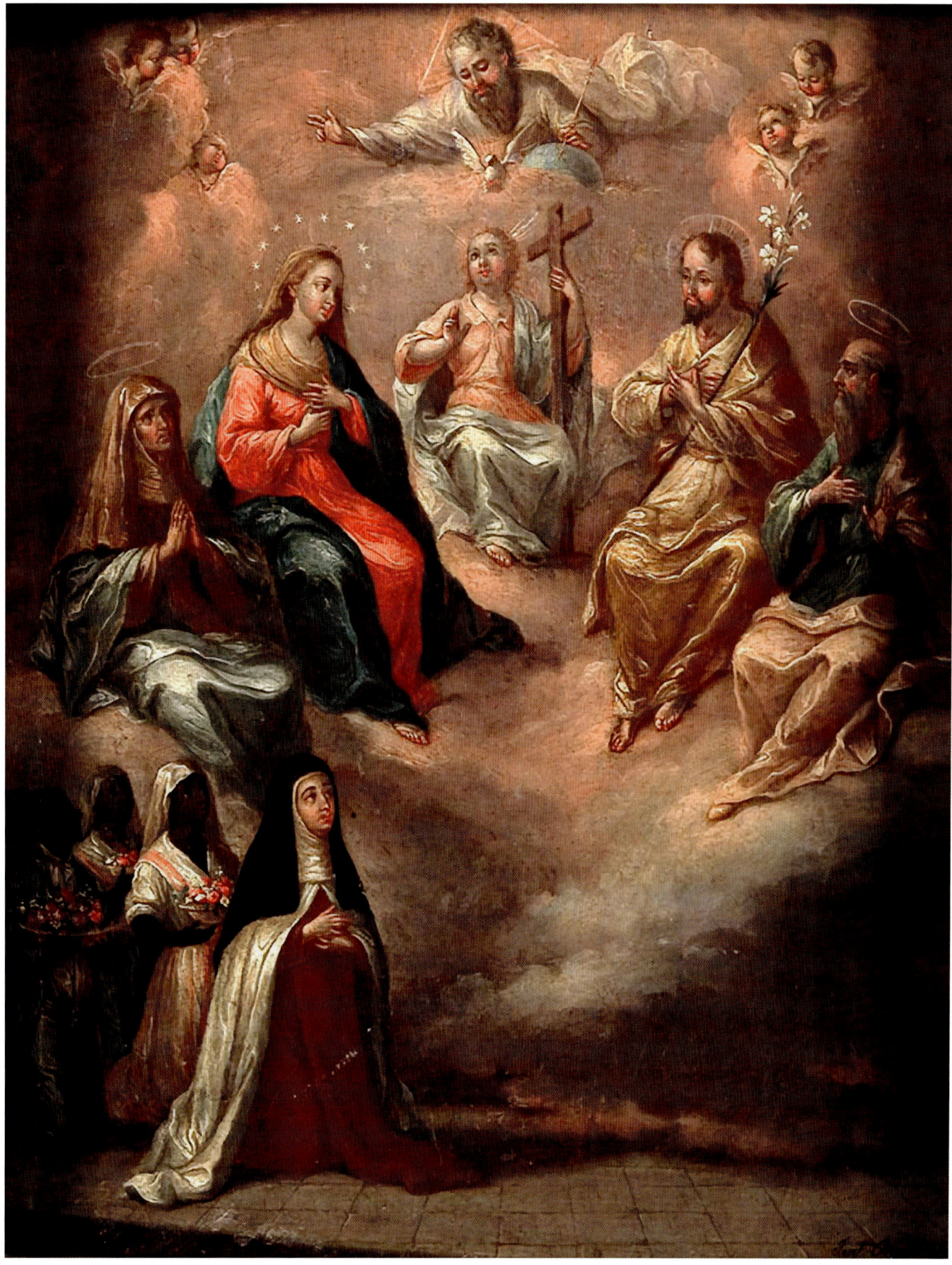

91

92 Francisco Oller. *The Old Ceiba Tree at Ponce*. Ca. 1887–1888. Oil on canvas. Ponce, Puerto Rico, Museo de Arte de Ponce.

schools named after him in Puerto Rico and the United States. His piety was also well known, and in 2004 the archbishop of San Juan requested of the Vatican that he be considered for canonization, which would make Cordero only the second Black saint in the Americas (the Afro-Peruvian St. Martín de Porres being the first and only) and also the second Puerto Rican to move through the process's initial stages (after the educator Carlos Manuel Rodríguez Santiago, the founder of the Catholic Center in the University of Puerto Rico, Rio Pedras). Although as of this writing he has not yet been granted sainthood, Pope Francis, in recognition of what are considered his heroic qualities, bestowed upon Rafael Cordero the title "Venerable."

Eventually Cordero's school admitted male children of all racial and economic strata. Oller's picture depicts the teacher as an elderly man, surrounded by eleven boys of both African and Caucasian ethnicities as well as those of mixed race. In the room that served as Cordero's classroom, religious paintings and images adorn the walls. At least one, a Madonna and child, may be a work by José Campeche. (His biographer tells us that Cordero owned such a painting.) We know that religion, as well as the basic subjects of reading and mathematics, were the staples of Cordero's pedagogical efforts. Tropical sunlight enters through the passageway to the inner courtyard of the house, still in existence today, and which was separated from Oller's studio by only a few blocks. The artist very likely had personal knowledge of the teacher as he died in June 1868 when Oller was thirty-five years old. Both Cordero and Oller had established reputations by that time and were part of the city's circle of known persons of the intellectual circles. Oller was also a teacher, having founded some ten schools for drawing and painting in San Juan and beyond.

There was certainly a feeling of admiration for Cordero on the artist's part, evident in the deeply sympathetic portrait he completed more than twenty years later.

The portrait of Rafael Cordero was not a unique instance of representations of Blackness in the work of Oller. Earlier in his career, he had executed a painting of an enslaved man being whipped by an overseer, perhaps one of the most direct testimonies to his abolitionist sympathies. (The painting itself is now lost, but it is known thanks to a photograph in the Bibliothèque nationale de France.)[13] The most well-known representations of Blacks by Francisco Oller appear in his monumental composition *El velorio* (*The Wake*), painted circa 1892–1893 (see fig. 59). This work, first shown in San Juan in 1893 and, later, in Havana before being sent to France for display in the Salon exhibition of 1895, depicts the wake of a tiny child in a small house in the central mountains of the island. The child is laid out on a modest table, dressed as an *angelito* (little angel) because it was thought that the soul of a baby or toddler would immediately go to heaven upon death. Many figures appear in this composition that combines mourning with music making, drinking, fighting, and gluttonous desire (on the part of the cleric and a white townsperson on the right). The scene is set within a jíbaro household. Inhabitants and visitors of varying degrees of Blackness participate in the proceedings as a white landowner on a donkey and his companion leave the scene as viewed through the door at the left of the composition. The composition's main focal points are the child and the tall Black man standing immediately before the inert corpse, formerly an enslaved man judging by his head wrap. This man, depicted in several compositions by Oller and known exclusively through photographs, and whose figure is based on a model

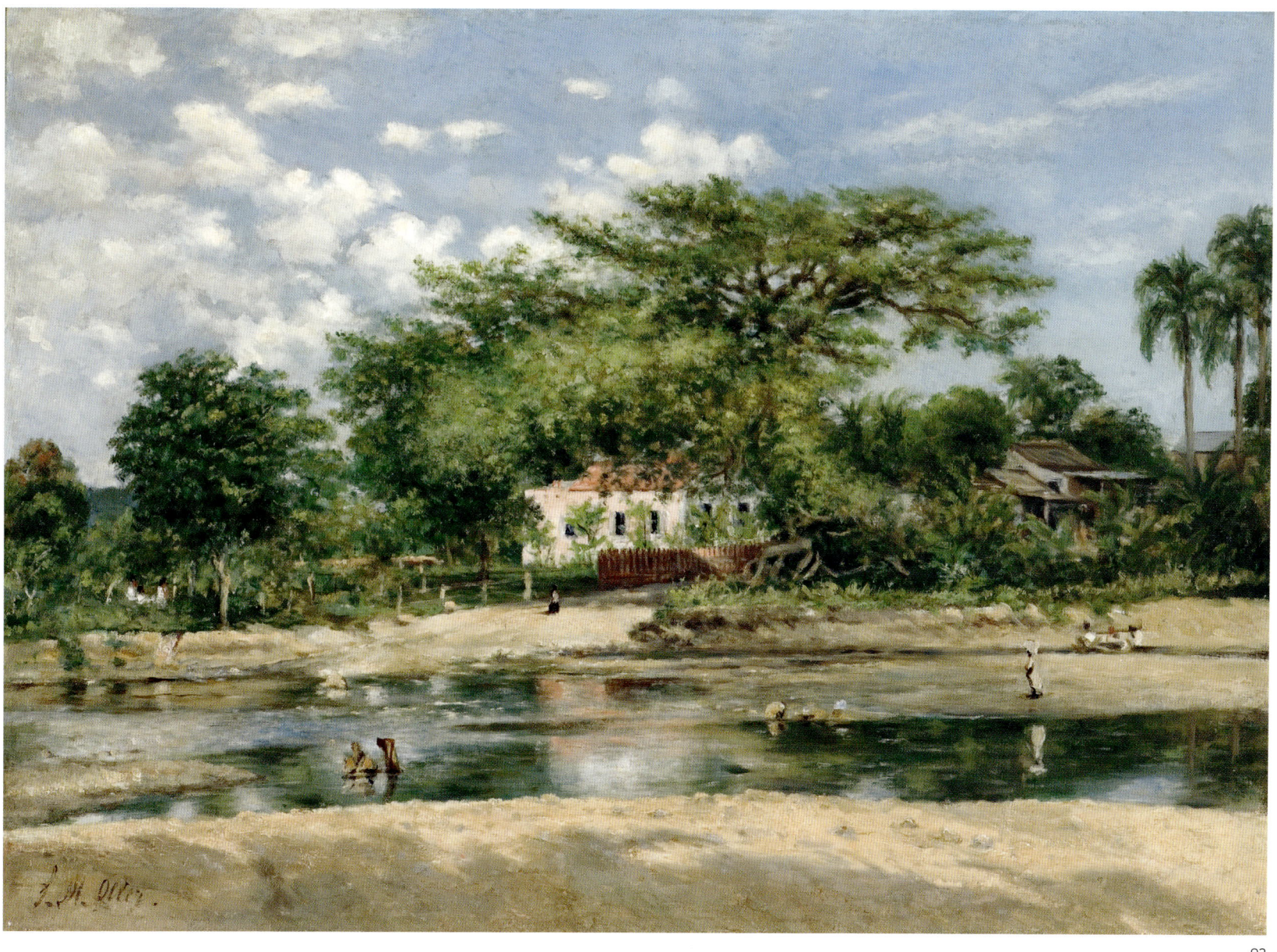

whose name is only recorded as *el negro Pablo*, is the only individual to look directly at the dead child. He is the sole participant in this scene of controlled mayhem—not unlike the "unruly household" pictures of Dutch seventeenth-century artists like Jan Steen (1626–1679), whose art Oller had seen in Europe—to directly contemplate the sorrowful purpose of this gathering. Here again, the artist's sympathy for Black dignity is manifest.

In images by Oller that could be read as traditional landscapes and carried with them strong reminiscences of the artist's work among his impressionist colleagues in France, Black bodies are often present as integral components of Puerto Rican society. Such is the case in *La ceiba de Ponce* (*The Old Ceiba Tree at Ponce*) of 1887–1888. The scene is set along the Río Portugués, which runs its course near Ponce, the island's second city, on the southern coast. We observe a modest house sheltered by an enormous tree. This is the ancient *ceiba* or silk cottonwood tree—still in existence—that was sacred to the Taíno, who gathered under its branches in precolonial times to worship. Several Afrodescendant

BLACK VISUALITIES IN PUERTO RICO AND THE DOMINICAN REPUBLIC

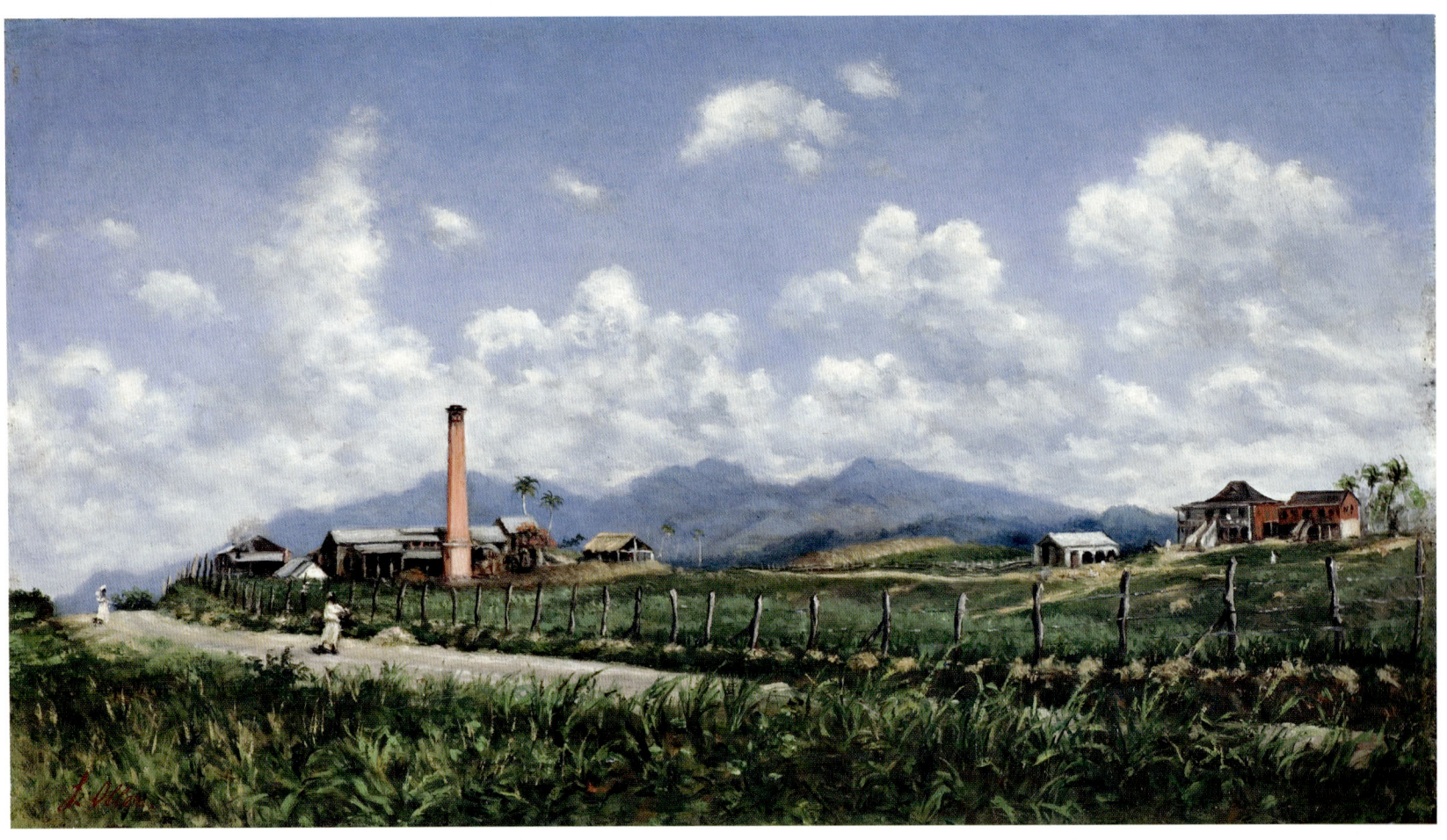
93

93 Francisco Oller. *Aurora Sugar Plantation*. 1898-1899. Oil on wood panel. Ponce, Puerto Rico, Museo de Arte de Ponce.

women wash clothes in the river while others wait on the shore in this tranquil composition.

In other works, Oller includes representations of Black people as workers in the sugar industry. Slave labor had, of course, been crucial to the development of the sugar, coffee, and cotton industries throughout the Caribbean Basin. Oller demonstrates that, despite their having been manumitted in 1873, Black workers continued to serve as the backbone of the island and mainland economies, especially in the coastal lowlands but also throughout the country. The 1898–1899 oil painting of the *Hacienda Aurora* portrays what appears to be a semi-abandoned *ingenio azucarero* (sugar plantation). Only the two lonely figures of Afro-Puerto Rican women (separated from the estate's land by a barbed wire fence) constitute the human presences in the painting. Many of these ingenios were reduced in size following 1873 and the disappearance of a portion of the enslaved labor force. The Aurora plantation also held personal significance for Oller, for it was there, at this estate near Corozal, west of San Juan, that Oller and his family sought refuge during the weeks of the American invasion of the island in late July 1898.

As was the case in Cuba and the Dominican Republic (as well as in the Anglophone and Francophone Caribbean), a number of the plantations in Puerto Rico were owned by Europeans who were sometimes absent altogether from their properties, leaving their care in the hands of managers and overseers. Such was not the case, however, with the Catalan entrepreneur José Gallart Forgas. His pride in his plantations manifested itself in the commission given to Francisco Oller for five "portraits" of the ingenios he owned, portraits which he intended to take back with him to Barcelona to demonstrate his real estate prowess. Oller only managed to finish one of these plantation pictures, the *Hacienda La Fortuna*, in 1885. In this arresting image of the *trapiche* (processing plant), the owner's house, and the slave quarters to the left, we observe a scene set on a morning in January, judging from the clear sky and the rising mist produced by the warm air drying the dew on the ground. Free workers of color, both female and male, carry on the work of the plantation. Yet there are relatively few laborers, and Oller's attention largely falls on the sky and the open area in the lower portion of the composition. Nonetheless, the Black figures are critical for our understanding of how the plantation functioned and the daily duties of its workers.[14]

At least two other paintings of the Forgas commission were executed by one of Oller's students, Pío Casimiro Bacener (1840–1900). Very little is known of Bacener, whose self-portrait now hangs in the Smithsonian American Art Museum in Washington, D.C. His mother was enslaved, and it is likely that he was born into an enslaved family, yet records show that by the time of his marriage in 1868, he had obtained his freedom. Bacener was a painter of modest talents, but his figure as a Black painter in a highly stratified society such as the small world of art and society in Puerto Rico in the mid- to late nineteenth century is significant. I could find references to no other Black artists in this time period. It is not until the mid-twentieth century that Afrodescendant painters and graphic artists come to the fore in Puerto Rico.

As indicated in the introduction to this essay, 1898 was a turning point for Puerto Rico. The American invasion and subsequent occupation of the island was accomplished in a matter of a few weeks, and for the most part it was peacefully carried out with a minimum of popular resistance. There was a more organized military conflict in Cuba, where the number of Spanish

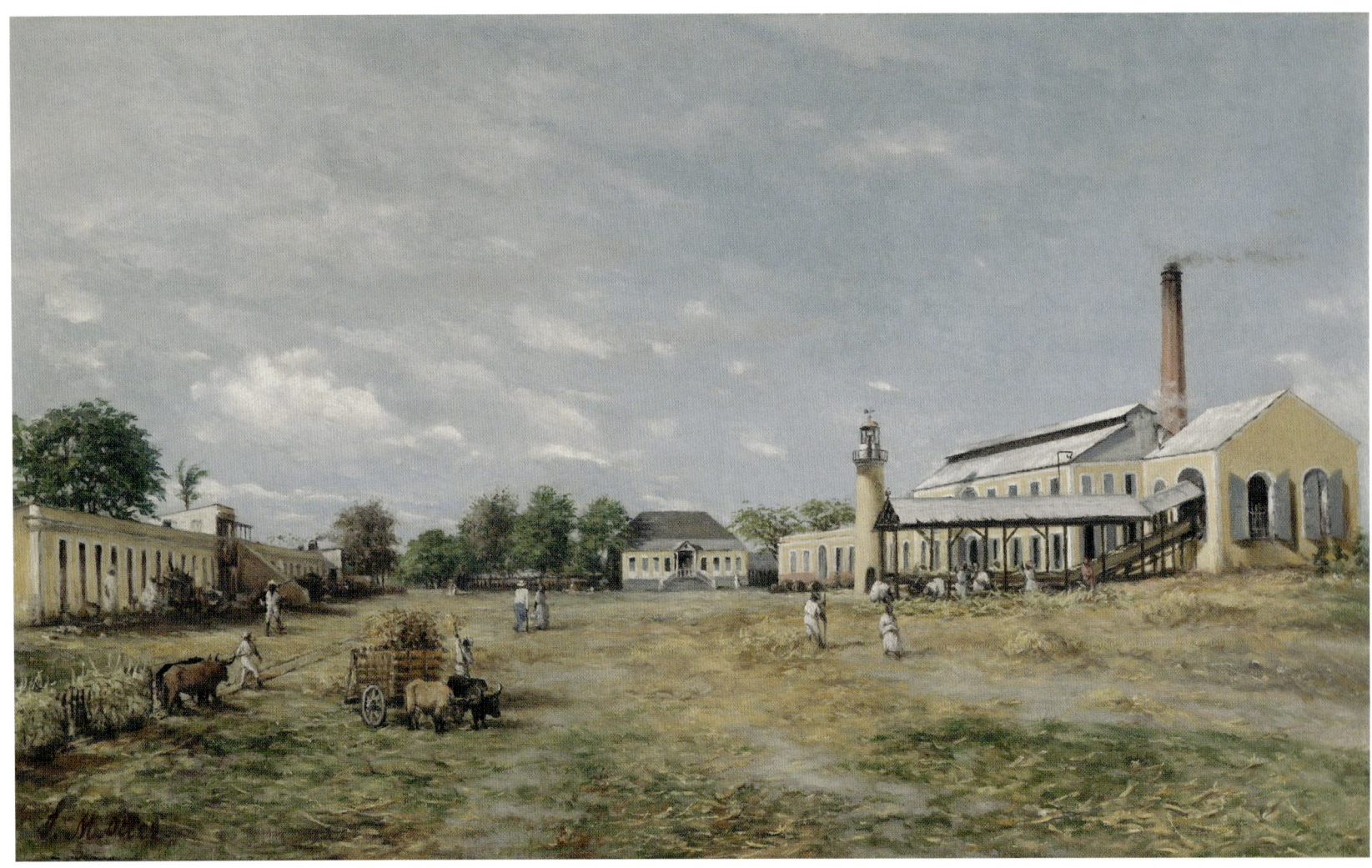
94

94 Francisco Oller. *La Fortuna Sugar Plantation*. 1885. Oil on canvas. New York, Brooklyn Museum.

95 Pío Casimiro Bacener. *Self-Portrait*. 1894. Oil on wood. Washington, DC, Smithsonian American Art Museum.

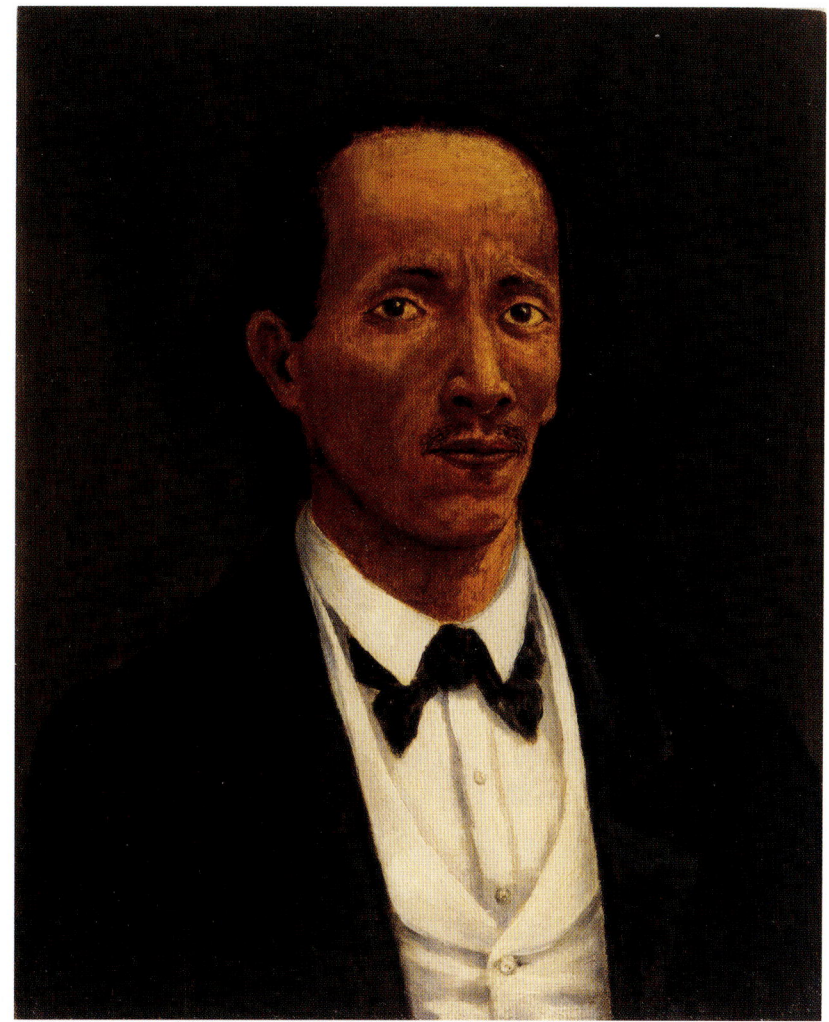

95

troops was greater, and it was also in Cuba where U.S. forces concentrated their armed activities. In addition, propaganda campaigns had been carefully confected both in the United States and in the islands that emphasized the "liberation" of Puerto Rico and Cuba from the depredations and neglect on Spain's part toward their last remaining Caribbean colonies.

Shortly after the six-week-long war, Puerto Rico became an American colony with the signing of the Treaty of Paris. Simultaneously, several books, distinctly victorious in tone, were published both to document the gains for the United States as a result of the 1898 war and to acclaim the benefits for the vanquished people under American occupation. Two of the most celebrated and well-illustrated of these books were both published in the pivotal year of 1898. The first was Trumbull White's four-volume *Our New Possessions*, an amply illustrated book with sections devoted to Puerto Rico, Cuba, the Philippines, and Hawaii. Although not a Spanish possession, Hawaii had also come into the American sphere of influence, and ultimately statehood, when the United States pried the island from its indigenous rulers.[15] White's text shared many of the same images (by anonymous photographers) with the one-volume compendium *Photographic History of the Spanish American War*.[16] The triumphal voice permeating these publications is noteworthy. Much space is dedicated to the military personnel who carried out the invasions. The dedication of Trumbull White's volume reads "To all Americans who go a-pioneering in our new possessions and to the people who were there before them." The "people who were there before" those "pioneering" Americans are often shown in photographs that record the conquered lands as domains of people of color, thus inferring that these were venues ripe for cultivation and conquest by the powers of the new imperialism. In addition, the photographs of the inhabitants of the new American possessions

BLACK VISUALITIES IN PUERTO RICO AND THE DOMINICAN REPUBLIC   185

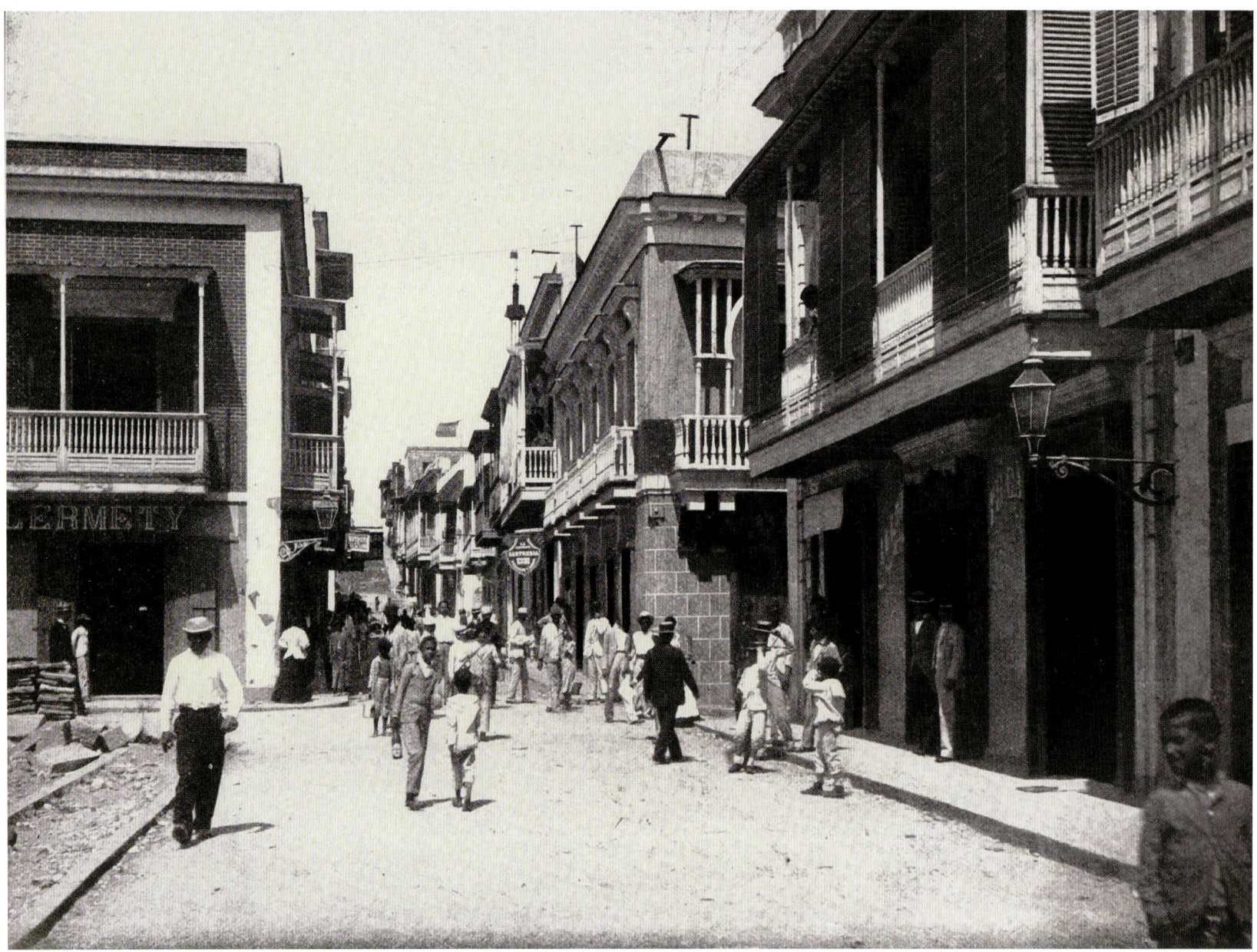

96 Unidentified photographer. *Street of the Cross, San Juan de Puerto Rico*. Ca. 1898. Photograph. Trumbull White, *Our New Possessions...* (Chicago, 1898).

97 Unidentified photographer. *Confection Vendors of Puerto Rico*. Ca. 1898. Photograph. Trumbull White, *Our New Possessions...* (Chicago, 1898).

98 Unidentified photographer. *A Colored Belle of Puerto Rico*. Ca. 1898. Photograph. Trumbull White, *Our New Possessions...* (Chicago, 1898).

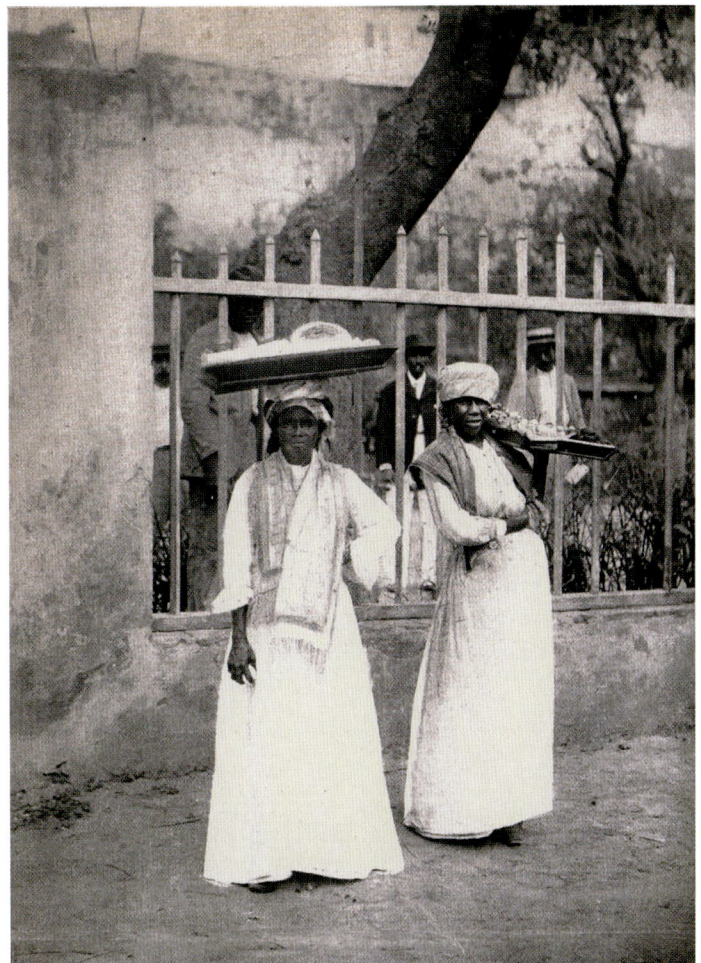

97

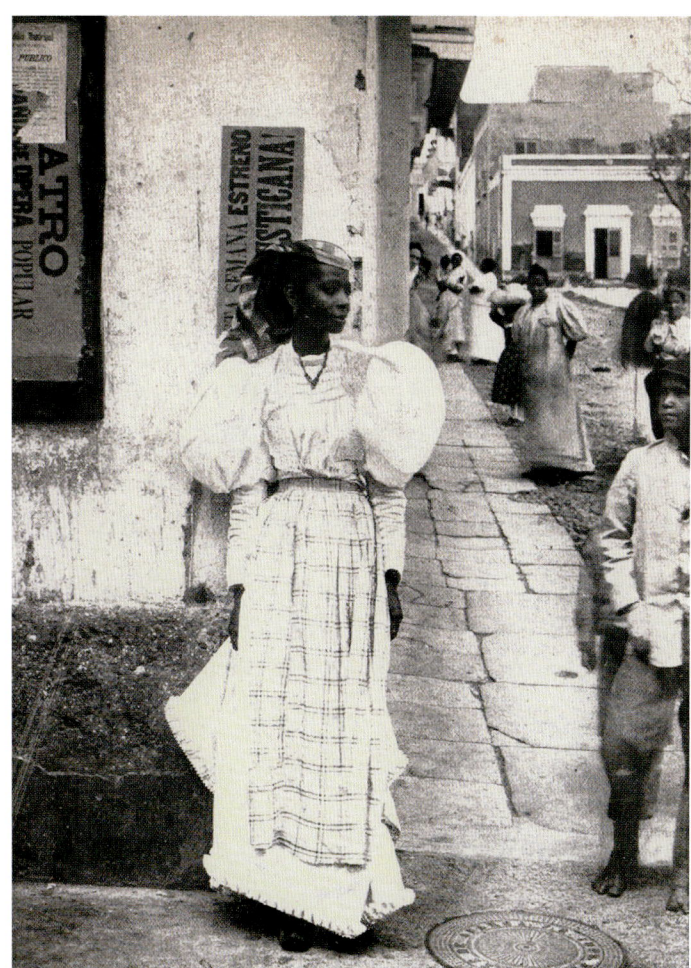

98

underscore the "exoticism" of their respective places, suggesting a platform for the creation of voyeuristic desire and an incipient market for tourism, which in the cases of Puerto Rico, Cuba, and Hawaii was to become one of the prime industries at the beginning of the twentieth century.

A look at several of the images of Afro-Puerto Ricans from *Our New Possessions* tells a revealing story. *Street of the Cross, San Juan de Puerto Rico* shows the Calle de la Cruz in Old San Juan, a main thoroughfare in the colonial heart of the capital, as the realm of Afrodescendant people of a variety of ages. *Confection Vendors of Puerto Rico* depicts two women of color, dressed in long skirts and shawls, sporting head wraps and, in one case, holding a tray of sweets on her head in a manner that would resonate with the (white Anglo) viewer as reminiscent of an African manner of object transport, while *A Colored Belle of Puerto Rico* illustrates an elegantly dressed young woman on the streets of San Juan. Accompanying these and all similar depictions of "life as lived by the people" are captions that articulate what is today recognized as a condescending and exoticizing attitude toward those (always unnamed) individuals who are the subjects of the camera's lens.

After the American invasion of Puerto Rico, San Juan's small art world fell into a state of stagnation not to be resuscitated until its resurgence with the rise of the generation of artists of the 1950s who are discussed below. Ramón Frade was one of the few artists of note working on the island after the death of Oller and before the artistic renascence of that decade. Yet he mostly worked in isolation in the small town of Cayey, creating nostalgic views of a vanished, somnolent island. He perpetuated the realist mode of Oller and belonged to a moment before the resurgence of Puerto

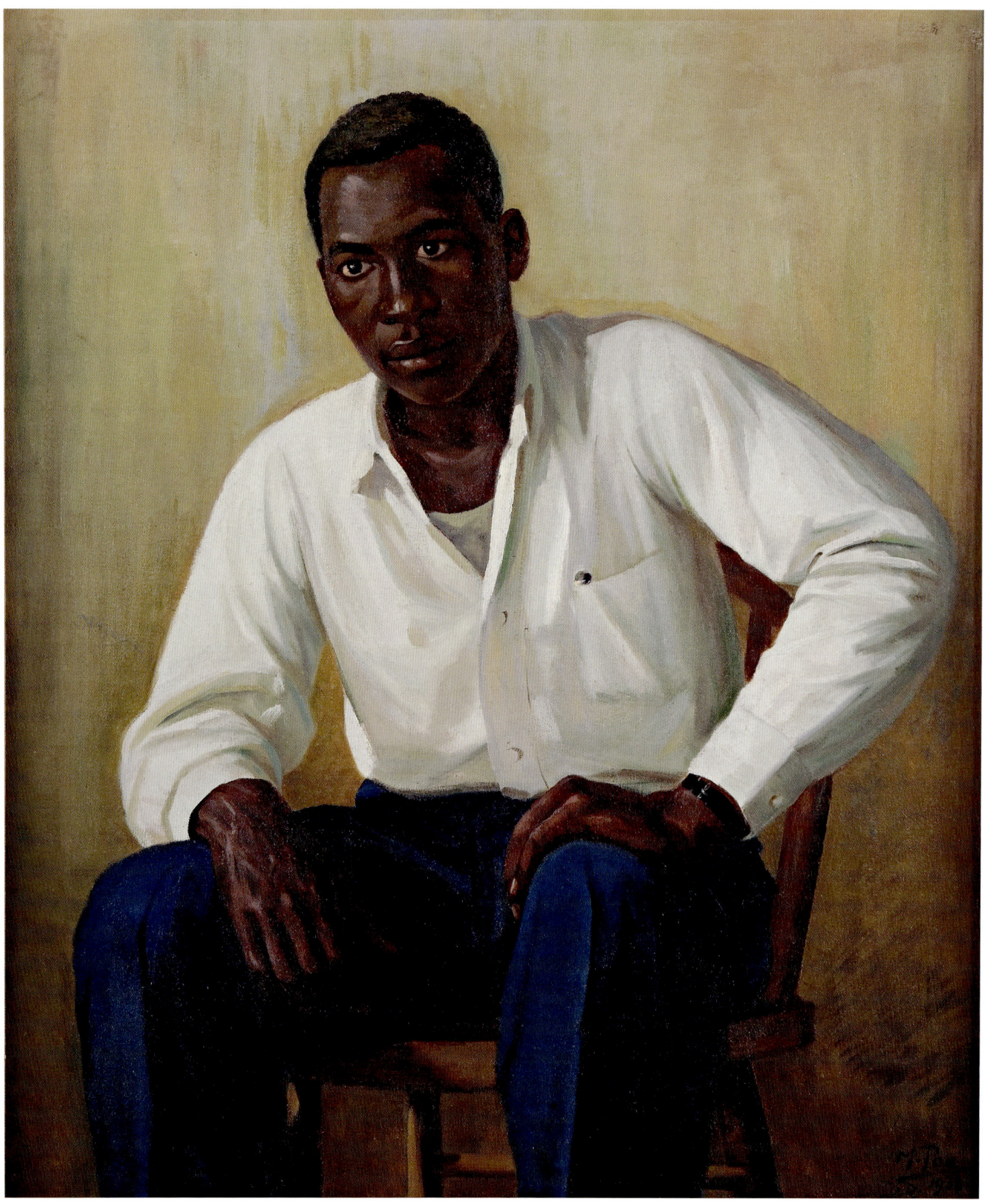
99

99 Miguel Pou y Becerra. *A Race of Dreamers (Portrait of Ciquí)*. 1938. Oil on canvas. Ponce, Puerto Rico, Museo de Arte de Ponce.

Rican art in the hands of the 1950s generation of modernist practitioners discussed below. Frade stated at one point that "Since all that is Puerto Rican is being swept away by the wind, … I seek to perpetuate it in paint."[17]

The country's second city, Ponce, became a provincial outpost of artistic activity in the 1920s and beyond. One of the few artists of genuine talent to emerge there from the late Spanish colonial era was Miguel Pou y Becerra (1880–1968). Like Oller, to whom Pou and all other Puerto Rican artists of this period were most indebted, Pou worked in a variety of genres. His studies at New York's Art Students League in the first decade of the century (he was the first Puerto Rican painter to make a career based on his studies in the United States) were defining for his later development as a landscapist and portraitist. Among Pou's most well-known works are his nostalgic evocations of the cityscape of Ponce and its horse-drawn carriages. Yet his portrait of a well-known baseball player of the 1930s named Ciquí (1938) is an impressive, informal evocation of a virile, young Afro-Puerto Rican man. The painting is created using tones of black, brown, and white. Pou's vigorous handling of the paint recalls his admiration for the art of members of New York's Ashcan School, including Robert Henri (1865–1929) and William Glackens (1870–1938). The art historian Marimar Benítez has stated that this is Pou's "best painting of a black person, a racial type that does not figure often in Puerto Rican painting."[18]

During the period between the First and Second World Wars, in which thousands of Puerto Ricans served in the U.S. armed forces, the economic fortunes of the island faltered and fell into a state of lassitude. Following World War II, an unprecedented period of migration from Puerto Rico began, with New York City and surrounding regions receiving the bulk of the newcomers. U.S. government authorities, together with Puerto Rican officials, headed by the first island-born governor, Luis Muñóz Marín, appointed in 1947, initiated an economic welfare project called *Operación Manos a la Obra* (Operation Bootstrap) designed to transform the still mainly agrarian island into a modern, industrialized economy. Although primarily directed at the business and technology sectors, Operation Bootstrap had a serious impact on the arts. In the island's history of the visual arts, the 1950s may be described as a period of reawakening and strengthening of the areas of painting, photography, and especially the graphic arts. The University of Puerto Rico, established in 1903 and located in the San Juan suburb of Río Piedras, became a focal point for art making. The campus's Museum of History, Anthropology and Art, with a collection that was begun in 1935—its most famous painting, the aforementioned *El velorio* by Francisco Oller—has served as a stimulus for thousands of visitors interested in the art and material culture of the country. In 1949, a government-supported initiative, the Division of Community Education, known in Puerto Rico by its acronym DIVEDCO for División de Educación de la Comunidad, was created; within it, the print workshop established a platform for artists interested in graphic arts. The following year, 1950, witnessed the founding of the Centro de Arte de Puerto Rico (CAP), a collective of a group of young artists interested in advancing the visual culture of their country and displaying the island's history as well as the richness of its ethnic diversity.

Among the outstanding artists associated with the modernizing movements on the island were the above-discussed Carlos Raquel Rivera as well as Lorenzo Homar (1913–2004) and Rafael

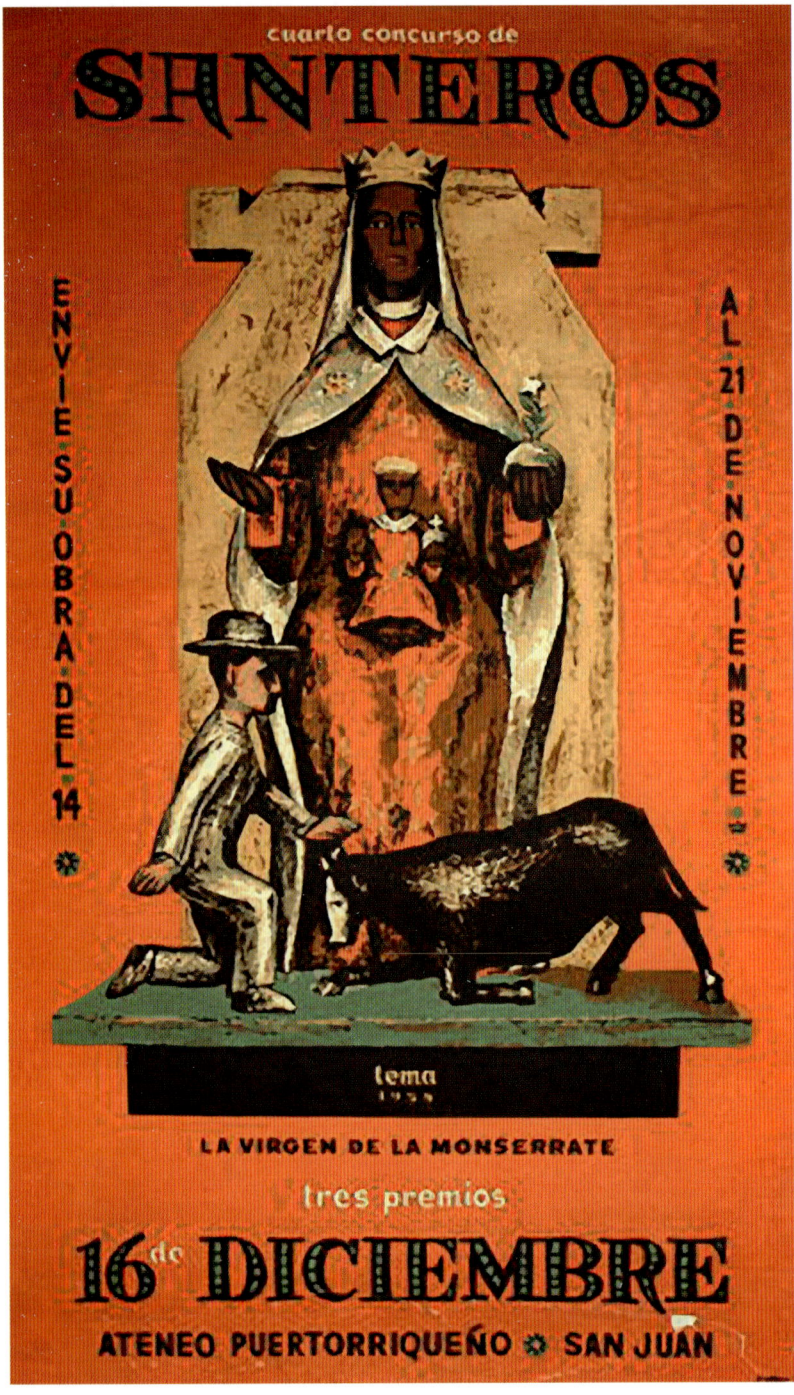

100

100 Lorenzo Homar. *Fourth Contest of Santeros*. 1955. Poster. Silkscreen.

Tufiño (1922–2008). All members of the CAP, an organization that effected a veritable transformation of the art scene in and beyond San Juan, were painters, yet their strong suit—and the art form for which this period in Puerto Rican art history is most noted—was print- and poster making.[19] This dedication to graphic work, which has persisted within the art context of the country, bore considerable fruit. In 1970 the San Juan Biennial of Latin American and Caribbean Graphic Art was established. It continues to function today as a Triennial, still serving as a major venue for exhibition and discussion of a wide variety of graphic arts.

Lorenzo Homar was born in Puerto Rico but trained as an artist in New York. His prints and posters are among the most well-known products to celebrate Puerto Rican culture, and within that category, Blackness and its importance within Puerto Rican society are commemorated in a variety of images. Many of his early posters functioned as announcements of educational films, exhibitions, theatrical or musical performances, or recent publications of Puerto Rican literature. A 1955 print, *Cuarto Concurso de Santeros*, announces the fourth annual competition organized by the Ateneo in San Juan to promote the work of *santeros* or carvers of popular wooden devotional images. The principal figure here is that of the Black Virgin of Montserrat, a Spanish advocation of the Virgin Mary venerated at the sixteenth-century basilica dedicated to her in the town of Hormigueros in the western part of the island. The Virgen de Hormigueros, as she is known locally, is represented as a wood *santo* figure. The dark-skinned Madonna is accompanied by a figure of a man and a bull, a reference to one of the miracles performed in the seventeenth century when a peasant encountered a wild bull that threatened his life. When he invoked the name of the Virgen de Hormigueros, the

101 Lorenzo Homar. *Paintings of José Campeche and His Workshop*. Poster. 1959. San Juan, Puerto Rico, Museo de Historia, Antropología y Arte de Río Piedras.

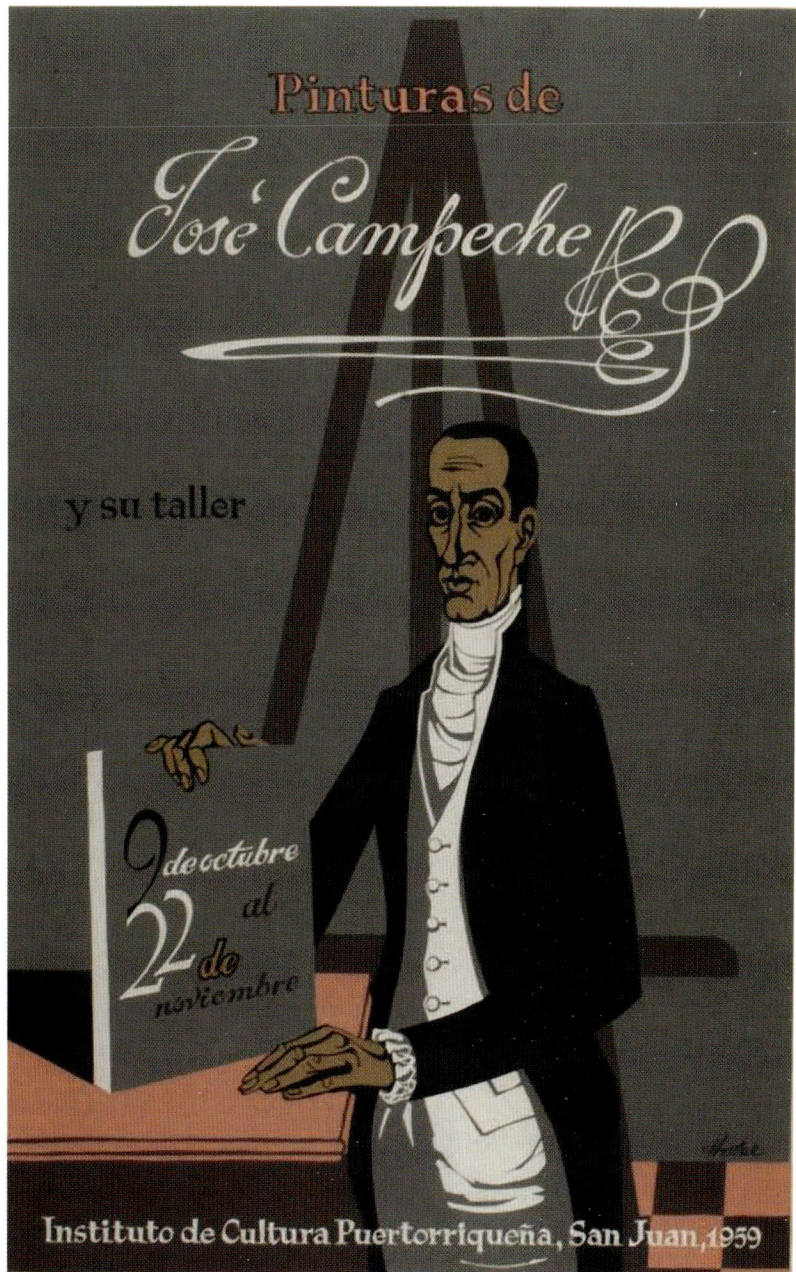

101

bull suddenly knelt down in front of him, and he was spared. An exhibition at the Instituto de Cultura Puertorriqueña (Institute of Puerto Rican Culture) in San Juan of the work of José Campeche and his workshop is celebrated in Homar's 1959 poster *Pinturas de José Campeche y su taller*, which depicts his own version of the Black painter's self-portrait discussed above. Campeche stands before his easel, but instead of holding a picture of the Virgin of Sorrows, he grasps a canvas on which are written the dates of the show.

Rafael Tufiño was born in Brooklyn, New York, to a Black Puerto Rican family that had emigrated to the United States before the great waves of settlement in mid-century New York. He returned with his parents to the island when he was four years old. Studies in San Juan and at the Academia de San Carlos in Mexico City with the painter and printmaker José Chávez Morado (1909–2002) were tremendously important for Tufiño. His experience in Mexico promoted Tufiño's developing interest in subject matter drawn from the lives of people around him in accordance with the Mexican School's tendencies toward social realism. Tufiño was a founding member of the CAP and highly influential in all phases of Puerto Rican painting and graphic arts well into the early years of the present century. His 1967 silkscreen poster *La plena*, which announced the release of a film produced by DIVEDCO, shows a three-quarter-length Black singer and musician dressed in a red shirt, starkly outlined by the bright yellow of the background. The *plena* is a traditional musical format for telling stories derived from the urban and rural folk culture of the country. Symbols of some of the characters in the best known of these songs are visible to the left and right of the singer's head.

Tufiño's painting expresses, in many instances, his innate iden-

BLACK VISUALITIES IN PUERTO RICO AND THE DOMINICAN REPUBLIC 191

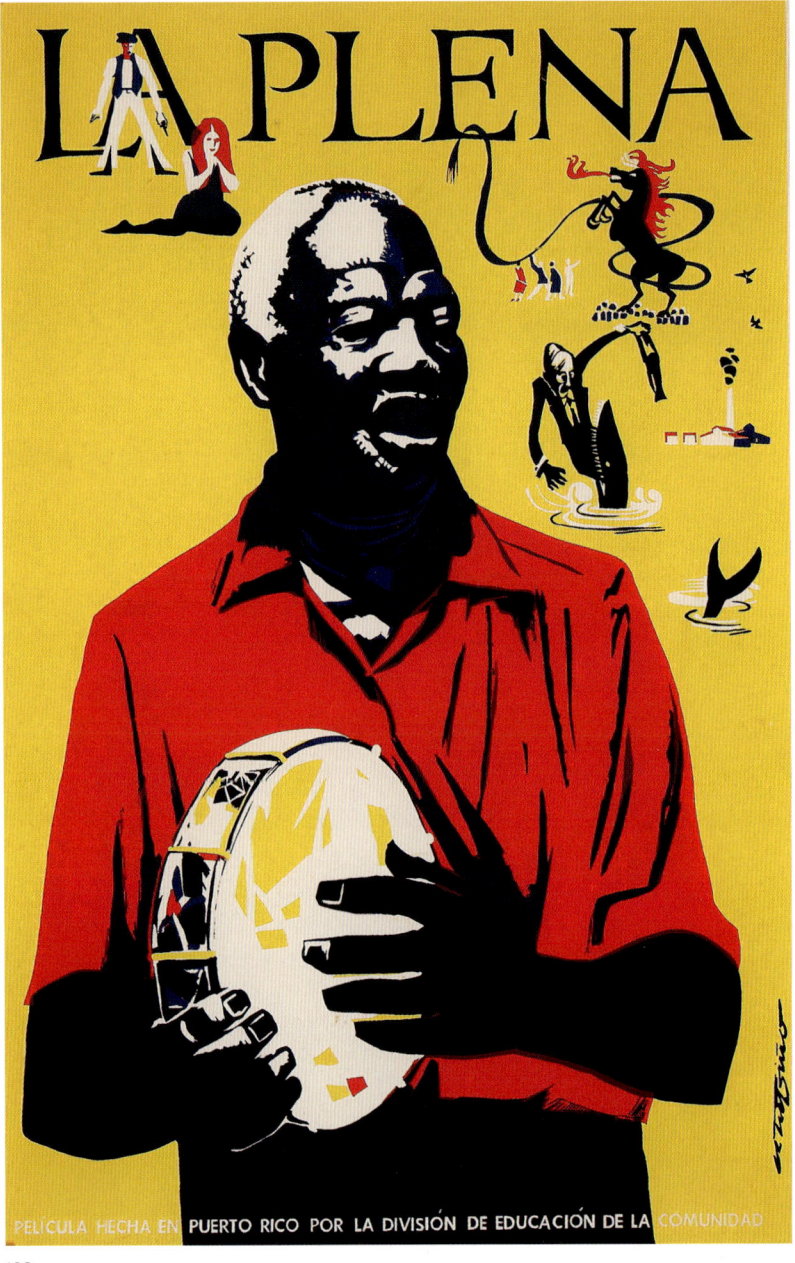

102

102 Rafael Tufiño. *La plena*. 1967. Poster. Serigraph. San Juan, Museo de Arte de Puerto Rico.

103 Rafael Tufiño. *Goyita*. 1953. Oil on masonite. San Juan, Instituto de Cultura Puertorriqueña.

tification with the Black ethnicities of the island. His most famous and arguably most affective work of art is his 1953 portrait of his mother. *Goyita* is a close-up portrayal of a middle-aged woman. The artist brings her upper torso and head so close to us that we have a direct, candid, and unmistakably clear encounter with her. She does not confront the viewer's gaze directly but instead looks off to a point slightly beyond the frame of the picture to her left. Goyita wears a red head wrap, a reference to her Afrodescendant slave roots. She stands before a humble townscape of one-story houses. Goyita has a determined, somewhat stern look on her face. There is in this work a curious, even haunting combination of pain and fortitude.

The Puerto Rican art historian Teresa Tió aptly describes the portrait of Goyita in a lengthy essay written for the artist's major retrospective exhibition, *Rafael Tufiño: Pintor del pueblo* (*Rafael Tufiño: Painter of the People*) organized by the Museo de Arte de Puerto Rico (San Juan) in 2001. It was also seen in early 2002 at El Museo del Barrio, New York.[20] It is worth including a quotation from this essay as it captures some of the essential qualities of this picture:

192   BLACK VISUALITIES IN PUERTO RICO AND THE DOMINICAN REPUBLIC

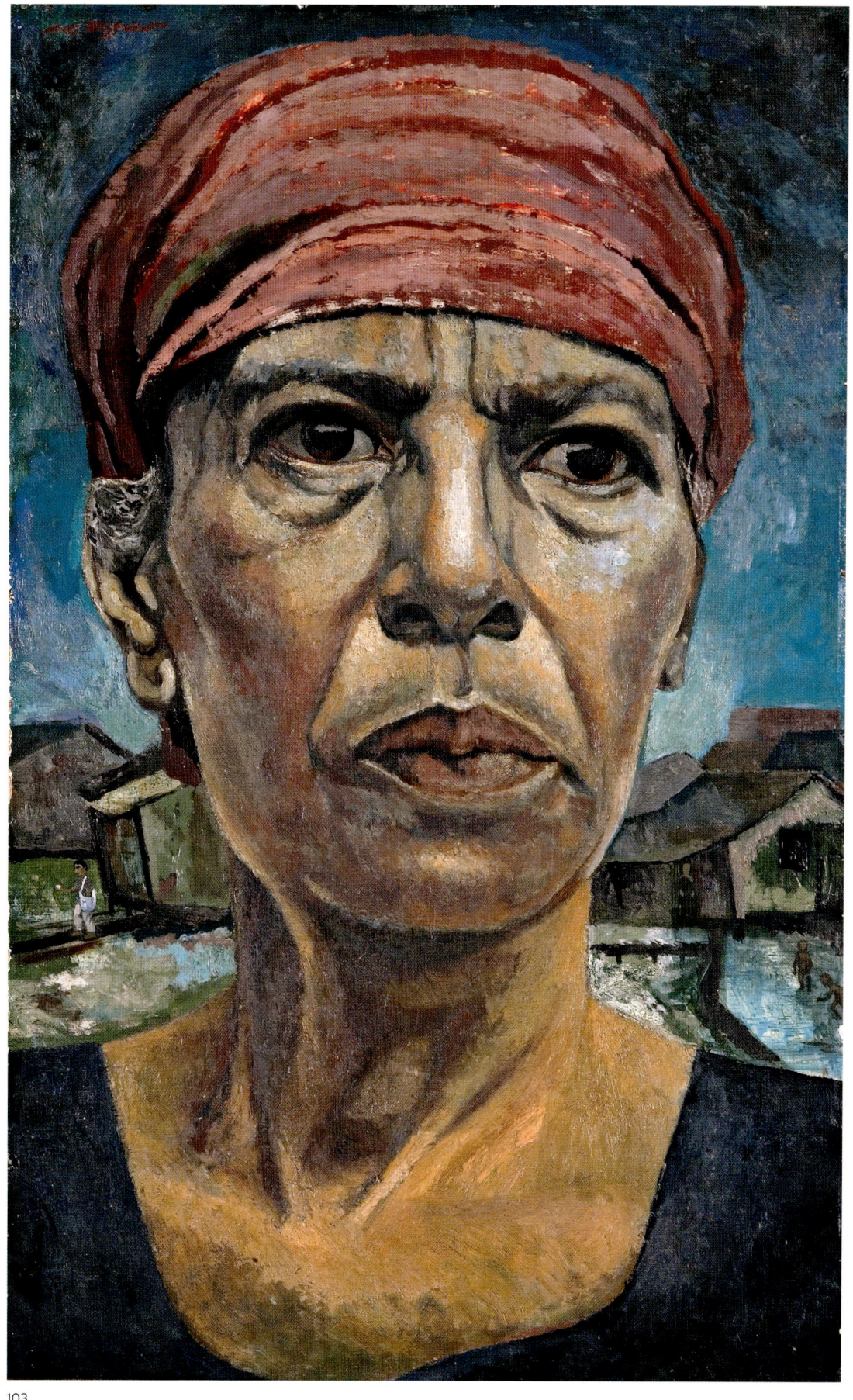

103

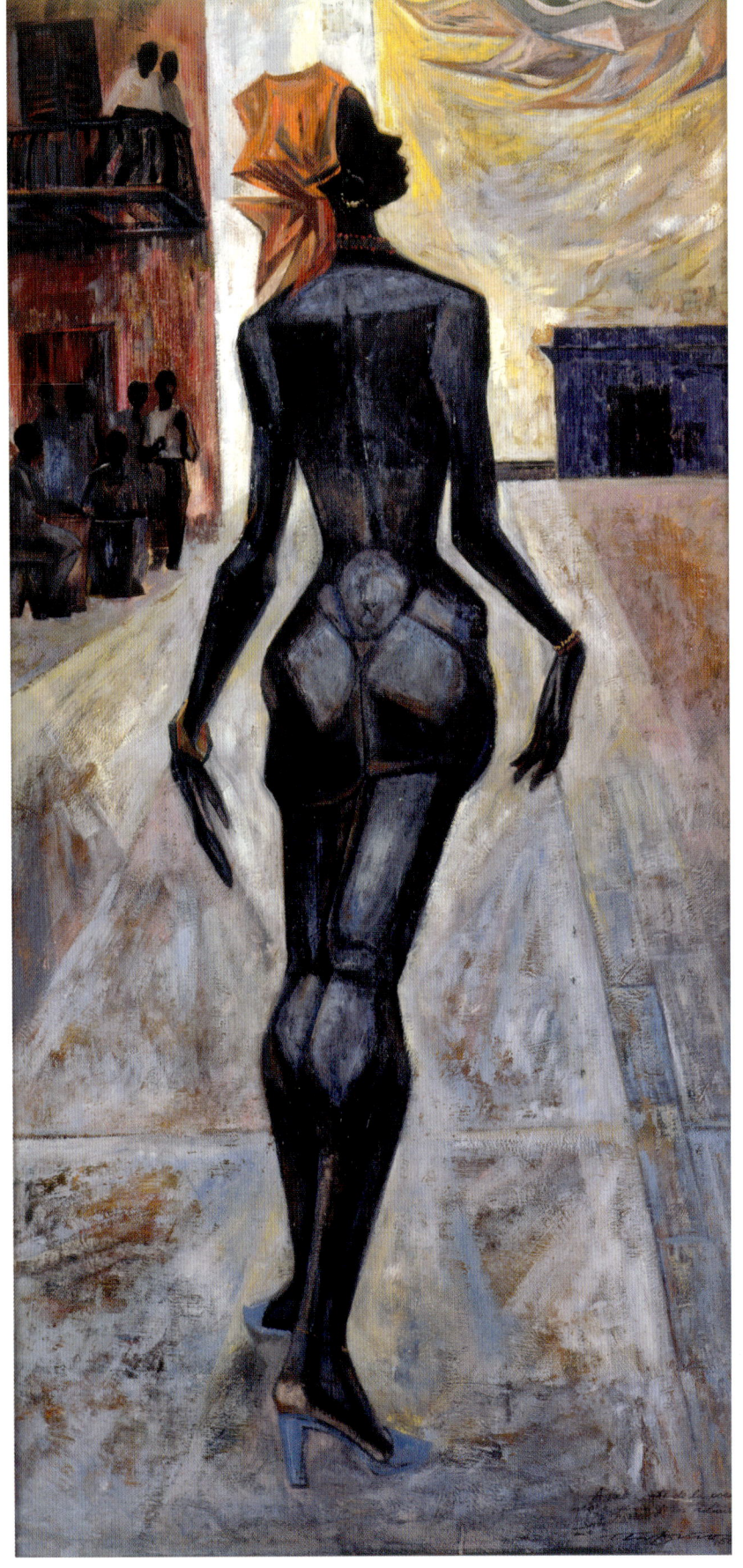

104

104 Rafael Tufiño. *Black Majesty*. 1958. Oil on canvas. San Juan, Puerto Rico, Cooperativa de Seguros Multiples.

This masterful portrait of [Tufiño's] mother is not the depiction of a certain woman. It has become, or better yet, we have made it an absolute icon of strength and determination. The landscape where her erect head appears, the barrio San José [in San Juan], portrays her reality of being a humble, hard-working woman. On the horizon there appears Tufiño, walking on the wooden planks with a bag of peanuts on his back. *Goyita* is the female version of the Black man of Oller's *El velorio*. Nonetheless, she is not looking at the dead child. She has fixed her gaze to another horizon, the horizon of life.[21]

In 1957 Tufiño's art was included in the *Exhibition of Puerto Rican Art* at the Riverside Museum, a now-defunct institution on Manhattan's Upper West Side that, until its closing in 1971, was very active in showing modern and contemporary art from Latin America and the Caribbean, among other places. At that same time, he created a portfolio of illustrations to accompany a poetry cycle by the foremost Puerto Rican creator of Afro-Antillean verses, Luis Palés Matos. *Canción festiva para ser llorada* (*Festive Song to Be Cried*) consists of ten sheets, each of which contains an illustration placed next to Palés's poetry. The first illustration intrigued Tufiño so much that he revisited its composition for his 1958 canvas *Majestad negra* (*Black Majesty*). In this painting, a young, statuesque woman is seen from the back as she walks down a street, her head raised proudly to the sky. She wears a short skirt and high-heeled shoes, and her head is wrapped in a red bandanna. We can see here that the artist has clearly internalized some of the lessons of international abstract expressionism, incorporating them within in relentlessly figurative visual language. Again, a quotation from Teresa Tió attests to the power of this image: "Tufiño has … achieved a thorough dominion of the poetic rhythm, in the acoustic means of the color and in the profiles of the figures against the light, so black that it is transformed into blue tonalities in the illuminated planes that enhance the movement of the image."[22]

I here return briefly to photography to end this consideration of Blackness in the arts of Puerto Rico in the mid-twentieth century. The Ukrainian-born photographer Jack Delano (1914–1997) came to the United States in 1923 and became an American citizen. By the mid-1930s he was employed by the U.S. Farm Security Administration (FSA) photography program. A contemporary and colleague of such renowned American photographers and FSA employees as Dorothea Lange (1895–1965), Arthur Rothstein (1915–1985), and Russell Lee (1903–1986), all of whom documented the rural and urban scene during the Great Depression, Delano and his wife, the artist Irene Delano (1919–1982), worked in Puerto Rico from the 1940s until the 1980s. Jack Delano located permanently to the island in 1946 and continued to work there until the early 1980s. Two of his photographs, one from the early phase of his career and the other from the later part, echo the compositions of work by Tufiño and offer a glimpse at Puerto Rican Black individuals with intimate insight. The 1946 *At a Religious Procession in San Juan on Saint John the Baptist Day* may remind us of the portrait of Tufiño's mother. It captures the subject's beauty, piety, and determination. The musicians in the 1981 photograph *Musicians at the Patron Saint's Festivities in the Town of Loíza Aldea* (a town on the coastal plain of northeastern Puerto Rico noted for its large Black population descended from the many people of color who were brought there enslaved

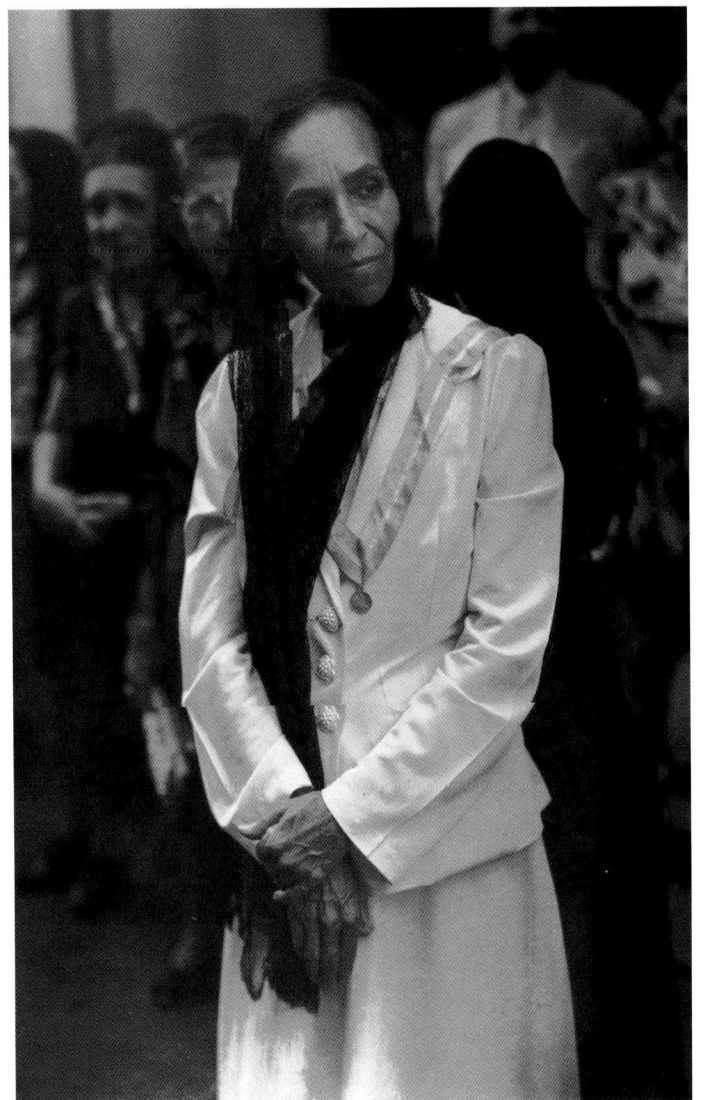

105

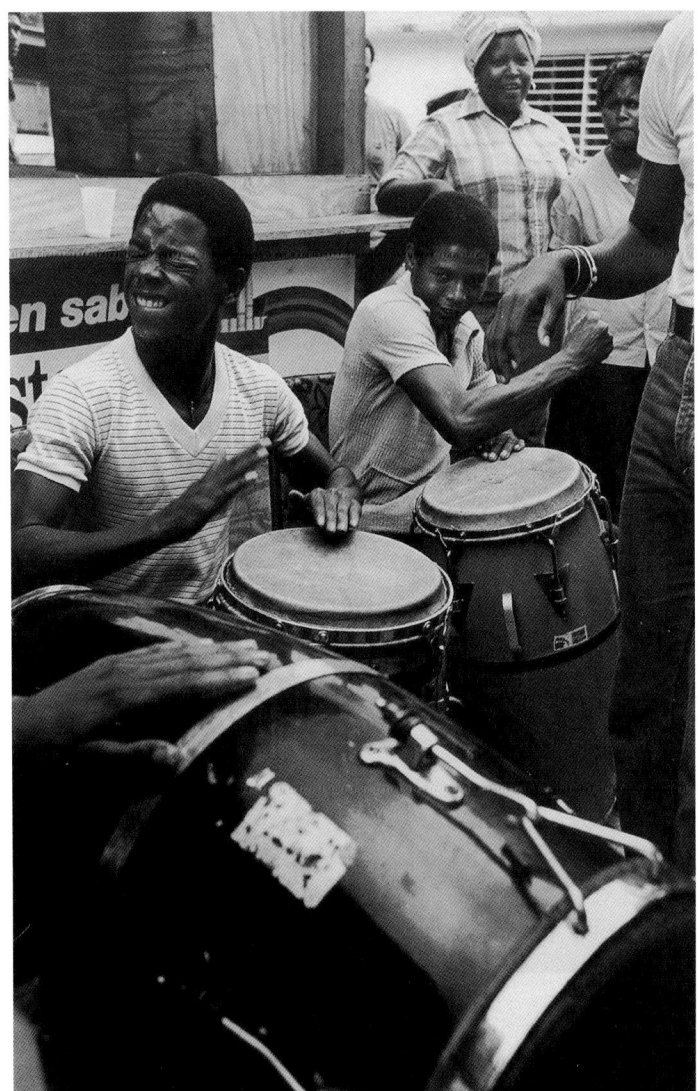

106

105 Jack Delano. *At a Religious Procession in San Juan on Saint John the Baptist Day*. 1946. Photograph.

106 Jack Delano. *Musicians at the Patron Saint's Festivities in the Town of Loíza Aldea*. 1981. Photograph.

107 Arnaldo Roche Rabell. *We Have to Dream in Blue*. 1986. Oil on canvas. Collection of John T. Belk III and Margarita Serapión.

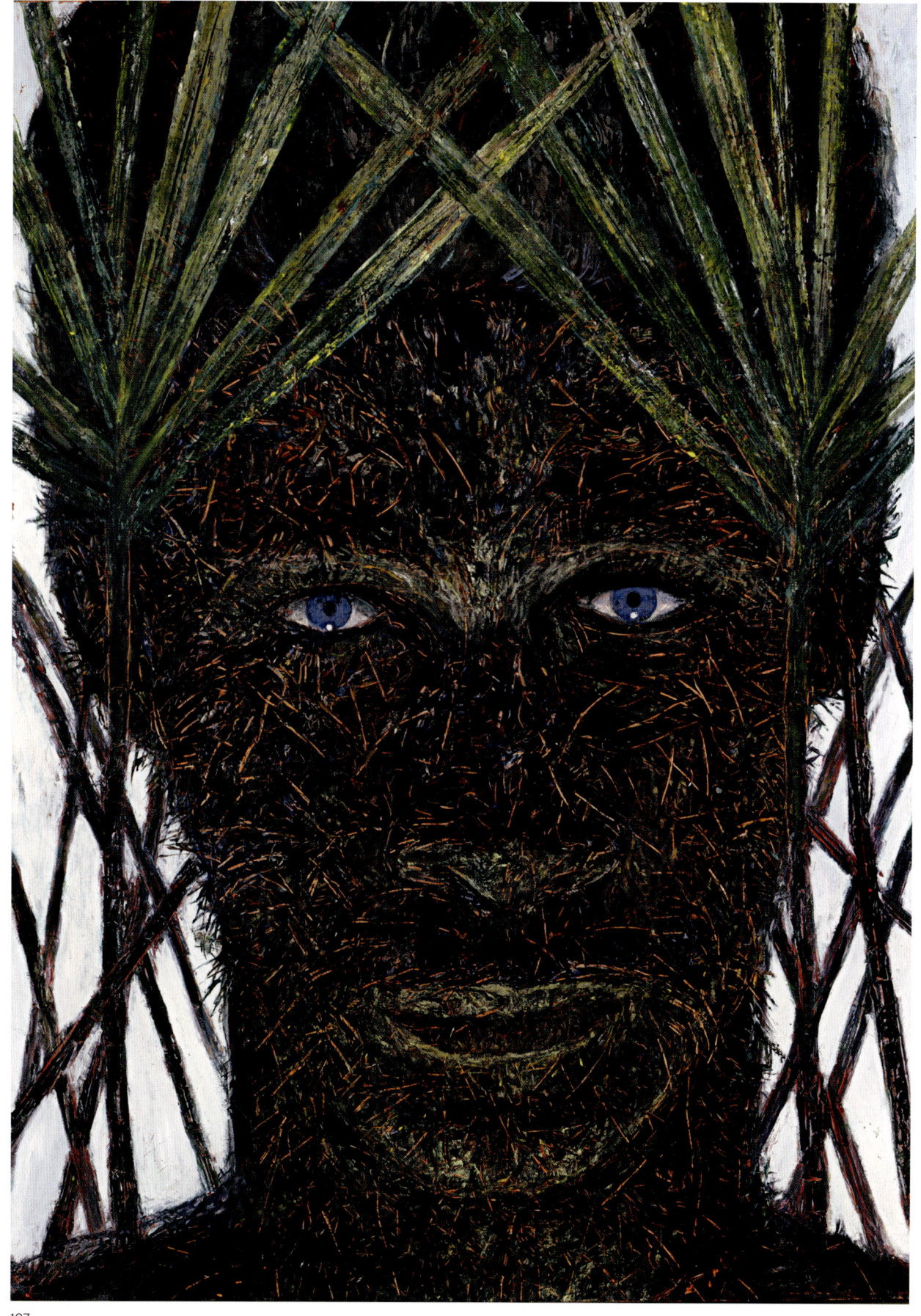
107

or who settled there as free persons of color) remind us of Tufiño's magisterial figure in the poster for *La plena*. Unlike the voyeuristic photographs of Black Puerto Ricans in the 1898 albums described earlier in this essay, the images by Jack Delano speak to the artist's affection for and intense identification with a wide swath of the island's population of all ethnicities.[23]

As an ending to this consideration of Puerto Rican art and the role of the image of the Black, we may consider a self-portrait by the Afro-Antillean artist Arnaldo Roche Rabell (1955–2018) that simultaneously represents self-affirmation and the questioning of the position of persons of color within the island's art world. The 1986 work *Tenemos que soñar en azul (We Have to Dream in Blue)* displays, as does Tufiño's portrait of Goyita, his own face in an ultra-close-up view. Roche stares directly out at us, his head emerging from a tangle of palm fronds, an effect achieved by the artist placing real fronds onto the wet canvas and pulling them away when the paint is not quite dry. His face is very dark, mottled, and somber. Blackness pervades this image, but the artist's bright blue eyes connect with those of his viewer. This portrait concentrates on the color of his eyes and presents his own questions of identity. Blue eyes are conventionally connected with whiteness and blondness, yet here they are a feature of a haunting, sober, and unforgettably self-aware Black face. Roche, who trained at the School of the Art Institute of Chicago, came of age in the artistic generation of the 1980s, with its interest in expressionistic (or neo-expressionist) form. In this and other related works, Roche makes ironic reference to the art world's preoccupation with gesture and rawness to assert Blackness and stresses the importance of both looking and dreaming comfortably within the spectrum of one's own skin tone.

Quisqueya

This term, meaning "mother of all lands," is the original Taíno name for the island that was originally dedicated to St. Dominic after it was first sighted at the end of Christopher Columbus's initial voyage of conquest. Santo Domingo, or Saint-Domingue in French, was the colonial denomination of the entire island, eventually becoming Aití (Haiti) and the Dominican Republic. Today the word *Quisqueya* indicates the western part of the landmass and is used by Dominicans to denote pride in their homeland.

Quisqueya also carries racial connotations, defining a "differentness" from "Haiti," a name and a term that to many Dominicans indicates Blackness as opposed to the deeper identification with both Spain and whiteness. This is of course a deeply problematic issue, as many writers have discussed, including the Dominican art historian Jeannette Miller. She and others have pointed out the paradoxical nature of racial identification in the western region of Hispaniola in terms of creating works of art. Miller states:

> A part of Dominican reality has been the idea of blackness, which similarly offers a starting point for modern artistic expression and is a factor for aesthetic change during the first half of the twentieth century. Blackness was both an internalized feeling and an avant-garde concept that challenged the old cultural standards defining beauty as white. Nonetheless, to accept their blackness was a complex process for Dominicans, one easier to understand if the Dominican struggle for independence from Haiti is recalled. The white element in the Dominican makeup represented their cultural identity in the face of "Haitianization": that is, a black country.[24]

In the above quotation, Miller refers specifically to the image of the Black in the growing definition of artistic modernization beginning around 1920 and continuing through the twentieth century that constitutes the subject of the following observations.

The dilemma of race and nationalism began to be articulated in this way at the end of the nineteenth century, when the concept of *El gran pesimismo dominicano* (The Great Dominican Pessimism) played a role in the writings of such critical social commentators as the Cuban-born Dominican essayist and novelist Federico García Godoy. Also discussing this theory in his writings was Eugenio María de Hostos, the Puerto Rican pedagogue, independence leader (whose portrait was painted by Francisco Oller), and essayist who settled in the Dominican capital and founded the first Escuela Normal (Teachers' College). Hostos, García Godoy, and others indicated a negative future for a racially and culturally "hybrid" nation.[25]

The Eurocentric element of Dominican art in the nineteenth and early twentieth centuries is predominant. Many artists who became well known in the small elite circles of Santo Domingo had studied in Spain or France. A census of Dominican painting circa 1900, for example, would reveal an emphasis on romantic landscapes and elegant portraits to adorn the salons of economically privileged citizens.

One of the pioneers of Dominican modernism, Celeste Woss y Gil (1891–1985), broke with this conservative tradition. Throughout her career, she created a series of images of nude women of color posing in her studio; in the Escuela Estudio, one of the private academies she founded in Santo Domingo in 1924 upon her return from two years of study at the Art Students League in New York; and in her Academia de Dibujo y Pintura, started in 1931. These were among the first organized art schools in the country. Woss y Gil also participated in the founding of the officially supported Escuela Nacional de Bellas Artes in 1942. Her importance as a teacher has been summed up in the words of the Afrodescendant Dominican artist Ada Balcácer (b. 1930), whose own art is remarked upon below. In 1995 she stated:

> One cannot consider the concept of activism on the part of Dominican women without taking into account the contribution of Celeste Woss y Gil; as a woman of advanced feminist ideas, creator and teacher who founded academies and centers of artistic teaching. Her pictorial work should be considered as stronger and freer than the men of her time and [she was] perhaps the model who inspired the movement of robust and powerful painting by women that went against the universal current of still lifes, scenes of motherhood and sweetly descriptive art.[26]

Woss y Gil's images of the *mulata* were called audacious or even scandalous when first exhibited in shows organized by her and her students, but they ultimately served as the basis for the initial depictions of Blacks in Dominican art and the reform, in terms of both non-academic style and subject matter, of the previously highly conservative nature of Dominican visual expression.

The daughter of Alejandro Woss y Gil, who twice served as president of the republic, Celeste Woss y Gil continued to create images of people of color throughout her long career. Her 1944 *El mercado* (*The Market*) shows two Black figures in straw hats arranging fruits and vegetables in an outdoor setting while other

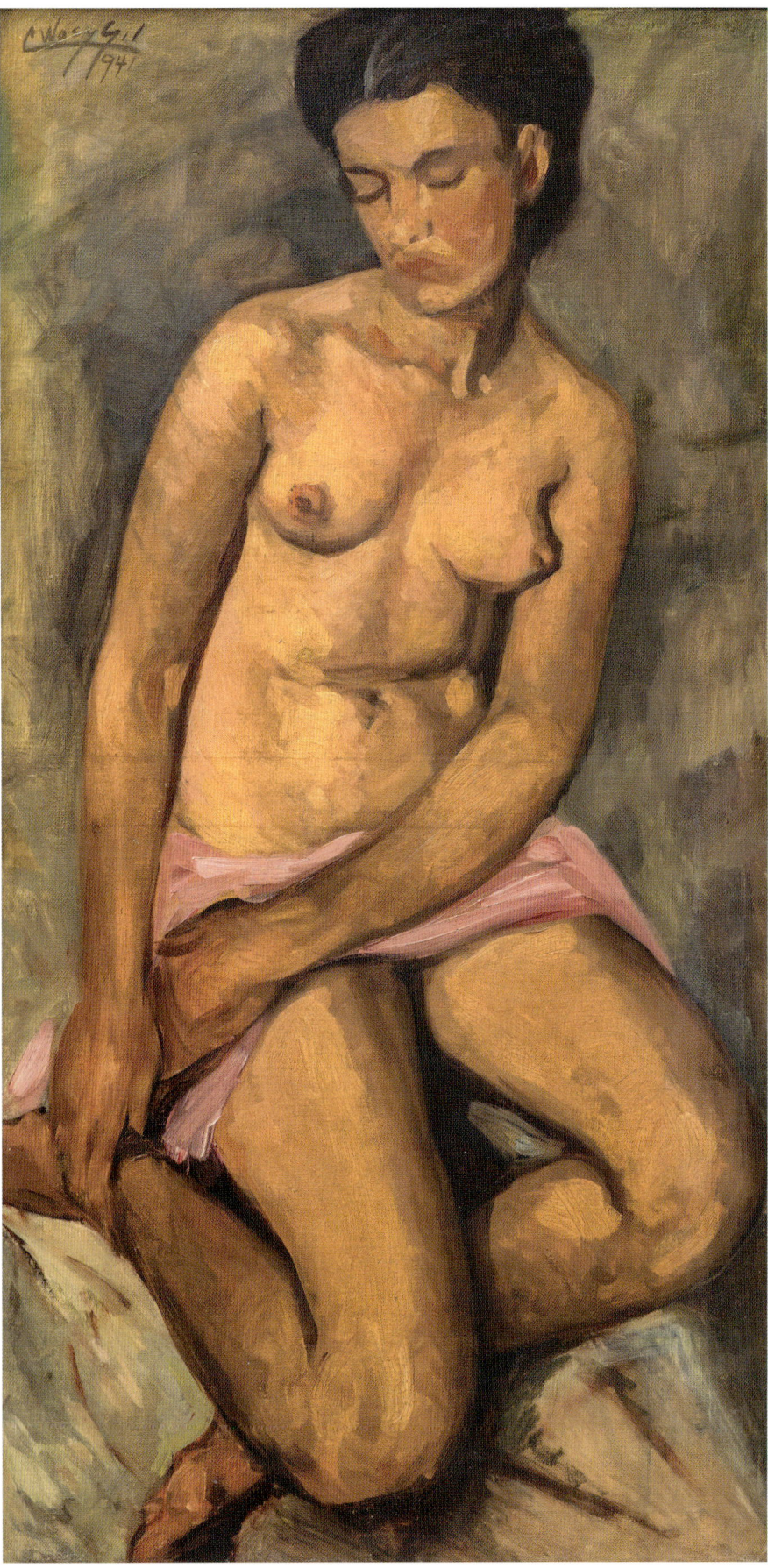

108 Celeste Woss y Gil. *Nude*. 1941. Oil on canvas. Santo Domingo, Dominican Republic, Museo de Arte Moderno.

109 Celeste Woss y Gil. *The Market*. 1945. Oil on canvas. Santo Domingo, Dominican Republic, Museo de Arte Moderno.

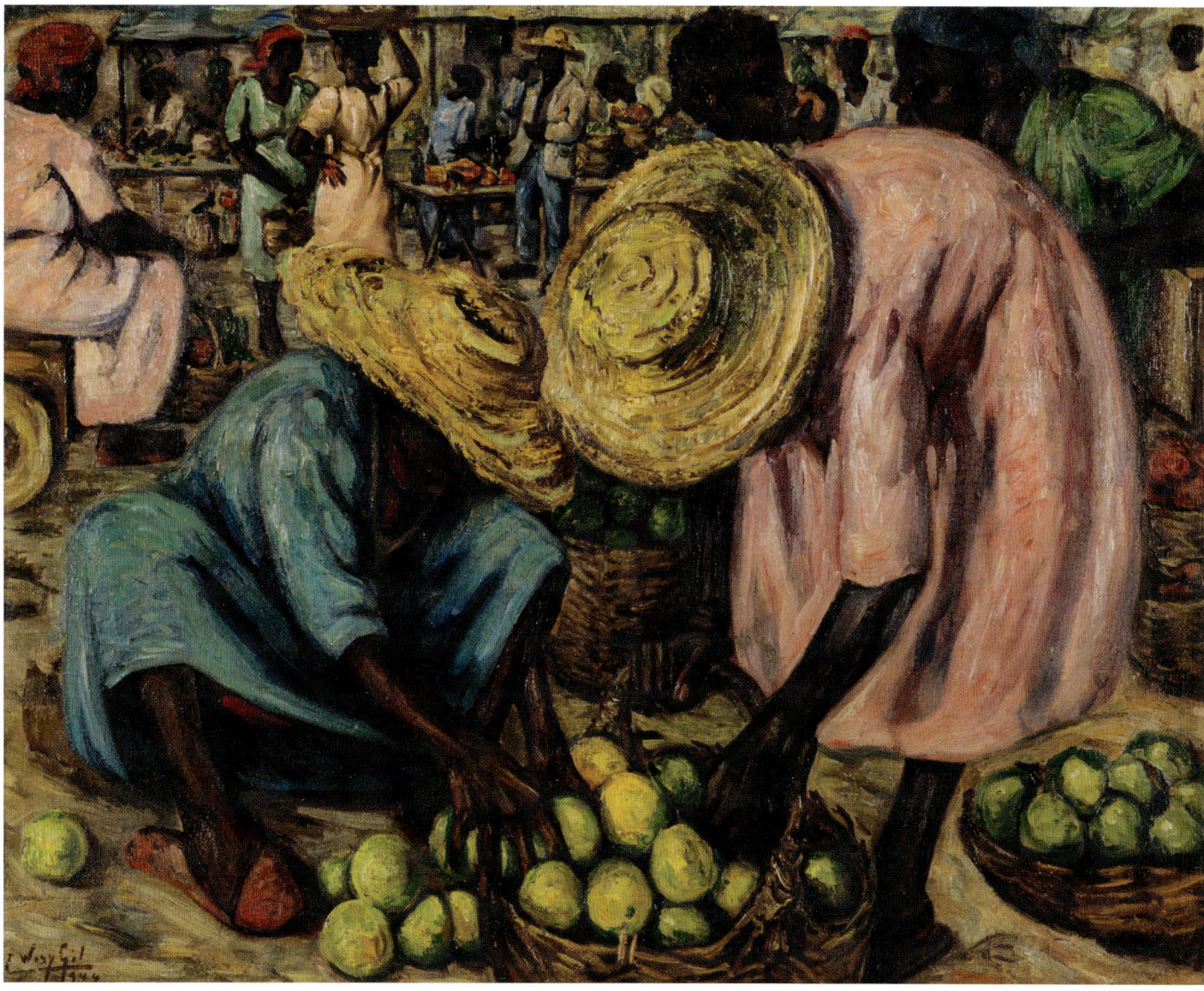

109

customers and vendors inhabit the background. This market scene recalls the numerous depictions of similar markets and other daily activities in neighboring Haiti depicted by Pétion Savain (1906–1973), one of the principal artists of the Haitian *inidgeniste* movement, an artistic and literary genre that arose in the 1930s and strived to evoke the "essential" nature of the people of Haiti. Depictions of the Black inhabitants of the countryside served as demonstrations of national pride and self-affirmation in the wake of the American invasion that had lasted from 1915 to 1934. Savain was one of the founders of the well-known Centre d'Art in Port-au-Prince in 1944, along with the American artist DeWitt Peters (1901–1966). It is not known if Woss y Gil knew the work of her Haitian contemporary, yet it is appropriate to mention this possible connection in the context of the Dominican Republic in the late 1930s and 1940s. This was a critical and tense time in Dominican-Haitian diplomatic and cultural relations. It was the moment of the previously mentioned 1937 "Parsley Massacre" of thousands of Haitians instigated by President Trujillo.

Another manifestation of the official Dominican stance against Blackness as a "national concept" was Trujillo's invitation to thousands of refugees fleeing the Spanish Civil War (1936–1939) to come to the republic and establish new lives in the countryside. That this was the core of a campaign to "whiten" the country and rid it of what was seen as the pernicious influence

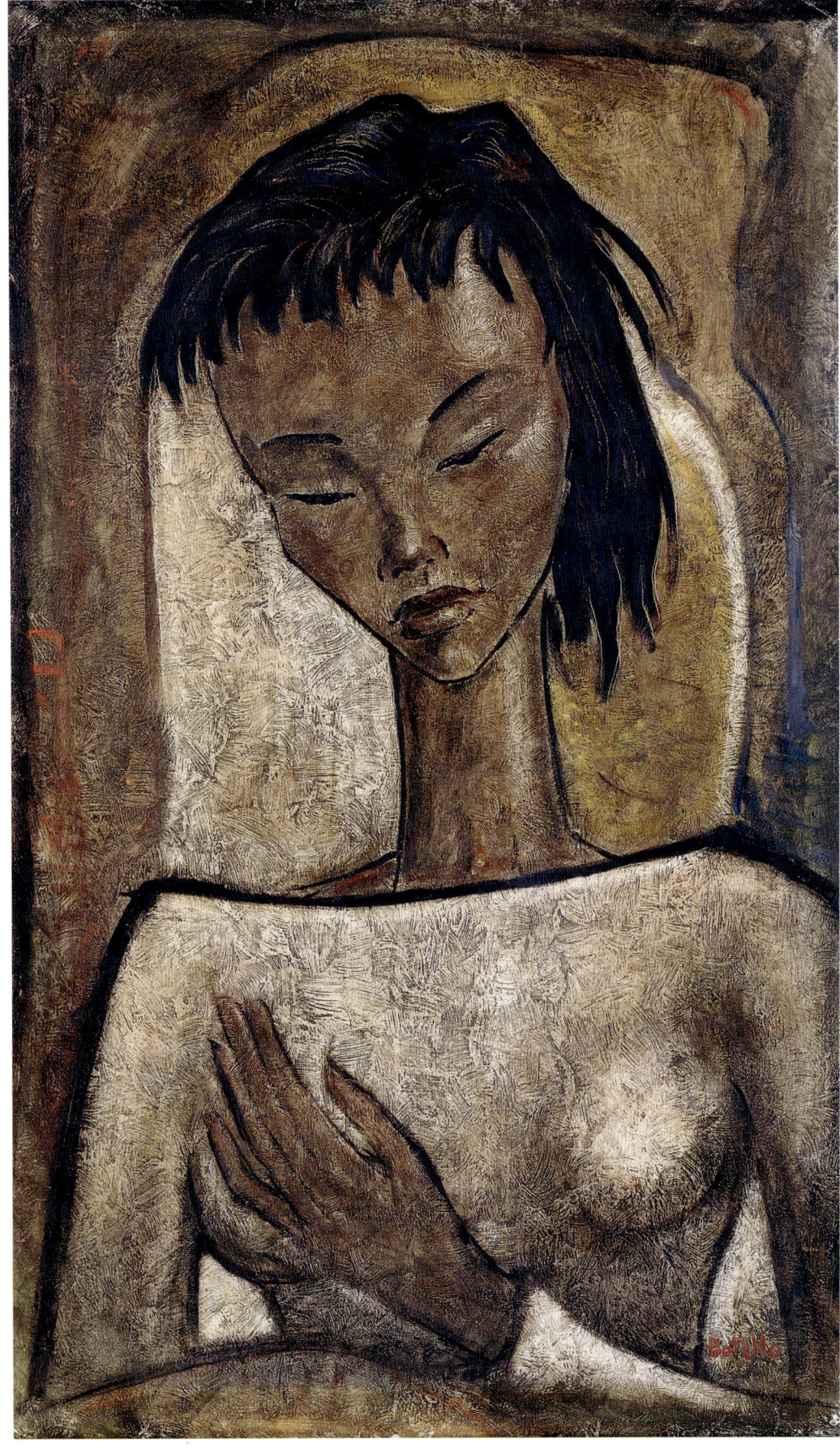

110 Angel Botello. *Haitian Woman*. Ca. 1950. Oil on board. Private collection.

111 Jaime Colson. *Merengue*. 1938. Oil on board. Santo Domingo, Dominican Republic, Museo Bellapart.

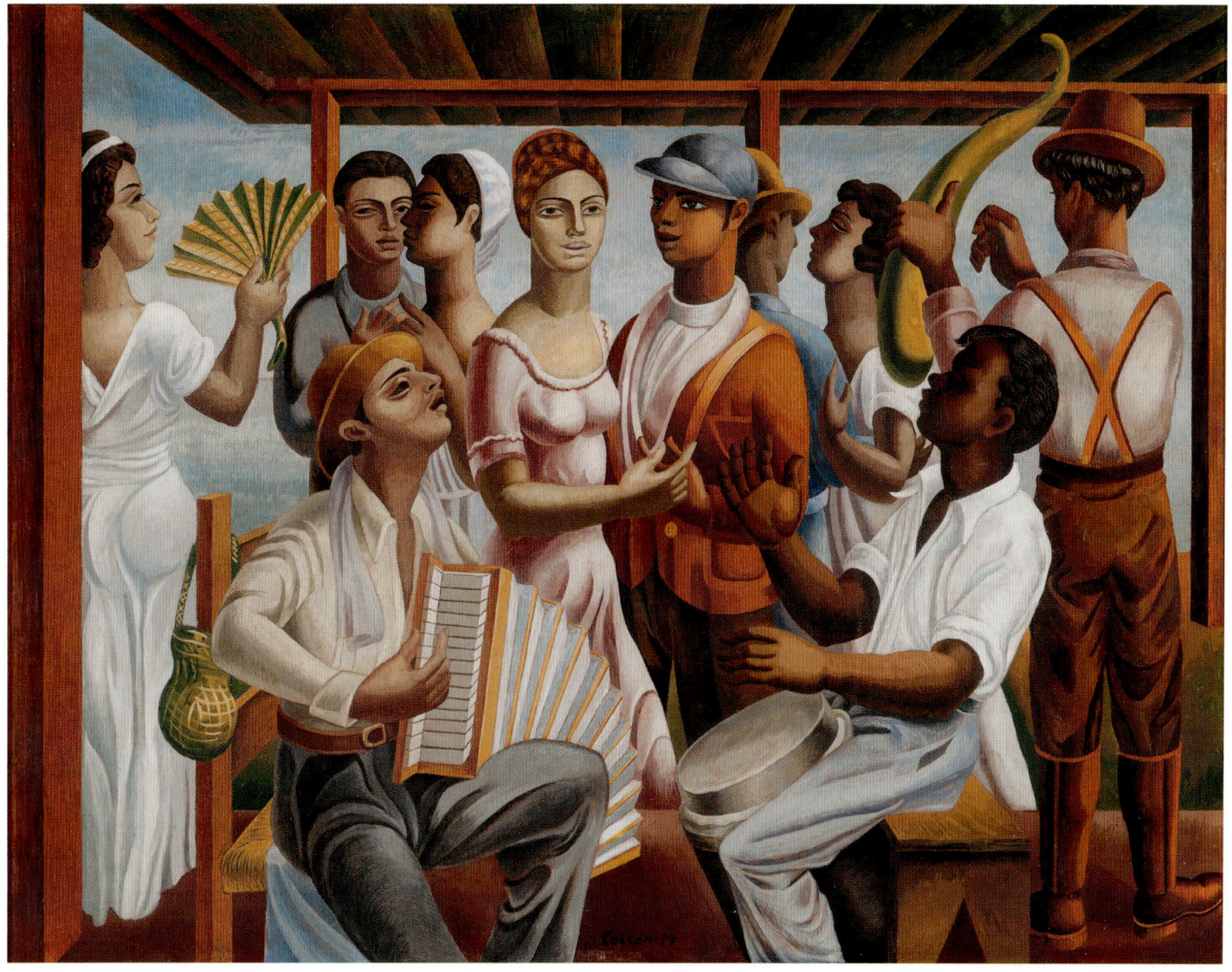
111

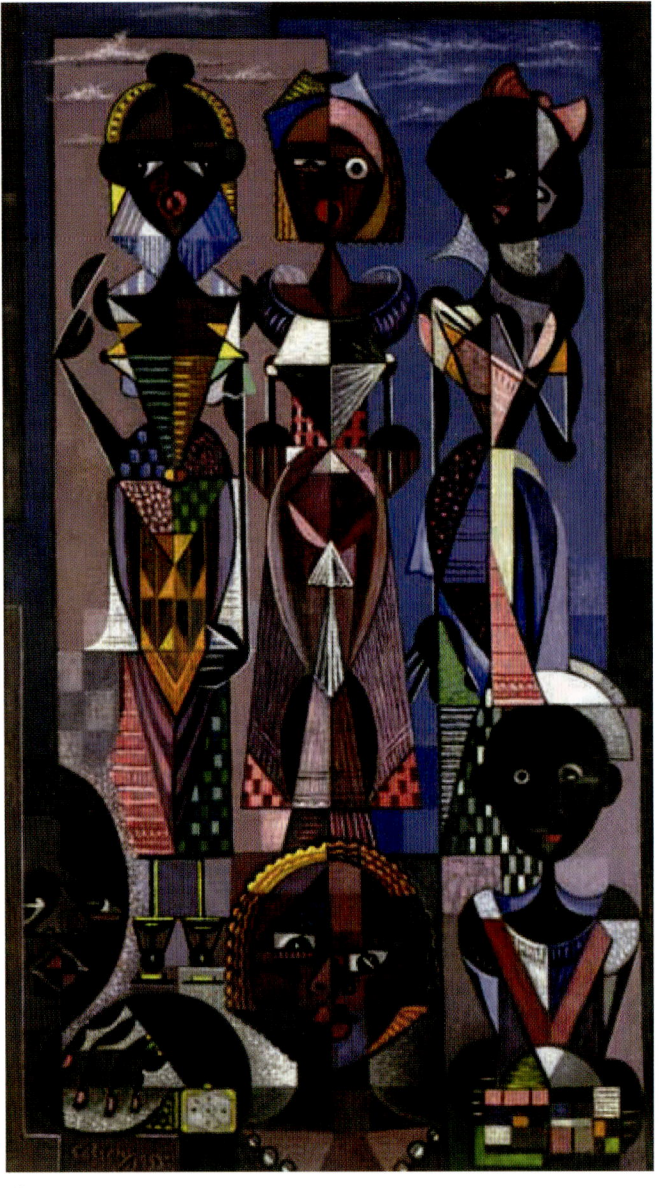

112

of its neighbor's Black identity was not stated outright. The plan failed, as most of the immigrants had not originally lived in rural areas but were urban-based workers or, more germane to our purposes, artists, musicians, writers, and intellectuals. A number of talented painters arrived in Santo Domingo between 1939 and 1940, making the capital, at least for a brief time, a hub of international artistic activity, as well as one of the Caribbean outposts of surrealism, especially after the 1941 visit of André Breton. Many of these Spaniards, including José Vela Zanetti (1913–1999) and José Gausachs (1889–1959), were attracted by those individuals they viewed as the "exotic" Afrodescendant inhabitants of the Dominican Republic, and they painted genre scenes and murals with Black Dominicans as their subjects.

Fleeing the Spain of Francisco Franco, Angel Botello (1913–1986) arrived in Santo Domingo in 1940. He traveled to Haiti as well as to Mexico between then and 1948, when he took up residence in Puerto Rico. He remained there for the rest of his life, becoming deeply embedded in the artistic and intellectual scene in San Juan. In both the Dominican Republic and during his travels in Haiti, he painted images of the Black female body that resonated with the interests on the part of his Dominican contemporaries for Blackness as subject matter for the "new" art in the capital. Botello's painting *Haitian Woman* is representative of this interest. As his career developed in Puerto Rico, Botello

110

112 Jaime Colson. *Fiesta in Guachupita*. 1955. Oil on wood. Santo Domingo, Dominican Republic, Museo Bellapart.

113 Gilberto Hernández Ortega. *Untitled*. 1976. Oil on canvas. Santo Domingo, Dominican Republic, Museo Bellapart.

114 Ada Balcácer. *Self-Portrait as a Young Painter without an Arm*. 2005-2010. Mixed media on canvas. Santo Domingo, Dominican Republic, Collection of the artist.

would develop a more experimental form of painting based on his continued interest in African sculpture as well as in Caribbean popular arts.[27]

Among mid-twentieth-century Dominican painters, Jaime Colson (1901–1975) was perhaps the most sophisticated—and peripatetic—proponent of an intriguingly personal mode of painting that combined references to cubism, futurism, and surrealism, a movement to which he had been introduced during his long periods of study and work in Europe and in Mexico City. Before continuing his travels to Paris, where the art of Fernand Léger (1881–1955) proved to be a particular source of inspiration in some of his paintings, he briefly returned to Santo Domingo in 1938 and began a body of work that took the Black figure as its principal subject. His most well-known image of this period is the 1938 *Merengue,* which represents a virtually encyclopedic view of racial mixing in the Dominican Republic. In addition, we observe a group playing instruments, representative of a pan-Caribbean taxonomy of forms of harmony as well as people performing a dance that has deep roots in the national personality.

A somewhat later painting, *Fiesta in Guachupita* from 1955, depicts stylized figures of five Afro-Dominican women and one man (at the lower left), also engaged in a musical performance. This work offers an interesting contrast to *Merengue* as it testifies to the artist's blending of his study of African art, which he had seen in the museums in Paris, with his interest in Dominican customs as practiced in the Santo Domingo neighborhood of Guachupita, a section of the city traditionally inhabited by Afrodescendant families.[28]

Considering the later-twentieth-century generation of Dominican artists and their continued interest in the Black body brings us to the work of two painters who studied with Celeste Woss y Gil later in her career. Gilberto Hernández Ortega (1923–1979) was one of the first major artists to emerge from the Escuela Nacional de Bellas Artes, where he took classes not only with Woss y Gil but also from the Spanish émigré artist Gausachs. He graduated in 1945. Throughout his career, he developed a distinct mode of expressionist and semi-abstract art. Virtually all of his works vibrate with a sense of urgency and quickly applied paint. The Black body plays a significant role and appears in many guises, from scenes of street life to images of religious figures as persons of color. Completed only three years before his death, an *Untitled* work of 1976 portrays a dark-skinned female figure seen in profile, facing to her right. Her facial features are exaggerated: her chin and nose are elongated; her neck is impossibly long. She wears an extravagant arrangement of flowers and fruits in her hair. Hernández Ortega has often been associated with surrealism, although I prefer to look at his work through the lens of the international avant-garde's interest in the expressionistic potential of idiosyncratic form. One of the artists whose work evidently touched the imagination of Hernández Ortega was the Cuban Afro-Chinese painter and printmaker Wifredo Lam (1902–1988), whose impact on cross-Caribbean visuality was definitive starting in the 1940s.

When discussing the presence of Blackness in Caribbean art of many venues, we must inevitably face the dilemma of questioning the artist's own identity as well as the audience for whom the works are destined. In the case of virtually every Dominican artist mentioned here, we are dealing with either a white, elite painter or one of mixed race, primarily from and working for the urban elites, the only socioeconomic class for whom the fine

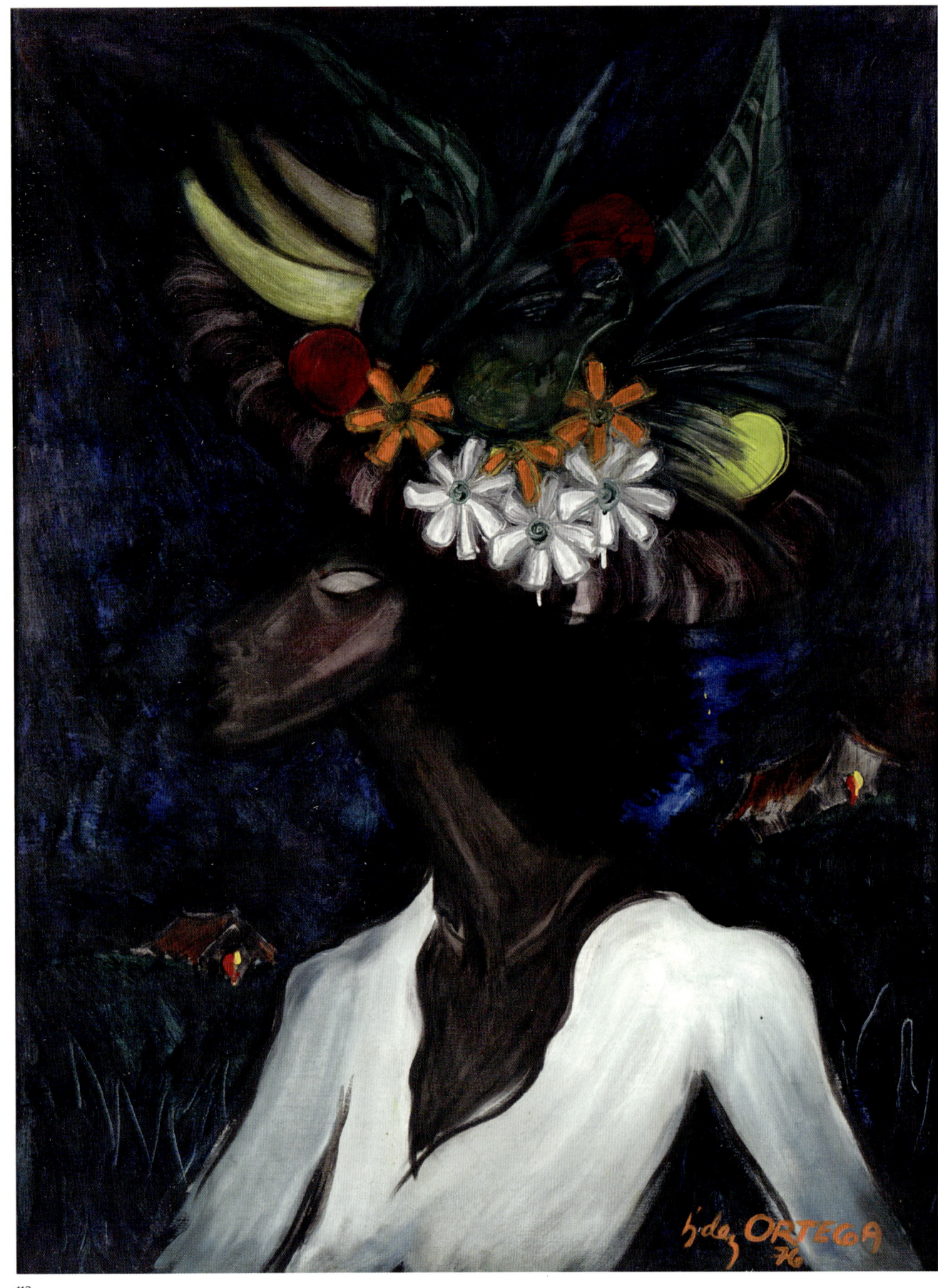

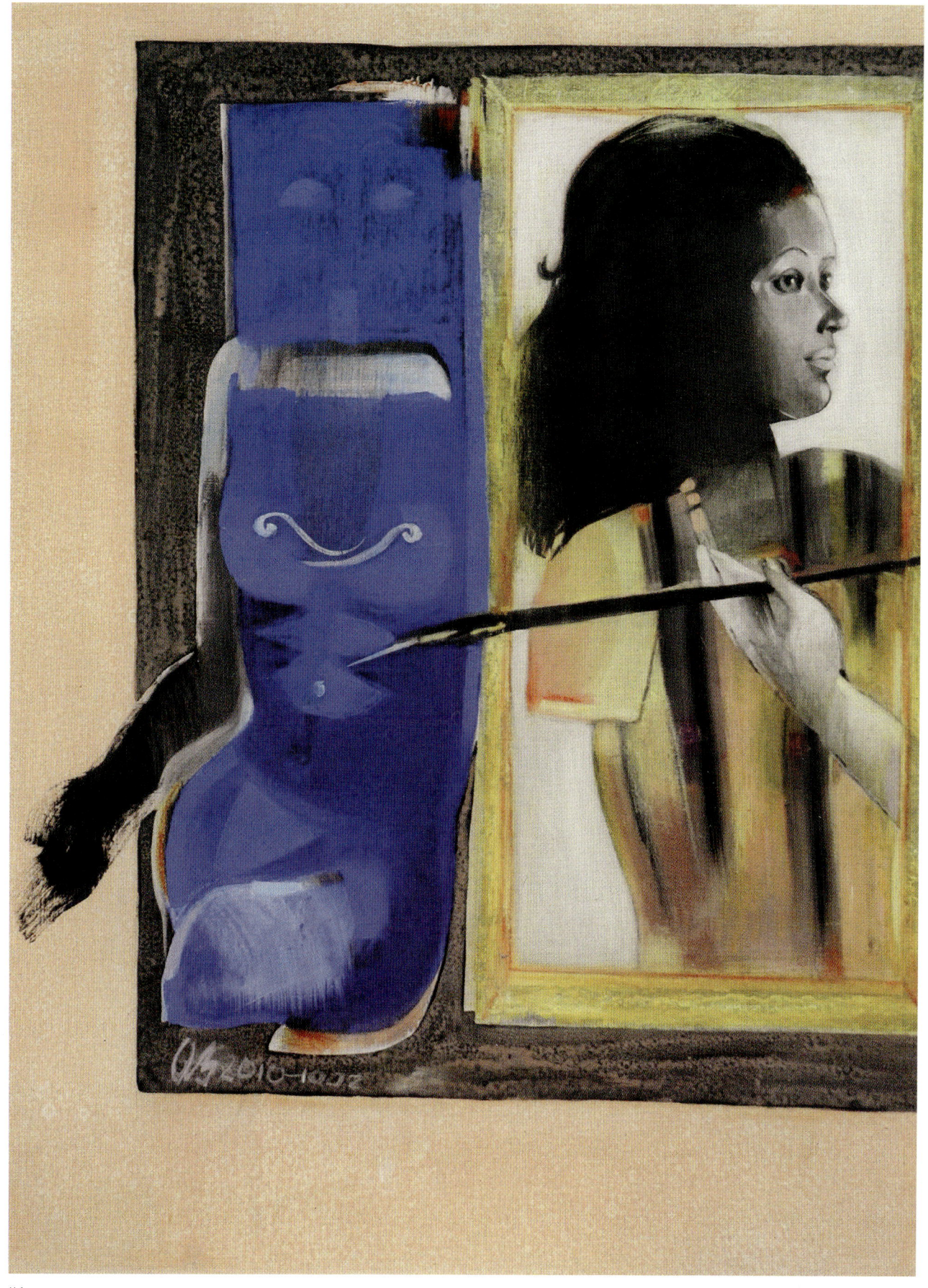

115 Juan Sánchez. *For Carmen María Colón*. 1986. Hand-colored lithograph with collage. Washington, DC, Smithsonian American Art Museum.

arts were intended, at least until the present century when there arose a greater consciousness of inclusion, not only of subject matter but of the public for whom the artist works. The disconnect between the white artist observing and depicting the Black body is evidently a fundamental one. Is it possible for a European-descended artist to "truthfully" portray Blackness? This is, of course, a highly charged subject and one in which the answer is either part of a theoretical discourse of multiple dimensions or unanswerable altogether. I do not pretend to suggest any definitive answers for this but instead turn to the assertion by the art historian Richard J. Powell, who articulated a theory regarding portraiture—and by extension, other subjects involving the Black body—suggesting that such images display a greater degree of empathy with the social circumstances from which the subject emerged than those representations of Blackness by non-Afrodescendant artists.[29] The following example is not meant specifically to be a "test" of this theory, but it will nonetheless serve as a signifier of Black agency in contemporary self-portraiture.

Ada Balcácer, whose words about her teacher Celeste Woss y Gil are quoted above, is an important case in point. Aside from Woss y Gil, Balcácer also studied with Hernández Ortega at the Escuela Nacional de Bellas Artes. She soon became a peripatetic artist, moving to San Juan and then for many years to New York and Miami, where she produced art in a variety of media, including mural painting. Her subject matter has veered between complete abstraction, in a gestural manner that utilizes the colors of the tropical surroundings in which she lives, and figuration.

Balcácer has worked in a serial fashion in her paintings and prints that often utilizes forms drawn from Dominican folk mythology. In her compelling 2005–2010 composition *Autorretrato de la joven pintora sin un brazo* (*Self-Portrait as a Young Painter without an Arm*), we observe a double portrait of the dark-skinned Balcácer. On the right side is a representational image of her head and torso. Her right hand reaches up seemingly out of the picture plane, holding an outsize brush that is painting a semi-abstract blue figure on the left of the picture, a nude self-portrait. Balcácer appears as a sixteen-year-old girl, commemorating the year that she lost her left arm in an accident. The mixed-media-on-canvas piece is an image both objective and proud as well as indicative of a strong sense of self-will and determination blended with one of tenderness and vulnerability.

Epilogue: The Diaspora

There can be no true comprehension of the arts of the Caribbean without an understanding of its broad extension into multiple corners of the world. Haitian artists in Brooklyn, Paris, or Montreal, Jamaican artists in London, or Cuban artists in Miami have created new, different, and geographically specific permutations of their art, or the art of the place where they or their families originated, that bring different visual vocabularies to the "Caribbean-ness" of art produced within the Basin itself. Thus, diasporic production is a key element in conceptualizing the constantly reconfigured concerns and ways of creating visual imagery. In the case of Puerto Rico and the Dominican Republic, the artists who left the island, or whose parents or grandparents immigrated elsewhere, form a "backbone" of the history of the island-based art forms that I have considered here. While I do not have the space to do justice to Latinx artists of Puerto Rican and Dominican heritage, it is imperative that the movements to which they belong be placed within at least a partial perspective.

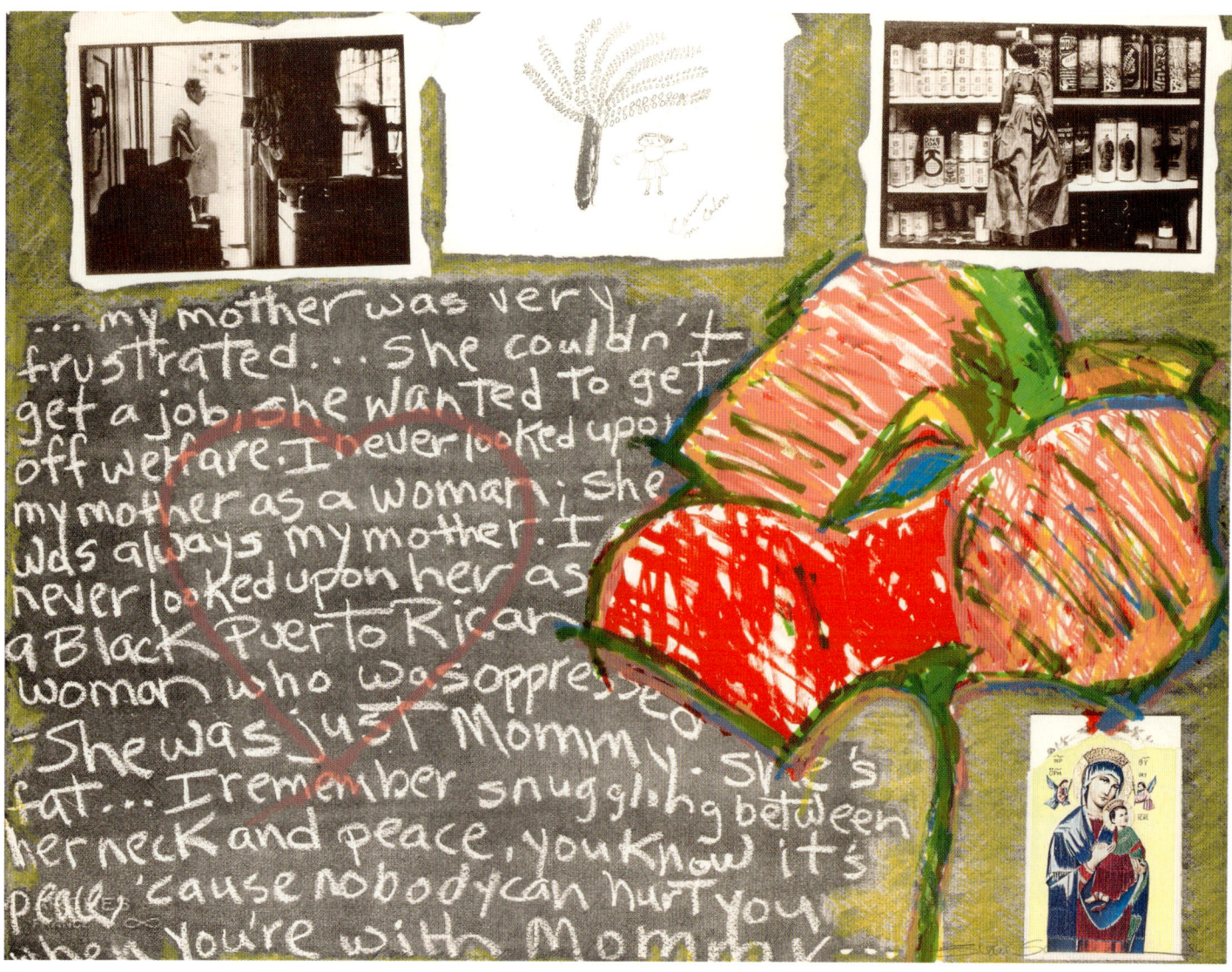

115

New York and surrounding areas have been the scene of important migrations of both communities. More recently, following the devastation of Hurricane María in 2017, Central Florida and Texas have been the venues of large-scale Puerto Rican migration. And more Dominican communities have been established in the Miami area in the recent past than before. Blackness, Afro-Puerto Rican, and Afro-Dominican themes and figures play a prominent role in this story. I will take only two examples that deserve large-scale studies in their own right.

Juan Sánchez was born in Brooklyn, New York, in 1954 to Afrodescendant Puerto Rican parents. After a youth of direct-action political activity influenced by the Young Lords, a Puerto Rican civil rights group begun in the late 1960s whose community-oriented social programs were at least in part inspired by the Black Panthers, Sánchez received an MFA degree from Rutgers University in New Jersey and began a successful career in which he has translated his motivations to promote social and political justice to underserved Latinx communities into strongly militant visual terms. His affective works in photo collage, serigraphs, paintings, posters, and other mixed-media modes of art making are integral parts of the identifying factors of contemporary Puerto Rican art outside of the island.

The island of Manhattan is Sánchez's realm; he is now a professor of art at Hunter College of the City University of New York. The Black Puerto Rican body is an inevitable presence in his art. It stands as a metaphor not only for the situation of people of

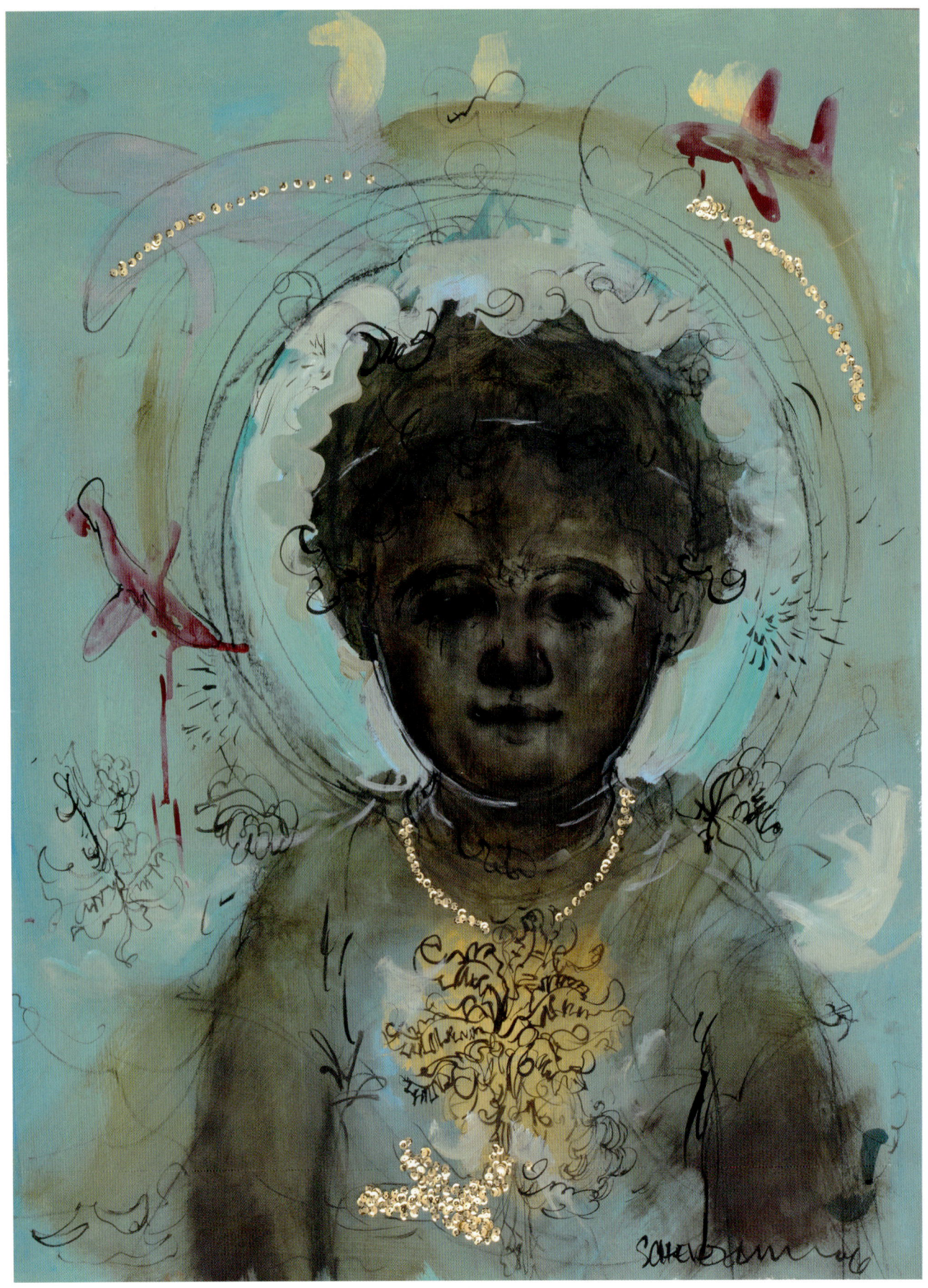

116 Scherezade García. *The Dominican York*. From the series *Island of Many Gods*. 2006. Mixed media. Washington DC, Smithsonian American Art Museum.

color of Puerto Rican descent living in the United States, but as a larger statement of the problematic existence of Afrodescendant communities in the country at large.

Dedicated to Sánchez's mother, *Para Carmen María Colón* (1986) is a lithograph of collaged elements including a photograph of the subject, the artist's mother, a photograph of a Black Spiritist doll (*muñequita*), and a religious image of the Virgin and child, as well as an explanatory text relating to his mother's personal and social struggles as a Black Puerto Rican woman. Other works by Sánchez incorporate symbols based on ancient Taíno petroglyphs found on the island or iconic works of Puerto Rican painting such as Ramón Frade's *El pan nuestro*, discussed earlier in this chapter (see fig. 88). Juan Sánchez's work on Blackness gives another, relentlessly urban and problematically North American cast to the polemics developed by Puerto Rican artists within the scope of this theme since the eighteenth century.

The Dominican-born New York resident Scherezade García (b. 1966) has engaged as much with her U.S. experience as she has with her identification with the Dominican Republic. Educated at the Altos de Chavón School of Design, Parsons School of Design in New York, and the City College of New York, García has, among many other initiatives, created an art and community activism project at the Dominican-Haitian border as part of her interest in reconciling the long-standing tensions and cultural and emotional disputes based on racial divisions between the two countries. She is the co-founder of the Dominican York Proyecto GRÁFICA, which takes its name from a phrase well known among Dominicans to describe either a person of Dominican birth living in New York or a U.S.-born individual of Dominican descent. In 2006 she created the *Island of Many Gods* of mixed-media works that constitute ruminations on race and displacement. *The Dominican York* from 2006 is an acrylic, charcoal, ink, and sequins on paper. We observe a young Black-skinned girl surrounded by a sea-blue background and hazy aureole. Airplanes swirl around her, indicative of the back-and-forth between New York and Santo Domingo. The young Black child is placid and unperturbed by the threats of displacement and possible disillusionment and disorientation by going from one place to another, either by choice or by necessity. This image takes on a deepening poignancy because this essay was being written in 2018, a year of controversy surrounding questions and often painful discussions of immigration to the United States—merely one chapter in an era of worldwide immigration controversies. This small Afrodescendant child thus simultaneously embodies locally specific and universal messages of the need for personal stability, openness to difference, and tolerance among all races.

9

THE IMAGE OF THE BLACK IN SELECT 20TH-CENTURY WORKS OF ART IN HAITI, MARTINIQUE, AND GUADELOUPE

JERRY PHILOGENE

Every colonized people—in other words, every people in whose soul an inferiority complex has been created by the death and burial of its local cultural originality—finds itself face to face with the language of the civilizing nation; that is, with the culture of the mother country. The colonized is elevated above his jungle status in proportion to his adoption of the mother country's cultural standards. He becomes whiter as he renounces his blackness, his jungle.
—Frantz Fanon, *Black Skin, White Masks* (1967)

This chapter is not a chronological presentation of Martinican, Haitian, and Guadeloupean art histories, artistic traditions, or artists. Rather, it is a rumination on the creative works of various artists from those locales as they visualize the complex ideas and tangled histories surrounding the "image of the Black." I draw my analysis from the tenets in several enormously influential texts by Martinican, Guadeloupean, and Haitian scholars, including *Ainsi parla l'Oncle* (1928) by Jean Price-Mars and *Cahier d'un retour au pays natal* (1939) by Aimé Césaire; from theoretical and linguistic concepts stemming from *Éloge de la créolité* (1989) by Jean Bernabé, Raphaël Confiant, and Patrick Chamoiseau; and from the imaginative *Traité du tout-monde* (1997) by Édouard Glissant. The theoretical and conceptual frameworks *Négritude*,[1] *indigénisme*, and *créolité*, Glissant's notion of *antillanité* and his encompassing and global *tout-monde*, expounded in these texts have had a tremendous impact on the literature and the visual arts of the Caribbean in general and these three Caribbean islands specifically. I use the above concepts to explore how they have influenced the visualization of Blackness in works of art by artists living in Haiti, Martinique, and Guadeloupe as well as by those creating art in their diasporas and how these concepts have expressly contributed to the discursivity of racial identities in these Francophone Caribbean spaces.

I begin in Haiti, examining works by self-taught artists and also by those who began their artistic training at the Centre d'Art, a major art gallery and school during the 1940s, as well as works by artists who studied in the United States and Europe and were associated with the Centre. I then focus on artists from Martinique and Guadeloupe, specifically on those working in the second half of the twentieth century and contemporarily in the twenty-first century, including the Martinican artists Serge Hélénon and Louis Laouchez, members of l'École Négro Caraïbe, founded in 1970, who were influenced by Césaire's writings. They sought to represent the "Black" in the Martinican man by depicting nonfigurative imagery in black and white colors accented by rich reds and earth ochres. Heavily influenced by the mask carvings and wooden figurative art of the Dogon from Mali, their works on paper and wooden collages, often made with found materials, sought to convey a supposedly utopian and idyllic Africa as it constituted their identities as Martinican artists living outside of Martinique. Ironically and aesthetically relevant, it is after their studies at l'École Nationale d'Arts Décoratifs de Nice, and while Laouchez was teaching in the Ivory Coast and Hélénon was teaching in Mali, that they initiated this group in Abidjan. L'École Négro Caraïbe's primary philosophy was captured in this statement: "… there is Africa as a quest, as a reference and its traces in the concrete topographic framework of the Antilles, convergences of a multiplicity of other traces, especially a Western one. Africa, as a primary reference, sticks to the skin first."[2]

For these artists, Africa was a utopian ideal, manifested as a referent of what it was to be Antillean. Thus, Africa as imagined on the skin of a Martinican was both essentially representative of Blackness and of a way of being and moving about the world. Similarly, Martinican artists who were part of Fwomajé, an artists' group founded in 1984 which explored Amerindian symbols in their work, were influenced by the cultural and artistic aesthetics of the African continent and the presence of "indigenous" individuals in the countryside. The group took its Creole name *fwomajé* from a "majestic tree that grows in the mountains of Martinique" that harbors spirits. Patricia Donatien-Yssa writes: "For the members of the group, the choice of this tree is very significant: its powerful roots that plunge deep into the soil; the straightness of its trunk covered with spikes, forcefully imposing itself; its sleek, red branches raised toward the sky; and its flowers like atoms sown into the far distance represented the artists' roots in the Martinican land…."[3]

One of Fwomajé's earliest members, Ernest Breleur, explored anthropomorphic forms and silhouettes to consider what might constitute a Martinican aesthetic, influenced in part by Césaire's directive to seek a cultural heritage that might modulate vulnerability, alienation, and displacement. I take as my point of departure the discourses about racialization that these written works produced and how such discourses became visualized, ultimately tracking the diverse and varied ways in which Blackness was manifested in selected works of art from Haiti, the first Black nation to gain its independence from France, to those of France's two *départements d'outre-mer,* Martinique and Guadeloupe. Of interest is how Blackness is imagined, configured, and reimagined aesthetically through the lens of the *figure*, how that figure (abstract or figurative, representational or nonrepresentational, absent or dematerialized) takes up what "Blackness" has come to symbolize for artists who conceive of themselves as connected to these three islands even when they are no longer physically tethered to them. Rather than emphasize *types raciaux,* I situate my analysis within a framework that investigates the "image of the Black" as it is mediated by representation, modernity, resistance, and history, themes that are essential in the aforementioned written pieces.

How does looking through the lens of Blackness shift our understanding of the object under exploration? How does the formation of Blackness steeped in a bilingual (French and Kreyòl/Creole) existence and a geopolitical and geoeconomic dependence (as in the case of Martinique and Guadeloupe) allow for a transhistorical understanding of racialization not bounded by territory or geographical specificity?[4] In this exploration, what emerges is a presentation consisting of a wide range of artists working in different geographical spaces, in different styles marked by different periods of artistic creativity, guided in part by political consciousness and resistance tactics, and also by acts of self-presentation, self-preservation, and visual agency.

A rich scholarship documenting Haitian artistic and expressive traditions written both in English and French exists in the registers of art histories of the African diaspora.[5] Until recently, this has not been the case for Martinique and Guadeloupe. The last two decades, however, have produced a steady and developing scholarship on the art and expressive traditions of both that is well documented in French, led by scholars, curators, and writers such as René Louise, Dominique Berthet, Dominique Brebion, and Patricia Donatien-Yssa.[6] Entering into the archives of Caribbean art and art of the African diaspora is a decisive and comprehensive body of scholarship that charts the beginning of Martinican art, not only encompassing the brief visit by the French post-impressionist painter Paul Gauguin in June of 1887, but also the creation of several art schools in Fort-de-France and the founding of the group of painters and sculptors of Atelier 45 after World War II and, later, Fwomajé, many of whom were trained in France. Thus, what has emerged in Martinique since the mid-twentieth century are artists, many of whom were students of members of Atelier 45 and Fwomajé, creating an archipelagic-wide and international conversation about art that incorporates Martinique with the wider Caribbean, Europe, the United States, and, to some degree, countries in Africa.

Simultaneously, in Guadeloupe, there is also documentation of Guadeloupean art and artistic expressions, including the paintings of the neoclassicist Guillaume Guillon-Lethière (1760–1832), born of a French colonial father and a mother of African and European ancestry in Sainte-Anne, Guadeloupe, and trained in France; the landscape drawings of Jules-Honoré Joseph Coussin (1773–1836), a Basse-Terre–born draftsman active in Guadeloupe during the early part of the nineteenth century; and landscape and portrait paintings of Armand Budan (1827–1874) and Évremond Auguste Léopold de Bérard (1824–1881), born in l'Anse-Bertrand and Sainte-Anne, respectively. During the twentieth century, we know that as part of his military service, the French artist Georges Rohner (1913–2000) spent 1934 to 1936 in Guadeloupe. In 1934, upon the completion of his military service, he was commissioned as part of the *tricentenaire du rattachement des Antilles à la France* to create several paintings *de la vie quotidienne en Guadeloupe* for the City Hall in Basse-Terre in his signature style—warm, flat colors with crisp backgrounds. The paintings consisted of four landscapes, two fishing scenes, a scene of the Basse-Terre harbor, and a portrait of the French abolitionist Victor Schoelcher.[7] In these commissioned paintings, there are no soft, lighter colors to allude to realistic shadows, just hints of browns to suggest shadowing of the tautly postured figures. While there is very little depth to the paintings, they do capture the landscape of Basse-Terre in the 1930s. In 1939, traveling in the United States for an international exhibition, the French painter Georges (Géo) François (1880–1968) was unable to return to France as a result of the outbreak of World War II. He instead traveled to Martinique and Guadeloupe via Cuba and from 1940 to 1943 produced several genre paintings and drawings capturing the quotidian life on both islands. By the end of

World War II, Christian Mas notes that French painters and realist landscapes dominated the archipelago, leaving little room for Guadeloupean artists to flourish. In 1946, Guadeloupe, along with Martinique, became an overseas department of France, yet that, he posits, provoked neither a rupture nor a revival in Guadeloupean art.[8]

By the start of the 1970s, Guadeloupean-born artists were influenced by European painting styles of the interwar and postwar period, particularly cubism, surrealism, expressionism, and abstraction, yet infused their work with a distinct *l'ideologie de la négritude*—an attention to Black roots.[9] Appropriately, the growing attention—one-person exhibitions, group exhibitions, and numerous essays—being paid to the work of contemporary artists from Martinique and Guadeloupe as well as those from Haiti contributes to an expanding scholarly concentration in the discipline of art of the Black diaspora.

Haiti

As Philippe Thoby-Marcelin, Gérald Alexis, and Michel-Philippe Lerebours have shown, Haitian art did not begin with the founding of the Centre d'Art in May 1944; rather, its foundation stems from a rich heritage built upon resistance and independence. It begins with the president of Haiti (1807–1811) and later King (1811–1820) Henri Christophe, who in 1816 surrounded himself with several painters under the supervision of Revinchal, known as the "King's Painter," and created a painting school at the Sans Souci Palace. The English painter Richard Evans spent several months teaching there while visiting the palace from 1816 to 1817. While there, Evans painted portraits of the royal family, and his portrait of King Henri Christophe in full military regalia was gifted to the British abolitionist William Wilberforce by Christophe.[10] Artists including the French painter Barincou Jeune and the American Charles Hardy settled in Port-au-Prince and were commissioned to paint portraits of generals in Alexandre Pétion's military entourage, many of which hung at Pétion's villa, Volant-Le-Thor. What follows are intermittent bursts of activity at art schools, where practicing portraitists, landscape artists, and painters of historical imagery were building and strengthening what would come to be known as Haitian art during the governments of Jean Pierre Boyer (1818–1843), Faustin Soulouque (1847–1849), Emperor of Haiti Faustin I (1849–1859), and Fabre Geffrard (1859–1867). Colbert Lochard (1804–1876) established a reputation as a painter and eventually became the director of the National School of Painting and Drawing in 1861; his son Archibald Lochard succeeded him as director.[11] With the advent of photography and chromolithography, portraiture and landscape painting declined in popularity in Haiti toward the latter part of the nineteenth century. Louis Rigaud, however, painted portraits of several Haitian heads of state, which, according to Michel-Philippe Lerebours, were commissioned by Frederick Douglass during Florvil Hyppolite's presidency (1889–1896).[12] Rigaud is perhaps most notable for his portrait of Toussaint L'Ouverture painted in 1877 in full French military regalia, the first by a Haitian artist and which abandoned the caricature of previous depictions of the revolutionary.[13]

Haiti would undergo important changes in its political and cultural life in the twentieth century. In the Americas, the period from 1925 to 1945 was marked by political, economic, and social turbulence and incessant conversations about nationalism, which ultimately expressed a desire by Black and brown people to construct an image of themselves.¹⁴ Fortuitously, while these artistic movements were occurring, in the literary realm, Jean Price-Mars's *Ainsi parla l'Oncle*, published in 1928, analyzed African traditions and popular beliefs in Haiti and their impact on Haitian subjectivity. As a galvanizing force, this classic study ushered in a cultural nationalism in the form of indigénisme that vehemently denounced U.S. imperialist forces occupying Haiti.¹⁵ As a fervent critique of the social and class divide between Haiti's white and brown ruling elites and the economically oppressed Black population, Price-Mars's work eloquently criticized the internal strife and conflict produced by the strict class codes and colorism so prevalent in occupied Haiti. In its potency and originality, *Ainsi parla l'Oncle* attempted to usher in an appreciation for African cultural traditions within the Black diaspora, especially in Haiti.

Price-Mars's critically acclaimed study of Afro-Haitian folklore accomplished its goal, signaling the emergence of new forms of Haitian culture and national values by placing the "folk" at the center of cultural analysis. While being extremely romantic in his views of the realities of the Haitian laboring class, Price-Mars called for a cultural nationalism that was truly inclusive and powerful, conscious of socioeconomic class stratifications and incorporating an appreciation of African and Haitian cultural traditions. Countries such as Cuba, Mexico, Brazil, and the United States were experiencing comparable cultural and art movements during the 1920s and 1930s, in which images of indigenous and Black peoples figured prominently as symbols of nationalism and cultural authenticity. Such movements upheld the images of the rural landscape populated by the "folk" as the location of an authentic culture. Cuba's *Afrocubanismo*, the Mexican mural movement, and Haiti's indigénisme as well as the United States' Harlem Renaissance were intended to be "new world" movements, embracing all culture considered African or indigenous.

Two years prior to the publication of Price-Mars's influential text, a group of writers and artists formed the Pont St. Géraud Group, meeting periodically to discuss the U.S. occupation of Haiti and the repressive regime of Louis Bornó. Among the group was Pétion Savain, a leading indigenist artist, writer, and teacher who had studied with the African American artist William Edouard Scott upon his visit to Haiti in March 1931 on a Julius Rosenwald Fellowship in Fine Arts.¹⁶ The group was guided in part by the artistic principles that would showcase the realities of Haitian rural life as *uniquely* Haitian, *expressively* Black, and *distinctively* folk. These aesthetic movements led the way for a more concentrated and internationally focused attention to the production of the expressive arts and the creation of Haitian modern art that came to fruition with the founding of the Centre d'Art in 1944.¹⁷ The International Exhibit of Modern Art, organized by UNESCO and held in Paris in November 1946, two years after the Centre's founding, was the first international exhibition to feature works of art by Haitian artists, who struck an interesting balance between being self-taught and academically trained, and many of whom would become leaders in so-called "primitive" and Haitian modern art.¹⁸ Among those closely associated with the Centre were the self-taught artists Hector Hyppolite (1894–1948), a *houngan* (male Vodou priest) from Montrouis, near Saint Marc; André Pierre (1914–2005), also a houngan, who resided in a family compound located in Croix-des-Missions on the outskirts of Port-au-Prince and whose brilliantly detailed and vividly colored paintings, rich with signs and symbols depicting the pantheon of

Vodou *lwa* (spirits), adds a complexity and new meaning to family portraiture; and Philomé Obin (1892–1986), a painter from the northern part of Haiti. In 1970, Obin, whose paintings often featured historical events and religious subjects, painted *Crucifixion de Charlemagne Péralte pour la Liberté* (*The Crucifixion of Charlemagne Péralte for Freedom*). With his signature flat brushstrokes, solid hues, and economical painting style, Obin emphasizes the martyrdom and saintlike status of the Haitian freedom fighter Charlemagne Péralte, a major leader of the resistance fighters known as *cacos,* who was murdered by U.S. Marines during the occupation of Haiti from 1915 to 1934. Situated in the center of the canvas, Péralte's body evokes the body of Jesus Christ as he lay dying, nailed to the cross, while next to Péralte is a crying woman dressed in black, perhaps Jesus's mother, Mary, or Obin's mother. Péralte's body, tied to a sky-blue door, floats on a bed of clouds, giving an almost celestial impression. The bold chromatic of the solid blues punctuated by areas of white that highlight his groin area and his mother's handkerchief and headscarf provide a well-balanced pictorial space. Obin has rendered the death of this Haitian citizen in terms that are both religiously poignant and politically and culturally charged, drawing connections to the apotheosis in classic religious paintings. Evoking tragic pathos and divine adoration, *Crucifixion de Charlemagne Péralte pour la Liberté* is a colorful pictorial retelling of Péralte's death, one that is pregnant with mysticism, quite different from the bloody murder recorded in a photograph by a U.S. Marine.

Artists such as Maurice Borno (1917–1955) and Luce Turnier (1924–1994), who had received traditional art school training outside of the United States, were also among the artists who participated in this defining moment in the art of the African diaspora. Turnier's *Jeune femme endormie* (1974) depicts a nude young woman asleep on her side. The warm browns and the simplicity of the composition, along with the abstract background and sculptural curves and lines of the woman's nude figure, tellingly indicate Turnier's engagement with a modernist tradition of figuration and the feminist aspirations embedded in her artwork. In Turnier's line and contour painting, which relies less on shading and more on heavier or lighter applications of painting, there is a serene and dignified sensuality embedded in the figure which suggests that, unlike the male members of the Centre, who depicted images of Erzulie, the *lwa* of love, sensuality, and protection, or of genre-type market women, Turnier's softly rendered study of this Black female figure places her as a forerunner among Caribbean modernist artists who depicted the image of Black women without the overtly sexualized and Vodou themes and images that were common and expected since the 1940s. What is conveyed is the internal energy of the sitter, even while in repose in this intimate compositional space.

In the following ten years, the Centre became an important and well-known gallery in the purchase of "authentic" and inexpensive Haitian art. Perhaps an overemphasis on self-taught artists resulting from increased tourism and numerous articles about "voodoo" and cheap Haitian art published in *Life, Vogue, Holiday, Harper's Bazaar, Time,* and *Newsweek* led to tensions between several of the academically trained artists and administrators at the Centre. As a result, the Foyer des Arts Plastiques was founded on August 11, 1950, by an art teacher and administrator at the Centre, Luckner Lazard (1928–1998).[19] Like many of the artists, Lazard rejected the hegemonic "primitive" label placed on the artists at the Centre. Lazard, along with Lucien

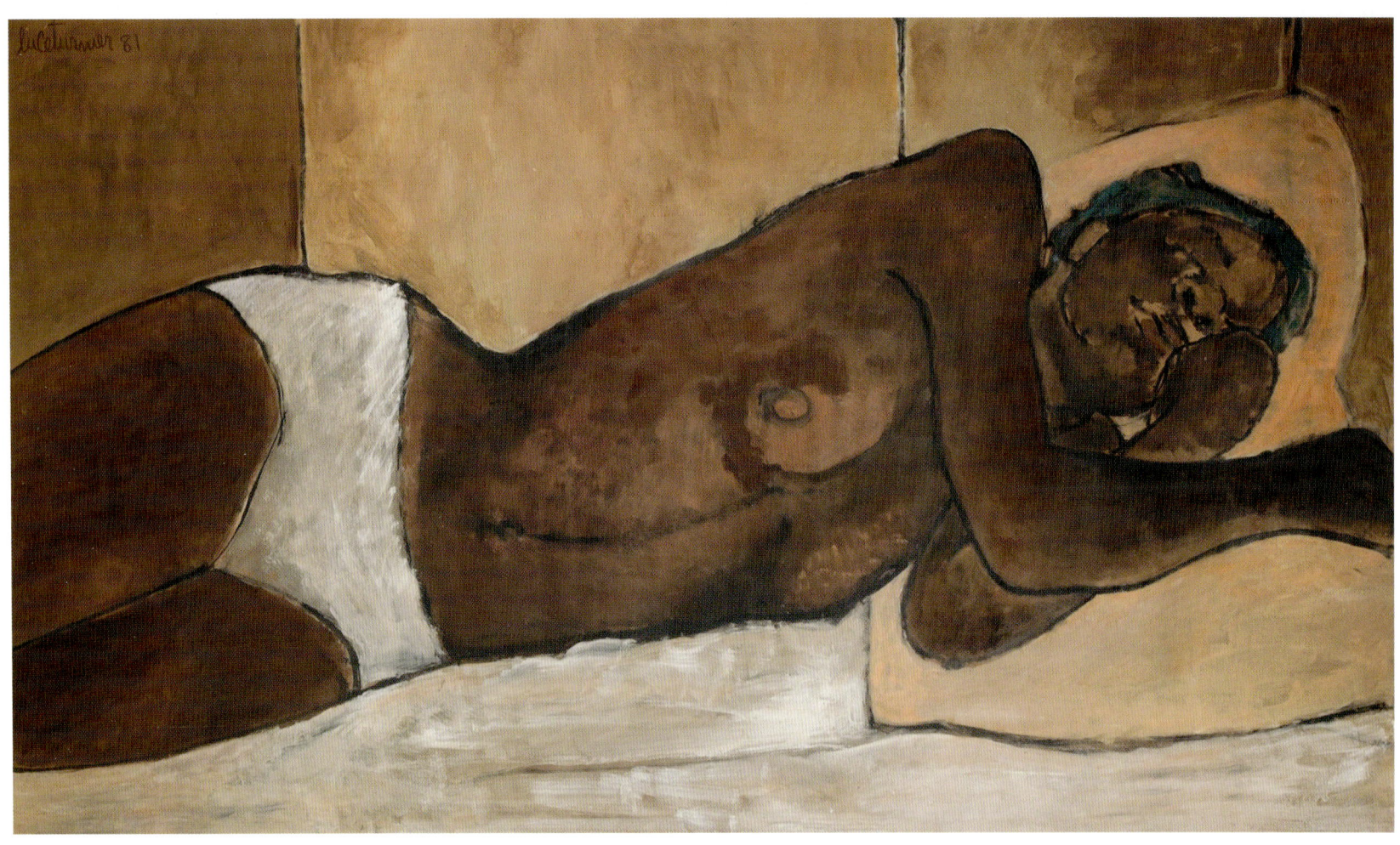
117

117 Luce Turnier. *Sleeping Young Woman*. 1974. Acrylic on masonite. Port-au-Prince, Le Musée d'Art Haïtien.

Price (1915–1963), Max Pinchinat (1925–1985), Roland Dorcély (1930–2017), Rene Exumé (1929–2016), and Dieudonné Cédor (1925–2010), wanted to put some distance between the "naïf" style that had become synonymous with Haitian art by 1950 by exploring the growing modernist trends in art they had learned from their travels and from the foreign artists (white American, African American, and Cuban) who had visited Haiti and taught at the Centre.[20] Interestingly, decades later in Martinique, creative differences and evolving differing aesthetic visions would also lead to the dissolution of an art collective.

In the early 1970s, another shift took place. The Saint-Soleil collective was founded in Soisson-la-Montagne, near Petionville in 1973, by Maud Robart (b. 1946) and Jean-Claude Garoute (Tiga) (1935–2006), later joined by Levoy Exil (b. 1944), Prosper Pierre-Louis (1947–1997), and Louisiane Saint Fleurant (1924–2005), creating a strong aesthetic environment which would lead to works of art replete with Vodou symbolism, abstracted and truncated figures, and with a keen attention to the daily lives of *paysans* (those who reside in the country). Like the image of the Black "folk" venerated by Jean Price-Mars, the image of the paysans in many of the works by the members of Saint-Soleil lend themselves to a nationalist bent.

Martinique
Martinicans and Guadeloupeans have a complex relationship with France and with the wider Caribbean. Sharing a language with Haiti, Réunion, and French Guiana, Martinique and Guadeloupe, like the northern side of Saint-Martin and the aforementioned, are départements d'outre-mer of France occupying a "curious tension-filled state of suspended animation between the periphery and the metropolis."[21] It's a precarious position for Martinicans and Guadeloupeans: lacking sovereignty over their own state, they are full French *citoyens,* yet they never fully *belong* to that nation, and are racialized as "other." Many of the artists in this chapter address the issues of colonialism and alienation in myriad ways, profoundly and creatively, offering a blistering critique of the postcolonial relationship between France and Martinique and France and Guadeloupe. Others veer away from political commentary and focus on personal issues affecting their daily lives as Black French citizens, issues expressed in Frantz Fanon's quote in the epigraph to this essay. At the heart of these paintings, sculptures, multimedia, photographic, and performance pieces, within the complexity of their surfaces, textures, colors, and images, is a deep and formal engagement with cultural legacies that are *au fond* about racialization and representation.

It is often difficult to pinpoint precisely when an art movement begins, given what might smolder beneath before it comes to the surface and is worthy of documentation. The travels of European and American artists to the Caribbean seeking artistic inspiration have been documented. The art historian Lindsay Twa discusses in *Visualizing Haiti in U.S. Culture, 1910–1950* (2014) the many African American artists who visited Haiti during the early part of the twentieth century, seeking creative inspiration from a Black country they believed to be pure and untouched by the racial and class oppression they faced in the United States.[22] Seeking an unrestricted freedom to nurture his inner "primitive" self, Paul Gauguin traveled to Martinique (and later to Tahiti) in search of artistic stimulus.[23] Gauguin had very little contact with other artists on the island, but both he and Charles Laval, his traveling companion, produced numerous drawings and genre paintings of the islands' landscape and people that had tremendous pictorial influence on their works (see *The Image of the Black in Latin American and Caribbean Art*, Book 1, Chapter 13).

According to the writer René Louise, Martinique offered its first drawing and painting classes in 1937 at the Lycée de Fort-de-France and Terres-Sainville.[24] Two years later, in 1939, the publication in Paris of the book-length poem *Cahier d'un retour au pays natal* by the poet and statesman Aimé Césaire brought to the Caribbean a movement that celebrated African cultural heritage: Négritude.[25] In *Cahier,* Césaire meditates on exile and a yearning to return to an imagined home while pondering the complex nature of cultural and racial identity of Black people living in a colonial setting. Like Fanon, Césaire was also interested in the "soul" that has been created by the "death and burial of its local cultural originality."[26] This inquiry into one's sense of self and belonging was echoed in the writings published in the Martinican literary and cultural journal *Tropiques* founded in 1941 by Césaire, René Ménil, Aristide Maugée, Lucie Thésée, and Suzanne Césaire. During its four-year run, *Tropiques* had a profound impact on the young artists who formed Atelier 45 in 1943, including Raymond Honorien (1920–1988), Marcel Mystille (1920–2008), and Germain Tiquant (1920–2011). Paying close attention to the writings of these authors, the members of Atelier 45 sought to express their Martinican identity in lush landscapes and still life. Their first show was held from April 3–28, 1945, at La Maison des Fleurs, Rue Victor Hugo, in Fort-de-France.

In the mid-twentieth century, several other art schools were established, beginning with the School of Applied Arts in 1943. The art historian Dominique Brebion explains that the "Municipal Center for the Fine Arts was founded in Fort-de-France in 1966" and "the Regional School of Plastic Arts and the Regional Institute of Visual Art in 1984 gave further structure to the visual arts in Martinique." Such schools supported the artists of Atelier 45 as well as the "first generation of modern artists who were attached to l'École Négro Caraïbe and Fwomajé." She writes further of "Ecole Negro Caraïbe, founded by Louis Laouchez (1934–2016) and Serge Hélénon (b. 1934), whose 1970 manifesto asserted the desire to find what is left of the African man in today's Martinique, and the groupe *fwomajé*—Victor Anicet (b. 1938), Ernest Breleur (b. 1945), Bertin Nivor (b. 1946), François Charles-Edouard (n.d.)—who were determined to promote a Caribbean aesthetic" through their exploration of "Amerindian symbols and Vodou or African imagery."[27]

Also, as part of their manifesto, the members of l'École Négro Caraïbe declared their own version of Glissant's encompassing notion of tout-monde, put forth in his *Poetics of Relation* (1990) and *Traité du tout-monde* (1997) and which imagines a phenomenological sense of *connection* to and *consciousness* of the world, not merely to a specific location at a specific moment. Laouchez writes: "We carry with us, as Serge Hélénon says, what is our original culture. We are not Africans, but Negroes of the diaspora, Negroes of all continents, Negroes of all backgrounds. Our identity, our difference can scare both the dominated and the domineering."[28] Their first exhibition, held in 1970 at the Centre Culturel Français d'Abidjan, showcased works of art that "participate in a revival of Negro art. Free of all the folklore and exoticism, it will draw its sources in the behavior and the actions of the black populations of the globe and permeate all the aspects and forms that reflect a Negro aesthetic originality in its essence."[29]

By the 1960s, several artists who had studied in France

returned to Martinique and began to question their racial and cultural identity. Heavily influenced by Négritude and the writings of Frantz Fanon, René Louise writes: "these visual artists begin by making sketches and studies of Black people. The sketches made at the beginning, revealed a lack of knowledge of the morphology of the race; portraits or sketches of nudes almost always approached the European type."[30] What became paramount was capturing the landscape of Martinique, as well as the stylistic tradition of the many French artists who had visited earlier. In "Writing the Self in the Antilles, Writing the Antilles: Writers and Anthropologists in Dialogue," Anna Lesne writes: "The reflection on a collective Martinique Creole identity, which was the central militant project of the Creolist movement until the end of the 1980s, gradually turned towards a reflection on *a way of being in the world* seen as unprecedented before the emergence of Creole societies and illuminating. ... [T]his idea takes a shape around the notion of individuation."[31] Perhaps as a way to understand one's way of being in the world as part of a collective, one's relationality, as would be proposed by Glissant, Ernest Breleur in 1989 published a manifesto in which he expressed the need to relinquish the anticolonialist and racially essentialist concerns which, he believed, hindered the creativity of his fellow artists in group Fwomajé. His thoughts mirrored those of several Martinican artists who were interested in having the freedom to explore a modern aesthetic that was not simply concerned with depicting racial representations or the local cultural traditions of Martinique. Rather, Breleur was interested in more universal and less parochial artistic practices that supported new artistic languages free from formulaic representations of conventional seascape and landscape imagery with bold bright colors that signaled Caribbean art.

Guadeloupe

Like the quest for identity in Martinique, an emphasis on the Creole language in Guadeloupe as a manifestation of an emerging Black political consciousness and a quest for a shared past was instrumental in creating a sense of cultural identity during the 1970s and 1980s. As an archipelago both in the geographical sense of the term and as a metaphorical understanding of its relation to the wider Pan-Caribbean, Guadeloupe is perhaps best seen in terms of Glissant's notion of tout-monde. Unlike the mostly literary movement of Négritude, initiated in France and led by the Martinican Césaire, the Senegalese Léopold Sédar Senghor, and the French Guianese Léon Damas in the 1930s and 1940s, which had Africa largely as its central focus; or *créolité* as theorized by the Martinicans Bernabé, Confiant, and Chamoiseau, whose existential theory was guided by the declaration, "Neither Europeans, nor Africans, nor Asians, we proclaim ourselves Creoles,"[32] Guadeloupe's concentration on language to explore its *âme* (soul) indicates the difference in the "historical, political, ideological cultural trajectories"[33] that were specific to Guadeloupe, often derisively referred to as the "sister island" to Martinique. In different ways, both embraced indigeneity as a postcolonial strategy to "speak back" to France, one in which a pan-African racial identity would be articulated not only in the embrace of a vernacular *langue* but also in the choice of prose, symbols, and imagery used in both literature and visual culture. For Glissant, the essentializing tendency of Négritude brought about a penetrative focus on language and langue that would be fully and deeply immersed in the Antilles, as antillanité, shifting the focus from Africa to the Caribbean and decidedly "a method and not a state of being.[34] Nonetheless, at the root of each ideo-

118 Didier William. *Ezili toujours konnen*. 2015. Ink and collage on panel.

logical current is the question, "What is Black identity?," and at its base is the interrogation of the figure, and its historical manifestation and existential presence.

Works of Art

> ... full knowledge of Creoleness will be reserved for Art, for Art absolutely.
> —Bernabe, Chamoiseau, and Confiant
> "In Praise of Creoleness" (1990)[35]

This section consists of an examination of works of art in a range of media including photography, sculpture, drawing, video, and performance art, as well as painting. These works include traditional portraiture by Luce Turnier and Robert Charlotte (b. 1966); the unconventional and experimental methods used in paintings by M. Florine Démosthène (b. 1971); the photographs of Shirley Rufin (b. 1985); the photograph-sculptures of Maksaens Denis (b. 1968); and the performances of Gwladys Gambie (b. 1988), Annabel Guérédrat (b. 1974) and Henri Tauliaut (b. 1966), and Jean-Ulrick Désert (b. 1960). What these works have in common is the centering of the figure, sometimes in an abstract unrecognizable form, "rendering it through expressive rather than descriptive forms, colors, and compositions," sometimes as an illusion or suggestion, intentionally producing an enigmatic, multivalent art and adopting a radical presence, at times figurative. These artists are engaged with global artistic communities that are not tethered to specific regional or national artistic styles or labels; rather, their aesthetic explorations use traditional artistic methods and invent visual languages that are embedded in Creole narratives, and most assuredly steeped in diasporic creativity.

In a conversation between the curators Johanna Auguiac-Célénice and Tumelo Mosaka for their November 2016 exhibition *Échos Imprévus: Turning Tide*, Mosaka states:

> I think the difference has been that in Martinique, we were engaged with how the idea of Negritude still applied to recent formulations of Black identity. Taking Aimé Césaire's formation of Black identity as inspiration, we were interested in examining ways artists from the Caribbean and the diaspora complicated this notion of Black identity by offering nuances and differences that also contradict existing understandings of Blackness as a unifying identity. Here in Guadeloupe the conversation has attempted to establish unequivocally different narratives addressing the legacy of colonialism rather than the specificity of race politics....[36]

Regardless of regional differences undeniably based on distinct colonial legacies, artistic traditions, and the status of governing, what is evident in the works of art discussed in this section is a deep and concentrated attention to form, style, color, space, texture, and medium as well as to the employment of the Black figure. These artists are committed to fashioning a future through the manipulation of conventional artistic styles and traditions that acknowledges coloniality but also imagines a freedom; a future where everything is called into question and that the strategic device to engage in it is the Black body and its representation; a future that asks *not* what is a Martinican, Haitian, or Guadeloupean artist, but accepts that they simply *are* and

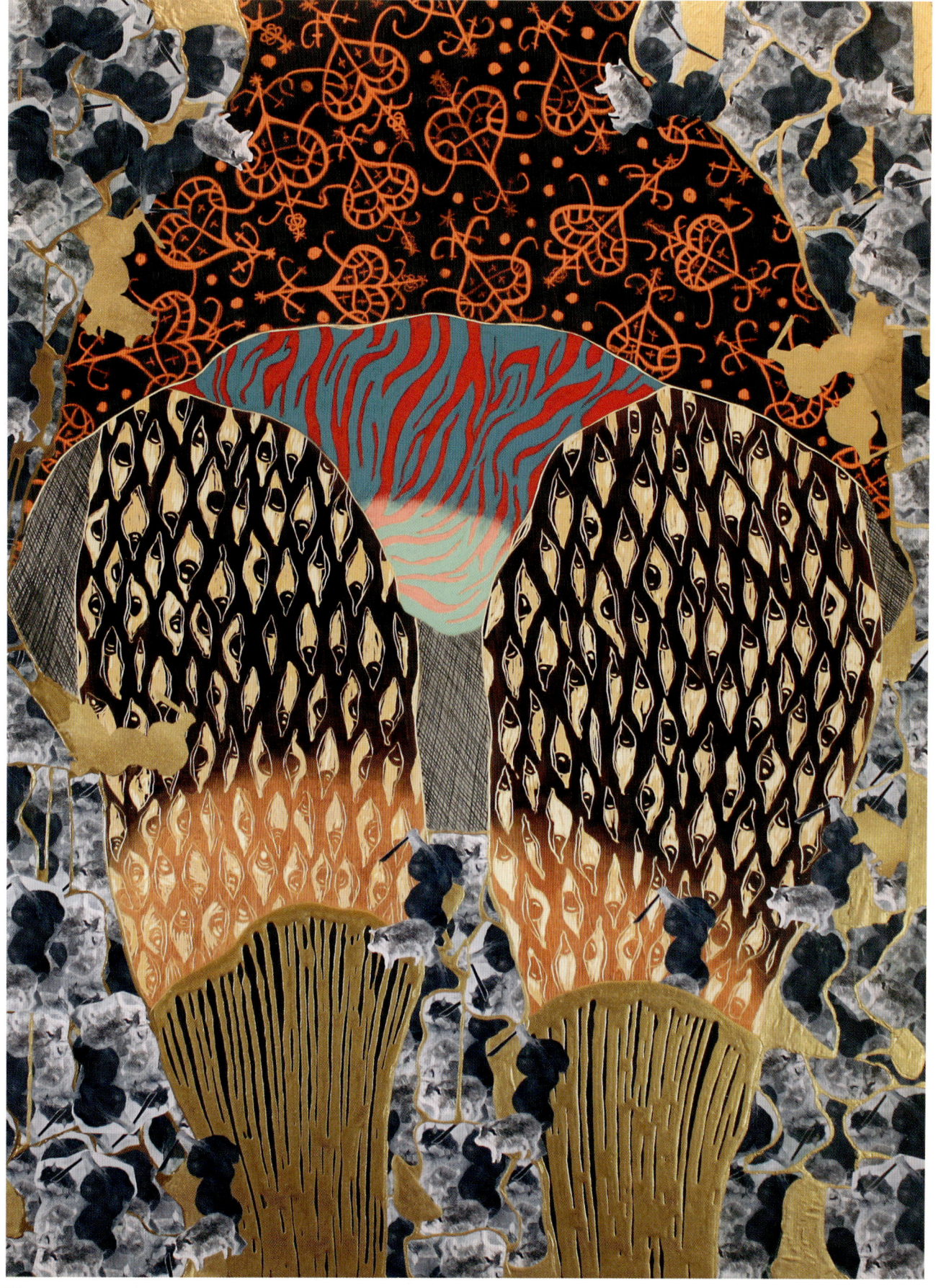

118

119 Didier William. *Menm pandan m'ap danse*. 2018. Collage, acrylic, ink, wood carving on panel. Collection of Carole Server.

imagines the alternative aesthetic perspectives and creative powers that are in their hands, and what that might mean in this postcolonial, neocolonial, and neoliberal moment. This might be the future of Blackness as imagined by Fanon, Price-Mars, Césaire, and Glissant.

According to Darby English, "the black body, objectified in its blackness, functions as a black representational space par excellence."[37] In different ways, artists have used the image of the Black body as a strategy of empowerment and as an artistic strategy for self-representation. Didier William (United States/Haiti), a painter based in Philadelphia, mischievously teases the formal and expressive elements of painting, a provocation that is captured in his creative vocabulary of bold colors and decorative patterning and abstraction, drawing from a variety of sources, such as the patterning of West African aesthetics or the patterning and decoration artists of the mid-1970s to the early 1980s. There is a palpable energy in the work from the vibrancy of mixed surfaces and a rhythmic interplay among colors, shapes, forms, and textures that produce conceptual, visually inventive spaces to contemplate identities, cultures, and the process of looking. At the center of his work is the figure that actively indexes a subjectivity, a presence. While a recognizable figure of Erzulie, the Haitian *lwa* of love and sexuality, is not evident in *Ezili toujours konnen* (2015), her *vévé* (a drawing that represents a *lwa*) brightly and vividly proclaims her presence. William's vévé-inspired patterning forms Erzulie's waist and draws our eyes to the top part of the painting; however, it is the carved-eye shapes forming her buttocks and legs, a familiar motif in William's oeuvre, that call our attention to the thickly applied paint that outline her legs. His paintings are large-scale and include carving, drawing, and staining. He uses water-based and oil-based paints that intentionally do not easily mix; they fracture and fissure and dry at different rates, then crack and fragment. What is created then is a blending, a *rasanblaj*—a space, according to the feminist anthropologist and performance artist Gina Athena Ulysse, that "blurs genres, shifting location, time and space to double-dutch the line between the sacred and the profane."[38] Eye shapes carved on the wooden panels create the stylistic intricacies that are equally apparent in *Menm pandan m'ap danse* (2018). In this black and white piece, the carved-eye–shaped figure poses enticingly and solidly on a stage beautifully surrounded by a patterned background. In its largeness, this ungendered figure takes center stage, literally and figuratively, revealing how the body can perform dynamics of power even at moments when it may be at odds with its environment. Ultimately, what is important for William is to make the bodies visible that have been absent from the visual archive.

The power dynamics of looking and seeing are also present in the mixed-media paintings of M. Florine Démosthène (Haiti/Ghana). In *Wounds #15* from *The Stories I Tell Myself* (2018), Démosthène explores the textured complexities of corporeality as both formal analysis and aesthetic endeavor. Her exploration of the Black female form is like the photographic work of the Martinican artist Shirley Rufin, whose manipulation of the formal and technical qualities of photography and photographic processing creates seductive imagery to highlight the medium's expressive and conceptual possibilities. In part, Rufin, like Démosthène, is interested in the exploitation and fetishization of the Black female body while simultaneously hinting at her strength. Démosthène's bold embrace of the interplay between a taboo subject, such as the Black female nude, and the aesthetic quality of materials

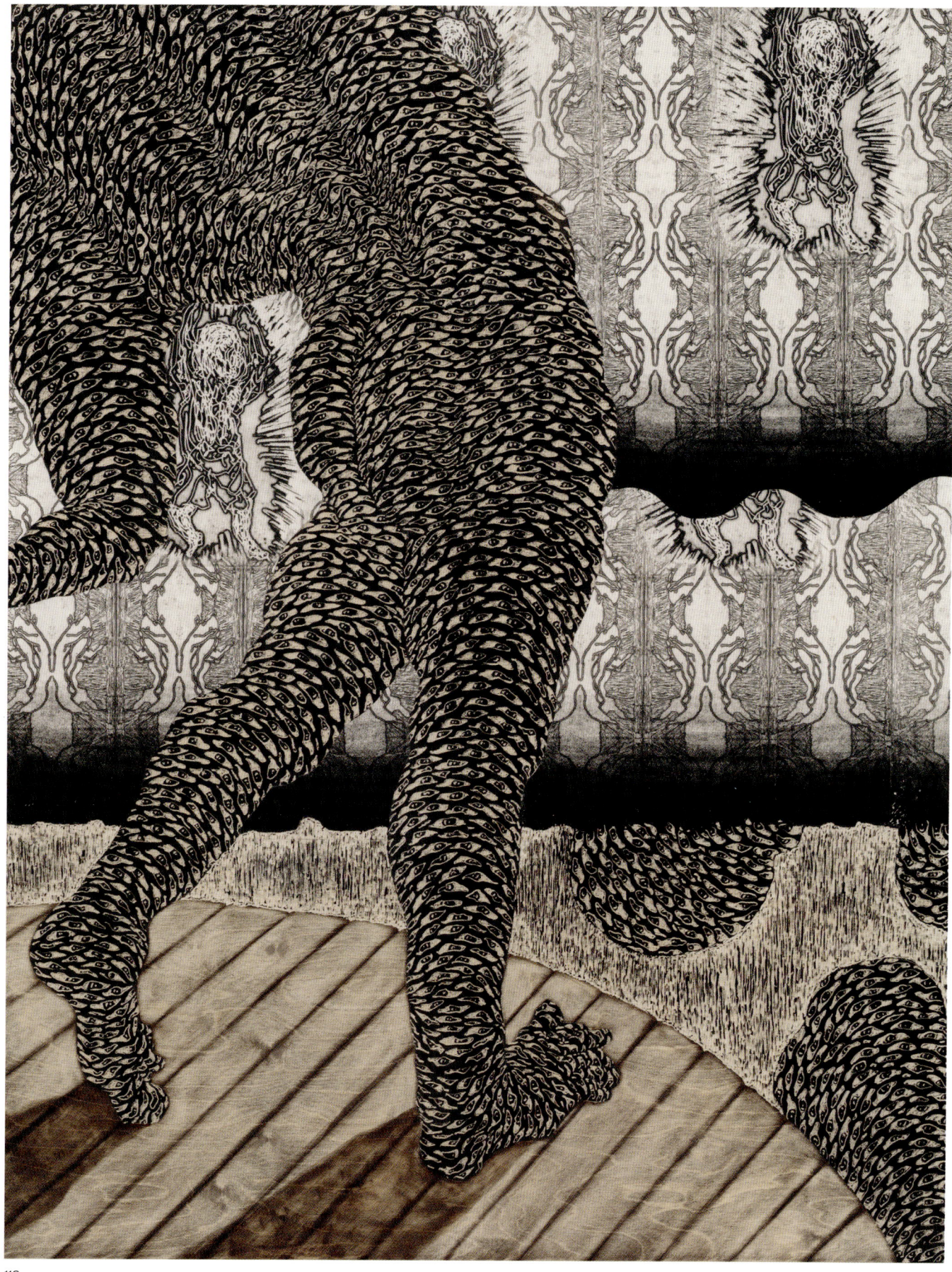

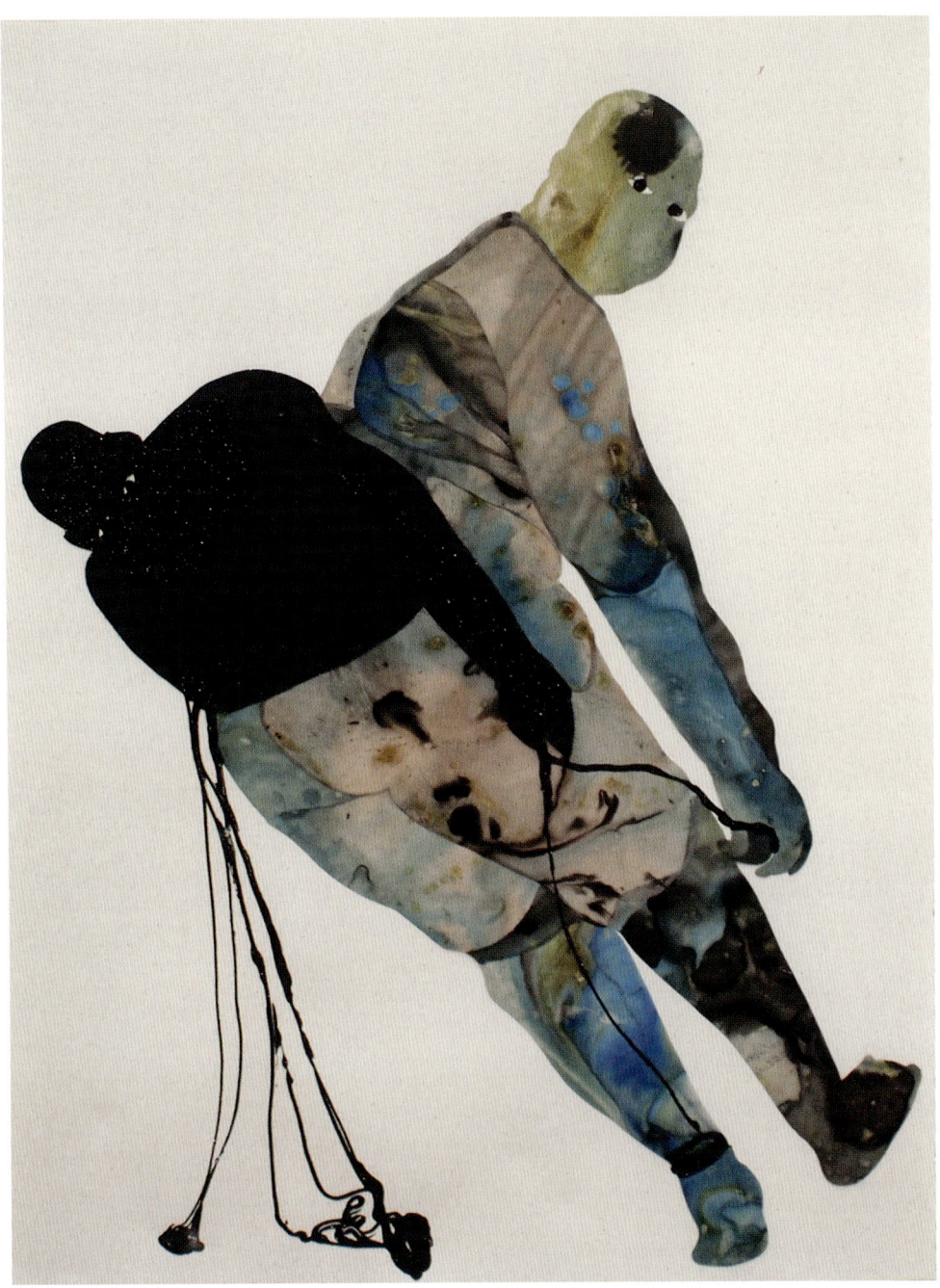

120

120 M. Florine Démosthène. *Wounds #15*. From the series *The Stories I Tell Myself*. 2018. Collage on paper. Private collection.

121 Shirley Rufin. *Avant C*. 2009. Black and white photograph, chemically treated. Digital print on Komacel support.

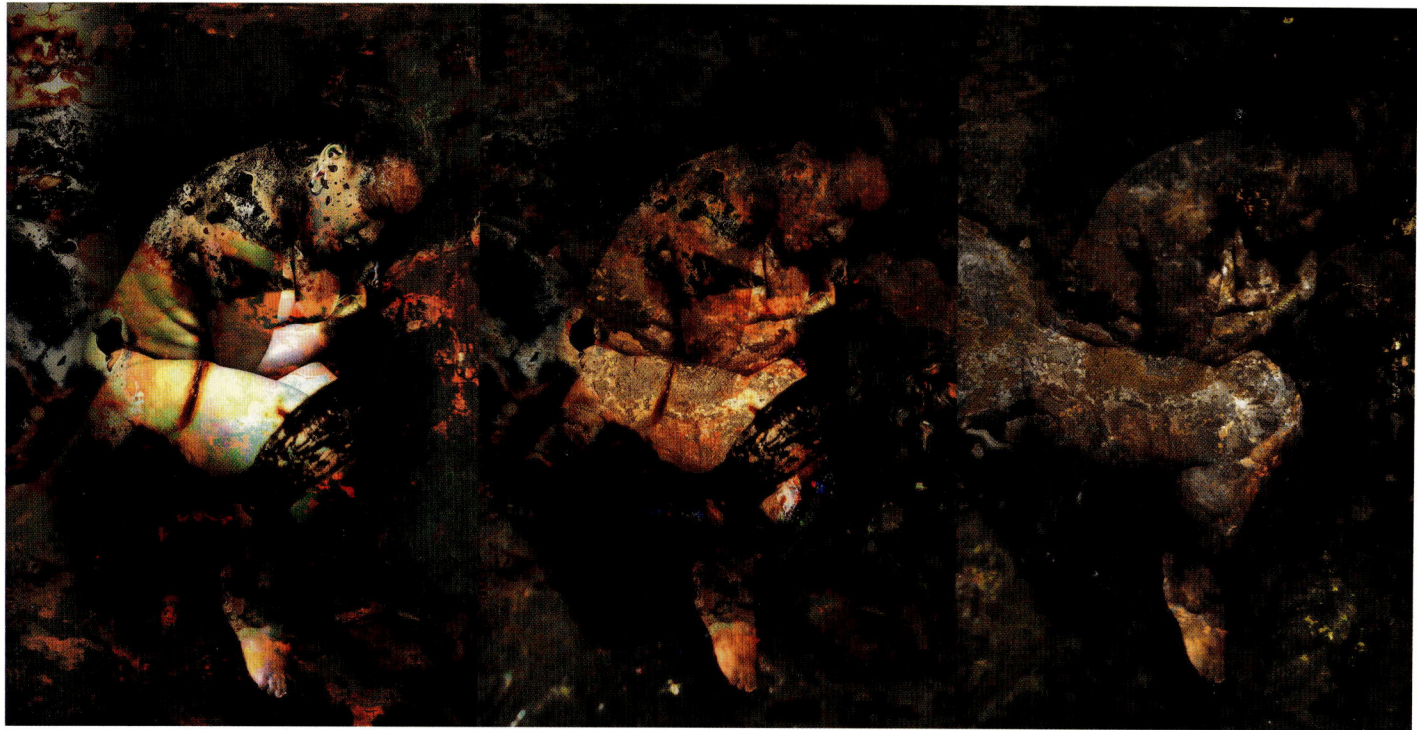

121

enables her to explore the visceral spaces between representation and abstraction, between belonging and alterity. There is love for the Black body in all its excess of materiality and fleshiness. Her work questions what it means to exist in a social world where one's body does not fit into clearly defined hegemonic frameworks of beauty, desire, and femininity. In *Avant C*, a triptych, Rufin has positioned an unidentified nude female in a fetal position and through manipulation in the darkroom has created a murky surface on the photographic paper, thus at the same time obscuring and elucidating the vulnerability implied by the pose of the nude female figure. It is as if she is in the womb, in the ultimate vulnerable state, seeking protection. However, it is not the choice to use a nude female figure that makes Rufin's artwork so profound, but her deft ability to manipulate and extend the purposes of photography and move beyond its mimetic and realist intentions to create a representational tool that challenges the viewer's understanding of the complexities of surface, shadow, color, and light. By inserting the Black female body as both

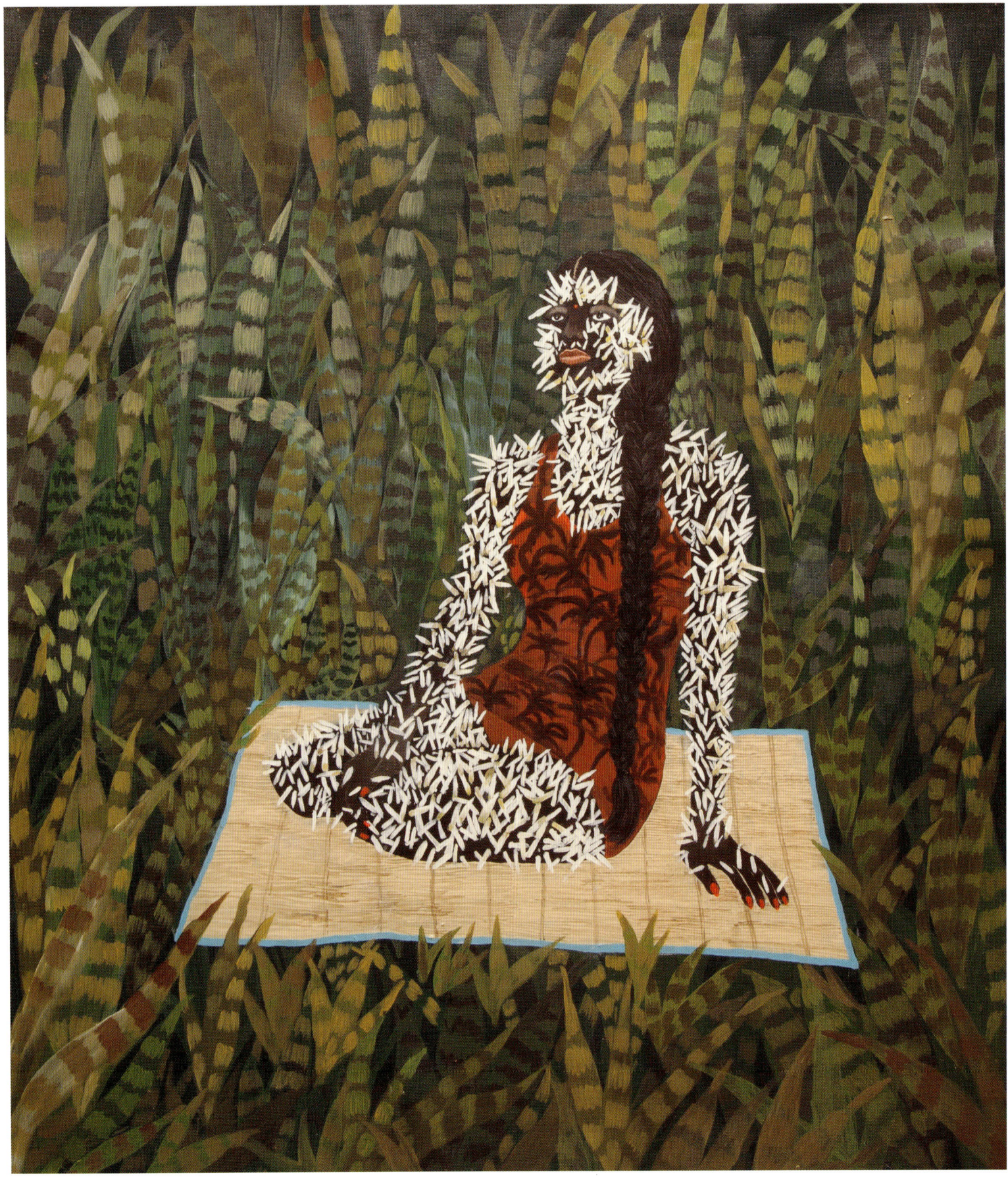

122

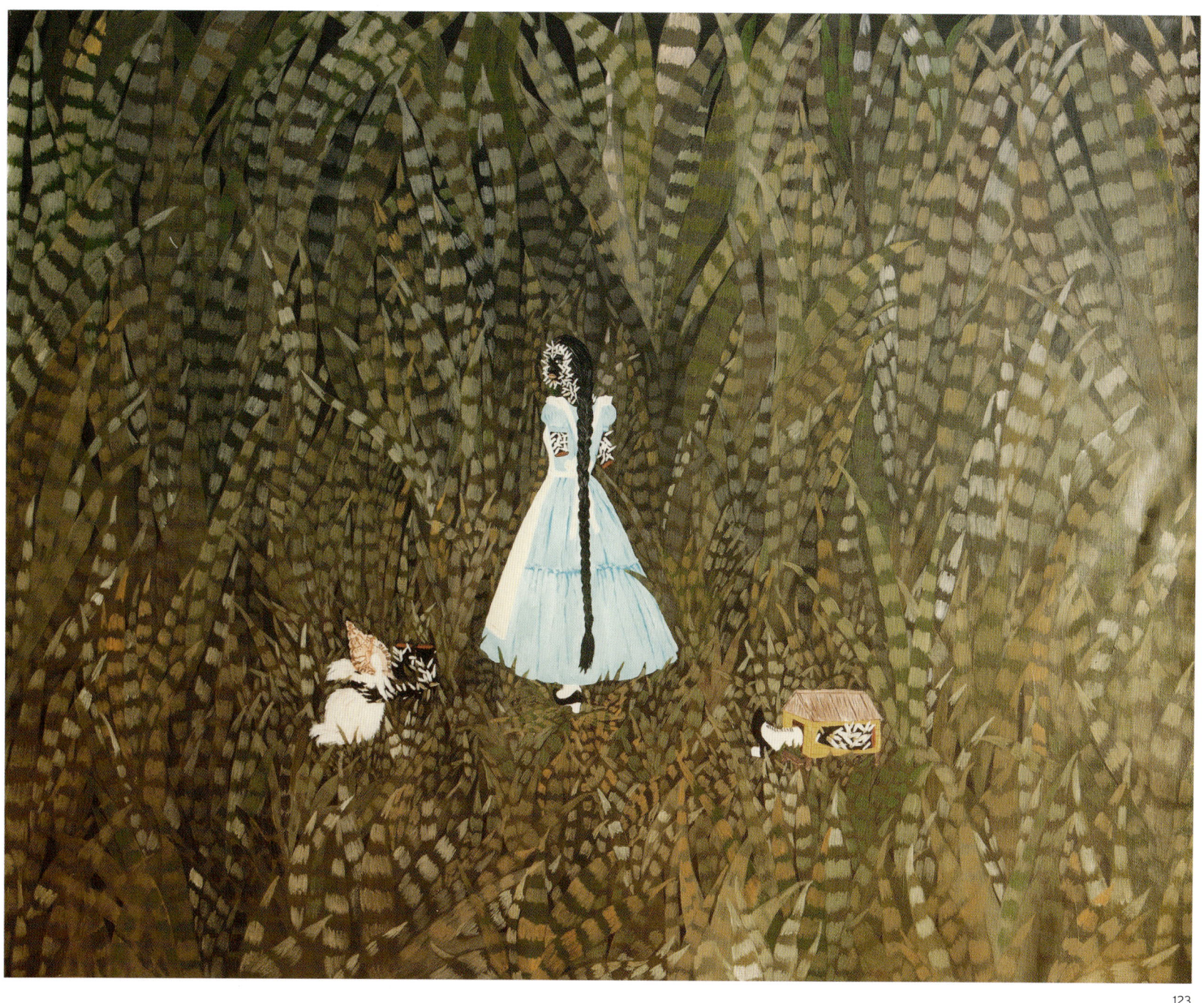

123

122 Kelly Sinnapah Mary. *Notebook of No Return to the Native Land.* 2018. Mixed-media textile installation.

123 Kelly Sinnapah Mary. *Notebook of No Return to the Native Land, Alice.* 2018. Mixed-media textile installation.

124 Mafalda Nicolas Mondestin. *Upside Down under the Frangipani*. From the *Marasa* series. 2016. Mixed media on paper.

protagonist and antagonist within the representational frame, Rufin shares with Démosthène the use of the body to question the simultaneous visibility and invisibility signaled by its Blackness, physicality, and sensuality. Démosthène's mixed-media paintings and drawings and Rufin's photographs are part of a Black feminist engagement with the meaning and representational strategy of the body, self-identity, sensuality, and, most importantly, agency.

Equally potent if less nebulous in texture and surface is the work of the Indo-Guadeloupean artist Kelly Sinnapah Mary (b. 1981) in her ongoing series *Notebook of No Return,* whose title is influenced by that of Aimé Césaire's epic poem *Cahier d'un retour au pays natal*. Like Césaire, Mary is interested in the concept of home both as an idyllic space and one that reinforces postcolonial trauma. As a multidisciplinary artist, her videos, drawings, material-based art pieces, site-specific installations, and paintings are visual critiques of the sexual and racial oppression of women. Known for her ongoing *Vagina* series (2013–) that seductively comments on symbolic and physical violence against women, she approaches provocative cultural and racial issues in poetic ways. In *Notebook of No Return* and *Notebook of No Return, Alice,* both conceived in 2018, Mary places the female figure, which can be read racially and ethnically as Indo-Caribbean, at the center of the canvas against a backdrop of foliage native to Guadeloupe. Attesting to the discrimination faced by members of the Indian community when they were brought to Guadeloupe as indentured servants in the late nineteenth century, Mary has adorned the gracefully sitting figure in *Notebook of No Return* with prickly skin. In *Notebook of No Return, Alice,* an elegantly dressed, long-haired, dark-skinned female, looks sideways at the viewer, indifferent to the fact that she is missing several limbs.

In these two works, the Indo-Caribbean body, one conceived in the manufactured space of paradise and the other in the imaginary space of the fairy tale, allows for the exploration of representations of the displaced, mangled Black figure, the violence executed upon it, and its future possibilities. While subversive in their depiction, the subjects of these paintings do not allow for a full departure from reality; instead, Mary's work echoes with a vibrancy that aesthetically necessitates a look at colonialism, enslavement, and oppression within the myth-making pictorial landscape, within the layered planes of imagery by adopting fantastical philosophies of time and space.

As in Mary's work, the Caribbean foliage serves as a backdrop for the contemplation of a fraught space imagined as home within the layered planes of imagery and myth-making in the acrylic paintings of Mafalda Nicolas Mondestin (b. 1982, Haiti/United States). *Causeries sous le sablier (Chit-chat under the Sandbox Tree)* and *Sens dessus dessous dans le frangipanier (Upside Down under the Frangipani)*, both from 2016, render the Black body in play and in relaxation. These paintings are sites for critical reflection and meditative contemplation. As the nude black-inked female bodies appear to float on the cream-colored, floral-patterned background, there is a sensually provocative quietness between the light background and the black skin of the figures, a certain playfulness between bodily skin and the skin of the glossy paper, almost a utopian existence in the space of Haiti, a space that was not meant to exist. What is revealed at the interstices of reflection and contemplation are snippets of vulnerability in an attempt at self-representation.

Self-representation and self-possession guide the photography of Robert Charlotte (Martinique), known for his 2014 portraits

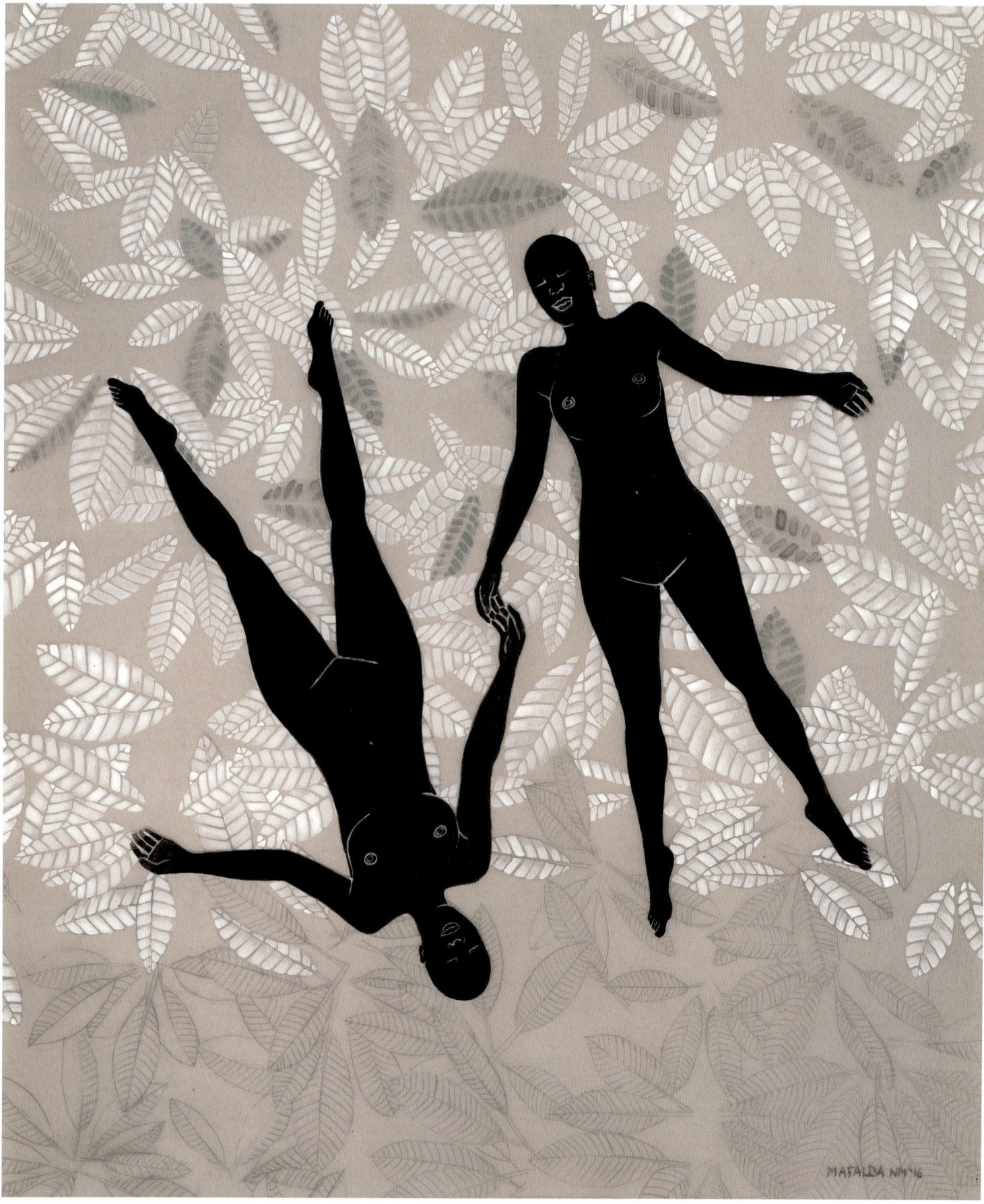

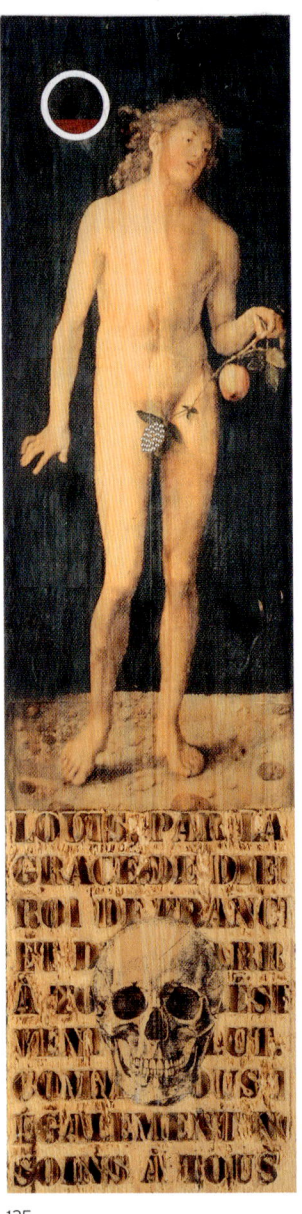 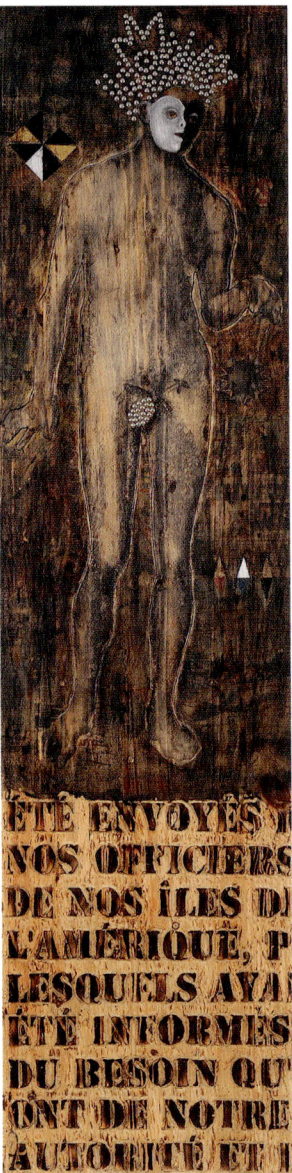 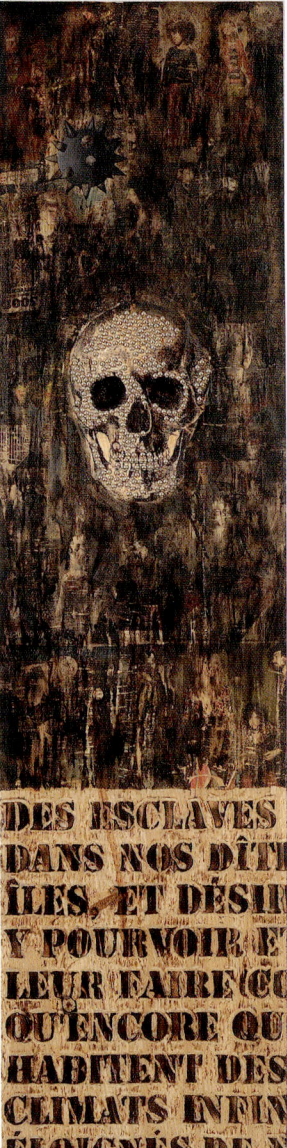 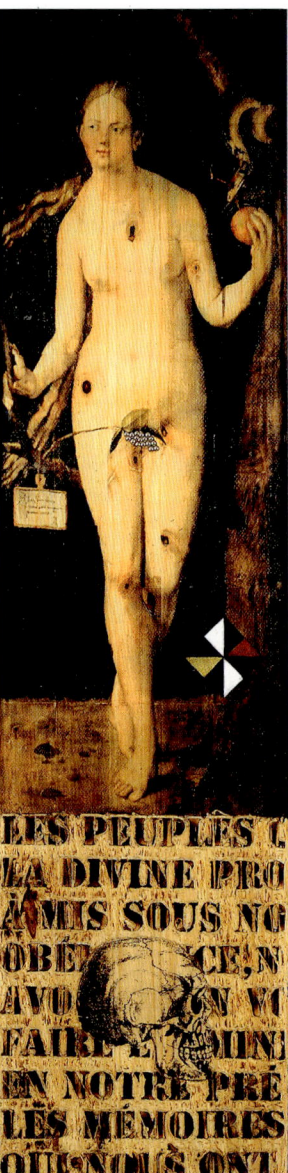 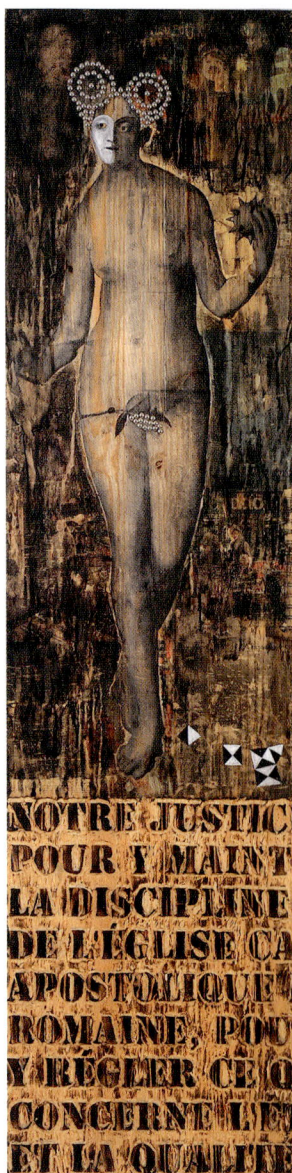

125   Bruno Pédurand. *The Heritage of Ham*. Panel 1. 2008. Oil and nails, details, Bible, etc., on wood. 5 panels. 200 × 50 cm. each. Courtesy of the artist.

126   Bruno Pédurand. *The Heritage of Ham*. Panel 2. 2008. Oil and nails, details, Bible, etc., on wood. 5 panels. 200 × 50 cm. each. Courtesy of the artist.

127   Bruno Pédurand. *The Heritage of Ham*. Panel 3. 2008. Oil and nails, details, Bible, etc., on wood. 5 panels. 200 × 50 cm. each. Courtesy of the artist.

128   Bruno Pédurand. *The Heritage of Ham*. Panel 4. 2008. Oil and nails, details, Bible, etc., on wood. 5 panels. 200 × 50 cm. each. Courtesy of the artist.

129   Bruno Pédurand. *The Heritage of Ham*. Panel 5. 2008. Oil and nails, details, Bible, etc., on wood. 5 panels. 200 × 50 cm. each. Courtesy of the artist.

of the descendants of the Garifuna, an Amerindian ethnic community living in St. Vincent, Honduras, and Belize. Charlotte creates portraits of individuals how they want to be seen—bold, dynamic, reserved, and always in control, in a way antithetical to the ways Black bodies are represented in economically struggling communities. A master of light, point of view, and composition, Charlotte poses his sitters against a studio background in ways that allow their vulnerabilities to come through while highlighting their resilience through their direct and bold gaze.

In *Vis-à-vis, sans titre* (2006–2009), a series of candid black and white and color studio portraits that he took of individuals from a working-class neighborhood in Fort-de-France, Charlotte combines the penetrative gaze of the camera with the sitters' clarity of individuality. In *Vis-à-vis, sans titre #19* (2006), a bejeweled couple decked out in classic urban chic against a photographer's black studio cloth possess an aura that only comes from those who value their own worth. The man has his right arm around the woman's shoulder while a thin cigar dangles from his other hand. She has both arms around his waist; her left hand is placed on his hip, and her right hand is touching his black fanny pack. Both look directly into the camera, she with an open, assertive stare and lightly pursed lips and he with confidence. To pose for a photo is both an act of empowerment and vulnerability. It is a submission to what Lauren DeLand calls "a process of self-fragmentation" that risks "the indefinite appropriation of one's image as proof to support any number of obscure and often oppositional convictions."[39] Nevertheless, in *Vis-à-vis, sans titre #19*, Charlotte takes full advantage of the urgency and vicissitudes of the medium to capture what William Henry Fox Talbot called photography in general: "the most transitory of things, a shadow, the proverbial emblem of all that is fleeting and momentary." Capturing a sartorial coolness that comes through the form-fitting "Fashion Pirate" emblem shirt of the woman and the meshed, sleeveless shirt the male sitter wears, Charlotte snaps the shot just as cigarette smoke comes through his nose; a habitual gesture becomes a decisive moment of self-representation and self-possession.

Born in Guadeloupe and based in Martinique, Bruno Pédurand (b. 1967) engages and examines the social and cultural contextual relevance of images, and his works of art are powerful expressions of the vexed histories of racial representation and colonial oppression. Inspired by the oil-on-panel paintings of Adam and Eve by the German Renaissance artist Albrecht Dürer, *L'héritage de Cham* (2008) is an amalgamation of Christian and Afro-Caribbean religious signs and symbols that come together to critique the violent legacies of colonialism and enslavement. Images of Adam and Eve and skulls are transferred onto five wooden planks. Under each plank, Pédurand, carving into the wood passages from Louis XIV's 1685 *Code Noir*—the royal decree that established regulations for the slave trade in the French colonial empire—creates a relief-textured pattern that recalls the branding that would be inflicted on the skin of enslaved people. Four Bibles, their covers overlaid with nails, rest on white-painted wooden pedestals placed in a semicircular formation. At the center is a black-painted pedestal holding several colored votive candles that faces the wooden panel with an image of a studded skull. Separately, the images on the wooden planks and the Bibles speak to the syncretism that exists between Afro-Caribbean religious imagery (Cuban Santería, Brazilian Candomblé, and Haitian Vodou) and Catholic icons, and Pédurand's deft weaving of pictorial and personal identity. As an installation, *L'héritage de*

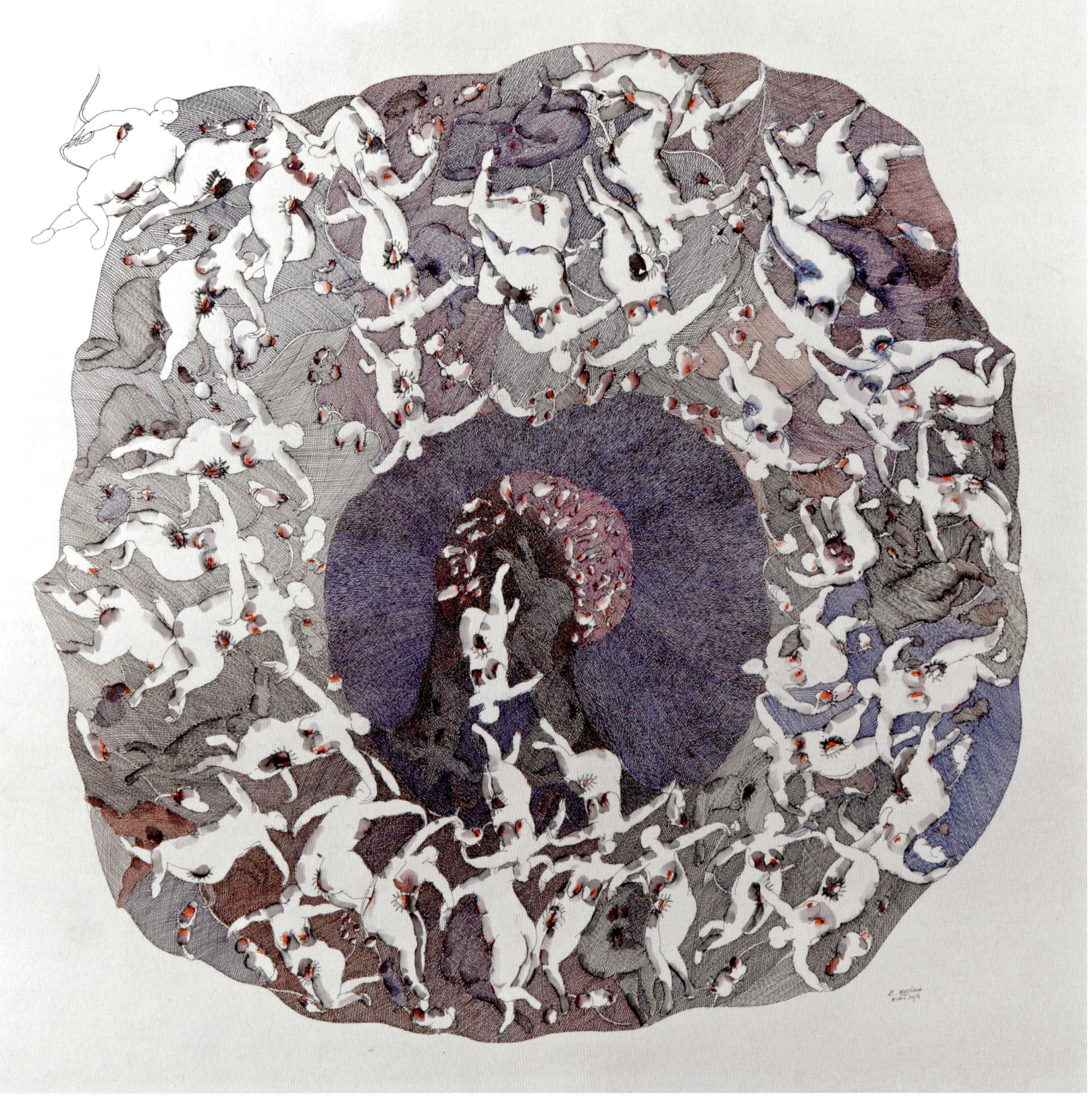

130

130 Ernest Breleur. *Untitled*. From the series *The Origin of the World*. 2014. Felt on paper.

131 Tessa Mars. *Conversation with Hector H*. 2015. Acrylic on canvas.

132 Hector Hyppolite. *Mistress Erzulie*. 1945–1948. Oil on masonite. Port-au-Prince, Musée d'Art Haïtien du Collège St. Pierre.

Cham conveys the racist legacy of the Catholic Church as a type of institution steeped in hierarchies of racialization ultimately codified on the body. Artfully, the genitalia of Adam and Eve are covered with silver studs in the shape of flowers, and their darker-tinted faces are half-covered with a white mask, while their heads are adorned with silver-studded crowns. The title of the installation references the story of Ham, whose son Canaan was cursed by Noah to be forever enslaved after Ham's encounter with his drunken, naked father. For Pédurand, the neocolonial enslavement of people of African descent recalls this biblical tale. What *L'héritage de Cham* brings to the forefront is both the interplay of history and religion and the mythology of race, which was also captured in Price-Mars's influential text *Ainsi parla l'Oncle*.

In the drawing series of one of the best-known Caribbean artists from Martinique, Ernest Breleur renders organic full-figured female bodies languidly floating in different poses, connected to each other by limbs and organic appendages extending from their bodies. *Origine* (2014), Breleur states, is about "the origin of the world, questioning the living body, sexuality and eroticism."⁴⁰ Using delicate strokes of black felt pen and a limited palette of blues and reds to create anthropomorphic cascading bodies entangled in sensual gestures and poses, these methodically composed drawings constitute Breleur's artistic language with imaginative networks of poetic organisms. He repeats the image of dancing, twisting women to create a circular composition of figures that suggests an interplay between external forces and the forces that reside in the human body and spirit. Breleur has captured exceptionally well the element that traverses specific geographic boundaries and speaks to Glissant's concept of tout-monde. A multitalented artist who works in painting, drawing, and installation, Breleur, using evocative images, takes a different approach to the legacy of colonialism in exploring its effect on the human form and the human condition.

Tessa Mars (b. 1985), born and living in Haiti, is another artist who uses the figure, particularly her own body, in many of her paintings. *Conversation avec Hector H/Conversation with Hector H* (2015) is an homage to the well-known painting by Hector Hyppolite, *Maîtresse Erzulie* (1945–1948). In Hyppolite's painting, the nude, brown-skinned Erzulie is presented in a vaguely erotic scene, sensually posed in profile. In his tight composition, Erzulie, the *lwa* of love and sexuality, is at the center of the painting, her full concentration fixed on the surrounding lush background filled with flamingos, flowers, butterflies, and a parrot. Mars's painting is a balance between positive and negative space. Hers is not a mimetic rendition of Erzulie. Erzulie's body has been replaced by Mars's lighter-skinned, nude, full-figured shape. She appears not in profile, but with her back to the viewer, gazing on the surrounding flora and fauna. Like Hyppolite's, Mars's color palette is rich and vibrant, but her colors are also electric, giving the painting an energy that intensifies its feminist intervention. There is a playfulness and candor in Mars's execution that does not belie the vexed pleasures of representation. As part of a series of four self-portraits, *Conversation avec Hector H/Conversation with Hector H* is a one-sided "conversation" between an older male painter whose name and oeuvre are inextricably associated with the characteristics of what is considered "Haitian art." It is a conversation with an undertone of respectful irony in which Mars inserts herself *within* the male-dominated artistic domain that formed at the Centre d'Art and the male-centered fictions of Haitian art history. Her body serves as a referent that signals

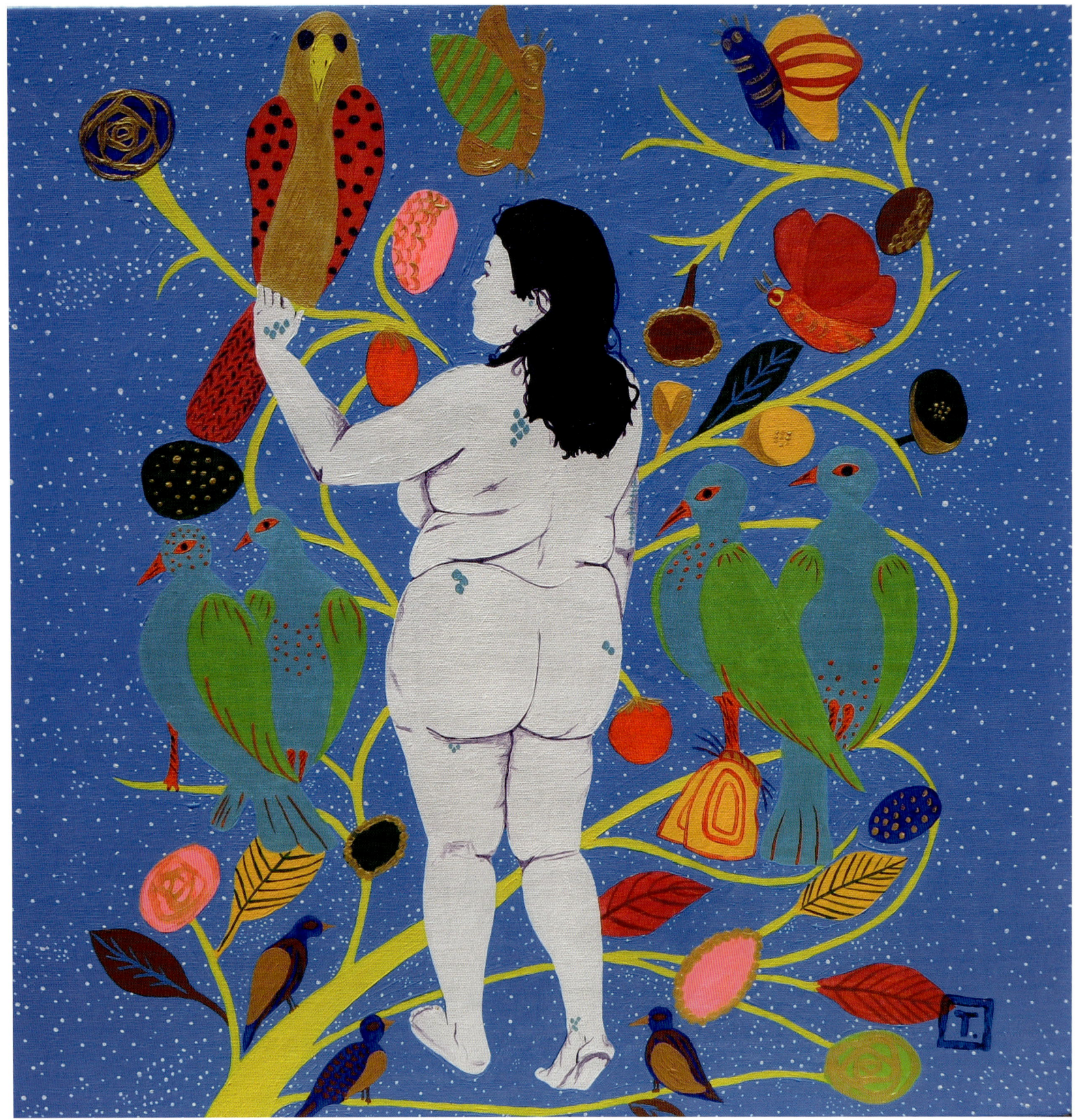

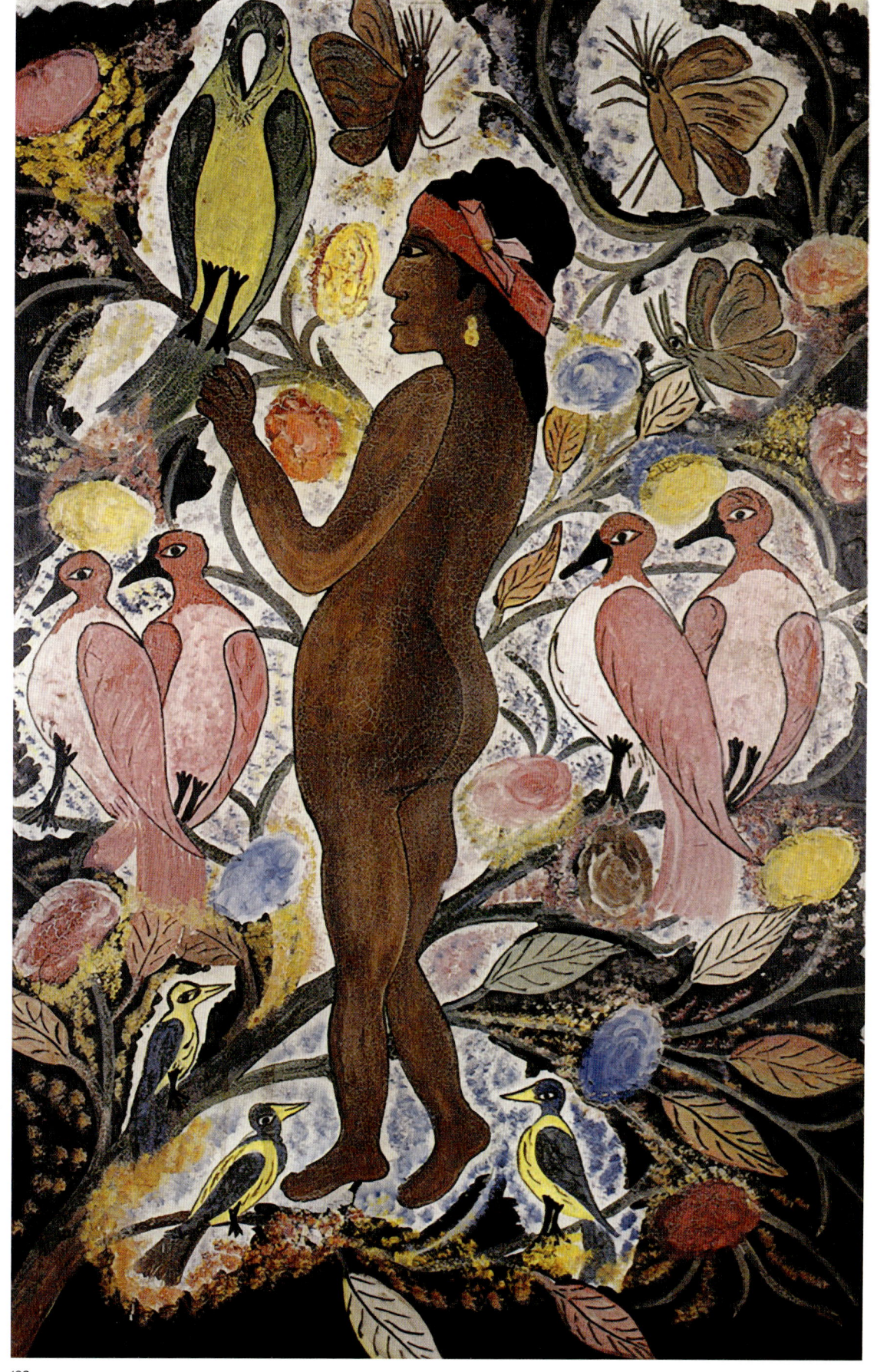

132

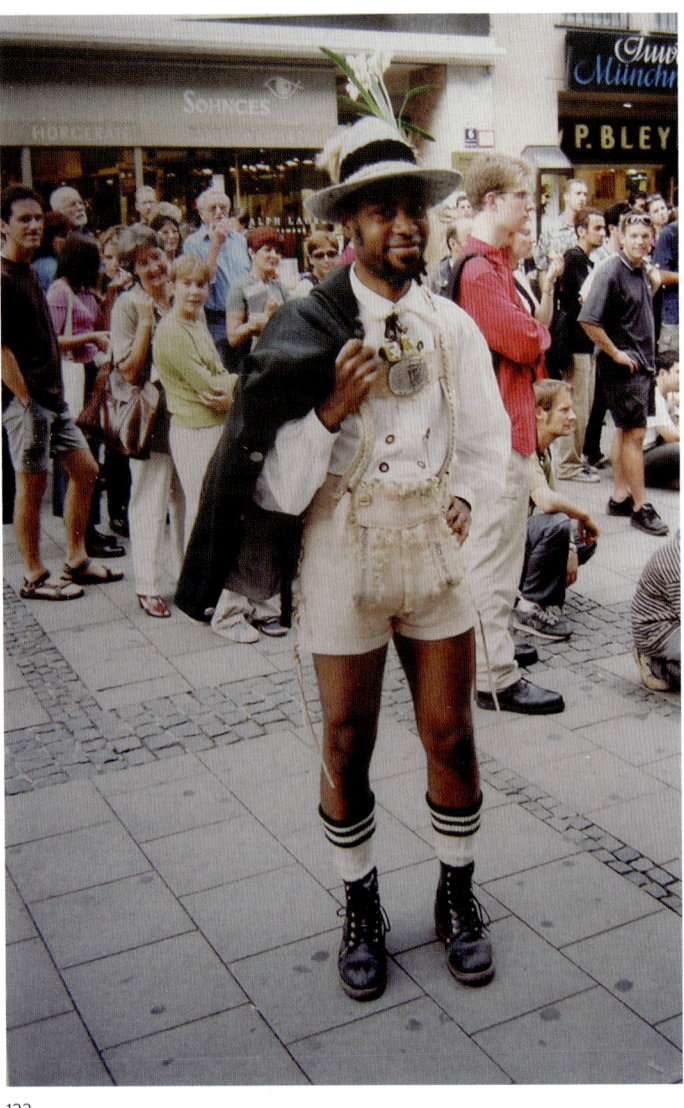

133

133 Jean-Ulrick Désert. *Negerhosen2000 (The Spectacle)*. 2000–present. 2001. Analog C-Print.

134 Jean-Ulrick Désert. *BLING*. 2018. Still from video.

135 Jean-Ulrick Désert. *BLING*. 2018. Still from video.

a visibility; like M. Florine Démosthène and Shirley Rufin, she exhibits a love for the full Black body in its excess of form, flesh, and materiality.

In his well-documented ongoing project *Negerhosen2000 (The Spectacle)* (2000–), the multidisciplinary artist Jean-Ulrick Désert (Haiti/Berlin) utilizes performance art, photography, installation, and ephemera to challenge the violent consequences of "walking while black." *Negerhosen2000* is imbued with the remnants of the histories of violence and is, in part, about reclaiming one's body from such violence. As a performative device, we may understand the figure of *Negerhosen2000* as a raconteur fluent in the hieroglyphic and vocabulary of visual culture. Like Frantz Fanon's encounter with the white child that commences the well-known chapter "The Fact of Blackness" in *Black Skin, White Masks*, *Negerhosen2000* as a performance act examines the precarious and unsettling nature in the encounter with the discomfort and unfamiliarity of Blackness, or confronts what Nicole Fleetwood calls the "troubling presence of blackness."[41] Désert continues to exhibit his visual and performative dexterity in the video-triptych *BLING–ECHO–GLORIA*, a project begun in 2018. *BLING* opens with a shirtless Désert with his back to the camera, facing a patterned gold lame-stripped curtain. As non-diegetic sound, the viewer hears rambunctious children talking, playing, and laughing happily. On the screen, Désert is donning the excessive gear of the controversial figure of Zwarte Piet, St. Nicholas's helper fêted in the Netherlands, Aruba, and Curaçao during St. Nicholas's Eve. As Désert systematically applies blackface and dons each accessory of the character—curly-haired wig, large silver hoop earrings, and large rhinestone-encrusted shades—the screen fades to black as he returns with a more elaborately

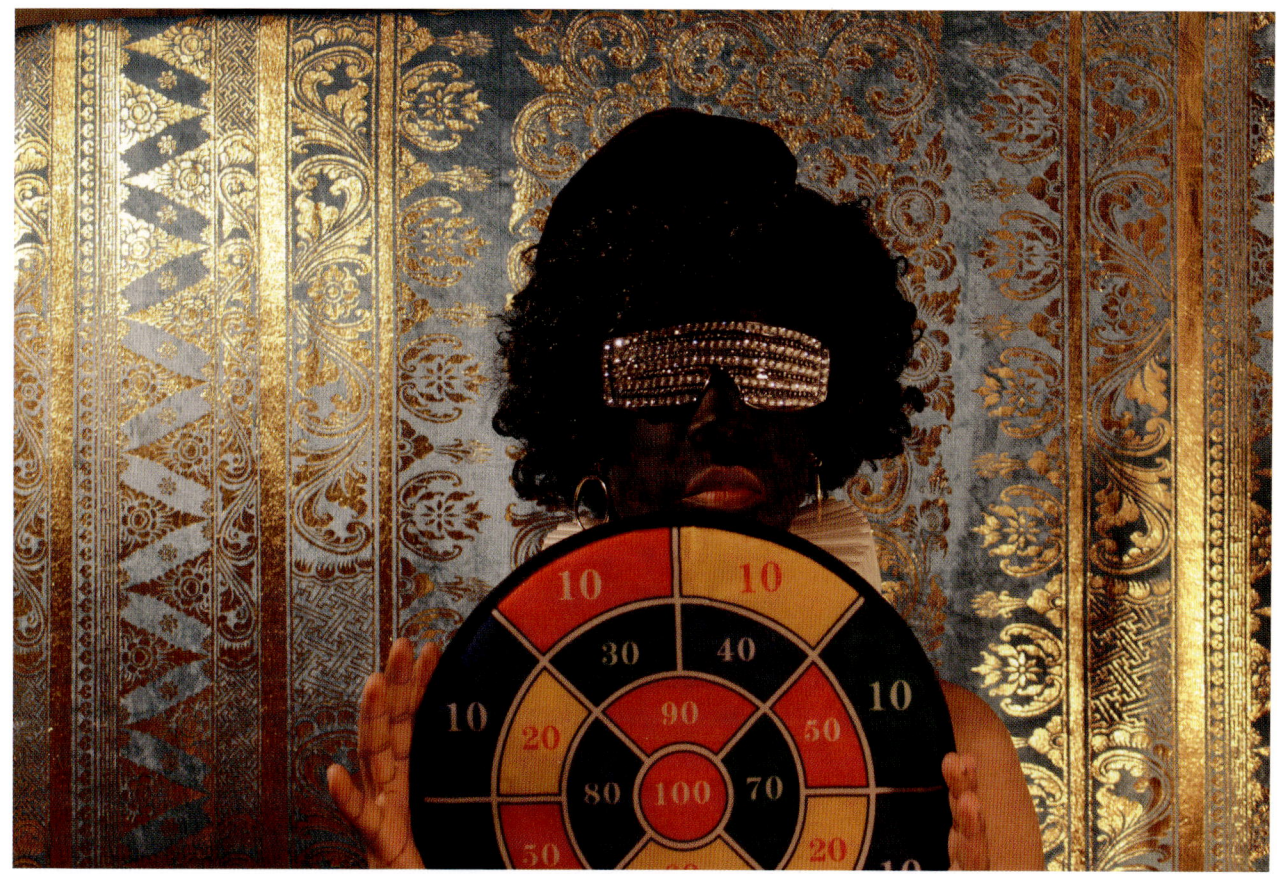

134

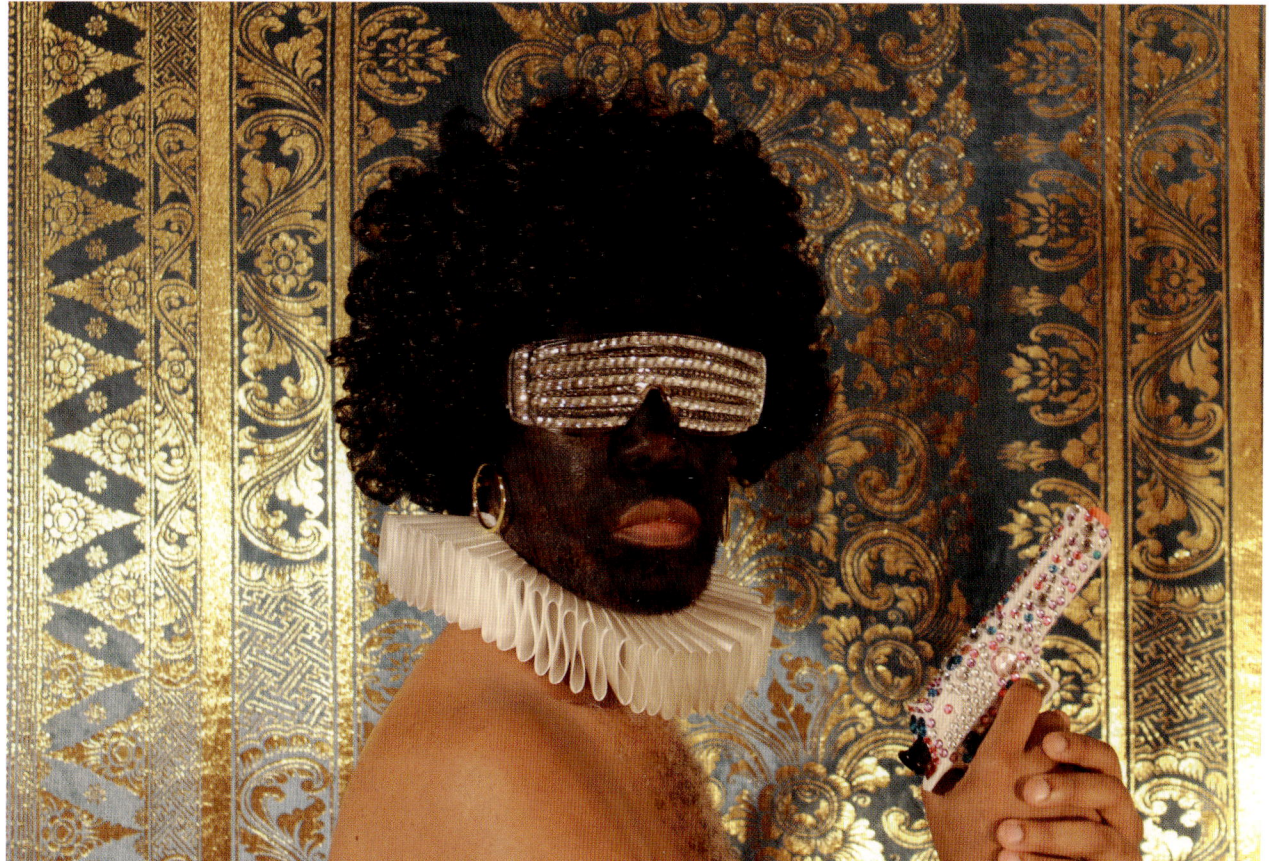

135

136 Jean-Marc Hunt. *Balloon*. 2014. Acrylic on canvas. Guadeloupe, Private collection.

outfitted version of Désert/Zwarte Piet. In the final scene, once again fading to black, we see Désert/Zwarte Piet with a similarly "blinged-out" gun pointed directly into his mouth. Once more, Désert is dealing with a thorny subject, using his Black queer body as a heuristic device to address the complex histories of racism and racial violence as they are acted on the Black body in general and the queer body of color specifically. This video is reminiscent of *Daily Mask* (2004), a three-and-a-half-minute 16mm film by the performance and installation artist Maren Hassinger, who applied black grease paint in a warlike pattern to her face to expose the racist elements in nineteenth- and twentieth-century minstrelsy and explore the ways Black identity is *always already* a performance. Instead of the sounds of buoyant children, ceremonial African drumming accompanies Hassinger's performative utterance.

Equally significant to the horrors of violence against the Black body is *Balloon* (2014), a painting by Jean-Marc Hunt (b. 1974) rendered in the style of neo-expressionism. Hunt, who was born in Strasbourg, France, now resides in Guadeloupe. In his large-scale paintings and broad gestural brushstrokes, Hunt's background as a graffiti artist is apparent. He begins a painting by filling areas on the canvas with bright, often clashing colors. After he has created a form, he fills in the negative space with white acrylic paint; no area on the canvas is left bare. He is adept at creating an alternative aesthetic that destabilizes what belongs on the canvas, how it is applied, and how we understand traditional forms of sculpture and painting. Unencumbered by distinct figurative cues, we see the distorted face of a young boy in the shape of a floating balloon, a dangling string wrapped around his throat. Hunt has not drawn the boy's full body; it is in the absence of the Black body that its potentially dangerous presence resonates, and through the material absence of a fully recognizable figure we come to understand the full weight of violence that is perpetuated on Black and brown bodies. In its graffiti-based style, *Balloon* allegorically refers to Eric Garner, an unarmed African American man killed on July 17, 2014, in Staten Island, New York. In a graphic, gruesome incident captured on video, a white uniformed New York City police officer, approaching Garner on suspicions of his selling cigarettes illegally, threw an allegedly resisting Garner to the ground, holding him there with the assistance of multiple officers in a chokehold that proved fatal. Garner's last words before he died, literally in the grips of the law, were "I can't breathe," which he repeated eleven times.[42] Deeply moved by this incident, Hunt attempts to capture, in the expression of a young boy, a sense of disbelief, confusion, and horror, gesturing to the despair felt by Garner at the moment of his death. As a discursive work of art filled with creative potential, *Balloon* captures a specific moment in time that had profound global resonance. Like Désert's *Negerhosen2000* performance, Hunt visualizes racial injustices and bodily trauma through the formal methods of expressive abstraction.

The art historian Rocío Aranda-Alvarado writes: "The body serves equally as sign for presence[,]… the permanence of its surface acting as a text that the artists develop through their work. The body becomes the living proof, made visible and reconsidered through the art object."[43] This indexicality, made possible through the performative aspect of the "living proof" body, is instrumental in the performances and creative collaborations between the dancer and choreographer Annabel Guérédrat (Martinique) and Henri Tauliaut (Guadeloupe/Martinique), a bio- and

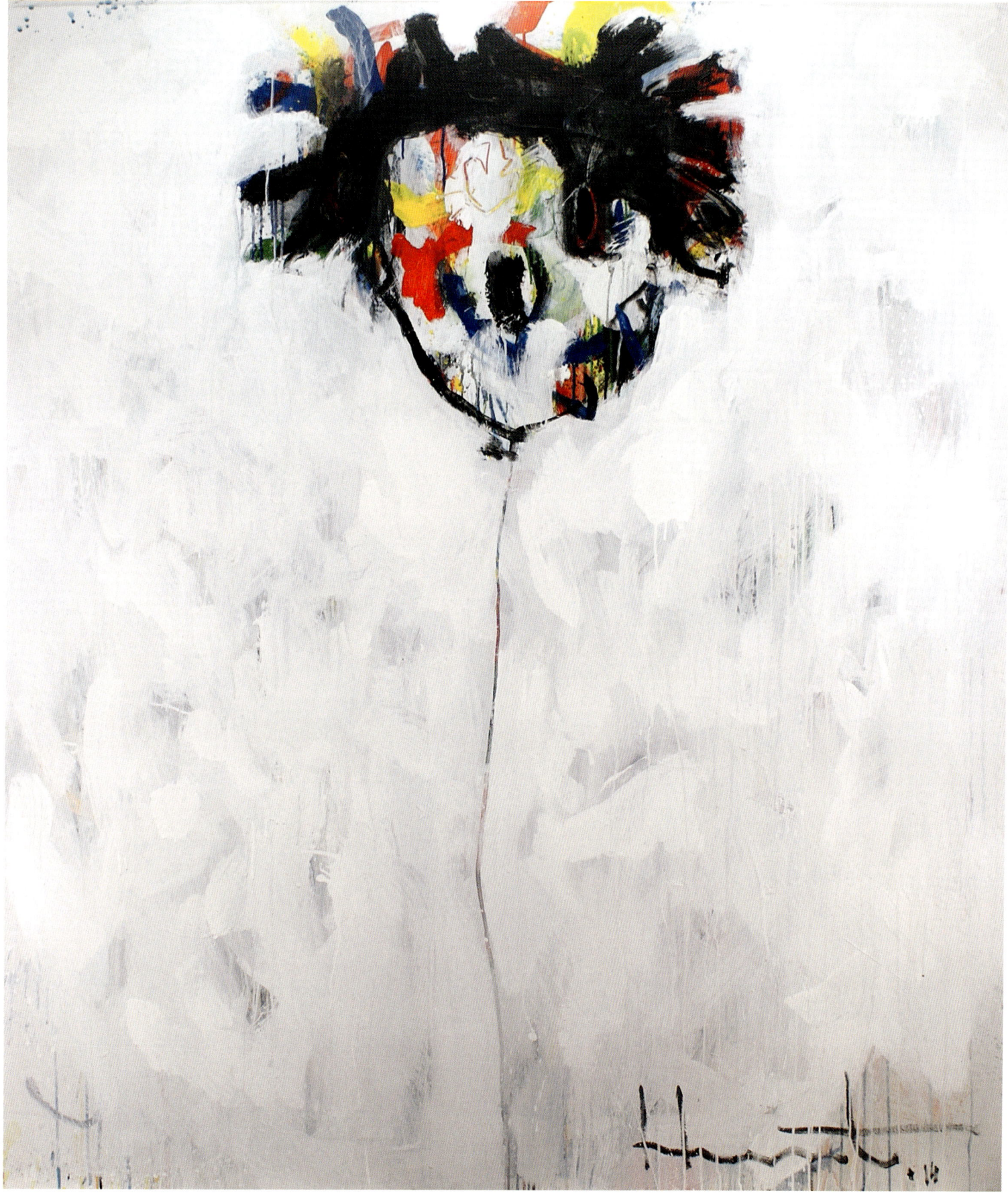

136

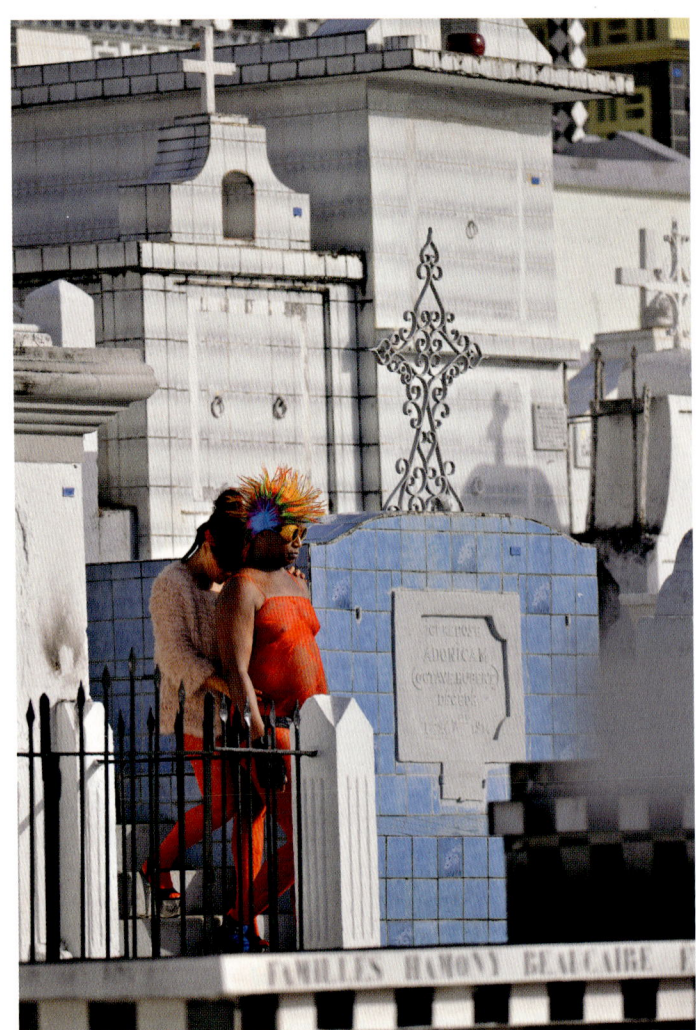
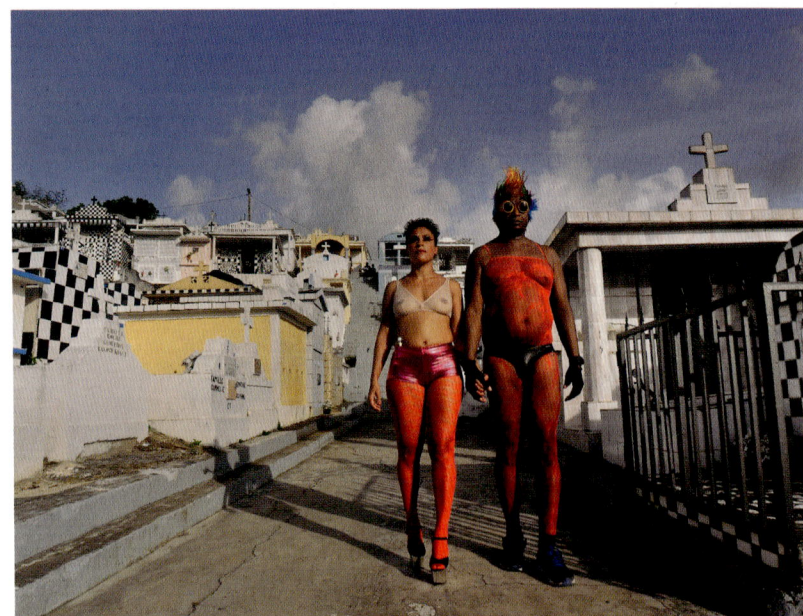

137 Annabel Guérédrat and Henri Tauliaut. *Nudes Descending a Staircase, #3.* 2013. Performance video.

138 Annabel Guérédrat and Henri Tauliaut. *Nudes Descending a Staircase, #3.* 2013. Performance video.

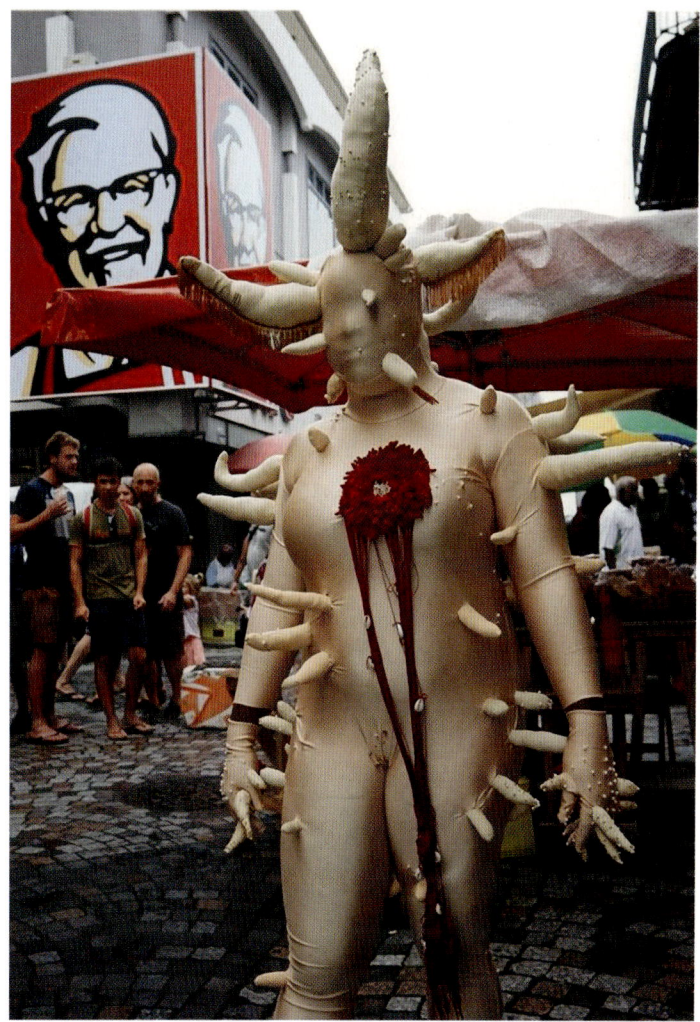

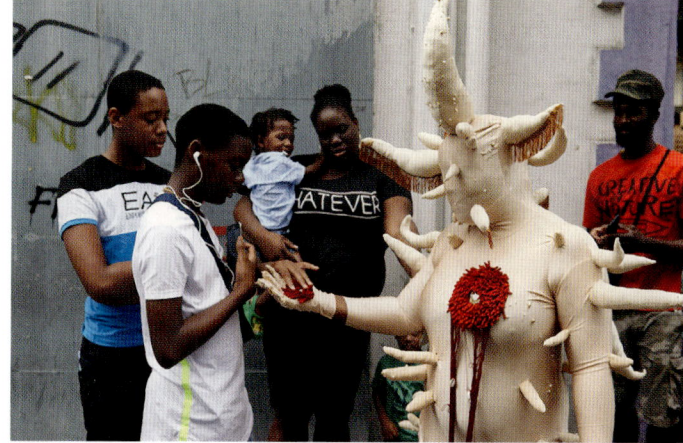

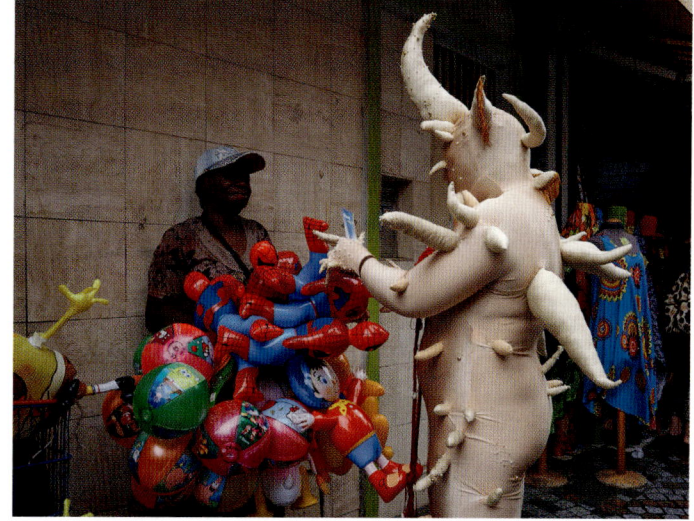

139 Gwladys Gambie. *Beautiful Monster*. April 2017. Performance. International Festival of Performance Art (FIAP) in Martinique.

140 Gwladys Gambie. *Beautiful Monster*. April 2017. Performance. International Festival of Performance Art (FIAP) in Martinique.

141 Gwladys Gambie. *Beautiful Monster*. April 2017. Performance. International Festival of Performance Art (FIAP) in Martinique.

142 Maksaens Denis. *Nude Descending a Staircase*. 2014. Digital photograph printed on cloth. Private collection.

digital artist.⁴⁴ Both have collaborated on performance art pieces that use their either nude or at times spectacularly outfitted bodies. In *Nus descendant l'escalier/Nudes Descending a Staircase, #3* performed at Cimetière de Morne-à-l'Eau in Guadeloupe, with beautiful arrangements of black and white tiles decorating the crypts, creating a spectacular resting place for the dead and a visually pleasing background for this performance, Guérédrat sports a short pink jacket, hot pink shorts over red tights, a cream-colored bra, and huge wedge heels. Tauliaut wears tight black leather shorts over full-body red tights, welder's glasses, and a spikey multicolored wig. As they slowly descend the stairs, they stop intermittently for Guérédrat to sprinkle the tombs with holy water, lending spirituality to an "afro punk" performance. Appropriately, two and a half minutes into the video documenting the performance, techno music begins to play and continues until the end. Their work is about building hybrid artistic worlds, revising gender and sexual identities, and interrogating relationships of power.⁴⁵ As part of the Festival International d'Art Performance, the painter Gwladys Gambie (Martinique) donned an off-white full-covering bodysuit adorned with variously sized appendages and walked the streets of Fort-de-France. On the mask covering her face, three large appendages were attached, one on each side of her face and the other on top of her head. *Beautiful Monster* (2017) is Gambie's interrogation of gender expectations and the presence of the body not as an alienated exotic artifact, but as an indexical performance that signals the power and strength of the Black female form. Like Désert's *Negerhosen2000* performance, Gambie's interactions with passersby elicited a combination of curiosity, suspicion, and perplexity. Many individuals attempted to speak to the titular Beautiful Monster while another recited the Lord's Prayer as Gambie walked by, hoping to ward off any evil spirits. Using the body as a strategic device, the performances of Désert, Guérédrat and Tauliaut, and Gambie are enmeshed in a visual vocabulary that is concerned with bringing Blackness into visibility through performative and interactive undertakings in which the body is adorned in spectacular fashion and engaged in peculiar acts, reminiscent of the performance art and interventionist art of African Americans Adrian Piper, Lorraine O'Grady, and William Pope.L. Thus, the Black body is no longer an unknown; rather, it is an active agent that attempts to strategically interject itself into the histories of racial, gender, sexual, and colonial oppression to activate other forms of knowing and creating new epistemologies to advance transformative change for the living.

In *Nu descendant l'escalier/Nude Descending a Staircase* (2014), which was included in the traveling exhibition *Relational Undercurrents*, Maksaens Denis (b. 1968, Haiti) references the iconic modernist painting by Marcel Duchamp with the same title. The exhibition curator Tatiana Flores writes that Denis "creates visually complex images that defy straightforward interpretation." This "digitally manipulated photograph printed on canvas, whose bright colors and garmented forms eclipse the bodies of several nude figures"⁴⁶ fragment and deconstruct what we presume nude male-identified bodies should look like. It is the fragmentation and the shattering of ideal gender expressions or gender identities displayed in the glittering of light and colors that is so potent in Denis's work. His repertoire of skills includes installation, sound projects, and experimental film and video. In *Untitled 02* (2011), Denis used X-ray films of his own body taken after a vicious homophobic attack in Haiti and affixed the digitally manipulated

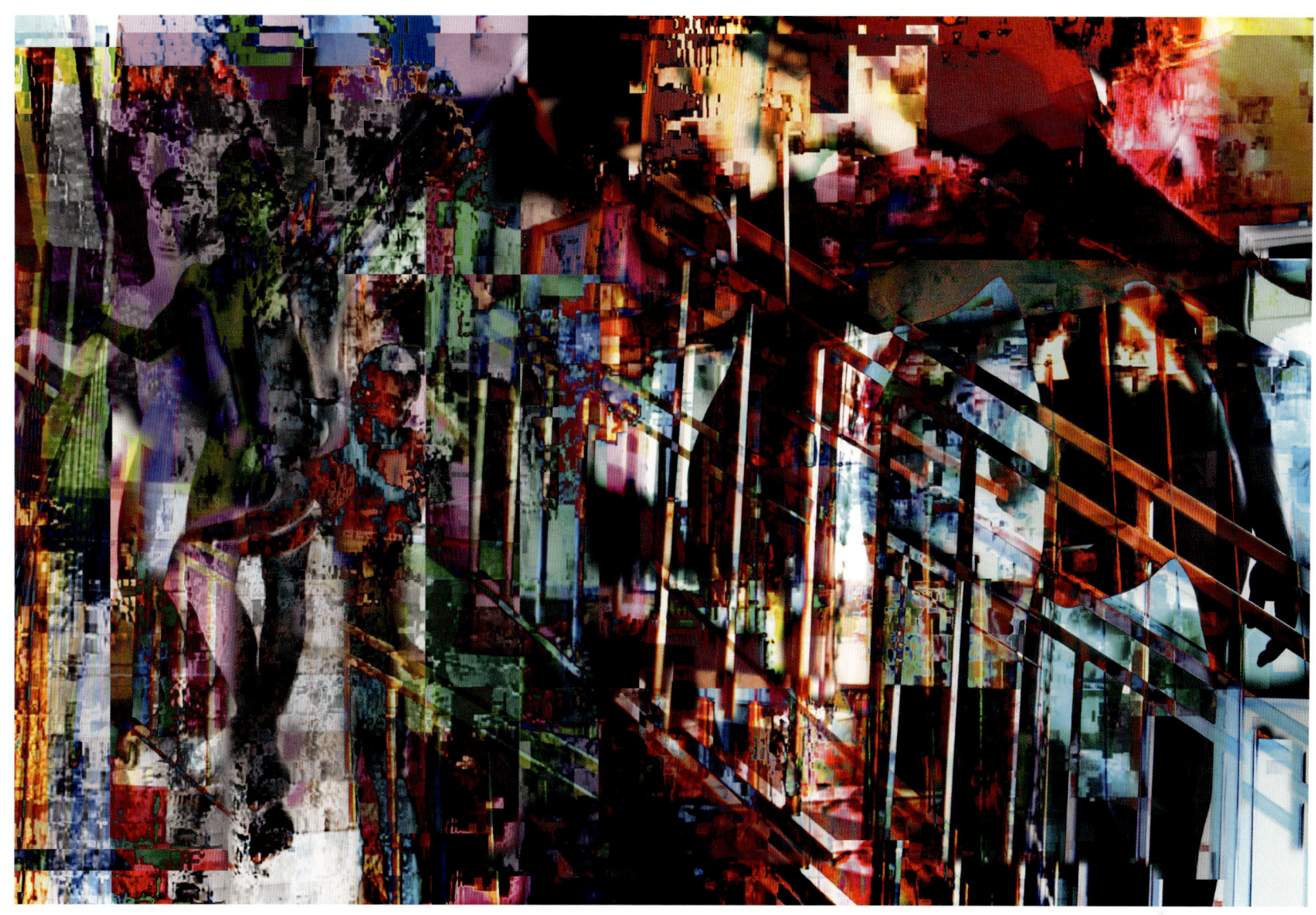

images onto Plexiglas enclosed within a brushed metal frame. In *Untitled 03* (2012), a reshaping of the 2011 piece, Denis has kept the original manipulated images, but has broken the Plexiglas and screwed the broken pieces onto wood. What we now have is a textured sculptural piece exploding with light, provocative in its materiality and equally provoking in what it implies. This is a harsh, raw piece that attests to the physical violence that he endured and the brutality and oppression that queer Black bodies living in the Caribbean endure. In *Untitled 02* and the reconfigured *Untitled 03*, Denis lays bare what is so often left unacknowledged. The X-ray films signal Denis's corporality while affirming the physical cruelty cast upon his body. Not a portrait in the conventional tradition of art history, Denis's sculptural artwork shares an aesthetic similarity with the work of the Cuban-born American artist Félix González-Torres. Both manipulate the conceptual nature of portraiture to convey the profound social and cultural undertones of autobiography in their wickedly smart works of art.

The goal of this chapter was not to be comprehensive in its explorations nor definitive in its speculations, but to present a broad overview of artistic moments and artists whose "artistic creation born under the legacies of colonialism, violence, and disenfranchisement becomes by necessity a representational act."[47] These "representational acts," filled with creative futurity, are dynamic enactments between the dialectical contradictions of postmodernity and the transformative nature of radical Black subjectivity. In addition, by broadly drawing my theoretical analysis from the tenets of several influential texts to explore how Blackness functions as evidence, as material, and as process in works of art allows for the exploration of the timelessness of radically different artistic and creative ideas, not bound by locale, yet influenced by time and place, and while not constituting a political agenda are influenced nonetheless by the politicization of race and ethnicity, and of the Black body itself.

10

RACE AND THE LATIN AMERICAN AVANT-GARDES, 1920s–1930s

ALEJANDRO DE LA FUENTE and RAFAEL CARDOSO

Le nègre est un élément réaliste.
—Oswald de Andrade, 1923

¿Quiénes somos, qué somos?
—José Vasconcelos, 1926

Students of the avant-garde literary, artistic, and cultural movements that swept Latin America in the 1920s and 1930s agree on some of the defining features of these movements: their emphasis on innovation, a reactive gesture against traditional cultural forms identified with so-called academicism; a wide range of aesthetic forms and proposals, often aligned with corresponding avant-garde currents in Europe; participation in transnational cultural, literary, and aesthetic debates, despite the prominence of local themes, informed by folkloric and nationalist concerns; the centrality of certain nodes of international art and culture, such as Paris; concerns about the role of arts and artists in public life; and the salience of manifestos as a literary and political device. One early example of such documents, the *Manifesto Pau-Brasil* (*Brazil Wood*), authored by the writer Oswald de Andrade (1890–1954) in 1924, already articulated many of the anxieties that characterized Brazilian modernists and other Latin American avant-garde intellectuals. The glorification of local cultural forms—"Pau-Brasil poetry, for export"; creative and aesthetic freedom—"no formula for the contemporary expression of the world"; the production of locally grounded, new cultural expressions as antidote to imported and obsolete forms—"native originality to neutralize academic conformity"; and the affirmation of generational and national identities—"merely Brazilians of our time."[1]

And, of course, also included was race, which was one of the central categories of the age. Avant-garde artists and writers not only had to deal with this concept but were active in the production and dissemination of multiple discourses of race and nation. The *Manifesto Pau-Brasil*, for instance, refers to Carnival in Rio de Janeiro as "the religious event of our race." Martí Casanovas (1894–1966), an art critic who worked with avant-garde artists in Cuba and Mexico, spoke about the need to capture the "racial essence" of Latin American nations and likewise of racial "feelings" and "meanings."[2] In 1928, just as *poesía mulata* (mulatto poetry) began to sweep Cuba, the poet and critic Mário de Andrade (1893–1945) wrote of "the imposition of the mulatto" during Brazil's colonial era as expressive of "a collective upsurge of Brazilian raciality."[3] Such discourses were frequently presented as new—"a premonition of what is to come," in typical avant-garde fashion—but were in fact a creative recycling of established metaphors of civilization, progress, culture, nation, climate, and understandings of human types.[4] The 1920s marked the high point of eugenics, a transnational scientific movement of racial "improvement" that found potent echoes in Latin America and shaped understandings and policies in areas as diverse as international relations, public health, education, penal regimes, urbanization, and culture.[5]

Despite its roots in the scientific racism of the nineteenth century, though, this was also a period of critical reinterpretation and potential ruptures. The shadow of the First World War cast doubts upon presumptions of European superiority, traditionally articulated through notions of race. In the eyes of many intellectuals in Latin America, the senseless slaughter witnessed between 1914 and 1918 recast Europeans as the real barbarians and primitives, raising doubts about the very meanings of race, civilization, and otherness. Sensing an opening, avant-garde writers and artists struck back at Europe and at a North Atlantic world that had consistently portrayed them as racially inferior and even degenerate. The time to out-modernize Europe had arrived. "I sincerely believe that America will provide the stream that will fertilize art in the 20th century… an art that will express passions not envisioned by the civilized European," the Cuban painter Eduardo Abela (1889–1965) declared in 1928. Not only were the "spiritual forces of Europe … basically exhausted," but salvation for its "civilization" could only come from mixture "with virgin races, filled with human essences."[6] From Brazil, Oswald de Andrade agreed in yet another manifesto, the *Manifesto antropófago* (*Anthropophagic*): "We want the Carahiba revolution. Bigger than the French revolution. […] Without us, Europe would not even have its wretched declaration of the rights of man. The golden age proclaimed by America. […] We already had communism. We already had the surrealist language."[7]

As the Abela quote illustrates, the counterpoint between the local and the international, between civilization and modernity, was frequently couched in the language of race. It could not be otherwise, as race had become a key epistemological construct to make sense of all sorts of social phenomena. Abela's celebration of mixture and of the redeeming attributes of "virgin races" was a direct response to dominant scientific discourses that since the nineteenth century equated racial mixture with "mongrelization" and "degeneration."[8] A potent counternarrative of Latin American manufacture began to posit racial hybridity as a positive quality, as is already evident in the early 1900s in the writings of authors like Manoel Bomfim, in Brazil, or Justo Sierra, in Mexico. Bomfim's *A América Latina: Males de origem* (*Latin America: Evils of Origin*), published in 1905, forcefully challenged the notion that the region's problems could be traced to racial causes.[9] As early as 1902, Sierra, in an explicit rebuttal of Gustave Le Bon's negative views about racial mixture, offered a spirited defense of "*la familia mestiza*," which he described as "the most dynamic element" in the history of the Mexican nation.[10] By the late 1920s, this new vision had become widely articulated in literary and art journals throughout the region and even received state backing in revolutionary Mexico. However much it subverted the paradigm of racial inferiority, though, it remained tied to the idea and the language of race.

The work of artists, writers, and intellectuals generally linked to avant-garde movements in Latin America was consequently

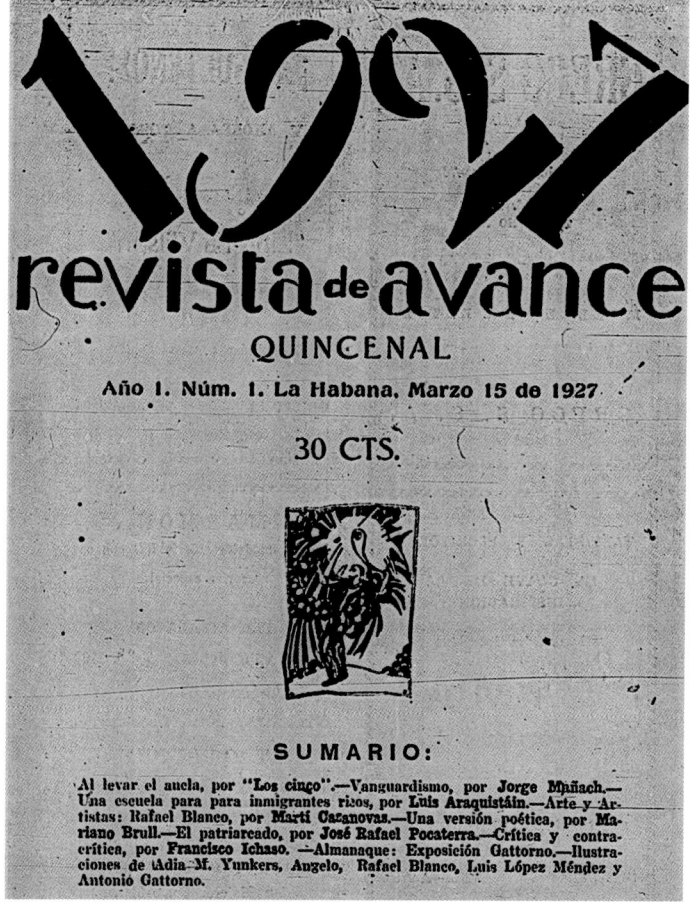

143 Cover of the journal *Avance*.

trapped in the spider web of Western European science and philosophy. As a result, it could not help but project deep ambiguities concerning individuals of African descent, their cultures and claims to citizenship. In countries with a long and brutal history of Atlantic slavery, racism was too deeply ingrained to be simply written off by optimistic reinterpretations. Afrodescendant artists and intellectuals often achieved minimal recognition, even while their counterparts from white elite backgrounds deployed Latin America's African and Amerindian heritage to get themselves noticed in Europe.[11] Processes of appropriation, representation, and cultural nationalization have been subjects of considerable debate, with scholars arguing over their nature, meanings, and social and ideological effects. Some authors characterize these as elite attempts to domesticate popular sectors by incorporating them into homogenized national cultures through filtering, stylization, and translation.[12] According to this view, popular sectors, including subordinate racial groups, are essentially objects of representation, "silent subalterns" who are robbed of their creativity and cultural practices.[13] Other scholars, however, emphasize the contentious and conflictive nature of such processes, which were defined to no small degree by the active participation and contributions of Black thinkers, journalists, and artists. Furthermore, these authors note, processes of incorporation and appropriation provided a doorway for popular artists and creators to irrupt into previously inaccessible social spaces, exercise some degree of control over cultural production, and personally profit from it.[14]

Elite Culture and Popular Culture

The debate, then, deals with the process of cultural production per se, as well as with its social and political implications. Part of the problem is that some authors approach cultural production through a corpus of texts, magazines, exhibits, and organizations that ignore the mobilization and cultural activities of the popular sectors. For instance, at the time *Revista de Avance*, which was as close to the official organ of the Cuban *vanguardia* as any publication could be, was being produced in Havana, Afro-Cuban intellectuals, professionals, activists, and journalists were voicing their concerns and views through a variety of cultural and recreational associations and the media, including, notably, the leading newspaper in the city, *Diario de la Marina*, where Gustavo Urrutia published an influential section devoted to Black culture. Other voices were heard through specialized publications such as the bulletin of the prestigious Club Atenas, an association of upwardly mobile Afro-Cuban professionals, entrepreneurs, and government officials, or in dedicated sections in the mainstream press, such as the "Problems of the Element of Color" published by *Unión Nacionalista*.[15] Similarly, in Brazil, the struggles of Afrodescendant intellectuals were largely ignored by the self-styled avant-gardes. In Rio de Janeiro, the writer Lima Barreto and the painter Arthur Timótheo da Costa grappled openly with issues of race in their innovative work of the 1910s and 1920s but remained outsiders to the rising currents of the modernist movement. São Paulo, the city that hosted the influential Semana de Arte Moderna (Modern Art Week) in 1922, was also home to a sizable Black press that, along with several literary clubs and associations, helped to channel "an unusual degree of intellectual production by self-identified *pretos* in the years of the Republic."[16] In Mexico, the literary and artistic vanguardia movements of the 1920s, from Estridentismo to ¡30–30!, cannot be understood without reference to the ideological and social conflicts of the Mexican Revolution, a process in which some of the country's most famous artists participated.[17] To what degree, then, is the subaltern "silent," as opposed to just not being heard by those who first recorded these histories?

It is also important to note that some of the writers, poets, musicians, and visual artists associated with the avant-gardes were themselves of African (or indigenous) descent, which influenced the aesthetic and thematic proposals of these movements. Some openly embraced a subaltern identity, as the painter Dr. Atl (Gerardo Murillo, 1875–1964) famously did in Mexico. His advocacy of folk art and interest in the Amerindian past proved to be vital influences on the younger generation that would revolutionize Mexican art in the 1920s and 1930s. In Cuba, the modernist poet Regino Boti devoted a book to one of the Afro-Cuban heroes of the war of independence, Guillermo Moncada, as well as a volume to study the works of the poet José Manuel Poveda, which received a glowing review in *Revista de Avance*. Both Boti and Poveda were described and known as "mulatto." Boti's work was followed by the militant poetry of Nicolás Guillén, Marcelino Arozarena, and Regino Pedroso, all of them authors of African descent.[18] Something similar happened in the visual arts, as exemplified by the works of the Afrodescendant artists Ramón Loy (1894–1986); Alberto Peña, better known as Peñita (1897–1938); and Teodoro Ramos Blanco (1902–1972), a sculptor. Unlike the Cuban poets cited above, who embraced the term "mulatto," others were less forthcoming about their ethnic origins. Although Mário de Andrade is known for championing the cultural contributions of the "mulatto" to Brazilian culture, he shied away from self-identification as such. His studies of Black musical forms remained decidedly ethnographic—the view of the educated outsider peering in—and he was more interested in folklore and rural traditions than the urban samba that was then coming into its own.[19]

The debate over *raza* (race) and *Négritude* was often complex, leading to conflicts over who could be properly identified under what racial epithet, as well as cultural misunderstandings based

144 Miguel Covarrubias. *Negro Drawings*. 1927. Illustration.

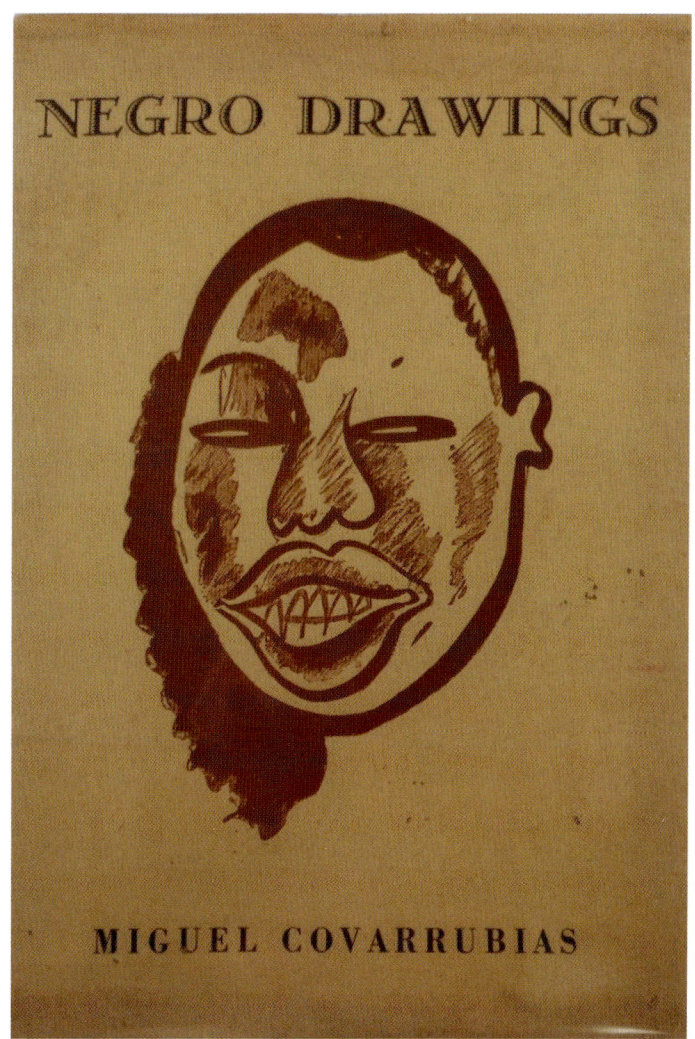

144

on the differing apprehension of terms that are homonymous (e.g., *negro* in Spanish and Portuguese and Negro in English) but resonate very differently in the various linguistic contexts in which these subjects were discussed over the 1920s and 1930s. The Harlem Renaissance poet Langston Hughes, for instance, was variously received in Spanish translation as *negro* or *mulato*, depending on the inflection that local critics wanted to attribute to his work.[20] Conversely, in the New York of the 1920s, any Latin American origin was presumed to provide insight into issues of Blackness. When the young Mexican illustrator Miguel Covarrubias published his book *Negro Drawings* (1927), he was hailed by the influential critic Frank Crowninshield as "the first important artist in America […] to bestow upon our Negro anything like reverent attention—the sort of attention, let us say, which Gauguin bestowed upon the natives of the South Seas." Despite his lack of Afrodescendant background, Covarrubias produced images of Black people perceived as particularly true and authentic by the smart social set that read publications like *Vanity Fair* and *The New Yorker*, which regularly featured his work. Crowninshield's recourse to the phrasing "our Negro" highlights how powerfully cultural appropriation played out as a factor in the representation of racial difference, as well as to how subtly the liminal status of Latin Americanness could serve to obfuscate positions that might otherwise prove contentious. Covarrubias possessed a unique ability to cross borders, not only as a Mexican artist in the United States but also as a graphic artist breaking into the elite domain of oil painting. Even while recognizing his potential as a painter, Crowninshield's introduction to the book labels him the "most promising and significant figure in the field of American black and white art," a statement that almost begs to be picked apart in the context of a book of "negro drawings" in which several of the works are paintings and none are produced by a Black artist, as the ambivalent title could imply.[21]

As the various literary and artistic avant-gardes across the region sought to break distinctions between popular and "high" cultural forms, they turned to Latin America's rich reservoir of vernacular cultural practices, techniques, media, aesthetics, and themes, which were of course associated with racially subordinate groups. As Tatiana Flores notes, whereas in Europe "primitive" art was the preserve of exotic peoples and distant folk traditions, Latin America was home to many of the groups that Europe perceived as exotic.[22] Primitivizing impulses in Latin America therefore often carried nationalist connotations. The tension between shifting conceptions of the national, the vernacular, and the local prompted discussions of authenticity and of which cultural forms could be rightly claimed by whom. When the hit musical group Oito Batutas traveled from Rio to Paris in 1922, they were widely perceived by the French press as representatives of Brazil and of the country's "racial soul."[23] Back home, however, conservative critics were unnerved by the fact that a majority of the eight members of the combo were Black or of mixed race. The best-selling writer Benjamim Costallat came to their defense in the daily newspaper *Gazeta de Notícias*: "I detest those good patriots who, wishing to give this land better publicity in Europe, deny the existence in Brazil of hot weather and blacks, two things they consider profoundly inelegant."[24] Although the Batutas were successful all over Brazil between 1919 and 1924, they went unnoticed by the modernists in São Paulo, who preferred to include more highbrow piano concerts in the musical program of the Semana de Arte Moderna. The cosmopolitan repertoire of the Batutas—mixing tango, waltz, ragtime, and foxtrot alongside *choro*, *maxixe*, *lundu*, and the newer style of samba—did not coincide with nationalist conceptions of how a Brazilian avant-garde should look and behave.[25]

Despite such tensions between elite and popular cultures, intellectuals, activists, and artists from subordinate groups were ideally located to contribute new visions of culture, race, and nation, as they could mediate the translation processes involved in cultural nationalization. As Doris Sommer has noted, Afrodescendant intellectuals and artists were versed in the art of processing contradictions, which is what the avant-garde writers and artists were trying to do globally as they sought to reconcile the European primitivizing gaze with their own projects of modernity.[26] Mexico is a good example. In the 1920s, the Secretaría de Educación Pública (SEP) launched several educational initiatives that were deeply informed by modernist and civilizing concerns about the indigenous population. For instance, the Secretaría sent "cultural missions" to rural Mexico to assess the problems of indigenous communities. In 1925, specialists from the National Museum and the Department of Fine Arts of the SEP conducted studies on the racial and cultural features of students at the Casa del Estudiante Indígena, an educational institution in Mexico City that became a testing ground for the possible assimilation and uplifting of allegedly pure "Indians." The SEP also sent visual artists to the countryside to study and eventually improve popular forms of craft production. But as Alexander Dawson has shown, this was never a one-way, univocal process. Government educational programs resulted in the formation of a group of "*indígenas capacitados*" (educated Indians) who became effective mediators between their *comunidades* and the state, as well as defenders of local cultural forms and expressions.[27] Furthermore, these intellectuals were particularly well versed in dealing with marginalization and degradation, which is precisely what the Latin American avant-gardes were contending with at the international level. Despite this parallel, the creativity and efforts of intellectuals of African and indigenous descent have tended to attract lesser historical scrutiny. The differences between the experience of elite and non-elite writers, poets, and artists underscore the importance of paying attention to concurrent spaces of cultural production and analyzing the social and class underpinnings of intellectual debates.

Regional and Transnational Networks

The emphasis on local themes and vernacular cultural practices notwithstanding, the avant-gardes were not just cosmopolitan, but in fact transnational, in the sense that the national was explored and defined within an international landscape, with Europe and the United States as the cardinal points of reference. As Micol Seigel has argued, the production of discourses of race and nation must be studied through global analytical lenses combined with an emphasis on the local that goes beyond the intellectual contributions of elites. Black intellectuals and performers, for instance, frequently used Parisian success to "shift the valence of blackness in popular culture" and to articulate metaphors of national belonging.[28] Many Black artists perceived Paris as a place of heightened artistic freedom and greater acceptance of their work, relatively unencumbered by the racial hierarchies that prevailed in the Americas. Indeed, the so-called negrophilia that swept Paris in the early decades of the twentieth century engendered unique opportunities for avant-garde practitioners to reinvent not only themselves, but also the ways in which ideas of racial and national identity were deployed within a fast-changing arena of cultural exchanges.[29]

Despite their nationalist concerns and inclinations, avant-garde magazines and journals paid systematic attention to cultural and artistic developments in other Latin American contexts. Cuba's *Revista de Avance*, for instance, regularly commented on some of the most important avant-garde publications from the region, such as *Amauta*, the leftist magazine of art and literature founded by the Peruvian writer José Carlos Mariátegui in 1926, or the literary journal *Martín Fierro* (Buenos Aires, 1924–1927). In 1927, *Avance* took note of the publication of the "avant-garde biweekly newspaper" *Vórtice* in Puerto Rico and greeted "the happy coincidence of the simultaneous emergence of avant-garde forces … in the two Antillean republics."[30] Systematic attention was given to some of the most important art and literary magazines of Mexico, such as the visual arts magazine *Forma* (1926–1928) published by the artist Gabriel Fernández Ledesma (1900–1983); the literary magazine *Contemporáneos* (1928–1931), which included numerous artists among its collaborators; and of course ¡30–30!: *Órgano de los Pintores de México* (1928–1930), which became the platform for a group of anti-academic and radical painters in the late 1920s.[31] *Avance* also published texts and illustrations by vanguardia writers and artists from other Latin American countries, including Miguel Angel Asturias from Guatemala, Carlos Oquendo de Amat from Peru, Ildefonso Pereda Valdés from Uruguay, and Mariano Azuela from Mexico. Mexicans were particularly well represented among its

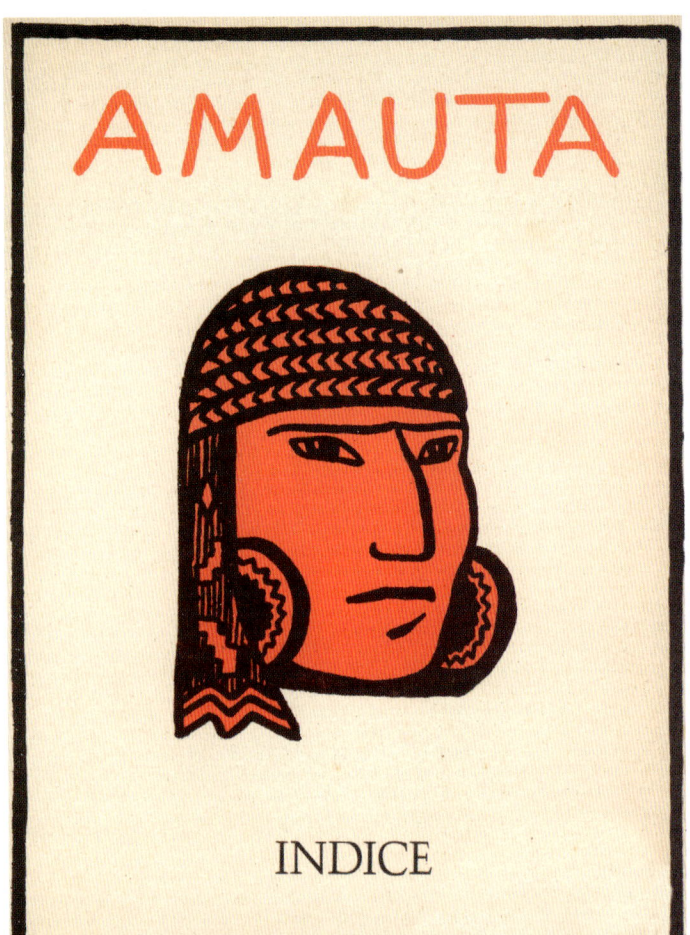

145 Cover of the journal *Amauta*.

illustrators, including such well-known artists as Diego Rivera (1886–1957), José Clemente Orozco (1883–1949), Gabriel Fernández Ledesma (1900–1983), Fernando Leal (1896–1964), and Carlos Mérida (1891–1984), who was Guatemalan, but was counted among the Mexican muralists.

None of this was exceptional. Just like *Avance* followed *Amauta*, *Amauta* recognized the existence of *Avance*, a journal that Mariátegui (1928) described as "inscribed with our affection."[32] Many of the same writers and artists published in both journals; and *Amauta*, like *Avance*, closely followed artistic, literary, and political events in Mexico. *Amauta* published texts by the writer and philosopher José Vasconcelos[33] (1882–1959) and, "in attention to the interest of our public for Mexican themes," reproduced a section of Azuela's *Los de abajo*,[34] with an illustration by Diego Rivera. The journal actually devoted several articles to Rivera, one of which included an autographed photograph of the artist with a dedication "*para Amauta*."[35] The art critic Martí Casanovas, one of the initial editors of *Avance*, also published in *Amauta*.[36] Born in Barcelona, Casanovas moved to Mexico because of political persecution in Cuba and became part of the artistic Mexican avant-garde, playing a leading role among the *treintatrentistas*.[37] Further south, in Argentina, the journal *Martin Fierro* also participated in these conversations. In fact, the first issue of *Amauta*, in September 1926, published an advertisement for *Martin Fierro*. Its issue 42 included poetry by the Mexican Alfonso Reyes (who also published in *Avance*), "six new poets of Mexico," and illustrations by Rivera, Orozco, and Máximo Pacheco (1907–1992),[38] as well as a text by the Uruguayan writer Pereda Valdés, the founder of the review *Los Nuevos* (1920) and a contributor to both *Avance* and *Amauta*. These avant-garde journals and magazines were at the center of truly transnational exchanges of ideas, programs, and artistic proposals that, despite their local differences, were implicated in a shared project of cultural and national affirmation.[39] Vasconcelos perhaps articulated best the central question of the literary and artistic avant-gardes in the pages of *Amauta*: "Who are we, what are we?"[40]

The great anomaly to this paradigm of regional exchange was Brazil. A reader perusing the main Brazilian avant-garde magazines of the 1920s—such as *Klaxon*, *Estética*, *Terra Roxa*, *Verde*, or *Revista de Antropofagia*—encounters few references to counterparts in other Latin American contexts. The exception that confirms the rule is the little-known magazine *América Latina*, published from 1919 to 1920, which, as its name suggests, was committed to pan-Americanism.[41] Rather, Brazilian modernists were obsessed with writings and publications in French and, to a lesser degree, English. The deep historical divide separating Portuguese-speaking Brazil from its Spanish-speaking neighbors continued to prevail. Even a movement as prominent as Mexican muralism only obtained notice in Brazil well into the 1930s, particularly after David Alfaro Siqueiros (1896–1974) visited Rio and São Paulo in 1933. Whenever such exchanges did take place, they often coincided with networks of international solidarity promoted by the various communist parties affiliated to the Third International. It is no coincidence that Siqueiros, a member of the Mexican Communist Party, gained quick acceptance among artists and intellectuals who were members or sympathizers of the Brazilian Communist Party, such as Di Cavalcanti (1897–1976), Oswald de Andrade, or Tarsila do Amaral (1886–1973).[42] Even then, however, such networks tended to mesh together via Paris, which, at that time, was still the place to which most of Latin America's avant-gardes looked for inspiration.[43]

The Paris Connection

Although the questions of identity posed by avant-garde practitioners were grounded in Latin American nationalist anxieties, they were, at least in some ways, of French manufacture. The very idea of a "Latin" America was largely concocted in nineteenth-century France as a means of countering the ascendency of British imperial dominion in the region; and notions of *Latinité* or *Latinidad* gained momentum as the United States came to assert increasing influence after the First World War.[44] Young writers and visual artists from across Latin America traveled to Paris, where they crisscrossed overlapping and frequently identical circuits of literary and artistic production.[45] In fact, it was in Paris that the first exhibitions of Latin American art were conceptualized and produced. The founding of the *Revue de l'Amérique Latine*, in 1922, provided an important forum for intellectuals from France and Latin America to gather around a unified project in Paris.[46] Over its ten-year existence, the journal published contributions from writers and thinkers as influential as Miguel Angel Asturias, Henri Barbusse, Jean Cassou, Blaise Cendrars, Joseph Conrad, Pierre Drieu de la Rochelle, Ventura García Calderón, Ramón Gómez de la Serna, Gabriela Mistral, and Alfonso Reyes, among many others, as well as building up a substantial corpus of translations of Latin American literature into French. In May 1923, the Maison de l'Amérique Latine was inaugurated (at 9, rue de Presbourg) with an exhibition of Latin American artists in which, among others, Tarsila do Amaral, Victor Brecheret, Alipio Dutra, Juan Manuel Gavazzo Buchardo, Alberto Lagos, and Anita Malfatti took part.[47] In quick succession, the Maison promoted a larger show, the *Exposition d'Art Américain-Latin*, which opened in March 1924 at the Musée Galliera.

146 Pedro Figari. *Candombe*. 1921. Oil on canvas. Museo de Arte Latinoamericano de Buenos Aires.

Described by its organizers as a moment of self-recognition for the "nearly one hundred million men" of the region, whose "similar ethnicity, religion, historical tradition, customs, and democratic ideals" informed the collective will to shape "humanity's future," the Musée Galliera exhibition included more than 260 works by forty-two artists from Latin America.[48] It was formed with preexisting works owned by local collectors and submissions from Latin American artists residing in Paris. The exhibition contained sections for painting, sculpture, and decorative arts, as well as a "retrospective section" that brought together pre-Columbian art and samples of material culture, including ceramics, textiles, feather-work, musical instruments, and even a collection of Cuban cigars, adding layers of presumed ethnographical and historical authenticity. Although avant-garde artists and works were not its focus, Victor Brecheret, Pablo Curatella Manes, Antonio Gattorno, Manuel Ortiz de Zárate, Emilio Pettoruti, and Xul Solar, among many others, exhibited works. The critic Raymond Cogniat, a Parisian observer of contemporary art from Latin America, was less than impressed with the overall quality of the show, expressing outrage at the number of "banal works" reminiscent of "illustrations for calendars."[49] Others complained about the lack of local and folkloric themes and deplored the obvious influence of European artistic currents and techniques. Very few of the works offered representations of Black individuals or indigenous peoples. Mexico was poorly represented by just two paintings, neither of which was part of its vibrant revolutionary art.[50]

The one artist who did offer renderings of Black culture and life in Latin America was the Uruguayan Pedro Figari (1861–1938), who exhibited two Candombe paintings that were in local private collections. An early modernist painter living in Buenos Aires at the time, where he participated in the Salon of Modern Art sponsored by the avant-garde journal *Martin Fierro* in 1925, Figari's works were well received by critics, who characterized them as "full of local color."[51] His paintings provide highly stylized depictions of Candombe practitioners dancing and playing music. Their compositions are filled with groups of small Black figures in colorful dress, simplified to the point where their bodies become almost abstract patterns. Facial features are often represented cartoonishly or not at all, and individuality is largely sacrificed to decorative effect. In these pictures, at their best, the swaying rhythms of color and shape convey a sense of collective belonging and ritualized harmony. At their worst, they become caricatural to the point of stereotype. Figari's paintings are early exemplars of a tradition of associating Blackness with a naïf style of representation that, in later decades, would prove extremely popular all over Latin America (for instance, in the works of Heitor dos Prazeres, in Brazil, or Pétion Savain, in Haiti). The *Revue de l'Amérique Latine* featured his work prominently, praising him for creating a truly "American national art." According to one critic, the artist was writing "the poem of the race."[52] Figari was so successful in Paris that he was given a solo exhibition at the prestigious Galerie Druet in December 1923 and became the subject of a 1926 pamphlet considering not only his artwork but his philosophical doctrines.[53]

Another possible Black representation was offered by one of the Paris-based Cuban painters at the Musée Galliera exhibition, Juan Emilio Hernández Giró (1882–1953), whose patriotic works were frequently inspired by historical events and figures linked to the Cuban war of independence (1895–1898), including some

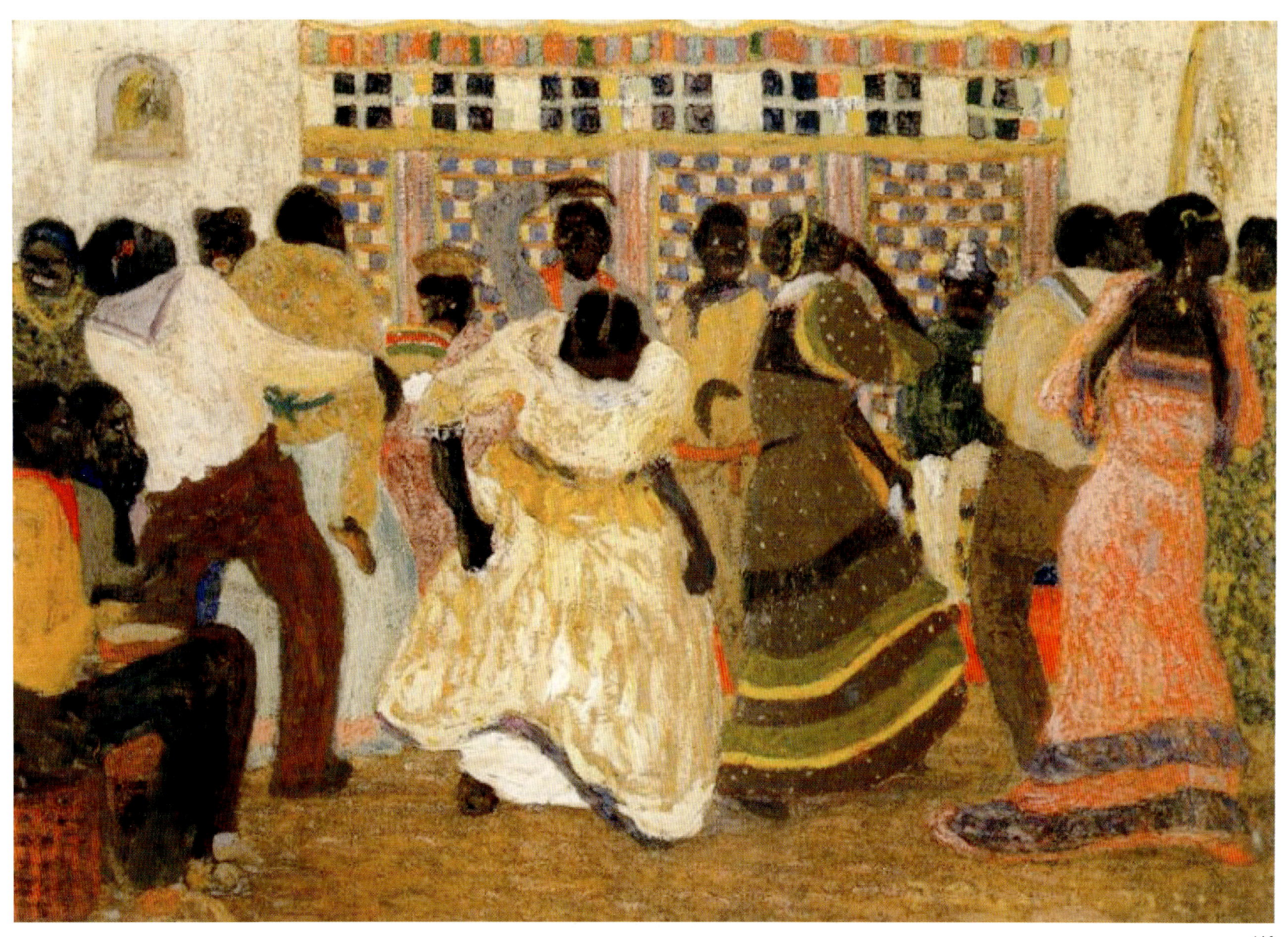

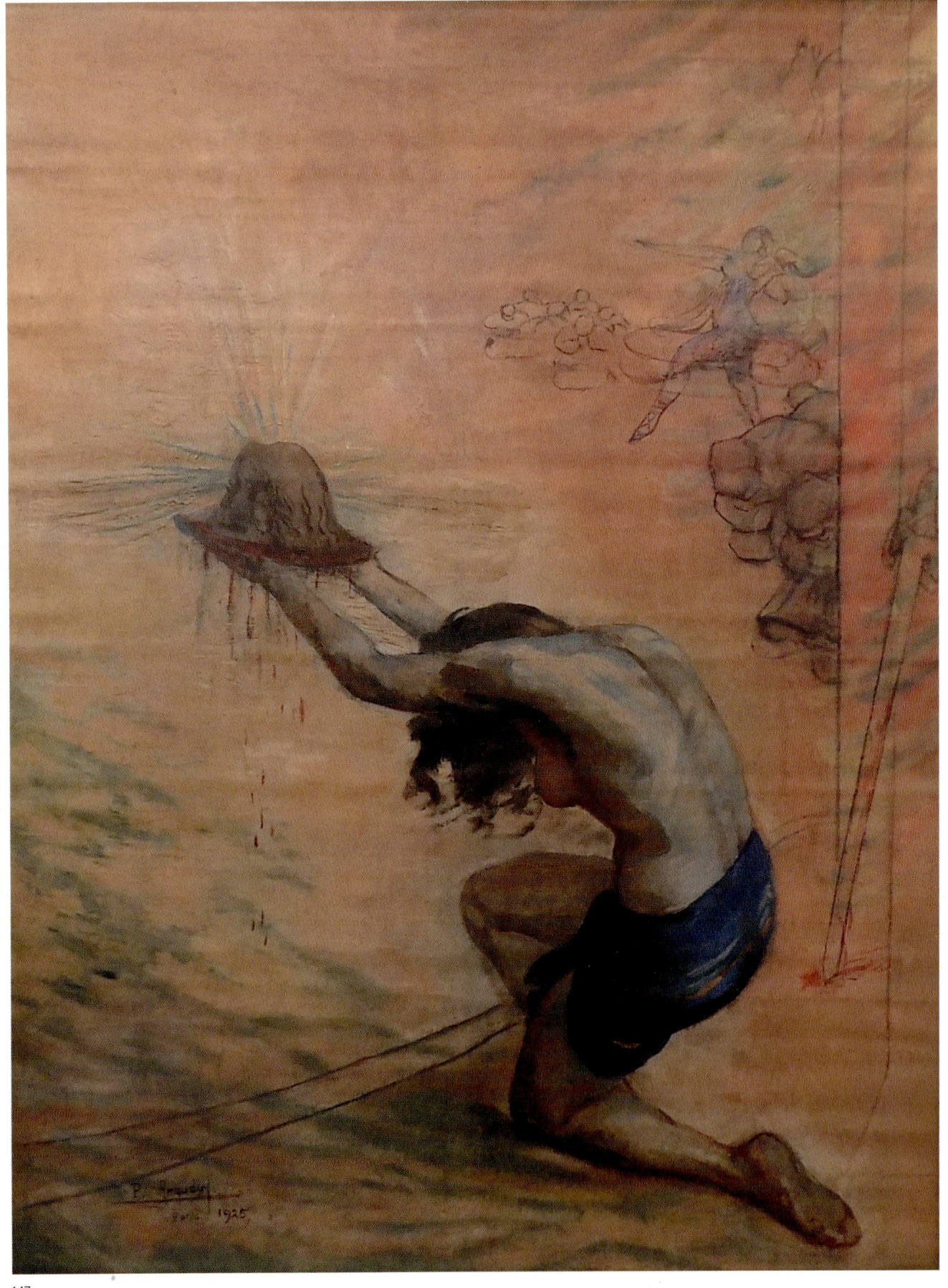

147

147 Pastor Argudín y Pedroso. *Offering*. Paris. 1925. Oil on canvas. Boston, Collection of Alejandro de la Fuente and Patricia González.

148 Manuel Ortiz de Zárate. *Pablo Picasso*. 1920-1925. Oil on wood. Paris, Musée Picasso.

149 Victor Manuel García. *Young Woman, Paris*. 1929. Oil on canvas. Boston, Collection of Alejandro de la Fuente and Patricia González.

of its most prominent Black heroes. One of his works shown in the exhibition, *The Vision of Maceo*, was devoted to the great Afro-Cuban activist, intellectual, and military strategist Antonio Maceo Grajales.[54] The Cuban representation also included works by the Afro-Cuban artist Pastor Argudín y Pedroso (1880–1968), an academically trained painter who resided in Paris between 1914 and 1931 and whose career and work remain mysteriously understudied. It is doubtful that any of his paintings in the exhibition made open reference to Blackness, as Argudín y Pedroso does not appear to have given serious attention to Afro-Cuban subjects and culture in his works.

It is somewhat ironic that Black subjects were not better represented at the *Exposition d'Art Américain-Latin*, for in the 1920s Paris was fascinated with *l'art nègre*. The voyeuristic "negrophilia" of the white avant-garde was deployed as a marker of its own modernity, informed by critical explorations of European colonial ventures in Africa and Oceania.[55] African "primitiveness" was embraced and imagined, as Patricia Leighten has written, to criticize civilization and "a decadent West."[56] This critique was fully compatible with the nationalistic impulses of Latin American artists and writers, who managed to find in their own countries and cultures the purported authenticity that Paris was seeking abroad. Indeed, French conceptualizations of primitiveness often included Latin America. As the conservator of the Musée Galliera, Henri Clouzot, stated, "the art of savage peoples is divided into three branches: American, Oceanian, and African."[57] To complicate matters further, Latin American intellectuals like the Chilean painter Manuel Ortiz de Zárate (1887–1946) or the Mexican gallerist Marius de Zayas (1880–1961) played strategic roles in shaping the way in which "primitive art" was viewed and displayed in conjunction with modern art in Paris and New York.[58] Suggestively, Ortiz de Zárate's portrait of Pablo Picasso, circa 1915, depicts its subject as a Black-faced mask, with huge blank eyes and a triangular yellow nose. By thus casting Picasso himself as a primitive, the Chilean artist returned the primitivizing gaze of Picasso's *Les Demoiselles d'Avignon*, painted in 1907, but first exhibited publicly in 1916, which excited Parisian audiences by linking pictorial modernism to African and Iberian traditions.

Paris would not only inspire a search for local themes and colors among Latin American artists, but some of the most iconic paintings of the Latin American avant-garde were produced there. Tarsila do Amaral's *A negra* (*The Negress*, 1923) represents an early example. As an almost caricatural depiction of a generic "negress," painted by a white artist from an elite background, it lays itself open to the charge of cultural appropriation. At the same time, the work reflects an intention to try and explore issues of ethnic identity that many artists only discovered once they found themselves away from their native lands and familiar circumstances.[59] In a letter to her family, circa 1923, Tarsila explained how she felt "ever more Brazilian" since her arrival in Paris.[60] This reinvention of the self as native and nativist is a running theme in the experience of Latin American artists in Europe. A few years later, the Cuban painter Victor Manuel García (1897–1969) would produce "the first classic of Cuban artistic modernity," his *Gitana tropical* (*Tropical Gipsy*, 1929), also in Paris. The painting portrays a racially mixed woman who, in Victor Manuel's own words, is "a mestiza, a mulatta, but I gave her the almond shape eyes of an Indian from Peru, Mexico."[61] Victor Manuel, who, like Tarsila, was known by his given name, appears to have explored this approach in other paintings produced during his

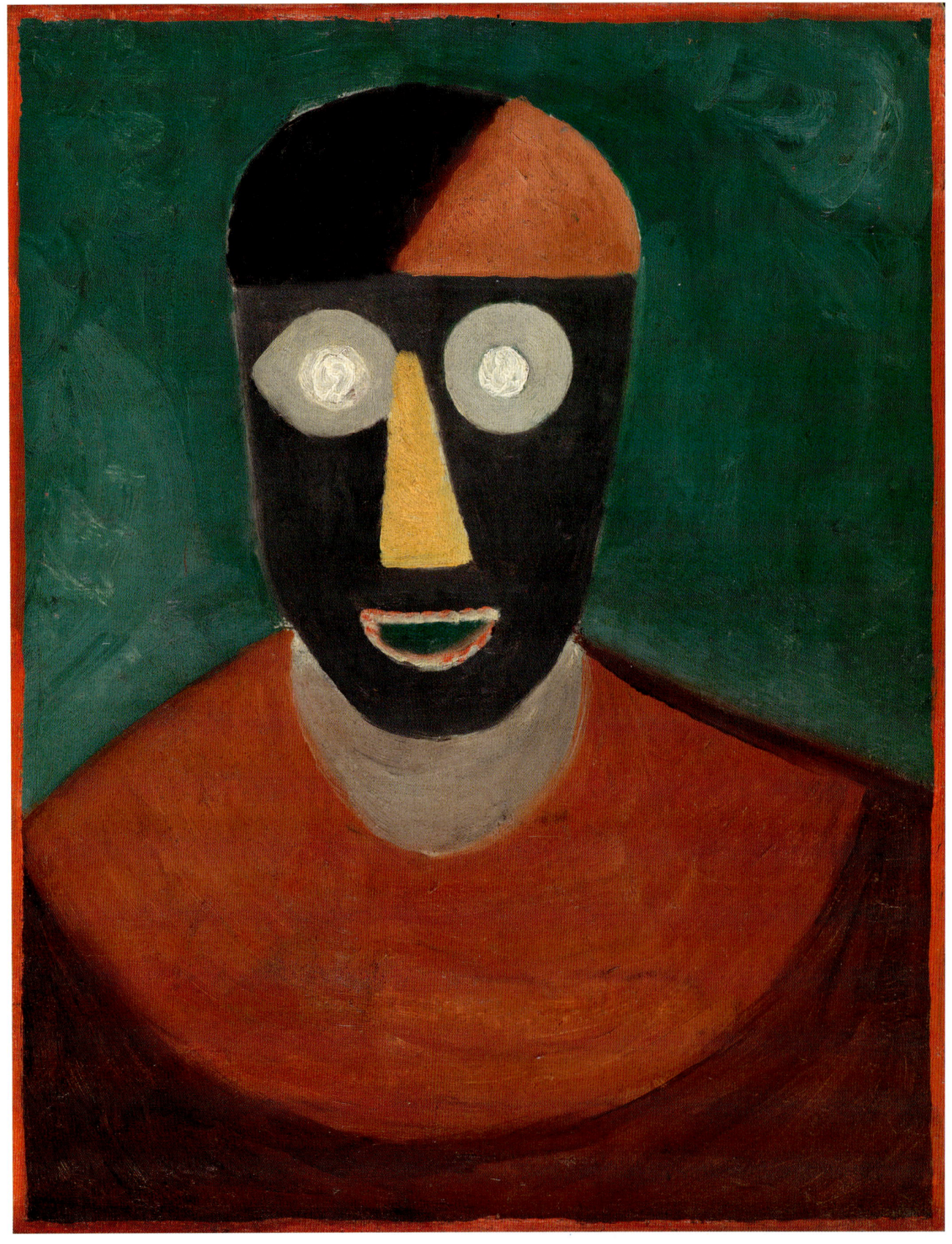
148

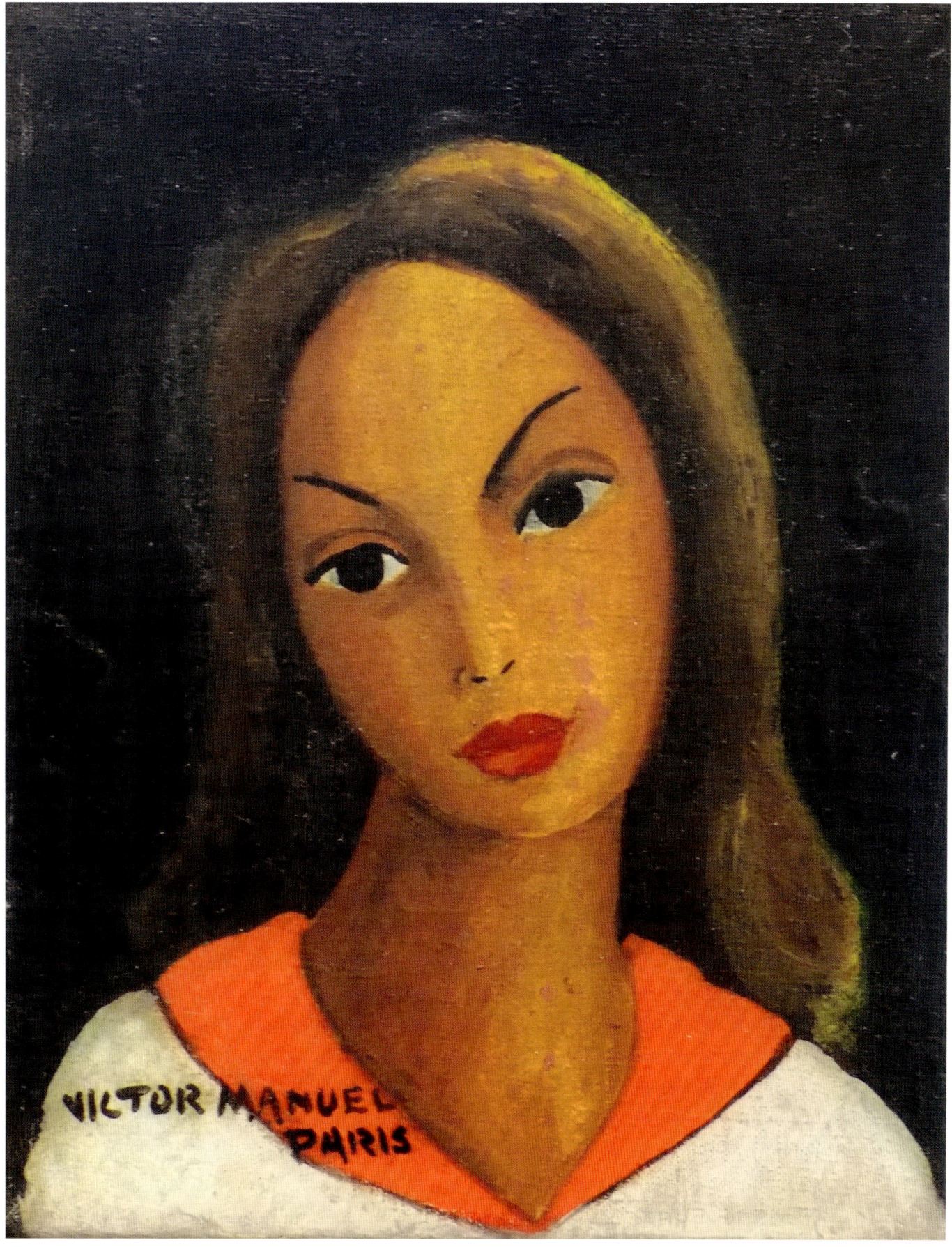

149

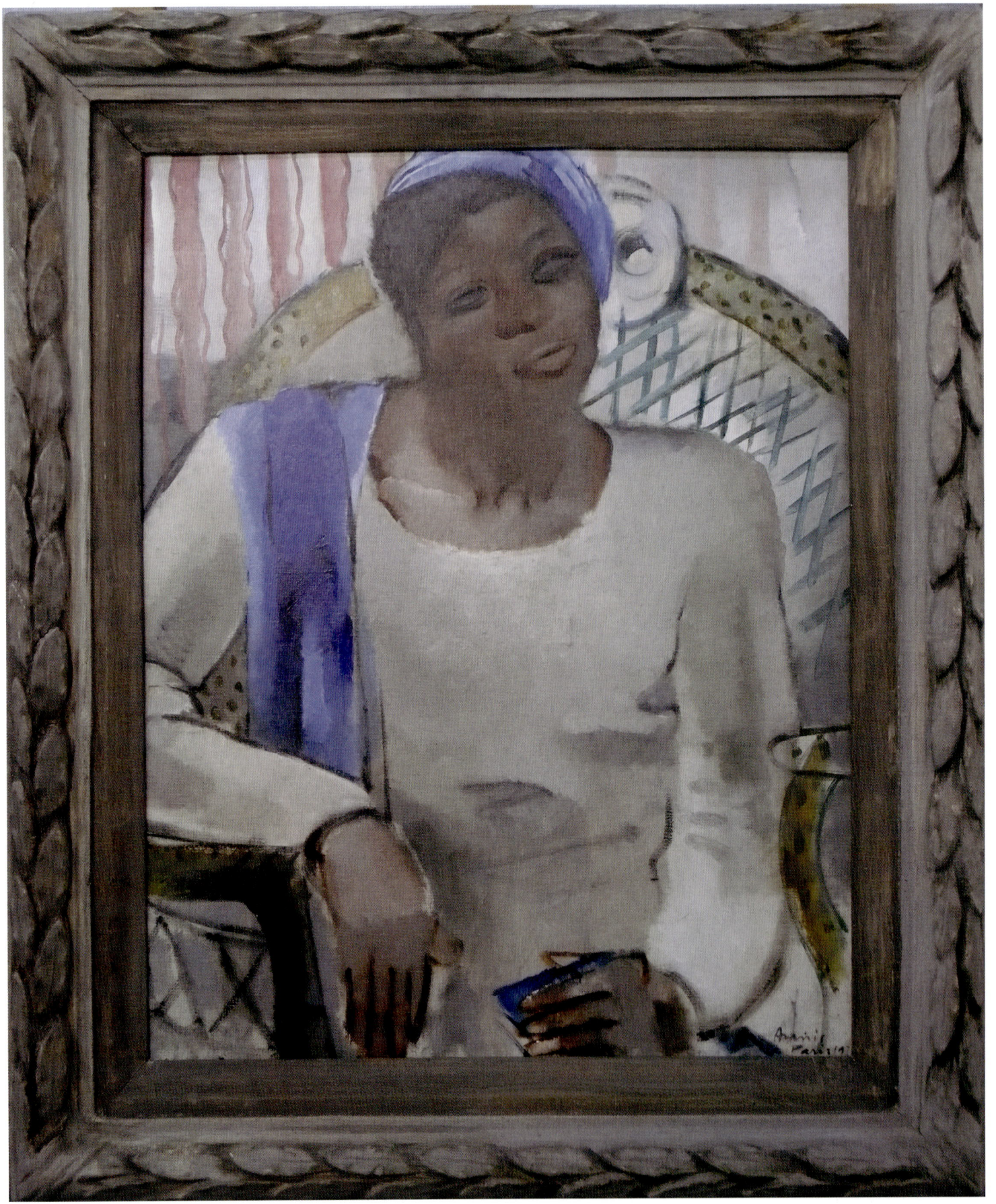

150

150 María Aranís Valdivia. *Black Woman*. 1931. Oil on canvas. Santiago, Chile, Museo Nacional de Bellas Artes.

149 trip to Paris, as illustrated by figure 149. A similar impulse seems to have animated the Chilean painter María Aranís (1903–1966), 150 whose *La negra* (1931) was also painted in Paris. Aranís was part of the Chilean literary and artistic avant-garde grouped around the Asociación de Artistas de Chile that sponsored the exhibit *Salón de los Independientes* in 1931.[62] The subsequent reception of such works—consumed in Paris for their exoticism and acclaimed back home for their modernity—betrays the misunderstandings, both deliberate and inadvertent, that marked relationships between Latin American avant-gardes and their European counterparts.

Exoticism and the Primitivized Self

The attraction of Paris was profoundly problematic, as it was tinged with primitivist fantasies and preconceptions about *peuplades savages* and their cultures, especially their "ritual art with religious and magic purposes."[63] As interpreted by many artists of the Cuban avant-garde, this call led them to the discovery and exploration of musical and dance practices that were closely linked to Afro-Cuban religions. These cultural forms had been previously denigrated as savage witchcraft with no place in a modernizing republic, as relics of a colonial past of obscurantism and slavery. By acknowledging and identifying these practices as key elements of Cuban culture, vanguardia artists contributed significantly to new formulations of Cubanness and of national culture; that is, they helped to produce new imaginaries that recognized the existence and contributions of individuals of African descent. A similar wish to reinterpret African religious traditions as objects of cultural value can be detected in a series of drawings and watercolor studies executed by the Brazilian poet Cecília Meireles (1901–1964) between 1926 and 1934. These works were first made public in Rio de Janeiro in 1933 and the following year were used to illustrate a lecture she delivered in Lisbon on Brazilian popular culture. They achieved immediate repercussion in Portugal and were published there as a booklet titled *Batuque, samba e macumba* in 1935, though they remained largely unknown in Brazil until many decades later.[64] Interest in Afro-Brazilian rituals slowly spread and can be detected in other works of the period such as Carlos Prado's *Batuque* (1935) or Pedro Correia de Araújo's *Jongo* (undated), both devoted to exploring the rhythms and 151 movements of Black bodies in a darkened compositional space.

The nature of such representations, however, was a subject of contention and debate. To many of the Paris-influenced vanguardia artists, Afro-Cuban contributions to national culture were circumscribed to music, rhythms, and sensual dance forms and were associated with mystical, occult powers.[65] Such perceptions could easily lead to highly stereotyped representations of Blacks, and especially of Black females, as oversexualized dancing subjects or as practitioners of primitive and colorful rituals. Indeed, in the thematic repertoire of the Cuban avant-garde concerning Black subjects, these elements—rituals, music, dance—are frequently intertwined. Disputes over authenticity ensued among intellectuals who focused on the African contribution to Latin American cultures. The Uruguayan writer Ildefonso Pereda Valdés (1899–1996), for instance, came to challenge the accuracy of his countryman Pedro Figari's depictions of Candombe, accusing him of misrepresenting rituals in a fanciful manner. Although he was white, Pereda Valdés took a keen interest in Black culture, authoring several books of poetry dedicated to Afro-Uruguayan themes in the 1920s. Among these was *Raza negra* (1929),

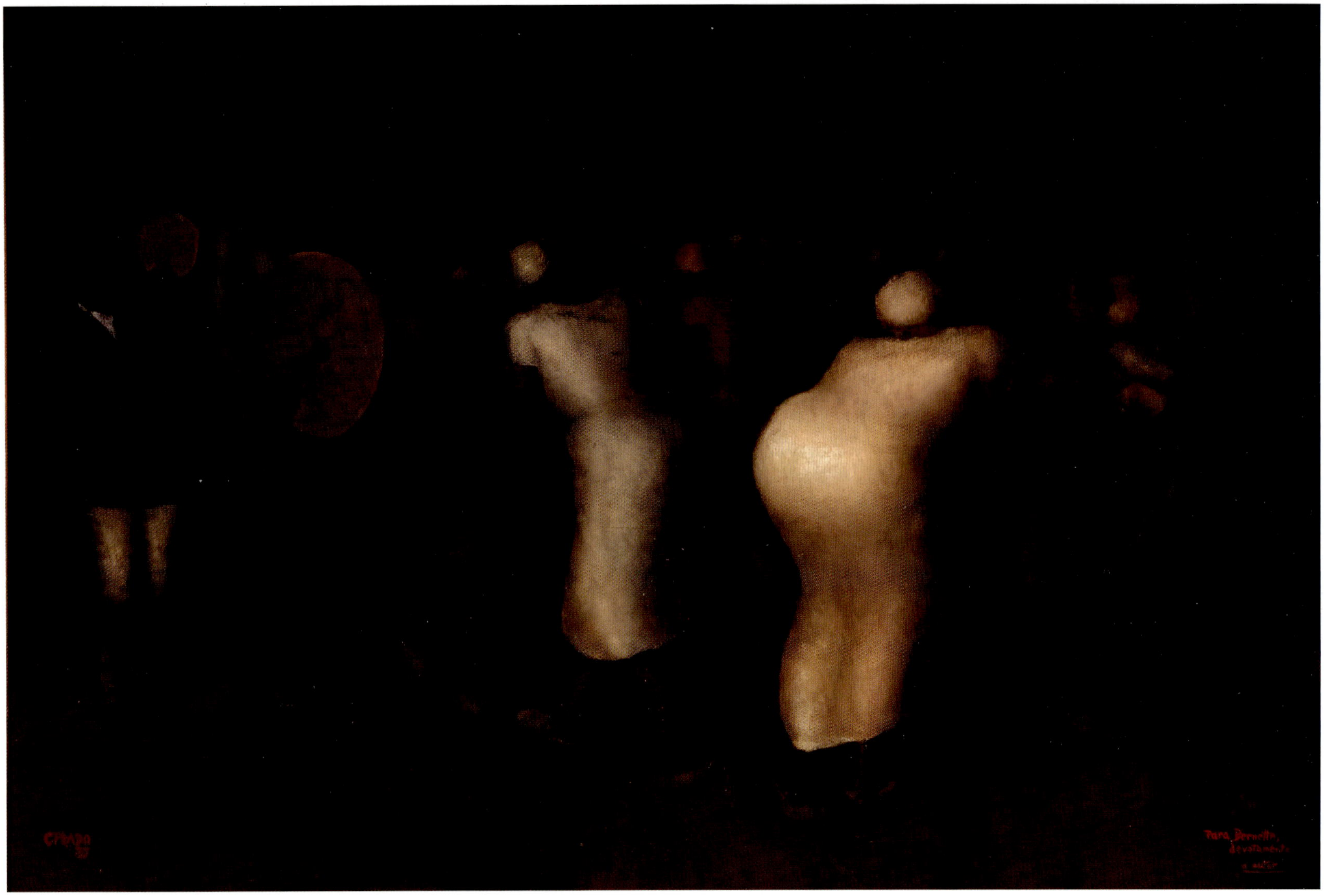

151

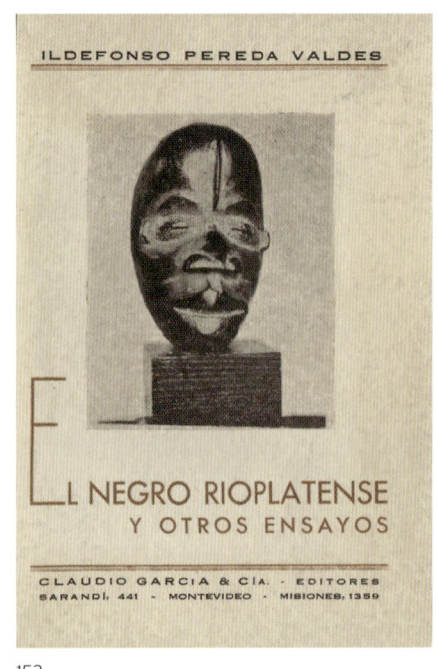

151 Carlos Prado. *Batuque*. 1935. Oil on canvas. Pinacoteca do Estado de São Paulo.

152 Ildefonso Pereda Valdés. *El Negro Rioplatense y otros ensayos* (Montevideo, Uruguay: Claudio Garcia & Cía., 1937).

153 Vicente do Rego Monteiro. *Combat*. 1927. Oil on canvas. Grenoble, France, Musée de Grenoble.

152

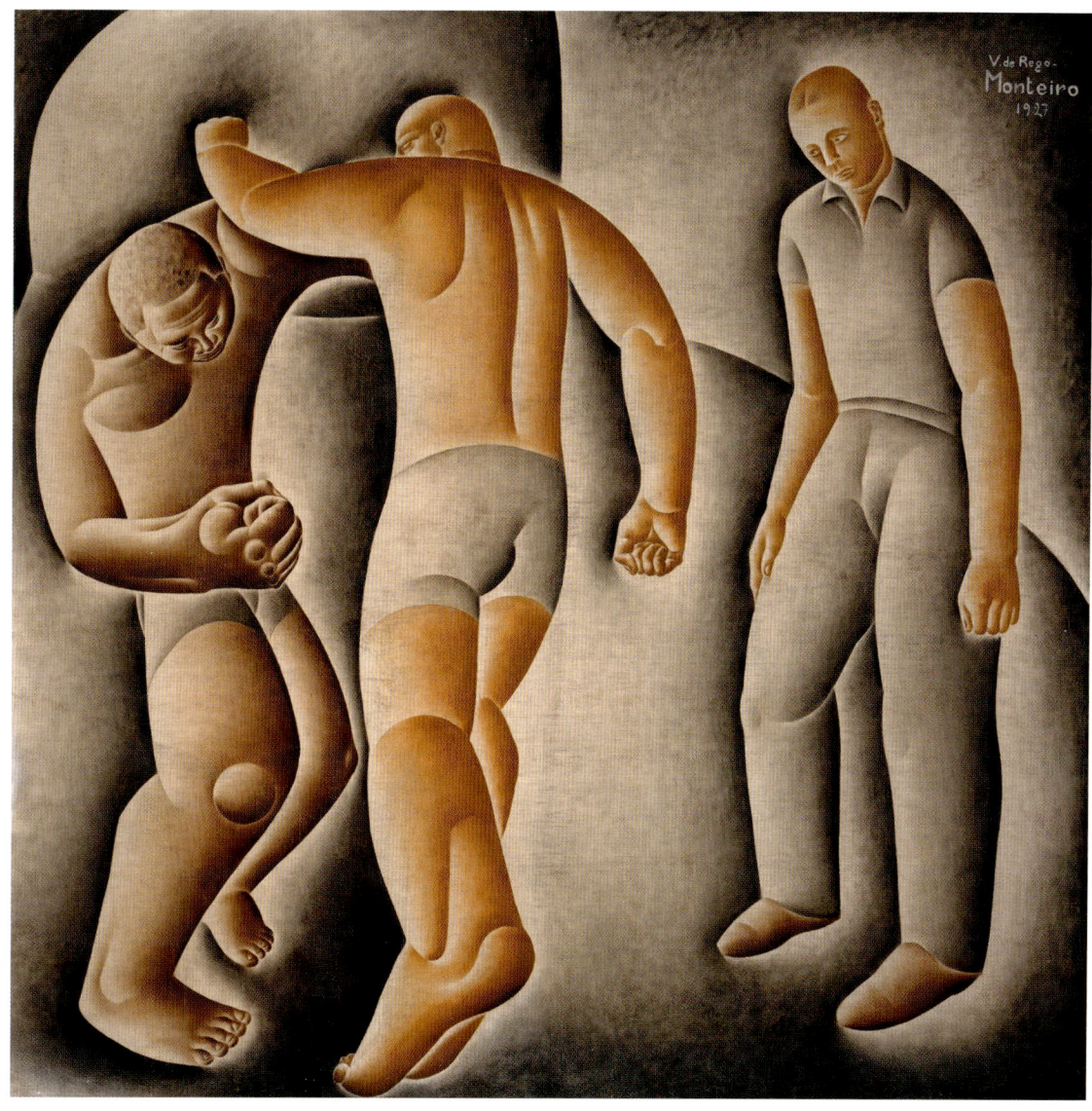

153

published by *La Vanguardia*, a periodical dedicated to defending "the interests of the black race."⁶⁶ Throughout the 1930s, Pereda Valdés's focus shifted from poetry to cultural anthropology, culminating in his study *Negros esclavos e negros libres* (1941), which examines the contributions of Afrodescendants to Uruguayan culture. His work was closely aligned with that of the psychiatrist and ethnologist Arthur Ramos across the Brazilian border, whose books *O negro brasileiro* (1934) and *O folklore negro do Brasil* (1935) renewed the study of race as a cultural category and showcased the myth of Brazil as "racial democracy."⁶⁷ The increased attention of white intellectuals to Blackness and Black culture became a worldwide phenomenon during the 1930s, as exemplified in the English-speaking world by Nancy Cunard's celebrated *Negro* anthology of 1934.

This is not to say that Latin American artists were always necessarily perceived through the lens of exoticism. The Brazilian artist who achieved the greatest success in Parisian avant-garde circles, Vicente do Rego Monteiro (1899–1970), managed largely to detach the reception of his work from ethnic or cultural stereotypes. During the mid-1920s, his paintings were regularly reproduced in Léonce Rosenberg's *Bulletin de l'Effort Moderne*; and, by 1929, the name "Monteiro" featured prominently on the cover of *Montparnasse* magazine, alongside Fernand Léger, Amedeo Modigliani, and Picasso, with no particular reference to his

RACE AND THE LATIN AMERICAN AVANT-GARDES, 1920s–1930s   265

154 Victor Manuel García. *Little Devil*. 1926. Pencil and crayon on paper. Havana, Museo Nacional de Bellas Artes de Cuba.

Brazilian origin. Edited by the critic Géo-Charles, *Montparnasse* soon became Rego Monteiro's greatest promoter, dedicating a four-page spread to him in November 1929 and reproducing several of his works in other issues.[68] By January 1930, his name appeared on the masthead as the publication's administrator. This was to be the last ever issue of the magazine, and it was entirely dedicated to an exhibition of artworks that Géo-Charles and Rego Monteiro subsequently took to Brazil, traveling through Recife, Rio de Janeiro, and São Paulo between March and June 1930.[69] Inverting the flow of European artists who staged primitivist ethnographies for a Parisian public, the exhibition *L'École de Paris au Brésil* aimed to overwhelm Brazilian audiences with a firsthand view of almost fifty artists representative of the so-called School of Paris, including Georges Braque, André Derain, Raoul Dufy, Albert Gleizes, Juan Gris, Léger, André Lhote, Henri Matisse, Picasso, and Maurice de Vlaminck. Contrary to recent evaluations that seek to exaggerate him into some sort of forerunner of postcolonial critiques,[70] Rego Monteiro can more reliably be seen as an extreme example of the complexity of transfers and exchanges taking place within international avant-garde networks. His selective recourse to "pictorial indigenism,"[71] particularly during the early years of his career, demonstrates that he was open to playing the native for a European audience at the same time that he liked to present himself as consummately modern and Parisian. There is no contradiction in this apparent paradox, since the primitivizing impulse was such an integral part of modernist sensibilities.

Two of the artists "most representative of our generation," as the avant-garde critic Martí Casanovas[72] referred to Eduardo Abela and Victor Manuel, illustrate early explorations of Afro-Cuban themes and culture. In his transformative first trip to Paris in 1925, Victor Manuel absorbed the city's fascination with primitive and exotic cultures and began to draft sketches of Black individuals as well as Afro-Cuban cultural icons. This dialogue would eventually lead to the development of a synthetic pictorial language later identified as foundational and authentically Cuban, but his initial forays into Blackness tended to be highly stereotypical and external. Illustrative of this moment are his *La mulata y la negrita* (*The Mulatto Woman and the Little Black Girl*), as well as *Diablito* (*Little Devil*), both from 1925–1926. *La mulata y la negrita* reflects the auto-primitivizing impulse with which many Latin American artists responded to Paris's negrophilia. It does so by connecting with prevalent discourses about *types*, according to which humans of various backgrounds could be neatly packed into discrete descriptive categories such as "Black" or "mulatto." These explorations showed little concern for the subjectivity or individuality of those represented, as if their phenotype and disposition provided enough information about them and about the group to which they allegedly belonged. The figures are surrounded by tropical foliage, to dispel any possible doubts about their location and cultural frame of reference.

In the same vein, *Diablito*, a drawing executed in Paris in 1926, depicts a dancing Íreme in highly stereotypical ways. The Íreme is a key liturgical figure in the rituals of the Abakuá, a secret male fraternal society that originated in the Cross-River basin between Nigeria and Cameroon. Enslaved people from this region, known in Cuba as Carabalí because of their embarkation point in Calabar, recreated their Ékpè (leopard) initiation lodges on Cuban soil in the nineteenth century, as mutual aid societies that provided much-needed networks of kinship and support.

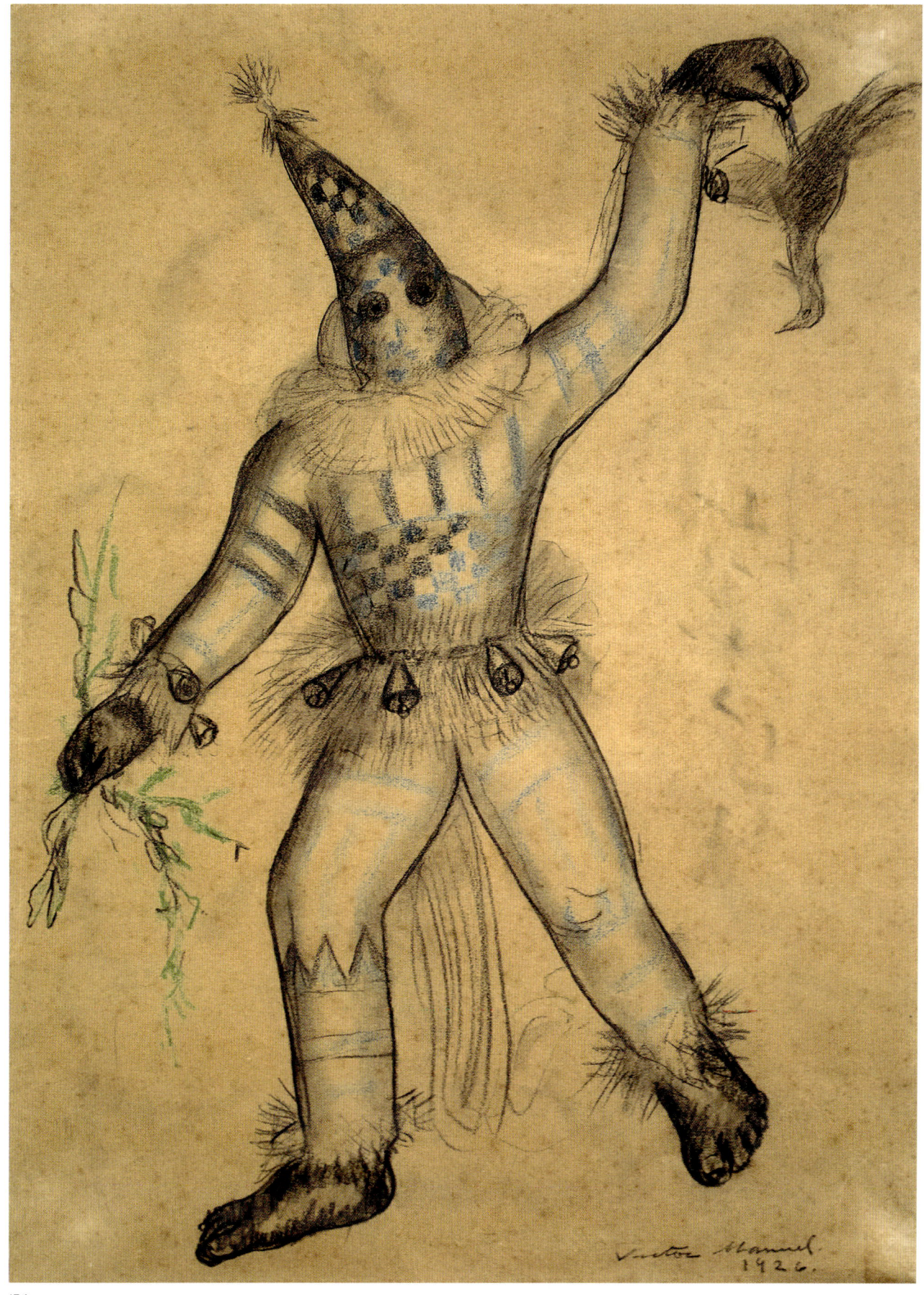
154

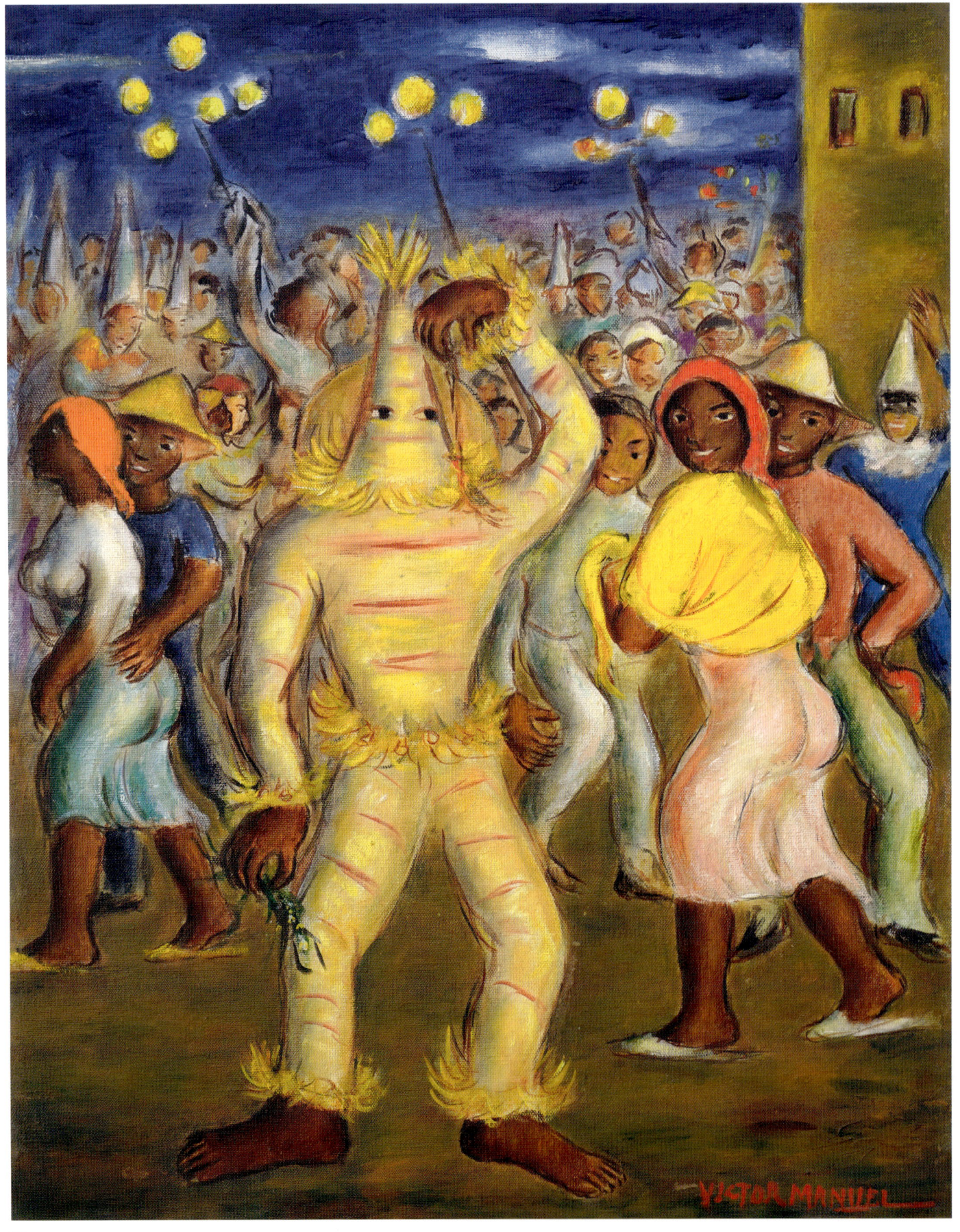

155

155 Victor Manuel García. *Carnival*. 1940s. Oil on canvas. Coral Gables, FL, Courtesy of Cernuda Arte.

At the sound of sacred drums, the Íreme communicate with the *ecobios* or lodge brothers through dance and hand gestures that are part of complex religious rituals by which they dispense blessings and well-being. Their garments are treated with much respect, and their identity, known to members of the lodge, is jealously protected.[73] Outsiders can easily perceive the Íreme as a carnivalesque, folkloric, and colorful dancing fetish devoid of any religious or ritual content. There is in fact a long tradition in Cuban painting, going back to nineteenth-century *costumbrismo*, that depicts them in this fashion. Victor Patricio Landaluze (1828–1889) included them among his Cuban *types* in Antonio Bachiller y Morales's *Tipos y costumbres de la Isla de Cuba* (1881) and devoted numerous watercolors to depict diablito costumes and dances. The exoticizing gaze informing these representations, of which *Diablito con gallo y tambor* (ca. 1880) is a fine example, is clearly echoed in avant-garde depictions such as Victor Manuel's, whose own *Diablito* holds branches in one hand and a sacrificial bird in the other. There is no indication that the artist understood or was even interested in the liturgical meanings of the various elements included in the composition. What is clear is that in his search for authentic Cuban elements, Victor Manuel turned to one of the most visible and picturesque icons of Afro-Cuban religiosity. The diablito would remain an important visual cue for the artist into the 1930s and 1940s, as exemplified by his later *Carnaval (Carnival)* (ca. 1940s), where the Íreme holds a central place among a large group of dancing subjects, many of whom appear to be of African descent.[74]

Victor Manuel's contemporary Eduardo Abela arrived in Paris in 1927 for a two-year stay. There, he would develop what the art critic Roberto Cobas Amate has described as "a brief but intense Afrocuban period," when he produced numerous paintings representing Black subjects and their culture.[75] One of the young writers of the vanguardia, Alejo Carpentier (1904–1980), reportedly influenced Abela, asking him to "afro-cubanize" himself under the logic that "to contemporary Cubans, the modern is Afro-Cuban."[76] In order to capture Cuba's "deep, autochthonous racial essence,"[77] Abela turned to popular traditions and to Afro-Cuban rituals and musical forms that had been previously ignored by academically oriented artists. These works typically present Blacks as musically oriented, dancing subjects whose movements, actions, and compositions are submerged in an atmosphere of deliberate mystery. Abela's paintings are populated by nocturnal, foggy figures that partake in enigmatic and ancestral rituals, as in *El gallo místico* (*The Mystical Rooster*, 1928), or in musical processions and festivities, as in *El triunfo de la rumba* (*The Triumph of the Rumba*, 1928). The deeper import of these expressions of popular culture and religiosity seems to escape the comprehension of the artist. Abela creates a ceremonial atmosphere that turns his lack of insider knowledge into an advantage, giving the paintings additional layers of exoticism. "Cuba seen from within abroad," commented a critic a propos an Abela exhibition in Paris in 1928.[78] One can almost hear the rhymes of "*La rumba*," the poem written by Abela's collaborator and editor of *Avance* José Zacarías Tallet the same year, in *El triunfo de la rumba*. The rhythmically oriented poem depicts rumba—a musical and dance form that encompasses a variety of Afro-Cuban influences—as a lascivious spectacle of sweaty bodies that engage in overtly sexual games, punctuated by "jungle smell" and by the odors of "urban shantytowns" and "slave barracks." Fernando Ortiz[79] described it as "white art with black motifs," a descrip-

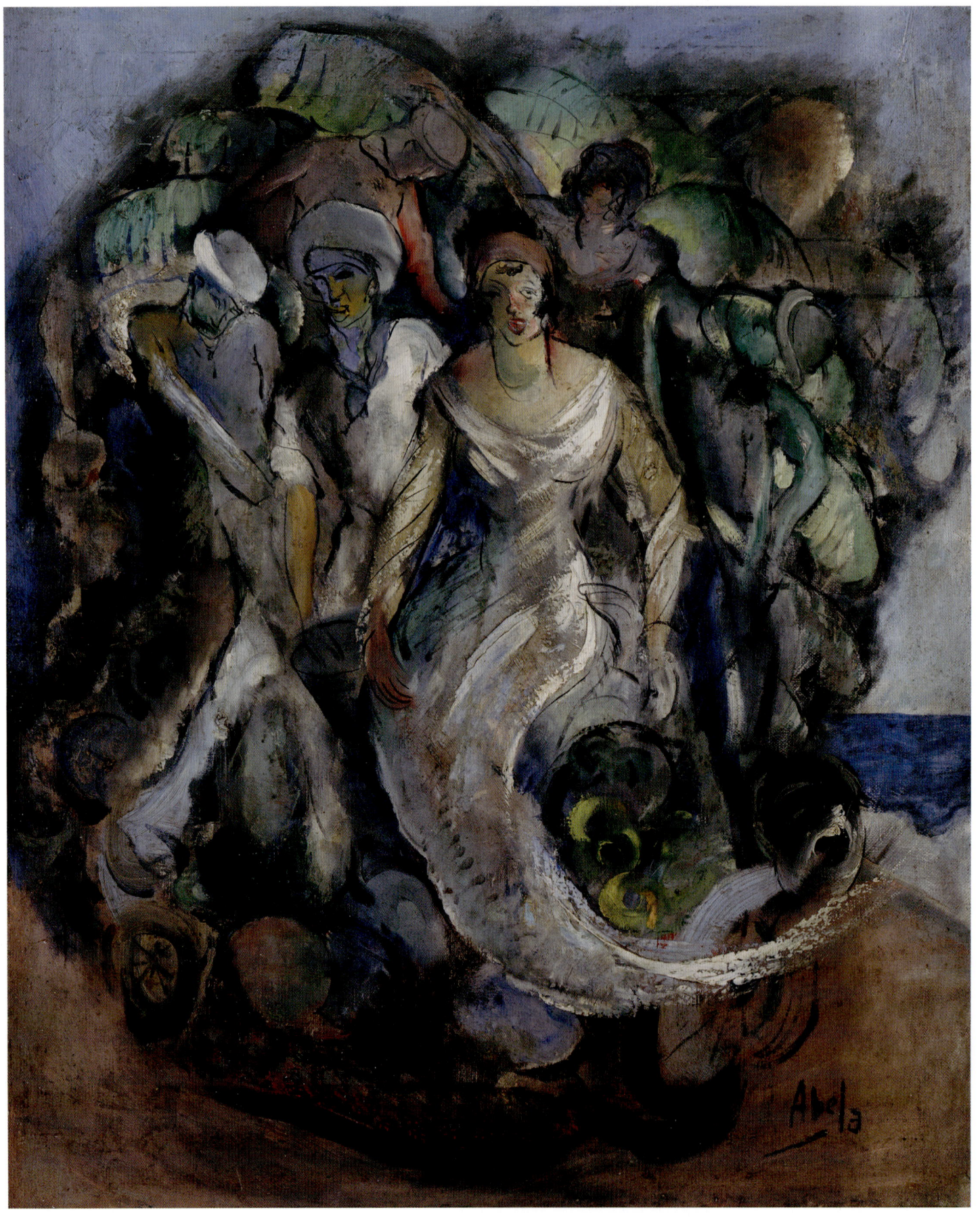

156

156 Eduardo Abela. *The Triumph of the Rumba*. 1928. Oil on canvas. Havana, Museo Nacional de Bellas Artes de Cuba.

tion that may well apply to Abela's representations. Years later, Abela himself would acknowledge that he stopped working on Afro-Cuban culture because he did not know how to develop the theme further.[80]

The trajectory of self-discovery followed by the painter Di Cavalcanti is similar to that of Victor Manuel or Eduardo Abela, and, remarkably, even some of their works bear formal comparison, though there is no evidence their paths ever crossed. After a period of two years in Paris, from 1923 to 1925, Di Cavalcanti returned to Brazil and began to produce a series of representations of carnival, samba, and the mostly Black and mixed-race characters who populated the streets and nightlife of his native Rio. As the artist himself phrased it in later years: "When I returned from my first trip to Europe, I felt the full lyrical force of Rio de Janeiro and determined that I would live the rest of my life from its magic."[81] Indeed, a period of intense creativity ensued culminating in the production of two large mural paintings for the João Caetano Theater, in Rio, between 1929 and 1931. Both depict multiple figures, mostly *moreno* or *mestizo*, engaged in musical activities. The men, in contemporary apparel, play musical instruments. The women, dressed in the attire typical of Afro-Brazilian rituals (such as Candomblé), dance, clap hands, and carry offerings of flowers. In his works of this period, the background frequently suggests the setting of the favelas, which were then a burgeoning presence in Rio's urban landscape. All too often, as in *Samba* (1927), one or more female figures are shown undressed amid groups of fully clothed men, generating a sense of unreality. In parallel, Di Cavalcanti produced numerous brothel and street scenes in which women of various shades, but especially Afrodescendant ones, subsist at the bottom of the social scale. Chromatically and stylistically, the artist's paintings of this period display an amalgam of post-cubist and *Neue Sachlichkeit* influences, but formal concerns are outweighed by their open celebration of popular culture and social criticism of the elites.[82]

The changes in subject and style of his paintings did not go unnoticed by his fellow veteran of the Semana de Arte Moderna, Mário de Andrade, in a May 1932 article hailing Di Cavalcanti's first exhibition in São Paulo since that event. The critic praised the artist for the newfound Brazilianness of his work, which contrasted with the "languid symbolism, very much of the imported variety" he had produced before. Especially praiseworthy, in Mário de Andrade's view, were "the admirable series of mulattas, of whom he has managed to reveal the hidden rosiness." According to the critic, Di Cavalcanti had become "the most exact painter of things national" precisely for choosing to depict "mulattas, blacks and carnivals."[83] This conflation of race and nation is characteristic of the turbulent political times, coming less than two years after the Revolution of 1930 that brought Getúlio Vargas to power and just months before the Constitutionalist Revolution of 1932, through which São Paulo attempted to secede from the Brazilian republic. As a supporter of both these movements, Mário de Andrade's position would soon come into conflict with that of Di Cavalcanti, who had joined the Brazilian Communist Party in 1928 and was therefore inclined to view the political struggle in decidedly less nationalistic terms. Yet at the particular juncture when he wrote those words, a consensus was taking shape across a broad ideological spectrum that affirmed a new Brazilian identity underpinned by the idea of racial mixture as a unifying force. The following year, 1933, would see the publication of Gilberto Freyre's *Casa grande e senzala* (later translated into English

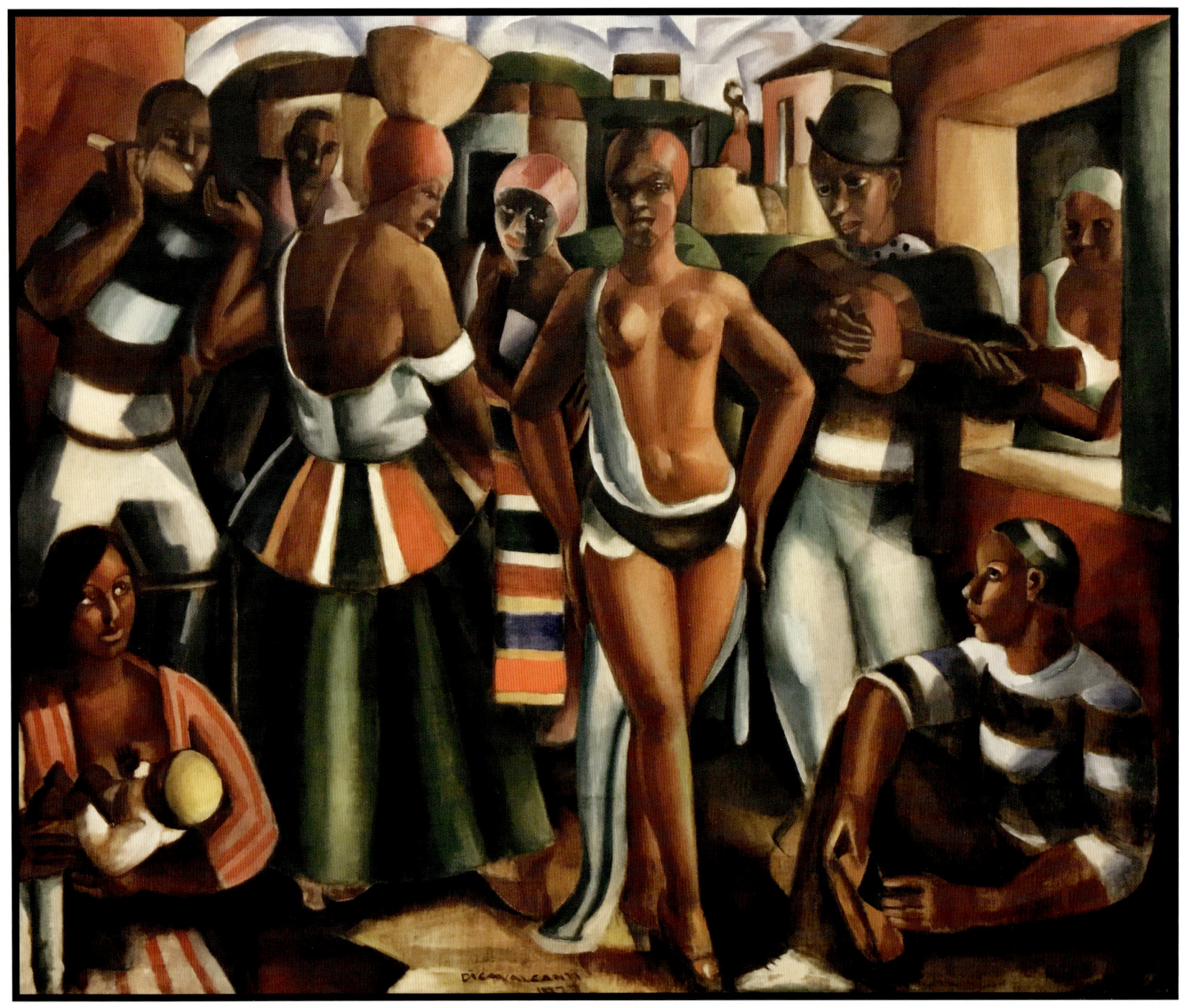

157 Emiliano Di Cavalcanti. *Samba*. 1927. Oil on canvas. Montevideo, Uruguay, Collection Latinamerican Art LLC.

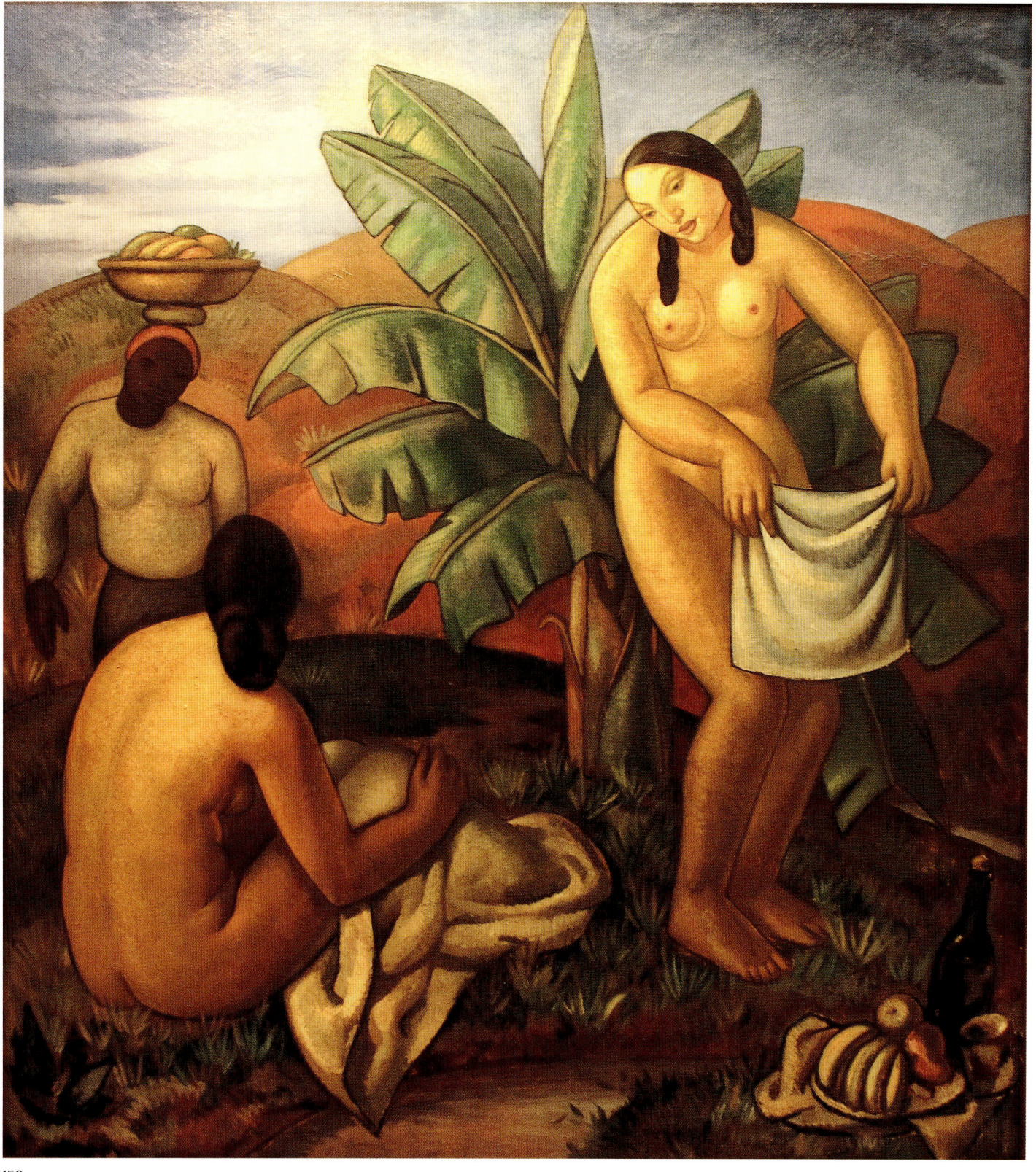

158

158 Antonio Gattorno. *Women by the River*. 1927. Oil on canvas. Havana, Museo Nacional de Bellas Artes de Cuba.

159 Tarsila do Amaral. *The Fruit Vendor*. 1925. Oil on canvas. Rio de Janeiro, Museu de Arte Moderna (MAM), Gilberto Chateaubriand Collection.

as *The Masters and the Slaves*), which famously articulated the thesis that racial mixing was the foundation of Brazilian culture.

Although disruptive and innovative in the sense that they re-centered national identity around popular cultural expressions of perceived African origins, avant-garde artists frequently relied on essentialist and prejudiced notions about Blackness in their appropriation and translation efforts. On the one hand, identifying national identity with street culture represented a seismic shift in how to imagine the region, away from hegemonic representations of Latin American nations as white and culturally European. Abela's rituals, Victor Manuel's carnivals, and Di Cavalcanti's depictions of samba and carnival, brothels, and favelas all illustrate this shift. By populating their compositions with vibrant Black and brown protagonists, these artists created a new and powerful iconography of modern Cuban and Brazilian life. On the other hand, by relying on primitivist and racialized stereotypes, such works contributed to subtly re-inscribe and reproduce racial and social hierarchies that placed Blacks at the bottom of society. Sometimes these representations were not even subtle, as illustrated by Antonio Gattorno's (1904–1980) *Mujeres junto al río* (*Women by the River*), of 1927. Painted after the inevitable study trip to Paris, where Gattorno worked between 1924 and 1926, *Women by the River* places three Gauguinesque women of different shades in an exotic tropical landscape. The lighter golden figures engage in leisure and bathe surrounded by provisions. The darker figure works, her social station graphically conveyed through the stereotypical image of a Black fruit vendor.

Another image of a fruit vendor, painted by Tarsila do Amaral in 1925, helps tease out some of the complexities of autoexoticism. Shown in the artist's solo exhibition of June 1926 at Galerie Percier in Paris, *O vendedor de frutas* (*The Fruit Vendor*, 1925), depicts a brown-skinned, blue-eyed young man, with a big straw hat balanced precariously on his head. He floats along a sea in a small boat full of tropical fruit, a parrotlike bird at his side. The background is filled with islands and palm trees and the colorful shapes of buildings that recall Brazil's colonial past. The boat is very small and round. The disproportionate size of the pineapple and oranges makes it look more like a fruit bowl than a real boat. The youth can thus be viewed as a fruit of nature, among others, more a sign of tropical abundance than an actual human being. His baffled expression, combined with the fact that only his torso and head are shown, adds to the sense that he is simply an object on display for the viewer's gaze, rather than a thinking and feeling subject. Unlike other paintings produced by Tarsila around this time, it lacks any of the markers of cubism or surrealism that might allow it to be categorized as an avant-garde work. It is slightly surprising, then, that this painting was selected for reproduction in the critic Raymond Cogniat's grand survey of Latin American art for the magazine *La Renaissance de l'Art Français et des Industries de Luxe*, published in August 1926.[84] With so many of her works then available in Paris—some bold statements, like *A negra*—why would the magazine choose to single out this naïf depiction of a visual cliché: the flora, fauna, and human variety of tropical nature? And why would Tarsila, a young woman attempting to make a name for herself as an avant-garde artist, even paint such a picture? Was it an attempt to explore the taste for naïf painting that had ensured Figari's success a few years earlier? Or was it intended as an ironic commentary on the expectations that French audiences had of how a Latin American artist should paint? If so, the irony went unnoticed. Reviews of Tarsila's show

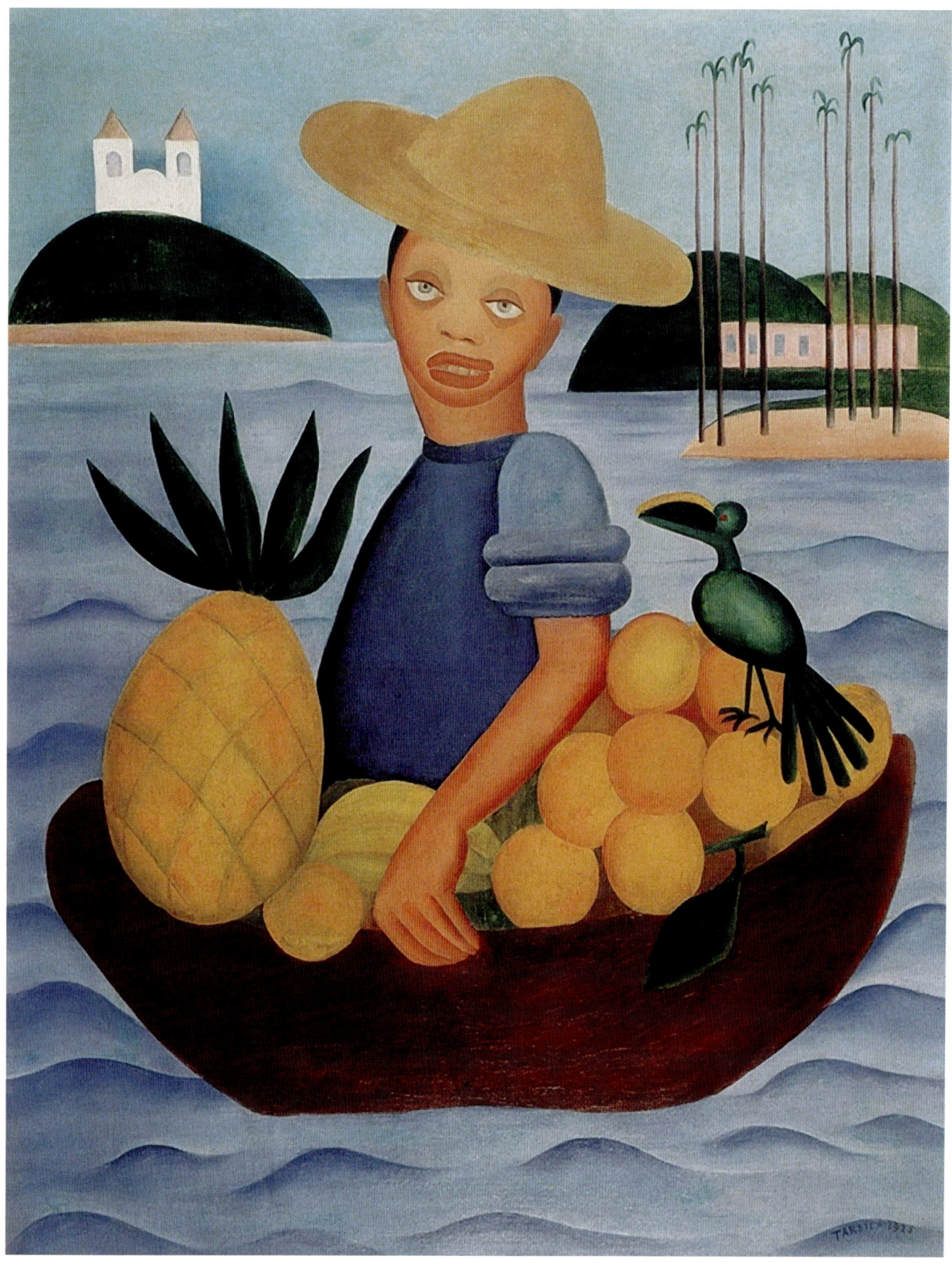

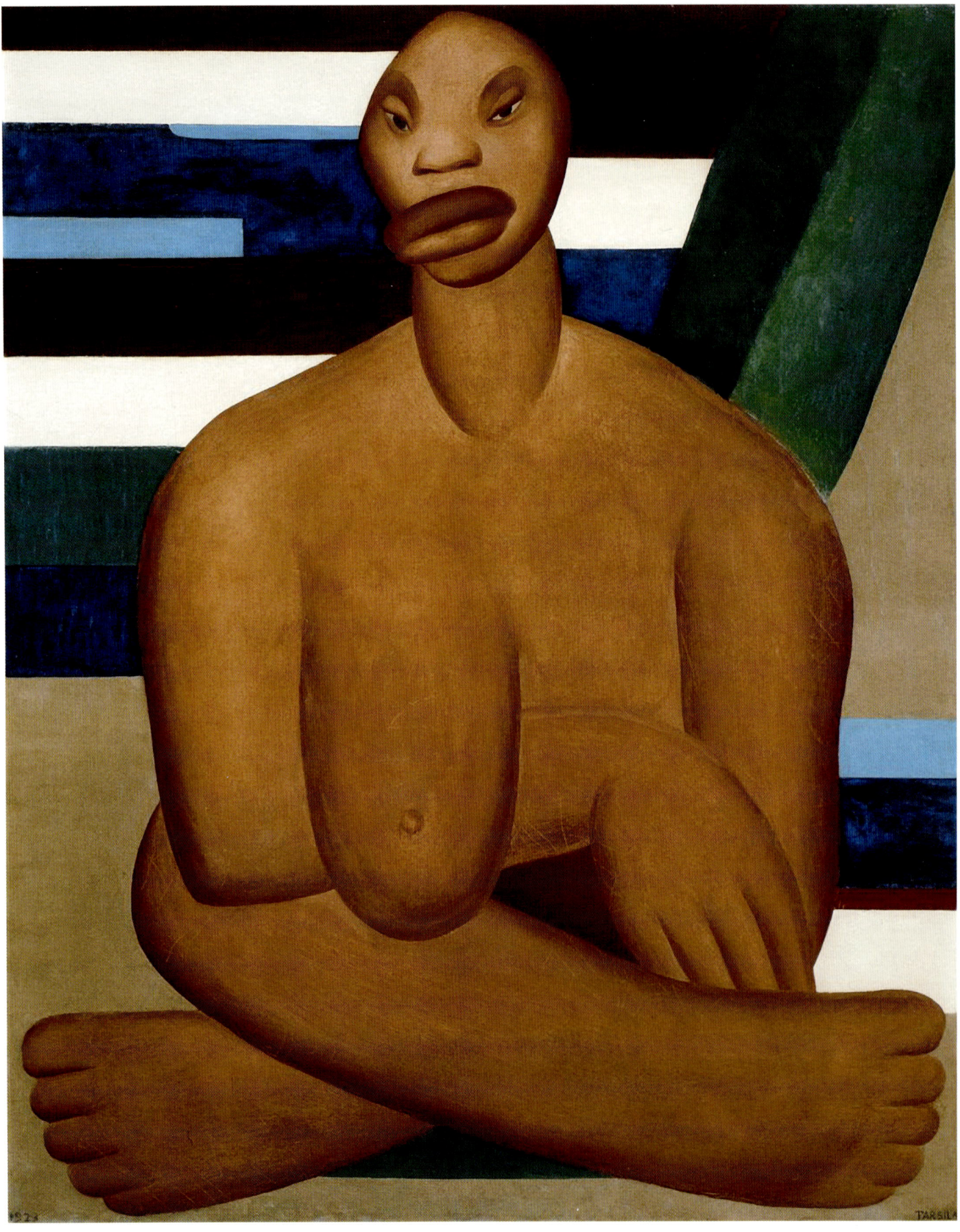
160

160　Tarsila do Amaral. *Black Woman*. 1923. Oil on canvas. Museum of Contemporary Art, University of São Paulo.

in the Parisian press tended to emphasize qualities like feminine delicacy, seductive exoticism, and colorful decorativeness but stopped short of taking her seriously as an avant-garde artist.[85]

Mexican Influences

The fruit vendors of Tarsila and Gattorno were not just convenient tropical figures; they were also workers, humble subjects who performed manual labor to make a living. Many radical avant-garde artists with communist sympathies identified their nations with the working brown masses, a link that found privileged artistic elaboration in Mexican muralism. Antonio Gattorno was enthusiastic about mural painting, and Diego Rivera is frequently mentioned as one of his most important influences.[86] Di Cavalcanti likewise referenced the Mexican muralists as the inspiration for his own mural works. This points to the importance of Mexico in the avant-garde pictorial movements of Cuba and other Latin American countries. As the poet and critic Armando Alvarez Bravo has written, "it was in Paris that the avant-garde found its raison d'être and its navigation charts," but it was in Mexico where those impulses were "reaffirmed."[87] The Mexicans came to embody the promises of renovation and creativity for the entire region—the avant-garde of the vanguardias. The Cuban writer Alejo Carpentier told approvingly of an anecdote according to which Diego Rivera shot at a gramophone so that he would not have to suffer Italian opera![88] The timing of the remark is interesting. Reminiscent of the iconoclastic bravado of the Italian Futurists, it was published shortly after F. T. Marinetti's 1926 tour of Argentina, Brazil, and Uruguay. In retrospect, Rivera's purported shot seems almost symbolic of a shift in the most radical energies of the avant-gardes. The decline of a European scene given over to an artistic "return to order" and living under the nascent shadow of fascism contrasts powerfully with the revolutionary forces at work in the Americas.

Mexican artists were perceived as the creators of a new visual language that not only captured the racial soul of their nation, but one that was at the service of popular sectors and the lower classes, many of them indigenous and mestizo.[89] "That is why, in the current moment of Mexico, art is the realization of collective realities and translates the dominant emotions of its people," noted the editors of *Avance*.[90] As Diego Rivera himself stated from the pages of *Amauta*, in Mexico it was possible to produce an art "capable of influencing the proletarian masses of the American continent."[91] The main journals of the vanguardia paid close attention to Mexican visual arts and helped disseminate their works and contributions. They celebrated the "new Mexican painting" as one that went straight to their "indigenous essence."[92] The Mexican people marched by the frescoes of the muralists and recognized themselves in them, thus providing a model that inspired artists all over the region.

When Siqueiros traveled to Argentina in 1933, he enlisted the collaboration of local artists like Lino Enea Spilimbergo, Antonio Berni, and Juan Carlos Castagnino, all of whom worked with the Mexican master to produce the mural *Ejercicio plástico* (*Plastic Exercise*), commissioned by Natalio Botana, owner of the newspaper *Crítica*. Though Berni soon fell out with Siqueiros, the revolutionary ideals of the muralists are discernible in many of his subsequent works, like *Desocupados* (*Unemployed*, 1934), *Manifestación* (*Demonstration*, 1934), and *Chacareros* (*Small Farmers*, 1935), which feature Black figures among other representatives of the working classes and *el pueblo* (the people).

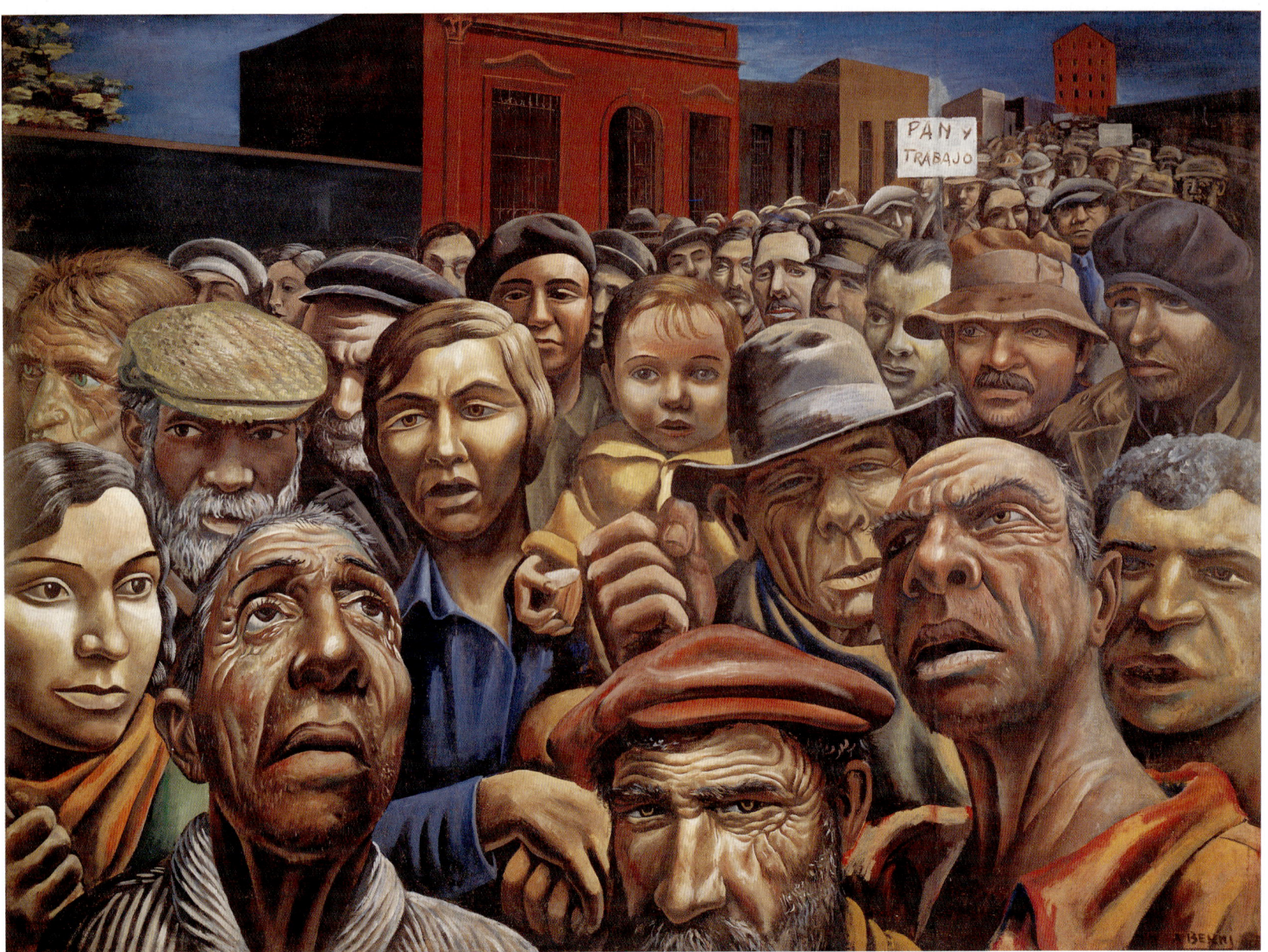

161

161 Antonio Berni. *Demonstration*. 1934. Tempera on burlap. Museo de Arte Latinoamericano de Buenos Aires.

162 Tarsila do Amaral. *Workers*. 1933. Oil on canvas. Acervo Artístico-Cultural dos Palácios do Governo do Estado de São Paulo.

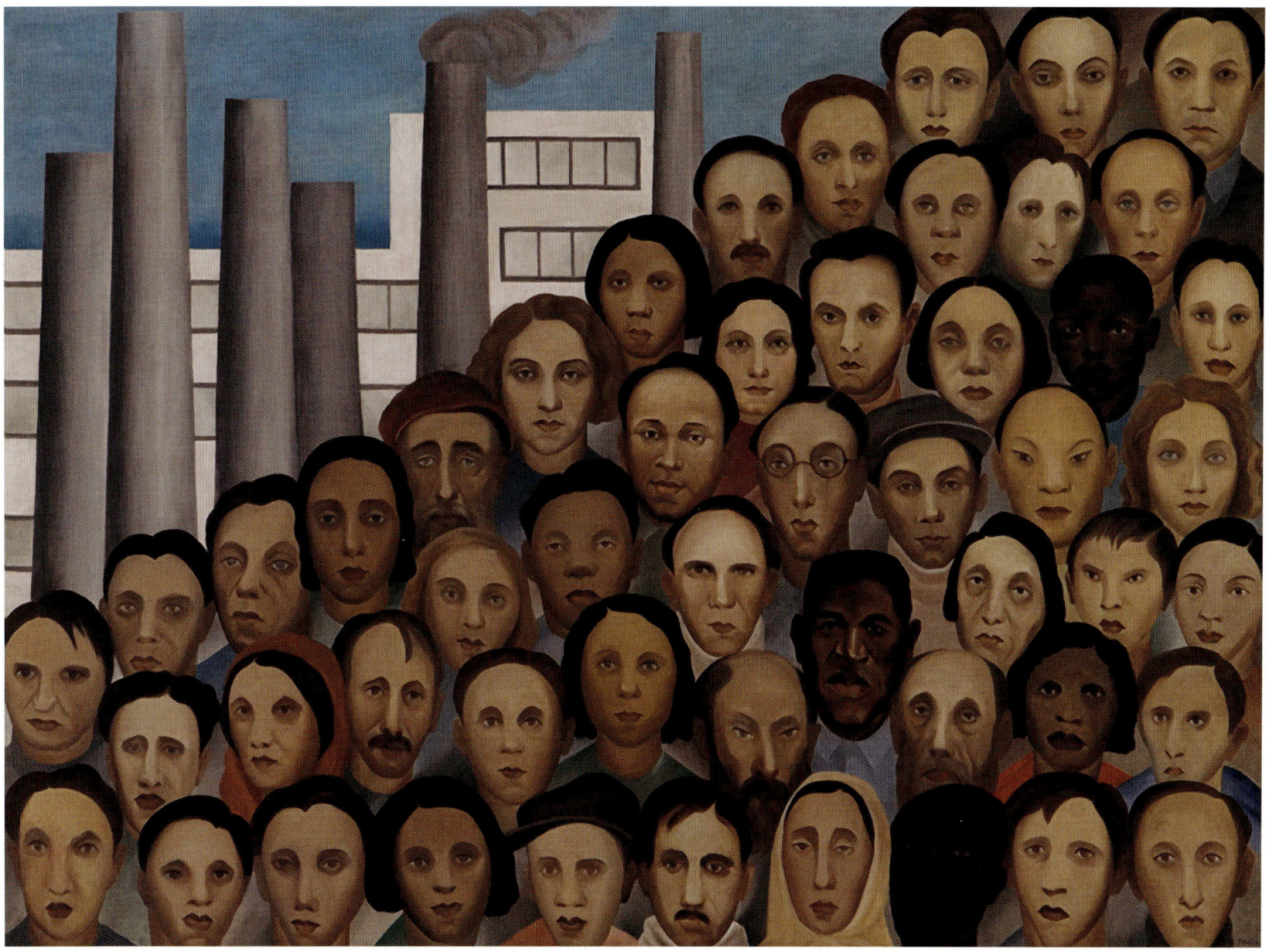

162 Tarsila do Amaral's *Operários* (*Workers*, 1933) is similarly careful to include a number of Black and brown faces among the imposing mass of its composition. Rivera, Ledesma, Orozco, and Leal became staple names among the Latin American avant-garde intelligentsia, including in Brazil. In a lecture of October 1935, inaugurating the politically radical exhibition *Mostra de Arte Social* in Rio de Janeiro, the critic Aníbal Machado (1894–1964) enjoined the Brazilian government to entrust the country's mural decorations to "the true artists," following the example of Rivera, Orozco, and Siqueiros in Mexico.[93]

Avant-garde painters heeded Mexico's artistic revolutionary calls and produced works that celebrated what Rivera called the "proletarian masses" of the region. Some of these artists traveled to Mexico to learn firsthand about and from the *muralistas*, who occasionally included Black subjects in representations of the working class or to highlight the slavelike condition of the peon.[94]

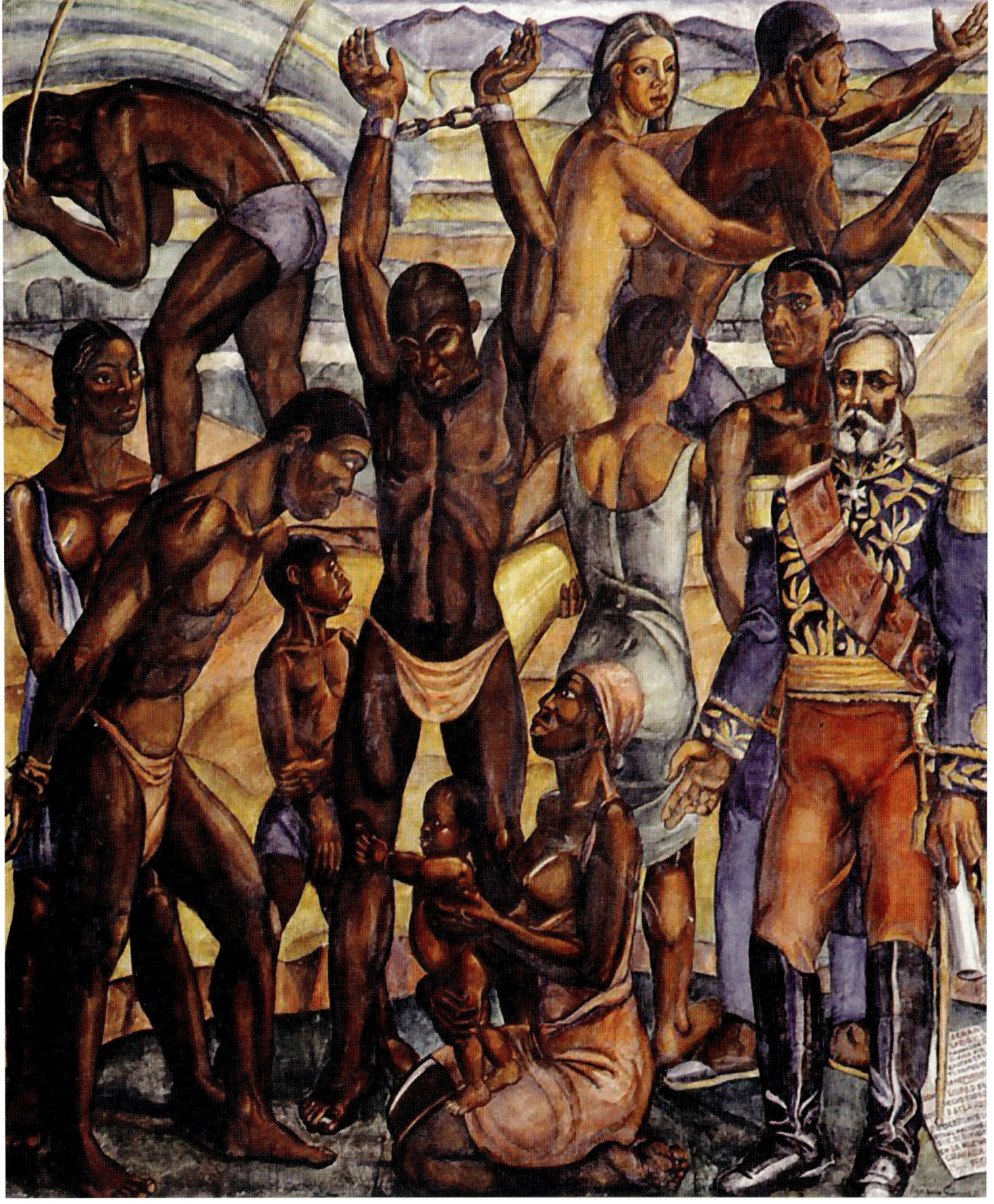
163

163 Ignacio Gómez Jaramillo. *The Freeing of the Slaves*. 1938. Fresco. Bogotá, Capitolio Nacional de Colombia, Congreso de la Republica de Colombia.

164 Mariano Rodríguez. *Couple with Oxen*. 1939. Oil on canvas. Aventura, FL, Private collection.

165 Cândido Portinari. *Mestizo*. 1934. Oil on canvas. Pinacoteca do Estado de São Paulo.

Among those traveling to Mexico was Ignacio Gómez Jaramillo (1910–1970), a Colombian painter who was part of the Bachué visual arts group (1920s–1940s). The group was named after a deity of the Muisca people and celebrated indigenous elements as a foundational contribution to Colombian culture.[95] Like many artists of his generation, Gómez Jaramillo studied in Europe, but he also traveled to Mexico, where, along with the artists in the Liga de Escritores y Artistas Revolucionarios (LEAR), he painted a mural graphically titled *La represión de los obreros* (*The Repression of the Workers*).[96] Back in Colombia, Jaramillo painted several frescoes in which individuals of African descent are prominently represented, including *La liberación de los esclavos* (*The Freeing of the Slaves*, 1938), part of his murals in Bogotá's National Capitol. The art historian Raúl Cristancho Álvarez describes this mural as "the first important work in Colombian visual arts that thematically is fully devoted to Afro-Colombians."[97]

One of the things Jaramillo absorbed in Mexico was the notion that el pueblo was incarnated first and foremost by "the mestizo people." This association, which acquired the status of state dogma under Mexican revolutionary education and artistic plans, was explored and represented by other muralists-influenced artists, such as Cuba's Mariano Rodríguez (1912–1990). By the early 1930s, Cuban thinkers, with important contributions from Afro-Cuban intellectuals such as Gustavo Urrutia, Juan Jiménez Pastrana, and Nicolás Guillén had begun to articulate a new vision that imagined the nation as a cultural and racial synthesis—Cuba as a mulatto country. Urrutia, for instance, wrote about *la raza cubana* (the Cuban race).[98] Guillén, in turn, anticipated in 1931 the dawn of a new, mestizo nation: "Cuba's soul is mestizo, and it is from the soul, not the skin, that we derive our definite color. Someday it will be called 'Cuban color.'"[99] A few years later, the pedagogue and historian Jiménez Pastrana spoke about "the mestizo reality of the Cuban soul."[100]

Such ideas and images gained currency throughout Latin America at this time. The Brazilian painter Cândido Portinari's (1903–1962) works *Mestiço* (*Mestizo*, 1934), *Negro com enxada* (*Black Man with a Hoe*, 1934) and *Café* (*Coffee*, 1935), among other iconic depictions produced circa 1933–1935, attest to the use of racial types to represent a presumed vital essence of national identity. In an article of December 1934, Oswald de Andrade established a clear link between such works and those of the Mexican muralists, arguing that Portinari's pictures needed to leave the confines of the canvas and proclaim a mural lesson: "They clamor for the walls that Siqueiros and his group have already managed to pry from the bourgeoisie in Mexico and in California and that Rivera saw destroyed by reaction in New York."[101] In 1936, Portinari was commissioned by the government to paint a series of murals for the new building of the Ministry of Education and Health, in Rio de Janeiro. The themes chosen corresponded to the various "economic cycles" through which Brazilian history could be interpreted as a series of commodities for export (for example, brazilwood, sugar, gold, coffee, rubber), and Portinari chose to depict these abstract cycles mainly through the figurative representation of laborers engaged in work. The conception and execution of the murals progressed slowly over eight years, during which time the Vargas regime descended into a full-blown dictatorship, the Estado Novo (New State), modeled on the national corporate states that were seen in many Catholic countries as a bulwark against communism and an antidote to the perceived failures of liberal democracy. Though the represen-

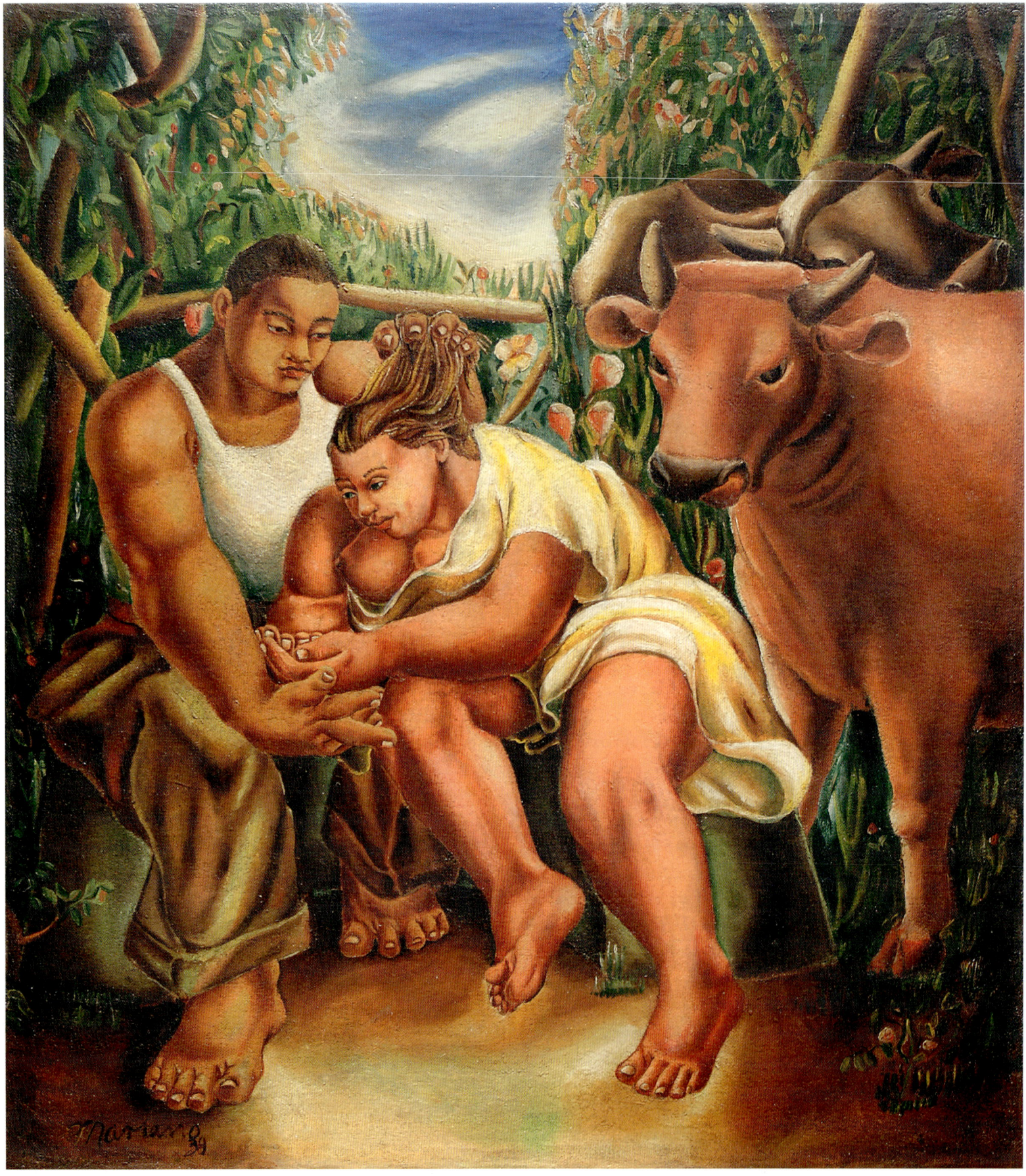
164

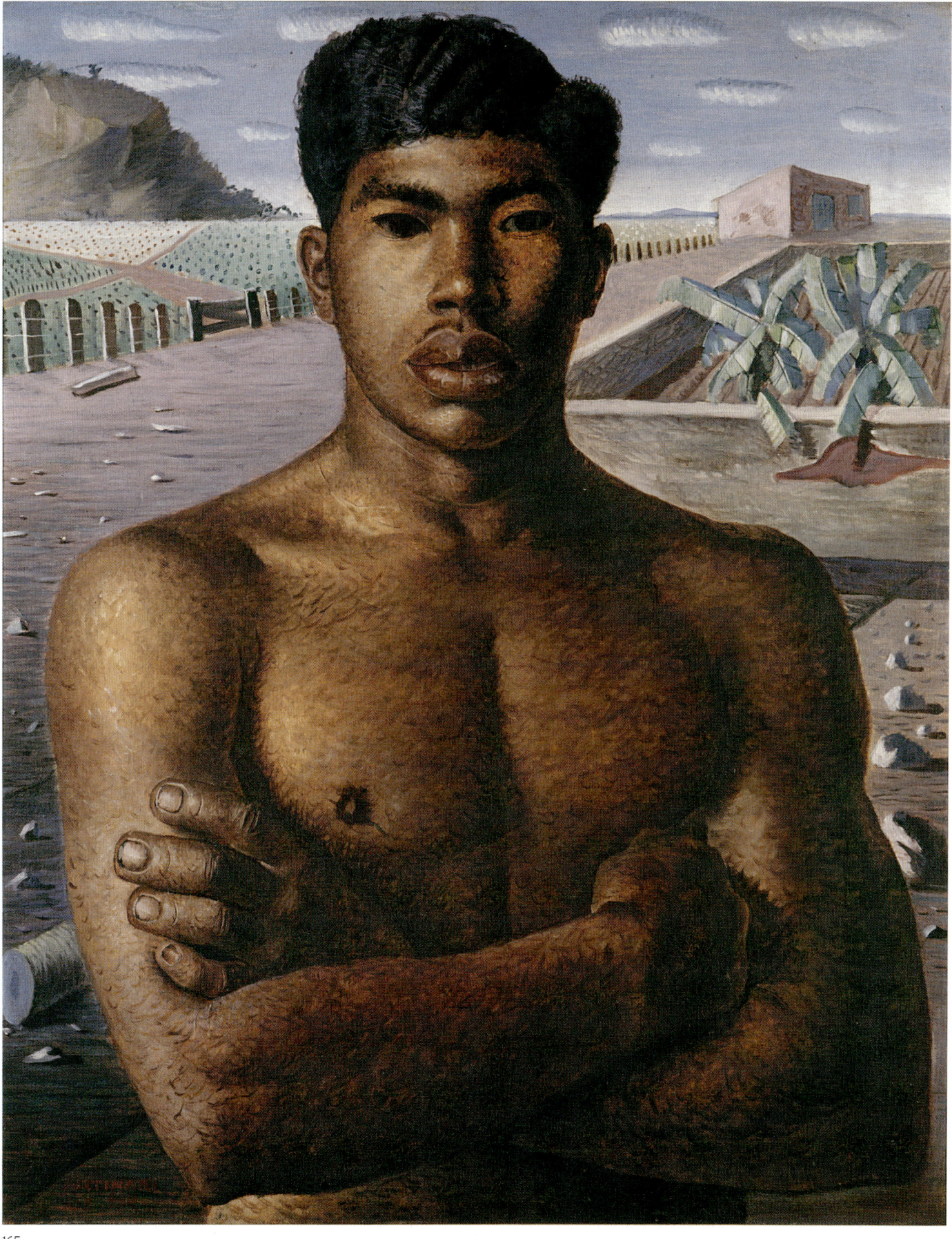

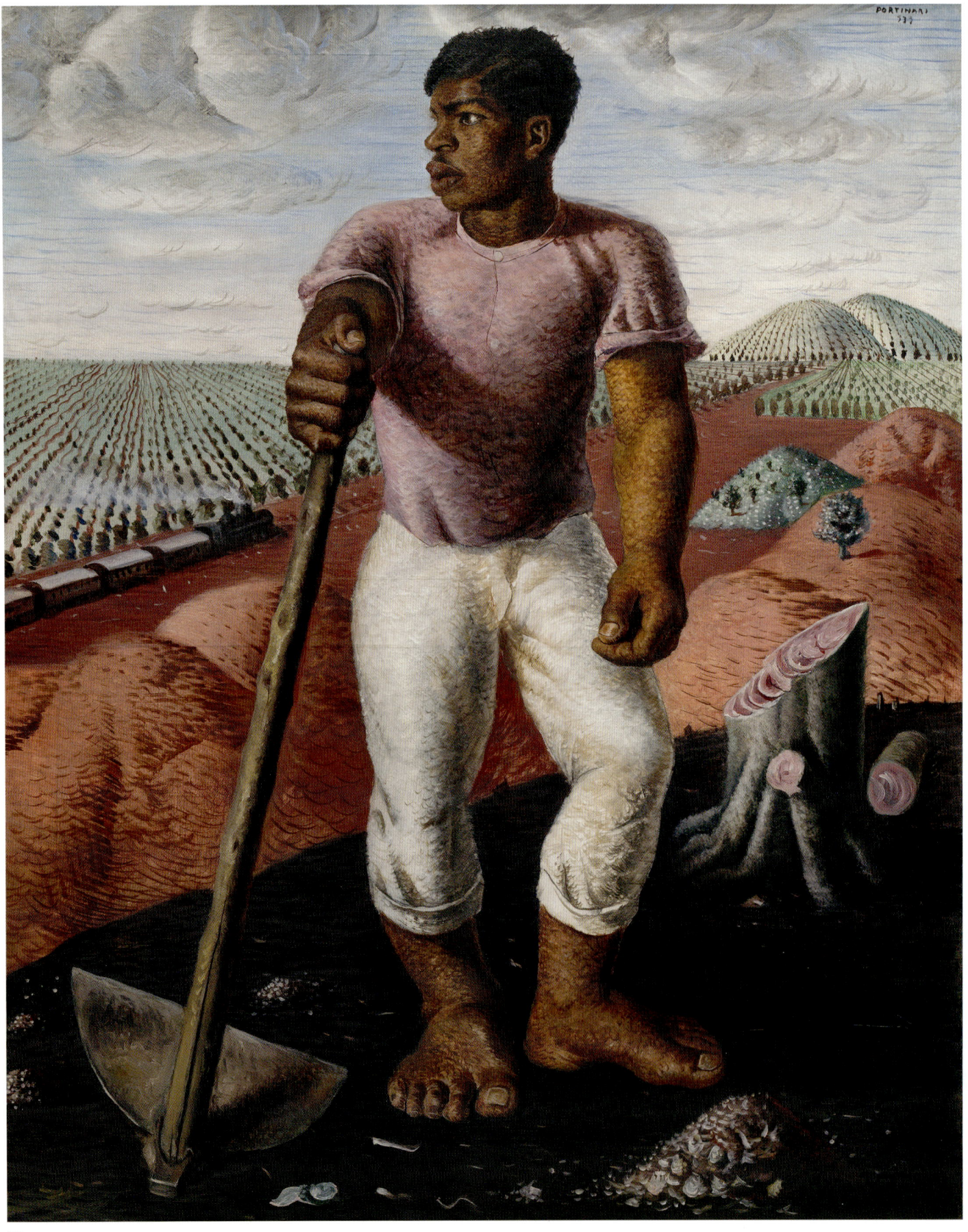

166

166 Cândido Portinari. *Black Man with a Hoe (Coffee Laborer)*. 1934. Oil on canvas. Museu de Arte de São Paulo Assis Chateaubriand.

167 Alberto da Veiga Guignard. *The Engaged Couple*. 1937. Oil on wood. Rio de Janeiro, Museus Castro Maya, Ibram/Minc.

168 Alberto da Veiga Guignard. *The Marine's Family*. ca. 1935. Oil on wood. Instituto de Estudos Brasileiros, Universidade da São Paulo.

tation of race and Blackness plays an important role in their compositions, the finished murals were emptied of the revolutionary implications envisaged by Oswald de Andrade. By 1939, the writer saw Portinari as a "reactionary" painter, whom he accused of staging a return to academic tradition.[102]

The imbrications of race and politics were by no means unambiguous, veering sharply from one context to another. In post-revolutionary Mexico, attempts to glorify a suppressed mestizo culture were initially aligned with a left-wing agenda of egalitarian policies and social justice. In Brazil, under the Estado Novo, representations of Blackness could convey very different meanings. Two paintings by Alberto da Veiga Guignard, *Os noivos* (*The Engaged Couple*, 1937) and *A família do fuzileiro naval* (*The Marine's Family*, circa 1935/1938) serve to illustrate this point. Both depict Black figures posing proudly in domestic interiors, in front of open doorways that look out onto scenery suggesting the hilly landscape of Rio de Janeiro. In the first painting, a uniformed marine stands next to his sitting bride, who wears a long dress trimmed with lace and a lace garland and holds a small bouquet. A large Brazilian flag is prominently displayed from the balcony. To its right, directly over the woman's head, is a framed picture with the image of the Sacred Heart of Jesus. The colorful composition further echoes the national green and yellow, blue and white in the patterns of the wallpaper and the woman's dress. Blackness is here explicitly linked to nationalism, the military, Catholicism, and traditional values of marriage and domesticity. Similar elements recur in the second painting: a family, the Brazilian flag, a woman in a long frilly dress, men (and even boys) in military uniforms. The stiff poses of the figures, reminiscent of old portrait photographs, add to the suggestion of uprightness, duty, and tradition. The symmetry of the compositions endows them with a sense of order and balance. These images could readily be interpreted as simple affirmations of identity and status—positive depictions of Black people as models of a new social order—which may well be what the artist intended. Nonetheless, in the context in which they were produced and shown, those meanings could be read very differently. Anticommunism was a key pretext for the seizure of power by Vargas in 1937; and the Estado Novo regime made strategic efforts to align the working masses with its own agenda of political centralization and social conservatism. Seen in this light, Guignard's almost naïf affirmations of Black Brazilian life acquire a more sinister bent.

Mestizaje, Hybridity, and the Idea of Blackness

The idea of a distinct identity arising out of the Latin American experience—"*La raza cósmica*" (*The Cosmic Race*), as penned by José Vasconcelos in 1925—once seemed like a straightforward affirmation of dignity and equality: the prophecy of a new human race, born of the mixture of all peoples. Over the 1930s, conflicts between nationalism and internationalism reached a boiling point, with debates about eugenics and racial purity playing a crucial part. After the Second World War and the Holocaust, the avowal of identities based on any category of racial distinction acquired sinister connotations that still resonate today in the abhorrence rightfully inspired by white supremacism. Still, the ideal of a cosmic race, based not on purity but total miscegenation and mixture, continues to reverberate in the collective imaginary of Latin American societies. Concepts of "hybrid cultures"[103] and even a "mestizo mind"[104] provide an intellectual challenge that demands to be unpacked historically.

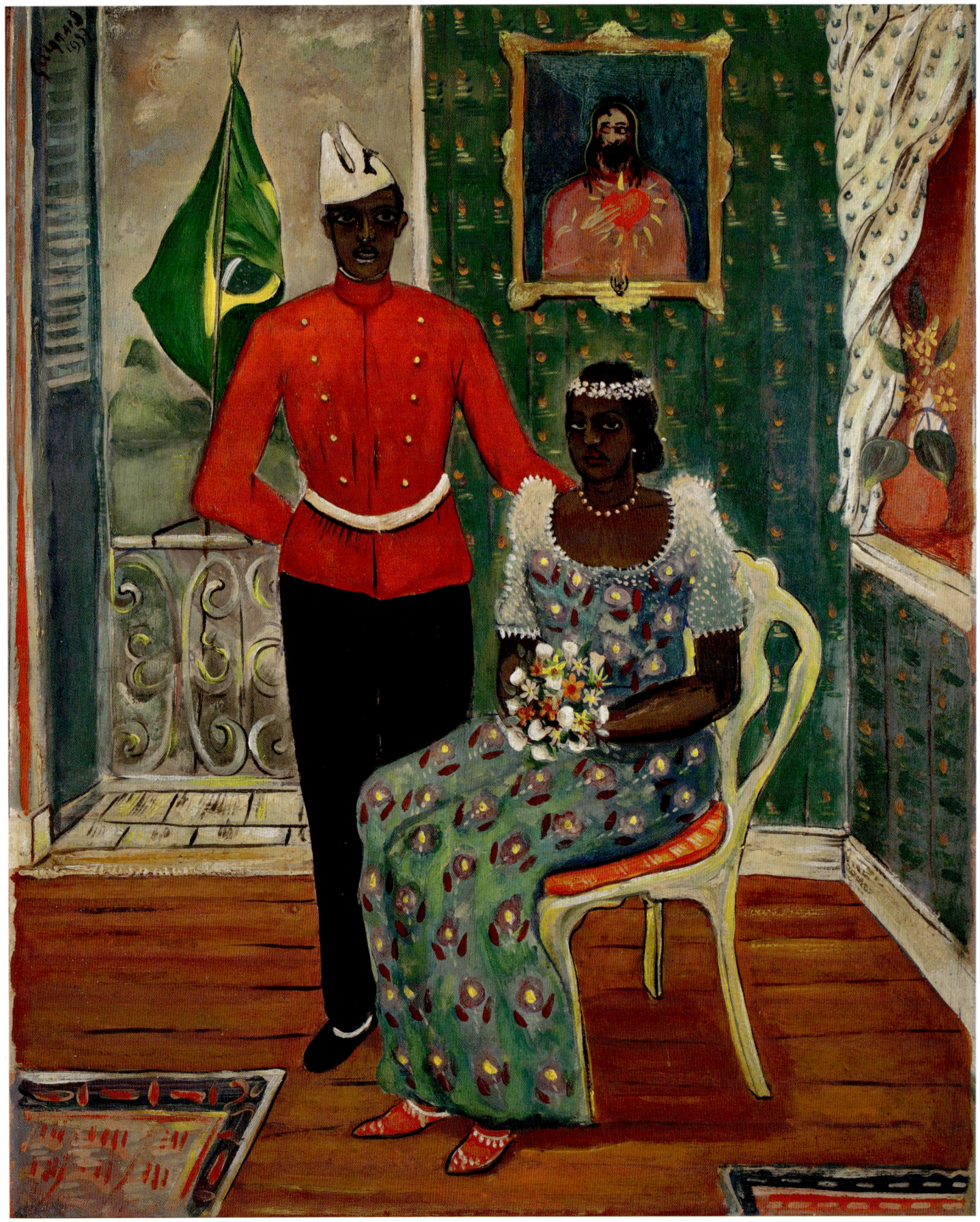

167

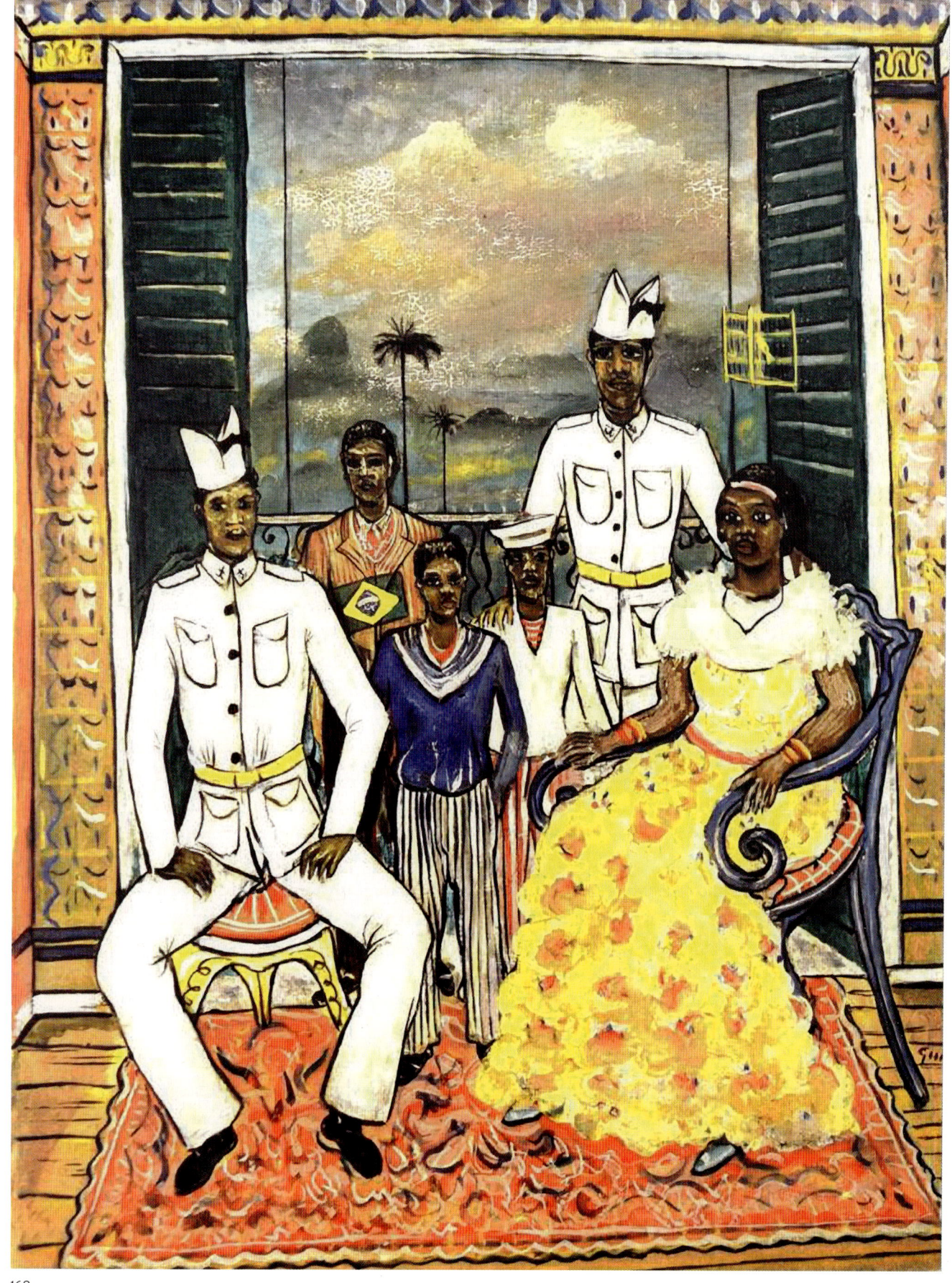

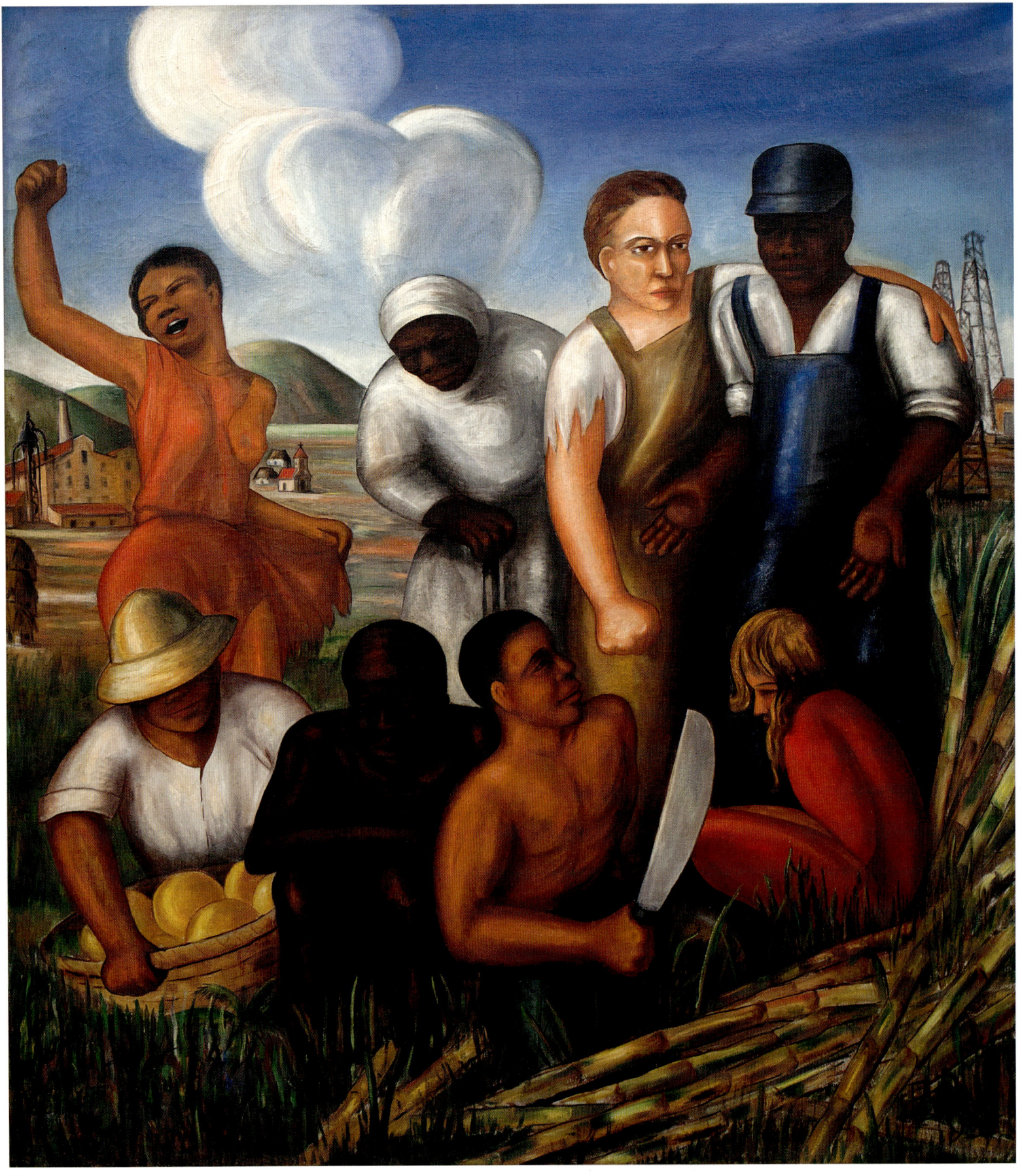
169

169 Alberto Peña (Peñita). *Workers*. 1934. Oil on canvas. Havana, Museo Nacional de Bellas Artes de Cuba.

170 Alberto Peña (Peñita). *Cuba on the March*. 1936. Oil on burlap. Coral Gables, FL, Cernuda Arte.

171 Alberto Peña (Peñita). *The Calling of the Ideal, or Martí*. 1936. Oil on canvas. Havana, Museo Nacional de Bellas Artes de Cuba.

Artists such as Portinari in Brazil or Mariano Rodríguez in Cuba tried to capture pictorially the mestizo essence of the new nation, to "represent in pictures that which is transcendentally Cuban" or particular to the cultural experience of a distinct national community.[105] Their shared emphasis on oversized hands and feet, often anchored in the earth, reflects a stylistic convention that points, of course, to muralism and further to Picasso, but that found vivid expression across the region. Mariano traveled to Mexico in 1936, where Juan Marinello, one of the editors of *Avance*, introduced him to the circle of Diego Rivera and where he studied with Manuel Rodríguez Lozano (1897–1971), at the time director of the Escuela Nacional de Artes Plásticas.[106] In Mexico he participated in the National Congress of Artists and Writers organized by LEAR, where he probably came across the Colombian painter Ignacio Gómez Jaramillo, who was part of the group. Mariano's early works display what he described as "muralist forms," with massive mestizo figures anchored in the Cuban countryside. These figures are typically barefoot, as in *Unidad* (*Unity*, 1938) and *Pareja con bueyes* (*Couple with Oxen*, 1939) (see fig. 164) to signal their humble social extraction, as well as Mariano's own communist sympathies. It is a synthesis that built on previous efforts to represent Cuba as a mestizo nation, notably exemplified by Victor Manuel's female portraits in the style of his famous aforementioned *Gitana tropical*.

An indirect connection exists between Victor Manuel and Mariano: the Afro-Cuban painter Alberto Peña. Peñita, as he was known, was a disciple of Victor Manuel, and he was also a teacher of Mariano, who took classes with him before going to Mexico. Influenced by Mexican muralism and revolutionary art, Peñita developed a body of work that represents a strong denunciation of social and racial injustices in Cuba.[107] His paintings are populated by manual workers of all shades, as illustrated by his *Trabajadores* (*Workers*, 1934), but Black subjects figure prominently, frequently as protagonists of labor struggles and of national history more generally. Some of these themes were prominently displayed at an art exhibit that he shared with the Afro-Cuban sculptor Teodoro Ramos Blanco (1902–1972) at the prestigious Club Atenas in 1936. Three of the paintings in that exhibit, *La protesta* (*The Protest*), *Cuba en marcha* (*Cuba on the March*), and *La llamada del ideal* (*The Calling of the Ideal*), portray forms of multiracial popular mobilization that seek to fulfill the foundational dreams of Cuban patriots, both white (José Martí, in the case of *The Calling*) and Black (Antonio Maceo in *The Protest*). Here, Peñita articulates a critical reading of the national ideologies of mestizaje and racial fraternity, suggesting, as he clearly does in *Cuba on the March*, that the future of justice and racial equality still needs to be constructed and that it can only be achieved through struggle and mobilization. Sugar workers, who he depicts as modern-day enslaved laborers in *Los nuevos esclavos del ingenio* (*The New Slaves of the Sugarmill*), are the architects of that envisioned future.

One of the most celebrated paintings in the Club Atenas exhibition, Peñita's *Mater Dolorosa*, represents an old, poor, tired Black woman who, despite her advanced age, still labors in order to survive. Peñita uses a Black female figure to denounce a society that cannot provide for those whose labor made the nation possible to begin with. "This poor woman," the critic Enrique Andreu wrote, "is not a woman: it is a piece of our history… This woman is the soul of the black race; the strength and the vigor of our race, that survives despite all adversities… until it fulfills its historic

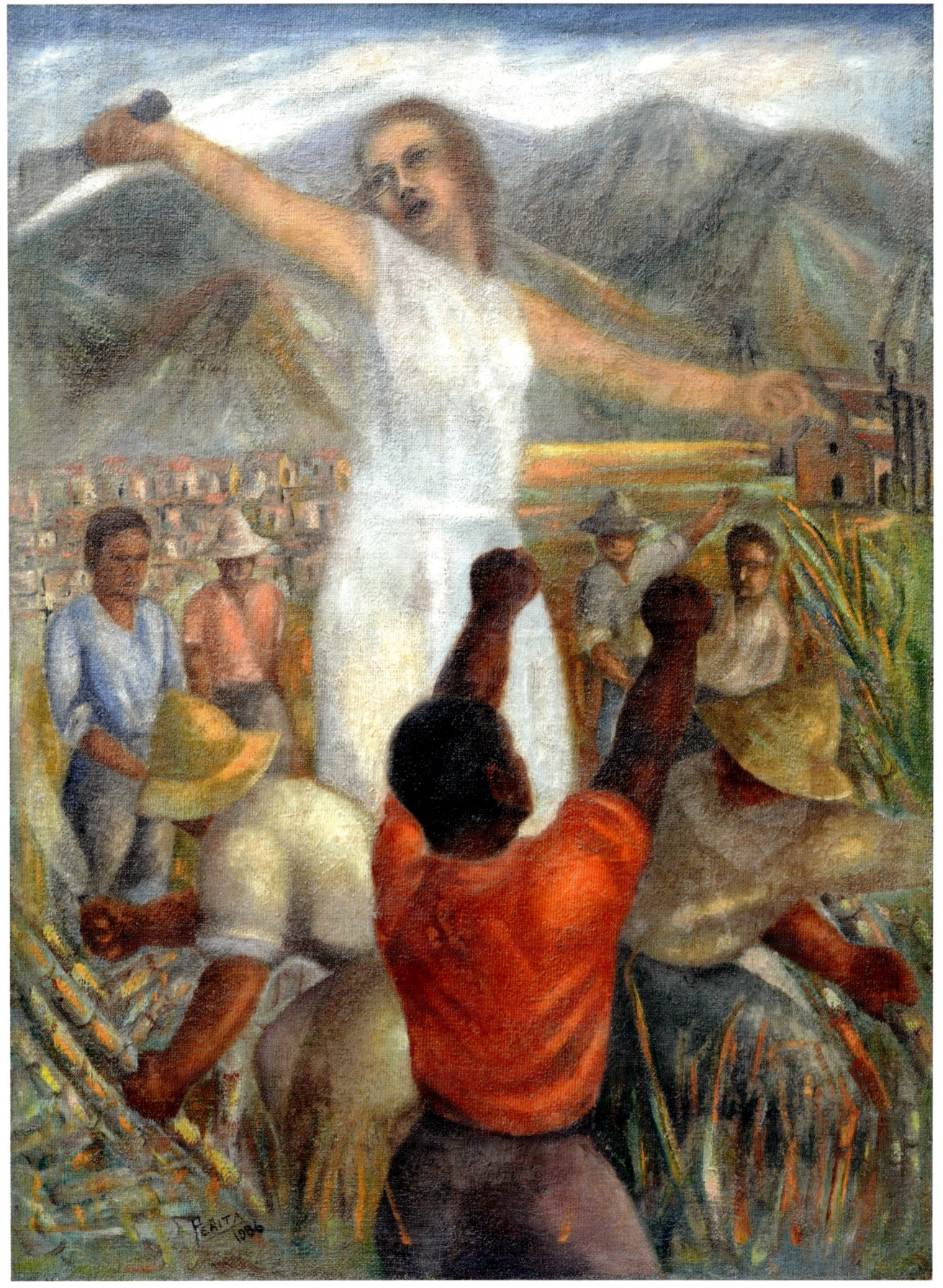

170

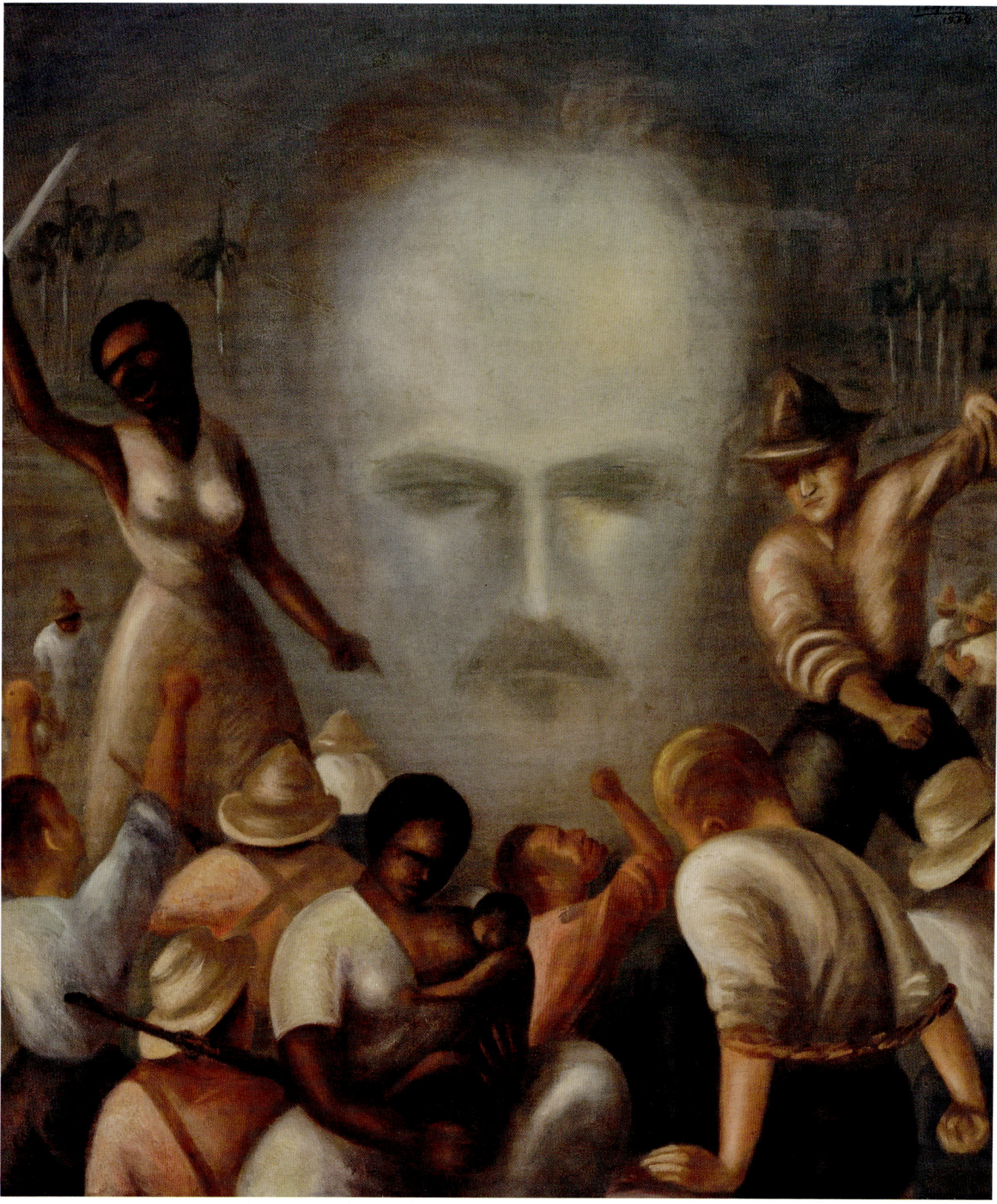

171

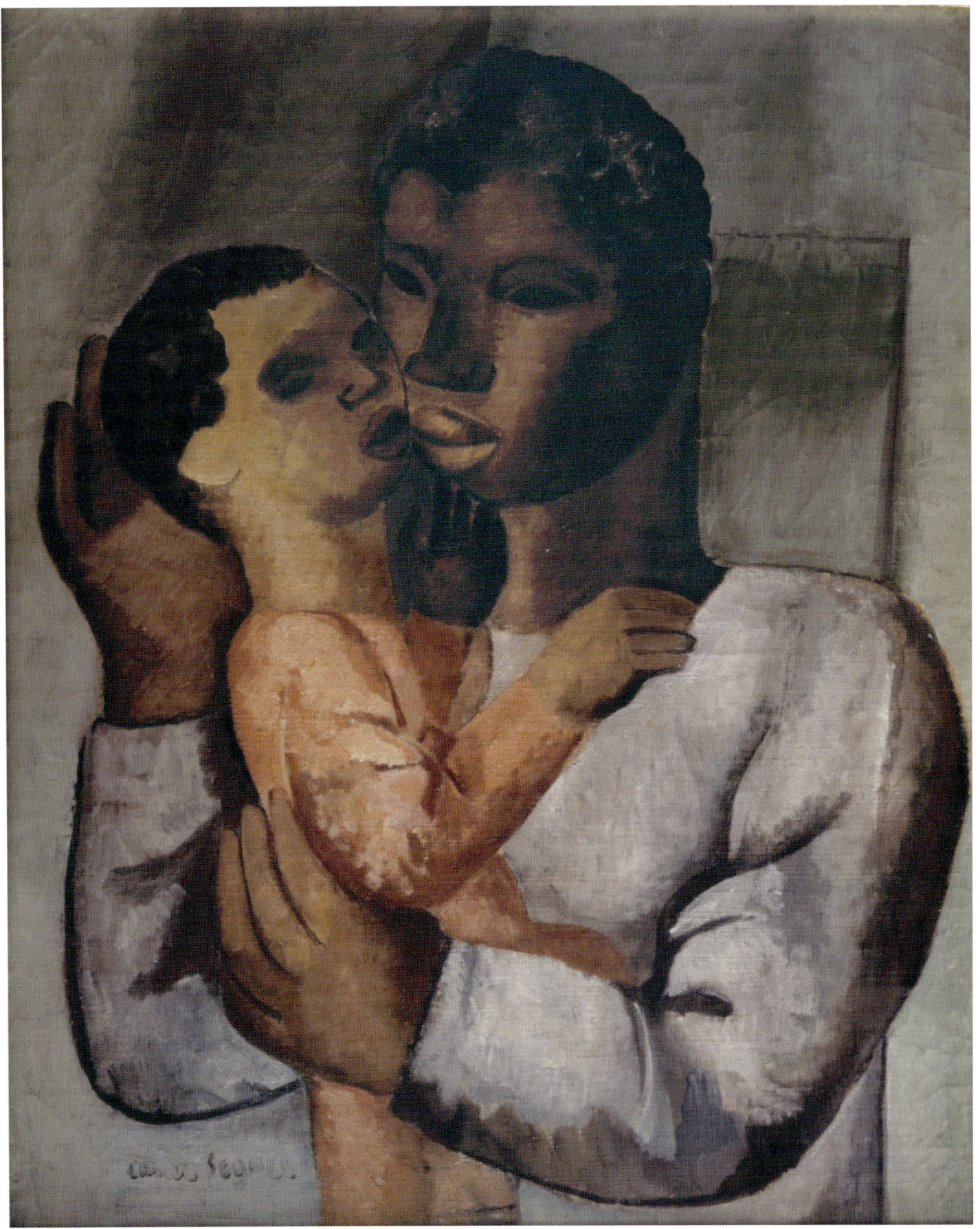

172

172 Lasar Segall. *Black Mother*. 1930. Oil on canvas. Private collection.

mission."[108] In *Sin trabajo* (*Unemployed*), Peñita resorts again to a Black female figure. The trope of Black womanhood used up by labor and abuse resonates deeply in the pictorial tradition of modern Latin America. It is present, just below the surface, in Tarsila's *A negra*, a work that alludes mutely to the tradition of Black nursemaids for white babies, a subject that was directly addressed by Lasar Segall (1891–1957) in the painting *Mãe preta* (*Black Mother*) of 1930.[109] It recurs in the tired faces of the prostitutes so often portrayed by Di Cavalcanti or Segall. It resurfaces, time and again, in the visual cliché of a woman balancing a large can of water on her head while she climbs the steps or slope of a hillside. This modern archetype of Brazilian life appears repeatedly in twentieth-century representations—from the popular illustrations of J. Carlos (1884–1950) to the woodcuts of Oswaldo Goeldi (1895–1961) and Renina Katz (b. 1925) to the paintings of Portinari and Carybé (1911–1997)—as a metonym for life in the favelas. Such images of long-suffering Black and brown women point to a deeper fissure in the social body, as exemplified in the Cuban painter Carlos Enríquez's (1900–1957) problematic *El rapto de las mulatas* (*The Abduction of the Mulatto Women*, 1938), where rape becomes a metaphor for nation making. The culture of machismo is such that the same avant-garde artists who championed the poor and oppressed were often quite willing to locate the idea of the nation on the sexualized bodies of Afrodescendant women.

A different brand of Black radicalism informed the work of the other artist in the 1936 Club Atenas exhibition, the sculptor Ramos Blanco. As the Afro-Cuban communist activist and writer Salvador García Agüero noted, the main concern of Ramos Blanco's work was to offer a new "concept and execution of blackness in art," one able to capture Black subjectivities beyond the picturesque and superficial representations of many vanguardia artists.[110] These explorations led to several superb pieces in marble, terracotta, and wood, such as *Vida interior* (*Internal Life*, 1934) and *Negra vieja* (*Old Black Woman*, 1936), a piece that was acquired by New York's MoMA in the 1940s. Speaking of this piece, Ramos Blanco distinguished between those artists who offered external representations of Blackness and his own work:

> Black form has been interpreted, or to be precise has been dealt with by great artists, but they have only achieved the exterior part, without content. They have given us the vessel, but visibly empty; they have lacked emotion and when they have tried to feel it, it has looked fake to us, as something neither felt nor experienced. Let us say that it was a matter of fashion or 'snobbism'.... How different is the effect when the form is interpreted—and now the expression is valid—by a sincere artist who is proud of his inspiration.... The touch is not about making a white or yellow form painted of black; you must feel it, model its expression, its rhythm, its beauty, its interior. And even if it is made of white marble, the form will be black because its essence is black.[111]

The choice of white stone for Ramos Blanco's *Internal Life* thereby sets up a strategic contrast with sculptures carved out of dark materials, including ebony, like several titled generically *Cabeza de negro* (*Head of a Black Man*) or *Cabeza de mujer* (*Head of a Woman*) made by the Venezuelan artist Francisco Narváez (1905–1982) in the 1930s. Their simplified shapes and showcas-

173 Teodoro Ramos Blanco. *Internal Life*. 1934. Marble. Havana, Museo Nacional de Bellas Artes de Cuba.

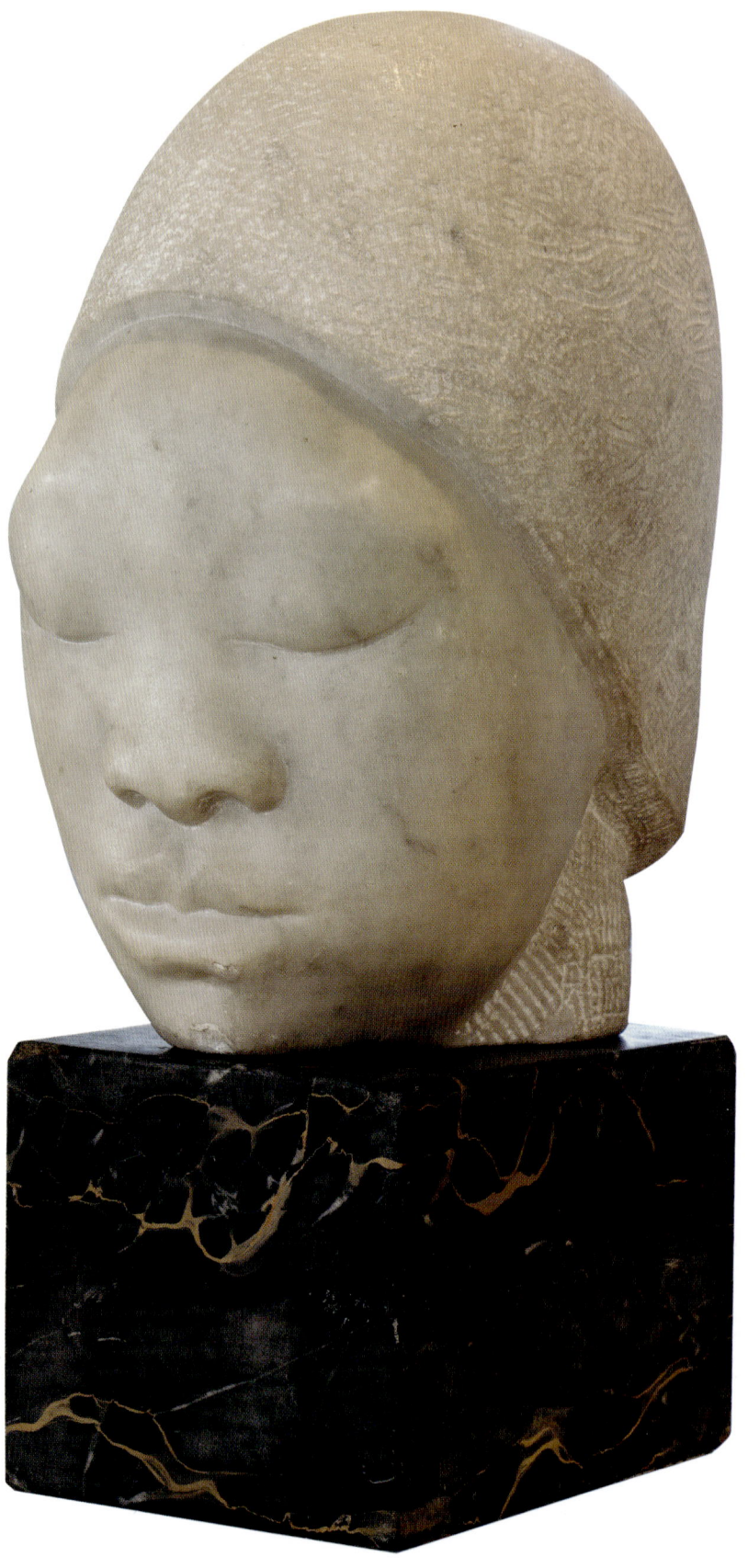

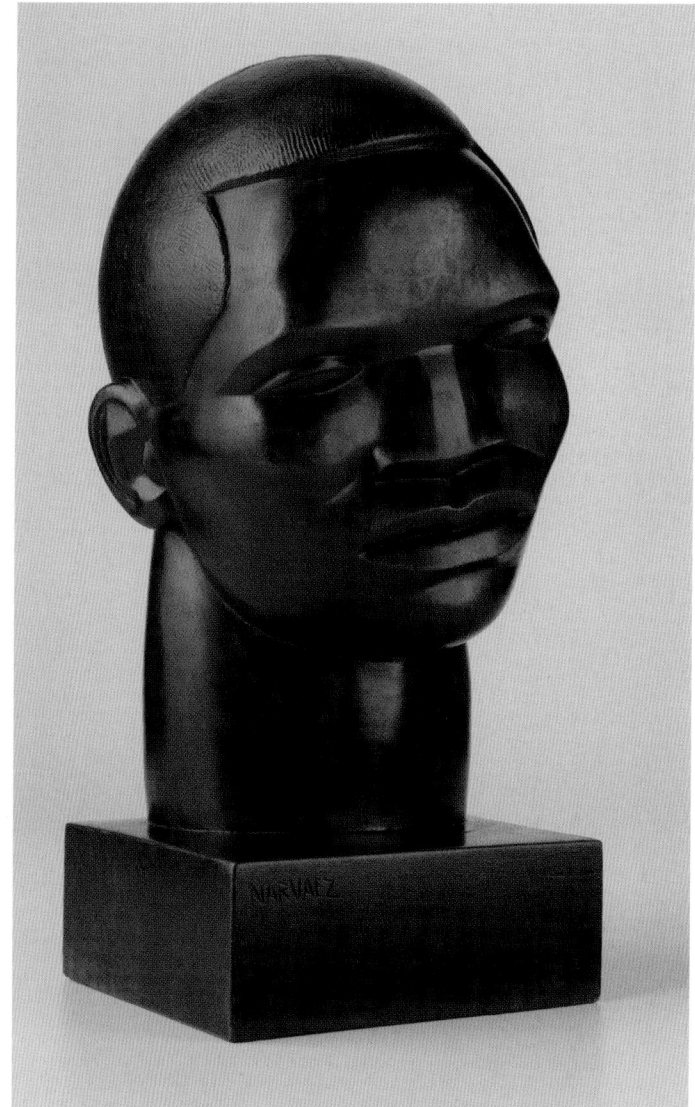

174 Francisco Narvaéz. *Head of a Black Man*. 1935. Carved ebony. Location unknown.

ing of material qualities echo the Romanian sculptor Constantin Brancusi's 1920s renditions of *La négresse blanche* (*The White Negress*, 1923), in marble and *La négresse blonde* (*The Blond Negress*, 1926) in polished bronze, thus suggesting how deeply convoluted issues of the representation of Blackness had become by then— Black artists shaping white heads of Black people; white artists shaping Black heads of Black people. Exactly what constituted Négritude, and who was authorized to claim it, were issues up for grabs in the 1920s and 1930s.

Ramos Blanco also executed numerous public monuments, starting with one devoted to Mariana Grajales, the mother of the Afro-Cuban leader Antonio Maceo, for which he won a national competition in 1928. The editors of *Avance* criticized Ramos Blanco's design as "mediocre," but the prize allowed him to travel to Europe and to complete the work in 1931.[112] He continued to render tribute to other prominent Afro-Cuban figures, including monuments to Juan Gualberto Gómez (1931) and the Pantheon at Cacahual, devoted to Antonio Maceo and Panchito Gómez Toro (1944). In 1943 he completed a bust of Haitian President Alexandre Pétion that was placed in Parque de la Fraternidad in Havana.[113] In the 1950s Ramos Blanco also executed several busts of Antonio Maceo that clearly portray the Afro-Cuban patriot and warrior as a subject with a rich intellect. The works of Peñita and Ramos Blanco exemplify how avant-garde representations of race

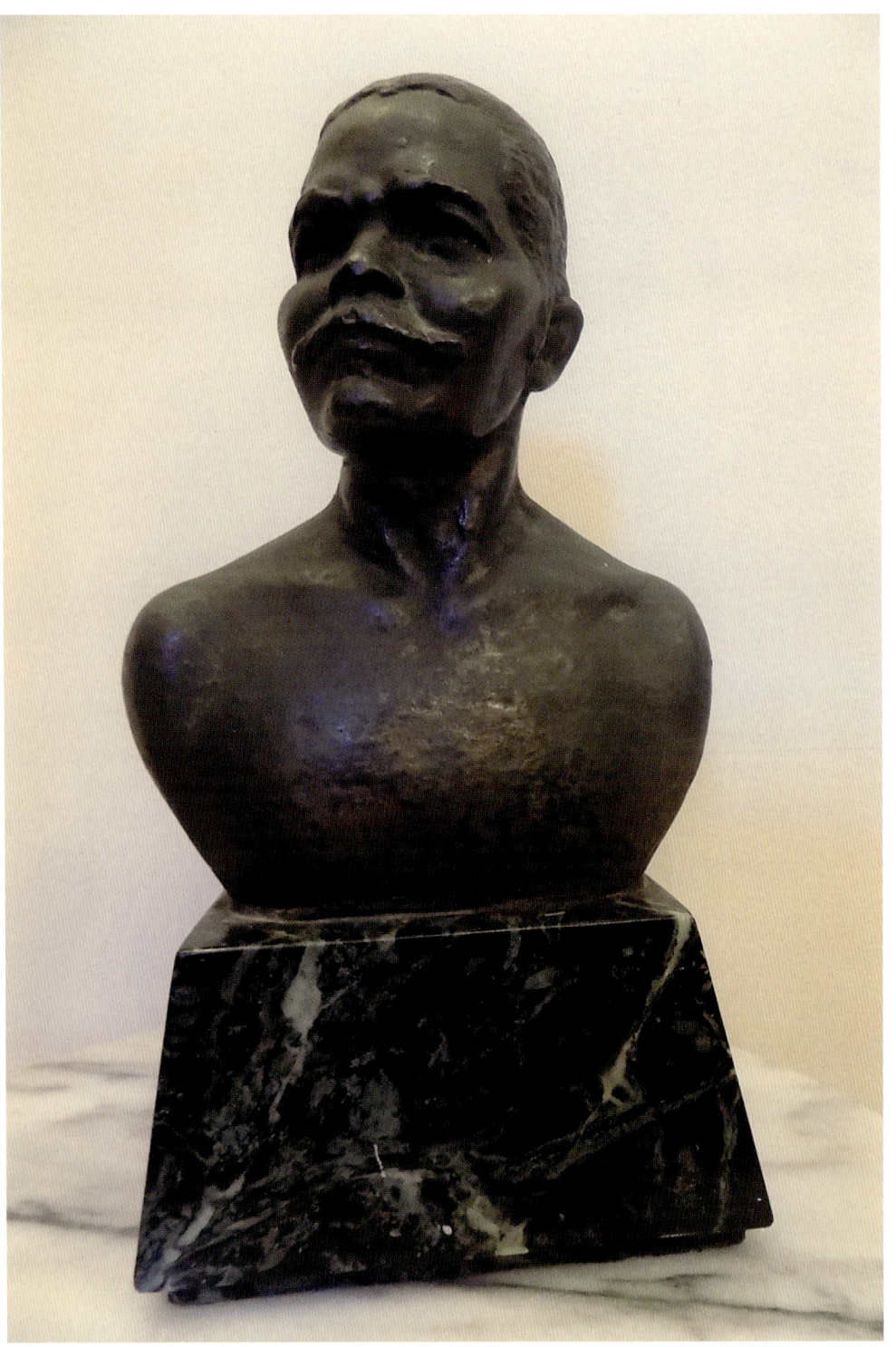

175

175 Teodoro Ramos Blanco. *Antonio Maceo*. 1950s. Bronze on green marble base. Boston, Collection of Alejandro de la Fuente and Patricia González.

and Blackness could be complex and contradictory. Some artists conveyed representations of Black subjects that bordered on caricatures. These caricatures reinforced ingrained preconceptions of Blacks as sexualized, magical, primitive, and musical beings. But there were other possibilities, as illustrated by Peñita and Ramos Blanco, whose works are a far cry from the voyeuristic auto-primitivism that guided the work of many artist of the vanguardias. And here lies, precisely, the importance of these literary and artistic movements. Despite their problematic approaches to race and Blackness, they created spaces that Afrodescendant artists could inhabit, providing new, critical insights into the Black experience.

White artists who somehow experienced oppression and marginality also came to engage with the representation of Blackness in unexpected ways. Lasar Segall, a painter and printmaker of Lithuanian Jewish origin who emigrated from Germany to Brazil in 1923, is perhaps the best example. The painting *Encontro* (*Encounter*, 1924), completed soon after his arrival in São Paulo, includes a self-portrait in which Segall depicts his skin considerably darkened, almost Black, in stark contrast with the light skin of the female figure in the composition. This action has been interpreted as an attempt to blend in with his new surroundings and an expression of self-identification with the other, deriving from his own experience as an immigrant and outsider.[114] The extent to which Segall's attitude differs from the exoticizing gaze of other European painters is open to debate. There is no shortage of depictions of racial types in his oeuvre—generic "negros" and "mulattos"—including woodcuts of the late 1920s that approximate Black faces with African masks, very much in the German expressionist mold in which he was formed as an artist. Paintings like *Menino com lagartixas* (*Boy with Geckos*, 1924) and *Bananal* (*Banana Grove*, 1927) repeat the visual cliché of associating Afrodescendant subjects with tropical flora and fauna. Yet in both these pictures, the sitters return the viewer's gaze with a notable degree of agency. Though engulfed by the foliage that fills the compositions, their subjectivity manages to filter through the artist's observation and rendering of difference.

Segall's painting *Morro vermelho* (*Red Hill*, 1926) provides an unusual representation of a Black mother, reminiscent of the Christian iconography of the Madonna and baby Jesus.[115] The mother and child are depicted in full-body length, framed by palm trees on both sides and other tropical vegetation in the foreground, with the blue sea and an orange sunset visible in the background. The largest part of the composition is covered by a receding red plane on which houses are stacked, favela-style— the red hill of the title more suggested than depicted. Though the position of her body indicates the woman is seated, nothing is shown upon which she might sit. Rather, she hovers over the landscape, disproportionately large in relation to the buildings, as if she were an apparition. Mother and child are almost fused into one. The contours of their clothing and skin overlap in planes of color that make it difficult, at first, to tell where one body ends and the other begins. The child's red smock echoes the color of the surrounding ground, as if he were made of the same stuff as the hill. Nestled in the mother's arms, it is almost as if she were cradling the hill itself and the houses that rest upon it. She is a saintly protector figure, not so unusual in the Catholic imaginary of Latin America, except for the fact that she is Black and the painter, Jewish. Segall's Madonna stares out at the viewer with a deadpan expression. She is young and strong and dignified, a

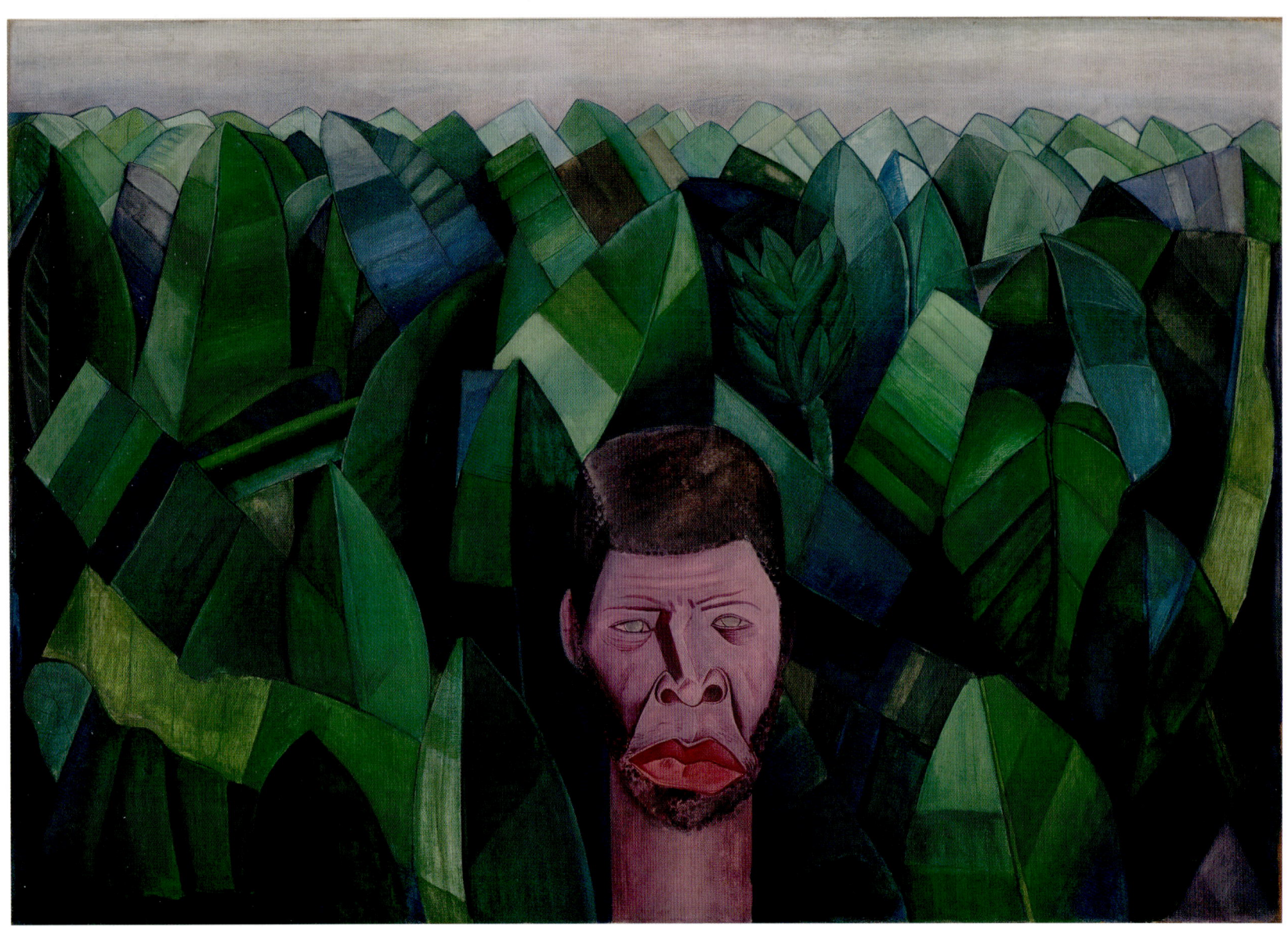

176

176 Lasar Segall. *Banana Grove*. 1927. Oil on canvas. Pinacoteca do Estado de São Paulo.

177 Lasar Segall. *Red Hill*. 1926. Oil on canvas. São Paulo, Private collection.

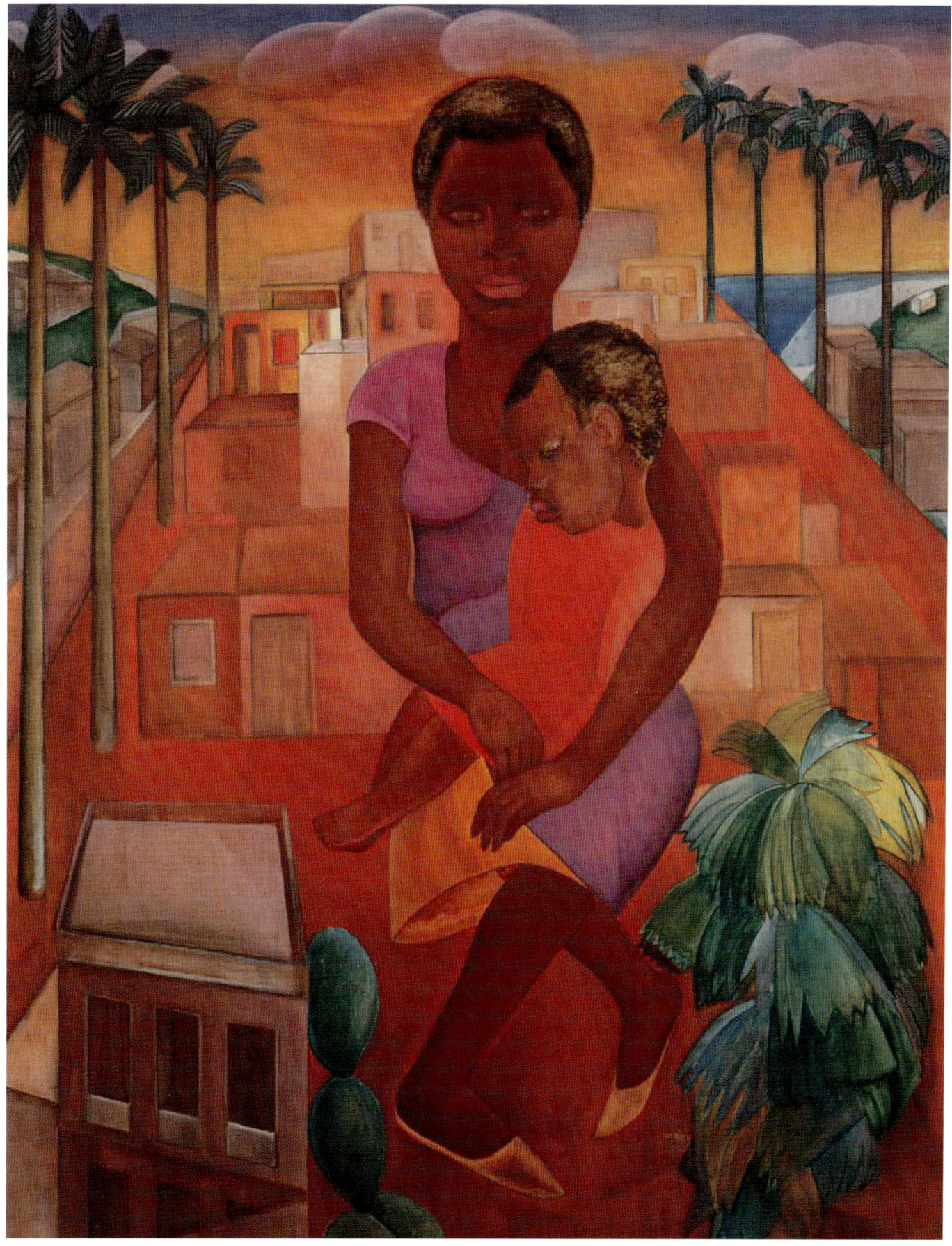
177

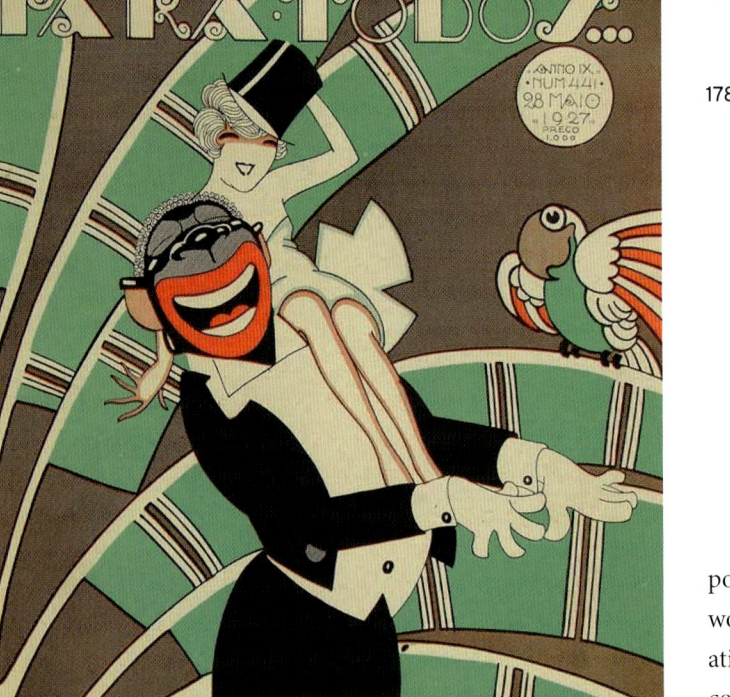

178 J. Carlos, cover of the periodical *Para Todos* (May 28, 1927).

powerful antidote to depictions of downtrodden Afrodescendant women so prevalent in the region's history. Elevated to the hieratic and symbolic stature of a religious icon, she embodies the cosmic ascension of the race.

The very exceptionality of the central figure in *Red Hill* begs a number of questions that open avenues for further research. Why should it be surprising to see a Black woman represented as a figure of inspiration and not oppression? What made an outsider like Segall capable of capturing the inner dimension of the very "other" Black subjects he represented, whereas many local and even Afrodescendant artists never went beyond the depiction of types and archetypes? Why should Black figures be seen primarily as "a realist element," as Oswald de Andrade phrased it in his 1923 lecture at the Sorbonne, cited in one epigraph to this text? Must the representation of Afro-Latinness always refer to a collective condition, as opposed to an individual one? Oswald de Andrade's statement was preceded by the contention that "The reaction against South American loquaciousness was staged in Brazil by black blood."[116] This somewhat cryptic remark implies that the silence and suffering of the Black experience operates as a counterpoint and corrective to the discursive excesses of high culture. It also infers, logically, that "black blood" is somehow separate from the essential nature of American identities, a later addition reacting against a preexisting order, rather than a constituent part of the cultural self. Oswald de Andrade affirms this explicitly, arguing in the lecture that Brazilian identity was initially formed by three elements: "the Indian, the Portuguese and the Latin priest. A little later, came the African negro."[117] Though arguable as a historical fact, this reading distinctly underplays the centrality of African heritage to Brazilian cultural identity. Taken in conjunction, Oswald's statements of 1923 consign Blackness to the margins, a mute emblem of nature and existence, seen but not heard, like tiny figures in the foreground of a landscape.

Throughout the iconographic tradition, both in Latin America and in Europe, Black figures appear frequently in incidental and supporting roles. More infrequently, as in the examples discussed here, they take on the role of protagonists. More often than not, though, they remain representatives of a type or a cause, rather than individuals fully developed in their human complexity. In considering the place of race in the representations generated by Latin America's avant-gardes, it is imperative to bear in mind the powerful undercurrent of mass culture—modernism's "repressed other," as famously phrased by Andreas Huyssen.[118] Awash in a sea of racist stereotypes, caricatures, cartoons, films, and the like, avant-garde artists faced the immense challenge of extracting Black subjects from the invisibility imposed upon them by centuries of enslavement and finding ways of making them visible, at whatever cost. Inevitably, many fell into the trap of confirming the very assumptions they sought to challenge. The task is an ongoing one. To deny distinctions based on race is to perpetuate inequality. To affirm them unequivocally deepens ancient divides. This is the dilemma we continue to face in discussions of race and its representation today.

11

IMAGE OF THE BLACK AND MORE: VISUAL THOUGHT AND CREATIVE EXPRESSION IN THE CARIBBEAN AND BRAZIL, 1939–1959

YOLANDA WOOD

> ... you are always in transit ...
> —George Lamming, *The Pleasures of Exile*

Past and Present, Thought and Discourse

This study is focused on the historical era between the outbreak of the Second World War in 1939 and the triumph of the Cuban Revolution on January 1, 1959. During that period, in which international hegemonies were reordered, a process of decolonization began that led to revolutionary action, and a line of thought developed that brought forth the image of the Black subject as a figure in early and contemporary history. Homi K. Bhabha defines the Black person as a "colonial subject who is historicized in the heterogeneous assemblage of the texts of history, literature, science, myth," and George Lamming writes that "[…] when we say Negro, there is no biological meaning whatsoever, nor is it used in the service of racial applause. When we say Negro, it is the name of a historical experience."[1] The self-recognition and appreciation of Black identity, so mistreated by colonial history, devalued and demonized by systems of domination, led to a conceptual florescence. An impressive diversity of creative expression became internationalized and circulated through new channels, resulting in cultural innovations and visionary crossings.

This generated ambiguities and ambivalences, an ontologizing of the production of meaning in interpretive systems, and the use of designations that revealed the permanent "interstitial zone" of cultural differences in the polemical contexts of the decolonizing process.[2]

The chronological endpoints mean little in and of themselves, but in that period, there was a resurgence of the role of Black subjects and their history around the Caribbean and the immense country of Brazil. Here I will attempt to define the relevance of a visual discourse that began while many of the island territories were still under colonial rule. Although World War II resulted in some changes in the status of colonies in Africa,[3] Asia, and some Caribbean islands—for instance, decolonization processes began that led to changes in the status of the French Overseas Territories in 1946 and for Puerto Rico in 1952, when it was redefined as a commonwealth (in Spanish *estado libre asociado*, or free associated state)—the general tendency was the persistence of colonial and neocolonial status through the commercial and financial restructuring and new power alignments brought about by the war through agencies such as the World Bank and the International Monetary Fund, which were meant to regulate and administer the global economy.[4] Such changes sharpened the social and racial contradictions in places where, as a result of their histories as dependent plantation societies during the era of the triangular Atlantic trade, a large population of enslaved people had been concentrated. That historical experience was part of the legacy of colonialism, which continued to be marked by discrimination and exclusion as expressions of violence, the structures of power, and complex interracial contradictions.[5]

The territories of the Greater Antilles that were already politically independent were still in a dependent economic relationship with the United States, which supported dictatorial figures that were regrettably emblematic of the twentieth century: Fulgencio Batista in Cuba; François Duvalier in Haiti; and Rafael Trujillo in the Dominican Republic. Brazil, meanwhile, continued to be guided by the nationalist tendencies of Getúlio Vargas until the end of World War II, renewed when he took power again in 1950, at a point when industrial and military investments by their huge neighbor to the north grew more important there.

In Brazil, Cuba, and other large Caribbean islands that had a greater degree of racial mixing—more than in Haiti, Jamaica, and the Lesser Antilles—a discourse of nationalism and national identity consolidated artistic processes that had already begun. In varying degrees according to the specific historical, cultural, and aesthetic-artistic factors in their ethno-racial makeup, all those "New Peoples," as Darcy Ribeiro defined them, highlighted the Afrodescendant component in their national identity.[6] A common liberating idea connected the present and the past not in a linear way, but instead as a conceptual framework that marked out an image of the Black subject in the national cultures—even though some were not yet republics with their own flags and constitutions.

The creative authenticity of these people was a significant aspect of their condition. It was a subjective "I" which defined itself from a position of exclusion to give voice and image to millions of silenced people and to their imaginations. Other Black, white, or mixed-race people were sensitive observers, and in addition to bringing to their art their own experiences, they turned to oral, documentary, and literary sources to re-create a connection of the present to the past with social and anthropological resources, poetic tropes, and new epistemological perspectives.

That decolonizing and declarative revaluation shows the construction of a discourse of new ideas that was generated from within. According to the interpretive proposals of the scholar Nelson Maldonado-Torres regarding the role of the Caribbean in the decolonizing turn, that discourse involved the subjects' awareness of themselves, their conditions of existence, and their ability to use social and cultural imaginaries to deconstruct the established system of power in order to decolonize knowledge and being, through a new logic of discourse and other ways of relating the subjects to themselves, to history, and to their own circumstances.

Through these critical changes, the relative intellectual isolation of those who were dispersed over the islands or in Europe while they completed their artistic education and maturation came to an end. The emergence of institutions and mechanisms of internal and international cultural circulation, such as conferences, journals, and other media, created points of contact.[7] During World War II, some people returned to their home territories or relocated to neighboring countries. These processes forged intellectual networks in the Americas, especially in the Caribbean and Brazil. Others made connections with African intellectuals such as Léopold Sédar Senghor (1906–2001); in Europe with André Breton (1896–1966), Claude Levi-Strauss (1908–2009), and others; or with artists in the United States, the home of the Harlem Renaissance movement, which was held in high esteem by intellectuals and artists in the Caribbean and Brazil, and was an important context for these developments. On the new cultural map of the postwar era, the United States acquired new hegemonic connotations. Some figures moved there, notably Breton, and several important exhibitions took place. The art of Africa and the African diaspora had been of interest in the West beginning with its use by the European vanguard during the first half of the twentieth century.[8] In 1946, the Pan-American Union established its Visual Arts Unit, and the Museum of Modern Art and other institutions gave special attention to the "black arts" of the Caribbean and Brazil. In those places of encounter and contestation, new conflicts of otherness and identity were evident in the discourses that crossed paths. In those critical frameworks, the image of the Black became prominent in the arts and much more.

Return in Order to Be: Image and Representation
In 1922, Edna Manley (1900–1987) arrived in Jamaica. Born in England to a Jamaican mother, she went to the island after receiving artistic training in London, where she was heavily influenced by cubism and art deco. Her marriage to Norman Manley, the co-founder of the People's National Party and later the island's premier, afforded her a prominent place on Jamaica's social and cultural scene. Her work slowly evolved toward a new iconography very interested in the physiognomy of Black men and women, emphasizing their inner strength, the body language of workers and market vendors, and the rituals of the Afro-Jamaican folk religion Pocomania. In 1940 she established the Jamaica School of Art and was a strong supporter of the Institute of Jamaica. By the early 1940s she had made fundamental contributions to the visual arts. "Beginning with *Negro Aroused*, carved in 1935 [see fig. 203], followed by *The Prophet*, *Young Negro*, *Pocomania*, and *The Diggers*, a new symbolic focus enters her work [...] The Jamaican press was enthusiastic, a public fund was started, and *Negro Aroused*, the key carving of the exhibition, was acquired for the Institute of Jamaica to form the nucleus of a permanent gallery."[9]

About these works, the artist and art historian David Boxer has written, "With their powerful insistent rhythms which frame the essential leitmotif of the head turned back, straining upward towards a vision, or downward in suppressed anger... [they] have truly become the icons of that period of our history, a period when the black Jamaican was indeed aroused, ready for a new social order, demanding his place in the sun."[10]

Manley's works established a new visual imagery that insisted on portraying Black subjects with their social identity. Her pieces were a great success when they were exhibited in Kingston in 1937, as well as in London the following year. The poet George Campbell (1918–2002), in his poem "Negro Aroused," wrote:

Negro Aroused! Awakened from
The ignominious sleep of dominance!
Freedom! Off with these shackles
That torment. I lift my head and scream to heaven
Freedom! Now my blood rushes through my veins
And boils up in my head at their insult.
The spirit of freedom is resurrected in me

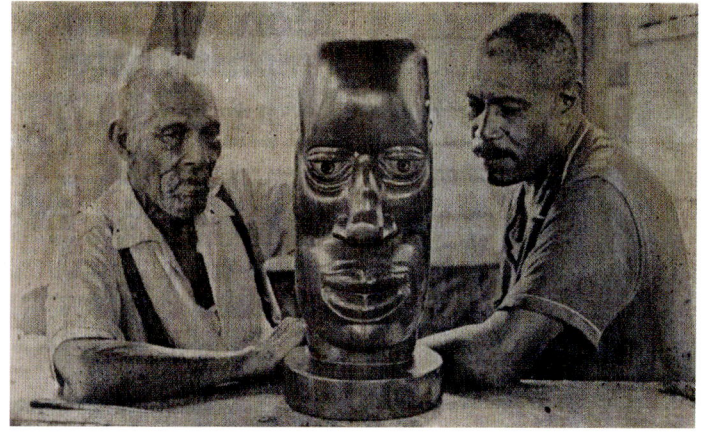

179 Unidentified photographer. *The Millers*. 1964. Published in *The Gleaner* and at the National Gallery of Jamaica Blog. Kingston, National Gallery of Jamaica.

I lift my head and cry to heaven defiance,
Freedom! Let them beat down this house,
Muscle built, stifle this screaming voice,
Let them! We are aroused![11]

That arousal was a sign of the times, as Jamaica was rocked by revolts and demands for political independence. Several original self-taught artists emerged during that period. The paintings of the barber John Dunkley (1891–1947) showed a world which, in the words of Boxer, "would have delighted the Surrealists had they known of them."[12] As Rex Nettleford wrote, with Dunkley and the Millers—David Sr. (1872–1969) and David Jr. (1902–1978)—the Intuitive movement was born with "the socio-political and cultural revolution of the late 1930s, when the artistic movement revealed national life and culture."[13] That tradition must have been a point of reference for the artistic projects of Edna Manley, as sensitive as she was to her surroundings, and these artists gained recognition as emerging figures in popular culture.

In that search for self-expression, the painters Albert Huie (1920–2010), David Pottinger (1911–2007), and Ralph Campbell (1921–1985), as well as the sculptor Alvin Marriott (1902–1992), looked to the customs and public life around them, with emphasis on the people who made up the majority of Jamaicans. For instance, Nine Night, the event depicted in Pottinger's work, is a traditional funerary rite involving music and singing.[14] Fully formed sculptures in wood, especially the busts by David Miller, Jr., portrayed an image of Afrodescendants with great expressive power and celebrated their somatic traits, a racial reification that brought forth a valued Black identity through an ethnic and artistic prototype. The carving *Paul Bogle* by Mallica "Kapo" Reynolds (1911–1989), inspired by the hero of Jamaica's Morant Bay rebellion, also revealed the expression of an ethnic group of color reclaiming its legacy. In the ideals of Marcus Garvey (1887–1940): "The immediate past has attempted to destroy the influence of the glory that is Africa, it has attempted to make us condemn and mistrust the vitality, the vigour, the rhythmic emotionalism that we get from our African ancestors."[15]

That renewed encounter with ancestral Africa was a gesture of historical reconciliation with their origins. For Garvey, Black nationalism based on self-determination and racial pride was an alternative to the exclusion of free Black men and women, the majority of Jamaica's population, who were denied their rights as citizens. The goal of getting "Back to Africa" emerged early in Garvey's program and was central to the Black Star Line, a shipping company he founded, and to those who believed they could return to their point of origin without knowing exactly where that point might be located.[16] When the promise of the shipping line was frustrated, the return acquired a symbolic dimension for the Rastafaris. In a movement that coincided with the emergence of Emperor Haile Selassie, whom the Rastafaris took to be the prophet of Africa's emancipation, the independent kingdom of Ethiopia became the promised land, the place of redemption for a social group that had been uprooted from its origins.

In the marginalized conditions in which Rastafarianism emerged, the body was always the essential locus of the messianic movement's image: "the dreadlock hair style, *I-tal* dietary rules, the ritual use of marijuana, the invention of *Nyahbinghi* music as a sacred rhythm for rituals."[17] All these attributes affected the bodies of people who essentially had nothing, and they used them as the iconographic basis for a Rasta visual culture that was

IMAGE OF THE BLACK AND MORE   305

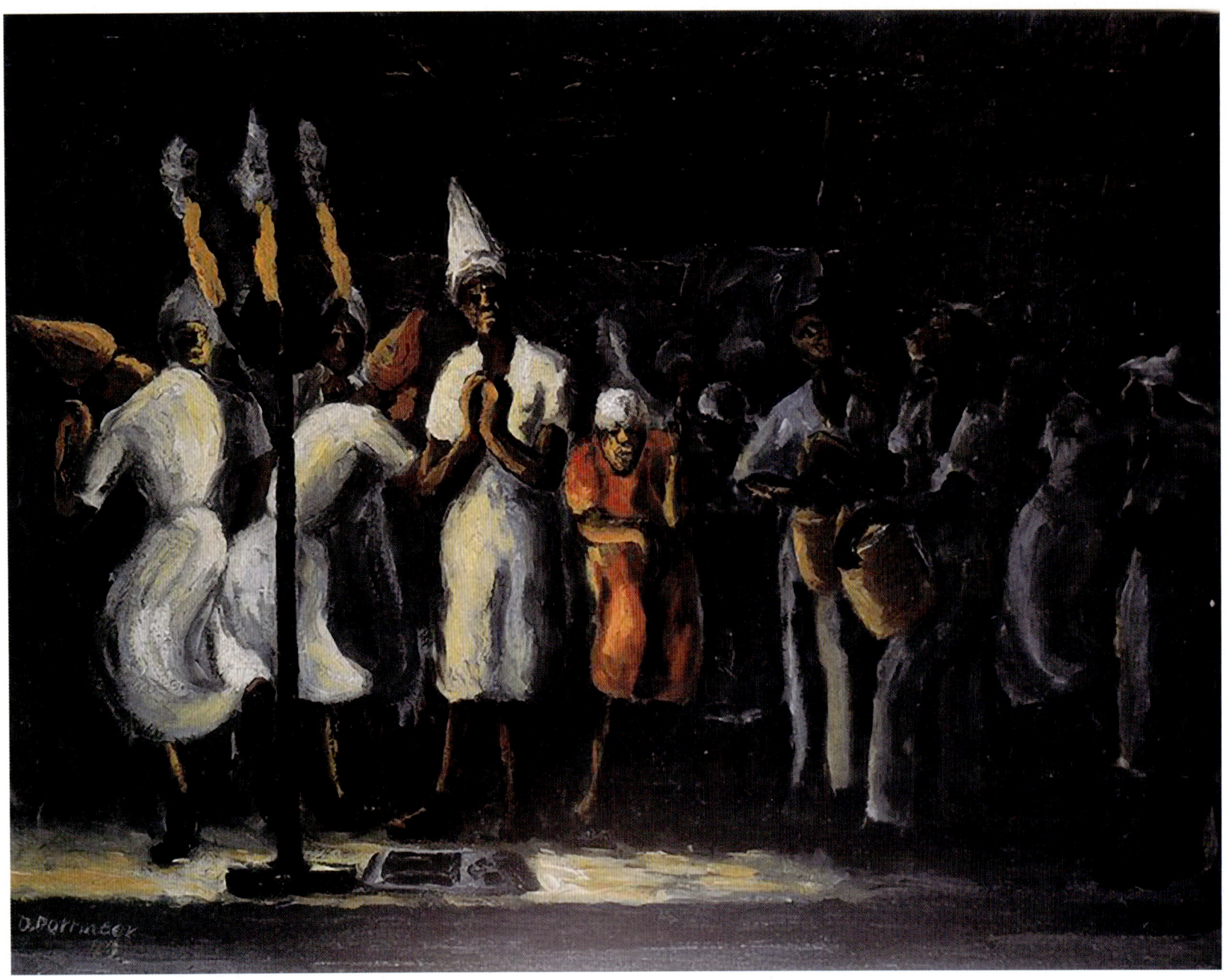

180

180 David Pottinger. *Nine Night*. 1949. Oil. Kingston, National Gallery of Jamaica.

181 Alvin Marriott. *Banana Man*. 1955. Wood. Kingston, National Gallery of Jamaica.

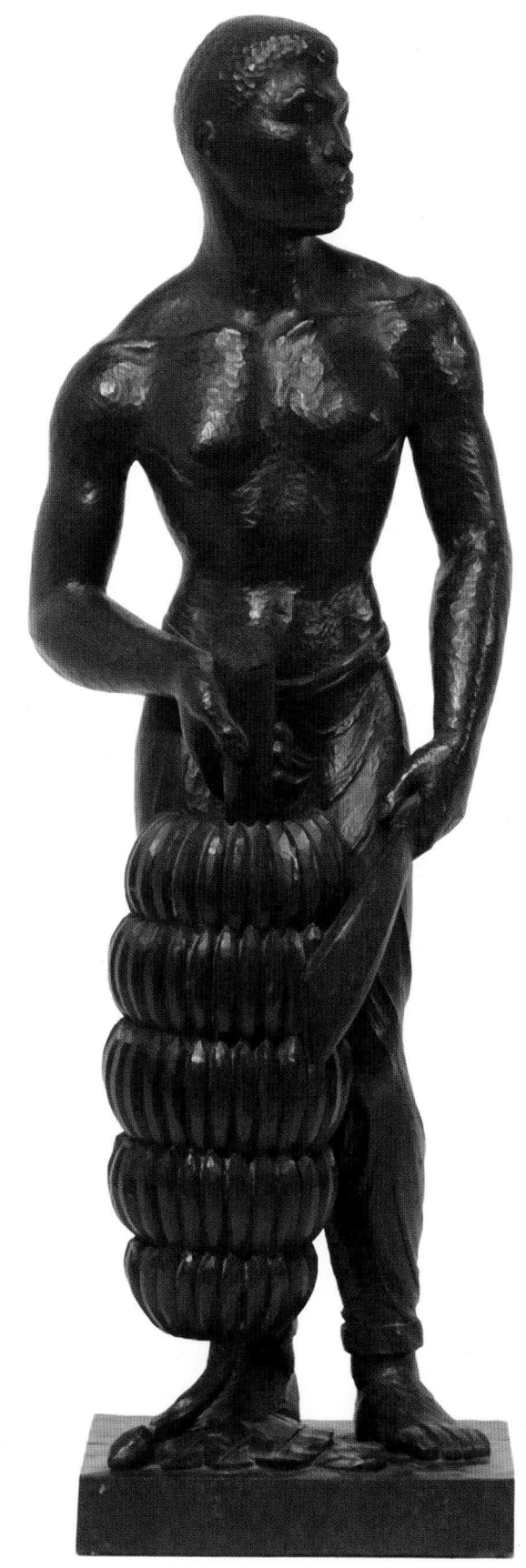

181

182 David Miller, Jr. *Girl Surprised*. 1949. Wood. Kingston, National Gallery of Jamaica.

extended even further with reggae music and its international reach in the following years. The return became a symbolic pilgrimage, an act of social and cultural resistance, and took on various forms in the multiplicity of Caribbean cultures.

In *Cahier d'un retour au pays natal* (*Notebook of a Return to My Native Land*, 1939), a poetic figure returned in the reverse trajectory, when the twenty-six-year-old Martinican Aimé Césaire, "the only great poet," according to Benjamin Péret, "of the French language to appear in the last twenty years," moved back to his island after finishing his studies in France amid the uncertainties of the start of the Second World War.[18] Martinique was still a French colony, and the poet evocatively described his status: "I don't belong to any nationality recognized by the foreign ministries."[19] As reflected in Césaire's writing, the trip was both real and allegorical, a return to one of the islands which, like the others in the Caribbean archipelago, were "stuck in the mud of this bay," an image of stagnation, immobility, and paralysis.[20] The writer returned to revisit his past while awaiting his future, a literary device recurrent in his text. *Cahier* was "an autobiographical book in which I try to take possession of my own self," a trip inward to reconnect, as Césaire said, with an Afrodescendant identity and with an Africa unknown to him. The vastness of the continent was revealed to him through dialogues with Léopold Senghor.[21] Like several Caribbean authors of the period, Césaire, although he had not yet been to Africa, ascribed to the continent a foundational role in his identity and his writing.

Négritude emerged in Césaire's verse like a shout in first-person singular, or in the plural of belonging to a group. He defined it as immersed in "the red flesh of the soil . . . the blazing flesh of the sky," as "neither tower nor cathedral."[22] He went on to write:

You know it is not hate for other races
That makes me work for this unique race.
What I want
Comes from a universal hunger,
From a universal thirst.[23]

René Depestre writes: "The concept of *negritude* has been, at a certain moment in the history of decolonization, the effective response of the exploited and humiliated black man in the face of the universal contempt of the white colonizer. . . . In its most acceptable and legitimate sense, it was fundamentally an awakening" to the double alienation of being black and being a colonial subject.[24] But also, he notes, it was a cultural revelation of the "originality of black African cultures and the aesthetic value of the black race," which in turn led "absurdly" to the appreciation of Afrodescendants as a particular human group with "an essence which only they have, and which has been called upon to provide Europe and the West in general *a sort of spiritual supplement* that Western civilization now needs."[25]

With Négritude inserted into the trends of Western European thought and taken up by Jean-Paul Sartre (1905–1980) in 1948 in his essay "Black Orpheus," it was then reinterpreted to give it an arcane and emotional tone that reified the racialized image of Black people. But Césaire said that Négritude was born in the struggle against alienation, not as some abstract notion, but as a concrete awareness that "we were black people, with a past. . . We were proud of our blackness, and . . . Africa was not a blank page in the history of humanity."[26] Négritude was a challenge and an act of political resistance against assimilation, against "the ideal of being a Frenchman with black skin."[27]

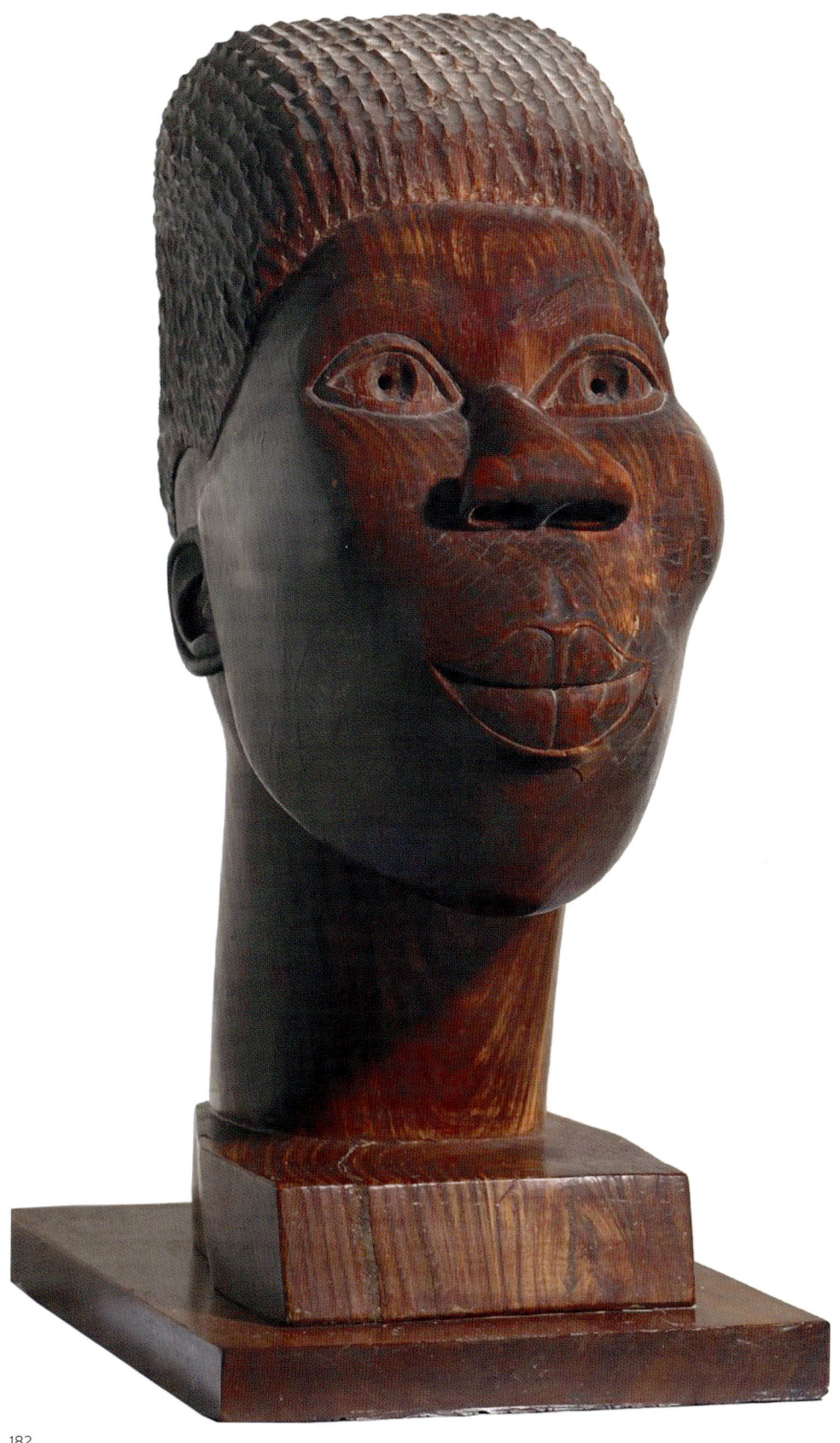

182

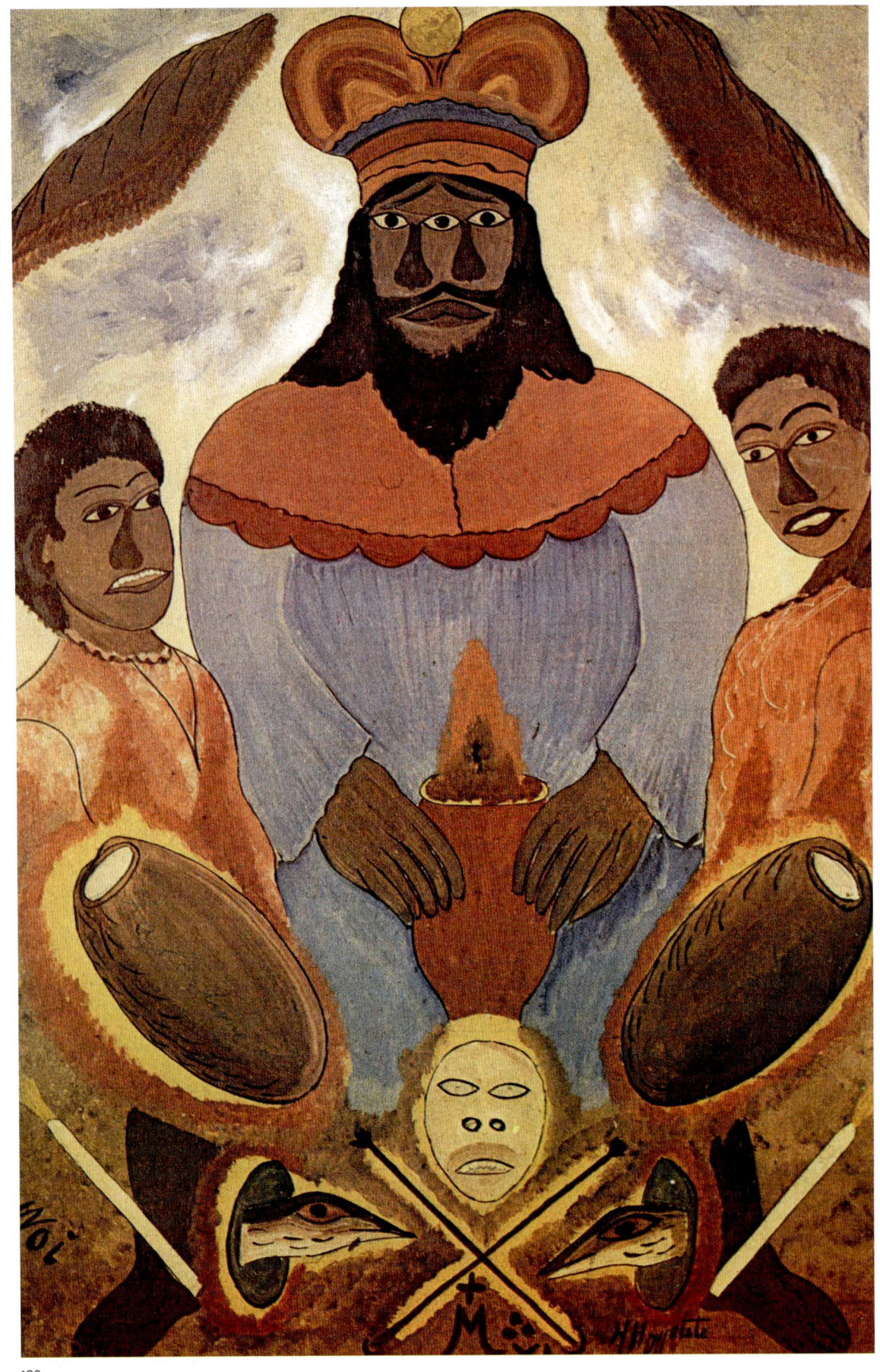

183

183 Héctor Hyppolite. *The Grand Master*. 1947. Oil on cardboard. Port-au-Prince, Musée d'Art Haïtien du Collège St. Pierre.

This conflict also left traces of exoticism that were generated from within, as explored by René Ménil in his essay "*De l´exotisme colonial*." The theme of a conflicted colonized personality was taken up by Frantz Fanon in his important 1952 study *Black Skin, White Masks*. The epistemological conflict of the colonized being was also explored by René Hibran in evaluating the problem of artistic representation in the development of Martinican art. He said that Black art lost its meaning in the era of enslavement, with the result being that in Martinique, the Black person's aesthetic was European. Hibran identified this as "an attitude of the spirit which denies a part of oneself, resulting in a changed and contradictory personality . . . and the inability to express oneself on an artistic level."[28] Therefore, "the artists of the future should look within and around themselves, and not elsewhere. It is not possible to revive Caribbean or Black art; that would be like speaking a dead language."[29] A project was launched to build an ethnic aesthetic that would permit artists to become aware of their own identities and not deny their various components. The School of Applied Arts was established in Martinique's capital, Fort-de-France, in 1943. The Atelier 45 and the group of Martinican artists began to promote artistic expression drawn from local surroundings, the common people, and the Creole charm of Martinican society, in which Black men and women were essential images in what had been a French plantation colony.

**Visual Image and Unknown Worlds:
Uncertainties about Haitian Art**

In 1944, the year of his death, the Haitian writer and political activist Jacques Roumain (1907–1944) published the novel *Los gobernadores del rocío* (*The Governors of the Dew*). The protagonist, Manuel, is one of the many Haitian emigrants who went to the sugarcane fields of Cuba to better their situation and would be brutally forced to return to their homeland in 1934 in the wake of the sugar market crash.[30] Manuel had not been in Haiti during its occupation by the United States from 1915 to 1934. For fifteen years, in Cuba, he had "flipped cane, every day . . . from first light to nightfall," where, he says, all the land "belongs to a white American, Mr. Wilson, . . . and the sugar mill, too, and everything around is his property." Everyone works for him while he sits in his garden. Manuel recalls the beatings from the Rural Guard that crunched his bones: "Damned Haitian, black shit."[31] Killing a Haitian or a dog was the same thing, the rural police said, and he thinks about the time he grabbed a guard's pistol and stuck it in his guts. Manuel personifies both the suffering and the rebelliousness of the most downtrodden, of the migrants who had no alternative but to go back from where they came.[32] The novel then moves to Haiti's interior, *le pays de dedans,* where environmental conflict, the real and symbolic drought, put all the author's narrative resources into tension to reveal the individual's struggle for survival, and the value of belief in the supernatural as the motive force of the social group. Space and time become permeable in this allegorical and magical portrayal.

During the months he spent in Haiti in 1943, the novelist and musicologist Alejo Carpentier (1904–1980) became interested in that deep world. A year later, the Centre d'Art was founded in Port-au-Prince, directed by the North American painter and English teacher DeWitt Peters (1901–1966). It became an emblematic institution for Haitian art and culture, with Haitian creativity displayed in all its splendor. The Centre d'Art became a point of contact for scattered artists and a showcase for creative talent.

184 Rigaud Benoit. *Ceremony under the Mapou Tree*. 1971. Oil on masonite. Private collection.

Local culture gradually took over, and the art of the people became increasingly evident in the Centre d'Art's work. From deep within Haiti's visual culture, an enigmatic and previously unknown style of painting emerged, which impressed the art world of the time. Through its visual codes and modes of expression, it was recognized as original and authentic in the island Caribbean.

These were the images that surprised André Breton and Pierre Mabille (1904–1952) during their trips to Haiti and touched the artistic sensibilities of the painters Carlos Enríquez (1900–1957) and Wifredo Lam (1902–1982), to mention only two of the Cuban artists who experienced Haiti in the 1940s. The art critic José Gómez Sicre (1916–1991) was eager to exhibit this art in Havana; another art critic, Selden Rodman (1909–2002), wrote about it in 1948 in *Renaissance in Haiti*; and the United States Information Service produced a documentary film, *Haiti 1950* (*L'Art en Haïti*), focused on the Centre d'Art and its artists.[33] During the 1940s, exhibitions in the United States and Europe generated all sorts of conjecture, confusion, and uncertainty about what label to put on painting so full of spontaneity and so rich with imagination. Because of a formal similarity with the work of Henri Rousseau (1844–1910), it was identified as *naïf*; since it was visually similar to images from other civilizations and the historical past, *primitif*; for its similarities to paintings by children and the so-called mentally deficient, *ingénu*; for some commentators, the "oneiric" visions, full of magic, could only be *surréaliste*.

What is certain is that what Carpentier called an "extraordinary pictorial florescence" did not escape the persistent values of a categorical and normative Western European aesthetic, with its system of classification by schools, trends, and movements.[34] This emerging art, with a modernity that was different because it was contradictory, entered into the international market. The various labels were well known, and they appealed to the imagination of potential buyers, including visitors to Haiti in a period of flourishing tourism.

Those artistic expressions which "it would be better to call spontaneous, from ordinary people," did not emerge from the Centre d'Art, but preceded it.[35] Within the Centre, artists were divided into either self-taught or modern, and the latter group began to take classes. The reality is that the division that was later seen in the promotion and critique of Haitian art originated in the Centre d'Art itself.

Héctor Hyppolite (1894–1948) was one of the great figures of Haitian popular art. Of low social origins, he had held the solemn position of *houngan*, or Vodou priest. Like Hyppolite, Rigaud Benoit (1911–1986) and André Pierre (1916–2005), among others, "were artists who arose from the common masses who . . . have seen their work exhibited in New York, Berlin, Havana, São Paulo, and many other cities."[36]

Vodou and painting were intertwined in the synthesis of the artistic image which functioned as symbolic meaning with socialized visual codes through the collective practice of the belief system. Although they were not the only themes portrayed, those strange visions, traveling through time from the deep feelings of the Haitian people, became puzzling and strongly enigmatic.

In the novel *El reino de este mundo* (*The Kingdom of This World*, 1949), Carpentier carried out a critical deconstruction of Haiti's past and present. He sought to understand the country's culture through a rereading of its history, which revealed itself in an intertwining of times and convergences that led to understanding. In reexamining the trajectory of the Haitian Revolu-

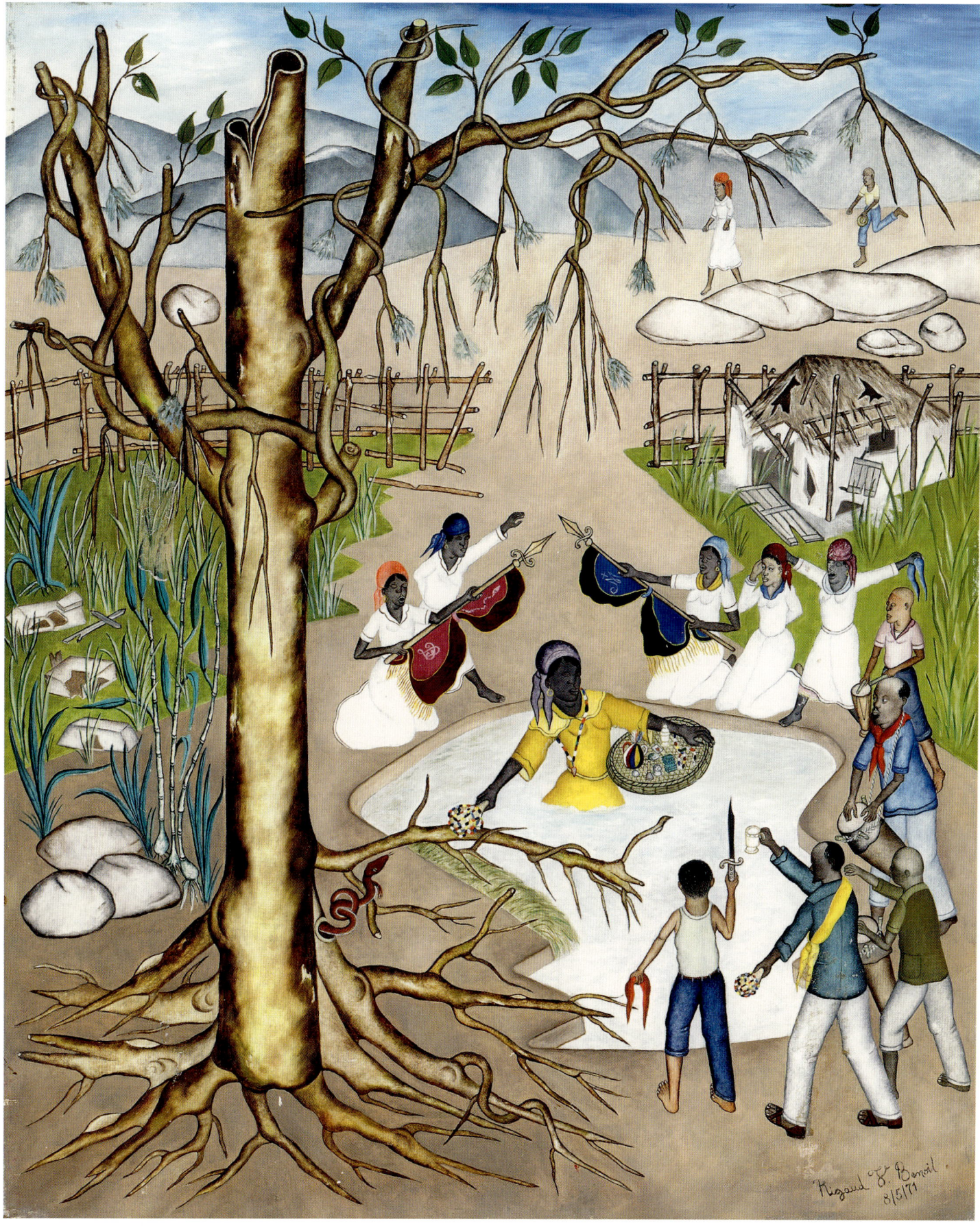

184

tion and its antecedents, he saw an unusual process, incredible because it was unthinkable, that helps explain the country that unfolded in the aftermath. In an extravagance of creative imagination, Carpentier combined a recounting of history with another reality, a mythical reality that permeates Haiti's culture. In Haiti, he noted, something "that we might call the marvelous real ... became particularly evident."[37] Expanding on the "marvelous real," he wrote, "I thought, furthermore, that the presence and validity of the marvelous real was not the unique privilege of Haiti, but was the patrimony of all the Americas."[38] It showed him "certain possible American synchronisms, recurring over time ... connecting the past to the present."[39]

It would have been difficult to imagine Haiti, a land of many symbiotic contrasts and strange incantations, as a propitious source for such a revelation, with the first revolution in the Americas combining antislavery and independence, the Black heroes, and the contradictory details of its history. Césaire described the nation that was founded by former enslaved people as "Haiti, where *negritude* first stood up."[40] It has been disdained by outsiders, condemned for daring to be free; a place where African identity lives on, latent in the belief in the safe return of its dead to the kingdom of Guinea and the persistence of ancestral beliefs in its Vodou rituals. Yet Carpentier saw it as the place where certain aspects of the culture of the Americas were revealed: the coexistence of the unusual and the real; of different times that were permeable and converged on their own, not through surrealist prestidigitation. A marvelous reality where the magical resides was part of Carpentier's conceptual debate with surrealism. Haiti showed Carpentier what would become a "hermeneutics of the Americas"—to borrow a phrase used by Ambrosio Fornet in a lecture on the topic—a concept to test and debate, but difficult to ignore. The central idea is the coexistence of the past with the present, resulting from the deeply discordant asynchronies of coloniality-modernity that violated and transformed their constituent patterns.

Existence in Simultaneous Times

In that world of contradictions, ideas that valued the race mixture of the Caribbean and Brazil flourished. While they recognized African origins and the racial pride of Afrodescendant people, those ideas reveal a complex interweaving of the socio-racial fabric resulting from the confluence, confrontation, and mixing of peoples and communities of diverse origins. It was not just Africa that could claim a different identity from the multiple original groups that came together.[41] To appreciate the African contribution to colonialized society was in itself a decolonizing act. But understanding the African cultural presence simultaneously with other cultural times in places where everyone came from somewhere else, confronting one another in hierarchies that racialized social interaction and profoundly influenced people's lives, added one more turn to the decolonizing screw. The situation became more complicated because, despite the differences that sharply divided societies, mixture took place that resulted in a very complex socio-racial mosaic in the Caribbean islands and Brazil. The prohibitions on interaction issued by colonial powers, or in the norms of discriminatory customs, were rules made to be broken, and varying degrees of mixture came to characterize the region.

Racial mixing was generally more pronounced in Spanish and Portuguese settlement colonies, where there was more immigration from Europe, in contrast to French and English plantation colonies, with their absentee planters and a majority population of enslaved Africans. In social practice and in critical subjectivity, white-Black mixing was the context for new concealments. Zuleica Romay notes that "historically the mixture of the extremes of the color scale has only served to sharpen the perception of differences," and that "black people are again put in a subordinate position, relative to those of mixed descent."[42] Thus, in some countries where mixture is placed on a psychosocial and artistic-literary pedestal as a characteristic of national identity, it has the effect of blocking out the presence of the component groups. Perhaps that's why Nicolás Guillén said "Cuba's soul is mixed," but that "a native poetry among us will by no means be complete if black people are left out."[43]

The great contribution of the Cuban anthropologist Fernando Ortiz (1881–1969) in his *Contrapunteo cubano del tabaco y el azúcar* (*Cuban Counterpoint of Tobacco and Sugar*, 1940) was to initiate an anthropological dialogue on those complex issues in specific cultural zones. At that time, the concepts of acculturation and deculturation were well established in scientific studies. Ortiz developed the concept of transculturation, a conceptual reconfiguration which understood cultural processes as "transitive," according to Bronislaw Malinowski, of "reciprocal influences."[44] He criticized Melville Herskovits's notion of acculturation, which Ortiz considered to be a limited and passive process of acquisition of another culture, or assimilation to the dominant culture.[45] Ortiz conceptualized a different dynamic which, although there might be loss or uprooting resulting in deculturation, emphasized the creation of new cultural phenomena. That means that the widely recognized racial mixing is not simply changing pigmentation through biological crossing, leading to a range of skin colors. In cultural mixing, the original components mix their times and imaginaries, and their various cultural matrixes interact. The idea that race mixture leads to transculturation became a very useful theoretical and methodological tool.

Ortiz himself made important use of this concept in the first of a series of books he published in the 1950s, *La Africanía de la música folklórica de Cuba* (*Africanness in Cuban Folkloric Music*), in which he focused on the importance of the African component in music, which had been barely examined until then. Ortiz noted that for such a study it was necessary to bring in not only musicology but religion, aesthetics, and other social phenomena, with scientific methods, because it involved "very complex transculturations which were difficult to analyze."[46] If a multidisciplinary approach was necessary for music, one of the most common cultural expressions of people in the Caribbean and Brazil, then the study of other art forms was similarly complex.

Ortiz used Robert R. Marett's *Psychology and Folklore* (1920), taking its concept of "cultural transvaluation," both vertical and horizontal, but always creating change. He then looked at important musical forms such as *contradanza, habanera, danzón, rumba, son,* and jazz. All these styles existed at the time he studied them, circulating beyond their folk origins through radio broadcasts, films, and stage shows. As Ortiz wrote, "At first they were appreciated not for their origins, but because they were exotic and different. But eventually that changed, and they were revalued as having universal appeal, even as their original value was retained."[47] Thus he insisted that while these musical forms originated with the common people, they must be studied like any social phenomenon, taking into careful consideration the integrity of the cultural group from which they originate, as well as

185 Emiliano Augusto Cavalcanti de Albuquerque e Melo (Di Cavalcanti). *Fishermen*. Ca. 1949-1950. Oil on canvas. Private collection.

the cultural elements in which they are transformed.

In cultural studies of Afrodescendant people, this conceptual framework is extremely valuable in the visual arts and the composition of images, because music in particular shows evidence of transculturation in instruments, dance, and especially in the rhythm that comes through in images in which gesture and the representation of performance are infused with new meanings. These features, as well as cultural mixing, particularly in the female figure and the *mulata*, come through in *El triunfo de la rumba* (*The Triumph of the Rumba*) (see fig. 156) and *La Comparsa* by the Cuban painter Eduardo Abela (1889–1965); in *Merengue* (see fig. 111) by the Dominican Jaime Colson (1901–1975); in *La plena* (see fig. 102), a mural by the Puerto Rican Rafael Tufiño (1922–2008); and in *Samba* (see fig. 157) and *Dança popular brasileira* (*Brazilian Popular Dance*) by the Brazilians Emiliano di Cavalcanti (1897–1976) and Cândido Portinari (1903–1962), respectively. All these styles of music and dance emerged in the social context of poverty and marginality, and from the culture of common people.

The title character of *Gabriela, cravo e canela* (*Gabriela, Clove and Cinnamon*), the 1958 novel by the Brazilian writer Jorge Amado (1912–2001), is a *mulata*.[48] Gabriela is a *retirante*, or migrant, who has crossed jungles and rivers to escape the intense drought of the interior of Brazil's Northeast. The novel is set in Amado's home state of Bahia, specifically in the town of Ilhéus, which is being transformed by the growth of cacao plantations and which Amado calls "a land of people from all over."[49] It begins with a procession in honor of St. George to fulfill a "fervent vow." Everyone was there, especially (and unusually, the author tells us) the richest and most notable people of the town, dressed in the costumes of their religious fraternities, to call down the waters to save the crops. But "Saint George, who was of course impressed by the volume of the prayers and promises . . . magnified the miracle and now the rains would not cease."[50] *Gabriela* is an urban novel, as were many of the Afro-Brazilian and Afro-Caribbean rhythms that evoke an image of Black music and dance in our countries. The illustrations in the first edition by Emiliano di Cavalcanti (who later did the cover art for the 1982 edition) were rendered with sharp contrasts in white and black that also provide social and cultural clues. The cover art of the first edition was by the São Paulo–born artist Clóvis Graciano (1907–1988), who took great interest in Black people as subject matter, exploring their image as musicians and dancers. Similar treatments can also be seen in the work of the self-taught artist Heitor de Prazeres (1898–1966), who presented scenes of common people and public festivities in which the expressive strength of body language is a distinctive marker of cultural mixture and hybridity, especially in dancing the samba. In the work of Hector Julio Páride Bernabó, known as Carybé (1911–1997), the powerful performative movement of *capoeira* stands out, as the lightness and linearity of the figures accentuate the intensity of the composition.

Brazil is a land of extreme symbiosis. In art, the world of its beliefs and rituals emerges in the mysteries of Candomblé ceremonies in the work of Djanira da Motta (1914–1979)—particularly notable for her mural *Candomblé* (1950–1951), painted to hang in the home of her friend, Jorge Amado.[51] Known by her first name, Djanira worked in a synthetic idiom using bold colors and sharply delineated figures. The most interesting feature of her work tends to be her use of techniques associated with folk art, and the dignity that comes through in the way Djanira portrayed

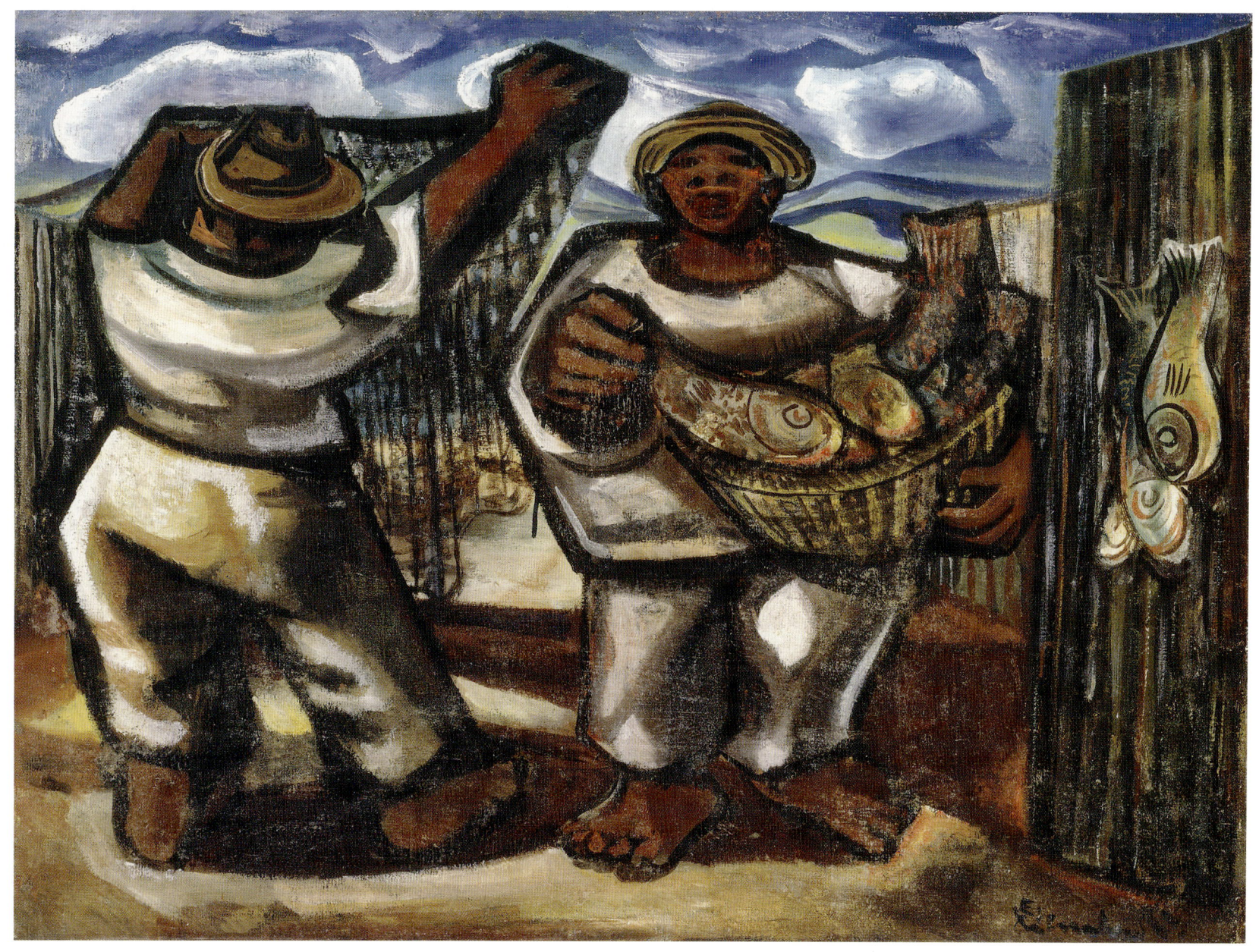

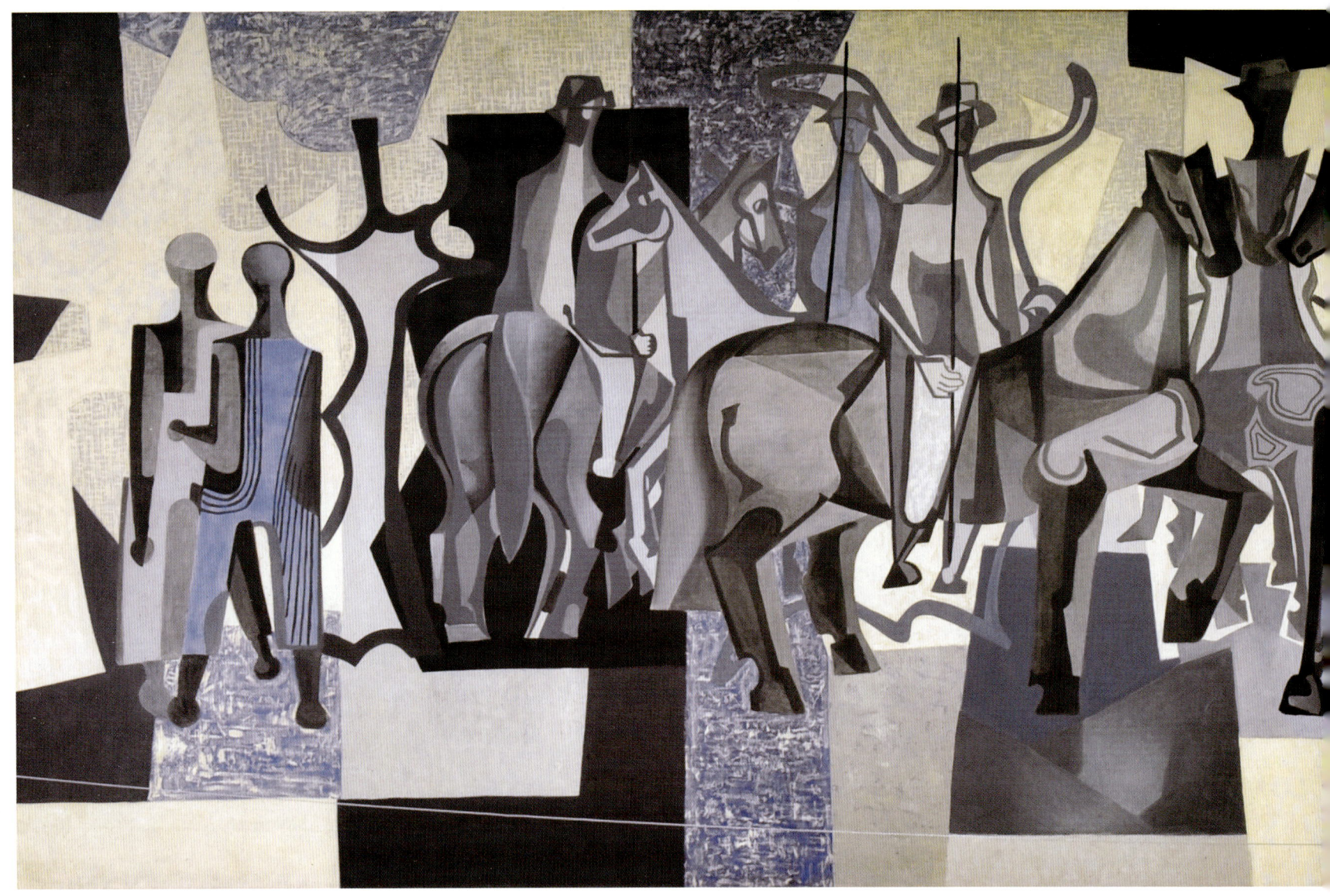

186 Emiliano Augusto Cavalcanti de Albuquerque e Melo (Di Cavalcanti). *People of Brasilia*. 1960. Oil on canvas. Brasilia, Palace of the Congress, Chamber of the Deputies.

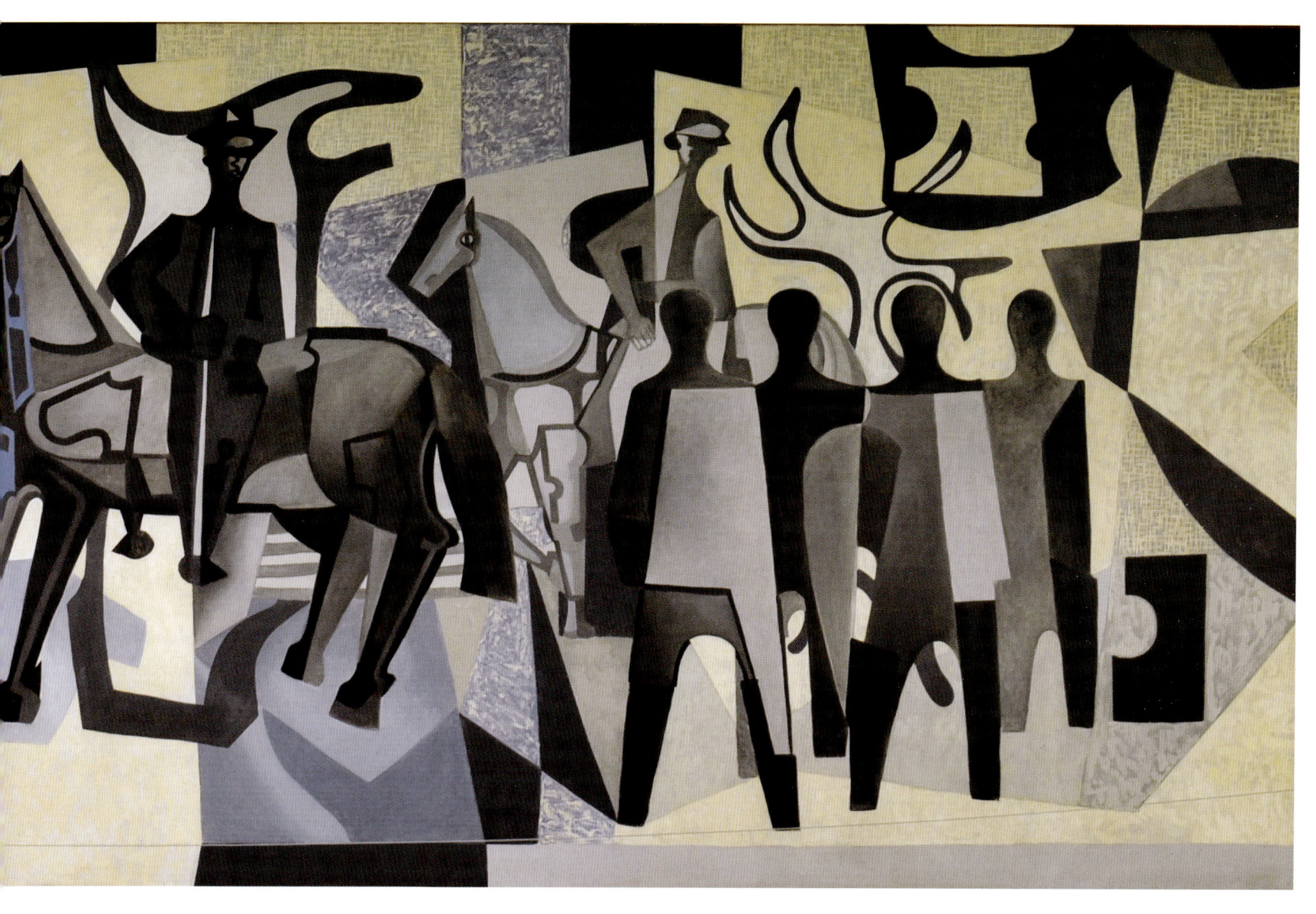

187 Clóvis Graciano. *Flag Dancers*. 1943. Tempera on canvas. Museu de Arte Contemporânea da Universidade de São Paulo.

188 Djanira da Motta e Silva. *Candomblé*. 1957. Tempera on wood. Salvador, Bahia, Brazil, Banco Itaú.

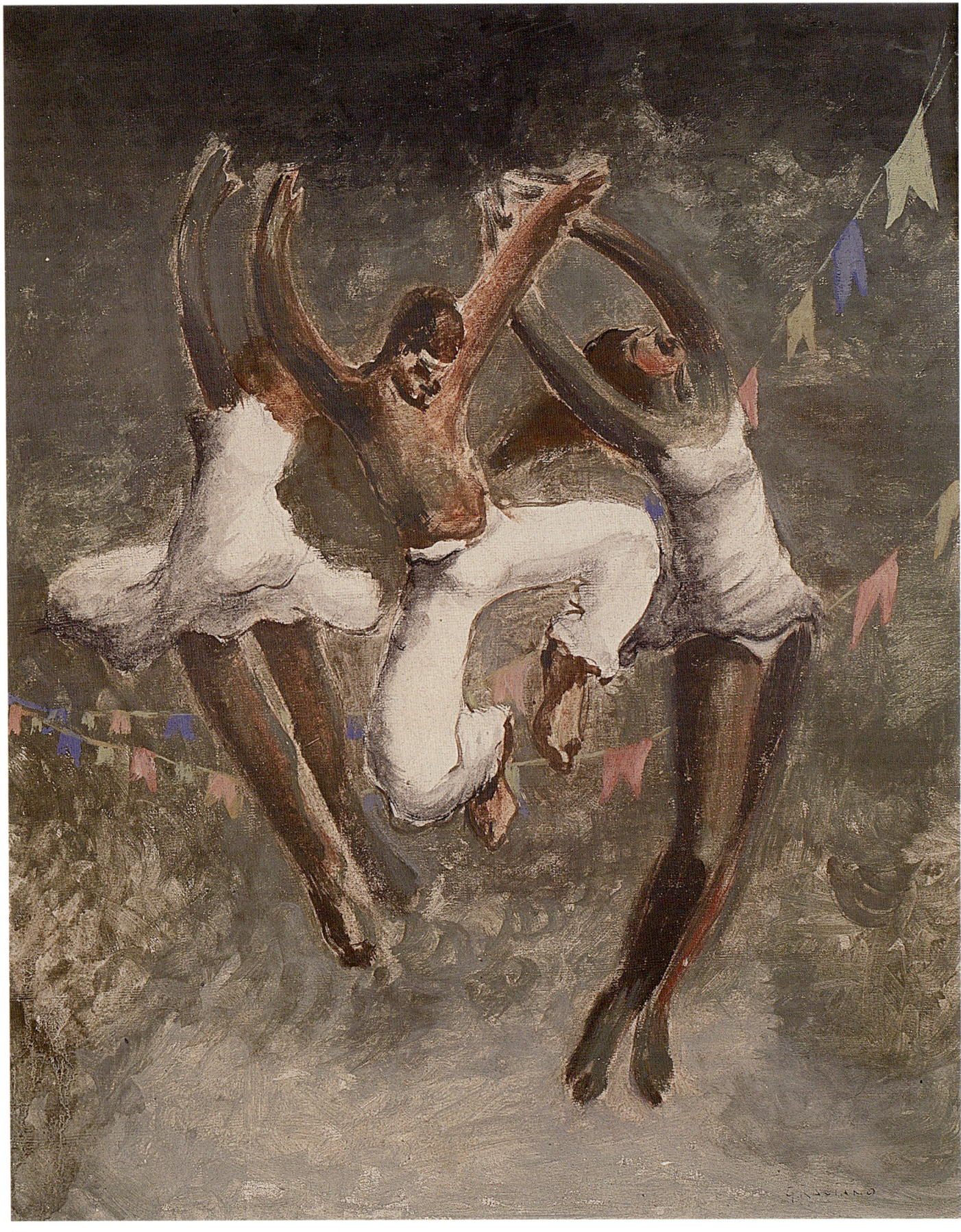

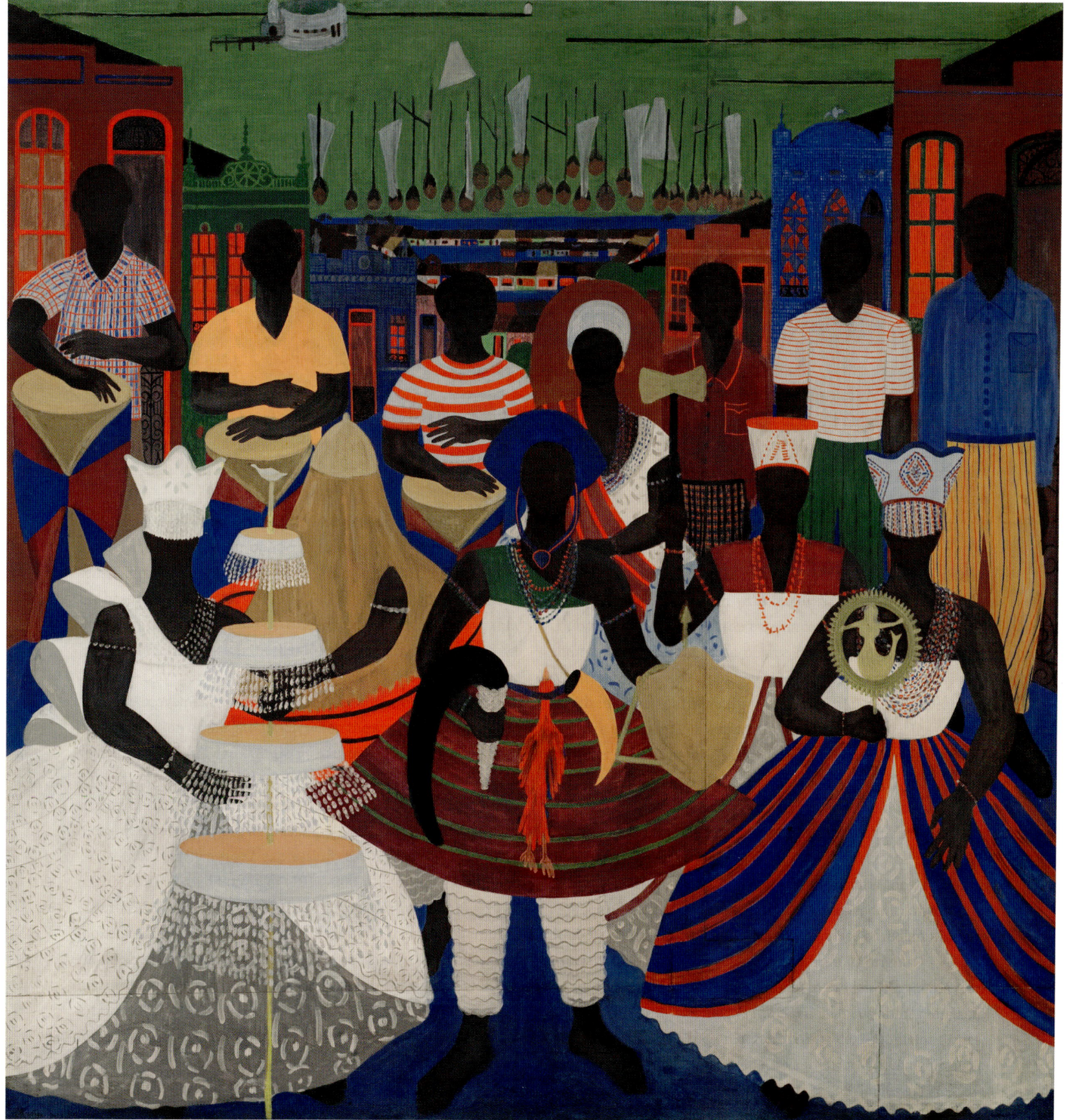

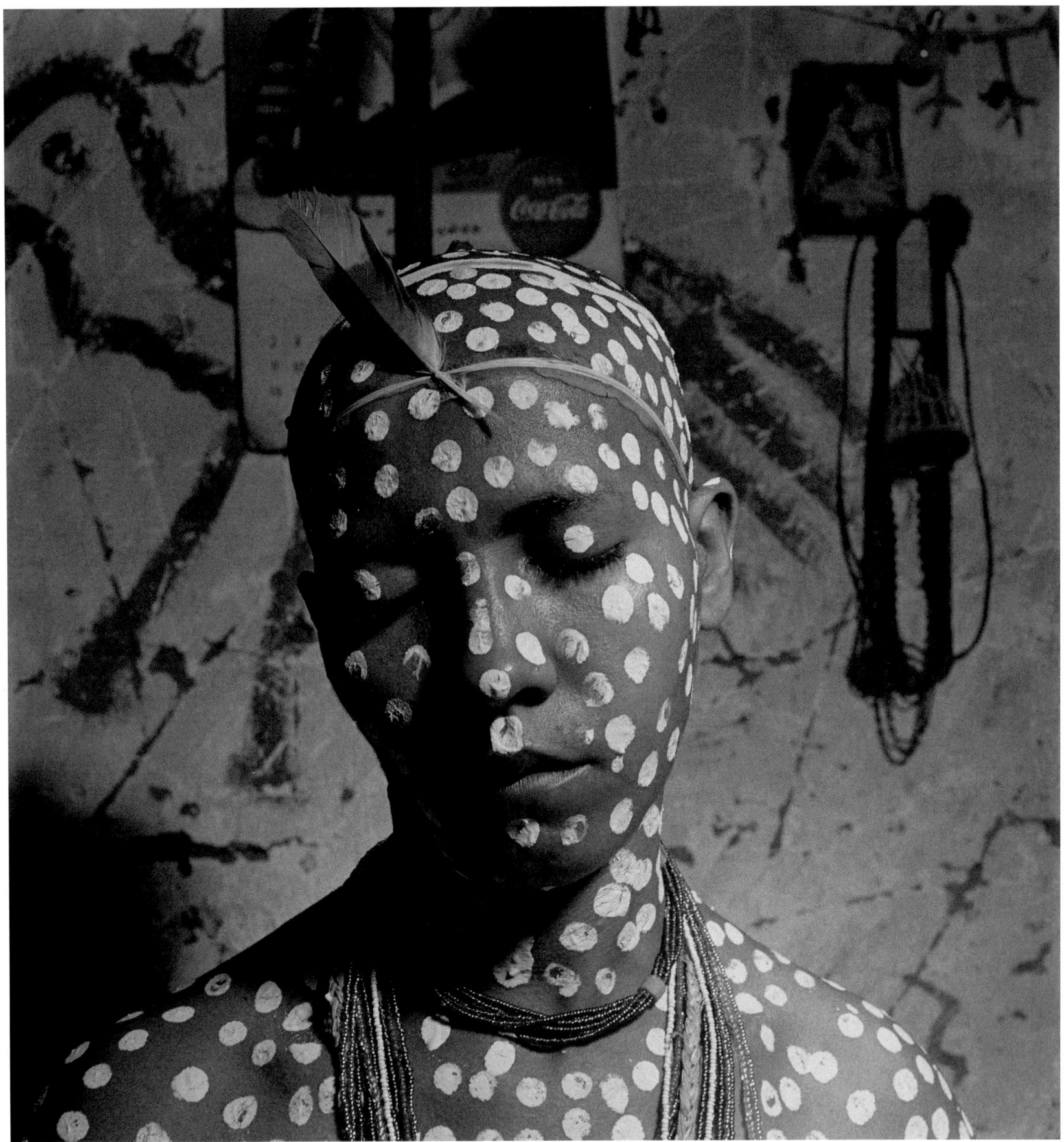

189

189 José Medeiros. *Initiation of a Daughter of a Priest in the Candomblé Precinct*. 1957. Photograph. Museu de Arte Moderna do Rio de Janeiro.

the costumes, attributes, and symbols related to the worship of *orixás,* the Afro-Brazilian gods.[52] This theme in Brazilian visual culture gained international recognition, especially through the photography of José Medeiros (1921–1990), a photojournalist for the magazine *O Cruzeiro*, founded by the Frenchman Jean Manzon (1915–1990). In his series on Candomblé initiation rituals, the force of the visual record is profoundly revealing of scenes the world had not previously witnessed.[53]

Another Look, Another Way of Seeing

These depictions of the world of Afro-Latin American rituals contrasted with the avalanche of images nurtured by the artistic novelty exemplified by the work of Pablo Picasso (1881–1973) in the early twentieth century. In that era, the discoveries of Ifé and Benin led to a search for a new artistic idiom in Europe. The purified visual devices of African art surprised and stimulated European sensibilities, and the so-called black arts opened new avenues of expression and helped resolve the crisis of Western art. But as African archaeological and ethnographic materials were adapted to Europe in form, those images and objects, filled with enigmas and unknown symbolic meanings, were stripped of their original cultural significance. Among the wide range of pieces in wood and bronze, masks had the most impact.[54] Europeans looking for new sources of inspiration found the frontal silence of African masks compelling, while their strangeness suggested an alternative concept of beauty. But in this appropriation, the mask was stripped of meaning, as its symbolic and mythical context, its original cultural value, were unknown. As Jean Laude states convincingly, "Sculptures and masks were brought to Europe with no documentation as to their meaning or purpose."

That, he adds, violated the fundamental connection in Western Europe between painting and writing: The African images had no supporting text.[55] The mask became a surface on which to explore visual solutions, in what Laude defines as questioning in search of the "autonomy of artistic forms."[56] The conceptual underpinnings and rationalist obsessions of cubism identified with African visual essentialism. The ways in which these elements penetrated the visual culture of Western Europe contributed to a new artistic consciousness that inspired modern art and extended in different ways into other styles and movements.

The Cuban artist Wifredo Lam was in Europe as these developments took place, and years later he reflected on them: "I was very irritated that in Paris African masks and idols were sold as decorations. … I decided to put black objects in function of their landscape, and their own world."[57] While he was still living in Spain, Lam slowly left behind the academic tradition in which he had been trained and began to explore the synthetic modes of the modern. In 1938 he painted *Dolor de España* (*Agony of Spain*), a significant example of his heightened consciousness and participation in the Spanish Civil War, and of his use of the mask as an expressive device. He was already close to Picasso and the Parisian vanguard, past his experimentation with cubism, but the polyfocal disassembly of figures and objects as a resource persisted in his work. He did not leave the teachings of the master behind, and the mask is perhaps the clearest indication. As Lam said, "I could become critical of European culture and represent the Third World within it, because I had earlier taken possession of that same culture."[58]

The human figure predominated in Lam's work, and the female form became the experimental basis for new directions.

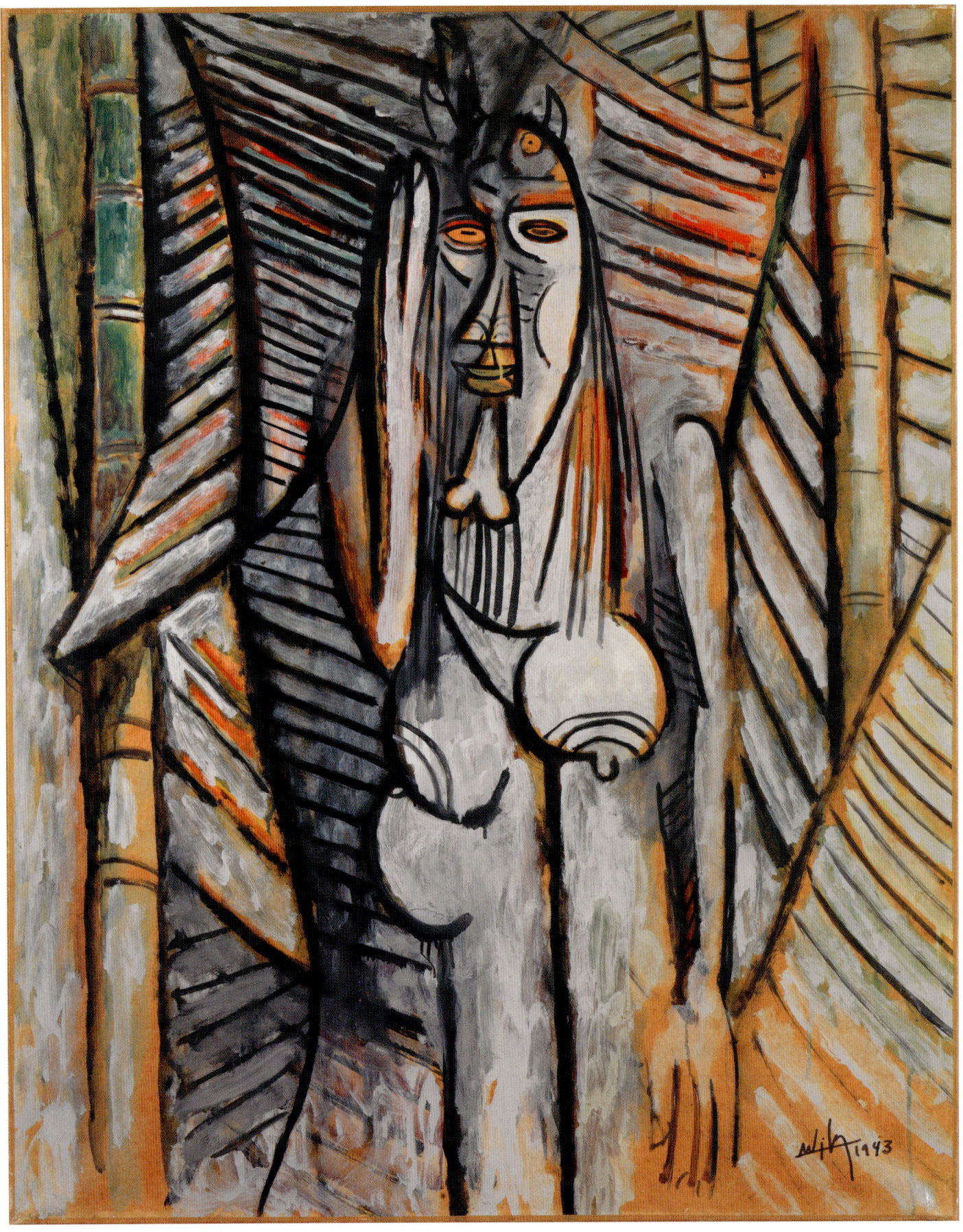

190 Wifredo Lam. *Rumor*. 1943. Paris, Musée national d'art moderne/Centre de creation industrielle Centre Georges Pompidou.

191 Wifredo Lam. *The Fiancée of Kiriwina*. 1949. Oil on canvas. Saint-Paul de Vence, France, Fondation Maeght.

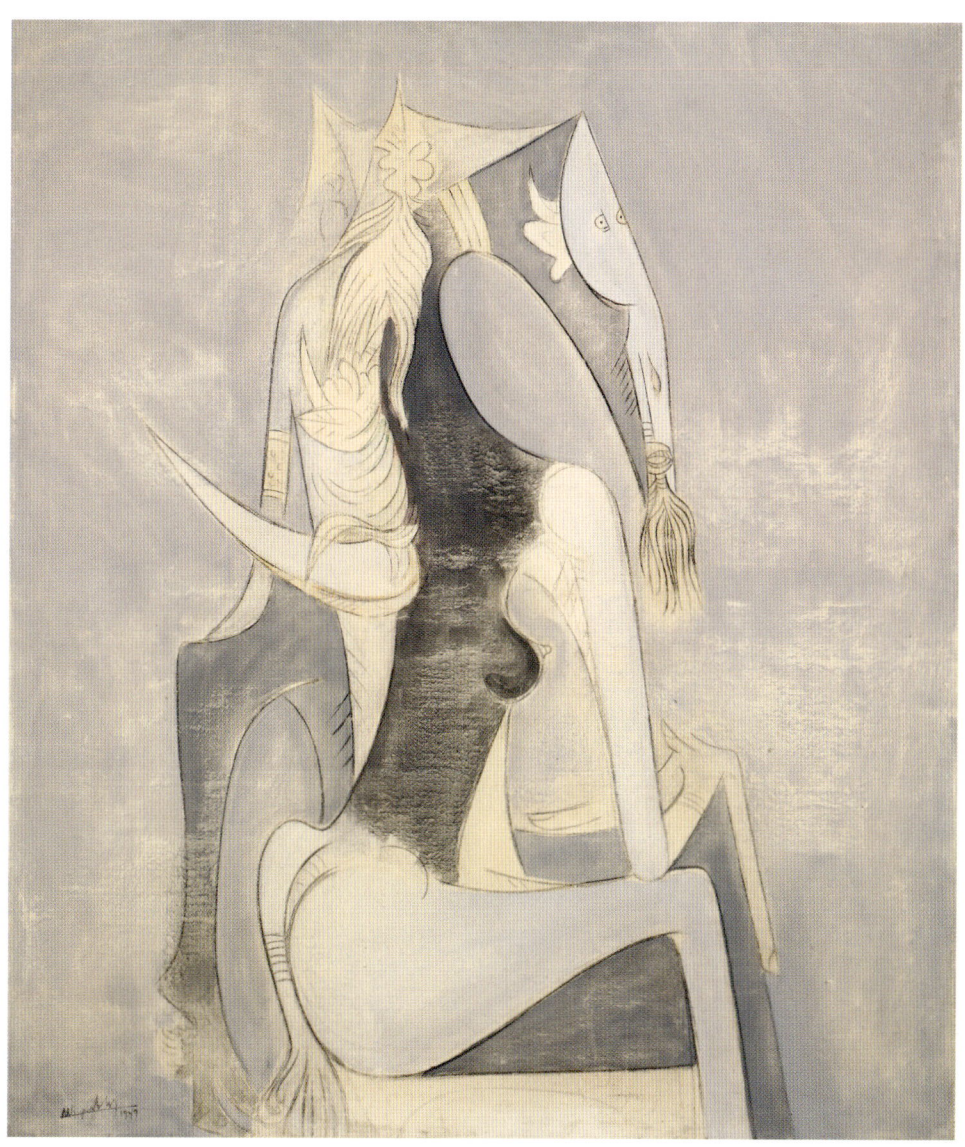

191

He used the mask as a resource for transfiguration, as shown in *Le bruit (Rumor)* and *Sin título (Untitled)*, both done in 1943 after the artist returned to his native Cuba in 1942, escaping Nazi-occupied Paris on a ship carrying many other intellectuals to the Americas.[59] In *Rumor*, the mask recovers its function as a fetish placed in a symbolic context. The hybridity of the figure suggests an image in metamorphosis and transformation, with its mythical content being redefined. The mask is reinstalled in the syncretic and transcultural imaginary of the Caribbean. Lam himself was the conjurer, the conscious artistic mediator between places and times, and cultures. The drawing *Sin título* is even more eloquent. A woman looks into a mirror (a common trope in Western European art), and sees the image of a horse. It prefigures a theme that Lam developed later—the image of the woman-horse. It is symbolically charged, implying a blending together of both African and Cuban beliefs. In Cuban Santería ritual, a "horse" is the adept that the deity "mounts" through spirit possession. While thus possessed, the horse will act, speak, and dance with the attributes of the deity. In Lam's vision of the woman-horse, the mask in the mirror reappropriates the hidden power and energy of a magical and symbolic reflection. In some of these pieces, the human is shown covered by the mask of an *íreme*, a mysterious figure in *Abakuá*, another of the powerful religious systems brought from Africa and still practiced in Cuba. But Lam did not copy an African model. Instead, he incorporated an ancestral legacy as an act of aesthetic and artistic legitimation.

The Afrodescendant presence in the visual forms of various countries came through in individual appropriations of the van-

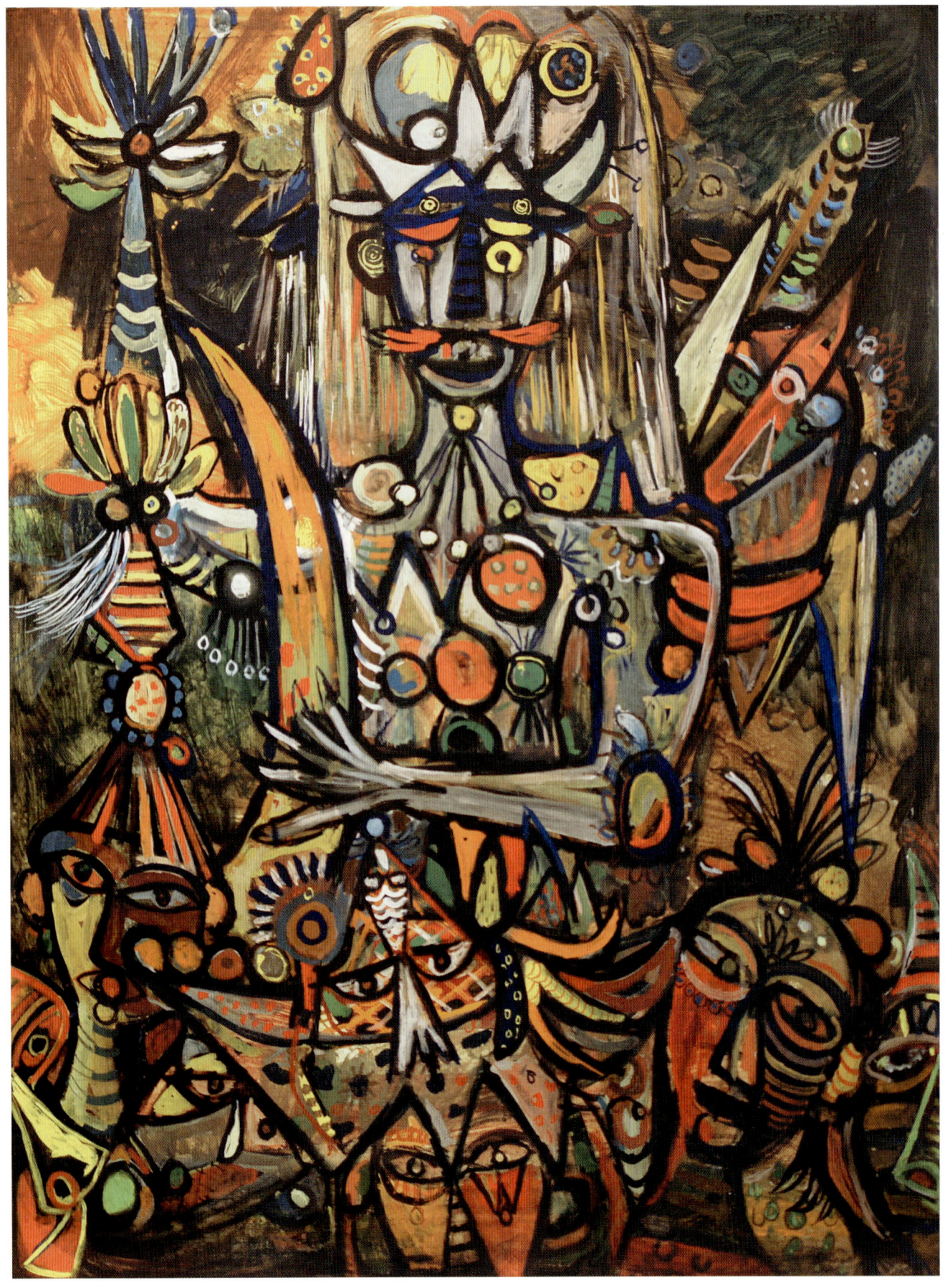

192

192 René Portocarrero. *Carnival Sorcerer*. 1945. Mixed media on board laid down on canvas. Private collection.

193 Lucien Price. *Study No. 6: Masks*. 1947. Pendiente Collection.

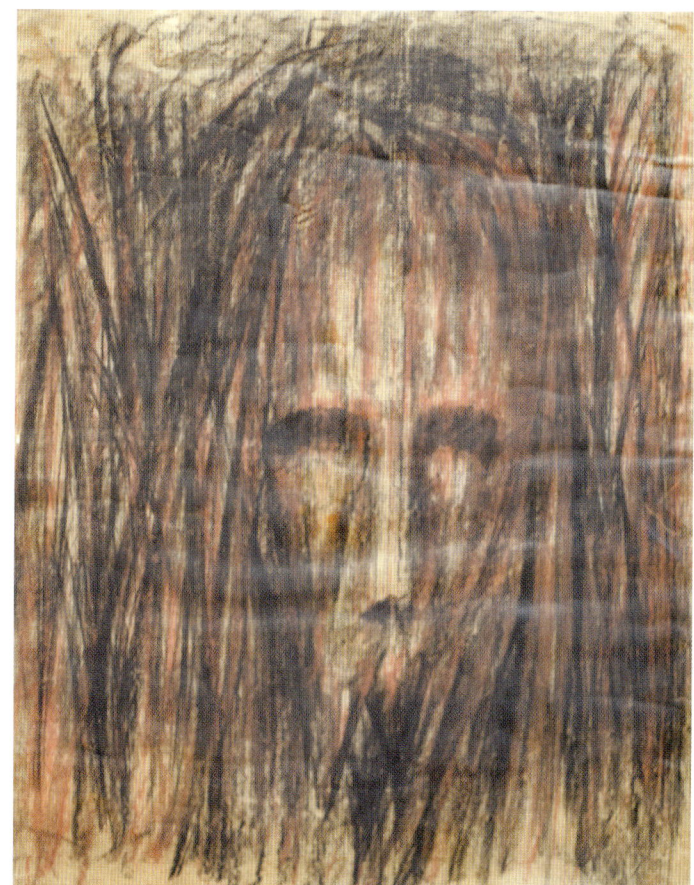
193

guardist idiom. Examples from the 1920s and 1930s include Tarsila do Amaral (1886–1973) in Brazil, Darío Suro (1917–1997) in the Dominican Republic, and Alberto Peña (1897–1938) in Cuba. But in the following years, the use of the mask was part of the revival of African ethnicity in the construction of cultural imaginaries of many other artists, such as René Portocarrero (1912–1985) in Cuba in his *Brujos* (*Sorcerers*) series in 1945, and whose second book, *Las máscaras* (1955), included a collection of twelve drawings; in the very original perceptions of the Haitian artist Lucien Price (1915–1963) in his *Étude no. 6: Masques* (*Study No. 6: Masks*) in 1947, and in some of the paintings of the Dominican Jaime Colson in which he enters into celebrations of Black people through a synthetic idiom of the mask, as in *Fiesta de Guachupita* (*Fiesta in Guachupita*) (see fig. 112) from 1955. Black people as figures gradually disappear as a motif, moving toward a more complete synthesis of their image as a visual symbol.

Penetrate the Jungle . . . Make the Invisible Visible

In the artistic imaginary of the Caribbean and Brazil, the occult powers made nature the repository of ancestral knowledge and spiritual territory. Of the many original belief systems, including those imposed by the colonial powers or those coming from Africa, the latter are present throughout the range of religions and cultures, although they are less visible in some mainland Latin American countries. Colonization put so much stress on the native peoples that their cultural systems were definitively destabilized. Territory was emptied and land taken as property. Then people were taken from their African homelands and brought by the millions. Both indigenous people and Africans were separated from their ancestral knowledge rooted in the land. The recovery of those cultural values was, and continues to be, one of the most important themes for the original people and all their descendants. It has been a way to put all the inverted roles in their proper order.[60] Like an archaeologist seeking hidden mysteries and protected values, the artist penetrates the inscru-

IMAGE OF THE BLACK AND MORE 327

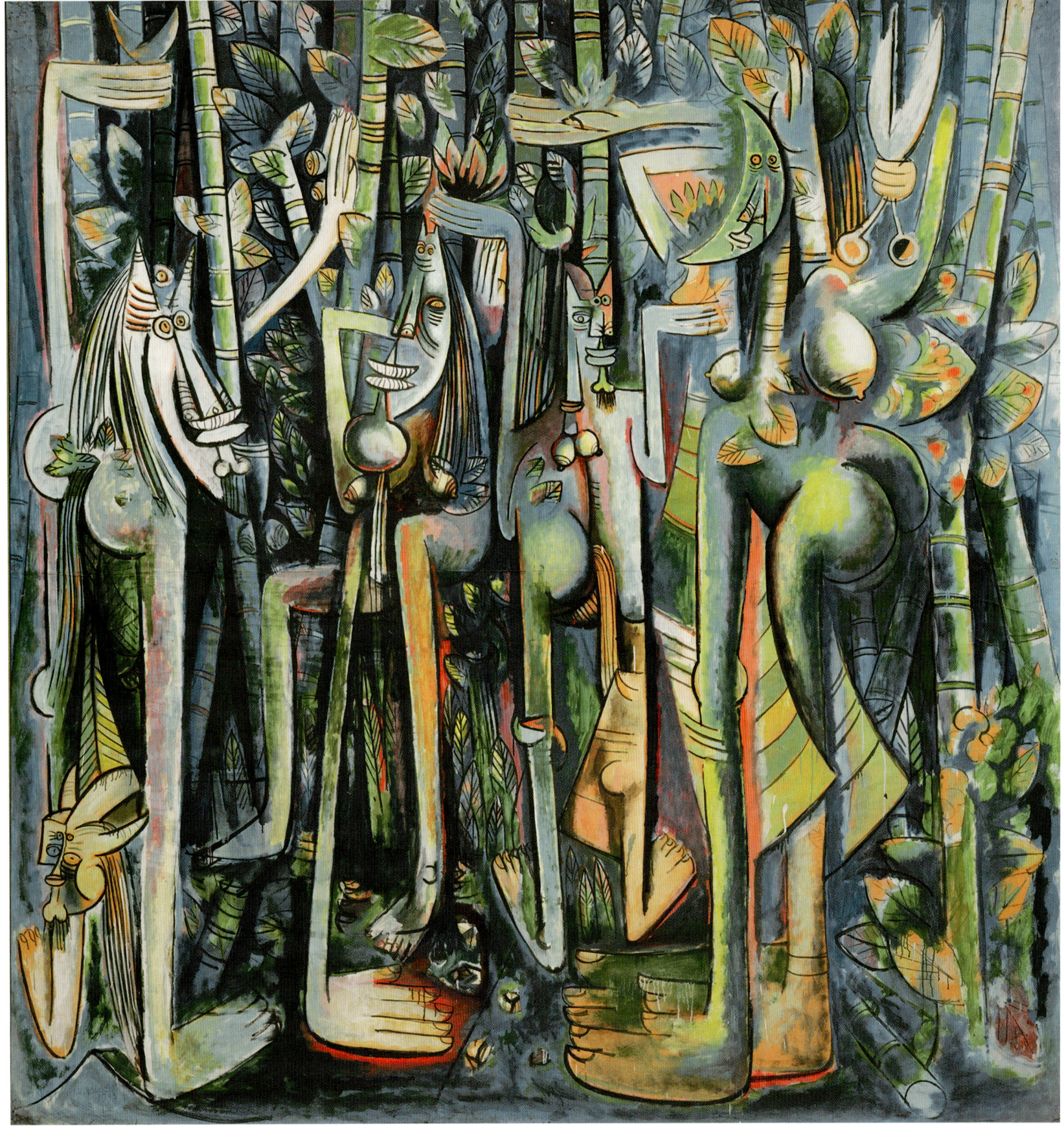

194 Wifredo Lam. *The Jungle*. 1943. Gouache on paper mounted on canvas. New York, Museum of Modern Art.

table obscure zones to rediscover the forces that once occupied the land and sea, forests and rivers, history and daily life. It was a sort of spiritual archaeology in which a transculturated Africa, now the source of new discourses, occupied the Americas in a reality that was marvelous because it was unthinkable, and all at the same time.

Wifredo Lam's *La jungla* (*The Jungle*) is a composite work, integrating natural and supernatural forces in metamorphosis, a sugarcane field inhabited by mythical beings that have settled in these lands.[61] The painting turns the source of the treasure that filled the colonizer's coffers into a space where the culture of the enslaved laborers takes refuge. This is a critical insight of great intellectual scope. More than just a place, therefore, the jungle is a metaphor for plantation and resistance, for confinement and liberation. Realities and times are piled on one another like a visual scheme plotting to connect people to the land, where they rediscover their mixed origins in a place where the visible and invisible coexist. It is a place of magical spells and the reverberations of nature that was believed to be silent.

The Museum of Modern Art in New York acquired *La jungla*, and there it remains. Artistically, Lam proceeded the way one constructs a *nganga,* the costume of the practitioners of the Palo Monte religion, by building up layers based on the earth, the source of all energies, where all the elements that go into the pot coexist, where everything is apparently mixed, but where each part has its own place.[62]

Commenting on *La jungla,* Aimé Césaire said that "Lam puts on the canvas the ceremony through which everything exists: the ceremony of the physical union of man with the world. … Lam celebrates the transformation of the world into myth and coexistence. … What definitively triumphs in this work is the spirit of creation in the Antilles."[63] Using visual symbols, the artist reconnected the fragmented worlds of the animal, vegetable, and human into the mythical and real. Through such ambiguous mutations, the figures become enigmatic and thus pay homage to all the possible and impossible magic in the realm of the imagination. Artists were again thought to be diabolical conjurers because of how their world appeared to be strange and unknown, in reality unrelenting.

The title of *La jungla* is itself a metaphor. In the islands, that sort of landscape is practically nonexistent compared to the tropical jungles of the interior of Brazil that, among other settings, inspired the anthropophagical vision of that country's modern artists. An array of decolonizing ideas put the Afrodescendant component into tension with other sources of Brazilian culture. The artistic reference point of 1928's *Anthropophagic Manifesto,* which announced "the birth of a new logic," was to devour and metabolize—a legitimation of the very idea of art in a colonial condition.[64] As they advanced, the conquerors imposed not only their language, but also their culture in all social and artistic spheres. But, George Lamming recognized, "It was not particularly the English language, but the discourse and idea as a way, a method, a necessary path toward zones of being that could not be reached in any other way."[65] With the conquerors, the type of Prospero from Shakespeare's *The Tempest* also arose to a position of power, as "colonization. . . is simply a tradition of habits that become the normal way of seeing."[66] What needed to be changed was what Lamming called a "normal way of seeing"; that is, what has been accepted and established. As Maryse Condé, an author from the island of Guadeloupe, has said, the irreverence of can-

195 Rubem Valentim. *Composition No. 5.* 1953. Oil on wood. Museu de Arte Contemporânea da Universidade de São Paulo.

nibalism was appropriated and reshaped, dismantling symbols, merging a variety of artistic techniques.[67] These provocative ideas emerged at an essential artistic-cultural moment in the decolonizing turn, and they make this declaration by Wifredo Lam understandable: "My painting is an act of decolonization, not physical, but mental."[68]

In the process of these critical turns, Caliban, the anagram for the Spanish spelling of "cannibal" in *The Tempest*, reappeared in George Lamming's *The Pleasures of Exile* (1960), and from the conceptual underpinnings of the character it is clear that this is not the Caliban that Prospero had in mind.[69] By turning Shakespeare's character into a symbolic representation of the people who arrived in the slave ships of the triangular trade, Lamming made a decolonizing change. The indigenous people are transmuted into the enslaved people brought from Africa—or rather, they are blended into a common image. In Lamming's words: "The slave whose skin suggests the savaged deformity of his nature, becomes identical with the Carib Indian who feeds on human flesh."[70]

As is well known, the genealogy of the cannibal extends through the Americas, with particular focus on the Caribbean and Brazil, starting with engravings and chronicles in the fifteenth and sixteenth centuries. Caliban is common to the historical and cultural development of those regions, and Lamming sees in him an essential blending between those who for the most part have been historically excluded: indigenous people and the descendants of enslaved people. He sees traces of this symbolic character in "the continued possibility of a profound revolutionary change, begun by Toussaint Louverture in the war for Haitian independence."[71] The Cuban writer Roberto Fernández Retamar (1930–2019) concurs with that sentiment, extending it to include, in addition to Louverture and many others, the last Inca ruler Túpac Amaru, the Guatemalan human rights activist Rigoberta Menchú, and Che Guevara.[72] This is Caliban's world, and Lamming thinks that emancipation is the paramount expression of Caliban's spirit, inspiring rebellions and promoting the idea of redemption in the face of Prospero the merchant and man of God.

Through words, images, and sounds, thinkers, artists, and poets proclaimed and sustained strong attachments to their own cultural expressions, which differed from those of the colonial metropole. They found support in a perspective that connected the past to the present, which in the language of the time also recognized continuities and ruptures between tradition and modernity. It was a process of intellectual synthesis laden with political and social polemics, renewals, and commitments in which an outstanding group of authors and researchers revised and enhanced appreciation of the African roots of the culture of the island Caribbean and Brazil, in the broader context of the Americas.

The Image of the Black, and More

By the beginning of the 1960s, creative Black people had produced a new discourse. They had created a world in which their imaginaries sustained a new artistic perception. Their praxis, whether self-taught or not, stood in confrontation with the established idioms as something previously unseen in the artistic panorama of the Caribbean and Brazil. After the Second World War, the Caribbean's relationship with the world changed markedly. Africa became an actor on the world stage, as did the Caribbean. Both regions participated in a complex decolonization

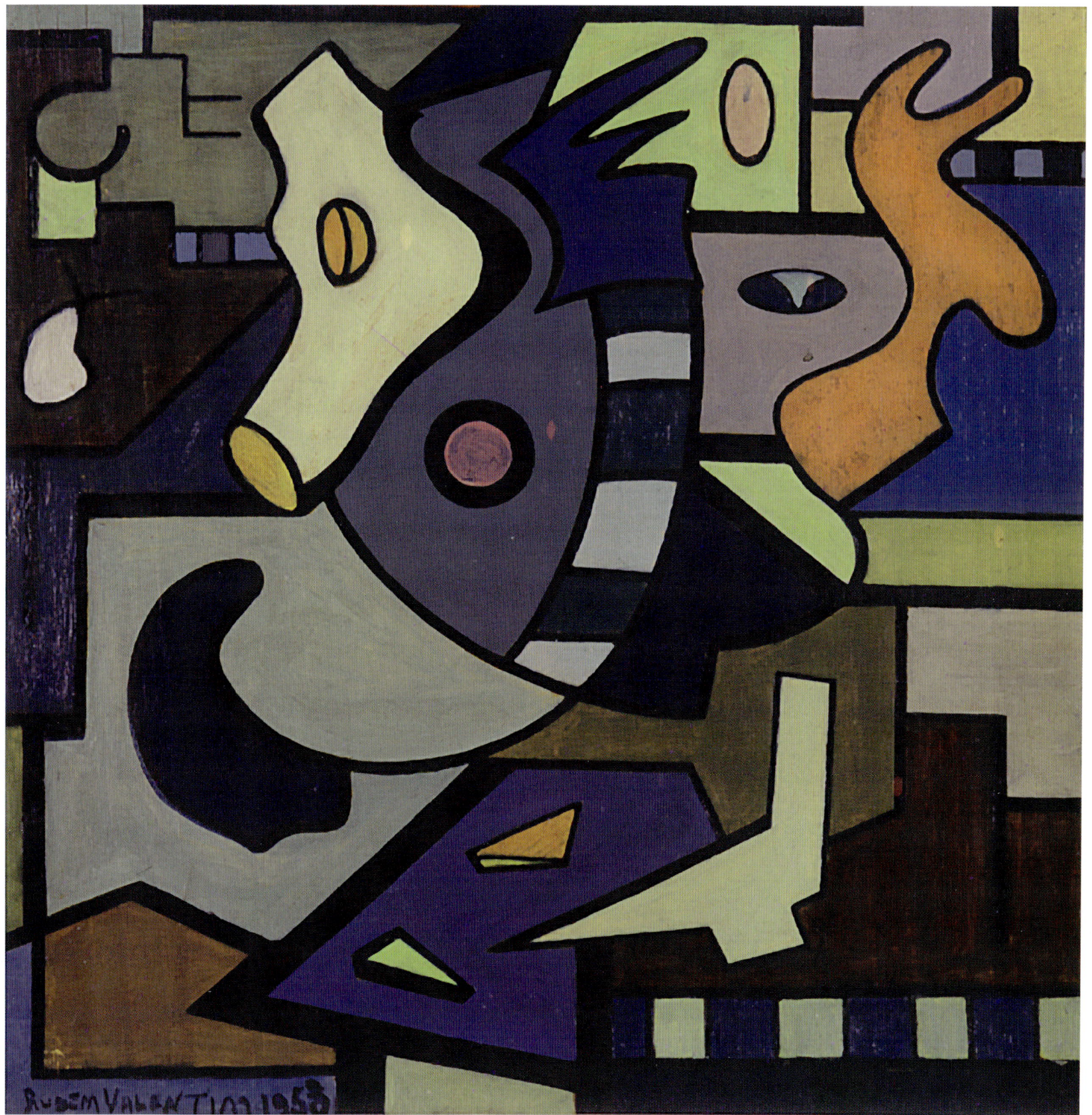

process, and developments since then have made them, like the rest of the world, participants in the web of globalization. The connections were intensified by new protests associated with Black movements on an international scale and the demand for the rights of minorities and the African, Caribbean, and Brazilian emigrant communities in the developed countries and the United States. At the same time, abstraction and other trends in the arts created new points of reference. Those who followed such innovations in the Caribbean and Brazil were not removed from the Africanness underlying their visual construction. Examples include the Cuban sculptor Agustín Cárdenas (1927–2001) with his rhythmic ideas expressed in various materials (see *The Image of the Black in Latin American and Caribbean Art*, Book 1, fig. 8*),* and the compositions of Rubem Valentim (1922–1991) in Brazil, profoundly inspired by a symbolic idiom based on the religious objects and symbols of the orixás, leading up to his extraordinary *emblemas* (emblems) in successive years. The works of both Cárdenas and Valentim refer back to images of Afrodescendants even more strongly through intensively expressive visual markers.

The new era coincided with other sociocultural circumstances in the Caribbean and Brazil resulting from their peripheral condition. Past and present seemed to be fused in an amalgam of dependent colonial history, pervasive poverty, cultural survivals, and social marginalization that was both individual and collective. What persisted was the richness and diversity of artistic expression, emancipatory thought in transit toward the challenge of decoloniality, and confidence that we will achieve it.

V

History and the Contemporary World

12

SOUND, FURY, AND FREEDOM: MONUMENTS AGAINST SLAVERY

ROBERTO CONDURU

In 1967, the Haitian sculptor and architect Albert Mangonès (1917–2002) created *Le marron inconnu de Saint-Domingue*, often shortened simply to *Le marron inconnu* (*The Unknown Fugitive Slave*) and also known as *Le nègre marron*. Installed in the Champs-de-Mars in Port-au-Prince, the monument celebrates the rebellion against slavery in Saint-Domingue, the portion of Hispaniola colonized by France, where in 1791 the revolution began that resulted in the independence of Haiti. The sculpture depicts an almost naked man in a very tense position. He kneels on his right knee; his left leg stretches behind him with a broken chain attached to the ankle; his right hand holds a cane-cutting machete resting on the ground. He arches his torso and tilts his head, extending his lips upward to blow through the *lanbi* (conch shell) he holds to his mouth with his left hand. In our imagination, we can hear the sound he produces for eternity, announcing Black people's fight against slavery and heralding their victory in their conquest of freedom.

There were innumerable previous efforts to end slavery in the Americas before the revolution in Haiti (1791–1804), ranging from those led by anonymous individual attempts to well-known collective and structured revolts. Some were even successful, but they were circumscribed temporarily or spatially, like those that resulted in the runaway-slave communities that existed outside of colonial control, called *cimarrones* in the Spanish colonies and *quilombos* in the Portuguese. Among the many such communities that existed in Brazil, the Quilombo dos Palmares resisted for more than a century before it was exterminated in 1697. Gaspar Yanga in Nueva España (now Mexico) and Benkos Biohó in Nueva Granada (now Colombia), however, defied the colonizers and secured freedom for themselves and their people in the early seventeenth century, constructing autonomous if somewhat restricted Maroon communities in the midst of colonized territories: San Lorenzo de los Negros (renamed Yanga in 1932) and San Basilio de Palenque, respectively.

Revolts and the establishment of independent settlements carried on throughout the seventeenth and eighteenth centuries, but none were as successful as Yanga's and Biohó's had been. Haiti's insurrection was a turning point for slavery and colonialism in the Americas. Although it was a unique event, the attainment of independence resulting from a rebellion of enslaved people was recognized worldwide as a major political event, challenging the persistence of economic and cultural colonialism to the present. Haiti achieved its independence in 1804; slavery didn't end in the Americas until 1888, when it was officially abolished in Brazil,

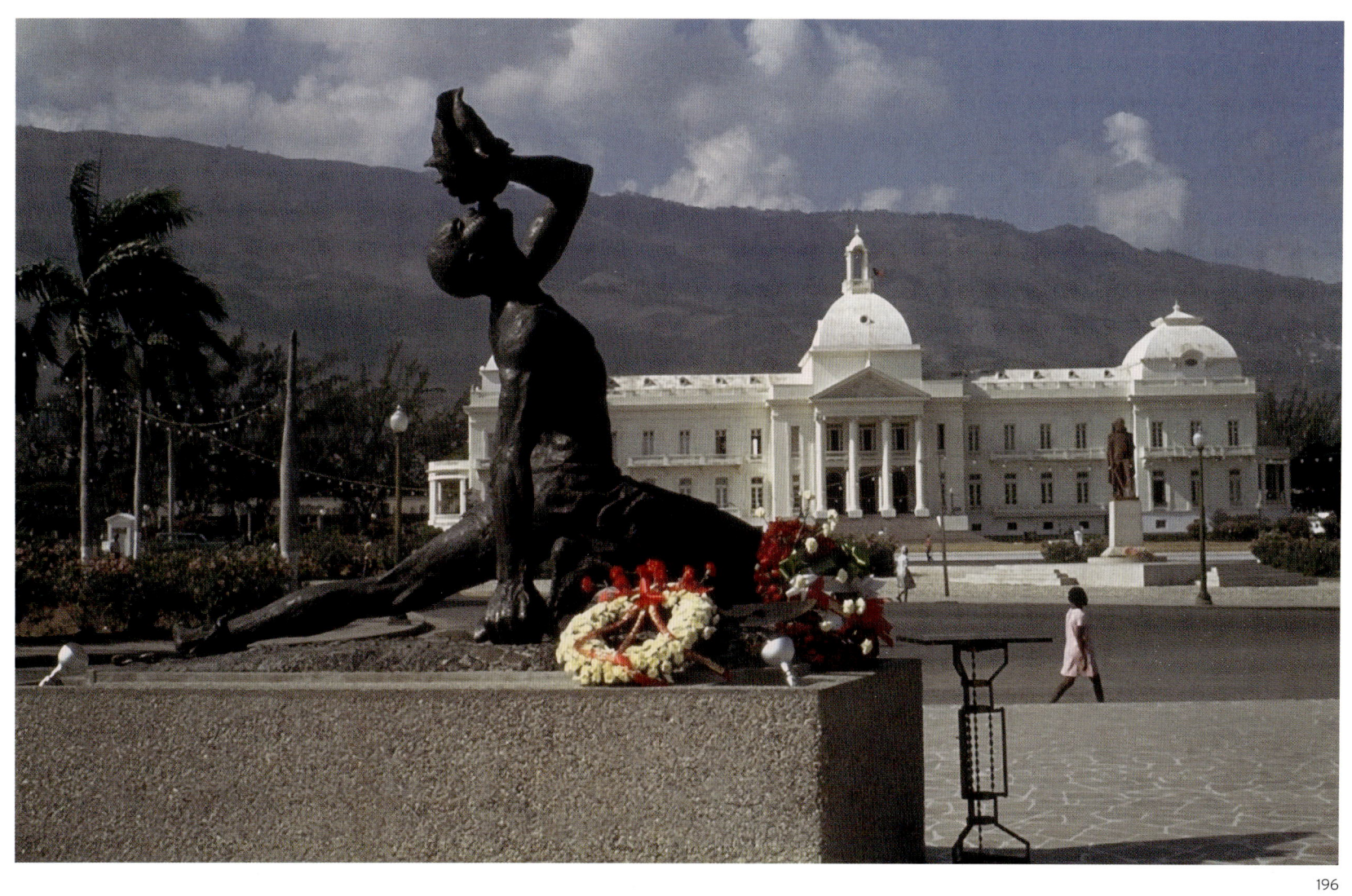

196 Albert Mangonès. *The Unknown Fugitive Slave*. 1967. Bronze. Port-au-Prince, Haiti, Champs-du-Mars.

but its baleful effects still contribute to the social inequality observed in all American countries. Full rights for Afrodescendants have yet to be effectively secured throughout the region; political autonomy and equality remain unachieved, particularly in, though not limited to, places like French Guyana, Martinique, and Puerto Rico.

In this sense, the Black Maroon of Mangonès's monument needs to exert himself continually to propagate as far as possible the sound of good news while calling on people to keep up the fight for freedom. The monument in Port-au-Prince proclaims past and present events, both the victorious battle for liberty in 1791 and the necessity of maintaining its effectiveness. It also announces the need to erect further monuments to commemorate and combat the ongoing effects of the slave trade and slavery while keeping up the struggle to maintain freedom and to celebrate African and Afrodescendant peoples and their cultural values. Indeed, in the last fifty years, there has been burgeoning construction of national and international monuments, memorial buildings, and sites related to the slave trade and slavery. The following text focuses on antislavery and pro-freedom monuments erected in Latin America and the Caribbean.

The (Anti-)Exemplary Black Body

Usually the monuments related to the slave trade and slavery have been erected according to the European tradition of monuments. Thus, many of them inscribe something new in the Americas' landscape: the good exemplarity of Black people and their actions. Among the many horrific situations experienced by enslaved Africans and Afrodescendants during the slavery period, there was the contradiction of sometimes being the majority of the population and at the same time being socially invisible, marginalized.

A small number of Black bodies portrayed not as enslaved people but rather as images close to European and Catholic models were represented in sculpture during the time of slavery, where Africans and their descendants appeared as Black angels, saints, and even as Jesus and Mary themselves. The standing *Cristo negro* (*Black Christ*) has been venerated since the end of the sixteenth century in Otatitlán, Mexico.[2] The image of Nossa Senhora da Conceição Aparecida (Our Lady of Conception Aparecida) is a Black Madonna whose veneration began in the early eighteenth century and culminated two centuries later when she was decreed the patroness of Brazil. Besides Black saints like St. Elesbaan and St. Ephigenia of Ethiopia, who were venerated in Brazil, Peru, and other American regions, there was a profusion of Black and mulatto angels hanging on altarpieces and decorative panels.[3] Whether it was an outcome of Catholicism's expansion among Africans and Afrodescendants or a way of co-opting them, the message was clear: to be exemplary, the Black body should deny African religions and values, convert to Catholicism, and embrace European culture.

Many drawings, prints, and paintings produced during the time of slavery depict aspects of captivity in the Americas: scenes of documentary or perversely picturesque characters to be consumed in Europe, feeding the appetite for the exotic. One of the few sculptural images representing servitude is the pair of lifesize cast-iron Blackamoors holding torches or lamps, from the Fonderies du Val d'Osne, in Haute-Marne, France, which could be found in the manor houses of coffee plantations like the one built between 1845 and 1853 in Fazenda Paraíso, in southeastern Brazil.[4]

Although images such as these permanently embodied the servitude and subjugation of Black people in elite environments, there was no public monument to the slave trade or slavery. Broadly speaking, the inclusion of enslaved figures in monuments in Europe passively endorsed slavery, and such images would have made no sense to enslaved people, whose suffering in captivity could not be mitigated by images supporting the institution.[5]

Some artifacts were intended not so much to exalt slavery as to demonstrate the perils enslaved people faced in trying to escape, disturbing the order of captivity in the colonies. Among the rare occasions in which the Black body got visual prominence was in the rites of public punishment. As depicted by Jean-Baptiste Debret (1768–1848) and Johann Moritz Rugendas (1802–1858), in one of these rituals, enslaved people were whipped while attached to a post in front of other people. In these rites (and in their rendering), deviant Black corporality was exhibited as a social antitype.

Following the Portuguese tradition in Brazil, the public loci for these punishments were designated as *pelourinhos* (Portuguese for "little pillory" [sing.], after the Medieval Latin *pilloria*). Stone columns or wooden posts symbolized Portuguese royal authority and were places of punishment for criminals, Maroons, and other people resistant to the colonial order. The pillory itself becomes a kind of monument, memorializing the colonial order and the anti-exemplarity of insurgent peoples.

Whipping posts, as well as other objects, buildings, and sites built to optimize the slave trade and slavery, were almost always destroyed after the end of slavery; they became not only useless, but socially uncomfortable. As signs of repression and torture, not of civilization and modernity, they automatically made visible what the ideologues of whitening American societies wanted to forget and to be forgotten. The eradication of slavery's material vestiges from cities and territories was an attempt to eliminate the slave trade and slavery from the memory and history of American countries, a process negated by most of the monuments discussed here.

But the cultural resonance of those pillories still persists, whether they are physically present or not. The best example is a neighborhood in the historic center of Salvador, Brazil's first capital, which is still popularly known as Pelourinho more than a century after the destruction of the city's whipping post, which was not even located there.

Few whipping posts still exist in Brazil. Of particular interest is the pillory in Minas Gerais Square in Mariana, a city in southeastern Brazil. Bordering the square is the Casa de Câmara e Cadeia (the public administration building), the Igreja de São Francisco de Assis (Church of St. Francis of Assisi), and the Igreja de Nossa Senhora do Carmo (Church of Our Lady of Mount Carmel). Since 1945, this urban architectural complex has been preserved as a national heritage site. Its pelourinho was erected by José Moreira Matos in 1750, destroyed in 1871, redesigned by José Wasth Rodrigues (1891–1957) in 1938, and rebuilt in 1981, using remaining pieces according to Rodrigues's project. With the symbols of Portuguese colonial rule evident (coat of arms, armillary sphere, scales of justice, and the sword of order), the renovated whipping post represents an attempt to restore the original configuration of one of the main squares built by the Portuguese in South America. As an instrument of maintenance of order and torture, however, it can also be read as an index of two of the most

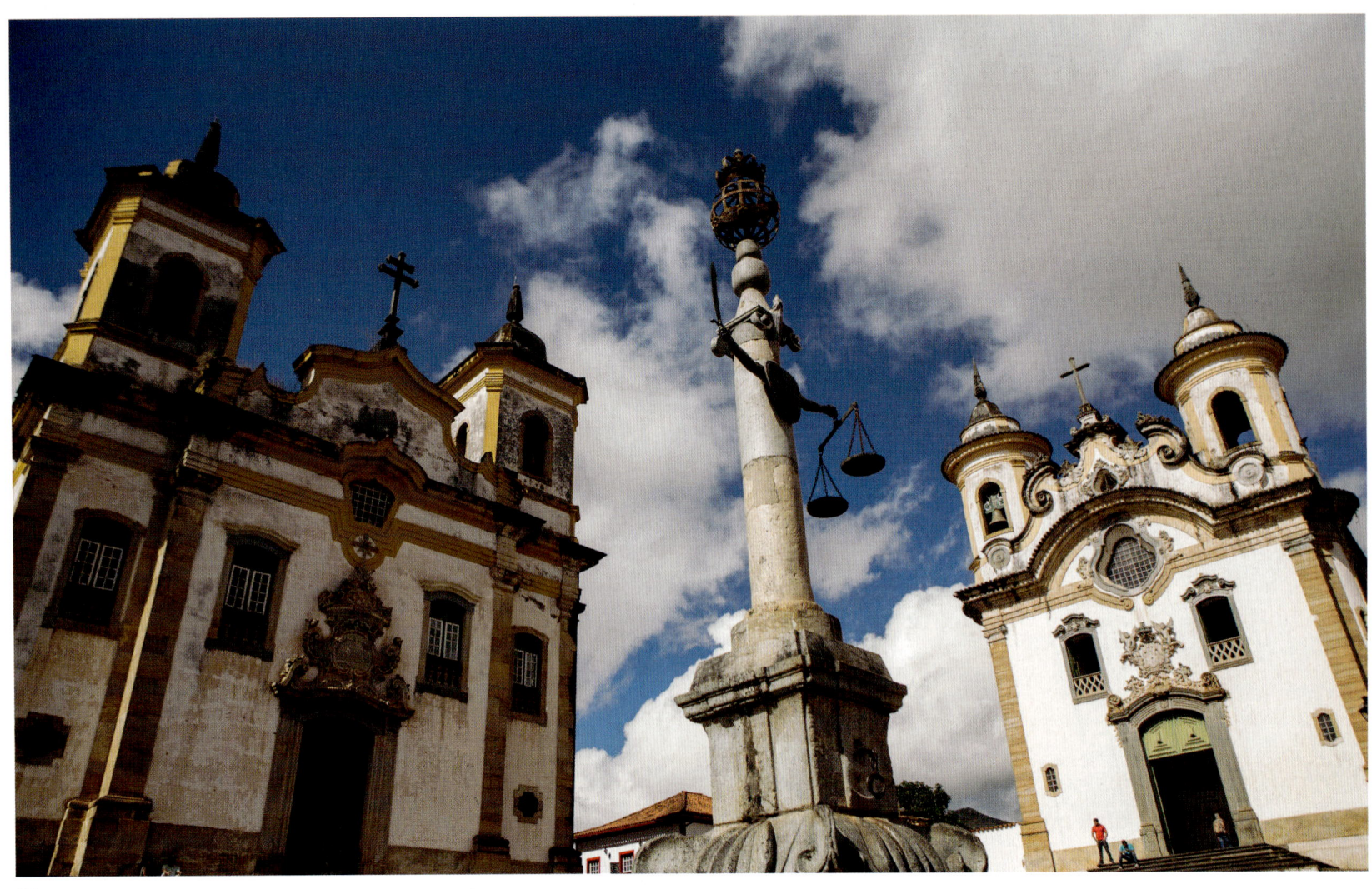

197

197 José Moreira Matos. *Pillory*. 1750. Dismantled in 1871, rebuilt in 1981. Mariana, Brazil, Minas Gerais Square.

198 Laurent Valère. *Cap 110*. 1998. Fifteen reinforced concrete statues. Anse Caffard, Le Diamant, Martinique.

undemocratic periods in Brazil's history: Getúlio Vargas's authoritarian government between 1937 and 1945, and the civil-military dictatorship in power from 1964 until 1985. While acting against the erasure of certain past historical practices of Brazilian cities, this pelourinho continues to evoke them, especially when tourists pose on it, as if to reenact the punishment of enslaved people.[6] In this sense, Mariana's pelourinho recalls the horrors of colonialism and captivity, allowing us to see it as a monument against freedom and to distance Minas Gerais Square from the historical sites with which the slave trade and slavery have been critically rethought in the last decades.

To Avoid Forgetting the Horror

There are also monuments in Latin America and the Caribbean that activate the collective memory, that aim to show explicitly the horrors of the slave trade and slavery. The memorial *Cap 110* was erected in southwest Martinique in 1998 as part of the celebration of the 150th anniversary of emancipation in the French West Indies. More specifically, though, the monument recalls a shipwreck that occurred in 1830 on the coast of Le Diamant, when a clandestine slave-trafficking boat struck the rocks of the Anse Cafard, killing some of its sailors and passengers, but mainly the African captives who were on board. Created by the Martinican artist Laurent Valère (b. 1959), fifteen figures made of white reinforced concrete form a triangular shape, a reference to the triangular slave trade, and face Diamond Beach and the Caribbean Sea at an angle of 110 degrees, in the direction of Africa's Gulf of Guinea, the departure point for many slave ships. Larger than human scale, the bent figures, which seem to have been deformed by the action of water, evoke feelings of pain and mourning of great intensity, calling to mind not only the people who died at Anse Cafard, but the more than a million who died during the Middle Passage.

Another interesting sculpture related to the slave trade is *Vicissitudes*, an underwater sculptural group installed in 2006 at the heart of the Molinère Bay on the island of Grenada, in the Caribbean Sea. The British-Guyanese sculptor Jason deCaires Taylor (b. 1974) says that "'Vicissitudes' is a sculpture about how we are all deeply affected by our environment."[7] Although he did not intend to create a tribute to people who died during the slave trade, this meaning has been read into his work, in which the circle of twenty-six statues of children of varied ethnic background is perpetually transformed into a coral reef. Despite deCaires Taylor's denial of an intention to depict enslaved people or the slave trade, *Vicissitudes* seems like a slave memorial, or at least resonates as such.

Death also surrounds *La esclavitud* (*Slavery*), originally known as *El esclavo* (*The Slave*), the monument conceived by the Argentinian sculptor Francisco Cafferata (1861–1890) and erected in 1881 in Buenos Aires.[8] A rare example of sculpture that depicts the condition of captivity, it forces us to confront its horror. The monument's recent title refers neither to a specific nor a generic enslaved person, but to slavery in general. Following in the tradition of Greco-Roman statuary, specifically *The Dying Gaul*, an Ancient Roman marble copy of a lost Hellenistic sculpture,[9] Cafferata depicts a man whose thin, naked, muscled body is reduced nearly to a state of exhaustion. The iron manacles around his wrists are generic symbols of captivity but are also instruments of torture, indicating that the man has just endured physical punishment. The hip, right arm, and the left leg

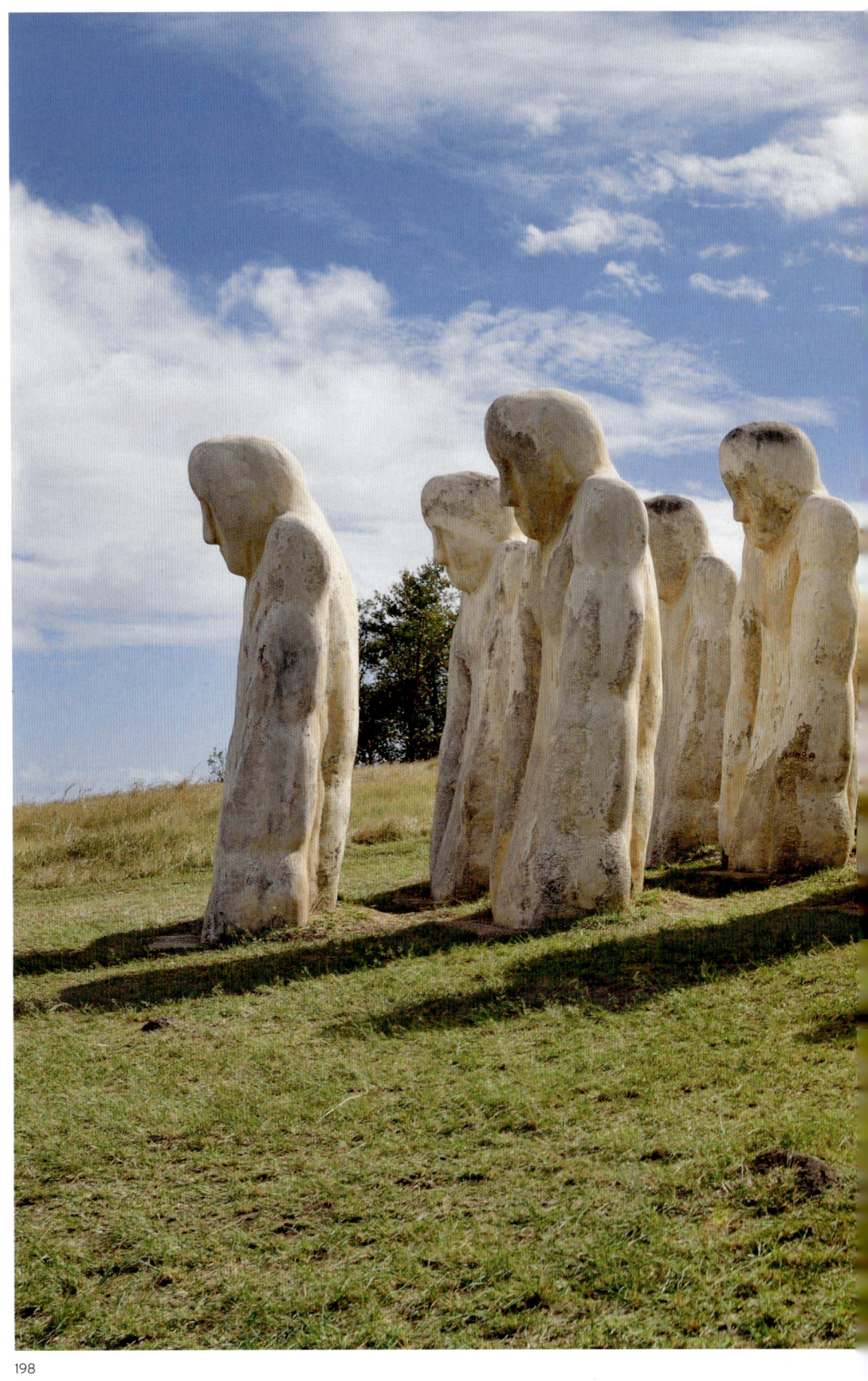

198

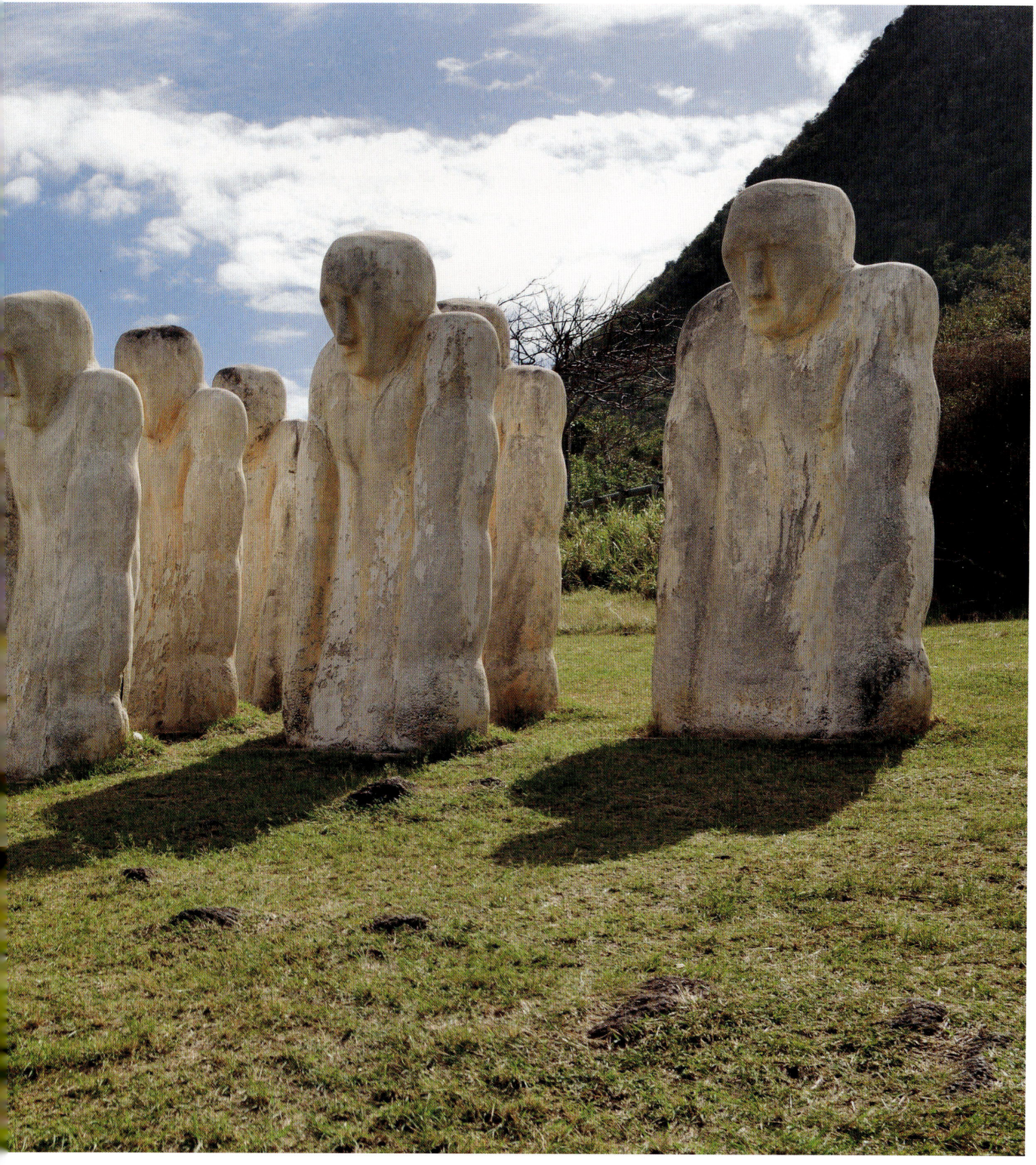

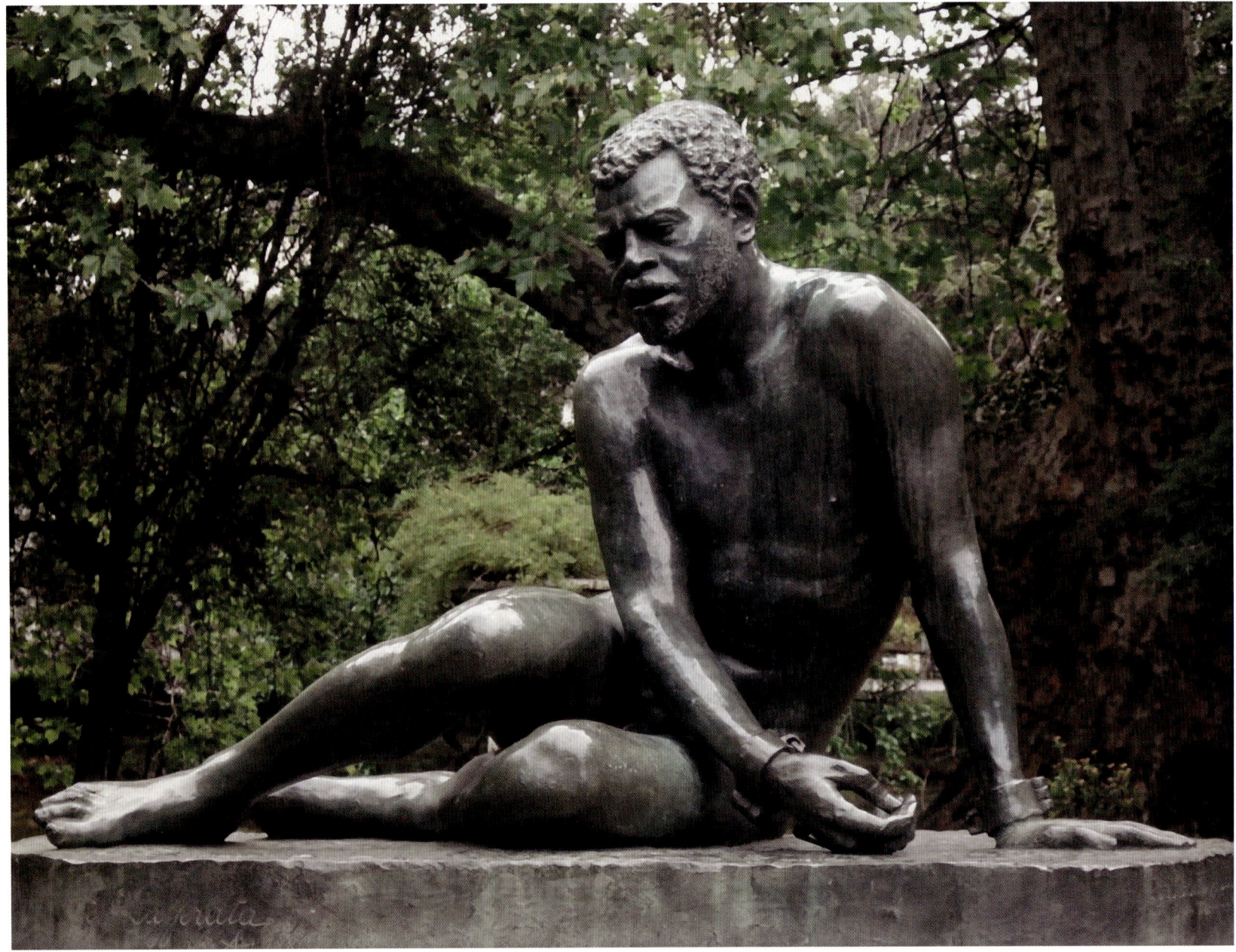
199

199 Francisco Cafferata. *Slavery*. 1881. Bronze. Buenos Aires, Argentina, Sicily Square, Parque 3 de Febrero.

200 Alberto Lescay. *Monument to the Runaway Slave*. 1997. Iron and bronze. Santiago de Cuba, Loma del Cimarrón.

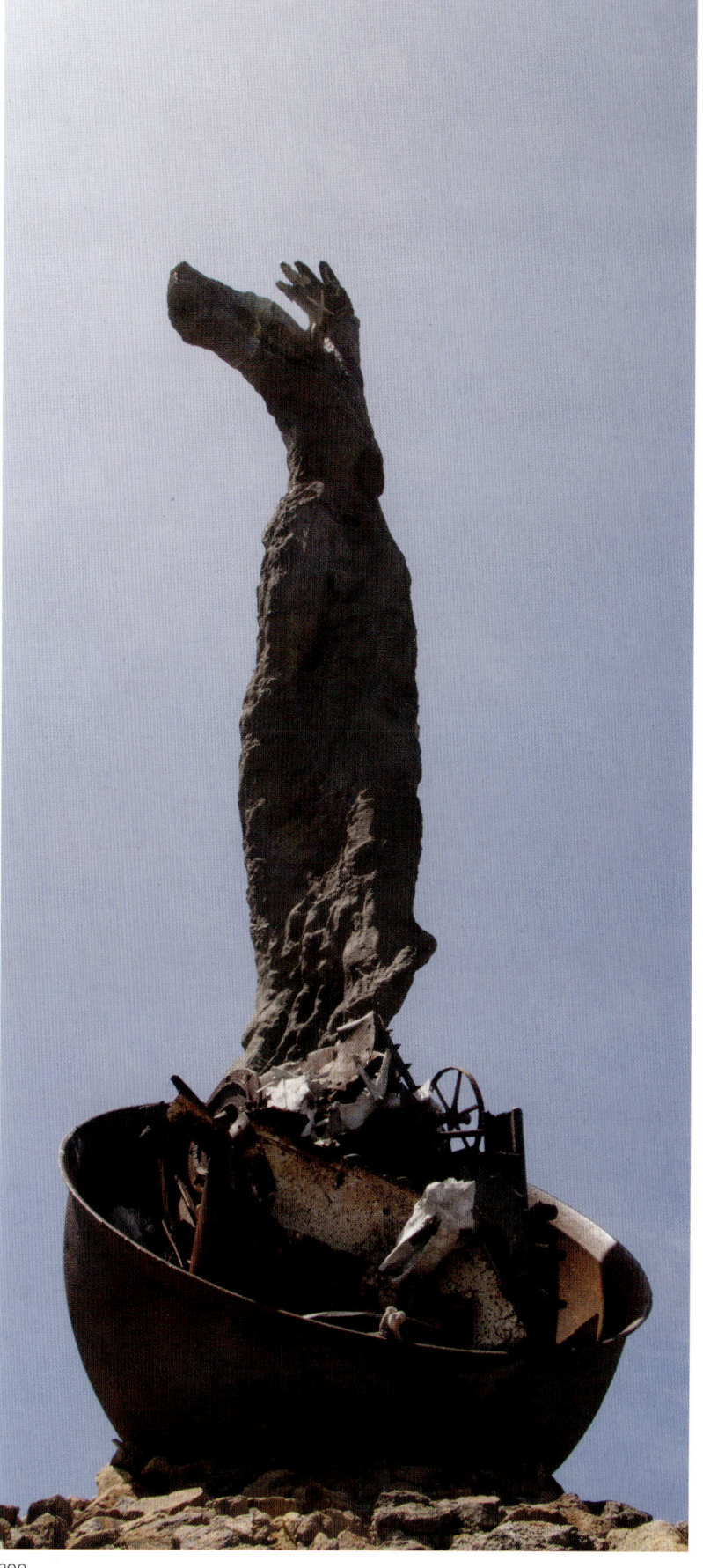

200

rest on the ground, and the right leg seems to move to the point of joining the other. The head tilts obliquely forward, and the trunk curves. The left arm seems to be the ultimate support that prevents the body from closing over itself. The facial expression is one of suffering, and the figure seems resigned and depressed, his half-open mouth indicating faint regret. Through him, we feel the physical and psychological effects of captivity.

Slavery in Argentina was abolished decisively in 1853 through the nation's first constitution, but the institution didn't end officially until 1861, when Buenos Aires joined the Confederation. Thus, the monument, upon its unveiling in 1881, represented a past condition, imploring people not to forget the horrors of slavery. The monument can also be read as a statement about the present condition of slavery, which had not yet ended in other regions: from the time of the unveiling of Cafferata's sculpture, it would take another five years before slavery ended in Cuba (1886) and seven before it ended in Brazil (1888). Representing captivity as a body breaking down, *La esclavitud* can be read as a representation of the ongoing process of dismantling slavery in the Americas. We can also read this monument in relation to a more extended future: it represents the end of slavery as an open, slow, and painful process that continues to affect the American nations. This poignant monument is full of meaning even today.

200 About suffering it is important to highlight the *Monumento al cimarrón* (*Monument to the Runaway Slave*). It was conceived by the Cuban artist Alberto Lescay (b. 1950) in 1997 and built in the mining region of El Cobre, in Santiago de Cuba, the site of the island's main but not only slave revolt. Understanding the *cimarrón* as an attitude toward existential freedom and even spiritual ascension, Lescay took a big cauldron used to boil sugarcane

SOUND, FURY, AND FREEDOM 343

201 Alicia Tafur. *Black Woman of the Fruit of the Peach Palm*. 1992. Bronze. Santiago de Cali, Colombia.

juice in the eighteenth century and transformed it both as a basis for an abstract volume with allusive corporeity and as a kind of *nganga*, a receptacle for offerings in the Afro-Cuban religion of Regla de Palo.[10] In the process of transmuting the sugarcane juice into pulp to be decanted and refined, from brown to white sugar, the fire makes it bubble. Lescay encourages people to renew the fire metaphorically as the cauldron is transformed into a nganga, evoking the Black body as consumed in captivity but also transcending it. With their offerings, people not only keep alive the memory of enslaved and rebel ancestors, but they also experience the suffering of the sacrificed Black body.

The Argentinian sculpture *La esclavitud*'s connection to the end of captivity in the Americas underscores the rarity of monuments actually erected in the campaigns against slavery. The French sculptor A. D. Bressae's *Alegoria a lei do ventre livre* (*Law of the Free Womb*, circa 1871) and the Brazilian sculptor Francisco Manuel Chaves Pinheiro's (1822–1884) *A emancipação do elemento servil* (*The Emancipation of the Servile Element*, 1875) were both designed in Brazil before slavery ended officially. Both are allegorical representations of the Brazilian law enacted in 1871 that granted freedom to all children born to enslaved women,[11] but neither of these monument projects was actually completed nor erected in an urban space; as such, they were unable to boost the campaign against slavery or anticipate publicly its certain but distant end.

Celebrating Social Types and Myths

La esclavitud is also exceptional in the period immediately following the end of slavery. Other monuments against slavery and in favor of freedom would still be long in coming. In that period, Black social types continued to be common in drawings, paintings, and engravings, but only much later did they begin to be transposed into sculpture and to be installed in public open spaces.

There have been few monuments celebrating the Black woman. She can be a robust figure, her platter overflowing with *chontaduros*—the iconic peach palm, a fruit from palm trees native to the tropical forests of South and Central America that is heavily associated with Pacific culture, as in the monument *La negra del chontaduro*, commissioned in 1992 by Club San Fernando and created by the Colombian artist Alicia Tafur (b. 1934) in Santiago de Cali, Colombia. The Black woman can also be generous and introspective, as in the Brazilian sculptor Júlio Guerra's (1912–2001) *Mãe preta* (*Black Mother*), installed in downtown São Paulo in 1954.[12] Guerra's sculpture was one of several monuments built in Brazil to celebrate the enslaved women who were obliged to nurse and breastfeed the children of their enslavers, to whom their own children belonged.[13] In another incarnation, the Black woman can be gracious and elegant, as is the *Nêga Fulô*, in the private garden the Brazilian artist Geraldo Simplício, known as Nêgo (b. 1943), carved directly on the ground around his house in Nova Friburgo, in southeastern Brazil, in the 1980s.

Intended neither as a monument nor as a celebration of Black women, the steel *Venus* cut by the São Paulo–based Brazilian sculptor José Resende (b. 1945) in 1992 was later nicknamed "*Negona*" ("*Big Black Woman*") upon its installation on Rosário Street in Rio de Janeiro.[14] Thus, the social renaming of this work presents the Black woman as a persistent social type in the Latin American and Caribbean imaginary. *Venus*/"*Negona*" is a Corten steel plate sectioned lengthwise down the middle to approximately

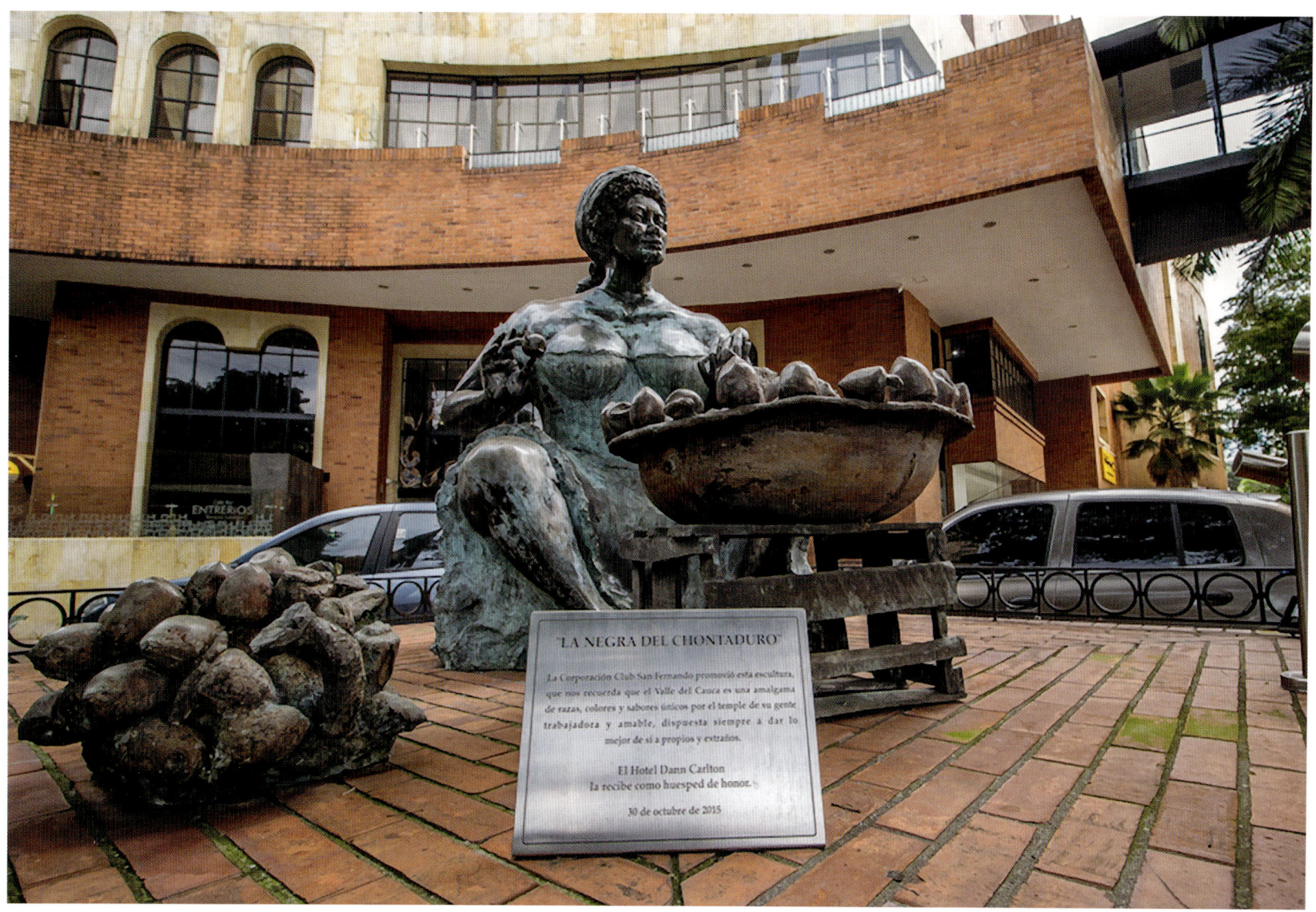

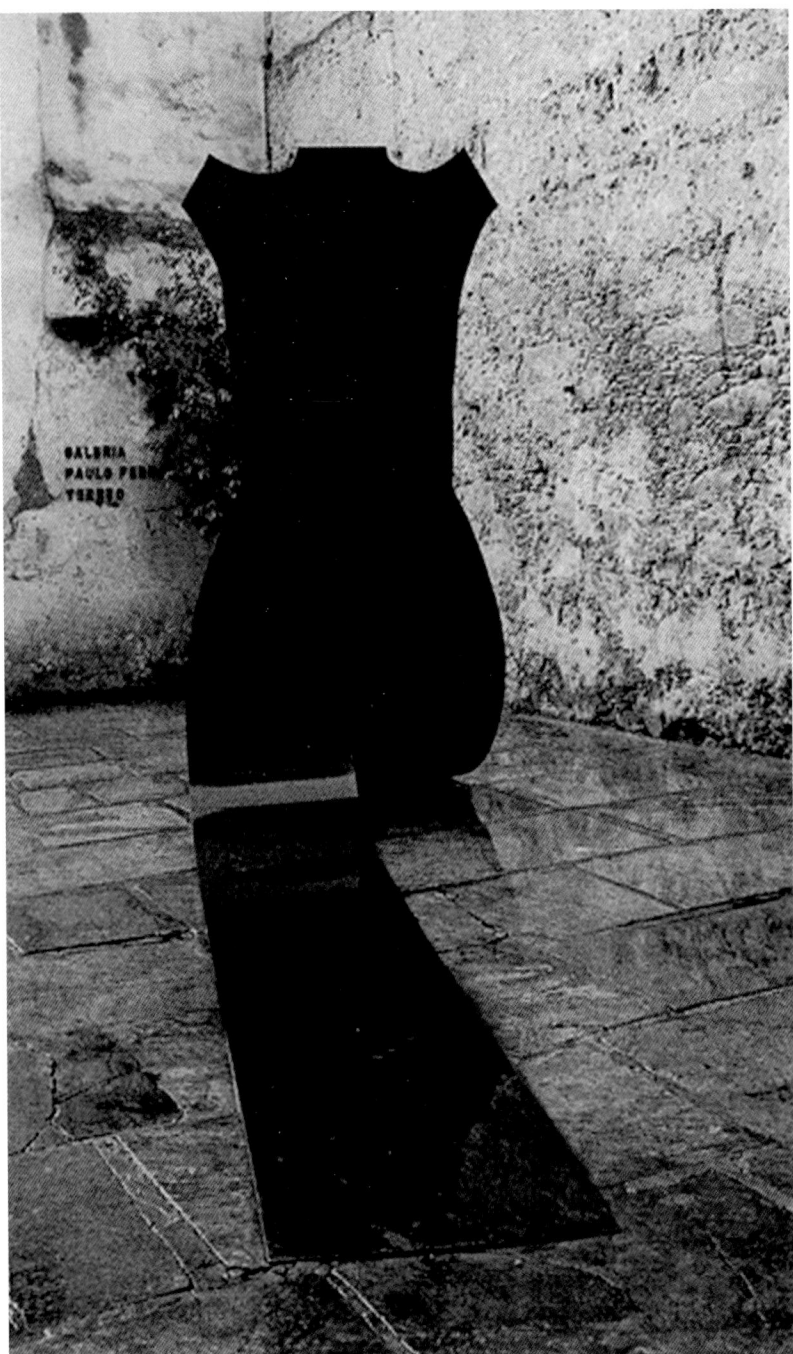

202

202 José Resende. *Venus/"Negona"* (*Venus/"Big Black Woman"*). 1991. Photograph by Miguel Rio Branco. Rio de Janeiro, Collection Paul Fernandes.

203 Edna Manley. *Negro Aroused*. Posthumously cast, 1991. Bronze. Kingston, Jamaica, intersection of Ocean Boulevard and King Street.

two-thirds, generating two strips that are laid out directly on the ground, but each extended in the opposite direction to the other, which makes the part not sectioned but, contoured in a way that alludes to the human body, rise. If the horizontal part is pressed down, the vertical part swings with lesser or greater intensity according to the force placed on it. This type of manipulation has occurred frequently in the urban space of Rio de Janeiro, and, along with the nickname given to it, elicits thoughts about how many Brazilian people's relationships with Black women often fuse feelings of affection and aggression, playfulness and violence, feelings that vary little, as well as the social roles of Black women as mother, lover, and servant in these and a small number of other monuments in Latin America and the Caribbean.

There are also monuments that feature archetypal Black men, such as *Preto velho* (*Old Black*) in Inhoaiba, a suburb of Rio de Janeiro, which celebrates a deity of the Afro-Brazilian religion Umbanda and is a symbol of the resilience and wisdom of Black elders. Created by the Brazilian sculptor Miguel Pastor (1930–1987) and erected in 1958, the seated bronze figure represents Joaquim Manuel da Silva (1854–1963), a formerly enslaved man who became a figure of respect in that region, known as Paizinho Preto (Black Daddy) or Tio Quincas (Uncle Quincas).[15] Another example is *Nego d'agua* (*Black from the Water*), installed in the São Francisco River in Juazeiro in northeastern Brazil, created by the Brazilian sculptor Ledo Ivo Gomes de Oliveira.[16] The monument depicts a legendary young man, tall and strong, who inhabits the bottom of Brazilian rivers and disturbs the work of fishermen.

If the men in these Brazilian monuments come from religion and myth, the figure in *Negro Aroused* in Jamaica derives from history, portraying not a specific person but a social group. Cre-

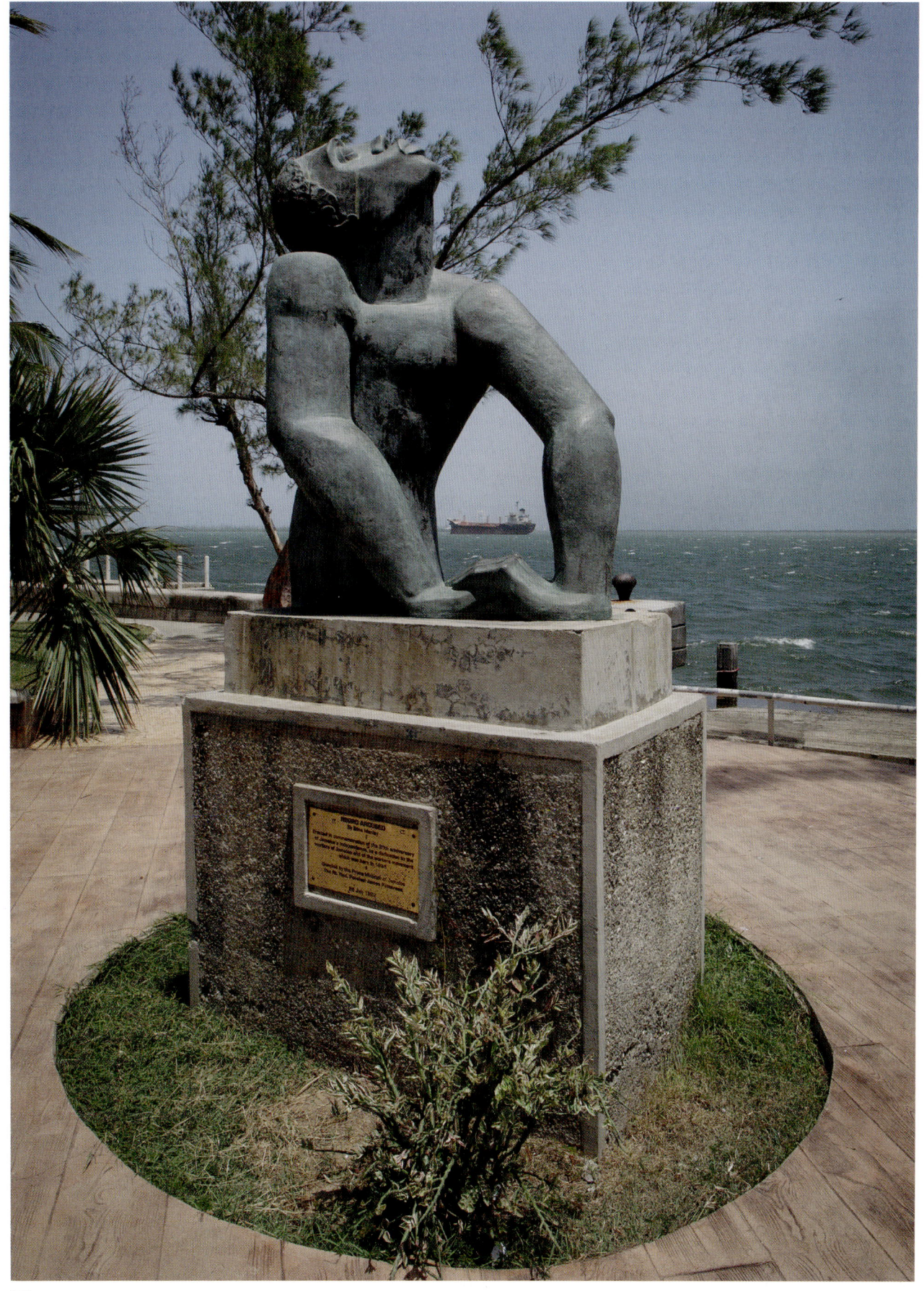

203

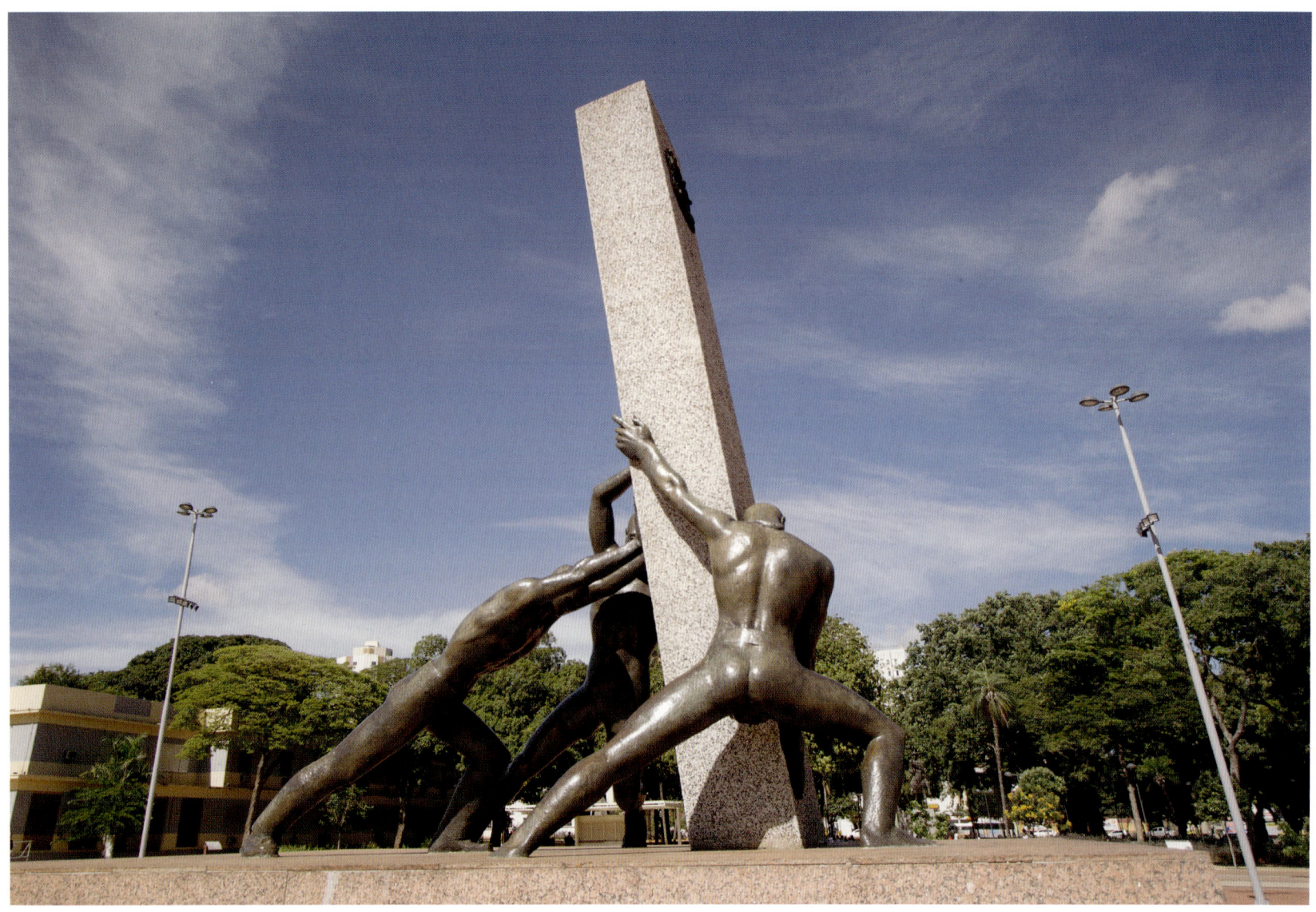

204

204 Neusa Morais. *Monument to Goiânia*, popularly known as *Monument to the Three Races*. 1968. Bronze and granite. Goiânia, Brazil, Dr. Pedro Ludovico Teixeira Square.

ated in 1935 by Edna Manley (1900–1987) as a wood sculpture, *Negro Aroused* presents a man with nonnaturalistic but harmonious body proportions who, with joined hands and extended arms, lifts his head and gazes skyward. Exhibited two years later, it was acquired by public subscription for the Institute of Jamaica collection (currently at the National Gallery of Jamaica). In 1938, one hundred years after the end of slavery in Jamaica, when its social and cultural effects still depressed the living conditions of Afrodescendant people, strikes and a rebellion against British colonial powers took place. Since that time, "*Negro Aroused* has become a symbol of the struggle of the people of Jamaica for independence, equality and human rights."[17] In the same year, a large-scale bronze copy was commissioned. In 1991, four years after Manley's death, a monument to the workers of Jamaica and the workers' movement, based on *Negro Aroused* and under construction since 1977, was finally cast in bronze from the artist's third version from 1982 and installed on Kingston's waterfront.

A controversial theme celebrated in monuments located in different latitudes and moments is the coexistence of the three main ethnic groups that have formed the Latin American and Caribbean nations: Native Americans, Europeans, and Africans. Two monuments—one in Goiânia, Brazil, and the other in Dorado, Puerto Rico—celebrate the myth of the harmonious relations of the three "races." In 1968, the Brazilian sculptor Neusa Morais (b. 1932) created *Monumento a Goiânia* (*Monument to Goiânia*), popularly known as *Monumento às três raças* (*Monument to the Three Races*), to be installed at the central civic square of Goiânia, a city built in the 1930s in central Brazil. Consisting of three bronze figures of men erecting a granite pillar inscribed with the city's coat of arms, it suggests the city as a work in progress that depends on the cooperation of the ethnic groups comprising its population.

In 1992–1993, on the occasion of the fifth centenary of the European conquest of the region later named America and of Borikén (now Puerto Rico), as well as the Dorado sesquicentennial, the Puerto Rican sculptor Salvador Rivera Cardona created *Monumento a las raíces puertorriqueñas* (*Monument to the Puerto Rican Roots*) to celebrate the tri-ethnic origins of the city, the state, and the Americas through three bronze figures of men, displaying symbols of their cultures.

In the Brazilian monument, the ethnic identities are not explicit because of the abstractness of the figures, but their ethnicities can be inferred from the degrees of nudity of each one: the Native American wears a thong; the African, shorts; and the European, trousers. In the Puerto Rican monument, by contrast, the ethnic groups are easily identifiable by the meticulous representation of their bodily features, clothing, and artifacts. The Native American wears a thong here, too, as well as a golden pendant called a *guanín*, grasping a spear with a fish and holding a stone collar.[18] The European wears a costume typical of a sixteenth-century European conquistador, with a sword tied to the hip and a book in his hand, and raises a Catholic cross. The African, with marks of body incisions, a metal collar on his neck, and a drum tied to his hip, holds a lit torch.

While insisting on the myth of harmonious coexistence, these monuments cannot hide the inequality between and inside those groups—inequality that they thus reinforce and help to maintain. Both monuments exclude women, privileging men as representatives of the ethnic groups. In the Puerto Rican monument, while the Native American and the European are identified as Taíno

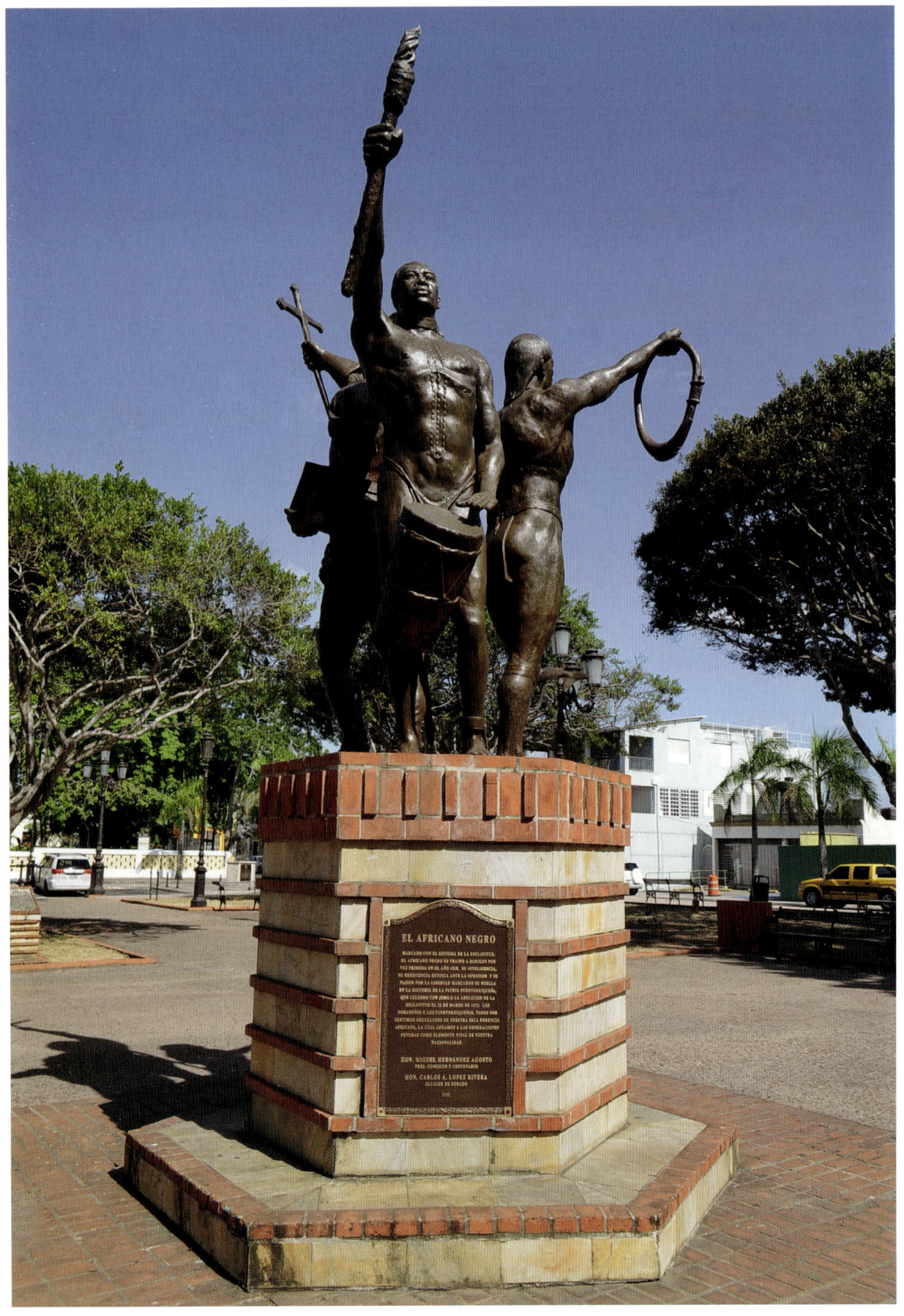

205 Salvador Riveira Cardona. *Monument to the Puerto Rican Roots*. 1992–1993. Bronze. Dorado, Puerto Rico, Plaza de Recreo.

and Spaniard, respectively, the third man is generically referred to as an "African negro," a broad definition that may stem from the mixing of ethnic groups with which slave traders and slaveholders tried to break social and family affinities. While the Spaniards and the Taíno people are represented by leaders, respectively a *conquistador* and a *cacique*, the African man has his enslavement specified by the metal collar around his neck, a sign of humiliation intended to thwart rebellion or disobedience of the enslaver. Although all three are cultural symbols of the past, those of the Spaniard tie him to modernity, while those of the Taíno and the African keep them closer to older cultures and to nature.

The monument in Goiânia does not precisely differentiate ethnicities, perhaps echoing the positive and mystified understanding of racial mixing that has animated Brazilian society since the 1930s, although the degrees of nudity of the three figures may suggest a prejudiced gradation of morality among them. In addition, their distinct social positions may be observed from the role of each man in the action: the figure representing Europe determines the direction in which the pillar rises, and thus, metaphorically, the construction of the city and, by extension, the state and country during and after colonization.

Although both monuments rely on the idea of the harmonious coexistence of the races, it is differently interpreted in each of them. If the sculptural group in Goiânia is centripetal, presenting men concentrating on completing a common task, the Dorado group is centrifugal, showing men individually performing the same action—exhibiting themselves and their respective cultures—but facing different directions from the same point. In 1960s Brazil, harmony in the city and society seemed to depend on the union and integrated action of subtly hierarchized ethnic groups, while in 1990s Puerto Rico, it seemed enough to recognize diverse ethnicities. In both places and times, however, the monuments only reinforce their unequal social situation.

Remembering the Fight for Freedom

Contrary to the fallacious ideas projected by these monuments, others erected in Latin America and the Caribbean keep alive the memory of the fight against enslavement of Africans and their descendants, celebrating their hard-won freedom, like the *Neg Mawon Emancipation Monument*, created by Franklyn Zamore and installed in the St. George parish in Roseau in the Dominican Republic in 2013.[19]

Like *Le marron inconnu de Saint-Domingue* in Port-au-Prince, the figure in the *Neg Mawon Emancipation Monument* does not represent a specific person, nor do the one female and two male figures created by the Cuban sculptor Enrique Moret (1910–1985) for the *Monumento al esclavo rebelde* (*Monument to the Slave Revolt*), which was installed by the Cuban architects José Raggi and Luis Rubio in the old Ingenio Triunvirato in Limonar in Matanzas in 1991.[20] Referring to unknown enslaved people, the Cuban, Dominican, and Haitian monuments are made up of archetypical figures, representing all Africans and their descendants in a positive light.

Sometimes the public understands the meaning of monuments differently from the artist, as we saw in the case of the underwater sculpture *Vicissitudes*, which was connected by the public to deaths during the slave trade. Similarly, Resende's *Venus* was perceived as "*Negona*," a big Black woman. The public can also personify figures meant to be anonymous. In the Dominican monument, the male figure does not represent a specific *neg*

SOUND, FURY, AND FREEDOM 351

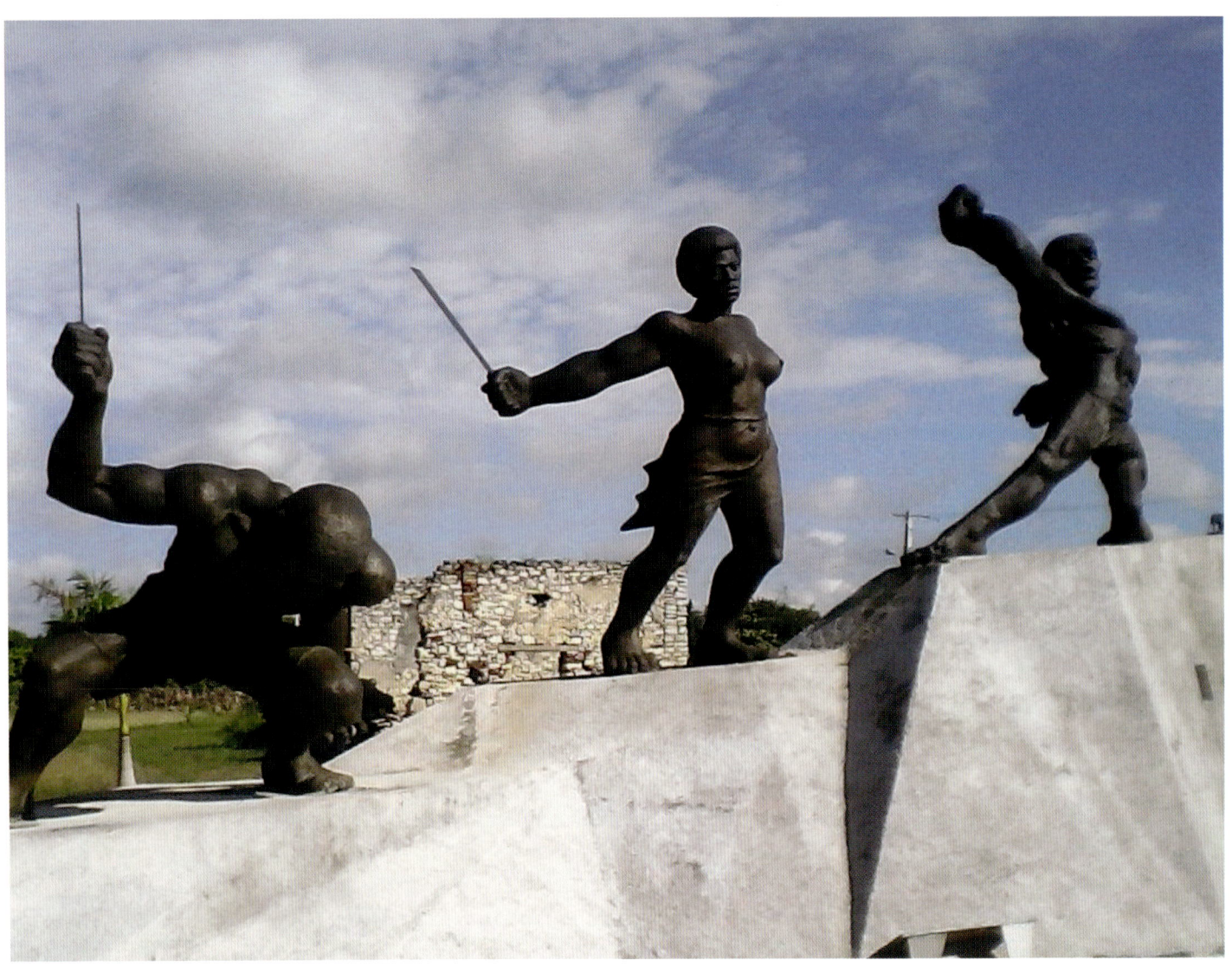

206

206 Enrique Moret Astruells. *Monument to the Slave Revolt*. 1976. Bronze. Matanzas, Cuba, Triunvirato.

207 Karl Broodhagen. *Emancipation Statue*. Unveiled in 1985. Bronze. Bridgetown, Barbados.

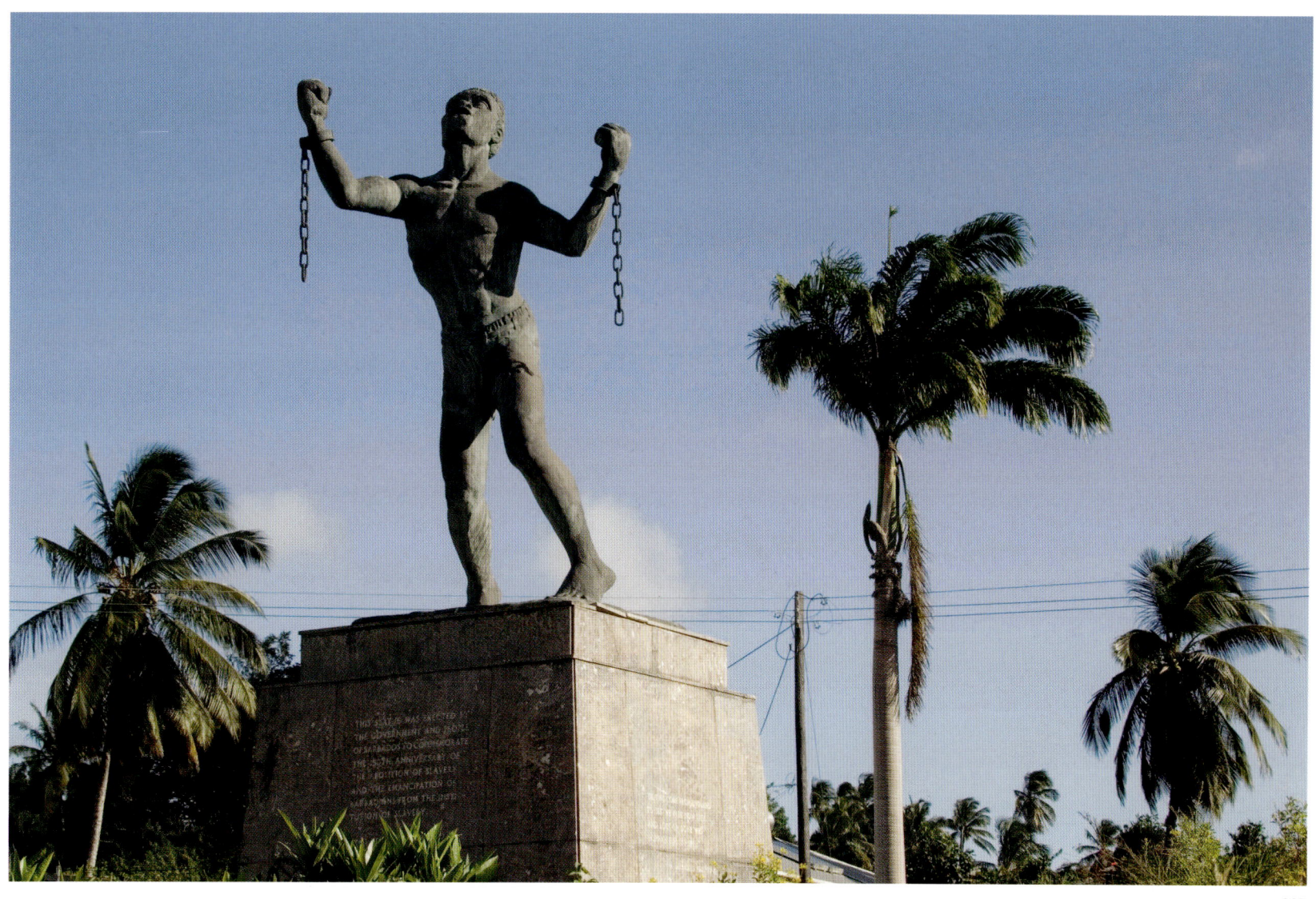

207

mawon but evokes local Black Maroon chiefs such as Balla, Jacko, Pharcel, and Quashie, as was suggested by Lennox Honychurch.²¹

207   Another example is the *Emancipation Statue*, created in 1985 by the Guyana-born Barbadian artist Karl Broodhagen (1909–2002) to celebrate the end of slavery in Barbados in 1830s. Instead of using its official title, in Barbados it is often referred to as "Bussa," the leader of the island's largest slave revolt, in 1816.

Also ambiguous are two other monuments in former Dutch colonies in the Caribbean. Here, sculptures that use singular human figures to represent slave revolts encourage viewers to visualize individuals in specific moments rather than as anonymous subjects acting collectively. Erected by the Guyanese artist Philip Moore (1921–2012) in 1976 in Georgetown, the *1763 Monument* celebrates the uprising of more than 2,500 enslaved people in Guyana. The monument is popularly called "Cuffy," in honor of the leader of the 1763 revolt, a Guyanese national hero.

208

SOUND, FURY, AND FREEDOM   353

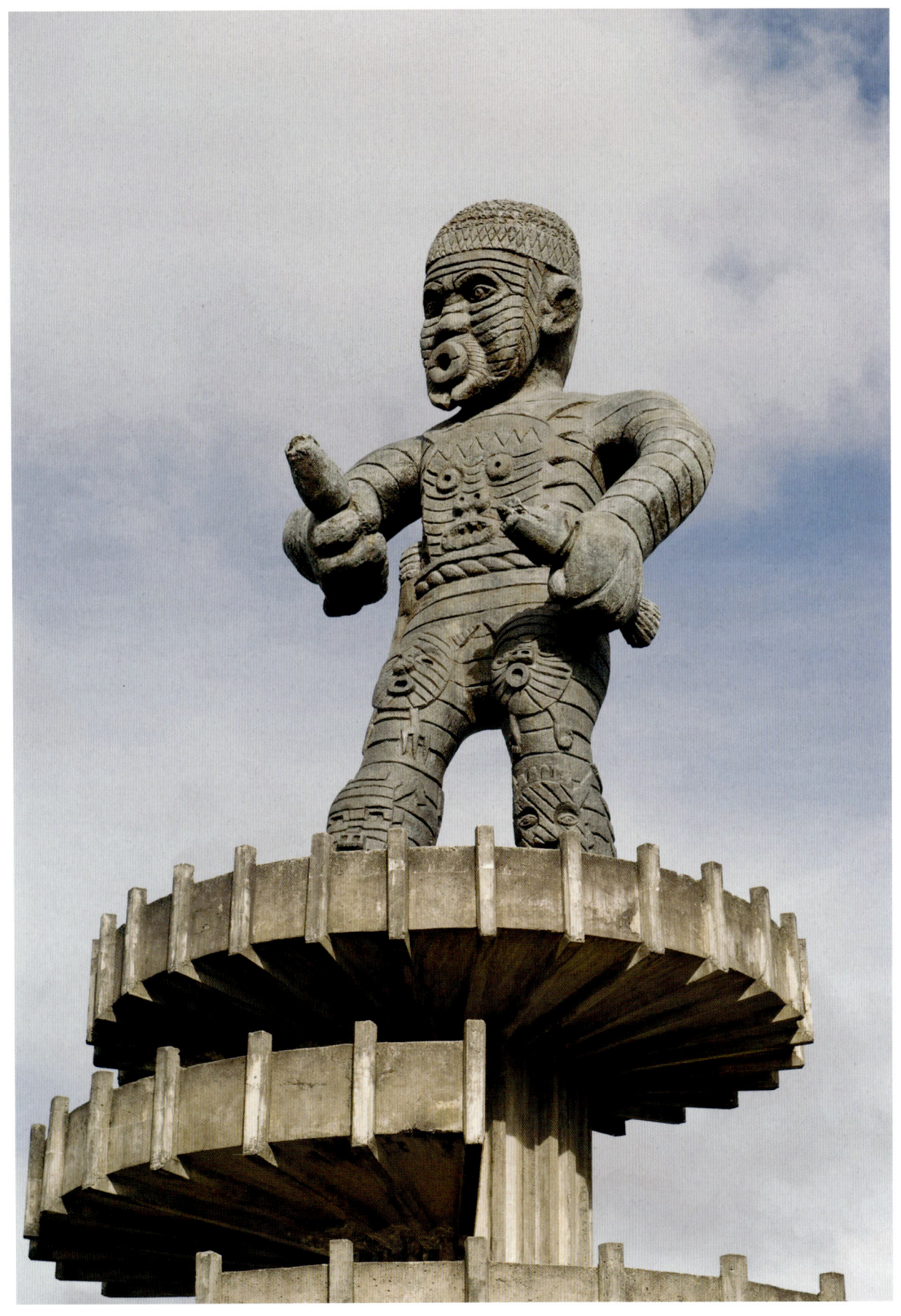

208

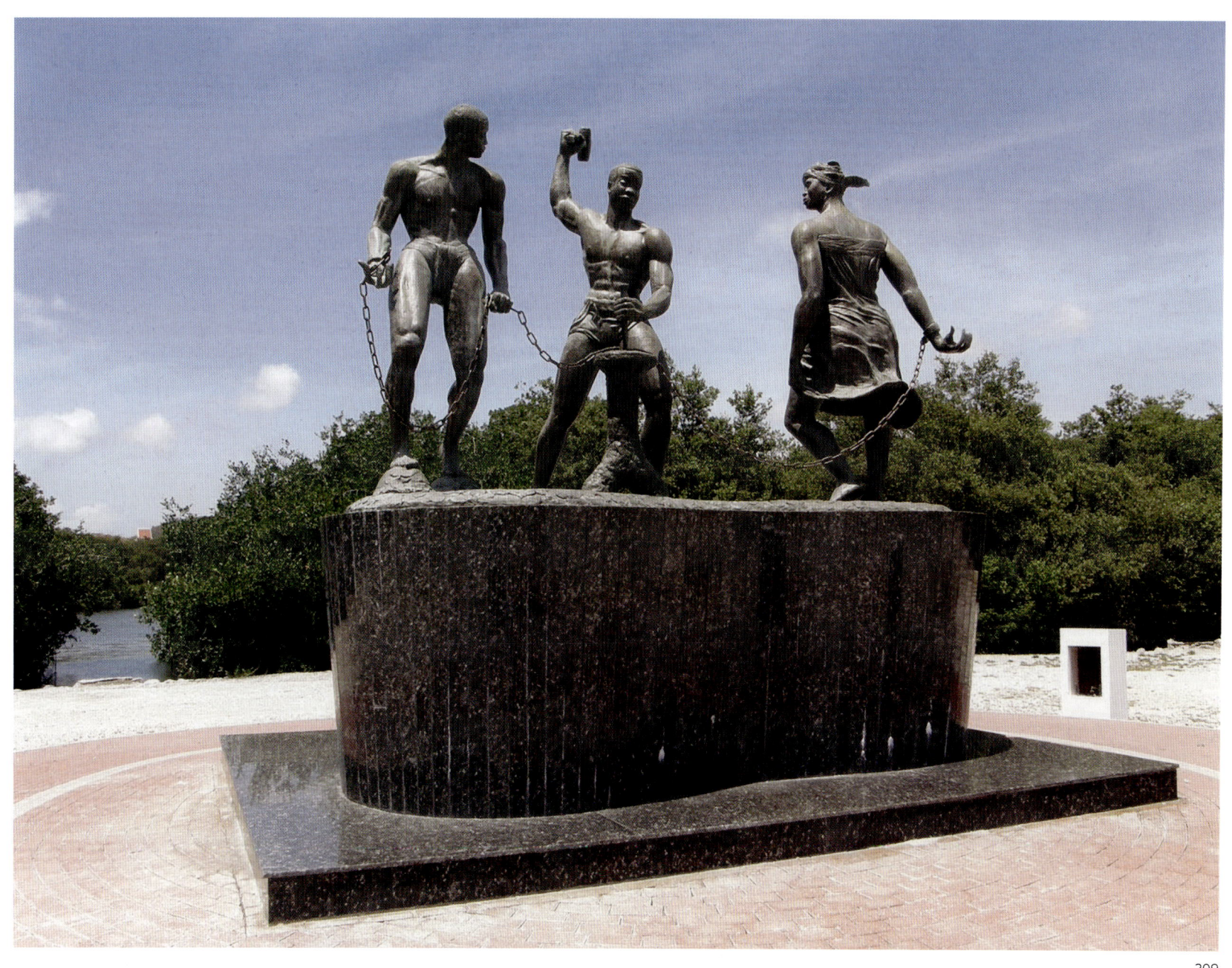

209

208 Philip Moore. *1763 Monument*. Unveiled in 1976. Bronze. Georgetown, Guyana, Square of the Revolution.

209 Nel Simon. *Unchained*. 1998. Bronze. Willemstad, Curaçao, Parke di Lucha pa Libertat.

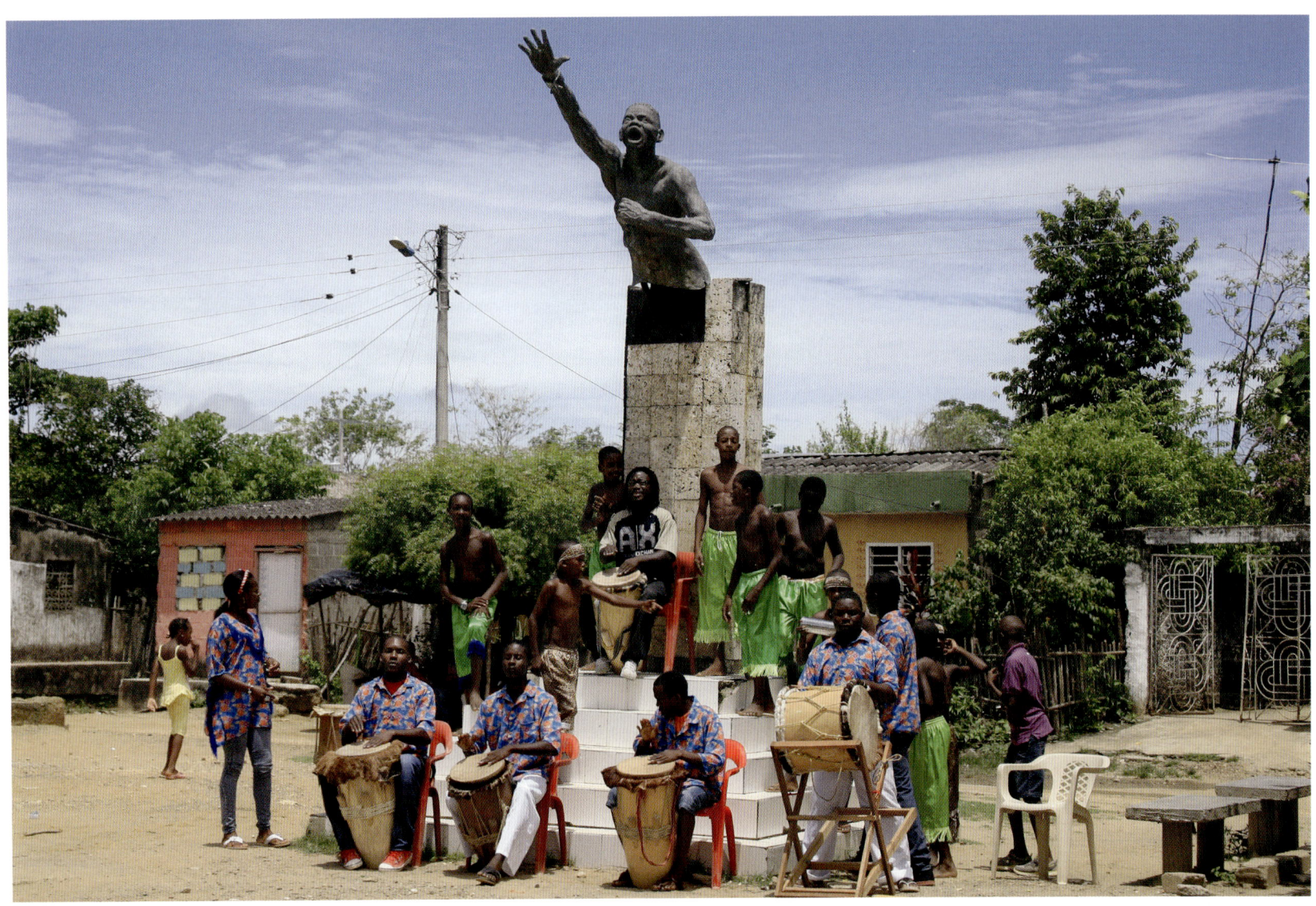

210

210 Unidentified photographer. *Residents playing traditional music in the street, June 1, 2013. Monument to Benkos Biohó*. 1998. Cartagena, Colombia, San Basilio de Palenque.

211 Erasmo Vásquez Lendechy. *The Yanga*. Dedicated 1973–1976. Bronze, marble. Veracruz, Mexico, Yanga Park.

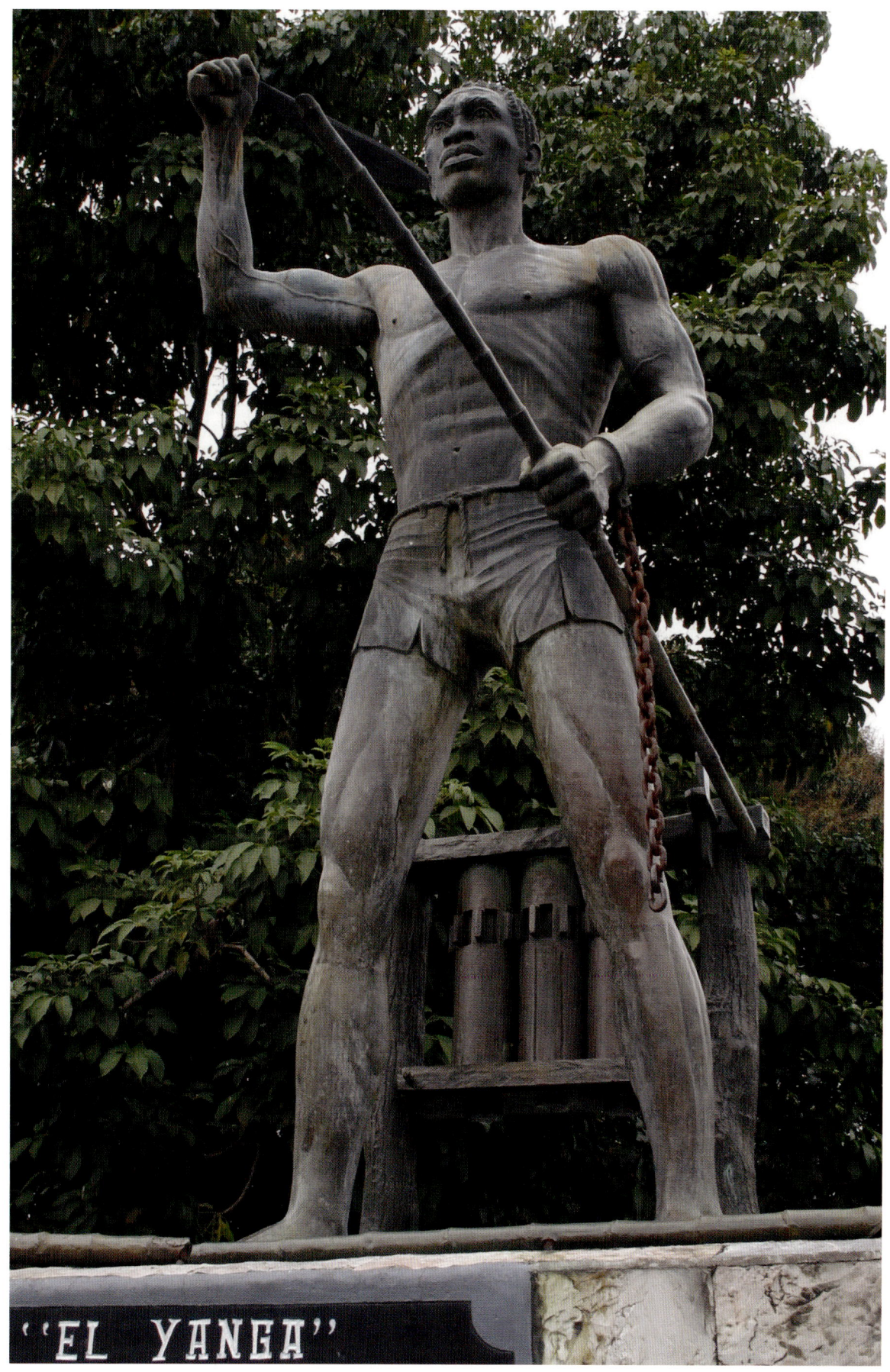

211

Similarly, in Curaçao, a monument memorializing the end of slavery, *Desenkadená* (*Unchained*), was created by the Curaçao-born sculptor Nel Simon (1938–2022) and installed in 1998 in the Parke Lucha pa Libertat ("Fight for Freedom"). The central figure, positioned between another man and a woman, is often identified as Tula, who led the 1795 slave revolt that began the Dutch colony's struggle for liberation.

Interpreting archetypal figures in monuments as specific individuals in Barbados, Curaçao, the Dominican Republic, and Guyana highlights those in which the focus is trained unambiguously on the decisive role of individuals. In addition to monuments dedicated to anonymous Black heroes, there are those that celebrate known heroes and communities. Two examples of the latter type are particularly compelling. The more recent was created in 1998 in Palenque de San Basilio, Colombia (formerly New Granada), to honor Benkos Biohó. Biohó was captured from his birthplace in present-day Guinea-Bissau in 1596. By 1599, he had led a revolt that secured his own and others' freedom from slavery, building a liberated Maroon settlement in the Montes de María region. Between 1605 and 1612, he established its independence in the midst of colonial territory but was betrayed by Spaniards, who captured and killed him in 1619 or 1621. Predating this monument by a little more than two decades is *El Yanga* (*The Yanga*), built between 1973 and 1976 in Mexico. It honors the "black African pioneer of black slaves' freedom," as inscribed on the monument. Gaspar Yanga was the leader of a Maroon settlement near Veracruz and is known for successfully resisting a Spanish attack on the settlement in 1609. In 1618 he reached a peace agreement with the colonizers, winning self-rule for the Maroon settlement, first called San Lourenço de los Negros, or San Lourenço de Cerralvo, and in 1932 renamed Yanga, in honor of the man who had become a national hero by the end of the nineteenth century.

Biohó's body is projected over the space from a stone pillar, his head lifted and eyes and mouth wide open, his right arm extended and hand also dramatically open, a chain dangling from the wrist. He seems to be asking for liberty, but the open chain links on his left hand make it clear that he has already liberated himself. In 2011, in an effort to be true to Biohó's story and to make his free condition more explicit, the chain on the right wrist was cut off, leaving only the cuff.[22] In *El Yanga*, Gaspar Yanga, too, is already liberated, his stance making evident that he is prepared to attack in order to defend his people: upright, stable, and firm, with a broken chain hanging from his left wrist, he holds an iron bar with his left hand while the right one is raised, gripping a machete, about to deal a blow. Biohó's figure is explicitly moving in space while Yanga's is self-contained. Both exhibit dramatic gestures—one expansive, the other restrained—celebrating or adopting a defensive posture after triumphing over slavery and winning freedom. The sculptures of Biohó, Yanga, and other Latin American and Caribbean Black heroes are inspiring not only in their setting and historical context, but they convey universal messages, reaching beyond their respective communities to all peoples who have known slavery or not, to the defenders of total freedom, and even to their opponents.

Some elements are common to these sculptures. While minimal clothing or nakedness indicate the subaltern social condition, and broken chains represent liberation from enslavement, machetes and lances, usually reinforced by dramatic gestures, attest to the need for violence in the fight for and maintenance of freedom.[23] Referring to the European artistic tradition, each of these monuments chooses among different moments as the special one in the process of liberation from slavery.

Less usual is the choice made by the sculptor Nel Simon at the Curaçao monument. *Desenkadená* concentrates the liberation of slavery in the symbolic act of breaking the chains. Erected where Tula would have been executed, the monument depicts not a generic moment of liberation of enslaved people that could have happened anywhere throughout the Americas and Africa—although it does have this resonance also—but a specific one. Tula breaks the chains with a sledgehammer over an anvil to free a man (possibly Bastian Karpata) and a woman (possibly Diana), both of whom helped him lead hundreds of enslaved individuals against the Dutch colonizers in 1795. Before Tula and Karpata were able to achieve freedom for themselves and other enslaved people, they were captured and killed. Although slavery was not abolished in Curaçao until 1863, following Tula's death, the enslaved people slowly began to gain some limited rights.

Like the monument to Benkos Biohó in Colombia, *Le marron inconnu* in Haiti, *Neg Mawon Emancipation Monument* in the Dominican Republic, and *Emancipation Statue* in Barbados all represent the moment that came soon after the breaking of chains. The Haitian and Dominican Maroons, as well as Biohó and Bussa in Barbados, communicate the conquest of freedom just after they have achieved it: the first figure gestures emphatically and seems to scream; the second and third blow through conch shells; and the last lifts up his head and arms. However, while Biohó and the Dominican Neg Mawon seem to be celebrating freedom and calling for others to rise up and join the fight, the Haitian Maroon still grips the machete, and the Barbadian hero has raised arms and clenched fists, suggesting that the fight goes on. We can apply to all these monuments what LeGrace Benson said about *Le marron inconnu*: these dramatic figures stand "for all the unrecorded individuals who dare to rise up to seize the land and the prosperity created by their own labor."[24]

The weapons and gestures in these sculptures bring us to other monuments that also focus on a moment when freedom is already won but not guaranteed, requiring that leaders remain vigilant, ready to defend aggressively their peoples. The Brazilian artist Márcia Magno (b. 1946) sculpted the figure of Zumbi, the last leader of Quilombo dos Palmares and a hero of Black Brazilian resistance, in a pose reminiscent of Yanga's, but less tense. On the monument, erected in Salvador in northeastern Brazil in 2008, Zumbi bends his left leg and supports it on his right, clutching in his right hand a machete tied to his hip and in his left a spear. He glances away, somewhere in the distance, as he stands guard to protect the quilombo from enemy attacks.

Another moment is represented in the *Monumento al esclavo rebelde* in Cuba. The figures, one female and two male, with their disproportioned, muscled, and tense bodies, brandishing machetes with dramatic gestures, refer to a moment prior to those in the other monuments: the fight to obtain freedom in colonial times. Such a moment, of course, can also be connected to ongoing efforts to maintain liberty.

Proposing Peace, Reaping Controversies
In opposition to the sort of dramatic imagery of the previous monuments, Laura Facey's *Redemption Song*, erected in 2003 in Emancipation Park in Kingston, Jamaica, portrays a different kind of emotion. Certainly Manley's *Negro Aroused* set a prec-

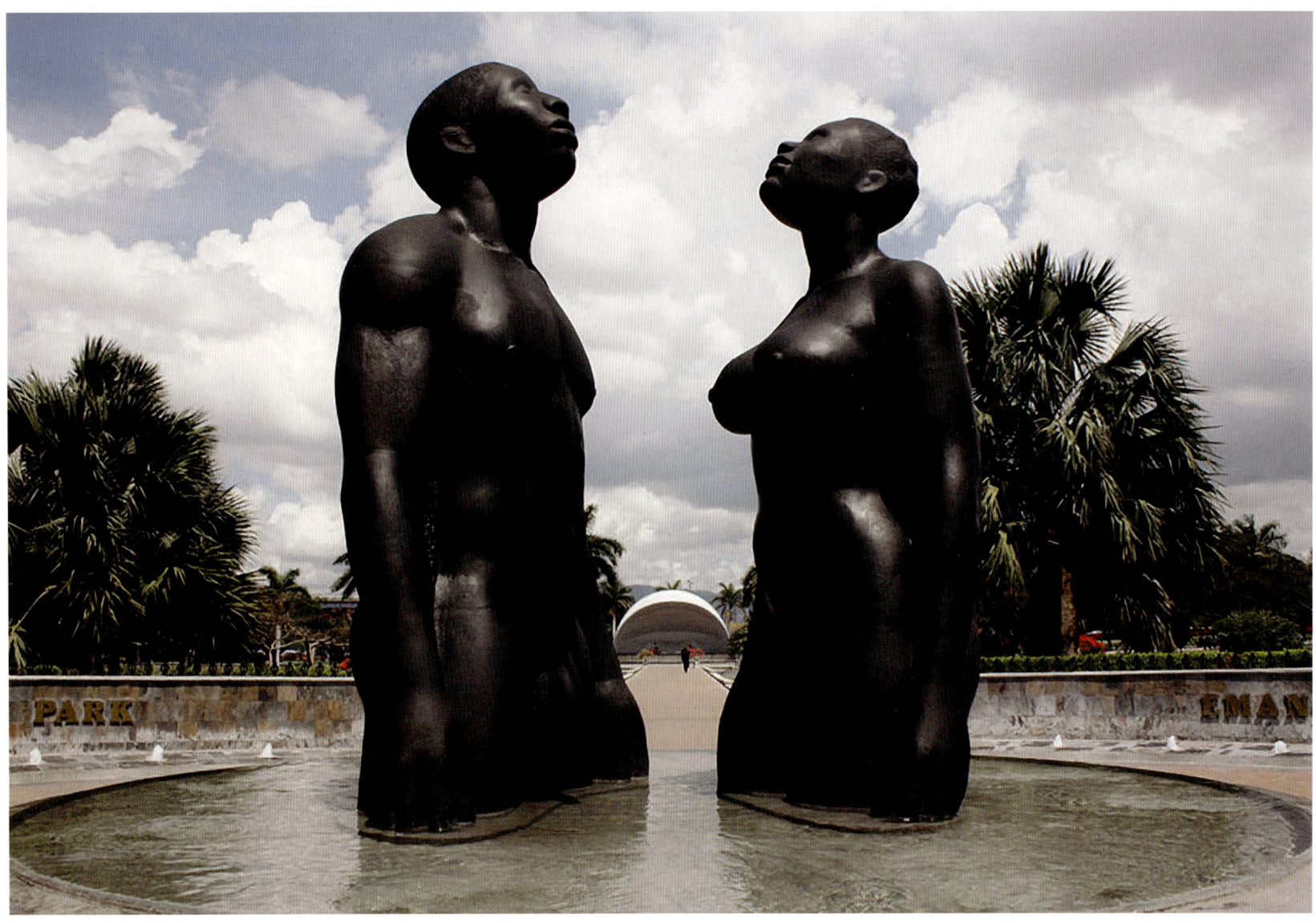

212

212 Laura Facey. *Redemption Song*. 2003. Bronze, cast iron. Kingston, Jamaica, Emancipation Park.

edent for Facey's choice of a peaceful and non-warlike grouping (see fig. 203). A nude woman and man emerge calmly from placid water and gaze skyward; *Redemption Song* refers to Marcus Garvey's idea that "none but ourselves can free our minds," appropriated by Bob Marley in the song from which the monument takes its name. The two bodies—at the height of maturity, comfortably upright, with heads slightly raised and eyes closed—suggest a woman and a man in a state of physical and mental equilibrium. Avoiding both the exaggerated corporality and the exalted state of other monuments, the artist suggests that emancipation was the result of introspection, reflection, consciousness, and balance.

Since its inauguration, however, the monument has generated controversy. There are criticisms of the figures' exuberant forms, particularly the size of penis, breasts, and buttocks, which seem to trade in sexual stereotypes associated with African descent. But their forms have naturalistic proportions, and their balanced opulence distances them from both the pathos of the Argentinian *La esclavitud* and the excessive muscularity of monuments like *Desenkadená* in Curaçao, *Monumento al esclavo rebelde* in Cuba, and *Emancipation Statue* ("Bussa") in Guyana. Nor do the poses of Facey's man and woman accentuate their sexuality; their trunks and limbs are naturally relaxed, seemingly in harmony with their minds. Presenting human bodies without moralism, the artist emphasizes the inextricable connection between body and mind that is central to many African ethnic groups, for example, in the Yoruba cult of *Orishas*. She thus reminds us that monuments cannot only motivate actions but can generate reflection.

The artist herself was questioned in relation to ethnic and phenotypic issues. Although Facey has African ancestry, she was not generally perceived as a Black artist, according to current beliefs about skin color; her credentials to gain the commission for the monument were called into question as they would not have been in the past. Many of the creators of the monuments discussed here are of African descent, among them Broodhagen, Lescay, Mangonès, Moore, Nêgo, and Valère. But there are some who are evidently not: Cafferata, Chaves Pinheiro, deCaires Taylor, Magno, Moret, Resende, and Tafur, among others. The primacy of African ancestry, which did not seem to be a requirement, became an important issue for the authorship of a monument related to the slave trade and slavery.

Honoring Black Heroes

In addition to the differences in the level of drama, Black exemplarity has been gaining variety through monuments dedicated to individuals. Besides homages to the heroes in the struggle against slavery, there are monuments to Black people who were involved in fights for national independence, revolution, or social transformation. These memorials are important for the inclusion of Black individuals in public memory and history. Besides celebrating revolutionaries and nationalists, such monuments demonstrate how Afrodescendants in the Americas have been almost solely responsible for securing, winning, and gaining their own freedom.

The monument to Falucho must be mentioned in relation to the memorialization of Black heroes in the struggles for independence in Latin America and the Caribbean. Falucho was the nickname of the legendary, even mythic Afro-Argentinian hero Antonio Ruiz, a soldier who fought in José de San Martín's Army of the Andes in the Argentine War of Independence in the 1810s.

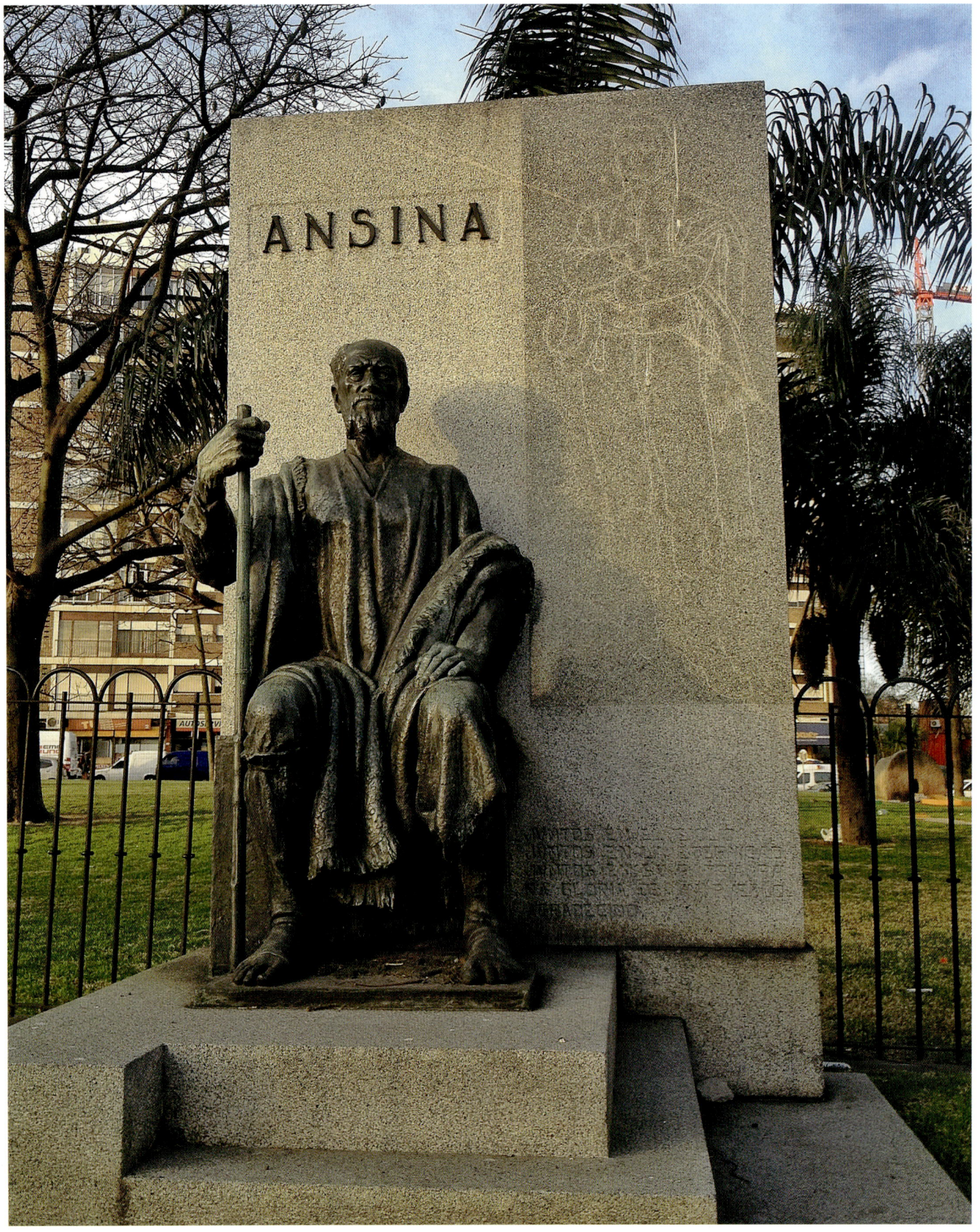

213

213 José Belloni. *Monument to Ansina (Joaquín Lenzina).* Unveiled in 1943. Bronze, granite. Montevideo, Uruguay, Rambla Republica Argentina.

Conceived by the Argentinian sculptor Lucio Correa Morales (1852–1923), who greatly altered Cafferata's initial plan of 1890, the monument was erected in Buenos Aires in 1897[25] and depicts Falucho in the exact moment in 1824 that "he gave his life before betraying the flag of the country," in its author's words (see fig. 76). His stance makes soldier and nation one. With his left arm folded on his chest, his hand on heart, his right arm clutching the flag to his body, he offers his body to the shooters, purportedly exclaiming immediately before death, "Long live Buenos Aires!"

In the Uruguayan capital of Montevideo, since 1943 a monument has stood to Ansina, an Afro-Uruguayan soldier of General José Gervasio Artigas's army, who accompanied and assisted the general in his exile in Paraguay after 1820. The Uruguayan sculptor José Belloni (1882–1965) based his depiction of the elderly Black man, noble and seated, on a photograph of Manuel Antonio Ledesma, another soldier of Artigas's army and who had been identified as Ansina. However, in the early 1950s Ansina was identified as the poet Joaquín Lenzina.[26] Belloni's monument was not the only one to superimpose these figures. As Alejandro Gortázar explains, "It was from the two above mentioned names (Lenzina and Ledesma) that two different Ansinas were created, one [Ledesma] submissive, symbol of fidelity and love of the hero, officially established by the State; and another [Lenzina] lawyer, author of the Artiguist gestation, polyglot and even leader in Afro issues within the Artiguist project, built by a set of 'counterhegemonic' intellectuals,"[27] an interpretation that legitimizes the superposition of the figures in the monument, not recommending its renaming, as it is intended to occur.[28]

The first monument erected in Havana, Cuba, to celebrate a Black hero of independence in the nineteenth-century wars against Spanish colonial rule was created in 1916 by the Italian sculptor Doménico Boni to honor Antonio Maceo. In addition to that monument, there are many busts and sculptures scattered throughout the country dedicated to the Cuban army general who fought in the wars of independence. Unusually, Cuba can boast two monuments to women who served admirably in the military during the Ten Years' War (1868–1878), an important period in Cuba's move toward independence: one to Maceo's mother, Mariana Grajales, created by the Cuban sculptor Teodoro Ramos Blanco (1902–1972) in 1931; and the other to Rosa La Bayamesa, a nurse and hospital organizer, sculpted by Lescay in 2000. These monuments are among the very few to memorialize Black women anywhere in Latin America and the Caribbean, highlighting the gender inequalities that exist alongside ethnic-racial ones in these regions.

Ramos Blanco also conceived the *Monumento a las razas* (*Monument to the Races*) that was erected in Santiago de Cuba in 1950. Celebrating Rafael María de Labra, Miguel Figueroa, and Juan Gualberto Gómez, important figures in the fight against slavery, the sculptural ensemble presents a Black couple symbolically offering their son to the memory of the famous antislavery leaders. A monument to another leader who fought for social equality was erected in 2008 in Rio de Janeiro, sculpted by Valter Brito; João Cândido, known as the "Black Admiral," was the leader of a revolt against corporal punishment and racism in the Brazilian navy in the beginning of twentieth century.

In addition to the monuments that celebrate Black persons as fighters for freedom and equality, many statues and monuments acknowledge important figures in the social and cultural realm. In Cuba there are statues of the musician Benny Moré and the

214 Deoscóredes Maximiliano dos Santos (Mestre Didi). *Ôpa n'Ílé: Ceptro (Cetro) da Terra (Scepter of the Earth)*. 1997. Polyester resin. Salvador, Brazil, Museu de Arte Moderna da Bahia.

artist Wifredo Lam (1902–1982). In Brazil, the poet Antônio Frederico de Castro Alves is memorialized in Salvador; the musician Alfredo da Rocha Viana Filho, known as Pixinguinha (after *bexiguento*, in reference to pockmarks) in Rio de Janeiro; and another musician, Naná Vasconcelos, in Recife. Monuments to athletes are also scattered throughout the Latin American landscape. In Uruguay, there are at least three monuments to Obdulio Varela, known as "*el Negro Jefe*" ("Black Chief"), the captain of the team that defeated Brazil to win the 1950 World Cup. In Brazil itself, there are many monuments to Pelé—born Edson Arantes do Nascimento—who carried Brazil to victory three times in the World Cup, in 1958, 1962, and 1970. In Palenque de San Basilio, Colombia, standing beside Biohó's monument is a statue of Antonio Cervantes, known as Kid Pambele, Colombia's greatest boxer.

Fighting for Freedom of Faith

From the beginning of the forced transposition of people from Africa to be enslaved, many African religions were reconfigured and adapted after their arrival in the Americas: Candombe in Uruguay;[29] Candomblé and Umbanda in Brazil; Lumbalú in Colombia; Quimbois in the French Antilles; Regla de Palo and Santería in Cuba; and Vodou in Haiti, among others. Although their names indicate differences due to local particularities, they share some principles and practices, preserving African values in the American colonial and postcolonial contexts. One common aspect of the African–Latin American religious communities is their special role in the resistance against the marginalization and persecution of Africans and Afrodescendants and the disqualification of their values and beliefs. These religions are intrinsically connected to nature and urban space, with many of its rituals needing to take place on beaches and near waterfalls, roads, streets, or squares, but those practicing them have rarely had full freedom to use sites beyond the walls of their communities.

It is not surprising, therefore, that public monuments honoring religious figures and themes began to appear in cities and countries long after the end of slavery with the decline of Catholic influence, though to a lesser extent than monuments honoring individuals and events in other social realms. Only from the middle of the twentieth century were monuments erected to Afro–Latin American and Caribbean deities and cosmogony, and they are important in the battle against the persecution that practitioners of these religions still suffer.

There are many monuments similar to *Preto velho* by Pastor in Rio de Janeiro, or to the one dedicated to Yemoja installed at Parque Rodó in Montevideo, in being sculptural representations of deities that project alternative moral and cultural references in public spaces. The different interpretations of the Yoruba deity Eshu by the Brazilian artist Mário Cravo, Jr. (1923–2018), exemplify how, in religious-themed monuments, artists have sometimes ventured beyond naturalistic figuration, in Cravo's case exploring modernist developments to move between nonnaturalist anthropomorphism, as in *Exú* (*Eshu*), installed in Salvador in 1984, and geometric abstraction, as in *Exú dos Ventos* (*Eshu of the Winds*), installed in Rio de Janeiro in 2000.

In addition to the iconic statues that embody permanently the presence of the African deities in Latin American and Caribbean imaginaries and fix them in the social space, some religious monuments are the products of artistic experimentation. This we have already seen in Cuba in the *Monumento al cimarrón* (see fig. 200), in which Lescay transformed a cauldron used to boil sugarcane

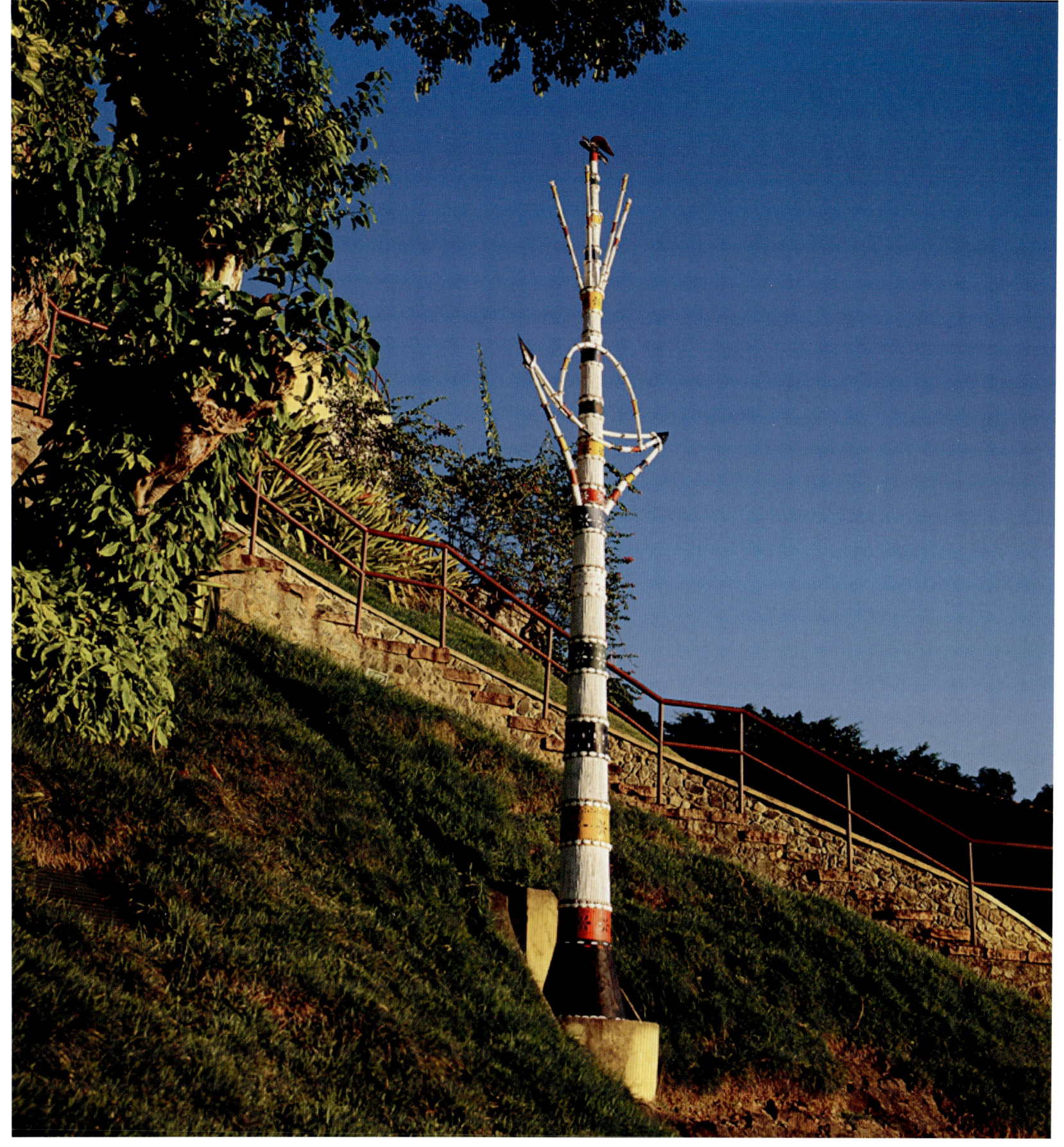

214

215 Rubem Valentim. *Syncretic Symbol of Afro-Brazilian Culture*. 1978. Reinforced concrete. São Paulo, Praça da Sé.

juice into a kind of nganga, configuring the sculpture's base as a receptacle for offerings, which makes the monument a collective and open work.

The Brazilian religious leader, writer, and visual artist Deoscóredes Maximiliano dos Santos (1917–2013), known as Mestre (Master) Didi, created two public monuments for his hometown: *Ôpa n'Ílé: Ceptro (Cetro) da terra* (*Scepter of the Earth*), installed in the sculptural park at the Museu de Arte Moderna da Bahia, in Salvador in 1997, and *Cetro da ancestralidade* (*Scepter of Ancestry*), in a square in Rio Vermelho, a neighborhood of the same city in 2001. In both monuments, he preserved forms and meanings he had learned from childhood in the *terreiros* (religious communities' sites) for the creation of ceremonial scepters for the Orishas Obaluaê and Nanã, but adopted materials (earth, resin, and fiberglass in the first monumental scepter, bronze in the second) that would guarantee their permanence in a public space.

Rubem Valentim's (1922–1991) *Marco sincretico da cultura afro-brasileira* (*Syncretic Symbol of Afro-Brazilian Culture*), built in reinforced concrete at Praça da Sé, the central square of São Paulo in southeastern Brazil in 1978, is not strictly a religious monument but is replete with religious resonances. Trying to reconcile Yoruba references (the Oranmyan Staff in Ife and the *oxê*, the double ax that is Shango's insignia), European iconography (Catholic Devil's stacks and Roman celebratory columns), and constructivist geometry, the Brazilian artist produced a contemporary totem, both universal and referring to particular cultural contexts, looking back to the past and toward the future, as a public manifestation of the syncretism he also explored in his paintings and objects.

The reference to syncretism evokes Moore's *1763 Monument*, Cuffy's statue in Guyana, which since its inauguration has perplexed much of the public, which was bemused by the proportions of the figure, the artifacts he holds, and the faces next to his body (possibly masks representative of other rebels), all derived from African artistic and cultural references.[30] In the sculptures conceived by Lescay, Master Didi, Valentim, and Moore, the European tradition of monuments survives, not in a pure form, but always incorporating principles, forms, and meanings from Afro–Latin American and Caribbean religions. African artistic languages marginalized during slavery and that survived in religious communities can be revitalized in urban spaces and the landscape.

Their recognition and acceptance, however, is relative. *Exú dos Ventos*, *Cetro da ancestralidade*, and *Preto velho* are among the many monuments related to Afro-Brazilian religions that have been vandalized. In 2007, the city of Belo Horizonte, in southeastern Brazil, reinstated the statue created in homage to Yemoja in 1982 by the Brazilian sculptor José Synfronini after it was repeatedly damaged. Juxtaposing metal plates cut with a geometry evocative of symbols of Orishas, the Brazilian sculptor Jorge dos Anjos (b. 1957) composed the *Portal da memória* (*Portal of Memory*), dedicated to many Orishas, and installed it on a small esplanade. In its re-installation, the Yemoja's statue rests on top of a pedestal emerging from the waters of the Pampulha lagoon.

Violence has not been restricted to religious monuments. The Jamaica-based artist Raymond Watson's (b. 1954) bust of Marcus Garvey, the famous Jamaican-born Black Nationalist, has generated all manner of controversy, from its installation to its removal, to its *re*-installation at the University of the West Indies in Mona.

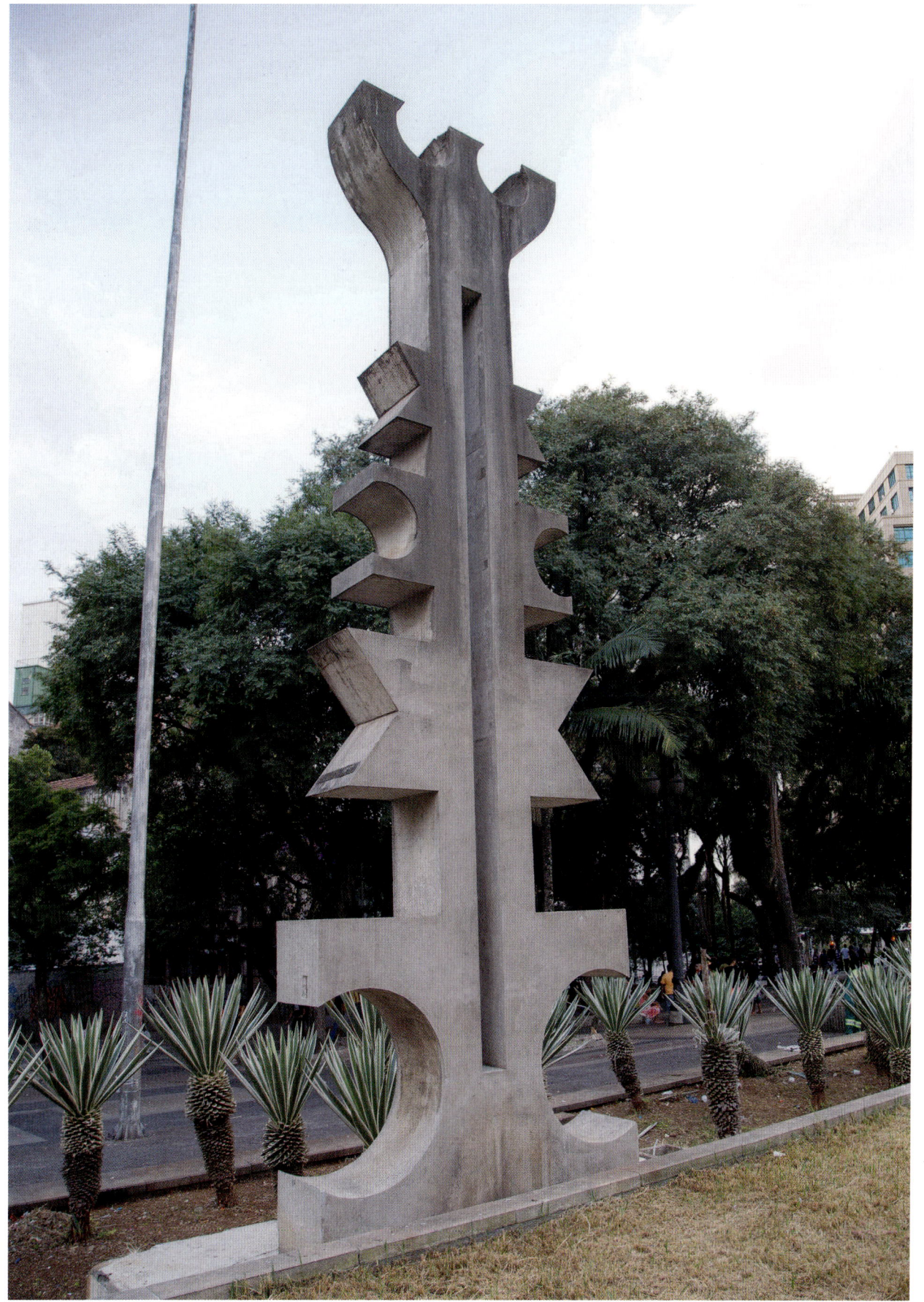

215

216 Darcy Ribeiro (conception); Romeu Alves (head); João Filgueiras Lima (base). *Zumbi dos Palmares*. 1986. Bronze and concrete. Rio de Janeiro, June 11 Square.

Everything from the sculpture's location to its likeness to Garvey proved contentious. According to Shalman Scott, a historian and the former mayor of Montego Bay, "the strong differences in the tide of opinions of a multiplicity of various groupings within the society have risen to a crescendo, resulting in deliberate damage to the Garvey monument."[31] Such vandalism is emblematic of the persistence of violence inflicted on Africans and their descendants since the beginning of their enslavement in the Americas, but it is also a response to attempts to inscribe other historical and cultural references in the collective space, thus reaffirming the need for these monuments.

Ambiguous Homage

The monument to Zumbi dos Palmares, a Black hero of resistance in Brazil, installed in Rio de Janeiro in 1986, has also been vandalized from time to time. But in terms of modes of representation, this monument is exceptional. Almost all the monuments discussed so far show a preference for conservative modes of representation; efforts to match celebration with new kinds of forms are rarer. Many monuments dedicated to Zumbi across Brazil are of the former kind, usually depicting him in more or less figurative and naturalistic busts and full-length figures. While it is not unusual to find him with broken chains, machetes, and even a *berimbau* (a musical instrument used to play *capoeira*, an Afro-Brazilian combat dance), in general he appears with spears, as in the monument erected to him in Salvador. An exception is the square named for Zumbi in Curitiba, in the south of Brazil, comprising fifty-four totems representing different African countries to celebrate the peoples of Africa. The monument to him in Rio de Janeiro is also connected to pan-Africanism.[32] Its ambiguities and the controversies it has sparked merit further attention.

A plate fixed to its base mentions only the Brazilian architect João Filgueiras Lima (1932–2014) as its creator, yet the Brazilian anthropologist, novelist, and politician Darcy Ribeiro (1922–1997) was certainly the central agent in its conception. As vice governor and secretary of culture of Rio de Janeiro at the time of its commission, Ribeiro made crucial decisions regarding the monument's final configuration.

The erection of the monument followed from a law passed in 1983 as a result of the efforts of the Brazilian Movimento Negro (Black Movement) to restore Zumbi as a major forerunner of Afrodescendants in the country. It was not, however, set up on the site originally planned—between the Monument to the Dead in World War II and the Modern Art Museum in Flamengo Park—but on President Vargas Avenue, one of the city's most heavily trafficked roads. Instead of standing in the company of national heroes, artists, and citizens in a beautiful park by the sea, Zumbi was connected to other Afro-Brazilian cultural references, although islanded amid buses and cars. The monument was installed at Praça Onze de Junho (June 11 Square), a stronghold of Black people after the end of slavery in Brazil, near a school honoring Tia (Aunt) Ciata, a famous Black female leader of the early twentieth century, and Passarela do Samba, an avenue flanked by bleachers built for the parades performed by the samba schools—two urban landmarks the same government did for the Afrodescendant community.

As there is no visual record of Zumbi, Ribeiro decided to represent him according to a sculpture belonging to the British Museum: the *Ife Head*, one of the three sculptures known as the crowned heads of Ife, two of which are probably "portraits of

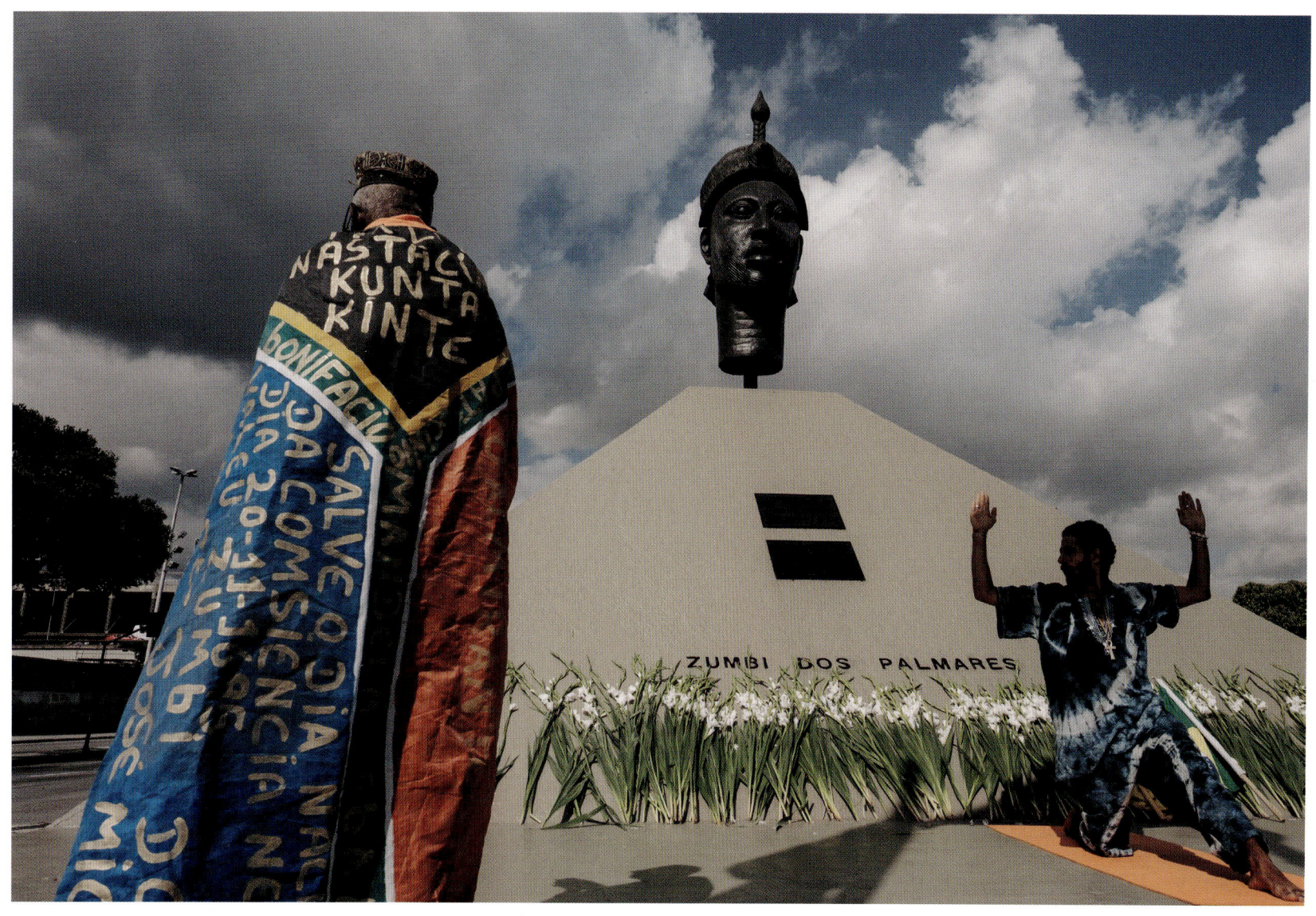
216

deceased rulers and form part of an ancestor cult."[33] Called the Oni of Ife, these rulers claimed descent from Oduduwa, the creator of the world for the Yoruba, and were often deified.

The form of that sculpture was enlarged from its original thirty-six centimeters to three meters and cast in eight hundred kilograms of bronze, a transformation that makes us think about the omissions in the monument's plaque. Besides not including Ribeiro's name, there is no reference to the *Ife Head* and not a single word about the Brazilian Romeu Alves (b. 1929), who sculpted the enlarged head and should be included as co-creator, nor about the workers who cast the piece and built the truncated pyramid. It is contradictory to silence the names of the workers responsible for a monument dedicated to a formerly enslaved Afro-Brazilian who later became a leader in the struggle for freedom and equality of all citizens.

The most surprising aspect of the anthropologist meddling in the artistic domain is the insensitivity to ethnic particularities. Ribeiro represents Zumbi as Yoruba, as a West African, when he was probably of Bantu origin, descended from people brought from the west coast of Central Africa. He is also connected to the north of Africa, more precisely to Egypt, by the pyramid designed by Lima that supports the head. The sculpture essentially associates Zumbi with regions far from the territory inhabited by his supposed African ancestors, and even farther from the region in which he was born and lived in South America. Thus, they connect him to a generic Africa, echoing the pan-Africanism that was then current in Brazil's Black Movement.

In reducing the leader of Palmares to a head and displaying it in a public space, Ribeiro recalls the way the Portuguese colonizers sought to discredit the late-seventeenth-century legend of Zumbi's immortality, bringing about the end of Palmares Quilombo and discouraging slave escapes, a point driven home brutally by the rod that connects the head to the pyramid, a reference to the pike on which Zumbi's head was stuck at a public square in Recife in 1695, making the monument itself a kind of trophy head.

If the monument refers to the European tradition of the bust, it can also be connected to the African tradition of the head. In that sense, Zumbi is presented as apart from the Palmares Quilombo, from slavery, or from the life of Black people in Brazil. He is an African and not just any African. Wearing a crown made of glass beads, a rosette, and a feathered crest, Zumbi is not depicted as enslaved, as an outlaw or a warrior, but as a ruler descending from the creator of the world of the Yoruba.

But the location of the monument links Zumbi specifically to Rio de Janeiro, and more generically Brazil, given the importance of the cult of *Ori* (head) in African religions practiced in Brazil. In this sense, the monument can be understood as an urban altar where Zumbi is deified and can be revered. In addition to expanding his historical meanings, the monument contributes to the evolution of the public presence of the Afro-Brazilian religions.

Even if the Black Movement was not initially on good terms with the government—certainly conflicts still persist—the site of the monument has become a place of political demonstrations against racism on behalf of citizenship, as well as the main space in Rio de Janeiro for Afro-Brazilian celebrations, especially those held on November 20, the date of Zumbi's death, and, since 2003, for Black Consciousness Day in Brazil.

Rio de Janeiro's monument to Zumbi is not the only one to provoke debates and be vandalized. Biohó's monument in Colombia, the *Redemption Song* monument, Marcus Garvey's bust in Jamaica, the *1763 Monument* (Cuffy's statue) in Guyana, and Ansina's statue in Uruguay have also been the subject of fraught discussion over form, subject, material, and/or artistic ownership. These disputes accentuate the controversies surrounding these monuments, which flare up because they exist in societies structured by racism, inequality, and marginalization.

Worldwide Fight

While monuments to Zumbi have been all but confined to Brazil in the way that the many monuments to Antonio Maceo are to Cuba, those celebrating François-Dominique Toussaint Louverture have been erected not only in his homeland but also abroad. In addition to those built in Haiti (Port-au-Prince, Haut-du-Cap, and Ennery), public monuments honor him in Benin (Allada, his family's place of origin, 1997–1998), Canada (Québec, 2010), Cuba (Santiago de Cuba), France (Massy, Bordeaux, and La Rochelle, in 1989, 2005, and 2015, respectively), and the United States of America (Miami, Florida, 2005). Connecting the Caribbean, North America, Europe, and Africa, these statues delineate an expansive geography that, besides retracing the triangular slave trade, project their meanings on a global scale.

Like these statues to Toussaint Louverture, monuments related to the slave trade and slavery in Latin America and the Caribbean are no longer restricted to these regions alone. By their very nature, sculptures are static, but they can activate a place and summon people to interact with them and the site, be it a gallery, a sculpture garden, or a park. Extending from the bottom of the sea to the top of a mountain, monuments against slavery and in favor of freedom from Latin America and the Caribbean, as well as across the continents, are global proclamations against slavery, the slave trade, and colonialism.

Certainly these monuments were not built from a single coherent movement. Many of them grew out of local anxieties, demands, and conquests. Some are also connected to UNESCO's "The Slave Route" project and its efforts to recognize and preserve memorial sites, monuments, and places linked to the slave trade and slavery. As explained on its website: "Initiated in April 1995 in Accra, [Ghana], this initiative is designed to encourage Member States to inventory, protect and promote these memorial sites and places and to include them in national and regional tourism itineraries."[34]

Sharing the same cause and articulated by some common elements (near-naked figures, broken chains, machetes, spears and conch shells, as well as grand and dramatic gestures), these monuments constitute an open circuit. Fixed to a specific site and often at great distance from one another, together they spur people to imagine an almost impossible physical mobility. Today social media allows navigation from one website to another as if from one physical site to another, making virtual transit possible between monuments and memorials, libraries, archives, museums, and other institutions.

In this global circuit, which links Latin America and the Caribbean to North America, Africa, Europe, and beyond, we can also include monuments like the one built in Savannah, Georgia, in the United States, to the Haitian soldiers who fought in the American Revolution. The monuments erected to Toussaint Louverture on different continents, as well as the memorial sites and monuments related to the slave trade and slavery that have been built in many countries, ask people to reflect on their

217 Jeannette Ehlers, La Vaughn Belle. *I Am Queen Mary (Mary Thomas)*. Unveiled 2018. Bronze figure and plaque. Copenhagen, Denmark, Langelinie Promenade, West Indian Warehouse.

nation's roles in the triangular slave trade and the persistence of its effects.

A special monument of European self-criticism over captivity and colonialism is *I Am Queen Mary*, a statue created by the Danish artist Jeannette Ehlers (b. 1973) and the Virgin Islands artist La Vaughn Belle (b. 1974).[35] Erected in Copenhagen in 2018 following the centennial anniversary of Denmark's sale of the Virgin Islands to the United States and commissioned "to memorialize Denmark's colonial impact in the Caribbean and those who fought against it," the monument is a tribute to Mary Thomas, one of four Black women who led the "Fireburn" of 1878, the largest labor revolt in Danish colonial history, which saw the burning of many plantations as well as the town of Frederiksted. The sculpture is installed in front of the former West Indian Warehouse in Copenhagen, which currently houses the Royal Cast Collection, in a position matching that of a copy of Michelangelo's *David*. Coral stones cut from the ocean by Africans enslaved in St. Croix form the plinth, on which rests the image of a woman who is a composite of the bodies of both artists, seated on a chair, holding a cane bill and a torch. The statue is an update in three dimensions of a famous photo of Huey P. Newton, the leader of the Black Panther Party. As in the tribute to Zumbi in Rio de Janeiro, the artists appropriated artistic and cultural references to design a monument that connects in its placing antislavery and anticolonial struggles on the shores of the Atlantic, echoing the voices of female resistance, from different moments and social domains.

Monuments not only unite meanings, places, and peoples, but also different times. Like *I Am Queen Mary*, many monuments discussed in this chapter look back to more or less distant periods in the past; they also illuminate the present and project it into the future. Some are focused mainly on the terror of the slave trade and slavery; others recall the fight against them, celebrating both known and unknown individuals. But all of them are monuments against the ongoing impact of the slave trade and slavery, as well as the exploitation of people's labor and other social inequalities. Despite older or contemporary modes of expression, they condense past, present, and future in their materiality, which is, with a few exceptions, static and unchanging.

In general, sculptures are silent. But with some imagination, we can hear the lament of the Argentinian enslaved man; the crackling fire on the *Monumento al cimarrón*; the metallic sounds of the beginning of freedom in *Desenkadená*; the hawkish blows of the Haitian *Nègre marron* and the Dominican *Neg Mawon*; the happy cries of Biohó, Bussa, and Cuffy; the menacing murmurs that lurk in the vigils of Yanga and Zumbi; and even the silent harmony that surrounds *Negro Aroused* and the absorbed couple in Jamaica—all sounds these monuments never rein in or restrain, whether against brutal oppression or in favor of liberty and peace.

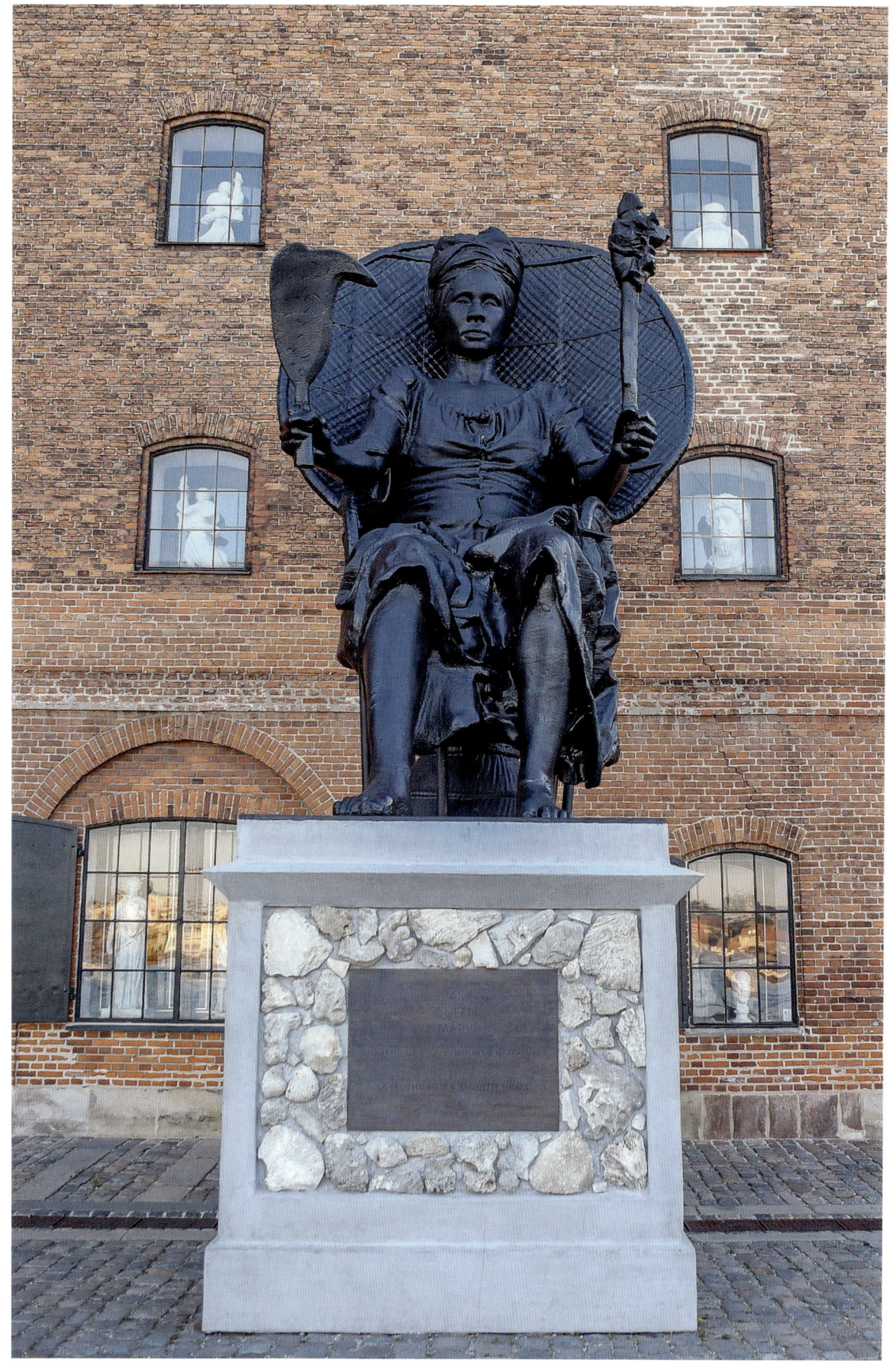

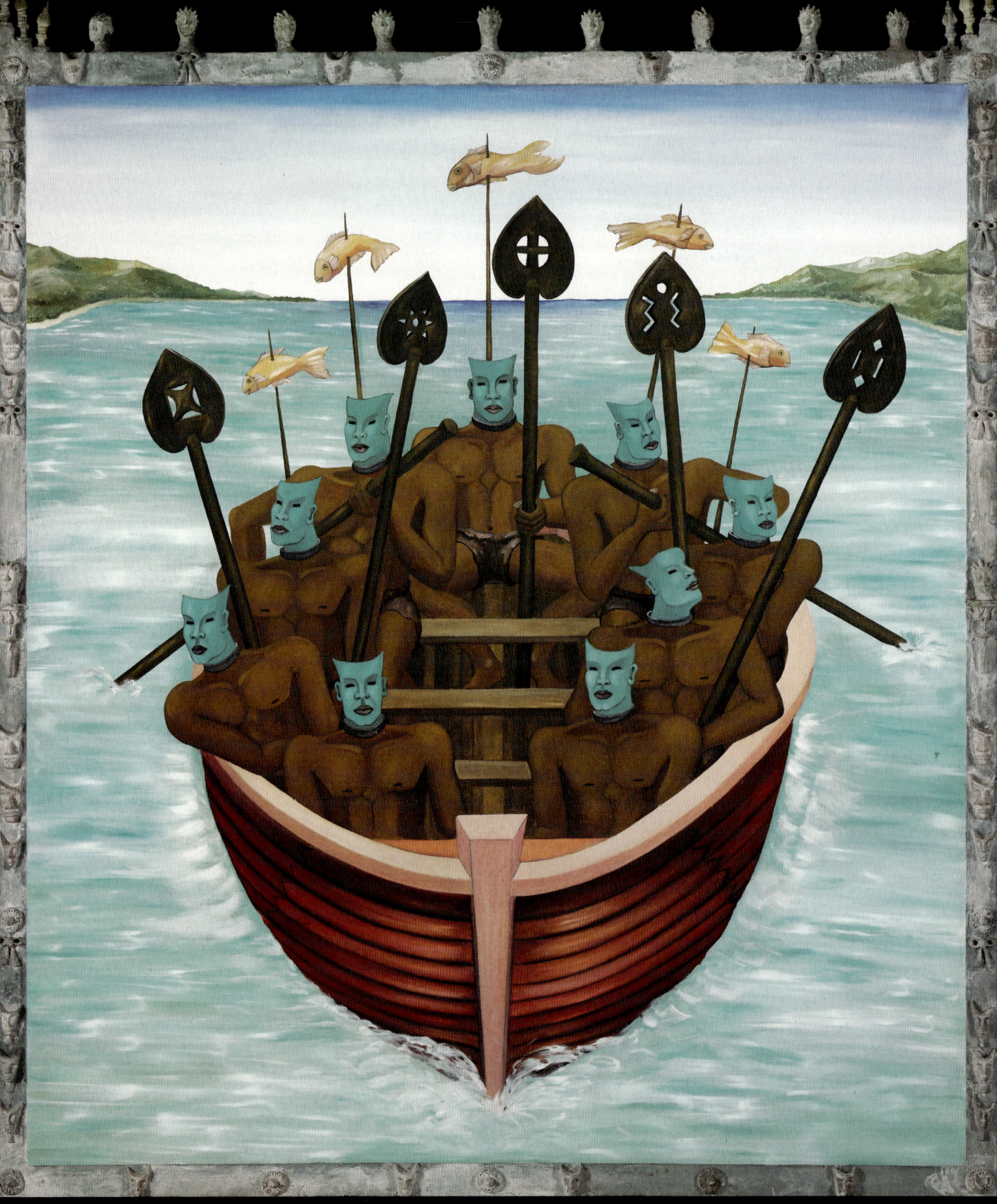

13

THE IMAGE OF THE BLACK IN 20TH-CENTURY ANGLO-AFRO-CARIBBEAN ART

PETRINE ARCHER

This chapter considers the art and histories of the English-speaking islands of the Caribbean—Jamaica, Trinidad, Barbados, The Bahamas, and mainland Guyana—in addition to the French-speaking Haiti, Martinique, and Guadeloupe. Presenting them thematically and mostly chronologically, it ties the work of these islands and their artists into a larger theoretical framework related to colonization, creolization, modernity, memory, identity, and, ultimately, "home."

Any discussion of how the Black image became prominent in the art of these islands is a complex exercise that calls for an understanding of the region's shifting power relations, its tangled historical beginnings, polyglot communities, distinct colonial legacies, and artistic traditions. Although all the islands have similar aboriginal beginnings with a shared native Indian heritage, the more recent history of art in the Caribbean has numerous stylistic threads and cultural quirks related to the tangible realities of colonialism, slavery, and indentured labor. The region's fragmentation makes any art survey challenging and a single narrative questionable.[1] Indeed, it is essential to explore the Caribbean visual arts comparatively to understand better the region's sense of place and collective identity. This then is a postmodern narrative that highlights the work of artists who for just a century have been applying themselves to a process of excavation and recovery.

Caribbean art today is the outcome of this search for identity. It is the result of the creativity and invention of artists who have no recourse but to validate their past from a vantage point in the present. In the face of colonial exclusion and invisibility, their art represents an attempt to reenvisage the past and the Black self in a likeness that can best represent their experiences of "arrested development" and survival.

This chapter mirrors the Caribbean artists' methodology, which skips between past and present and fills the gaps of memory with the products of their imagination. Marrying history and twentieth-century imagery seems appropriate now because so much of the region's contemporary art foregrounding the Black image is preoccupied with the retelling of history and reconstructing the past.[2] As the cultural theorist Stuart Hall points out, Caribbean identity is "always a question of producing in the future an account of the past."[3]

The Caribbean formed part of what has been called "Plantation America," the vast swaths of land repopulated with Africans shipped by the millions mainly from West and Central Africa to work as enslaved people.[4] This forced migration was both traumatic and transformative. Depicting this Middle Passage journey

218 Edouard Duval-Carrié. *Altar to the Nine Slaves*. 1992. Oil on canvas. Miami, Little Haiti, Collection of the artist.

219 Alex Burke. *The Spirit of the Caribbean*. 1999. Forty-seven dolls made of various fabrics and other materials. Paris, Collection of the artist.

is almost a rite of passage itself for artists in the Caribbean diaspora who use memory to reimagine its horrors. María Magdalena Campos-Pons, Keith Piper, Charles Campbell, David Boxer, Kcho (Alexis Leiva Machado), Edouard Duval-Carrié, and Thierry Alet have all navigated this route. Rafts, boats, ships, or just the vicissitudes of the ocean all prefigure in their "rememberings," which recount this narrative of displacement so central to any understanding of the Caribbean's Black identity. Only rarely is that journey envisaged in terms of drowning; rather, vessels are wombs for rebirth and spiritual awakening. Duval-Carrié's *Rétable des neuf esclaves* (*Altar to the Nine Slaves*) (1992) depicts the enslaved as boat people in a modest canoe rather than a slave ship. As blue-faced Vodou gods, they are steering their own vessel and in charge of their own destiny. The centerpiece of this nine-paneled altar is surrounded by other portraits in which the enslaved individuals are represented as winged angels grappling with the vagaries of a new land.

Alex Burke's *Les otages* (*The Spirit of the Caribbean*) (1999) is more macabre. Removing any sense of physical agency, he presents human forms that are tightly bound with scraps of colorful cloth. The mummified forms are faceless, armless beings. Unable to cry, fight, or swim, they are propped up or laid out in ways that suggest their tightly packed passage west. Despite being mute, these oversize Vodou-like dolls radiate an immutable presence because of their refusal to be silenced or just die. In this defiant zombielike state, they share a haunting sense of spiritual survival and continuity.

The Middle Passage represented a rupture and slave-ship rebirthing into a life of compromise and despair, accommodation and survival. The contingency of Africans' New World lives shaped their formation of imagined communities and identities based on transposed cultural forms and a forced consciousness of their race and its restrictions. As a result of this wrenching, a return to an African homeland would be impossible. The rigors of plantation life undermined their creativity in textile making, carving, and pottery that might have sustained their links to Africa. Within generations, they could no longer trace a direct line to an African past, save through the intimacy of their spiritual lives. In Haiti, this became increasingly important, as Christian rituals were displaced with African ones that allowed for Vodou and alternative belief systems. Other islands shared similar rituals only with different names such as Obeah in Jamaica and Trinidad or Santería in Cuba.

Enslaved people, as a silent Black majority ruled by a white and later colored minority, were outwardly forced to embrace their new Caribbean environment and Creole citizenship that was syncretic and heavily influenced by their European colonizers. The photographer Leah Gordon has reenvisioned the deeply racialized, hierarchical system that governed the daily fortunes of Black people in Haiti before the revolution. She calls the series of photographs *Caste* (2010), referencing the classification system introduced by the French colonialist Moreau de Saint-Méry (see *The Image of the Black in Western Art,* vol. III, pt. 3, pp. 295–298), with categories ranging from *Noir* through *Sacatra, Griffe, Marabou, Mulâtre, Marmelouque, Quarteronnée,* and *Sang-Melée* to *Blanche*: varying shades of Blackness that carried with them physical, moral, and intellectual attributes. Her images are beautiful, almost stately forms that confound their historical origins. Gordon uses contemporary models dressed in historical garb against stark backgrounds that parody famous Renaissance

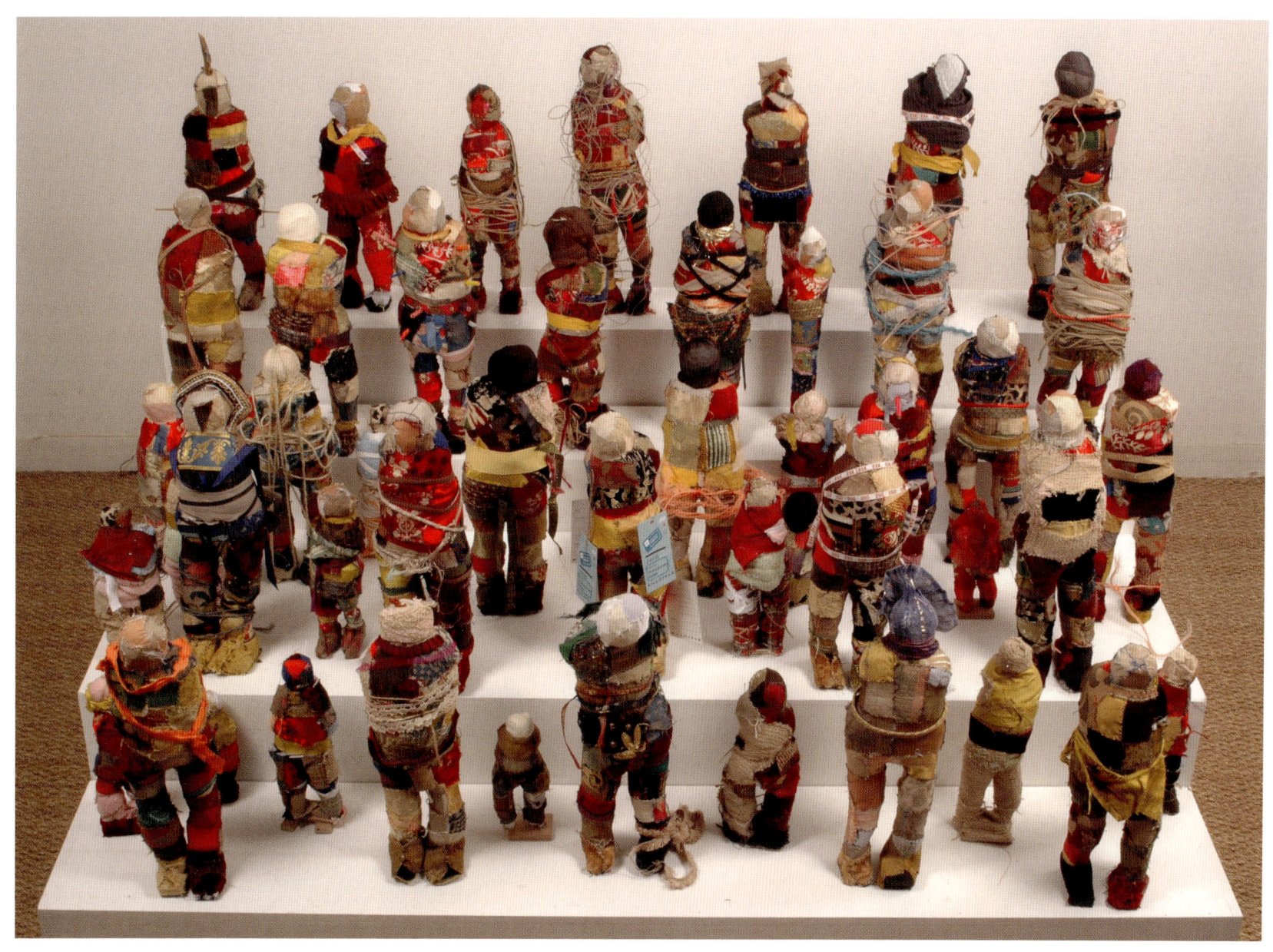

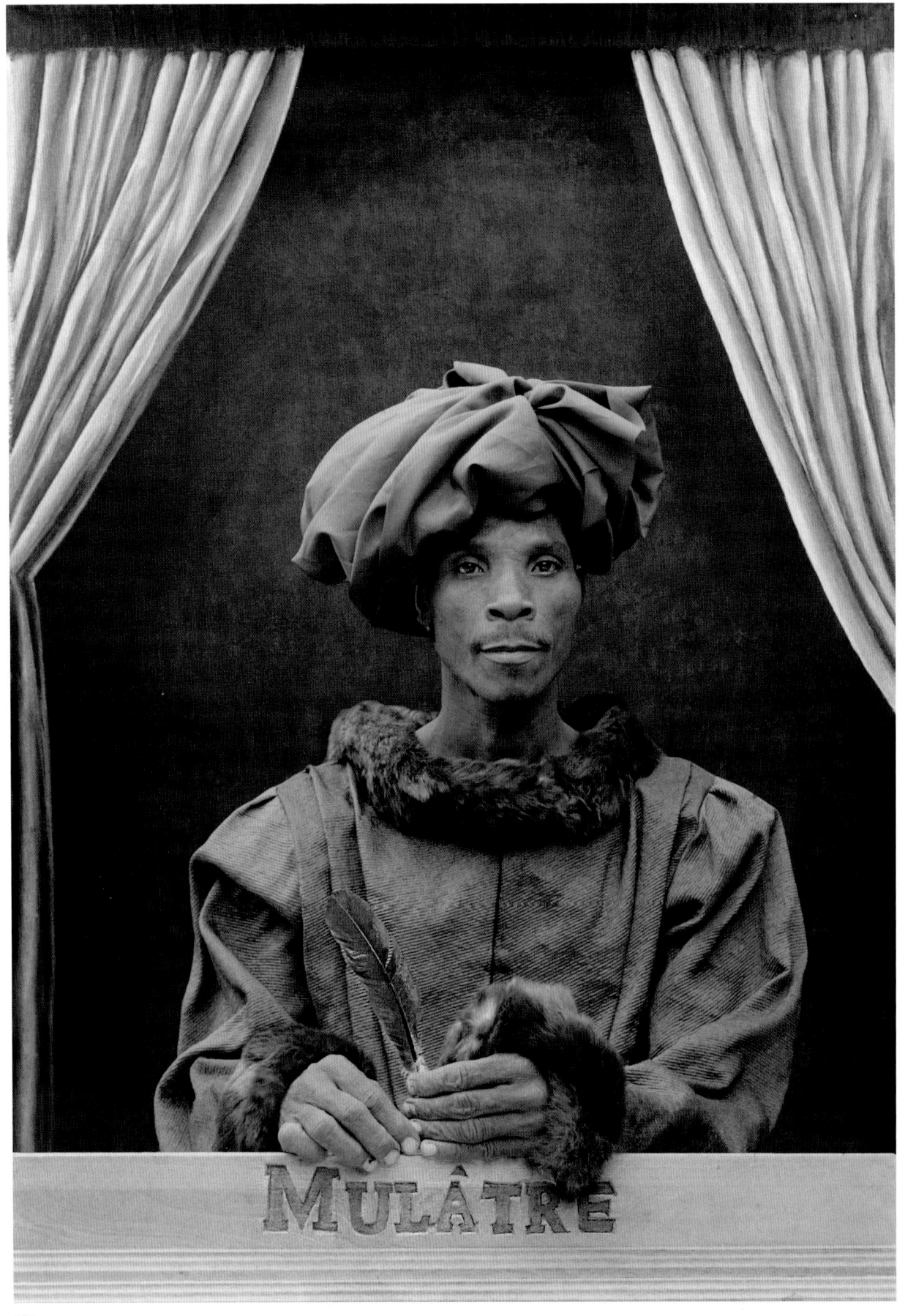

220

220 Leah Gordon. *Mulatto Woman*. From the *Caste* series. 2010. One of nine black-and-white photographs. London, Riflemaker Gallery.

portraits but also belie the rudimentary conditions in which they were created in post-earthquake Haiti: "We did the shoot in a slum: it looks so neat in the photos, but the set was made from an old trestle table, some models had to stand on blocks, and the backdrop kept blowing away. Amazingly, the camera created these beautiful moments of peace amid all that."[5]

Haiti's caste system with its "nine degrees of the skin" was mirrored throughout the region, only with different nomenclature that ensured that Black skin remained a mark of inferiority and even bestiality. The grinding poverty, sense of displacement, existence on the lowest rungs of society, and the desire to return to Africa deterred the identification of formerly enslaved men and women with the Caribbean as home. *Sugar Cane Alley* (1983), the Martinican film directed by Euzhan Palcy set in the 1930s, graphically depicts how an older generation of Africans still pined for their motherland even as they slaved to secure a place for their children in French society. The traditional *cric-crac* story exchanged between young José and his mentor Medouze keeps alive the memory of revolt and the frustration of assimilation:

> We were sold to cut cane for the whites, crick crac
> I was a young boy like you Medouze
> All the blacks came from the hills with sticks
> Machetes, guns and torches
> They invaded the town of St. Pierre
> They burned all the homes
> For the first time, blacks saw whites shake with fear,
> lock themselves in their mansions and die
> That was how slavery ended, crick crac
> and the old man said
> I think I ran around all Martinique
> When my feet refused to go on
> I looked ahead and behind
> I saw I was back in the Black Shack Alley again
> It was back to the cane fields
> We were free but our bellies were empty
> The Master had become the Boss
> So I stayed on like all the other blacks
> in this cursed country.

These tensions between victory and loss, yearnings for home versus a sense of no return, and a recognition that so little really changes resulted in art forms with hidden modalities, methods of signing and signifying that operated on multiple levels, what Erica James has called "metapictures" that communicate nuanced, multilayered, and sometimes contradictory readings.[6]

Haitian flags are a good example of these coded forms; portraits created from bric-a-brac and sequins outwardly depict saints such as St. Peter, St. Anthony, or Our Lady of Sorrows while displaying markings that signify Legba, Dambala, Erzulie, or other Yoruba gods and goddesses. These *veve* would only be known to the initiated or secret society members who could carry on their worship of traditional Catholic forms without compromising their African beliefs.

By 1900, the Caribbean population would be characterized by disaffection and migratory restlessness at all levels of its racially stratified society. For its upper classes, absentee landlordism was intensified following the revolution in Haiti: the wealthy, as before, preferred to manage their properties from a safe distance for fear of further uprisings or reprisals. After emancipation, their

221 Kathleen Hawkins. *Plantation Workers on Their Way Home*. Undated. Watercolor. St. Michael, Barbados, National Art Collection of Barbados.

lands were administered by mixed-race Creoles or mulattos distinguished by their birth in the islands and education elsewhere. Jewish refugees as well as other traders from the Middle East added to this middle tier of caretakers and merchants, while the steady influx of indentured laborers from India and China in places such as Trinidad and Guyana, Surinam and Jamaica made the lower classes less homogenous. The beginning of the twentieth century was marked by constant shifts in the population with large numbers, mostly of men, moving in and out of the region in search of work on plantations in South and Central America or on construction sites in places like Panama and the Canal Zone.[7] Caribbean culture was therefore more outward looking than inward, more fragmented than centered.

Initially, the production of fine art in the islands was a luxury pastime that fell to women of privilege. They chose craft as a complement to their feminine character. As Félix Angel tells us, skills in the applied and decorative arts "were particularly welcomed in places such as the colonies, where a delicate touch could do much to alleviate the drudgery and uncertainties of daily life. However, becoming a professional artist and producing fine art lay outside the nature of things for women in colonial society."[8]

The training, vision, and preoccupations of these artists of the Creole class were essentially European, reflecting their places of learning and metropolitan styles in Paris, London, or Spain that they initially strove to emulate. Kathleen Hawkins was the first Barbadian to be awarded an associateship of the Royal College of Art in London. Typically, on her return to the island she took up teaching, devoting herself to that profession for thirty years and creating images in a range of media for their educational value. Her work was renowned for its nostalgia. She preferred to capture aspects of the island's peasant life that she believed to be vanishing. She intentionally avoided dating her works so that they might be perceived as fragments of the past and documents that could elucidate the island's history.[9] Her *Plantation Workers on Their Way Home*, date unknown, speaks to this art form that sentimentalized the depiction of Black people while containing them within a plantation landscape and tropes of docility. The work reflects a time when the plantocracy were redefining their emancipated Black populace and their territories as peaceful, productive, and free from revolt, especially since the banana industry and tourism were poised for growth.[10] In this sense, these twentieth-century images continue the itinerant tradition of an earlier century. For all the artist's earnest intentions, this weary couple is locked in time and place. Captured with the backdrop of a sugar factory, they are objectified, showing little advance in their personhood or social status.

The *mouvement indigéniste*, a term coined in Haiti by the writer Jacques Roumain in about 1925, contrasted sharply with this idea of temporal fixity and social stasis. This group valued Haitian culture and its African origins and the use of Haitian dialect and local subjects. Unlike the *école indigéniste*, Roumain favored a term that allowed for progression and change. The mouvement indigéniste's ideas initially applied to literature but eventually had parallels in the visual arts as the region's artists and intellectuals turned their attention inward, looking for inspiration from local subject matter.[11]

This movement was not entirely insular nor removed from Western influence. Rather, this appreciation for folk culture was in step with postwar interests in the primitive shared by Europe's avant-garde who despised bourgeois complacency. Especially

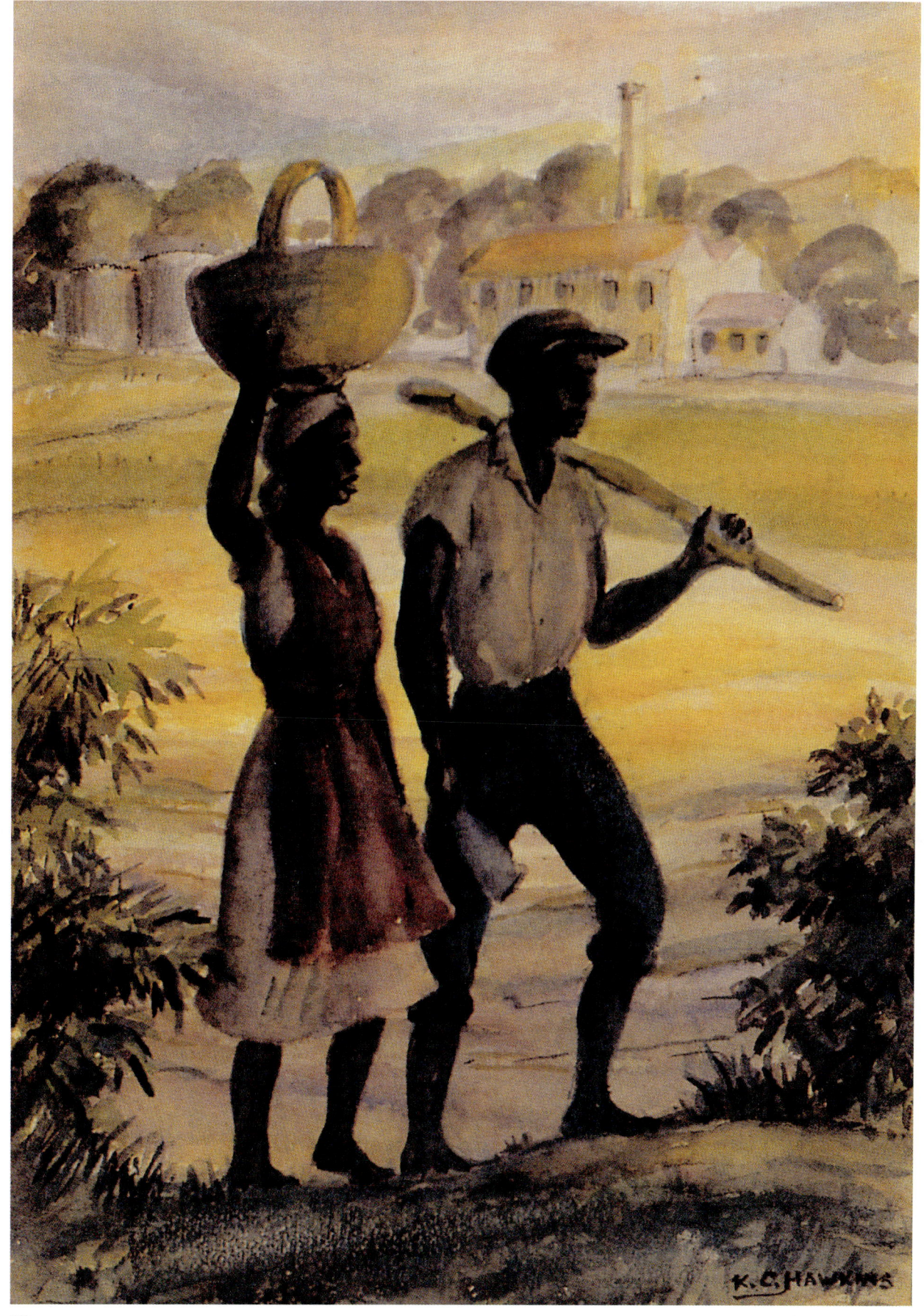

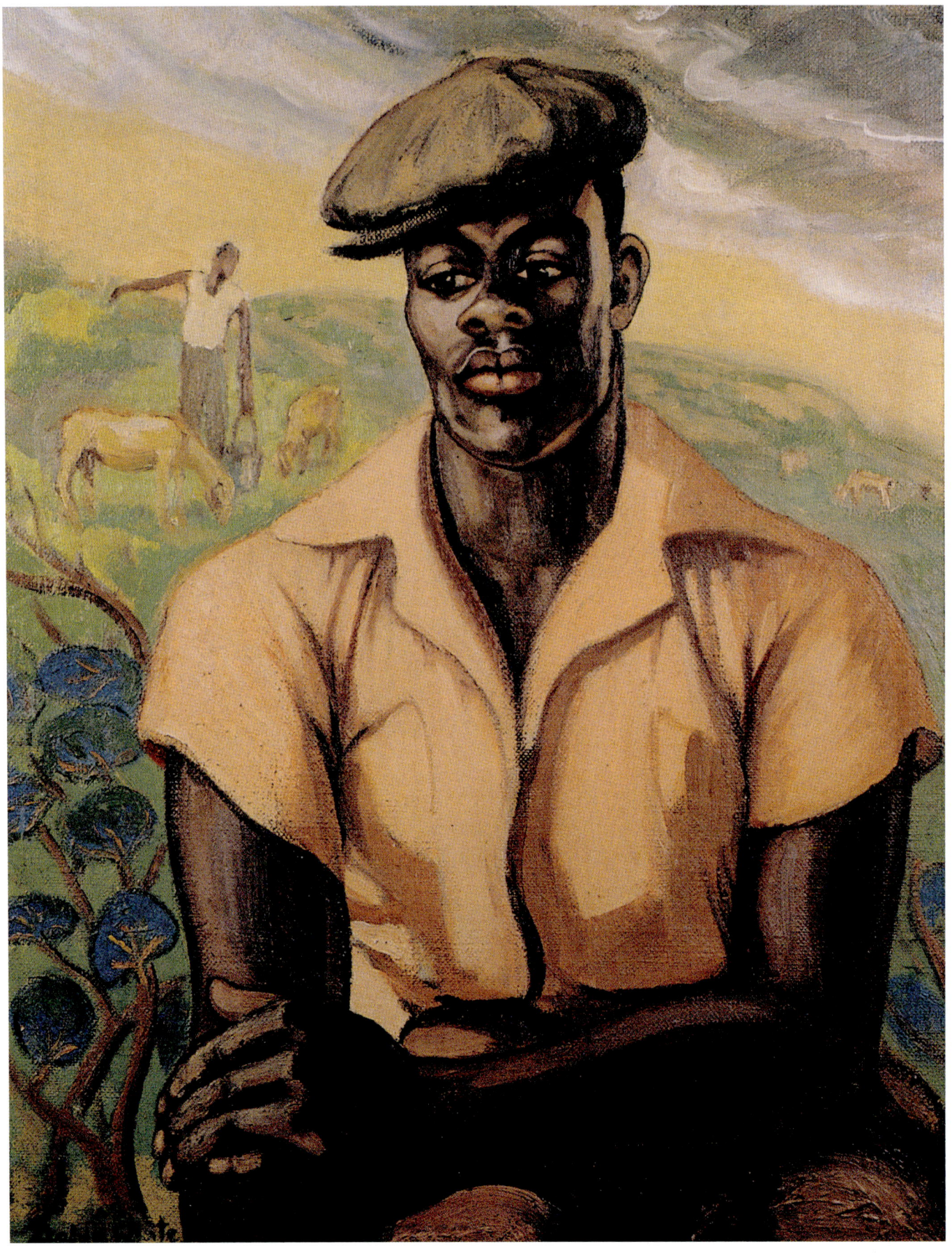

222

222 Golde White. *Black Man in a Cap*. Undated. Oil on canvas. Washington, DC, Private collection.

after the First World War and the mechanized carnage many of these young artists witnessed, they promoted other cultures and a return to new beginnings based on simpler values and idyllic existence originally envisaged in Paul Gauguin's paintings of Martinique and later Tahiti. Looking at this trend, we can recognize how the Caribbean and its art were perceived as being already modern. It was framed within a modernist discourse when avant-garde artists, disenchanted by the spoils of imperialism and inspired by the art of other cultures, posited new ways of seeing.

Following in the footsteps of Gauguin, a handful of European writers and artists made their way to the Caribbean in search of a primitive lifestyle. In 1929, William B. Seabrook published *The Magic Island,* describing his travels and "baptism of blood" in Haiti. Documenting Vodou beliefs and rituals, this book was enormously influential in surrealist circles, especially with the dissident Michel Leiris, who seems to have patterned his own journal about travels in Africa, *L'Afrique fantôme,* on Seabrook's occult research. *The Magic Island* depicted Haiti as savage, exotic, and mysterious, applauding its history of defiance that had ousted the French colonial rule to become the first Black republic. Its author's research involved adventurous fieldwork, the taking of secret oaths, and living intimately with Haitians to learn their customs.[12]

The portrait painter Augustus John also visited Jamaica in 1937.[13] Inspired by a spiritualist reading and the lure of "rum, treacle, white devilry and black magic," the British artist spent two months painting, using local models and exploring the island, even offering encouragement to local artists. John lamented that Jamaica had been blighted by colonialism that had "subdued its natural exuberance into a sober monotony." Like Seabrook, he relished the *Pokomanya* revivalist meetings he attended, conducted by the shepherd and sculptor Mallica Reynolds, known as Kapo, and was "deeply stirred."[14] While there, he painted *Two Jamaican Girls* (1937; Liverpool, Walker Art Gallery), an impressionist-styled portrait that set the trend for a number of itinerant expatriates including John Wood and Vera Cummings, who spent extended periods in the island painting local subjects. Meanwhile, Edna Manley drew on a small collection of works by modern British painters such as Vanessa Bell and Duncan Grant in the Bloomsbury Group as teaching tools for her classes.[15]

A similar sentiment is true for the surrealist André Breton, who escaped to Martinique from imprisonment as an anarchist in war-torn France in 1941. Breton used the island as a brief refuge and a source of inspiration for his book, *Charmeuse de serpents* (*Snake Charmer*), titled after the fantasy primitive painting by the self-taught artist Henri Rousseau.[16] For the month he was there, Breton believed he was in paradise and confided this to his surrealist friend, André Masson, who shared his onward journey to New York.[17] His short stay inspired the poem "*Un grand poète noir,*" which also provided a platform for the young writer Aimé Césaire and his new work *Cahier d'un retour au pays natal* (1939), a seminal work for the *Négritude* movement a decade later.[18]

The Caribbean also attracted diaspora artists such as Edna Manley in Jamaica, Richmond Barthé there and in Haiti, and Wifredo Lam in Cuba. They were not immune to ideas of the primitive. But more important, they came in search of Black identity to islands where they felt some cultural connection.

With the creation of works such as Edna Manley's *Beadseller* (1922) and Golde White's *Black Man in a Cap* (undated), we can speak of an art form rooted in local subject matter by art-

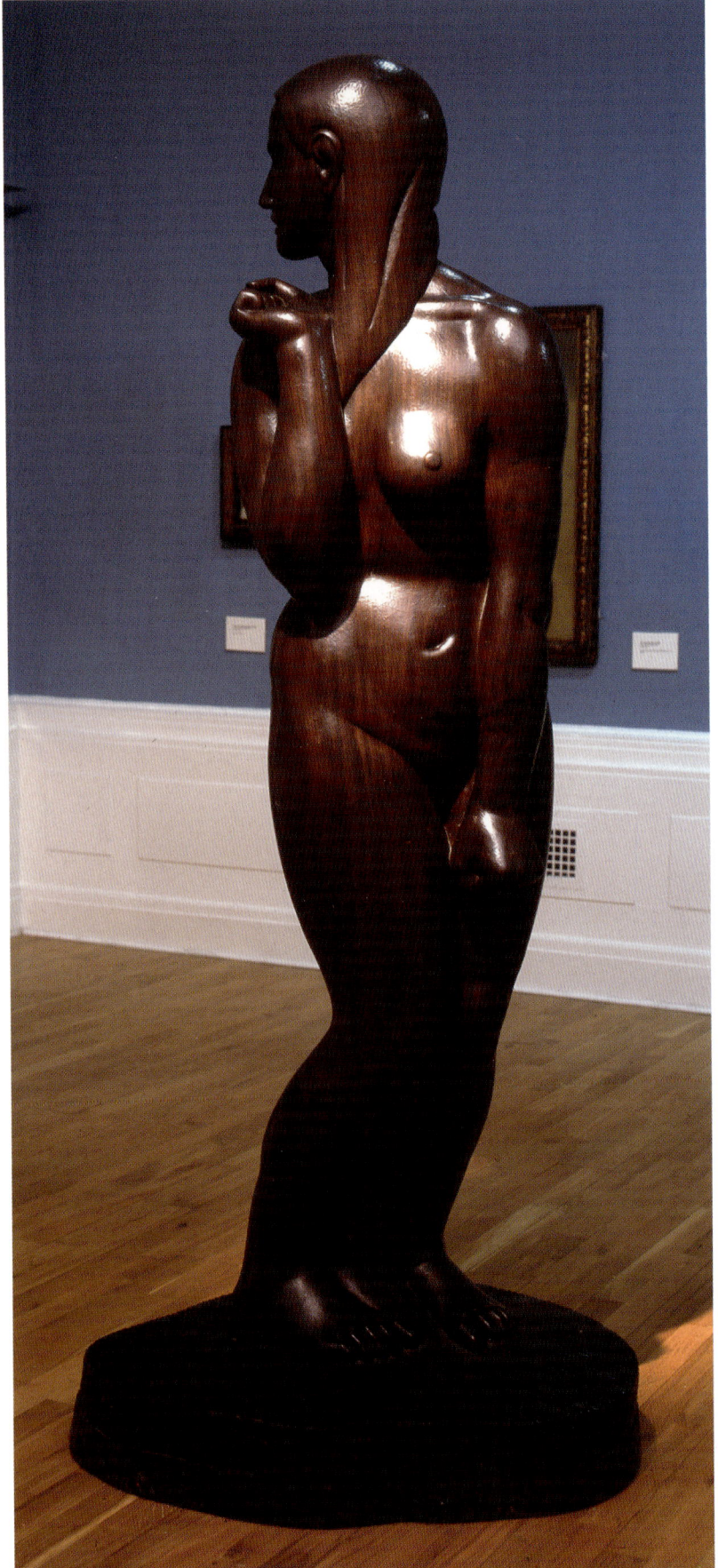

223 Edna Manley. *Eve*. 1929. Mahogany. Sheffield, England, Graves Art Gallery.

224 Ronald Moody. *Midonz (Goddess of Transmutation)*. 1937. Elm wood. London, Tate Britain.

ists who identified with the Caribbean as home. Ironically, like Lam in Paris, this appreciation for local culture had come from their study experiences abroad and their exposure to avant-garde thinking. Kobena Mercer notes that in Paris, "French West Indian students sent to the metropolis to be trained as middle class professionals not only laid claim to their blackness as an empowering act of cultural affirmation but also went back to the Caribbean with altered perceptions of the region's 'indigenous folk' cultures as a potential route towards the higher reality or sur-reality that would transform the experience of everyday life."[19]

Trends in Britain affected students there, too. Both White and Manley had studied in London when academicism was under attack from members of the arts and crafts movement as well as from modern movements such as post-impressionism and cubism that filtered through from Europe. "A typical student... would therefore have to correspond to incompatible regimes. There would be the diet of national 'academic' [exercises]... featuring anatomical drawing, architectural drawing, flower painting, drawing or modelling from nature, while at the same time responding to the vague iconoclasm of Vorticism and the refinements of pure abstraction."[20] This ambivalence is evidenced in Manley's earliest Jamaican works created in the 1920s. Fresh from St. Martin's School of Art, her styles ranged from the conventional to the cubist as she experimented with forms that could best suit her new environment and Caribbean subject matter. In the next decade, with the creation of works such as *Eve* (1929), *Beulah* (1933), and *Pocomania* (1936), she settled on robust, organic figures inspired by Picasso, Henry Moore, and Barbara Hepworth but wholly focused on the Black physiognomy.

Eve is an Edenic Amazon mother carved out of solid mahog-

384 THE IMAGE OF THE BLACK IN 20TH-CENTURY ANGLO-AFRO-CARIBBEAN ART

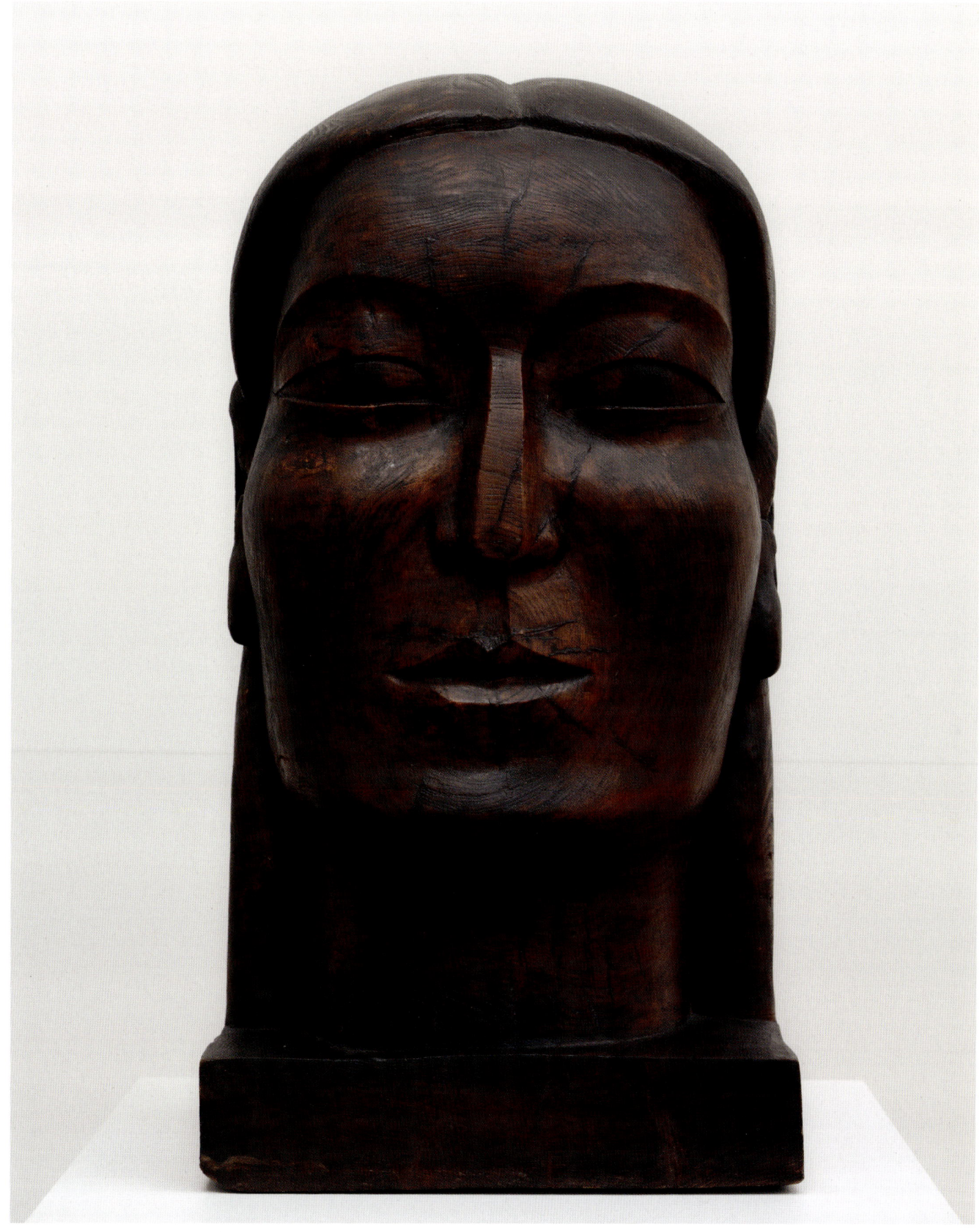

225 Osmond Watson. *Peace and Love*. 1969. Kingston, National Gallery of Jamaica.

any. In keeping with the modernist sentiments of that era, she shares much in common with Pablo Picasso's nudes that some twenty years before had laid the foundation for cubism and his watershed abstract work *Les Demoiselles d'Avignon* (1907). *Eve* most closely resembles his 1906 pair of nudes who stand in profile facing each other but gaze backward coyly. *Eve* offers the same gesture, lifting her hand toward her mouth and suggesting self-doubt or shame as she looks behind her. She is massive. Her whole body is bulbous, and with deep brown tones that suggest her African origins. Yet her facial features and hair bear no distinctive phenotype. Like the work of Manley's fellow Jamaican Ronald Moody, this *Eve* stands for a universal woman, a prototype predating constructs of race.

These pioneering images, along with the iconic *Negro Aroused* (1935) (Kingston, National Gallery of Jamaica) (see fig. 203), provoked racial awareness and promoted Black imagery. They expressed antipathy toward colonialism and concern for the nonwhite world's independence. These interests coincided with shifts in political power from colonial administrations to a growing middle class attracted by cultural nationalist sentiments and the New Negro philosophies that swept through America's cities in the 1930s. Ronald Moody exhibited *Midonz* (1937) alongside the work of other Harlem Renaissance artists in the Harmon Foundation's *Contemporary Negro African Art* exhibition (1939). This large female Buddha head with pronounced features put the interior life of Black people at the center of discussions about spiritual awareness and human development already cultivated in Paris after World War I, especially among the surrealists. Although Moody had left Jamaica in 1923, he carried with him an acute sense of cultural memory and place that would echo through the silence of his gargantuan forms. Moody's intuitive harnessing of Egyptian and pre-Columbian forms predicted the marriage of forms that would become a feature of the Caribbean aesthetic, later witnessed in imagery such as Philip Moore's *1763 Monument* (Guyana) (see fig. 208), or LeRoy Clarke's *In the Maze, There Is a Single Line to My Soul* (1986, Trinidad) (see fig. 245).

The twentieth century witnessed the first grassroots challenge to colonial authority through the efforts of Marcus Garvey and his Pan-African Universal Negro Improvement Association (UNIA). This Black separatist organization, based in Harlem but with strong roots in Garvey's homeland of Jamaica, and a network of migrants who had worked in Honduras, Venezuela, Costa Rica, Nicaragua, Panama, and on ships throughout the Caribbean, promoted a Back to Africa program that found traction with his largely underprivileged Black audiences in cities throughout the African diaspora. Garvey's movement appealed largely to working-class men and women. With rudimentary education and limited instruction in art making, many of the Caribbean's earliest self-taught artists developed their craft from practical skills that relied on their hands. They were woodworkers, cabinetmakers, welders, sign painters, and even barbers. Stanley Greaves recalls that he first became aware of art from his father:

> I think it was [from] growing up in a house where my father did signboards, like J. Smith: Carpenter, or Tinsmith or Tailor, for friends of his. I used to help him: he drew the outlines and I would fill them in. He also did headstones for graves. That's where I learned the distinction between roman and italic lettering, and Germanic capitals. I think I got riveted through seeing images. My father used to retouch

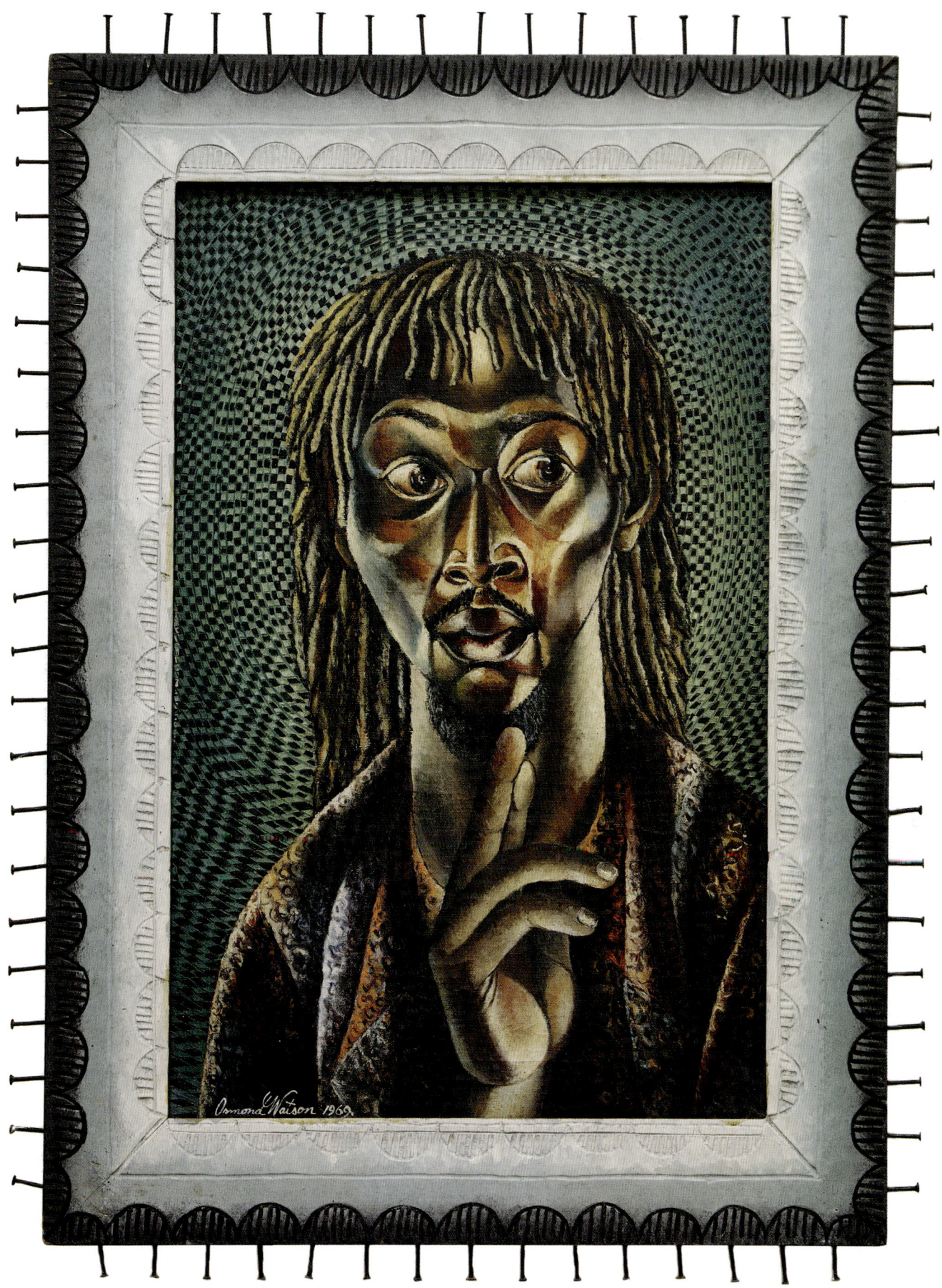

225

226 Albert Huie. *The History Lesson*. 1943. Kingston, Jamaica, Private collection.

and repair the certificates of societies like the Freemasons and the Scottish Lodge. He also repaired the aprons that Freemasons wore, with images of the square and compass and the eye looking out of a pyramid. I found the symbols extremely mysterious, and my mind was compelled to find out what all these things meant.[21]

Garvey aimed to raise Black consciousness through an understanding of Black history and by promoting African culture. He was particularly drawn to the art of Egypt, teaching that it represented Black people's earliest contribution to world culture. Garvey recognized the importance of positive images, particularly for Black men who since slavery had been treated as boys. He gave these working-class masons, soldiers, and factory workers an image of themselves that was purposeful and ambitious. His use of military garb and other regal paraphernalia was a way to reinstate their manliness and sense of self-worth.[22] It also helped reestablish their connection to Africa as stakeholders and defenders of a new homeland, envisioned initially in Liberia but later replaced by Ethiopia. Although many of the artists who responded to his challenge were largely self-taught, their images of themselves and their communities would underpin the movement for racial pride and self-awareness that marked Black activism in the twentieth century.

Black people painting images of themselves in the Caribbean then is an entirely modern phenomenon. When the Jamaican artist Osmond Watson painted his iconic *Peace and Love* in 1969, he was responding directly to Garvey's earlier clarion call that his UNIA members should see God through "the eyes of Blackness" and that artists should create Black Christs and Madonnas to educate Black children.[23] In the 1940s, Watson had witnessed Garvey's influence on Kingston's street-side preachers who spread a message of Black "upliftment." Watson was also aware of other itinerants like Leonard P. Howell and Joseph Hibbert, forerunners of a bourgeoning Rastafari movement, who as early as 1935 sold coronation photographs of His Imperial Majesty Haile Selassie, the recently enthroned emperor of Ethiopia, considering him to be Christ incarnate.

Watson's painting of *Peace and Love* fulfilled the promise of a lineage of Caribbean-based artists, including Pétion Savain (Haiti), Albert Huie (*The History Lesson,* 1943, Jamaica), and Karl Broodhagen (Barbados), who had already captured this message of race pride in their work. But few of them could match Watson's technical skills, spiritual conviction, and unique artistic vision that aptly depict Garvey's canonization of Jesus Christ as the "Black Man of Sorrow." Watson's modest background—his street-smart "grounations,"[24] local art school training, a British Council scholarship to St. Martin's in London, and his eventual rejection of European methods in favor of Africanized forms—meant he was perfectly suited to articulate visually the image of race consciousness and divine Blackness that the orator and reformer Marcus Garvey had hoped for almost a half century earlier.[25]

Created in the artist's characteristic style that synthesized his modern art school training with his growing interest in Black portraiture, Watson demonstrates an understanding of his inner divinity and the Rastafari's *I and I* principle that recognizes their spiritual union with God. Mimicking but also mocking Christian icons, Watson employs his own image where we might expect to see Christ's. Depicted in multiple brown skin tones, this Black Christ's face is dramatically defined by a cubist-style angularity

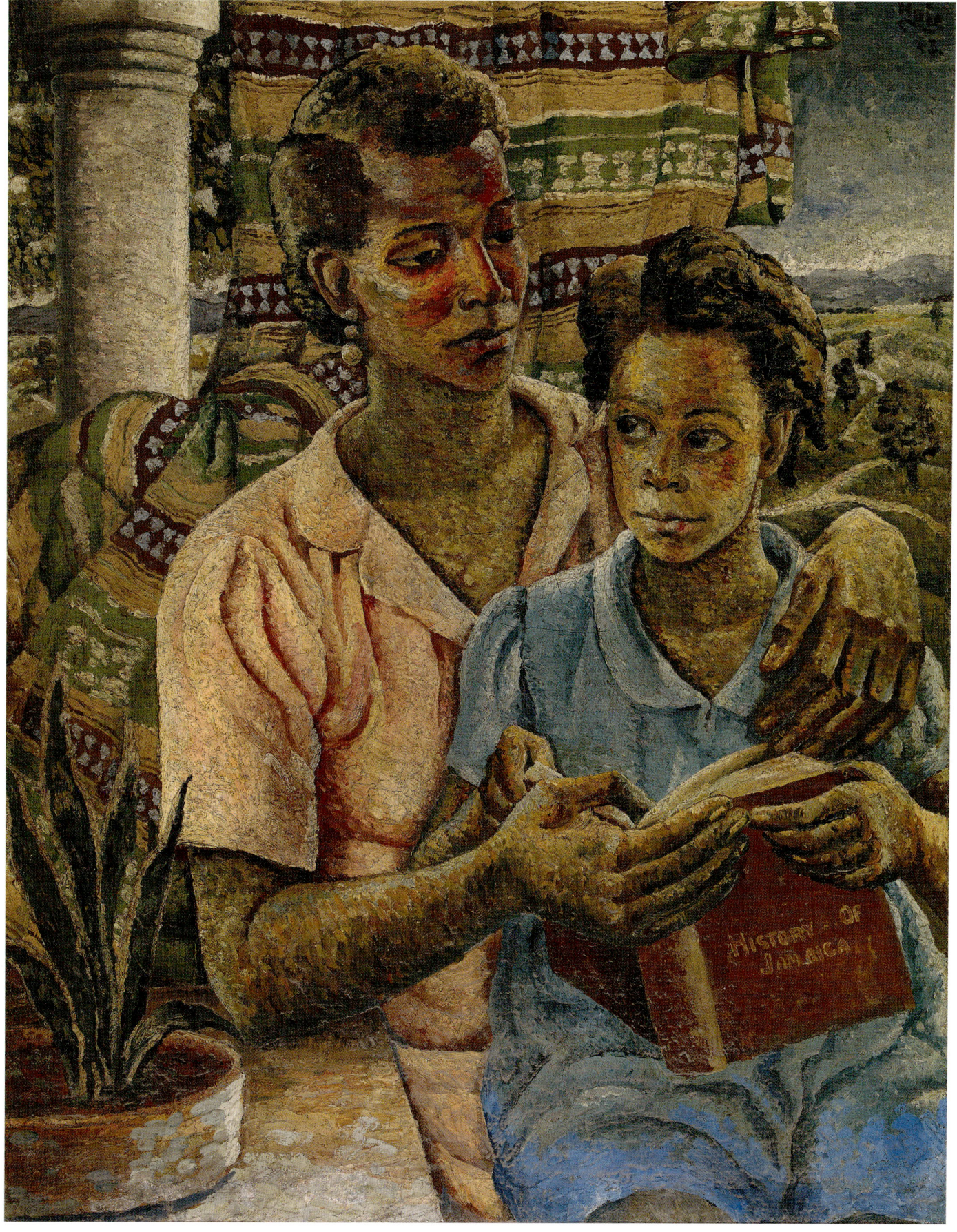

227 Karl Broodhagen. *Patricia*. Undated. Terracotta. Collection of the artist.

that also challenges the long-held stigma that the hues of Black skin do not reflect light and are therefore difficult to paint.

Christ's eyes, almost perfectly oval and smoked with tinges of red, bulge as they turn away from the viewer and focus outside the frame, while his pursed lips reinforce the blessing of his hand raised in a benediction of peace and love. It is Christ's hair, however, that confounds the modern viewer. Christ's perfectly groomed but woolly-looking locks, like a halo surrounding his head, sanctify this image and reinforce the artist's message about race and inner divinity. Blue patterning heightens the aura and brings to mind the jeweled quality of Byzantine icons. Meanwhile, the carved frame bordered with nails speaks to Christ's persecution and also hints at Watson's awareness of the Congo Nkisi's traditional use of nails when creating objects of power. Combined, these elements represent a shift from the Christian missionary promotion of a blond-haired, blue-eyed Christ—an image on many living room walls that was the spiritual staple of the colonized Caribbean—toward a new aesthetic rooted in an Old Testament past and Africa.

The Caribbean's Black diaspora imagery traces its lineage back to Haiti's revolution in 1789, slave rebellions of the nineteenth century, and the spread of Garveyism and its later manifestation in Rastafari after 1930. Unlike the educated Creole middle class, self-taught artists across the Caribbean developed their imagery within this social ethos. Among these artists were Hector Hyppolite of Haiti (*Magique noir*, ca. 1946–1947), Mallica "Kapo" Reynolds of Jamaica (*Revival Goddess Dina*, ca. 1968), Amos Ferguson of The Bahamas (*Woman Lying on a Couch*, 1960, private collection), Ivan Payne of Barbados (*Maube Seller,* undated), and Honoré Chosrova of Martinique (*Séance,* 1988). Most culti- vated their styles through trial and error, or, like Chosrova, from correspondence courses and evening classes in Paris. Other art school–trained artists such as Christopher Gonzáles of Jamaica (*Mountain Head* [*Woman of Zion*], 1980, private collection), Maxwell Taylor of The Bahamas (*Love and Responsibility*, 1997); and Joseph Sainte-Croix Rene-Corail, of Martinique, called Khokho (*Untitled,* 1963) also consciously drew on this Black worldview, harnessing their art school techniques selectively and combining them with a more conscious African aesthetic.

These works share strong matriarchal imagery that militates against the sexualized and fecund stereotypes regularly placed on Caribbean women since the days of Paul Gauguin.[26] These women are wizened, with heads tied and aging bodies. The Black Madonnas suggest stability, industry, and spiritual strength. In Stanley Greaves's *The Annunciation* (from the *There's a Meeting Here Tonight* series, 1993, Guyana), the grandmother stands next to a youth, prepared to carry the burden of his folly. The artist also draws on iconography peculiar to Caribbean pop culture: a microphone, an oil drum, and the deejay youth's cap bearing the American flag turned backward on his head. These spiritual and secular symbols have inherited meaning from the Caribbean diaspora's long march to freedom. For generations starved of visual stimuli or tokens from home, these are surreal, imaginative constructs that share a local collective intelligence.

In time, social acceptance of Rastafari and the popularity of works by Ras Dizzy (*The Rasta Says*, 1987), Everald Brown (*Victory over Satan*, 1968), or Ras Daniel Heartman, all of Jamaica, has meant that these homegrown art forms, combined with their ubiquitous images of the reggae musician Bob Marley, Haile Selassie, and biblical symbols such as the Star of David, the lilies

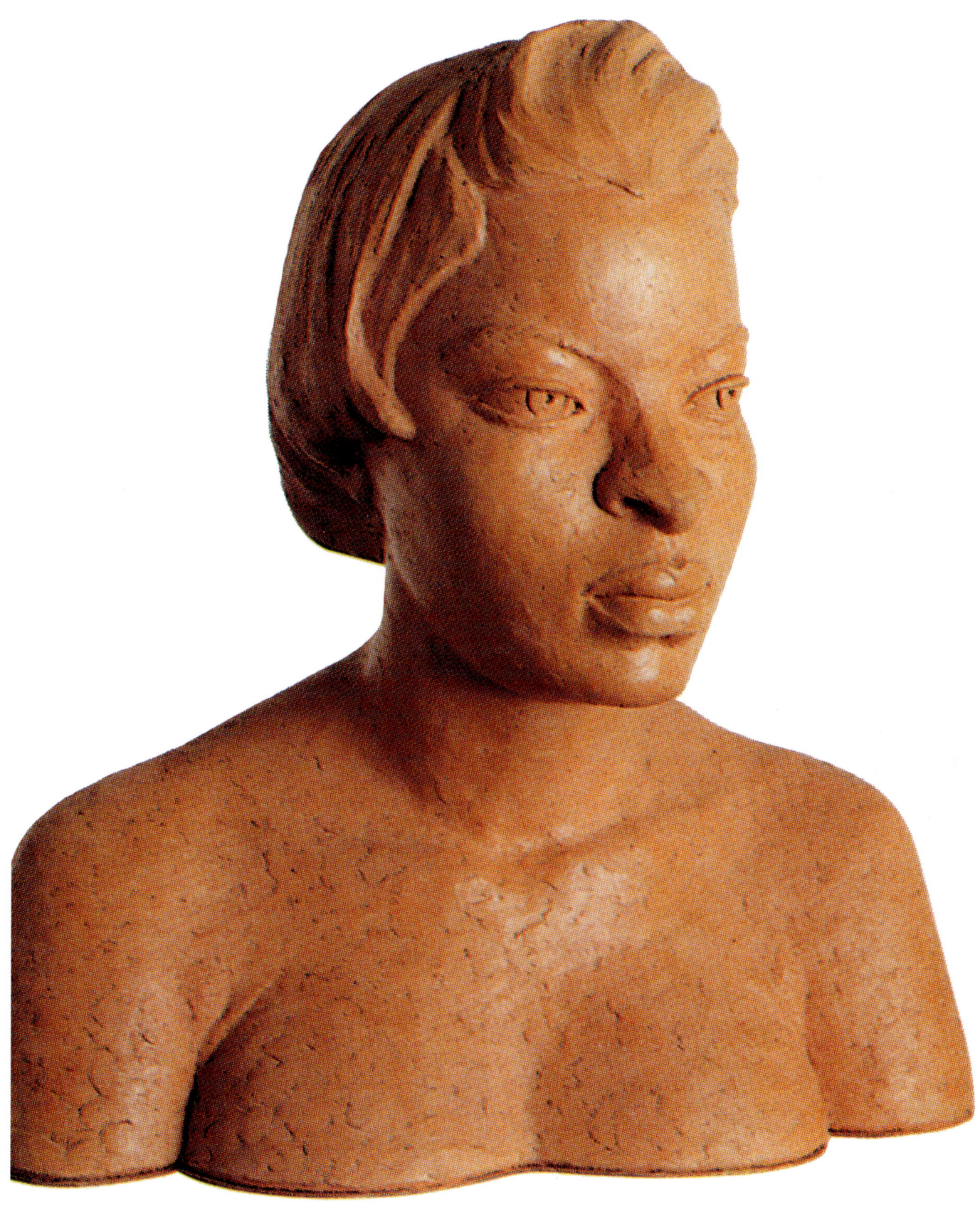

227

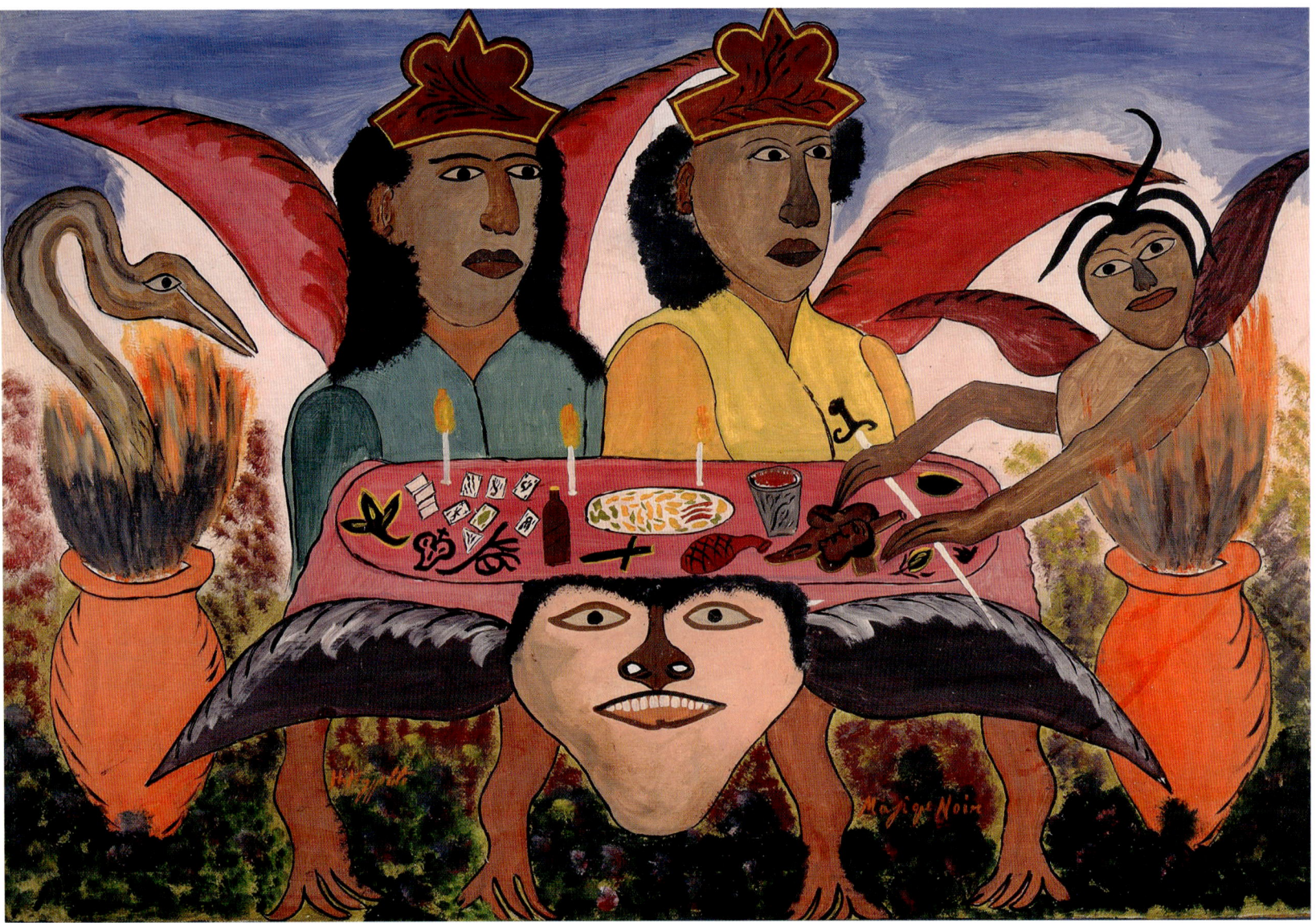

228

228 Hector Hyppolite. *Black Magic*. Ca. 1946–1947. Oil on board. Wisconsin, Milwaukee Art Museum.

229 Kapo (Mallica Reynolds). *Revival Goddess Dina*. Ca. 1968. Lignum vitae. Kingston, National Gallery of Jamaica.

230 Ivan Payne. *Maube Seller*. Undated. Mahogany. Kingston, Jamaica, Private collection.

231 Honoré Chosrova. *Séance*. 1988. Location unknown.

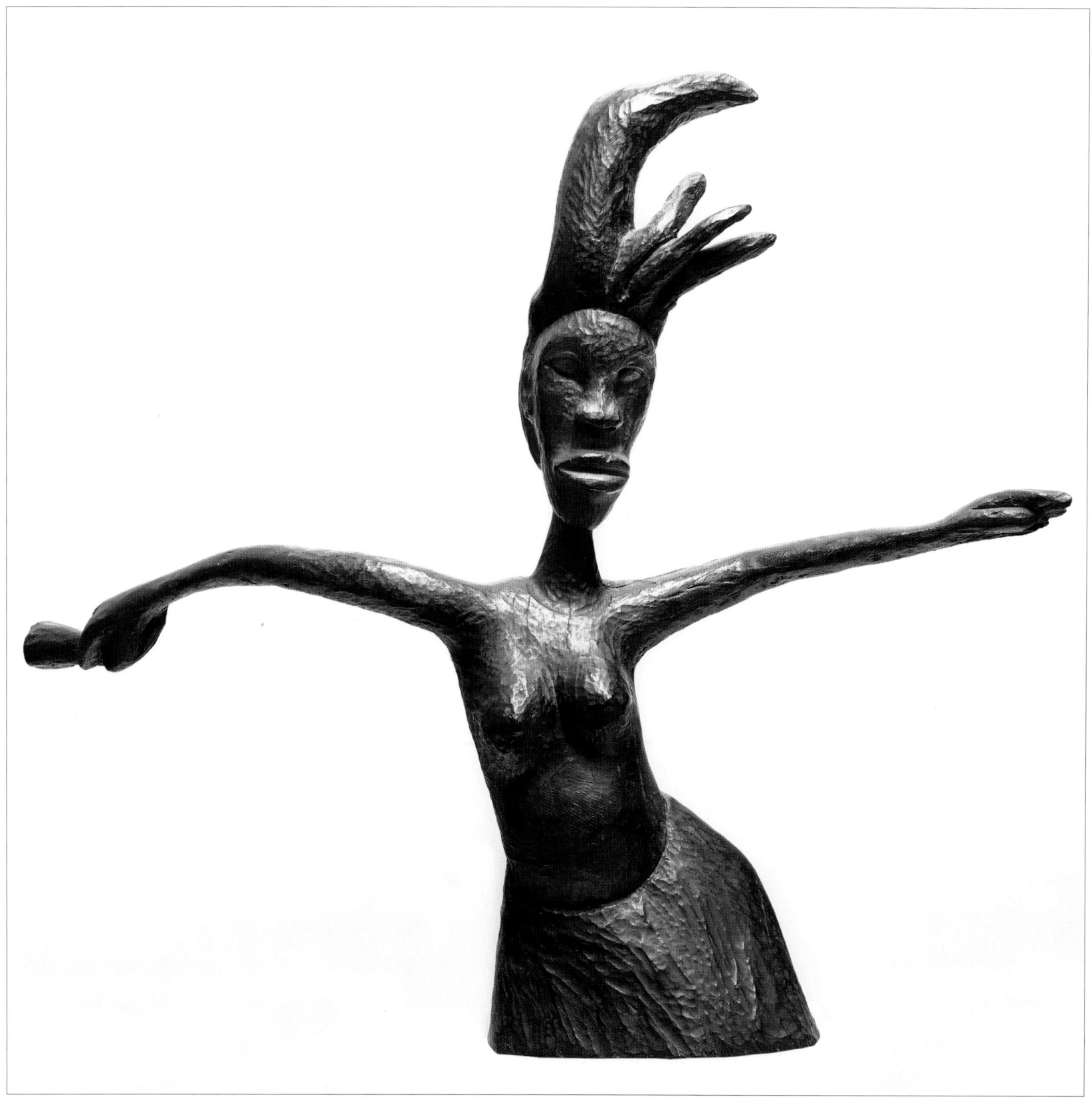

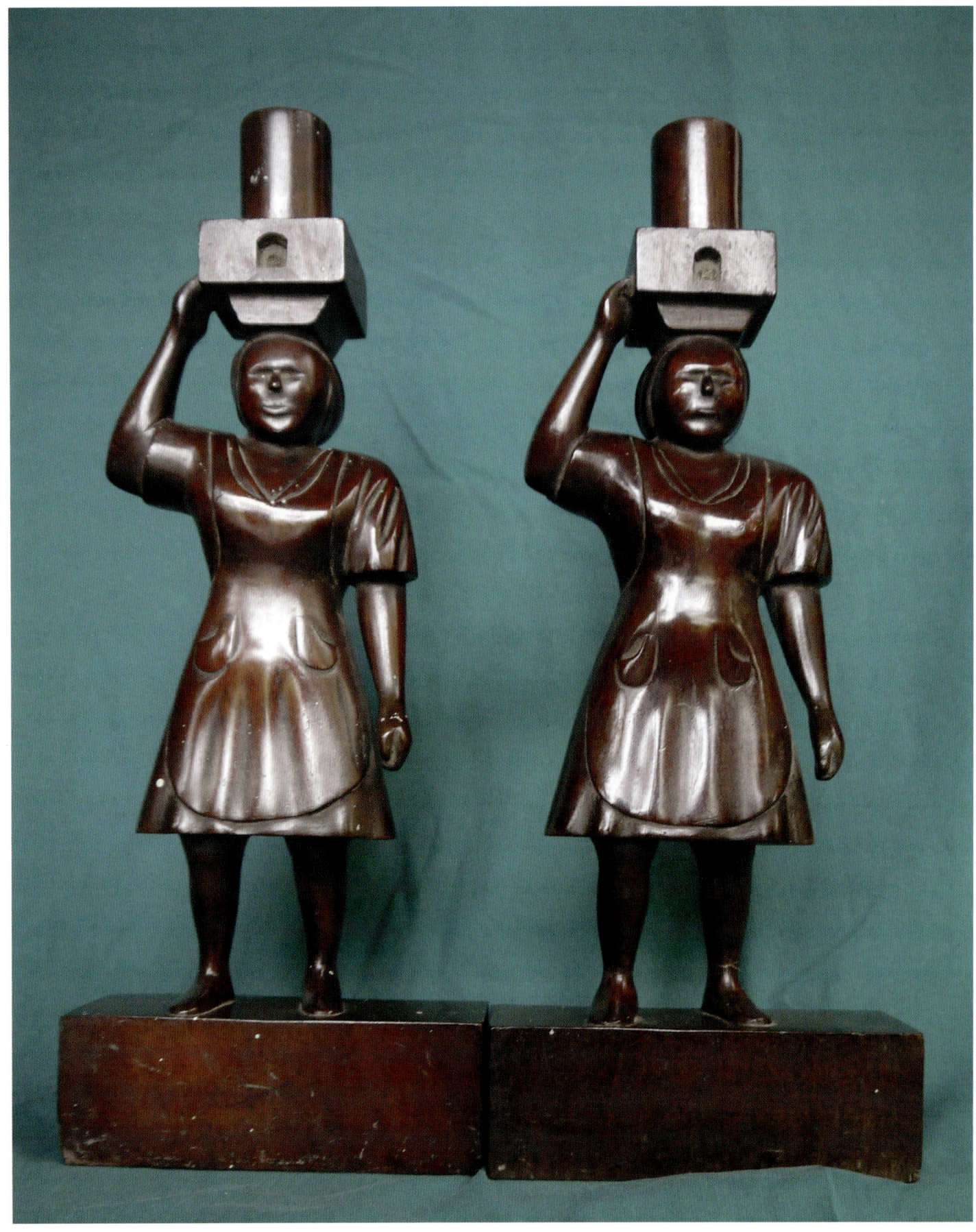

230

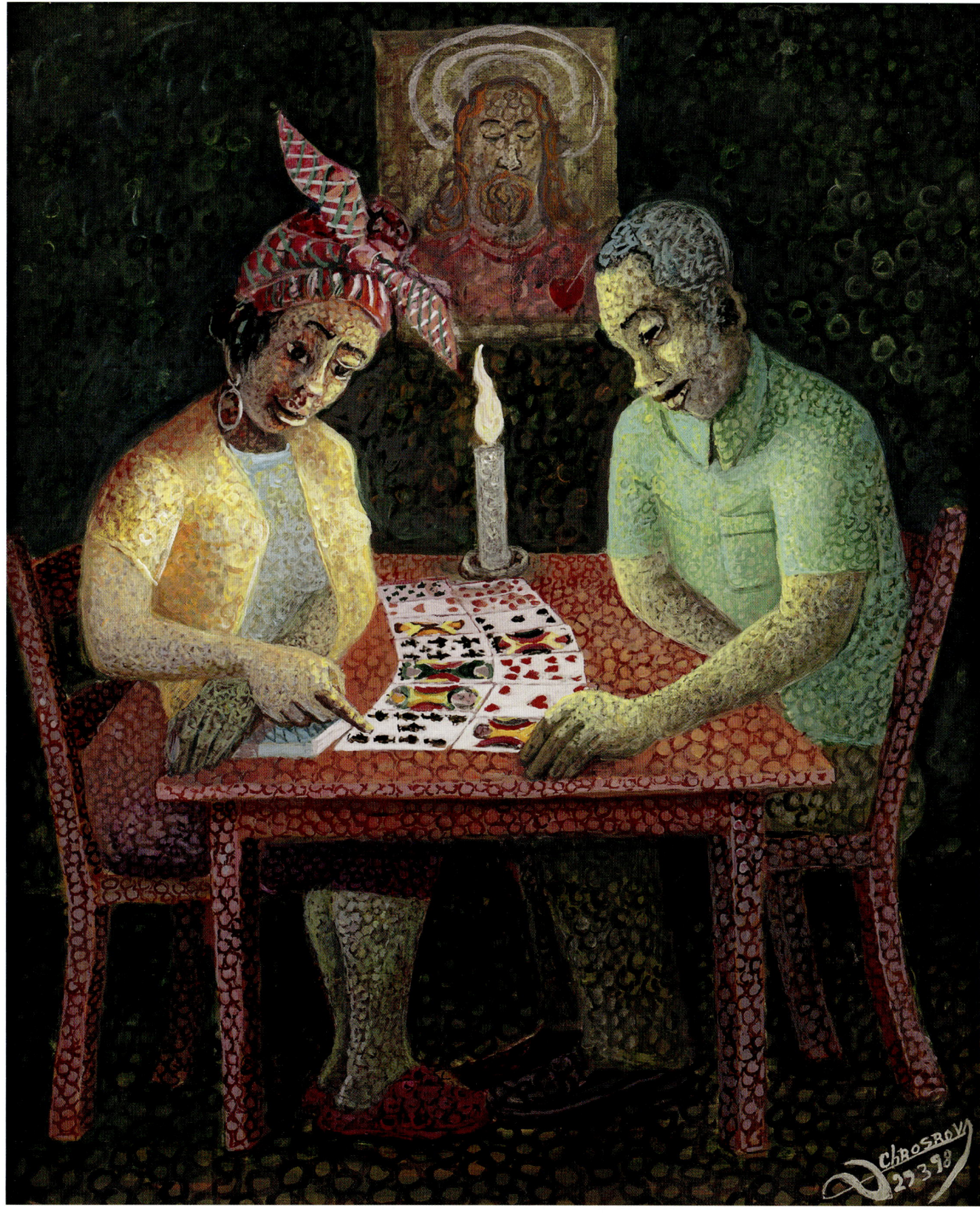

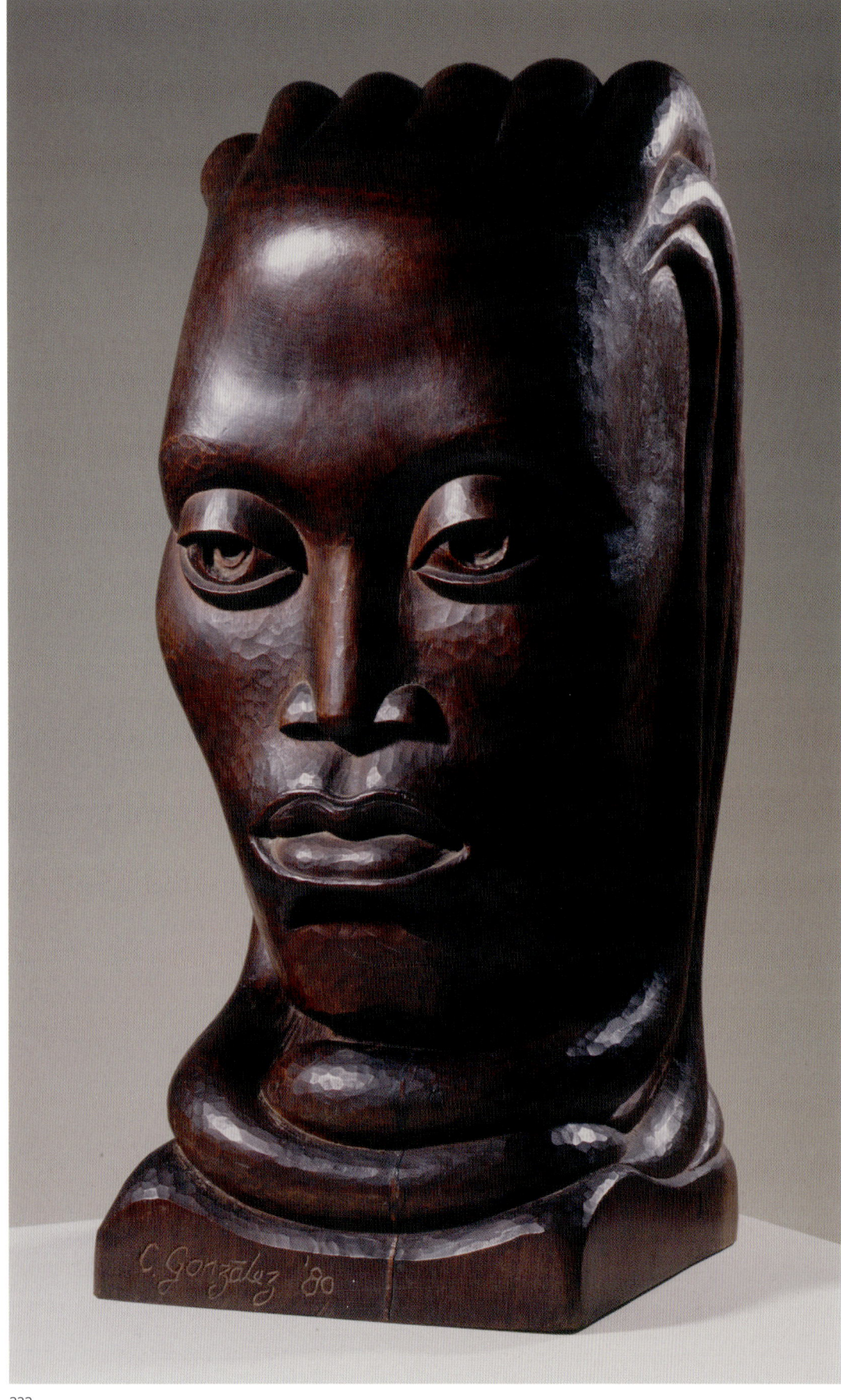

232 Christopher Gonzáles. *Mountain Head (Woman of Zion)*. 1980. Kingston, Jamaica, Collection of Mrs. Sheila Graham.

233 Maxwell Taylor. *Love and Responsibility*. 1997. Woodcut. The Bahamas, The Dawn Davies Collection.

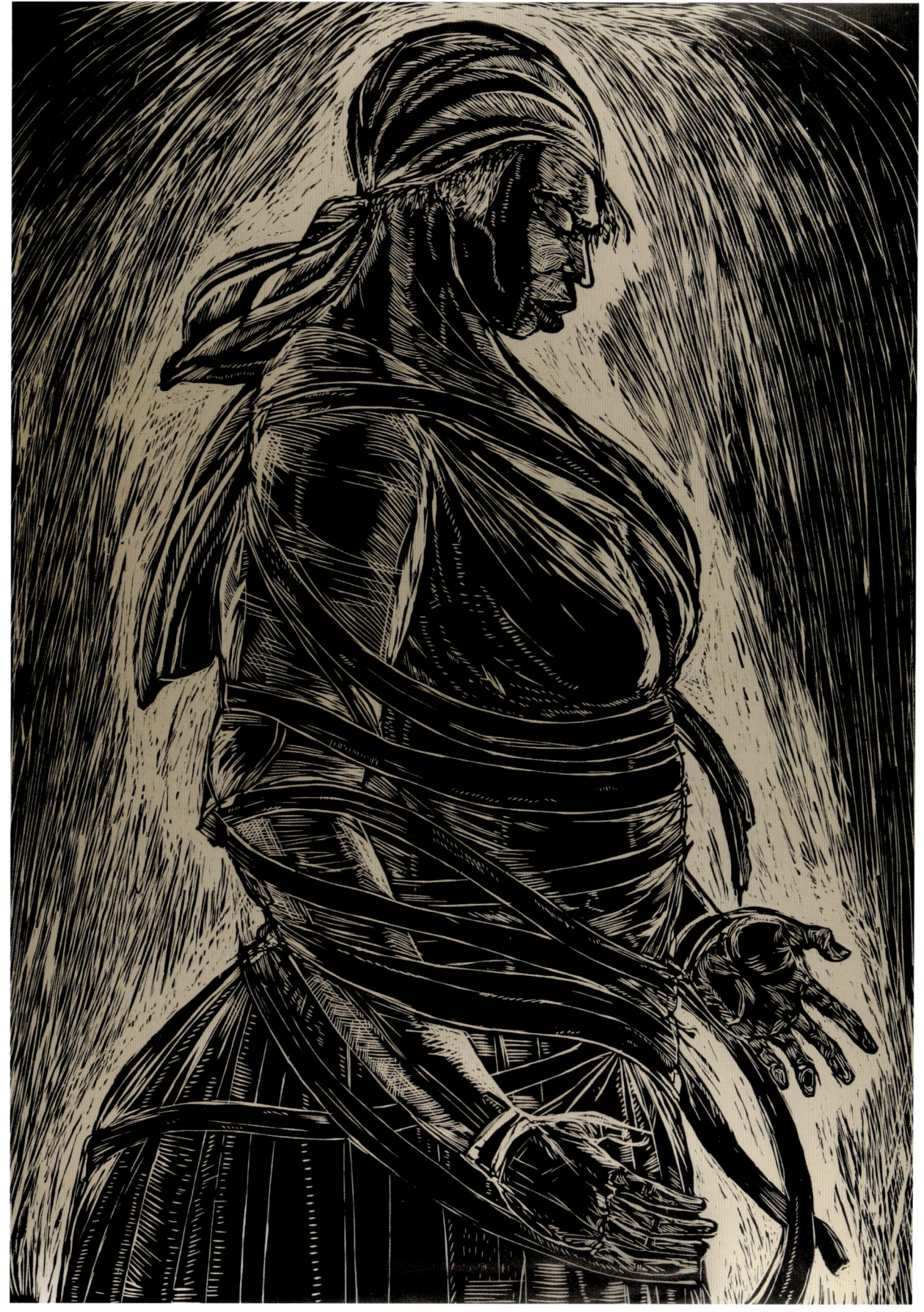

of the field, the Lion of the Tribe of Judah, and the Stem of Jesse, have become part of the Caribbean diaspora's visual lexicon. They appear on LP album covers, garments, and Rasta memorabilia.

Karl Parboosingh was one of Jamaica's earliest trained artists to portray Rastas and their symbolism (*Ras Smoke I*, 1972). But the contemporary conjurer of these visual iconographies is Ras Ishi Butcher, who is devoted to the scouring of the Black man's four-hundred-year history in the Caribbean (*Blazin 1*, 2003–2004). His paintings, which employ Egyptian hieroglyphs, colonial emblems, stripped-down cartoon forms, grotesquerie, portraiture, and codified racial ideograms, repeat themselves throughout his oeuvre, morphing with each new series to extend their meaning and the viewer's understanding of his visual repertoire. Ras Ishi's work collates, collages, and summarizes the doubled, tripled, and multiplied meanings that have riddled the Black man's sojourn in the Caribbean diaspora since he disembarked. His body of work serves as an ongoing visual diary that includes gang workers, chattel houses, colonials in panama hats, and local vegetation that tell a story about how that history has defined the Black man's relocation. His paintings are punctuated statements that in their graphic, flattened, and overlaid posterlike presentation constantly repeat his slogans for change.

Even as Black people were mobilizing for repatriation to Africa, the region's middle-class Creoles sought to go beyond their European influences to accommodate African, Asian, and Native American histories. They took inspiration from local subjects as well as Pan-African movements such as the Harlem Renaissance and its ideas of a New Negro.[27] The nationalist movements of the twentieth century were cultural as well as political. They coalesced around clusters of middle-class artists, writers, and intellectuals keen to reconnect the region with its Taíno origins and its Asian and African heritage while supporting independence from their mother countries.

Norman and Edna Manley were at the center of nationalist decolonization debates in Jamaica during the 1940s. Educated and married in England, they immersed themselves in politics and local culture after returning to Jamaica. In the run-up to the island's political independence, their home was a hub for artists, poets, and intellectuals keen to promote Jamaican self-government and a homespun artistic and literary aesthetic.[28] With artists and writers such as Roger Mais, George Campbell, and Koren der Harootian, they articulated a new social contract for the country that emphasized political independence and cultural nationalism. Through the Institute of Jamaica, they promoted a homegrown culture and the establishment of a national art collection started in 1937 with the purchase of Edna Manley's *Negro Aroused* (1935).

Similar scenarios supporting local culture occurred throughout the region in the late 1920s and early 1930s. Museums and collections such as the British Guyana Arts and Crafts Society and the Barbados Museum and Historical Society laid a foundation for national exhibitions and competitions. Instruction in local art forms would follow with the founding of national art schools such as the School of Applied Arts in Martinique in 1941 or the Junior Centre in Jamaica after 1940. In Haiti, the establishment of the Centre d'Art by DeWitt Peters in 1944 provided a more formal structure for a handful of self-taught artists to create, showcase, and sell work that they had been producing for almost a decade. Meanwhile in Trinidad, the Society of Trinidad Independents was formed in 1929 around Amy Leong Pang; in

1943, Leong Pang and Sybil Atteck established the Trinidad Art Society (now the Art Society of Trinidad and Tobago) upon her return from studies in London; Lima, Peru; and St. Louis, Missouri. Both groups promoted freedom of expression and the promotion of a national identity. They began under the patronage of the colonial administration with exclusive salons, but later the Trinidad Art Society broadened its base, even accommodating self-taught artists.[29]

By the 1940s, the Caribbean had become an accommodating cultural hub where Black ideas about Africa and idealistic European notions related to folk culture and primitivism could safely interact. The region was what Kobena Mercer has called a "contact zone" where artists of different ethnicities were entangled in cross-cultural dialogue that provided the impetus for Black modernism. Mercer even suggests that key words from that era such as *amalgam* can be viewed as "a synonym for cross-cultural mixing; we begin to observe that many of the metaphor-concepts put into play by the postcolonial turn of the 1980s—hybridity, syncretism, creolisation—were first registered in debates of the 1940s that saw cross-cultural exchange as a source of fresh esthetic possibilities brought about by the global conditions of modernity."[30] In short, ideas about race and multiculturalism first raised in the Caribbean set the stage for postmodern thinking a half century later.

Antonio Benítez-Rojo postulates the idea of being and even becoming as an essential option for the survival of a community with no common past. This notion of survival was built into a type of Creole poetic discourse that informed representational politics during the 1940s. The ferment produced Caribbean intellects like C. L. R. James, Norman Manley, and later Eric Williams, who promoted political development rooted in cultural nationalism. They were strongly supported by a "brown skin" middle class who recognized that as a colored minority with a history that could not slot back easily into Europe or Africa, they had nowhere else to go.

Their bid for political ascendancy in the pre-independence years came out of a recognition that the Caribbean would be home, and they began to define their identities in Creole terms that reflected their checkered cultural backgrounds. They encouraged Caribbean people to recognize how their European, African, Asian, and Native American heritages made them distinctly Caribbean, the result of a gene pool of races that could be unified through mottos such as Jamaica's "Out of Many, One People" or Trinidad's "Together we aspire, together we achieve." Sybil Atteck's *Panmen* (ca. 1960, Trinidad Citizens for Conservation) illustrates this ethos, depicting a group of men playing the steel pan, some with the pans strung around their necks, others standing beating oil drums. The artist uses this unique, locally created instrument as a unifying symbol of nation and modernity.

The Creole classes' defining of the larger Black population that they represented was benevolent. The Black man was framed in romantic and enlightened ideas about the "noble savage" that reflected their own negrophilia sentiments. This was characterized by the poetic idealization of the tropical island existence, the Spanish *paradiso*, and a growing interest in the craft and culture of Black urban and rural peasant folk. Institutional patronage of the Haitian artist Georges Liautaud or later, the Bahamian Tyrone Ferguson, both initially blacksmiths and welders who were intuitively drawn to sculpture, speaks to their retention of ironworking from ancient West African traditions. Liautaud's imagery

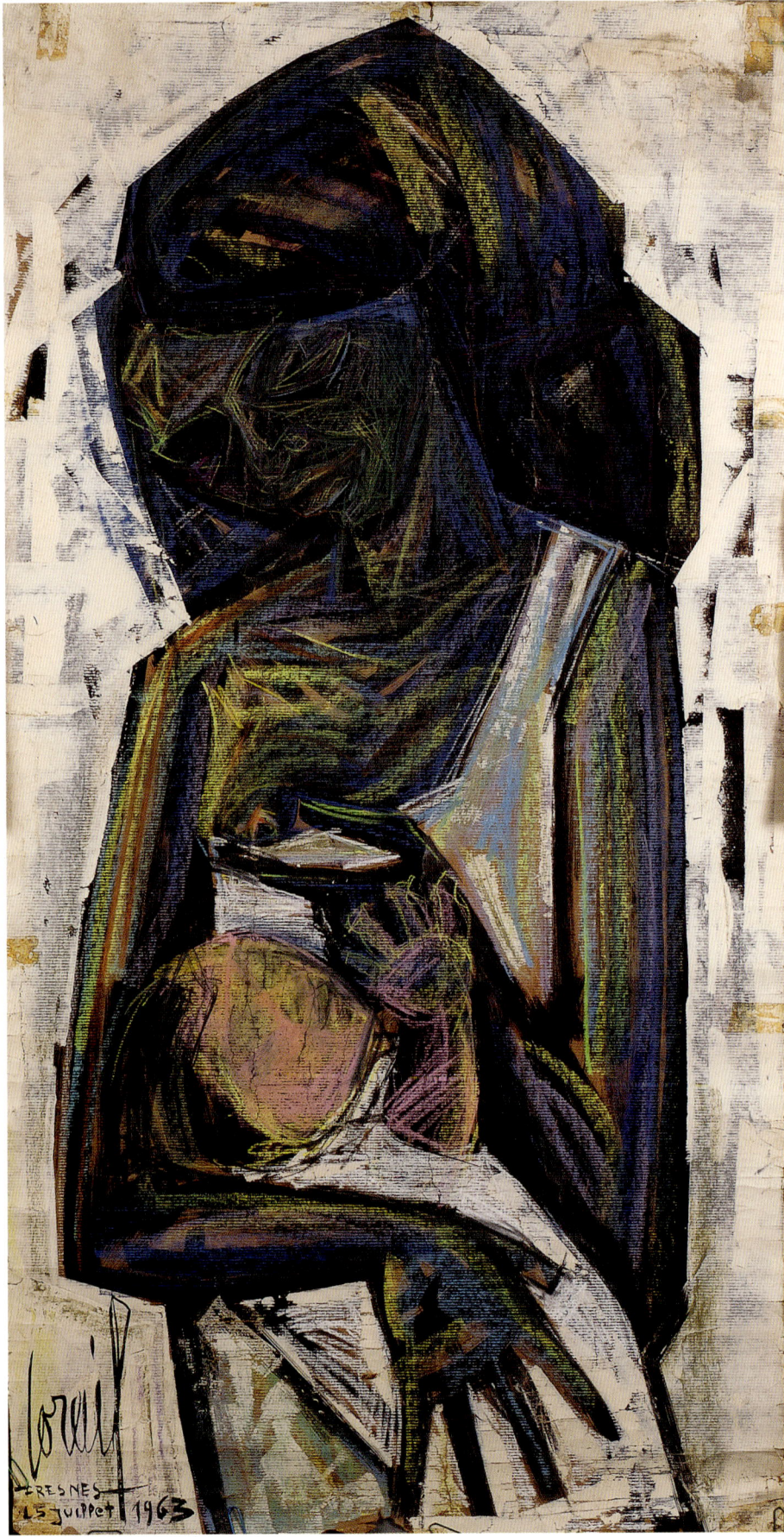

234 Khokho (Joseph Sainte-Croix René-Corail). *Untitled*. 1963. Location unknown.

235 Stanley Greaves. *The Annunciation*. From the series *There's a Meeting Here Tonight*. 1993. Barbados National Art Gallery.

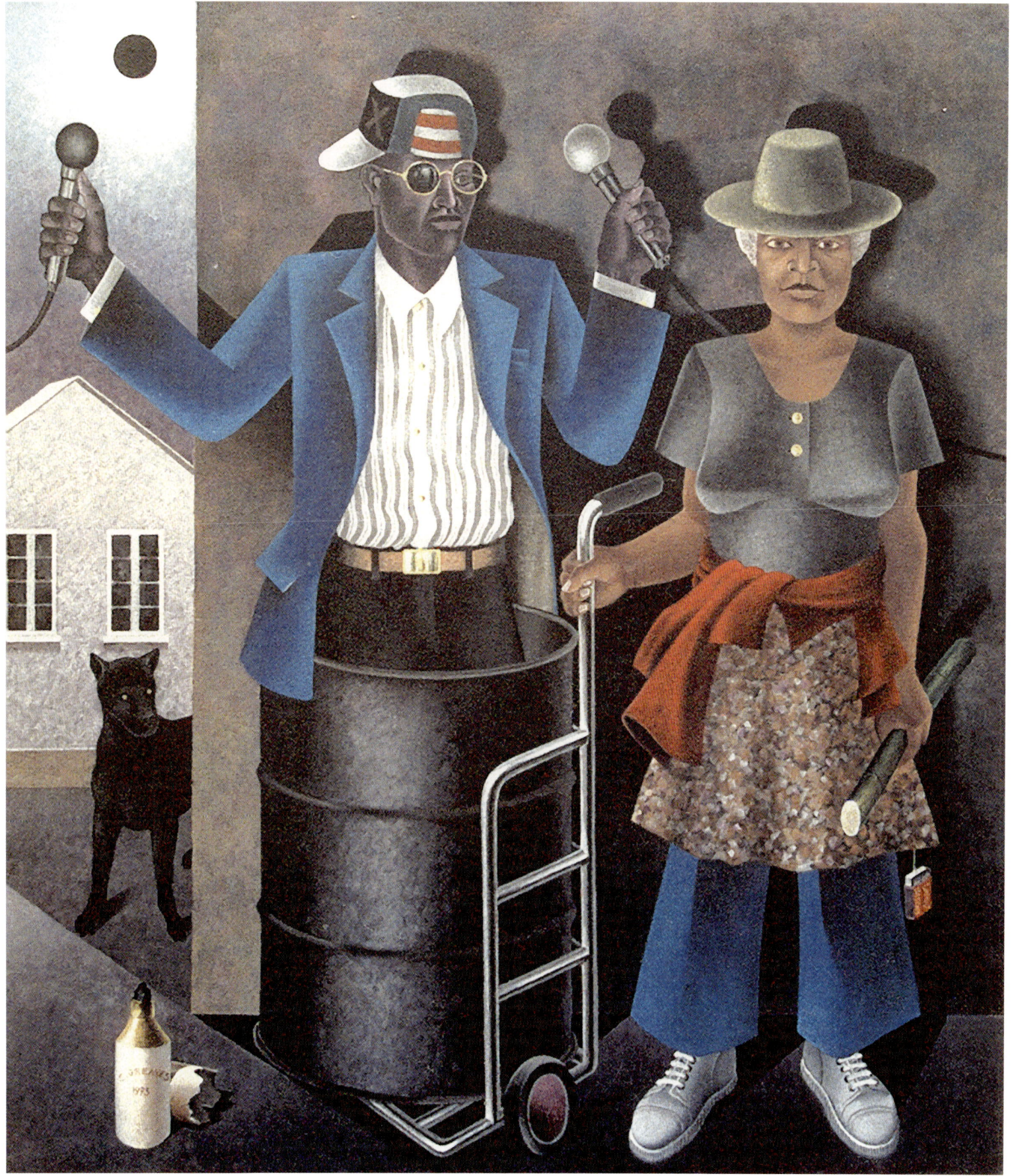

235

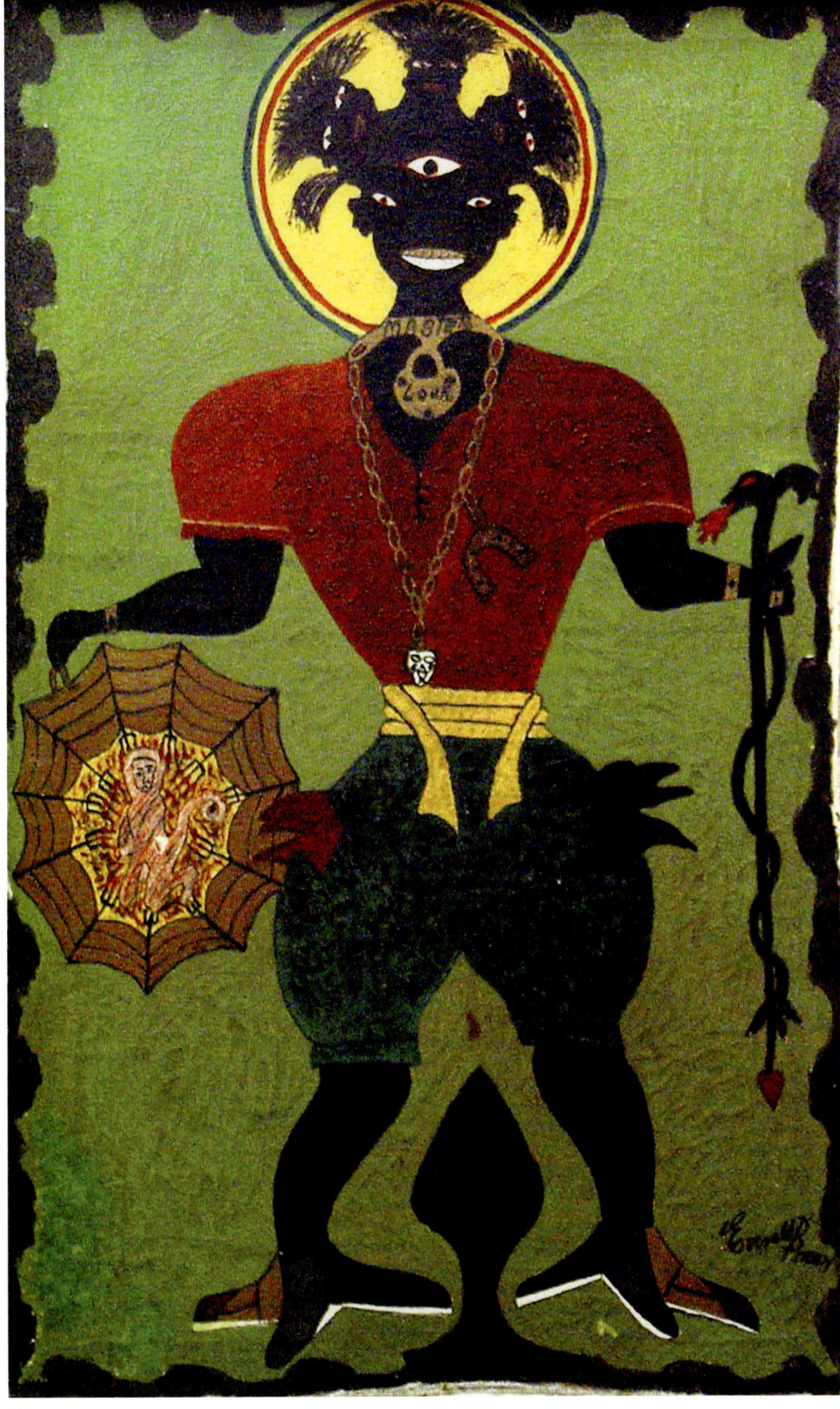

236 Everald Brown. *Victory over Satan*. 1968. Jamaica, Private collection.

237 Karl Parboosingh. *Ras Smoke 1*. 1972. Kingston, National Gallery of Jamaica.

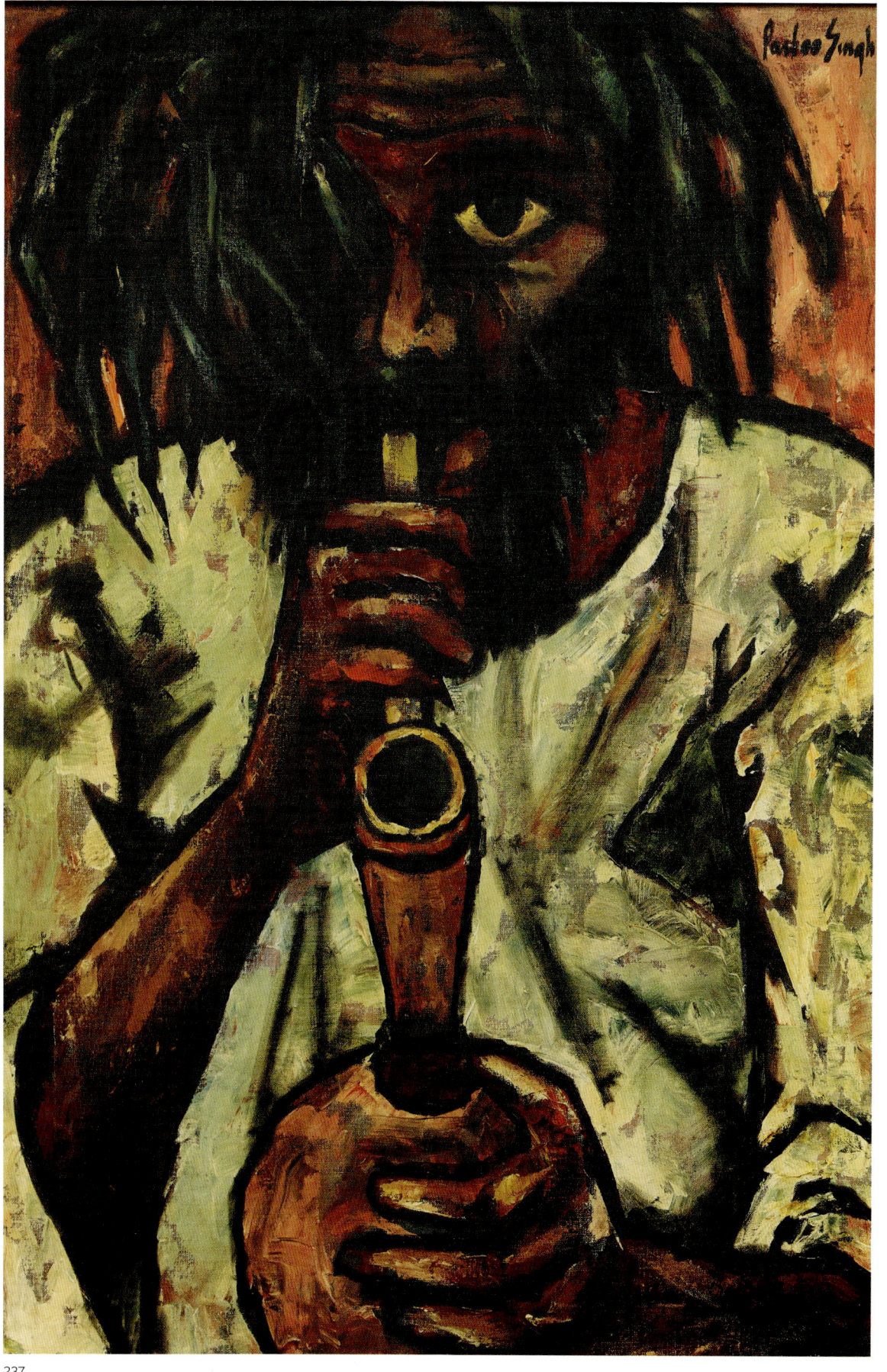
237

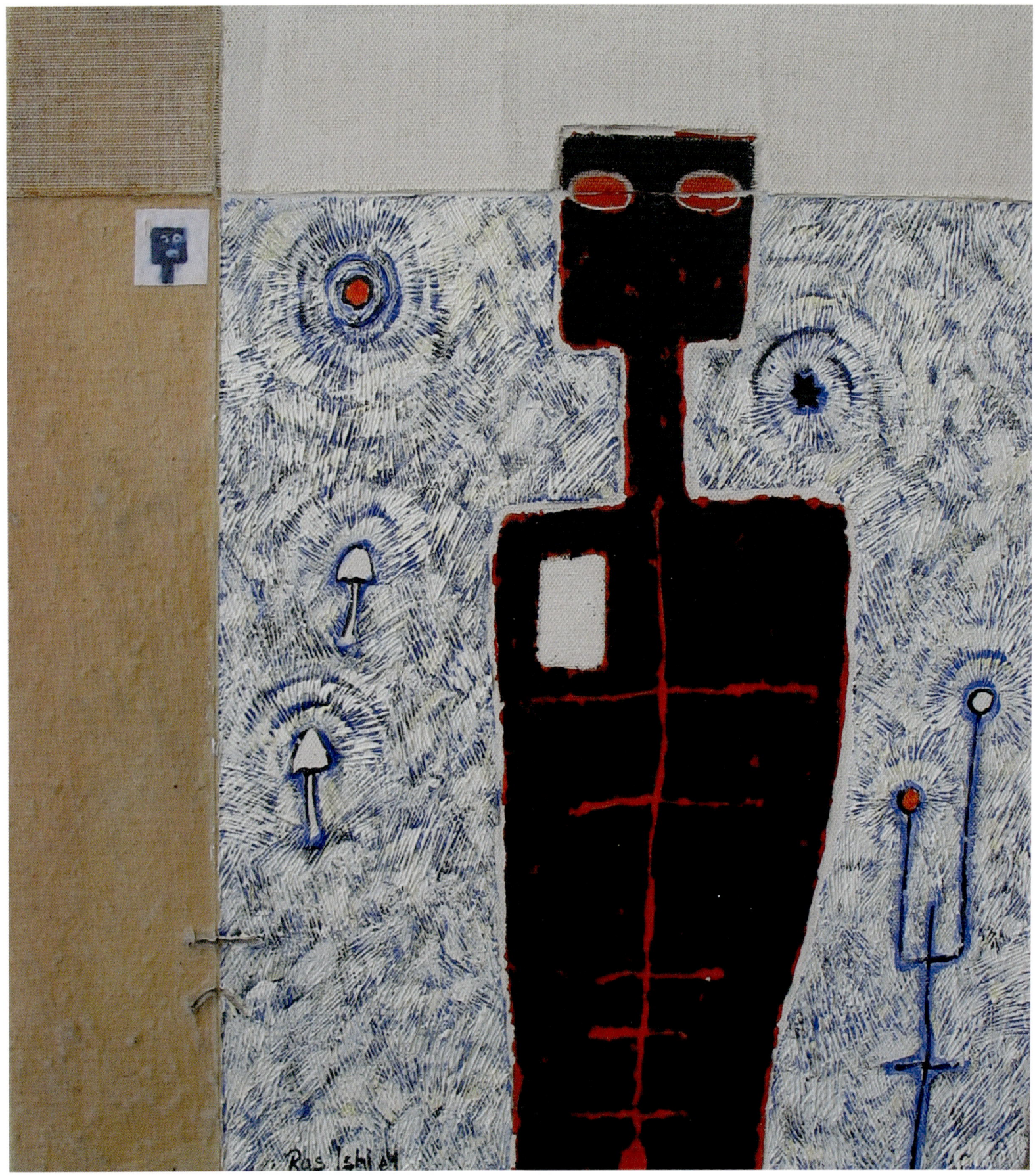

238 Ras Ishi Butcher. *Blazin 1*. 2003-2004. Mixed media. Barbados, Collection of Crawford Billings Associates.

239 Georges Liautaud. *Danbala*. Ca. 1959. Cut and forged metal. Wisconsin, Milwaukee Art Museum.

240 Brent Malone. *Junkanoo Ribbons*. 1984. Oil on canvas. Kingston, National Gallery of Jamaica.

developed out of the crosses he designed to decorate graves in Haiti. His ornate work captured the attention of DeWitt Peters who encouraged him to work at the Centre d'Art and expand his use of materials. Liautaud would go on to create enigmatic *Loas*, figures cut from the flattened metal of oil drums, inscribed with veve markings. He established a style mimicked by others, although not with the same sense of spiritual profundity, a circumstance that has led many to question the role of patronage and its manipulation of folk forms.

Middle-class support for volunteer art classes at the Institute of Jamaica fostered young talents such as Albert Huie, Ralph Campbell, Henry Daley, and Osmond Watson in classes that would become formalized into an art program offered at the Jamaica School of Art. Guyana was the same. E. R. Burrowes established the Working People's Free Art Classes there, encouraging young men such as Stanley Greaves and Donald Locke to develop their skills and create imagery rooted in their own culture. These informal classes would be incubators for talented artists who used the British Council's scholarships to study abroad as an alternative to a more mundane career path in the civil service.

In the 1950s and 1960s, many of the region's artists received formal training in Britain as a result of these study grants: Carlisle Chang (Trinidad); Albert Huie, Ralph Campbell, and Barrington Watson (Jamaica); and Donald Locke and Stanley Greaves (Guyana). Most trained at reputable British art institutions such as Goldsmith's College, Royal College of Art, and St. Martin's School of Art, each developing his own representational styles influenced by post-impressionism, realism, and cubism, respectively. Then, like Brent Malone of The Bahamas, they returned to teach at their local colleges and institutions in the Caribbean. Their art referenced an aesthetic that was historically African and more latently Caribbean in an environment of post-independence optimism.[31]

Barrington Watson's *Mother and Child* (1958) aptly illustrates how his academic training at the Royal Academy in London could be harnessed to serve local Caribbean ends and to develop an iconography better suited to the region's collective psyche. Here, this classical theme is translated into the intimate setting of the bedroom of the artist's own mother. This more humanized and domesticated Madonna glances fondly toward the son she is potty-training. The theme is elevated beyond the mundane by its salon-size scale and Watson's masterly attention; the artist treats the subject of national significance and suggests that the particularities of Caribbean people's daily lives can take priority over the glorified images and ideas imported from elsewhere.[32] A similar sentiment is communicated through Alexandre Bertrand's *Untitled* (undated), in which a young mother and child walk hand in hand along a rural path. The two baguettes in the young mother's other hand and the simple diaper worn by the toddler underscore the value of companionship even in the face of ingrained poverty.

This type of imagery related to cultural nationalism, which remained the main ideological sentiment behind the Caribbean's artistic movements and their products up to and beyond independence. As a result, viewers still warm to such images of themselves, their portraits, genre scenes, and landscapes; such images relate to their daily lives, and this serves to locate them within the Caribbean experience. Mainstream artists such as Barrington Watson, Trinidad's Boscoe Holder, and The Bahamas' Brent Malone enjoy popularity because they held a flattering mirror of a contented society to the growing middle class. Yet this type of genre painting mixed too easily with more kitsch tourist

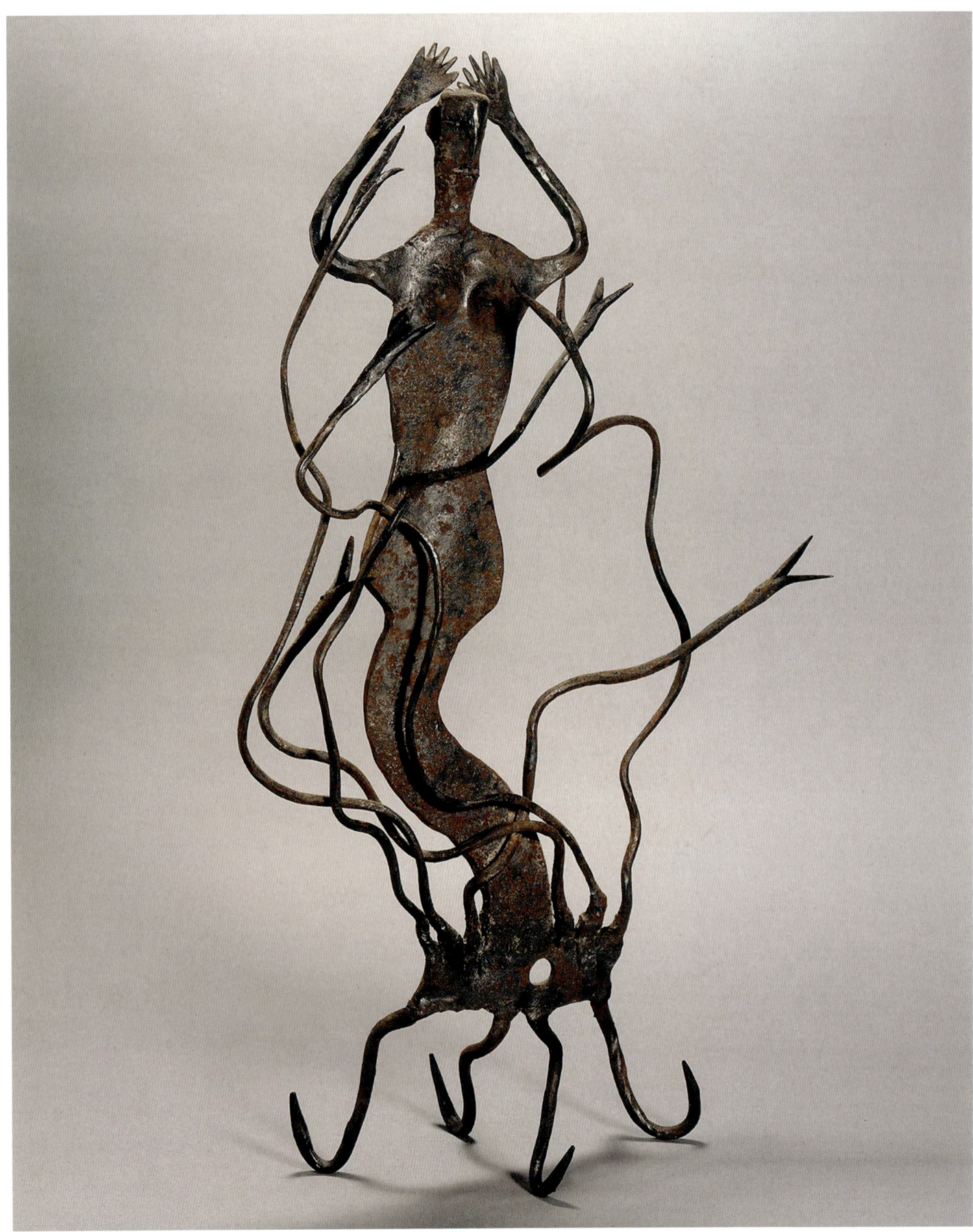

239

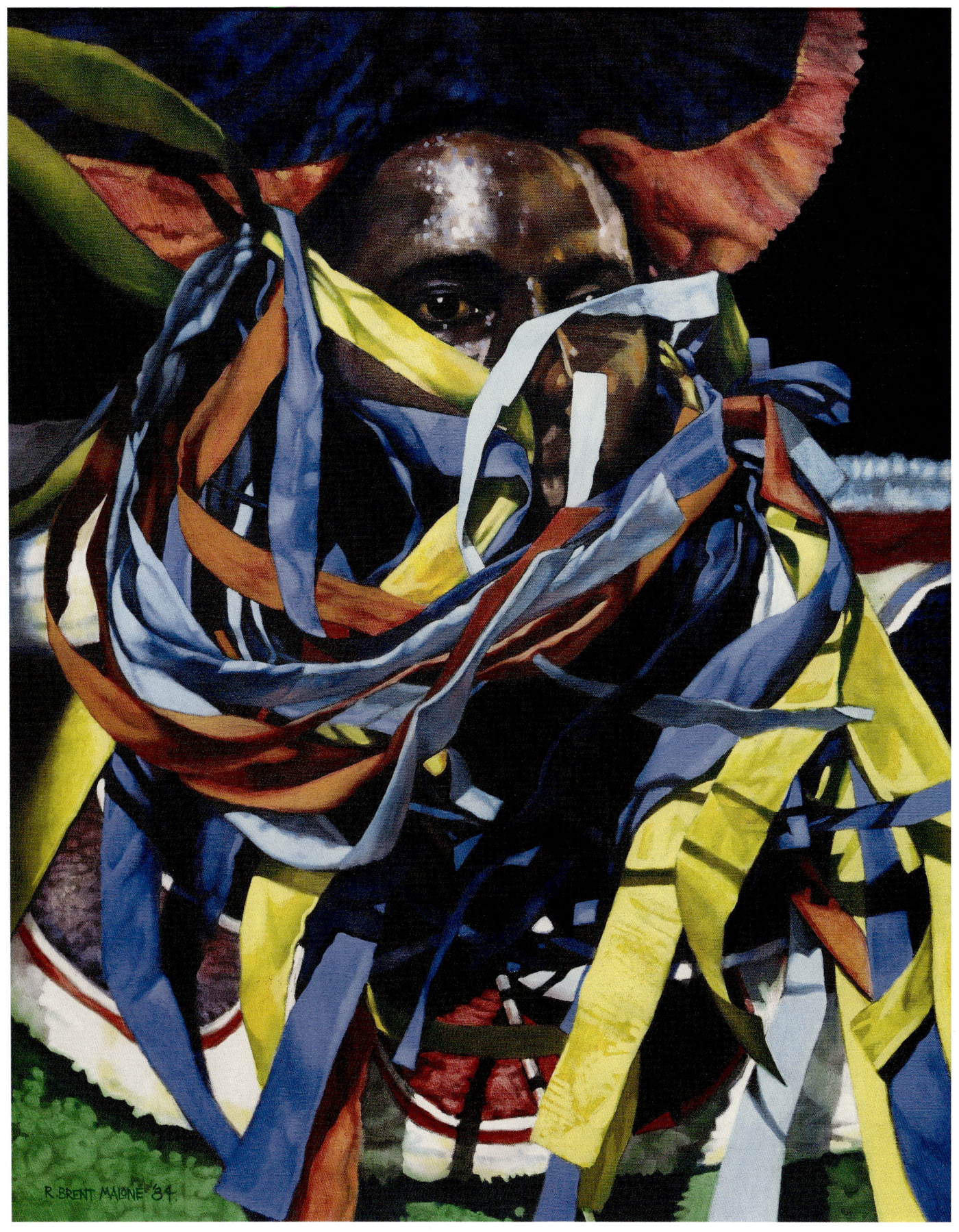

240

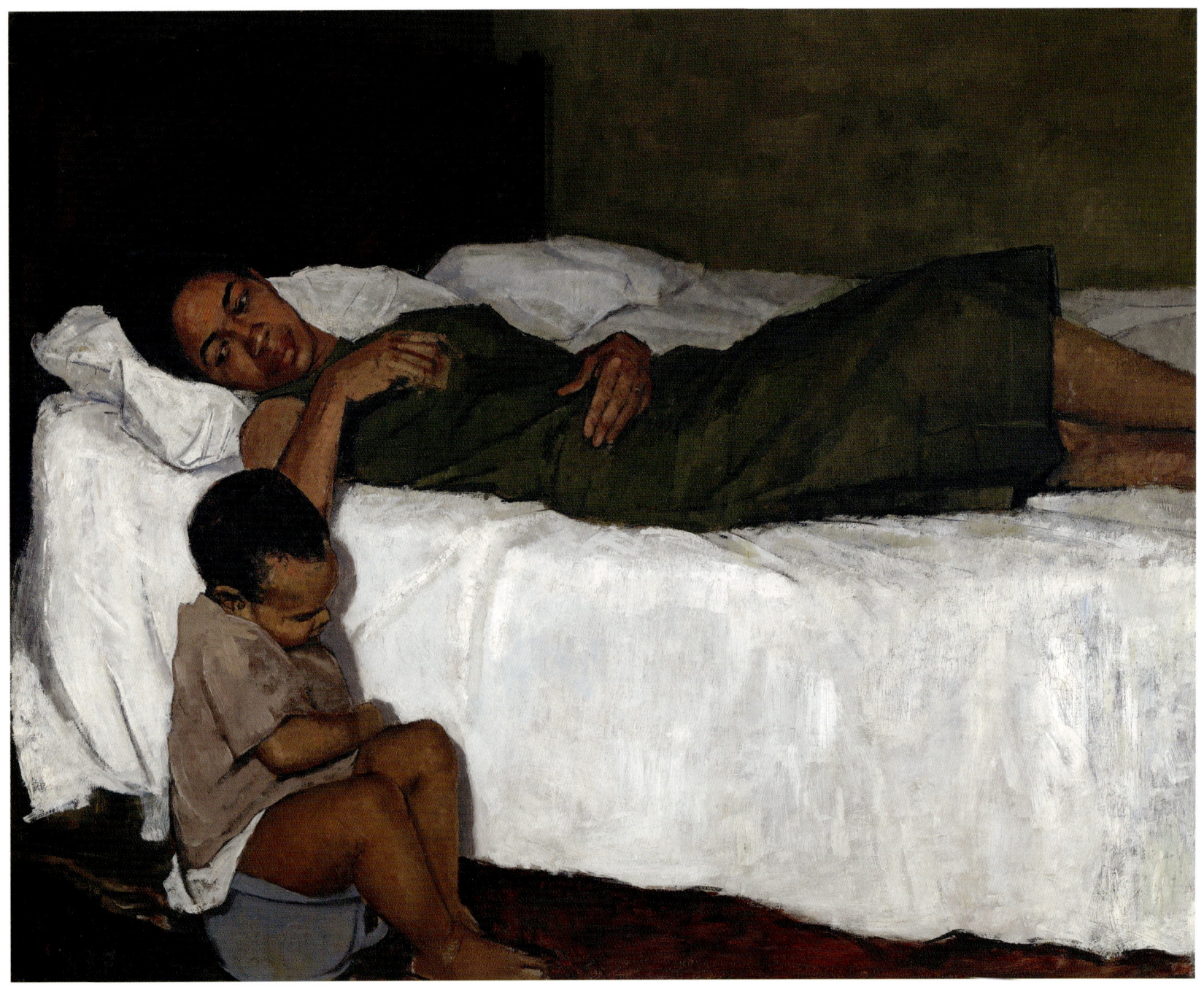

241

241 Barrington Watson. *Mother and Child*. 1958. Oil on canvas. Kingston, National Gallery of Jamaica.

242 Alexandre Bertrand. *Untitled*. Undated. Oil on canvas. Private collection.

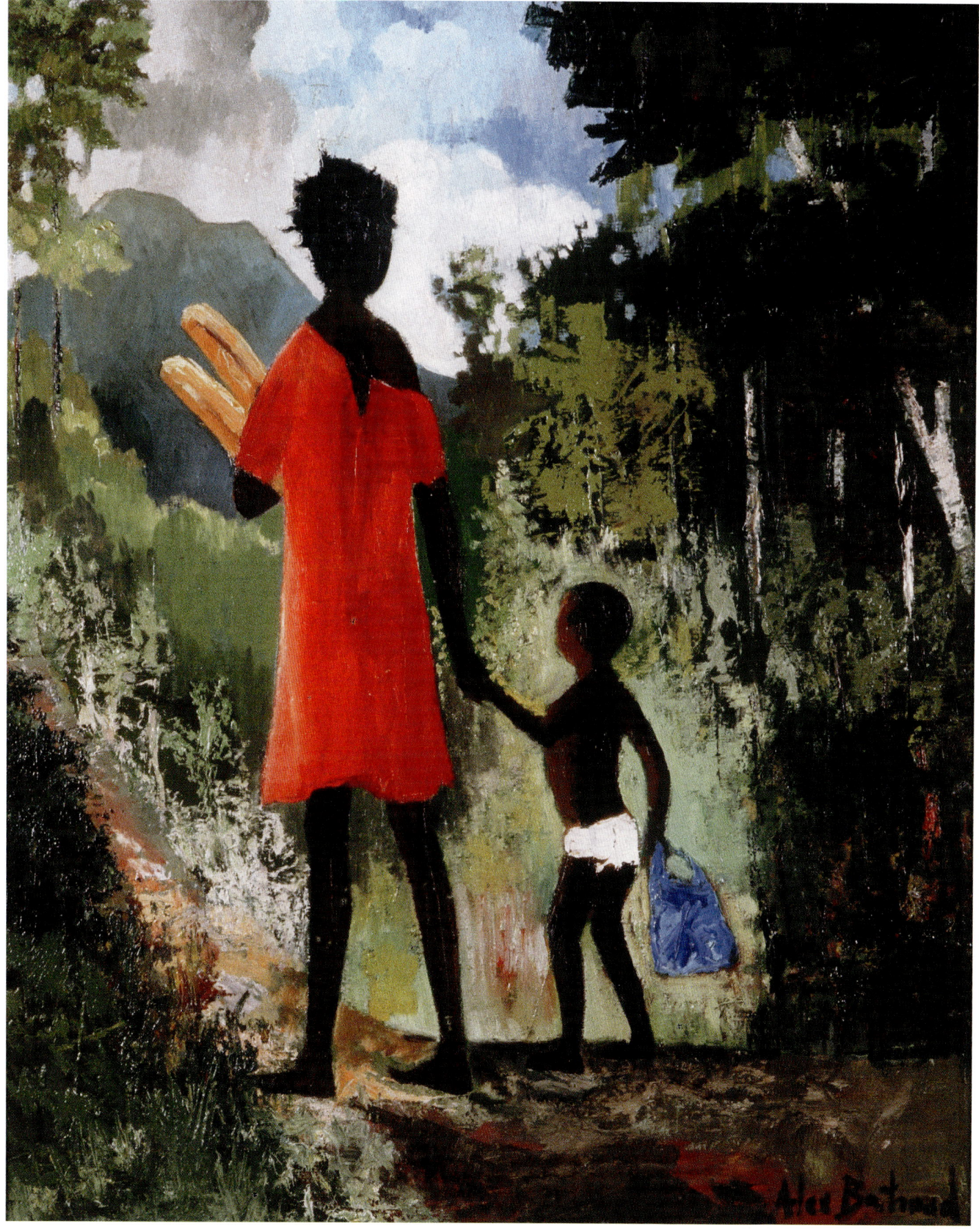

242

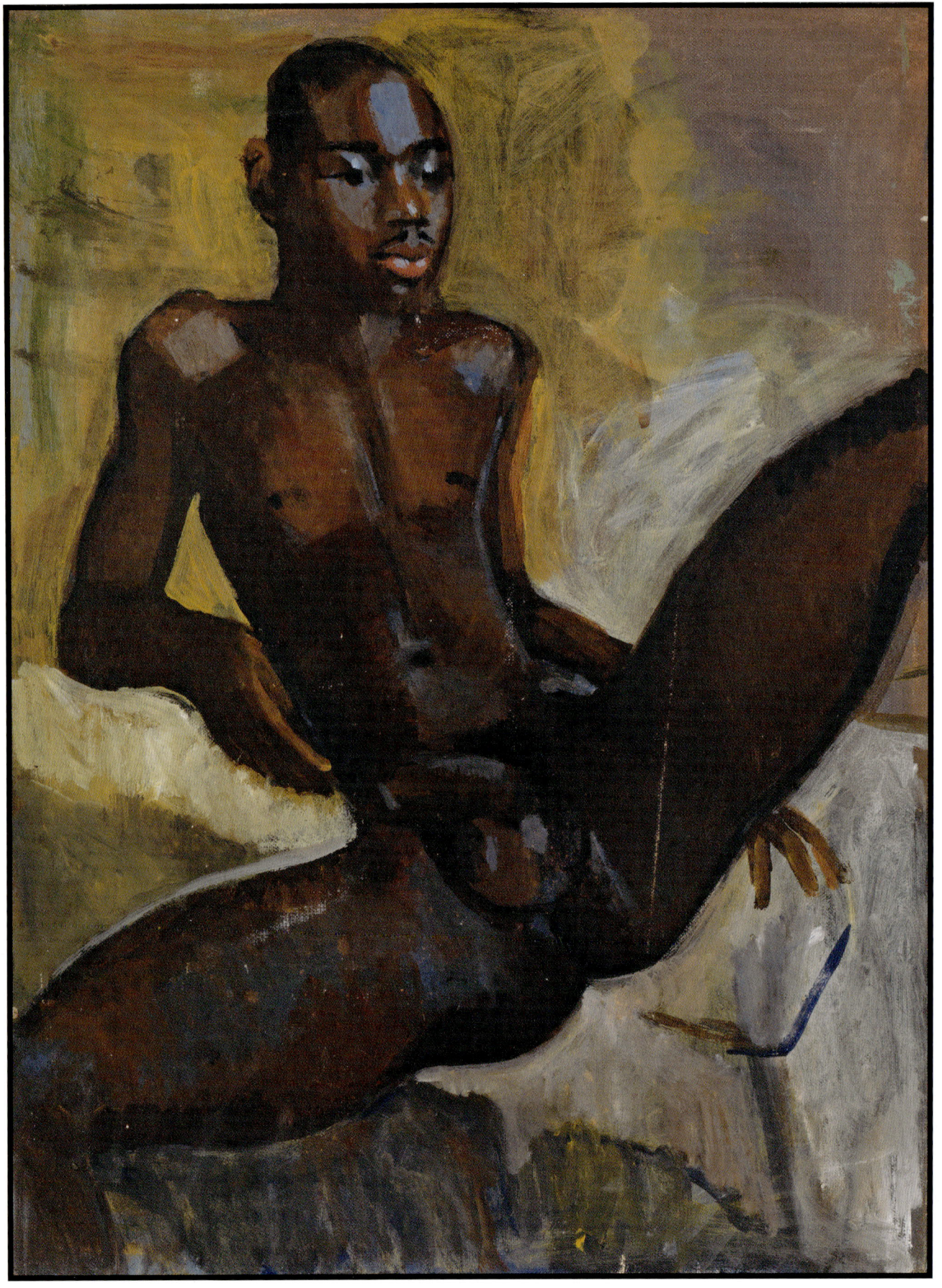

243

243 Boscoe Holder. *Untitled Male Nude*. Undated. Oil on canvas.

art that played out the stereotypes of an island existence. Palm-strewn beaches, bustling markets, and rural areas populated with sturdy Black men and sinewy women were part of the region's iconography shared by both high and low art forms. In this sense, Holder's portraits of dancers go against the grain of commodification. These more intimate paintings referencing his "other" life as a dancer, as in his *Untitled Male Nude* (undated), alludes to another aspect of Caribbean reality related to gender and difference that is often elided. His frank painting of the male form in ways that are beautiful, eroticized, and even feminized broaches a subject rare for that era.

Abstraction, allegory, and satire were pictorial options for artists to maintain their precarious balance as social commentators. In Haiti and Jamaica, where political affiliation might lead to victimization, satire proved a useful tool for communicating their truths without compromise. Among the masters of this kind of disguise are Milton George in *The Art of Being Polite on a Red Background* (1986) or *The P.M. Speaks at 8* (1988); Edouard Duval-Carrié in *J.C. Duvalier as Mad Bride* (1979); Stanley Greaves in *The Annunciation* (1993), seen earlier in this chapter; and Eugene Hyde in *Casualties Series* (1978).

Women artists also used these strategies of allegory effectively as ways of making statements about their role in society and feminism. During the 1980s, windows and doors were their preferred symbols of unrest and longing. But the landmark exhibition *Lips, Sticks and Marks*, mounted by seven women in 1998, introduced the female body as a site of contest.[33] Although this show made significant statements about women's worlds, a more lasting perception was that in exploring their Caribbeanness, these seven women, none of whom was Black, opened up another space for young white Caribbean artists prepared to use art to reevaluate their historical identities and their legacies of slavery. In the new millennium, with the waning of regional exhibitions and dwindling opportunities to exhibit abroad, their contribution to the arts also triggered discussion about what constitutes the national art forms and whether the Black aesthetic, so visible in the work of self-taught artists, represents a truer reflection of regional identity than the Westernized or "whitewashed" forms of art school–trained artists.[34]

Debates have been most strident around public monuments, especially those related to slavery and emancipation, where the majority viewers of African descent have claimed a greater stake in how their lives and freedoms are envisioned. Regularly, school-trained artists have designed these monuments with a vision that differs conceptually and sometimes even materially from how the Black majority perceives itself. The statue of the abolitionist Victor Schoelcher in Martinique (1904) (see vol. IV, pt.1, fig. 173), the monument associated with the slave revolt leader Bussa in Barbados (1985) (see fig. 207), and the memorial of the Coramantee slave Prince Klaus in St. John, Antigua (1983), have all proved controversial. The most recent case has been Laura Facey's *Redemption Song* (2003), a monument erected in Kingston's Emancipation Park to mark the bicentenary of that event in Jamaica (see fig. 212).

Redemption Song is a larger-than-life depiction of a naked man and woman facing each other with heads turned heavenward. Cast in bronze with a darkened skin tone, the artist has honed their bodies to ensure that they communicate their racialized features. But many argue that the artist's depiction of female and male with pendulous breasts and penis, respectively, is

244 Aubrey Williams. *Revolt*. 1960. Oil on canvas. Georgetown, Guyana, The National Gallery of Art, Castellani House.

offensive. Some contend that their posed inertness, with hanging, listless arms, is too passive for a work of this nature. Others argue that these figures should have been clothed and given active gestures that represent the victory of emancipation and recognized that enslaved women and men viewed the representation of their nakedness as a memory of their disinheritance and impoverishment. Most question whether a white artist could have the moral or racial sensitivity to depict such an important moment in Black history with conviction. They argue publicly that the decision to award the commission to a white Jamaican artist is indicative of a small white and brown social elite's control and legislation of culture and raises the question, "Who has the authority to memorialize this event?"[35]

Similar issues arise in carnival, a public sphere that is historically a marketplace for the fluid and complex exchange of identities. After more than two hundred years, carnival remains a popular annual festival, especially in Cuba, Trinidad, and Haiti, where its celebrations remain highly charged performances that use parody, satire, and caricature to critique contemporary society. The cultural historian Gerard Aching in *Masking and Power* explains their inherent ambiguity since "amidst the annual revelry in which different classes and sectors of Caribbean societies simultaneously took to the streets, the festivities also became events through which colonial authorities exercised, measured, and reaffirmed their power employing exhibited techniques of crowd control."[36]

This controlled "uncontrolled" space seems all the more relevant today where islands have adopted carnival for the purposes of tourism and where sponsorship facilitates visibility. But in an era in which glitz and skimpy costume parades dictate media visibility, the ultimate subversion is *J'ouvert,* in which people dressed as devil bands or *Jab-Jab* rope throwers coated in black soot and molasses, often padlocked to one another, run amok through the streets beating tin pans and other crude percussion. The increasing popularity of J'ouvert, especially with the young, suggests the appeal of these outsider characters who maraud on the edge of society's moral boundaries.

The choice to blacken one's skin still further, as Aching tells us, "facilitates a strategic 're-appropriation' of blackness beyond which no further mimicry is feasible."[37] But even more, the act of affirming one's Blackness also calls out whiteness, bringing it into plain sight. Leah Gordon, a British-born photographer living in Haiti, has experienced this kind of self-recognition. It is the route she has had to take to understand her cultural inheritance and her privileges as the daughter of a white working-class family from Manchester, also implicated in the Atlantic slave trade. Her powerful images of Jab-Jab youths in Haiti pulsate with juvenile malevolence even as they speak to the reclamation of old identities and the country's own demonization.

The region's artists as cultural agents, middle class or otherwise, have played an important role in nation building. The most effective are those able to underpin their day-to-day realities with a sense of cultural memory. As social inheritors of slavery, and with only fragile links to the past, these artists use their imagination as a creative resource. Their formations of a new Caribbean identity are those that exist in an abstract mental realm harnessed through memory and intuition, such as Karl Broodhagen's *Emancipation Statue* ("Bussa") (1985) in Barbados and Aubrey Williams's *Revolt* (1960) in Guyana, the latter eventually employing the language of abstraction and expressionism to explore

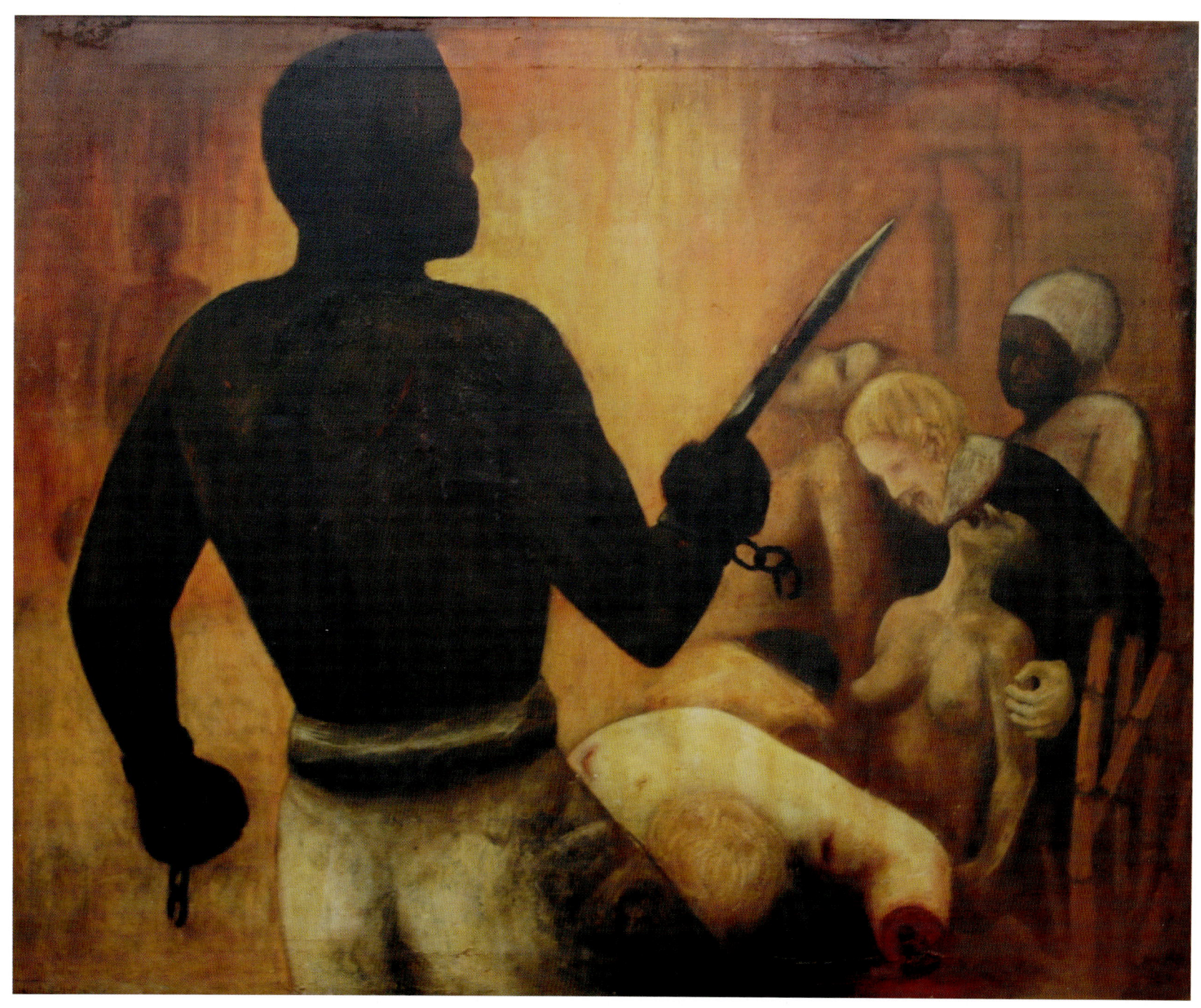

244

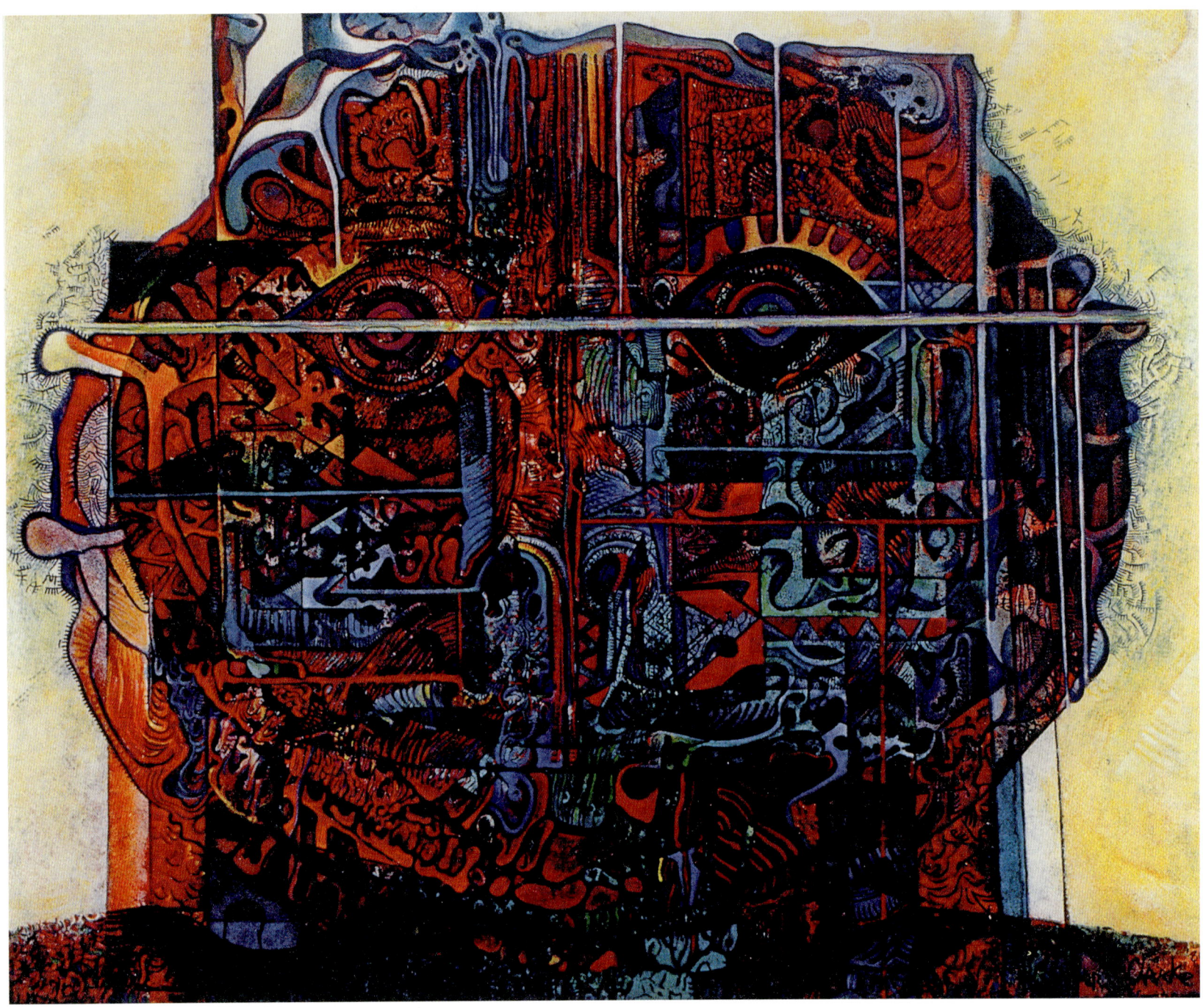

245

245 LeRoy Clarke. *In the Maze, There Is a Single Line to My Soul*. 1986. Port of Spain, Trinidad, Estate of the artist.

these dark recesses. With a past shrouded by dislocation, absence, and forgetting, Caribbean identity would need to be constructed outside of history.

Leon Wainwright describes Williams's *Revolt* as an anachronism.[38] This representation of a slave revolt in the Dutch colony of Berbice, now a county of Guyana, harks back to 1763 and is styled in a manner that defies Williams's contemporary explorations with abstraction. The image shows a robust figure (not unlike the artist himself) standing menacingly over the maimed body of a naked white woman and a cowering white man. Williams's figure brandishes a cutlass and wears broken chains, popular symbolism of the day that Wainwright sees as standing "not so much for the deliverance of emancipation, but the winning of freedom."[39] The painting's graphic narrative even in pigment tells a story so powerful from the artist's imagination that it was rejected by the organization to which it was initially given, Guyana's Royal Agriculture and Commercial Society. Yet its permanent place in the National Collection at the National Gallery of Art, Castellani House, in Georgetown, demonstrates how the timeless principles behind its painting have outlived a more temporal understanding of history's inherent distortions and ideologies.

The temporal elision is even more profound when we recognize that Williams painted this event in Britain in 1960, a time when he and many other Black immigrants were facing renewed prejudice for their presence there. By inserting himself into this rebellious scene, he makes a bold statement about his own feelings of resentment in the face of oppression. As Wainwright explains elsewhere: "Painting had a dynamic potential for Williams as a vehicle for his wide exploration of interior and exterior life. He used his art practice to engage and change modern art's concerns with philosophy and aesthetics. He was attracted to the idea that modernism could be a way of criticizing centers of power, and could itself undermine the idea that there should be a single best way of seeing and showing the world."[40]

The 1960s was a volatile period that deeply affected Caribbean artists at home and abroad. Among the events that provided the backdrop to the turbulent decade were the Bay of Pigs attempted invasion of Cuba; civil rights marches and deaths; student riots in the United States, France, and Vietnam; decolonization; and the spread of the Black Power movement. The Caribbean was not immune to any of these events.

In Martinique, the painter Joseph René-Corail, nicknamed Khokho, was at the center of the movement for French decolonization. He was considered radical for his communist views, his conscientious objection to completing the French National Military Service, and his activism in supporting independence from France. After becoming involved in the Organization of Anti-Colonial Martinican Youth (OJAM), he was deemed a political prisoner. Arrested in Martinique, he was imprisoned in Paris until his acquittal in December 1963. Upon his return, he took up a professorship at the School of Applied Arts and devoted the rest of his life to the promotion of Martinique's culture, creating many of the island's public monuments from clays, metals, cloths, and woods such as bamboo.

René-Corail continued his activism in the Martinique Independence Movement (MIM), setting himself at odds with the status quo and Martinique's historical relationship as a department of France. Khokho created his mother-and-child painting (*Untitled*, 1963), shown earlier in this chapter, while imprisoned in Fresnes. He is viewed as a cultural icon in Martinique and

246 Omari Ra. *Bois Caiman's Foreign Policy: Retro Reconstruction Globe Shrugged*. 2006. Mixed media on cloth. Kingston, Jamaica, Collection of the artist.

Guadeloupe, where some still have ambivalent feelings about political autonomy and self-determination.

LeRoy Clarke's status in Trinidad is similar. He returned to Trinidad after studying and working in New York in the 1970s. His experiences in the United States when the civil rights and Black Power movements were on the rise strengthened the message of race consciousness in his work even as he acknowledged his sense of Caribbeanness. His complex portrait *In the Maze, There Is a Single Line to My Soul* (1986) harnesses both African and Native American imagery while still being informed by an Afro-Cobra aesthetic.[41] It also references Sun Ra's musical abstraction of the late 1960s when the inner mind, like outer space, was envisaged as a place of refuge from white iniquities and planet Earth, and the Black person was viewed in futuristic terms.

This head's multifaceted, compartmentalized forms are at once ancient and modern. Clarke allows the viewer access to the inner workings of the Black mind, its thinking and feeling centers, and depicts them as an interaction of the fixed and the fluid. Its robotic, almost digitized, compartments are intersected with juicy molten globs of liquid, lava, and membrane that pulsate and mutate through the mind. Yet in the midst of these myriad thoughts is a single line that dissects the form right through its line of vision. The title's reference to the soul, so much a part of that era's pop vernacular, distinguishes this mind-blown, spaced-out self-portrait as nevertheless whole and spiritually rooted. Clarke is a self-professed Obeah man, believing that his nation's embrace of its culture and its Blackness is the way to reclaim the past and liberate its people.

This act of re-creation places Caribbean artists in a valued position as seers and healers who are allowed to dream in the past, present, and future. In the troubled 1970s and 1980s after independence, against a background of political turbulence and economic hardship, another generation of artists such as Omari Ra of Jamaica and Ras Akyem I Ramsay and Ras Ishi Butcher of Barbados (*Ital Princess,* 1986) gave visual form to their pan-African identities as they hopscotched through history to recover a lost heritage. Harnessing imagery inspired by rituals, mutinies, and enslaved heroes, they affirmed a Black spiritual tradition that harshly criticized the white West even as they posited new models for survival.

Omari Ra places his own larger-than-life portraits at the center of historical dramas. In self-portraits with characteristically convoluted titles such as *Bois Caiman's Foreign Policy: Retro Reconstruction Globe Shrugged* (2006), he paints himself into history, replacing the faces of slave leaders, such as Tacky or Jack Mansong, with his own distinctly African facial features. These gargantuan heads completely fill his oversize surfaces. With little else to distract the eye, the viewer is forced to confront his Blackness painted in monochrome tones of red or green with dramatic chiaroscuro lighting. In his imagery devoted to the Bois Caiman rebellion, two massive portraits are placed side by side. Despite their physical resemblance, they do not relate to each other. They appear like smudged photographs of Black military heroes. Apart from their enhanced racialized features, their only distinction is their tightly fastened military garb that bears veve markings rather than the gold-braided emblems favored by Garvey. Omari Ra's portraits are created knowingly. Like visual dubplates, they riff on the imagery and iconography of Black activists and artists gone before. They bring history up to date, affirming a Black spiritual heritage that harshly critiques the white West.

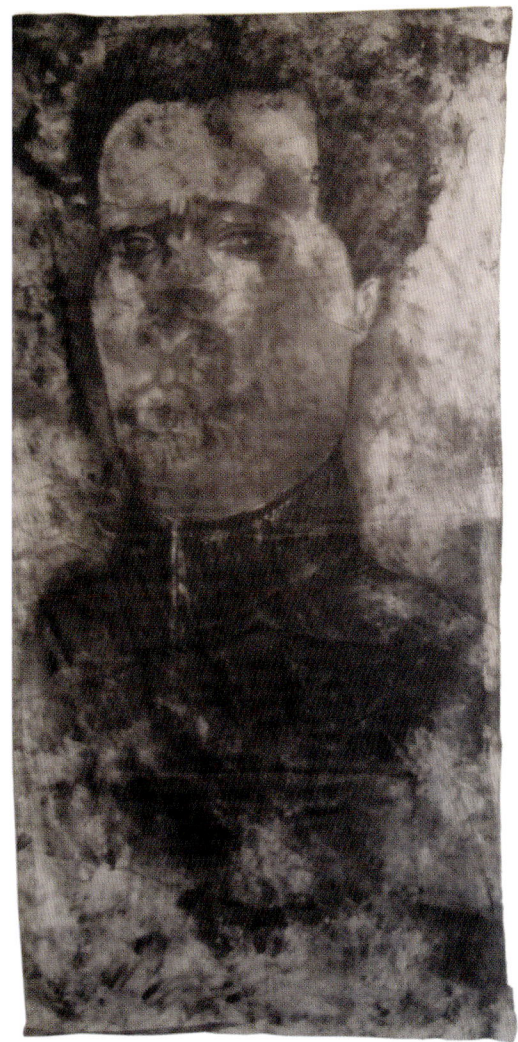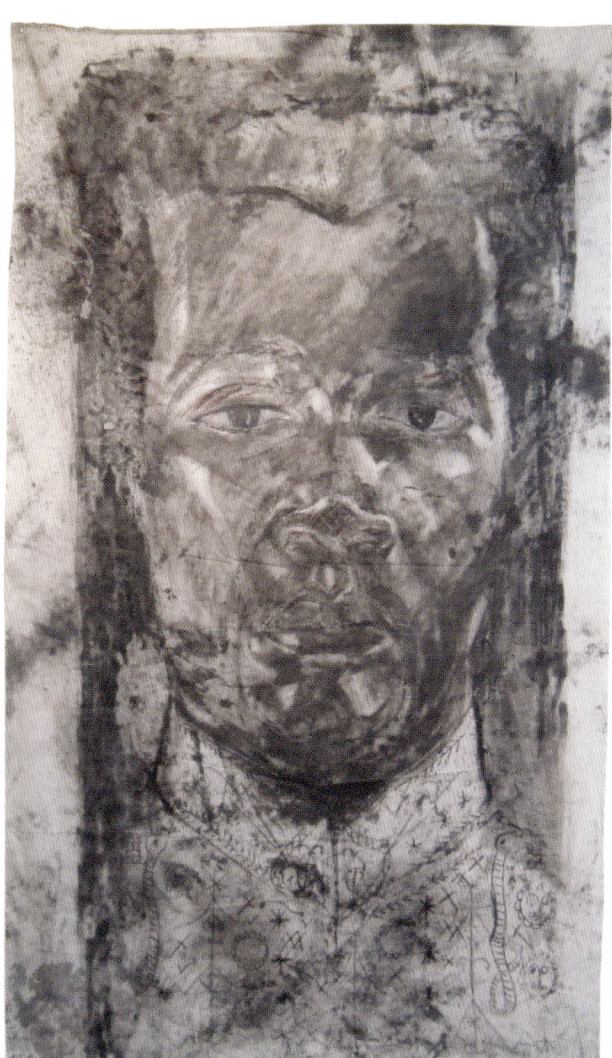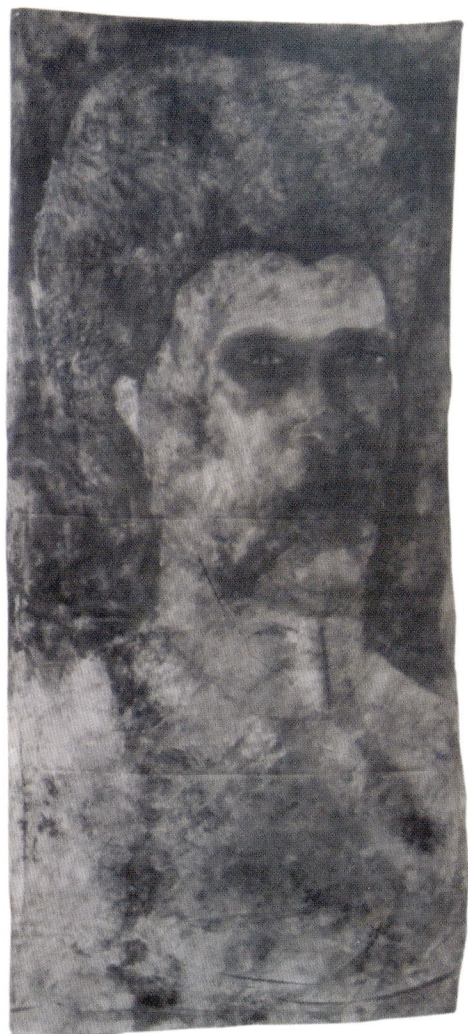

246

247 Christopher Cozier. *The Castaway*. From the series *Tropical Night*. Late 2005-ongoing. Drawings. Ink, rubber stamps, and graphite.

248 Albert Chong. *Seated Presence*. From the *Throne Series*. 1990. Silver gelatin print. Colorado, Collection of the artist.

249 Joscelyn Gardner. *Veronica frutescens (Mazerine)*. From the series *Creole Portraits*. 2009. Hand-painted stone lithograph on frosted mylar.

Not all these artists employ such strident strategies. Some approach the problem of the Black person's existence in the region from the perspective of *not* calling attention to the pain of his extended exile from Africa. Barbadian artists Ras Akyem I Ramsay's *Untitled No. 2* (undated) and Ras Ishi Butcher's *Blazin 1* (2003–2004), both of whom were mentored by LeRoy Clarke, posit new models for survival that take a more persuasive but also more problematic approach to the Black body. In their understanding of Caribbeanness they have avoided the Black separatist message of Ra to portray instead the Caribbean man in his present-day existence. Their images are stripped-down, winnowed forms that hint at Jean-Michel Basquiat in their scarred vulnerability, but show an even greater influence of the digital age that postdates him. Ras Akyem's images are the most disturbing. His bloated, disfigured, amputated, nerve-wracked forms trouble any idyllic reading of place and identity.

It is against this backdrop of independent vision and anticolonialism that we can begin to view the Caribbean art of the postmodern era. The Caribbean diaspora's restless migratory patterns since slavery have left island communities in constant motion, a people of the sea, forever looping back to points of entanglement rather than to our origins.

That everyone in the Caribbean descends from people who came from somewhere else has set in motion a repeating pattern as they have scattered around the globe to urban communities in London, New York, Toronto, and Miami as migrant workers in search of opportunities and a better life, making the island nations what Stuart Hall calls "twice diasporized." Those who return—and most do—are what the cultural theorist Annie Paul has in their defense labeled "alterNATIVES," or natives who, like Trinidadian artists Christopher Cozier or Steve Ouditt, have been altered by their contact with the wider world or by their education abroad, but who still continue to contribute a great deal to their home countries by virtue of their double vision.[42] Any contemporary cultural history of the region must take account of these trends and tensions, which are at once both global and local and which generate imagery such as Cozier's *The Castaway* (2006) that speaks to these wider issues.

In the 1990s, a greater awareness of postmodern trends and a connection with Jamaica's wider diaspora communities in Britain, Canada, and the United States saw many artists reappraising their personal cultural histories and revisiting the sites of their ancestral origins, be they indigenous Indian cultures, Asian, African, or European, or, in the case of Cozier, their sense of nomadic "unbelonging," which led to his depiction of the Black person as an amphibian survivor with a mast on his back that keeps him afloat.[43] These artists are trying to understand and communicate the experience of being Caribbean, and explore their own sense of place within the African diaspora.

Albert Chong's *Seated Presence* is perhaps the most personal work from his *Throne Series* (1990). Here the artist captures his own blurred, naked image, seated but open to the camera's scrutiny. Superimposed over his body are artifacts, coals, skulls, and antelope horns that speak to preoccupations with Santería and the artist's sense of inner power and divinity. The work references his multicultural Asian-African-Caribbean roots as well as his peculiarly Catholic accommodation of symbolic spiritual forms. Through his photographs and assemblages, Chong seamlessly blends the artistic and the spiritual while quietly critiquing traditional religious iconography. From a close examination of his

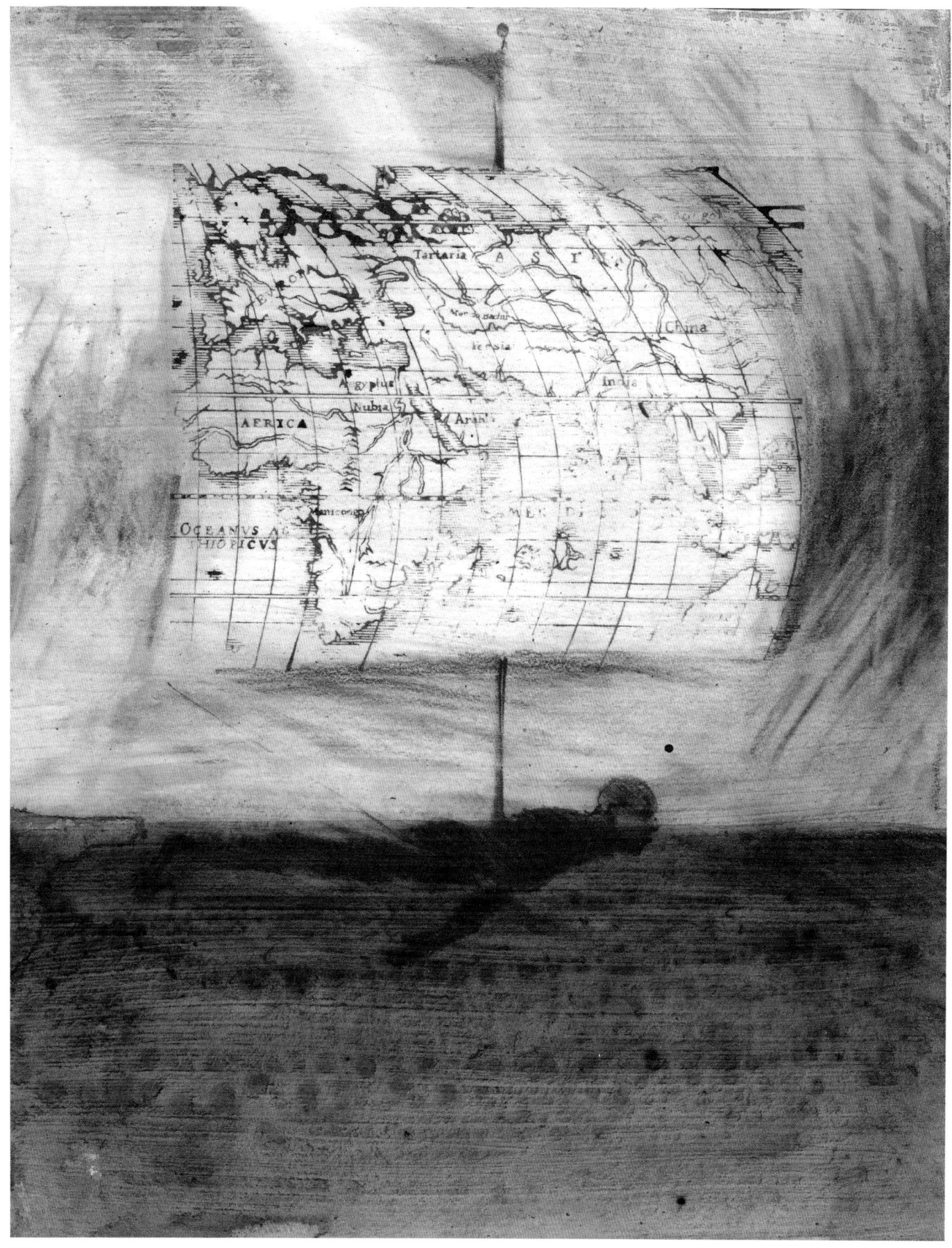

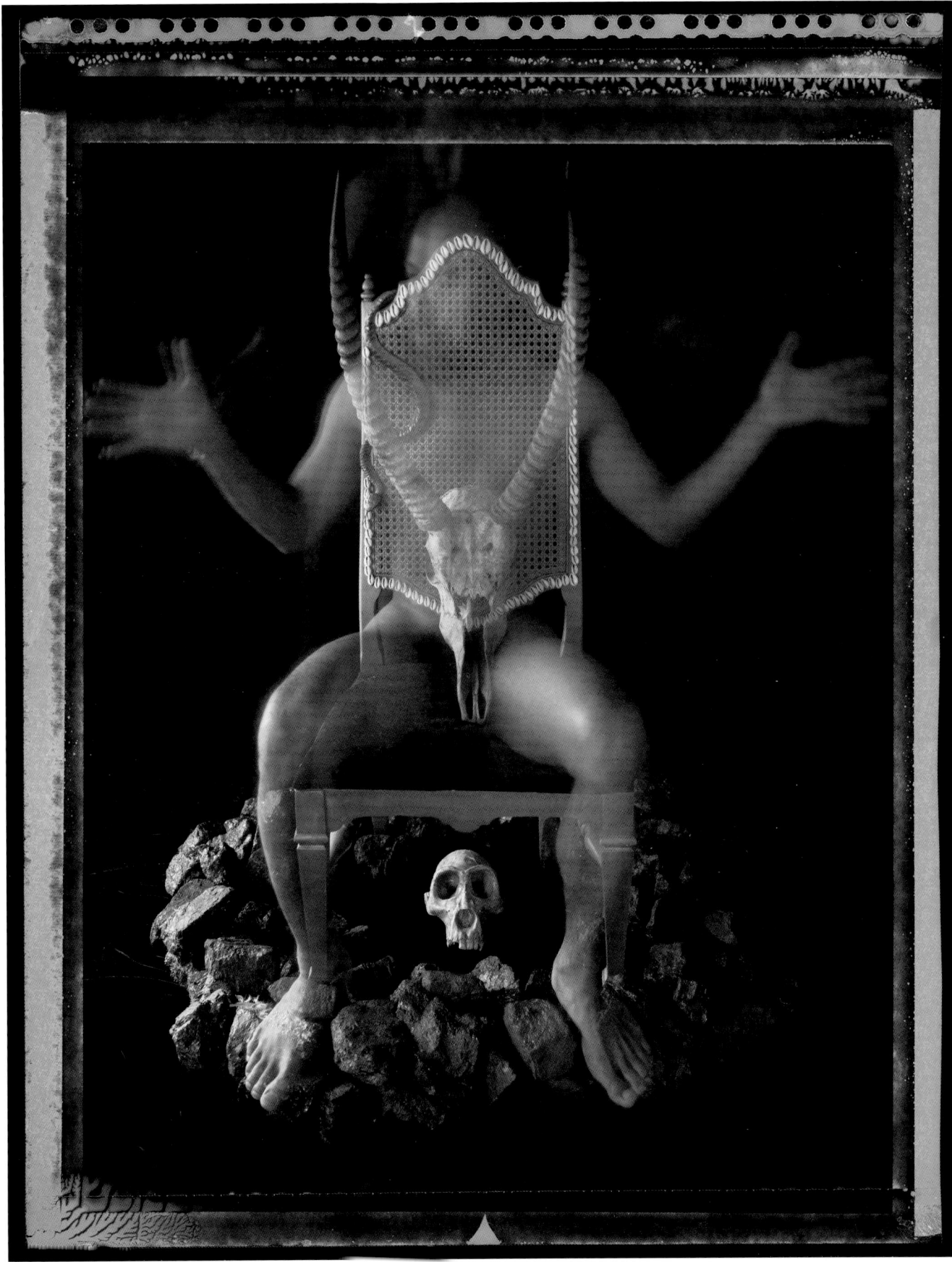

248

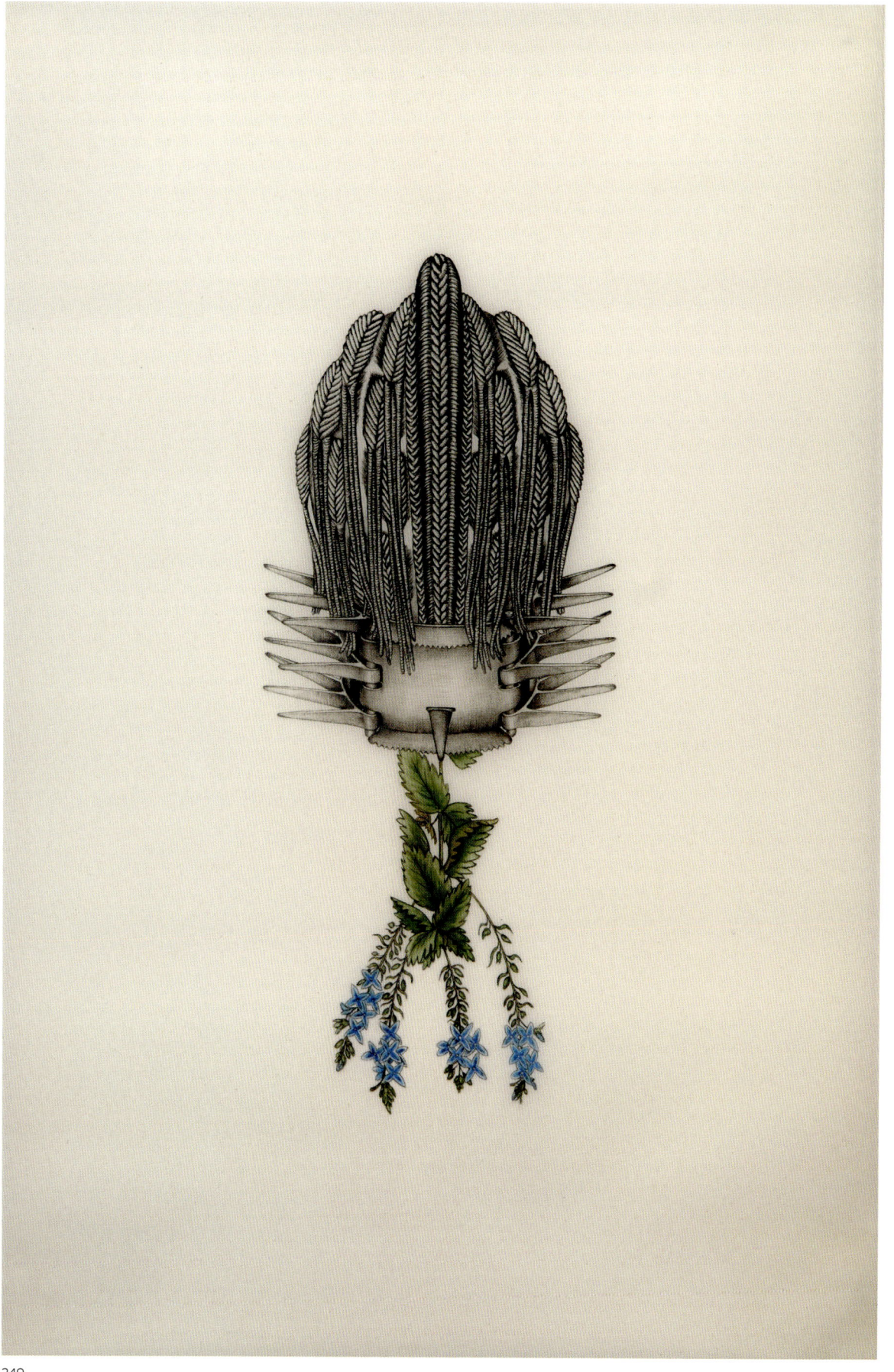

249

250 Roberta Stoddart. *Earl*. From the series *In the Flesh*. 2006. Port of Spain, Trinidad, Private collection.

ideas and processes we learn not just about this artist as a keeper of memories but also about multiple Caribbean identities. The cultural work Chong carries out through the production of these images is important to the African diaspora and ancestors of slavery, since these identities exist in an abstract mental realm that is necessarily constructed in the present and subject to its vagaries.

Globalization and its attendant postmodern sentiments have encouraged the search for a new language that better suits the region's diversity and cultural complexity. This "new worldism" is evidenced in an interest in the region's indigenous cultures and a more clearly defined sentiment for Africa. This process of creolization, where both Black and white people recognize their commonality and cultural indebtedness, has also triggered an exploration of the past from both sides of the racial and class divide. There have been many attempts to confront and redress the more shameful aspects of the Caribbean's history. As a descendant of the planter class, Joscelyn Gardener has embarked on a project that puts a face to this process. Her series of prints titled *Creole Portraits* references the region's "disordered past" with depictions of the braided heads of enslaved women from Barbados's Egypt Estate intertwined with tools of torture such as iron collars, bridle, and shackles. In her later series, *Bleeding and Breeding*, the same heads are woven with the imagery of botanical plants that these women used to self-abort after being impregnated by their enslavers.

Prepared to own her guilt, Gardner chooses subjects that allow her to explore plantation life and its atrocities. Explaining in her website's artist statement that she uses "a postcolonial feminist methodology to probe colonial material culture... to explore my (white) Creole identity," she "aim[s] to articulate the intertwined historical relationship shared by black and white women in the Caribbean by recognizing that under patriarchy and colonialism the lives of all Caribbean women have been shaped by 'mastership.'" Her "project also aims to address the repression and dissociation that operate in relation to the topic of slavery and white culpability in the wider postcolonial world."[44]

Roberta Stoddart's imagery is less ambivalent but equally challenging. In her hyperrealist style, she employs psychological tension in her work that echoes issues of race, gender, and sexuality. In her *In the Flesh* series, she explores the human psyche and its desire for place by depicting homeless people and vagrants in painstaking detail. In *Earl*, her painting of a young albino man suffering from a skin disease that destroys Black pigment, she questions notions of Blackness and the prejudices of a Black society that has itself experienced discrimination. Earl is culturally Black but physically white, or even colorless, and Stoddart exploits his lack of facial/racial identity by painting his skin, "warts and all," with a cruel, calculating eye.

Younger artists such as Ebony G. Patterson and Peter Rickards are engaging with similar issues related to the social dislocation that came with Jamaican independence. These artists recognize that old models of social organization within the church, state, and society are shifting and being replaced by post-nationalist forms with different spatial and spiritual codes of belonging.[45]

Patterson has introduced these secular trends in her work by exploring gender ambivalence in Jamaica. This subject, which has absorbed her energies for the past decade, requires an understanding of slavery, colonial history, local attitudes toward authority and violence as well as spirituality and worship. But Patterson's images are far from analytical or dreary. Rather, they

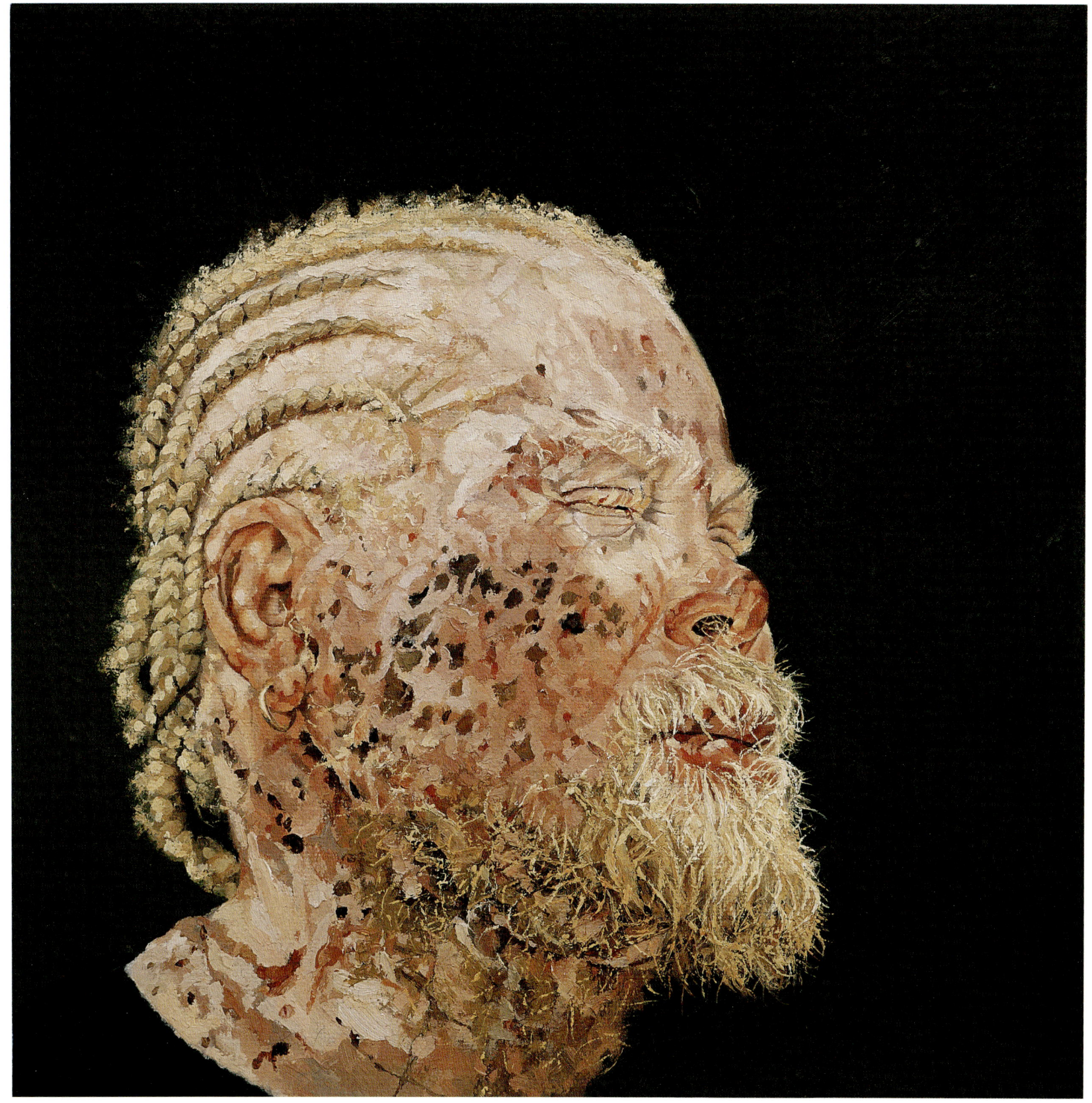

250

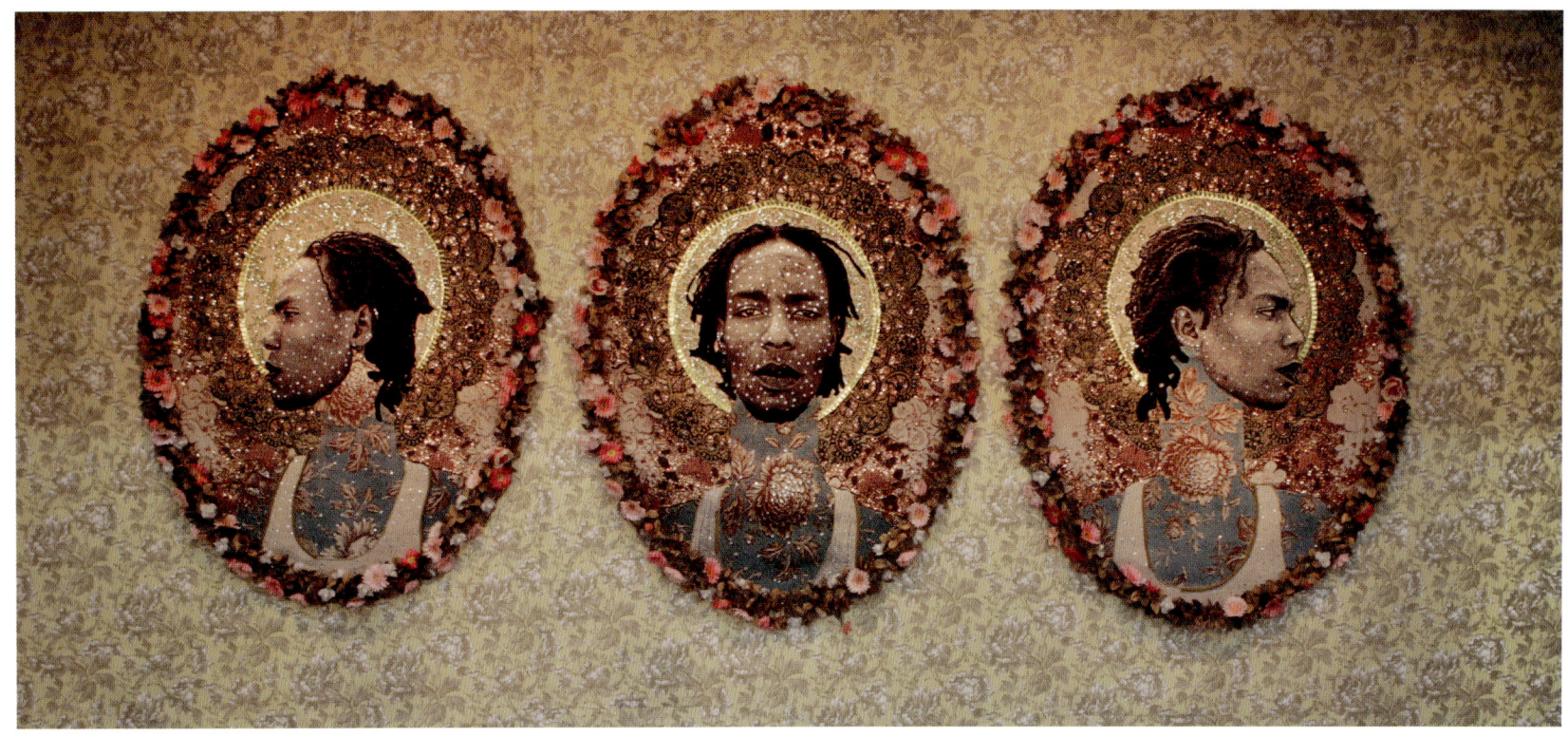
251

251 Ebony G. Patterson. *Di Real Big Man*. 2010. Mixed media. Hand-embellished photo tapestry with garlands on wallpaper. Variable dimensions. Kingston, National Gallery of Jamaica.

are adrenaline-pumped, color-saturated, richly textured, and highly patterned works that shout for her viewers' attention. Over the years her work has shed any cultural insecurity arising from her formal art school training, and in her dance hall subject matter, she has liberated her palette to make her work gaudier, more lavish, and more "ghetto fabulous." Through these paintings, Patterson questions why young Black men, especially those related to Jamaica's dance hall culture, are regularly viewed in terms of aggression. To counter these perceptions, she rebalances their male macho personas with feminine touches and homoerotica.

Patterson's portraits of Jamaican ghetto leaders known as "dons" and their "disciplez," who practice skin bleaching, are sanctified in her portraits, their stark faces embellished with rouged lips, halos, and other marks of beatification. Bleached of color, their complexions speak to a complete shift in the racial register and a debunking of nationalist narratives that prioritize art and spirituality over commerce and the marketplace. Although surrounded by glitz and glamour, these portraits no longer reflect the angst of race or the moralizing consciousness of Revivalism or Rastafari. They are a new breed of rude boys worshipping consumerism whose faces stare back at their African heritage—blankly.

These ideas and events are still unfolding, but they suggest that a younger generation of artists must consider and compete with the more glaring aspects of the Caribbean's popular culture, especially dance hall, ghetto fabulous fashions, street art, and the aesthetics of bling funerals, for a stake in the nation's visual memory. In this new hyped environment, art has morphed into other forms of media such as Facebook and Twitter that venerate celebrity status and a more materialist consumer culture. They also provide anonymity and the possibility of choosing an identity outside the construct of race.

After more than a century, Caribbean artists are responding to definitions of Blackness in multifarious ways. Their imagery provides more options for identity beyond the phenotypical, and they illustrate a narrative unrestrained by the problematic history that once shaped the destiny of their islands. These artists are confident in their choices, recognizing that the rich recipe of their callaloo culture can produce valuable ways of thinking and seeing that can be models for a "post-Black," post-racialized world.

14

THE ART OF BLACK MOBILIZATION, 1960s–2010s

ALEJANDRO DE LA FUENTE

> Art must be transformed into a weapon for struggle, a tool for liberation… including the dramatic problem of racial discrimination.
> —*Primer Congreso de las Culturas Negras de las Américas* (Cali, 1977)

Hundreds of activists, community leaders, intellectuals, scholars, and government officials from all over the Americas gathered in Santiago de Chile from December 5–7, 2000, to attend a regional meeting in preparation for the World Conference against Racism, Racial Discrimination, Xenophobia and Related Intolerance that would take place in Durban, South Africa, a year later. The final declaration of the regional conference included a scathing critique of Latin American states and societies, which were characterized as the historical products of centuries of colonialism, slavery, and other forms of servitude. Participants denounced that the enslavement of Africans and indigenous peoples resulted in the persistence of "systemic discrimination that still affects large sectors of the population." An ambitious Plan of Action called on all states to develop effective mechanisms to address these social ills, to eradicate racism and discrimination, to eliminate poverty, and to "promote more participatory and inclusive societies."[1]

The public, official acknowledgement that racism, discrimination, and other forms of social exclusion afflict Latin American societies represented a major shift in state discourses concerning race and nation in the region. For decades, the region's politicians had regularly denied the existence of institutional or even informal racism and discrimination in their societies; embraced ideologies of racial mixture and harmony; discouraged any form of racially defined mobilization; and rejected demands framed in terms of racial justice. Frequently in contrast to the United States, the societies of Latin America were depicted as models of racial coexistence and racial democracy. African cultural contributions were rhetorically celebrated as key ingredients of national cultures, but confined to politically safe spaces through processes of nationalization and folklorization that denied their continuing vitality and strength among popular sectors. Artists and other cultural producers trying to formulate demands for racial justice and equality found little state support, if not outright repression.

Participants in the regional conference challenged this official culture of silence and denial: "Ignoring the existence of discrimination and racism, at both the State and the society level, contributes directly and indirectly to perpetuating the practices of racism, racial discrimination, xenophobia and related intolerance."

In an effort to correct this denial, the final declaration contained numerous references to culture and to cultural rights, including the protection of the cultural heritage of Afrodescendants as well as the promotion of "greater knowledge of and respect for" their cultural and artistic expressions.[2] States were required to provide institutional and financial support for these purposes, an agenda that acknowledged the importance of cultural production as part of wider efforts against racism and exclusion in the region.

The attention to culture as a key element in the struggle for recognition and racial justice built on decades of Afrodescendant activism and on the tenacious efforts of numerous artists to gain recognition, visibility, and respect for their own creation and for cultural forms of perceived African origin. Many of the activists traveling to Santiago de Chile began their work in organizations, clubs, study groups, and community institutions devoted to the study and development of Black culture. Black participation in national life was frequently linked to their perceived cultural contributions and to the contentious incorporation of popular expressions into mainstream culture. Spaces for Black political mobilization (indeed for any form of mobilization) became severely restricted with the rise of authoritarian regimes in the 1960s, so culture became the preferred space for activists to articulate Black pride and identity and to make demands for equality.

Culture was also the terrain where activists articulated their earliest critiques of dominant discourses of racial democracy and *mestizaje*. This happened through processes of Black cultural revival, as in Peru in the 1950s through the 1970s, or through the affirmation and celebration of Black cultural forms that could not be reduced to folkloric ingredients of a mixed national culture, as in Brazil, Colombia, and Cuba during the 1960s and 1970s.

In Peru, cultural revival efforts were linked to the formation in the 1950s of an Afro-Peruvian dance company named after the Afro-Peruvian painter Pancho Fierro (ca. 1807–1879), and especially to the activities of the musician and activist Nicomedes Santa Cruz (1925–1992) who, along with his sister Victoria Santa Cruz (1922–2014), spearheaded the revalorization and popularization of Black musical and dance forms that were previously forgotten.[3] Their dance and performance ensemble Cumanana "was both a cultural revival and a core of black activism."[4]

Another cultural cauldron of Black activism was the Teatro Experimental do Negro (TEN), created by the activist, cultural promoter, and visual artist Abdias do Nascimento (1914–2011) in Rio de Janeiro in 1944. TEN sought to work toward the "social valorization of blacks in Brazil, through education, culture, and art."[5] Its plays provided a platform for Black actors and for the development of a theatrical discourse based on Black aesthetics and Afro-Brazilian culture. At the same time, TEN was a space for antiracist activism and social justice. As a cultural project, one of its main goals was to combat racism, and the company attracted a large number of young Afro-Brazilian activists who sought to influence public debate concerning race in Brazil and to participate in the political life of the country.[6]

Visual artists were active contributors to cultural projects that looked to highlight the centrality of Blacks and Black cultures in nation-making processes in Latin America. Many of them found inspiration in the decolonization processes that swept the African continent between the 1950s and 1970s. For example, one of the earliest collaborators of Nascimento in TEN was the Afro-Brazilian painter Wilson Tibério (ca. 1920–2005), who spent most of his career in Europe, but who also lived and worked in

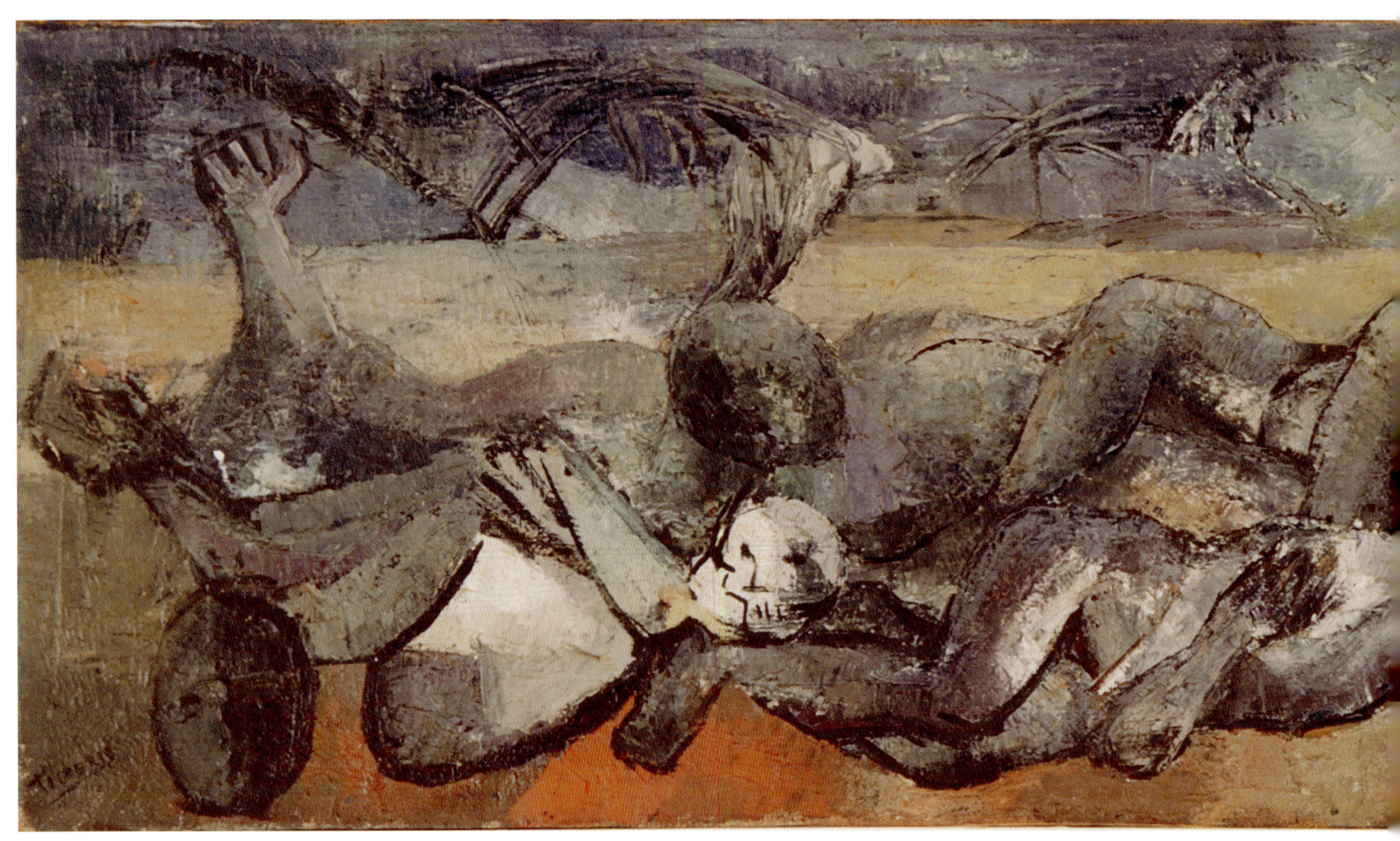

252 Wilson Tibério. *Massacre in South Africa*. Undated. Oil on canvas. Paris, Estate of the artist.

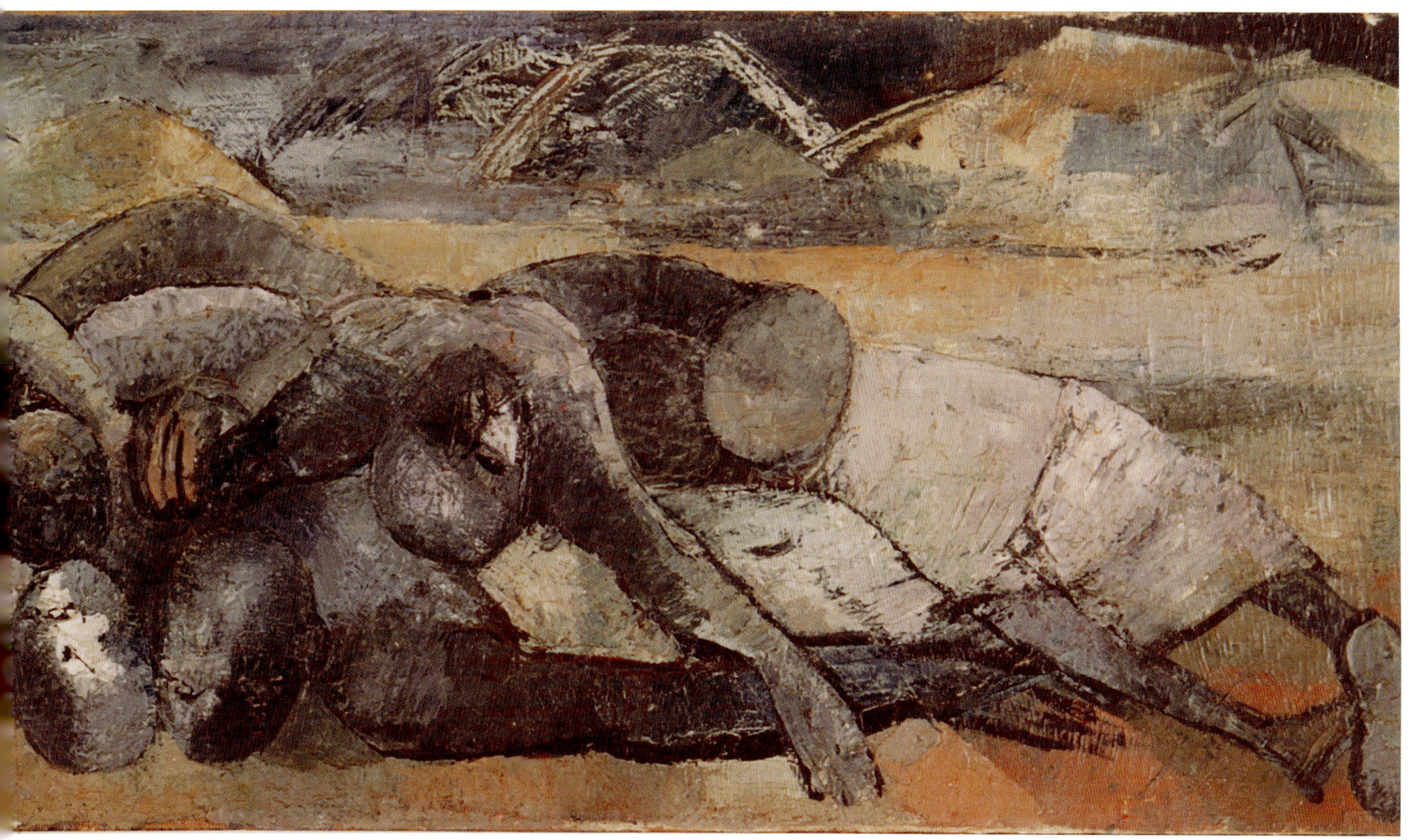

several African countries such as Senegal, Côte d'Ivoire, Benin, and Burkina Faso. Tibério's early paintings, populated by people of African descent who casually go about their daily activities, capture Brazilian urban life.[7] In the 1950s and 1960s, under the influence of the ideological and cultural movement of *Négritude*, his work became increasingly critical of French colonial practices and sympathetic to African decolonization efforts. In 1960, a year marked by the independence of numerous African countries, Tibério settled in Abidjan, Côte d'Ivoire, learned about local cultures and folkways, and worked on a personal exhibition that would open a year later.[8] In his own words, struggles for independence and justice in Africa and Brazil served as inspiration for much of his works.[9] Other Latin American artists, Black and white, were inspired by similar political ideas, which linked racial struggles in Latin America to global movements against racism and colonialism. The civil rights movement in the United States and the struggle against apartheid in South Africa found powerful echoes across Latin America and contributed to the proliferation of popular cultural forms that challenged dominant discourses of racial harmony in the region. In Peru, Nicomedes Santa Cruz attributed the "renaissance" of Black culture to "a universal movement with its origins in the recent independence of African countries and the struggle that Africa and Afro-America preserve against neocolonialism and racial discrimination."[10] In

Brazil, organizations such as the Sociedade de Intercambio Brasil-Africa (SINBA, created in 1974) and the Instituto de Pesquisas das Culturas Negras (IPCN, 1975) sought to draw connections with and lessons from African anticolonial struggles and to construct spaces for Black cultural autonomy.[11] Among the cultural products that gained the attention and sympathy of the IPCN was soul music, a politicized, counterhegemonic diasporic musical genre and aesthetic that young Afro-Brazilians embraced as a way to articulate new markers of racial pride and identity.[12] Some of these aesthetic representations also reached Cuba, where a new generation of Afro-Cuban intellectuals, activists, and artists was contesting official representations of Black culture as folklore, as well as official denials of racial discrimination.[13] Meanwhile, Colombia witnessed in 1976 the creation of SOWETO, a study group integrated by Black university students, named in honor of the South African township that rose up against apartheid.[14]

These transnational cultural, political, and aesthetic influences found fertile ground in a variety of international conferences and forums where intellectuals, activists, and artists came together to debate questions of Black culture and identity and to devise strategies against racism and colonialism. International events such as the World Black and African Festivals of Arts and Cultures (FESTAC) in Senegal (1966) and Nigeria (1977) provided opportunities for visual artists from across the diaspora to exhibit their work and to participate in diasporic conversations on race, culture, and justice.

Among those exhibiting at the 1966 Festival in Dakar were the Afro-Brazilian artists Agnaldo Manoel dos Santos (1926–1962), Heitor dos Prazeres (1898–1966), and Rubem Valentim (1922–1991). Wilson Tibério was in attendance; so were Prazeres and Valentim. The Brazilian government organized an even larger art exhibit for Nigeria in 1977, curated by the white art critic Clarival do Prado Valladares. Twelve artists, all of African descent, were represented.[15] They belonged to different generations, worked in a variety of styles, and had different artistic trajectories. Some, like the sculptors Francisco Biquiba Guarany (ca. 1884–1985), Valentim, and Boaventura Silva Filho, known artistically as Louco (1929–1992), or the painter José de Dome (José Antônio dos Santos, 1921–1982), were self-taught artists, some of them of rather humble origins. Others, such as Octávio Araújo (1926–2015) and Emanoel Araújo (1940–2022) were formally trained in national and international academies. Other Latin American countries with large Afrodescendant populations also participated in FESTAC 1977, including Colombia, Venezuela, Panama, and the Dominican Republic.[16] Cuba was not invited to Dakar in 1966, but the country did send a delegation to Nigeria, including Afro-Cuban artists such as the sculptors Rogelio Rodríguez Cobas (1925–2014) and Ramón Haití Eduardo (1932–2008), as well as the painter Manuel Mendive Hoyo (b. 1944).[17]

Events such as the Festivals of Dakar and Lagos sought to promote Black and African cultures and Black and African artists, writers, and performers at the same time.[18] According to the African American painter Arthur Monroe (1935–2019), more than seventeen thousand artists from fifty-seven countries participated in FESTAC 1977, when Lagos became "a mecca" for Black artists from all over the diaspora—"black Americans, Cubans, Jamaicans, or Brazilians, an African in the eyes of his brethren on the continent."[19]

Behind these celebrations of unity, however, lay serious conflicts concerning race, culture, authenticity, and representation.

Countries such as Cuba and Brazil participated with official delegations in these festivals because their foreign affairs bureaucracies saw them as propitious venues to achieve broader geopolitical goals. Both countries sought to increase their influence on the African continent, and both presented themselves internationally as champions of racial harmony and democracy. There were important differences, however. Whereas under military rule, Brazil was a protagonist in the Cold War crusade against communism, Cuba served as a nexus for international radical networks of Black and anticolonial solidarity. But both countries saw race and Black culture as useful tools in their foreign policy.[20]

The official endorsement of ideologies of racial harmony by the governments of countries such as Brazil and Cuba had contradictory effects on Black cultural production and art. On the one hand, this led to official support for cultural projects and popular folklore, including participation in international events such as FESTAC. African contributions were acknowledged as part of national art. On the other hand, such contributions were confined to the categories of folkloric roots and deprived of life and vitality.[21] They were purposefully divorced from the daily struggles of the popular sectors or from any demands for racial justice and equality. Cultural expressions were channeled to what a distinguished scholar of Afro-Brazilian mobilization has called "culturalism," which reduces cultural practices to their "material, expressive, artifactual elements," so "Afro-Brazilian and Afro-Diasporic symbols and artifacts become reified and commodified; culture becomes a thing, not a deeply political process."[22]

Some Afrodescendant artists and intellectuals contested these official narratives and tried to wrest control of Black cultural production away from state institutions and to carve out autonomous spaces for Black culture. In reaction to the exclusion of TEN and other racially conscious artists from the official delegation to the 1966 Festival in Dakar, Abdias do Nascimento published a letter addressed to his "brothers of blood and artistic militancy." The letter denounced the Brazilian official ideology of racial integration and offered a scathing critique of the Cultural Department of Itamaraty, the Brazilian Ministry of Foreign Affairs. According to Nascimento, the commission in charge of selecting the participants in the festival consisted exclusively of white people and did not consult with any Black artists. "Everything was done in the old paternalistic molds, decisions were made, defining what is or isn't black art or that which they think is Afro-Brazilian art, with the absolute marginalization and disdain for the militants."[23] In charge of the visual arts section was the white art critic Valladares, who was honored by the Senegalese government with a position in the festival's jury.[24]

Among the artists who, according to Nascimento, had been unjustly bypassed for Dakar was the Afro-Brazilian painter Wilson de Azevedo Sérgio (dates of birth and death unknown). Little is known about his career or his work. In the 1950s, Azevedo worked in architectural design in Rio de Janeiro and presented some of his paintings in the IV Salão Paulista de Arte Moderna (1955). The Tourist Department of Rio acquired some of his works, apparently to decorate the city during the Carnival season. Like Nascimento, Azevedo complained publicly about the process of selection by Itamaraty. In his view, the work of those selected, like the primitive painter Prazeres, would not "transmit anything to Africans," and he resented the exclusion of those whom he characterized as "black artists of modern tendencies." He even threatened to organize a strike by Black artists in the

253 Abdias do Nascimento. *The Horse and the Saint: Yemanjá*. 1975. Acrylic on canvas. The State University of New York at Buffalo, IPEAFRO Collection.

streets of Rio, complaining that whereas the United States was sending three hundred artists to Dakar, Brazil was sending only two.[25]

Nascimento criticized Brazilian racial democracy again at FESTAC 1977. A political exile living in the United States at the time, he attended the event, but as part of the American delegation. He contested Itamaraty's official discourse of Brazil as "the only country in the world that has managed to build a multiracial society without clash or conflict"[26] and spoke of a whitening of Brazil that amounted to a "massacre" against Afro-Brazilians.

By the time he went to Lagos, Nascimento had developed a substantial body of paintings that celebrated Brazil's African connections through Candomblé. A self-taught artist who did not turn to the visual arts until his arrival in the United States in 1968, Nascimento managed to gain significant recognition and success for his artistic work. Several major galleries and art spaces specializing in African American art embraced the artist and organized solo exhibits of his work. Through these exhibits, Nascimento helped to communicate to American audiences the centrality of African cultures in Brazil and to construct a transnational Pan-African pantheon of deities and influences built around the Orixás, which he saw as "living beings" that shaped people's daily lives. Nascimento's visual artistic production declined after his return to Brazil in 1981, when he devoted most of his time and energy to political activism (he served two terms in Congress) and to educational and cultural projects such as the Instituto de Pesquisas e Estudos Afro Brasileiros (IPEAFRO),[27] which he created in 1981.[28]

Nascimento was not the only artist who used his work to celebrate and promote the Afro-Diasporic ritual cultures of Latin America. This discursive strategy represented a critique of state folklorization attempts, highlighted the vitality of African-based cultural forms, and underlined what Nascimento called "the spiritual vitality of the black race."[29] In Brazil, following Mariano da Cunha's lead, one would have to include artists usually grouped under the "primitive" and "popular" labels, whose work reflects African influences not only thematically, but in terms of formal expressions.[30] Also in this group would be artists whose production is squarely placed within ritual art, such as the sculptor Mestre Didi (Deoscóredes Maximiliano dos Santos, 1917–2013) and those who articulate their Afro-Brazilian religious grounding through new formal solutions and visual languages, such as Valentim and the São Paulo artist Niobe Xandó (1915–2010).[31] In the 1980s, Ronaldo Rego (b. 1935) developed an important body of work celebrating Umbanda,[32] a syncretic Afro-Latin American religion created in the twentieth century that incorporates Amerindian, European, and African elements.[33]

These artists partook in what could be broadly characterized as a shared cultural project that was shaped by transnational conversations and influences. But their political, discursive, and aesthetic proposals were widely different. Nascimento championed Négritude and other ideologies of Pan-African unity. His representations of the Orixás used a figurative modernist language. In turn, the sculptor Rubem Valentim used geometric abstraction and the visual language of constructivism to convey the richness of his Afro-Bahian religious universe. Unlike Nascimento, he claimed to find inspiration in the "cultural complex of Bahia," a city that he characterized as a "great collective synthesis translated into the fusion of European, African, and Amerindian ethnic and cultural elements" (see fig. 215). That is, Valentim's vision of

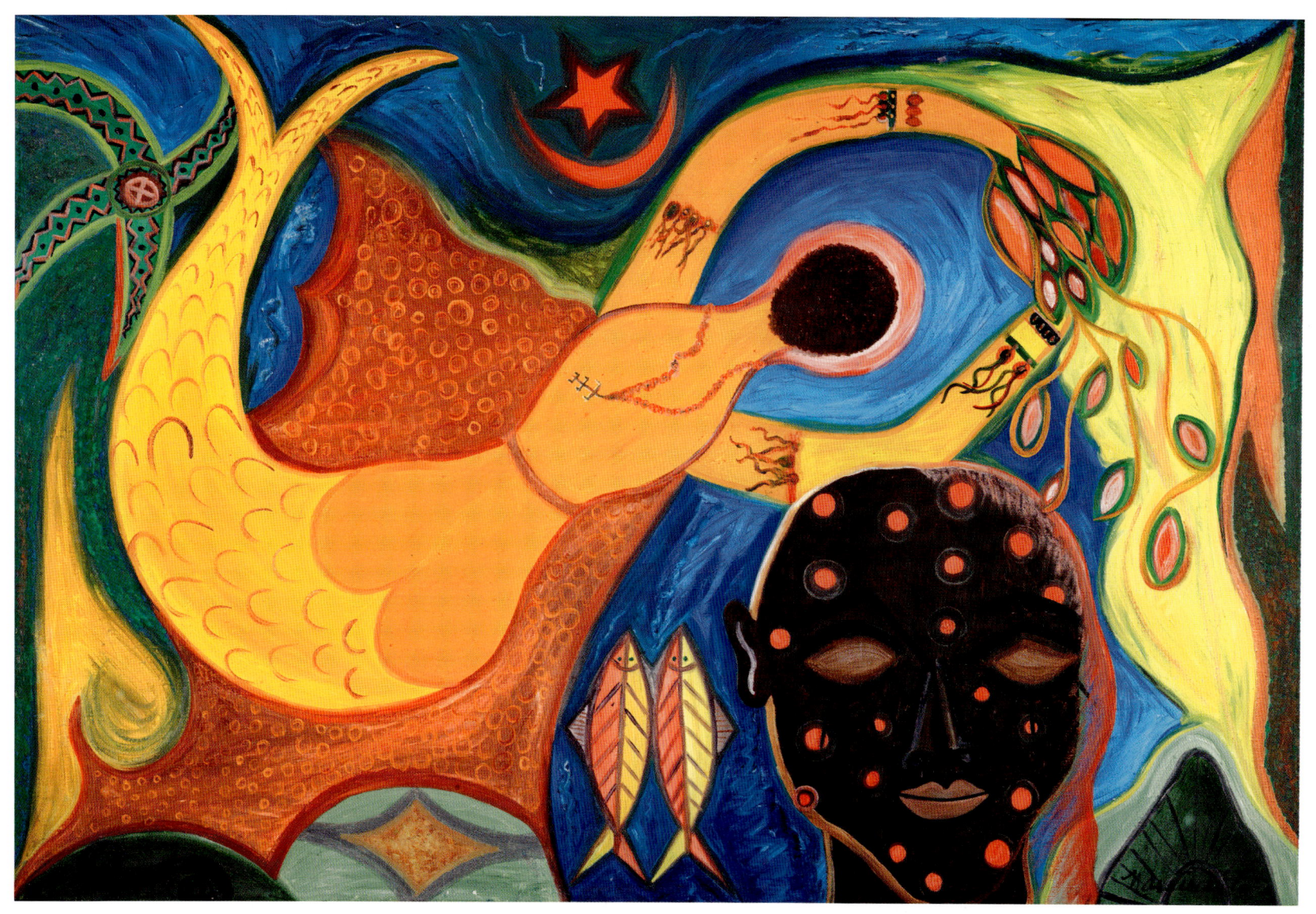

254 Ruben Galloza. *Afro-Uruguay*. Mural. Montevideo, Afro-Uruguayan Social and Cultural Association (ACSUN).

Afro-Brazilian culture was based on notions of mixture that were closer to dominant ideas about race and nation in Brazil.[34]

Artists interested in the recovery, construction, and dissemination of Black culture in Latin America fell somewhere between these discursive positions, although most of them found inspiration in religious practices and beliefs of perceived African origin. Such was the case of the self-taught Afro-Uruguayan painter Rubén Galloza (1926–2002), the son of a Black domestic servant who grew up in the working-class neighborhood of Barrio Sur in Montevideo and who, as a young man, participated in the civil rights struggles for racial equality and cultural recognition in mid-twentieth-century Montevideo.[35] Galloza was a tireless promoter of Candombe who devoted most of his artistic work to reconstruct and disseminate the religious practices and popular culture of Afro-Uruguayans.[36] The recovery of African cultural elements was also important to the Afro-Colombian painter Cogollo (Heriberto Cuadrado Cogollo, b. 1945).[37] After settling in Paris in the late 1960s, Cogollo began a process of research and discovery of African cultural influences without Western filters that would result in the creation of a personal catalog of "Afro-Caribbean symbols."[38] In 1973, on the occasion of a personal exhibit at Galerie Suzanne Visat in Paris, Cogollo defined himself as an African sorcerer who had the ability to see and represent the entrails of others. The cover of the catalog reproduced his *El hombre de mañana* (*The Man of Tomorrow*, 1970), a defiant surrealist Afrodescendant subject with a raised fist.[39]

Cuban artists also participated in this search for a visual culture associated with Blackness and Africa. Like the Brazilians, those interested in the promotion of Afro-Cuban culture worked in a tense and contradictory environment. On the one hand, the revolutionary government created several institutions to research, preserve, and incorporate popular cultural expressions into what the Afro-Cuban ethnomusicologist Rogelio Martínez Furé described as "the new socialist culture . . . but without betraying its folkloric essence."[40]

On the other hand, the new socialist culture was perceived to be incompatible with African-based expressions and practices. The main goal of the new educational system was to overcome what the Cultural Congress of Havana in 1968 characterized as "cultural underdevelopment." It was to create a technically sophisticated, modern, Western man cleansed of traditional cultural influences. Santería and other African-based religious practices were described as "no more than folkloric manifestations, valuable as a historical record of cultural processes but *paralyzing hindrances* on the road to true progress."[41] They had to be eliminated. In the early 1970s, artistic production was subordinated to the needs of the educational system and to political propaganda, effectively blurring "the line between art, education, propaganda, and publicity."[42] A central element of state propaganda was that the Cuban government had eradicated racism and discrimination in the island, so most references to the topic were articulated as denunciations and critiques of American society. Events such as the Tricontinental Conference (1966) and organizations like OSPAAAL (Organization of Solidarity with the People of Asia, Africa and Latin America) inspired a visual corpus that linked racism to imperialism and colonialism, thus deflecting attention away from national problems. Articulated in Cuba mostly through a vibrant school of graphic design that produced hundreds of political "solidarity" posters, this corpus also included paintings by Cuban and international artists.[43] Wilson Tibério,

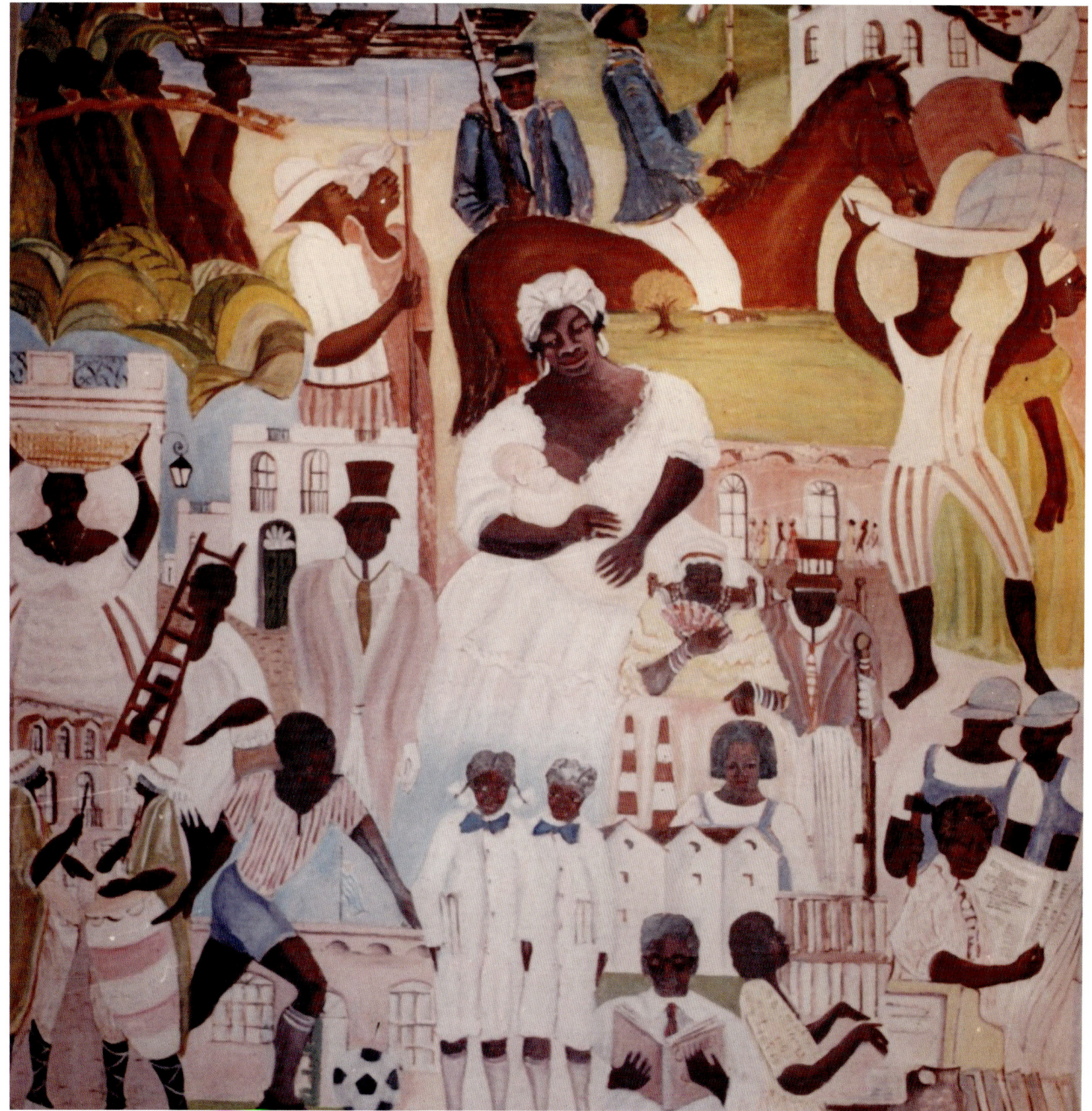

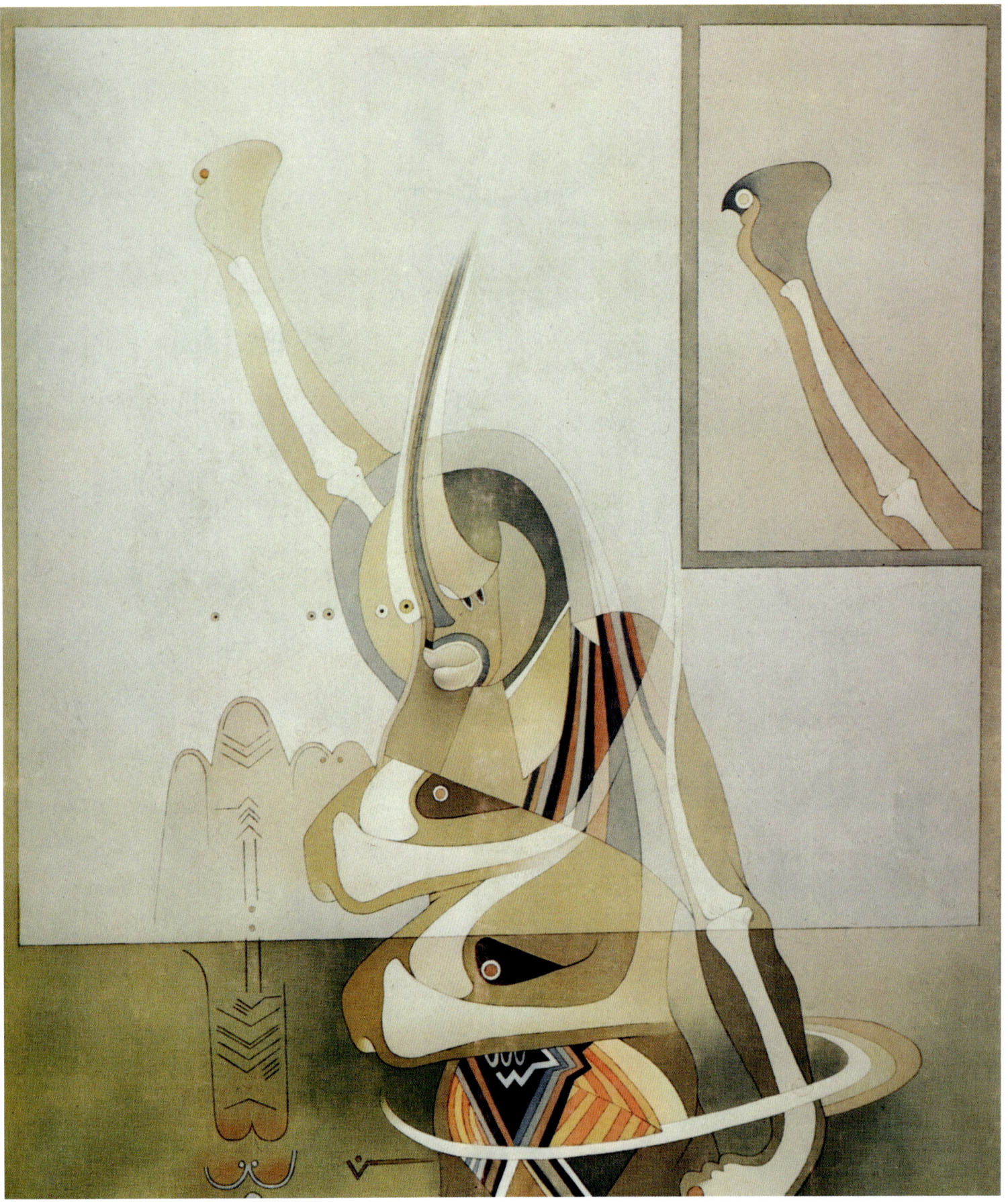

255

255 Heriberto Cuadrado Cogollo. *The Man of Tomorrow*. 1970.

for instance, created a painting titled *Tricontinental*, while one of Niobe Xandó's prints from 1970 celebrated *Black Power*. Cuban artists interested in debating domestic issues of race and identity gravitated, like their Brazilian peers, toward the exploration of African connections, particularly in religion. Paradoxically, just as authorities were discouraging Santería and other African-based religious practices, a group of fairly young visual artists was starting to develop an important corpus that, through the incorporation of ritual and iconographic elements taken from the Yoruba-based Santería, from the Congo-inspired Palo Monte, or from the rituals associated with the male esoteric society known as the Abakuá, sought to construct a Cuban popular culture that was inextricably linked to Africa.[44] Like Nascimento, these artists experienced these religions as key and vibrant influences in the daily lives of ordinary Cubans. They subscribed to the view, articulated by the Afro-Cuban activist Walterio Carbonell, that African religions were at the center of "national culture," played "a progressive role in the politics and culture" of the nation, and continued to impact people's material and spiritual lives: "The people worship their generous gods.... Religion and music are of capital importance in the spiritual life of black people."[45]

Prominent among the young artists whose work was heavily influenced by Afro-Cuban religiosity were the painter Manuel Mendive and the sculptor and engraver Rafael Queneditt Morales (1942–2016). By 1970, Mendive's work was already openly celebratory of the Orishas, and the most important pieces of this period, such as *Babalú Ayé*, *Obba*, and *Oyá*, all from 1967, were dedicated to them.[46] Queneditt's work—which, like Valentim's, was influenced by constructivist and abstract influences—was also dedicated to the deities of Santería, as illustrated by some of his earliest engravings such as *Oyá* (1970), *Ochosi* (1970), *Baba-lu-aye* (1971), *Echo* (1971), *Shangó y los eggunes* (1972), and *Obbatalá* (1973).[47] The work of the Afro-Cuban sculptors Cobas and Haití Eduardo, both of whom attended FESTAC 1977, can also be included in this group, even though they were older than Mendive and Queneditt. Their art was heavily influenced by two major figures in Afro-Cuban art, the sculptor Agustín Cárdenas (1927–2001) (see *The Image of the Black in Latin American and Caribbean Art*, Book 1, fig. 8) and the painter Wifredo Lam (1902–1982), both of whom were living in Paris at the time. The imposing early totems of Cobas owed much to Cárdenas, but he later developed a rather personal body of work that placed the ingenuity and creativity of people of African descent at the center of Western technological developments, as illustrated by his later *Satellite* series. Haití's sculptures, in turn, have been described as volumetric incarnations of Lam's fantastic creatures.[48]

These artists faced an increasingly hostile official environment in the early to mid-1970s, when they had vanishingly few opportunities to exhibit their work. As Cuban cultural policy became increasingly dogmatic and exclusionary, visual representations of Afro-Cuban traditions lost favor. The work of the multiracial art collective *Origen* (1974–1979), founded by Mariano Suárez del Villar (1929–1996) with the participation of Miguel de Jesús Ocejo (1940–2006) and Pablo Toscano (1940–2003), illustrates how rarefied the official space in which to explore Afro-Cuban religions had become.[49] Suárez del Villar and Toscano were of African descent; Ocejo was a white self-taught artist who grew up in Santiago de Cuba, where Afro-Cuban and Afro-Caribbean cultural influences predominate. Each of them developed a visual language that was influenced by surrealism and that consequently

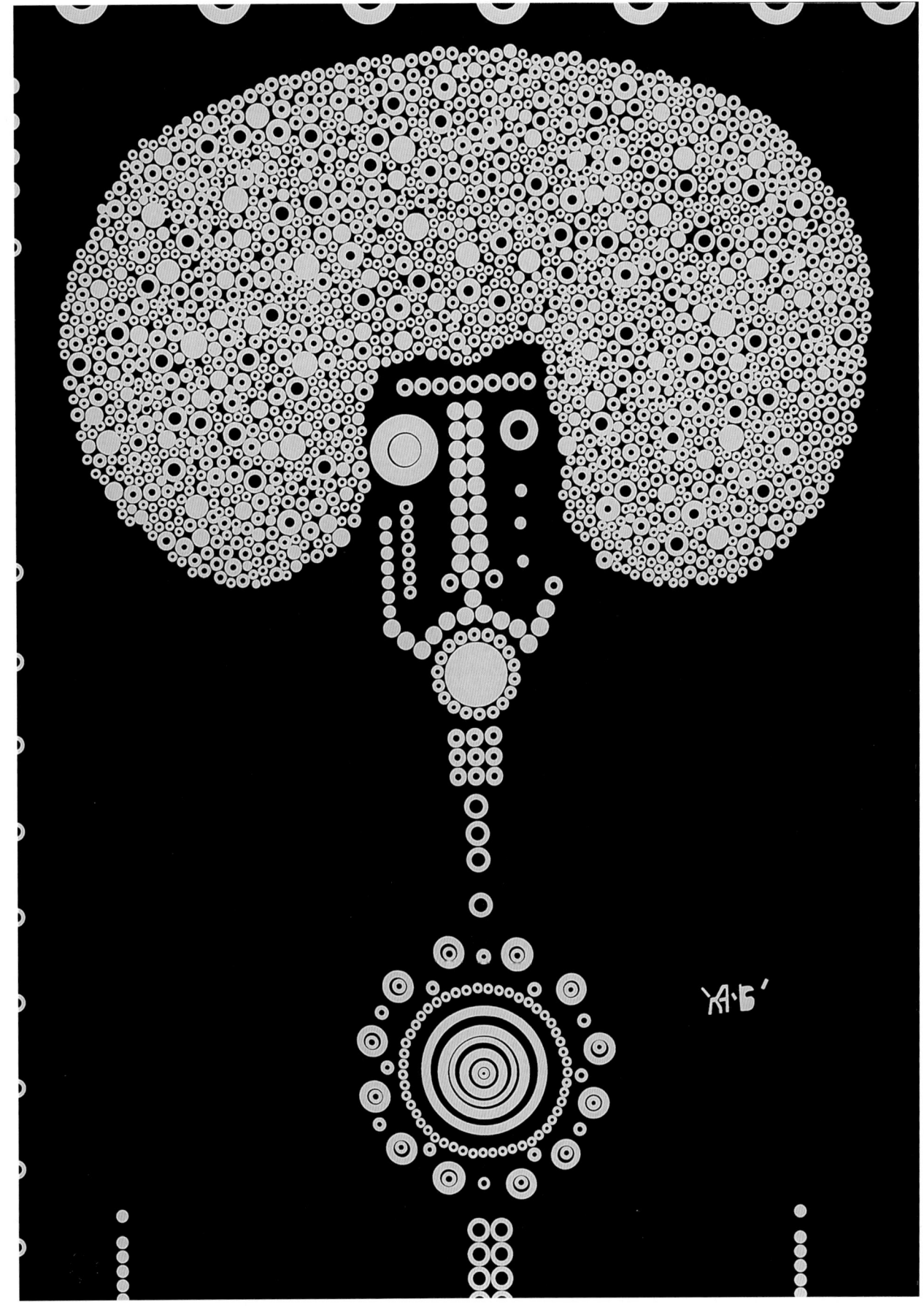

256

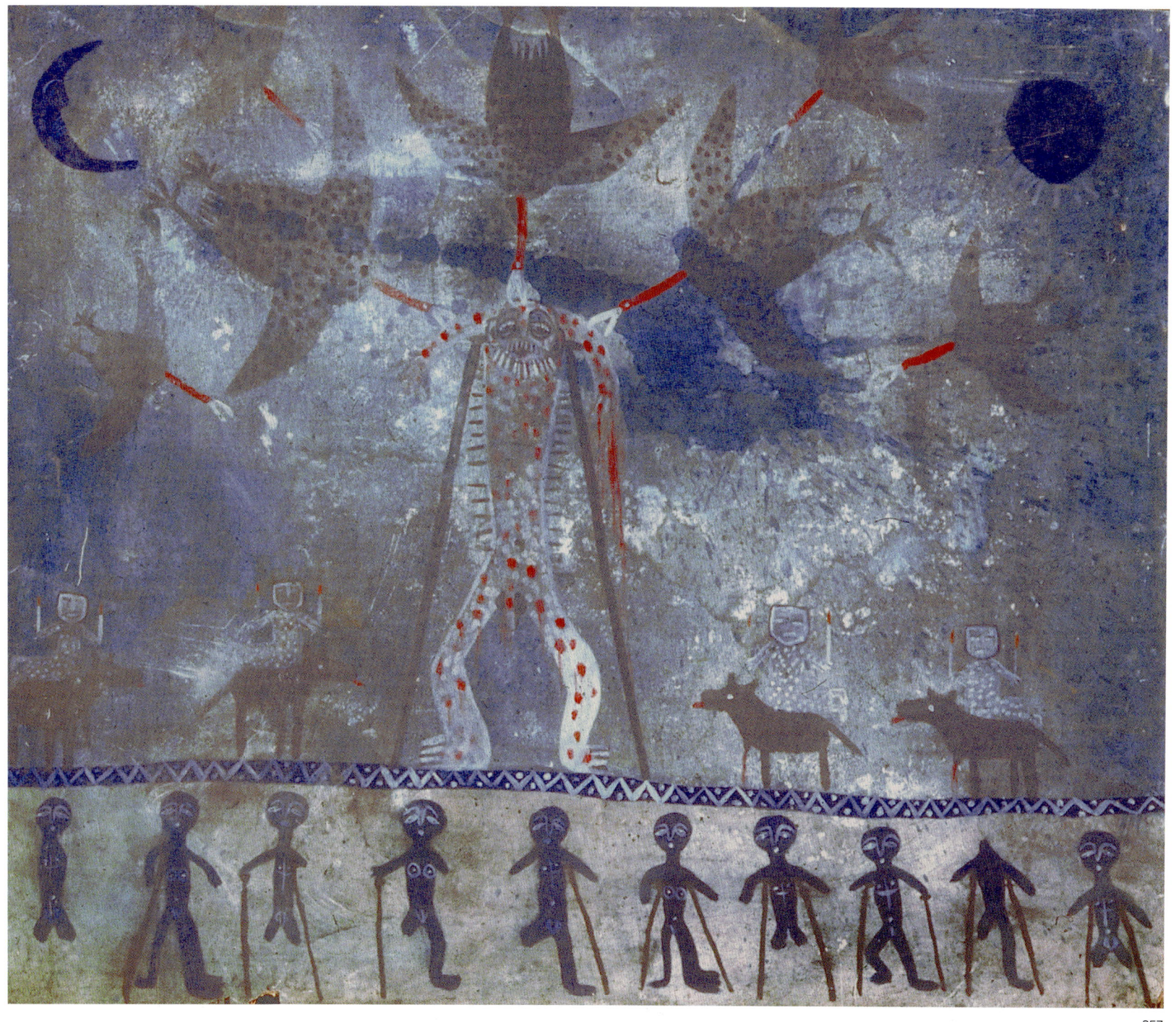

256 Niobe Xandó. *Black Power I*. 1970. Serigraph. São Paulo, Museu de Arte Moderna.

257 Manuel Mendive. *Babalú Ayé*. 1967. Mixed media on wood. No longer exists.

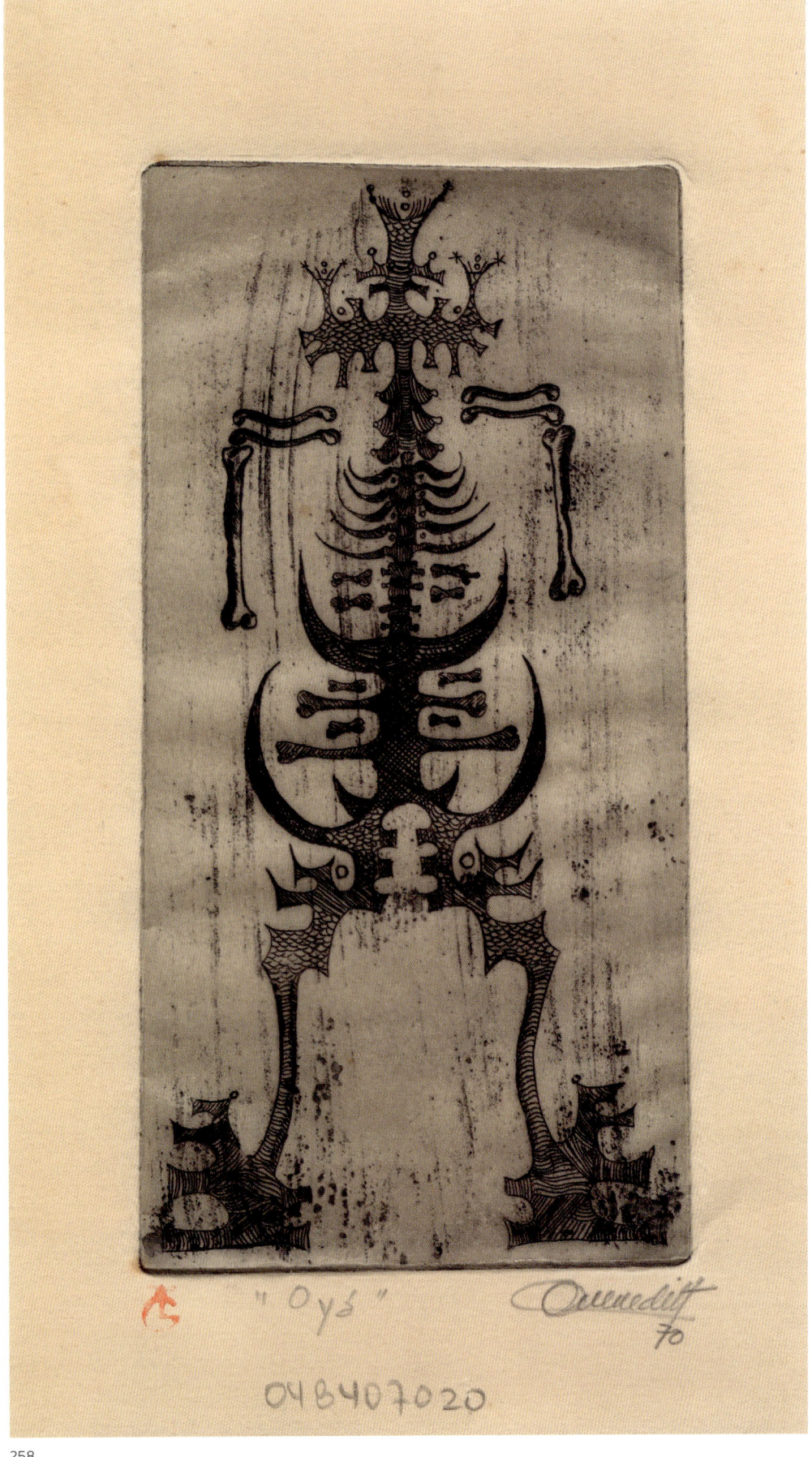

258 Rafael Queneditt Morales. *Oyá*. 1970. Copper engraving. Location unknown.

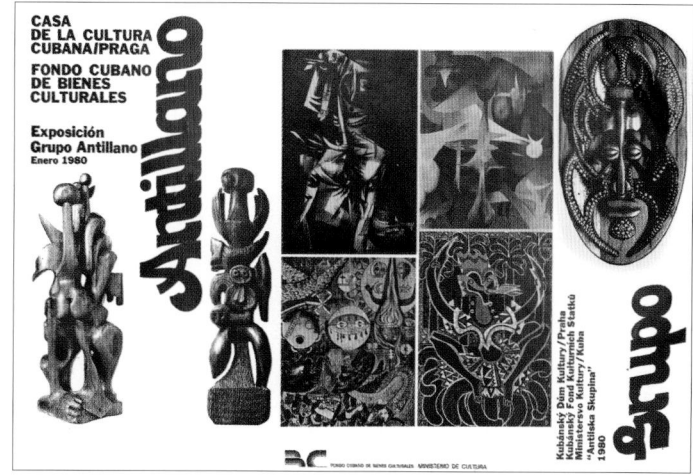

259 Esteban Ayala, designer. *Grupo Antillano*. 1980. Exhibition poster.

deviated from orthodox representations linked to socialist realism. The collective sought to represent Cuba's cultural fusion through a new language, highlighting in the process the importance of African religiosity, but insisting on the fact that their project was to create a *secular* visual culture that "demystified" religious rituals. Despite their best efforts to align their work with official cultural policy, however, they faced charges of promoting Black consciousness and producing religious art.[50]

The context for Black cultural production improved in the late 1970s, as Cuba expanded its geopolitical footprint on the African continent, built new political alliances in the Caribbean, and took institutional steps to provide artistic production with some degree of autonomy. Taking advantage of this propitious moment, Rafael Queneditt created Grupo Antillano (1978–1983), a multiracial art collective that would articulate a vision of Cuban national culture that, as their foundational manifesto stated, was solidly anchored in African and Afro-Caribbean references. In this search, they claimed to build on a generation of previous artists, among them Wifredo Lam (who became honorary president of the group and exhibited with them) and the deceased Afro-Cuban artist Roberto Diago (1920–1955). Three of the group's collaborators, Clara Morera (b. 1944), Adelaida Herrera (1941–2016), and Julia Valdés (b. 1952), were women, a feat worth noting in what otherwise was a heavily male-dominated cultural environment.

Grupo Antillano placed Santería and other African religious and cultural practices at the very center of Cuba's national formation, a position that openly contested official characterizations of such practices as primitive obstacles in the construction of a modern socialist society. It engaged the sympathy and support of a large group of collaborators, including some of the leading Black intellectuals in Cuba at the time. The group built a true Afro-Cuban cultural movement, and their exhibits became cultural, academic, and social events that transcended the visual arts.[51] Those exhibits were also a searing critique of Cuban art academies, where new trends in Western art found a privileged space, and of a cultural bureaucracy that insisted on relegating Black culture to the spaces of folklore.

These explorations of African cultural influences and of Pan-African themes and topics led in the 1980s and 1990s to a more direct critique of Latin American racial democracies. The congresses of Black Culture in Cali (1977), Panama (1980), and Brazil (1982) helped to articulate these concerns. At these events, activists and artists debated not only how to promote Black culture in the Americas, but also how to use art and culture more generally to combat racism and racial discrimination in the region. In countries such as Brazil, where processes of democratic opening created new opportunities to make demands for racial justice, activists, artists, and curators organized exhibits and events that challenged established narratives of racial democracy and highlighted the continuing subordination of Black people.

A leading example of these events is the landmark exhibit *A mão afro-brasileira* (*The Afro-Brazilian Touch*) organized by the artist, curator, and activist Emanoel Araújo in 1988. Organized on the occasion of the centennial of emancipation in Brazil, the exhibit did not link "Afro-Brazilian" art to any particular expression, theme, or school, but to the artists' ancestry. All the participants, including the curator, were widely perceived to be Black. As Araújo explained, his goal was to highlight the "cultural contributions of blacks and their descendants to our arts since the

THE ART OF BLACK MOBILIZATION, 1960s–2010s 441

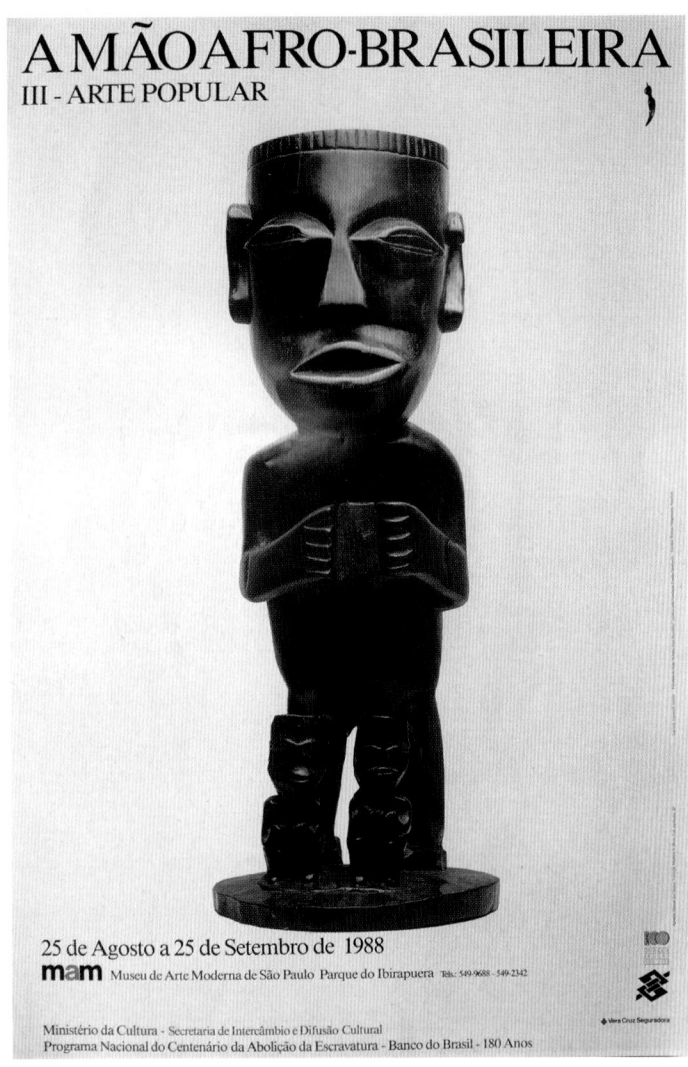

260

260 Emanoel Araújo. *The Afro-Brazilian Touch*. 1988. Poster for the eponymous exhibition curated by Emanoel Araújo.

261 Juan Roberto Diago. *A Piece of My History*. From the series *Here What You Can't Do Is Die*. 2003. Mixed media on metal. Boston, Collection of Alejandro de la Fuente and Patricia González.

arrival of the first groups of slaves in Portuguese America."[52] The exhibit and its accompanying volume openly called for a new, Afrocentric and revolutionary art history of Brazil.[53] Araújo would go on to organize other important exhibits of Afro-Brazilian art in the 1990s and 2000s,[54] and he would organize a new version of his own exhibit, *A nova mão afro-brasileira*, in 2014. In contrast to the original exhibit, *A nova mão afro-brasileira* highlights the work of a selected group of contemporary artists, including highly acclaimed artists such as Rosana Paulino (b. 1967) and the photographer Eustáquio Neves (b. 1955).[55]

Two additional curatorial projects are also connected to broader patterns of Black mobilization: *Viaje sin mapa* (2006) in Colombia and *Queloides* (1997–2012) in Cuba. Curated by Mercedes Angola and Raúl Cristancho Álvarez, two faculty members at the Universidad Nacional de Colombia, *Viaje sin mapa* sought to offer the first comprehensive survey of "afro representations in Colombian contemporary art." Probably not coincidentally, the exhibit took place at a time when debates concerning how to count people of African descent in the Colombian national census were raging.[56] *Viaje sin mapa* was presented at the Luis Angel Arango Library in Bogotá, its main goal to neutralize the invisibility that has traditionally affected Black artists in Colombia. Cristancho went on to organize, along with Luz Adriana Maya Restrepo, *¡Mandinga Sea! África en Antioquia* (2013–2014), an ambitious exhibition that sought to trace the impact of West African cultures in Antioquia and that looked at representations of Blackness from the colonial period to the present.[57]

In Cuba, *Queloides* represented the angst of a group of young,

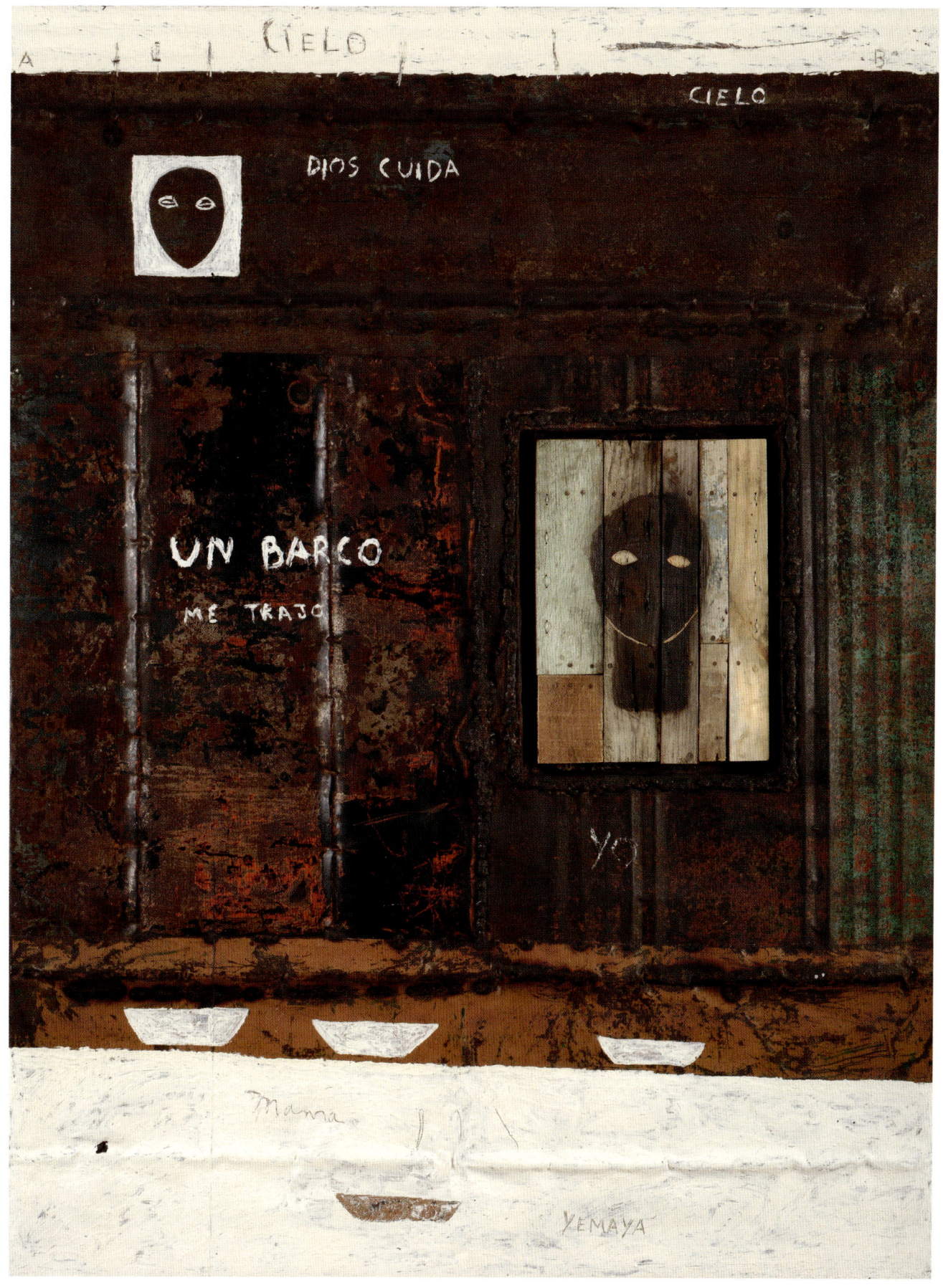

261

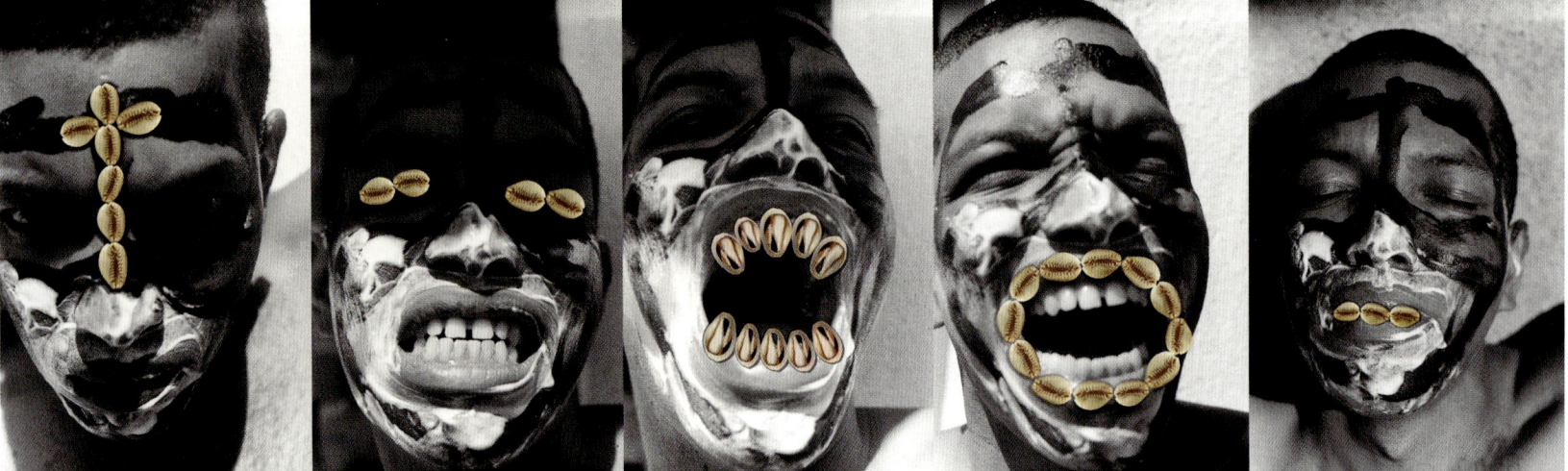

262

mostly Black artists as they experienced the collapse of the Cuban socialist welfare state in the 1990s.[58] Queloides (keloids) are raised, pathological scars; the title makes reference both to the traumatic effects of racism and to the widespread belief that Black skin is especially susceptible to developing these scars. The first exhibit, *Queloides I Parte* (1997), was organized by the artist Alexis Esquivel (b. 1968) and by the art critic and visual artist Omar-Pascual Castillo (b. 1971). A second, larger edition of the exhibit took place at the Centro de Desarrollo de Artes Visuales in Havana in 1999, thanks to the curatorial intervention of the Afro-Cuban writer and art critic Ariel Ribeaux Diago (1969–2005). These exhibits received very limited state support and were ignored by the Cuban media, despite being unprecedented events in Cuban art. Because of this, in 2010, the Afro-Cuban artist Elio Rodríguez Valdés (b. 1966) and I organized a new edition of the exhibit under the title *Queloides: Raza y racismo en el arte cubano contemporáneo* (*Keloids: Race and Racism in Cuban Contemporary Art*). It was the first and only time that the terms "race" and "racism" appeared in an art exhibit in Cuba.[59] The artists participating in each of these exhibits have varied, but five of them—Alexis Esquivel, Elio Rodríguez, Manuel Arenas (b. 1964), René Peña (b. 1957), and Douglas Pérez (b. 1972)—have participated in all of them.

Roberto Conduru's assertion that politics has become an increasingly important topic in Afro-Brazilian art is applicable to other countries in the region, as all these exhibits illustrate.[60] This political emphasis is articulated through several thematic axes across national boundaries, a clear illustration that racist ideologies and practices are not nationally bound and that the work of these artists is connected with and contributes to broader patterns of Afrodescendant mobilization. The work of some of these artists is literally a scream, a cry for help and recognition, as in *Grito* (*Scream*), a large, mural-like canvass executed by a young, perplexed, and angry Juan Roberto Diago (b. 1971) in 1997. Diago has developed a body of work that represents a militant invocation of Africa as the source of an ethnic and cultural identity that cannot be erased by mixture or by processes of cultural nationalization (see, for instance, his *Un pedazo de mi historia* [*A Piece of My History*], 2003).[61] A similar concern is found in the work of other Afrodescendant artists in Latin America, such as the Colombian Javier Mojica Madera (b. 1966), whose *Yo soy Babalú* (*I Am Babalú*, 2006) was exhibited in both *Viaje sin mapa* and *¡Mandinga Sea!* and in the *Valongo: Letters to the Sea* series (2015) produced by the Afro-Brazilian photographer Eustáquio Neves to honor the memory of the enslaved Africans who arrived in Rio de Janeiro through the wharf of Valongo,

262 Javier Mojica Madera. *I Am Babalú*. 2006. Digital photograph. Antioquia, Colombia, Museum. Donated 2013.

263 Eustáquio Neves. From the series *Good Appearance*. 2005. Photography, mixed media.

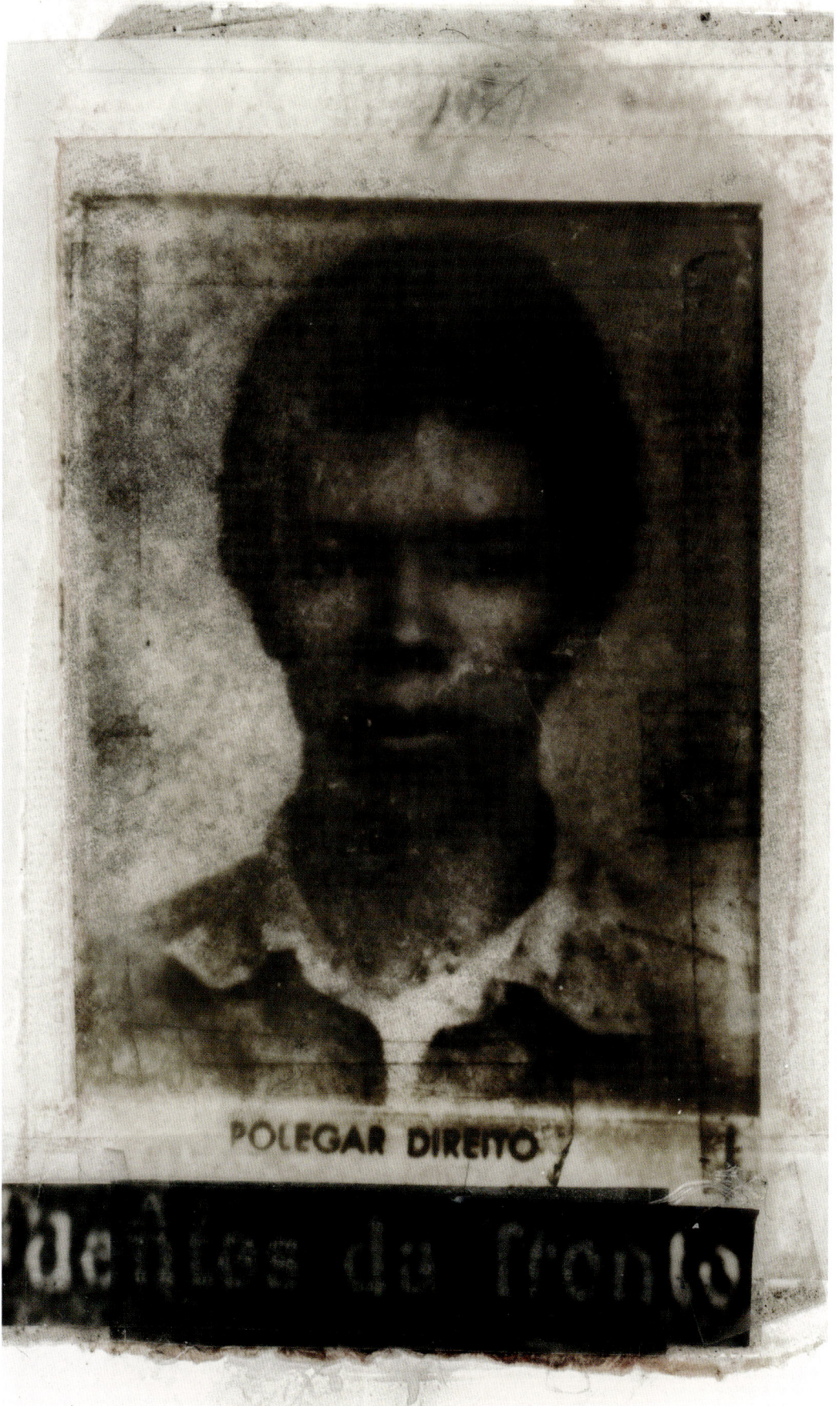

263

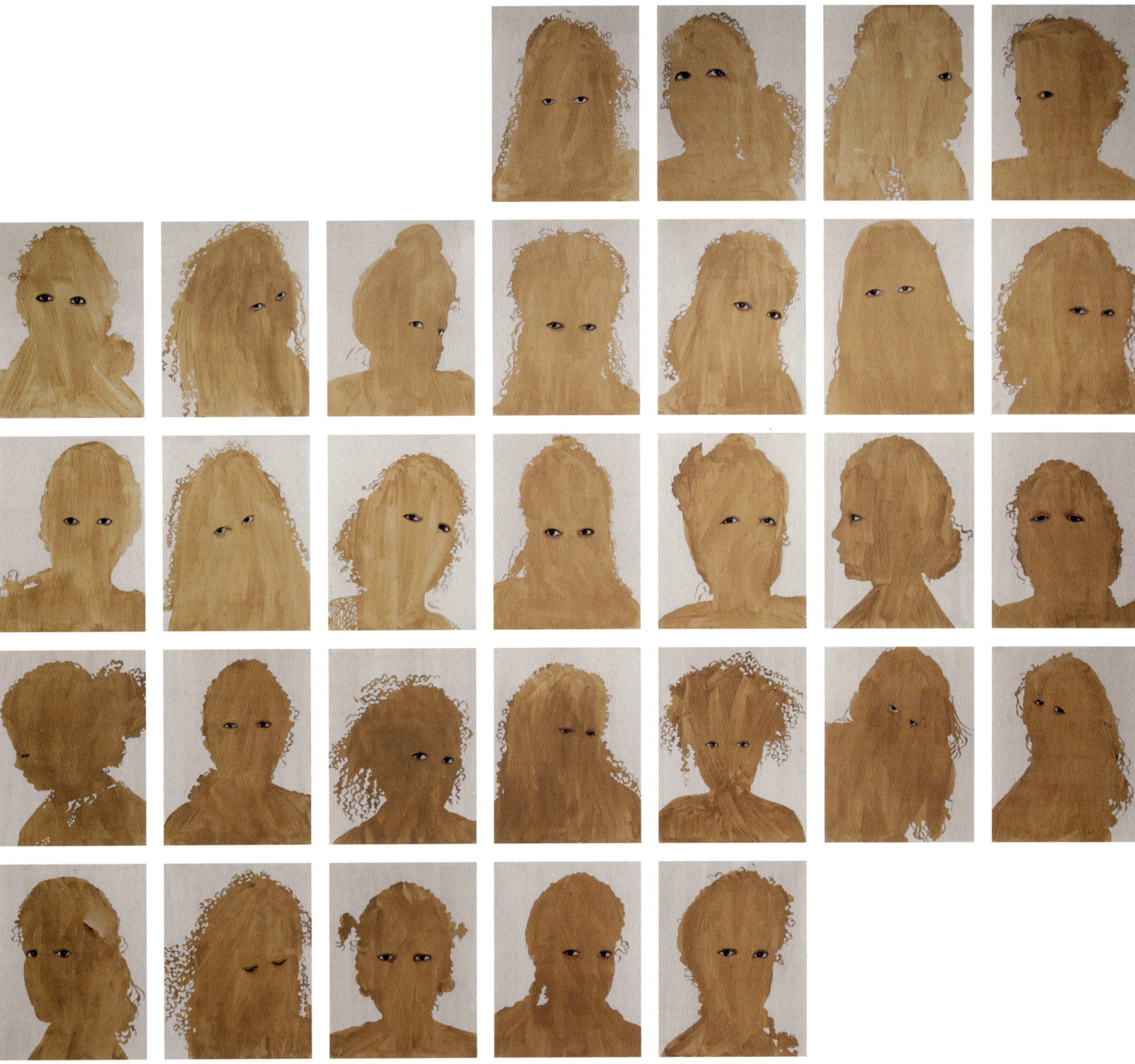

264

264 Firelei Báez. *Can I Pass? Introducing the Paper Bag to the Fan Test for the Month of June.* 2011. Gouache, ink, and graphite on paper. Pleasanton, CA, Collection of Tad Freese.

which was declared a World Heritage Site by UNESCO in 2017.[62] The contemporary reverberations of Valongo are at the center of an important exhibit, *Do Valongo à favela: Imaginário e periferia* (*From Valongo to favela: Imaginary and Periphery*, 2014) that connects the slave wharf with the history of exclusion and urban poverty so central to the lives of many Afro-Brazilians.[63]

Some artists use their work to confront, deconstruct, and highlight the persistence of racist stereotypes that continue to sustain exclusionary and discriminatory practices in Latin America. Neves's *Boa aparência* (*Good Appearance*, 2005) series, for example, refers to the widespread practice of using aesthetic racialized qualifiers to exclude people of African descent from different occupations.[64] References to "*buena presencia*" or "*buena apariencia*" appear in numerous job advertisements across the region, from Peru to the Dominican Republic and Cuba.[65]

Evaluations of beauty are typically linked to gendered phenotypical features such as skin color and "hair quality," a theme broached by the Dominican painter Firelei Báez (b. 1981) in her installation *Can I Pass? Introducing the Paper Bag to the Fan Test for the Month of June* (2011) and by many others.[66] Visual artists have also explored how Black gendered subjects are constructed through stereotypes concerning Black masculinity (René Peña [b. 1957]) and interracial sex; for example, Armando Mariño (b. 1968) in his *Gozando de la libertad* (*Enjoying Freedom*, 2002). Others, such as the multimedia artists Rosana Paulino (b. 1967) from Brazil and María Magdalena Campos-Pons (b. 1959) from Cuba, explore the female body as a site for memories of enslavement and violence, "a connective, redemptive component linking present and past, personal and collective experiences."[67] Artists have also denounced how the female Black body is deployed to feed the racialized fantasies that sustain the tourist industry in the Caribbean and other areas with large Afrodescendant populations, a revolving cycle of violence that transforms Black women into exotic objects of sexual desire, as illustrated in the work of Elio Rodríguez Valdés.

In order to denounce racism and exclusion, numerous artists offer a critical reexamination of national histories and the inability of people of African descent to write their own histories. They denounce the invisibility of Afrodescendants in national tales, with the consequent whitening of national histories. That is why in 2011, to celebrate the bicentennial of independence in Cartagena, a performance by the Afro-Colombian artist Nelson Fory (b. 1986) invited citizens to reflect on the erasure of popular actors in the making of the nation by placing Afro wigs on monuments dedicated to white patriots. "My art is strictly political," Fory noted. "We are represented in statues. They are all white criollo colonizers."[68] Alexis Esquivel makes a similar argument in many of his works. His *Picnic nacional* (*National Picnic*, 1996), for instance, is populated by a group of white patriots—all easily identifiable by Cubans. The only Black person invited, Juan Gualberto Gómez, is stopped by the police and presumably asked to furnish identity papers. In Nicaragua, the Afro-Nicaraguan self-taught feminist artist and poet June Beer (1933–1986) engaged in a similar project of historical rewriting and reconstruction by transforming the country's most important hero, Augusto César Sandino, into a *Black Sandino* (1983), a move that sought to place "the black and indigenous peoples of the Caribbean Coast at the center of [a] revolutionary project" that otherwise marginalized Blackness.[69]

A different kind of historical critique is offered by artists who

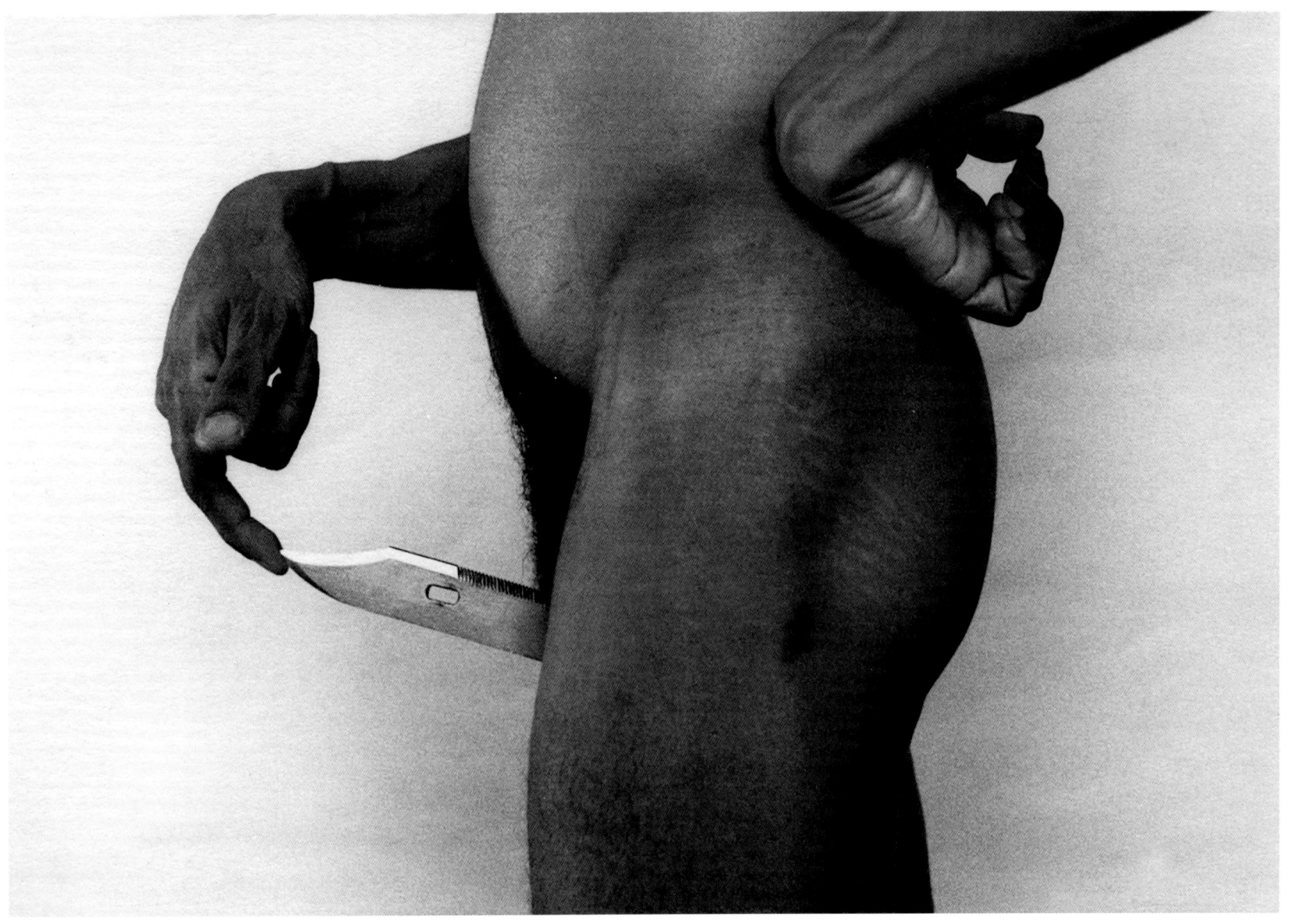

265 René Peña. *Untitled*. 1994. Gelatin silver print. Boston, Collection of Alejandro de la Fuente and Patricia González.

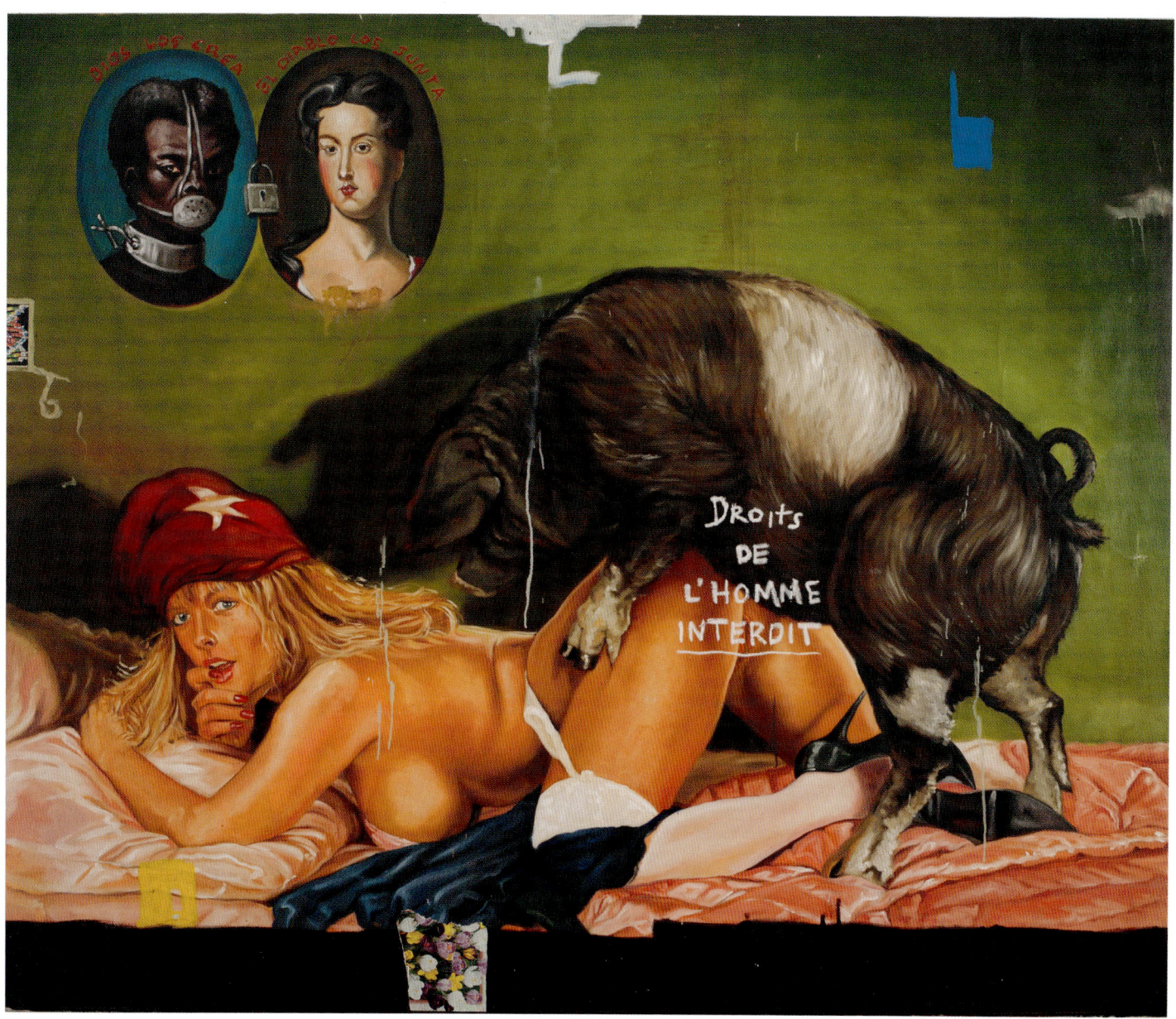

266 Armando Mariño. *Enjoying Freedom*. 2002. Oil on canvas. Boston, Collection of Alejandro de la Fuente and Patricia González.

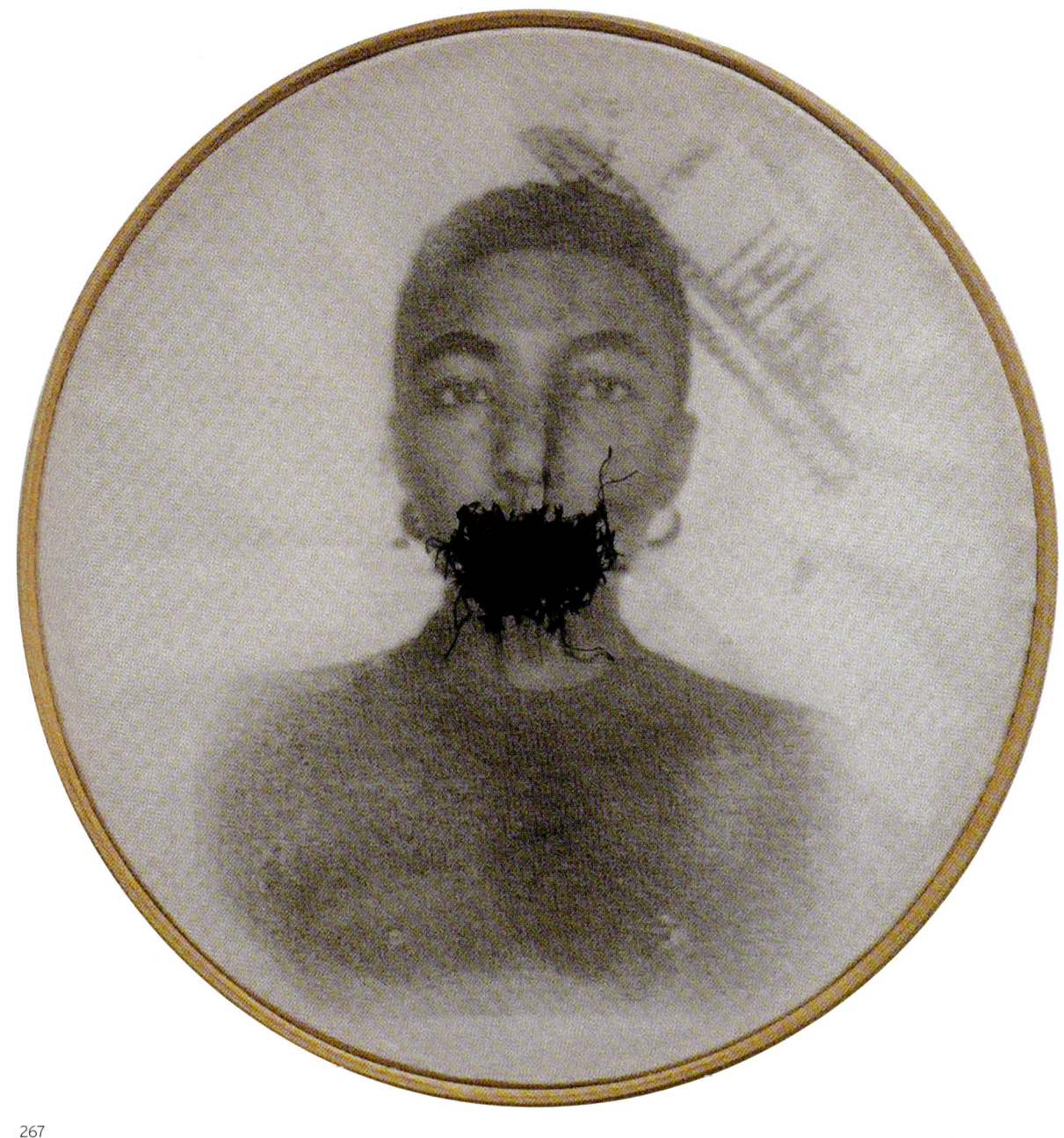

267

267 Rosana Paulino. From the series *Embroidery Hoops*. 1997. Mixed media: photographic image transferred to fabric, mounted on embroidery hoop.

268 María Magdalena Campos-Pons. *Untitled*. From the series *When I Am Not Here/Estoy Allá*. 1994. Photograph. Boston, Collection of Alejandro de la Fuente and Patricia González.

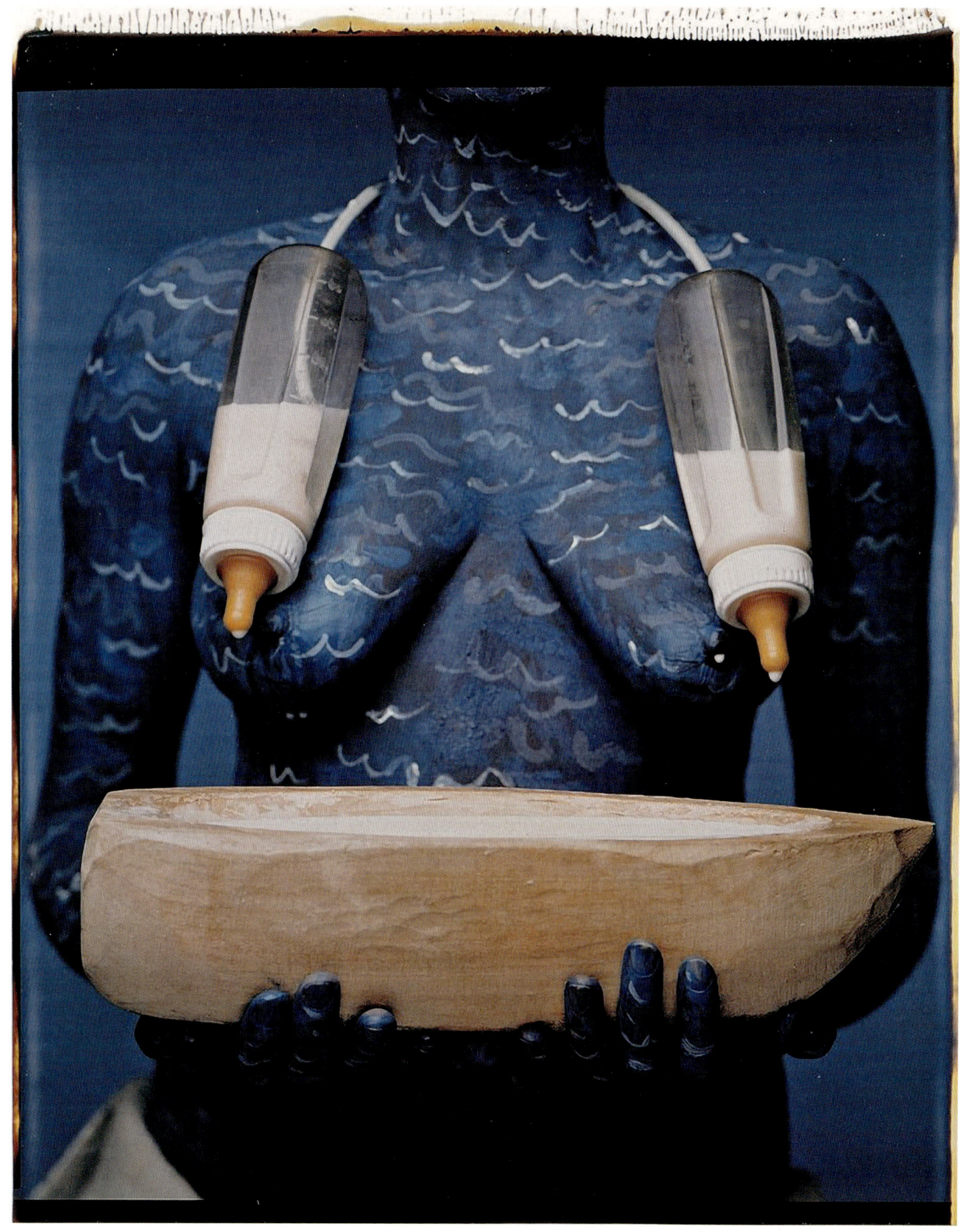

268

451

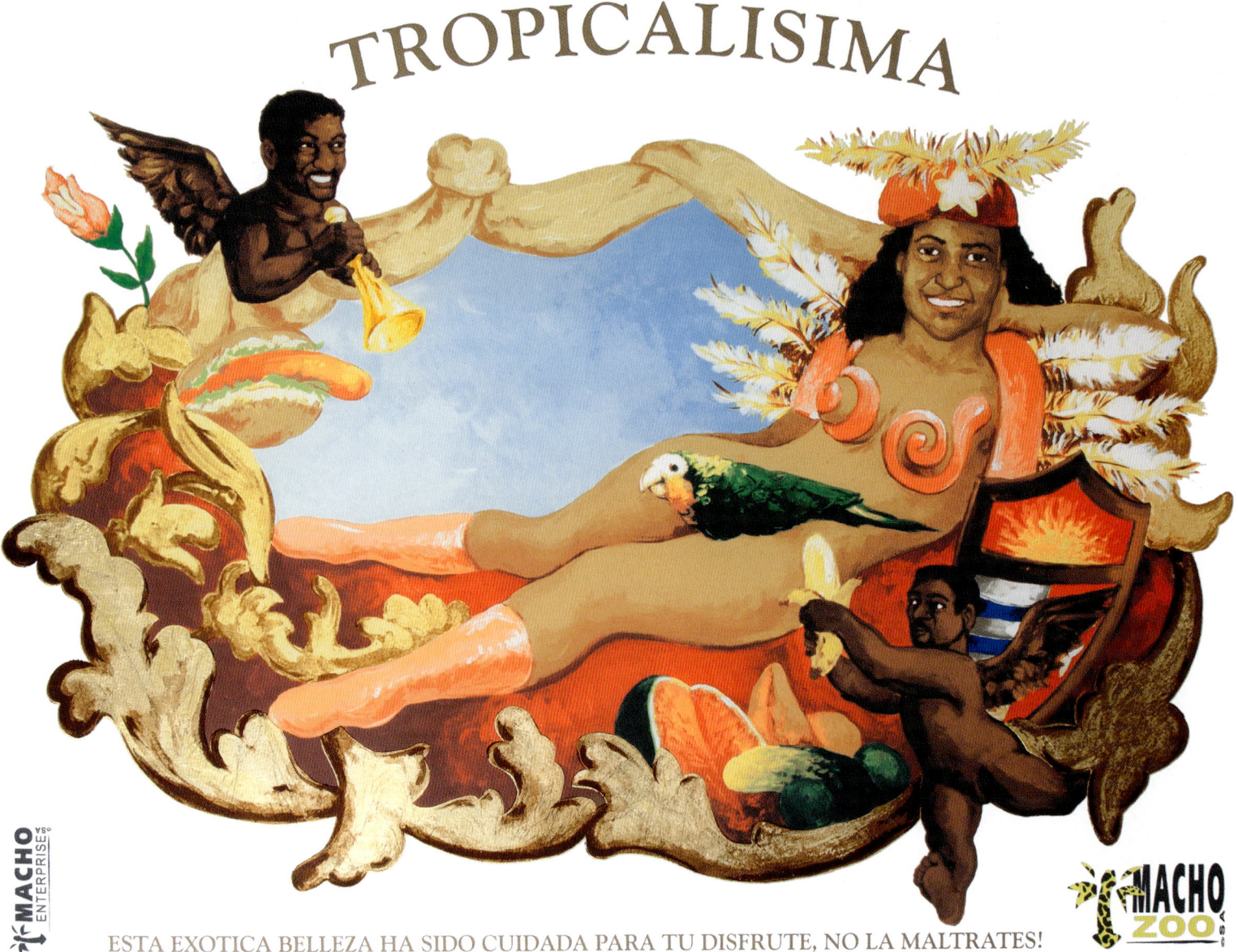

269 Elio Rodríguez Valdés. *Very Tropical*. 2007. Silkscreen illuminated on paper.

270 Nelson Fory. From the series *Our History, Sir!* 2011. Photograph.

make use of well-known traditional images and visual idioms to suggest the permanence—or the permanent relevance—of the past. They collapse time to propose new historical narratives built on continuities, in which the present is past. Rosana Paulino achieves this by reclaiming and intervening in racist anthropological photographs, such as those commissioned by the scientist Louis Agassiz, who visited Brazil in the 1860s. Elio Rodríguez does it by appropriating the traditional design of tobacco *marquillas*, which were frequently used in the nineteenth century to construct disparaging and highly sexualized images of Afro-Cubans.⁷⁰ Another artist who participated in the *Queloides* project, Douglas Pérez, achieves the same end by making use of nineteenth-century *costumbrista* visual cues.

Collectively, the work of these militant artists and of the curatorial projects mentioned before have achieved at least two important goals. First, they have created opportunities for artists interested in issues of race and identity, including a growing group of Afrodescendant artists, to share and disseminate their work in Latin America and beyond. Notably, this includes the work of a small but growing number of female Afrodescendant artists, who have traditionally been grossly underrepresented in the region's art scene. Second, the artists participating in these exhibits have articulated potent critiques of Latin American societies and contributed to making racism and discrimination socially visible. Their work can be located in, and understood as, contributions to current debates concerning race, gender, and justice in the region. In a sense, the dream of the Afro-Colombian writer and activist Manuel Zapata Olivella, the organizer of the Primer Congreso de las Cultura Negra de las Américas, has been realized: art did become, as he had hoped, a tool for Black liberation.

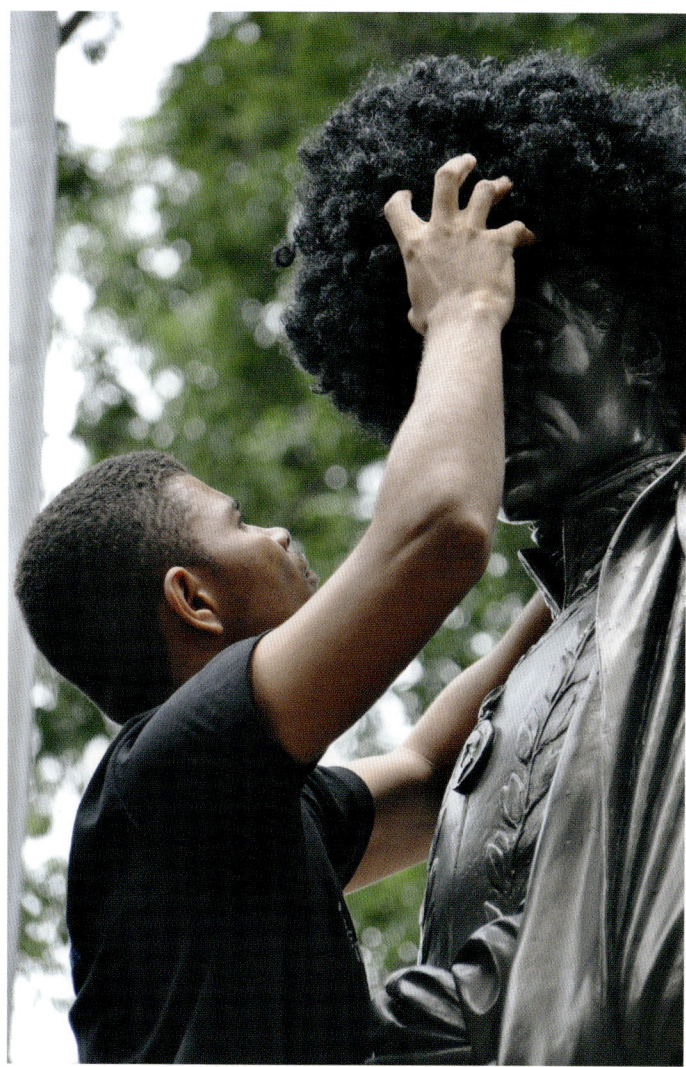

270

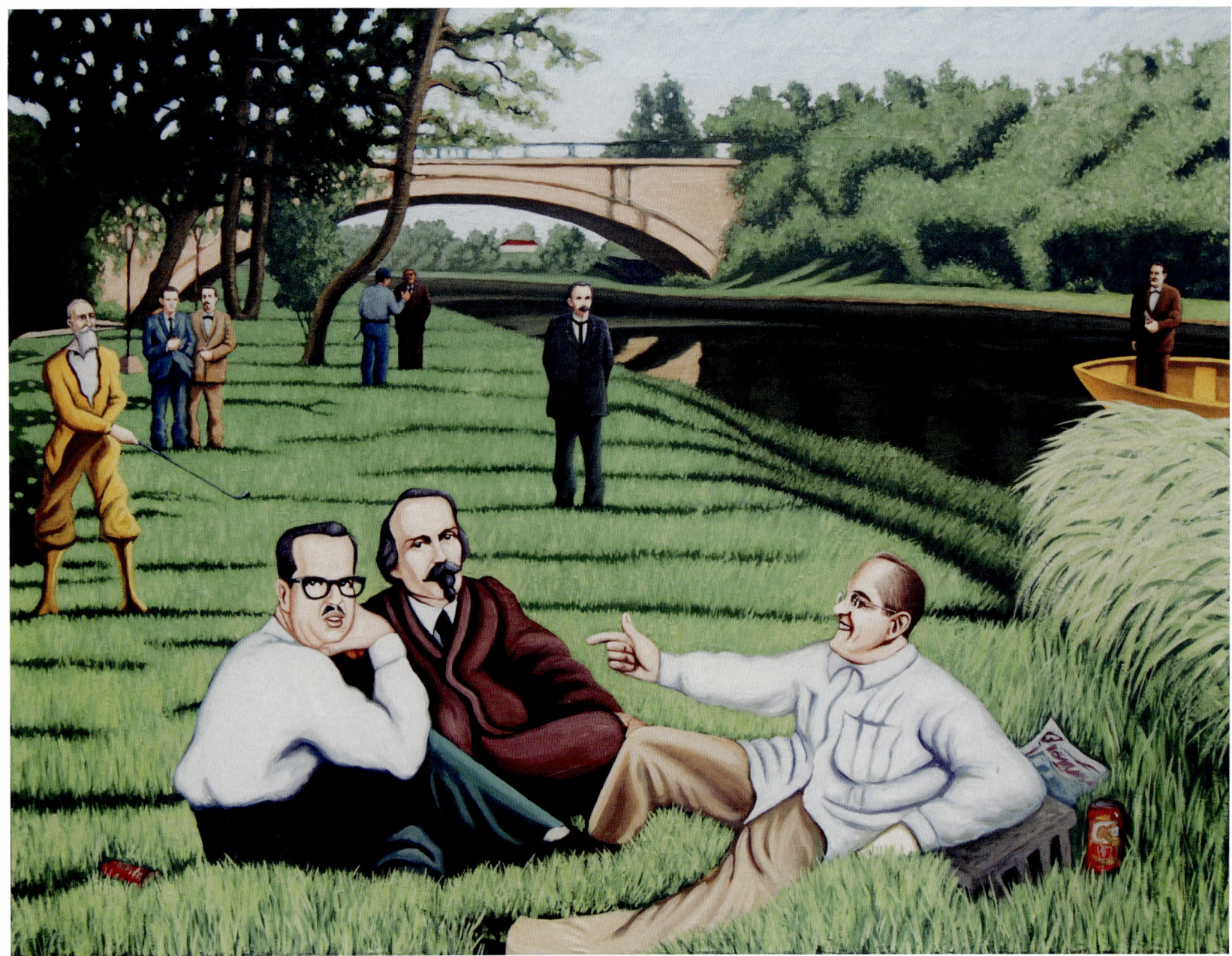

271

271 Alexis Esquivel. *National Picnic*. 1996. Oil on canvas. Boston, Collection of Alejandro de la Fuente and Patricia González.

272 June Beer. *Black Sandino*. 1983. Oil on canvas. Private collection.

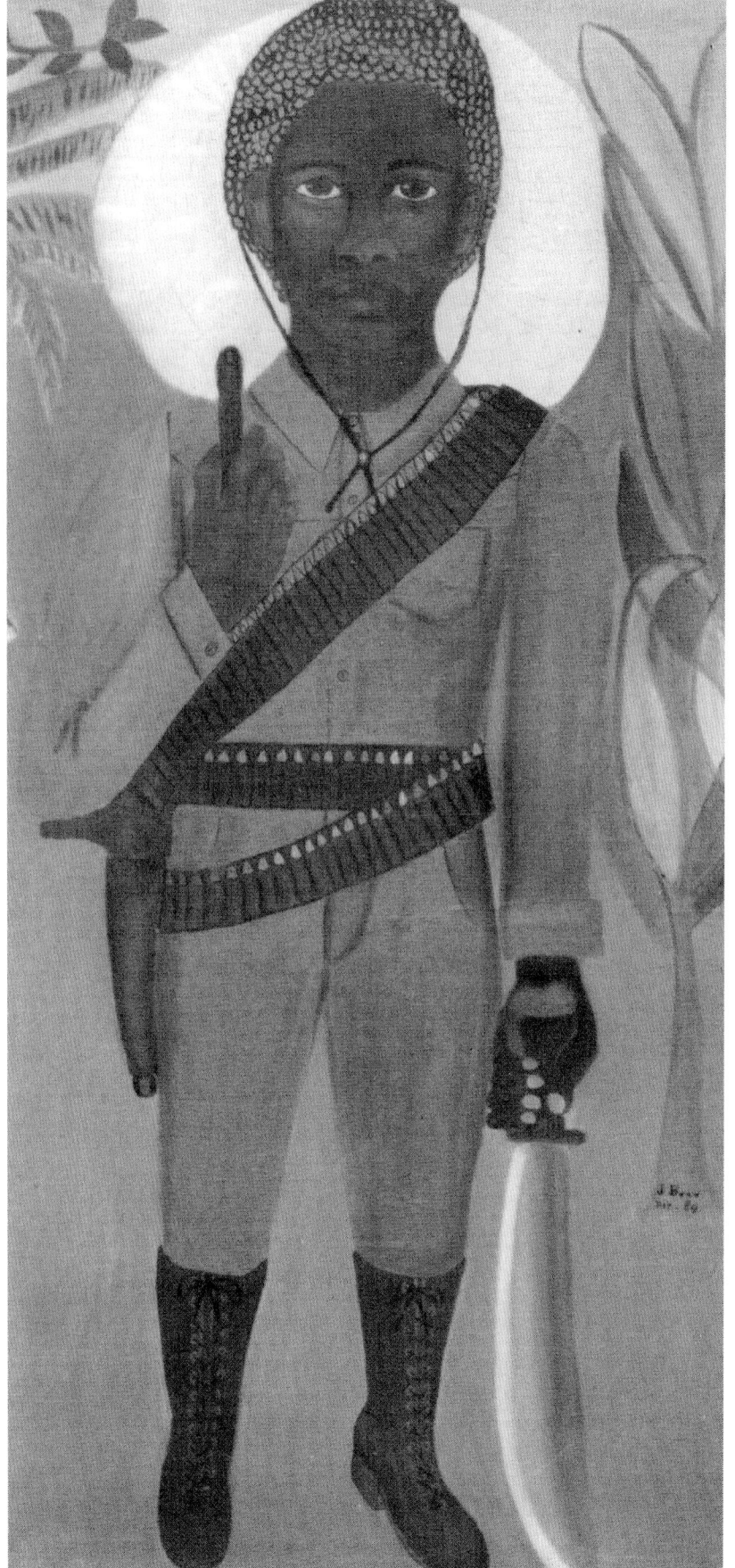

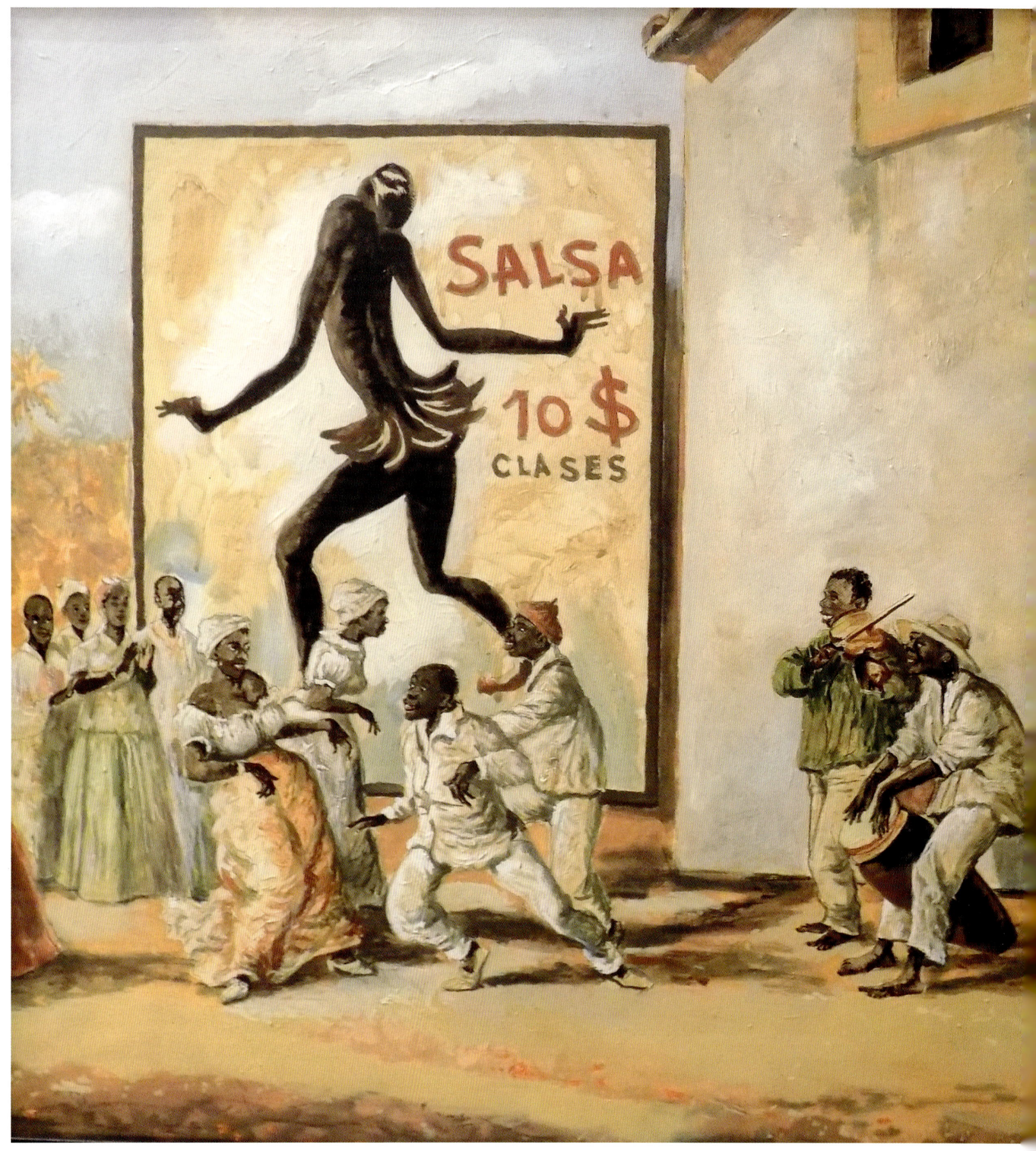

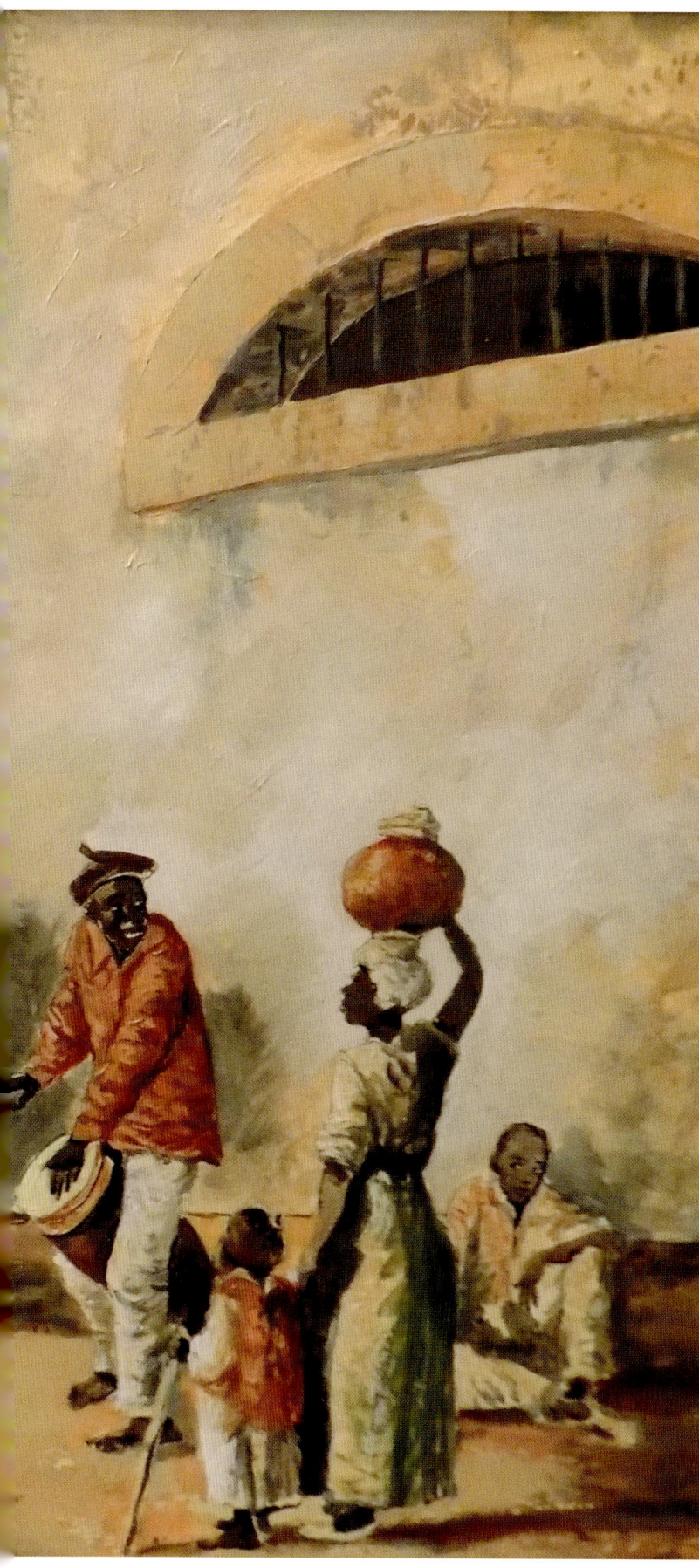

273 Douglas Pérez. *The Academy*. 2016. Oil on canvas. Boston, Collection of Alejandro de la Fuente and Patricia González.

15

SURFACE VIEWING: ON BLACKNESS, SKIN, AND PHOTOGRAPHY IN CONTEMPORARY JAMAICAN ART

KRISTA THOMPSON[1]

In September 2017, just as Apple released its new iPhone, an image circulated on social media spoofing the use of facial recognition to unlock the device. Apple's Face ID, the meme insinuated, was not available in Jamaica. Two photographs of the Jamaican dancehall musical artist Vybz Kartel appeared as visual explanation for the iPhone's inability to function in "the region." The photographs, presented side by side, taken years apart, highlighted the transformations in the appearance of Kartel's face, neck, and hair. In the first image, a dark-skinned man with short, freshly barbered hair appears in dark shades, wearing a patterned shirt. In the second, more recent image, in "before and after" time-lapse fashion, Kartel's skin is considerably lighter, or "brighter." Braided black locks frame his face. His skin appears to be patterned with tattoos on his neck and face. The lighter color of Kartel's face was the result of skin bleaching, a process—as I will detail—of visually manipulating the surface of the skin. In publicly endorsing and defending skin bleaching, Kartel proclaimed that his skin represented a "colouring book."[2] The digital images of the musician, with a kind of mocking humor, suggested that because of such dramatic facial transformations in Jamaica, epitomized by but not limited to Kartel, the technologies of facial recognition that rely on certain consistencies of appearance of the face would not be available on the island.

This essay explores understandings of Blackness as readable or unreadable on the surface of the body, which have been popularized in part in dancehall culture in contemporary Jamaican society and have informed contemporary art on and beyond the island. Although presented in jest by the creator of the meme, the Kartel photograph comparison implies that, through skin bleaching and other forms of bodily modification, notions of race and Blackness as legible on the body were seen as changeable and unstable. The suggestion, too, that facial recognition technologies would not function in Jamaica also underscores how visual technologies like photography, which have been so central to illustrating and perpetuating notions of race in different geographic locations since the 1840s, are reconfigured in the popular imagination on the island.[3] I make the case that the idea of Blackness has been reimagined in contemporary Jamaican society and contemporary art by playing with the surface of the body and the surface of the photograph. Indeed, I maintain that in contemporary dancehall culture, the skin is manipulated *as* a photographic surface.

Further, I take up Kartel's provocative suggestion that his body was a "colouring book," his assertion that the surface of his

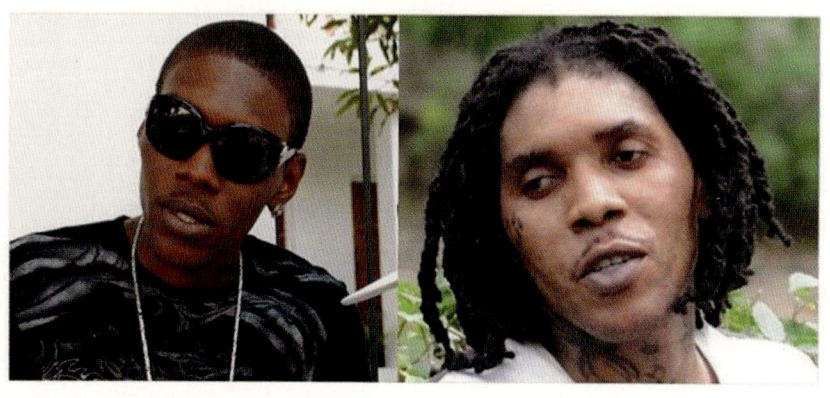

274

body constituted art, a place for visual production, imagination, and creation. The term *colouring book* also suggests a pedagogic function of skin, how skin color in Jamaica could delineate or prescribe a set of social boundaries in which people were expected to operate. Kartel's own skin bleaching specifically and expressive practices in dancehall more broadly have informed the artistic concerns and media choices of a number of contemporary artists who precisely engage and extend the idea of the surface of the body as a site of photographic, artistic, and social reinvention. I examine the work of artists who, as the art critic Annie Paul points out, are part of a new generation of artists from the island who have embraced popular cultural forms in their studio practice in the twenty-first century: Camille Chedda, Andrea Chung, Leasho Johnson, Ebony G. Patterson, Oneika Russell, and Paul Anthony Smith.[4] I also consider how an attention to the surface of the photograph and the body informs an understanding of history and its relationship to photography in Jamaica.

I focus on Jamaica and on photography because I want to be precise about media, place, and time in my consideration of "the image of the Black," to cite the title of this book series. I understand race, as Barnor Hesse characterizes it, as "an inherited western, modern-colonial practice of violence, assemblage, superordination, exploitation and segregation. Race is constitutively and unequally relational, regulatory and governmental, demarcating the colonial rule of Europe over non-Europe."[5] Following in the work of scholars who want to understand not simply that race is socially constructed, I am interested in "what is socially constructed as race."[6] I see race as a technology. To draw on the work of Wendy Hui Kyong Chun, race may be conceived as a technology because it is "a carefully crafted, historically inflected system of tools, mediation or enframing" that gives race its "social materiality" and social life.[7] I am also attentive to how the technology of race employs other technologies, like photography, to map "the colonial constituted practice of race," aimed at reproducing "social inequalities of domination and subordination, superiority and inferiority," onto human bodies.[8] In Jamaica, I demonstrate, the technologies of photography gave the technology of race its social materiality, both reproducing ideals of Black Jamaican subjects in photographs and modeling an understanding of race as legible on the surface of bodies of people of African descent. The artists I consider respond to, highlight, or refuse the intertwined ways the surface of the Black body and photography have been used as technologies of race on the island.

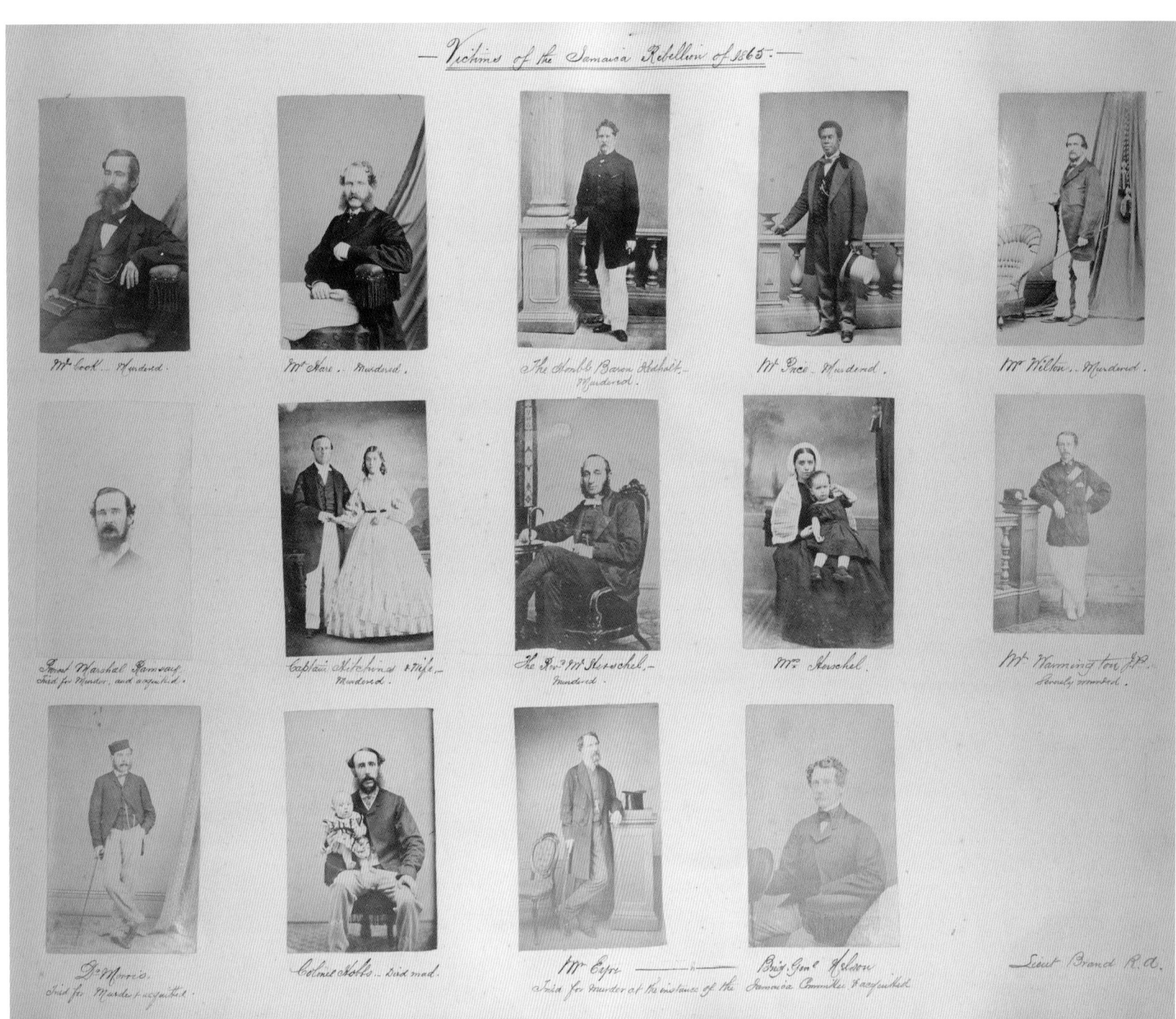

274 Image of Vybz Kartel that circulated on social media, September 2017.

275 Alexander Dudgeon Gulland. *Victims of the Jamaica Rebellion of 1865*. 1865. Albumen photographs. Princeton, NJ, Princeton University Library.

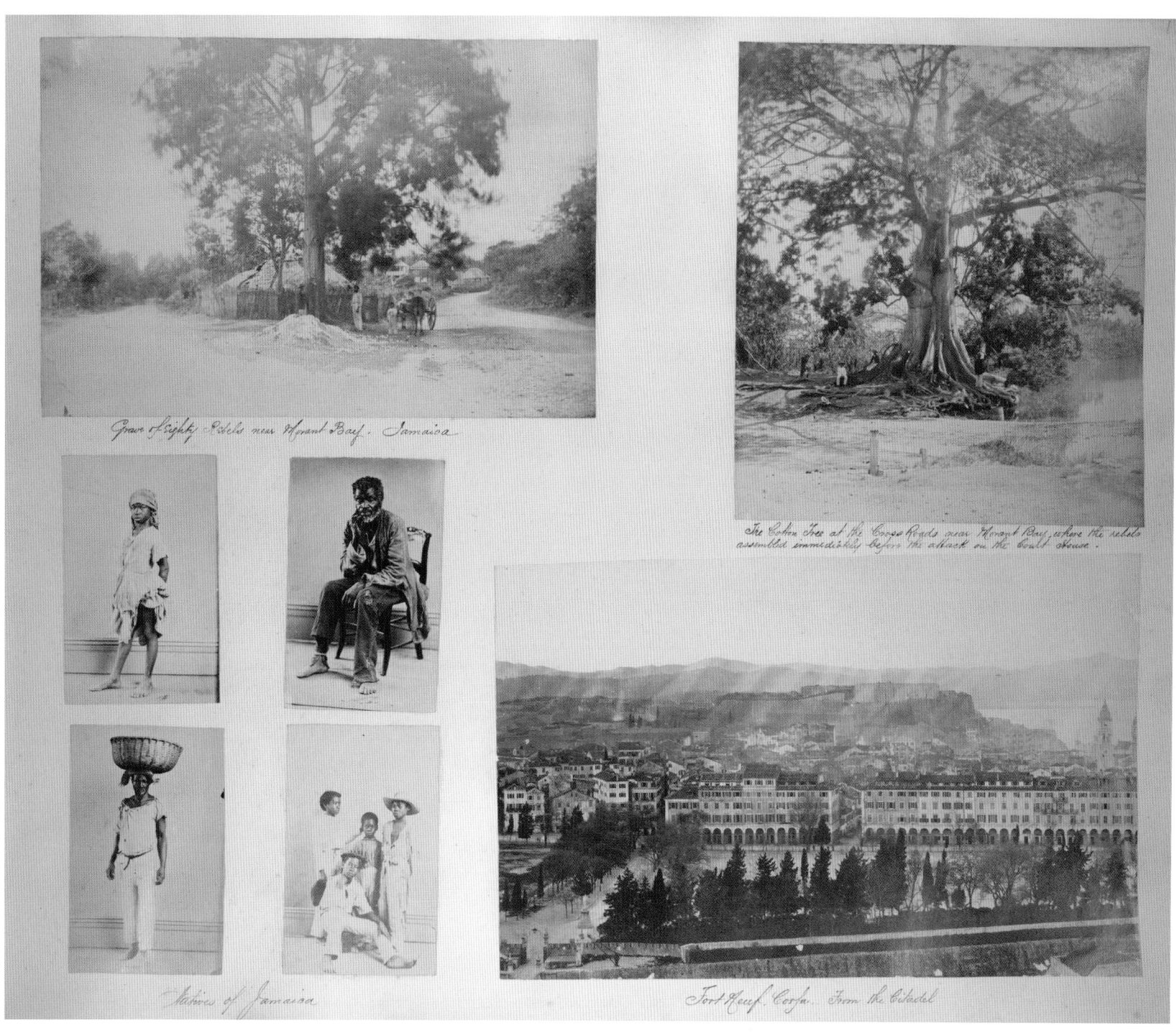

276 Alexander Dudgeon Gulland. *Natives of Jamaica*. 1865. Albumen photographs. Princeton, NJ, Princeton University Library.

277 Unidentified photographer. *Paul Bogle (often identified as)*. Undated. Tintype (reproduction). Kingston, National Library of Jamaica.

To understand the history of the images of Black Jamaicans as circulated through photography, a brief, necessarily surface history of photography on the island is useful. The medium was available in the British colony as early as 1841, soon after persons working on some of the earliest forms of photography made them available in a variety of locations, including England, France, and Brazil. A photographer named Adolphe Duperly opened the first daguerreotype studio in Kingston in 1841, just seven years after Emancipation.[9] Studio photographs from the mid-nineteenth century suggest that the studio portraits became popular in Jamaica among British colonial officials and locally born white and brown men—Christian and Jewish—in the British colony.[10] (In Jamaica, *brown* is a racial designation associated with the upper classes and with the light skin color of mixed-race Jamaicans. This group typically benefited socially and economically because of their appearance.) These photographs—many of which are cartes de visite and cabinet photographs—largely feature men displaying their status and authority through fine clothes, accoutrements, and accessories, such as top hats, canes, books, and umbrellas.[11] Many of these photographs locate their subjects in domestic spaces, foregrounded against props like architectural balustrades and curtains. Mimi Sheller argues that these recreated three-dimensional interior scenes highlight "the spatiality of citizenship"; that the photographic performance of Britishness needed to take place in a particular mise-en-scène.[12] On the rarer occasions when Black sitters appeared in studio photographs of the mid-nineteenth century, they were classed as "native types." They typically occupied shallow, nondescript studio settings barefoot and dressed in ways that emphasized their lack of social standing.

Given the relatively few photographs of Black subjects during the mid-nineteenth century, we might describe images of Black Jamaicans during the period as represented through their photographic absence. During that period in Jamaica, figures deemed significant to the island's Black population—from enslaved persons who lived just before the advent of photography to Black rebel leaders of the insurgency known as the Morant Bay Rebellion (1865)—were often not represented photographically. Their photographs could also be withdrawn from public view for decades or go missing from colonial criminal and national archives.[13] This occlusion was even more acute for Black women or non-cisgendered subjects. In this way, photography was long "unavailable in the region" for many Black Jamaicans outside the domain of "native types."

This history of photographic absence, to cite just one example, surrounded Paul Bogle, a key leader of the Morant Bay Rebellion. A reproduction of a tintype widely circulated as Bogle was revealed to the general public by his descendants in 1959, almost one hundred years after their ancestor's 1865 execution by the British colonial government. Unlike the contemporaneous white and brown subjects pictured in the cartes de visite, Bogle's physical appearance and photographic likeness were relatively unknown to the larger public during the time that he lived.

In the absence of a photograph, one of the most detailed and most cited newspaper descriptions of Bogle, aimed at the rebel's capture, lingered on Bogle's skin. It read: "Paul Bogle is a very black man, with shining skin, bearing heavy marks of smallpox on his face, and more especially on his nose; teeth good, large mouth with red, thick lips; about five feet eight inches in height, broad across the shoulders, carries himself indolently, and has no

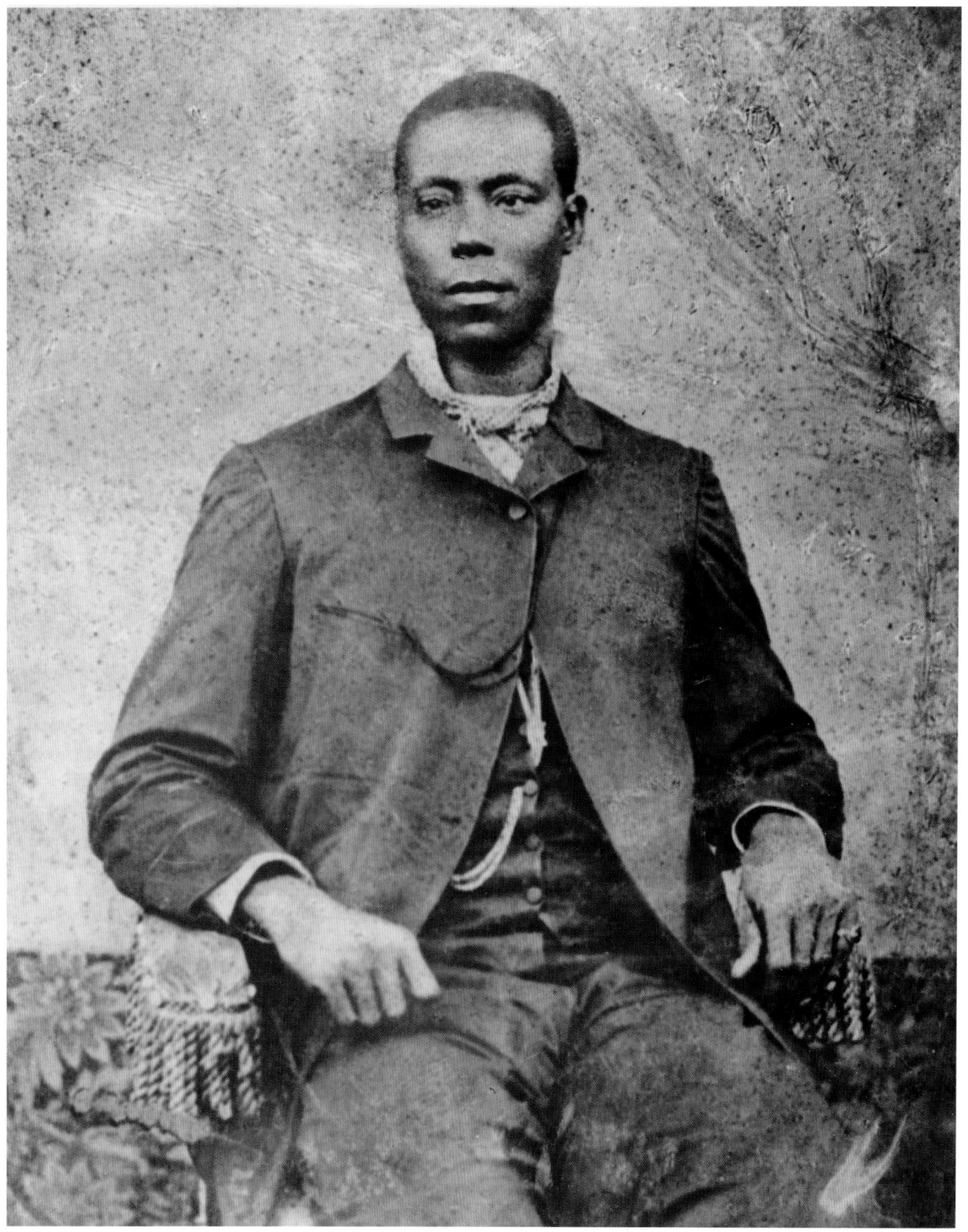

whiskers."[14] The characterization of Bogle focused on the surface of his skin, its shininess, its redness, its infliction with smallpox, and the visual excessiveness of Bogle's Blackness. If clothing, studio props, and settings marked men as having distinction and worth in the cartes de visite described above, Bogle's skin—the surface of his body—was cast as his defining trait. His skin functioned in this way like a studio photograph, a surface on which his character was purportedly graphed. Significantly, the face of the male figure in the photograph often identified as Bogle does bear marks across the surface of his face reminiscent of the heavy pox described in the newspaper account. The marks, which continue into the background of the photograph, were likely created by photochemical processes that transformed the entire surface of the photograph. The Bogle image is one explicit instance of the complicated ways in which the surface of Black bodies functioned as a technology of race, one that became intertwined materially with photography. In other words, the photograph of Bogle represented the surface of his Black body through the textured surface of the image, which was marked by its use and ongoing photochemical transformations.

In light of this outline of a longer colonial, and photographic, history in which Black skin was an index of a lack of character and social standing, I want to return to the issue of skin bleaching in contemporary dancehall, highlighted in the photographs of Kartel. The process of skin bleaching has a long and geographically disparate history. It can also be understood as a response to the technologies of race in Jamaica and many other former slave plantation societies, in which race was seen as legible on the body and used to bestow social privilege and class mobility on those deemed as having fairer skin.[15] Such social hierarchies based on skin color were reinforced and reproduced through photographic technologies.

Here I am interested in the practice of skin bleaching in contemporary Jamaican society specifically. In the late 1990s and again in 2007, skin bleaching was so widespread that the island's Ministry of Health initiated public health campaigns against the dangers of using skin-lightening chemicals on the body's surface, what they called "killing the skin."[16] People used a variety of chemicals, from manufactured products like Ambi, Nadinola, and Neoprosone to homemade recipes composed of toothpaste, bleach, cornmeal, curry powder, or milk powder, to semi-permanently transform the color of their skin, particularly their faces. Some people bleached in order to gain the social advantages associated with appearing less Black.[17]

The practice of skin bleaching was popularized in part in contemporary dancehall culture.[18] Dancehall, which encompasses music, dance, fashion, and visual technologies, first came to prominence in the early 1980s. The music and modes of self-fashioning enunciated the desires of a new Black modern subject, one that celebrated individualism, consumerism, and "slackness," an overt approach to sexuality that ignored middle-class rules of decorum.[19] In the 2000s, skin bleaching in dancehall gained renewed attention when a number of dancehall artists, most notably Vybz Kartel and Lisa Hype, publicly endorsed the practice. Hype even offered recipes of sorts for transforming the skin's surface in her song "Proud ah Mi Bleaching," and Kartel eventually marketed his own line of bleaching products. Kartel would maintain his skin was "pretty like a colouring book," drawing on art—in a widely accessible form, a coloring book—to underscore his right to re-color, reinvent, and reconfigure the surface of his body.[20] Like the outlines of a drawing in a coloring book, his skin invited inscription, play, and creativity. The artist credited skin bleaching for his heterosexual sex appeal at a time when critics took him to task for engaging in what had been associated with a female beauty rite.[21] Kartel's suggestion that bleaching enhanced his hypermasculinity in a dancehall culture which is simultaneously—as several scholars have argued—both staunchly homophobic and queer, highlights the gendered dimensions of skin bleaching.[22] Because of the ways in which it disrupts norms of race, gender, and class, as Winnifred Brown-Glaude argues, skin bleaching has been widely viewed in the local press as a social problem and framed within discourses of pathology and self-hate.[23]

Rather than aspiring to whiteness as an ideal or representing a social malady, I want to highlight a point that Brown-Glaude and Natasha Barnes have made: skin bleachers may be seen as claiming and reconfiguring ideals of race as legible on the body's surface, showing these ideals as changeable and manipulatable.[24] To quote Brown-Glaude, "bleachers betray or at least destabilize popular conceptions of blackness that rely on an understanding of the body as given, fixed, permanently and naturally marked by race."[25] In other words, race as technology that relies on reading the surface of the body as index is destabilized in the practice.

When skin bleachers use chemicals to change the surface of their skins, bleaching not only affects the physical appearance of the skin's color but makes the body into a medium that absorbs and reflects light.[26] Bleaching literally makes skin light-sensitive. In this process, skin becomes sensitized in the same way that paper is sensitized to produce a photographic print. In effect, people who bleach their skin make the surface of their bodies into a form of corporeal photograph. As such, skin bleaching may be interpreted as a photographic technology that is both part of and against the complex histories and technologies throughout which race has been constituted through the bodily and photographic surfaces.

This overview provides some background against which the work of Chedda, Chung, Johnson, Patterson, Russell, and Smith may be considered. They make the body's surface and photographic surfaces intrinsic parts of the form, content, and production of their work. In doing so, they encourage a type of surface viewing, an attention to the materiality of the surface of the work which foregrounds the surface as a formative site of artistic and social meaning. Manipulating, effacing, tearing into, or overemphasizing the surface of the work (in ways that refuse a transparent seeing through the surface), they encourage an engagement with the intertwined histories of the surface of photography and ideals of race, gender, social status, history, and, to return to Sheller, the "spatialization of citizenship" on the island. Taking up Stephen Best and Sharon Marcus's characterization of surface reading, this type of viewing seeks less to reveal what's hidden or kept secret behind the surface than to "make visible what is invisible only because it's too much on the surface of things."[27] Surface viewing is taken up here not only as a process of visual engagement with the work and all too legible histories of race, but the artwork examined in the remainder of the essay necessitates prolonged engagements with the tools, media, and modes of surface viewing that contributed to formulations of race and antiblackness. In the spirit of surface viewing, I focus largely on one work by each artist and offer a critical description of the piece, foregrounding matters raised by the material surfaces of the work.[28]

278 Paul Anthony Smith. *Port Antonio Market #3*. 2013. Unique picotage on inkjet print with spray paint mounted on museum board. Private collection.

Paul Anthony Smith

The artist Paul Anthony Smith (b. 1988) quite literally materially pulls together the surface of the photograph and the surface of skin, as evident in a series of photographs that the artist took in Port Antonio, on the northeast coast of Jamaica, in 2013. Smith uses a process he describes as "picotage" to press into and pull at the surface of photographs using a tool more commonly used in ceramics. In many of his images, the surface of the figure, in particular their skin and clothing, are transformed through picotage. In Smith's photograph *Port Antonio Market #3* (2013), a male figure, centrally positioned in a blue and gray scene of a market, seems a granular shadow, an apparition, a specter that partly evades or refuses photographic capture. With the exception of the eyes and mouth (abbreviated, as in a child's drawing, to three cavernous black ovals), the figure's clothing and skin are represented through black and white marks that follow their own patterns across the surface of the image. A closer viewing of the surface of the work reveals that the marks, produced through picotage, form a kind of braille across the image across the photograph's surface. The result is a surface that "feels like Velcro, but much thicker and rough," because, as the artist explains, "I'm digging into the photographs, and they are sharp on the ends."[29] Small punctures, where the photographic paper has been turned outside in, give the figure its rough form and shadowy, shallow pictorial depth.

The figure in *Port Antonio Market #3* foregrounds the way that people identified as Black were too often subsumed, overdetermined, or not seen because of the technologies of race. The sharp, open edges of picotage visually disrupt the ways that Black skin, dress, and the surface of the photograph might be understood to turn, to index, the subject pointed to in its surface. In the context of Jamaica, the sites of racial fixing in and beyond the island are evacuated of color and stable surface in the work. The surface of the body and photograph are conjoined and ruptured, pulled together and apart through Smith's tool. The image brings into relief the mutual constitutiveness of these bodily and photographic surfaces. The work makes material the entanglement of the photographic and racialized surfaces.

The source for *Port Antonio Market #3* is an enlargement of a photograph that Smith took in Port Antonio with a disposable digital camera during a visit to his hometown. Many of the subjects of his photographs were people he knew or with whom he had a history.[30] Among some of the familiar faces that Smith would see when he returned to Jamaica, he would observe people whose bodies had been transformed by skin bleaching. He noted how the area around the eyes and mouth became the most obvious parts of the face where bleaching was discernible.[31] The darkness around their eyes created the appearance of a mask. More broadly, Smith was interested in the transformation of skin through scarring or body modification to mark a coming of age across cultures, with ceremonial rituals of the Kuba people of Central Africa being one example and the mask designs and patterns on Songye/Kifwebe masks being another. Smith was attentive to how these markings often denoted a central transition point in social rites of passage by rendering the new social status on the bodies' surface.

Returning to the strident figure in Smith's *Port Antonio Market #3*, the representation of clothing or photography studio accessories are also subsumed in the picotage of Smith's figure, which denies a parsing out of clothing or other props that might

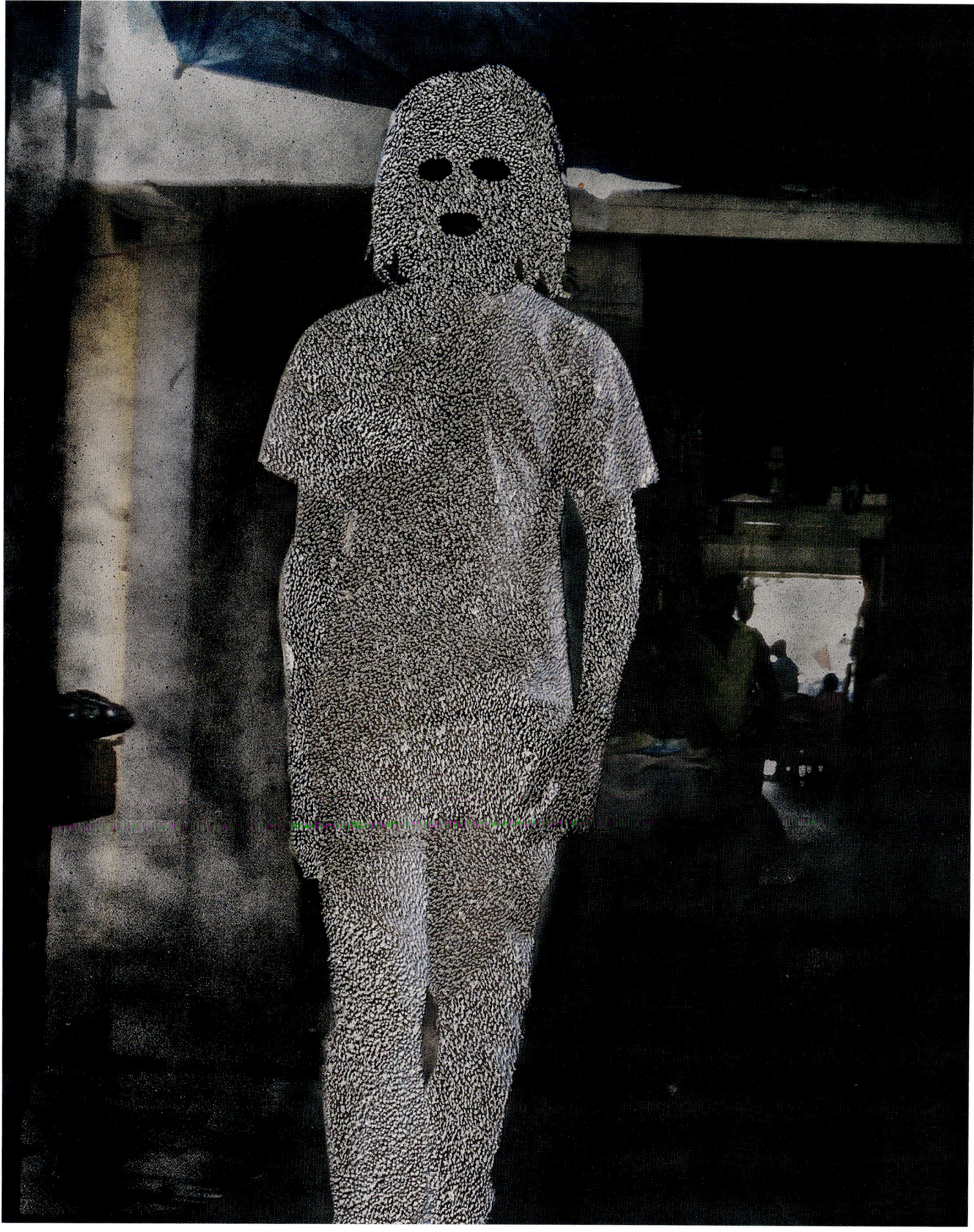

279 Ebony Patterson. *Untitled Lightz 1*. 2013. Mixed media on paper. Kansas City, MO, Collection of Bill and Christy Gautreaux.

index social distinction. The textured marks across the body also disrupt the very representation of space in the photograph. The figure appears to exceed the spatial confines of the photograph but seems to be on the verge of disintegrating, resettling, returning to the surface of the image. It occupies a plane beyond the material confines of the photograph, beyond the pictured space of the photograph. The form's separation from the background or spatial ambiguity may be contrasted with the way that the white and brown (and rarely Black) sitters in nineteenth-century cartes de visite utilized the space of the studio as a ground to indicate their social standing, racial distinction, and spatialized citizenship. Conversely, space was denied to Black subjects in "native photographs" or in the purported photograph of Bogle, in which the figure of the man and the studio background collapse. Smith's photographic space might create, might set the image of the Black Jamaican in another space of representational formation and possibility.

Port Antonio Market #3 may be considered within a longer photographic history in Jamaica, precisely because it pictures a town that was one of the first places marketed in the island's photographic campaigns in the late nineteenth century. The artist scanned and enlarged his own 4×6 inch prints of Port Antonio and manipulated the images, causing them to appear older, "from 40 years ago, just by the different processes of using technology."[32] His contemporary series of photographs made to look older raises questions about the relationship between his pictured subjects and historical representations of the island. His technique of working in picotage, too, calls attention to absences in the photographic record, as the punctures in the work literally constitute and visualize absences. What histories are accessible or vacated through historical photographs of Jamaica? Smith's work might be seen as countering trypophobia, an aversion to the sight of irregular patterns, small holes, or bumps. The sharp edges of picotage encourage one to look at these holes, to linger on the form and meaning of photographic absences. The work might also foreground different types of sight needed to bring Black subjects and histories into view.

Ebony G. Patterson

The artist Ebony G. Patterson (b. 1981) also highlights points of intersection between the surface of the body and photography in contemporary Jamaican society, particularly in dancehall culture. *Untitled Lightz I* (2013) is one example of how the artist has used collage and the embellished, eye-catching surface of her work to draw on and highlight the bodily and sartorial surfaces that are so intrinsic in visual and aesthetic practices of dancehall and understandings of the location of race, class, and gender in Jamaican society more generally. In the larger-than-life 81 × 148 inches multimedia work on paper, ten figures (or it is their shadows?) appear, with an emphasis on the skin of their faces and on the vibrant colors and patterns of their clothing. Some recall silhouettes, seemingly weightless cutouts, delineated by a single piece of floral-patterned cloth laid on the surface of the work. Toward the foreground of the image, four of the figures are more visually defined in sartorial splendor, constituted through contrasting patterns and textures. The use of white and black paint to render their skin makes them stand out in the colorful work. Unlike the vibrant colors that visually saturate the piece, their faces, sculpted in white paint, are devoid of color. The faces are more three-dimensional in form than any other part of the work. Staring out at

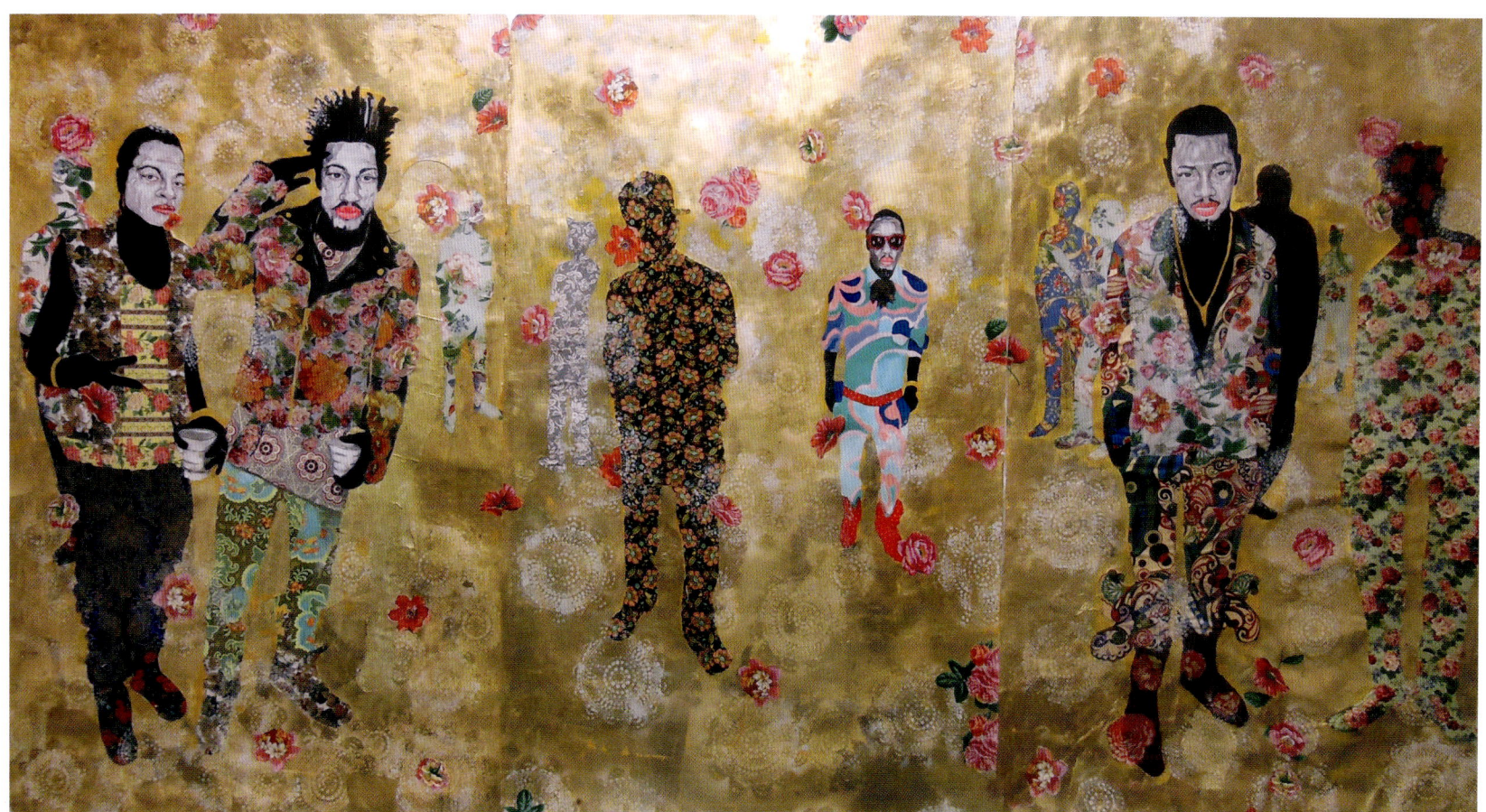

279

the viewer, with pronounced pink and red lips, their visages seem both caught in harsh lights and the sources of illumination in the piece. In stark contrast, their bodies are Kerry James Marshall Black. The surfaces of their skins appear as voids in the work. The figures look out beyond the picture plane, seeming to anticipate the gaze of the viewer, assuming poses, gesturing, waiting.

The surfaces of the work are further highlighted through the representation and production of light in the piece. The figures inhabit an ambiguous gold ground. Space is defined through or is ambiguously defined by light, by white light, yellow light, golden light, both shimmering and matte, and by decorative white imprints across the surface of the work that seem to reflect, to represent, light's effects. Depth and three-dimensional space are suggested only by the size of figures that appear to recede in the center of the image dissolving into the background of the image, and by the cascading flowers that suggest both gravity and lightness in the work.

Untitled Lightz I is part of a broader body of Patterson's work informed by dancehall culture. Since 2007, her work has been attentive to dancehall participants' use of certain aesthetic practices, from eye-catching fashions to skin bleaching, to change their surface appearance and social standing in the space of the dancehall.[33] The artist has been particularly interested in what she describes as the "metrosexual" dimensions of these practices, how these practices transform gendered expectations surrounding the performance of masculinity.[34] I cast a spotlight on *Untitled Lightz I* because the piece also engages a particular visual technology that is popular in dancehall, known locally as video light. The white faces of the figures in *Untitled Lightz I* do not only refer to the "colouring book" of bleached skin, but more specifically to the appearance of lightened skin as it meets the light from a video camera. In other words, the white faces call attention to the interface of technologies of photography and Black skin.

Video light refers to the use of a video camera, which is typically mounted by a very bright light and screens in the space of dancehall and the performative, representational, social, and

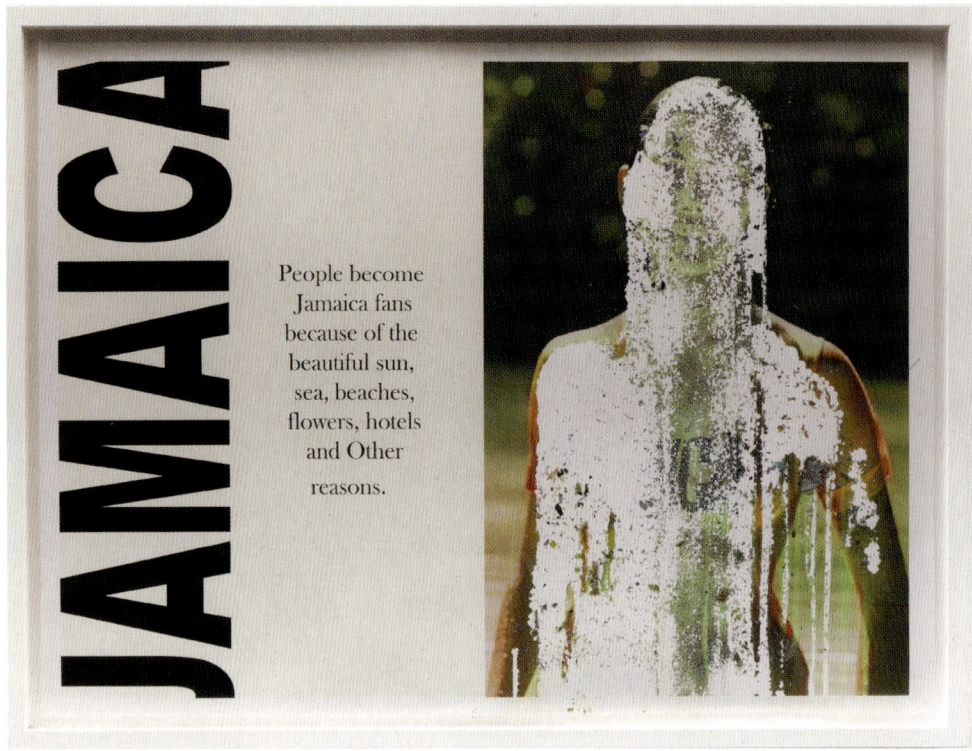

280

economic practices surrounding the light.³⁵ Videographers use the camera to scope around the dancehall venue spotlighting different attendees, often lingering on dancers or those dressed in a spectacular way, sometimes projecting the image of dancehall goers onto screens in the space or recording the proceedings for future audiences. More immediately and importantly, the camera's harsh white light bestows a certain social cache in the space of the dancehall. Dancehall participants will go to various lengths, often dancing or dressing in innovative or sexually provocative ways, to be in the video light. The recent rise in the practice of skin bleaching among women and men in Kingston's dancehalls is in part a response to the desire to be in video light. Some dancehall participants made their faces and other exposed parts of their bodies lighter in an effort to be more visible for the camera. They sought to make their skin more legible to videographic technologies long designed to focus on white skin. In *Untitled Lightz I*, the representation of bleached faces as sites of light and legibility, the depiction of Black skin on the body of the figures as representational absence, the focus on representing and using different materials to reflect light, and the interplay of visual excess and absence, all suggest an engagement with exploring the effects of videographic technologies on (primarily) Black male bodies in the space of dancehall.

Returning to the idea of spatial citizenship mentioned by Sheller, *Untitled Lightz I* presents figures in pictorial space reconfigured by the visual technologies of dancehalls and its surface aesthetics. Unlike the mid-nineteenth photographs in Jamaica in which clothing, accessories, and the studio setting were key to representing social standing in photographs, the work provocatively suggests how in contemporary dancehall the surface of the body itself is the site and space of representation and reimagined notions of social status and worth.

Andrea Chung

Andrea Chung (b. 1978) also explores the constitutive intersections of skin and photography in Jamaica through her artistic process, one that incorporates bleach as a part of the work. Chung's art engages another aspect of the history of photography in Jamaica, images that played a role in the island's tourism campaigns after its independence in 1962. In *Bleach* (2008), Chung transforms an iconic photographic image featured in a Jamaica Tourist Board ad from the 1970s. The work, measuring 25 × 34 ³⁄₁₆ inches, is composed of two halves. On the left side of the image, the word *JAMAICA* runs vertically, partly cut off at both ends, in a bold, uppercase font now synonymous with the country's tourism brand. On the right side of the work, the re-

280 Andrea Chung. *Bleach*. 2008. Bleached digital print. Collection of the artist.

mains of a photograph appear. The figure that once occupied the center of the photograph appears simultaneously dissolved and peeling off of the surface of the photograph. A granular, white and gray-black texture partly veils the form. At the edges of the photograph's eviscerated surface, the figure's prior photographic form is legible, haunting the image, refusing to be absented. The image appears to shift between presence and absence, between materially disappearing states. Only the background of the photograph, a landscape with gently rippling water, remains largely intact. The words, "People become Jamaica fans because of the beautiful sun, beaches, flowers, hotels and Other reasons," appear like a poem, occupying the space in between brand Jamaica and the near-absented female figure.

I will not reproduce the photograph from the Jamaican Tourist Board's poster from which Chung draws on the right side of her work. *Bleach* hints at the way that the photograph haunts an ideal of Jamaica since it was first circulated in 1972, whether or not it is physically reproduced. An American advertising agency hired by the Michael Manley government created the image, which the Jamaican *Gleaner* newspaper described "as the most powerful travel poster ever."[36] The photograph, taken in Port Antonio, circulated as a poster in six versions and as part of a television commercial. Notably, the photograph pictured an Indo-Trinidadian woman, Sintra Bronte, with light brown skin, as the touristic face of Jamaica. The firm originally intended to feature a Chinese Jamaican woman in an effort to market the island as an "exotic east" that was close to the United States. After two weeks of searching, "no such girl was found," the *Gleaner* reports.[37] Instead, the agency used Bronte, who was visiting Jamaica at the time, as "the Other" reason to visit Jamaica, presenting the woman and the landscape in explicitly sexualized and exoticized ways.

Chung took a glossy digital scan of the iconic photograph from a travel magazine and sprayed bleach on it. She saw bleach (the agent of contemporary skin bleaching) as a tool long used by Black laborers for the purposes of cleaning or laundering.[38] It is the bleach that turned the figure into its ghostly white form, making parts of the image dissolve and drip down the surface of the work. The figure's skin and clothing in particular—which formed an Other skin in the image—was chemically transformed by the bleach. It stripped the ink from parts of the image and eventually made the interior of the photograph come to the surface of the work, flaking up and peeling off. The woman's form became white in some areas, translucent in others. Chung's use of a chemical that also whitens foregrounds the ideals of race that seem to be at work in the 1970s campaign, one that privileged fair skin as representative of Jamaica. The image may have been intended to jettison how the island was racially imagined in the post-independence period. The near-phantom image arguably calls attention precisely to the bodies that are absented in the photographic choice, the Jamaican photographic subjects who could not be found. The image's blurred form is about what is not legible and the persons who could not come to photographic visibility.[39] The photograph thus represents a number of displacements: Jamaica for the "exotic east"; the erotic female body for the island; the Indo-Trinidadian for the Chinese Jamaican; and the light-skinned subject for Jamaica. Chung's artistic process brings to the surface the ongoing histories of violent whitewashings as the skin of the iconic figure and photograph's surface continue to chemically transform the work.

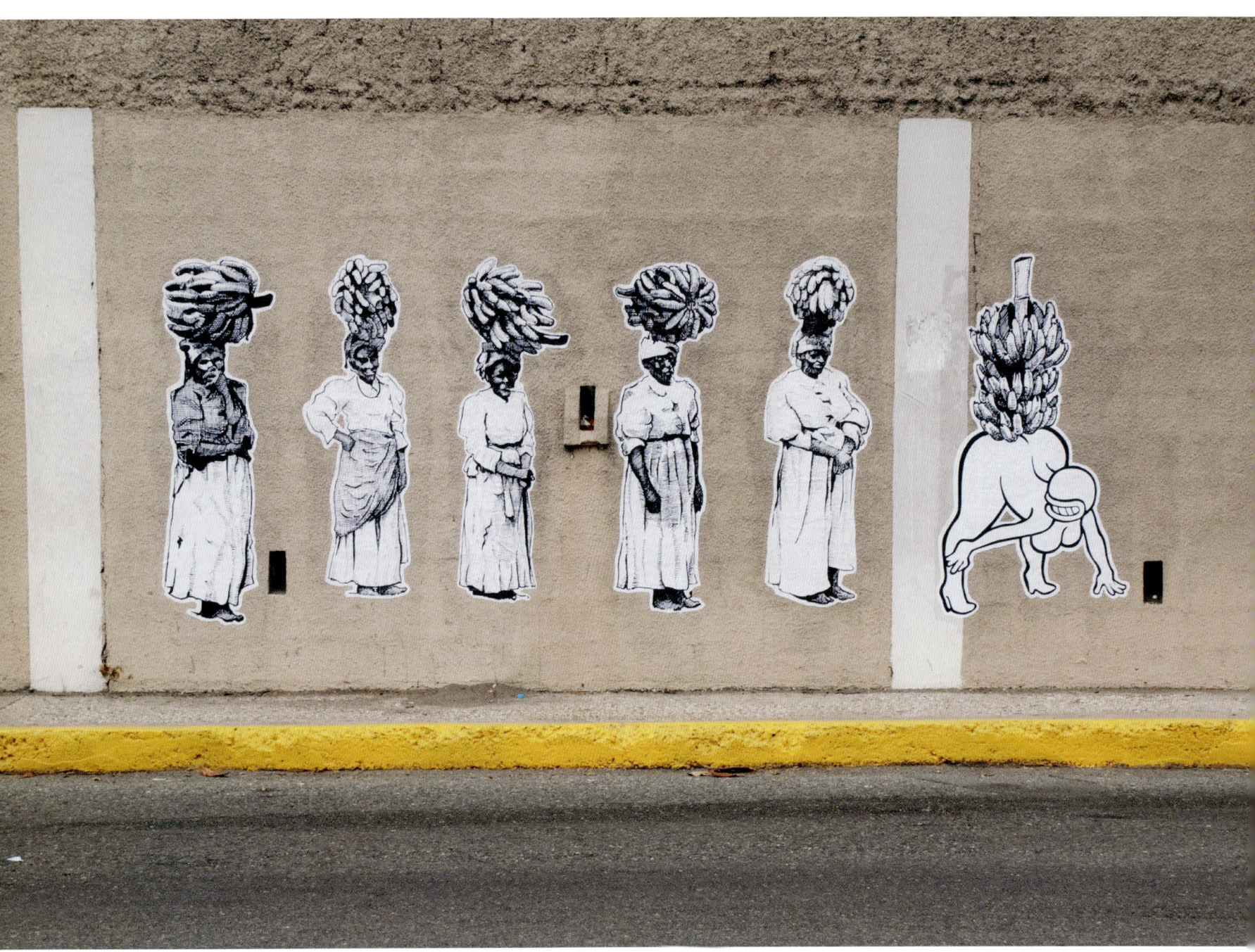

281 Leasho Johnson. *Back-fi-a-bend*. 2015. Paper and yeast paste on wall. Kingston, Jamaica.

Leasho Johnson

Leasho Johnson's (b. 1984) work engages the intersection of technologies of race and photography in the tourism industry and in the spaces of dancehall. In *Back-fi-a-bend* (2015), the artist combines a reproduction of a historical photograph created in the service of the tourism industry with a bending cartoon-like figure in the style of Japanese anime and Tokyoplastic animation and graphic design. The piece, drawing its title from a Vybz Kartel song,[40] foregrounds the relationship and dissidence between the images of Black Jamaicans as represented in turn-of-the-twentieth-century photographs and the presentation of the body, often for cameras, by contemporary Black female dancehall participants.

In one part of *Back-fi-a-bend*, five dark-skinned women, each balancing a load of bananas on their heads, appear to float across the spatially ambiguous surface of a cement wall. They form part of what Johnson describes as a street work, a part of the artist's practice that involves displaying art on highly visible public walls and buildings, typically without permission. The nearly life-size figures come from a photograph produced by the A. Duperly and Sons photography firm in 1896 and was part of the large corpus of images created for tourism at the end of the nineteenth century. The image circulated in two versions across many photographic forms: as a photographic print, as a postcard, as an illustration in numerous editions of A. Duperly and Sons' book *Picturesque Jamaica* (1891) and in *Stark's Jamaica Guide* (1898), and as postcards often becoming more granular over time with each reproduction. In Johnson's enlargement, the photograph's history of circulation and transformation seems evident in the textured appearance of the female figures from the photograph on a cement wall. Affixed with a yeast paste that became very hard, the banana carriers form a type of skin on the urban landscape.

Versions of the Duperly photograph reveal shifts in bodily posture, arms akimbo or resting on chins, which speak to historical forms of Black women's labor. The women's comportment for the camera as well as their expressions of judgment or exhaustion gesture toward the ways Black Jamaicans were often made to perform, to labor, as disciplined and picturesque subjects for the camera in the tourism industry. Johnson lifts the figures from their roadside setting and places them on a wall in contemporary Jamaica to highlight the continued ways that the social, economic, and visual demands of tourism can encourage the self-conscious performance of certain ideals of Blackness.

Unlike the photographic procession of the women with bananas, who all appear within a segment of the wall defined by two white columnlike structures, one white cartoonlike figure breaks outside the structural confines. The figure appears gendered but not human. The visage of the figure is evacuated, except for wide lips and teeth that appear across the entirety of its lower face. One arm of the figure reaches for the ground and the other for its lower leg, in a pose the artist says references the sexualized postures of some women in contemporary dancehalls, often before the video light. One videographer describes this practice of exposing as much of the body as possible to the camera through sexualized performances as appearing "skinless" or "skinout."[41]

Johnson sees dancehall as an aspect of culture that the state typically does not feature in tourism campaigns. To Johnson, the dancehall figure expresses a certain freedom not allowable in tourism, outside of constraints of respectable behavior.[42] The space of dancehall, in his estimation, allows Black Jamaican iden-

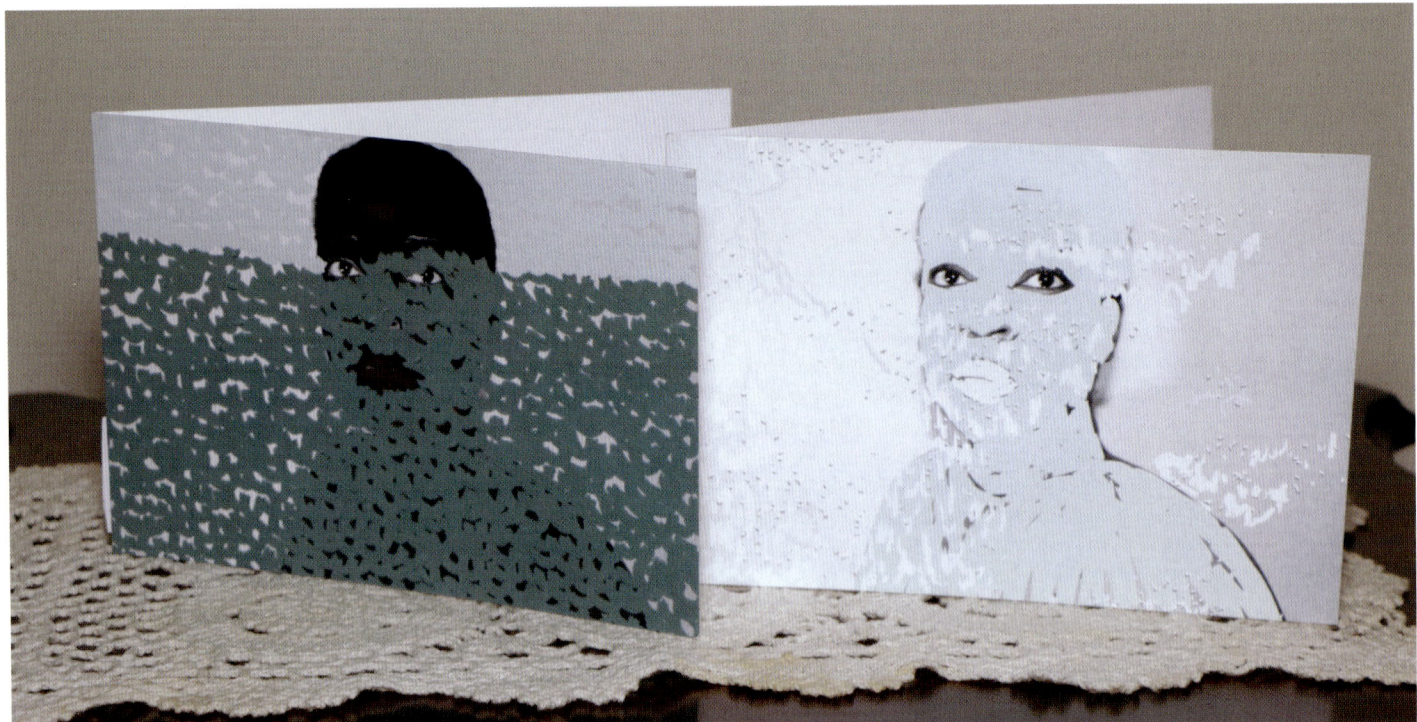

tity to assume an unconstrained form. The inclusion of bananas on the lower back of the dancing figure, however, suggests perhaps another demanding form of bodily female labor for the camera in dancehalls.

Back-fi-a-bend was removed from the wall on which it appeared by those critiquing the indecency of the work after a few days. Its censorship suggests a reluctance to make space for forms of visibility associated with dancehall and contemporary artistic expressions that highlight these practices. Indeed, the high wall on which Johnson's work appears foregrounds the literal and figurative barriers based on class, race, and gender that continue to structure how different citizens occupy physical and representational space in contemporary Jamaican society.

Oneika Russell and Camille Chedda
The works considered so far engage distinct threads of the histories that bind together the technologies of race, photography, and dancehall. Other artists working in Jamaica (although not addressing dancehall explicitly) also encourage an interrogation of the intertwined histories of photography, skin, and surface. Oneika Russell (b. 1980) in *Notes to You* (2014) and *Preservations* (2014) installed small notecards throughout the historic building Devon House in Kingston. Some of the pieces feature outlines drawn from historical photographs and embroidered into the surface of the work. Other small cards feature drawings and collages of Black faces and upper bodies covered in colorful circular marks or covered over by patterns that appear both on the skin of the figures and run across the surface of the card. Inside the note-

282 Oneika Russell. *Notes to You*. 2014. Installation. Devon House, Kingston, Jamaica.

283
284

cards, the artist includes short handwritten texts. One of the notes reads, "you learned to keep you head down and your heart shut and your scope small,"[43] underscoring the pedagogical function of the surface viewings of the Black bodies in Jamaica historically. The visual artist Camille Chedda's (b. 1985) *Wholesale Degradables* (2014–2015) also calls attention to the facial surface of the body and artwork. The work comprises a rectangular grid of the faces of people who have died at the hands of police in the Jamaica Constabulary Force.[44] Chedda painted the faces on plastic grocery bags with acrylic paint, based on photographs that the artist had found on social media and in newspaper archives. Chedda uses historical figures killed by colonial authorities, including the Paul Bogle image, when no photograph could be found. Viewers experience the faces on or through the white, crinkled, and disintegrating surface of the bag. The changeable, degradable, flaking skin of the pictured subjects speak materially to the fragility of subjects seen as Black in contemporary Jamaican society.[45]

Chedda, Chung, Johnson, Patterson, Russell, and Smith make materially manifest how the surfaces of skin and photography have configured the idea of race and Blackness as visually legible and socially consequential in the context of Jamaica. Drawing on photographs from the mid-nineteenth century to present-day videographic practices in dancehall, the artists interrogate how photography has functioned to give race its social materiality, to return to Kyong Chun, at different historical moments. Smith, Patterson, Chung, Johnson, Russell, and Chedda, through artistic engagement with the surface of their work—whether through picotage, collage and gold embossing, bleaching, or yeast pasting, embroidery, or painting on plastic respectively—encourage a critical engagement with the history of surface viewing. Their artwork foregrounds, disrupts, refuses, or tears into the histories and visual techniques that produced antiblack understandings of race in and beyond Jamaica. They offer the surfaces of their work as critical new sites on which to render the edges of these histories legible, tangible, and, crucially, changeable. The work foregrounds how technologies of race that have been transformed and reconfigured in popular aesthetic and visual practices like that of contemporary dancehall. The artwork, too, highlights the surface as a site to come to terms with absence, with holes, with phantom presences, with whitewashing as constitutive parts of the history of photography of people of African descent in the island. Finally, if in the early forms of photography in Jamaica people white and brown used accessories and studio backdrops suggestive of the space they occupied as citizens, each of these artists' works—which reconfigure space, the relationship of figure to ground—forge new sites of social possibility beyond, to echo Hesse, the social inequalities of domination and subordination, superiority and inferiority constituted by technologies of race.

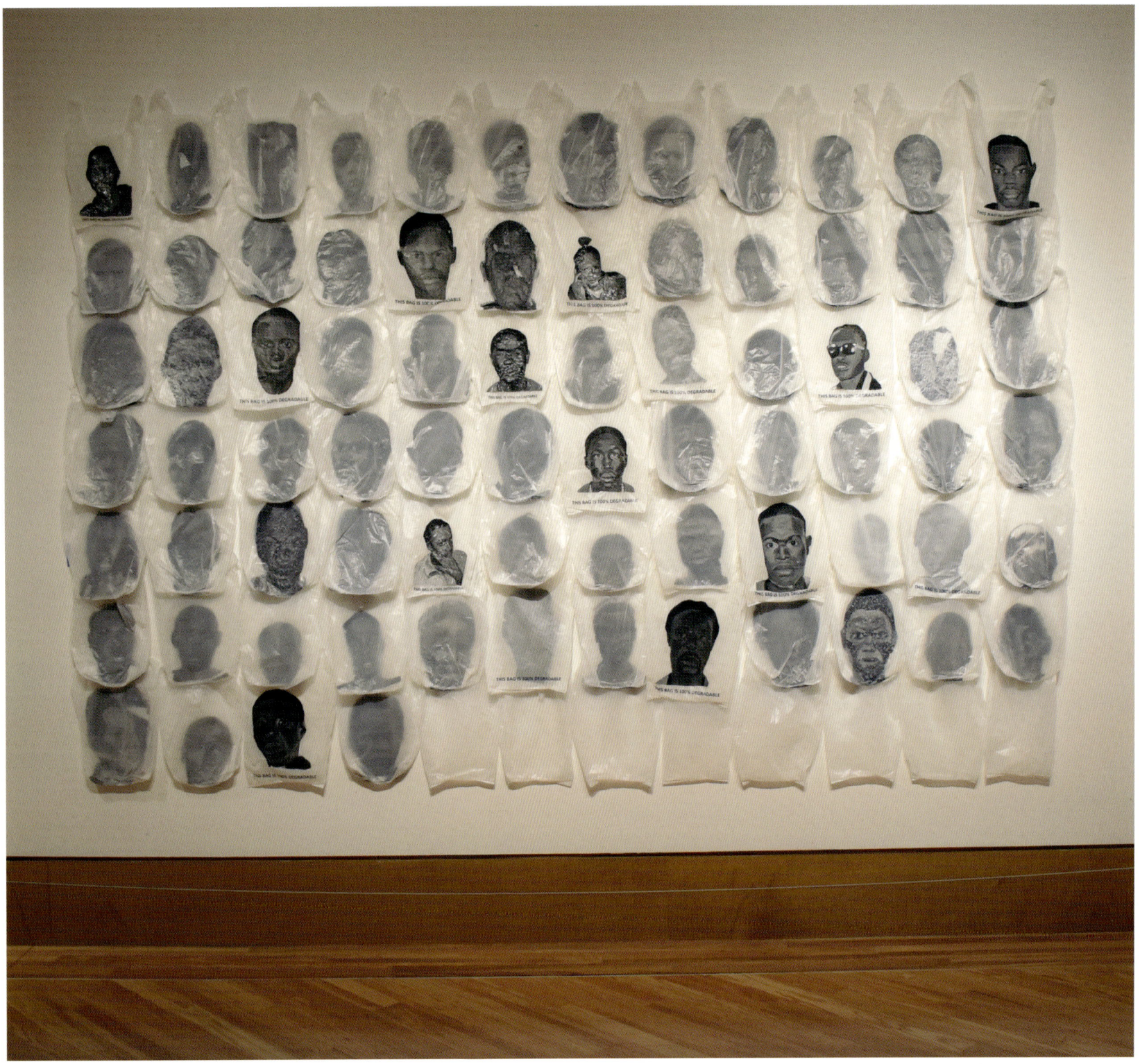

283 Camille Chedda. *Wholesale Degradables*. 2014-2015. Acrylic on disposable plastic bags.

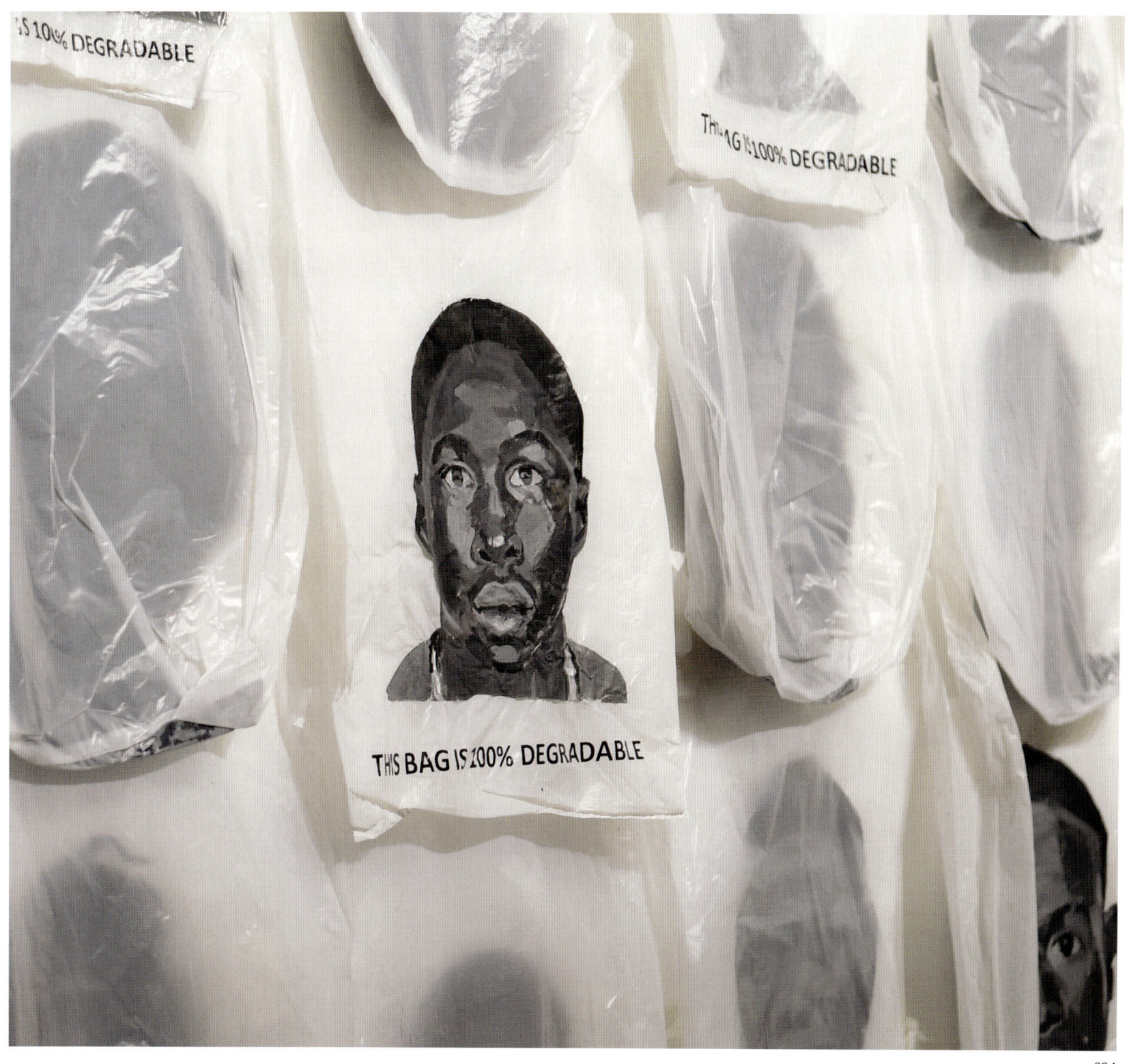

284 Detail. Camille Chedda. *Wholesale Degradables*. 2014-2015. Acrylic on disposable plastic bags.

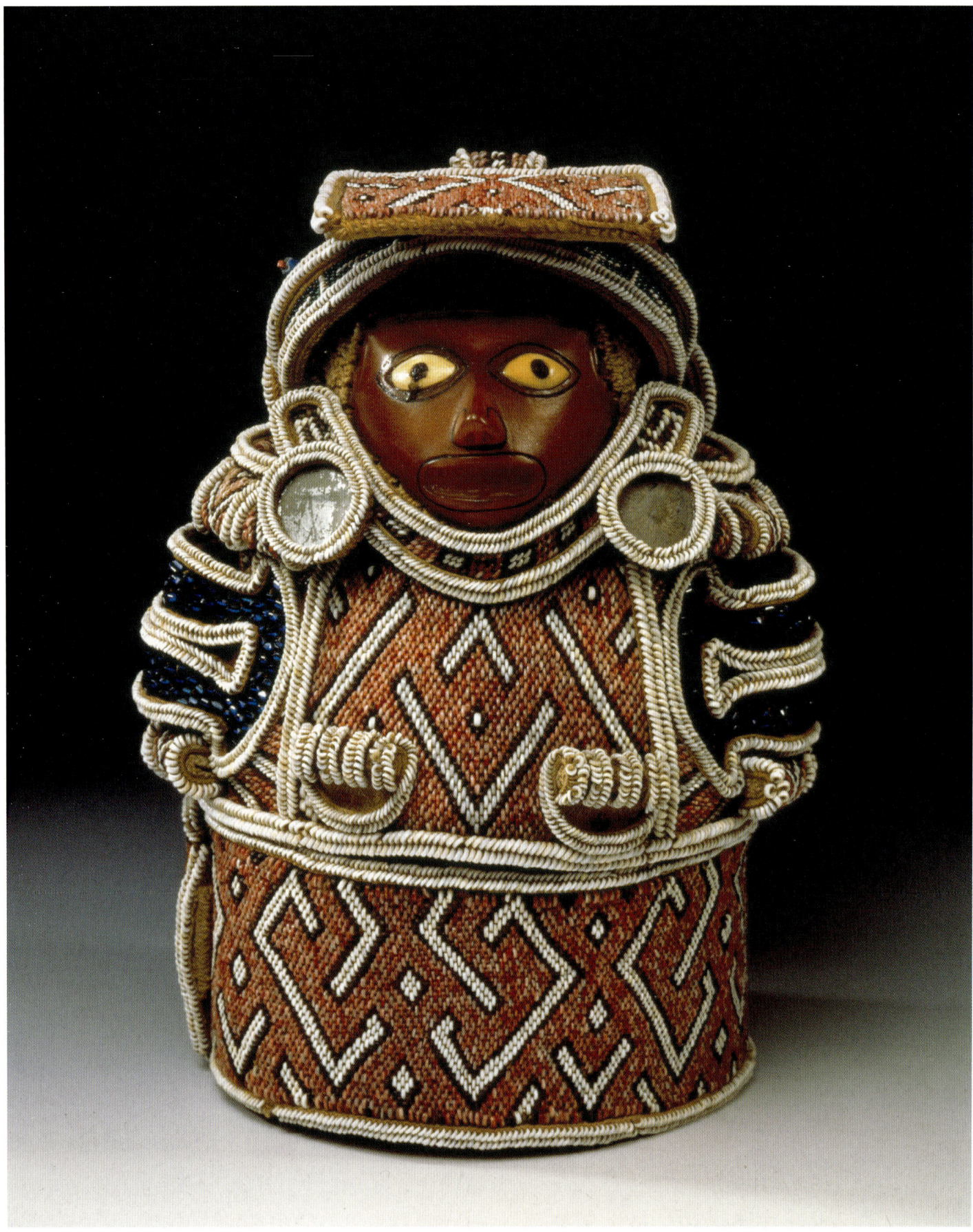

285

16

PRISMATIC BLACKNESS:
ART, BEING, AND AESTHETICS IN THE GLOBAL CARIBBEAN

ERICA MOIAH JAMES

A Zemi is an object that represents something beyond itself. Its form embodies a supernatural or god figure to the Taíno, the people Columbus encountered in the Caribbean in 1492. The Pigorini Zemi (Rome, Luigi Pigorini National Museum of Prehistory and Ethnography) materializes a discourse of creolized aesthetic formation in the midst of profound societal transformation in ways few works of art can. In recent scholarly work, it has been cited as an example of an object produced at a point of contact in global flows, or as Caribbean Creole aesthetics in action.[1] But it is also important to recognize it as an expressive form generated within a uniquely cultured spatio-temporal plane: the opening of the Americas to pre-modern Europe and the rest of the world by a "Caribbean" artist.

The Pigorini Zemi consists of a human face carved out of African rhinoceros horn, sewn onto a torso shaped by a genus of cotton found in the Americas prior to hybridization with Europe. Its diamond-shaped eyes are inlaid bone with incised pupils filled with black resin. The black pigment enhances the carved features of the face, permitting a truer representational reading of the form. A flattened forehead typical of the Taíno people is topped by black fibers sewn in clumps to suggest human hair. Viewed from the side, the face appears to be rendered screaming or in a state of shock. It is also a Janus-headed figure. On the reverse of the human face is a skull with eye sockets made of green Venetian beads further articulated by orbs of tightly wound cotton that enclose and hold in place two glass mirrored discs that serve as eyes. Remaining material suggests that the skull's eye sockets were once faced in a silver, reflective substance that transformed the eyes into mirrors, adding dimensionality as well as symbolic complexity. The ears are pierced by mirrored discs from Venice, faced in the same reflective material as the interior eyes and arranged to reflect, flatly and directly, the image of the person or landscape before the object. The beaded geometric body patterns are remarkably similar to those found in Kuba art and aesthetics from the southeast Congo. Scientific analyses indicate that the white beads are made of Caribbean conch shell and the red contrast beads are Caribbean coral. The green and blue beads that accentuate the figure's tunic are Venetian.

Soon after contact with Columbus, an unidentified artist gathered the Venetian trade beads and mirrors, African rhinoceros horn along with local gold, coral, and conch shell beads. Using known and newly introduced techniques, this artist produced a volumetric creolized sculpture for use within a local belief system. It is quite unlike anything seen before in Taíno art.[2] And

285 Unidentified artist. *Zemi (Taíno effigy figure)*. Back view. Ca. 1510-1515. Shell beads and other materials. Rome, Museo Nazionale Preistorico ed Etnografico "Luigi Pigorini."

286 Geoffrey Holder. *Self-Portrait*. Ca. 1945. Bridgetown, Barbados Museum & Historical Society.

though it may first appear to be representative of a Taíno man, and is indeed a Taíno art object, the headpiece and clothing worn on the Janus-headed figure re-creates aspects of the helmets and dress worn by Spanish soldiers during the age of Columbus. This suggests that rather than self-representation, the Pigorini Zemi is a creolized form that represents the European as *Other* from the *point of view of the Americas*. As a generative Caribbean art object, it materializes intimacies of contact among Europe, Africa, and the Caribbean, and, through the evocation of the Janus form, prophesies the European as the face of death.

Following the Martinican writer and philosopher Édouard Glissant, the Zemi objectifies the foundational ethos that centers an understanding of global Caribbean art; a recognition that one's "being is in a state of perpetual change";[3] that creolization is a sign of change; that creolized objects like the Zemi gather materials, ideas, processes, philosophies, and histories of art making from everywhere and, through resignification and form, emerge through this process as new objects whose meaning cannot be framed by a single story. Creolization sees the Caribbean as a conceptual idea and the Zemi as a theoretical form whose creation process is echoed by all self-identified artists of Caribbean descent wherever they choose to work in the world.

Global Caribbean art history deploys a generative discursive model mindful of the uses and limits of deconstructing these creolized objects into multiple parts. It works to never lose sight of the art image, object, or experience and the implications of its wholeness within context. The Zemi enunciates its parts and affirms its objecthood. It is a global Caribbean artwork that takes into account the ongoing creative history of the world, acknowledging that in "this very moment the whole world is creolizing itself, and there are no longer nations or races that are untouched by others."[4] Therefore, to speak of global Caribbean art is to enter a diaspora tethered by shared histories and cultures at the crossroads of the world.

This chapter explores manifestations of global Caribbean art and its engagement with ontological and conceptual Blackness in New York City, London, Paris, and the contemporary Caribbean. It begins in Trinidad, in the 1950s, with the migration of two brothers, one to London and the other to New York, and ends in the present day. It crafts this narrative by considering how the concept of Blackness was challenged or enlarged in relation to Caribbean identities as these artists moved through formal and informal collectives, artist initiatives, and institutions in global metropoles, but also in the Caribbean itself after the 1980s, when artists, resident in or returning to the geographic area, began to confidently declare their seat at the global art table from within the region.

Port of Spain, Trinidad, 1950

> I'd say, one day a mist is going to lift and I am going
> to see America at the end of the horizon. I used to feel that
> it was there. . . . I knew I was going.
> —Geoffrey Holder [5]

In 1952, the Trinidad-based Holder Brothers Dancers auditioned for the American dancer and choreographer Agnes de Mille in Puerto Rico, after which their leader, Geoffrey Holder (1930–2014), and a pared-down number from the troupe were invited to come to New York to audition for Sol Hurok. They arrived in New

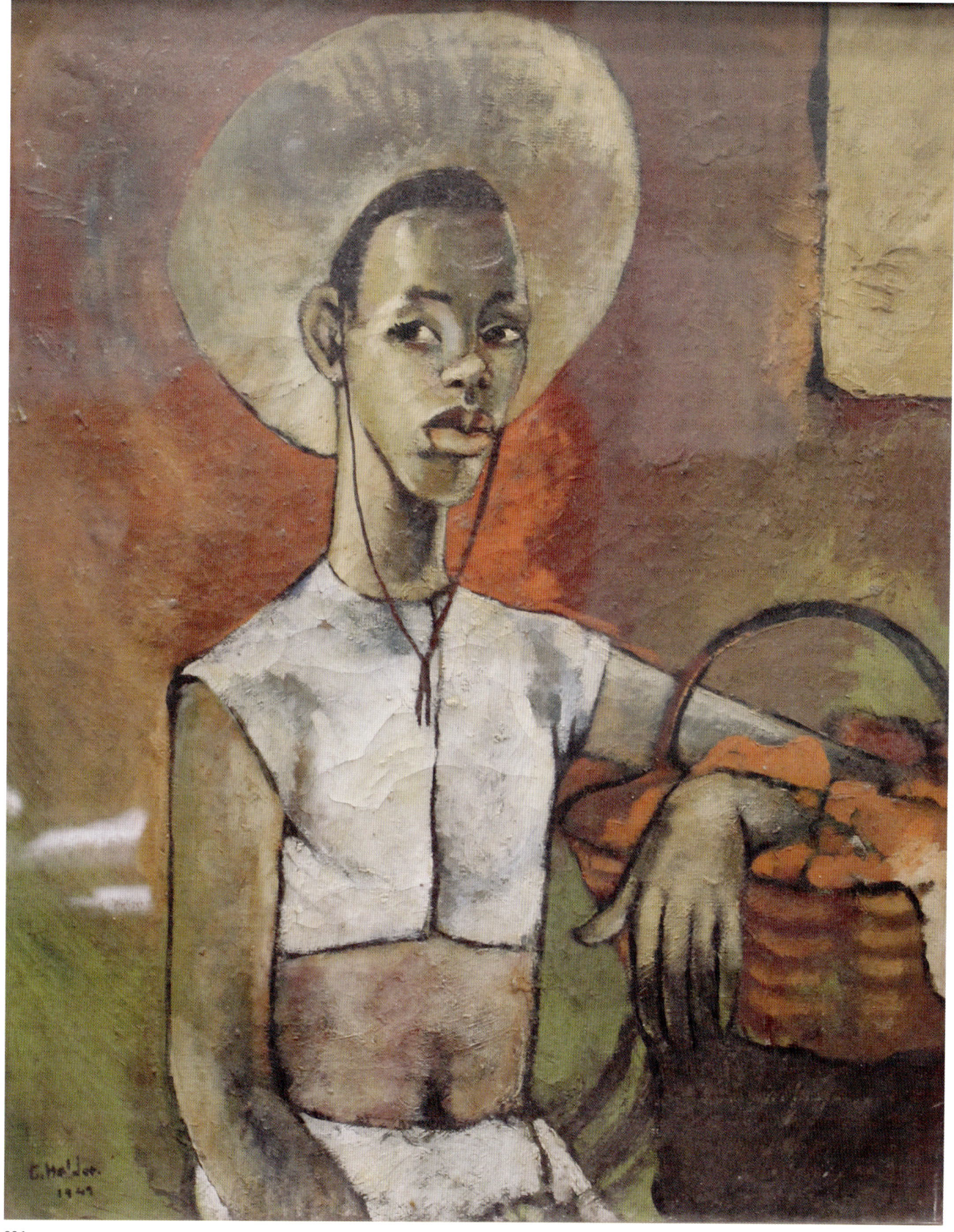

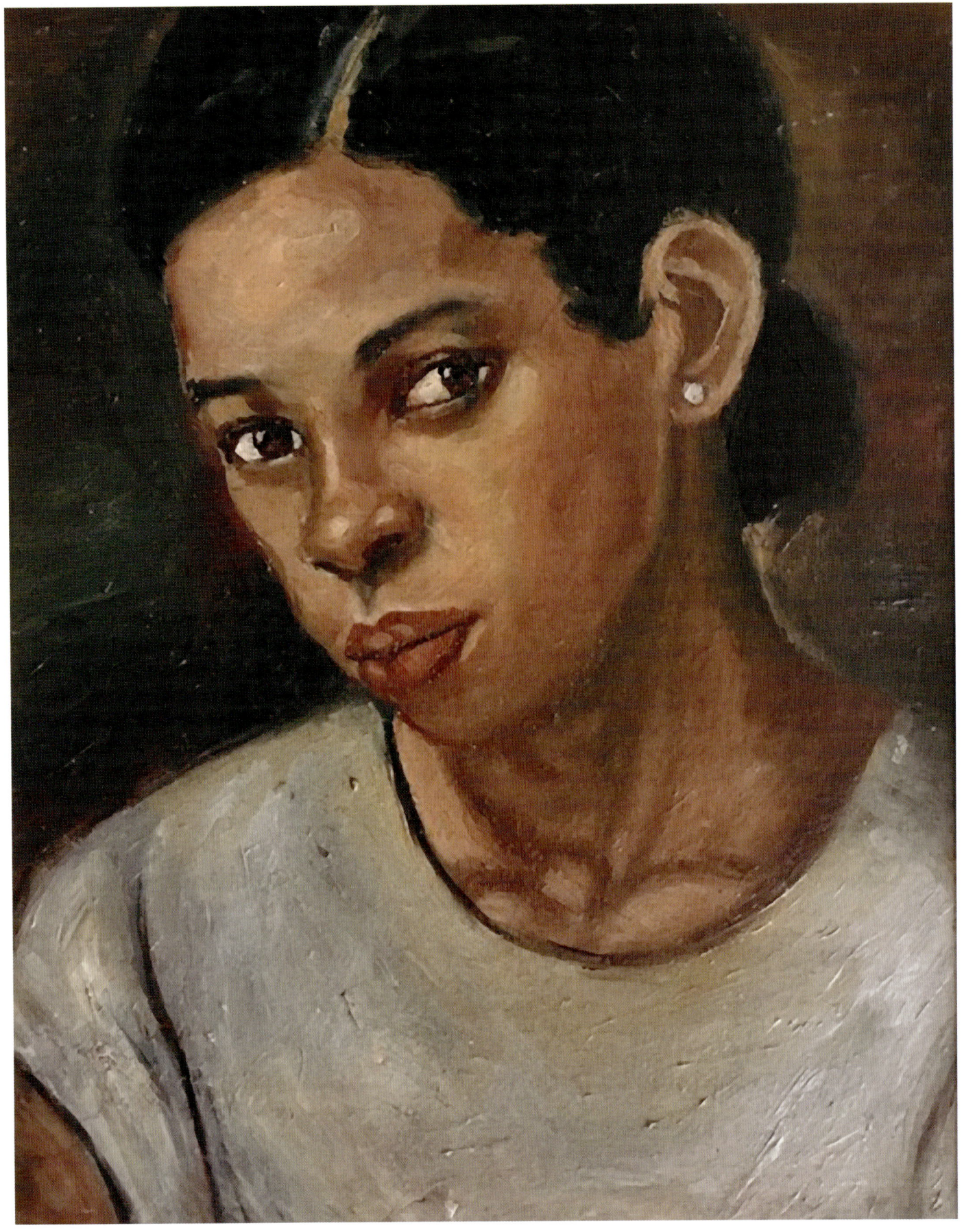

287 Boscoe Holder. *Mother*. 1938. Boscoe Holder Estate.

York City in the spring of 1953. Holder's brother, Boscoe (1921–2007), had left for London three years prior in the hope of finding a larger audience for his creative expression. They were part of a new wave of postwar, opportunity-seeking migrants from the Caribbean who made their way to global cities in the 1950s and 1960s.

The Trinidad the Holder brothers left was then, as now, a racially and ethnically diverse place that people of multiple ethnicities—among them African, Indian, Chinese, Syrian, Portuguese, and Venezuelan—divided further by class, called home. It was a society deeply influenced by these cultures, enmeshed in a colonial system further organized by Victorian values and aesthetics.

The Holders lived for what they dreamed rather than adjust to their circumstances. When their father bought a piano, Boscoe taught himself to play it. The brothers also taught themselves to paint and draw. Geoffrey stuttered and was bullied in school, but in an early self-portrait, he painted the image of himself that he saw: a young man who was proud, beautiful, and somewhat shy. Boscoe wanted to dance; after he learned all the local folk dances from the various traditions himself, he taught them to Geoffrey. In many ways, Boscoe, the elder of the two, cleared the path for himself and his brother as they performed and exhibited across Trinidad, most notably at the yearly exhibitions hosted by the Trinidad Art Society, which earned them their reputation as performers and painters. Their paintings, using expressionistic brushstrokes and featuring the island's landscape and people, became so well known that the Trinidadian government sent anyone expressing an interest in art depicting what was then seen as *authentic* Trinidad to their house. It soon became clear, however, that the Holders were reaching for something beyond mere representation.

In the rich tradition of interregional migrations, their father had migrated to Trinidad from Barbados, their mother from Martinique. Though both islands became important spaces of respite for Boscoe early in life, Martinique particularly provided an aesthetic avalanche that heightened his already extraordinary observational skills for aesthetic detail. Perhaps because of his joint interest in dance and painting, Boscoe viewed visualities first through a body's movement, the way in which an individual projected her or his body in space, or carried it, and only then through adornment. In Martinique, he was mesmerized by the way the body moved in a quadrille or *bélé*, or glided straight back, chin up, through the streets as if the person was doing the street a favor. This foundational aesthetic in motion was expanded by the eruptions between the colorful madras cloth, the full tonal range of Black skin, jewelry, and head kerchiefs worn by the women. He had always been drawn to confidence in carriage and expressions of natural individuality as seen in an early portrait of his *Mother* (1938), who gazes directly at the audience with only a hint of shyness. After his sojourn in Martinique, Boscoe began to express even more vividly a heightened version of this aesthetic. His eye was not limited to representations of women. He actively sought a certain *je ne sais quoi* in everyday Black Caribbean men as seen in *Man in Straw Hat* (1961) and *Carnival Costume* (1993).

In 1952, Geoffrey took fifteen dancers from his Holder Brothers dance company to the First Caribbean Festival of the Arts in Puerto Rico. It was his first time off of an English-speaking Caribbean island, the first time he was able to see Trinidad in relief. There he met and saw artists and dancers perform from elsewhere in the region, among them the great Haitian dancers Louis

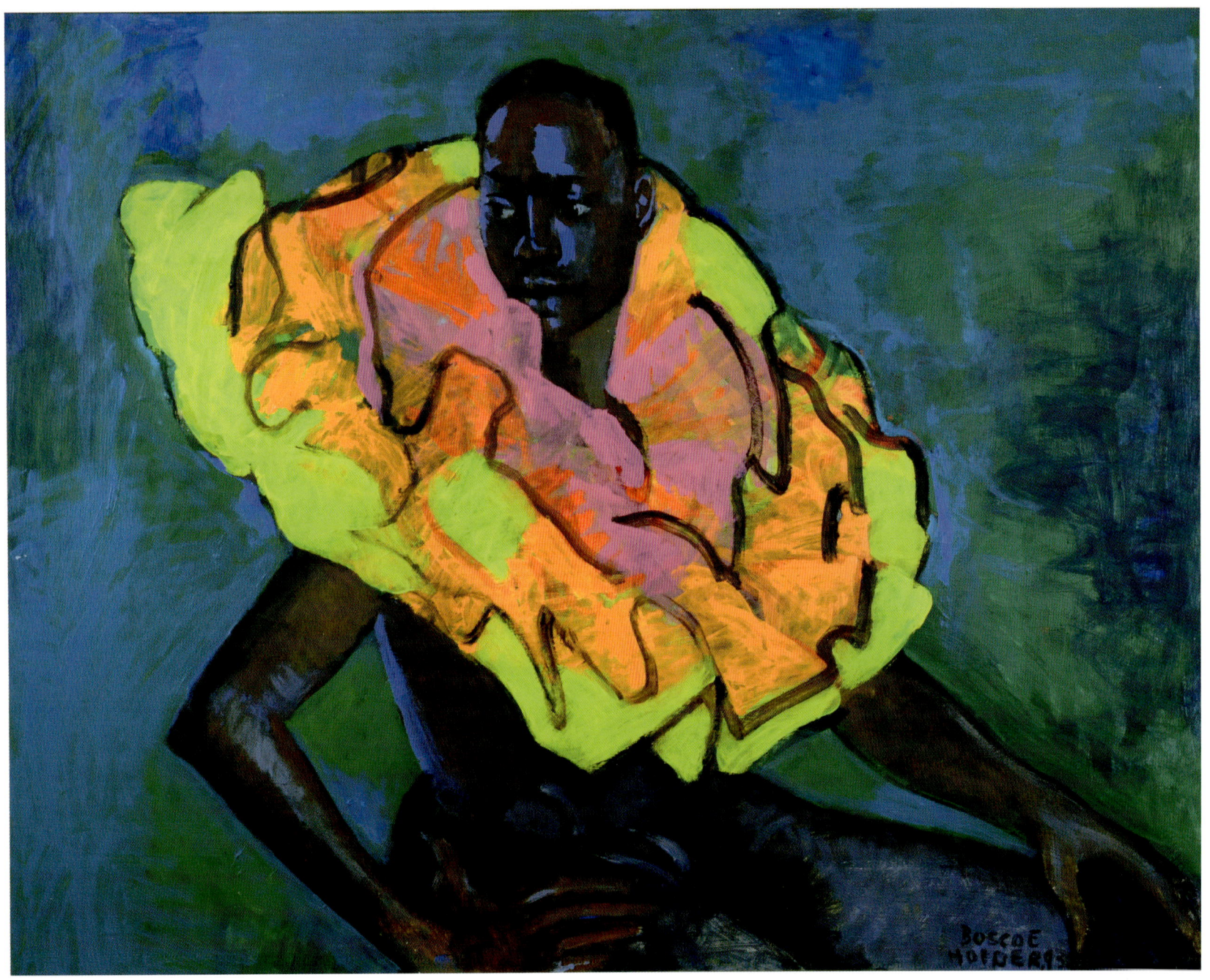

288 Boscoe Holder. *Carnival Costume*. 1993. Acrylic on canvas. Mahwah, Ramapo College of New Jersey.

Celestin and Jean-Léon Destiné.⁶ If Martinique served as a transformative aesthetic landscape for Boscoe Holder, Geoffrey intimates that this festival served as his full awakening as to who he was and what he believed artistically as a Caribbean creative in space and time. From this point on, he would express an abiding faith in a creative process defined by crossing intellectual, artistic, and conceptual boundaries in ways Caribbean people lived but took for granted. For him, learning to create in the fire of creolizing Vodou beliefs and practices, Christianity, Buddhist theosophy, and notions of the folk in service to a sublime aesthetic opened his thinking in transformative ways. He was never the same.

While Boscoe looked at the body and the specificity of a Martinican-inspired creolizing aesthetic, Geoffrey came to it through his recognition of the complexity of Caribbean cultural expression as a model for conscious creativity during an early iteration of the Caribbean Festival of the Arts. What is important to note is that through different means, they both came to understand and deploy the artistic ethos that generated the Zemi. When Boscoe traveled to London and Geoffrey to New York, they took these ideas with them. For Geoffrey, New York was a city that had been mapped for him five years earlier during Boscoe's yearlong visit and attendance at the Art Students League. Taken with the energy of the city, the younger Holder reflected on that time of arrival: "… I knew I could make it here. I just backed myself up against the wall and saw the whole thing and I knew that this was my place. I belonged here."⁷

New York: The Art Students League

In 1947, Boscoe Holder arrived in New York City and enrolled at the Art Students League for what he claimed was all of three days. Founded in 1875, the League was a welcoming space for those who at the time were not considered part of mainstream art movements: women, Black people, immigrants, and other artists of color. There was no vetting process, and fees were kept low enough for most people to afford a class. Though it accepted foreign students for full courses of study, it offered no degrees or diplomas; instead, it provided excellent instruction by artists from diverse backgrounds to amateur artists and those seeking to become professionals. By the 1950s, its teachers were legendary and its alumni were leaders of the New York avant-garde. The League had become a beacon for those dreaming of becoming artists from around the world.

As Katherine E. Manthorne proposes, art schools like the League were contact zones for rising Latin American artists in the first decades of the twentieth century.⁸ During the First World War, the Brazilian artist Anita Malfatti (1889–1964) and the Puerto Rican artist Miguel Pou y Becerra (1880–1968) attended. Artists from the Spanish-speaking Caribbean who attended during the interwar years of the 1920s included the Dominican Celeste Woss y Gil (1890–1985); the Cubans Marcelo Pogolotti (1902–1988) and Amelia Peláez (1896–1968); the Mexican Jean Charlot (1898–1979); and another Puerto Rican artist, Lorenzo Homar (1913–2004). This cohort expanded over the years to include the Dominican Tito Enrique Cánepa (1916–2014) and the Brazilian Cândido Portinari (1903–1962) in the 1930s and the Colombian Enrique Grau (1920–2004) and the Cuban Emilio Sánchez (1921–1999) in the 1940s.

But the importance of the League, commingled with the city of New York, was not limited to artists from Latin America and the Spanish-speaking Caribbean, who were *Caribbean white*. (To be described as "Caribbean white" means that one's whiteness is tied to status; more than likely, the person being described is of mixed racial heritage.) The seminal Haitian artists Pétion Savain (1906–1973) and Geo Remponeau (1916–2012) also attended in the early 1940s, along with the Black Cuban sculptor Teodoro Ramos Blanco (1902–1972) and lesser-known figures such as the Black Bahamians Horace Wright (1915–1976) and Don Russell (1921–1962), who would return to the Caribbean and introduce art instruction in public schools. These artists and others, including the Cuban artist Carlos Enríquez (1900–1957) and his wife, the American Alice Neel (1900–1984), as well as the Uruguayan Joaquín Torres-García (1874–1949) and the Mexican Miguel Covarrubias (1904–1957), were part of vibrant nationalist, pan-Caribbean and Pan-African circles in New York with substantial groupings in Brooklyn, Queens, and Harlem.

Into this mix Boscoe Holder arrived, claiming an inability to pay for classes, though, given his lifelong resistance to anything remotely resembling an instructional class, one doubts that attending the League was ever his true intention. The city of New York was a classroom he could master. He went on to survive, and one might say thrive, in the city for an entire year, gaining a teaching position at the Katherine Dunham School, playing piano, and demonstrating the Trinidadian temerity to organize a performing troupe—the eponymous Boscoe Holder Dancers—and build a performance résumé in the short time they were together.

While Holder was taking the city by storm, managing to avoid immigration authorities in the process, an eighteen-year-old woman who had arrived in New York a year earlier from rural Jamaica intending to study at the Art Students League began to make her way in the city also. Mavis Pusey (1928–2019) arrived in New York with an interest in fashion design. Enrolling in the famous Traphagen School of Fashion in New York City, she attended the school for two years before financial constraints forced her to drop out. Forever changed by the atmosphere and experience in the city, she made her way initially by building on her fashion knowledge and taking a job at a bridal boutique. In the 1950s, she began classes at the Art Students League with the legendary Harry Sternberg and Will Barnet. Like many other teachers, Barnet had studied at the League in the 1930s with Stuart Davis. He and Sternberg saw themselves as painters, printmakers, and social realist artists. Pusey would later assume this dual identity, but rather than adhering to a representational form of social realism, she would demonstrate how it might be possible to think through similarly urgent ideas using abstraction.

Though Pusey initially wanted to continue working in fashion while attending the League, her teachers encouraged her to pursue the fine arts when it became clear that her skills and imagination as an artist were nothing short of phenomenal. Titles of early works such as *Justice—The Art of Law* hint at an interest in the social realism of her mentors. As she matured as an artist, Pusey moved into abstraction, where the topics of race and social justice on first glance appear to be absent. The mythologies of American abstraction as a politically free form make them harder to see. A close reading of her work, however, demonstrates Pusey's interest in a referential abstraction. In paintings like *Nexus* (ca. 1968) and *Solitude* (1963), an element of the body in an action, drained of specificity of context and finite references to a raced body, is clearly present. What pulls forward in her paintings and prints are Pusey's drawing skills and appreciation for precision. The lines in her prints and paintings, always emphatically black, exhibit a sonic quality that vibrate beyond a two-dimensional plane. On occasion, as she does in the painting *Re-Gentrification,* Pusey guides viewers into a politicized space where in the late 1960s and early 1970s the city descended into debt and violence, precipitating what became known as "white flight" from certain neighborhoods. Though Pusey's eye was firmly cast in an abstract mode, her subject in part was the city of New York. In the midst of its chaos, degradation, and change, she found rhythms to pull on and amplify through the work. Blackness was present, not through direct representation but through occupation or the Black migrant presence. This would be seen again decades later in the work of another Jamaican artist migrant to the city, Nari Ward (b. 1963). In the work of Pusey and Ward, one understands the spaces rendered as being occupied by Black and brown people. One can also think of Pusey's oeuvre as representational Blackness in a different sense, where a Black Jamaican girl *from country* simultaneously marks her presence and participation in the history of American abstraction and global Caribbean art.

The presence of Blackness as a conceptual idea in the work of Caribbean painters in New York was extended later in the decade when, in 1957, Hervé Télémaque (1937-2022) arrived in New York from Haiti in anticipation of the rise of François Duvalier. Like many before him, Télémaque immediately became a member of the Art Students League. While there, he studied under Julian Edwin Levi, a semi-abstract painter who seemed a perfect mentor for the artist at this time. He also paid visits to artists like Larry Rivers and developed a circle of friends that included the poet Robert Magowan, the artist and designer Clifford LaFontaine, and the avant-garde filmmaker Maya Deren, whom he admits helped him to see Haiti from an entirely new perspective.[9]

Though Télémaque destroyed many pieces from this period, what remains provides a glimpse into the creolizing process Boscoe and Geoffrey Holder were both so viscerally drawn to in different ways years before. His paintings testify to a creative mind fully engaged with new possibilities generated at this point of contact. In works like *Quand j'appris la nouvelle* (1960) and *Histoire sexuelle* (1960), one can almost see and feel his brush moving across the canvas with fury, soaking up and spitting out the disjunctions between the Caribbean migrant body and the space he now occupies. One of the push factors that would cause him to leave New York was what he once described as the "ambient racism" he experienced there.[10] In these works, figures emerge from the expressionist strokes, riding spooked red horses that explode into a million disembodied parts, or, as in the painting *Toussaint Louverture in New York* (1960), in which we see the revolutionary general walking in the opposite direction from a pale white horse whose hind quarters appear to explode in an island of red. Above him, a grenade with wheels in the colors of the Haitian flag sits at a parking meter, filled with the possibility of explosion. Though the imagery unfolds like a dream, it is clear that if Louverture saw the need to depart this toxic environment even in this unreal urban landscape, Télémaque would follow the directive. In 1962 he left the League and New York and settled in Paris.

What Pusey and Télémaque's presence and experiences in New York make clear is that the complexion of artists traveling to study or work outside the Caribbean had expanded more broadly to include Black individuals; that in most cases, these students became islands of color in classrooms that were mostly white; and despite the politically progressive ethos of the League, the New York art world still reflected the prejudices and bigotries of

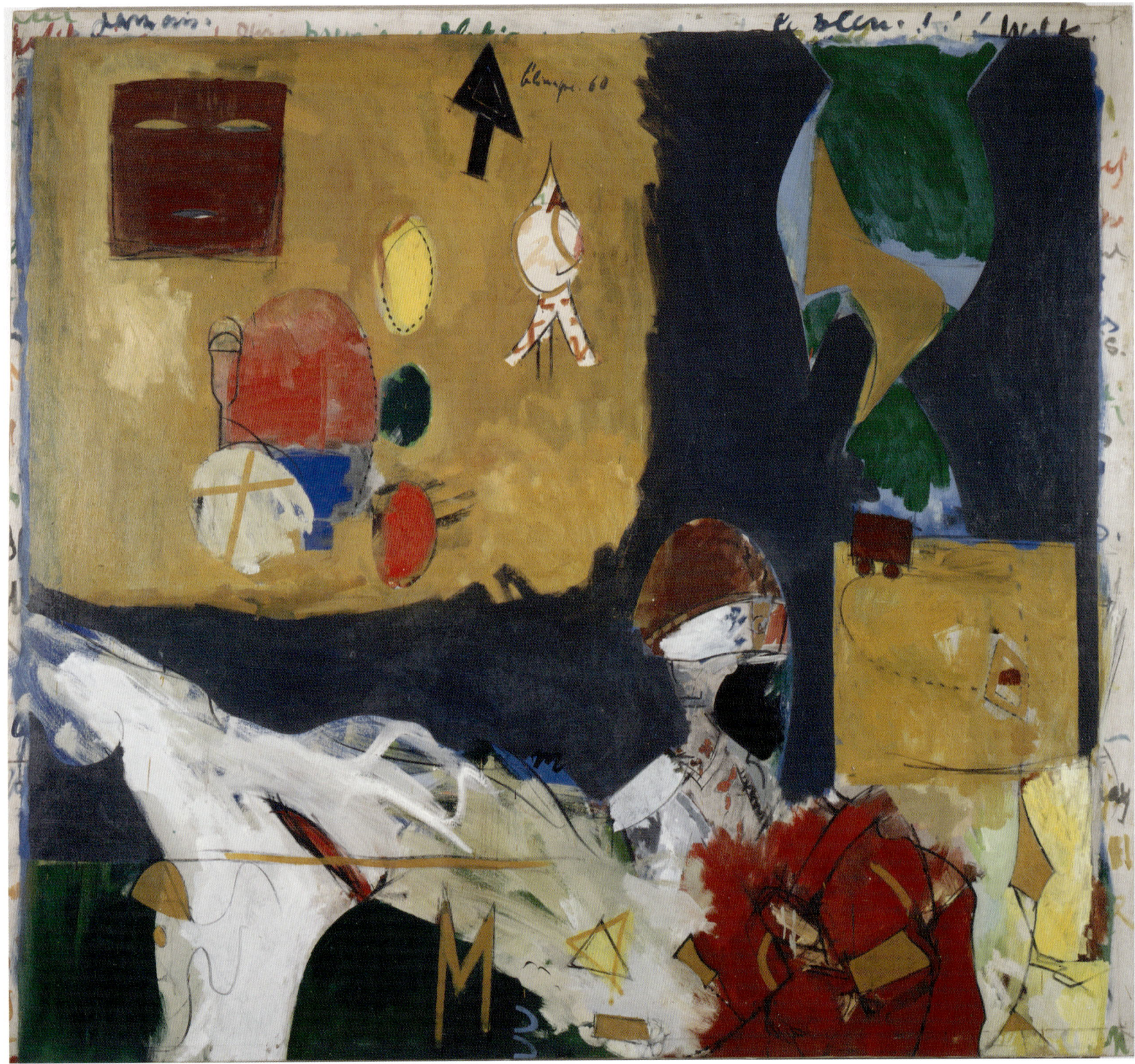

289 Hervé Télémaque. *Toussaint Louverture in New York*. 1960. Oil on canvas. Dole du Jura, France, Musée des Beaux-Arts.

American society.

In 1968, Maxwell Taylor (b. 1938) arrived at the Art Students League from The Bahamas. Like Télémaque, though for more personal reasons, he came to New York out of desperation, hoping to become a part of something larger than what he saw possible for himself in Nassau. Approaching his thirties and feeling the need for more formal training, he had found himself in The Bahamas viewed as the leader of a generation of modern artists that would set a new course for Bahamian art. This burden of leadership arose partly because Taylor was one the first local artists to turn his eye to the plight of the Black Bahamian masses as subject. His early works such as *Untitled (Pregnant and Alone)* (1960) and *Rum* (1960) presented Black men and women, the working poor, in cryptic arrangements activated by a side eye, intense gaze or frown, narratively positioned by the work's titles. The small wooden houses in tightly arranged yards where the majority of the Black population resided also became a major part of his oeuvre. It was work so different from the endless mass-produced paintings of seascapes, royal poincianas, and market women tailored to the tourist's eye that Taylor often found himself showing work that was heaped with praise but with no commercial prospects. His work did not relay the image country leaders wanted to project out into the world, and it was not seen as affirming toward the local Black population.

The New York art world Taylor entered in 1968 was not enthusiastic about representational art either, but for different reasons. Realism had been "tainted by its association with leftwing politics of the 1930s," and abstraction was seen not only as avant-garde but "ideologically neutral."[11] Unlike Pusey and Télémaque, Taylor was an artist whose work centered on representations of Black people in a direct way. At the League, he had the fortune to study printmaking with the Chinese émigré artist Seong Moy and the American artist, printmaker, and sculptor Edmond Casarella. They, along with the Brazilian artist and teacher Roberto De Lamonica, became great mentors for Taylor as he navigated this new world.[12]

As a foreign student at the League, Taylor was expected to attend day classes on a full-time basis; he worked as a janitor at the school to defray his tuition costs. Prior to arriving in New York, Taylor had only been exposed to the work of European artists, but his constant presence at the League—as student and employee—allowed him to meet artists from around the world as well as African American artists such as Hughie Lee-Smith (1915–1999) and Alvin Hollingsworth (1928–2000), who attended in the evenings. He also got a chance to study with Richard Mayhew (b. 1924) and exhibited in a show at the Brooklyn Museum where the renowned African American muralist Hale Woodruff (1900–1980) had chosen the work. Though Caribbean, Taylor identified with African Americans as artists and human beings in an America struggling to achieve the dreams of the civil rights movement and engaged in an unpopular war.

In addition to regular instruction at the League, Taylor also visited museums as if they held a secret he needed to know. It was during one of these visits that he encountered an exhibition of Leonard Baskin's monumental prints. Baskin was not an abstract artist, and against the prevailing winds affirmed a belief that art should be, and to some extent needed to be, political. Rather than crumble under the weight of opposing perspectives around him, Taylor was energized by the discourses. His work during his time at the League and into the 1970s demonstrates the range of skills

290 Maxwell Taylor. *Inhibited*. 1978. New York, Collection of the Bob Blackburn Printmaking Workshop.

earned by a master printer, fully attuned to the political struggles in the world around him. Though rare, Taylor's abstract works like *Green Route* (1970) are fully realized. When Taylor turned his attention to the political, Sternberg's influence can be clearly seen in works like *1967 Crisis* (1968) or *Another One* (1969), where a mother embraces her murdered child's body on the streets. At other times the work was more subtle, more in conversation with Moy and Baskin, including *Dark Angel* (1969–1970) *or (Untitled) Digital Head* (1971). On his own in New York, Taylor, like Pusey, also turned to the city for his inspiration. He found it particularly among the African Americans who had left the South, and the Black and brown Caribbean migrants who, like him, had left their island. The influence shows in works like *Express to Work* (1978) or *Inhibited* (1978). Though abstraction would always be an element in his work, Taylor emerged from the League reaffirming his commitment to the representational Black form.

New York: Robert Blackburn's Printmaking Workshop

While it is unlikely that that Pusey, Télémaque, and certainly Taylor ever met at the League, Pusey and Taylor may have encountered each other and many first- and second-generation Caribbean artists at the Robert Blackburn Printmaking Workshop. Taylor began to work for the artist Robert "Bob" Blackburn (1920–2003) in 1969 while still attending classes at the League. A fellow Leaguer had suggested that they meet, and one day Blackburn, the New Jersey–born son of Jamaican parents, rode his bicycle all the way to East New York to do just that. Taylor was intrigued by Blackburn's proposal to teach printmaking across the boroughs, as well as by his offer to use the equipment at the workshop for his personal work. Taylor would stay on at the workshop for the next eight years, and prints there periodically as of this writing.

The ethos of the workshop was much like the League's. It declared itself an inclusive and innovative space, "a cooperative printmaking workspace … committed to inspiring and fostering a racially, ethnically, and culturally diverse artistic community."[13] Blackburn believed in the spirit of openness, and over the years many Caribbean artists who came through the workshop became a fundamental part of its extended family.

At an early age, Blackburn, a first-generation American, demonstrated an interest in art making and was taught printmaking by Riva Helford at the Harlem Community Arts Center. For many immigrants and immigrant families who made their way from the South, and for those who arrived during the Caribbean diaspora in the 1910s and 1920s, Harlem offered a place of possibility within limits. Community centers played vital roles in the cultivation of art practices among Black people, and Blackburn was certainly not alone. Other children of Caribbean migrants were able to take advantage of these spaces, and a few, like Ernest Crichlow (1914–2005), the child of Barbadian parents, and Ronald Joseph (1910–1992), who had migrated from St. Kitts with his family to New York at the age of four, became Blackburn's lifelong friends. The collective spirit of Harlem arts was further established by these artists through their participation in the WPA mural project in the community, where Crichlow and Blackburn first met.

Blackburn established the workshop in 1948 with the help of his teacher at the Art Students League, Will Barnet, the same instructor who would later mentor Pusey. It started with one lithography press and developed slowly, but Blackburn's friends, Romare Bearden (1911–1988) and Jacob Lawrence (1917–2000),

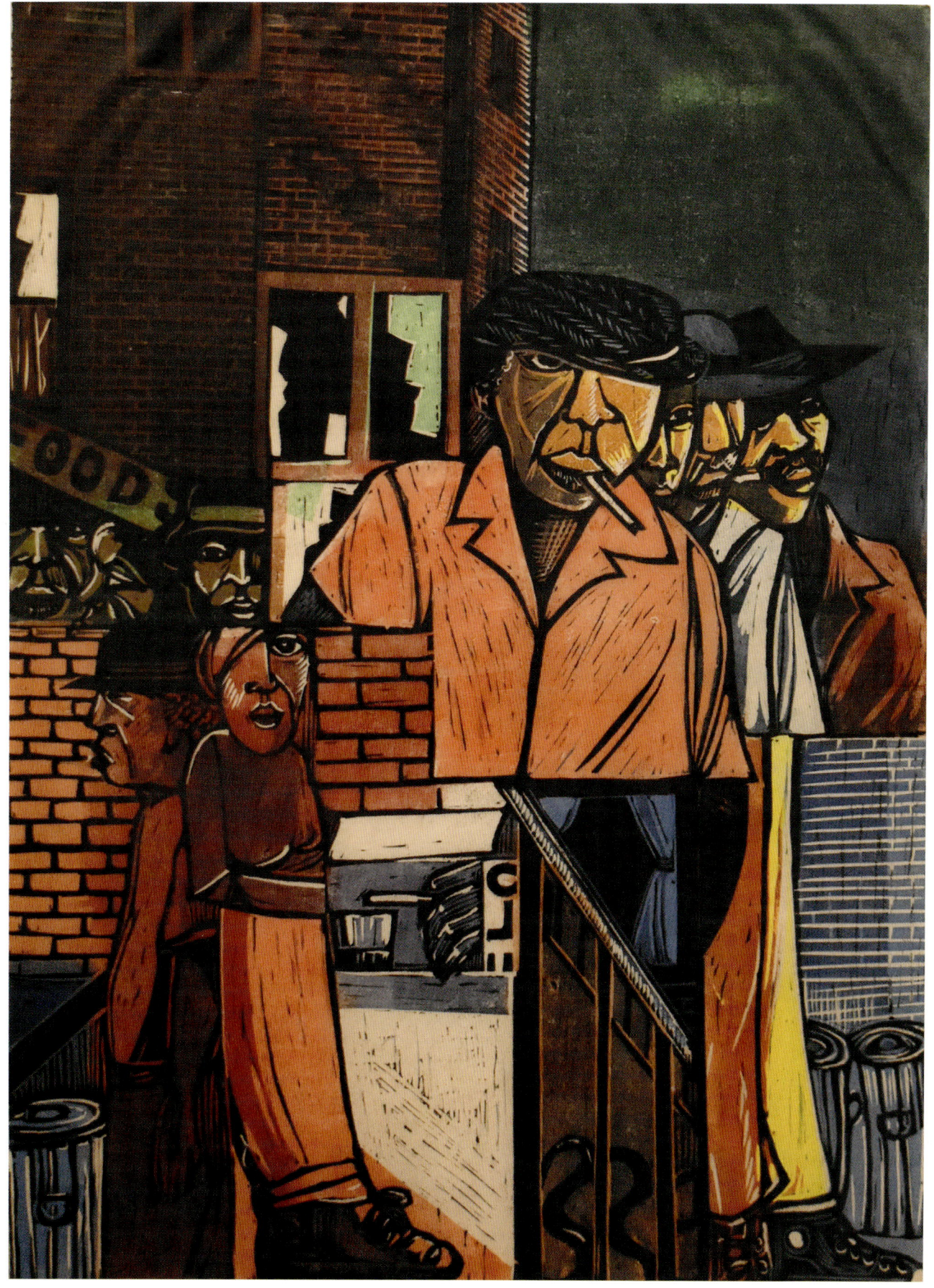

291 Mavis Pusey. *Frozen Vibration*. 1968. Color screen print. New York, Collection of the Bob Blackburn Printmaking Workshop.

made frequent use of the press, giving life to the idea of the workshop as it grew. Pusey also became a friend, printing at the workshop from the late 1960s through 1973, during the time Taylor was involved. The works Pusey completed there, such as *Frozen Vibration* (1968), *Paris Mai-Juin 68* (1968), *Decaying 7* (ca. 1970), *Operation 7* (1973), and *Contact* (1972), are sonic expressions in a two-dimensional plane. They extend her interest in the decaying city and demonstrate Pusey's extraordinary artistic vision and technical skills in etching, aquatint, dry point, and various other hard ground techniques. Like the paintings, the prints evince a level of precision through use of a limited palette in compositions that are linear, clean, sharp, and nothing short of beautiful.

A number of Caribbean artists in addition to Pusey, Taylor, and Blackburn's friends Bearden, Lawrence, Crichlow, and Joseph came through the workshop, among them the Jamaican artists Vernal Reuben (b. 1911), whose work was included in *About Face*, the first major exhibition of Jamaican art to travel to Germany and Britain in 1962–1963, and Mallica "Kapo" Reynolds (1911–1989); the Puerto Ricans Néstor Otero (1948–2021), Candida Alvarez (b. 1955), Diógenes Ballester (b. 1956), and Maritza Davila (b. 1952); the Cubans Hugo Consuegra (1929–2003) and Emilio Cruz (1938–2004); the Virgin Islander Ademola Olugebefola (b. 1941); the Bahamian R. Brent Malone (1941–2004); the Dominicans Luanda Lozano (b. 1973) and Pepe Coronado (b. 1965); the Surinamese Carlos Henny Blaaker (b. 1961), who also attended the League, as well as first-generation American artists of Caribbean descent such as Herbert Gentry (1919–2003) and Whitfield Lovell (b. 1959). This is a small sampling of an extensive list of well-known and lesser-known Caribbean artists drawn to the workshop over the years and into today, a list that includes the rising Dominican American artist Kenny Rivero (b. 1981). What is even more remarkable about the workshop is how Blackburn's commitment to affirming presence through the archive has been sustained. He ensured that artists ran at least two additional prints for the workshop, and now a complete set of these prints is held at the Library of Congress, providing a seminal record of work completed within this vibrant artist community.

The Art Students League and the Robert Blackburn Printmaking Workshop served as important contact zones for Caribbean artists arriving in New York, enabling them to gain a foothold in the artistic life of the city and obtain much needed training and mentorship often unavailable to them in their home countries. Rather than affirming a single global Caribbean aesthetic or inserting a marker into the work that identified it as essentially "Caribbean," those who made the journey remained individuals of Caribbean descent making art by drawing on what was around them. In this respect, artistic life in the New York art world of the 1950s, 1960s, and 1970s for most artists of Caribbean descent remained largely archipelagic, with connections made on an institutional level or through personal associations, with the depth of critical conversation often limited to form and process. At the same time, an entirely different global Caribbean arts community was emerging in London. If New York could be described as archipelagic in this period, then London was pangaeaic, or supercontinental. Like Harlem and Paris in the 1920s and 1930s, for artists from the English-, French-, and Spanish-speaking Caribbean, London in the 1960s became a place where our current understanding of the Caribbean and the conceptual threads of global Caribbean art and cultural studies coalesced.

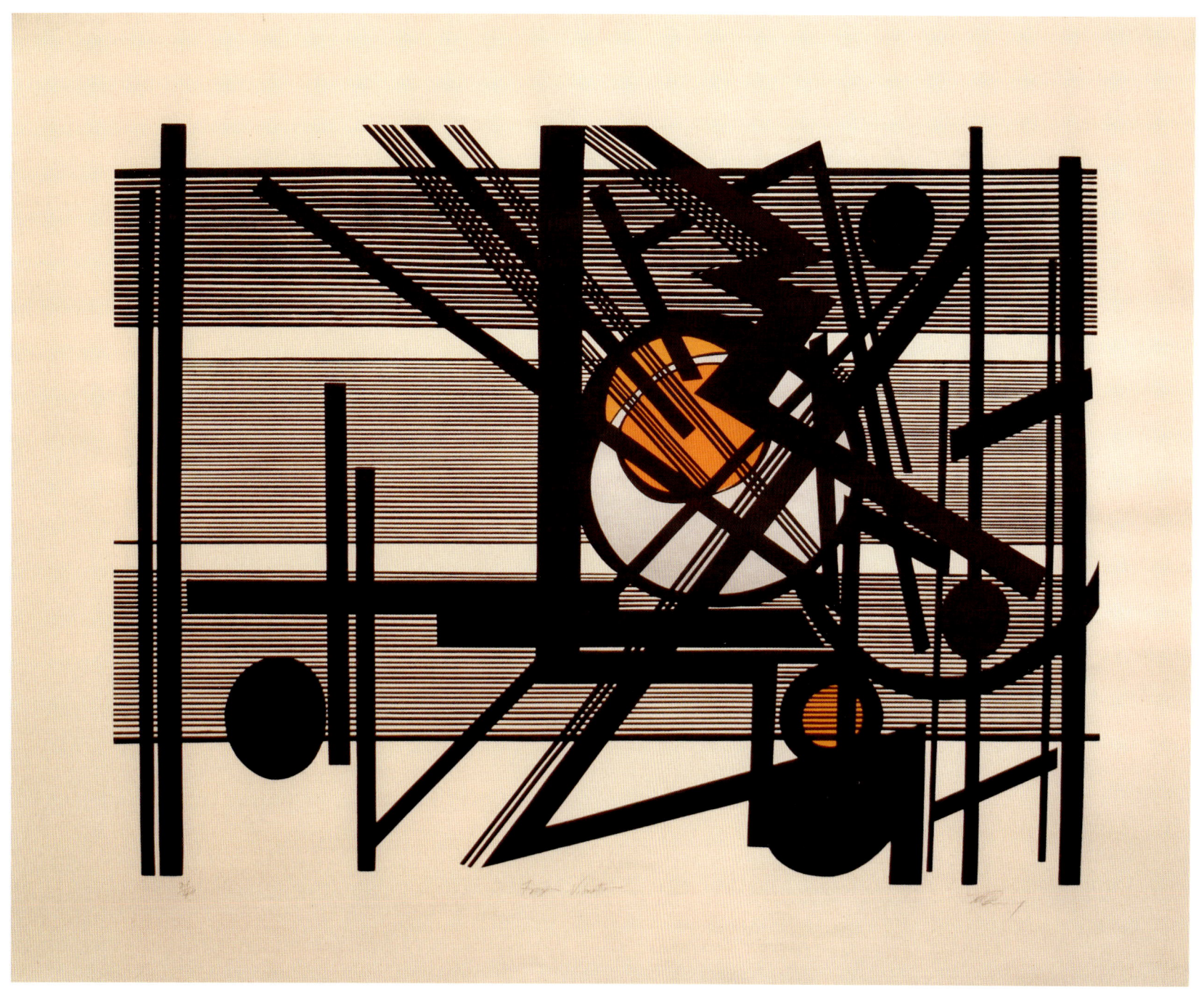

291

London: The Caribbean Artists Movement

For what it's worth, London made me Black . . .
—Andrew Salkey[14]

When Max Taylor arrived in London in 1962 to enroll in St. Martin's College of Art, his experience with racism proved so traumatic that he decided to leave. He elected to travel around Europe for a few months instead and returned to the Caribbean to start over. While London was not for him, for many others it proved to be as energizing as a decentralized New York would be for Taylor and his cohort. By the late 1960s, artistic activity for an exceptional critical mass of Caribbean creatives gathered in London galvanized around the Caribbean Artists Movement (CAM), an organization whose vision toward the arts and letters would help shape an understanding of the circum-Caribbean as the critical space it is today.

While Caribbean people had been in Great Britain for centuries, CAM emerged out of waves of concentrated migration from the West Indies. The symbolic first wave was marked by the arrival of the *Empire Windrush* at the port of Tilbury, Essex, on June 21, 1948. Of the more than one thousand passengers aboard, about eight hundred were registered as being of Caribbean descent. Most in that number were Jamaicans who intended to remain in Britain.[15] The *Windrush* was closely followed by the arrival of the *Orbita* and other ships. Between 1948 and 1970, when the border was finally closed, almost a half million Caribbean people had migrated to Britain. Most were responding to the call for the labor needed to rebuild the country in the war's aftermath. The 1949 Nationalities Act granted the immigrants, already British citizens, lifetime residence in Britain. Carpenters, plumbers, and people with myriad skills made the journey, but among them were also writers, artists, and poets. The writers George Lamming (1927–2022) from Barbados and Samuel Selvon (1923–1994) from Trinidad arrived in 1950. V. S. Naipaul (1932–2018), Geoffrey Holder's classmate in Trinidad, and the Barbadian Edward Kamau Brathwaite (1930–2020) also arrived as students that year, both not insignificantly on government scholarships. The Jamaican Stuart Hall (1932–2014) came as a Rhodes scholar in 1951; the Jamaican-Panamanian Andrew Salkey (1928–1995) and the Trinidadian Althea McNish (1924–2020) came in 1952. Ivan Van Sertima (1935–2009) arrived from Guyana in 1959, and John La Rose (1927–2006) from Trinidad via Venezuela in 1961. C. L. R. James (1901–1989), who had first arrived in 1932 only to leave in 1938, returned in 1962 after his dream of a West Indian Federation failed. In ways unlike any other metropolitan space in the world at that time, and not without some measure of colonial irony, London, through CAM, became a test site of Caribbean unity after the federation experiment ended.

Britain became a place where people separated on various islands across the region could finally meet other islanders, often for the first time. Where in the geographic Caribbean nationalities like Jamaican, Trinidadian, and St. Lucian had dominated, in Britain those differences dissolved at the edges and melded into a broader Caribbean identity. This Caribbeanness was further solidified through changing public and political attitudes toward the migrants. The steady arrival of Black and brown citizens from colonies and former colonies stoked the fears of politicians and in turn the public, who feared that Britain was losing its identity. Such racially grounded fears were enacted through police brutality and racial discrimination in housing; the 1958 Nottingham riots; the "Rivers of blood" speech delivered by Member of Parliament Enoch Powell in 1968; and shifting immigration policies through the 1962, 1968, and finally 1971 versions of the Commonwealth Immigrants Act, which eventually closed Britain's borders to immigrants from former British colonies in the Caribbean, Asia, and Africa.

In the midst of this, Caribbean cultural institutions such as BBC Radio's *Caribbean Voices* thrived, and new ones blossomed, among them the *West Indian Gazette*, the first Black newspaper in Britain, founded by the Trinidadian radio personality Claudia Jones; The Notting Hill Carnival; and the aforementioned Caribbean Artists Movement (CAM).[16] CAM was founded in London in 1967 by Brathwaite, Salkey, and La Rose, stemming from poet and writer Brathwaite's desire to be a part of a community of Caribbean artists, writers, and thinkers now assembled in London. CAM meetings were held once a month from March 1967 for the next three years at the West Indian Students' Center in Collingham Gardens, in London's Earls Court section.[17] These meetings were supplemented by special symposia, talks, informal gatherings, and travel to Caribbean-centered meetings in the region. CAM allowed for the concretization of the idea of Caribbeanness as a critical and creative state of being that transcended the national and cohered around similar though not identical experiences of slavery, plantation society, indentured servitude, colonialism, and neocolonialism.

Also important to note, first, CAM came together at the tail end of a transformative period for diasporic Blackness, through civil rights, decolonization, Pan-Africanism, and the beginning of the period of "the post" (revolution, independence, colonial).

This period was marked by the work of *Présence Africaine*, a Pan-African journal begun in 1947 by the Senegalese writer Alioune Diop (1910–1980) in Paris, a publication committed to expanding the Black archive and in so doing to affirming history to shape the future. Gaining knowledge and expressing creativity were positioned as anticolonial actions as powerful as a sword. In many ways, La Rose's vision for CAM was deeply aligned with the values of *Présence Africaine* within the specificity of a global Caribbean imaginary. According to Anne Walmsley, as La Rose evolved politically, he became more aware of the ways in which Trinidadians were "deprived of information which would have provided them a sense of continuity with the past, so that each generation starts as if nothing had happened before . . ."[18] Like Diop, La Rose believed that there was a need to publish and generate an archive of the present in order to keep "continuities alive." This ethos was shared by CAM's founders and became central to the organization. From the beginning, CAM ensured that the conversations and activities of the group would be collected in a newsletter for distribution within the Caribbean. It was always understood that the geographic Caribbean had to be included in the conversation.

Second, CAM adhered to a multilingual, pan-Caribbean concept of the region. The necessity for this approach had become clear to La Rose years earlier when he heard an Eric Williams lecture given in Port of Spain in 1952 titled "Four Poets of the Greater Antilles."[19] The talk introduced him to the work of Nicolás Guillén (Cuba), Jacques Roumain and Jean Brierre (Haiti), and Luis Palés Matos (Puerto Rico). It was the first time La Rose recalls hearing the poetry of Aimé Césaire. The experience transformed the way he saw his world, the work that was possible in it, and deeply influenced the organization character as a Pan-Caribbean thinking space.[20]

Third, though filled with luminaries, the organization attracted creatives from all walks of life. Though several Caribbean writers and visual artists worked exclusively in their fields in London during the late 1960s, many others worked as domestics and factory workers by day, yet saw themselves in larger terms as writers, musicians, and artists. CAM provided a space for them to be seen as the creatives they believed themselves to be.

Fourth, CAM took on an interdisciplinary, artistic character almost from the beginning. Founded by writers and scholars with a deep appreciation for Caribbean aesthetic production and interventions from various disciplines, an interdisciplinary rather than multidisciplinary approach accounted for the diverse interests of those gathered. The artists and writers were often also historians, sociologists, economists, and anthropologists. This was evidenced in the expanding leadership corps, which grew to include the sociologist and novelist Orlando Patterson (b. 1940) from Jamaica; the literary scholar Kenneth Ramchand (b. 1939) from Trinidad; and the scholar and literary critic Gordon Rohlehr (1942–2023), the author and theoretician Wilson Harris (1921–2018), and the visual artist Aubrey Williams, all from Guyana.

Aubrey Williams (1926–1990) had arrived London in 1952. In CAM he was tasked with leading the discourse on visual art. His efforts were supported by the presence and participation of Ronald Moody (1900–1984), a Jamaican artist who by the time CAM began had been living in London for almost fifty years. Like many Caribbean people whose family had the means to send their children to Britain for university or professional training, Moody left Jamaica in 1923 for London to train in dentistry at Kings College. After earning his qualifications in 1928, Moody began life as an artist and sculptor. As he gained recognition for his work, he moved to Paris in 1936, earning a one-man show there in 1937 and another in Amsterdam the following year. When the Nazi occupation of Paris began in 1940, Moody escaped and returned to Britain.

From the outset, Moody's work pushed against easy framing. As a colonial Jamaican, one may have expected him to be interested in Western art histories and practices and, finding little to no representation in the work, dismiss it as inauthentic. In his own words, though, Moody was "not greatly moved by the works of the renaissance… (but) the sort of inner feeling of movement and stillness of Egyptian and Eastern art…. [T]he important thing for me, at any rate, was the *imagination*; in the sense that all our institutions and way of living turn upon an inner source."[21] The quality of stillness of which he speaks centers Moody's work. It is a stillness that imparts a knowledge, a confidence of being that remains intact despite persecution of the body and of the ideological erasure of bodies whose complex identities defy typical frames. In *Midonz* (1937) (see fig. 224) and *Tacet* (1938), Moody expresses stillness through a hybridity of references reimagined in a whole form. The materiality of *Midonz*—its weight, massing, and density; the precision of the carving; its monumentality; its pupil-less eyes—suggests a tuning out of the world and a turning inward through a deep meditative state that is constant and unshakable in the midst of chaos. As works of art, *Midonz* and *Tacet* suggest that through one's inner resources, one finds the power to triumph over the signatory limits of the flesh.

After Moody returned to London, the city and his world

gradually became more diasporic. He exhibited work at Harmon Foundation shows in the United States; he met and befriended artists like the Nigerian Uzo Egonu (1931–1996), who had arrived in 1945 to study at London's Camberwell School of Arts and Crafts;[22] and he became a mentor to his fellow Jamaican artist and novelist Namba Roy (1910–1961). Unlike Moody, Roy was not from Jamaica's moneyed brown and Black elite class. He was purportedly from the Maroon village of Accompong and had lived a mysterious but seemingly colorful life. In 1938, the bon vivant Carl Van Vechten, who did portraits of all the Black and brown people who "mattered" and who came through Harlem at the time, photographed Roy under unknown circumstances. During World War II, Roy served in the British Merchant Navy. Discharged after being severely wounded in 1944, he chose to remain in London rather than return to Jamaica or the United States. By the early 1950s, guided in part by connections and conversations with Moody, he had two solo shows of his work at the Archer Gallery, London.[23] Roy's commitment to aesthetic Blackness through representations of filial relation among Black people, most often mothers and children, often rendered in fine ivory, won him a great deal of praise. *Jesus and His Mammy* (1956) and *Accompong Madonna* (1958) are two fine examples of Roy's work. The intimate sculpture *Jesus and His Mammy*, of a Black Mary leaning over her child, Jesus, to form a protective cocoon as he asks her a question, visualizes a much needed tenderness in a relationship historically fraught by slavery and oppression. Both works pointedly appropriate the Madonna and child genre as metaphor for contemplation within a Black racial imaginary. After Roy's death, and with Boscoe Holder present in London but rarely exhibiting (he recorded only eight exhibitions of work there between 1951 and 1968), Moody was viewed as the elder statesman of Caribbean art, becoming a vocal presence at CAM's special meetings on the visual arts.

Aubrey Williams was a generation younger than Moody, and his stated reasons for his travel to Britain followed a somewhat similar course. When Williams took six months' leave from his job as an agronomist in the 1950s, his official reason was further study in agricultural engineering. That he entered St. Martin's School of Art shortly after arriving affirmed that his reasons for leaving always centered on art.

By the time CAM was formed, Williams lived in an interstitial space with regard to the British art establishment and the Caribbean. Because of his association with the New Vision Group and also his having won the Commonwealth Prize for Painting in 1964, he was seen in part as a "Commonwealth artist," a representative of empire.[24] Despite this recognition and a deep social circle that included the artists Frank Bowling (b. 1934), who arrived in London in 1953, and Donald Locke (1930–2010), and the intellectual Jan Carew (1920–2012), all Guyanese-born, as well as the Jamaican writer Sylvia Wynter (b. 1928), Williams felt "terribly isolated, physically and intellectually" in London. Though hailed in many circles, Williams, unlike Télémaque in Paris, remained on the outside looking in, unable to break through the British art establishment's racial boundaries.[25] As a result, he was keen to respond to Brathwaite, Salkey, and La Rose's invitation to the group, and CAM became an important step in his search for an intellectual community capable of challenging him. Williams committed himself to cultivating a discourse on Caribbean art through it. At CAM's Symposium of West Indian Artists in June 1967, he, along with Moody, McNish, Errol Lloyd (b. 1943), and Karl "Jerry"

PRISMATIC BLACKNESS 497

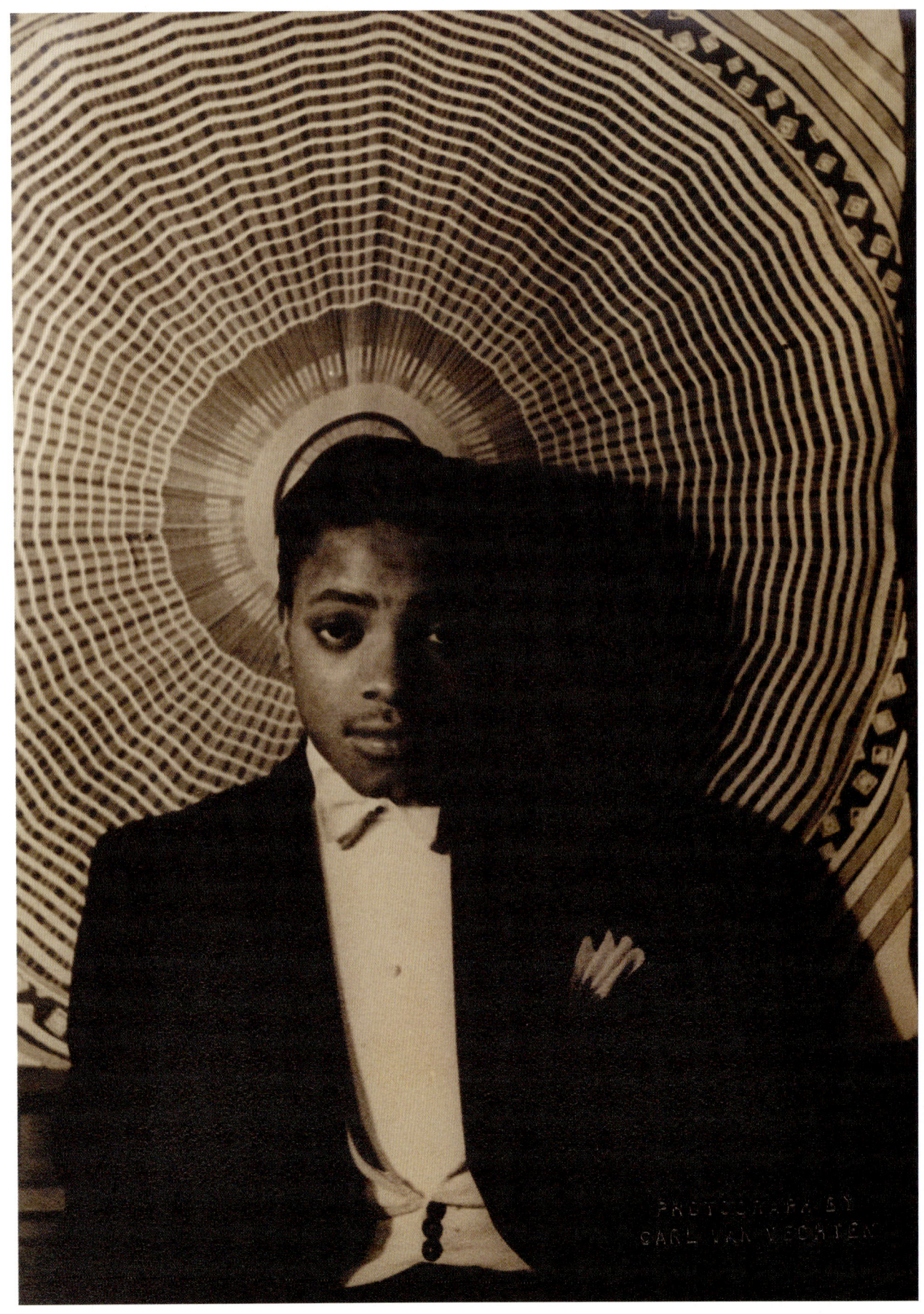

292

292 Carl Van Vechten. *Namba Roy*. 1934. Gelatin silver print. Miami Beach, The Wolfsonian-Florida International University.

293 Namba Roy. *Accompong Madonna*. Ca. 1958. Plastic wood. Kingston, National Gallery of Jamaica.

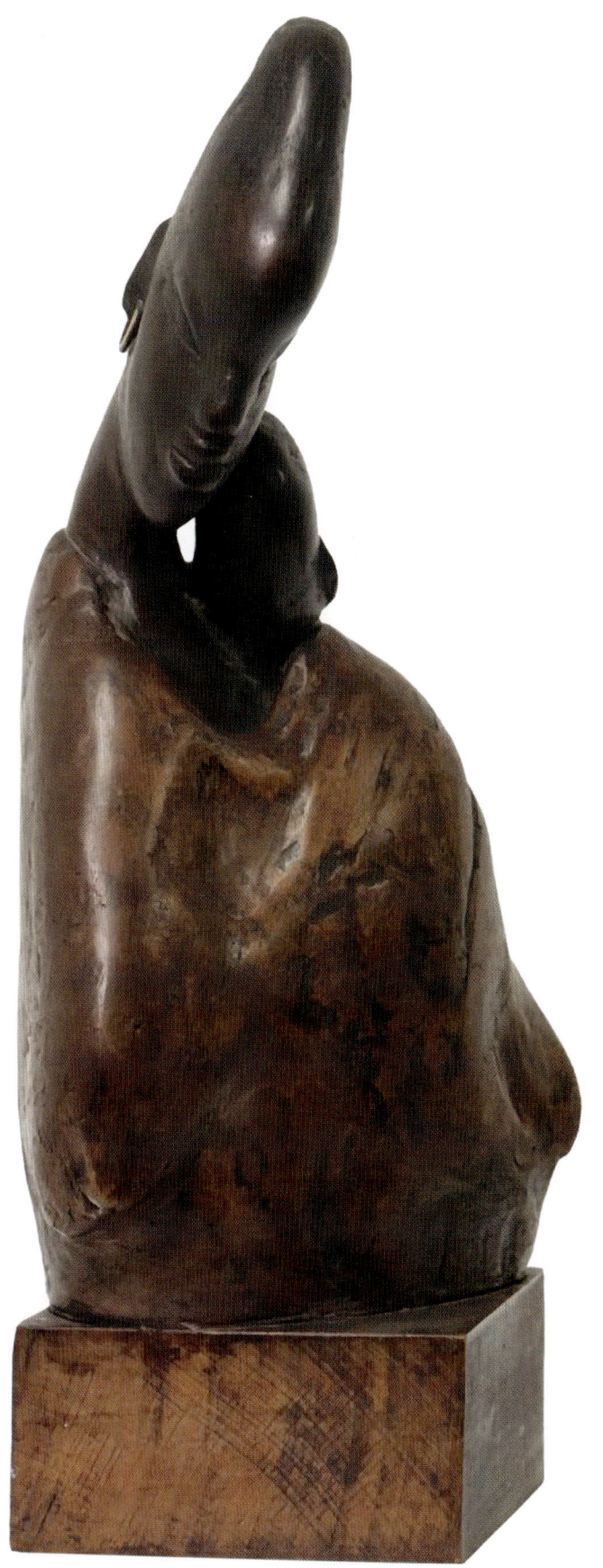

293

294 Aubrey Williams. *Visual Idea*. 1963. Oil on canvas. Location unknown.

Craig (b. 1937) shared their work for the very first time with a community they had long wished to engage.

Frank Bowling took a very different path from Williams's. He recognized himself as Caribbean but at the time rejected attempts to see and define his work through cultural and racial identities. Seeking freedom from these limits, Bowling left London for New York just as CAM was coming on stream, beginning a fifty-year period when he moved back and forth between these cities, forging a singular career never fully recognized in the discourse of either space until very recently. Bowling's circular but necessary pursuit was a key conceptual presence in his work, of which the majestic *Night Journey* (1969–1970) stands as a key example (see *The Image of the Black in Latin American and Caribbean Art*, Book 1, fig. 9).

The keynote speaker at the first CAM conference in September 1967 was Brathwaite's mentor, Elsa Goveia (1925–1980). In her talk, she called for the need for Caribbean artists to think about folk wisdom and culture, societal needs, and an artist's responsibility in the face of those needs. She criticized abstract art as not being conducive to meeting those needs, believing that Caribbean art had to be socially and politically revolutionary, an achievement that was only possible through narrative. Aubrey Williams was deeply disturbed by her closed position. As an artist whose works appeared nonrepresentational—he was reluctant to call himself an abstract artist—and who drew on his entire human experience, he believed that his paintings were no less socially committed than narrative art, and that his art spoke to the soul of man in necessary ways.[26] Williams's works from the period such as *Visual Idea* (1963) and *Towakaima* (1965) resist narrow interpretation. They are affective and emotive and map an interior space that approximates to the soul. The work suggests that he and Goveia differed on what constituted revolution and the ways it could be enacted for Black Caribbean people through art.

In his speech at the second CAM conference in 1968, Stuart Hall spoke of the Caribbean's intimate knowledge of Europe and argued that the central experience in the formation of the West Indian personality was not Africa but "slavery, plantation life and colonialism."[27] While some CAM leaders believed that being in London gave Caribbean people the distance to critically engage the Caribbean experience, Hall proposed that this ability did not emerge from a reflection on the past, but, having entered a diasporic space, "the West Indian had been obliged to define himself in global terms, in terms of movements of Black peoples throughout the world."[28] Hall's argument was for an understanding of Caribbean identity as global. Much like the philosopher Édouard Glissant of Martinique, Hall believed that once one's experience of the world had been enlarged, one is unable to return to a prior state of knowledge or being. Though CAM's contribution to the visual arts culminated in the exhibition *Caribbean Artists in England* in 1971 at the Commonwealth Institute, this position, and Hall himself, would have a major impact on second- and third-generation Caribbean visual artists in Britain. CAM would become a strategic model for artists in the 1980s and 1990s who came together in multiple cooperatives with different life spans. Many, like CAM itself, petered out after doing their work.

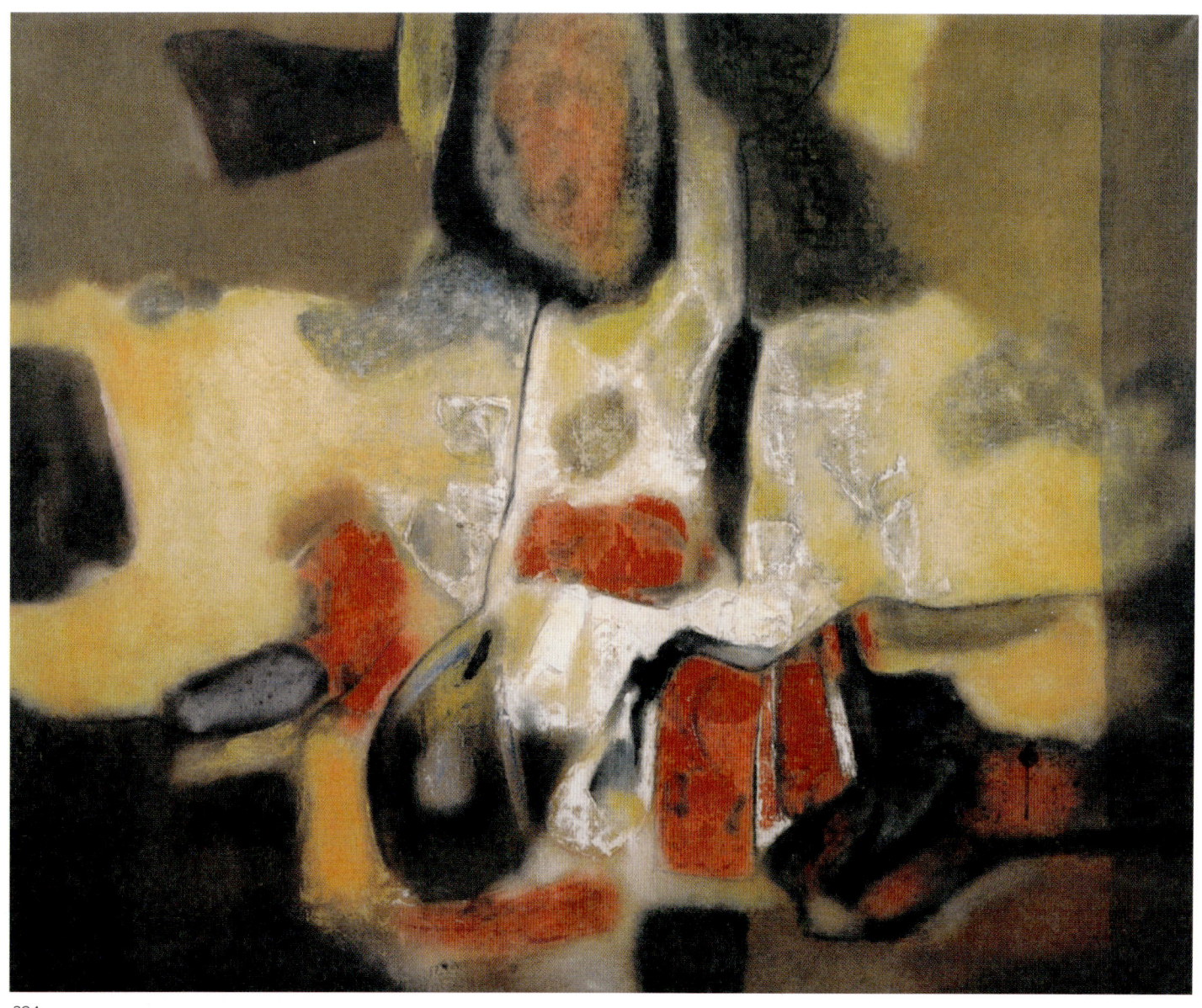
294

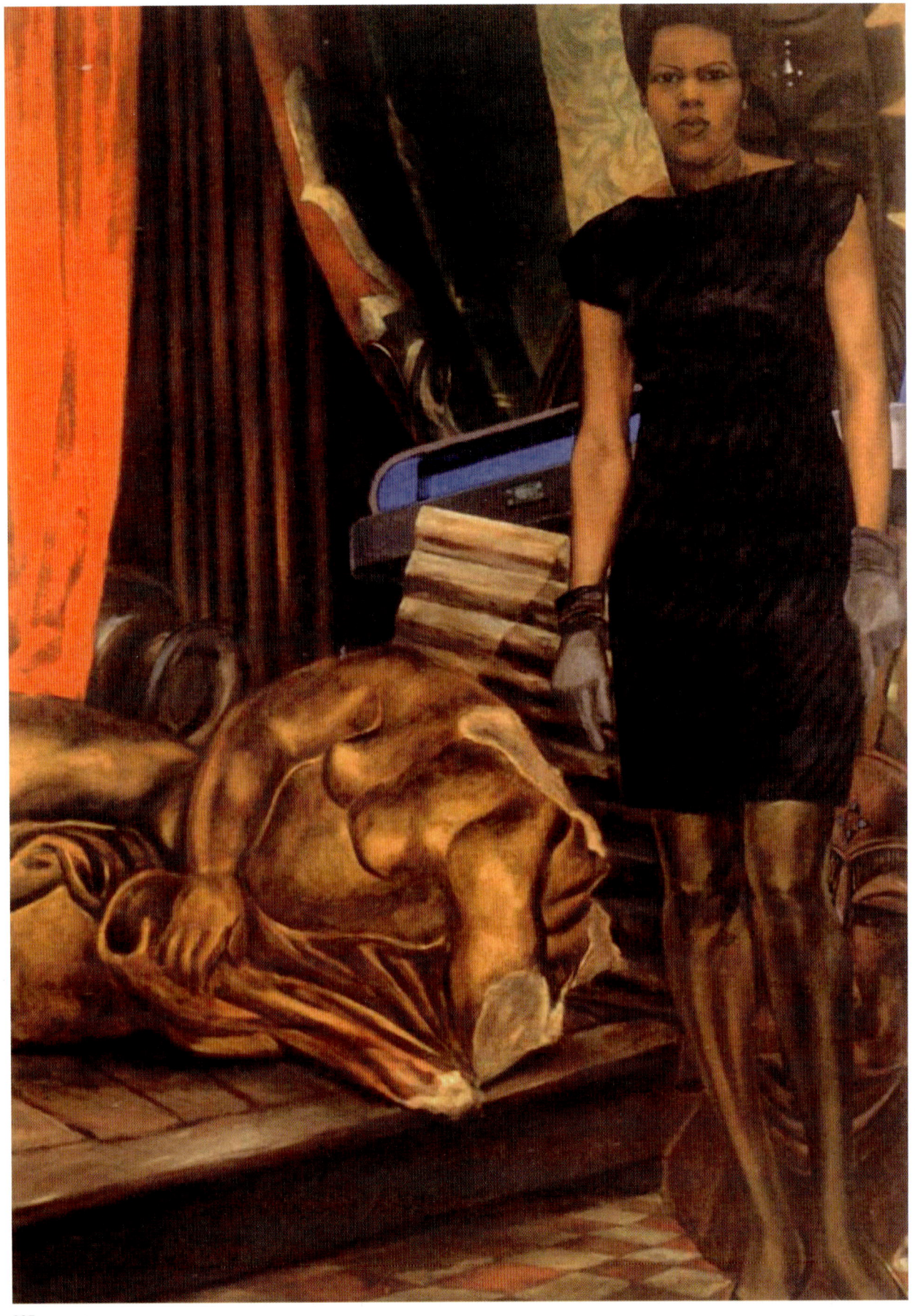
295

295 Eugene Palmer. *Index*. 1993. Oil on canvas. Private collection.

London in the Wake of CAM

> I don't know how long one can depend on recollections.
> —Michael Anthony[29]

In the wake of CAM and the growing emphasis on Blackness in Great Britain defined by non-whiteness, Caribbean identity understandably became an element within this larger prism of difference. While migrants in the arts continued to make their way to Britain, they, along with the children of migrants born in Britain, would anchor a new generation of British Caribbean artists under a larger umbrella of Blackness. Perhaps ironically, it is under this umbrella that the social divisions of color active in the Caribbean became less meaningful. Andrew Salkey understood the condition well, openly acknowledging how migration to London made his Blackness more legible to himself.

After the Brixton riots erupted in 1981, the discourse in London fully shifted from the Caribbean to social activism for those who had chosen to remain, and to questions of belonging or inhabiting the seemingly incompatible notions of Blackness and Britishness simultaneously. To this was added the urgency of feminism and later sexuality during the onslaught of AIDS. This generation understood the need to craft its own narrative through exhibition and scholarship and were theoretically bolstered by the work of Stuart Hall. Exhibition spaces became central to the challenge of belonging for Black artists, and women led the way. *Five Black Women* at London's Africa Centre and *Black Woman Time Now* at Battersea Arts Center, both from 1983, and the *Thin Black Line* at the Institute for Contemporary Arts, London, in 1985, all curated by the Zanzibar-born 2017 Turner Prize winner Lubaina Himid (b. 1954), introduced the world to a diverse group of Black women artists whose work included critical reflections on their place in a multicultural Britain. Three of the titular five Black women were either Caribbean by birth or descent, and all of Himid's exhibitions consisted of women artists of Caribbean, Asian, and African birth or descent with the intended declaration of their presence; Britain was their home. In the art that emerged, Blackness was sometimes imaged literally, but always within a meta visual discourse that drew in the possibilities of signification through form. Increasingly, Blackness became abstracted and grappled with as a critical concept within the work, reflective of the lived reality of being Black in London. The Caribbean might be engaged directly and at other times merely a trace in the work, but it was always part of a more expansive discourse.

Curation became a powerful and effective tool for contextualizing and engaging the art of this generation. It was the curator who positioned the work in relation to the canon and set the terms of encounter, as seen in shows such as *Black Art an' Done* at the Wolverhampton Art Gallery in 1981, curated by Eddie Chambers (b. 1960) and Keith Piper (b. 1960), which featured a new generation of artists of Caribbean descent, among them Donald Rodney (1961–1998), Marlene Smith (b. 1964), Claudette Johnson (b. 1959), and Wenda Leslie (birthdate unavailable); *From Two Worlds* at London's Whitechapel Art Gallery in 1986, curated by Nicholas Serota (b. 1946) and Gavin Jantjes (b. 1948); and the seminal *The Other Story*, curated by Rasheed Araeen (b. 1935) at London's Hayward Gallery in 1989. What these artists as curators insisted on was space at the center of British art. Whether a conscious or collective decision, it is important to note that though almost everyone involved in the Black arts movement of the 1980s and 1990s began as artists, they soon branched out to take control of various aspects of the system, first by curating, then through scholarship, then by institution building and directing, and finally by providing the theoretical basis from which to address the work within a space of multiplicity. They sought to control the narrative around the work from the CAM generation of Denis Williams (1923–1998; b. Guyana); Aubrey Williams; Frank Bowling; Errol Lloyd; Tam Joseph (b. 1947, Dominica); Winston Branch (b. 1947, St. Lucia) and George "Fowokan" Kelly (b. 1943, Jamaica); to Vanley Burke (b. 1951, Jamaica), Ingrid Pollard (b. 1953, Guyana), Eugene Palmer (b. 1955, Jamaica); the recently "discovered" Denzil Forrester (b. 1956, Grenada); Joy Gregory (b. 1959, Oxfordshire, of Jamaican parentage); Roshini Kempadoo (b. 1959, Crawley, Sussex, of Guyanese parentage); Isaac Julien (b. 1960, London, of St. Lucian parentage); the aforementioned Donald Rodney (born in London to Jamaican parents); and Sonia Boyce (b. 1962, London, of Grenadian and Barbadian parentage).

With the passage of time, it is difficult to think of histories of British art without these artists, partly because the slightly younger generation—including Hew Locke (b. 1959), the Edinburgh-born son of the Guyanese sculptor Donald Locke; Barbara Walker (b. 1964) and Hurvin Anderson (b. 1965), both born in Birmingham to Jamaican parents; and the Academy Award–winning director Steve McQueen (b. 1969), who was born in London of Grenadian and Trinidadian parentage—entered a different art landscape because of them. The painter and art historian Eddie Chambers has noted how the work of these artists, unlike the earlier generation, is seen independently of each other as opposed to as part of a cohort and thus has been able to signify in different registers simultaneously. As a result, they appear to be living the freedom Bowling once sought without having to set aside their Caribbeanness. Chambers also questions whether the degree of engagement with their work might indicate that the need for collective action based on race and cultural heritage, so much a part of the 1980s, has passed.[30]

The Caribbean Festival of Arts (CARIFESTA)

Though the narrative of the modern-day CARIFESTA ostensibly begins in Guyana, its model builds on the first version mounted in Puerto Rico in 1952, the same event that introduced Geoffrey Holder to Haitian art and completely transformed the way he viewed the capacity of Caribbean creolization as an infinite creative process. Puerto Rico's location in the Caribbean, its role in the history and study of the region, and its intentional development of the CARIFESTA model, has not been fully studied and recognized. However, it is important to know that the Institute of Caribbean Studies at the University of Puerto Rico–Rio Piedras, founded in 1958, is the oldest academic body continuously committed to multilingual, pan-Caribbean scholarship. In addition, the library at UPR–Rio Piedras holds the Alfred Nemours Archive of Haitian History, the very archive that C. L. R. James called upon to write *The Black Jacobins* (1938) while still in the possession of its donor. It was a pivotal acquisition made by Richard Morse when he was the director of the institute in the early 1960s and includes two of the most outstanding representations of Blackness in the region, portraits of the Haitian Revolution leader Henri Christophe (King Henry I of Haiti) and his son, Jacques-Victor Henry, anointed by his father the prince royal, completed from life in 1816 and acquired from the family

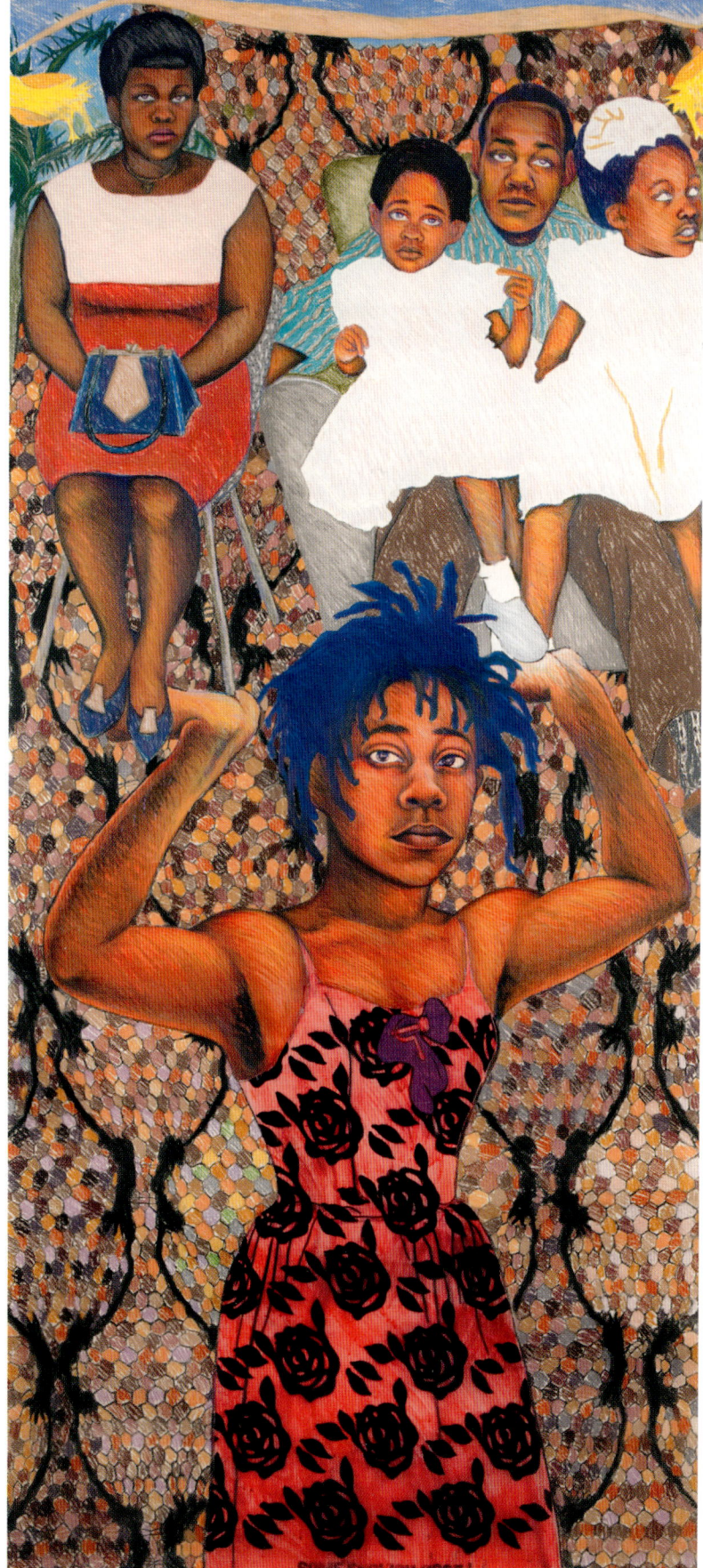

296 Sonia Boyce. *She Ain't Holdin' Them Up, She's Holdin' On (Some English Rose)*. 1986. Crayon, chalk, pastel, and ink on paper. England, Middlesborough Institute of Modern Art.

estate of William Wilberforce by Nemours in 1909. (For Richard Evans's *Portrait of Henri Christophe, King of Haiti, 1818*, see *The Image of the Black in Western Art*, vol. IV, pt 1, p. 86, fig. 58. The portrait is housed at the Musée du Panthéon National Haïtien in Port-au-Prince.)

It is unknown whether any other key members of CAM made the trip to Puerto Rico in 1952, but all of its core leaders attended Guyana's republican celebrations in 1970 and the Convention of Writers and Artists that accompanied them. Brathwaite and CAM formally proposed a revival of the pan-Caribbean arts festival at the Guyana convention. Two years later, however, when the event finally occurred, organizers attached to the government, much to Brathwaite's dismay, claimed to have never heard of CAM, sadly demonstrating the group's concern about continuity.

Notable, though, is that visual art featured prominently in Guyana's CARIFESTA. The festival included an international art exhibition with work from fourteen countries; solo exhibitions by the celebrated Guyanese artists Stanley Greaves (b. 1934), Aubrey Williams, and Philip Moore (1921–2012); and a show on Jamaican art curated by Edna Manley (1900–1987).[31]

CARIFESTA's first three iterations—in Georgetown, Guyana, in 1972; Kingston, Jamaica, in 1976, and Havana, Cuba, in 1979—were very much in keeping with CAM's values, which were central to a contemporary global view of Caribbean culture, but not Blackness. That view encompassed Caribbean studies, Caribbean visual and performing arts, and Caribbean literatures and theories. Where Caribbean identity in the context of Britain came under the umbrella of Blackness, in the Caribbean, Black Africa is recognized as fundamental to the modern Caribbean; it is constitutive of national and regional identities.

For CARIFESTA 1976, the topical forums cultivated by CAM in London were drawn on to produce the volume *Carifesta Forum: An Anthology of 20 Caribbean Voices,* edited by the Canadian-born Jamaican novelist John Hearne. This anthology provides the makings of a Caribbean cultural studies canon. It opens with an excerpt from C. L. R. James's *Beyond a Boundary*, Martinique's Aimé Césaire's *Discourse on Colonialism*, and Cuba's Nicolás Guillén's *National Identity and Mestizaje*, followed by contributions from the Haitian poet and activist Réné Depestre (b. 1926); the Cuban writers George Lamming and Roberto Fernández Retamar (1930–2019); the St. Lucian poet and future winner of the Nobel Prize in Literature Derek Walcott (1930–2017); the Jamaican scholars Sylvia Wynter and Rex Nettleford (1933–2010); the Trinidadian V. S. Naipaul; the Surinamese poet Robin Dobru (1935–1983); the Guyanese writers Jan Carew, Wilson Harris, and Gordon Rohlehr and artist Denis Williams; the Puerto Rican playwright and short story writer René Marqués (1919–1979); the Barbadian Brathwaite; the Mexican novelist Carlos Fuentes (1928–2012) and poet Octavio Paz (1914–1998); and the Colombian novelist and future winner of the Nobel Prize in Literature Gabriel Garcia Marquéz (1927–2014). It is truly an extraordinary text. The sole visual artist among the group was Guyana's Denis Williams, whose contribution, "Identity in Guyanese Plastic Art," had been written in consideration of the African presence in Guyanese culture after his mural *Memorabilia II* (1976) and Philip Moore's *1763 Monument* ("Cuffy") (see fig. 208) had been installed in Georgetown in celebration of the tenth anniversary of Guyanese independence a few months prior.

Considering Aubrey Williams's place in the CAM and his visibility throughout the Caribbean at the time, the choice of Denis Williams (a close friend of Aubrey's) to carry the mantle for the plastic arts was telling. Denis Williams's father's family, as well as Moore's, were from Berbice, a place whose Black settlers were the direct descendants of former enslaved Africans.[32] In the essay, Williams, who in 1945 received a British Council Scholarship to study at the Camberwell School of Art (CSA) in London and is considered by many to be the first Black painter to gain a measure of acclaim there, considers the creative output of Africa, the process of loss experienced in the Middle Passage, the dominance of European values in plantation society, and the complexity of Guyanese culture with the immigration of Portuguese, East Indians, and Chinese to the country. He also questions the power of the national to suture diversity under a single nationalistic aesthetic.

To that point, Williams had led a fascinating life. Rather than remain in London after CSA and professional acclaim, in 1957 he began a long journey back to Guyana via myriad points in Africa, first in Sudan as a teacher of painting and drawing in the Department of Fine and Applied Art in Khartoum (1957–1962) and then traveling extensively in Northern Rhodesia, Kenya, Uganda, Tanganyika, and Zanzibar. He then took a post as a lecturer at the University of Ife in Nigeria (1962–1966) where he, along with the architect and scholar Julian Beinart, conducted the first Oshogbo Art Workshop.[33] Finally, after spending shorter periods at the University of Nigeria, Lagos, and Makerere University, Uganda, he returned to Guyana. Known for portraiture during his youth in Guyana and in London, including his famous portrait of George Lamming, Williams transitioned into an abstract artist at the height of his career. His early work was visibly engaged with that of the Black Cuban modernist Wifredo Lam (1902–1982),

297 Denis Williams. *Pauline, 1970.* 1973–1974. Tempera on canvas on plywood. Courtesy Williams Estate.

298 Gilles Elie-Dit-Cosaque. *Twinkl/Zétwal* (*Stars*). 2009. Film. 52 min.

but by the mid-1950s, works like *Painting in Six Related Rhythms* (1955) represented the maturation of his personal style. By the 1970s, the hard edge of *Rhythms* had softened into a representational abstraction in works like *Pauline* (1974). With it, Williams completed a journey that reaffirmed the Caribbean's place as a part of a discursive global circuit of art and ideas, marked by contacts, exits, engagements, and returns.

Black is Beautiful. *Noire est belle.*
When Hervé Télémaque left New York in 1961, he headed directly to Paris. Though the city would never regain its prewar status as the center of the art world, the ongoing place of Paris in the Black diasporic imaginary remains unmapped and not fully rendered. For many Black artists and writers, from the American Henry Ossawa Tanner (1859–1937) to the South African artists Ernest Mancoba (1904–2002) and Gerard Sekoto (1913–1993), and the Ethiopian Alexander "Skunder" Boghossian (1937–2003), postwar Paris, and France more broadly, provided a place of respite for those seeking to escape the specific imprint of Pan-American racism and colonial violence. As the work of Petrine Archer has shown, Black residence in France did not signal the absence of racism there, but marked it as a place of possibility and political refuge in a diasporic community open to residence and participation in multiple social and intellectual circles simultaneously.

Like New York and London, in 1930s Paris, many residents of former and current French colonial departments like Haiti, Martinique, Guadeloupe, Senegal, and Côte d'Ivoire were drawn to the city for educational and artistic opportunities. An important gathering point was the home of the Martinican intellectual Paulette Nardal (1896–1985), whose Black diasporic friends included "Countee Cullen, Nicolas Guillen, Marian Anderson, Alain Locke, Claude McKay, Roland Hayes, Clara Sheperd, Léopold Senghor, and Eslanda Robeson," Aimé Césaire, René Maran, and his wife, Collette, and many others.[34] Nardal became particularly known for her stance on Blackness and her constant use of the catchphrase "Black is beautiful!" in English. It is no surprise that the *Négritude* movement, influenced by the Harlem Renaissance and embedded within a global Black consciousness, was born in her living room.

In 1931 Nardal formalized her worldview of Blackness by establishing the journal *La Revue du Monde Noir*. This effort and the critical life of Négritude it engendered were later extended by the Senegalese writer Alioune Diop, who, as noted earlier, founded the journal *Présence Africaine* in Paris in 1947. While affirming Paris as his base, Diop would go on to become one of the principal organizers of the international First Congress of Negro Writers and Artists in Paris in 1956, and in 1966 he organized the First World Festival of Negro Arts in Dakar, Senegal, the country where his friend, the poet-turned-politician Léopold Senghor, was now president.

This is the critical environment into which the Black Cuban modernist Wifredo Lam entered in 1938. The city would become his primary residence after his sojourn in Cuba, Martinique, and Haiti during the Second World War. For artists like Lam, and later Geoffrey Holder and Télémaque, Paris became a place to forge a life within one's own enlarged vision of diasporic Blackness while establishing self-authored relationships with the Caribbean. In the decades since, it has played a similar role in the life and practice of artists such as the Martinican-born Alex Burke (b. 1944) and Jean-François Boclé (b. 1971), both based in Paris, as well

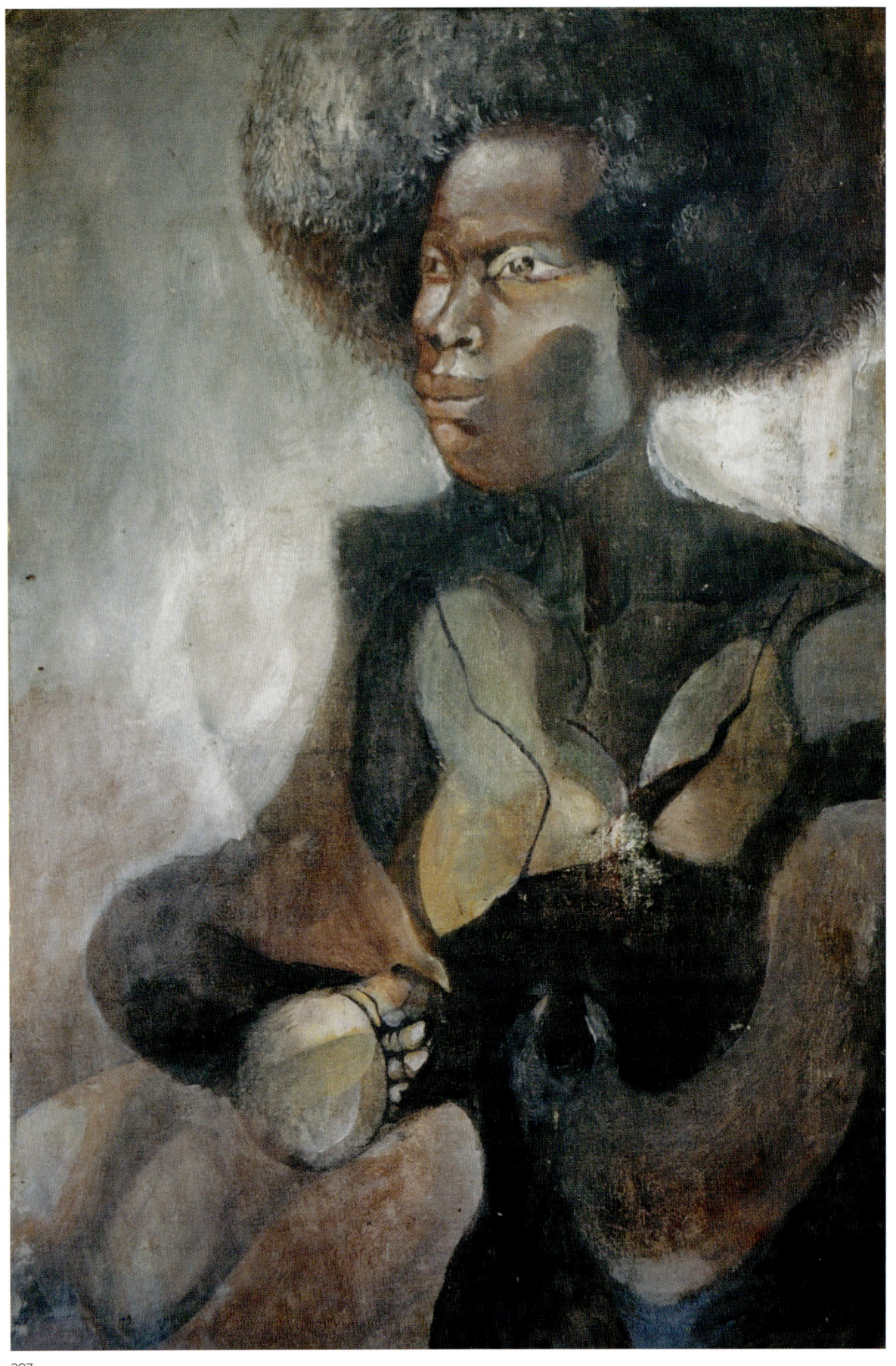
297

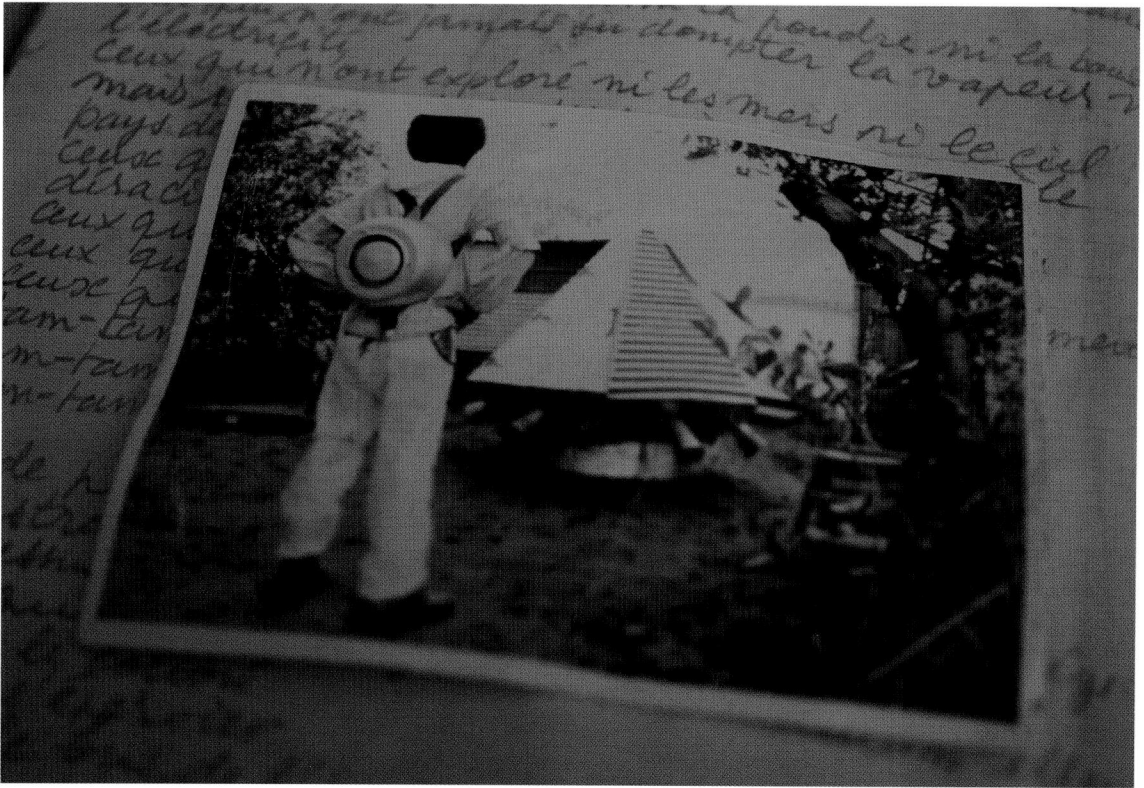
298

as the Martinican-born Marc Latamie (b. 1952) and the Haitian artist Edouard Duval-Carrié (b. 1954), who both spent many years in Paris before relocating to New York and Miami, respectively. The range and critical and formal depth of work represented by these artists is extraordinary, but each of their practices remains intimately engaged with and expressive of conceptual ideas centered on the Caribbean.

This approach is poignantly and beautifully observed today in the work of the Paris-born artist of Martinican descent Gilles Elie-Dit-Cosaque (b. 1968). Raised on comics and free radio in Paris, Cosaque searches through his work in photography, painting, drawing, and film for something elusive yet universal in the global Black imaginary. His film *Zétwal (Stars)* (2009) tells the story of Robert Saint-Rose, the first Martinican to devise a rocket ship that would take him into outer space. The story is told documentary-style through archival photograph and interview footage recording the memories of those who knew Saint-Rose. Even as one watches the story unfold, Cosaque inserts a punctum in the narrative: rather than using fossil fuel, Saint-Rose's spaceship is designed to be fueled by Aimé Césaire's poetry. This conceptual shift immediately gives one pause. Rather than encourage audiences to consider the impossibility of the endeavor, it asks them to consider the implications of Cosaque's Black futurist vision beyond the limits of the postcolonial and science. The beauty of *Zétwal* lies not in the dream of space travel but in the restorative work of the idea. One is never clear whether Saint-Rose really existed. It is an ambiguity the artist cultivates, allowing the work to endlessly form and reform, akin to the way the Caribbean pushes and pulls at the absoluteness of linear time, and continually perforates the boundaries of space and time erected around it.

PRISMATIC BLACKNESS

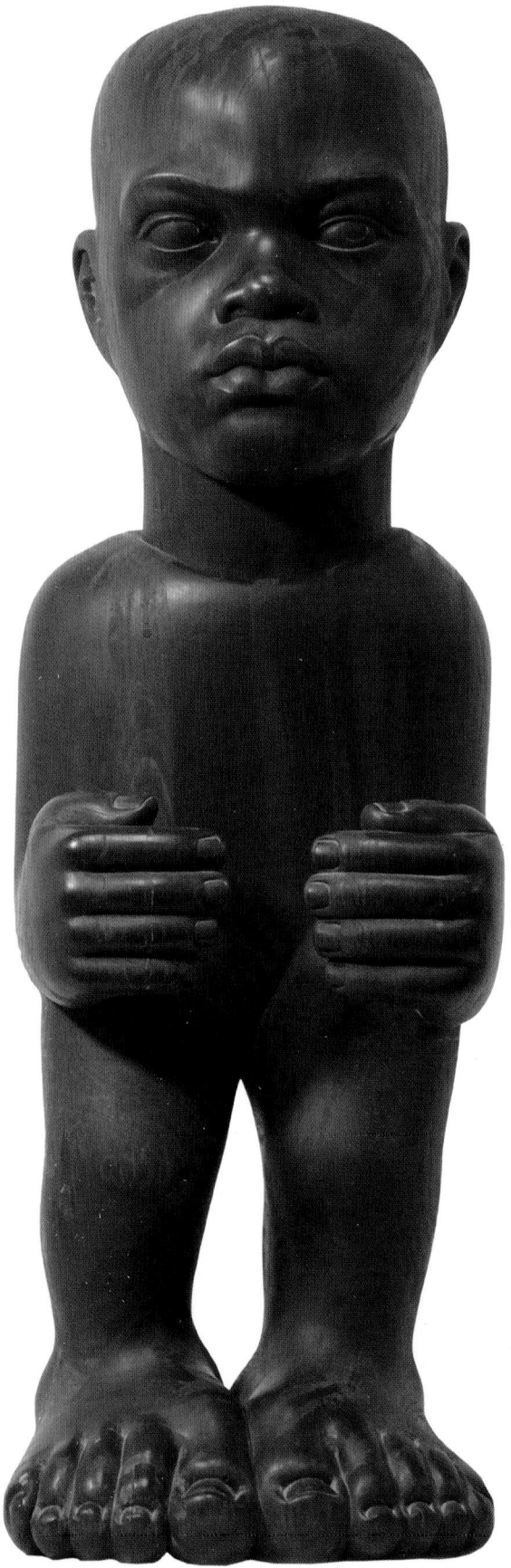

299

299 Winston Patrick. *Youth*. 1973. Kingston, National Gallery of Jamaica.

300 Renee Cox. *River Queen*. From the series *Queen Nanny of the Maroons*. 2004. Digital inkjet print on watercolor paper.

Global Circuits

> … there is no "them" out there.
> —Christopher Cozier[35]

In 1967, Aubrey Williams received a personal note from Wifredo Lam, "inviting him to spend six weeks in Cuba … (working) alongside artists of different nationalities."[36] Lam wanted Williams to work on the Collective Mural of Cuba, a project he conceived while still supportive of the goals of the revolution. According to the curator Lowery Stokes Sims, Lam wanted the mural to show the world that art could be made in the Caribbean.[37] Embedded at the time in the work of CAM in London, Williams does not appear to have traveled to the island, but Lam's action in Cuba represented an important gesture on the part of Caribbean artists working in New York, London, Paris, and other global centers to retain physical connections with the region.

Denis Williams returned to Guyana that same year, and Boscoe Holder would repeat Denis's peripatetic journey back to Trinidad in 1970 after stays in Sweden and Guadeloupe. Holder and other Caribbean artists such as the Trinidadian LeRoy Clarke (1938–2021) and the Jamaicans Karl "Jerry" Craig and Winston Patrick (b. 1946), who had attended the National Academy of Fine Arts in New York in the 1960s, and the Bahamian R. Brent Malone, who had spent the early 1960s in Britain and Europe. For these artists, there was something in the physical Caribbean space that fed them in ways impossible to obtain in the metropole. Malone remarked how following his London sojourn, he had initially regretted returning to The Bahamas, thinking he had made a terrible mistake. However, an experience he had a

299

510   PRISMATIC BLACKNESS

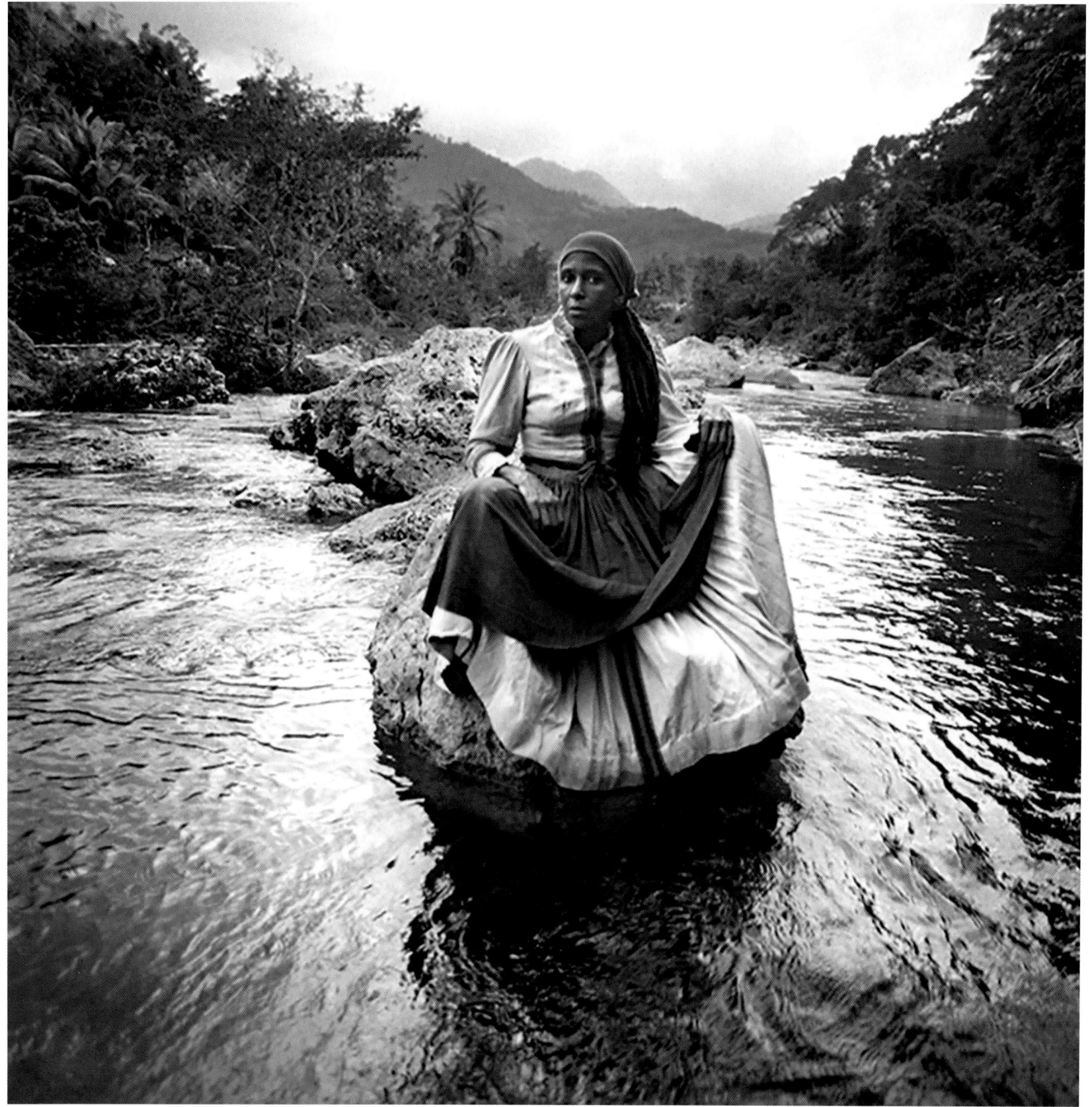

300

301 Visual documentation of LeRoy Clarke's residency at the Studio Museum in Harlem. Early 1970s.

few years after his return helped him see things clearly. He had traveled to Europe in search of *something*, scouring the museums of Paris and London in hopes of finding it. At a Junkanoo festival in Nassau, he finally saw that all that he ever needed in terms of a monumental subject was already there.[38]

Many other artists, including Télémaque, Moody, Aubrey Williams, and Maxwell Taylor, would follow Lam's example and develop a relationship with the region while remaining resident in Paris, London, and New York. Each navigated the historic decentralization of art centers that began to occur in the 1980s in different ways. The decade of the 1980s saw a critical mass of trained artists enter global spaces. Many chose to return to the Caribbean, stimulating art movements that mirrored the rise of Black artists in Britain in the 1980s and 1990s. This was an important period of consolidation for global Caribbean art practices partly because through these artists, the Caribbean, as Lam had hoped, reentered the conversation as a site of postmodern production. The reasons for this are complex. In part, it emerged through increased wealth as mass tourism and oil allowed more and more young people to seek an arts education regionally or internationally. Another factor was the intensifying political violence and resulting economic limitations in places like Haiti and the Dominican Republic. Deep fissures were also being exposed between Cuba's revolutionary dreams and its lived realities. Devastating hurricanes, changing economic policies toward the region, and political corruption that limited the hopes of independence also forced a massive movement of Caribbean people to Europe, though in lesser numbers than had done in previous generations, and increasing numbers to the United States.

Artists of Caribbean birth or descent emerging in the 1980s and 1990s flooded New York, among them the aforementioned Martinican artist Marc Latamie and the Bahamian-Trinidadian artist Janine Antoni (b. 1964); the Jamaicans Renee Cox (b. 1960) and Nari Ward; and the Trinidadian Christopher Cozier (b. 1959). Once again, institutions and relationships with communities of artists played a major role in grounding Caribbean artists in the city, allowing a number of them to completely disappear into "universality." For some, New York became a place where gallerists handled their work on the international stage and they became a part of the contemporary American art canon. For Latamie, it would become a place to work and emerge as needed, to share pointedly evocative art focused on global production, trade networks, and their imbrication with histories of Caribbean landscape, violence, and memory.

Few places became as important a site for Caribbean artists in this period as the Studio Museum in Harlem (SMH), particularly its artist-in-residence program. In 1971 Trinidad's LeRoy Clarke became the first to occupy this position. The program emerged out of the work of the Smokehouse Group, an important collective of abstract artists who created large murals in and with the Harlem community between 1968 and 1970. The group was led by the Yale-trained abstract artist William T. Williams (b. 1942) and included the sculptor Melvin Edwards (b. 1937), Billy Rose (birthdate unavailable), and Guy Ciarcia (b. 1942). Wanting to continue to support Black artists working in Harlem after the Smokehouse Group dissolved, William T. Williams drafted the proposal for a residency program at the museum. It remains part of the museum's mission to this day. Clarke remained in the program for several years, and since that time, a number of other key global Caribbean artists have been honored with the residency,

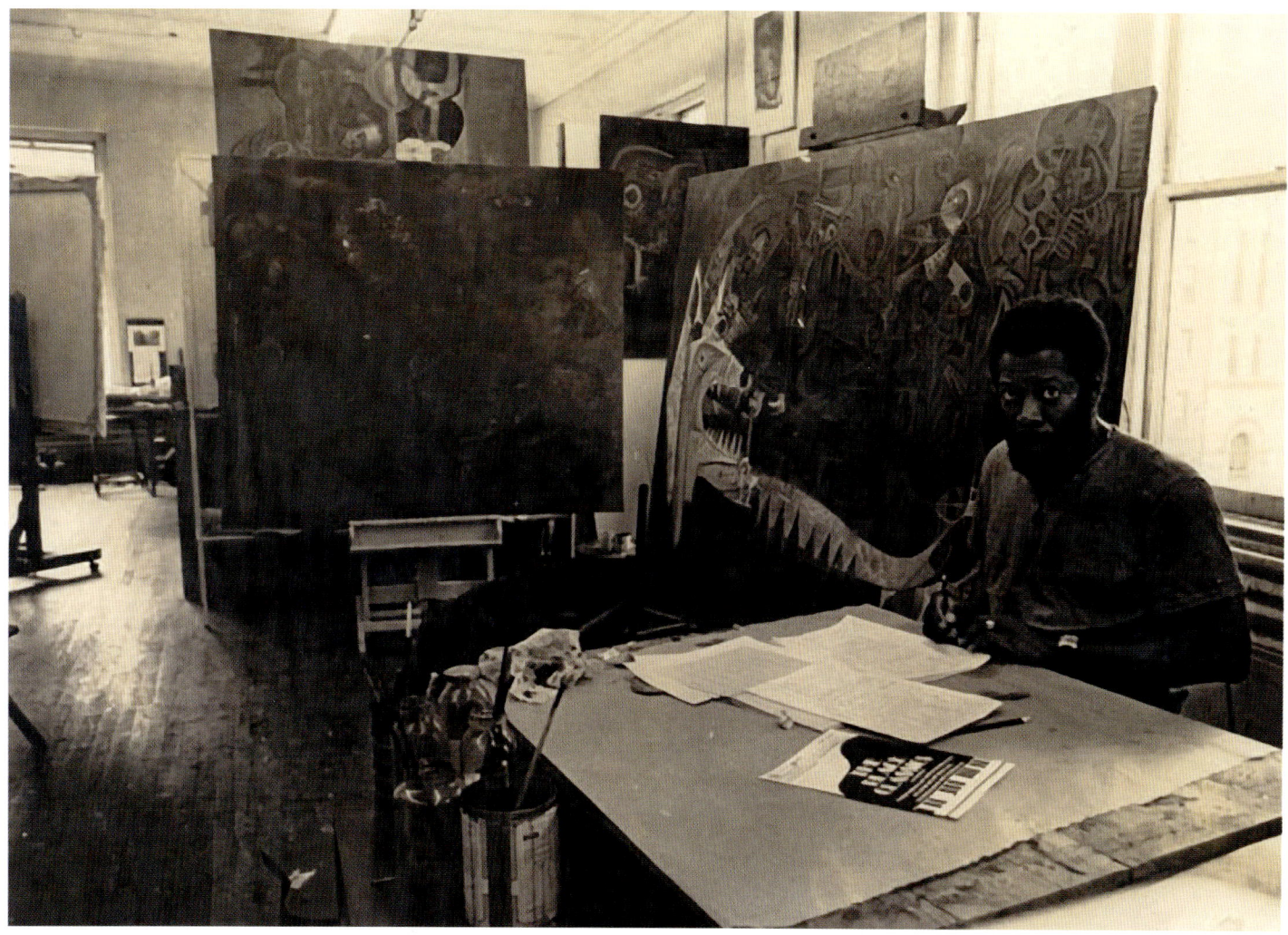
301

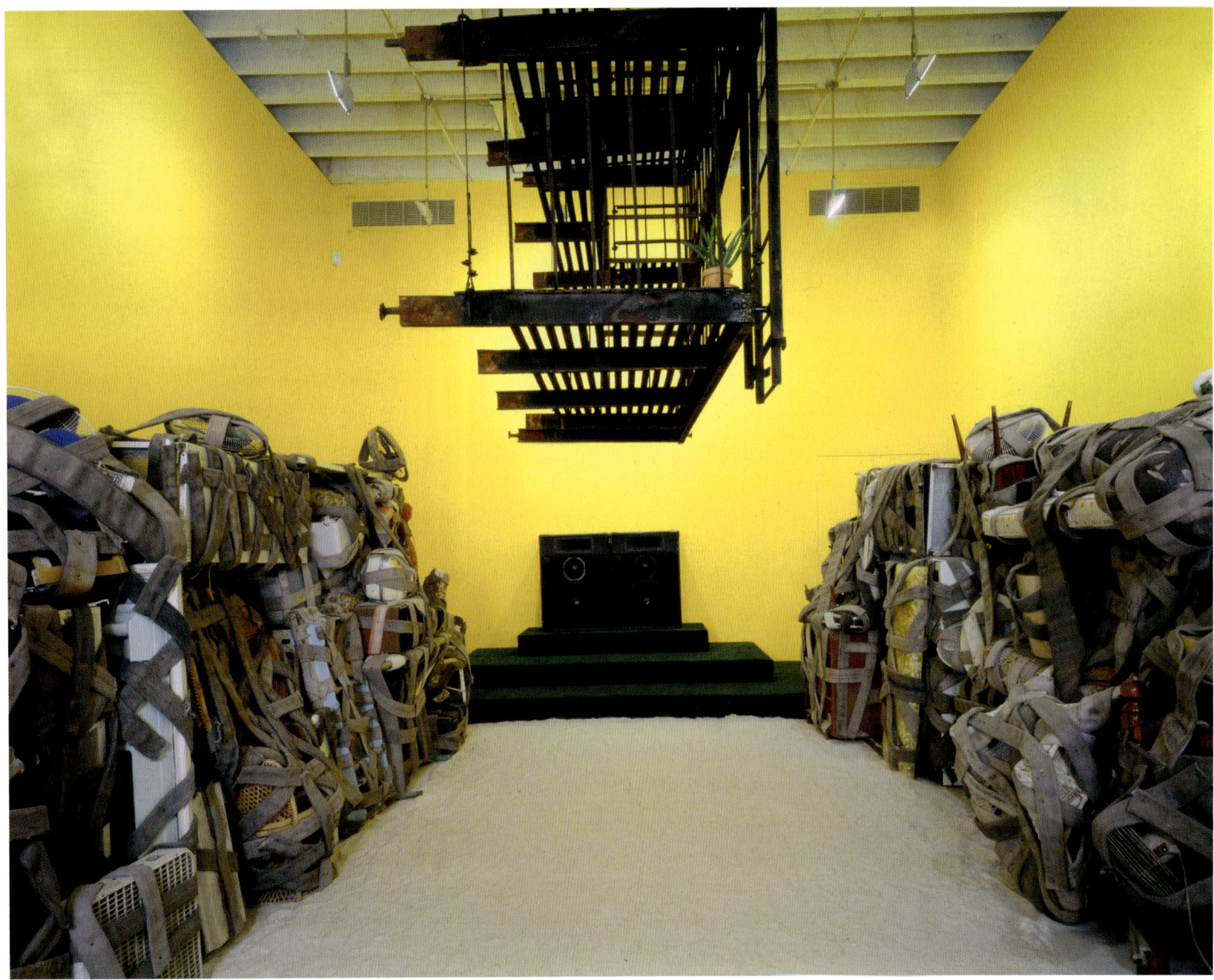

302 Nari Ward. *Happy Smilers: Duty Free Shopping*. 1996. Installation. Awning, soda bottles, fire hose, fire escape, audio recording, speakers, etc.

including the Jamaican artists Nari Ward, Petrona Morrison (b. 1954), and Dave McKenzie (b. 1977), in 1993, 1994, and 2004, respectively; the Trinidadian Nicole Awai (b. 1966) in 2000; and Andy Robert (b. 1984) of Haiti in 2016.

For Ward, the residency helped launch his professional career. In early works such as *Happy Smilers: Duty Free Shopping* (1996), we see a migrant artist, grappling with the space he now occupies in a three-dimensional experiential collage; a storefront that takes the essential form of a Jamaican restaurant in the diaspora; a bright yellow barrel awning over a green wall, with the words "Happy Smilers" flanked by images of pineapples etched in black. Liter bottles of tropical-flavored soda hang from the awning, and calypso music emanates from an unseen source. The walls of the work consist of household elements bound with decommissioned fire hoses, made to resemble shipping pallets of goods shipped around the world. In the middle of the space, a fire escape hangs precariously above the maze of goods, with a potted aloe plant sitting on a step. In context, the fire escape becomes a super object, a northern city's stand-in for a sacred ceiba tree, a potomitan in Haitian Creole, allowing passage between worlds while evoking feelings of alienation on the part of the urban migrant from the earth and the Caribbean migrants' frequent state of limbo. In this configuration, the aloe plant acts as a point of connection and salvation, used to heal all manner of things in the Caribbean: if it can make it, so can we.

If one searches for features uniting much of the work by global Caribbean artists from this period, the connection is immaterial. Rather than form, color, or technique, what binds them is the high level of criticality that asks the viewer to confront subjects and situations often forbidden in the region and beyond, in the context of a definitive turn to conceptual art and ideas. For contemporary artists, the Caribbean enters the work in different densities, but the process of creolization remains present in their practice, foundational to the larger conceptual ideas that ground the work.

The artist Christopher Cozier finished his postgraduate studies at Rutgers University in the late 1980s. Like Ward, who would benefit from the advice and mentorship of William T. Williams and the African American artist David Hammons (b. 1943), Cozier and his wife, the Trinidadian artist Irénée Shaw (b. 1963), cultivated fruitful relationships with mentors including the American painters Joan Semmel and Leon Golub. Cozier also worked as a studio assistant for Howardena Pindell (b. 1943) after graduate school, gaining important insight into the complexities of the New York art world at the time. The longer he remained in the city, however, the more he saw himself as an "inarticulate voyeur" there, and, against the advice of his mentors, Cozier decided to return to Trinidad in 1989.

In conversation with a lot of the work being produced in the global Caribbean at the time, Cozier began to craft a multimedia practice focused on ideas. Upon his return, he saw more clearly that like him, other Trinidadian artists, including John Stollmeyer (b. 1962), Wendy Nanan (b. 1955), Francisco Cabral (b. 1945) and Peter Minshall (b. 1941), were also interested in using materials and form through drawing, sculpture, installation performance, and Mas[querade] to create deeply rooted artwork that probed the complexity of Caribbean people in space and time. Notably, he recognized that they had been doing this work for a long time with little fanfare, and doing it anyway. Minshall's *Mancrab* (1983) is a modern Pigorini Zemi in its thrilling

303 Peter Minshall. *Mancrab on Dimanche Gras Night*. 1990. Video still from Carnival performance.

capacity to tell an epic history of the region through multiple media within the performance realm of Mas. Cozier's work seeks a similar critical density in a less narrative form, as can be seen in works such as the performance works *Conversation with a Shirt Jac* (1991) and *Blue Soap* (1994) and the installation *Attack of the Sandwich Men* (2002). He would later initiate his ongoing *Tropical Night* series of drawings that includes one of the most reproduced images in the history of contemporary art in the Caribbean, having appeared on more than thirty covers of scholarly books and magazines across the world (see fig. 247).

In London in the 1980s, artists branched out to take up roles that would push forward the work of Black artists. Lubaina Himid and David A. Bailey (b. 1952) became curators. Eddie Chambers became an archivist, curator, art historian, and university professor. Mark Sealy (b. 1960) became an institutional leader, eventually taking over Autograph APB, founded in 1988 as the Association of Black Photographers. Kobena Mercer (b. 1960) is an art writer, academic, critic, and historian. In the Caribbean, Cozier assumed many of these roles in addition to that of artist. As a result, he has played a unique role in framing the conversation around contemporary arts in the global Caribbean, as a curatorial consultant and curator for massive international exhibitions of Caribbean art such as *Infinite Island* (2007), *Wrestling with the Image* (2010), and *Relational Undercurrents* (2017), as well as regional efforts such as *Span Paramaribo* (2010) and the *Jamaican Biennial* (2016). He has also had a crucial impact on the cultivation of critical platforms such as the literary and scholarly journal *Small Axe*, published by Duke University Press, as well as the experimental space Alice Yard, which encourages artists, art writers, and scholars the world over to become a part of the story, and the arts organization Caribbean Contemporary Arts (CCA7), both of which are located in Port of Spain. For Cozier, "the critical space for Caribbean art is larger than the geographic island and nation. It is diasporic, meaning it exists in many places at once… wherever Caribbean people have settled and continue to imagine and respond to the world around them."[39] For global Caribbean artists like Cozier, John Beadle (b. 1964), Sheena Rose (b. 1985), Oneika Russell (b. 1980), and others who returned or who crafted a life where they practice in multiple locations and sites, *there is no "them" out there.* This shift in perception was expressed early on by a simultaneous shift in the ways many artists began to seek training.

Though many students had felt it necessary to travel abroad for art education through the earlier decades of the twentieth century, in the 1980s and 1990s, regional schools, such as the Edna Manley College of the Visual and Performing Arts (EMC) in Kingston, Jamaica, and the Instituto Superior de Arte (ISA) in Havana, Cuba, had grown to a level of renown where they began to attract regional and diasporic artists to their programs, as well as local students. While the scope of the exchange between the students and professors such as Petrona Morrison and Cecil Cooper (1946–2016) at EMC, and Belkis Ayón (1967–1999) at the ISA, requires extensive study, two remarkable examples of the impact of regional art schools, involving the artists Marcel Pinas and Ebony G. Patterson, are worth noting, as is the ethos communicated by the instructors.

In the 1990s, Suriname began a long recovery from the devastation of the prior decade: a revolution and brutal military coup in 1980; the assassination of fifteen prominent opponents of the military in 1982; a violent civil war in 1986 that pitted Maroons

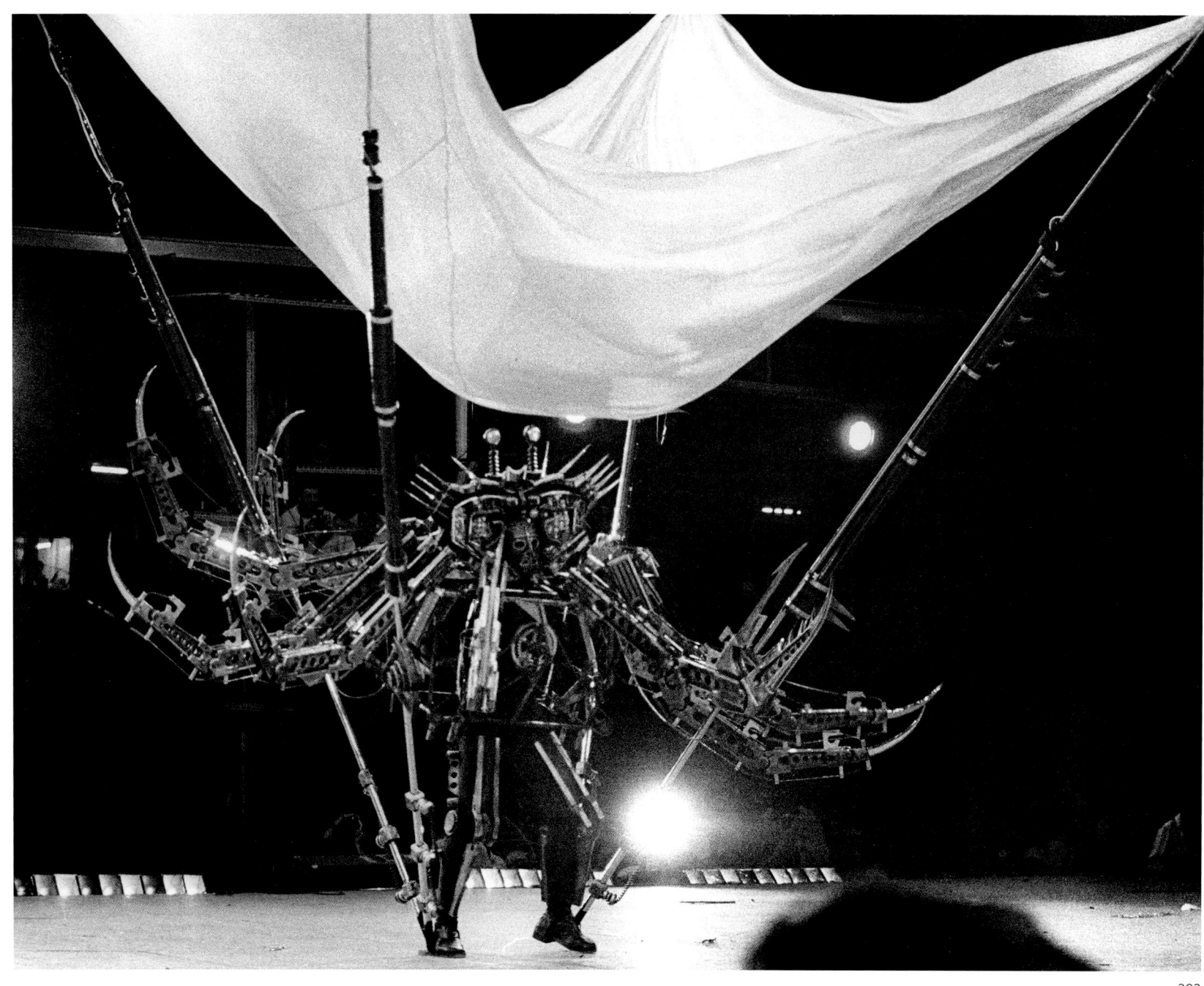

303

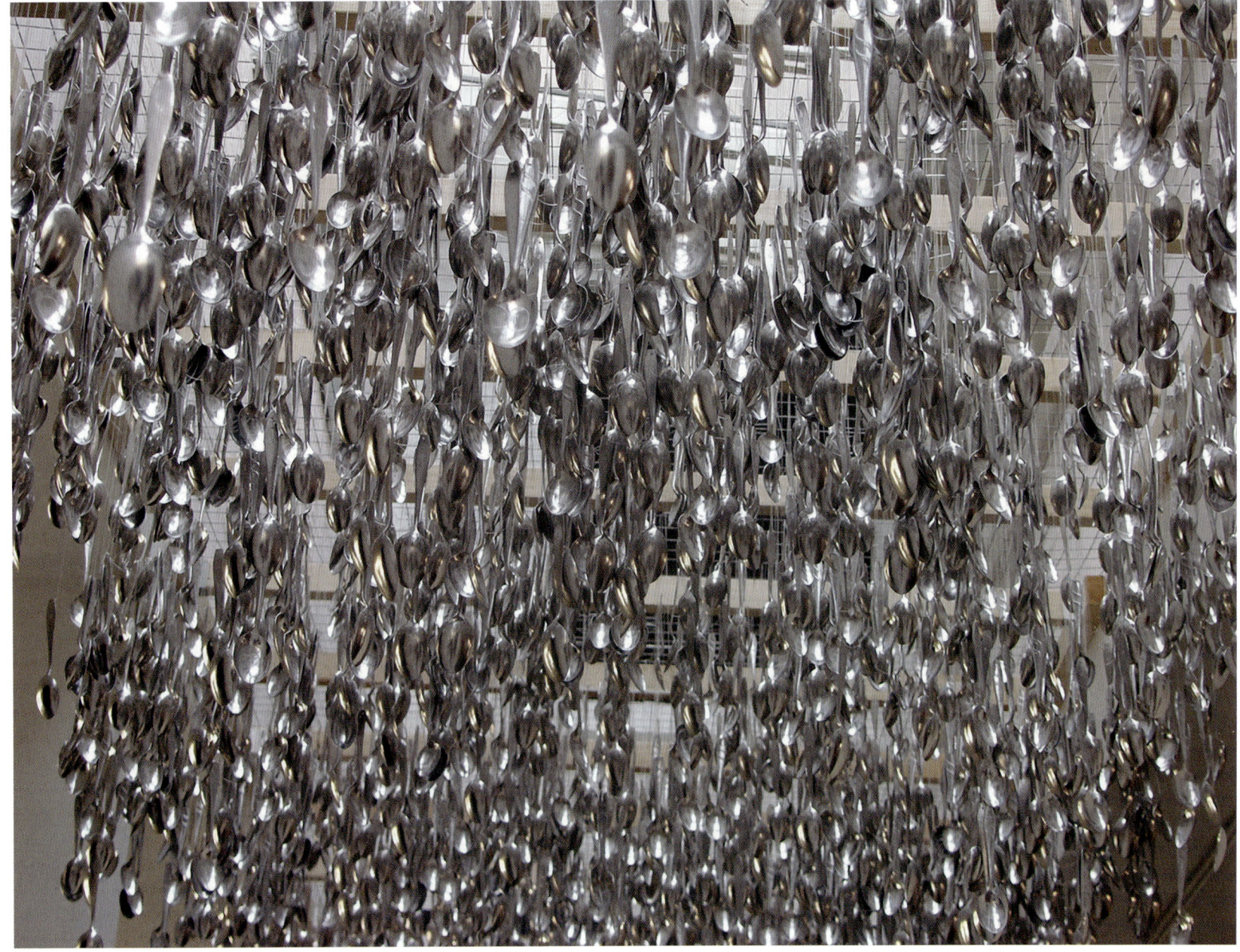

304

304 Marcel Pinas. *Sanfika*. 2009. Installation. Several thousand suspended spoons, each engraved with an Afaka sign from the language of the artist's birthplace.

against the military; and the accompanying military dictatorship that ruled the country with a heavy hand. During this period, Suriname became isolated from much of the world. Yet at the same time, there was remarkable movement in the arts, with many young artists rising from communities deeply affected by the events of the 1980s. Rather than seek professional training in Europe as one might have expected, Marcel Pinas (b. 1971), along with fellow Surinamese artist George Struikelblok (b. 1973), received scholarships to attend the EMC in Jamaica. Up to this point, their education had been immersed in European art, and they were unsure what to expect in Jamaica. For Pinas, however, attending EMC became a transformative event in his practice, largely because of his encounters with Cooper and Morrison.

Pinas is a Ndyuka Maroon. The Ndyukas were deeply affected during the civil war, forced to flee their lands to French Guiana to stave off elimination by the army. Living through this traumatic experience, Pinas was painfully aware of the realities of cultural loss. However, at school in Jamaica, Pinas was challenged to look inward for his visual resources. Having been raised in an environment where Europe occupied the peak of art hierarchies, where the destruction of one's local culture had been state-ordered and the threat of violence was real, this was not easy. But challenged by Cooper and Morrison, Pinas began to look to the graphic language of his people, Afaka, to formulate a visual language for his work. He describes it as having a mirror held up to you and seeing the full dimension of yourself for the first time.[40] Pinas's initial paintings were abstract, and he soon expanded to installations using iconic materials from Ndyuka life as material. His work represented the Black image not literally but linguistically and culturally, each as a marker of Black presence.

Pinas's encounter with Cooper and Morrison was echoed in the experience of the Jamaican-born artist Ebony G. Patterson (b. 1981). For Patterson, Cooper and Morrison, as well as Stanford Watson (b. 1959) and Natalie Butler, became crucial mentors for her while she was a student at Edna Manley. She states: "(T)hey saw me as a human being and since they were interested in my totality as a person, they were able to nurture me as an artist. I felt that when I went to graduate school, I carried all of them with me."[41] For both Patterson and Pinas, the way their teachers modeled the discipline and hard work required to be an artist was central to their personal development. As they taught, the students also saw them working and exhibiting. Patterson recalls Cooper arriving for early-morning meetings with his feet drenched with paint after having worked all night. In process, these teachers "demonstrated how to live this thing; how to make it happen and also how to support others in that, to help people along the way."[42] That ethos that Pinas encountered at EMC—that as one learns, one must help others along the way—became essential to his practice when he returned to Suriname with the intention of utilizing art to transform his community in Moengo. Though he was responsible for establishing a wildly successful cultural festival there, the way in which the people of his community became a part of his work, both symbolically and as co-producers, was extraordinary. In 2012, at the Havana Biennial, Pinas installed *Sanfika* (2009), an exhibition comprising ten thousand Ndyuka-designed spoons in the very spot where Wifredo Lam had executed his mural forty-six years before. Every element used in his installations is made by or comes from his community, including the carved spoons that make up *Sanfika*, the slingshots that comprise *Feti* (2009), and the plates and cups that are

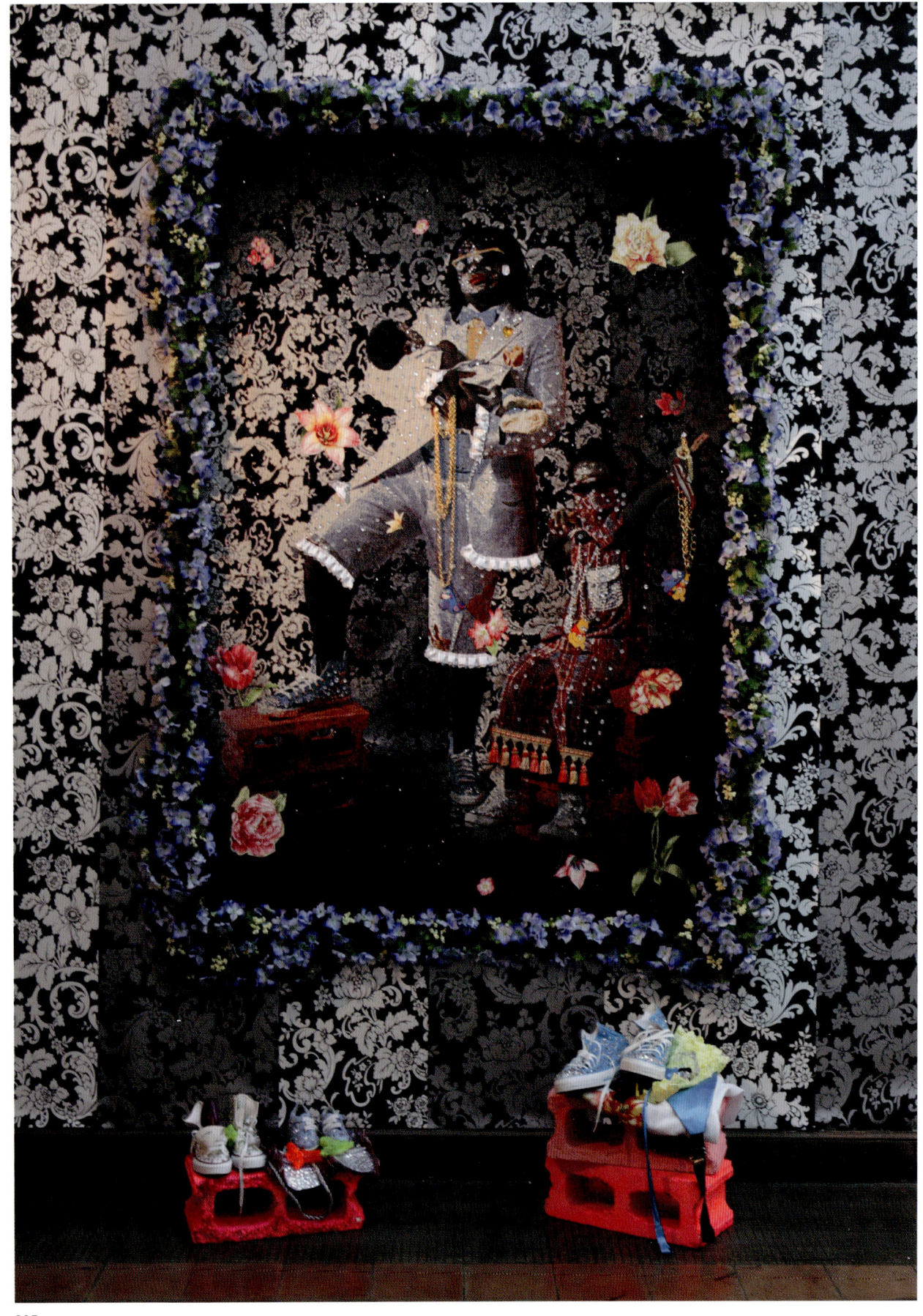

305

305 Ebony G. Patterson. *Daadi + Yutez.* 2010. Mixed media. Photo tapestry with glitter, appliqués, rhinestones, toys, etc. Private collection.

elements of *Piekien Kukuu* (2016). The installation in Havana ironically affirmed Lam's desire that art be made in the Caribbean, but in different ways. Pinas is not interested in primarily convincing the world of Ndyuka creativity, but seeks to cultivate and affirm the artistry that was always present in his culture that was almost destroyed.

For Patterson, the interior work demanded by her teachers meant looking to herself and to Jamaica for monumental subjects. This would lead to her exploration of violence, masculinity, and sexuality through dancehall, don culture, and the phenomenon of skin bleaching in works such as *Blood Breda Crew* (2008) and the *Gangstas for Life Series*, as well as an important series of works in the mid-2000s where she reconsidered iconic paintings from the Jamaican canon through her generational lens. *Daadi + Yutez* (2010), a riff on Barrington Watson's iconic *Mother and Child* (1959), and *Counting Money Haha* (2010), which reimagines the Jamaican icon Albert Huie's 1938 painting *Counting Lesson,* are examples of this work.

Like the Manley School, the ISA attracted local and international teachers and students. It would become the training ground for countless Cuban artists who came to prominence in the 1990s as well as for international artists like the Malian great Abdoulaye Konate (b. 1953). Two Barbadian artists, Ras Ishi Butcher (b. 1965) and Ras Akyem I Ramsay (b. 1953), achieved a level of success in regional exhibitions in the 1990s, and through these shows became aware of the contemporary art landscape. In their view, when the opportunity arose for further study, Cuba was the place producing the most cutting-edge work in the region. Seeking to immerse themselves in the environment that had cultivated the level of excellence they had witnessed in the work of Cuban artists, they chose to attend the Instituto Superior de Arte in the late 1990s. Both artists were consciously driven and deeply embedded spiritually and intellectually in Rastafarianism's centering of liberatory Blackness. Cuba provided them with a level of freedom to push these ideas further, and, as had been the case with Cecil Cooper, artists and teachers at the ISA such as Belkis Ayón modeled a level of commitment and discipline to craft that was invaluable. Like Cooper, Ayón would be seen on campus drenched in the evidence of her labor, her hands and arms covered in ink after printing for hours on end.

For Ishi, the heart of his work became clear as early as 1975, when a group of *bredren* from Jamaica called the Sons of Thunder visited his high school. In his words, he immediately "identified with their concept of 'whole blackness.'"[43] The experience triggered a self-reflexive journey that enabled him to think through the violence enacted upon the Black body, both self-inflicted and from external forces in his work. While Ras Ishi's work focuses on the representational capacity of the Black Bajan (Barbadian) woman, Ras Akyem's art more clearly positions the Black male as protagonist, empowered to directly confront situations that seek to imprison his mind, body, and spirit and forge a more self-directed path, as seen in works such as *Dead-Stone* (2005). For both of these artists, these institutions allowed for synergies they believe would not have been experienced had they studied elsewhere. They played and continue to play a fundamental role in the way the Caribbean is imagined today, by Caribbean artists refusing to become peripheral in their own discourse.

A Global Archipelago

> What good are roots if you can't take them with you?
> —Kwame Anthony Appiah[44]

Today, whether based on home islands, neighboring islands, or in cities across the world, Caribbean artists have come to know each other in unprecedented ways as part of a global imaginary. The division between home and away continues to dissolve as opportunities to collaborate, exhibit together, discuss work, and connect through virtual conversations, shared exhibitions, conferences, symposia, and residencies both inside and outside the region become possible. This has been led in large part by a growing network of formal and informal artist-led organizations and by the sheer number of artists practicing around the world. These artists have joined in the discourse not by accident of birth, but as the result of a choice to directly engage a Caribbean critical apparatus. The conversation includes artists like the Puerto Rican multimedia and public artist Miguel Luciano (b. 1972), who, in works like *Plátano Pride* (2006), transforms objects associated with the region into super signifiers, destabilizing stereotypes using dry, cutting wit, as does the work of Sheena Rose; Alberta Whittle (b. 1980), an artist of Barbadian-Scottish parentage; and Joanne Petit-Frére (b. 1987), a visual artist born in New York of Haitian descent. In a similar vein, the artwork of the Dominican-Haitian artist Firelei Báez magnifies the presence and power of women, as in *Sans-Souci* (2015) and her *Ciguapa* series, which features the female trickster figure from Dominican culture. Báez is leading a new generation of Dominican artists, the majority of whom are women, who have emerged in the wake of luminaries like Jorge Pineda (b. 1961) and Tony Capellán (1955–2017), whose art deeply penetrated the peculiarities of Dominican life in relation to the world, and, in the case of Pineda, probed the concept of boundaries, including the country's relationship with its neighbor Haiti and the entanglements of race, family, history, and power referenced therein. The work of the New York–based artists Kenny Rivero, Lucia Hierro (b. 1987), and Joiri Minaya (b. 1990) is also part of this contemporary Dominican landscape.

As global Caribbean art continues to enunciate itself across the world, the city of Miami has emerged as an important locus in the critical discourse. The Haitian artist Edouard Duval-Carrié arrived in Miami in 1992 from Paris and has become an important voice through his contemporary practice and curatorial work centered at the Little Haiti Cultural Center in the Miami community known by that name. Duval-Carrié is not alone in making Miami the location of his studio practice. Both established and rising stars such as Vickie Pierre (birthdate unavailable), Adler Guerrier (b. 1975), Asser Saint-Val (b. 1974), and Morel Doucet (b. 1990), all of Haitian descent, as well as the Jamaican Jacqueline Gopie (b. 1960), have worked in Miami for years and forged practices that haven taken their work far beyond its boundaries.

Despite the burgeoning artistic activity, the character of Miami as an art space more generally and as a global Caribbean art space specifically remains to be determined, partly because of the general sense that, aside from the mega fair Art Basel and the impressive collection of contemporary art at the Pérez Art Museum Miami (PAMM), the city lacks a sustained engagement with the arts of the Caribbean and Latin America, despite its Latin culture and playful description as the "capital of the Caribbean." Reasons cited for this apparent incongruity have been the lack of money

306 Miguel Luciano. *Plátano Pride*. 2006. Chromogenic photograph. New York, Brooklyn Museum.

307 Alexandre Arrechea. *The Weight of Emptiness*. 2005. Digital media.

invested in the arts; the scarcity of critical writing; the seasonal nature of art activities; the smaller number of collectors and galleries than one finds in cities like New York, Berlin, and London; and the continuing draw of other locations for artists who, as they begin their professional lives in the South Florida city, search for larger, more established artistic communities with greater career opportunities. As time passes, however, it is becoming clearer that for a younger, rapidly expanding, immigrant-based city like Miami, those models may not be completely relevant for much longer. Despite the notable increase in current and proposed institutions in the city, the arts have taken on the decentralized character of the city itself and cater to a somewhat migratory population, its artists drawn to and also propelled by the anonymity and free flow Miami affords between the space and the world.

Besides the impact of artists primarily from Haiti, Miami's artistic landscape has been shaped most consistently by Cuban artists whose relationship with the city has shifted over the past fifty years. Large numbers of artists and intellectuals, such as the author and folklorist Lydia Cabrera (1899–1991) and Antonia Eiriz (1929–1995), began to arrive in Miami after the Cuban Revolution, either to stay indefinitely or to relocate to other American and global cities, while others arrived in the latter part of the twentieth century as refugees during the Mariel boatlift in 1980 or through other means. Artistic arrivals in the 1960s, 1970s, and 1980s included Juana Valdes (b. 1963), whose work centers on abstracted ruminations of Blackness, gender, and spaces of belonging. Current residents include Rosa Naday Garmendia (b. 1963), Tomás Esson (b. 1963), José Bedia (b. 1959), and Alexandre Arrechea (b. 1970). How much time these artists spend in Miami is unknown, but they are often joined throughout the year by other artists from across Latin America and the Caribbean who are drawn to the city by numerous residencies and exhibition opportunities and relatively inexpensive places to work.

Beyond the locus of cities like Miami, artist residents of the global Caribbean can be found across the world. The archipelago has gone global. Los Angeles has become home to the Bahamian artist April Bey (birthdate unavailable) and the Jamaican Andrea Chung (b. 1978); Atlanta, the base for the Jamaican artist Cosmo Whyte (b. 1982) and the Bahamian Lillian Blades (b. 1973). In some cases, because of the necessity of increased mobility, some artists like Lavar Munroe (b. 1982), originally from The Bahamas, have become peripatetic, while his critical focus on the dystopic afterlives of postcolonial, post-independence violence and manhood in the Caribbean continues uninterrupted. Other artists hide in plain sight, such as the Jamaican photographer Ruddy Roye (b. 1969), who first gained international attention through social media. Roye's work focuses on the nuances of Blackness and violence in the United States. He travels extensively to bear witness to Black life and death, being and mourning, to document the lives of those afflicted after the television cameras and the national and international media outlets have departed the scene. His Trinidad-based counterpart, the Jamaican-born Marlon James (b. 1980), has also had opportunities to show his photo-based work widely in both popular and fine art formats. A series of portraits James recently completed centered on the phenomenon of skin bleaching in Jamaica. Originally commissioned by the journal *Small Axe*, the series was featured in an article in the American fashion magazine *Marie Claire* and demonstrates the global network commonly drawn upon by artists in the region to share work.

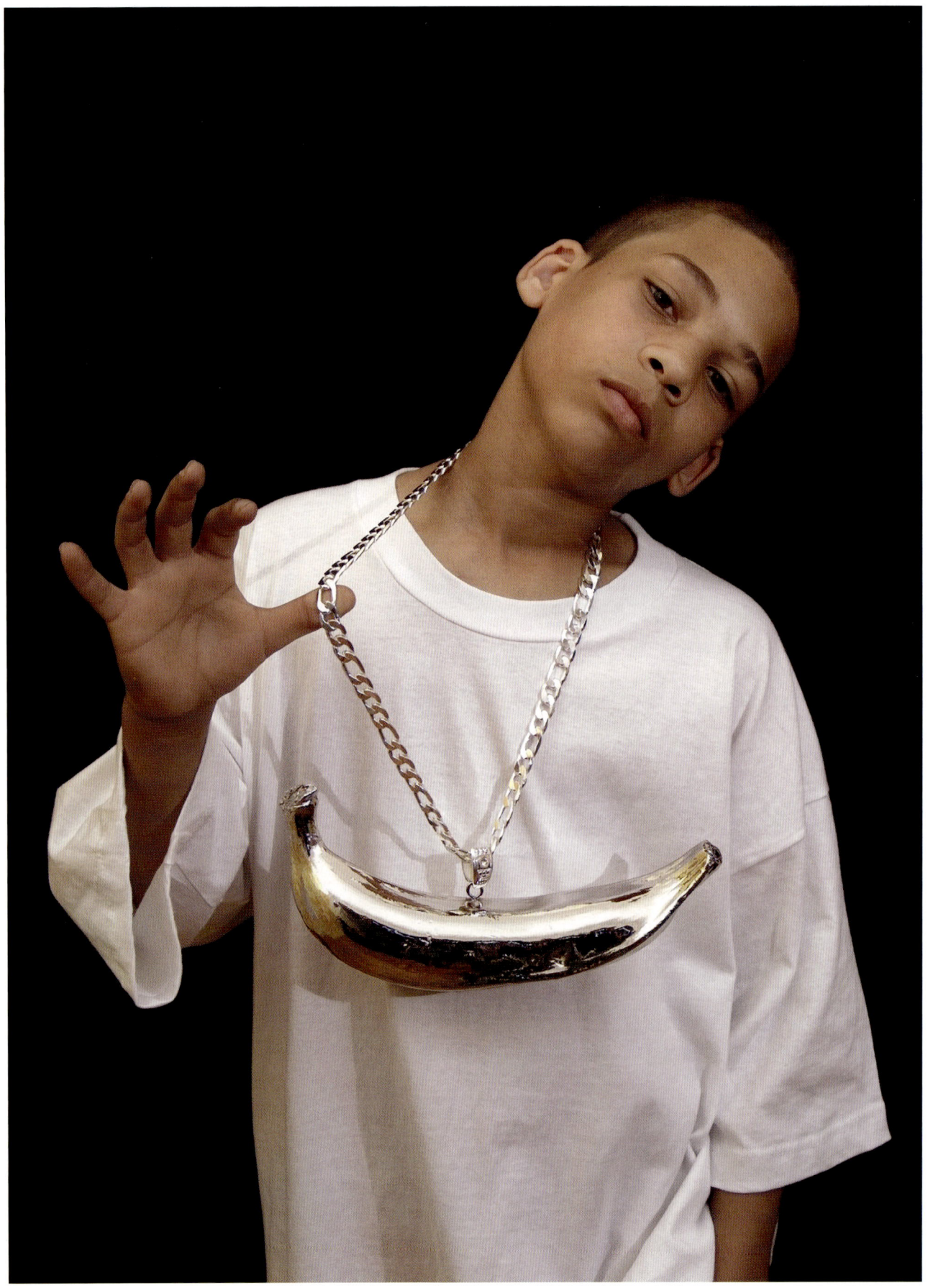

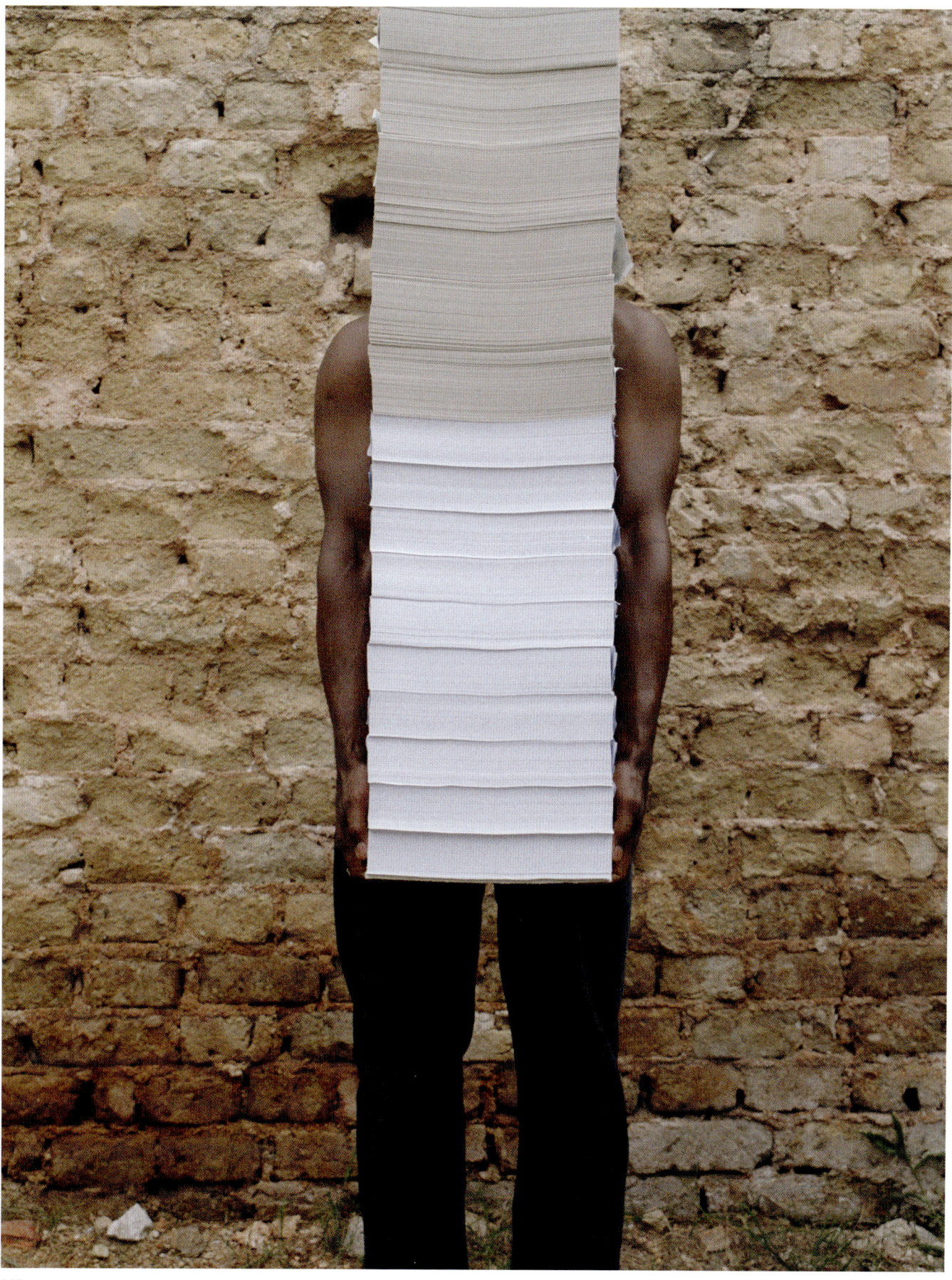

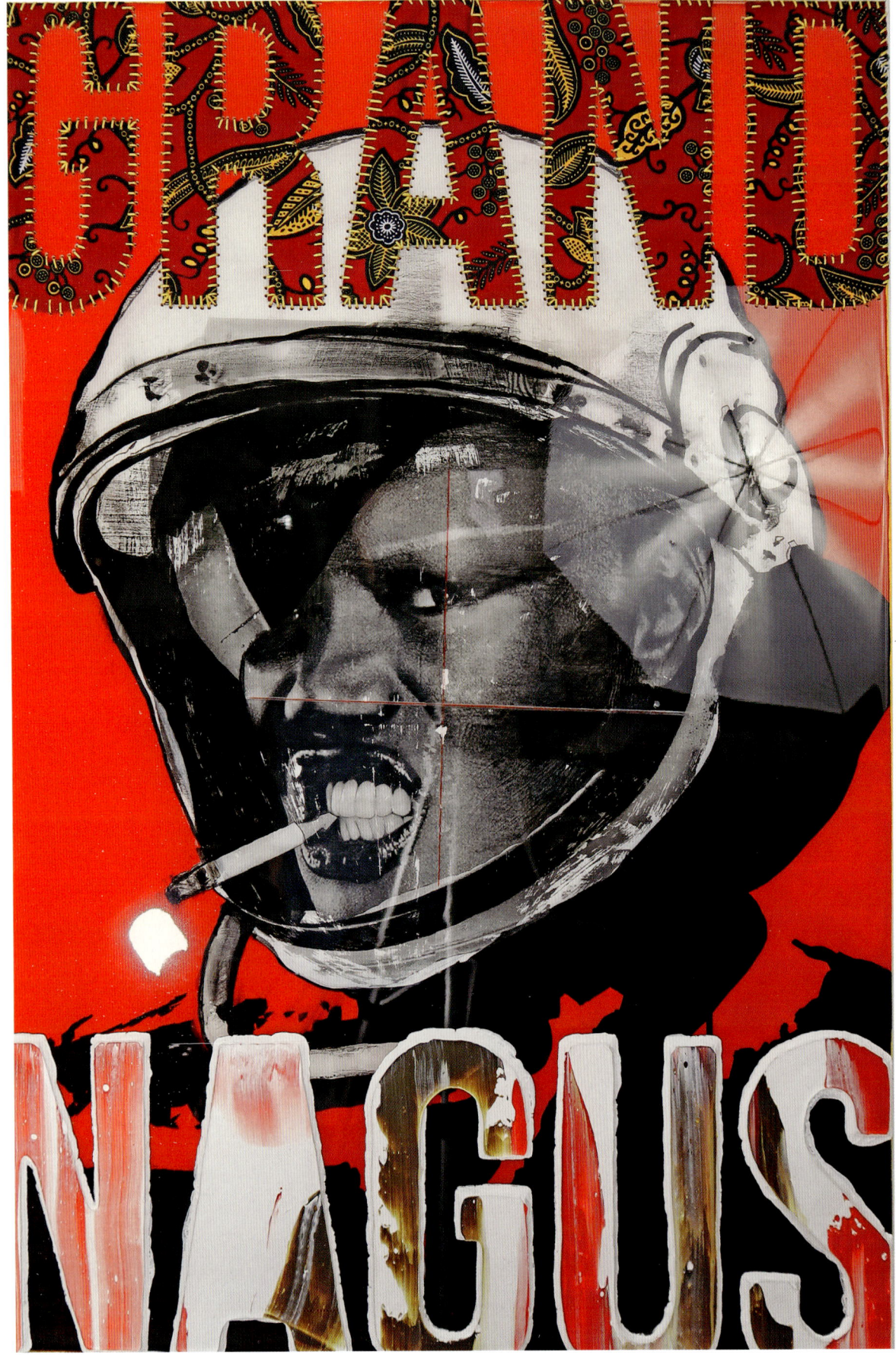

308

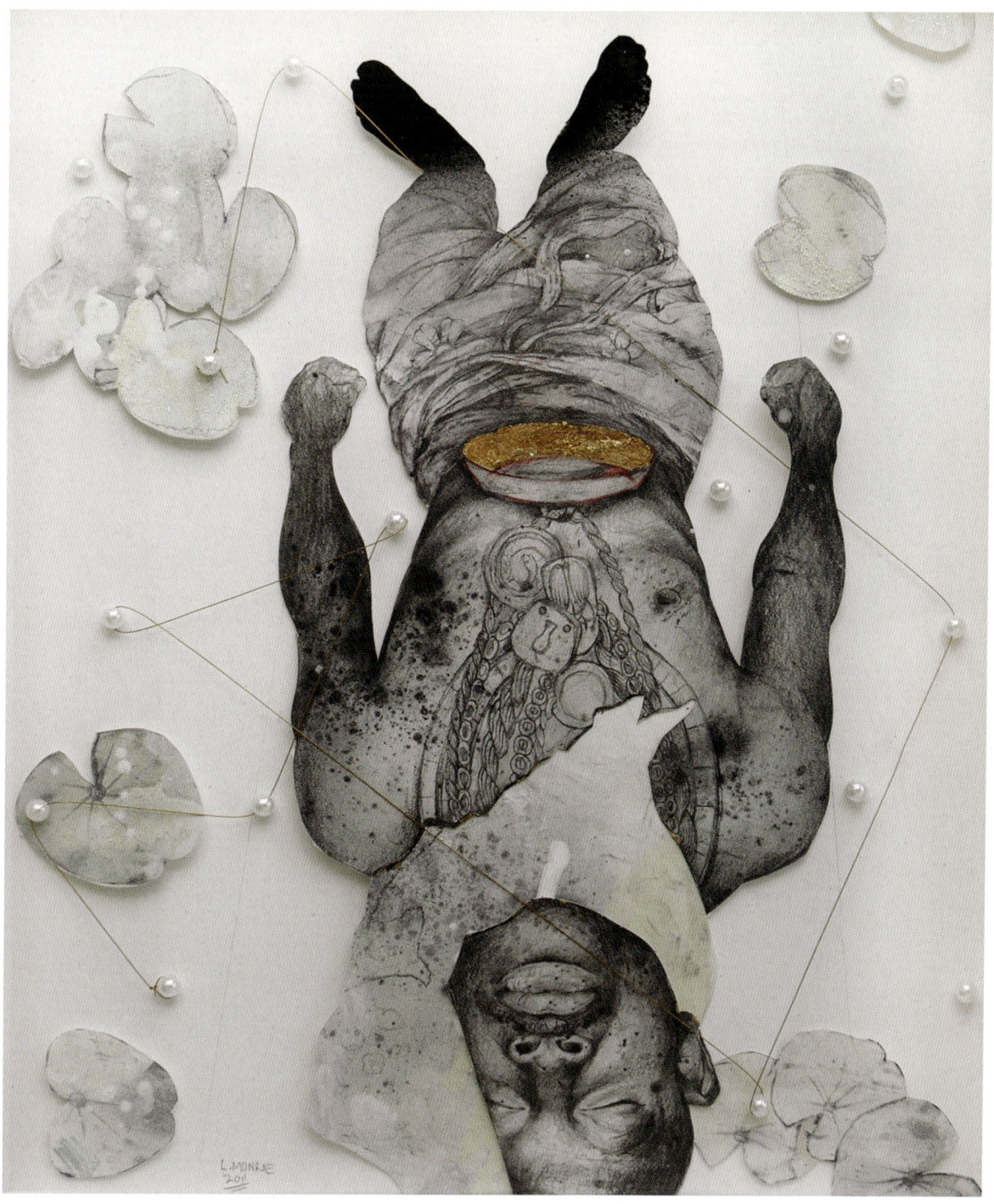

308 April Bey. *By the Grace of the Grand Nagus*. 2018. Ghanaian Hitarget Chinese fabric sewn into resin on panel, acrylic paint. Private collection.

309 Lavar Munroe. *Floater* (study). 2011. Graphite drawing, acrylic paint, pearls, copper, and 24k gold leaf on cut paper. The Bahamas, The Dawn Davies Collection.

310 Joscelyn Gardner. *Coffee Arabica (Clarissa)*. 2011. Hand-colored stone lithograph on frosted mylar.

In Japan, one can commune with Trinidad-born Marlon Griffith (b. 1976), whose *Powder Box Schoolgirl* series (2009) came to life there and was later produced in his homeland. In Amsterdam one can do studio visits with Patricia Kaersenhout (b. 1966) and Remy Jungerman (b. 1959), both of Suriname, and Felix De Rooy (b. 1952) of Curaçao, among others. In London, visits with Blue Curry (b. 1974) and Lynn Parotti (b. 1968), both born in The Bahamas, land you back in the Caribbean. The same is true in Berlin with Jean-Ulrick Désert (b. 1960) of Haiti and in Hamburg with Nicholas Morris (b. 1967) of Jamaica. Fellow Jamaican Joscelyn Gardner's seminal *Creole Portraits* series came to life in Toronto, but the series pieces together historical ways of image making in the Caribbean, merging histories of botanical illustration with the haptic, life-affirming action of hair braiding, to depict the lives of women whose individual presence was marked only by notes of their assaults in their enslavers' diaries.

This dissolution of "here and there" due to an increased mobility paradoxically sutures a global Caribbean arts community bolstered in part by formal and informal art institutions working to ensure that the discourse does not privilege location. In the last twenty years, encouraged by the success and focus of global institutions like Autograph and INIVA in London, and early incarnations of the Havana Biennial, the global Caribbean has become the site of an artist-led conversation evidenced in the upstart nature of Haiti's Ghetto Biennale and the expansion of the National Gallery of Jamaica's recent series of biennials that reached out to include the diaspora. Important work has also taken place in privately operated, artist-run, or artist-centered spaces throughout the region, all driven by the expressed desire to expand the critical discussion and connect with the global community, while nurturing the place where one is planted. Over the years, they have included large spaces like the Contemporary Arts Center (CCA7, 1997–2006); Alice Yard, the collaboration of Christopher Cozier, Nicholas Laughlin, and Sean Leonard (1999–present); Insituto Buena Bista (IBB), managed by the artist Tirzo Martha in Curaçao; L'Artocarpe in Guadeloupe; Elvis Fuentes's Foundation Ateliers in Aruba; Deborah Anzinger and NLS I Jamaica; John Cox and Heino Schmid's Popopstudios in The Bahamas (1999–2016); Groundation Grenada; Hillside House in The Bahamas, led by Antonius Roberts; Fresh Milk in Barbados, established by Annalee Davis; Marcel Pinas's Tembe Art Studio in Suriname; Espace d'art contemporain 14°N 61°W in Martinique; the artists' collective Quintapata in the Dominican Republic; and Diaspora Vibe Incubator in Miami.

In the essay "Between Narratives and Other Spaces," Christopher Cozier muses how the desire for national narratives, as part of the project of nation, is a monument of history rather than a "critical activity."[45] What Cozier is concerned with is the tendency to treat the Caribbean, with its history of federation, as a nationalistic body, and discuss its art in terms of an endless search for a singular essence or aesthetic. The Caribbean aesthetic was an idea that committed members of the CAM generation, particularly Kamau Brathwaite, grappled with for years. The expectation that a single aesthetic could be found represents a limit in the theories gifted to the present by that extraordinary generation. Any attempt to place Caribbean artistic production and history in such a narrow box is akin to gathering smoke. Based on a nationalistic viewpoint, as Cozier observed, it places the contemporary artist in a peculiar yet eerily familiar position: the need to

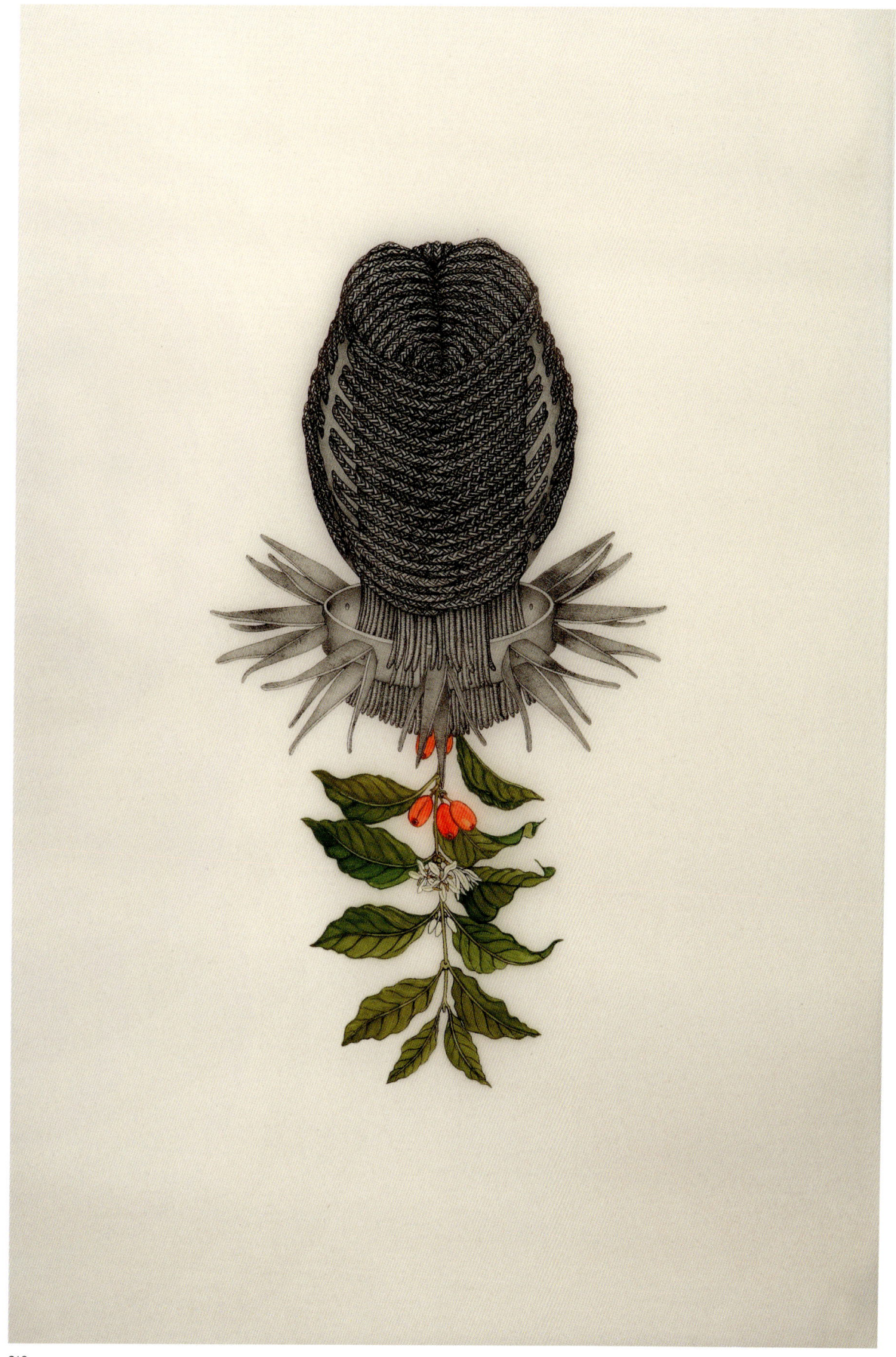

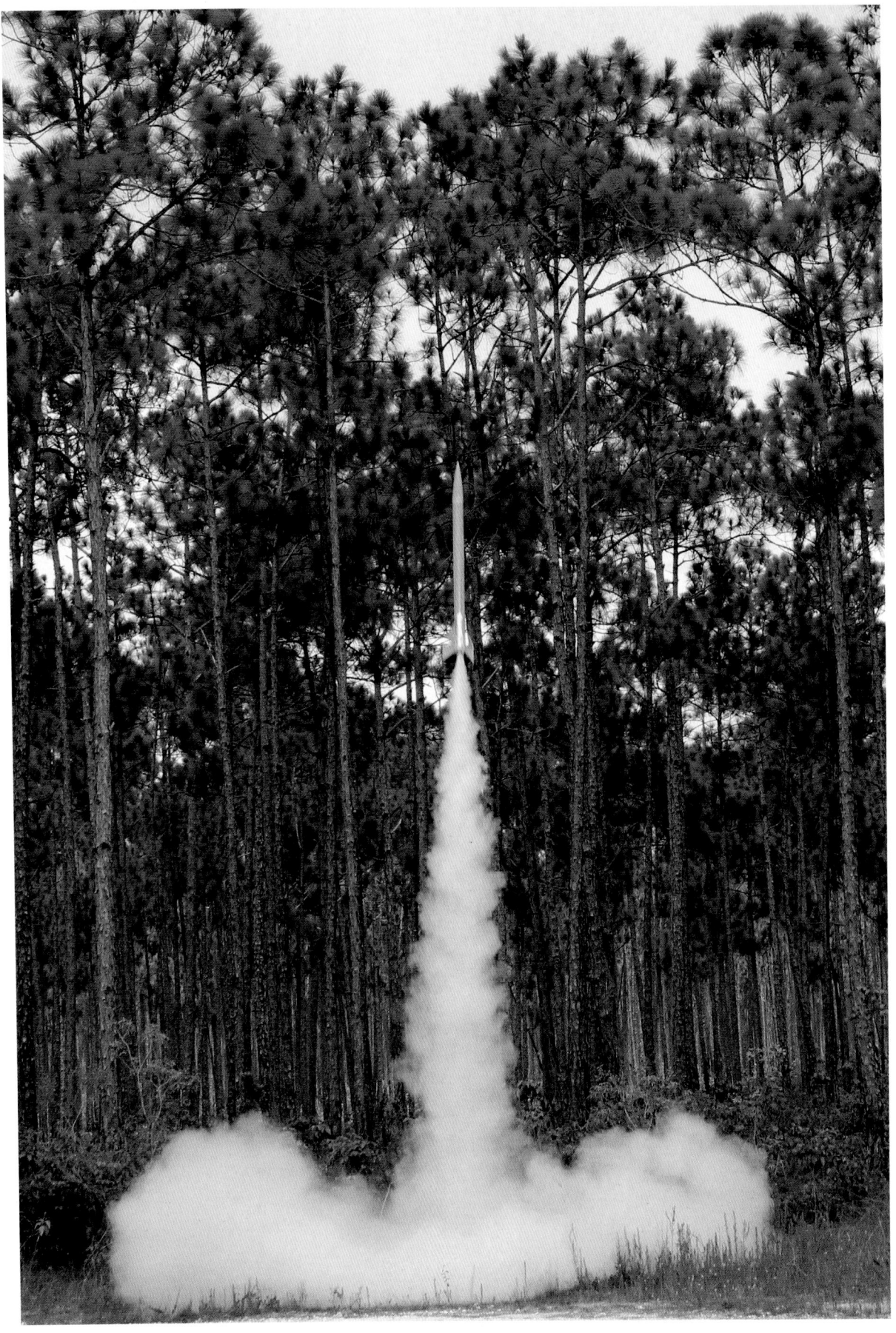

311

311 Tavares Strachan. *Blast Off*. 2008-2009. Video of glass rocket launched with sugarcane fuel. Exhibited, Venice Biennale, 2013.

resist a new postcolonial frame that mimics the one they thought they had escaped.[46]

In his early work *The Color of the Sun* (2003), the artist Tavares Strachan (b. 1979) attached a light meter to his mother's house in The Bahamas and transmitted the reading over the internet to his dorm room at the Rhode Island School of Design, where a corresponding light had been wired to respond in relative intensity to re-create, in his room, sunshine. Through material, process, and form, Strachan's is a work that escapes the inscription Cozier and contemporary artists seek to avoid, because, like the global Caribbean itself, it is without a center or defined boundaries. In its release of that tangible center, the work creates an aesthetic experience that is poignant, beautiful, and deeply meaningful, dematerializing space and further dissolving real and conceptual boundaries through the elements of light and heat.

The intentionality of this work is reaffirmed in the work *Blast Off* (2008–2009). For the piece, Strachan made a series of rockets out of glass made with a type of pure sand called aragonite found in the Caribbean. With a small group, he traveled to the local pine forests and launched the rockets one by one into space. The resulting images are a bit disjunctive; no one expects rocket launches to occur in pine barrens in small countries in the absence of space programs. Therefore, to even approach the work requires a reconsideration of material, process, and signification in relation to the Caribbean in ways that recall the work of an unknown Taíno artist five hundred years before. It is an artistic intervention centered in global Caribbean art practices where an artist draws from all he or she knows to render conceptually the limitless capacity of Black being, even when the literal image of Black people is no longer present.

NOTES

ILLUSTRATIONS

INDEX

NOTES

Preface

1. The essays on *casta* paintings by Thomas Cummins in *The Image of the Black in Western Art*, volume III, part 3, and on the Caribbean by the late Petrine Archer in volume V, part 1, have been edited for and reprinted in the present volume.

2. David Bindman and Henry Louis Gates, Jr., *The Image of the Black in Western Art* (Cambridge, MA: Belknap Press of Harvard University Press, 2010–2014), viii–ix. (The text of the preface is repeated in every volume of the series.)

3. David Bindman, Suzanne Blier, and Henry Louis Gates, Jr., *The Image of the Black in African and Asian Art* (Cambridge, MA: Belknap Press of Harvard University Press, 2017), ix.

Introduction

1. Fernando Ortiz, "*Por la integración cubana de blancos y negros*," *Revista Bimestre Cubana* 51 (1943): 258.

2. Alfonso Franco Silva, *La esclavitud en Sevilla y su tierra a fines de la edad media* (Seville, Spain: Diputación Provincial, 1979); José L. Cortés López, *La esclavitud negra en la España peninsular del siglo XVI* (Salamanca, Spain: Universidad de Salamanca, 1989); William Phillips, *Historia de la esclavitud en España* (Madrid: Playor, 1990); Debra Blumenthal, *Enemies and Familiars: Slavery and Mastery in Fifteenth-Century Valencia* (Ithaca, NY: Cornell University Press, 2009).

3. John K. Thornton, *A Cultural History of the Atlantic World, 1250–1820* (New York: Cambridge University Press, 2012), 22.

4. Manuel Lobo Cabrera, *La esclavitud en las Canarias Orientales en el siglo XVI: Negros, moros y moriscos* (Santa Cruz de Tenerife: Ediciones del Cabildo Insular de Gran Canaria, 1982).

5. Robin Blackburn, *The Making of New World Slavery: From the Baroque to the Modern, 1492–1800* (London: Verso, 1997), 52; Vicenta Cortés Alonso, *La esclavitud en Valencia durante el reinado de los Reyes Católicos, 1479–1516* (Valencia, Spain: Ayuntamiento, 1964); A. C. de C. M. Saunders, *A Social History of Black Slaves and Freedmen in Portugal, 1441–1555* (New York: Cambridge University Press, 1982).

6. Matthew Restall, "Black Conquistadors: Armed Africans in Early Spanish America," *The Americas* 57, no. 2 (2000): 172.

7. Consuelo Varela, *La caída de Cristóbal Colón: El juicio de Bobadilla* (Madrid: Marcial Pons, 2006), 142, 155, 246. Some of the documents concerning Juan Moreno are transcribed on the website by City University of New York, Dominican Studies Institute, First Blacks in the Americas: The African Presence in the Dominican Republic, http://firstblacks.org/en/summaries/arrival-01-free-and-enslaved/.

8. Restall, "Black Conquistadors"; Fernando Ortiz, *Los negros esclavos* (Havana: Editorial de Ciencias Sociales, 1975), 81–82.

9. Carlos E. Deive, *La esclavitud del negro en Santo Domingo, 1492–1844*, 2 vols. (Santo Domingo, Dominican Republic: Museo del Hombre Dominicano, 1980), 1:18–22.

10. Alex Borucki, David Eltis, and David Wheat, "Atlantic History

and the Slave Trade to Spanish America," *American Historical Review* (April 2015): 433–461; Hugh Thomas, *The Slave Trade: The Story of the Atlantic Slave Trade, 1440–1870* (New York: Simon & Schuster, 1997).

11. John Thornton, *Africa and Africans in the Making of the Atlantic World, 1400–1680* (New York: Cambridge University Press, 1998), 184–192.

12. Antonio Carreira, *Cabo Verde: Formaçao e extinçao de uma sociedade escravocrata (1460–1878)* (Praia, Cape Verde: Instituto Cabo-Verdeano do Livro, 1983); B. Barry, "Senegambia from the Sixteenth to the Eighteenth Century: Evolution of the Wolof, Sereer and 'Tukuloor,'" in *Africa from the Sixteenth to the Eighteenth Century*, ed. B. A. Ogot (Paris: UNESCO, 1992), 262–299.

13. Enriqueta Vila Vilar, *Hispanoamérica y el comercio de esclavos* (Seville, Spain: EEHA, 1977); Antonino Vidal Ortega, *Cartagena de Indias y la región histórica del Caribe, 1580–1640* (Seville, Spain: Universidad de Sevilla, 2002); David Wheat, *Atlantic Africa and the Spanish Caribbean, 1570–1640* (Chapel Hill: University of North Carolina Press, 2016). Jorge Felipe Gonzalez provided additional research into these numbers.

14. Herbert S. Klein, *African Slavery in Latin America and the Caribbean* (New York: Oxford University Press, 1986), 36–37.

15. Stuart B. Schwartz, *Sugar Plantations in the Formation of Brazilian Society: Bahia, 1550–1835* (New York: Cambridge University Press, 1985), 65–72.

16. Stuart B. Schwartz, ed. *Tropical Babylons: Sugar and the Making of the Atlantic World, 1450–1680* (Chapel Hill: University of North Carolina Press, 2004).

17. Laurent Dubois and Richard Lee Turits, *Freedom Roots: Histories from the Caribbean* (Chapel Hill: University of North Carolina Press, 2019), 53–92.

18. Borucki, Eltis, and Wheat, "Atlantic History and the Slave Trade to Spanish America," 433–461.

19. Alejandro de la Fuente and Ariela J. Gross, *Becoming Free, Becoming Black: Race, Freedom, and Law in Cuba, Virginia, and Louisiana* (New York: Cambridge University Press, 2020).

20. James Sweet, *Recreating Africa: Culture, Kinship, and Religion in the African-Portuguese World, 1441–1770* (Chapel Hill: University of North Carolina Press, 2003); Michael Gomez, *Exchanging Our Country Marks: The Transformation of African Identities in the Colonial and Antebellum South* (Chapel Hill: University of North Carolina Press, 1998); Paul Christopher Johnson and Stephan Palmié, "Afro-Latin American Religions," in *Afro-Latin American Studies: An Introduction*, ed. Alejandro de la Fuente and George Reid Andrews (New York: Cambridge University Press, 2018), 438–485.

21. João José Reis, *Slave Rebellion in Brazil: The Muslim Uprising of 1835 in Bahia* (Baltimore: Johns Hopkins University Press, 1993); Manuel Barcia, *The Great African Slave Revolt of 1825: Cuba and the Fight for Freedom in Matanzas* (Baton Rouge: Louisiana State University Press, 2012), 100; María del Carmen Barcia Zequeira, *La otra familia: Parientes, redes y descendencia de los esclavos en Cuba* (Havana: Casa de las Américas, 2003); Aisnara Perera Díaz and María de los Angeles Meriño Fuentes, *El cabildo carabalí viví de Santiago de Cuba: Familia, cultura y sociedad (1797–1909)* (Santiago de Cuba: Editorial Oriente, 2013); Philip A. Howard, *Changing History: Afro-Cuban Cabildos and Societies of Color in the Nineteenth Century* (Baton Rouge: Louisiana State University Press, 1998).

22. Matthew Restall, *The Black Middle: Africans, Mayas, and Spaniards in Colonial Yucatan* (Stanford, CA: Stanford University Press, 2013); Herman L. Bennett, *Africans in Colonial Mexico: Absolutism, Christianity, and Afro-Creole Consciousness, 1570–1640* (Bloomington: Indiana University Press, 2003).

23. Leslie King-Hammond, "Identifying Spaces of Blackness: The Aesthetics of Resistance and Identity in American Plantation Art," in *Landscape of Slavery: The Plantation in American Art*, ed. Angela D. Mack and Stephen G. Hoffius (Columbia: University of South Carolina Press, 2008), 58.

24. Tatiana Flores, "Disturbing Categories, Remapping Knowledge," in *The Routledge Companion to African American Art History*, ed. Eddie Chambers (New York: Routledge, 2019), 134–145.

25. Edward Long, *The History of Jamaica or, General Survey of the Antient and Modern State of that Island* (London: T. Lowndes, 1774), 2: 260. The genesis of the caste system in Spanish America is analyzed in María Elena Martínez, *Genealogical Fictions: Limpieza de Sangre, Religion, and Gender in Colonial Mexico* (Stanford, CA: Stanford University Press, 2008).

26. Lara E. Putnam, *Radical Moves: Caribbean Migrants and the Politics of Race in the Jazz Age* (Chapel Hill: University of North Carolina Press, 2003); Frank A. Guridy, *Forging Diaspora: Afro-Cubans and African Americans in a World of Empire and Jim Crow* (Chapel Hill: University of North Carolina Press, 2010), 61–106; Andrea J. Queeley, *Rescuing Our Roots: The African Anglo-Caribbean Diaspora in Contemporary Cuba* (Gainesville: University Press of Florida, 2015).

27. Krista A. Thompson, "Preoccupied with Haiti: The Dream of Diaspora in African American Art, 1915–1942," *American Art* 21, no. 3 (2007): 74–97.

1. The Configuration of the Afro-Brazilian Body, 1800–1900: Race, Slavery, Agency, and Celebration

1. M. I. Finley, *Ancient Slavery and Modern Ideology* (London: Chatto and Windus, 1980), 11.

2. For an overview of the representation of Black bodies in early Brazilian photography, see Boris Kossoy, *Dicionário histórico-fotográfico brasileiro: Fotografos e Ofício da Fotografia no Brasil (1833–1910)* (Rio de Janeiro: Instituto Moreira Sales, 2002); George Ermakoff, *O negro na fotografia brasileira do século XIX* (Rio de Janeiro: George Ermakoff Casa Editorial, 2004).

3. For a detailed account of the spread of the *bolsa* across the early Brazilian diaspora and its popularity with enslaved people, see James H. Sweet, *Recreating African Culture Kinship and Religion in the African-Portuguese World, 1441–1770* (Chapel Hill: University of North Carolina Press, 2003), 179–182.

4. For *axé* and its transference from Africa to Brazil, see William Bascom, *Sixteen Cowries: Yoruba Divination from Africa to the New World* (Bloomington: Indiana University Press, 1993); Mikelle Smith Omari-Tunkara, *Manipulating the Sacred: Yorùbá Art, Ritual, and Resistance in Brazilian Candomblé* (Detroit: Wayne State University Press, 2005), 35–44.

5. For accounts stressing the social permeability of Umbanda and its astonishing growth in São Paulo, see Roger Bastide and Florestan Fernandes, *Relações raciais entre pretos e brancos em São Paulo* (São Paulo: Editora Anhembi, 1955); Armando Cavalcanti Bandeira, *Umbanda: Evolução histórico-religiosa* (Rio de Janeiro: n.p., 1961); Esther J. Pressel, "Umbanda in São Paulo: Religious Innovation in a Developing Society," in *Religion, Altered States of Consciousness, and Social Change*, ed. Erika Bourguignon (Columbus: Ohio State University Press, 1973); Serge Bramly, *Macumba: The Teachings of María-Jose, Mother of the Gods* (New York: St. Martin's Press, 1977); Renato Ortiz, *A Morte Branca do feiticeiro negro: Umbanda na sociedade de clases* (São Paulo: Editora Brasilense, 1977); Diana De Groat Brown, *Umbanda: Religion and Politics in Urban Brazil* (New York: Columbia University Press, 1994).

6. These figures have all been commented on in detail. See Marcus Wood, "The Museu do Negro in Rio and the Cult of Anastácia as a New Model for the Memory of Slavery," *Representations* 113, no. 1 (2011): 111–149.

7. Marcus Wood, "Celebrating the Middle Passage: Atlantic Slavery, Barbie and the Birth of the Sable Venus," *Atlantic Studies* 1, no. 2 (2005): 123–130; Marcus Wood, *Black Milk: Imagining Slavery in the Visual Cultures of Brazil and America* (New York: Oxford University Press, 2013).

8. The classic European anthropological discussion of the "Protean" nature of Umbanda and Candomblé deities and their ability to accrete onto Catholic icons is Roger Bastide, *The African Religions of Brazil* (Baltimore: Johns Hopkins University Press, 1978). See particularly pp. 268–275. For bizarre incarnations of Iemanjá, see Wood, "Celebrating the Middle Passage: Atlantic Slavery, Barbie and the Birth of the Sable Venus."

9. For a populist overview of the global history of the Black Madonna, see Ella Rozett, http://interfaithmary.net/pages/blackmadonna.html. For the Brazilian Nossa Senhora da Conceição Aparecida (Our Lady of the Apparition of the Immaculate Conceptions), see Malgorzata Oleszkiewicz-Peralba, *The Black Madonna in Latin America and Europe: Tradition and Transformation* (Albuquerque: University of New Mexico Press, 2007); Michael D. Murphy and J. Carlos González Faraco, "Identifying the Virgin Mary: Disarming Skepticism in European Vision Narratives," *Anthropos* (2011): 511–527; Lucia Chiavola Birnbaum, *Black Madonnas: Feminism, Religion, and Politics in Italy* (Boston: Northeastern University Press, 1993).

10. https://en.expertissim.com/wood-black-madonna-brazil-18th-century-12194953.

11. See the facsimile of the 1750 edition of *The Illustrated Litany of Loretto in Fifty-Six Titles* (Dublin: James Duffy and Sons, 1878), plate O, *Mater Divina Gratia*.

12. Doris Green, "Traditional Dance in Africa," in *African Dance: An Artistic, Historical, and Philosophical Inquiry,* ed. Kariamu Welsh Asante (Trenton, NJ: Africa World Press, Inc., 1994), 13–28; Esilokun Kinni-Olusanyin, "A Panoply of African Dance Dynamics," in Welsh Asante, *African Dance*, 29–38; Robert W. Nicholls, "African Dance: Transition and Continuity," in Welsh Asante, *African Dance*, 41–63.

13. The best, and as far as I know only, scholarly analysis of Sacy's cultural genesis and of his racist distortions within popular illustrated Brazilian fictions of the twentieth century is Elise Dietrich, "Ziraldo's *A Turma do Pererê*: Representations of Race in a Brazilian Children's Comic," *Afro-Hispanic Review* 29, no. 2, *The African Diaspora in Brazil* (Fall 2010), 143–160, http://www.jstor.org/stable/41349346. This article also does a fine job of locating Sacy-Pererê's cultural genesis firmly within Brazil before 1888.

14. For popular accounts of these strange narrative amalgams of Sacy's myth, see http://www.yerbamateblog.com/legend-saci-perere; for a highly entertaining documentary providing a series of filmed oral histories of Sacy, see *Somos Todos Sacys* at https://vimeo.com/11609651.

15. For a spectacular account of Sacy as slave migrant, see the documentary based on the Brazilian music group who have named themselves Sacy Pererê, http://www.amberfilm.de/sacyperere.htm.

16. For Sacy's red cap and revolutionary iconography, see Dietrich,

"Ziraldo's *A Turma do Pererê*: Representations of Race in a Brazilian Children's Comic," who states: "'*e barrete frigio*,' or Phrygian cap, was initially worn in Brazil by Portuguese fishermen and later came to signify involvement in the Republican movement in the late nineteenth century, inspired similar hats worn by participants in the French Revolution," 156n1.

17. The most solid study which collected oral narratives from all over São Paulo in the early twentieth century is the anonymous *O Saci-Pererê: Resultado de um inquérito* (São Paulo: Estado de São Paulo, 1917).

18. I quote from the first scholarly edition: *The Voyage and Travayle of Sir John Maundeville Knight*, ed. John Knight (London: Pickering and Chatto, 1877), 119–120.

19. *Voyage*, 119–120n.

2. Abolition and Post-Abolition in the Visual Culture of Latin America: Colombia, Brazil, Argentina, and Peru

1. Magdalena Candioti, "*Regulando el fin de la esclavitud: Diálogos, innovaciones y disputas jurídicas en las nuevas repúblicas sudamericanas, 1810–1830*," *Jahrbuch für Geschichte Lateinamerikas* 52 (2015): 149–172.

2. Marcus Wood, "Emancipation Art, Fanon and the 'Butchery of Freedom,'" in *Slavery and the Cultures of Abolition: Essays Marking the Bicentennial of the British Abolition Act of 1807*, ed. Brycchan Carey and Peter J. Kitson (Woodbridge, England: Boydell & Brewer Ltd., 2007), 20.

3. Carolina Vanegas Carrasco, "*Arte y política a mediados del siglo XIX en la Nueva Granada: El caso del 'Bolívar de Tenerani*,'" in José Cirillo, Teresa Espantoso Rodríguez, and Carolina Vanegas Carrasco, *II seminário internacional sobre arte público en Latinoamérica: Arte público y espacios políticos: Interacciones y fracturas en las ciudades latinoamericanas* (Vitória, Brazil: UFES, Comart, 2011), 235.

4. Ibid., 231.

5. See Fernán E. González, "*La guerra de los Supremos (1839–1841) y los orígenes del bipartidismo*," *Boletín de Historia y Antigüedades* 97, no. 848 (March 2010).

6. Simón Bolívar, *Discurso en el Congreso de Angostura* (San José de Costa Rica: García Monge, [1819] 1922), 99.

7. For example, Alonso Carrió de la Vandera (Concolorcorvo), *El Lazarillo de ciegos caminantes: Desde Buenos Aires hasta Lima* (Buenos Aires, Argentina: ed. Argentinas, Solar, [1773] 1942).

8. On the iconography of Bolívar, see Beatriz González, Margarita González, and Daniel Castro, *El Libertador Simón Bolívar, creador de Repúblicas: Iconografía revisada del Libertador*, Serie cuadernos iconográficos, no. 4 (Bogotá: Ministerio de Cultura, Museo Nacional de Colombia, 2004).

9. In an earlier project, I suggested that given the numerous representations of Afrodescendants in profile, artists, Europeans in particular, might have used the diagram by Albrecht Dürer (included in a treatise published in 1528, after his death) to compose the head of an African, or, failing that, the images by Pieter Camper. Although the diagrams by Dürer and Camper differ somewhat, Camper mentions Dürer several times in his treatise in reference to Africans and comments on the close similarities of the facial angles in both diagrams. See María de Lourdes Ghidoli, *Estereotipos en negro: Representaciones y autorrepresentaciones visuales de afroporteños en el siglo XIX* (Rosario, Argentina: Prohistoria Ediciones, 2016), 46–47. On Camper, see David Bindman, *Ape to Apollo: Aesthetics and the Idea of Race in the 18th Century* (London: Reaktion Books, 2002), 201–209.

10. He was a student of Bertel Thorvaldsen (1770–1844), a Danish sculptor based in Rome.

11. For an exhaustive analysis of Angelo Agostini and the abolition of slavery in Brazilian satirical graphic art, see Marcus Wood, *Black Milk: Imagining Slavery in the Visual Cultures of Brazil and America* (Oxford: Oxford University Press, 2013), 132–187.

12. Historiography is divided on President Francisco Solano López, Paraguay's second constitutional ruler, and thus on the War of the Triple Alliance. For liberal historians (those who wrote the official accounts and those who hold that view today), he was a dictator who took Paraguay into the war, and thus to destruction. For the so-called revisionists (in the past and today), he was his country's greatest hero.

13. Bolívar, *Discurso en el Congreso de Angostura*; Bernardo de Monteagudo, *Obras políticas* (Buenos Aires, Argentina: La Facultad, 1916).

14. Daryle Williams, *Culture Wars in Brazil: The First Vargas Regime, 1930–1945* (Durham, NC: Duke University Press, 2001), 147.

15. Viviane Rummler da Silva, "*Pintores fundadores da Academia de Belas Artes da Bahia: João Francisco Lopes Rodrigues (1825–1893) e Miguel Navarro y Cañizares (1834–1913)*" (master's thesis, Universidade Federal da Bahia, 2008), 273.

16. Ibid., 284.

17. Ibid., 316. Here Silva suggests that the object is a quill pen for signing the law. I do not agree, because the object is too large, and the law had already been signed. The palm leaf is a symbol of salvation and redemption.

18. Kleber Antonio de Oliveira Amancio, "*A representação visual do negro na primeira república*," in ANPUH, *Anais do XXVII Simpósio Nacional de História* (July 2013), http://www.snh2013.anpuh.org/resources/anais/27/1364939709_ARQUIVO_Onegronaartebrasileiradaprimeirarepublica_2.pdf.

19. For the identification of some of those portrayed in the painting, see Silva, "*Pintores fundadores*," 318–319. One of the figures in civilian dress is José de Patrocinio, of African descent, a main leader of the

abolitionist movement.

20. On these religious connotations, it is interesting to note that Pope Leo XIII issued an encyclical on May 5, 1888, congratulating Brazil for abolishing slavery, and in September of that year he awarded Princess Isabel the Golden Rose, a papal honor recognizing deeds the church deemed notable.

21. Williams, *Culture Wars in Brazil,* 147.

22. See Sidney Chalhoub, *Visões da liberdade: Uma história das últimas décadas da escravidão na Corte* (São Paulo: Companhia das Letras, 2011).

23. See the detailed analysis of this work in Ghidoli, *Estereotipos en negro,* 154–169.

24. Ricardo D. Salvatore, *Wandering Paysanos: State Order and Subaltern Experience in Buenos Aires during the Rosas Era* (Durham, NC: Duke University Press, 2003), 243.

25. González Bernaldo suggests that it might have been hung in Rosas's residence to remind visitors of his connection to the Afrodescendant population. See Pilar González Bernaldo de Quirós, *Civilidad y política en los orígenes de la Nación Argentina: Las sociabilidades en Buenos Aires, 1829–1862* (Buenos Aires, Argentina: FCE, 2008), 217.

26. Ricardo D. Salvatore, "Integral Outsiders: Afro-Argentines in the Era of Juan Manuel de Rosas and Beyond," in *Beyond Slavery: The Multilayered Legacy of Africans in Latin America and the Caribbean,* ed. Darién J. Davis (Lanham, MD: Rowman and Littlefield, 2007), 57–80.

27. In Argentina, the May Revolution of 1810 is celebrated on May 25.

28. For details on the Law of the Free Womb in Argentina, see Liliana Crespi, "*Ni esclavo, ni libre: El status del liberto en el Río de la Plata desde el periodo indiano al republicano*," in "*Negros de la Patria*": *Los afrodescendientes en las luchas por la independencia en el antiguo Virreinato del Rio de la Plata,* ed. Silvia C. Mallo and Ignacio Telesca (Buenos Aires, Argentina: Editorial SB, 2010), 15–38; and Magdalena Candioti, "*Abolición gradual y libertades vigiladas en el Río de la Plata: La política de control de libertos de 1813,*" *Corpus* 6, no. 1 (2016), https://corpus-archivos.revues.org/1567.

29. Roberto Amigo, "*Prilidiano Pueyrredón y la formación de una cultura visual en Buenos Aires,*" in *Prilidiano Pueyrredón* (Buenos Aires, Argentina: Banco Velox, 1999), 51.

30. Ibid., 51.

31. Ghidoli, *Estereotipos en negro,* 75–79.

32. In 1853 the constitution of Santa Fe abolished slavery in the Argentine Confederation, but the separate province of Buenos Aires did not include that measure in its constitution of 1854. Only with unification in 1861, and the acceptance of the constitution by Buenos Aires, was slavery abolished there. See George Reid Andrews, *The Afro-Argentines of Buenos Aires, 1800–1900* (Madison: University of Wisconsin Press, 1980), 57.

33. "*El arte argentino en la semana que corre,*" *Correo del Domingo,* September 10, 1865.

34. Ibid.

35. José León Pagano, *Prilidiano Pueyrredón* (Buenos Aires, Argentina, Academia Nacional de Bellas Artes, 1945), 90. Italics added.

36. Santiago Manuel Gimenez, "*Imágenes raciales en Buenos Aires: Una mirada desde la antropología histórica a lo 'negro' y lo 'blanco' en la Galería de Ladrones de la Capital (1880–1887) y el semanario Caras y Caretas (1898–1905),*" (master's thesis, Universidad de Buenos Aires, Argentina, 2017), 62–66.

37. "*El arte argentino en la semana que corre.*"

38. Ibid. Italics in original.

39. Andrews, *The Afro-Argentines*; Alejandro Frigerio, "'*Negros' y 'Blancos' en Buenos Aires: Repensando nuestras categorías raciales,*" in *Buenos Aires negra: Identidad y cultura,* comp. Leticia Maronese (Buenos Aires, Argentina: CPPHC, 2006), 77–98; Lea Geler, *Andares negros, caminos blancos: Afroporteños, Estado y Nación: Argentina a fines del siglo XIX* (Rosario, Argentina: Prohistoria Ediciones, 2010).

40. On the liberal revolution of 1854, see Jorge Basadre, *Historia de la República del Perú,* vol. 3 (Lima: Editorial Peruamérica, 1964); Carmen McEvoy, "*El legado castillista,*" *Histórica* 20, no. 2 (1996): 211–241; and more recently, Victor Peralta Ruiz, "*La guerra civil peruana de 1854: Los entresijos de una revolución,*" *Anuario de Estudios Americanos* 70, no. 1 (2013): 195–219.

41. See Ricardo Kusunoki Rodriguez and Ramón Mujica Pinilla, *La rebelión de los lápices: El Perú del siglo XIX en caricaturas* (Lima: Biblioteca Nacional del Perú, 2012).

42. Natalia Majluf, "*Estudio Introductorio: Francisco Laso, escritor y político,*" in Francisco Laso, *Aguinaldo para las señoras del Perú y otros ensayos, 1854–1869* (Lima, Peru: Institut Français d'Études Andines/Museo de Arte de Lima, 2003), 45.

43. Gonzalo Portocarrero, "*Las tres razas de Francisco Laso,*" in *Oído en el silencio: Ensayos de crítica cultural* (Lima: Red para el Desarrollo de las Ciencias Sociales en el Perú, 2010), 400.

44. Majluf, "*Estudio Introductorio.*"

45. "*Crónica de la capital: Cuadros de pintura,*" *El Comercio,* April 15, 1859. Cited in Majluf, "*Estudio Introductorio,*" 41.

46. On racial categories and their persistence in Buenos Aires, see Eva Lamborghini, Lea Geler, and Florencia Guzman, "*Los estudios afrodescendientes en Argentina: Nuevas perspectivas y desafíos en un país 'sin razas,'*" *Tabula Rasa,* no. 27 (July-December 2017): 67–101; Lea Geler, "African Descent and Whiteness in Buenos Aires: Impossible

Mestizajes in the White Capital City," in *Rethinking Race in Modern Argentina*, ed. Paulina Alberto and Eduardo Elena (Cambridge: Cambridge University Press, 2016), 213–240; Frigerio, "'*Negros*' y '*Blancos*' en Buenos Aires."

47. In this incident, recounted in Genesis 9: 20–27, Noah became drunk, and his son Ham committed the offense of seeing him naked. Noah then issued a curse that Ham's son Canaan and all his descendants would be enslaved by the descendants of Noah's other sons.

48. Tatiana H. P. Lotierzo and Lilia K. M. Schwarcz, "*Raça, gênero e projeto branqueador: 'A redenção de Cam,' de Modesto Brocos*," *Artelogie*, no. 5 (October 2013), http://cral.in2p3.fr/artelogie/spip.php?article254.

49. This iconography is exhaustively analyzed in Tatiana Helena Pinto Lotierzo, *Contornos do (in)visível: A redenção de Cam, racismo e estética na pintura brasileira do último oitocentos* (master's thesis, Universidade de Sao Paulo, 2013).

50. Rafael Cardoso, "The Problem of Race in Brazilian Painting, c. 1850–1920," *Art History* 38, no. 3 (June 2015): 488–511, 499.

3. The Image of the Black in the Formation of Latin American Nations

1. Hans-Joachim König, "*La función de las imágenes en el proceso de construcción de las naciones latinoamericanas*," in *La nación expuesta: Cultura visual y procesos de formación de la nación en América Latina*, ed. Sven Schuster (Bogotá, Colombia: Editorial Universidad del Rosario, 2014), 1.

2. Natalia Majluf, "*De cómo reemplazar a un rey: Retrato, visualidad y poder en la crisis de la independencia (1808–1830)*," *Historica* 37, no. 1 (2013): 75.

3. Ibid.; König, "*La función*," 2014.

4. Rebecca Earle, "*Sobre héroes y tumbas*: National Symbols in Nineteenth-Century Spanish America," *Hispanic American Historical Review* 85, no. 3 (2005).

5. Rodrigo Gutiérrez Viñuales, "*Construyendo las identidades nacionales: Próceres e imaginario histórico en Sudamérica (siglo XIX)*," in *La construcción del héroe en España y México (1789–1847)*, ed. Manuel Chust and Víctor Mínguez (Valencia, Spain: Publicacions de la Universitat de Valencia, 2003), 281–282.

6. In Mexico, for example, the liberals considered Hidalgo the father of independence; for the conservative faction, that role was played by Iturbide, and their choices were reflected in their portraits. By choosing Hidalgo, a more conservative figure, to be their dignitary, other liberal leaders, such as Morelos, were relegated for being too liberal. See Inmaculada Rodríguez Moya, *El retrato en México: 1781–1867: Héroes, ciudadanos y emperadores para una nueva nación* (Castellón, Spain: Universitat Jaume 1, 2006).

7. Gutiérrez, "*Construyendo*," 284.

8. Ibid., 287.

9. Rebecca Earle, "'*Padres de la Patria*' and the Ancestral Past: Commemorations of Independence in Nineteenth-Century Spanish America," *Journal of Latin American Studies* 34, no. 4 (2002): 778.

10. Ibid., 780.

11. Ibid., 783.

12. Ibid., 784.

13. Fredy Enrique Martínez, "*La fiesta de la Libertad: Celebraciones cívicas y manumisión de esclavos en la Gran Colombia*," *Revista Colombiana de Educación*, 59 (July–December 2010): 249.

14. Ibid., 253.

15. Jaime Olveda Legaspi, "*La abolición de la esclavitud en México, 1810–1917*," *Signos Históricos* 15, no. 29 (January–June 2013): 26–27.

16. Ibid., 27.

17. Carlos María de Bustamante, *Diario histórico de México, 1822–1848, de Carlos María de Bustamante* [CD-ROM], ed. Josefina Zoraida Vázquez and Héctor Cuauhtémoc Hernández Silva (El Colegio de México: Centro de Investigaciones y Estudios Superiores en Antropología Social, 2001), September 16, 1827.

18. The artist received lands in Veracruz as ordered by King Ferdinand VII. See Sonia Lombardo de Ruiz, *Trajes y vistas de México en la mirada de Theubet de Beauchamp* (Mexico City: Instituto Nacional de Antropología e Historia, 2009).

19. Ibid., 2009.

20. See María José Esparza Liberal, *La cera en México: Arte e historia* (Mexico: Fomento Cultural Banamex, 1994); Francisco Cabrera, *Agustín Arrieta: Pintor costumbrista* (Mexico: Universidad Autónoma de Puebla, Comisión V Centenario, 1991); Various authors, *Los mexicanos pintados por sí mismos: Tipos y costumbres nacionales* (Mexico: Editorial: Murguia, 1854); Various authors, *Los cubanos pintados por sí mismos* (Havana: Imprenta de Barcina, 1852).

21. Natalia Majluf, "*Pancho Fierro, entre el mito y la historia*," in Natalia Majluf and Marcus B. Burke, *Tipos del Perú: La Lima criolla de Pancho Fierro* (Madrid: Ediciones El Viso, 2008).

22. Maribel Arrelucea Barrantes, "*Raza, género y cultura en las acuarelas de Pancho Fierro*," *Arqueología y Sociedad*, no. 23 (2011): 267–293.

23. Helen Melling, "'Colourful Customs and Invisible Traditions': Visual Representations of Black Subjects in Late Colonial and 19th Century, Post-Independence Peru (1750s–1890s)" (PhD diss., King's College, London, 2014), 189–190.

24. Ibid., 190.

25. Ibid.

26. Rafael Cardoso Denis, "Academicism, Imperialism, and National

Identity: The Case of Brazil's Academia Imperial de Belas Artes," in *Art and the Academy in the Nineteenth Century,* ed. Rafael Cardoso Denis and Colin Trodd (New Brunswick, NJ: Rutgers University Press, 2000), 53.

27. Juan Carlos Arellano González, "*El pueblo de 'filibusteros' y la 'raza de malvados': Discursos nacionalistas chilenos y peruanos durante la Guerra del Pacífico (1879–1884),*" *Diálogo Andino,* no. 48 (2015): 73.

28. María Lucrecia Johansson, "*Paraguay contra el monstruo antirrepublicano: El discurso periodístico paraguayo durante la Guerra de la Triple Alianza (1864–1870),*" *Historia Crítica,* no. 47 (May–August 2012): 73.

29. Ibid., 78.

30. Ibid., 89.

31. Roberto Goiriz, *Historia del humor gráfico en Paraguay* (Alcalá de Henares, Spain: Milenio Publicaciones, 2008), 31–32.

32. In Brazil, different illustrated publications were published, mainly in Rio de Janeiro, to deal with political, economic, and social themes, with less racist content and which include heroic portraits of Black soldiers such as those who return home to see their mother being whipped on a trunk (Nobuyoshi Chinen, "*A imagem do negro no humor gráfico brasileiro do século XIX até meados do século XX,*" *Via Atlântica,* no. 18 (2010): 64.

33. Arellano, "*El pueblo,*" 242.

34. Rodrigo Ruz Zagal, Luis Galdames Rosas, Michel Meza Aliaga, and Alberto Díaz Araya, "*Caricaturas del Perú negro en magazines chilenos: Referentes iconográficos y alteridad (1902–1932),*" *Chungara, Revista de Antropología Chilena* 49, no. 3 (2017): 398.

35. Ibid., 398.

36. Ibid., 399.

37. Tomás Perez Vejo quoted in Santiago Robledo Páez, "*Pintura histórica y retratos de próceres en Colombia durante el siglo XIX: Ausencia de apoyo público e importancia de las iniciativas privadas,*" *Historia y Sociedad,* no. 34 (2018): 79.

38. Isis Pimentel de Castro, "*Os embates entre o empiricismo e a idealização na tradição artística oitocentista: Uma análise das telas de batalhas de Pedro Américo e Vítor Meireles,*" *Sæculum, Revista de História* 19 (July–December 2008): 58.

39. Cardoso, "Academicism," 61.

40. Juan Ortiz Escamilla, "*Identidad y privilegio: Fuerzas armadas y transición política en México, 1750–1825,*" in *Conceptualizar lo que se ve: François-Xavier Guerra, historiador: homenaje,* ed. Erika Pani and Alicia Salmerón (Mexico: Instituto Moro, 2004), 323–349.

41. In Mexico, José María Morelos, Vicente Guerrero, Juan Álvarez, and José Francisco Gordiano Guzmán were leaders of the Independent movement. See Jaime Olveda, *Gordiano Guzmán, un cacique del siglo XIX* (Mexico: SEP/INAH, 1980); María Dolores Ballesteros Páez, "*Vicente Guerrero: Insurgente, militar y presidente afromexicano,*" *Revista Cuicuilco* 18, no. 51 (2011): 23–41.

42. See Claudio Linati, Pl. 33: *Garde Civique D'Alvarado (descendante), en Trajes civiles, militares y religiosos de Mexico* (1828) (Mexico: Imprenta Universitaria, 1956); Anton Goering, *Tropas venezolanas acampadas,* 1870, watercolor, 30 × 45 cm, Colección Corina Röhl de Brillembourg; Francisco Fierro, *Soldado negro a caballo,* 1830–1860, watercolor, 27.5 × 18.5 cm, Museo de América; Auguste Le Moyne, *Soldado,* 1835, watercolor, 19.3 × 1.1 cm, Museo Nacional de Colombia; and Juan Manuel Blanes, *Lancero de la época de Rivera,* undated, oil on cardboard, 36 × 24.5 cm, Colección Horacio Porcel, Buenos Aires, Argentina.

43. Rodrigo Gutiérrez Viñuales, "*Bajo el ala de las academias: El Neoclasicismo y el historicismo en la pintura iberoamericana del XIX,*" in *Pintura, escultura y fotografía en Iberoamérica, siglos XIX y XX* (Madrid: Ediciones Cátedra, 1997).

44. Ibid., 4.

45. Jens Andermann, "*Orden visual y economía política: Museo y colección como aparatos de Estado,*" in *La nación expuesta: Cultura visual y procesos de formación de la nación en América Latina,* ed. Sven Schuster (Bogotá, Colombia: Editorial Universidad del Rosario, 2014), 35.

46. Adelaida de Juan and Miguel Angel Rojas Mix, *Dos ensayos sobre plástica cubana* (Santiago de Chile: Editorial Andres Bello, 1972), 9.

47. Tomás Pérez Vejo, "*Pintura de historia e identidad nacional en España*" (PhD diss., Universidad Complutense de Madrid, 2002), 17.

48. Ibid., 22.

49. Ibid., 23.

50. The commissioners had certain freedom to impose censorship. The painting *La Batalla de Boyacá (The Battle of Boyacá)* by Andrés de Santamaría was rejected because the liberating army was represented by ragged soldiers, without the associated grandeur, but it was a more realistic image of soldiers that crossed the Andes in such conditions. From Marta Fajardo de Rueda, "*Francisco Antonio Cano: Escultor y maestro de la Escuela Nacional de Bellas Artes,*" *Calle 14: Revista de Investigación en el Campo del Arte,* no. 3 (July–December 2009): 109.

51. Daniel Castro and Paola Londoño, *En el páramo: Historia hecha pintura* (Bogotá, Colombia: Casa Museo Quinta de Bolívar, 2011). Exhibition catalog, 1–2.

52. Nanda Leonardini, "*Identidad, ideología e iconografía republicana en el Perú,*" *ARBOR Ciencia, Pensamiento y Cultura* 185, no. 740 (November–December 2009): 1259–1270.

53. Ibid., 1262.

54. Ibid., 1265. The representation of San Martin also mimics the Proclamation of Independence painted by Ignacio Merino (Fernando Villegas Torres, "*Recreando imaginarios: Del general José de San Martín*

a Augusto B. Leguía," Mana Tukukuq ILLAPA, no. 12 (2015): 62.

55. Villegas Torres, "*Recreando*," 62.

56. See the arrival of Hernán Cortés to Tenochtitlán in the Azcatitlan Codex.

57. Carlos Masotta, "*Imágenes recientes de la 'Conquista del Desierto': Problemas de la memoria en la impugnación de un mito de origen,*" RUNA 26 (2006): 227.

58. Ibid., 233.

59. José Luis Grosso, *Indios muertos, negros invisibles: Hegemonía, identidad y añoranza* (Córdoba, Spain: Encuentro Grupo Editor, 2008), 22.

60. Peter Wade, *Race and Ethnicity in Latin America* (New York: Pluto Press, 2010), 31.

61. Ibid., 31.

62. Ibid., 33.

63. Mónica Quijada, "*De la colonia a la república: Inclusión, exclusión y memoria histórica en el Perú,*" Histórica 18, no. 2 (1994): 366.

64. Ibid., 372.

4. *Costumbrismo*: Mapping Blackness in the New Nations of Mexico, Colombia, and Peru

1. Nancy P. Appelbaum, Anne S. Macpherson, and Karin Alejandra Rosemblatt, "Introduction: Racial Nations," in *Race and Nation in Modern Latin America* (Chapel Hill: University of North Carolina Press, 2003), 1–31.

2. Christina A. Sue and Tanya Golash-Boza, "Blackness in Mestizo America: The Cases of Mexico and Peru," *Latino(a) Research Review* 7, no. 1–2 (2009): 33.

3. Peter Wade, *Blackness and Race Mixture: The Dynamics of Racial Identity in Colombia* (Baltimore: Johns Hopkins University Press, 1993); George Reid Andrews, *Afro-Latin America, 1800–2000* (New York: Oxford University Press, 2004).

4. Helen Melling, "'Colourful Customs and Invisible Traditions': Visual Representations of Black Subjects in Late Colonial and Nineteenth Century, Post-Independence Peru (1750s-1890s)" (PhD diss., King's College London, 2015).

5. Natalia Majluf, "The Creation of the Image of the Indian in Nineteenth-Century Peru: The Paintings of Francisco Laso (1823–1869)" (PhD diss., University of Texas at Austin, 1996), 104.

6. Mey-Yen Moriuchi, *Mexican Costumbrismo: Race, Society and Identity in Nineteenth-Century Art* (University Park: Pennsylvania State University Press, 2018), 28–29.

7. Natalia Majluf and Marcus B. Burke, *Tipos del Perú: La Lima criolla de Pancho Fierro* (New York: Hispanic Society of America, 2008), 28.

8. George Reid Andrews, "On Seeing and Not Seeing," in *Afro-Latin America: Black Lives, 1600–2000* (Cambridge, MA: Harvard University Press, 2016).

9. Ilona Katzew, *Casta Painting: Images of Race in Eighteenth-Century Mexico* (New Haven, CT: Yale University Press, 2004); Magali Carrera, *Imagining Identity in New Spain: Race, Lineage, and the Colonial Body in Portraiture and Casta Paintings* (Austin: University of Texas Press, 2003).

10. Moriuchi, *Mexican Costumbrismo*, 70; María Dolores Ballesteros Páez, "*De castas y esclavos a ciudadanos: Las representaciones visuales de la población capitalina de origen africano del periodo virreinal a las primeras décadas del México independiente*" (master's thesis, Instituto de Investigaciones, 2010).

11. Claudio Lomnitz-Adler, *Exits from the Labyrinth: Culture and Ideology in the Mexican National Space* (Berkeley: University of California Press, 1992).

12. Erica Segre, *Intersected Identities: Strategies of Visualisation in Nineteenth- and Twentieth-Century Mexican Culture* (New York: Berghahn Books, 2007), 39.

13. Ben Vinson III and Bobby Vaughn, *Afroméxico, el pulso de la población negra en México: Una historia recordada, olvidada y vuelta a recordar* (Mexico City: Centro de Investigación y Docencia Económicas, 2004), 38. The passage is translated as "since the diminished numbers of those remaining on the Pacific and Atlantic coasts are entirely insignificant…."

14. The Swiss traveler-artist Johann Salomon Hegi (1814–1896) also incorporates a number of Black types in his watercolors of Veracruz, but they remain absent from his representations of the capital. See María Dolores Ballesteros Páez, "*Los 'otros' mexicanos: Las representaciones visuales de la población de origen africano de México en la pintura costumbrista europea,*" in *Representaciones y prácticas sociales: Visiones desde la historia moderna y contemporánea*, coord. Rodrigo Laguarda (Mexico: Instituto Mora, 2012), 40.

15. Moriuchi, *Mexican Costumbrismo*, 53–54.

16. María Dolores Ballesteros Páez, "*Los afrodescendientes en el arte veracruzano y cubano del siglo XIX,*" Cuadernos Americanos: Nueva Epoca 2, no. 156 (2016): 24.

17. Moriuchi, *Mexican Costumbrismo*, 8.

18. Edward Sullivan, "José Agustín Arrieta (1802–1879), *El costeño,* 2012. Auction catalog. http://www.sothebys.com/en/auctions/ecatalogue/2012/latin-american-art-n08907/lot.18.html.

19. Ibid.

20. Javier López Morton, "*Del mundo de las subastas: La Mulata*" (May 27, 2014); "*Esperanza de volverte a ver: La Mulata parte 2* (June 24, 2104), https://javierlmorton.wordpress.com/2014/05/27/del-mundo-de-

las-subastas-la-mulata/.

21. Beatriz Balanta Rodríguez, "*El ensamblaje visual del cuerpo negro: El caso de la Comision Corografica de la Nueva Granada,*" *Tabula Rasa: Revista de Humanidades,* no. 17 (2012): 43–61; Nancy P. Appelbaum, *Mapping the Country of Regions: The Chorographic Commission of Nineteenth-Century Colombia* (Chapel Hill: University of North Carolina Press, 2016); Olga Restrepo Forero, "*Un imaginario de la nación: Lectura de láminas y descripciones de la Comisión Corográfica,*" *Anuario Colombiano de Historia Social y de la Cultura,* no. 26 (1999): 30–58.

22. Appelbaum, *Mapping the Country of Regions,* 2.

23. Wade, *Blackness and Race Mixture,* 53–54; Brooke Larson, *Trials of Nation Making: Liberalism, Race, and Ethnicity in the Andes, 1810–1910* (Cambridge: Cambridge University Press, 2008), 77.

24. Black types feature to a very limited extent in the works of Colombia's primary costumbrista artist, Ramon Torres Mendez. Restrepo Forero observes that his repertoire was confined to types of the capital and only extended to incorporate those from other regions as a result of the influence of the Chorographic Commission (Restrepo Forero, "*Un imaginario de la nación,*" 39).

25. Wade, *Blackness and Race Mixture.*

26. Sue and Golash-Boza, "Blackness in Mestizo America," 33; Wade, *Blackness and Race Mixture,* 34–36.

27. Larson, *Trials of Nation Making,* 75.

28. Celina de las Mercedes López Rodríguez, "*Ficciones raciales: Representaciones de raza y género a través de la literatura y las artes visuales en Colombia, 1830–1875,*" (PhD diss., Georgetown University, 2013); Larson, *Trials of Nation Making*; Appelbaum, *Mapping the Country of Regions.*

29. Tamara J. Walker, "Black Skin, White Uniforms: Race, Clothing, and the Visual Vernacular of Luxury in the Andes," *Souls* 19:2 (2017): 202–204.

30. Arrelucea Barrantes, "*Raza, género y cultura en las acuarelas de Pancho Fierro,*" 286; Melling, "'Colourful Customs and Invisible Traditions,'" 128–130.

31. Appelbaum, *Mapping the Country of Regions,* 69.

32. A contemporary response to this image can be seen in the works of the Colombian artist Liliana Angulo. See "*Retrato de Lucy Rengifo,*" in Sol Astrid Giraldo Escobar, *Retratos en blanco y afro: Liliana Angulo* (Bogotá, Colombia: Ministerio de Cultura, 2014).

33. Appelbaum, *Mapping the Country of Regions,* 89.

34. Julio Arias Vanegas, *Nacion y diferencia en el siglo XIX colombiano: Orden nacional, racialismo y taxonomias poblacionales* (Bogotá, Colombia: Uniandes, 2005), 57; Appelbaum, *Mapping the Country of Regions,* 84.

35. Appelbaum, *Mapping the Country of Regions,* 86.

36. Manuel Maria Paz, 1853.

37. Balanta Rodríguez, "*El ensamblaje visual del cuerpo negro,*" 53.

38. Manuel Maria Paz, 1853.

39. This is equally applicable to Gauthier's illustrations of the region's indigenous population; Appelbaum, *Mapping the Country of Regions,* 94.

40. Eduardo Restrepo, "'*Negros indolentes*' en las plumas de corógrafos: Raza y progreso en el occidente de la Nueva Granada de mediados del siglo XIX," *Nómadas* 26 (2007): 28–43.

41. Manuel Maria Paz, 1853.

42. Appelbaum, *Mapping the Country of Regions,* 102.

43. The Andean "Indian" only emerges as a subject of literary and political interest after the War of the Pacific in Peru. In costumbrista iconography of Lima, they feature to a much lesser extent than Afro-descendant types.

44. Melling, "'Colourful Customs and Invisible Traditions.'"

45. Majluf and Burke, *Tipos del Perú,* 18.

46. Alejandro de la Fuente, "Afro-Latin American Art," in *Afro-Latin American Studies: An Introduction*, ed. Alejandro de la Fuente and George Reid Andrews (New York: Cambridge University Press, 2018), 356.

47. Deborah Poole, *Vision, Race, and Modernity: A Visual Economy of the Andean Image World* (Princeton, NJ: Princeton University Press, 1997); Maribel Arrelucea Barrantes, "*Géneros, razas y nación en el siglo XIX: La mirada de Pancho Fierro o las miradas a Pancho Fierro,*" in *Presencia y persistencia: Paradigmas culturales de los afrodescendientes* (Lima, Peru: Centro de Desarrollo Étnico, 2013), 211–231; Melling, "'Colourful Customs and Invisible Traditions.'"

48. Tamara J. Walker, *Exquisite Slaves: Race, Clothing, and Status in Colonial Lima* (Cambridge: Cambridge University Press, 2017); Melling, "'Colourful Customs and Invisible Traditions,'" 2015.

49. de la Fuente, "Afro-Latin American Art," 373.

50. Melling, forthcoming.

51. Wade, *Blackness and Race Mixture*; Jean Muteba Rahier, *Blackness in the Andes: Ethnographic Vignettes of Cultural Politics in the Time of Multiculturalism* (London: Palgrave Macmillan, 2016).

52. Appelbaum, *Mapping the Country of Regions,* 9.

53. Balanta Rodríguez, "*El ensamblaje visual del cuerpo negro,*" 47; Walker, "Black Skin, White Uniforms"; Moriuchi, *Mexican Costumbrismo,* 28–29.

5. The War on Blackness ca. 1888: Religious Expression, Repression, and Resistance in Brazil

A special thanks to Alejandro de la Fuente and David Bindman for the invitation to participate in this volume, to Roberto Conduru for mentorship and intellectual collaboration on this topic over so many years, and to Rafael Cardoso for many helpful insights. I am deeply grateful to Arthur Valle (Universidade Federal Rural do Rio de Janeiro) for generously providing his personal photographs of the Afro-Brazilian objects from Rio's National Museum/UFRJ in the wake of the devastating 2018 fire.

1. For a discussion of the National Museum fire and losses, see Meilan Solly, "Around 2,000 Artifacts Have Been Saved From the Ruins of Brazil's National Museum Fire," *Smithsonian Magazine*, February 15, 2019, https://www.smithsonianmag.com/smart-news/around-2000-artifacts-have-been-saved-ruins-brazils-national-museum-fire-180971510/.

2. For a discussion of the African and Afro-Brazilian collections at the National Museum, see the institution's website, http://museunacional.ufrj.br/destaques/africa. For a larger history of the Africana collections, see the curator and anthropologist Mariza de Carvalho Soares's important study "Collectionism and Colonialism: The Africana Collection at Brazil's National Museum (Rio de Janeiro)," in *African Heritage and Memories of Slavery in Brazil and the South Atlantic World*, ed. Ana Lucia Araujo (Amherst, NY: Cambria Press, 2015), 17–44.

3. Manuel Covo, "L'Révolution haïtienne entre études révolutionnaires et Atlantic History," in *L'Atlantique révolutionnaire: Une perspective ibéro-américaine*, ed. Clément Thibaud et al. (Paris: Éditions Les Perséides, 2013), 259–288.

4. Thomas E. Skidmore, "Abolition and Its Aftermath: The Brazilian Way," in *Contemporary Afro-Brazil: A Multidisciplinary Anthology*, ed. Bonnie S. Wasserman (San Diego, CA: Cognella, 2019), 29–30.

5. Thomas H. Holloway, *Policing Rio de Janeiro: Repression and Resistance in a 19th-Century City* (Stanford, CA: Stanford University Press, 1993), 24. For the 1890 Penal Code, see https://www2.camara.leg.br/legin/fed/decret/1824-1899/decreto-847-11-outubro-1890-503086-publicacaooriginal-1-pe.html.

6. Holloway, *Policing Rio de Janeiro*, 9.

7. Holloway, *Policing Rio de Janeiro*, 8. There is a long history of defining colonial sorcery in Brazil. For one of the more recent anthologies, see *Sorcery in the Black Atlantic,* ed. Luis Nicolau Parés and Roger Sansi (Chicago: University of Chicago Press, 2011).

8. The 1890 Penal Code (Decree of October 11, 1890, Rio de Janeiro: Imprensa Nacional) is discussed in Ulisses N. Rafael and Yvonne Maggie's landmark study, "Sorcery Objects under Institutional Tutelage: Magic and Power in Ethnographic Collections," *Vibrant: Virtual Brazilian Anthropology* 10, no. 1 (2013): 281.

9. Rafael and Maggie detail, Article 156 of the 1890 Penal Code, 281–282.

10. See the essay by Ana Paula Höfling, "Capoeiras of Bahia," in *Axé Bahia: The Power of Art in an Afro-Brazilian Metropolis*, ed. Patrick A. Polk et al. (Los Angeles: Fowler Museum at UCLA, 2018), 148–159. Exhibition catalog.

11. Maya Talmon-Chvaicer, *The Hidden History of Capoeira: A Collision of Cultures in the Brazilian Battle Dance* (Austin: University of Texas Press, 2008), 8.

12. Thomas H. Holloway, "'A Healthy Terror': Police Repression of *Capoeiras* in Nineteenth-Century Rio de Janeiro," *Hispanic American Historical Review* 69, no. 4 (November 1989): 665–666.

13. Rogério Budasz, "Black Guitar-Players and Early African-Iberian Music in Portugal and Brazil," *Early Music* 35, no. 1 (February 2007): 12.

14. James H. Sweet, *Recreating Africa: Culture, Kinship, and Religion in the African-Portuguese World*, 1441–1770 (Chapel Hill: University of North Carolina Press, 2003), 220, 144–146. For a larger history of *lundu* and other African musical forms in Brazil, see Peter Fryer, *Rhythms of Resistance: African Musical Heritage in Brazil* (Hanover, NH: University Press of New England, 2000).

15. Martha Tupinambá de Ulhôa and Luiz Costa-Lima Neto, "Memory, History and Cultural Encounters in the Atlantic: The Case of *Lundu*," *The World of Music (New Series)* 2, no. 2, *Transatlantic Musical Forms in the Atlantic World* (2013): 63–65.

16. Ibid., 56.

17. See Cécile Fromont, "Becoming the Black Rome: Bahia, Africa, and the African Atlantic," in *Axé Bahia: The Power of Art in an Afro-Brazilian Metropolis*, ed. Patrick A. Polk et al. (Los Angeles: Fowler Museum at UCLA, 2018), 54–67. Exhibition catalog.

18. For an excellent overview of Candomblé, see Nathaniel Samuel Murrell, "Dancing to the Orixás' Axé in Candomblé," in *Contemporary Afro-Brazil: A Multi-Disciplinary Anthology*, ed. Bonnie S. Wasserman (San Diego, CA: Cognella, 2019), 64–85.

19. For foundational texts on Candomblé, see Roger Bastide, *African Civilizations in the New World*, trans. Peter Green (New York: Harper and Row, 1972); Reginaldo Prandi, *Herdeiras do axé: Sociologia das religiões afro-brasileiras* (São Paulo: Editora Hucitec, 1996); Paul Christopher Johnson, *Secrets, Gossip, and Gods: The Transformation of Brazilian Candomblé* (Oxford: Oxford University Press, 2002); and J. Lorand Matory, *Black Atlantic Religion: Tradition, Transnationalism, and Matriarchy in the Afro-Brazilian Candomblé* (Princeton, NJ: Princeton University Press, 2005).

20. Murrell, 66–67. For the famous uprising in Brazil, see João José Reis, *Slave Rebellion in Brazil: The Muslim Uprising of 1835 in Bahia*,

trans. Arthur Brakel (Baltimore: Johns Hopkins University Press, 1993).

21. Paul Christopher Johnson, "Law, Religion, and 'Public Health' in the Republic of Brazil," *Law & Social Inquiry* 26, no. 1 (Winter 2001): 9–33.

22. One of the key early works by Raimundo Nina Rodrigues includes *O animismo fetichista dos negros baianos*, *Revista Brazileira*, published in four chapters in 1896/1897; Rodrigues, *Os africanos no Brasil* (São Paulo: Companhia Editora Nacional, 1988) (originally published posthumously in 1932).

23. Roger Sansi-Roca, "The Hidden Life of Stones: Historicity, Materiality, and the Value of Candomblé Objects in Bahia," *Journal of Material Culture Studies* 10, no. 2 (2005): 145.

24. Stefania Capone, "Nazaré, Maria Júlia da Conceição 'Mãe Maria Julia,'" in *Dictionary of Caribbean and Afro-Latin American Biography*, ed. Franklin W. Knight and Henry Louis Gates, Jr., Oxford African American Studies Center, http://www.oxfordaasc.com/article/opr/t456/e1504.

25. For an important study on the use and reception of photography within Bahian Candomblé, see Lisa Earl Castillo, "Icons of Memory: Photography and Its Uses in Bahian Candomblé," *Stockholm Review of Latin American Studies,* no. 4 (March 2009): 15–16.

26. For a discussion of Afro-Brazilian jewelry in the period, see "Jewelry," in *Brazil: Body and Soul*, ed. Edward J. Sullivan (New York: Guggenheim Museum, 2001), 272, exhibition catalog; Laura Cunha and Thomas Milz, *Joias de Crioula: Jewelry of the Brazilian Crioula* (São Paulo: Editora Terceiro Nome, 2011); and Raul Lody, *Dicionário de Arte Sacra e Técnicas Afro-Brasileiras* (Rio de Janeiro: Impresso no Brasil, 2003).

27. For a discussion of *pencas* and their ties to earlier tradition of *mandinga* pouches, see Amy Buono, "Historicity, Achronicity, and the Materiality of Cultures in Colonial Brazil," *Getty Research Journal* 7 (2015): 25–26.

28. See Matory, *Black Atlantic Religion*, ch. 1, and J. Lorand Matory, "Candomblé: Making the Saint, Making History, Making Spirited Things," in *Axé Bahia: The Power of Art in an Afro-Brazilian Metropolis*, ed. Patrick A. Polk et al. (Los Angeles: Fowler Museum at UCLA 2018), 80. Exhibition catalog.

29. Kim D. Butler, *Freedoms Given, Freedoms Won: Afro-Brazilians in Post-Abolition São Paulo and Salvador* (New Brunswick, NJ: Rutgers University Press, 1998), 200.

30. Ibid., 55–56.

31. Bruno Carvalho, *Porous City: A Cultural History of Rio de Janeiro* (Liverpool, England: Liverpool University Press, 48).

32. For an overview of Malta's photographs, see Viviane da Silva Araujo, "*Exotismos próximos: Reflexões sobre a cidade moderna na imagem das primeiras favelas cariocas*," *Revista Espaço Acadêmico* 14, no. 166 (March 2015): 1–13.

33. This is described and detailed in Araujo, "*Exotismos próximos*," 7.

34. João do Rio, "*Os livres acampamentos da miséria*," in *Vida vertiginosa* (São Paulo: Martins Fontes, 2006), 132–133.

35. See Amy Chazkel, *Laws of Chance: Brazil's Clandestine Lottery and the Making of Urban Public Life* (Durham, NC: Duke University Press, 2012).

36. Holloway, *Policing Rio de Janeiro*, 31–32.

37. For the iconography of Candomblé objects, see Lody, *Dicionário de Arte Sacra.*

38. To understand what constitutes an image in Afro-Brazilian religious practice, see Roger Sansi, "Objects and Images in Brazilian Religions," in *Handbook of Contemporary Religions of Brazil*, ed. Bettina Schmidt and Steven Engler (Leiden, The Netherlands: Brill Publishers, 2017), 515–534.

39. Silke Karg, "*Afro-brasilianische Kultobjekte aus Rio Grande do Sul – die Sammlung Pietzcker*," *Baessler-Archiv* 55 (2007): 19–41. Many thanks to Dr. Viola Koenig, the former director of the Ethnology Museum in Berlin, for bringing this collection to my attention and for providing images.

40. Alex Borucki, "The Slave Trade to the Río de la Plata, 1777–1812: Trans-Imperial Networks and Atlantic Warfare," *Colonial Latin American Review* 20, no. 1 (April 2011): 81–107.

41. For general histories of the museum, see Yvonne Maggie, *Medo do feitiço: Relaçoes entre magia e poder no Brasil* (Rio de Janeiro: Arquivo Nacional, 1992); Alexandre Fernandes Corrêa, *O museu mefistofélico e a distabuzação da magia: Análise do tombamento do primeiro patrimônio etnográfico do Brasil* (Sao Luis/MA, Brazil: EDUFMA, 2009).

42. Johnson, *Secrets, Gossip, and Gods*.

43. Fernandes Corrêa, *O Museu Mefistofélico e a distabuzação da magia*, 409. For a list of the original objects in the "Black Magic" collection, see Arthur Valle, "*Religiões afro-brasileiras e repressão policial nas primeiras décadas do séc. XX: Testemunhos no acervo do Museu da Policia Civil do Estado do Rio de Janeiro*," *Revista do Arquivo Geral da Cidade do Rio de Janeiro* (2020).

44. Rafael and Maggie, "Sorcery Objects under Institutional Tutelage," 291.

45. Instituto do Patrimônio Histórico e Artístico Nacional (originally SPHAN), "*Derecto-Lei n. 25, de 30 de Novembro de 1937*," http://portal.iphan.gov.br/uploads/legislacao/Decreto_no_25_de_30_de_novembro_de_1937.pdf.

6. The Unrepresentable: Navigating Black Agency during Times of Transition

1. For details on the book in which this print appears, see Deborah Jenson, "Jean-Jacques Dessalines and the African Character of the Haitian Revolution," *William and Mary Quarterly* 69, no. 3 (July 2012): 615–638.

2. Slavery was abolished in Puerto Rico in 1873.

3. Edward J. Sullivan, "The Black Hand: Notes on the African Presence in the Visual Arts of Brazil and the Caribbean," in *The Arts in Latin America, 1492-1820*, ed. Joseph J. Rishel and Suzanne Stratton-Pruitt (New Haven, CT: Yale University Press, 2006), 51. For more on Campeche, see René Taylor, *José Campeche and His Time* (Ponce, Puerto Rico: Museo de Arte de Ponce, 1988).

4. For more on this, see José Antonio Saco, "*Las artes están en manos de la gente de color*," in *Memoria sobre la vagancia en Cuba* [1829] (Havana: Ministerio de Educación, Dirección de Cultura, 1946), 93–104.

5. Anselmo Romero's "*El Guardiero*" was first published in 1853 in *La Revista de La Habana*. It is reproduced in Salvador Buenos's anthology *Costumbristas cubanos del siglo XIX* (Venezuela: Biblioteca Ayacucho, 1985), 319–323.

6. The docile slave is comparable to what Sterling A. Brown termed "the Contented Slave" in his groundbreaking typological survey of Black types in American literature. See "The Negro Character as Seen by White Authors," *The Journal of Negro Education* II, no. 2 (April 1933): 179–203.

7. Edward J. Sullivan, *From Spain to San Juan and Back: Francisco Oller and Caribbean Art in the Era of Impressionism*, chapter 3 (New Haven, CT: Yale University Press, 2014), 53.

8. In some parts of Latin America and Spain, the death of an infant was cause for celebration since the child's spirit was thought to go directly to heaven.

9. For a detailed and excellent overview of Oller's transnational career and a thoughtful analysis of *The Wake*, see Sullivan, *From Spain to San Juan and Back*, 80.

10. For more on this painting, see Benigno Trigo, "Anemia and Vampires: Figures to Govern the Colony, Puerto Rico, 1880 to 1904," *Comparative Studies in Society and History* 41, no. 1 (January 1999): 104–123, and as cited by Nicholas Mirzoeff, *The Right to Look: A Counterhistory to Visuality* (Durham, NC: Duke University Press, 2011).

11. Oller described the painting as such: "Astonishing criticism of a custom that still exists in Puerto Rico among country people and which has been propagated by the priests. On this day, the family and friends have kept vigil all night over the dead child, extended on a table with flowers and laces. The mother is holding back her grief, on her head she wears a white turban; she does not weep for fear her tears might wet the wings of this little angel on his flight to heaven. She laughs and offers a drink to the priest, who with eager eyes gazes up at the roast pig whose entry is awaited with enthusiasm. Inside this room of indigenous structure, children play, dogs romp, lovers embrace and the musicians get drunk. This is an orgy of brutish appetites under the guise of a gross superstition. Two figures in the midst of the general disorder: the old countryman … pants rolled up … who comes to bid farewell to the dead child who is gone forever." Taken from *Francisco Oller: A Realist-Impressionist* (Ponce, Puerto Rico: Museo de Arte de Ponce, 1983), 193.

12. For an excellent discussion of the Academia de San Alejandro, the Templete, and Jean Baptiste Vermay, see Paul Niell, "Founding the Academy of San Alejandro and the Politics of Taste in Late Colonial Havana, Cuba," *Colonial Latin American Review* 21, no. 2 (August 2012): 293–318.

13. Artists working in nineteenth-century Cuba are ripe for further study. Agnes Lugo-Ortiz's investigation of the patronage and racial politics behind Nicolas Escalera's religious paintings for the Church of Santa María del Rosario in Havana is an excellent example of the kinds of detailed studies that are necessary. See Agnes Lugo-Ortiz, "Between Violence and Redemption: Slave Portraiture in Early Plantation Cuba," in *Slave Portraiture in the Atlantic World*, ed. Agnes Lugo-Ortiz and Angela Rosenthal (Cambridge: Cambridge University Press, 2013), 201–226.

14. For a facsimile of the production, see J. G. Cantero and E. Laplante, *Los ingenios de Cuba*, ed. Levi Marrero (Barcelona: La Modern Poesía, 1984).

15. For more on Laplante, see Charles Burroughs, "The Plantation Landscape and Its Architecture: Classicism, Representation, and Slavery," in *Buen Gusto and Classicism in the Visual Cultures of Latin America, 1780-1910*, ed. Paul B. Niell and Stacie G. Widdifield (Alburqueque: University of New Mexico Press, 2013), 114–135. For more on related estate portraits in the United States, see John Michael Vlach, *The Planter's Prospect: Privilege and Slavery in Plantation Paintings* (Chapel Hill: University of North Carolina Press, 2002).

16. Some of the photographs are reproduced in *Salon and Picturesque Photography in Cuba, 1860-1920: The Ramiro Fernández Collection* (Daytona Beach, FL: Museum of Arts and Sciences, 1988).

17. Plantation owners in other parts of the Spanish Caribbean were known to commission estate portraits that included representations of enslaved Africans and/or their descendants. For example, in 1885, the Spaniard José Gallart commissioned the Puerto Rican artist Francisco Oller to depict one of his thriving *ingenios*. See Richard Aste, "Art of the Spanish American Home at the Brooklyn Museum," in *Behind Closed Doors: Art in the Spanish American Home, 1492–1898*, ed. Richard Aste (New York: Monacelli Press, 2013), 40–44. Exhbition catalog.

18. While the figure's large buttocks are clearly accentuated by her bustled dress, the meaning of this iconography and its relationship to Black female sexuality in the nineteenth century cannot be overlooked. In his study of the iconography of female sexuality in the nineteenth century, which centered on the exaggerated buttocks of the so-called Hottentot women from southern Africa, Sander Gilman has argued that the Black woman's buttocks became a sign of her supposed primitive, lascivious sexuality. Landaluze taps into this international reference here. See Sander L. Gilman, "Black Bodies, White Bodies: Toward an Iconography of Female Sexuality in Late Nineteenth-Century Art, Medicine, and Literature," *Critical Inquiry* 12, no. 1, "*Race," Writing, and Difference* (Autumn 1985): 204–242.

19. Fernando Ortiz, "The Afro-Cuban Festival 'Day of the Kings,'" annotated and translated by Jean Stubbs, in *Cuban Festivals: A Century of Afro-Cuban Culture*, ed. Judith Bettelheim (New York: Garland Publishers, 1993), 9.

20. The painting is in the collection of Instituto de Cultura Puertorriqueña, San Juan, Puerto Rico. For more on Chartrand, see Raúl R. Ruiz, *Esteban Chartrand: Nuestro romántico* (Havana: Editorial Letras Cubanas, 1987).

21. Books with extensive reproductions of *marquillas* include Antonio Núñez Jimenez, *Cuba en las marquillas cigarreras del siglo XIX* (Havana: Ediciones Turísticas de Cuba, 1985); Antonio Núñez Jimenez, *El libro del tabaco* (Nuevo León, Mexico: Pulsar International, undated); and Antonio Núñez Jimenez, *Marquillas cigarreras cubanas* (Madrid: Ediciones Tabapress, 1989).

22. The most common marketing gimmick was to issue *marquillas* in a series so as to encourage purchasers to collect an entire set. Some marquillas also printed music on their back sides or could be used as parlor games. One company, La Honradez, allowed anyone who paid a fee to sit for one of their artists and have their likeness represented on a limited run of marquillas. See Narciso Menocal, *Cuban Cigar Labels: The Tobacco Industry in Cuba and Florida: Its Golden Age in Lithography and Architecture* (Miami: Cuban National Heritage, 1995), 7.

23. Alison Fraunhar makes this point. See her dissertation, "Re-visioning the Mulata in Cuban Visual Culture" (PhD diss., University of California at Santa Barbara, March 2005), 130. Fraunhar also extensively analyzes marquillas in her *Mulata Nation: Visualizing Race and Gender in Cuba* (Jackson: University Press of Mississippi, 2018).

24. Benjamin Céspedes, *La prostitución en la ciudad de La Habana* (Havana: Establecimiento Tipográfico, 1888), 171.

25. Robert Farris Thompson, *Flash of the Spirit. African and Afro-American Art and Philosophy* (New York: Vintage Books, 1984).

26. David H. Brown, "Pictures, Performances, and the Police: Changing Contexts for Costumbrista Arts," in *The Light Inside: Abakúa Society Arts and Cuban Cultural History* (Washington, DC: Smithsonian Books, 2003), 129–148.

27. For more on this early phase in Ortiz's career, see Robin Dale Moore, "Representations of Afro-Cuban Expressive Culture in the Writings of Fernando Ortiz," *Latin American Music Review* 15, no. 1 (Spring–Summer 1994): 32–54.

28. Judith Bettelheim, "Caribbean Espiritismo (Spiritist) Altars: The Indian and the Congo," *The Art Bulletin* 87, no. 2 (June 2005): 323.

29. Africa Céspedes, "Sr. Director de *La Fraternidad*," *La Fraternidad*, November 10, 1888, 4.

30. For more on this journal, see Carmen Montejo Arrechea, "Minerva: A Magazine for Women (and Men) of Color," in *Between Race and Empire: African-Americans and Cubans before the Cuban Revolution*, ed. Lisa Brock and Digna Castañeda Fuertes (Philadelphia: Temple University Press, 1998), 33–47. The author notes that Africa Céspedes, also mentioned in this essay, was a regular contributor and that the artist Torriente donated his services because he wanted to "help the colored race."

7. Individual and Type: The Limits of Self-Representation in the Era of Portraiture, 1800–1880

1. Natalia Majluf, "*En busca de José Gil de Castro: Rastros de una (auto)biografía*," in *José Gil de Castro, pintor de libertadores*, ed. Natalia Majluf (Lima, Peru: Museo de Arte de Lima, 2014), 25. Among the exceptions for the early nineteenth century, see the delicate pencil portrait of Pedro Lovera, generally misidentified as that of his mentor Juan Lovera, in Carlos F. Duarte, *Juan Lovera, el pintor de los próceres* (Caracas, Venezuela: Fundación Pampero, 1985), 144–151.

2. These arguments are considered in Majluf, "*En busca de José Gil de Castro: Rastros de una (auto)biografía*."

3. See Lilia Moritz Schwarcz, Adriano Pedrosa, and Tomás Toledo, "Portraits," in *Histórias afro-atlânticas/Afro-Atlantic Histories,* vol. 1, ed. Adriano Pedrosa and Tomás Toledo (Sao Paulo: Instituto Tomie Ohtake, Museo de Arte de Sao Paulo Assis Chateaubriand, 2018), 244–249. Exhibition catalog.

4. See the entries on Bolívar's portraits by Natalia Majluf and Laura Malosetti in *José Gil de Castro, pintor de libertadores.*

5. See, for example, Marixa Lasso, *Myths of Harmony: Race and Republicanism during the Age of Revolution, Colombia 1795–1831* (Pittsburgh, PA: University of Pittsburgh Press, 2007). For a general introduction to these issues in the Peruvian context, see Carlos Aguirre, *Breve historia de la esclavitud en el Perú: Una herida que no deja de sangrar* (Lima, Peru: Fondo Editorial del Congreso del Perú, 2005), and Maribel Arrelucea Barrantes and Jesús A. Cosamalón Aguilar, *La presencia afrodescendiente en el Perú: Siglos XVI-XX* (Lima, Peru:

Ministerio de Cultura, 2015).

6. The Argentine president Bernardino Rivadavia was of African descent, as his portrait by Manuel Pablo Núñez de Ibarra clearly demonstrates, though other images of him, such as the miniature at the Museo Lázaro Galdiano in Madrid, tend to dissimulate his ethnicity. I thank Roberto Amigo for generously sharing these images and his suggestions in the process of writing this text. For a general survey of portraiture in Latin America, see *Retratos: 2,000 Years of Latin American Portraits*, ed. Marion Oettinger, Jr. (New Haven, CT: Yale University Press, 2004).

7. María Dolores Ballesteros Páez, "*Vicente Guerrero: Insurgente, militar y presidente afromexicano*," *Cuicuilco* 18, no. 51 (May–August 2011): 26ff.

8. María José Esparza Liberal, "*Retrato del pueblo y de sus hombres ilustres*," in María José Esparza Liberal and Isabel Fernández de García-Lascurain, *La cera en México: Arte e historia* (Mexico: Fondo Cultural Banamex A.C., 1994). For a detailed account of the different portraits of Guerrero produced in the nineteenth century, see Irma Pérez Cárdenas, "*El patrocinio cultural de Mariano Riva Palacio Díaz (1803–1880)*" (Ph.D. diss., Universidad Nacional Autónoma de México, 2017), 139–159.

9. In October 1849, upon Álvarez's request, Mariano Riva Palacio commissioned the artist Severiano Hernandez to paint a portrait of Vicente Guerrero to hang in the regional congress. See "*El patrocinio cultural de Mariano Riva Palacio Díaz (1803–1880)*," 156–159.

10. For an account of this painting, see Pérez Cárdenas, "*El patrocinio cultural de Mariano Riva Palacio Díaz*," 135–139. The author notes that Álvarez's portrait was donated by Guerrero's son-in-law to the national museum.

11. Ballesteros Páez, "*Vicente Guerrero: Insurgente, militar y presidente afromexicano*," 29.

12. On Romero, see Claudia Arancibia F., "*Un soldado de la Independencia*," *Revista de Historia Militar*, Santiago 4 (December 2005): 14–16. Very well documented, though revealing in its prejudices, is the biography included in Guillermo Feliú Cruz's *La abolición de la esclavitud en Chile: Estudio histórico y social*, 2nd ed., prologue by Domingo Amunátegui Solar (Santiago, Chile: Editorial Universitaria, 1973), 117ff.

13. Feliú Cruz, *La abolición de la esclavitud en Chile*, 153–158. See also Mercedes Marín del Solar, *Canto fúnebre a la memoria del ciudadano José Romero en el día de sus exequias celebradas en el convento de Agustinos* (Santiago, Chile: Imprenta del 'Conservador,' 1858).

14. A carte de visite photograph based on the print was distributed by the studio J. A. Ovalle & Ca. Fotógrafos of Santiago in the early 1860s. See [*José Romero "Zambo Peluca"*], Sala Medina, Biblioteca Nacional, Santiago. Available at Biblioteca Nacional Digital de Chile, http://www.bibliotecanacionaldigital.cl/bnd/632/w3-article-312034.html.

15. Lea Geler, "'*¡Pobres negros!*' Algunos apuntes sobre la desaparición de los negros argentinos," in *Estado, región y poder local en América Latina, siglos XIX–XX: Algunas miradas sobre el estado, el poder y la participación política*, ed. Pilar García Jordán (Barcelona: TEIAA, Universitat de Barcelona, 2007), 125n6; María de Lourdes Ghidoli, *Estereotipos en negro: Representaciones y autorrepresentaciones de visuales de afroporteños en el siglo XIX* (Rosario, Argentina: Prohistoria, 2016), 200.

16. Ghidoli, *Estereotipos en negro*, 179. On the anonymous character of the figure of Falucho, see the discussion in Geler, "'*¡Pobres negros!*'"

17. Ghidoli, *Estereotipos en negro*, 180.

18. See Deborah Poole's analysis of the opposition between the individuality of upper-class Creole women of Lima and the anonymity of Indians and Afrodescendants in Manuel Atanasio Fuentes's *Lima*, an important illustrated book published in 1866. Deborah Poole, *Vision, Race, and Modernity: A Visual Economy of the Andean Image World* (Princeton, NJ: Princeton University Press, 1997), 158ff.

19. For a fascinating study of one of the very rare and early exceptions to this rule, see Tom Cummins, "Three Gentlemen of Esmeraldas: A Portrait Fit for a King," in *Slave Portraiture in the Atlantic World*, ed. Agnes Lugo-Ortiz and Angela Rosenthal (Cambridge: Cambridge University Press, 2013), 119–145. For a discussion of the portrait of Manuel de Salzes illustrated here, see Juan Manuel Martínez Silva, Marisol Richter, and Cynthia Valdivieso, "*Don Manuel de Salzes y doña Francisca Infante: Representación, memoria y devoción en el Reino de Chile*," in *El sistema de las artes: VII Jornadas de Historia del Arte*, ed. Raquel Abella et al. (Santiago, Chile: Museo Histórico Nacional, 2014): 195–200. For further information on this painting, see the database entry http://www.surdoc.cl/registro/2-7.

20. I thank Ricardo Kusunoki for referring me to this image and for sharing with me his ideas on late-eighteenth-century portraiture.

21. Literally, "thanks for the exclusion," or a process of purchasing or being issued a royal decree that enabled the bearer to elevate his status to that of a white person.

22. Alejandro E. Gómez, "*Las revoluciones blanqueadoras: Elites mulatas haitianas y 'pardos beneméritos' venezolanos, y su aspiración a la igualdad, 1789–1812*," *Nuevo Mundo Mundos Nuevos* [online], Colloques, http://journals.openedition.org/nuevomundo/868.

23. Duarte, *Juan Lovera*, 71.

24. Enrique López Albújar, *De mi casona* [1924] (Lima, Peru: Ediciones Peisa, 1998), 28.

25. On this discourse, see the critical discussion in Ghidoli, *Estereotipos en negro*. Feliú Cruz's *La abolición de la esclavitud en Chile*, however, uncritically extends such nineteenth-century narratives

in his account of José Romero's biography.

26. These figures appear in a number of collections, but notably in the later series of watercolors by Fierro. See especially Helen Melling's discussion of Black citizens in "'Colourful Customs and Invisible Traditions': Visual Representations of Black Subjects in Late Colonial and 19th Century, Post-Independence Peru (1750s–1890s)" (PhD diss., King's College London, 2015), 228ff. See also Natalia Majluf, "*La creación del costumbrismo: Las acuarelas de la donación Juan Carlos Verme*," in *La creación del costumbrismo: Las acuarelas de la donación Juan Carlos Verme*, ed. Natalia Majluf (Lima, Peru: Museo de Arte de Lima, 2016), 28.

27. Ghidoli, *Estereotipos en negro*, 219–224. On this tension between portraiture and typology, see especially Angela Rosenthal and Agnes Lugo-Ortiz, "Introduction: Envisioning Slave Portraiture," in *Slave Portraiture in the Atlantic World*, ed. Agnes Lugo-Ortiz and Angela Rosenthal (Cambridge: Cambridge University Press, 2013), 8–14.

28. Magally Alegre Henderson, "Androginopolis: Dissident Masculinities and the Creation of Republican Peru (Lima, 1790–1850)," (PhD diss., Stony Brook University, 2012), 212ff.

29. Fierro has only recently emerged as a tangible historical figure through the biographical information provided by genealogical studies. See especially Gustavo León y León Durán, *Apuntes histórico genealógicos de Francisco Fierro: Pancho Fierro* (Lima: Fondo Editorial de la Biblioteca Nacional del Perú, 2004). For the discursive construction of Fierro as part of the urban myth of Creole Lima, see Natalia Majluf, "*Pancho Fierro, entre el mito y la historia*," in Natalia Majluf and Marcus B. Burke, *Tipos del Perú: La Lima criolla de Pancho Fierro* (Madrid: Ediciones El Viso and The Hispanic Society of America, 2008), 18ff.

30. On the standardized nature of the carte-de-visite format in relation to racial depictions and Latin America, see Poole, *Vision, Race, and Modernity*, 139ff. See also the chapter "*Las buenas maneras: Fotografía y sujeto burgués en América Latina durante el siglo XIX*," in José Antonio Navarrete, *Fotografiando en América Latina: Ensayos de crítica histórica* (Caracas, Venezuela: Fundación para la Cultura Urbana, 2009): 35–47; and Beatriz González-Stephan, "*Cuerpos in/a-propiados: Carte-de-visite y las nuevas ciudadanías en la pardocracia venezolana postindependentista*," *Memoria y Sociedad* 17, no. 34 (January–June 2013): 14–32.

31. My selection of images here follows largely that presented by Melling in "'Colourful Customs and Invisible Traditions,'" 310–320.

32. For Brazil, see Marcelo Eduardo Leite, "*La población negra en São Paulo y su auto-representación en las cartes-de-visite producidas por el estudio Photographia Americana (1875–1885)*," *Revista Chilena de Antropología Visual*, no. 18 (2011), http://www.Rchav.cl/leite.html.

33. See Geoffrey Batchen's nuanced theoretical consideration of carte-de-visite portraits in "Dreams of Ordinary Life: Cartes-de-visite and the Bourgeois Imagination," in *Photography: Theoretical Snapshots*, ed. J. J. Long, Andrea Noble, and Edward Welch (London and New York: Routledge, 2009), 80–97, esp. 88.

34. Nicole Hudgins, "A Historical Approach to Family Photography: Class and Individuality in Manchester and Lille, 1850–1914," *Journal of Social History* 43, no. 3 (April 2010): 559–586.

35. On the subject of dress as a means of control of enslaved individuals, see Tamara J. Walker, "'He outfitted his family in notable decency': Slavery, Honour and Dress in Eighteenth-Century Lima, Peru," *Slavery and Abolition* 30, no. 3 (2009): 383–402, DOI: 10.1080/01440390903098011.

8. Black Visualities in Puerto Rico and the Dominican Republic: 19th and 20th Centuries

1. See José Trías Monje, *Puerto Rico: The Trials of the Oldest Colony in the World* (New Haven, CT: Yale University Press, 1997).

2. Many authors have described this event. Perhaps the most evocative description of the killing of thousands of Haitians at the Dominican border is that in the novel by Edwidge Danticat, *The Farming of Bones* (New York: Soho Press, 1998). The Parsley Massacre was so named because Dominican forces would ask prisoners to pronounce the word for *parsley* in Spanish, and if their Kreyol accent betrayed them, they would be killed.

3. Marimar Benítez, "The Special Case of Puerto Rico," in Luis R. Cancel et al., *The Latin American Spirit: Art and Artists in the United States, 1920–1970* (New York: Harry N. Abrams, 1989), 77.

4. See Carlos Solís Magaña, "Criollo Pottery from San Juan de Puerto Rico," in *African Sites: Archaeology of the Caribbean*, ed. Jay B. Haviser (Princeton, NJ: Markus Weiner Publishers, 1999), 131–141.

5. Teodoro Vidal, *Los Espada: Escultores sangermeños* (San Juan, Puerto Rico: Alba, 1994).

6. Arturo Dávila et al., *Campeche: Mito y realidad* (San Juan: Museo de Arte de Puerto Rico, 2010), 138. Exhibition catalog.

7. Ibid.

8. Cayetano Coll y Toste, "*El pintor Campeche*," *Boletín Histórico de Puerto Rico*, 3 (1916): 310.

9. Quoted in Osiris Delgado Mercado, *Francisco Oller y Cestero (1833–1917): Pintor de Puerto Rico* (San Juan: Centro de Estudios Superiores de Puerto Rico y El Caribe, 1983), 221–222.

10. See Edward J. Sullivan, *From San Juan to Paris and Back: Francisco Oller and Caribbean Art in the Era of Impressionism* (New Haven, CT: Yale University Press, 2014).

11. See Ibid., chapter 3, for a discussion of this painting, the life of Rafael Cordero, and the history of pedagogy in Puerto Rico.

12. Lorenzo Puente Acosta, *Biografía del Maestro Rafael Cordero*

(San Juan, Puerto Rico: Imprenta de Acosta, 1868).

13. Illustrated in Haydée Venegas, "Francisco Oller: Profile of a Puerto Rican Painter," in *Francisco Oller: A Realist-Impressionist* (Ponce, Puerto Rico: Museo de Arte de Ponce, 1983), 127. Exhibition catalog.

14. For a history of the development of sugar plantations in Puerto Rico, see Lizette Cabrera Salcedo, *De los bueyes al vapor: Caminos de la tecnología del azúcar en Puerto Rico y el Caribe* (San Juan: La Editorial, Universidad de Puerto Rico, 2010).

15. Trumbull White, *Our New Possessions: Four Books in One: A Graphic Account, Descriptive and Historical, of the Tropic Islands of the Sea which Have Fallen under Our Sway* (Chicago: Star Publishing Co., 1898).

16. *Photographic History of the Spanish-American War: A Pictorial and Descriptive Record of Events on Land and Sea with Portraits and Biographies of Leaders on Both Sides* (New York: Pearson Publishing, 1898).

17. Benítez, 74.

18. Ibid., 76.

19. Teresa Tió Fernández, *El cartel de Puerto Rico* (San Juan: Instituto de Cultura Puertorriqueña, 1985).

20. *Rafael Tufiño: Pintor del pueblo* (San Juan: Museo de Arte de Puerto Rico, 2001). Exhibition catalog. It is worth noting that this exhibition was also shown at El Museo del Barrio in New York. Created in 1969 by Puerto Rican artists in the *barrio* (neighborhood) of the Puerto Rican diaspora in Manhattan, this museum has been the principal institution in the United States for the dissemination of knowledge of works by artists from all parts of the Spanish-speaking Americas. El Museo now functions as a museum of Latin American and Caribbean art.

21. Tió Fernández, "Rafael Tufiño: The Art of Self," in *Rafael Tufiño*, 206.

22. Ibid., 207.

23. See the compilation of Delano's photographs of Puerto Rico in Jack Delano, *Puerto Rico Mío: Four Decades of Change* (Washington, DC: Smithsonian Books, 1989).

24. Jeanette Miller, "An Approach to Dominican Art: 1920–1970," in Elizabeth Ferrer, Suzanne Stratton, and Edward J. Sullivan, *Modern and Contemporary Art of the Dominican Republic* (New York: Americas Society: The Spanish Institute, 1996), 39. Exhibition catalog.

25. Ibid., 50n8; and José Ramón López, *El gran pesimismo dominicano* (Santo Domingo, Dominican Republic: Universidad Católica Madre y Maestra, 1975).

26. Ada Balcácer, "El activismo de la mujer en el arte dominicano," in *Mujer y arte dominicano hoy: Homenaje a Celeste Woss y Gil* (Santo Domingo, Dominican Republic: Casa de Bastidas, 1995), 51.

27. See José del Castillo and Anne W. Chevako, *Botello: Angel Botello Barros* (San Juan, Puerto Rico: Galería Botello, 1988).

28. *Jaime Colson: Pinturas—Peintures—Paintings* (Coral Gables, FL: Palette Publications, 1996).

29. Richard J. Powell, *Cutting a Figure: Fashioning Black Portraiture* (Chicago: University of Chicago Press, 2008), 41–65.

9. The Image of the Black in Select 20th-Century Works of Art in Haiti, Martinique, and Guadeloupe

1. Launched in Paris in the 1930s as an ideology based in the affirmation of a Black racial identity, *Négritude* galvanized a generation of intellectuals to embrace a shared sense of African heritage and self-pride and self-determination with the intention of combatting the demoralization of French imperialism. Occurring in the United States a decade prior to Négritude was the Harlem Renaissance, a moment of profound cultural, political, and artistic creativity that also sought to celebrate a race consciousness rooted in Africa and Blackness to challenge racial oppression and violence in the nation. The Harlem Renaissance was spearheaded by the philosopher and scholar Alain Locke, who felt that art would be the catalyst toward Black liberation and self-determination.

2. Th. Mpoyi-Buatu, "*Deux peintres de l'école négro-caraïbe à Paris*," *Présence Africaine*, Nouvelle série, no. 124, "*Aspects de la médecine en Afrique*"/"Some Aspects of Medicine in Africa" (4e Trimestre 1982), 232. The original in French reads, "*Il y a donc l'Afrique comme quête, comme référence et ses traces dans le cadre topographique concret des Antilles, c'est-à-dire aux convergences d'une multiplicité d'autres traces, notamment occidentales. L'Afrique, comme référence première, colle d'abord à la peau.*" All translations of quotes are by the author unless otherwise specified.

3. Patricia Donatien-Yssa, "Fwomajé and Totem: The Beginnings and Consolidation of an Artistic Language in Martinique," trans. Nadève Ménard, *Small Axe* 13, no. 3 (November 2009): 119. Interestingly, the mysticism of nature is also captured in the work of Vodou-inspired Haitian artists. Specifically, the mapou tree, thought to have mystical and life-giving powers, is often represented in the work of the Haitian contemporary *drapo* artist Myrlande Constant.

4. While most Guadeloupeans and Martinicans are bilingual, easily speaking French and Creole, most Haitians speak only Creole. However, French and Creole are the official two languages in Haiti.

5. For a history of the formation of the plastic arts in Haiti, see Philippe Thoby-Marcelin, "Magic in Paint," *Americas* (December 1949); Philippe Thoby-Marcelin, *Art in Latin America Today: Haiti* (Washington, DC: Pan American Union, 1959); Michel-Philippe Lerebours, *Haïti et ses peintres de 1804 à 1980* (Port-au-Prince, Haiti: L'Imprimeur I.,

1989); Michel-Philippe Lerebours, "The Indigenist Revolt: Haitian Art, 1927–1944," *Callaloo* 15, no. 3 (Summer 1992); and Gerald Alexis, *Peintres haïtiens (Haitian Painters)* (Paris: Éditions Cercle d'Art, 2000).

6. René Louise, *Peinture et sculpture en Martinique* (Paris: Editions Caribéennes, 1984). See also Anne and Hervé Chopin, *Les peintres martiniquais (Painters from Martinique)* (Paris: HC Éditions, 1998). Since 2007, several encyclopedic texts have been published. See *La peinture en Martinique,* ed. Gerry L'Étang, with Renée-Paule Yung-Hing, with preface by Alfred Marie-Jeanne (2007); and *Anthologie de la peinture en Guadeloupe des origines à nos jours*, ed. Roger Toumson, with foreword by Victorin Lurel (2009).

7. Christian Mas, "*1848–1960: Constitution d'une identité picturale*," in *Anthologie de la peinture en Guadeloupe des origines à nos jours*, ed. Roger Toumson (Consell régional de Guadeloupe: HC Éditions, 2009), 61.

8. Ibid., 65. The French reads: "*En conclusion la peinture en Guadeloupe est marquée dans l'entre-deux guerres, par la présence de peintres français. Ceux-ci composent des tableaux où le paysage apparaît comme un genre autonome. Dans l'ensemble, peu de place est laissée aux artistes locaux. La fin de la Seconde Guerre mondiale, les débuts de la départementalisation ne suscitent ni une rupture ni un renouveau dans l'art guadeloupéen.*"

9. "*Paradoxes esthétiques des Caraïbes: Un cas d'espèce*," introduction to *Anthologie de la peinture en Guadeloupe des origines à nos jours*, ed. Roger Toumson (Consell régional de Guadeloupe: HC Éditions, 2009), 11.

10. For a thorough and illuminating account of nineteenth-century Haitian portraiture, see Erica Moiah James, "Decolonizing Time: Nineteenth-Century Haitian Portraiture and the Critique of Anachronism in Caribbean Art," *Nka Journal of Contemporary African Art* 2019, no. 44 (May 2019): 8–23.

11. For a detailing of the Haitian and itinerant artists who were working in Haiti during the nineteenth century, please see Michel-Philippe Lerebours's *Bref regard sur deux siècles de peinture haïtienne (1804–2004)* (Port-au-Prince: Éditions de l'Univesité d'État d'Haïti, 2018).

12. Frederick Douglass was consul general of the United States in Haiti from 1889 to 1891. Yale University's Peabody Museum of Natural History owns fifteen paintings, currently undergoing restoration, including several of Toussaint Louverture painted by Louis Rigaud. Lerebours, *Bref regard sur deux siècles de peinture haïtienne (1804–2004)*, n20, 31. Unfortunately, many of these paintings are lost. The Sans Souci Palace was looted after Christophe committed suicide in 1820. The villa Volant-Le-Thor, the Senate, and House of Representatives where many of these portraits were housed burned in 1864, 1866, and 1867, respectively.

13. The painting is currently in the collection of the Yale Peabody Museum of Natural History.

14. In *Cuban Art and National Identity: The Vanguardia Painters 1927–1950*, Juan A. Martinez writes, "[i]n Havana the vanguardia painters developed their full-grown artistic vision during the 1930s. In that tumultuous decade of economic depression and political instability in Cuba, the years 1935, 1937, and 1938 are important landmarks in the development of modern Cuban art." Martinez, *Cuban Art and National Identity* (Gainesville: University Press of Florida, 1994), 16. Rocío Aranda-Alvarado writes about the role of the racialized figure in modern art in the "new world" between 1925 and 1945. She argues that during this period, artists in the "new world" worked toward the creation of a culturally, nationally, and racially specific image that would "stand as a symbol for a new national identity and, simultaneously, for modernity as a whole." Aranda-Alvarado, "New World Primitivism in Harlem and Havana: Constructing Modern Identities in the Americas, 1924–1945" (PhD diss., City University of New York, 2001), 267–290.

15. *Indigénisme* was an important movement in Haiti during the 1920s and 1930s. Haiti was occupied by the United States from July 28, 1915, to August 1, 1934. Many scholars have argued that indigénisme was a direct result of the racial oppressive occupation of the United States as well as the socioeconomic oppressive tactics of the Haitian elite.

16. Prior to this, Pétion Savain and his students Yvonne Sylvain and Georges Remponeau were active in Port-au-Prince during the mid-1900s. Savain was the author of the novel *La Case de Damballah/Damballah's House* (1939), a novel he illustrated with linocuts which explored Vodou ceremonies, Haitian folklore, and rural peasant life. Savain would have eight exhibitions in Haiti from 1931 to 1939. In 1938, his *Marché dans la campagne/Market on the Hill*, 1938/1939 was chosen to represent Haiti in the International Business Machines Corporation competition held in 1939 at the Golden Gate International Exposition in San Francisco. Savain went on to study painting at the Art Students League in New York in the early 1940s.

17. The Centre was founded in May 1944 by the American watercolorist DeWitt Peters and several Haitian artists and writers: Gérald Bloncourt, Maurice Borno, Jean Chenet, Raymond Coupeau, Antoine Derenoncourt, Raymond Lavelanette, Albert Mangonès, Georges Remponeau, and Philippe-Thoby Marcelin.

18. The self-taught artists who were included in this landmark exhibition were Louverture Poisson, Philomé Obin, Luckner Lazard, Rigaud Benoit, Sénèque Obin, Préfète Duffaut, André Pierre, Jasmin Joseph, and Wilson Bigaud. See Lerebours, *Bref regard sur deux siècles de peinture haïtienne*, n44.

19. The members of the Foyer published a "declaration" in *Le*

Nouvelliste in August 1950 denouncing the Centre and publicly disassociating themselves from the Centre and its American administrators. The letter was signed by Max Pinchinat, Lucien Price, Jean Chenet, Néhémy Jean, and Georges Remponeau, among others. In the opening paragraph, they state "*nous soussignés reconnaissons par la présente que nos liaisons passées avec le Centre d'Art sont et demeurent entièrement abolies et ceci pour des raisons dont nous rejetons toute la charge sur la Direction du dit Centre* ("We, the undersigned, hereby acknowledge that our past association with the Centre d'Art are and remain abolished and this can only be blamed on the Centre's management.") Eventually, some fifty-eight artists left the Centre to form Le Foyer des Arts Plastiques.

20. Cuban artists such as Carlos Enríquez (1945), Wifredo Lam (1946), and Cundo Bermúdez (1947) visited the Centre at different times. The Centre also saw visits from William Edouard Scott (1931), Aaron Douglas (1938), Jason Seley (1942), James Porter (1946), Richmond Barthé (1948), Harlan Jackson (1948–1951), Eldzier Cortor (1949–1951), and Ellis Wilson (1950–1951).

21. Veerle Poupeye, "Trading across the Black Atlantic: Globalization and the Work of Marc Latamie," *Australian and New Zealand Journal of Art* 3, no. 2 (2002): 83.

22. Lindsay J. Twa, *Visualizing Haiti in U.S. Culture, 1910–1950* (London: Ashgate Publishing, 2014). In her informative and well-researched book, Twa provides a roadmap of African American and white American artists who visited and worked in Haiti during the first part of the twentieth century. It is a significant contribution toward the study of Haiti's involvement in the history of art of the Black diaspora. See also Krista A. Thompson, "Preoccupied with Haiti: The Dream of Diaspora in African American Art, 1915–1942," *American Art* 21, no. 3 (Fall 2007): 74–97; and Margaret Rose Vendryes, "Brothers under the Skin: Richmond Barthé in Haiti," *Journal of Haitian Studies* 10, no. 2 (Fall 2004): 116–134.

23. At the writing of this essay, the exhibition *Gauguin and Laval in Martinique* was at the Van Gogh Museum in Amsterdam. This exhibition featured drawings and paintings by Charles Laval and Paul Gauguin from their time in Martinique, begun in June 1887. According to Britt Salvesen, "In March he and his new friend Laval decided to 'flee Paris': they set sail in April and by May were working in the city of Colón in jobs related to the building of the Panama Canal. Far from being the Utopia they had anticipated, however, Panama was ugly and insalubrious, with high mortality rates resulting from rampant tropical diseases. … In June, the two artists left for the island of Martinique, a French colony since the mid-seventeenth century, where they planned 'to live like savages' in a cabin … in St.-Pierre. Even though Laval contracted yellow fever, and Gauguin suffered a serious bout of dysentery and malaria, Gauguin described Martinique as 'a Paradise' and … persisted with his art." … Upon his return to Paris by mid-November 1887, Gauguin articulates a new persona, one purportedly found in the "Paradise" of Martinique. In a letter to his wife, according to Salvesen, Gauguin writes, "'You must remember that I have a dual nature, [that of] the Indian and [that of] the sensitive civilized man. The latter has disappeared [since my departure], which permits the former to take the lead.'" This "fundamental dualism of his character" is due, Gauguin claimed, to his mother's Peruvian heritage which gave him the right to "define himself as both European and foreign, civilized and primitive, and to create for himself a space in which to assert an unchallenged originality." In a letter to Theo van Gogh, his dealer of less than two years, he writes: "'You know that by birth my background is Indian, Inca, and all that I do reflects this. It's the foundation of my personality. I am seeking to set something more natural over against corrupt civilization, with the primitive as my starting point.'" All quotes from Britt Salvesen, *Gauguin: Artists in Focus,* ed. Douglas W. Druick and Peter Kort Zegers (New York: Harry N. Abrams, Inc., 2001), 24, 37.

24. The original French reads: "*C'est à partir de 1937 que l'on commence à s'enseigner le dessin et la peinture au Lycée de Fort-de-France. Le professeur, M. Bailly, d'origine française, et le petit-fils du gouverneur Bailly. A cette même époque, M. Peu enseigne le dessin dans une école des Terres-Sainville, et M. Sixtain, à l'école de Perrinon. Parallèlement, des cours de dessin seront dispensés au Séminaire Collège.*" See Louise, *Peinture et sculpture en Martinique,* 7–8.

25. By the 1920s, Paris had become an incubator for many young Francophone Caribbean intellectuals whose insightful inquiries into the colonial and postcolonial world would originate watershed cultural movements such as Négritude. Also at this moment, Paris was the center for many modernist and avant-garde art movements as well as theoretical and philosophical currents. Art nègre had become a fascination for artists interested in cubism and surrealism. See Petrine Archer Straw, *Negrophilia: Avant-Garde Paris and Black Culture in the 1920s* (London: Thames and Hudson; 2000), Brent Hayes Edwards, *The Practice of Diaspora: Literature, Translation, and the Rise of Black Internationalism* (Cambridge, MA: Harvard University Press, 2003); and Michel Fabre, *From Harlem to Paris: Black American Writers in France, 1840–1980* (Champaign: University of Illinois Press, 1991).

26. Frantz Fanon, *Black Skin, White Masks,* trans. Charles Lam Markmann (New York: Grove Press, 1967), 18.

27. Dominique Brebion, "Memory and the Contemporary Visual Arts of the Francophone Caribbean," *Small Axe* 13, no. 3 (November 2009): 107–108. See also Donatien-Yssa, "Fwomajé and Totem: The Beginnings and Consolidation of an Artistic Language in Martinique," and Louise, *Peinture et sculpture en Martinique*. All are excellent sources

to ascertain the artists, stylistic periods, and academic art institutions in Martinique. Each in varying ways provide the political, social, and cultural contexts in which Martinican art was produced.

28. Louis Laouchez, *l'École Négro-Caraïbe*. The original in French reads: "*Nous transportons avec nous, comme dit Serge Hélénon, ce qui est notre culture originelle. Nous ne sommes pas africains, mais nègres de la diaspora, nègres de tous les continents, nègres de tous les milieux. Notre identité, notre différence peuvent faire peur aussi bien aux dominés qu'aux dominateurs.*" https://louislaouchez.com/.

29. Pierre Brana, *Martin Miguel, Serge Hélénon: Le parti pris du bâti*, Château Lescombes: Centre d'Art Contemporain de Eysines, 11 janvier–12 mars 2017 (Eysines, France: Korus Impression, 2017), 2–31, 15. Exhibition catalog, http://www.performarts.net/performarts/index.php?option=com_content&view=article&id=2575:bati&catid=2:expositions&Itemid=21. The French reads, "*…participerait en fait à un renouveau de l'art nègre. Dégagée de tout folkore et exotisme, elle va puiser ses sources dans le comportement et les agissements des populations noires du globe et s'imprègne de tous les aspects et formes qui reflètent une originalité esthétique nègre en son essence.*"

30. Louise, *Peinture et sculpture en Martinique,* 14. The French reads, "*Ces plasticiens commencent par réaliser des croquis et des études morphologiques de la race noire. Les croquis réalisés au début, mirent en évident une méconnaissance de la morphologie de la race: portraits ou croquis de nus rapprochaient presque toujours du type européen.*"

31. Anna Lesne, "Writing the Self in the Antilles, Writing the Antilles: Writers and Anthropologists in Dialogue" ("*S'écrire aux Antilles, écrire les Antilles: Écrivains et anthropologues en dialogue*"), *L'Homme* 207–208, no. 3 (2013): V. Italics mine.

32. Jean Bernabé, Patrick Chamoiseau, and Raphaël Confiant, "In Praise of Creoleness," trans. Mohamed B. Taleb Khyar, *Callaloo* 13, no. 4 (Autumn 1990): 886.

33. Ellen M. Schnepel, *In Search of a National Identity: Creole and Politics in Guadeloupe* (Madison: University of Wisconsin Press, 2004), 11.

34. Édouard Glissant, *Poetics of Relation*, trans. Betsy Wing (Ann Arbor: University of Michigan Press, 1997), 1996.

35. Bernabé, Chamoiseau, and Confiant, "In Praise of Creoleness," 893.

36. *Échos Imprévus: Turning Tide*, Région Guadeloupe: Mémorial ACTe, November 19–April 30, 2017, 14. Exhibition catalog.

37. Darby English, *How to See a Work of Art in Total Darkness* (Cambridge, MA: MIT Press, 2007), 32.

38. Gina Athena Ulysse, "Vodou as Idea: On Omise'eke Natasha Tinsley's 'Ezili's Mirrors,'" *Los Angeles Review of Books*, September 28, 2018, https://lareviewofbooks.org/article/vodou-as-idea-on-omiseeke-natasha-tinsleys-ezilis-mirrors/#!. See also Ulysse, "Seven Keywords for this Rasanblaj," *Anthropology Now* 8, no. 3 (2016): 122–125, DOI: 10.1080/19428200.2016.1242921, where she provides the following definition: "Rasanblaj: n., assembly, compilation, enlisting, regrouping (of ideas, things, people, spirits…)."

39. Lauren DeLand, "Black Skin, Black Masks: The Citational Self in the Work of Glenn Ligon," *Criticism* 54, no. 4 (Fall 2012): 507–537, 517–518.

40. "Ernest Breleur's drawings as a visual metaphor questioning the corporeal," interview by Dominique Brebion, *Aica Caraïbe*, July 4, 2014, https://aica-sc.net/2014/07/04/ernest-breleurs-drawings-as-a-visual-metaphor-questioning-the-corporeal/.

41. Nicole R. Fleetwood, *Troubling Vision: Performance, Visuality, and Blackness* (Chicago: University of Chicago Press), 3.

42. In another notoriously fatal encounter, this time in the Powderhorn Park community in Minneapolis on May 25, 2020, an unarmed African American man, George Floyd, who was arrested for allegedly using counterfeit money for a purchase, uttered the very same words as Garner—"I can't breathe"—as a white police officer kneeled on his neck for seven minutes and forty-six seconds. Floyd's murder sparked national and international protest against police brutality.

43. Rocío Aranda-Alvarado, "Bodies of Color: Images of Women in the Works of Firelei Báez and Rachelle Mozman," *Small Axe* 21, no. 1 (March 2017): 58–70, 57.

44. Guérédrat and Tauliaut co-organized the inaugural Festival International d'Art Performance (FIAP) in Fort-de-France, Martinique, from April 17–23, 2017.

45. Raphael Cuir, "Annabel Gueredrat and Henri Tauliaut," Festival International d'Art Performance, 19. Exhibition catalog.

46. Tatiana Flores, "Inscribing into Consciousness: The Work of Caribbean Art," in *Relational Undercurrents: Contemporary Art of the Caribbean Archipelago*, ed. Tatiana Flores and Michelle A. Stephens (Durham, NC: Duke University Press, 2017), 78. Exhibition catalog.

47. Ibid., 72.

10. Race and the Latin American Avant-Gardes, 1920s–1930s

1. Oswald de Andrade, "*Manifesto da poesia Pau-Brasil*," *Correio da Manhã* 9147 (March 18, 1924), 5. ["Manifesto of Pau-Brasil Poetry," trans. Stella M. de Sá Rego, *Latin American Literary Review* 14, no. 27 (1986), 184–187].

2. Martí Casanovas, "*Arte & artistas: Rafael Blanco*," *Revista de Avance* 1, no. 1 (1927): 7.

3. Mário de Andrade, *Aspectos das artes plásticas no Brasil* (Belo Horizonte, Brazil: Itatiaia, 1984), 13–18; Alejandro de la Fuente, *A Nation for All: Race, Inequality, and Politics in Twentieth-Century Cuba* (Chapel

Hill: University of North Carolina Press, 2001), 182.

4. Martí Casanovas, "*Arte nuevo*," *Revista de Avance* 1, no. 7 (1927): 157.

5. Nancy Leys Stepan, "*The Hour of Eugenics*": Race, Gender, and Nation in Latin America (Ithaca, NY: Cornell University Press, 1991); Alexandra Minna Stern, *Eugenic Nation: Faults and Frontiers of Better Breeding in Modern America* (Berkeley: University of California Press, 2005).

6. Eduardo Abela, "*Indagación: ¿Qué debe ser el arte americano?*," *Revista de Avance* 2, no. 29 (December 15, 1928): 361.

7. Oswald de Andrade, "*Manifesto antropófago*," *Revista de Antropofagia* 1, no. 1 (May 1928), 3, 7. ["Cannibalist Manifesto," trans. Leslie Bary, *Latin American Literary Review* 19, no. 38 (1991)].

8. Stepan, "*The Hour of Eugenics*," 85–119.

9. Manoel Bomfim, *A América Latina: Males de origem* (Rio de Janeiro: Topbooks, 2005). See also Rafael Cardoso, "The Brazilianness of Brazilian Art: Discourses on Art and National Identity, c.1850–1930," *Third Text* 26, no. 1 (2012): 21–25; Paula Rejane Fernandes, "*América Latina aos olhos de Manoel Bomfim: Análise da obra 'A América Latina: Males de origem*,'" *Dimensões* 29 (2012): 100–118.

10. Justo Sierra, *Evolución política del pueblo mexicano* (Caracas, Venezuela: Biblioteca Ayacucho, 1977), 299.

11. Rafael Cardoso, "The Problem of Race in Brazilian Painting, c. 1850–1920," *Art History* 38 no. 3 (2015): 500–508.

12. Michael George Hanchard, *Orpheus and Power: The Movimento Negro of Rio de Janeiro and São Paulo, Brazil, 1945–1988* (Princeton, NJ: Princeton University Press, 1994); Alexandra Isfahani-Hammond, *White Negritude: Race, Writing, and Brazilian Cultural Identity* (New York: Palgrave Macmillan, 2008); Vera M. Kutzinski, *Sugar's Secrets: Race and the Erotics of Cuban Nationalism* (Charlottesville: University of Virginia Press, 1993); Vicky Unruh, "Modernity's Labors in Latin America: The Cultural Work of Cuba's Avant-Gardes," in *The Oxford Handbook of Global Modernisms*, ed. Mark A. Wollaeger and Matt Eatough (New York: Oxford University Press, 2012), 341–366.

13. Francine Masiello, "Rethinking Neocolonial Esthetics: Literature, Politics, and Intellectual Community in Cuba's *Revista de Avance*," *Latin American Research Review* 28, no. 2 (1993): 28.

14. de la Fuente, *A Nation for All*; John Charles Chasteen, *National Rhythms, African Roots: The Deep History of Latin American Popular Dance* (Albuquerque: University of New Mexico Press, 2004); George Reid Andrews, *Blackness in the White Nation: A History of Afro-Uruguay* (Chapel Hill: University of North Carolina Press, 2010); Marc A. Hertzman, *Making Samba: A New History of Race and Music in Brazil* (Durham, NC: Duke University Press, 2013).

15. de la Fuente, *A Nation for All*; Melina Pappademos, *Black Political Activism and the Cuban Republic* (Chapel Hill: University of North Carolina Press, 2011).

16. Paulina L. Alberto, *Terms of Inclusion: Black Intellectuals in Twentieth-Century Brazil* (Chapel Hill: University of North Carolina Press, 2011), 29.

17. Tatiana Flores, *Mexico's Revolutionary Avant-Gardes: From Estridentismo to ¡30–30!* (New Haven, CT: Yale University Press, 2013); Vicky Unruh, *Latin American Vanguards: The Art of Contentious Encounters* (Berkeley: University of California Press, 1994).

18. Juan Marinello, "*Notas acerca de José Manuel Poveda por Regino E. Boti y Héctor Poveda*," *Revista de Avance* 2, no. 23 (1928): 160; Luciano Cruz-Morgado, "Image, Expression, and Meaning of the *Mulato* in Four Moments of Cuban Literature (1868–1948)," (PhD diss., University of Kentucky, 2008); Miriam DeCosta-Willis, "Marcelino Arozarena's Journey to His Roots," *Afro-Hispanic Review* 17, no. 1 (1998): 12–18; Debbie Lee, "Regino Pedroso and the Creation of a Triple Consciousness," *Journal of Hispanic Higher Education* 2, no. 3 (2003): 225–240; Georgina Arozarena Himely, "*Marcelino Arozarena: Griot del Caribe*," *Afro-Hispanic Review* 31, no. 1 (2012): 233–252.

19. Mário de Andrade, *Taxi e crônicas do Diário Nacional* (São Paulo: Duas Cidades/Secretaria de Cultura, Ciência e Tecnologia, 1976), 103, 322; Maria Luisa Nunes, "Mario de Andrade in 'Paradise,'" *Modern Language Studies* 22, no. 3 (1992): 70–75; Hermano Vianna, *O mistério do samba* (Rio de Janeiro: Jorge Zahar/Ed. UFRJ, 1995), 106–107.

20. Vera M. Kutzinski, *The Worlds of Langston Hughes: Modernism and Translation in the Americas* (Ithaca, NY: Cornell University Press, 2012), 56–66; Gayle Rogers, *Incomparable Empires: Modernism and the Translation of Spanish and American Literature* (New York: Columbia University Press, 2016), 180–185.

21. Miguel Covarrubias, *Negro Drawings* (New York: Alfred A. Knopf, 1927).

22. Flores, *Mexico's Revolutionary Avant-Gardes*, 164–165.

23. Hertzman, *Making Samba*, 108; Rafael José de Menezes Bastos, "*Les Batutas, 1922: Une anthropologie de la nuit parisienne*," *Vibrant* 4, no. 1 (2007): 28–55.

24. Lira Neto, *Uma história do samba: "As origens*," vol.1 (São Paulo: Companhia das Letras, 2017), 125.

25. Carlos Sandroni, *Feitiço decente: Transformações do samba no Rio de Janeiro (1917–1933)* (Rio de Janeiro: Jorge Zahar/Ed. UFRJ, 2001); Vianna, *O mistério do samba*, 115–120; Maria Alice Rezende de Carvalho, "*O samba, a opinião e outras bossas… na construção republicana do Brasil*," in *Decantando a República: Inventário histórico e politico da canção popular moderna brasileira*, ed. Berenice Cavalcante, Heloisa Starling, and José Eisenberg (Rio de Janeiro: Nova Fronteira & São Paulo: Fundação Perseu Abramo, 2004); Neto, *Uma história do samba*,

119–125, 140–152.

26. Doris Sommer, "Literary Liberties: The Authority of Afrodescendant Authors," in *Afro-Latin American Studies: An Introduction*, ed. Alejandro de la Fuente and George Reid Andrews (New York: Cambridge University Press, 2018), 319–347.

27. Alexander Dawson, *Indian and Nation in Revolutionary Mexico* (Tucson: University of Arizona Press, 2004).

28. Micol Seigel, *Uneven Encounters: Making Race and Nation in Brazil and the United States* (Durham, NC: Duke University Press, 2009), 117.

29. Tyler Stovall, *Paris Noir: African Americans in the City of Light* (New York: Houghton Mifflin, 1996); Petrine Archer-Straw, *Negrophilia: Avant-Garde Paris and Black Culture in the 1920s* (London: Thames and Hudson, 2000); Fionnghuala Sweeney and Kate Marsh, ed., *Afromodernisms: Paris, Harlem and the Avant-Garde* (Edinburgh, Scotland: Edinburgh University Press, 2013).

30. "*Almanaque: Vórtice*," *Revista de Avance* 1, no. 7 (1927): 179.

31. Flores, *Mexico's Revolutionary Avant-Gardes*; David Craven, *Art and Revolution in Latin America* (New Haven, CT: Yale University Press, 2002).

32. José Carlos Mariátegui, "*Notas: '1928' y la 'Oda al Bidet*,'" *Amauta* 3, no. 17 (1928): 91.

33. José Vasconcelos, "*El nacionalismo en la América Latina*," *Amauta* 1, no. 4 (1926): 13–16 and 2, no. 5 (1926): 22–24.

34. Mariano Azuela, "*Los de abajo*," *Amauta* 2, no. 11 (1928): 30–31.

35. Esteban Pavletich, "*Diego Rivera: El artista de una clase*," *Amauta* 2, no. 5 (1927): 5–9.

36. Martí Casanovas, "*Cuadro de la pintura mexicana*," *Amauta* 3, no. 19 (1928): 37–50.

37. Flores, *Mexico's Revolutionary Avant-Gardes*.

38. Alfonso Reyes, "*Verso y prosa*" and "*Seis poetas nuevos de México*," *Martín Fierro* 4, no. 42 (June 10–July 10, 1927), 351, 353.

39. Marcela Naciff, "*Martín Fierro, Revista de Avance y Amauta: Hacia una literaturización vanguardista de la identidad latinoamericana*" (PhD diss., Arizona State University, 2012).

40. Vasconcelos, "*El nacionalismo en la América Latina*," 13.

41. Angela de Castro Gomes, *Essa gente do Rio…: Modernismo e nacionalismo* (Rio de Janiero: Fundação Getúlio Vargas, 1999), 46.

42. Renata Gomes Cardoso, "*Arte da América Latina na crítica de Raymond Cogniat, 1926*," *Revista Eletrônica da ANPHLAC* 19 (2015): 43.

43. Ana Paula Cavalcanti Simoni, "*Le modernisme brésilien, entre consécration et contestation*," *Perspective* 2 (2013); Agustín Arteaga, ed., *Mexique 1900–1950: Diego Rivera, Frida Kahlo, José Clemente Orozco et les avant-garde* (Paris: Réunion des Musées Nationaux, 2016). Exhibition catalog.

44. Nancy P. Appelbaum, Anne S. Macpherson, and Karin Alejandra Rosemblatt, ed., *Race and Nation in Modern Latin America* (Chapel Hill: University of North Carolina Press, 2003); Walter D. Mignolo, *The Idea of Latin America* (Oxford: Wiley-Blackwell, 2005).

45. Ana Paula Cavalcanti Simioni, "*Le voyage à Paris: L'Académie Julian et la formation des artistes peintres brésiliennes vers 1900*," *Cahiers du Brésil contemporain* 57–58/59–60 (2004–2005): 261–281; Michele Greet, "1920s Transatlantic Encounters: Latin American Artists in Paris," *Global Studies Review* 2, no. 3 (2006); Isabel Plante, "*Les Sud-américains de Paris*: Latin American Artists and Cultural Resistance in Robho Magazine," *Third Text* 24, no. 4 (2010): 445–455.

46. Adriana Castillo de Berchenko, "*La Revue de l'Amérique Latine en los años 20*," *América: Cahiers du CRICCAL*, no. 4–5 (1990): 21–26.

47. Gomes Cardoso, "*Arte da América Latina*," 256–257.

48. Michele Greet, "Occupying Paris: The First Survey Exhibition of Latin American Art," *Journal of Curatorial Studies* 3, nos. 2–3 (2014): 216–217.

49. Raymond Cogniat, "*Exposition d'art Américain-latin au Musée Galliera*," *Revue de l'Amérique Latine* 3, no. 7 (1924): 435–436.

50. Greet, "Occupying Paris," 220.

51. Greet, "Occupying Paris," 226; "*Salon de arte moderno argentino-uruguayo*," *Martin Fierro* 2, nos. 14–15 (January 1925): 95.

52. Charles Lesca, "*Pedro Figari, peintre uruguayen*," *Revue de l'Amérique Latine* 2:5 (1923): 167.

53. Raymond Cogniat, "*Exposition de Pedro Figari à la Galerie Druet*," *Revue de l'Amérique Latine* 2, no. 6 (1923): 357–358; Désiré Roustan, *Simple note sur l'art et les doctrines de M. Pedro Figari* (Paris: Éditions de la Revue de l'Amérique Latine, 1926).

54. Raymond Cogniat, "*Exposition d'art Américain-latin au Musée Galliera*," *Revue de l'Amérique Latine* 3, no. 7 (1924): 5.

55. Daniel Sherman, *French Primitivism and the Ends of Empire, 1945–1975* (Chicago: University of Chicago Press, 2011).

56. Patricia Leighten, "The White Peril and *L'Art nègre*: Picasso, Primitivism, and Anticolonialism," *The Art Bulletin* 72, no. 4 (1990): 610.

57. Henri Clouzot and André Level, *L'art nègre et l'art océanien* (Paris: Devambez, Éditeur, 1919), 9.

58. Laurick Zerbini, "Sur les traces des arts africains, XIXe-XXIe siècles," in *La construction du discours colonial: L'empire français au XIXe et XXe siècles*, ed. Oissila Saaïdia and Laurick Zerbini (Paris: Karthala, 2009), 75–77.

59. Rafael Cardoso, "White Skins, Black Masks: '*Antropofagia*' and the Reversal of Primitivism," in *Artworks Adrift/Das verirrte Kunstwerk*, ed. Uwe Fleckner and Elena Tolstichin (Berlin: De Gruyter, 2020).

60. Aracy Amaral, *Tarsila—sua obra e seu tempo* (São Paulo: Ed. 34/Edusp, 2010).

61. Ramón Vázquez Díaz, *Víctor Manuel* (Madrid: Ediciones Vanguardia Cubana, 2010), 92, 97.

62. Enrique Mosella, *Salón de los Independientes: Museo Nacional de Bellas Artes (Parque Forestal)* (Santiago de Chile: Asociación de Artistas de Chile, 1931).

63. Clouzot and Level, *L'art nègre et l'art océanien*, 33.

64. Cecília Meireles, *Batuque, samba e macumba: Estudos de gesto e de ritmo, 1926–1934* (São Paulo: Martins Fontes, 2003); Márcia Ramos de Oliveira, "Batuque, samba e macumba nas palavras e pincéis de Cecília Meireles," *História em Revista* 10 (2004); Roberto Conduru, *Pérolas negras—primeiros fios: Experiências artísticas e culturais nos fluxos entre África e Brasil* (Rio de Janeiro: EdUERH, 2013), 310–312.

65. Michael Taussig, *Shamanism, Colonialism, and the Wild Man: A Study in Terror and Healing* (Chicago: University of Chicago Press, 1987); Peter Wade, *Race and Ethnicity in Latin America*, 2nd ed. (London: Pluto Press, 2010).

66. Marvin A. Lewis, *Afro-Uruguayan Literature: Post-Colonial Perspectives* (Lewisburg, PA: Bucknell University Press, 2003); Andrews, *Blackness in the White Nation*.

67. Maria José Campos, *Arthur Ramos, Luz e sombra na antropologia brasileira* (Rio de Janeiro: Biblioteca Nacional, 2004).

68. Géo-Charles, "Monteiro," *Montparnasse* 15, no. 57 (1929): 7–10.

69. Moacir dos Anjos, Jr., and Jorge Ventura Morais, "Picasso 'visita' o Recife: A exposição da Escola de Paris em março de 1930," *Estudos Avançados* 12, no. 34 (1998): 313–335.

70. Edith Wolfe, "Paris as Periphery: Vicente do Rego Monteiro and Brazil's Discrepant Cosmopolitanism," *The Art Bulletin* 96, no. 1 (2014): 98–119.

71. Michele Greet, *Beyond National Identity: Pictorial Indigenism as a Modernist Strategy in Andean Art, 1920–1960* (University Park: Pennsylvania State University Press, 2009).

72. Casanovas, "*Arte & artistas: Rafael Blanco*," 6–9.

73. David H. Brown, *The Light Inside: Abakuá Society Arts and Cuban Cultural History* (Washington, DC: Smithsonian Institution Press, 2003); Ivor Miller, *Voice of the Leopard: African Secret Societies and Cuba* (Jackson: University Press of Mississippi, 2009); Israel Moliner, "Abakuá," in *The Encyclopedia of Caribbean Religions,* ed. Patrick Taylor and Frederick I. Case (Champaign: University of Illinois Press, 2012), 1–9.

74. Vázquez Díaz, *Víctor Manuel,* 82–83.

75. Roberto Cobas Amate, "*Eduardo Abela: Pintor cubano y universal*," in *Abela*, ed. José Veigas Zamora and Beatriz Gago Rodríguez (Madrid: Fundación Arte Cubano, 2010), 17.

76. Ibid., 16.

77. Casanovas, "*Arte & artistas: Rafael Blanco*," 7.

78. Adolfo Zamora, "Eduardo Abela, pintor cubano," *Revista de Avance* 3, no. 30 (1929).

79. Fernando Ortiz, "*Más acerca de la poesía mulata: Escorzos para su estudio*," *Revista Bimestre Cubana* 37 (1936): 27.

80. José Seoane Gallo, *Eduardo Abela cerca del cerco* (Havana: Editorial Letras Cubanas, 1983).

81. Emiliano Di Cavalcanti, *Reminiscências líricas de um perfeito carioca* (Rio de Janeiro: Civilização Brasileira, 1964), 33.

82. Rafael Cardoso, "Ambivalências políticas de um perfeito modernista: Di Cavalcanti e a arte social," in *No subúrbio da modernidade – Di Cavalcanti 120 anos*, ed. José Augusto Ribeiro (São Paulo: Pinacoteca do Estado, 2017), 41–53. Exhibition catalog.

83. Mário de Andrade, *Taxi e crônicas do Diário Nacional*, 528.

84. Cogniat, "Les peintres de l'Amérique Latine," 470; Gomes Cardoso, "Arte da América Latina na crítica de Raymond Cogniat, 1926."

85. Cardoso, "White Skins, Black Masks."

86. Jorge Mañach, "Triunfos de la pintura hispánica," *Revista Hispánica Moderna* 2, no. 3 (1936): 36–39; Narciso G. Menocal, "An Overriding Passion: The Quest for a National Identity in Painting," *The Journal of Decorative and Propaganda Arts* 22 (1996): 186–216.

87. Armando Alvarez Bravo, "The Cuban 'Vanguardia,'" in *Remembering Cuba through Its Art*, ed. Diego Costa Peuser (Miami: Arte al Día, 2004), 91. Exhibition catalog.

88. Alejo Carpentier, "Diego Rivera," *Revista de Avance* 1, no. 9 (1927): 232–235.

89. Casanovas, "*Cuadro de la pintura mexicana*."

90. "*Leal… Rivera*," *Revista de Avance* 1, no. 9 (1927), insert between pages 228–229.

91. Pavletich, "Diego Rivera."

92. "*Orozco… Fernandez Ledesma*," *Revista de Avance* 1, no. 8 (1927), insert between pages 204–205.

93. Raúl Antelo, *Parque de diversões—Aníbal Machado* (Belo Horizonte, Brazil: UFMG & Florianópolis, Brazil: UFSC, 1994).

94. Dawn Ades, "The Image of the Black in Latin America," in *The Image of the Black in Western Art*, ed. David Bindman and Henry Louis Gates, Jr., vol. V, pt. 1 (Cambridge, MA: Belknap Press of Harvard University Press, 2014), 227–256.

95. Melba Pineda Garcia, "*Rómulo Rozo, la diosa Bachué y el indigenismo en Colombia (1920–1950)*," *Baukara* 3 (2013): 41–56.

96. Juanita Solano Roa, "The Mexican Assimilation: Colombia in the 1930s—The Case of Ignacio Gómez Jaramillo," *Historia y Memoria* 7 (2013): 79–111.

97. Luz Adriana Maya Restrepo and Raúl Cristancho Álvarez, ed., *¡Mandinga Sea! África en Antioquia* (Bogotá, Colombia: Ediciones Uniandes, 2015), 28. Exhibition catalog.

98. Gustavo Urrutia, "*La raza cubana*," *Diario de la Marina*, Havana

(June 26, 1928).

99. Nicolás Guillén, *Obra poética* (Havana: Instituto Cubano del Libro, 1972), 1:114.

100. Juan Jiménez Pastrana, "*Balance del carnaval en el Prado*," *Nuevos Rumbos* 1, no. 5 (1946): 7–8.

101. Annateresa Fabris, *Portinari, pintor social* (São Paulo: Perspectiva, 1990), 8–10, 85–86.

102. Ibid., 14, 26; Annateresa Fabris, *Cândido Portinari* (São Paulo: Edusp, 1996), 51–68.

103. Néstor García Canclini, *Hybrid Cultures: Strategies for Entering and Leaving Modernity* (Minneapolis: University of Minnesota Press, 2005).

104. Serge Gruzinski, *The Mestizo Mind: The Intellectual Dynamics of Colonization and Globalization* (London: Routledge, 2002).

105. Narciso G. Menocal, "An Overriding Passion," 209.

106. José Viegas Zamora, *Mariano: Catálogo razonado: Pintura y dibujo, 1936–1949*, vol. 1 (Madrid: Ediciones Vanguardia Cubana, 2010); Xavier Moyssén, "Manuel Rodríguez Lozano," in *Encyclopedia of Latin American and Caribbean Art*, ed. Jane Turner (New York: Grove's Dictionaries, 2000), 608.

107. Enrique Andreu, "*La muerte de Peñita*," *Estudios Afrocubanos* 2, no. 1 (1938): 115–117; Salvador Garcia Agüero, "*Un comentario final*," *Revista Bimestre Cubana* 38 (1936): 126–132.

108. Enrique Andreu, "*El pintor Alberto Peña y su obra*," *Revista Bimestre Cubana* 38 (1936): 114.

109. Alberto, *Terms of Inclusion: Black Intellectuals in Twentieth-Century Brazil*, 69–75; Marcus Wood, *Black Milk: Imagining Slavery in the Visual Cultures of Brazil and America* (Oxford: Oxford University Press, 2013), 1–4; Cardoso, "White Skins, Black Masks."

110. García Agüero, "*Un comentario final*," 126.

111. Alejandro de la Fuente, "Afro-Latin American Art," in *Afro-Latin American Studies: An Introduction*, ed. Alejandro de la Fuente and George Reid Andrews (New York: Cambridge University Press, 2018), 392.

112. M. L. D., "*Un concurso*," *Revista de Avance* 2, no. 25 (1928): 228.

113. José Veigas Zamora, *La escultura en Cuba: Siglo XX* (Santiago de Cuba: Editorial Oriente, 2005).

114. Vera D'Horta Beccari, *Lasar Segall e o modernismo paulista* (São Paulo: Brasiliense, 1984), 81; Sergio Miceli, *Nacional estrangeiro: História social e cultural do modernismo em São Paulo* (São Paulo: Companhia das Letras, 2003), 163.

115. Tadeu Chiarelli, *Segall realista: Algumas considerações sobre a pintura do artista* (São Paulo: Centro Cultural FIESP, 2008), 11–12.

116. Oswald de Andrade, "*Manifesto antropófago*," 200.

117. Ibid., 197.

118. Andreas Huyssen, *After the Great Divide: Modernism, Mass Culture, Postmodernism* (London: Macmillan, 1986), 16.

11. Image of the Black and More: Visual Thought and Creative Expression in the Caribbean and Brazil, 1939-1959

1. Homi K. Bhabha, *El lugar de la cultura* (Buenos Aires, Argentina: Manantial, 1994), 64; George Lamming, *Los placeres del exilio* (Havana: Casa de las Américas, 2007), 24.

2. Bhabha, on "the cultural interstice of the borders of contact," 271.

3. That led to multiple crossings of ideas and political movements on both sides of the Atlantic, connected to pan-African thought, including the ideas of such founding figures as W. E. B. Du Bois, Frederick Douglass, and Booker T. Washington.

4. Pablo Carriedo Castro, "*Guerra fría y cultura: Un panorama sobre la libertad y el compromiso del escritor en la mitad del siglo XX*," *Nómadas: Revista Crítica de Ciencias Sociales y Jurídicas* 12, no. 2 (2005), unpaginated, https://www.redalyc.org/articulo.oa?id=18153298019.

5. Walter Rodney has noted that fascism strengthened "institutional racism" against Jews and Black Africans in that period. Rodney, *Cómo Europa subdesarrolló a África* (Havana: Ciencias Sociales, 2011), 263.

6. "The New Peoples also received an important genetic component from Afrodescendants, variable from country to country depending on the importance of black slavery, which also created mulattos and mestizos." Darcy Ribeiro, "*La civilización emergente*," *Nueva Sociedad* 73 (July–August 1984): 28, https://static.nuso.org/media/articles/downloads/1187_1.pdf.

7. The journal *Présence Africaine,* founded by the Senegalese intellectual Alioune Diop in 1947, organized the First Congress of Black Writers and Artists at the Sorbonne in Paris in 1956. Pablo Picasso created the poster for it. Among the participants were Richard Wright from the United States, Aimé Césaire and Frantz Fanon from Martinique, J. Price-Mars from Haiti, Léopold Sédar Senghor from Senegal, and Jacques Rabemananjara from Madagascar.

8. Pierre Mabille, "Wifredo Lam," *Tropiques* no. 6–7 (February 1943), vol. II, *Réproduction anastaltique* (París: Éditions Jean-Michel Place, 1978), 61–63.

9. David Boxer and Veerle Poupeye, *Jamaican Art, 1922–1982* (Kingston: National Gallery of Jamaica and Smithsonian Institution, 1982), typescript, unpaginated.

10. David Boxer, "Edna Manley: From Quiet Carvings to Shattered Light," *Américas* 32, nos. 6, 7 (June-July 1981), 37.

11. George Campbell, *First Poems* (Kingston, Jamaica: City Printery, 1945), cited by Boxer and Poupeye, *Jamaican Art, 1922–1982*, unpaginated.

12. Ibid., unpaginated.

13. Karl "Jerry" Craig, Introduction, and Rex Nettleford, "Caribbean Cultural Identity," in *Shared Visions: Celebrating the 50th Anniversary of the University of the West Indies* (Kingston, Jamaica: Canoe Press University of the West Indies, 1997), 6. Exhibition catalog.

14. See Isabel Leymarie, *Del tango al reggae: Músicas Negras de América Latina y el Caribe* (Zaragoza, Spain: University of Zaragoza, 2015), 119.

15. Norman Manley, "National Culture and the Artist," in *Manley and the New Jamaica*, cited by Boxer and Poupeye, *Jamaican Art, 1922–1982*.

16. See the documentary *El barco prometido* directed by Yazmín Ross, a journalist, writer, and director born in Mexico's Caribbean coast, who has lived in Costa Rica since 1989. She is the author of *La flota negra* for the Italian photographer and filmmaker Luciano Capelli. https://www.youtube.com/watch?v=-aNLw8OWVkE.

17. Alberto Romero Contreras, "*La cultura rastafari y sus principales manifestaciones identitarias,*" *Pacarina del Sur: Revista de Pensamiento Crítico Latinoamericano* 3, no. 10 (January-March 2012), http://www.pacarinadelsur.com/home/mascaras-e-identidades/383-la-cultura-rastafari-y-sus-principales-manifestaciones-identitarias.

18. Prologue to Césaire, *Cahier d'un retour au pays natal*, trans. Lydia Cabrera, illus. Wifredo Lam, 1st ed. (Havana: Molina and Compañia, 1942).

19. Aimé Césaire, *Retorno al país natal*, trans. Lydia Cabrera and Lourdes Arencibia (Havana: Colección SurEditores, 2011), 43.

20. Ibid., 13.

21. Quoted by René Depestre, *Buenos días y adiós a la negritud* (Havana: Casa de las Américas, 1987), 51.

22. Césaire, *Retorno al país natal*, 50.

23. Ibid., 53.

24. Depestre, 39.

25. Ibid., 41 (italics added).

26. Aimé Césaire, "*Entrevista*," in Depestre, *Buenos días y adiós a la negritud*, 59.

27. Ibid., 57.

28. René Hibran, "*Le problème de l´art à La Martinique,*" *Tropiques* no. 6–7 (February 1943): 40.

29. Ibid., 41.

30. On this theme, see the documentary *Reembarque* (2014) by the Cuban filmmaker Gloria Rolando, https://new.artsmia.org/event/durades-dialogue-film-reembarquereshipment-with-gloria-rolando-and-robert-byrd/.

31. Jacques Roumain, *Gobernadores del rocío y otros textos* (Caracas, Venezuela: Biblioteca Ayacucho, 2004), 146–147, https://biblioteca.org.ar/libros/211568.pdf.

32. See Yolanda Wood, "*West Indies Ltd. y el Caribe de Nicolás Guillén,*" in *Caribe: Universo visual* (Havana: Félix Varela, 2017).

33. *Haiti 1950* (*L'art en Haïti*) is available at https://www.youtube.com/watch?v=5Mr1USFY3mY.

34. Alejo Carpentier, "*Panorama del arte haitiano*" (1957), in *Letra y solfa: Artes visuales* (Havana: Editorial Letras Cubanas, 1993), 200.

35. Carpentier, "*Panorama del arte haitiano*" (1957), 200–203.

36. Ibid., 201.

37. This prologue, entitled "*Lo real maravilloso de América,*" was published before the first edition of Carpentier's novel *El reino de este mundo*, in the Caracas newspaper *El Nacional*, April 8, 1948. Araceli García-Carranza, *Bibliografía de Alejo Carpentier* (Havana: Editorial Letras Cubanas, 1984), 21.

38. Prologue to the first edition of *El reino de este mundo*, in "*De lo real maravilloso americano,*" *Tientos y diferencias* (Montevideo, Uruguay: Editorial Arca, 1967), 97. On the theoretical basis for the extension of the marvelous real to the Americas, see Leonardo Padura, "*Ver a América,*" in *Un camino de medio siglo: Alejo Carpentier y la narrativa de lo real maravilloso* (Havana: Editorial Letras Cubanas, 1994), 95–180.

39. Padura, "*Ver a América,*" 95.

40. Césaire, *Retorno al país natal,* 28.

41. See Darcy Ribeiro, "*Los pueblos nuevos,*" in *Las Américas y la civilización* (Havana: Casa de las Américas, 1992), 163–290.

42. Zuleica Romay Guerra, *Elogio de la altea o las paradojas de la racialidad* (Havana: Casa de las Américas, 2012), 65.

43. Nicolás Guillén, "*Prólogo,*" in *Sóngoro cosongo*, 1993, http://www.cervantesvirtual.com/obra-visor/songoro-cosongo-1931-0/html/ff47ec48-82b1-11df-acc7-002185ce6064_2.html.

44. "His studies of the economic, social, and cultural aspects of the reciprocal influences between Africans and Latin Americans always impressed me as model work." Bronislaw Malinowski, "*Opiniones sobre Fernando Ortiz,*" in *Órbita de Fernando Ortiz* (Havana: UNEAC, 1973), 321.

45. Melville Herskovits, *Les bases de l'anthropologie culturelle* (Paris: Payot, 1952).

46. Fernando Ortiz, *La Africanía de la música folklórica de Cuba* (Havana: Editorial Letras Cubanas, 2001), IX.

47. Ibid., XV.

48. On this theme, see the paintings of the same name by Cândido Portinari (1944) and Clóvis Graciano (1945).

49. Jorge Amado, *Gabriela, clavo y canela* (Mexico: Editorial Diana, 1990), 60.

50. Ibid., 15.

51. "Djanira da Motta e Silva," https://www.ebiografia.com/djanira/.

52. A description of this festival of the "daughters of the saints,"

the *iaô* of the *Iansá*, focusing on the attributes and qualities specific to the various *orixás*, is in Amado, *Gabriela, clavo y canela*, 308–309.

53. The work of Pierre Verger is important in establishing the photographic record of Candomblé rites and ceremonies. Born in France, Verger moved to Salvador da Bahía in 1946. He traveled to Africa in 1956, and after being initiated as a *babalao*, or priest, of the Ifá religion, he took the name Fátúmbi. In 1954 he published *Dieux d'Afrique: Culte des Orishas et Vodouns à l'ancienne Côte des Esclaves en Afrique et à Bahia, la Baie de Tous les Saints au Brésil*, the first of several works on the religious world of Candomblé and African and Afro-Bahian culture. Verger traveled widely, and in the 1940s and 1950s visited several Caribbean countries. The theme of religiosity with African origins shows in his photographs in Haiti and Cuba, where he met Lydia Cabrera and Fernando Ortiz. See Yolanda Wood and Kirenia Rodríguez, *Pierre Fatumbi Verger y el Caribe: Conexiones caribeñas* (Havana: Casa de las Américas, 2011), and the website of the Pierre Verger Foundation in Salvador da Bahía, www.pierreverger.org/.

54. See Yolanda Wood, "*Resignificación de un legado africano: La máscara*," in *Caribe: Universo visual* (Havana: Editorial Félix Varela, 2017).

55. Jean Laude, *Les arts de l'Afrique noire* (Paris: Edité par Le Livre de Poche, 1966), 6.

56. It also led to the accumulation of large collections, an active market, and exhibitions at the end of the nineteenth century and subsequently. There were important shows in Marseille in 1923, Paris in 1925, and others such as the 1931 International Colonial Exhibition in Paris. There were also many studies of this topic in centers of international art.

57. Gerardo Mosquera, *Exploraciones en la plástica cubana* (Havana: Editorial Letras Cubanas, 1983), 184.

58. Ibid., 186.

59. On the transatlantic voyage, Lam established a friendship with Césaire during the leg from Martinique to Cuba, and he provided the illustrations for the Spanish translation of *Cahier d'un retour au pays natal*, published in Havana under the direction Lydia Cabrera.

60. See Yolanda Wood, *Islas del Caribe: Naturaleza-arte-sociedad* (Havana: Editorial UH and CLACSO, 2012).

61. See Édouard Glissant, "*Iguanas, azores, deidades delirantes: El arte primordial de Wifredo Lam*," *Artecubano*, no. 2 (2008).

62. On Palo Monte, the *nganga*, and their attributes, see *The Encyclopedia of Caribbean Religions*, vol. 2, ed. Patrick Taylor and Frederick I. Case (Champaign: University of Illinois Press, 2013), 661–666.

63. Cited by Antonio Núñez Jiménez in *Wifredo Lam* (Havana: Editorial Letras Cubanas, 1982), 163.

64. Spanish version: https://nanopdf.com/download/manifiesto-antropofago-5af60c8678984_pdf; English translation: https://sibila.com.br/english/anthropophagic-manifesto/2686.

65. Lamming, *Los placeres del exilio*, 183.

66. Ibid., 258.

67. Maryse Condé, *Palabras al catálogo, Latitudes 2004: Art contemporain: Terres de l'Atlantique: Guadeloupe, Martinique, Saint-Pierre-et-Miquelon, Cuba, Haiti, Jamaique, République dominicaine, Trinidad & Tobago / [organisé par la Mairie de Paris]; avant-propos de Maryse Condé*. Paris: OCEA. Exhibition curated by Régine Cuzin.

68. Gerardo Mosquera, *Exploraciones en la plástica cubana* (Havana: Editorial Letras Cubanas, 1983), 184.

69. Lamming said he wrote the text in 1959.

70. Lamming, *Los placeres del exilio*, 21.

71. Ibid., 23.

72. See Roberto Fernández Retamar, "Caliban," *Casa de las Américas*, no. 68 (September–October 1971).

12. Sound, Fury, and Freedom: Antislavery and Pro-Freedom Monuments

1. The author thanks Beatriz Balanta, Julio Biar, David Bindman, Rafael Cardoso, Petrina Dacres, Alejandro de la Fuente, Alberto Martin Chillón, and Lisa Pon for their contributions.

2. Verónica Espinosa Garduño, "*Memoria colectiva en torno ao culto ao Cristo Negro en el Santuario de Otatitlán, Veracruz (S.XX)*" (diss., Universidad Nacional Autonoma de Mexico, 2016).

3. Anderson José Machado de Oliveira, "*Devoção e identidades: Significados do culto de Santo Elesbão e Santa Efigênia no Rio de Janeiro e nas Minas Gerais no Setecentos*," *TOPOI* 7, no. 12 (June 2006): 60–115; Roberto Sánchez, "The Black Virgin: Santa Efigenia, Popular Religion, and the African Diaspora in Peru," *Church History* 81, no. 3 (September 2012): 631–655.

4. Cristiano Mascaro et al., *Fazendas do Império* (Rio de Janeiro: Edições Fadel, 2010), 201.

5. On the various meanings of the enslaved figures sculpted by Michelangelo for the tomb of Pope Julius II, see Maria Ruvoldt, "Michelangelo's *Slaves* and the Gift of Liberty," *Renaissance Quarterly* 65, no. 4 (Winter 2012): 1029–1059. It is also worth noting the presence of Moorish captives in the four corners of the pedestals of two monuments not erected to celebrate slavery in the Americas: the equestrian statue of King Henry IV of France in Paris, designed by Pierre de Franqueville and completed by Francesco Bordoni between 1614 and 1618, and the statue of Ferdinand I in Livorno, Italy, created by Pietro Tacca between 1617 and 1624. Jean Michel Massing, "The Mediterranean Scene," in *The Image of the Black in Western Art*, ed. David Bindman and Henry Louis Gates, Jr., vol. III, pt. 2 (Cambridge, MA: Harvard University Press,

2011), 191–197. See also Anthea Brook, "From Borgo Pinti to Doccia: The Afterlife of Pietro Tacca's Moors for Livorno," in *The Slave in European Art*, ed. Elizabeth McGrath and Jean Michel Massing (London; Turin: The Warburg Institute; Nino Aragno Editore, 2012), 165–191.

6. Elias Fernandes, "*O pelourinho denuncia Mariana*," Ponto Final (September 2017), https://saci2.ufop.br/servico_clipping?id=4055.

7. Jason deCaires Taylor, "The Underwater Museum," https://maptia.com/jasondecairestaylor/stories/the-underwater-museum.

8. María de Lourdes Ghidoli, "'*Falucho vale poco en comparación a su raza*': *Variaciones en torno a un monumento*," in *Estudios Afro-latinoamericanos: Nuevos enfoques multidisciplinarios: Actas de las Terceras Jornadas del GEALA*, ed. María de Lourdes Ghidoli and Juan Francisco Martinez Peria (Buenos Aires, Argentina: Ediciones del CCC, 2013), 180–181.

9. Also known as *The Dying Galatian* or *The Dying Gladiator*, the sculpture belongs to Musei Capitolini in Rome.

10. María de Los Angéles Pereira, "*Artistas cubanos en la urdimbre temporal del Caribe: Representación, memoria e identidade en la escultura comtemporánea*," in *Nosotros, los mas infieles: Narraciones criticas sobre el arte cubano (1993–2005)*, ed. Andrés Isaac Santana (Murcia, Spain: CENDEAC, 2007), 887–888.

11. Fátima Alfredo, "*Francisco Manuel Chaves Pinheiro e sua contribuição à imaginária carioca oitocentista*," *19&20* 5, no. 2 (April 2010), http://www.dezenovevinte.net/artistas/fmcp_fa.htm; Paulo Knauss, "Gaze Game: Indians and Africans in the 19th Century Sculpture between France and Brazil," *História* (São Paulo) 32, no. 1 (January/June 2013): 122–143, http://www.scielo.br/pdf/his/v32n1/en_08.pdf.

12. About Mãe Preta and that monument, see Paulina L. Alberto, *Terms of Inclusion: Black Intellectuals in Twentieth-Century Brazil* (Chapel Hill: University of North Carolina Press, 2011), 69–109.

13. Other monuments were erected in Sorocaba, Passo Fundo, and Três Rios.

14. Roberto Conduru, *Arte Afro-Brasileira* (Belo Horizonte, Brazil: C/Arte, 2007).

15. Vera Dias, *Preto Velho—Monumento em Inhoaiba, Campo Grande*, http://ashistoriasdosmonumentosdorio.blogspot.com/2014/05/preto-velho-monumento-em-inhoaiba-campo.html; Ana Lucia Araujo, *Shadows of the Slave Past: Memory, Heritage, and Slavery* (New York: Routledge, 2014), 166.

16. "Negro d'Água, uma das Lendas do Velho Chico," *Geovale do rio São Francisco*, April 7, 2015, http://geovaledoriosaofrancisco.blogspot.com.br/2015/04/nego-dagua-uma-das-lendas-do-velho-chico.html.

17. Debbie J. Challis, "A Fusion of Worlds—Negro Aroused (1935) by Edna Manley," UCL Museum & Collections Blog, March 15, 2014, https://blogs.ucl.ac.uk/museums/2014/03/15/a-fusion-of-worlds-negro-aroused-1935-by-edna-manley/.

18. About these stone collars, see José R. Oliver, *Caciques and Cemí Idols: The Web Spun by Taíno Rulers between Hispaniola and Puerto Rico* (Tuscaloosa: University of Alabama Press, 2009), 121–140.

19. "Emancipation statue unveiled," Dominica News Online, August 2, 2013, http://dominicanewsonline.com/news/homepage/news/culture/emancipation-statue-unveiled/.

20. The author thanks María de Los Angéles Pereira and Alejandro de la Fuente for providing the details regarding the monument's installation.

21. "Emancipation statue unveiled," Dominica News Online.

22. "*Palenque corta cadenas de Benkos Biohó en Día Afrocolombianidad*," *El Tiempo*, May 21, 2011, https://www.eltiempo.com/archivo/documento/CMS-9416084.

23. About some uses of broken chains in representations of emancipation, see Marcus Wood, *The Horrible Gift of Freedom: Atlantic Slavery and the Representation of Emancipation* (Athens: University of Georgia Press, 2010).

24. LeGrace Benson, "Trauma and Victory: Absence and Memory in Haitian Art," in *Slavery in Art and Literature: Approaches to Trauma, Memory and Visuality*, ed. Birgit Haehnel and Melanie Ulz (Berlin: Frank & Timme, 2010), 171.

25. Ghidoli, "'*Falucho vale poco en comparación a su raza*,'" 175–190.

26. Ana Frega, "Afro-descendants and the Founding Story of the Nation: Monuments and Commemorative Dates," https://webarchive.unesco.org/web/20220403203319/http://www.unesco.org/new/fileadmin/MULTIMEDIA/HQ/CLT/images/Frega_Eng.pdf.

27. Alejandro Gortázar, "*Ansina: ¿Un héroe afro–uruguayo?*," *Sujetos*, May 10, 2011, https://sujetos.uy/2011/05/10/ansina-un-heroe-afro-uruguayo/.

28. Carmen Cova, "*Uruguay: Cambiarán nombre a Monumento de 'Ansina' por error de identidad*," *Segundo Enfoque*, March 23, 2018, https://www.taringa.net/+noticias/uruguay-cambiaran-nombre-a-monumento-de-ansina-por-error-de-identid.

29. About religiosity in Argentinian and Uruguayan Candombe, see Carla Tudanca, "*¿Candombe como religión o religión como candombe? ¿Qué rasgos de religiosidad podemos encontrar en la tradición del candombe de procedencia afrouruguaya en Buenos Aires?*," × *Jornadas de Sociología*, Facultad de Ciencias Sociales, Universidad de Buenos Aires, Argentina, 2013.

30. "1763 Monument," *Stabroek News*, May 1, 2016, https://www.stabroeknews.com/2016/features/05/01/1763-monument/.

31. Shalman Scott, "The damage to Marcus Garvey's statue and what he meant to Jamaica," *Jamaica Observer*, November 19, 2017, https://

www.jamaicaobserver.com/columns/the-damage-to-marcus-garveys-statue-and-what-he-meant-to-jamaica/.

32. About this monument, see Mariza de Carvalho Soares, "*Nos atalhos da memória—Monumento a Zumbi*," in *Cidade vaidosa: Imagens urbanas do Rio de Janeiro*, ed. Paulo Knauss (Rio de Janeiro: Sette Letras, 1999), 117–135; Roberto Conduru, "Releasing Mistakes? Appropriation and Ambiguity in the Monument to Zumbi dos Palmares in Rio de Janeiro," in *Proceedings of the 34th World Congress of Art History*, ed. Shao Dazhen, Fan Di'an, and LaoZhu, vols. I-III (Beijing: The Commercial Press, 2019), 1652–1655, http://www.ciha.org/content/terms-proceedings-34th-world-congress-art-history.

33. Editha Platte, *Bronze Head from Ife* (London: The British Museum Press, 2010), 19.

34. See "The Slave Route: Preservation of Memorial Sites and Places," UNESCO, https://webarchive.unesco.org/web/20180704133222/http://www.unesco.org/new/en/social-and-human-sciences/themes/slave-route/spotlight/preservation-of-memorial-sites-and-places/.

35. "I Am Queen Mary," https://www.iamqueenmary.com/.

13. The Image of the Black in 20th-Century Anglo-Afro-Caribbean Art

1. With regard to the English-speaking Caribbean, the first publication to document successfully the art history of the region was Veerle Poupeye's *Caribbean Art*, a fairly specialized evaluation of art that raised the bar for art books in the region. See Veerle Poupeye, *Caribbean Art,* World of Art Series (London: Thames and Hudson, 1998).

2. See Michel-Rolph Trouillot, *Silencing the Past: Power and the Production of History* (Boston: Beacon Press, 1995).

3. Stuart Hall, "Cultural Identity and Diaspora," *Framework: The Journal of Cinema and Media*, no. 36 (1989): 68–81.

4. Poupeye, *Caribbean Art*, 12.

5. Sarah Phillips, "Leah Gordon's best photograph," *The Guardian*, June 20, 2012.

6. Erica Moiah James, "Speaking in Tongues: Metapictures and the Discourse of Violence in Caribbean Art," *Small Axe: A Journal of Criticism* 16, no. 1 (March 2012): 119–143.

7. Annette Insanally, Mark Clifford, and Sean Sheriff, ed., *Regional Footprints: The Travels and Travails of Early Caribbean Migrants* (Mona and Kingston, Jamaica: Latin American-Caribbean Centre, The University of the West Indies, 2006), 10.

8. Félix Angel, curator, *Parallel Realities: Five Pioneering Artists from Barbados = Realidades paralelas: Cinco artistas pioneros de Barbados*, Washington, DC: Inter-American Development Bank, Cultural Center, May 2–July 16, 1999. Exhibition catalog.

9. Alissandra Cummins, Allison Thompson, and Nick Whittle, *Art in Barbados: What Kind of Mirror Image?* (Kingston, Jamaica: Ian Randle Publishers, 1999), 43.

10. Krista A. Thompson, *An Eye for the Tropics: Tourism, Photography, and Framing the Caribbean Picturesque,* Objects/Histories series (Durham, NC: Duke University Press, 2006).

11. Kersuze Simeon-Jones, *Literary and Sociopolitical Writings of the Black Diaspora in the Nineteenth and Twentieth Centuries* (Lanham, MD: Lexington Books, 2010), 122.

12. *Magic Island* sensationalized the new ethnographic approaches promoted by field workers such as James George Frazer, Marcel Mauss, and Claude Levi-Strauss. But as the cultural historian J. Michael Dash has noted, Seabrook seems to have been more concerned with protecting Haiti from cultural contamination than with seeing it develop as a modern nation. See J. Michael Dash, *Haiti and the United States: National Stereotypes and the Literary Imagination,* 2nd ed. (Basingstoke, England: Palgrave Macmillan, 1998), 34ff.

13. Augustus John, *Autobiography* (London: Jonathan Cape, 1975), 293–302.

14. Ibid.

15. As previously noted in Petrine Archer-Straw, ed., *Fifty Years—Fifty Artists, 1950–2000: The School of Visual Arts* (Kingston, Jamaica: Ian Randle Publishers, 2002), 22.

16. André Breton and André Masson, *Martinique: Charmeuse de serpents* (Paris: Jean-Jacques Pauvert, 1972 [1948]).

17. André Masson, *La mémoire du monde* (Geneva, Switzerland: Skira, [1974]).

18. Aimé Césaire, *Cahier d'un retour au pays natal*, introd. André Breton (Paris: Bordas, 1947).

19. Kobena Mercer, "Cosmopolitan Contact Zones," in *Afro Modern: Journeys through the Black Atlantic*, ed. Tanya Barson and Peter Görschluter (Liverpool, England: Tate Liverpool, January 29–April 25, 2010). Exhibition catalog, 44.

20. Cummins, Thompson, and Whittle, *Art in Barbados*, 14, 16.

21. Anne Walmsley, "Stanley Greaves," *BOMB: Art and Culture: Artists, Writers, Architects, Directors and Musicians: The Americas Issue* 86 (Winter 2004): 38–45.

22. For a more complete and compelling reading of Marcus Garvey's aesthetic, see Robert A. Hill, "Making Noise: Marcus Garvey Dada, August 1922," in *Picturing Us: African American Identity in Photography,* ed. Deborah Willis (New York: W. W. Norton and Co., 1995).

23. *The Marcus Garvey and Universal Negro Improvement Association Papers,* ed. Robert A. Hill, vol. V: *September 1922–August 1924* (Berkeley: University of California Press, 1986), 603, 625.

24. *Grounations* is popularly used among the Rastafari community to suggest their understanding of Black culture. The word is most often used

to celebrate April 21 annually, in honor of Haile Selassie's visit to Jamaica in 1966.

25. Veerle Poupeye, "Osmond Watson: Defining Painter and Sculptor of Modern Jamaican Culture," *The Guardian,* December 1, 2005, 38.

26. Paul Gauguin stayed in Martinique from April until June 1887. He had gone in search of "exotic landscapes" but left after falling sick. He would later settle in Tahiti, where he created a body of work more in keeping with his "primitive" ideas. See Paul Gauguin, *Noa Noa: The Tahitian Journal,* trans. O. F. Theis (New York: N. L. Brown, 1920).

27. As evidenced in Esther Chapman's play *The West Indian* (1936), see Petrine Archer-Straw, "Cultural Nationalism: Its Development in Jamaica, 1900–1944" (master's thesis, University of the West Indies, 1986), 124.

28. For a detailed account of the significance of the Manleys and their home at Drumblair, see Rachel Manley, *Drumblair: Memories of a Jamaican Childhood* (Kingston, Jamaica: Ian Randle Publishers, 1996).

29. Geoffrey Maclean, "The Art of Trinidad and Tobago," in *Season of Renewal: Celebrating 50 Years of Independence and Caribbean Partnership* (Mona and Kingston, Jamaica: The Museum, University of the West Indies, June 7–11, 2012). Exhibition catalog, 74–83.

30. Mercer, "Cosmopolitan Contact Zones" in *Afro Modern,* 41.

31. The cultural theorist Stuart Hall has discussed the problems of this type of synthesizing in relation to Jamaica's coat of arms; see Stuart Hall, "Negotiating Caribbean Identities," *New Left Review,* no. 209 (January–February 1995): 5.

32. Like *Negro Aroused* (1935), this work was purchased for the National Gallery of Jamaica, Kingston, by patrons concerned for its posterity. A limited-edition print of its imagery was made as part of a fundraising campaign to acquire the work. Conversation with Valerie Facey, Manor Park, Kingston, May 22, 2012.

33. The Art Foundry, *Lips, Sticks and Marks,* St. Philip, Barbados, August 23–October 25, 1998. Exhibition catalog. This exhibition was co-curated by artists in the show: Alida Martinez and Osaira Muyale of Aruba; Annalee Davis and Joscelyn Gardner of Barbados; Roberta Stoddart of Jamaica; and Susan Dayal and Irénée Shaw of Trinidad and Tobago.

34. See Petrine Archer-Straw, "Paradise, Primitivism, and Parody," in *Créolité and Créolization, Documenta 11—Platform 3,* ed. Okwui Enwezor et al., St. Lucia, January 13–15, 2002. Exhibition catalog, 63–76.

35. Annie Paul and Krista A. Thompson, "Caribbean Locales/Global Artworlds," *Small Axe: A Journal of Criticism* 8, no. 2 (September 2004): viii.

36. Gerald Aching, *Masking and Power: Carnival and Popular Culture in the Caribbean,* Cultural Studies of the Americas series, vol. 8 (Minneapolis: University of Minnesota Press, 2002), 4.

37. Ibid., 17.

38. Leon Wainwright, "Aubrey Williams: A Painter in the Aftermath of Painting," *Wasafiri* 24, no. 3 (September 2009): 65–79.

39. Ibid., 68.

40. Leon Wainwright, "Aubrey Williams: Atlantic Fire," in *Aubrey Williams: Atlantic Fire,* ed. Reyahn King, Liverpool and London: National Museums and October Gallery, 2010. Exhibition catalog, 46–55.

41. For the Afro-Cobra movement, see Adrienne L. Childs, "Activism and the Shaping of Black Identities," in *The Image of the Black in Western Art,* ed. David Bindman and Henry Louis Gates, Jr., vol. V, pt. 2 (Cambridge, MA: Belknap Press of Harvard University Press, 2014), 131–178.

42. Annie Paul, "Subjects Matter: The Repeating AlterNATIVE and the Expat Gaze," in *Arts Education for Societies-in-Crisis,* ed. Rawle Gibbons and Dani Lyndersay (St. Augustine, Trinidad and Tobago, 2007), 31–53.

43. See Petrine Archer in *New World Imagery: Contemporary Jamaican Art,* ed. David Boxer et al. (London: National Touring Exhibitions, South Bank Centre, 1996). Exhibition catalog.

44. www.joscelyngardner.org/artist-statement.

45. See, for instance, Louis Chude Sokei, "Post-Nationalist Geographies: Rasta, Ragga, and Reinventing Africa," *African Arts* 27, no. 4 (Autumn 1994): 80–84, 96; or Deborah A. Thomas, *Modern Blackness: Nationalism, Globalization, and the Politics of Culture in Jamaica,* Latin America Otherwise series (Durham, NC: Duke University Press, 2004).

14. The Art of Black Mobilization, 1960s–2010s

1. U.N. General Assembly, *Report of the Regional Conference of the Americas, Santiago, Chile, 5–7 December 2000,* https://digitallibrary.un.org/record/440441?ln=en.

2. Ibid.

3. Heidi Carolyn Feldman, *Black Rhythms of Peru: Reviving African Musical Heritage in the Black Pacific* (Middletown, CT: Wesleyan University Press, 2006).

4. Tanya Maria Golash-Boza, *Yo Soy Negro: Blackness in Peru* (Gainesville: University Press of Florida, 2012), 4.

5. Abdias do Nascimento, "Teatro experimental do negro: Trajetória e reflexões," *Estudos Avançados* 18, no. 50 (2004): 210.

6. Paulina L. Alberto, *Terms of Inclusion: Black Intellectuals in Twentieth-Century Brazil* (Chapel Hill: University of North Carolina Press, 2011); Michael George Hanchard, *Orpheus and Power: The Movimento Negro of Rio de Janeiro and São Paulo, Brazil, 1945–1988* (Princeton, NJ: Princeton University Press, 1994); Nascimento, "Teatro experimental do negro."

7. Kleber Antonio de Oliveira Amancio, "*O autorretrato de Wilson Tibério*," *Encontro Escravidão e Liberdade no Brasil Meridional* (Universidade Federal de Santa Catarina, May 2013), http://www.escravidaoeliberdade.com.br/site/images/Textos.6/kleberamancio.pdf.

8. Francielly Rocha Dossin, "*Wilson Tibério (1916–2005): Primeiras notas biográficas sobre 'O Negro Mago do Pincel,'*" *Anais do 24o Encontro da Associação Nacional de Pesquisadores em Artes Plásticas* (September 2015), http://anpap.org.br/anais/2015/; Carlos Roberto Saraiva da Costa Leite, "*Wilson Tibério: A negritude de um gênio das artes plásticas*," *Dasartes* (August 21, 2015), https://www.geledes.org.br/wilson-tiberio-a-negritude-de-um-genio-das-artes-plasticas/.

9. N. Chabani Manganyi, *A Black Man Called Sekoto* (Johannesburg: Witwatersrand University Press, 1996).

10. Feldman, *Black Rhythms of Peru,* 117.

11. Alberto, *Terms of Inclusion.*

12. Hanchard, *Orpheus and Power*; George Reid Andrews, *Afro-Latin America, 1800–2000* (New York: Oxford University Press, 2004); Alberto, *Terms of Inclusion*; Christopher Dunn, *Contracultura: Alternative Arts and Social Transformation in Authoritarian Brazil* (Chapel Hill: University of North Carolina Press, 2016).

13. Carlos Moore, *Castro, the Blacks, and Africa* (Los Angeles: UCLA Center for Afro-American Studies, 1988).

14. Tianna S. Paschel, *Becoming Black Political Subjects: Movements and Ethno-Racial Rights in Colombia and Brazil* (Princeton, NJ: Princeton University Press, 2016).

15. Roberto Conduru, "*Negrume multicor: Arte, África e Brasil para além de raça e etnia*," *Acervo* 22, no. 2 (2009): 29–44.

16. Morgan Kulla, "The Politics of Culture: The Case of Festac," *Ufahamu: A Journal of African Studies* 7, no. 1 (1976): 166–192.

17. Judith Bettelheim, *AFROCUBA: Works on Paper, 1968–2003* (San Francisco: International Center for the Arts, San Francisco State University, 2005).

18. Kulla, "The Politics of Culture"; Ife Enohoro, "The Second World Black and African Festival of Arts and Culture: Lagos, Nigeria," *The Black Scholar* 9, no. 1 (September 1977): 26–33.

19. Arthur Monroe, "FESTAC 77—The Second World Black and African Festival of Arts and Culture: Lagos, Nigeria," *The Black Scholar* 9, no. 1 (September 1977): 34.

20. Jerry Dávila, *Hotel Trópico: Brazil and the Challenge of African Decolonization, 1950–1980* (Durham, NC: Duke University Press, 2010); Moore, *Castro, the Blacks, and Africa.*

21. Alberto, *Terms of Inclusion*; Katherine J. Hagedorn, *Divine Utterances: The Performance of Afro-Cuban Santería* (Washington, DC: Smithsonian Books, 2001).

22. Hanchard, *Orpheus and Power,* 21.

23. Abdias do Nascimento, "*Carta aberta a Dacar*," *Tempo Brasileiro: Revista de Cultura* 4, no. 9/10 (April–June 1966): 100.

24. Elisa Larkin Nascimento, "*O movimento social afro-brasileiro no século XX: Um esboço sucinto*," in *Cultura em movimento: Matrizes africanas e ativismo negro no Brasil*, ed. Elisa Larkin Nascimento (São Paulo: Selo Negro Edições, 2014).

25. This reconstruction of the activities of Azevedo is based on the following: "*Arte moderna no carnaval*," *Correio da Manhã,* Rio de Janeiro, January 12, 1958; "*Pintor diz que Itamarati não deu oportunidade para negro nôvo expo rem Dacar*," *Jornal do Brasil* (Rio de Janeiro, November 12, 1965); "*Pintor va reunir artistas negros no Atêrro para protestar contra Itamarati*," *Jornal do Brasil* (January 11, 1966); "*Artes negras levam pintores a acampar*," *Diario de Noticias* (Rio de Janeiro, January 11, 1966). I am grateful to the art historian Kleber Amancio for sharing these sources with me.

26. Dávila, *Hotel Trópico,* 234.

27. The IPEAFRO website features many of Nascimento's paintings: http://ipeafro.org.br/acervo-digital/imagens/museu-de-arte-negra/obras-abdias-nascimento/.

28. Kimberly Cleveland, *Black Art in Brazil: Expressions of Identity* (Gainesville: University Press of Florida, 2013).

29. Ibid., 48.

30. Mariano Carneiro da Cunha, "*Arte afro-brasileira*," in *História geral da arte no Brasil*, ed. Walter Zanini, Cacilda Teixeira da Costa, and Marilia Saboya de Albequerque, vol. 2 (São Paulo: Instituto Walther Moreira Salles and Fundação Djalma Guimarães, 1983): 973–1033.

31. Marta Heloísa Leuba Salum, "*Cem anos de arte afro-brasileira*," in *Mostra do redescobrimento: Arte afro-brasileira,* ed. Nelson Aguilar (São Paulo: Associação Brasil 500 Anos Artes Visuais, 2000), 112–121; Conduru, "*Negrume multicor.*"

32. Cleveland, *Black Art in Brazil.*

33. Paul Christopher Johnson and Stephan Palmié, "Afro-Latin American Religions," in *Afro-Latin American Studies: An Introduction*, ed. Alejandro de la Fuente and George Reid Andrews (New York: Cambridge University Press, 2018), 438–485.

34. Conduru, "*Negrume multicor,*" 32–33.

35. George Reid Andrews, *Blackness in the White Nation: A History of Afro-Uruguay* (Chapel Hill: University of North Carolina Press, 2010).

36. Tomás Olivera Chirimini, "Candombe, African Nations, and the Africanity of Uruguay," in *African Roots/American Cultures: Africa in the Creation of the Americas,* ed. Sheila S. Walker (Lanham, MD: Rowman & Littlefield, 2001), 259–274; Vannina Sztainbok, "National Pleasures: The Fetishization of Blackness and Uruguayan Autobiographical Narratives," *Latin American and Caribbean Ethnic Studies* 3, no. 1 (2008): 61–84.

37. Michel Fabre, "Herberto [sic] Cuadrado Cogollo (1945–), Afro-Colombian," *Callaloo*, 8/10 (1980): 19–26; Franklin Rosemont and Robin D. G. Kelley, ed., *Black, Brown, and Beige: Surrealist Writings from Africa and the Diaspora* (Austin: University of Texas Press, 2009); Álvaro Medina, *El arte del Caribe colombiano* (Cartegena, Colombia: Gobernación del Departamento de Bolívar, 2000).

38. Eduardo Márceles Daconte, *Los recursos de la imaginación: Artes visuales del Caribe colombiano* (Barranquilla, Colombia: Artes Gráficas Industriales, 2010), 255.

39. Heriberto Cuadrado Cogollo, *Cogollo: Le monde d'un nohor* (Paris: Galerie Suzanne Visat, 1973).

40. Rogelio Martínez Furé, *Diálogos imaginarios* (Havana: Editorial Arte y Literatura, 1979), 248, 249.

41. Alejandro de la Fuente, ed., *Queloides: Race and Racism in Cuban Contemporary Art* (Pittsburgh: Mattress Factory and University of Pittsburgh Press, 2010); Alejandro de la Fuente, *Grupo Antillano: The Art of Afro-Cuba* (Pittsburgh: Fundación Caguayo and University of Pittsburgh Press, 2013); Lillian Guerra, *Visions of Power in Cuba: Revolution, Redemption, and Resistance, 1959–1971* (Chapel Hill: University of North Carolina Press, 2012).

42. Ambrosio Fornet, "*El quinquenio gris: Revisitando el término*," *Criterios* (2007), https://rebelion.org/el-quinquenio-gris-revisitando-el-termino/.

43. Richard Frick, ed., *The Tricontinental Solidarity Poster* (Switzerland: Comedia-Verlag Bern, 2003).

44. For more information on these religions, see Johnson and Palmié, "Afro-Latin American Religions."

45. Walterio Carbonell, *Crítica: Cómo surgió la cultura nacional* (Havana: Biblioteca Nacional José Martí, 2005 [1961]), 119–120.

46. Guillermina Ramos Cruz, *Lam y Mendive, arte afrocubano* (Barcelona: Ediciones Linkgua, 2009).

47. de la Fuente, *Grupo Antillano*; Bettelheim, *AFROCUBA*.

48. Bettelheim, *AFROCUBA*.

49. de la Fuente, *Grupo Antillano*; Ramos Cruz, *Lam y Mendive*.

50. de la Fuente, *Grupo Antillano*.

51. de la Fuente, *Grupo Antillano*; Ramos Cruz, *Lam y Mendive*; Bettelheim, *AFROCUBA*.

52. Emanoel Araújo, *A mão afro-brasileira: Significado da contribuição artística e histórica*, vol. 1 (São Paulo: Imprensa Oficial do Estado de São Paulo / Museu Afro Brasil, 2010), 15.

53. Emanoel Araújo, *A nova mão afro-brasileira* (São Paulo: Museu Afro Brasil, 2014).

54. Cleveland, *Black Art in Brazil*.

55. Araújo, *A nova mão afro-brasileira*.

56. Mercedes Angola Rossi and Raúl Cristancho Álvarez, *Viaje sin mapa: Representaciones afro en el arte contemporáneo colombiano* (Bogotá, Colombia: Banco de la República, 2006); Tianna Paschel, "'The Beautiful Faces of My Black People': Race, Ethnicity and the Politics of Colombia's 2005 Census," *Ethnic and Racial Studies* 36, no. 10 (2013): 1544–1563.

57. Luz Adriana, Maya Restrepo, and Raúl Cristancho Álvarez, *¡Mandinga Sea! África en Antioquia* (Bogotá, Colombia: Ediciones Uniandes, 2015).

58. Alejandro de la Fuente, "The New Afro-Cuban Cultural Movement and the Debate on Race in Contemporary Cuba," *Journal of Latin American Studies* 40, no. 4 (2008): 697–720; de la Fuente, *Queloides*.

59. de la Fuente, *Queloides*; Odette Casamayor Cisneros, "*Queloides: Inevitables, lacerantes: En torno a la exposición Queloides: Raza y racismo en el arte cubano contemporáneo*," *Artecubano: Revista de Artes Visuales* 2 (2011): 22–29; Ana Belén Martín-Sevillano, "Crisscrossing Gender, Ethnicity, and Race: African Religious Legacy in Cuban Contemporary Women's Art," *Cuban Studies* 42 (2011): 136–154.

60. Conduru, "*Negrume multicor*."

61. Alejandro de la Fuente, *Diago: The Pasts of This Afro-Cuban Present* (Cambridge, MA: Ethelbert Cooper Gallery and Harvard University Press, 2017).

62. Ana Paula Orlandi, "In Conversation with Eustáquio Neves, 'Letter to the Sea,'" *C&América Latina* (March 5, 2018), http://amlatina.contemporaryand.com/editorial/brazilian-photographer-eustaquio-neves/.

63. Clarissa Diniz and Rafael Cardoso, ed. *Do Valongo à favela: Imaginário e periferia* (Rio de Janeiro: MAR, 2016).

64. Cleveland, *Black Art in Brazil*.

65. Tanya Katerí Hernández, *Racial Subordination in Latin America: The Role of the State, Customary Law, and the New Civil Rights Response* (New York: Cambridge University Press, 2013); Andrews, *Afro-Latin America*; David Howard, *Coloring the Nation: Race and Ethnicity in the Dominican Republic* (Oxford: Signal Books, 2001); Alejandro de la Fuente, *A Nation for All: Race, Inequality, and Politics in Twentieth-Century Cuba* (Chapel Hill: University of North Carolina Press, 2001).

66. Maria Elena Ortiz, *Firelei Báez: Bloodlines* (Miami: Pérez Art Musuem, 2016).

67. Marguerite Itamar Harrison, "Through the Eyes of Brazil's African Daughters: Vision and Memory in the Artwork of Rosana Paulino and in the Short Fiction of Marilene Felinto," *Revue Lusotopie* 12, no. 1–2 (2005): 127.

68. Juan Roberto Mascardi, "*Los próceres de Cartagena usan pelucas afro*," Hipermedula.org (2011), http://hipermedula.org/2011/08/colombia-cronicada/.

69. Frank A. Guridy and Juliet Hooker, "Currents in Afro-Latin American Political and Social Thought," in *Afro-Latin American Studies: An Introduction*, ed. Alejandro de la Fuente and George Reid Andrews (New York: Cambridge University Press, 2018), 212. See also Betty LaDuke, "June Beer's Story," *Heresies: A Feminist Publication on Art and Politics* 20 (1986): 54–57; María Dolores Torres, "June Beer (Bluefields, RACS, 1935–1986)" and "Datos biográficos de June Beer," *Revista de Temas Nicaragüenses* 96 (April 2016): 7–13.

70. Evelyn Carmen Ramos-Alfred, "A Painter of Cuban Life: Victor Patricio de Landaluze and Nineteenth-Century Cuban Politics (1850–1889)," (PhD diss., University of Chicago, 2011).

15. Surface Viewing: On Blackness, Skin, and Photography in Contemporary Jamaican Art

1. Thanks to Huey Copeland and Jerry Philogene for their comments on an earlier draft of this essay.

2. Kartel released an album titled *Colouring Book* in July 2001. Winnifred Brown-Glaude, "Don't Hate Me 'Cause I'm Pretty: Race, Gender and The Bleached Body in Jamaica," *Social and Economic Studies* 62, no. 1/2 (2013): 53–78.

3. The literature on race and photography in the nineteenth century is extensive. For a sampling, see *Only Skin Deep: Changing Visions of the American Self*, ed. Coco Fusco and Brian Wallis (New York: International Center of Photography/Harry N. Abrams, Inc., 2003); Shawn Michelle Smith, *American Archives: Gender, Race, and Class in Visual Culture* (Princeton, NJ: Princeton University Press, 1999); Elizabeth Edwards, *Evolving Images: Photography, Race and Popular Darwinism* (New Haven, CT: Yale University Press, 2009).

4. Annie Paul, "'Dancehall A Mi Everything': Art and Music in 21st Century Jamaica," in *Jamaican Routes*, ed. Selene Wendt (Norway: Galleri F15, 2016), 59–71.

5. Barnor Hesse, preface to *Conceptual Aphasia in Black: Displacing Racial Formation*, ed. P. Khalil Saucier and Tryon P. Woods (Lanham, MD: Lexington Books, 2016), viii.

6. Hesse, vii. See Saucier and Woods, ed., *Conceptual Aphasia in Black*; Irene Tucker, *The Moment of Racial Sight: A History* (Chicago: University of Chicago Press, 2012); Osagie K. Obasogie, *Blinded by Sight: Seeing Race through the Eyes of the Blind* (Stanford, CA: Stanford University Press, 2013); Stuart Hall, "The Spectacle of 'the Other': Cultural Representation and Signifying Practices," in *Representation: Cultural Representations and Signifying Practices* (London: Sage, 1997); Nadine Ehlers, *Racial Imperatives: Discipline, Performativity, and Struggles against Subjection* (Bloomington: Indiana University Press, 2012).

7. Wendy Hui Kyong Chun, "Introduction: Race and/as Technology; or, How to Do Things to Race," *Camera Obscura: Feminism, Culture, and Media Studies* 24, no. 1 (2009): 7. On the "social materiality and social practice" of race, see Hesse, vii.

8. Hesse, viii. On race as technology, see Chun, 8.

9. On the early history of photography in Jamaica, see David Boxer, "The Duperlys of Jamaica," in *Duperly: An Exhibition of Works by Adolphe Duperly, His Sons, and Grandsons Mounted in Commemoration of the Bicentenary of His Birth*, ed. National Gallery of Jamaica (Kingston: National Gallery of Jamaica, 2001), 6; Gillian Forrester, "Noel B. Livingston's Gallery of Illustrious Jamaicans," in *Victorian Jamaica*, ed. Tim Barringer and Wayne Modest (Durham, NC: Duke University Press, 2018), 357–394.

10. Forrester, "Noel B. Livingston's Gallery of Illustrious Jamaicans," 393; Mimi Sheller, *Citizenship from Below: Erotic Agency and Caribbean Freedom* (Durham, NC: Duke University Press, 2012), 114–142.

11. For a discussion of the albums containing these photographs, see Sheller and Forrester.

12. Sheller, *Citizenship from Below*, 129.

13. For an example of this see, Krista Thompson, "'I WAS HERE BUT I DISAPEAR': Ivanhoe 'Rhygin' Martin and Photographic Disappearance in Jamaica," *Art Journal* 77, no. 2 (2018): 80–99.

14. "Paul Bogle," *Colonial Standard & Jamaica Despatch*, October 18, 1865.

15. Diane J. Austin-Broos, "Race/Class: Jamaica's Discourse of Heritable Identity," *New West Indian Guide* 68, no. 3–4 (1994): 213–233; Natasha Barnes, *Cultural Conundrums: Gender, Race, Nation, and the Making of Caribbean Cultural Politics* (Ann Arbor: University of Michigan Press, 2006); Gina A. Ulysse, *Downtown Ladies: Informal Commercial Importers, a Haitian Anthropologist, and Self-Making in Jamaica* (Chicago: University of Chicago Press, 2007).

16. Donna P. Hope, "From Browning to Cake Soap: Popular Debates on Skin Bleaching in the Jamaican Dancehall," *Journal of Pan African Studies* 4, no. 4 (2011): 165–194.

17. Athaliah Reynolds, "'Proud a Mi Bleaching': 'Skin-Bleachers' Defend Their Action Despite Health and Cultural Warnings," *Sunday Gleaner*, November 15, 2009.

18. Hope, "From Browning to Cake Soap."

19. On "modern blackness," see Deborah A. Thomas, "Modern Blackness; or, Theoretical 'Tripping' on Black Vernacular Cultures," in *Modern Blackness: Nationalism, Globalization, and the Politics of Culture in Jamaica* (Durham, NC: Duke University Press, 2004), 230–262. On the notion of slackness, consult Carolyn Cooper, "Slackness Hiding from Culture: Erotic Play in the Dancehall," in *Noises in the Blood: Orality, Gender, and the "Vulgar" Body of Jamaican Popular Culture* (Durham, NC: Duke University Press, 1995), 136–173. Cooper writes, "Slackness is a metaphorical revolt against law and order; an undermining of

consensual standards of decency. It is the antithesis of Culture" (141).

20. Vybz Kartel, "Pretty Like a Colouring Book?," *Jamaica Journal* 33, no. 3 (2001): 24.

21. In the tune "Look Pon We," Kartel reiterated a similar sentiment: "Di girl dem love off mi brown cute face, di girl dem love off mi bleach-out face." See discussion of Kartel and skin bleaching in Hope, "From Browning to Cake Soap," 180–182.

22. Nadia Ellis, "Out and Bad: Toward a Queer Performance Hermeneutic in Jamaican Dancehall," *Small Axe: A Caribbean Journal of Criticism* 15, no. 2 (2011): 7–23.

23. See Brown-Glaude's analysis of newspaper stories about skin bleaching in the *Gleaner*: Winnifred Brown-Glaude, "The Fact of Blackness? The Bleached Body in Contemporary Jamaica," *Small Axe: A Caribbean Journal of Criticism* 11, no. 3 (2007): 34–51.

24. Barnes, *Cultural Conundrums*.

25. Brown-Glaude, "The Fact of Blackness?," 35.

26. See Krista Thompson, "Video Light: Dancehall and the Aesthetics of Spectacular Un-visibility in Jamaica," in *Shine: The Visual Economy of Light in African Diasporic Aesthetic Practice* (Durham, NC: Duke University Press, 2015), 112–168.

27. Best and Marcus quote Foucault here. See *Foucault Live: Collected Interviews, 1961–1984*, ed. Sylvère Lotringer, trans. Lysa Hochroth and John Johnston (New York: Semiotext(e), 1989), 57–58; Sharon Marcus and Stephen Best, "Surface Reading: An Introduction," *Representations* 108, no. 1 (2009): 1–21.

28. On critical description, see Best and Marcus, 11.

29. Paul Anthony Smith, interview with the author, July 7, 2015.

30. Ibid. Smith often chose to take photographs of them from afar, wanting to avoid too self-conscious performances for the camera. Sometimes he cropped the images, making the peripheral figures central in the photograph.

31. Ibid.

32. Ibid.

33. See my discussion of Patterson's work in Krista Thompson, *Shine: The Visual Economy of Light in African Diasporic Aesthetic Practice* (Durham, NC: Duke University Press, 2015).

34. See *Bad at Sports* podcast, episode 546: Ebony G. Patterson, April 18, 2016, https://badatsports.com/2016/episode-546-ebony-g-patterson/. The term *metrosexual* typically refers to a heterosexual urban man in post-industrial and capitalist cultures who spends a significant amount of time and money on his appearance. See, too, Nadia Ellis, "Obscure; or, The Queer Light of Ebony G. Patterson," in *Caribbean Queer Visualities: A Small Axe Project*, ed. David Scott, Erica Moiah James, and Nijah Cunningham (New York: Small Axe Inc., 2016), 18–27.

35. See Thompson, "Video Light," 112–168.

36. Dave Rodney, "Sintra Back on the Block with Her World Famous Wet T-Shirt Poster," *The Gleaner*, August 11, 2015, http://jamaica-gleaner.com/article/outlook/20150816/sintra-back-block-her-world-famous-wet-t-shirt-poster.

37. Ibid.

38. Andrea Chung, interview with the author, September 21, 2018.

39. Ibid.

40. Patricia Joan Saunders, "'Church inna Session': Leasho Johnson, Mapping the Sacred through the Profane in Jamaican Popular Culture," in *Caribbean Queer Visualities: A Small Axe Project*, ed. David Scott, Erica Moiah James, and Nijah Cunningham (New York: Small Axe Inc., 2016), 86–99.

41. Night Rider, videographer, quoted in Beth-Sarah Wright, "Emancipative Bodies: Woman, Trauma and a Corporeal Theory of Healing in Jamaican Dancehall Culture" (PhD diss., New York University, Graduate School of Arts and Science, 2004).

42. Leasho Johnson, interview with the author, July 11, 2017.

43. This work was installed as part of the Jamaica Biennial, 2014. Oneika Russell, Skype interview with the author, July 19, 2017. For a description of this work, see Selene Wendt, "Wake the World and Tell the People," in *Jamaican Routes*, ed. Selene Wendt (Norway: Galleri F15, 2016), 48–52.

44. Camille Chedda, interview with the author, November 27, 2019.

45. For another type of engagement with surface viewing, see Petrona Morrison's photographs of skin and DNA in her *Mapping* series (2017) and *ID* series (2018–2019).

16. Prismatic Blackness: Art, Being, and Aesthetics in the Global Caribbean

1. Jill H. Casid and Aruna D'Souza, ed., *Art History in the Wake of the Global Turn* (Williamstown, MA: Sterling and Francine Clark Art Institute; New Haven, CT: Yale University Press, 2014); Edward J. Sullivan, *From San Juan to Paris and Back: Francisco Oller and Caribbean Art in the Era of Impressionism* (New York: Brooklyn Museum; New Haven, CT: Yale University Press, 2014) are examples of this scholarship.

2. This analysis is based on the author's direct study of the Zemi at the Pigorini Museum, Rome, May–June 2013, and builds on the scholarship of Dicey Taylor, Marco Biscione, and Peter G. Roe, "Epilogue: The Beaded Zemi in the Pigorini Museum," in *Taíno: Pre-Columbian Art and Culture from the Caribbean*, ed. Fatima Brecht et al. (New York: El Museo del Barrio; Monacelli Press, 1997), 158–169.

3. Manthia Diawara, "A Conversation with Édouard Glissant aboard the RMS Queen Mary 2," trans. Christopher Winks, in *Afro Modern: Journeys through the Black Atlantic*, ed. Tanya Barson and Peter Gorschlüter (Liverpool, England: Tate Publishing, 2010), 58–63.

4. Ibid., 61.

5. Jennifer Dunning. *Geoffrey Holder: A Life in Theater, Dance and Art* (New York: Harry N. Abrams, Inc., 2001), 35.

6. Ibid., 32.

7. Ibid., 42.

8. Katherine E. Manthorne, "Art School as Contact Zone: Latin American Students and Their Teachers," in *Nexus New York: Latin/American Artists in the Modern Metropolis*, ed. Deborah Cullen (New York: Museo Del Barrio; New Haven, CT: Yale University Press, 2009), 48–63.

9. *Hervé Télémaque: Trottoirs d'Afrique à l'acrylique* (Paris: Galerie Louis Carré & Cie, 2001), 46.

10. Hervé Télémaque, in conversation with the author. Duke University, Durham, NC, June 2017.

11. Leonard Baskin, *Proofs and Process* (New York: Galerie St. Etienne, October 9, 2007–January 5, 2008). Exhibition catalog.

12. Erica Moiah James, *Max Taylor: Paperwork 1960–1992* (Nassau: National Art Gallery of The Bahamas, 2009). Exhibition catalog.

13. Robert Blackburn Printmaking Workshop, flyer.

14. Evelyn A. Williams, *The Art of Denis Williams* (Leeds, England: Peepal Tree Press, 2012), 19.

15. Lucy Rodgers and Maryam Ahmed, "Windrush: Who Exactly Was on Board?," BBC News, April 27, 2018.

16. Mora J. Beauchamp-Byrd, "London Bridge: Late 20th Century British Art and the Routes of 'National Culture,'" in *Transforming the Crown: African, Asian, and Caribbean Artists in Britain, 1966–1996*, ed. Mora J. Beauchamp-Byrd (New York: Caribbean Cultural Center; Chicago: University of Chicago Press, 1997), 27. Exhibition catalog.

17. Anne Walmsley, "Caribbean Artists Movement, 1966–1972: A Space and a Voice for Visual Practice," in *Transforming the Crown*, 47.

18. Anne Walmsley, *The Caribbean Artists Movement, 1966–1972: A Literary and Cultural History* (London: New Beacon Books, 1992), 36.

19. Ibid., 37.

20. The belief in a conceptual Caribbean rather than a Latin America or Latin America and the Caribbean was something La Rose championed. In January 1968, he, along with C. L. R. James and Andrew Salkey, attended the First Cultural Congress of Havana. Aimé Césaire and René Depestre also attended. The Congress's theme was "Colonialism and Neo-Colonialism in the Cultural Development of Peoples" in Asia, Africa, and Latin America. At the Congress, La Rose proposed that the term *Latin America* be abolished. In his mind, not only did it not account for the English-speaking Caribbean at all, but the colonial frame of reference performed a *colonial act* on this constituency. It erased a necessary element in the region's understanding of itself from the archive and contemporary discourse. See Walmsley, *The Caribbean Artists Movement*, 138.

21. Walmsley, *The Caribbean Artists Movement*, 82.

22. Beauchamp-Byrd, 21.

23. "Jamaican Sculptor Wins Praise in London," *Jet*, February 12, 1953; Walmsley, "A Space and a Voice for Visual Practice," in *Transforming the Crown*, 16.

24. Guy Brett, "A Tragic Excitement," in *Aubrey Williams* (London: iNIVA, 1998), 24. Exhibition catalog. Also, Walmsley, *The Caribbean Artists Movement*, 47.

25. Brett, 28; Anne Walmsley, "Chronology," in *Aubrey Williams* (London: iNIVA, 1998), 79. Exhibition catalog.

26. Aubrey Williams, "The Predicament of the Artist in the Caribbean," in *Guyana Dreaming: The Art of Aubrey Williams*, comp. Anne Walmsley (London: Dangaroo Press, 1990), 15–20; Walmsley, *The Caribbean Arts Movement*, 99.

27. Walmsley, *The Caribbean Arts Movement*, 163.

28. Ibid.

29. Michael Anthony, quoted in Walmsley, *The Caribbean Artists Movement, 1966–1972*, 103. The Trinidadian writer (b. 1932) made this statement fourteen years after migrating to Britain, not certain he would ever return to the island. Up to that point, Anthony had only published novels set in Trinidad and questioned how long his memories of his distant homeland could feed or sustain his art. He returned to Trinidad in 1970.

30. Eddie Chambers, *Black Artists in British Art: A History since the 1950s* (New York: I. B. Tauris & Co., 2014), 167.

31. Walmsley, *The Caribbean Artists Movement*, 273.

32. Evelyn A. Williams, *The Art of Denis Williams*, 2.

33. Ibid., 143.

34. Emily Musil Church, "In Search of Seven Sisters: A Biography of the Nardal Sisters of Martinique," *Callaloo* 36, no. 2 (Spring 2013): 367.

35. Christopher Cozier and Claire Tancons, "No More Than a Backyard on a Small Island," *Fillip*, no. 16 (Spring 2012): 45.

36. Walmsley, "Chronology," 80.

37. Lowery Stokes Sims, *Wifredo Lam and the International Avant-Garde, 1923–1982* (Austin: University of Texas Press, 2002), 152, 158–160.

38. See *R. Brent Malone: Reincarnation—A Retrospective Exhibition (1954-2004)*, curated by Erica Moiah James (Nassau: The National Art Gallery of The Bahamas, 2015). Exhibition catalog.

39. Cozier and Tancons, 47.

40. Marcel Pinas, in conversation with the author, May 2, 2018, Miami, FL.

41. Ebony Patterson, in conversation with the author, July 2018, Miami, FL.

42. Ibid.

43. Nancy Rogers Yaeger, "Ras Ishi: Son of Thunder," *Caribbean Beat*, no. 10 (Summer 1994), https://www.caribbean-beat.com/issue-10/son-thunder-ras-ishi.

44. Kwame Anthony Appiah, quoting Gertrude Stein, in *The Ethics of Identity* (Princeton, NJ: Princeton University Press, 2010), 297n14.

45. Christopher Cozier, "Between Narratives and Other Spaces," *Small Axe: A Caribbean Journal of Criticism* 3, no. 2 (September 1999): 19.

46. Ibid.

ILLUSTRATIONS

Introduction

P. 20 Map with population data ca. 1800. Geographical boundaries reflect the current distribution of states as depicted by Natural Earth Data (https://www.naturalearthdata.com/). Population percentages are from George Reid Andrews, *Afro-Latin America, 1800–2000* (New York: Oxford University Press, 2004). Maps composed by Jeffrey Blossom of Center for Geographic Analysis, Harvard University.

P. 21 Map with population data ca. 2010. Geographical boundaries reflect the current distribution of states as depicted by Natural Earth Data (https://www.naturalearthdata.com/). Population figures are from Economic Commission for Latin America and the Caribbean (CEPAL, https://www.cepal.org/en), the CIA World Factbook (https://www.cia.gov/the-world-factbook/), and 2010 U.S. Census data. Maps composed by Jeffrey Blossom of Center for Geographic Analysis, Harvard University.

Chapters 1-16

1 Unidentified artist. *Escrava Anastácia (The Slave Anastácia)*. Undated. Impromptu altar. Beads, quartz crystal. Rio de Janeiro, Museu do Negro, Igreja de Nossa Senhora do Rosário e São Benedito dos Homens Pretos. Digital photograph, 2008.

2 Unidentified artist. *Iemanjá Fertility Goddess*. Ca. 1850. Coal tar. Pernambuco, Brazil.

3a, 3b Unidentified artist. *Iemanjá/Calunga*. Ca. 1820–1830. Two views. Wood, polychrome gesso, fiber. Height: 64.5 cm. Private collection.

4 Marcus Wood. *Calungas and Black Dancers*. Photograph. Recife, Brazil, Night of the Silent Drums. Image, 2007.

5 Unidentified artist. *Sacy-Pererê*. Ca. 1970. Molded and painted plaster.

6 Michael Wolgemut, workshop. *A Sciopod*. Woodcut. Hartmann Schedel, *Nuremberg Chronicle* (Nuremberg, Germany: Anton Koberger, 1493). London, British Library. Shelfmark IC.7452.

7 Unidentified artist. *Sacy Shoe Polish*. Ca. 1930. Advertisement. Lithograph.

8 Josiah Wedgwood. *Am I not a Man and a Brother?* Ca. 1787. Antislavery medallion. Black jasperware on white ceramic background. Front view. Washington, DC, Smithsonian National Museum of American History. Behring Center. Act. no. 68.150.

9 Pietro Tenerani. *The Abolition of Slavery*. Front relief, base of monument to Simón Bolívar. 1846 (inaugurated). Bronze. Bogotá, Colombia, Plaza de Bolívar.

10 Pietro Tenerani, after. *The Abolition of Slavery*. Front relief, monument to Simón Bolívar. Steel engraving. 27.3 × 27.4 cm. From Filippo Gerardo, *Intorno alla statua de Bolívar* (1845). Bogotá, Museo Nacional de Colombia.

11 Karl Friedrich Voigt. *Simón Bolívar, Liberator of the Slaves*. 1846. Commemorative medal. Obverse: Bolívar with thankful formerly enslaved family. Reverse: Statue of Bolívar from his monument, Bogotá,

Colombia. Issued in bronze and silverplate versions. Formerly Bowers & Merena (auctioneers), Russell B. Patterson Collection. March 1985, lot 1543.

12 Angelo Agostini. *De volta do Paraguai* (*Back from Paraguay*). Illustration with epigraph. Published in *A Vida Fluminense* 3, no. 128 (June 11, 1870).

13 A. D. Bressac. *Alegoria à lei do ventre livre* (*Allegory on the Law of the Free Womb*). Ca. 1871. Polychromed plaster. 171 × 131 cm. Rio de Janeiro, Museu Histórico Nacional.

14 Miguel Navarro y Cañizares. *Alegoria à lei do ventre libre* (*Allegory on the Law of the Free Womb*). 1871. Oil on canvas. Salvador, Bahia, Brazil, Basilica do Bonfim. Museu dos Ex-votos.

15 Miguel Navarro y Cañizares. *Alegoria à lei áurea* (*Allegory on the Golden Law*). 1888. Oil on canvas. 65.5 × 55.6 cm. Salvador, Bahia, Brazil, Escola de Belas Artes da Universidade Federal de Bahia.

16 D. Plot. *Las esclavas de Buenos Aires demuestran ser sibres y gratas a su noble libertador* (*The Female Slaves of Buenos Aires Show That They Are Free and Grateful to Their Noble Liberator*). 1841. Oil on cloth. 73 × 149 cm. Buenos Aires, Argentina, Museo Histórico Nacional.

17 Prilidiano Pueyrredón. *Patio porteño en 1850* (*Patio in Buenos Aires in 1850*). Ca. 1860. Oil on copper. 30 × 43 cm. Buenos Aires, Argentina, Museo Nacional de Bellas Artes. Acc. no. 3182.

18 Prilidiano Pueyrredón. *Esquina porteña* (*Buenos Aires Street Corner*). 1865. Oil on canvas. 1.02 × 1.28 m. Private collection.

19 Prilidiano Pueyrredón. *El naranjero* (*The Orange Vendor*). 1865. Oil on canvas, 153.6 × 122 cm. Private collection. Auction, Buenos Aires, Argentina, La Casa Bullrich, Gaona y Wernicke, April 2017.

20 León Williez, editor. Manuel María del Mazo, illustrator. *¡¡Rompe estas cadenas!! ¡¡Levanta al indígena de la postración!! ¡¡Conquistemos la inmortalidad!!* (*Break These Chains!! Raise the Indigenous People from Oppression!! Let Us Conquer Immortality!!*). From the *Serie Adefecios* (*Nonsense* series). 1855. Lithograph. 31 × 43.7 cm. Museo de Arte de Lima.

21 Francisco Laso. *Las tres razas, o la igualdad ante la ley* (*The Three Races, or Equality before the Law*). Ca. 1859. Oil on canvas. 81 × 106 cm. Museo de Arte de Lima.

22 Modesto Brocos y Gomez. *A redenção de Cam* (*The Redemption of Ham*). 1895. Oil on canvas. 199 × 166 cm. Rio de Janeiro, Museu Nacional de Belas Artes.

23 Theubet de Beauchamp. *Vista de la plaza de México el 16 de septiembre de 1827* (*View of Mexico Square, September 16, 1827*). 1827. Watercolor. 11 × 17.5 cm. Madrid, Real Biblioteca. © Patrimonio Nacional Real Biblioteca (Madrid), GRAB/261.

24 Francisco "Pancho" Fierro. *Procesión cívica de los negros (1821)* (*Civic Procession of the Blacks* [1821]). Undated. Watercolor on paper. 22.9 × 18.2 cm. Lima, Peru, Pinacoteca Municipal Ignacio Merino de la Municipalidad Metropolitana de Lima. Colección Ricardo Palma.

25 Unidentified artist. *Sobre lo blanco negro* (*Black over White*). Illustration. *Cabichui* 1 (1867), no. 29, p. 2.

26 Santander Pereira. Illustration. 1927. *Revista Sucesos*, no. 1307.

27 Pedro Américo. *Batalha do Avaí* (*Battle of Avaí*). 1874–1877. Oil. 6 × 11 m. Rio de Janeiro, Museo Nacional de Bellas Artes.

28 Hercules Morelli. *La caridad cristiana coronando el busto de Francisco Carvallo, fundador de la escuela y hospital de Belén* (*Christian Charity Crowning the Bust of Francisco Carvallo, Founder of the School and Hospital of Belén*). 1857. Oil on canvas. 90 × 71 cm. Havana, Museo Nacional de Bellas Artes de Cuba.

29 Francisco Antonio Cano. *Paso del ejército libertador por el Páramo de Pisba* (*Passage of the Liberating Army through the Páramo de Pisba*). 1922. Oil. 195 × 379 cm. Bogatá, Colombia, Colección Casa Museo Quinta de Bolívar. MinCultura.

30 Juan Lepiani. *Proclamación de la independecia del Perú* (*Proclamation of the Independence of Peru*). 1904. Oil. 255.9 × 397.9 cm. Lima, National Museum of Archaeology, Anthropology and History of Peru.

31 Juan Manuel Blanes. *La conquista del desierto* (*The Conquest of the Desert*). 1896. 4 × 11 m. Buenos Aires, Argentina, Museo Histórico Nacional.

32 Claudio Linati, design. *Costeño: Nègre des environs de Veracruz (Santa Fe) dans son costumes de Dimanche* (*Man from the Coast: Black Man from the Vicinity of Veracruz [Santa Fe] in His Sunday Clothes*). 1828. Hand-colored lithograph. *Costumes civils, militaires et réligieux du Mexique: Dessinés d'après nature* (Brussels, Belgium: C. Sattanino; printed by the Lithographie royale de Jobard, 1828), plate 12.

33 Édouard Pingret. *Músico de Veracruz* (*Musician from Veracruz*). Ca. 1850. Oil on cardboard. 40 × 39 cm. Colección Banco Nacional de México.

34 José Agustin Arrieta. *El costeño* (*Young Man from the Coast*). After 1843. Oil on canvas. 89 × 71 cm. New York, Hispanic Society of America. Museum Department Purchase, 2013. Accession no.: LA2391.

35 Felipe Santiago Gutiérrez. *Retrato de mulata* (*Portrait of a Mulatto Woman*). 1875. Bogotá, Colombia, Proyecto Bachué.

36 Carmelo Fernández. *Mujeres blancas, provincia de Ocaña* (*White Women, Ocaña Province*). 1850. Watercolor. 22 × 31 cm. Bogotá, Biblioteca Nacional de Colombia. Colección de la Comisión Corográfica.

37 Manuel Maria Paz. *Venta de aguardiente en el pueblo de Lloró, provincia de Chocó* (*Sale of Liquor in the Village of Lloró, Province of Chocó*). 1853. Watercolor. 24 × 31 cm. Bogotá, Biblioteca Nacional de Colombia. Colección de la Comisión Corográfica.

38 Léon Gauthier. *Modo de lavar oro, provincia de Barbacoas* (*How

Gold Is Washed, Province of Barbacoas). 1853. Watercolor. 30 × 24 cm. Bogotá, Biblioteca Nacional de Colombia. Colección de la Comisión Corográfica.

39 Francisco "Pancho" Fierro. *Danzando al son de los diablos* (*Dancing to the Sound of the Devils*). Undated. Watercolor on paper. 23.4 × 18.1 cm. Lima, Peru, Pinacoteca Municipal Ignacio Merino de la Municipalidad Metropolitana de Lima. Colección Ricardo Palma.

40 Léonce Angrand. *La chichería* (*Woman Selling Chicha*). 1837. Watercolor. 19.3 × 28.5 cm. Paris, Bibliothèque nationale de France.

41 Francisco "Pancho" Fierro. *Cuadrilla de negros festejando el 28 de julio de 1821* (*Group of Blacks Celebrating the 28th of July, 1821*). Undated. Watercolor on paper. 23.3 × 18.2 cm. Lima, Peru, Pinacoteca Municipal Ignacio Merino de la Municipalidad Metropolitana de Lima. Colección Ricardo Palma.

42 *Kumbukumbu: Africa, Memory, and Heritage.* Installation at the National Museum of Brazil/UFRJ, Rio de Janeiro (pre-fire).

43 Augustus Earle. *Capoeira*. 1824. Watercolor. 16.5 × 25.1 cm. Canberra, National Library of Australia. Rex Nan Kivell Collection NK12/103.

44 Johann Moritz Rugendas. *Danse landu* (*Lundu Dance*). 1835. Lithograph. In Rugendas, *Malerische Reise in Brasilien* (*Artistic Travels in Brazil*) (Paris: Englemann & Cie., 1835), plate 96.

45 Unidentified photographer. *The Iyalorixá Eugênia Anna dos Santos (Mãe Aninha)* (*The Iyalorixá Eugênia Anna dos Santos [Mother Aninha]*). Ca. 1890. Photograph. Washington, DC, National Anthropological Archives, Papers of Ruth Schlossberg Landes.

46 Unidentified artist. *Pencas de balangadãs* (*Amulets*). 19th century. Gold and other materials. 41.7 × 7 cm. Vitória, Salvador, Brazil, Carlos Costa Pinto Museum.

47 Augusto Malta. *Casebres no Morro do Santo Antonio* (*Shanties in the Morro de Santo Antonio*). 1914. Photograph. G. Ermakoff Casa Editorial Ltd.

48 Afro-Brazilian objects. Rio de Janeiro, National Museum of Brazil / UFRJ (pre-fire). Xangô figure. Photo courtesy of Arthur Valle, Universidade Federal Rural do Rio de Janeiro.

49 Afro-Brazilian objects. Ca. 1880. Berlin, Ethnological Museum. Wilhelm Pietzker Collection. Photo courtesy of Prof. Dr. Viola König, Freie Universität Berlin.

50 Afro-Brazilian object. Ca. 1880. Berlin, Ethnological Museum. Wilhelm Pietzker Collection. Photo courtesy of Prof. Dr. Viola König, Freie Universität Berlin.

51a Afro-Brazilian object. Ca. 1880. Berlin, Ethnological Museum. Wilhelm Pietzker Collection. Photo courtesy of Prof. Dr. Viola König, Freie Universität Berlin.

51b Afro-Brazilian object. Ca. 1880. Berlin, Ethnological Museum. Wilhelm Pietzker Collection. Photo courtesy of Prof. Dr. Viola König, Freie Universität Berlin.

52 Haitian Vodou Bizango statues and other objects awaiting processing. Photo Sarah Scaturro, © Smithsonian Institution https://www.cooperhewitt.org/2011/08/23/haiti-cultural-recovery-project-part-1/.

53 Haitian Vodou drum, confiscated in 1916. Photograph. Philadelphia, Penn Museum, University of Pennsylvania. Film NC35–21128.

54 Ilê Axé Opô Afonjá Museum, Salvador, Bahia, Brazil.

55 Manuel López López Iodibo. *Desalines* [*sic*]. Engraving. Louis Dubroca, *Vida de J. J. Dessalines, gefe de los Negros de Santo Domingo* (*Life of J. J. Dessalines, Leader of the Negroes of Santo Domingo*) (Mexico: Oficina de D. Mariano de Zúñiga y Ontiveros, 1806). Providence, RI, Brown University, John Carter Brown Library, Archive of Early American Images.

56 José Campeche. *Governor Miguel Antonio de Ustariz*. Ca. 1789–1790. Oil on canvas. 60 × 41.5 cm. San Juan, Instituto de Cultura Puertorriqueña.

57 Juan Jorge Peoli. *The Caretaker*. 1853. Lithograph. *La Revista de La Habana*. Havana, Biblioteca José Martí.

58 Francisco Oller. *The School of Master Rafael Cordero*. 1890–1892. Oil on canvas. 99.1 × 158.8 cm. San Juan, Ateneo Puertorriqueño.

59 Francisco Oller. *El velorio* (*The Wake*). Ca. 1893. Oil on canvas. 2.69 × 4.12 m. San Juan, Museo de Historia, Antropología y Arte de la Universidad de Puerto Rico, Río Piedras.

60 Eduardo Laplante. *Ingenio San José de la Angosta* (*Sugar Mill Owned by Conde de Fernandina in Cuba*). 1857. Lithograph. Justo G. Cantero, *Los ingenios: Colección de vistas de los principales ingenios de azúcar de la Isla de Cuba* (Havana: Litografía de L. Marquier, 1857), 82.

61 Eduardo Laplante. *Casa de calderas del ingenio Asunción* (*Boiler House of the Asunción Sugar Plantation*). Lithograph. Justo G. Cantero, *Los ingenios: Colección de vistas de los principales ingenios de azúcar de la Isla de Cuba* (Havana: Litografía de L. Marquier, 1857), 43.

62 Victor Patricio de Landaluze. *Judith Liberates Cuba from the Separatist Rebellion*. Published in *La Sombra* I, no. 26 (March 29, 1874). Havana, Biblioteca Nacional José Martí.

63 Victor Patricio de Landaluze. *Corte de caña* (*Cutting Sugar Cane*). 1874. Oil on canvas. Havana, Museo Nacional de Bellas Artes de Cuba.

64 Victor Patricio de Landaluze. *Día de Reyes en la Habana* (*Epiphany in Havana*). Early to mid-1870s. Oil on canvas. 51 × 61 cm. Havana, Museo Nacional de Bellas Artes de Cuba.

65 Victor Patricio de Landaluze and Esteban Chartand, after. *Cimarron* (*Runaway Slave*). 1875. Wood engraving. *La Ilustración*

Española y Americana XIX, no. 35 (September 22, 1875). Regenstein Library, University of Chicago.

66 La Charanga de Villergas (cigarette factory). *"Si Me Amas Serás Feliz"* (*"If You Love Me, You Will Be Happy"*). 1860s. Color lithograph. From the series *Vida y muerte de la mulata* (*Life and Death of the Mulata*), no. 4. Havana, Biblioteca Nacional José Martí.

67 La Charanga de Villergas (cigarette factory). *"¿Caridad, Quieres Mecha … Siaa?"* (*"Caridad, Want Me to Light You Up?"*). 1860s. Color lithograph. From the series *Vida y muerte de la mulata* (*Life and Death of the Mulata*), no. 12. Havana, Biblioteca Nacional José Martí.

68 *Álbum formado de cubiertas para cigarrillos de varias marcas de la Habana* (Album of cigarette covers with different Havana brands). 1864. Seville, Spain, Archivo General de Indias.

69 Víctor Patricio de Landaluze. *El ñáñigo* (*Spirit Dancer*). 1881. Lithograph. Antonio Bachiller y Morales, *Tipos y costumbres de la Isla de Cuba* (Havana: Miguel de Villa, [1881]). New York Public Library.

70 C. D. Fredricks. *Cabildo Group Carte de Visite*, Havana. 1860. New York, Schomburg Center for Research in Black Culture, Photographs and Prints Division, The New York Public Library Digital Collections.

71 Torriente. *Úrsula de Valverde,* editor of the Cuban periodical *Minerva* in 1888–1889. Photographic reproduction. *Minerva* (1888). Havana, Instituto de Literatura y Lingüísticas.

72 José Gil de Castro. Reverse of the *Portrait of Manuel Larenas y Álvarez Rubio.* 1829. Oil on canvas. 83 × 63 cm. Santiago, Chile, Museo Histórico Nacional. Reg. no. 3–186. Inv. no. 000760 755.

73 José Francisco Rodríguez. *Vicente Guerrero.* Ca. 1828. Wax. 8 × 6.5 cm. Mexico City, Museo Nacional de Historia, INAH. Morton Subastas.

74 Carlos Guevara. *Juan Álvarez.* 1853. Oil on canvas. 102 × 83 cm. Mexico City, Museo Nacional de Historia, INAH. Wikipedia Commons.

75 Unidentified artist. *José Romero.* Ca. 1850–1865. Oil on canvas. 85.5 × 69 cm. Santiago, Chile, Museo Histórico Nacional. 3–91.

76 Lucio Correa Morales. *Public Monument to Antonio Ruiz ("Falucho").* 1897. Bronze. Buenos Aires, Argentina.

77 Unidentified artist. *Virgin with Donors Don Manuel de Salzes y de Doña Francisca Infante.* 1767. Oil on canvas with gold leaf. 107 × 86 cm. Santiago, Chile, Museo Nacional de Bellas Artes.

78 Juan Lovera. *Lino Gallardo.* 1830. Oil on canvas. Caracas, Venezuela, Galería de Arte Nacional. Wikipedia Commons.

79 Unidentified artist. *Eladia Gallardo.* Ca. 1822. Oil on canvas. 46 × 36 cm. Caracas, Venezuela, Galería de Arte Nacional.

80 Ildefonso Páez. *Micaela Vilela de López, Piura.* 1853. Oil on canvas. 87 × 70 cm. Museo de Arte de Lima. Donation in memory of Manuel López Arrese.

81 Francisco Javier Cortés, attributed. *Juan José Cabezudo ("Comesuelas") and His Friend.* Ca. 1827. Watercolor on paper. 24.6 × 19.4 cm. Museo de Arte de Lima. Gift of Juan Carlos Verme.

82 Courret Studio (Lima). *El vivandero Juan José Cabezudo ("Comesuelas")* (*The Cook Juan José Cabezudo ["Comesuelas"]*). Ca. 1860. From a gelatin silver print. 22 × 18 cm. Lima, Biblioteca Nacional del Perú, Archivo Courret.

83 Courret Studio (Lima). *Francisco "Pancho" Fierro.* Ca. 1870–1879. Gelatin silver print. Lima, Biblioteca Nacional del Perú, Archivo Courret. Wikipedia Commons.

84 Courret Studio (Lima). *Familia Silva* (*The Silva Family*). Ca. 1890. Gelatin silver print. Lima, Biblioteca Nacional del Perú, Archivo Courret.

85 Courret Studio (Lima). *Natalia Paz Soldán.* Ca. 1890. Gelatin silver print. Lima, Biblioteca Nacional del Perú, Archivo Courret.

86 Carlos Raquel Rivera. *El huracán del norte* (*The Hurricane of the North*). 1955. Linocut on paper. 30.8 × 40.6 cm. Boston, Museum of Fine Arts. Gift of anonymous collector to the MFA, 1966. Acc. no. 66.186.

87 Rafael Tufiño. *Carlos Raquel Rivera.* 1957. Oil on wood. 77.2 × 55.9 cm. San Juan, Museo de Arte de Puerto Rico.

88 Ramón Frade. *El pan nuestro* (*Our Daily Bread*). 1905. Oil on canvas. 152.4 × 96.5. San Juan, Instituto de Cultura Puertorriqueña.

89 Unidentified artist. *Los Tres Reyes Magos* (*The Three Kings*). Carved and polychromed wood. Washington, DC, Smithsonian American Art Musueum. 1997.97.0538.

90 Ramón Atiles. *Portrait of José Campeche* (copy of a now-lost self-portrait by Campeche). Undated. Oil on canvas. 100.3 × 80.6 cm. Alpine, NJ, Collection of Mrs. Carmen Ana Unanue.

91 José Campeche y Jordan. *Ex voto of the Holy Family.* Ca. 1809. Oil on wood. 25.7 × 13.1 cm. San Juan, Instituto de Cultura Puertorriqueña.

92 Francisco Oller. *La ceiba de Ponce* (*The Old Ceiba Tree at Ponce*). Ca. 1887–1888. Oil on canvas. 48.9 × 69.2 cm. Ponce, Puerto Rico, Museo de Arte de Ponce. The Luis A. Ferré Foundation, Inc. Accession no. 59.0008.

93 Francisco Oller. *Hacienda Aurora* (*Aurora Sugar Plantation*). 1898–1899. Oil on wood panel. 32 × 55.6 cm. Ponce, Puerto Rico, Museo de Arte de Ponce. The Luis A. Ferré Foundation, Inc. Bequest of Dolores Forteza, widow of Saldana, in memory of Victor Saldana. Accession no. 83.1252.

94 Francisco Oller. *Hacienda La Fortuna* (*La Fortuna Sugar Plantation*). 1885. Oil on canvas. 50.8 × 101.6 cm. New York, Brooklyn Museum. 2012.19.

95 Pío Casimiro Bacener. *Self-Portrait.* 1894. Oil on wood. 30.2 × 24.7 cm. Washington, DC, Smithsonian American Art Museum. 1996.91.12.

96 Unidentified photographer. *Street of the Cross, San Juan de Puerto Rico*. Ca. 1898. Photograph. Trumbull White, *Our New Possessions: A Graphic Account Descriptive and Historical of the Tropical Islands of the Sea…* (Chicago: Star Publishing Co., 1898), vol. II (Puerto Rico).

97 Unidentified photographer. *Confection Vendors of Puerto Rico*. Photograph. Ca. 1898. Trumbull White, *Our New Possessions: A Graphic Account Descriptive and Historical of the Tropical Islands of the Sea…* (Chicago: Star Publishing Co., 1898), vol. II (Puerto Rico).

98 Unidentified photographer. *A Colored Belle of Puerto Rico*. Photograph. Ca. 1898. Trumbull White, *Our New Possessions: A Graphic Account Descriptive and Historical of the Tropical Islands of the Sea…* (Chicago: Star Publishing Co., 1898), vol. II (Puerto Rico).

99 Miguel Pou y Becerra. *A Race of Dreamers (Portrait of Ciquí)*. 1938. Oil on canvas. 87 × 71.1 cm. Ponce, Puerto Rico, Museo de Arte de Ponce. The Luis A. Ferré Foundation, Inc. Accession no. 85.1647.

100 Lorenzo Homar. *Cuarto Concurso de Santeros (Fourth Contest of Santeros)*. 1955. Poster. Silkscreen. 81.3 × 47.9 cm. Event held at San Juan, Ateneo Puertorriqueño, December 16, 1955.

101 Lorenzo Homar. *Pinturas de José Campeche y su taller (Paintings of José Campeche and His Workshop)*. 1959. Poster. Silkscreen. 73.7 × 47.6 cm. San Juan, Universidad de Puerto Rico, Museo de Historia, Antropología y Arte de Río Piedras. Donation of Smith Klein Beecham (GlaxoSmithKline). Accession no. 3.2008.0849.2.

102 Rafael Tufiño. *La plena*. 1967. Poster. Serigraph. 71.4 × 49.4 cm. San Juan, Museo de Arte de Puerto Rico.

103 Rafael Tufiño. *Goyita*. 1953. Oil on masonite. 65.1 × 41 cm. San Juan, Instituto de Cultura Puertorriqueña.

104 Rafael Tufiño. *Majestad negra (Black Majesty)*. 1958. Oil on canvas. 122 × 61 cm. San Juan, Puerto Rico, Collection of the Cooperativa de Seguros Multiples.

105 Jack Delano. *At a Religious Procession in San Juan on Saint John the Baptist Day*. 1946. Photograph.

106 Jack Delano. *Musicians at the Patron Saint's Festivities in the Town of Loíza Aldea*. 1981. Photograph.

107 Arnaldo Roche Rabell. *Tenemos que soñar en azul (We Have to Dream in Blue)*. 1986. Oil on canvas. 213 × 152 cm. Collection of John T. Belk III and Margarita Serapión.

108 Celeste Woss y Gil. *Desnudo (Nude)*. 1941. Oil on canvas. 97 × 50 cm. Santo Domingo, Dominican Republic, Museo de Arte Moderno.

109 Celeste Woss y Gil. *El mercado (The Market)*. 1945. Oil on canvas. 74.9 × 94.5 cm. Santo Domingo, Dominican Republic, Museo de Arte Moderno. Photographer: Mariano Hernández.

110 Angel Botello. *Haitiana (Haitian Woman)*. Ca. 1950. Oil on board. 78.7 × 48.2 cm. Private collection. Photo © Christies Images—Puerto Rican, in copyright.

111 Jaime Colson. *Merengue*. 1938. Oil on board. 52 × 68 cm. Santo Domingo, Dominican Republic, Museo Bellapart.

112 Jaime Colson. *Fiesta en Guachupita (Fiesta in Guachupita)*. 1955. Oil on wood. 100 × 67 cm. Santo Domingo, Dominican Republic, Museo Bellapart.

113 Gilberto Hernández Ortega. *Untitled*. 1976. Oil on canvas. 117 × 88 cm. Santo Domingo, Dominican Republic, Museo Bellapart.

114 Ada Balcácer. *Autorretrato de la joven pintora sin un brazo (Self-Portrait as a Young Painter without an Arm)*. 2005–2010. Mixed media on canvas. Santo Domingo, Dominican Republic, Collection of the artist.

115 Juan Sánchez. *Para Carmen María Colón (For Carmen María Colón)*. 1986. Hand-colored lithograph with collage. From the portfolio Guariquen: Images & Words Rican/structed. 56.5 × 76.2 cm. Washington, DC, Smithsonian American Art Museum. Museum purchase made possible by the Joan Mitchell Foundation. Accession no. 2013.58.1.2. Copyright 1986, Juan Sánchez.

116 Scherezade García. *The Dominican York*. From the series *Island of Many Gods*. 2006. Acrylic, charcoal, ink, and sequins on paper. 76.2 × 57.1 cm. Washington, DC, Smithsonian American Art Museum. Museum purchase made possible by the R. P. Whitty Company and the Cooperating Committee on Architecture. Object number 2013.28.1. © 2006, Scherezade García.

117 Luce Turnier. *Jeune femme endormie (Sleeping Young Woman)*. 1974. Acrylic on masonite. 66 × 101.6 cm. Port-au-Prince, Le Musée d'Art Haïtien.

118 Didier William. *Ezili toujours konnen*. 2015. Ink and collage on panel. 91.4 × 122 cm. Image courtesy of Anna Zorina Gallery.

119 Didier William. *Menm pandan m'ap danse*. 2018. Collage, acrylic, ink, wood carving on panel. 162.6 × 127 cm. Collection of Carole Server. Image courtesy of Anna Zorina Gallery.

120 Florine Démosthène. *Wounds #15*. From the series *The Stories I Tell Myself*. 2018. Collage on paper. 55 × 76 cm. Private collection.

121 Shirley Rufin. *Avant C*. 2009. Black and white photograph, chemically treated. Digital print on Komacel support. 150 × 300 cm.

122 Kelly Sinnapah Mary. *Notebook of No Return to the Native Land*. 2018. Mixed-media textile installation.

123 Kelly Sinnapah Mary. *Notebook of No Return to the Native Land, Alice*. 2018. Mixed-media textile installation.

124 Mafalda Nicolas Mondestin. *Sens dessus dessous dans le frangipanier (Upside Down under the Frangipani)*. From the *Marasa* series. 2016. Mixed media on paper. 35.6 × 43.2 cm. Collection of Xavier Dalencour.

125 Bruno Pédurand. *L'héritage de Cham* (*The Heritage of Ham*). Panel 1. 2008. Oil and nails, details, Bible, etc., on wood. 5 panels. 200 × 50 cm each. Courtesy of the artist.

126 Bruno Pédurand. *L'héritage de Cham* (*The Heritage of Ham*). Panel 2. 2008. Oil and nails, details, Bible, etc., on wood. 5 panels. 200 × 50 cm each. Courtesy of the artist.

127 Bruno Pédurand. *L'héritage de Cham* (*The Heritage of Ham*). Panel 3. 2008. Oil and nails, details, Bible, etc., on wood. 5 panels. 200 × 50 cm each. Courtesy of the artist.

128 Bruno Pédurand. *L'héritage de Cham* (*The Heritage of Ham*). Panel 4. 2008. Oil and nails, details, Bible, etc., on wood. 5 panels. 200 × 50 cm each. Courtesy of the artist.

129 Bruno Pédurand. *L'héritage de Cham* (*The Heritage of Ham*). Panel 5. 2008. Oil and nails, details, Bible, etc., on wood. 5 panels. 200 × 50 cm each. Courtesy of the artist.

130 Ernest Breleur. *Untitled*. From the series *L'origine du monde* (*The Origin of the World*). 2014. Felt on paper. 150 × 150 cm. Copyright Jean-Luc de Lagarigue. Courtesy Maëlle Galerie.

131 Tessa Mars. *Conversation avec Hector H/Conversation with Hector H*. 2015. Acrylic on canvas. 65.3 × 65.3 cm. Collection of Xavier Dalencour.

132 Hector Hyppolite. *Maîtresse Erzulie* (*Mistress Erzulie*). 1945–1948. Oil on masonite. 86 × 57 cm. Port-au-Prince, Musée d'Art Haïtien du Collège St. Pierre.

133 Jean-Ulrick Désert. *Negerhosen2000* (*The Spectacle*). 2000–present. Daily stroll through the main thoroughfare leading to Munich's Marienplatz. 2001. Analogue C-Print. 70 × 100 cm.

134 Jean-Ulrick Désert. *BLING*. 2018. Still from video.

135 Jean-Ulrick Désert. *BLING*. 2018. Still from video.

136 Jean-Marc Hunt. *Balloon*. 2014. Acrylic on canvas. 170 × 150 cm. Guadeloupe, Private collection.

137 Annabel Guérédrat and Henri Tauliaut. *Nus descendant l'escalier, #3* (*Nudes Descending a Staircase, #3*). 2013. Performance video.

138 Annabel Guérédrat and Henri Tauliaut. *Nus descendant l'escalier, #3* (*Nudes Descending a Staircase, #3*). 2013. Performance video.

139 Gwladys Gambie. *Beautiful Monster*. April 2017. Performance. International Festival of Performance Art (FIAP) in Martinique. Co-directed by Annabel Guérédrat and Henri Tauliaut.

140 Gwladys Gambie. *Beautiful Monster*. April 2017. Performance. International Festival of Performance Art (FIAP) in Martinique. Co-directed by Annabel Guérédrat and Henri Tauliaut.

141 Gwladys Gambie. *Beautiful Monster*. April 2017. Performance. International Festival of Performance Art (FIAP) in Martinique. Co-directed by Annabel Guérédrat and Henri Tauliaut.

142 Maksaens Denis. *Nu descendant l'escalier* (*Nude Descending a Staircase*). 2014. Digital photograph printed on cloth. 40 × 60 cm. Private collection. Courtesy of the artist.

143 Cover of the journal *Avance*.

144 Miguel Covarrubias. *Negro Drawings*. 1927. Illustration.

145 Cover of the journal *Amauta*.

146 Pedro Figari. *Candombe*. 1921. Oil on canvas. 73 × 104 cm. Museo de Arte Latinoamericano de Buenos Aires.

147 Pastor Argudín y Pedroso. *Ofrenda* (*Offering*). 1925. Oil on canvas. 111.8 × 86 cm. Boston, Collection of Alejandro de la Fuente and Patricia González.

148 Manuel Ortiz de Zárate. *Pablo Picasso*. 1920–1925. Oil on wood. 41 × 32.7 cm. Paris, Musée Picasso.

149 Victor Manuel García. *Muchacha* (*Young Woman*). 1929. Oil on canvas. 30 × 25 cm. Boston, Collection of Alejandro de la Fuente and Patricia González.

150 María Aranís Valdivia. *La negra* (*Black Woman*). 1931. Oil on canvas. 66 × 54.3 cm. Santiago, Chile, Museo Nacional de Bellas Artes.

151 Carlos Prado. *Batuque*. 1935. Oil on canvas. 80 × 120.7 cm. Pinacoteca do Estado de São Paulo.

152 Ildefonso Pereda Valdés. *El Negro Rioplatense y otros ensayos* (Montevideo, Uruguay: Claudio Garcia & Cla., 1937). Courtesy of the Latin American and Caribbean Collections, George A. Smathers Libraries, University of Florida.

153 Vicente do Rego Monteiro. *O combate* (*Combat*). 1927. Oil on canvas. 130 × 130 cm. Grenoble, France, Musée de Grenoble.

154 Victor Manuel García. *Diablito* (*Little Devil*). 1926. Pencil and crayon on paper. 34 × 25 cm. Havana, Museo Nacional de Bellas Artes de Cuba.

155 Victor Manuel García. *Carnaval* (*Carnival*). 1940s. Oil on canvas. 61 × 49 cm. Coral Gables, Forida, Courtesy of Cernuda Arte.

156 Eduardo Abela. *El triunfo de la rumba* (*The Triumph of the Rumba*). 1928. Oil on canvas. 65 × 54 cm. Havana, Museo Nacional de Bellas Artes de Cuba.

157 Emiliano Di Cavalcanti. *Samba*. 1927. Oil on canvas. 158.5 × 197.5 cm. Montevideo, Uruguay, Collection Latinamerican Art LLC.

158 Antonio Gattorno. *Mujeres junto al rio* (*Women by the River*). 1927. Oil on canvas. 193 × 117 cm. Havana, Museo Nacional de Bellas Artes de Cuba.

159 Tarsila do Amaral. *O vendedor de frutas* (*The Fruit Vendor*). 1925. Oil on canvas. 108.5 × 84.5 cm. Rio de Janeiro, Museu de Arte Moderna (MAM), Gilberto Chateaubriand Collection.

160 Tarsila do Amaral. *A negra* (*Black Woman*). 1923. Oil on canvas. 100 × 82 cm. Museum of Contemporary Art, University of

São Paulo.

161 Antonio Berni. *Manifestación* (*Demonstration*). 1934. Tempera on burlap. 180 × 249.5 cm. Museo de Arte Latinoamericano de Buenos Aires.

162 Tarsila do Amaral. *Operários.* (*Workers*). 1933. Oil on canvas. 150 × 205 cm. Acervo Artístico-Cultural dos Palácios do Governo do Estado de São Paulo.

163 Ignacio Gómez Jaramillo. *La liberación de los esclavos* (*The Freeing of the Slaves*). 1938. Fresco. 344 × 305 cm. Bogotá, Capitolio Nacional de Colombia, Congreso de la Republica de Colombia. Fresco whitewashed soon after completion; uncovered in 1959.

164 Mariano Rodríguez. *Pareja con bueyes* (*Couple with Oxen*). 1939. Oil on canvas. 55 × 50 cm. Aventura, FL, Private collection.

165 Cândido Portinari. *Mestiço* (*Mestizo*). 1934. Oil on canvas. 81 × 65 cm. Pinacoteca do Estado de São Paulo. Purchased by the state of São Paulo, 1935.

166 Cândido Portinari. *Negro com enxada* (*Black Man with a Hoe*). 1934. Oil on canvas. 100 × 81 cm. Museu de Arte de São Paulo Assis Chateaubriand. MASP.00519. Gift of José Maria Whitaker, 1964. Photo by Eduardo Ortega. Painting later renamed *O lavrador de café* (*Coffee Laborer*).

167 Alberto da Veiga Guignard. *Os noivos* (*The Engaged Couple*). 1937. Oil on wood. 58 × 48 cm. Rio de Janeiro, Museus Castro Maya, Ibram/Minc. Photographer Jaime Acioli.

168 Alberto da Veiga Guignard. *A familia do fuzileiro naval* (*The Marine's Family*). Ca. 1935. Oil on wood. 58 × 48 cm. Instituto de Estudos Brasileiros, Universidade da São Paulo.

169 Alberto Peña (Peñita). *Trabajadores* (*Workers*). 1934. Oil on canvas. 144 × 128 cm. Havana, Museo Nacional de Bellas Artes de Cuba.

170 Alberto Peña (Peñita). *Cuba en marcha* (*Cuba on the March*). 1936. Oil on burlap. 114 × 87 cm. Coral Gables, FL, Cernuda Arte.

171 Alberto Peña (Peñita). *La llamada del ideal, o Marti* (*The Calling of the Ideal, or Martí*). 1936. Oil on canvas. 95 × 81 cm. Havana, Museo Nacional de Bellas Artes de Cuba.

172 Lasar Segall. *Mãe preta* (*Black Mother*). 1930. Oil on canvas. 73 × 60 cm. Private collection.

173 Teodoro Ramos Blanco. *Vida interior* (*Interior Life*). 1934. Marble. 30 × 17 × 23.5 cm. Havana, Museo Nacional de Bellas Artes de Cuba.

174 Francisco Narváez. *Cabeza de negro* (*Head of a Black Man*). 1935. Carved ebony. 50.8 × 22.9 × 22.2 cm. Location unknown. Formerly New York, Phillips. Sale: *Latin American Art*. Estate of Francisco Narvaéz, November 22, 2016, lot 22.

175 Teodoro Ramos Blanco. *Antonio Maceo*. 1950s. Bronze on green marble base. 25 × 15 × 8 cm. Boston, Collection of Alejandro de la Fuente and Patricia González.

176 Lasar Segall. *Bananal* (*Banana Grove*). 1927. Oil on canvas. 87 × 127 cm. Pinacoteca do Estado de São Paulo. Purchased by the state of São Paulo, 1928.

177 Lasar Segall. *Morro vermelho* (Red Hill). 1926. Oil on canvas. 115 × 95 cm. São Paulo, Private collection. Photo: Isabella Matheus.

178 J. Carlos, cover of the periodical *Para Todos* (May 28, 1927).

179 Unidentified photographer. *The Millers*. 1964. Published in *The Gleaner* and at the National Gallery of Jamaica Blog. Kingston, National Gallery of Jamaica.

180 David Pottinger. *Nine Night*. 1949. Oil. Kingston, National Gallery of Jamaica.

181 Alvin Marriott. *Banana Man*. 1955. Wood. Kingston, National Gallery of Jamaica.

182 David Miller, Jr. *Girl Surprised*. 1949. Wood. Kingston, National Gallery of Jamaica.

183 Héctor Hyppolite. *Le Grand Maître* (*The Grand Master*). 1947. Oil on cardboard. 94 × 64 cm. Port-au-Prince, Musée d'Art Haïtien du Collège St. Pierre.

184 Rigaud Benoit. *Ceremonie sous le mapou* (*Ceremony under the Mapou Tree*). 1971. Oil on masonite. 60.4 × 50.2 cm. Private collection. Photo © Christies Images - Haitian. Sold November 24, 1993.

185 Emiliano Augusto Cavalcanti de Albuquerque e Melo (Di Cavalcanti). *Pescadores* (*Fishermen*). Ca. 1949–1950. Oil on canvas. 74 × 101.3 cm. Private collection.

186 Emiliano Augusto Cavalcanti de Albuquerque e Melo (Di Cavalcanti). *Candangos* (*People of Brasilia*). 1960. Oil on canvas. 283 × 881 cm. Brasilia, Palace of the Congress, Chamber of the Deputies.

187 Clóvis Graciano. *Dança de bandeirolas* (*Flag Dancers*). 1943. Tempera on canvas. 57 × 46.5 cm. Museu de Arte Contemporânea da Universidade de São Paulo. Doação Francisco Matarazzo Sobrinho. 1963.1.328.

188 Djanira da Motta e Silva. *Candomblé*. 1957. Tempera on wood. 250 × 243 cm. Salvador, Bahia, Brazil, Banco Itaú. Photo: Iara Venanzi.

189 José Medeiros. *Iniciaço de uma filha de santo num terreiro de Candomblé* (*Initiation of a Daughter of a Priest in the Candomblé Precinct*). 1957. Photograph. Museu de Arte Moderna do Rio de Janeiro. Gift of the artist.

190 Wifredo Lam. *Le bruit* (*Rumor*). 1943. Paris, Musée national d'art moderne/Centre de creation industrielle Centre Georges Pompidou. Gift of the French State. Copyright estate of Wifredo Lam/SODRAC (2007).

191 Wifredo Lam. *La fiancée de Kiriwina* (*The Fiancée of Kiriwina*). 1949. Oil on canvas. 124 × 109 cm. Saint-Paul de Vence, France, Fondation Maeght.

192 René Portocarrero. *Brujo de carnaval (Carnival Sorcerer)*. 1945. Mixed media on board laid down on canvas. 93 × 70 cm. Private collection.

193 Lucien Price. *Étude no. 6: Masques (Study No. 6: Masks)*. 1947. Pendiente Collection.

194 Wifredo Lam. *La jungla (The Jungle)*. 1943. Gouache on paper mounted on canvas. 239.4 × 229.9 cm. New York, Museum of Modern Art. Inter-American Fund. 140.1945

195 Rubem Valentim. *Composição no. 5. (Composition No. 5)*. 1953. Oil on wood. 40 × 40 cm. Museu de Arte Contemporânea da Universidade de São Paulo.

196 Albert Mangonès. *Le nègre marron inconnu de Saint-Domingue (The Unknown Fugitive Slave of Saint-Domingue)*. 1967. Bronze. Length: 3.6 m. Height: 2.4 m. Port-au-Prince, Haiti, Champs-du-Mars.

197 José Moreira Matos. *Pillory*. 1750. Dismantled in 1871, rebuilt in 1981, after project of José Wasth Rodrigues, 1938. Mariana, Brazil, Minas Gerais Square.

198 Laurent Valère. *Cap 110*. 1998. Fifteen reinforced concrete statues. Anse Caffard, Le Diamant, Martinique.

199 Francisco Cafferata. *La esclavitud (Slavery)*. 1881. Bronze. Buenos Aires, Argentina, Sicily Square, Parque 3 de Febrero.

200 Alberto Lescay. *Monumento al cimarrón (Monument to the Runaway Slave)*. 1997. Iron and bronze. Height: 9.6 m. Santiago de Cuba, Loma del Cimarrón.

201 Alicia Tafur. *La Negra del chontaduro (Black Woman of the Fruit of the Peach Palm)*. 1992. Bronze. 1.6 × 1.6 m. Santiago de Cali, Colombia.

202 Jose Resende. *Venus/"Negona" (Venus/"Big Black Woman")*. 1991. Photograph by Miguel Rio Branco. Rio de Janeiro, Collection Paul Fernandes.

203 Edna Manley. *Negro Aroused*. Posthumously cast, 1991. Bronze. Kingston, Jamaica, intersection of Ocean Boulevard and King Street. AFP Photo/Mladen Antonov.

204 Neusa Morais. *Monumento a Goiânia (Monument to Goiânia)*, popularly known as *Monumento às três raças (Monument to the Three Races)*. 1968. Bronze and granite. 700 × 310 × 470 cm. Goiânia, Brazil, Dr. Pedro Ludovico Teixeira Square (formerly Civic Square).

205 Salvador Riveira Cardona. *Monumento a las raíces puertorriqueñas (Monument to the Puerto Rican Roots)*. 1992–1993. Bronze figures on masonry base. Dorado, Puerto Rico, Plaza de Recreo.

206 Enrique Moret Astruells. *Monumento al esclavo rebelde (Monument to the Slave Revolt)*. 1976. Bronze. Matanzas, Cuba, Triunvirato.

207 Karl Broodhagen. *Emancipation Statue*. Unveiled in 1985. Bronze. Bridgetown, Barbados.

208 Philip Moore. *1763 Monument*. Unveiled in 1976. Bronze. 4.57 m, including base. Five bronze plaques mounted on base. Georgetown, Guyana, Square of the Revolution.

209 Nel Simon. *Desenkadená (Unchained)*. 1998. Bronze, figures over lifesize. Willemstad, Curaçao, Parke di Lucha pa Libertat.

210 Unidentified photographer. *Residents playing traditional music in the street, June 1, 2013, Monument to Benkos Biohó*. 1998. Cartagena, Colombia, San Basilio de Palenque.

211 Erasmo Vásquez Lendechy. *El Yanga (The Yanga)*. Dedicated 1973–1976. Bronze, marble. Veracruz, Mexico, Yanga Park.

212 Laura Facey. *Redemption Song*. 2003. Bronze, cast iron. Height: ca. 3 m. Kingston, Jamaica, Emancipation Park.

213 José Belloni. *Monumento a Ansina (Joaquín Lenzina). (Monument to Ansina [Joaquín Lenzina])*. Unveiled in 1943. Bronze, granite. Montevideo, Uruguay, Rambla Republica Argentina.

214 Deoscóredes Maximiliano dos Santos (Mestre Didi). *Ôpa n'Ílé: Ceptro (Cetro) da terra (Ôpa n'Ílé: Scepter of the Earth)*. 1997. Polyester resin. 320 × 200 × 80 cm. Salvador, Brazil, Museu de Arte Moderna da Bahia.

215 Rubem Valentim. *Marco sincrético da cultura afro-brasileira (Syncretic Symbol of Afro-Brazilian Culture)*. 1978. Reinforced concrete. Height: 8.2 m. São Paulo, Praça da Sé.

216 Darcy Ribeiro (conception); Romeu Alves (head, after 14th- to-15th-century Ife bronze); João Filgueiras Lima (base). *Zumbi dos Palmares*. 1986. Bronze and concrete. Height: 3 m (head). Rio de Janeiro, June 11 Square.

217 Jeannette Ehlers, La Vaughn Belle. *I Am Queen Mary (Mary Thomas)*. Unveiled in 2018. Bronze figure and plaque, plinth incorporating coral stones from St. Croix, Virgin Islands. Height: ca. 7 m. Copenhagen, Denmark, Langelinie Promenade, West Indian Warehouse.

218 Edouard Duval-Carrié. *Rétable des neuf esclaves (Altar to the Nine Slaves)*. 1992. Oil on canvas. Central Panel: 200 × 180 cm. Two side panels: 140 × 120 cm each; nine small panels depicting Haitian boat migrants: 60 × 60 cm each. Little Haiti, Miami, Collection of the artist.

219 Alex Burke. *Les otages (The Spirit of the Caribbean)*. 1999. Forty-seven dolls made of various fabrics and other materials. Dimensions variable. Paris, Collection of the artist.

220 Leah Gordon. *Mulâtre (Mulatto Woman)*. From the *Caste* series. 2010. One of nine black-and-white photographs. London, Riflemaker Gallery.

221 Kathleen Hawkins. *Plantation Workers on Their Way Home*. Undated. Watercolor. 34.4 × 25.5 cm. St. Michael, National Art Collection of Barbados & the Barbados Gallery of Art.

222 Golde White. *Black Man in a Cap*. Undated. Oil on canvas. 50 × 40 cm. Washington, DC, Private collection.

223 Edna Manley. *Eve.* 1929. Mahogany. 198.5 × 86 × 60 cm. Sheffield, England, Graves Art Gallery. Gift, 1937. VIS.2749.

224 Ronald Moody. *Midonz (Goddess of Transmutation).* 1937. Elm wood. 69 × 38 × 49.5 cm. London, Tate Britain. Purchased 2010. T3324.

225 Osmond Watson. *Peace and Love.* 1969. Kingston, National Gallery of Jamaica.

226 Albert Huie. *The History Lesson.* 1943. Kingston, Jamaica, Private collection, Judy Ann MacMillan.

227 Karl Broodhagen. *Patricia.* Undated. Terracotta. Height: 43.2 cm. Collection of the artist.

228 Hector Hyppolite. *Magique noir (Black Magic).* Ca. 1946–1947. Oil on board. 64.8 × 95.3 cm. Wisconsin, Milwaukee Art Museum. Gift of Richard and Erna Flagg. M1991.127.

229 Mallica "Kapo" Reynolds. *Revival Goddess Dina.* Ca. 1968. Lignum vitae. Height: 78.7 cm. Kingston, National Gallery of Jamaica.

230 Ivan Payne. *Maube Seller.* Undated. Mahogany. Height: 37.6.cm. Kingston, Jamaica, Private collection.

231 Honoré Chosrova. *Séance.* 1988. Location unknown. Reproduced in *La peinture en Martinique,* ed. Gerry L'Étang, Renée-Paule Yung-Hing (Fort de France: Conseil Regional de Martinique, HC Editions, 2007), 241.

232 Christopher Gonzáles. *Mountain Head (Woman of Zion).* 1980. Kingston, Jamaica, Collection of Mrs. Sheila Graham.

233 Maxwell Taylor. *Love and Responsibility.* 1997. Woodcut. 121.9 × 91.4 cm. The Bahamas, The Dawn Davies Collection.

234 Khokho (Joseph Sainte-Croix René-Corail). *Untitled.* 1963. Location unknown. Reproduced in *La peinture en Martinique,* ed. Gerry L'Étang, Renée-Paule Yung-Hing (Fort de France: Conseil Regional de Martinique, HC Editions, 2007), 241.

235 Stanley Greaves. *The Annunciation.* From the series *There's a Meeting Here Tonight.* 1993. Barbados National Art Gallery.

236 Everald Brown. *Victory over Satan.* 1968. Jamaica, Private collection.

237 Karl Parboosingh. *Ras Smoke 1.* 1972. Kingston, National Gallery of Jamaica.

238 Ras Ishi Butcher. *Blazin 1.* 2003–2004. Mixed media. 121 × 152.4 cm. Barbados, Collection of Crawford Billings Associates.

239 Georges Liautaud. *Danbala.* Ca. 1959. Cut and forged metal. 66.36 × 31.43 cm. Wisconsin, Milwaukee Art Museum. Gift of Richard and Erna Flagg. M1991.168.

240 Brent Malone. *Junkanoo Ribbons.* 1984. Oil on canvas. 84 × 76 cm. Kingston, National Gallery of Jamaica. Estate of R. Brent Malone. Image courtesy of Roland Rose and the National Art Gallery of The Bahamas.

241 Barrington Watson. *Mother and Child.* 1958. Oil on canvas. Kingston, National Gallery of Jamaica.

242 Alexandre Bertrand. *Untitled.* Undated. Oil on canvas. Private collection. Reproduced in *La peinture en Martinique,* ed. Gerry L'Étang, Renée-Paule Yung-Hing (Fort de France: Conseil Regional de Martinique, HC Editions, 2007).

243 Boscoe Holder. *Untitled Male Nude.* Undated. Oil on canvas. 63.5 × 49 cm. Reproduced courtesy of Christian Holder, the Artist's Estate/VW (VeneKlasen/Werner), Berlin.

244 Aubrey Williams. *Revolt.* 1960. Oil on canvas. 134.5 × 166.5 cm (frame). Georgetown, Guyana, The National Gallery of Art, Castellani House. Photo Georgetown, Guyana, The National Gallery of Art, Castellani House. Copyright Estate of Aubrey Williams. All rights reserved, DAC 2013.

245 LeRoy Clarke. *In the Maze, There Is a Single Line to My Soul.* 1986. Port of Spain, Trinidad, Estate of the artist.

246 Omari Ra. *Bois Caiman's Foreign Policy: Retro Reconstruction Globe Shrugged.* 2006. Mixed media on cloth. Two panels, 256.5 × 147 cm each; two panels, 241 × 121 cm each. Kingston, Jamaica, Collection of the artist.

247 Christopher Cozier. *The Castaway.* From the series *Tropical Night.* Late 2005–ongoing. Drawings. Ink, rubber stamps, and graphite. 22.9 × 17.8 cm each. Image courtesy of the artist.

248 Albert Chong. *Seated Presence.* From the *Throne Series.* 1990. Silver gelatin print. Colorado, Collection of the artist. Photo courtesy of the artist.

249 Joscelyn Gardner. *Veronica frutescens (Mazerine).* From the series *Creole Portraits.* 2009. Hand-painted stone lithograph on frosted mylar. 91.4 × 61 cm. Photo courtesy of the artist.

250 Roberta Stoddart. *Earl.* From the series *In the Flesh.* 2006. Port of Spain, Trinidad, Private collection.

251 Ebony G. Patterson. *Di Real Big Man.* 2010. Mixed media. Hand-embellished photo tapestry with garlands on wallpaper. Variable dimensions. Kingston, National Gallery of Jamaica. Image courtesy of the artist and Monique Meloche Gallery.

252 Wilson Tibério. *Massacre na Africa do Sul (Massacre in South Africa).* Oil on canvas. 44 × 127 cm. Paris, Estate of the artist.

253 Abdias do Nascimento. *O cavalo e o santo: Yemanjá (The Horse and the Saint: Yemanjá).* 1975. Acrylic on canvas. 102 × 152 cm. The State University of New York at Buffalo, IPEAFRO Collection.

254 Ruben Galloza. *Afro-Uruguay.* Mural. Montevideo, Asociación Cultural y Social Uruguay Negro (Afro-Uruguayan Social and Cultural Association, ACSUN).

255 Heriberto Cuadrado Cogollo. *El hombre de mañana (The Man of Tomorrow).* 1970. Digital scan provided by Alejandro de la Fuente.

256 Niobe Xandó. *Black Power I*. 1970. Serigraph. 100 × 70 cm. São Paulo, Museu de Arte Moderna.

257 Manuel Mendive. *Babalú Ayé*. 1967. Mixed media on wood. 121 × 151 cm. No longer exists.

258 Rafael Queneditt Morales. *Oyá*. 1970. Copper engraving. 25.4 × 15.2 cm. Location unknown.

259 Esteban Ayala, designer. *Grupo Antillano*. 1980. Exhibition poster.

260 Emanoel Araújo. *A mão afro-brasileira* (*The Afro-Brazilian Touch*). 1988. Poster for the eponymous exhibition curated by Araújo.

261 Juan Roberto Diago. *Un pedazo de mi historia* (*A Piece of My History*). From the series *Aquí lo que no hay es que morirse* (*Here What You Can't Do Is Die*). 2003. Mixed media on metal. 198.1 × 149.9 cm. Boston, Collection of Alejandro de la Fuente and Patricia González.

262 Javier Mojica Madera. *Yo soy Babalú* (*I Am Babalú*). 2006. Digital photograph. Antioquia, Colombia, Museum. Donated 2013.

263 Eustáquio Neves. From the series *Boa aparência* (*Good Appearance*). 2005. Photography, mixed media.

264 Firelei Báez. *Can I Pass? Introducing the Paper Bag to the Fan Test for the Month of June*. 2011. Gouache, ink, and graphite on paper. 325.1 × 243.8 cm (overall). Pleasanton, CA, Collection of Tad Freese. Courtesy of the artist and James Cohan, New York.

265 René Peña. *Untitled*. 1994. Gelatin silver print. 40.4 × 49.8 cm. Boston, Collection of Alejandro de la Fuente and Patricia González.

266 Armando Mariño. *Gozando de la libertad* (*Enjoying Freedom*). 2002. Oil on canvas. 179 × 218.4 cm. Boston, Collection of Alejandro de la Fuente and Patricia González.

267 Rosana Paulino. From *Bastidores* (*Embroidery Hoops* series). 1997. Mixed media: photographic image transferred to fabric, mounted on embroidery hoop.

268 María Magdalena Campos-Pons. *Untitled*. From the series *When I Am Not Here/Estoy Allá*. 1994. Photograph (made from Polaroid Polacolor Pro 24 × 20 in. film plates). 61 × 51 cm. Boston, Collection of Alejandro de la Fuente and Patricia González.

269 Elio Rodríguez Valdés. *Tropicalísima* (*Very Tropical*). 2007. Silkscreen illuminated on paper. Edition of 10. 80 × 100 cm.

270 Nelson Fory. From the series ¡*La historia nuestra, caballero!* (*Our History, Sir!*). 2011. Photograph of the artist's intervention with a monument of white authority in Cartagena, Colombia.

271 Alexis Esquivel. *Picnic nacional* (*National Picnic*). 1996. Oil on canvas. 150 × 200 cm. Boston, Collection of Alejandro de la Fuente and Patricia González.

272 June Beer. *Black Sandino*. 1983. Oil on canvas. Private collection.

273 Douglas Pérez. *La academia* (*The Academy*). 2016. Oil on canvas. 50 × 70 cm. Boston, Collection of Alejandro de la Fuente and Patricia González.

274 Image of Vybz Kartel that circulated on social media, September 2017. Image from author.

275 Alexander Dudgeon Gulland. *Victims of the Jamaica Rebellion of 1865*. 1865. Albumen photograph. From *Photography album documenting the Morant Bay rebellion in Jamaica (1865), the Indian Northwest Frontier Hazara Campaign (1867–1870), views of Malta, Ireland, Guernsey, Spain, and Elsewhere*. Princeton, NJ, Graphic Arts Collection, (GAX) 2009–0016E, Department of Rare Books and Special Collections, Princeton University Library, p. 45 (online pagination).

276 Alexander Dudgeon Gulland. *Natives of Jamaica*. 1865. Albumen photograph. From *Photography album documenting the Morant Bay rebellion in Jamaica (1865), the Indian Northwest Frontier Hazara Campaign (1867–1870), views of Malta, Ireland, Guernsey, Spain, and Elsewhere*. Princeton, NJ, Graphic Arts Collection, (GAX) 2009–0016E, Department of Rare Books and Special Collections, Princeton University Library, p. 45 (online pagination).

277 Unidentified photographer. *Paul Bogle (often identified as)*. Undated. Tintype (reproduction). Kingston, National Library of Jamaica.

278 Paul Anthony Smith. *Port Antonio Market #3*. 2013. Unique picotage on inkjet print with spray paint mounted on museum board. 78.1 × 52.7 cm. (framed). Private collection. © Paul Anthony Smith. Courtesy of the artist and Jack Shainman Gallery, New York.

279 Ebony G. Patterson. *Untitled Lightz 1*. 2013. Mixed media on paper. 205.7 × 375.9 cm. Kansas City, Missouri, Collection of Bill and Christy Gautreaux. Courtesy of the artist and Monique Meloche Gallery.

280 Andrea Chung. *Bleach*. 2008. Bleached digital print. 63.5 × 86.8 cm. Collection of the artist.

281 Leasho Johnson. *Back-fi-a-bend*. 2015. Paper and yeast paste on wall. Kingston, Jamaica. Photograph by the artist.

282 Oneika Russell. *Notes to You*. 2014. Installation. Devon House, Kingston, Jamaica.

283 Camille Chedda. *Wholesale Degradables*. 2014–2015. Acrylic on disposable plastic bags.

284 Detail. Camille Chedda. *Wholesale Degradables*. 2014–2015. Acrylic on disposable plastic bags.

285 Unidentified artist. *Zemi* (Taíno effigy figure, from Hispaniola). Back view. Ca. 1510–1515. Shell beads and other materials. Rome, Museo Nazionale Preistorico ed Etnografico "Luigi Pigorini." Photo: Rome, Archivo Fotografico del Museo Preistorico Etnografico Luigi Pigorini.

286 Geoffrey Holder. *Self-Portrait*. Ca. 1945. Bridgetown, Barbados Museum & Historical Society.

287 Boscoe Holder. *Mother*. 1938. Boscoe Holder Estate. Reproduced courtesy of Christian Holder.

288 Boscoe Holder. *Carnival Costume*. 1993. Acrylic on canvas. Mahwah, Ramapo College of New Jersey, Morris/Svehla Collection.

289 Hervé Télémaque. *Toussaint Louverture in New York*. 1960. Oil on canvas. 177 × 195 cm. Dole du Jura, France, Musée des Beaux-Arts.

290 Maxwell Taylor. *Inhibited*. 1978. New York, Collection of the Bob Blackburn Printmaking Workshop.

291 Mavis Pusey. *Frozen Vibration*. 1968. Color screen print. 83.8 × 57.8 cm. New York, Collection of the Bob Blackburn Printmaking Workshop.

292 Carl Van Vechten. *Namba Roy*. 1934. Gelatin silver print. 24.2 × 17.6 cm. Miami Beach, The Wolfsonian–Florida International University. Gift of Daniel Morris. 2019.2.29.

293 Namba Roy. *Accompong Madonna*. Ca. 1958. Plastic wood. Height: 53.3 cm. Kingston, National Gallery of Jamaica. Gift of the Maroons of Accompong, 1981.

294 Aubrey Williams. *Visual Idea*. 1963. Oil on canvas. Location unknown. Image credit: The known image of this was taken by Rasheed Araeen and is image #39.3 in Kwesi Owusu, ed., *Black British Culture and Society: A Text Reader* (London: Routledge, 2000).

295 Eugene Palmer. *Index*. 1993. Oil on canvas. 213 × 152 cm. Private collection.

296 Sonia Boyce. *She Ain't Holdin' Them Up, She's Holdin' On (Some English Rose)*. 1986. Crayon, chalk, pastel, and ink on paper. 218 × 99 cm. England, Middlesborough Institute of Modern Art.

297 Denis Williams. *Pauline, 1970*. 1973–1974. Tempera on canvas on plywood. 60 × 60 cm. Courtesy Williams Estate.

298 Gilles Elie-Dit-Cosaque. *Twinkl/Zétwal* (*Stars*). 2009. Film. 52 min.

299 Winston Patrick. *Youth*. 1973. Kingston, National Gallery of Jamaica.

300 Renee Cox. *River Queen*. From the series *Queen Nanny of the Maroons*. 2004–2005. Digital inkjet print on watercolor paper. Edition of 5. 106.7 × 106.7 cm. (image); 111.8 × 111.8 cm. (sheet).

301 Visual documentation of LeRoy Clarke's residency at the Studio Museum in Harlem. Early 1970s. Most concern his preparation for his exhibition at SMH in 1972.

302 Nari Ward. *Happy Smilers: Duty Free Shopping*. 1996. Installation. Awning, soda bottles, fire hose, fire escape, salt, household elements, audio recording, speakers, and aloe vera plant. Variable dimensions. Image credit: Image courtesy of the artist and Lehmann Maupin NY and Hong Kong.

303 Peter Minshall. *Mancrab on Dimanche Gras Night*. 1990. Video still from Carnival performance. Photo credit: Mark Lyndersay.

304 Marcel Pinas. *Sanfika*. 2009. Installation. Several thousand suspended spoons, each engraved with an Afaka sign from the language of the artist's birthplace. 250 × 1000 cm. Image courtesy of the artist.

305 Ebony G. Patterson. *Daadi + Yutez*. 2010. Mixed media. Photo tapestry with glitter, appliqués, rhinestones, trimming, clothing, toys, and ratchet. Variable dimensions. Private collection. Image courtesy of the artist and Monique Meloche Gallery.

306 Miguel Luciano. *Plátano Pride*. 2006. Chromogenic photograph. 101.6 × 76.2 cm. New York, Brooklyn Museum. Gift of the artist. 2008.15.

307 Alexandre Arrechea. *The Weight of Emptiness*. 2005. Digital media. Edition of 3, and artist's proof. Height: 63.5 cm.

308 April Bey. *By the Grace of the Grand Nagus*. 2018. Ghanaian Hitarget Chinese fabric sewn into resin on panel, acrylic paint. 76.2 × 61 cm. Private collection. Image courtesy of the artist.

309 Lavar Munroe. *Floater* (study). 2011. Graphite drawing, acrylic paint, pearls, copper, and 24k gold leaf on cut paper. 45.7 × 34.9 cm. The Bahamas, The Dawn Davies Collection. Image courtesy of Jackson Petit from Nassau, The National Art Gallery of the Bahamas.

310 Joscelyn Gardner. *Coffee Arabica* (*Clarissa*). 2011. Hand-colored stone lithograph on frosted mylar. Photo credit: John Tamblyn.

311 Tavares Strachan. *Blast Off*. 2008–2009. Video of glass rocket launched with sugarcane fuel. Exhibited, Venice Biennale, 2013.

INDEX

Page numbers in italics indicate illustrations.

Abela, Eduardo, 248, 266, 269, 271, 274
    La Comparsa, 316
    The Mystical Rooster, 269
    The Triumph of the Rumba, 269, *270*, 316
Aching, Gerard, 412
Acosta, José Julián, 178
Adandozan, king of Dahomey, 103
Africa, 15–19, 22, 109, 213, 302, 304–5, 308, 314, 323–30, 370, 375–76, 379, 386, 388, 429–31, 434, 437, 441–42, 447
Afro-Brazilian objects, *115–19*
Agassiz, Louis, 453
Agostini, Angelo, 27
    Back from Paraguay, 47, *48*
album of cigarette covers with different Havana brands, *143*, 144
Alet, Thierry, 376
Alexis, Gérald, 215
Allegory of Charles IV and the Spanish Empire (unidentified artist), 79
Alvarez, Candida, 492
Álvarez, Juan, 152
Alvarez Bravo, Armando, 277
Alves, Romeu, *Zumbi dos Palmares* (with Darcy Ribeiro and João Filgueiras Lima), 368, *369*, 370
Amado, Jorge, *Gabriela, Clove and Cinnamon*, 316
Amaral, Tarsila do. *See* Tarsila do Amaral
Amaru, Túpac, 330
Amauta (journal), cover of, *254*
Americo, Pedro, *Battle of Avaí*, 75, *76–77*
Amigo, Roberto, 56
amulets, 111, *111*
Anderson, Hurvin, 504
Anderson, Marian, 507
Andrade, Mário de, 123, 247, 250, 271
Andrade, Oswald de, 247, 248, 255, 281, 285, 300
Andreu, Enrique, 289
Angel, Félix, 380
Angola, 16, 17, 18
Angola, Mercedes, 442
Angrand, Léonce, 96, 101
    Woman Selling Chicha, 96, *99*
Anicet, Victor, 220
Aninha, Mãe. *See* Santos, Eugênia Anna dos
Anjos, Jorge dos, *Portal of Memory*, 366
Anthony, Michael, 503
Antoni, Janine, 512
Anzinger, Deborah, 528
Appiah, Kwame Anthony, 522
Araeen, Rasheed, 503
Aranda-Alvarado, Rocío, 240
Aranís Valdivia, María, *Black Woman*, 262, *263*
Araújo, Emanoel, 430, 441–42
    The Afro-Brazilian Touch, 441, *442*
Araújo, Octávio, 430
Archer, Petrine, 507
Arenas, Manuel, 444
Argentina, 53, 56, 61–62, 84, 339, 343, 361, 363
Argudín y Pedroso, Pastor, *Offering*, *258*, 259
Arozarena, Marcelino, 250
Arrechea, Alexandre, 523
    The Weight of Emptiness, *525*
Arredondo, Esteban, 161
Arrieta, José Agustín, *Young Man from the Coast*, 90, *91*
Artigas, José Gervasio, 363
Art Students League, New York, 485–87, 489, 490, 492
Asturias, Miguel Angel, 253, 255
Atiles, Ramón, *Portrait of José Campeche* (copy), *176*, 177
Atteck, Sybil, 399
    Panmen, 399
Auguiac-Célénice, Johanna, 222
Avance (journal), cover of, *249*
Awai, Nicole, 515
Ayala, Esteban, *Grupo Antillano* exhibition poster, 441, *441*

Ayón, Belkis, 516, 521
Azevedo Sérgio, Wilson de, 431
Azuela, Mariano, 253, 254

Bacener, Pío Casimiro, 183
  Self-Portrait, 183, *185*
Bachiller y Morales, Antonio, *Tipos y costumbres de la Isla de Cuba*, 269
Báez, Firelei, 522
  Can I Pass? Introducing the Paper Bag to the Fan Test for the Month of June, 446, *447*
  Ciguapa series, 522
  Sans-Souci, 522
Bahamas, 15, 375, 489
Bahia, 19
Bailey, David A., 516
Balanta Rodriguez, Beatriz, 95
Balcácer, Ada, 199, 208
  Self-Portrait as a Young Painter without an Arm, *207*, 208
Baldorioty de Castro, Ramón, 178
Balla (Black Maroon chief), 353
Ballester, Diógenes, 492
Ballesteros Páez, María Dolores, 152
Barbados, 18, 375
Barbary Coast, 15
Barbusse, Henri, 255
Barnes, Natasha, 465
Barnet, Will, 486, 490
Barreto, Lima, 250
Barthé, Richmond, 383
Basarás, Joaquín Antonio de, 69
Baskin, Leonard, 489, 490
Basquiat, Jean-Michel, 418
Bastide, Roger, 29
Batista, Fulgencio, 303
Beadle, John, 516
Bearden, Romare, 490, 492
Beauchamp, Theubet de, *View of Mexico Square, September 16, 1827*, 69, *70–71*
Bedia, José, 523
Beer, June, *Black Sandino*, 447, *455*
Beinart, Julian, 506
Bell, Vanessa, 383
Belle, La Vaughn, *I Am Queen Mary (Mary Thomas)* [with Jeannette Ehlers], 372, *373*
Belloni, José, *Monument to Ansina (Joaquín Lenzina)*, *362*, 363, 371
Benítez, Marimar, 172, 189
Benítez-Rojo, Antonio, 399

Benoit, Rigaud, *Ceremony under the Mapou Tree*, 312, *313*
Benson, LeGrace, 359
Bérard, Évremond Auguste Léopold de, 214
Bernabé, Jean, 212, 221–22
Berni, Antonio, 277
  Demonstration, 277, *278*
  Small Farmers, 277
  Unemployed, 277
Berthet, Dominique, 214
Bertrand, Alexandre, *Untitled*, 405, *409*
Best, Stephen, 465
Bettelheim, Judith, 144
Bey, April, 523
  By the Grace of the Grand Nagus, *526*
Bhabha, Homi K., 302
Bight of Benin, 17, 19, 109
Bight of Biafra, 17, 19
Biohó, Benkos, 334, 358, 359
Biquiba Guarany, Francisco, 430
Blaaker, Carlos Henny, 492
Blackburn, Robert "Bob," 490, 492
Black Christ (unidentified artist), 336
Black over White (unidentified artist), *73*, 73
Blades, Lillian, 523
Blanes, Juan Manuel, 75
  The Conquest of the Desert, *82–83*, 84
Boclé, Jean-François, 507
Boghossian, Alexander "Skunder," 507
Bogle, Paul, 462, 464, 475
Bolívar, Simón, 43, 45, 47, 69, 150
Bolivia, 75
Bomfim, Manoel, 248
Boni, Doménico, 363
Bornó, Louis, 216
Borno, Maurice, 217
Bosch, Juan, 172
Botana, Natalio, 277
Botello, Angel, 204–5
  Haitian Woman, *202*, 204
Botello, Juan, 24
  The Pinetree Forest, 24
Boti, Regino, 250
Bowling, Frank, 497, 500, 504
  Night Journey, 500
Boxer, David, 304, 305, 376
Boyce, Sonia, 504
  She Ain't Holdin' Them Up, She's Holdin' On (Some English Rose), 505
Boyer, Jean Pierre, 215

Branch, Winston, 504
Brancusi, Constantin
  The Blond Negress, 295
  The White Negress, 295
Braque, Georges, 266
Brathwaite, Edward Kamau, 494, 495, 497, 500, 505, 506, 528
Brazil, 18–19, 23, 24, 27–41, 47, 50–51, 67, 73, 75, 79, 84, 103–23, 247, 250, 252, 255, 265–66, 271, 274, 281, 285, 300, 303–4, 316, 323, 336–37, 339, 344, 349, 351, 359, 366, 368, 370, 427, 430–32, 441–42, 447
Brebion, Dominique, 214, 220
Brecheret, Victor, 255, 256
Breleur, Ernest, 213, 220, 221, 235
  Untitled, from the series *The Origin of the World*, *234*, 235
Bressae, A. D., *Allegory on the Law of the Free Womb*, 47, *49*, 50, 51, 67, 344
Breton, André, 24, 204, 304, 312, 383
  Snake Charmer, 383
Brierre, Jean, 495
British West Indies, 23
Brito, Valter, 363
Brocos, Modesto, *The Redemption of Ham*, 66, 67
Bronte, Sintra, 471
Broodhagen, Karl, 361, 388
  Emancipation Statue, 353, *353*, 359, 411, 412
  Patricia, *391*
Brown, Everald, *Victory over Satan*, 390, *402*
Brown-Glaude, Winnifred, 465
Budan, Armand, 214
Burke, Alex, 507
  The Spirit of the Caribbean, 376, *377*
Burke, Vanley, 504
Burrowes, E. R., 405
Bussa (slave revolt leader), 353, 359, 411
Bustamante, Carlos María de, 69
Butcher, Ras Ishi, 398, 416, 521
  Blazin 1, 398, *404*, 418
Butler, Kim, 113
Butler, Natalie, 519

Cabezudo, Juan José ("Comesuelas"), 161, 163
Cabo Verde Islands, 17
Cabral, Francisco, 515
Cabrera, Lydia, 523
Cafferata, Francisco
  Slavery, 339, *342*, 343, 361

581

Campbell, Charles, 376
Campbell, George, 398
  "Negro Aroused" (poem), 304–5
Campbell, Ralph, 305, 405
Campeche y Jordán, José, 22, 126, 174, 177, 180
  Ex voto of the Holy Family, 177, *179*
  Governor Miguel Antonio de Ustáriz, 126, *127*, 128
Campos-Pons, María Magdalena, 376
  Untitled, 447, *451*
Canary Islands, 15
Cândido, João, 363
Cánepa, Tito Enrique, 485
Cañizares, Miguel Navarro y
  Allegory on the Golden Law, 51, *52*
  Allegory on the Law of the Free Womb, 47, 50–51, *50*
Cano, Francisco Antonio, *Passage of the Liberating Army through the Páramo de Pisba*, 79, *80*
Capellán, Tony, 522
Carbonell, Walterio, 437
Cárdenas, Agustín, 332, 437
Cardoso, Rafael, 67
Carew, Jan, 497, 506
Caribbean, 15–16, 18–19, *20*, *21*, 22–24, 124, 126, 169, 172, 205, 208, 303–4, 330, 375–425, 479–531
Carlos, J., 293
  cover of the periodical *Para Todos*, *300*, 301
Carpentier, Alejo, 269, 277, 311, 312
  The Kingdom of This World, 312, 314
Carrasco, Vanegas, 43
Carybé (Hector Julio Páride Bernabó), 293, 316
Casanovas, Martí, 247, 254, 266
Casarella, Edmond, 489
Cassou, Jean, 255
Castagnino, Juan Carlos, 277
casta paintings, 24, 69, 126
Castilla, Ramón, 62
Castillo, Omar-Pascual, 444
Castillo, Teófilo, 98
Castro, Fidel, 172
Castro Alves, Antônio Frederico de, 364
Cédor, Dieudonné, 219
Celestin, Louis, 483, 485
Cendrars, Blaise, 255
Centre d'Art, Port-au-Prince, 201, 212, 215–17, 219, 235, 311–12, 398, 405
Cervantes, Antonio (Kid Pambele), 364

Césaire, Aimé, 24, 33, 212, 213, 220, 221, 222, 224, 314, 329, 495, 506, 507, 509
  Notebook of a Return to My Native Land, 220, 230, 308, 383
Césaire, Suzanne, 220
Céspedes, Africa, 146
Céspedes, Benjamin de, *Prostitution in the City of Havana*, 141, 144
Chambers, Eddie, 503, 504, 516
Chamoiseau, Patrick, 212, 221–22
Chang, Carlisle, 405
Charanga de Villergas, La (cigarette factory)
  "Caridad, Want Me to Light You Up?," 141, *142*
  "If You Love Me, You Will Be Happy," 141, *142*
Charles III, king of Spain, 174
Charles-Edouard, François, 220
Charlot, Jean, 485
Charlotte, Robert, 222, 230, 233
  Vis-à-vis, sans titre, #19, 233
  Vis-à-vis, sans titre series, 233
Chartrand, Esteban, *Runaway Slave* (wood engraving after Chartrand and Victor Patricio de Landaluze), 140–41, *140*
Chaves Pinheiro, Francisco Manuel, *The Emancipation of the Servile Element*, 344, 361
Chávez Morado, José, 191
Chedda, Camille, 459, 465
  Wholesale Degradables, 475, *476*, *477* (detail)
Chile, 75
Chong, Albert, *Seated Presence*, 418, *420*, 422
Chosrova, Honoré, *Séance*, *390*, 395
Christophe, Henri, 215, 504
Chung, Andrea, 459, 465, 470–71, 523
  Bleach, 470–71, *470*
Ciarcia, Guy, 512
Ciata, Tia (Aunt), 368
Ciquí (baseball player), 189
Ciseri, Antonio, *Ecce Homo*, 79
Clarke, LeRoy, *417*, 418, 510, 512, *513*
  In the Maze, There Is a Single Line to My Soul, 386, *414*, 416
Cleto Noa, Juan, 178
Clouzot, Henri, 259
Cobas Amate, Roberto, 269
Codazzi, Agustín, 95
Cogniat, Raymond, 256, 274
Cogollo, Heriberto Cuadrado, 434

The Man of Tomorrow, 434, *436*
Coll y Toste, Cayetano, 177
Colombia, 16, 43, 45, 69, 79, 85–86, 91–95, 102, 281, 430, 442, 447
Colored Belle of Puerto Rico, A (unidentified photographer), 187, *187*
Colson, Jaime, 205
  Fiesta in Guachupita, *204*, 205, 327
  Merengue, *203*, 205, 316
Columbus, Christopher, 15, 16, 169, 174, 479
Condé, Maryse, 329
Conduru, Roberto, 444
Confection Vendors of Puerto Rico (unidentified photographer), 187, *187*
Confiant, Raphaël, 212, 221–22
Congo, 16, 18
Conrad, Joseph, 255
constructivism, 437
Consuegra, Hugo, 492
Cooper, Cecil, 516, 519, 521
Cordero, Rafael, 128, 178, 180
Coronado, Pepe, 492
Correa, Juan (the younger), 22
Correa Morales, Lucio, *Public Monument to Antonio Ruiz ("Falucho")*, *154*, 155, 361, 363
Correia da Araújo, Pedro, *Jongo*, 263
Cortés, Hernán, 16
Cosaque, Gilles Elie-Dit-, *Twinkl/Zétwal (Stars)*, 509, *509*
Costa, Arthur Timótheo da, 250
Costa-Lima, Luiz, 106
Costallat, Benjamin, 252
Costa Rica, 23
costumbrismo paintings, 56, 62, 68–69, 72, 85–102, 126, 128, 134, 141, 144, 161, 269, 453
Courret Studio
  The Cook Juan José Cabezudo ("Comesuelas"), 161, 163, *163*
  Francisco "Pancho" Fierro, 163, *163*
  Natalia Paz Soldán, 164–65, *165*
  The Silva Family, 164, *164*
Coussin, Jules-Honoré Joseph, 214
Coutinho, Gonzalo Vaez, 18
Coutinho, João Rodrigues, 18
Covarrubias, Miguel, 251–52, 486
  Negro Drawings, 251, *251*
Cox, John, 528
Cox, Renee, 512
  River Queen, 511
Cozier, Christopher, 418, 510, 512, 515–16,

528, 531
   Attack of the Sandwich Men, 516
   Blue Soap, 516
   The Castaway, 418, *419*, 516
   Conversation with a Shirt Jac, 516
   Tropical Night series, 516
Craig, Karl "Jerry," 497, 500, 510
Cravo, Mário, Jr., 364
Crichlow, Ernest, 490, 492
Cristancho Álvarez, Raúl, 281, 442
Crowninshield, Frank, 251–52
Cruz, Emilio, 492
Cuba, 15, 16, 18–19, 23, 79, 84, 124–47, 169, 172, 178, 183, 185, 187, 250, 263, 266, 269, 281, 325, 343–44, 363, 430–31, 434, 437, 441, 442, 444, 447, 521
cubism, 205, 323, 384, 386, 405
Cullen, Countee, 507
Cummings, Vera, 383
Cunard, Nancy, *Negro*, 265
Cunha, Manuel da, 22
Cunha, Mariano da, 432
Curaçao, 358, 359
Curatella Manes, Pablo, 256
Curry, Blue, 528

Daley, Henry, 405
Damas, Léon, 221
Daumier, Honoré, 27
David, Jacques-Louis, *The Coronation of the Emperor and Empress*, 134
Dávila, Arturo, 177
Davila, Maritza, 492
Davis, Annalee, 528
Davis, Stuart, 486
Dawson, Alexander, 252
Debret, Jean-Baptiste, 27, 47, 337
deCaires Taylor, Jason, *Vicissitudes*, 339, 361
de la Fuente, Alejandro, 101
De Lamonica, Roberto, 489
DeLand, Lauren, 233
Delano, Irene, 195
Delano, Jack, 195, 198
   At a Religious Procession in San Juan on Saint John the Baptist Day, 195, *196*
   Musicians at the Patron Saint's Festivities in the Town of Loíza Aldea, 195, *196*
de Mille, Agnes, 480
Démosthène, M. Florine, 222, 224, 227, 230, 238
   Wounds #15, 224, *226*
Denis, Maksaens, 222
   Nude Descending a Staircase, 244, *245*
   Untitled 02, 244, 246
   Untitled 03, 246
Depestre, René, 308, 506
Derain, André, 266
Deren, Maya, 487
De Rooy, Felix, 528
Désert, Jean-Ulrick, 222, 528
   BLING, 238, *239*, 240
   Negerhosen2000 (The Spectacle), 238, *238*, 240, 244
Dessalines, Jean-Jacques, 124
Destiné, Jean-Léon, 485
Diago, Juan Roberto, 441
   A Piece of My History, *443*, 444
   Scream, 444
Di Cavalcanti, Emiliano, 255, 271, 274, 277, 293, 316
   Fishermen, 316, *317*
   People of Brasilia, 318–19
   Samba, 271, *272*, 316
Djanira da Motta (known as Djanira), 316
   Candomblé, 316, *321*
Diop, Alioune, 495, 507
Dobru, Robin, 506
Dome, José de (José Antônio dos Santos), 430
Dominican Republic, 23, 169–74, 183, 198–211, 522
Donatien-Yssa, Patricia, 213, 214
Dorcély, Roland, 219
Doucet, Morel, 522
Douglass, Frederick, 215
Dr. Atl (Gerardo Murillo), 250
Drieu de la Rochelle, Pierre, 255
Duchamp, Marcel, *Nude Descending a Staircase*, 244
Dufy, Raoul, 266
Dunkley, John, 305
Duperly, Adolphe, 462, 473
Dürer, Albrecht, 233
Dutra, Alipio, 255
Duval-Carrié, Edouard, 509, 522
   Altar to the Nine Slaves, 374, 376
   J.C. Duvalier as Mad Bride, 411
Duvalier, François, 303, 487
Dying Gaul, The (ancient sculpture), 339

Earle, Augustus, *Capoeira*, 106, *107*

Echenique, José Rufino, 62
Eckhout, Albert, 27
Edna Manley College of the Visual and Performing Arts (EMC), Kingston, Jamaica, 516, 519
Edwards, Melvin, 512
Egonu, Uzo, 497
Ehlers, Jeannette, *I Am Queen Mary (Mary Thomas)* [with La Vaughn Belle], 372, *373*
Eiriz, Antonia, 523
Eladia Gallardo (unidentified artist), 157, *159*
EMC. *See* Edna Manley College of the Visual and Performing Arts (EMC), Kingston, Jamaica
Ender, Thomas, 27
English, Darby, 224
Enríquez, Carlos, 312, 486
   The Abduction of the Mulatto Women, 293
Escobar, León, 161
Escobar, Vicente, 22, 128
Escuela Nacional de Bellas Artes, Santo Domingo, 199, 205, 208
Esquivel, Alexis, 444
   National Picnic, 447, *454*
Esson, Tomás, 523
Evans, Richard, 215
   Portrait of Henri Christophe, King of Haiti, 505
Exil, Levoy, 219
Exumé, Rene, 219

Facey, Laura, *Redemption Song*, 359, *360*, 361, 371, 411–12
Fanon, Frantz, 33, 42, 212, 220, 221, 224, 311
   Black Skin, White Masks, 238, 311
Faustin I, emperor of Haiti, 215
Ferdinand VII, king of Spain, 69
Ferguson, Amos, *Woman Lying on a Couch*, 390
Ferguson, Tyrone, 399
Fernandes Corrêa, Alexandre, 122
Fernández, Carmelo, *White Women, Ocaña Province*, 92, *93*
Fernández Carrillo, Enrique, 144
Fernández Ledesma, Gabriel, 253, 254
Fernández Retamar, Roberto, 330, 506
Ferreira, Luís, 27
Ferrez, Marc, 27
Fierro, Francisco "Pancho," 69, 72, 75, 86, 96, 98, 101, 102, 161, 163, 427

Civic Procession of the Blacks, 72, *72*
Dancing to the Sound of the Devils, 96, *98*
Group of Blacks Celebrating the 28th of July, *100*, 101
Figari, Pedro, 256, 263, 274
   Candombe, 256, *257*
Figueroa, Miguel, 363
Filgueiras Lima, João, *Zumbi dos Palmares* (with Darcy Ribeiro and Romeu Alves), 368, *369*, 370
Finley, M. I., 27
Fleetwood, Nicole, 238
Flores, Tatiana, 244, 252
Fonseca e Silva, Valentim da (Mestre Valentim), 22
Forgas, José Gallart, 183
Fornet, Ambrosio, 314
Forrester, Denzil, 504
Fory, Nelson, *Our History, Sir!* series, 447, *453*
Frade, Ramón, 187, 189
   Our Daily Bread, 172, *173*, 211
France, 213–15, 219, 221, 255–56, 259, 263, 266, 269, 274, 277, 323, 507, 509
Francis (pope), 180
Franco, Francisco, 204
François, Georges (Géo), 214
Fredricks, C. D., *Cabildo Group Carte de Visite*, 144, *146*
Freyre, Gilberto, 271
Fuentes, Carlos, 506
Fuentes, Elvis, 528
Fuentes, Manuel Atanasio, *Lima; or Sketches of the Capital of Peru*, 101
futurism, 205, 277

Gallardo, Eladia, 157
Gallardo, Lino, 157
Galloza, Ruben, 434
   Afro-Uruguay, 434, *435*
Gálvez Egúsquiza, José, 62
Gambie, Gwladys, 222
   Beautiful Monster, *243*, 244
García, Scherezade, 211
   The Dominican York, *210*, 211
   Island of Many Gods series, 211
García, Victor Manuel. *See* Victor Manuel García
García Agüero, Salvador, 293
García Calderón, Ventura, 255
García Godoy, Federico, 199

Garcia Marquéz, Gabriel, 506
Gardner, Joscelyn
   Bleeding and Breeding, 422
   Coffee Arabica (Clarissa), 528, *529*
   Creole Portraits series, 422, 528
   Veronica frutescens (Mazerine), *421*
Garmendia, Rosa Naday, 523
Garner, Eric, 240
Garoute, Jean-Claude (Tiga), 219
Garrido, Juan, 16
Garvey, Marcus, 23, 305, 361, 366, 368, 371, 386, 388, 390, 416
Gattorno, Antonio, 256, 277
   Women by the River, *273*, 274
Gauguin, Paul, 214, 219, 251, 274, 383, 390
Gausachs, José, 203, 205
Gauthier, Léon, *How Gold Is Washed, Province of Barbacoas*, 95, *97*
Gavazzo Buchardo, Juan Manuel, 255
Geffrard, Fabre, 215
Gentry, Herbert, 492
Géo-Charles, 266
George, Milton
   The Art of Being Polite on a Red Background, 411
   The P.M. Speaks at 8, 411
Gerardo, Filippo, 43
Gerónimo de Bruselas, 174
Gil de Castro, José, 22, 148, 150, 152, 155
   reverse of *Portrait of Manuel Larenas y Álvarez Rubio*, 148, *149*
Glackens, William, 189
Gleizes, Albert, 266
Glissant, Édouard, 212, 220, 221, 224, 235, 480, 500
Goeldi, Oswaldo, 293
Goering, Anton, 75
Golub, Leon, 515
Gomes, Diogo, 15
Gomes de Oliveira, Ledo Ivo, *Black from the Water*, 346
Gómez, Juan Gualberto, 295, 363, 447
Gómez de la Serna, Ramón, 255
Gómez Jaramillo, Ignacio, 281, 289
   The Freeing of the Slaves, *280*, 281
Gómez Sicre, José, 312
Gómez Toro, Panchito, 295
González, Christopher, *Mountain Head (Woman of Zion)*, 390, *396*
González-Torres, Félix, 246

Gopie, Jacqueline, 522
Gordon, Leah, 412
   Caste series, 376, 379
   Mulatto Woman, *378*
Gortázar, Alejandro, 363
Goveia, Elsa, 500
Graciano, Clóvis
   Flag Dancers, 316, *320*
Grajales, Mariana, 295, 363
Grant, Duncan, 383
Grant, Ulysses S., 171
Grau, Enrique, 485
Greater Antilles, 169, 303
Great Jolof, 15
Greaves, Stanley, 386, 388, 405, 505
   The Annunciation, 390, *401*, 411
Gregory, Joy, 504
Grenada, 18
Griffith, Marlon, *Powder Box Schoolgirl* series, 528
Gris, Juan, 266
Guadeloupe, 212–15, 221–22, 230, 375
Guérédrat, Annabel, 222, 240, 244
   Nudes Descending a Staircase, #3 (with Henri Tauliaut), *242*, 244
Guerra, Júlio, *Black Mother*, 344
Guerrero, Vicente, 152
Guerrier, Adler, 522
Guevara, Carlos, *Juan Álvarez*, *151*, 152
Guevara, Che, 330
Guillén, Nicolás, 250, 281, 315, 495, 506, 507
Guillon-Lethière, Guillaume, 214
Gulland, Alexander Dudgeon
   Natives of Jamaica, 461, *462*
   Victims of the Jamaica Rebellion of 1865, *460*, 462
Gutiérrez, Felipe Santiago, *Portrait of a Mulatto Woman*, 91–92, *91*
Gutiérrez, Rodrigo, *The Senate of Tlaxcala*, 83
Guyana, 375, 415

Haile Selassie, emperor of Ethiopia, 305, 388, 390
Haiti, 18, 23, 24, 105, 109, 124, 169, 171, 178, 198, 201, 203, 211, 212–19, 235, 311–12, 314, 334, 336, 375, 376, 379, 380, 383
Haitian Vodou Bizango statues, *120*
Haitian Vodou drum, *121*
Haití Eduardo, Ramón, 430, 437
Hall, Stuart, 375, 418, 494, 500, 503

Hammons, David, 515
Hardy, Charles, 215
Harootian, Koren der, 398
Harris, Wilson, 496, 506
Hassinger, Maren, *Daily Mask*, 240
Hawaii, 185, 187
Hawkins, Kathleen, 380
   Plantation Workers on Their Way Home, 380, *381*
Hayes, Roland, 507
Hearne, John, 506
Heartman, Ras Daniel, 390
Hegel, G. W. F., 42
Hélénon, Serge, 212–13, 220
Helford, Riva, 490
Henri, Robert, 189
Henry, Jacques-Victor, 504
Henschel, Alberto, 27
Hepworth, Barbara, 384
Hernández Giró, Juan Emilio, 256
   The Vision of Maceo, 259
Hernández Ortega, Gilberto, 205, 208
   Untitled, 205, *206*
Herrera, Adelaida, 441
Herskovits, Melville, 315
Hesse, Barnor, 459, 475
Hibbert, Joseph, 388
Hibran, René, 311
Hidalgo, Miguel, 69
Hierro, Lucia, 522
Himid, Lubaina, 503, 516
Hispaniola, 16, 18, 169, 171, 198
Hogarth, William, 35, 141
Holder, Boscoe, 405, 411, 483, 485–87, 497, 510
   Carnival Costume, 483, *484*
   Man in Straw Hat, 483
   Mother, *482*, 483
   Untitled Male Nude, *410*, 411
Holder, Geoffrey, 480, 483, 485, 487, 494, 504, 507
   Self-Portrait, *481*, 483
Hollingsworth, Alvin, 489
Holloway, Thomas, 106
Homar, Lorenzo, 189–91, 485
   Fourth Contest of Santeros, 190, *190*
   Paintings of José Campeche and His Workshop, *191*
Honorien, Raymond, 220
Honychurch, Lennox, 353
Hostos, Eugenio María de, 199

Howell, Leonard P., 388
Hueso, Maestro, 161
Hughes, Langston, 251
Huie, Albert, 305, 405
   Counting Lesson, 521
   The History Lesson, 388, *389*
Hunt, Jean-Marc, 240
   Balloon, 240, *241*
Hurok, Sol, 480
Huyssen, Andreas, 300
Hyde, Eugene, *Casualties Series*, 411
Hype, Lisa, 464
Hyppolite, Florvil, 215
Hyppolite, Hector, 216, 312
   Black Magic, 390, *392*
   The Grand Master, *310*, 312
   Mistress Erzulie, 235, *237*

Iberia, 15, 22. *See also* Portugal; Spain
Iemanjá/Calunga (unidentified artist), 33, *34*, 35–37
Iemanjá Fertility Goddess (unidentified artist), 32, *32*
Ilê Axé Opô Afonjá Museum, Salvador, Bahia, Brazil, 104, *122*
impressionism, 177, 181
Ingres, Jean-Auguste-Dominique, 178
Instituto Superior de Arte (ISA), Havana, Cuba, 516, 521
Isabel, princess of Brazil, 51
Iyalorixá Eugênia Anna dos Santos (Mãe Aninha), The (unidentified artist), *110*, 111, 113
Izaguirre, Leandro, *The Torture of Cuauhtémoc*, 84

Jacko (Black Maroon chief), 353
Jamaica, 18, 23, 178, 304–5, 308, 349, 359, 361, 375, 383, 398, 411–12, 458–75
James, C. L. R., 399, 494, 504, 506
James, Erica, 379
James, Marlon, 523
Jantjes, Gavin, 503
Javier Cortés, Francisco (attributed), *Juan José Cabezudo ("Comosuelas") and His Friend*, 161, *162*
Jiménez Pastrana, Juan, 281
João, prince regent of Portugal, 103
John, Augustus, 383
   Two Jamaican Girls, 383

Johnson, Claudette, 503
Johnson, Leasho, 459, 465, 473–74
   Back-fi-a-bend, *472*, 473–74
Johnson, Lyndon B., 172
Jones, Claudia, 495
Joseph, Ronald, 490, 492
Joseph, Tam, 504
José Romero (unidentified artist), 152, *153*, 155
Juana Inés de la Cruz, 177
Julien, Isaac, 504
Jungerman, Remy, 528

Kaersenhout, Patricia, 528
Karpata, Bastian, 359
Kartel, Vybz, 458–59, *459*, 464–65, 473
Katz, Renina, 293
Kcho (Alexis Leiva Machado), 376
Kelly, George "Fowokan," 504
Kempadoo, Roshini, 504
Khokho (Joseph Sainte-Croix René-Corail), 415
   Untitled, 390, *400*, 415
King-Hammond, Leslie, 22
Klaus, Prince, 411
Knight, John, 41
Konate, Abdoulaye, 521
Kumbukumbu: Africa, Memory, and Heritage (exhibition), 103, *104*
Kyong Chun, Wendy Hui, 459, 475

La Bayamesa, Rosa, 363
Labra, Rafael María de, 363
LaFontaine, Clifford, 487
Lagos, Alberto, 255
Lam, Wifredo, 24, 205, 312, 323, 325, 330, 364, 383, 437, 441, 506, 507, 510, 512, 519, 521
   Agony of Spain, 323
   The Fiancée of Kiriwina, 325, *325*
   The Jungle, *328*, 329
   Rumor, *324*, 325
   Untitled, 325
Lamming, George, 302, 329–30, 494, 506
Landaluze, Victor Patricio de, 134, 137, 140–41, 144, 269
   Epiphany in Havana, 137, *138–39*, 140
   Judith Liberates Cuba from the Separatist Rebellion, 134, *135*
   Runaway Slave (wood engraving after Landaluze and Esteban Chartrand), 140–41, *140*

Spirit Dancer, 144, *145*
Sugarcane Cutting, 136–37, *137*
Lange, Dorothea, 195
Laouchez, Louis, 212–13, 220
Laplante, Eduardo, 134, 141
    Boiling House of Asunción Sugar Plantation, *133*, 134
    Sugar Mill Owned by Conde de Fernandina in Cuba, *132*, 134
La Rose, John, 494, 495, 497
Laso, Francisco, 62
    The Three Races, or Equality before the Law, 62, *64–65*, 65, 67
Latamie, Marc, 509, 512
Latin America, 15–16, 18, *20*, *21*, 22–24, 68–84, 124, 247–50, 255–56, 426, 429, 434, 441
Laude, Jean, 323
Laughlin, Nicholas, 528
Laval, Charles, 219
Lavalle, José Antonio de, 98
Lawrence, Jacob, 490, 492
Lazard, Luckner, 217, 219
Leal, Fernando, 254
Le Bon, Gustave, 248
Ledesma, Manuel Antonio, 363
Lee, Russell, 195
Lee-Smith, Hughie, 489
Léger, Fernand, 205, 265, 266
Leighten, Patricia, 259
Leiris, Michel, 383
Le Moyne, Auguste, 75
Lenzina, Joaquin, 363
Leonard, Sean, 528
Leong Pang, Amy, 398–99
Lepiani, Juan, *Proclamation of the Independence of Peru*, 79, *81*, 83
Lerebours, Michel-Philippe, 215
Lescay, Alberto, 361, 363, 364
    Monument to the Runaway Slave, 343, *343*, 344, 364, 372
Leslie, Wenda, 503
Lesne, Anna, 221
Levi, Julian Edwin, 487
Levi-Strauss, Claude, 304
Lhote, André, 266
Liautaud, Georges, 399, 405
    Danbala, 405, *406*
Linati, Claudio, 75, 88
    Man from the Coast: Black Man from the Vicinity of Veracruz (Santa Fe) in His Sunday Clothes, 87, 88–89
    Negre etendu dans son hamac, 89
Lisboa, Antônio Francisco (Aleijadinho), 22
Lloyd, Errol, 497, 504
Lochard, Archibald, 215
Lochard, Colbert, 215
Locke, Alain, 507
Locke, Donald, 405, 497
Locke, Hew, 504
Lombroso, Cesare, 144
London, England, 494–504
Long, Edward, 23
López, Agustín, 157
López Albújar, Enrique, 157
López de Santa Anna, Antonio, 152
Lopéz López Iodibo, Manuel, *Desalines [sic]*, 124, *125*
Lotierzo, Tatiana, 67
Louco (Boaventura Silva Filho), 430
Louise, René, 214, 220, 221
Louis XIV, king of France, 233
Lourdes Ghidoli, María de, 161
Lovell, Whitfield, 492
Lovera, Juan, *Lino Gallardo*, 157, *158*
Lower Guinea, 17
Loy, Ramón, 250
Lozano, Luanda, 492
Luciano, Miguel, *Plátano Pride*, 522, *524*
Luis (brother of Charles III, king of Spain), 174

Mabille, Pierre, 312
Maceo Grajales, Antonio, 259, 289, 295, 363, 371
Madagascar, 16, 19
Madrazo, Federico de, 178
Maggie, Yvonne, 123
Magno, Márcia, 359, 361
Magowan, Robert, 487
Mais, Roger, 398
Majluf, Natalia, 62, 86, 98
Maldonado-Torres, Nelson, 303
Malfatti, Anita, 255, 485
Malinowski, Bronislaw, 315
Malone, Brent, 405, 492, 510, 512
    Junkanoo Ribbons, 405, *407*
Malta, Augusto, *Shanties in the Morro de Santo Antonio*, *112*, 113–14
Mancoba, Ernest, 507
Mangonès, Albert, *The Unknown Fugitive Slave*, 334, *335*, 336, 359, 361, 372

Manley, Edna, 304–5, 383, 384, 398, 505
    Beadseller, 383
    Beulah, 384
    Eve, 384, *384*, 386
    Negro Aroused, 304, 346, *347*, 349, 359, 372, 386, 398
    Pocomania, 384
Manley, Michael, 471
Manley, Norman, 304, 398, 399
Mansong, Jack, 416
Manthorne, Katherine E., 485
Manzon, Jean, 323
Marcus, Sharon, 465
Marett, Robert R., *Psychology and Folklore*, 315
Mariátegui, José Carlos, 253
Marín del Solar, Mercedes, 155
Marinello, Juan, 289
Marinetti, F. T., 277
Mariño, Armando, *Enjoying Freedom*, 447, *449*
Marley, Bob, 361, 390
Marqués, René, 506
Marriott, Alvin, 305
    Banana Man, 305, *307*, back jacket
Mars, Tessa, 235
    Conversation with Hector H., 235, *236*, 238
Marshall, Kerry James, 469
Martha, Tirzo, 528
Martí, José, 289
Martín de Porres, 180
Martínez Furé, Rogelio, 434
Martinique, 24, 178, 212–15, 219–22, 312, 339, 375, 383, 415, 483
Mary, Kelly Sinnapah, 230
    Notebook of No Return to the Native Land, *228*, 230
    Notebook of No Return to the Native Land, Alice, *229*, 230
Mas, Christian, 215
Masson, André, 383
Matisse, Henri, 266
Maugée, Aristide, 220
Maya Restrepo, Luz Adriana, 442
Mayhew, Richard, 489
Mazo, Manuel María del, from the *Nonsense* series, 62, *63*
McKay, Claude, 507
McKenzie, Dave, 515
McNish, Althea, 494, 497
McQueen, Steve, 504
Medeiros, José, *Initiation of a Daughter of a*

Priest in the Candomblé Precinct, 322, 323
Meireles, Cecília, 263
Melbye, Fritz, 24
Melling, Helen, 72
Menchú, Rigoberta, 330
Mendive Hoyo, Manuel, 430
    Babalú Ayé, 437, *439*
Ménil, René, 220, 311
Mercer, Kobena, 384, 399, 516
Mérida, Carlos, 254
Mexico, 16, 18–19, 22, 68–69, 83–86, 88–91, 248, 250, 252–54, 277, 281
Miami, Florida, 522–23
Miller, David, Jr., 305, *305*
    Girl Surprised, 305, *309*
Miller, David, Sr., 305, *305*
Miller, Jeannette, 198–99
Millers, The (unidentified photographer), 305, *305*
Minaya, Joiri, 522
Minshall, Peter, 515
    Mancrab on Dimanche Gras Night, 515–16, *517*
Mistral, Gabriela, 255
Mitre, Bartolomé, 155
Modigliani, Amedeo, 265
Mojica Madera, Javier, *I Am Babalú*, 444, *444*
Moncada, Guillermo, 250
Mondestin, Mafalda Nicolas
    Chit-chat under the Sandbox Tree, 230
    Upside Down under the Frangipani, 230, *231*
Monroe, Arthur, 430
Montiel, José Justo, *Negrito fumando*, 91
Moody, Ronald, 386, 496–97, *497*, 512
    Midonz (Goddess of Transmutation), *385*, 386, 496
    Tacet, 496
Moore, Henry, 384
Moore, Philip, 505
    1763 Monument, *354*, 361, 366, 371, 386, 506
Mora, José María Luisa, 88
Morais, Neusa, *Monument to Goiânia (Monument to the Three Races)*, *348*, 349, 351
Moré, Benny, 363
Moreau de Saint-Méry, M. L. E., 376
Moreira Matos, José, *Pillory*, 337, *338*
Morelli, Hércules, *Christian Charity Crowning the Bust of Francisco Carvallo*, 78, *79*
Moreno, Juan (Juan Prieto), 16

Morera, Clara, 441
Moret Astruells, Enrique, *Monument to the Slave Revolt*, 351, *352*, 361
Moriuchi, Mey-Yen, 89
Morris, Nicholas, 528
Morrison, Petrona, 515, 516, 519
Morse, Richard, 504
Mosaka, Tumelo, 222
Motta, Djanira da. *See* Djanira da Motta
Moy, Seong, 489, 490
Mozambique, 16, 19
Muñóz Marín, Luis, 189
Munroe, Lavar, 523
    Floater (study), *527*
Murillo, Gerardo. *See* Dr. Atl
Museum of Black Magic, Rio de Janeiro, 121–23
Mystille, Marcel, 220

Naipaul, V. S., 494, 506
Nanan, Wendy, 515
Nardal, Paulette, 507
Narváez, Francisco
    Head of a Black Man, 293, 295, *295*
    Head of a Woman, 293
Nascimento, Abdias do, 427, 431–32, 437
    The Horse and the Saint: Yemanjá, *433*
naturalism, 177
Neel, Alice, 486
Nêgo (Geraldo Simplício), 344, 361
Négritude, 212, 220–22, 250, 295, 308, 314, 383, 429, 432, 507
Nettleford, Rex, 305, 506
Neue Sachlichkeit, 271
Neves, Eustáquio, 442
    Good Appearance series, *445*, 447
    Valongo: Letters to the Sea series, 444
Newton, Huey P., 372
New York, New York, 485–92, 512
Nicaragua, 23, 447
Nigeria, 17, 19
Nina Rodrigues, Raimundo, 110, 123
Nivor, Bertin, 220

Obin, Philomé, 217
    The Crucifixion of Charlemagne Péralte for Freedom, 217
Obregón, José María, *The Discovery of Pulque*, 83
Ocejo, Miguel de Jesús, 437

O'Grady, Lorraine, 244
O'Higgins, Bernardo, 148
Oiticica, Hélio, 27
Olaya, José, 150
Oller, Francisco, 128–29, 177–78, 180–81, 183, 187, 189, 199
    Aurora Sugar Plantation, *182*, 183
    La Fortuna Sugar Plantation, 183, *184*
    The Old Ceiba Tree at Ponce, 181, *181*, 183
    The School of Master Rafael Cordero, 128, *130*, 178
    The Wake, 128–29, *131*, 180–81, 189, 195
Olugebefola, Ademola, 492
Oquendo de Amat, Carlos, 253
Orozco, José Clemente, 254
Ortiz, Fernando, 15, 269, 315
    Africanness in Cuban Folkloric Music, 315
    The Afro-Cuban Underworld, 144
Ortiz de Zárate, Manuel, 256, 259
    Pablo Picasso, 259, *260*
Otero, Néstor, 492
Ouditt, Steve, 418
Ovando, Nicolás de, 16

Pacheco, Máximo, 254
Páez, Ildefonso, *Micaela Vilela de López, Piura*, 157, *160*, 161
Pagano, José León, 61
Palcy, Euzhan, *Sugar Cane Alley*, 379
Palés Matos, Luis, 195, 495
Palmer, Eugene, 504
    Index, 502
Panama, 16, 23
Paraguay, 73, 75
Parboosingh, Karl, *Ras Smoke 1*, 398, *403*
Paret y Alcázar, Luis, 126, 174, 177
Páride Bernabó, Hector Julio. *See* Carybé
Paris, France. *See* France
Paris, José Ignacio, 43
Parotti, Lynn, 528
Pastor, Miguel, *Old Black*, 346, 364
Patrick, Winston, 510
    Youth, 510
Patterson, Ebony G., 422, 425, 459, 465, 468–70, 475, 516, 519, 521
    Blood Breda Crew, 521
    Counting Money Haha, 521
    Daadi + Yutez, *520*, 521
    Di Real Big Man, 422, *424*, 425
    Gangstas for Life Series, 521

Untitled Lightz 1, 468–70, *469*
Patterson, Orlando, 496
Paul, Annie, 418, 459
Paul Bogle (often identified as) [unidentified photographer], 462, *463*, 464, 468, 475
Paulino, Rosana, 442, 453
    Embroidery Hoops series, 447, *450*
Payne, Ivan, *Maube Seller*, 390, *394*
Paz, Manuel María
    Aspecto esterior de las casas de Nóvita, provincia del Chocó, 95
    Sale of Liquor in the Village of Lloró, Province of Chocó, *94*, 95
Paz, Octavio, 506
Pedro II, emperor of Brazil, 50–51
Pedroso, Regino, 250
Pédurand, Bruno, 233
    The Heritage of Ham, *232*, 233, 235
Peláez, Amelia, 485
Pelé (Edson Arantes do Nascimento), 364
Peña, Alberto (Peñita), 250, 289, 295, 297, 327
    The Calling of the Ideal, or Martí, 289, *291*
    Cuba on the March, 289, *290*
    Mater Dolorosa, 289
    The New Slaves of the Sugarmill, 289
    The Protest, 289
    Unemployed, 293
    Workers, *288*, 289
Peña, René, 444
    Untitled, 447, *448*
Peoli, Juan Jorge, *The Caretaker*, 128, *129*
Péralte, Charlemagne, 217
Pereda Valdés, Ildefonso, 253, 254, 263, 265
    El Negro Rioplatense y otros ensayos, *264*, 265
    Raza negra, 263, 265
Pereira, Santander, illustration for *Revista Sucesos*, *74*, 75
Pereira Passos, Francisco, 113
Péret, Benjamin, 308
Pérez, Douglas, 444
    The Academy, 453, *456–57*
Peru, 18, 62, 68–69, 72, 75, 79, 83–86, 88, 95–102, 427, 429
Peters, DeWitt, 201, 311, 398, 405
Pétion, Alexandre, 215, 295
Petit-Frére, Joanne, 522
Pettoruti, Emilio, 256
Pharcel (Black Maroon chief), 353
Picasso, Pablo, 259, 265, 266, 289, 323, 384, 386
    Les Demoiselles d'Avignon, 259, 386
Pierre, André, 216, 312
Pierre, Vickie, 522
Pierre-Louis, Prosper, 219
Pietzker, Wilhelm, 115
Pinas, Marcel, 516, 519, 521, 528
    Feti, 519
    Piekien Kukuu, 521
    Sanfika, *518*, 519
Pinchinat, Max, 219
Pindell, Howardena, 515
Pineda, Jorge, 522
Pingret, Édouard, *Musician from Veracruz*, 89, *89*
Piper, Adrian, 244
Piper, Keith, 376, 503
Pissarro, Camille, 24, 178
Pliny, 40, 41
Plot, D., *The Female Slaves of Buenos Aires Show That They Are Free and Grateful to Their Noble Liberator*, 53, *54–55*
Pogolotti, Marcelo, 485
Pollard, Ingrid, 504
Ponce de León, Juan, 16, 174
Pope.L, William, 244
Portinari, Cândido, 281, 285, 289, 293, 485
    Black Man with a Hoe, 281, *284*
    Brazilian Popular Dance, 316
    Coffee, 281
    Mestizo, 281, *283*
Portocarrero, Gonzalo, 62
Portocarrero, René
    Carnival Sorcerer, *326*, 327
    Las máscaras, 327
    Sorcerers series, 327
portraiture, 148–65
Portugal, 15, 17–18, 106, 289. See also Iberia
post-impressionism, 384, 405
Pottinger, David, 305
    Nine Night, 305, *306*
Pou y Becerra, Miguel, 189, 485
    A Race of Dreamers (Portrait of Ciquí), *188*, 189
Poveda, José Manuel, 250
Powell, Enoch, 495
Powell, Richard J., 208
Prado, Carlos, *Batuque*, 263, *264*
Prado Valladares, Clarival do, 430
Prazeres, Heitor dos, 256, 316, 430, 431
Price, Henry, 95

Price, Lucien, 217, 219
    Study No. 6: Masks, 327, *327*
Price-Mars, Jean, 212, 219, 224, 235
    Ainsi parla l'Oncle, 216
Puente Acosta, Lorenzo, 178
Puerto Rico, 16, 23, 124, 126, 128–29, 146–47, 169–98, 203, 208–11, 349, 351, 504
Pueyrredón, Prilidiano
    Buenos Aires Street Corner, 56, *58–59*, 61–62, 67
    The Orange Vendor, 56, *60*, 61–62, 67
    Patio in Buenos Aires in 1850, 56, *57*, 61–62, 67
Pusey, Mavis, 486–87, 490, 492
    Contact, 492
    Decaying 7, 492
    Frozen Vibration, 492, *493*
    Justice—The Art of Law, 486
    Nexus, 486
    Operation 7, 492
    Paris Mai-Juin 68, 492
    Re-Gentrification, 487
    Solitude, 486

Quashie (Black Maroon chief), 353
Queneditt Morales, Rafael, 437, 441
    Oyá, 437, *440*
Querino, Manuel, 29
Quesada, Francisco, 155

Ra, Omari, 416
    Bois Caiman's Foreign Policy: Retro Reconstruction Globe Shrugged, 416, *417*
Rafael, Ulisse, 123
Raggi, José, 351
Ramchand, Kenneth, 496
Ramos, Arthur, 265
Ramos Blanco, Teodoro, 250, 289, 293, 295, 297, 363, 486
    Antonio Maceo, 295, *296*
    Internal Life, 293, *294*
    Monument to the Races, 363
    Old Black Woman, 293
Ramsay, Ras Akyem I, 416, 521
    Dead-Stone, 521
    Untitled No. 2, 418
Raquel Rivera, Carlos, 169, 189
    The Hurricane of the North, *168*, 169
Ras Dizzy, *The Rasta Says*, 390
realism, 177, 405

Rego, Ronaldo, 432
Rego Monteiro, Vicente do, 265–66
   Combat, 265, *265*
Reinel, Pedro Gomes, 18
Remponeau, Geo, 486
René-Corail, Joseph Sainte-Croix. *See* Khokho
Resende, José, *Venus/"Big Black Woman,"* 344, 346, *346*, 351, 361
Residents playing traditional music in the street, June 1, 2013 (unidentified photographer), 356, *358*
Reuben, Vernal, 492
Revinchal, 215
Reyes, Alfonso, 254, 255
Reynolds, Mallica "Kapo," 383, 492
   Paul Bogle, 305
   Revival Goddess Dina, 390, *393*
Ribeaux Diago, Ariel, 444
Ribeiro, Darcy, 303
   Zumbi dos Palmares (with Romeu Alves and João Filgueiras Lima), 368, *369*, 370
Rickards, Peter, 422
Rigaud, Louis, 215
Rio, João do, 114
Rio de Janeiro, Brazil, 113–23
Rivafrecha Campeche, Tomás de, 174
Rivera, Diego, 254, 277, 281, 289
Rivera Cardona, Salvador, *Monument to the Puerto Rican Roots*, 349, *350*, 351
Rivero, Kenny, 492, 522
Rivers, Larry, 487
Robart, Maud, 219
Robert, Andy, 515
Robert Blackburn Printmaking Workshop, New York, 490, 492
Roberts, Antonius, 528
Robeson, Eslanda, 507
Roche Rabell, Arnaldo, *We Have to Dream in Blue*, *197*, 198
Rodman, Selden, 312
Rodney, Donald, 503, 504
Rodríguez, José Francisco, *Vicente Guerrero*, *150*, 152
Rodríguez, Mariano, 281, 289
   Couple with Oxen, 281, *282*, 289
   Unity, 289
Rodríguez Cobas, Rogelio (Cobas), 430, 437
Rodríguez Lozano, Manuel, 289
Rodríguez Santiago, Carlos Manuel, 180
Rodríguez Valdés, Elio, 444, 453

Very Tropical, 447, *452*
Rohlehr, Gordon, 496, 506
Rohner, Georges, 214
Romay, Zuleica, 315
Romero, José, 152, 155
Roosevelt, Franklin D., 171
Rosas, Juan Manuel de, 53, 56, 61, 161
Rose, Billy, 512
Rose, Sheena, 516, 522
Rosenberg, Léonce, 265
Rothstein, Arthur, 195
Roumain, Jacques, 380, 495
   The Governors of the Dew, 311
Rousseau, Henri, 312, 383
Roy, Namba, 497
   Accompong Madonna, 497, *499*
   Jesus and His Mammy, 497
Royal Academy of San Carlos, Mexico City, 79, 191
Roye, Ruddy, 523
Rubio, Luis, 351
Rufin, Shirley, 222, 224, 230, 238
   Avant C, 227, *227*
Rugendas, Johann Moritz, 27, 47, 96, 101, 105, 337
   Lundu Dance, 106, *108*
   San Juan en Amancaes, 96
Ruiz, Antonio "Falucho," 155, 361, 363
Russell, Don, 486
Russell, Oneika, 459, 465, 516
   Notes to You, 474–75, *474*
   Preservations, 474–75

Saco, José Antonio, 128
Sacy-Pererê (unidentified artist), 30, 38–41, *38*
Sacy Shoe Polish (unidentified artist), 41, *41*
Saint-Domingue, 18, 105, 198, 334
Saint Fleurant, Louisiane, 219
Saint-Val, Asser, 522
Salkey, Andrew, 494, 495, 497, 503
Salvador, Brazil, 109–13
Salvatore, Ricardo, 53
San Alejandro Academy, Havana, 79, 129
Sánchez, Emilio, 485
Sánchez, Juan, 209, 211
   For Carmen María Colón, 209, 211
Sandino, Augusto César, 447
Sandoval, Alonso de, 17
San Martín, José de, 69, 83, 361
Santa Cruz, Nicomedes, 427, 429

Santa Cruz, Victoria, 427
Santander, Francisco de Paula, 43, 79
Santos, Agnaldo Manoel dos, 430
Santos, Deoscóredes Maximiliano dos (Mestre Didi), 366, 432
   Ôpa n'Ílé: Scepter of the Earth, *365*, 366
   Scepter of Ancestry, 366
Santos, Eugênia Anna dos (Mãe Aninha), *110*, 111, 113
Sartre, Jean-Paul, 33, 308
Savain, Pétion, 201, 216, 256, 388, 486
Schmid, Heino, 528
Schoelcher, Victor, 214, 411
School of Applied Arts, Martinique, 220, 311, 398, 415
Scott, Shalman, 368
Scott, William Edouard, 216
Seabrook, William B., *The Magic Island*, 383
Sealy, Mark, 516
Segall, Lasar, 293, 297, 300
   Banana Grove, 297, *298*
   Black Mother, 292, 293
   Boy with Geckos, 297
   Encounter, 297
   Red Hill, 297, *299*, 300
Segre, Erica, 88
Seigel, Micol, 253
Sekoto, Gerard, 507
Selvon, Samuel, 494
Semmel, Joan, 515
Senghor, Léopold Sédar, 221, 304, 308, 507
Serota, Nicholas, 503
Shakespeare, William, *The Tempest*, 329–30
Shaw, Irénée, 515
Sheller, Mimi, 462, 465, 470
Sheperd, Clara, 507
Sierra, Justo, 248
Silva, Joaquim Manuel da, 346
Silva Filho, Boaventura. *See* Louco
Simon, Nel, *Unchained*, 355, 358, *359*, 372
Simplício, Geraldo. *See* Nêgo
Sims, Lowery Stokes, 510
Siqueiros, David Alfaro, 255, 277, 281
Slave Anastácia, The (unidentified artist), 30, *31*
Smith, Marlene, 503
Smith, Paul Anthony, 459, 465, 466, 468
   Port Antonio Market #3, 466, *467*, 468
social realism, 486
Solar, Xul, 256

Soldán, Natalia Paz, 164–65
Sommer, Doris, 252
Souloque, Faustin, 215
Spain, 15–16, 23, 124, 126, 169, 198, 203. See also Iberia
Spilimbergo, Lino Enea, 277
Stahl, Augusto, 27
Steen, Jan, 181
Sternberg, Harry, 486, 490
St. Kitts, 18
Stoddart, Roberta, *Earl*, 422, *423*
Stollmeyer, John, 515
Strachan, Tavares
   Blast Off, *530*, 531
   The Color of the Sun, 531
Stradanus, Johannes, 134
Street of the Cross, San Juan de Puerto Rico (unidentified photographer), *186*, 187
Struikelblok, George, 519
Suárez del Villar, Mariano, 437
Suárez y Romero, Anselmo, "The Caretaker," 128
Sullivan, Edward, 91
Sun Ra, 416
Suriname, 516, 519
Suro, Darío, 327
surrealism, 203, 205, 305, 437
Sweet, James, 106
Synfronini, José, 366

Tacky (slave leader), 416
Tafur, Alicia, *Black Woman of the Fruit of the Peach Palm*, 344, *345*, 361
Talbot, William Henry Fox, 233
Tallet, José Zacarías, 269
Tanner, Henry Ossawa, 507
Tarsila do Amaral (known as Tarsila), 255, 277, 327
   Black Woman, 274, *276*, 293
   The Fruit Vendor, 274, *275*
   The Negress, 259
   Workers, *279*
Tauliaut, Henri, 222, 240, 244
   Nudes Descending a Staircase, #3 (with Annabel Guérédrat), *242*, 244
Taylor, Maxwell, 489–90, 494, 512
   1967 Crisis, 490
   Another One, 490
   Dark Angel, 490
   Express to Work, 490

Green Route, 490
Inhibited, 490, *491*
Love and Responsibility, 390, *397*
Rum, 489
(Untitled) Digital Head, 490
Untitled (Pregnant and Alone), 489
Télémaque, Hervé, 487, 489, 490, 507, 512
   Histoire sexuelle, 487
   Quand j'appris la nouvelle, 487
   Toussaint Louverture in New York, 487, *488*
Tenerani, Pietro, 43
   The Abolition of Slavery, 43, *44*, 45, 47
   The Abolition of Slavery (engraving after Tenerani), 45, *45*
Thésée, Lucie, 220
Thoby-Marcelin, Philippe, 215
Thomas, Mary, 372
Thornton, John, 15, 17
Three Kings, The (unidentified artist), 174, *175*
Tibério, Wilson, 427, 429, 430
   Massacre in South Africa, *428–29*
   Tricontinental, 434, 437
Tió, Teresa, 192, 195
Tiquant, Germain, 220
Toribio Ureta, Manuel, 62
Torres-García, Joaquín, 486
Torriente, *Úrsula de Valverde*, 146, *147*
Toscano, Pablo, 437
Toussaint Louverture, François-Dominique, 215, 330, 371
Triay, José, 141
Trinidad, 375, 483
Trujillo, Rafael Leonidas, 171–72, 201, 303
Tufiño, Rafael, 189–92, 195, 198
   Black Majesty, *194*, 195
   Carlos Raquel Rivera, 169, *170*
   Goyita, front jacket, 192, *193*, 195
   La plena, 191, *192*, 198, 316
Tula (slave revolt leader), 358, 359
Tupinambá de Ulhôa, Martha, 106
Turnier, Luce, 222
   Sleeping Young Woman, 217, *218*
Twa, Lindsay, 219

Ulysse, Gina Athena, 224
United States, 75, 124, 169, 171–72, 185, 255, 303
Upper Guinea, 17
Urrutia, Gustavo, 250, 281
Uruguay, 265, 363

Ustáriz, Miguel Antonio de, 126, 128

Valdes, Juana, 523
Valdés, Julia, 441
Valentim, Rubem, 430, 432, 437
   Composition No. 5, *331*, 332
   Syncretic Symbol of Afro-Brazilian Culture, 366, *367*
Valère, Laurent, *Cap 110*, 339, *340–41*, 361
Valverde, Úrsula de, 146
Van Sertima, Ivan, 494
Van Vechten, Carl, 497
   Namba Roy, 497, *498*
Varela, Obdulio, 364
Vargas, Getúlio, 109, 121–22, 271, 285, 303, 339
Vasconcelos, José, 247, 254, 255, 285
Vasconcelos, Naná, 364
Vásquez Lendechy, Erasmo, *The Yanga*, 357, 358
Veiga Guignard, Alberto da
   The Engaged Couple, 285, *286*
   The Marine's Family, 285, *287*
Vela Zanetti, José, 204
Velázquez, Diego, 16
Venezuela, 23
Verger, Pierre, 29
Vermay, Jean-Baptiste, 129
Vespucci, Amerigo, 134
Viana Filho, Alfredo da Rocha (known as Pixinguinha), 364
Victoria, Guadalupe, 69
Victor Manuel García (known as Victor Manuel), 266, 271, 274, 289
   Carnival, *268*, 269
   Little Devil, 266, *267*, 269
   The Mulatto Woman and the Little Black Girl, 266
   Tropical Gipsy, 259
   Young Woman, 261, *263*
Vilela, Micaela, 157, 161
Virgin with Donors Don Manuel de Salzes y de Doña Francisca Infante (unidentified artist), 155, *156*
Vlaminck, Maurice de, 266
Voiage and Travayle of Sir John Maundeville, Knight, The (unidentified writer), 40–41
Voigt, Karl Friedrich, *Simón Bolívar, Liberator of the Slaves*, 45, *46*

Wainwright, Leon, 415
Walcott, Derek, 506
Walker, Barbara, 504
Walmsley, Anne, 495
Ward, Nari, 487, 512, 515
    Happy Smilers: Duty Free Shopping, *514*, 515
Wasth Rodrigues, José, 337
Watson, Barrington, 405
    Mother and Child, 405, *408*, 521
Watson, Osmond, 405
    Peace and Love, 387, *388*, 390
Watson, Raymond, 366
Watson, Stanford, 519
Wedgwood, Josiah, 42
    Am I not a Man and a Brother? 42, *43*
White, Golde, 384
    Black Man in a Cap, *382*, 383
White, Trumbull, *Our New Possessions*, 185
Whittle, Alberta, 522
Whyte, Cosmo, 523
Wilberforce, William, 215, 505
William, Didier, 224
    Ezili toujours konnen, *223*, 224
    Menm pandan m'ap danse, 224, *225*
Williams, Aubrey, 496, 497, 504, 505, 506, 510, 512
    Revolt, 412, *413*, 415
    Towakaima, 500
    Visual Idea, 500, *501*
Williams, Denis, 504, 506–7, 510
    Memorabilia II, 506
    Painting in Six Related Rhythms, 507
    Pauline, 507, *508*
    Rhythms, 507
Williams, Eric, 399, 495
Williams, William T., 512, 515
Williez, León, 62
Wolgemut, Michel, workshop, *A Sciopod*, *40*, 41
Wood, John, 383
Wood, Marcus, 42
Woodruff, Hale, 489
Woss y Gil, Alejandro, 199
Woss y Gil, Celeste, 199, 201, 205, 208, 485
    The Market, 199, 201, *201*
    Nude, 199, *200*
Wright, Horace, 486
Wynter, Sylvia, 497, 506

Xandó, Niobe, 432
    Black Power I, 437, *438*

Yanga, Gaspar, 334, 358

Zamore, Franklyn, *Neg Mawon Emancipation Monument*, 351, 359, 372
Zapata Olivella, Manuel, 453
Zayas, Marius de, 259
Zemi (Taíno effigy figure) [unidentified artist], *478*, 479–80
Zumbi (Quilombo dos Palmares leader), 359, 368, 370–71